SEXUAL ASSAULT TRIALS

Third Edition

VOLUME 1

Paul DerOhannesian II

QUESTIONS ABOUT THIS PUBLICATION?

For questions about the **Editorial Content** appearing in these volumes or reprint permission, please call:

Michelle L. Aubin .... 1-800-424-4200 Ext. 3071
E-mail .... Michelle.L.Aubin@LexisNexis.com
Outside the United States and Canada please call .... (518) 487-3000

For assistance with replacement pages, shipments, billing or other customer service matters, please call:

Customer Services Department at .... (800) 833-9844
Outside the United States and Canada, please call .... (518) 487-3000
Fax number .... (518) 487-3584
Customer Service Website .... http://www.lexisnexis.com/custserv/

For information on other Matthew Bender Publications, please call
Your account manager or .... (800) 223-1940
Outside the United States and Canada, please call .... (518) 487-3000

ISBN 0-8205-7466-X
LCCN 98-88607

Editorial Offices
744 Broad Street, Newark, NJ 07102 (973) 820-2000
201 Mission St., San Francisco, CA 94105-1831 (415) 908-3200
www.lexis.com

Statement on Fair Use

Matthew Bender recognizes the balance that must be achieved between the operation of the fair use doctrine, whose basis is to avoid the rigid application of the copyright statute, and the protection of the creative rights and economic interests of authors, publishers and other copyright holders.

We are also aware of the countervailing forces that exist between the ever greater technological advances for making both print and electronic copies and the reduction in the value of copyrighted works that must result from a consistent and pervasive reliance on these new copying technologies. It is Matthew Bender's position that if the "progress of science and useful arts" is promoted by granting copyright protection to authors, such progress may well be impeded if copyright protection is diminished in the name of fair use. (See *Nimmer on Copyright* §13.05[E][1].) This holds true whether the parameters of the fair use doctrine are considered in either the print or the electronic environment as it is the integrity of the copyright that is at issue, not the media under which the protected work may become available. Therefore, the fair use guidelines we propose apply equally to our print and electronic information, and apply, within §§107 and 108 of the Copyright Act, regardless of the professional status of the user.

Our draft guidelines would allow for the copying of limited materials, which would include synopses and tables of contents, primary source and government materials that may have a minimal amount of editorial enhancements, individual forms to aid in the drafting of applications and pleadings, and miscellaneous pages from any of our newsletters, treatises and practice guides. This copying would be permitted provided it is performed for internal use and solely for the purpose of facilitating individual research or for creating documents produced in the course of the user's professional practice, and the original from which the copy is made has been purchased or licensed as part of the user's existing in-house collection.

Matthew Bender fully supports educational awareness programs designed to increase the public's recognition of its fair use rights. We also support the operation of collective licensing organizations with regard to our print and electronic information.

TABLE OF CONTENTS

VOLUME 1

CHAPTER 1
PRETRIAL ISSUES, DISCOVERY, AND MOTIONS

Table of Contents

CHAPTER 2
FAIR TRIAL, FREE PRESS, AND DEALING WITH PUBLICITY

Table of Contents

CHAPTER 3
JURY SELECTION

Table of Contents

CHAPTER 4
OPENING STATEMENT

Table of Contents

CHAPTER 5
DIRECT AND CROSS-EXAMINATION OF COMPLAINING WITNESS

Table of Contents

Table of Contents

Table of Contents

Table of Contents

CHAPTER 7
CONSENT

Table of Contents

CHAPTER 8
IDENTIFICATION AND IDENTIFICATION DEFENSE

Table of Contents

Table of Contents

CHAPTER 10
HEARSAY

Table of Contents

CHAPTER 11
EXPERT TESTIMONY

Table of Contents

Table of Contents

Table of Contents

VOLUME 2

CHAPTER 12
MEDICAL EVIDENCE AND TESTIMONY

Table of Contents

Table of Contents

CHAPTER 13
DNA AND SCIENTIFIC EVIDENCE

Table of Contents

CHAPTER 14
PAINTING THE PICTURE: THE USE OF REAL AND DEMONSTRATIVE EVIDENCE

Table of Contents

CHAPTER 15
SUMMATION

Table of Contents

CHAPTER 16
JURY INSTRUCTIONS

Table of Contents

PREFACE

Since the first edition, tremendous changes have taken place in many areas of sexual assault. Developments in both statutory and decisional law reflect not only the increased number of sexual assault cases that enter the courtroom, but also the changes in societal attitudes and knowledge concerning sexual assault itself. The advent of the internet has meant new evidentiary issues in child pornography and related prosecutions.

The third edition tracks emerging and developing issues in sexual assault. It not only updates the original text but also adds many additional sections including those devoted to Crawford and an expanded discussion of hearsay issues and expert psychological testimony, digital photographs and authenticating of computer evidence, child pornography issues, such as the discovery of child pornography images and the determination of age in those images, and expanded discussion of many areas such as disclosure of information under Brady and issues surrounding the use of polygraph.

Sexual assault litigation requires the expertise of other fields, such as psychology, social work, and medicine. Because of the dynamic nature of sexual assault litigation, current knowledge, principles, and approaches can easily become outmoded or overtaken by events. In that regard, this text offers a beginning for analysis of some of the issues addressed. Medical, scientific, and social science principles are advancing rapidly in many areas, such as the interpretation of physical findings in the examination of assault victims, the psychological aspects of sexual abuse, the sensitive interviewing of child witnesses, DNA and related technology.

This text does not seek to imply any particular standard in the area of sexual assault litigation, but hopes to highlight issues and approaches in sexual assault trials. There are contradictory holdings not only between jurisdictions but also within jurisdictions. The belief is that an informed, knowledgeable and vigorous prosecution and defense will yield the goal of the most just and reliable outcomes in sexual assault trials. This is necessary to the integrity of the criminal justice system. In many situations, there will be no substitute for judgment. It is also necessary for the growth and development of the law. In this field, it is critical that practitioners remain up-to-date. Therefore, future supplements to the third edition should be carefully reviewed.

Paul DerOhannesian II

ACKNOWLEDGEMENTS

The third edition would not have been possible without the support, encouragement and commitment of Matthew Bender, which was reflected in the hard work of Kathryn Calista, Manager, Practice Area Strategy and Development, and Editor, Michelle Aubin. The original idea for this book came from Regena Sanders, Senior Acquisitions Editor of The Michie Company. Ms. Sanders helped navigate the manuscript through the choppy waters of concept to final product. Her patience, guidance, and tempered perseverance provided essential support in the completions of this project. I am extremely fortunate to have had the benefit of the legal editing skills of Richard Patterson, Esq. of Indianapolis, Indiana, who so constructively reviewed the original manuscript.

Many individuals are responsible for providing ideas and experience, which are illustrated in the trial issues set forth in this book. One person stands out as a prime professional influence: the late Daniel Dwyer, Esq., who was my mentor and friend -first as a law student and then throughout my years as a prosecutor. I wish to acknowledge his guidance and support without which I would not have been able to develop the skills and knowledge that made this book possible. Hopefully, he would be pleased to acknowledge his role in this book.

Two attorneys, Susan Via, Esq. and Susan Perlis Marx. Esq., provided a critical eye to portions of the original manuscript and shared some of their insight, thoughts and encouragement. Over the years, many prosecutors and defense attorneys, too numerous to mention, have in one way or another contributed to the third edition. Their professional collegiality is appreciated.

No less daunting than the preparation of the content of this book was the actual production of the manuscript. Maria DePaul, aided by Kristin Bruno, provided many months of technical assistance and support. Maria's work has been particularly noteworthy in the production of the third edition and the voluminous changes and additions that were made. Jennifer Zegarelli, Esq., my associate, also ably contributed to the text of the third edition as well as assisting in the editing process. Without their efforts and willingness to work long and extended hours, the final manuscript would not have been produced. Their smiles and patience while under the stress of completing the manuscript helped keep the project on an even keel.

On a day-to-day basis, I would not have been able to complete the original work underlying the third edition without the support of my family, particularly my wife Melissa, and my two children, Paul and Danielle. I must acknowledge my late father, Paul, with whom I practiced law. His inspiration and professional encouragement are fondly remembered and deeply appreciated. There is no doubt, however, that without the strong support and understanding of my family, I would have been unable to dedicate the long hours necessary to the completion of the first and subsequent editions.

CHAPTER 1

PRETRIAL ISSUES, DISCOVERY, AND MOTIONS

§ 1.1 Interviewing the client.

The initial interview with a client accused of a sexual assault can help guide the defendant's attorney in choosing avenues of pretrial discovery, investigation, and eventually to a trial defense. A good question at the beginning of an interview is to ask the client to tell the attorney about himself, his background, work history, and what the client thinks is important for the attorney to know. Later, the attorney can ask more specific questions about a defendant's background, but this initial interview will allow the attorney to see how the client defines himself. The question is also nonthreatening and allows the attorney to ascertain the communication skills of the client and to see what kind of impression the client may make as a witness. It also provides information essential to both bail and pretrial release.

Part of the client's background would include medical and mental health history. The attorney should also be aware of the client's alcohol, drug history, or criminal background. These areas may be relevant not only to bail or sentencing decisions, but also to the charges themselves. Does the client have a favorable work history? Who can provide character references for bail, possible character testimony for trial, or letters of support at sentencing?

Attorneys are divided on the issue of whether to ask clients if they have committed the crime. It is helpful to ask the client to tell the lawyer what he knows about the complainant in the case and the relationship, if any, he has had with that complainant. If the client offers that he did not commit the offense, ask him if he knows who did. It is also helpful to ask the client what, if anything, he knows about the investigation, and what proof he thinks there is against him. To the extent possible, allow the client to explain why he believes he is accused.

The client may be aware of who may be potential witnesses both against him and for him. A question to ask the client during the initial interview and an issue that looms large in many sexual assault trials is whether the client has any idea why he is being accused of the sexual assault charges. Why is this person making this accusation if it is not true? This is a question the jury or prosecution would raise. The defendant can guide the attorney in answering this question, if there is an answer, and developing the information to support the defendant's answer.

In a child sexual assault case, it is important to ask the client how the child complainant knows about the details of sexual activity if it did not occur. The defendant's answers can be helpful in directing the defendant's attorney to witnesses and investigatory avenues and pretrial motions to pursue. As a general rule, knowing the child's environment may help answer this question or explain other aspects of the case. The answers to these questions will help the attorney develop a theory and theme for the case.[1]

Ask the client to whom he has spoken about the case or investigation. Clients should be advised not to speak to anyone about the case; however, there may be situations where the attorney and the client will decide to make certain public statements, but this must be a very carefully made decision. This is discussed further in the chapter on pretrial publicity.[2] Clients should be warned of the pitfalls of contacting an alleged victim. Foremost, there may be an order of protection, which prohibits such contact. A violation of the order can further damage the client's legal position and possibly lead to a loss of pretrial freedom. It is also possible that a client's contact with a potential witness or victim may lead to the accusation that the client has threatened or made admissions to the witness. Many witness tampering statutes are extremely broad and cover a variety of activities that a client may not realize can form the basis of further charges.[3]

---

[1] See § 3.3.

[2] See §§ 2.29–30.

[3] See, e.g., 18 U.S.C. § 1512: (b) Whoever knowingly uses intimidation or physical force, or threatens another person, or attempts to do so, or engages in misleading conduct toward another person, with intent to — (1) influence, delay, or prevent the testimony of any person in an official proceeding; (2) cause or induce any person to — (A) withhold testimony, or withhold a record, document, or other object, from an official proceeding; (B) alter, destroy, mutilate, or conceal an object with intent to impair the object's integrity or availability for use in an official proceeding; (C) evade legal process summoning that person to appear as a witness, or to produce a record, document, or other object, in an official proceeding; or (D) be absent from an official proceeding to which such person has been summoned by legal process; or (3) hinder, delay, or prevent the communication to a law enforcement officer or judge of the United States of information relating to the commission or possible commission of a Federal offense or a violation of conditions of probation, parole, or release pending judicial proceedings; shall be fined not more than $250,000 or imprisoned not more than ten years, or both. (c) Whoever intentionally harasses another person and thereby hinders, delays, prevents, or dissuades any person from — (1) attending or testifying in an official proceeding; (2) reporting to a law enforcement officer or judge of the United States the commission or possible commission of a Federal offense or a violation of conditions of probation, parole, or release pending judicial proceedings; (3) arresting or seeking the arrest of another

Try to ascertain what pressures the client may be under from family, fellow workers, or other persons and also what support he may expect from these individuals. If the defendant has support from his wife or family members, this can be demonstrated at a trial and send a powerful message to the jury.

In conducting the initial interview with the client, it is best that no other person, including the client's spouse, be present. The presence of a third person may break the attorney-client privilege, and that person may be subject to subpoena. There are several notable exceptions to the spousal confidential communication privilege that may apply in the sexual assault scenario; these include crimes against a spouse or a child and crimes that are deemed not to be in the best interest of the marriage or the spouse. In these situations, it is possible that the spouse may be subpoenaed to testify concerning otherwise confidential communications. It is also possible that the attorney can be subpoenaed concerning the communications because of the presence of a third party. This could even result in the subsequent disqualification of the attorney from the proceedings.

Some clients may know they did something wrong but will not acknowledge any culpability. It is also possible for a client to be somewhat "out-of-step" with legal or societal norms. The client may have a misunderstanding of the law, such as the notion that mistaking the age of the complainant is a valid defense to a child sexual assault charge. Therefore, sometimes the initial interview may involve an explanation of legal principles.

At the end of the interview, the client should note his or her responsibilities and duties, such as what not to say or do, what documents or evidence to gather, or information to provide the attorney. The possibility that the client will still be under investigation or "targeted" should also be discussed.

§ 1.2 Interviewing of and defendant's access to complainants and complainant's parents.

While a defendant may be precluded from contacting a complainant by court order, or may wish to avoid being accused of threatening the witness or making admissions to the complainant, the defendant's attorney has a right to interview the complainant subject to some important limitations.

The complainant is a very important source of information in a sexual assault prosecution. Ordinarily, a complainant in a sexual assault case will not want to speak to the defendant's representatives. A witness has the right to decline to

---

person in connection with a Federal offense; or (4) causing a criminal prosecution, or a parole or probation revocation proceeding, to be sought or instituted, or assisting in such prosecution or proceeding; or attempts to do so, shall be fined not more than $25,000 or imprisoned not more than one year, or both. (d) In a prosecution for an offense under this section, it is an affirmative defense, as to which the defendant has the burden of proof by a preponderance of the evidence, that the conduct consisted solely of lawful conduct and that the defendant's sole intention was to encourage, induce, or cause the other person to testify truthfully.

speak with an investigator or attorney. Because witnesses do not belong to any party, the prosecution may not "suggest" to witnesses, much less "advise" or require them under a plea agreement, "not to talk to anyone unless . . . the prosecutor [is] present."[4] It may also be improper for prosecutors to instruct witnesses to not discuss their grand jury testimony with others.[5] Most courts hold that ordering an interview of a sexual abuse complainant is within the broad discretion given to courts in maintaining control over discovery.[6] However, some courts find there is no authority for a court to order an interview of a sexual assault complainant.[7]

Some courts find that a defendant is entitled access to prospective witnesses, including a complainant, and when specific prejudice can be shown from the denial of access to a witness, the court may take appropriate remedial measures.[8] A trial court may provide a defendant with access to child witnesses and place restrictions on the interview, such as precluding the defendant or any other person, from being present other than a victim/witness advocate.[9] A court may also order access to a child complainant's parent.[10] A trial court may not prohibit a defendant from personally contacting a sexual assault victim to protect the victim from "embarrassment," "harassment," "adverse publicity," or a violation of the

---

[4] Gregory v. United States, 369 F.2d 185, 188–89 (D.C. Cir. 1966). *See also* United States v. Soape, 169 F.3d 257, 270 (5th Cir. 1999); Kines v. Butterworth, 669 F.2d 6 (1st Cir. 1981) ("[W]hen the free choice of a potential witness to talk to defense counsel is constrained by the prosecution without justification, this constitutes improper interference with a defendant's right of access to the witness." *Id.* at 9); United States v. Rodgers, 624 F.2d 1303, 1311 (5th Cir. 1980) (holding prosecutors improperly "suggested" that witnesses "speak with defense lawyers only if [government] lawyers were also present"); United States v. Cook, 608 F.2d 1175 (9th Cir. 1979) ("As a general rule, . . .[b]oth sides have the right to interview witnesses before trial. Exceptions to this rule are justifiable only under the 'clearest and most compelling circumstances.' " *Id.* at 1180) (internal citations and quotation marks omitted).

[5] United States v. Clemones, 577 F.2d 1247, 1251 (5th Cir. 1978) (holding it improper for "assistant United States Attorney handling the case [to] instruct some 30 to 35 witnesses appearing before the grand jury that the proceedings were secret and that they should not discuss their testimony with anyone other than their attorneys or government agents").

[6] State v. Miller, 195 W.Va. 656, 466 S.E.2d 507 (1995) (holding a trial court properly denied defendant's lawyer's request to interview sexual abuse complainant since matters of pretrial discovery are within the discretion of the trial court).

[7] Knight v. State, 207 Ga. App. 846, 429 S.E.2d 326 (1993) (defendant has no right to a pretrial interview of a child complainant); Eakes v. State, 665 So. 2d 852 (Miss. 1995) (trial court lacked authority to order three child witnesses to alleged sexual abuse and victim's doctor to speak with defense attorney prior to trial).

[8] United States v. Medina, 992 F.2d 573, 579 (6th Cir. 1993), *cert. denied sub nom.;* Wilson v. United States, 510 U.S. 1109 (1994).

[9] Commonwealth v. Giacobbe, 56 Mass. App. Ct. 144, 775 N.E.2d 759 (2002).

[10] State v. Swoboda, No. C4-99-1455, 2000 Minn. App. LEXIS 182, at *8 (Feb. 29, 2000) ("The state failed to show that the district court abused its discretion by requiring E.E.'s mother to make herself available to provide the defense psychologist with background information relating to the alleged abuse." *Id.*).

victim's privacy.[11] Of course, if there is a showing of possible danger to the safety of the victim, limitation in the contact with a victim may be appropriate. The access to child sexual assault complainants, and some impaired adult complainants, may be controlled by the parent or guardian of the child or impaired adult. The child may also be in the custody of a social services agency. Several courts have held that a social services agency which has custody of a child sexual assault victim has a right to decline a defendant's request to interview or examine a child.[12] Even if a court orders access to a complainant, the complainant has a right to refuse to be interviewed, or to request a representative of the district attorney be present.[13]

Any interview with a material witness should be well-documented, possibly recorded or witnessed by a third person, in case the witness's statements need to be presented at trial. Consideration should be given to the fact that if the attorney conducts the interview, he or she may be a witness if the witness' statements are at issue.

There is nothing that precludes the defendant's representatives from attempting to speak to a complainant concerning the allegations, but the defendant's representatives must not engage in unethical or illegal activities, such as criminal impersonation, to overcome a complainant's desire to not speak about the case. Some jurisdictions will make the complainant available to the defendant's attorney or representative for an interview. Also, some jurisdictions, for example, Indiana, Florida, and Vermont, permit the pretrial deposition of witnesses,

---

[11] Reid v. Superior Court, 55 Cal. App. 4th 1326, 64 Cal. Rptr. 2d 714 (6th Dist. 1997).

[12] United States v. Rouse, 111 F.3d 561, 566–68 (8th Cir.) (*en banc*), *cert. denied*, 522 U.S. 905 (1997) (finding no need shown to make child victims available so that defendant's expert could demonstrate role of suggestive interviewing techniques and environmental pressures); Hewlett v. State, 520 So. 2d 200, 203–04 (Ala. Crim. App. 1987); Thornton v. State, 264 Ga. 563, 449 S.E.2d 98, 109–10 (1994); Commonwealth v. Adkinson, 442 Mass. 410, 416–19, 813 N.E.2d 506 (2004) (holding decision to allow child to be interviewed by defense expert or counsel on child sexual abuse case belongs to social services agency with custody of child); State *ex rel.* O'Leary v. Lowe, 307 Or. 395, 400–04, 769 P.2d 188, 190–93 (1989) (*en banc*); State v. Dison, 1997 Tenn. Crim. App. LEXIS 93 (Jan. 31, 1997).

[13] *See, e.g.*, Commonwealth v. Rivera, 424 Mass. 266, 271–72, 675 N.E.2d 791, 796 (1997), *cert. denied*, 525 U.S. 934 (1998); People v. Estrada, 1 A.D.3d 928, 767 N.Y.S.2d 552 (2003), *appeal denied*, 1 N.Y.3d 627, 808 N.E.2d 1285, 777 N.Y.S.2d 26 (2004):

> Finally, we reject the further contention of defendant that he was denied a fair trial based on the refusal of a potential prosecution witness to talk to defendant's attorney, allegedly because the prosecutor had told the witness not to discuss the case with anyone. Defendant's attorney sought a letter from the prosecutor excepting defense counsel from that alleged prohibition. The prosecutor denied giving such an instruction and refused counsel's request. Because witnesses have a constitutional right to refuse to talk to defense counsel [citation omitted], and because there is no evidence that the prosecutor gave such an instruction, we conclude that there is no merit to defendant's contention.

including the complainant. At times, pretrial depositions of witnesses are not available for victims under a particular age.[14]

§ 1.3 Areas of investigation.

An attorney or investigator should understand that most evidence in a sexual assault prosecution will come from one of three sources: the scene, the complainant, or the defendant. If an attorney is representing a defendant, the attorney should be able to control the flow of information or evidence from a defendant once the attorney has entered the picture. The police will be restricted in their contact with the defendant at this point. Nonetheless, law enforcement officials may still obtain a search warrant of the defendant's premises or person regardless of a defendant's representation by counsel, and may also obtain court orders for non-testimonial evidence. Subpoenas can be used to gather non-testimonial evidence. Is there evidence that must be promptly obtained before it is lost or destroyed, such as police communications or tapes? Will the scene change if not promptly documented?

Law enforcement officials also can contact individuals with whom the defendant may have discussed or is discussing matters pertaining to his or her case. Ordinarily, defendants or suspects should be advised not to engage in any communications with any individuals concerning the investigation.

If available, the scene of the alleged incident should be documented as soon as possible. Even if the scene has already been processed by law enforcement officials, the defendant's attorney should still obtain as much information as possible from the scene or elsewhere.[15] The scene can be photographed or videotaped and provide the basis for a discussion with the client during subsequent interviews. Even after a scene has been processed by law enforcement officials, there may be evidence left behind that was overlooked by investigators, or evidence that the investigators saw but did not consider significant to the case. Also, evidence discovered at the scene by the defendant's own experts sometimes leads to theories not initially considered by the defense or prosecution. Examination of the scene may also determine whether there were other individuals in the area who might be potential witnesses.

Of course not only should the defense obtain statements of witnesses in the prosecution's possession, but it should also seek to interview those witnesses. The issues surrounding the interview of a complainant are discussed in the following section. Other witnesses would include neighbors where the crime took place or of the complainant or defendant, as well as friends and family of the

---

[14] N.H. Rev. Stat. § 517.13. The statute does not apply to a victim who was less than 16 years of age at time of trial, but who had attained age 16 at the time of the discovery request. *See* State v. LaPorte, 134 N.H. 73, 587 A.2d 1237 (1991).

[15] See § 1.12 with respect to a defendant's request for access to a scene when it is the complainant's residence.

defendant who may not have been interviewed by law enforcement officials but may have information favorable to the defense about the crime or defendant. The client may not know this information or may not be in a position to approach these or other witnesses once the client is the target of the investigation.

Nevertheless, any witness has the absolute right to refuse to be interviewed and the right to refuse to say anything. A witness can also be advised by an attorney that he or she is under no obligation to speak to anyone.[16]

One key area for review is the medical evidence or lack of medical evidence in the case. A defendant should be prepared to have a position with respect to the medical evidence in the case.

It is important to review the investigatory procedures in a case, not only with respect to the failure to discover important areas of evidence, but also to determine whether the manner of the investigation denied the defendant the right of due process, such as through the use of repeated, suggestive questioning of young witnesses.[17] This is an area that expert witnesses can sometimes help to develop. Experts can assist in documenting inadequacies in the forensic investigation of a case as well as in the interview process. As will be seen in many of the areas discussed in this book, the interview process has become a major subject of review in many child sexual assault cases.[18]

The conviction of Margaret Kelly Michaels, in a highly-publicized sexual abuse case involving children at a day-care center, was reversed and remanded for a hearing to determine whether the investigation and interview process was unduly "tainted" or whether it "suggested" the statements of the child witnesses. In a decision that affects not only pretrial motions and practice, New Jersey's Supreme Court held that a defendant who can establish "sufficient evidence of unreliability" of children's statements has the right to a pretrial taint hearing to determine whether investigatory or interview techniques "were so suggestive that they give rise to a substantial likelihood of irreparably false recollection of material facts bearing on defendant's guilt."[19] A developing issue in child sexual

---

[16] United States v. Medina, 992 F.2d 573, 579 (6th Cir. 1993), *cert. denied sub nom.* Wilson v. United States, 510 U.S. 1109 (1994).

[17] *See, e.g.*, State v. Bullock, 791 P.2d 155 (Utah 1989), *cert. denied*, 497 U.S. 1024 (1990). *See also* discussion of *People v. Michaels, infra.*

[18] *See, e.g.*, State v. Michaels, 136 N.J. 299, 642 A.2d 1372 (1994); People v. Hudy, 73 N.Y.2d 40, 535 N.E.2d 250, 538 N.Y.S.2d 197 (1988) (reversing defendant's conviction due to trial court's failure to permit cross-examination of investigating officers concerning the manner in which complainants were first questioned. Questioning of the investigators "concerned more than the credibility of the people's witnesses in general and went instead to a possible reason for fabrication by these impressionable witnesses, i.e., the investigator's suggestive comments." *Id.* at 57, 535 N.E.2d at 260, 538 N.Y.S.2d at 207).

[19] *Id.* at 320–21, 642 A.2d at 1383. After reviewing many court decisions and articles, the court concluded:

We therefore determine that a sufficient consensus exists within the academic,

assault prosecutions is the possible suggestiveness of the investigatory interview of child witnesses. This is discussed in § 11.40-41.

§ 1.4 Basic areas of discovery.

It should be remembered that there is no constitutional right to discovery and that the rules or analyses applicable to the pretrial access of information may differ from those applicable to a defendant's trial right of information since a defendant at trial has certain constitutional rights, such as confrontation and compulsory process, which are absent during pretrial proceedings.[20] A court may be limited in ordering disclosure not authorized by statute.[21] In discussing a defendant's right to certain records and information, such as counseling or mental health records, a court may well take the view that a defendant's pretrial right of access to such information is more limited than the defendant's access to that information at trial.[22] California's Supreme Court has explained that a defendant cannot have a pretrial right of access to privileged material as follows:

> Nevertheless, defendant asks us to hold that the Sixth Amendment confers a right to discover privileged psychiatric information before trial. We do not, however, see an adequate justification for taking such a long step in a direction the United States Supreme Court has not gone. Indeed, a persuasive reason exists not to do so. When a defendant proposes to impeach a critical prosecution witness with questions that call for privileged information, the

professional, and law enforcement communities, confirmed in varying degrees by courts, to warrant the conclusion that the use of coercive or highly suggestive interrogation techniques can create a significant risk that the interrogation itself will distort the child's recollection of events, thereby undermining the reliability of the statements and subsequent testimony concerning such events.

Id. at 212, 642 A.2d at 1379. As to the issues to be reviewed at such a pretrial hearing, the court stated:

> Without limiting the grounds that could serve to trigger a taint hearing, we note that the kind of practices used here — the absence of spontaneous recall, interviewer bias, repeated leading questions, multiple interviews, incessant questioning, vilification of defendant, ongoing contact with peers and references to their statements, and the use of threats, bribes, and cajoling, as well as the failure to videotape or otherwise document the initial interview sessions — constitute more than sufficient evidence to support a finding that the interrogations created a substantial risk that the statements and anticipated testimony are unreliable, and therefore justify a taint hearing.

Id. at 321, 642 A.2d at 1383.

[20] Weatherford v. Bursey, 429 U.S. 545, 1559 (1977).

[21] Miller v. Schwartz, 72 N.Y.2d 869, 528 N.E.2d 507, 532 N.Y.S.2d 354 (1988) (noting that there is no constitutional right to discovery and that the law of discovery is basically a creature of legislative policy. *Id.* at 870, 528 N.E.2d at 355, 532 N.Y.S.2d at 354).

[22] Goldsmith v. State, 337 Md. 112, 651 A.2d 866 (1995) ("[W]e must keep in mind that an accused has limited pretrial discovery rights, which may not outweigh a witness' privilege, whereas the accused's right to obtain and present exculpatory evidence at trial is entitled to far greater constitutional protection." *Id.* at 121, 651 A.2d at 870–71.).

trial court may be called upon, as in *Davis v. Alaska*, to balance the defendant's need for cross-examination and the state policies the privilege is intended to serve. [citation omitted]. Before trial, the court typically will not have sufficient information to conduct this inquiry; hence, if pretrial disclosure is permitted, a serious risk arises that privileged material will be disclosed unnecessarily.[23]

Many areas of discovery in sexual assault litigation parallel those areas of other criminal proceedings. In addition, sexual assault litigation presents specific concerns that should be addressed as part of the discovery process. The following represents basic items and areas to consider when making demands to produce or motions for discovery. The list is by no means intended to be all-inclusive, but only a guideline. The circumstances of the case, the law of the particular jurisdiction, and the predilections of the particular judge will ultimately determine whether these items need to be provided.

1. Any written, recorded, or oral statement of the accused and/or a co-defendant to be tried jointly, made other than in the course of a criminal transaction to a public servant engaged in law enforcement activity or to a person then acting under his direction or in cooperation with him, or to a private citizen, or to any inmate of any correctional facility where the defendant has been lodged.

2. A transcript of testimony relating to the criminal action or proceeding pending against the accused given by the accused, by a co-defendant and/or a co-participant in the crime, or by any witness or person who may be considered an accomplice, which was given by the accused, co-defendant, co-participant, or accomplice before a grand jury.

3. A statement as to whether immunity was given in connection with the presentation of an indictment to the grand jury or any connection with the presentation of any aspect of the proof relating to charges contained within the indictment.

4. A description of any promise, reward or inducement given to any informant or witness in return for information or testimony concerning the investigation in this case.

5. Any written report or document, or portion thereof, concerning a physical or mental examination, or scientific test or experiment, relating to the criminal action or proceeding made by or at the request of, or at the direction of, a public servant engaged in law enforcement activity.

6. The records of all medical examinations of the complainant performed in connection with the case.

---

[23] People v. Hammon, 15 Cal. 4th 1117, 938 P.2d 986, 65 Cal. Rptr. 2d 1 (1997), *cert. denied*, 118 S. Ct. 1071 (1998).

7. All medical records of the complainant obtained from any source in connection with the case.

8. All pharmacy records relating to the complainant obtained from any source.

9. Any and all photographs, drawings, or sketches relating to the criminal action or proceeding made by or completed by a public servant engaged in law enforcement activity, or by someone engaged in law enforcement to create such items.

10. All photographs of the complainant in the possession of the prosecution.

11. Copies of all photographs taken of the accused by law enforcement officials in the possession of the prosecution.

12. Any property or tangible physical evidence obtained from the accused or co-defendant, or from any vehicle or premises in which the defendant has had an interest.

13. All physical evidence or property seized at the scene of the alleged offense.

14. All physical evidence or property that the prosecution intends to offer at trial.

15. Any tapes or other electronic recordings that formulate the basis for the arrest of the defendant, whether or not the prosecutor intends to introduce them at trial.

16. Tape recordings and transcripts of any recorded calls or 911 calls to the police that relate to the indictment.

17. All written statements, videotapes, or tape recordings of all statements created or submitted to the prosecution in connection with this case, including all handwritten notes or statements made by and/or interviews of the complainant in connection with this case.

18. Copies of all tape recordings of all interviews from which transcripts have been prepared in connection with the case.

19. Copies of all tape recordings of all interviews from which transcripts have not been prepared in connection with the case.

20. All interview tape recordings, videotapes, transcripts, memoranda, and notes of all persons interviewed in any capacity and for any reason in connection with the case.

21. All notes of interviews with the complainant.

22. Records and documentation pertaining to contacts between the complainant and any person acting in the capacity of law enforcement, child protection, social workers, court services, or attorneys representing any party to litigation, civil or criminal, that relate to the charges.

23. A copy of all investigation reports made by any law enforcement agency involved in the investigation and prosecution of the case.

24. A copy of all records or reports made, filed, and maintained in the regular course of business of the law enforcement agency investigating the matter set forth in the indictment.

25. All notes by all police officers who conducted, or were present during, interviews with any and all witnesses in connection with the case.

26. The criminal history and FBI criminal history sheet of the accused.

27. All specific instances of the accused's prior uncharged criminal, vicious, or immoral conduct that the prosecution intends to use at trial for purposes of impeaching the credibility of the accused upon cross-examination.

28. The criminal history and FBI criminal history sheet for all witnesses and for the complainant in this case.

29. The arrest records, state criminal history records, corrections and prison record, FBI record, fingerprint record, and Drug Enforcement Administration record of each and all prosecution witnesses.

30. The names and addresses of all witnesses the prosecution intends to call at the time of trial.

31. The names and addresses of all persons known to have information concerning the subject matter of the indictment, whether it be inculpatory or exculpatory in nature, and who the prosecutor does not anticipate calling as witnesses at the time of the trial.

32. All polygraph examinations conducted of the complainant or defendant, including all questions asked, all supporting documentation, and all analysis thereof.

33. Records and reports of any similar complaints made by any of the alleged victims in this case concerning crimes of rape, sodomy, or sexual abuse.[24]

34. Anything required to be disclosed, prior to trial, to the accused by the prosecutor pursuant to the constitution of this state or the United States.

The more particular discovery aspects of DNA evidence[25] and an identification defense[26] are discussed in further detail in the chapters dealing with those topics.

---

[24] The propriety in using this type of evidence is discussed in § 5.46.

[25] *See* Chapter 13.

[26] *See* Chapter 8.

§ 1.5 Right to statements and reports of a federal agent in state proceedings.

Ordinarily, a defendant is entitled to the notes, reports, or statements of a witness. Increasingly, particularly in Internet child exploitation cases, a federal agent is involved as a witness in a state proceeding. However, the usual rules pertaining to a defendant's right to a witness's statements or reports detailing a witness's statements may not apply.

The right to a witness's statements and discovery in general is not of constitutional dimension. Thus, the investigation notes or reports of an FBI agent in a sexual abuse case need not be provided, since a federal regulation[27] precludes production or disclosure of information in a Department of Justice file in which the United States is not a party and the approval of the Department of Justice has not been obtained.[28] Because the prosecution is precluded from obtaining the information, just as it may be precluded from obtaining privileged records of a complainant, the defendant may not mandate production of the federal agents' notes or reports from the prosecution in a state proceeding to which the United States is not a party. The duty to disclose can not be greater than the power to acquire it.[29]

§ 1.6 Discovery of child pornography images.

Ordinarily, a defendant is entitled to discovery of physical evidence in the possession of the prosecution, including copies of photographs made or obtained by the prosecution. Child pornography images, however, are contraband in and of themselves. This raises the issue of whether the prosecution can or should make available copies of the child pornography. On the one hand, the defense needs to review the images. On the other hand, copies of the images may be easily made, particularly electronic images, which could further disseminate the images. When tangible evidence like drugs is provided to the defense, it is not possible to "duplicate" the drugs, but it is possible to determine how much has been consumed by the defense analysis. Sometimes copies of the images will not be enough and the hard drive of the computer will need to be examined. Several federal[30] and state[31] courts find that a defendant is not necessarily

---

[27] 28 CFR 16.22(a).

[28] People v. Button, 276 A.D.2d 229, 232, 722 N.Y.S.2d 629 (2000), *appeal denied*, 96 N.Y.2d 757, 748 N.E.2d 1079, 725 N.Y.S.2d 283 (2001).

[29] People v. Santorelli, 95 N.Y.2d 412, 741 N.E.2d 493, 718 N.Y.S.2d 696 (2000), *cert. denied*, 532 U.S. 1008 (2001).

[30] United States v. Horn, 187 F.3d 781, 792 (8th Cir. 1999), *cert. denied*, 529 U.S. 1029 (2000); United States v. Kimbrough, 69 F.3d 723 (5th Cir. 1995), *cert. denied*, 517 U.S. 1157 (1996); United States v. Husband, 246 F. Supp. 2d 467, 468 (E.D. Va. 2003).

[31] State v. White, 2001 Del. Super. LEXIS 513 (Dec. 28, 2001) (trial court denied defendant's request for delivery of child pornography to the defense; the defense had to inspect the evidence in a police facility or another facility to which parties could agree); State v. Ross, 792 So. 2d

entitled to copies of child pornography, since it is "contraband" and the defense and any defense experts are limited to viewing the images while they are under the prosecution's control. Many of these cases reviewed a trial court's order denying discovery under an abuse of discretion standard.

Other courts find a defendant is entitled to copies of child pornography, usually subject to a protective order limiting dissemination of the materials and requiring return of the images. When the contents of the hard drive are central to a case, there may be a more compelling argument for the defense to have a copy of the computer images and examine the hard drive containing the images, even if they are alleged to be pornographic.[32]

---

699 (Fla. Ct. App. 2001) (The court followed the reasoning of *Kimbrough* and analyzed that child pornography is illegal contraband and that such contraband cannot be distributed to, or copied by, the defense, and that the prosecution's offer to make the child pornography available for inspection but not to allow them to be copied was reasonable). It further observed:

> Here, the State did not maintain that the photo images could not be reviewed by Ross, just that the State should not be ordered to relinquish control over them. Ross has failed to demonstrate any prejudice or harm which would be caused by the procedures proposed by the State for review of these materials. The only potential harm specifically alleged by Ross was the potential that he would be required to reveal the identity of his consulting experts, information, which is normally protected by the work product privilege. That concern can be adequately addressed by the trial court fashioning procedures, which would allow Ross' consulting experts to review the photo images without their identity being disclosed.

Id. at 702. *See also*, Rogers v. State, 113 S.W.3d 452, 459 (Tex. Ct. App. 2003) (without deciding whether federal prosecutor's threat to prosecute defense counsel if he obtained copy of hard drive containing child pornography violated defendant's rights, court held that defendant was given adequate access to child pornography images to assist in defense).

[32] Taylor v. State, 93 S.W.3d 487, 502–04 (Tex. Ct. App. 2003) (The court compared a defendant's right to analyze the child pornography with a defendant's right to examine drug evidence):

> The contents of the hard drive were necessarily the central issue in this trial. The failure to order a copy of the hard drive produced, after request by counsel, had several results. Most importantly, defense counsel had no opportunity to discover for himself the errors referenced above. Those errors had the potential to be of critical importance to Taylor's defense, but without the opportunity to examine those errors in a less haphazard manner than the "on-the-fly" efforts made on cross-examination, we do not have sufficient information for more than an analysis of probabilities, rather than facts.

> The failure to provide a copy of the hard drive also meant counsel did not have a copy of the photographs, which the State alleged to be pornographic, which necessarily impacted his ability to prepare a defense to the claim.

> Cocaine can be analyzed, and the result conclusively shows whether the substance is contraband. That is not the case with photographs that may or may not be lewd. That is most clearly shown by the fact that we must conclude the jury decided one of the photographs was not pornographic. Counsel should have been provided with the information requested.

> We conclude that under these facts this error had a substantial or injurious effect on the jury's verdict.

Id. at 504.

According to one court, the defendant in such a situation should have a copy of the hard drive to be examined at a place of the defendant's choosing with a representative of the state present.[33] Courts ordering copies of the images to be provided to the defense find no barrier to such disclosure in the legal prohibition against producing and possessing child pornography:

> Nothing in the plain language of [California's child pornography possession statute] prohibits the copying of the images for use by the defense in preparing for trial. The People's interpretation of the statute — that the deputy district attorney would violate the law if he copied the images for the defense — not only defeats the purpose of the law and exalts absurdity over common sense, but it is also logically flawed. If the exemption in [California's child pornography possession statute] allows the prosecutor to duplicate and distribute the images for prosecution purposes as the People readily concede, then the prosecutor can duplicate and distribute the images with impunity to any of the players in the criminal action — to the court pretrial as the prosecutor did on the motion here, to the jury at trial and/or to the defense as part of the prosecutor's discovery duties. In addition, to the extent there is any genuine concern about the disposition of the material provided to the defense, the court can issue a protective order limiting disclosure to counsel and their agents or order the return of the images to the court for destruction at the conclusion of the case . . . .
>
> Finally, requiring the defense to view — and apparently commit to memory — the "thousands" of images at the computer crimes office obviously impacts [the defendant's] right to effective assistance of counsel and his right to a speedy trial.[34]

The fact that a criminal statute barring possession of child pornography does not provide immunity to defense attorneys does not necessarily justify denying defense counsel a copy of child pornography.[35] Nevada's Supreme Court holds that a defendant's right to effective assistance of counsel "trumps" any statutory restriction on possessing child pornography when a defendant seeks a copy of child pornography, which is prosecution evidence.[36] One Federal District in *United States v. Hill*, court has also found that "competent representation"

---

[33] *Id.* at 503.

[34] Westerfield v. Superior Court, 99 Cal. App. 4th 994, 998, 121 Cal. Rptr. 2d 402, 404–05 (2002).

[35] Cervantes v. Cates, 206 Ariz. 178, 76 P.3d 449 (2003), *review denied*, 2004 Ariz. LEXIS 32 (Mar. 16, 2004) (vacating trial court's decision to deny defendant a copy of child pornography seized as evidence, but noting court could impose safeguards on the copying and use of the materials). *Cates* was subsequently overruled by § 13-3553. *See also* State v. Butler, 2005 Tenn. Crim. App. LEXIS 302 (Mar. 30, 2005) (holding "that the possession, copying, or distribution of child pornographic materials does not constitute a violation of Tennessee's sexual exploitation of a minor statutes so long as it occurs in the context of the prosecution or defense of a case under the statute." *Id.* at *33).

[36] State v. Second Judicial Dist. Court, 89 P.3d 663 (Nev. 2004).

requires providing a defense attorney copies of child pornography.[37] At least one other federal district court has followed the *Hill* analysis.[38] The parties' stipulation outlining the handling of the materials is set forth in Appendix A.

§ 1.7 Discovery of child welfare records and *Pennsylvania v. Ritchie*.

In sexual assault trials, many complaining witnesses have had the opportunity to see counselors, therapists, or child protective workers. Information concerning these contacts is in records that may be deemed confidential due to physician-patient privilege, psychotherapist-patient privilege, or state law providing for the confidentiality of child welfare records. Sometimes the existence of such records will be ascertainable by review of statements, investigation reports, and medical records. In states permitting the pretrial deposition of witnesses, the existence of such records can be ascertained through the deposition process.

---

[37] United States v. Hill, 322 F. Supp. 2d 1081 (C.D. Cal. 2004):

The government analogizes the zip disks to narcotics, arguing that their inspection and analysis by defendant's expert should take place in the government's lab under government supervision. This analogy is inapt. Analysis of a narcotics sample is a fairly straightforward, one-time event, while a thorough examination of the thousands of images on the zip disks will take hours, even days, of careful inspection and will require the ability to refer back to the images as the need arises.

The court concludes that defendant will be seriously prejudiced if his expert and counsel do not have copies of the materials. Defense counsel has represented that he will have to conduct an in-depth analysis of the storage media in order to explore whether and when the various images were viewed, how and when the images were downloaded, and other issues relevant to both guilt and sentencing. The court is persuaded that counsel cannot be expected to provide defendant with competent representation unless counsel and his expert have ready access to the materials that will be the heart of the government's case.

The government's proposed alternative — permitting the defense expert to analyze the media in the government's lab at scheduled times, in the presence of a government agent — is inadequate. The defense expert needs to use his own tools in his own lab. And, he cannot be expected to complete his entire forensic analysis in one visit to the FBI lab. It took defense counsel between two and three hours to quickly scroll through the 2,300 images in the Encase report, so it is likely to take the expert much longer than that to conduct a thorough analysis. Defendant's expert is located in another state, and requiring him to travel repeatedly between his office and the government's lab — and obtain permission each time he does so — is unreasonably burdensome. Moreover, not only does defendant's expert need to view the images, his lawyer also needs repeated access to the evidence in preparing for trial.

Id. at 1091–92.

[38] United States v. Frabizio, 341 F. Supp. 2d 47 (D. Mass. 2004) (holding that the defendant could obtain discovery of the child pornography and that "there is no reason to think that defense counsel or her expert cannot be trusted to abide by the proposed protective order . . . [and] the government's concerns about the risk of further dissemination are adequately addressed by the proposed protective order, and the government's concern about re-victimization will be implicated regardless of where defense counsel and her expert view the images." *Id.* at 50).

The Supreme Court has provided some guidance in the area of defense access to confidential records in *Pennsylvania v. Ritchie*.[39] In *Ritchie*, the defendant subpoenaed the state child welfare agency's records pertaining to his daughter, the complainant in the case. The defendant argued that without the child welfare agency records he did not know which types of questions would best expose the weakness in the complainant's testimony.[40] The records were produced and possessed by a government agency; no statutory privilege shielded the records. The Supreme Court did not decide whether denying a defendant access to the child welfare records violated a defendant's right of confrontation or right to compulsory process. Rather, the Supreme Court held that under the due process clause of the Fourteenth Amendment, the state welfare agency's records should be turned over to the trial court for an *in camera* review. Then the court would determine which, if any, information or records should be turned over to the defense. The Court would not permit the defendant to have access to all of the files since there is a legitimate state interest in the confidentiality of the records. In this regard, the Court noted:

> A defendant's right to discover exculpatory evidence does not include the unsupervised authority to search through the Commonwealth's files. . . . [T]his Court has never held — even in the absence of a statute restricting disclosure — that a defendant alone may make the determination as to the materiality of the information. . . . [D]efense counsel has no constitutional right to conduct his own search of the state's files to argue relevance.[41]

The *Ritchie* case declared that the information must be material to the guilt of the accused.[42] Based on *Ritchie*, many courts after denying a defendant access to child welfare records, will include in the record for appellate review the records reviewed *in camera* so that an appellate court can determine whether or not the information is favorable to the accused and material to his guilt or punishment.[43] A defendant may waive his right to raise the propriety of a judge's denial of access to a complainant's psychological records by failing to include the records in the appellate record.[44]

The *Ritchie* opinion also drew a distinction between a defendant's use of confidential information already in the defendant's possession, as in *Davis v. Alaska*,[45] and the defendant seeking to obtain discovery of records not in the defendant's possession.[46] The Court's analysis of the defendant's right to access

---

[39] 480 U.S. 39 (1987).

[40] *Id.* at 51.

[41] *Id.* at 59.

[42] *Id.* at 57–58.

[43] *See, e.g.*, State v. Hardy, 293 N.C. 105, 128, 235 S.E.2d 828, 842 (1977).

[44] State v. Cramer, 44 P.3d 690 (Utah 2002).

[45] 415 U.S. 308 (1974) (defendant's constitutional right of confrontation violated by prohibiting defendant from cross-examining witness concerning the witness's criminal record).

[46] *Ritchie*, 480 U.S. at 54:

of the child welfare records was based upon the due process clause and not the confrontation or compulsory process clause.[47]

The Court noted that it is possible that information that may be immaterial upon the original examination by the court may become more important as a trial progresses, and that a court would be obligated to release further information as a trial progressed.[48]

Many courts have utilized the *in camera* review process to determine whether to release child welfare records.[49]

[I]n this case the confrontation clause was not violated by the withholding of the CYS file; it would only have been permissible for the judge to have prevented Ritchie's lawyer from cross-examining his daughter. Because defense counsel was able to cross-examine all of the trial witnesses fully, we find that the Pennsylvania Supreme Court erred in holding that the failure to disclose the CYS file violated the confrontation clause.

[47] *Id.* at 54–56.

[48] *Id.* at 60.

[49] Honeycutt v. State, 245 Ga. App. 819, 538 S.E.2d 870 (2000); State v. Brossette, 634 So. 2d 1309 (La. Ct. App.), *cert. denied*, 640 So. 2d 1344 (1994) (finding defendant's rights are protected by the court's *in camera* review of child protective service (CPS) records for exculpatory information). The court discussed further the defendant's request for information in the CPS records:

The defendant also argues that the trial court erred in ruling in chambers that evidence of the Child Protection Agency's actions taken subsequent to the accusation being made was not admissible. The defendant contends this ruling erroneously restricted the evidence which he should have been able to present to the jury concerning the possible coaching of Ashley, the benefits she received following the accusations, her removal from the home, and her relationship with the Child Protection Agency workers. In addition, the defendant asserts the information was relevant to show the degree of pressure put upon Michelle Brossette, the victim's mother, to testify against her husband, the defendant. Defendant apparently wished to impeach the credibility of the victim and the Child Protection Agency. The trial court ruled that defendant's allegations were not sufficient to show a pattern on the part of the Child Protection Agency which would affect the credibility determinations to be made by the jury.

Defendant fails to set forth any evidence which would substantiate the allegations raised. Mere speculation as to what occurred between the victim, her mother, and the Child Protective Agency is sufficient to make such claims admissible. Additionally, we fail to see what relevance such unsubstantiated evidence has to the issue at hand, whether the defendant raped his stepdaughter. Without any substantiation, the trial court correctly decided not to allow any evidence of the post-accusation conduct of the parties and the Child Protection Agency.

Id. at 1317–18; State v. Perry, 552 A.2d 545 (Me. 1989); State v. Gagne, 136 N.H. 101, 612 A.2d 899 (1992); People v. Love, 307 A.D.2d 528, 762 N.Y.S.2d 162 (2003) (court properly denied defendant access to social services records, where court conducted *in camera* review and failed to make offer of proof concerning possible false allegations in the records); People v. Walden, 236 A.D.2d 779, 653 N.Y.S.2d 875, *appeal denied*, 90 N.Y.2d 865, 683 N.E.2d 1066, 661 N.Y.S.2d 192 (1997) (Department of Social Services records were properly reviewed *in camera* by court. Defendant has no right to discovery of those records which were not in possession of prosecutor);

The specificity of a defendant's request to examine records or files can be a significant factor in reviewing the propriety of a trial court's decision to withhold the confidential records from the defense.[50]

The failure of a trial judge to review child welfare records, medical and psychotherapeutic files *in camera* may be reversible error.[51] There is authority that a trial judge cannot delegate the review of confidential records to the prosecuting attorney since such records contain information to which a district attorney does not have access.[52] As a threshold matter, it may be necessary to determine whether a proper privilege exists and applies to the records sought[53] and many courts require that a defendant make a preliminary showing that social service records are likely to contain material and relevant information before conducting an *in camera* review of such records.[54] This showing is also often

State *ex rel.* Renfro v. Cuyahoga County Dep't of Human Servs., 54 Ohio St. 3d 25, 560 N.E.2d 230 (1990) (holding that state child abuse records do not have absolute confidentiality and are best reviewed by an *in camera* inspection when there is reason to do so); State v. Dison, 1997 Tenn. Crim. App. LEXIS 93 (Jan. 31, 1997) (no showing by defendant that he was entitled to review state social service records); State v. Cramer, 2002 UT 9, 44 P.3d 690 (2002) (*in camera* review process of complainant's medical records did not violate defendant's rights under Utah constitution).

[50] *Ritchie*, 480 U.S. at 58, n. 15.

[51] State v. Paradee, 403 N.W.2d 640 (Minn. 1987) (reversing defendant's conviction for court's failure to review county welfare records); State v. Wilson, 118 N.C. App. 616, 456 S.E.2d 870, *appeal denied*, 341 N.C. 424, 461 S.E.2d 768 (1995); State v. Kelly, 118 N.C. App. 589, 456 S.E.2d 861 (1995).

[52] Commonwealth v. Barroso, 122 S.W.3d 554 (Ky. 2003) (Kentucky's Supreme Court ruled trial court must conduct *in camera* review of psychotherapy records since defendant's compulsory process right prevails over a witness' statutory claim of privilege; procedure keeps witness' privilege intact since it does not require her to waive it.); State *ex rel.* Dugan v. Tiktin, 313 Or. 607, 837 P.2d 959 (1992).

[53] Commonwealth v. Pelosi, 441 Mass. 257, 805 N.E.2d 1 (2004) (requiring such a step under Massachusetts framework for review of a complainant's psychotherapy records).

[54] State v. Kulmac, 230 Conn. 43, 56–59, 644 A.2d 887, 895–96 (1994); State v. Brossette, 634 So. 2d 1309 (La. Ct. App.), *cert. denied*, 640 So. 2d 1344 (La. 1994); Commonwealth v. Zane Z., 51 Mass. App. Ct. 135, 743 N.E.2d 867 (2001), *rev'd on other grounds* (finding defendant failed to establish "a factual basis to support his claim that the [Department of Social Services] records are likely to be relevant to the [defendant's] theory." *Id.* at 146, 743 N.E.2d 867); State v. Gagne, 136 N.H. 101, 612 A.2d 899 (1992) (holding that in a case where Children's Youth Services records involved defendant "in order to trigger an *in camera* review of confidential or privileged records, the defendant must establish a reasonable probability that the records contain information that is material and relevant to his defense." *Id.* at 105, 612 A.2d at 901); People v. Bush, 14 A.D.3d 804, 788 N.Y.S.2d 258, *appeal denied*, 4 N.Y.3d 852, 830 N.E.2d 325, 797 N.Y.S.2d 426 (2005) (holding that because the defendant's application to review the complainant's Department of Social Services records "was supported solely by speculation in an attorney's affidavit, without even an indication of the basis for that speculation," the trial court did not abuse its discretion in refusing to sign a judicial subpoena for the records); People v. Walden, 236 A.D.2d 779, 653 N.Y.S.2d 875, *appeal denied*, 90 N.Y.2d 865, 683 N.E.2d 1066, 661 N.Y.S.2d 192 (1997) (discovery rules do not allow access to social services records; "[d]efendant failed to show that

required with respect to counseling records. Usually asserting that the records may contain inconsistencies in the complainant's account or may provide cross-examination material is insufficient.

> The threshold showing to trigger an *in camera* review is not unduly high . . . [but the defendant] must present a plausible theory of relevance and materiality sufficient to justify review of the protected documents [citation omitted] but he is not required to prove that his theory is true.[55]

A consent for child welfare records signed by a child's guardian does not necessarily open the door to access child welfare records nor negate the requirement that defendant establish that the privileged materials are favorable to the defense and, thus, requiring an *in camera* review.[56]

Other courts find no need for an *in camera* review and provide the defendant access to the child welfare agency files, including records covered by another privilege, such as medical and counseling records.[57] The identity of the individual reporting the suspected abuse may remain confidential if there is concern for the reporter's safety.[58]

Child welfare records may contain information on many persons concerning many matters to which a prosecutor would have no rightful access. Since these records can be quite voluminous, an *in camera* review can consume considerable judicial time. Many confidential records are not available to the prosecution; however, if the police obtain confidential child welfare documents, the prosecutor will be responsible for such evidence in the possession of the police. If the prosecution does not possess the records, the prosecutor cannot disclose the records. If a complainant or witness has made statements that are part of confidential records to which the prosecutor does not have direct access, there is no duty on the part of the prosecutor to produce the notes of the interview

---

there was material exculpatory evidence in the possession or control of the People, that the People failed to turn such evidence over to defendant, and that the use of such evidence at trial would have created a reasonable possibility of acquittal."); State v. Thompson, 139 N.C. App. 299, 533 S.E.2d 834 (2000) ("With respect to N's medical records, however, the trial judge never performed an *in camera* inspection nor sealed the records for appellate review. But just because defendant asks for an *in camera* inspection does not automatically entitle him to one. Defendant still must demonstrate that the evidence sought to be disclosed might be material and favorable to his defense." *Id.* at 306–07, 533 S.E.2d at 840); State v. Clabo, 905 S.W.2d 197 (Tenn. Crim. App.), *appeal denied*, 1995 Tenn. LEXIS 312 (June 5, 1995) (defendant's request for child and family services records on the theory that they may help to impeach the victims or weaken their credibility did not establish a material need for the records).

55 State v. Graham, 142 N.H. 357, 363, 702 A.2d 322, 325–26 (1997) (remanding case to trial court for determination of reasons for court's decision to not conduct *in camera* review and whether defendant made sufficient showing of need for such records).

56 State v. Bassine, 188 Or. App. 228, 71 P.3d 72 (2003).

57 Commonwealth v. Lloyd, 523 Pa. 427, 567 A.2d 1357 (1989); Commonwealth v. Kennedy, 413 Pa. Super. 95, 604 A.2d 1036, *appeal denied*, 531 Pa. 638, 611 A.2d 711 (1992).

58 *Kennedy*, 413 Pa. Super. at 101, 604 A.2d at 1309.

or statements. The proper remedy would be to subpoena the confidential records for an *in camera* review of relevant material, such as statements of witnesses.[59] The court may decline to release child welfare records if they contain information already supplied the defendant.[60] A complainant's prior allegations of sexual abuse resulting in a child protective investigation involving the same time frame as the sexual assault charges in the indictment, and which resulted in an unfounded complaint and suggested prior false allegations of sexual assault, could be disclosed to a defendant regardless of a state statute providing that unfounded reports are not admissible in any judicial or administrative proceeding.[61] A provision of a state statute that renders unfounded complaints inadmissible in a judicial or administrative proceeding may be unconstitutional.[62]

Information in social services records demonstrating that a complainant may have fabricated allegations or lied about material components of the crime should be disclosed to a defendant.[63] Social services records may be admissible as

---

[59] *See, e.g.,* State v. Graville, 304 Or. 424, 746 P.2d 715 (1987).

[60] State v. Ball, 2004 SD 9, 675 N.W.2d 192 (2004), *rev'd on other grounds* (holding while complainant's statements in child protective records were relevant, they were not different from her statements in defendant's possession and court was within its discretion in not releasing the confidential social services records).

[61] People v. McFadden, 178 Misc. 2d 343, 683 N.Y.S.2d 694 (1998) ("However, statutory confidentiality of D.S.S. records is not always sacrosanct, and upon the basis of a proper showing they may be released upon court order after an *in camera* inspection." *Id.* at 345, 683 N.Y.S.2d at 695 (1998)).

[62] *Id.*

[63] State v. William C., 267 Conn. 686, 841 A.2d 1144 (2004) (the court reversed defendant's conviction due to failure to disclose social services records to defendant and remanding for trial court to decide which portions would be admissible as business records). The court determined:

> As our review of the trial transcript, in particular the testimony of the victim, and the records of the department that the defendant sought to admit into evidence demonstrates, much of the evidence contained within the department's files is qualitatively different from the other evidence used to impeach the victim at trial. Most glaringly, while much of the defendant's cross-examination of the victim centered upon the victim's misbehavior and propensity to lie in a general sense or in other instances, the information contained in the department's records evince, if believed by the trier of fact, a pattern of vacillations with regard to the very allegations of abuse for which the defendant was standing trial. Moreover, we are mindful that the records contain entries that indicate that the victim had remarked to several other individuals that she had begun to question whether her allegations of abuse were legitimate or whether she had imagined the incidents. At trial, the victim testified that she recalled making such a statement to her foster mother, but denied making such a statement to anyone else. When asked whether she had intimated such doubts to the individuals mentioned in the records, the victim responded in the negative. The records, therefore, would have been a particularly strong source of impeachment evidence as to the victim's credibility. Additionally, numerous entries in the records reference the victim's inconsistent statements with regard to the details of abuse, her statements that she would lie if she thought it necessary, and statements of the victim's physician as to the victim's capacity to distort reality and come to believe her

business records.[64] The burden is on the opponent to object to the portion which may be inadmissible hearsay, irrelevant, not connected to the "business," or improper opinion evidence.[65] When the child welfare records do not contain exculpatory or impeaching evidence, they will not be released.[66]

§ 1.8　Discovery of complainant's psychiatric or counseling records.

Counsel may also wish to obtain the psychological and psychiatric records of a complainant. This demand may be set forth as follows:

(1)　The names and addresses of all psychotherapists, including psychiatrists, psychologists, or other mental health professionals who have given treatment to the complainant. This should include any drug rehabilitation counseling or any other type of counseling.

(2)　All medical and psychiatric records or drug treatment records pertaining to any complainant identified in the indictment that do or may bear on the testimony and testimonial capacity, memory, or recollective ability or credibility of the witness.

(3)　All psychological testing of complainant, including raw data upon which any interpretation is based.

(4)　All progress notes, intake evaluations, reports, discharge summaries, and letters relating to any assessment or therapy session of the complainant by any mental health professional.

The principles of *Ritchie* provide some guidance in the area of psychological or psychiatric records; however, *Ritchie* dealt with the state's compelling interest in maintaining confidentiality of its welfare agency's investigations into child abuse. In matters of private counseling, the state's interest will not be present. On the other hand, *Ritchie* involved government records which are "confidential" records, while a complainant's psychotherapy records may be "privileged" and thus enjoy somewhat greater protection.[67]

---

distortions. These subjects are all highly relevant to the defendant's theory at trial: that the victim had concocted, intentionally or not, consciously or not, the allegations of abuse. This was not a case in which the state had numerous witnesses testify as to the allegations of abuse. The heart of the state's case against the defendant was the testimony of the victim and the testimony of witnesses to whom the victim had detailed her allegations of abuse.

64 *Id.*

65 *Id.* at 706, 841 A.2d at 1155–56.

66 State v. James G., 268 Conn. 382, 402–04, 844 A.2d 810, 823–24 (2004) (upholding trial court's withholding of confidential school and Department of Children and Families records, since they did not contain exculpatory or impeaching evidence or relate to child's ability to relate the truth).

67 Dill v. People, 927 P.2d 1315 (Colo. 1996) ("In sum, the information in question is not collected by the state, is disclosed only to a psychologist, and requires a higher level of confidentiality in order to achieve the open communication upon which successful therapeutic treatment depends." *Id.* at 1324); Goldsmith v. State, 337 Md. 112, 651 A.2d 866 (1995).

There is a view that the psychotherapist patient privilege can not be breached, even if the defendant establishes a reasonable probability that the privileged records contain information necessary to the defense.[68] This principle finds support in the Supreme Court's decision in *Jaffee v. Redmond*,[69] which states that disclosure of patient counseling records could not be overcome in the interest of justice. The court stated:

> Making the promise of confidentiality contingent upon a trial judge's later evaluation of the relative importance of the patient's interest in privacy and the evidentiary need for disclosure would eviscerate the effectiveness of the privilege. As we explained in *Upjohn Co. v. United States, 449 U.S. 383 (1981)*, if the purpose of the privilege is to be served, the participants in the confidential conversation "must be able to predict with some degree of certainty whether particular discussions will be protected. An uncertain privilege, or one which purports to be certain but results in widely varying applications by the courts, is little better than no privilege at all."[70]

Jaffee was not a criminal case and did not reach the issue if a criminal defendant can compel a third party to produce exculpatory information.

Massachusetts' Supreme Court has gone so far as to refer to a "victim's constitutionally protected right of confidentiality."[71]

The records may not be privileged if the person providing the counseling is not covered by the definition of the statutory privilege. The privilege may belong only to a licensed therapist or rape crisis counselor. A threshold question is whether the records are covered by a privilege. Nonetheless, a defendant's trial right of confrontation and compulsory process (as opposed to the pretrial discovery phase) may at times override the claim of privilege.[72] Federal law and regulations require a court order for drug, substance abuse, or alcohol treatment records.[73]

Most courts will follow the approach and analysis of *Ritchie*, however, and hold that privileged records may be subpoenaed but should be reviewed by a trial court to determine if there is any information that is relevant to the defense.

A generalized assertion by a defendant that the complainant's counseling records are needed to attack the credibility of the accuser or to develop possible areas of impeachment is insufficient in most jurisdictions to justify an *in camera*

---

[68] State v. Famiglietti, 817 So. 2d 901 (Fla. Ct. App. 2002).

[69] 518 U.S. 1 (1996).

[70] *Id.* at 17–18, quoting 449 U.S. at 393.

[71] Commonwealth v. Tripolone, 425 Mass. 487, 489, 681 N.E.2d 1216, 1218 (1997) ("We continue to see whatever right to confidentially [sic] in a criminal proceeding that an alleged victim may have as being subject to the balancing of the defendant's rights and the alleged victim's rights that we discussed in our *Fuller* opinion." *Id.* at 489, 681 N.E.2d at 1218.).

[72] *Id.* Goldsmith, *supra* note 66.

[73] 42 U.S.C. § 290dd-2(a); 42 C.F.R. § 2-13(a).

review of the confidential records. The rule developed by a significant number of courts is that unless a defendant can establish sufficient grounds to justify examining the victim's counseling records, a defendant is not entitled to a review of confidential records.[74] The lack of references to any abuse by a defendant

---

[74] Hammon v. United States, 695 A.2d 97 (D.C. 1997) (involving a defendant's request for court to examine a witness' juvenile files); Dill v. People, 927 P.2d 1315 (Colo. 1996) (an *in camera* inspection of victim's psychological records is not required when there is only an assertion that statements in the records may be helpful to the defense or inconsistent with complainant's trial testimony. "The vague assertion that the victim may have made statements to her therapist that might possibly differ from the victim's anticipated trial testimony does not provide a sufficient basis to justify ignoring the victim's right to rely upon her statutory privilege." *Id.* at 1325. Court noted that *Ritchie* standard not applicable since information in question not provided to a state agency); State v. Peseti, 101 Haw. 172, 65 P.3d 119, 128 (2003); People v. Foggy, 121 Ill. 2d 337, 521 N.E.2d 86, *cert. denied*, 486 U.S. 1047 (1988) (holding more than a general request is necessary to trigger the need for an *in camera* inspection of record); Richardson v. Commonwealth, 161 S.W.3d 327 (Ky. 2005) (noting defendant failed to establish that psychological records contained exculpatory evidence); Goldsmith v. State, 337 Md. 112, 651 A.2d 866 (1995) (holding that a defendant's assertion that the complainant's psychotherapy records were relevant for assessment of the victim's credibility was not a sufficient foundation for disclosing the records, and that the defendant had failed to establish that disclosure of the records would likely yield relevant information); Commonwealth v. Tripolone, 425 Mass. 487, 681 N.E.2d 1216 (1997); Commonwealth v. Fuller, 423 Mass. 216, 667 N.E.2d 847 (1996) (Massachusetts' Supreme Court holds that "likely to be relevant" standard for review of rape crisis records is too broad since "disclosure, even in the limited form of an *in camera* inspection, should not become the general exception to the rule of confidentiality." It felt that there should be a routine *in camera* inspection of rape crisis records, and concluded that "[a] judge should undertake an [in camera] review of [privileged] records. . . only when a defendant's motion of production of the records has demonstrated a good faith, specific, and reasonable basis for believing that the records will contain exculpatory evidence which is relevant and material to the issue of the defendant's guilt. By 'material evidence' we mean evidence which is not likely to meet criteria of admissibility, but which also tends to create a reasonable doubt that might not otherwise exist." *Id.* at 226, 667 N.E.2d at 855. Court gave the example of a complainant fabricating or a showing of bias or a complainant having difficulty distinguishing fantasy from reality); Commonwealth v. Pelosi, 55 Mass. App. Ct. 390, 771 N.E.2d 795 (2002) (holding defendants did not sufficiently establish that child's counseling records should be disclosed because they might show mother's bias, evidence of suggestive interview techniques, or that information was not otherwise available. Defendant also had the opportunity to cross-examine mother, children, and counselors about interviewing techniques and circumstances of disclosure); People v. Stanaway, 446 Mich. 643, 681–82, 521 N.W.2d 557, 576 (1994), *cert. denied*, 513 U.S. 1121 (1995) (Michigan's Supreme Court holds that it is insufficient to claim that the records are necessary to search for possible prior inconsistent statements since this is a general assertion the records may contain useful evidence); State v. Hummel, 483 N.W.2d 68, 72 (Minn. 1992) (holding that defendant failed to justify an *in camera* review of victim's mental health records); State v. Gonzales, 121 N.M. 421, 426–27, 912 P.2d 297, 302–03 (1996) (When the defendant makes a showing that privileged records may reasonably be expected to provide information material to the defense, the court should conduct an *in camera* review of the records, and the failure to produce the records will result in suppressing victim's testimony. However, "[a] general assertion that inspection of the records is needed for a possible attack on the victim's credibility is insufficient to meet this threshold showing." *Id.* at 426, 912 P.2d at 302); People v. Buchholz, 23 A.D.3d 1093, 805 N.Y.S.2d 763 (2005) ("Contrary to the contention of defendant, County Court properly precluded him from presenting the testimony of

as opposed to explicit denial of abuse is not a reason to provide defendant with a victim's privileged psychotherapy records.[75]

Sometimes this requirement has been phrased so that the party seeking confidential information must establish a "factual predicate" that there is some information in the confidential records that would establish "the unreliability of either the criminal charge or the complaining witness."[76] When such a factual showing cannot be made, a subpoena for confidential records may be quashed.[77] Other courts have held that "a defendant must establish a reasonable likelihood that the privileged records contain exculpatory information" before being entitled to such records.[78] California's Supreme Court has noted that:

> It is not adequate to simply contend that "all psychological records will provide evidence of the existence or nonexistence of said molestations" or "are necessary to prove the victim's lack of credibility, her propensity to

a psychologist who treated his daughter. Defendant failed to present a sufficient factual predicate to overcome the psychologist/patient privilege." *Id.* at 1094, 805 N.Y.S.2d at 765); People v. Arredondo, 226 A.D.2d 322, 642 N.Y.S.2d 630, *appeal denied*, 88 N.Y.2d 964, 670 N.E.2d 1350, 647 N.Y.S.2d 718 (1996) ("It was a proper exercise of discretion for the trial court to have denied defendant's request for disclosure of the psychological records of the complainant since he failed to sustain his burden of showing a factual predicate that the records could establish the unreliability of the victim or provide a motive to falsify." *Id.* at 322, 642 N.Y.S.2d at 631); People v. Lussier, 205 A.D.2d 910, 613 N.Y.S.2d 466, *appeal denied*, 83 N.Y.2d 1005, 640 N.E.2d 154, 616 N.Y.S.2d 486 (1994), *cert. denied*, 513 U.S. 1078 (1995) (ruling that trial court had properly precluded a psychological report by the victim's school psychologist when the defense had raised issue only of victim's general credibility and "that defendant failed to sustain his burden of showing a factual predicate that the record could establish the unreliability of the victim or provide a motive to falsify"); State v. Roy, 194 W. Va. 276, 460 S.E.2d 277 (1995):

> Although we refuse to adopt a blanket rule denying a criminal defendant access to all information protected by statute, we believe the defendant has the initial burden to demonstrate a need for an *in camera* inspection. We hold that before any *in camera* inspection of statutorily protected communications can be justified, the defendant must show both the relevancy. . . and a legitimate need for access to the communications. . . . This preliminary showing is not met by bald and unilluminating allegations that the protected communications could be relevant or that the very circumstances of the communications indicate they are likely to be relevant or material to the case. Similarly, an assertion that inspection of the communication is needed only for a possible attack on credibility is also rejected.

Id. at 284, 460 S.E.2d at 286).

[75] State v. Reed, 173 Or. App. 185, 21 P.3d 137 (2001) (finding trial court's *in camera* review properly found no reason to disclose victim's psychotherapy records to defense since the records did not tend to exonerate the defendant; court noted defendant was free to comment on witness' failure to report the abuse earlier).

[76] *In re* Covenant House/Under 21, 169 A.D.2d 723, 564 N.Y.S.2d 473 (1991) (In this sexual assault trial, the defendant subpoenaed records from an agency that assists runaway and homeless youth whose records are deemed confidential by state statutory and regulatory provisions.).

[77] *Id.*

[78] *Goldsmith*, 337 Md. at 133, 651 A.2d at 877. *See also* State v. Roy, 194 W. Va. 276, 460 S.E.2d 277 (1995).

fantasize and imagine events that never occurred." Such a holding would essentially result in an *in camera* hearing in any case where the complaining witness had received psychiatric/psychological counseling.[79]

Likewise, Massachusetts' Supreme Court has ruled that there should not be a standard that "would result in virtually automatic *in camera* inspection for an entire class of extremely private and sensitive privileged material."[80]

A victim's psychiatric records are properly withheld from a defendant when an *in camera* review reveals no evidence of delusions, failure of recollection, sexual fantasies, or false reports of sexual assault.[81]

---

[79] People v. Hammon, 15 Cal. 4th 1117, 1121, 938 P.2d 986, 988, 65 Cal. Rptr. 2d 1, 3 (1997), *cert. denied*, 522 U.S. 1125 (1998), *citing* trial court's decision.

[80] Commonwealth v. Fuller, 423 Mass. 216, 224, 667 N.E.2d 847, 854 (1996).

[81] United States v. Antone, 981 F.2d 1059, 1061 (9th Cir. 1992); United States v. Butt, 955 F.2d 77, 81 (1st Cir. 1992); Gunter v. State, 313 Ark. 504, 512–13, 857 S.W.2d 156, 161 (1993); State v. James G., 268 Conn. 382, 402–04, 844 A.2d 810, 823–24 (2004) (upholding trial court's withholding of confidential school and Department of Children and Families records, since they did not contain exculpatory or impeaching evidence or relate to her ability to relate the truth); State v. Slimskey, 257 Conn. 842, 779 A.2d 723 (2001) (reversing defendant's conviction due to trial court's failure to disclose to defendant the complainant's school records, including psychological or psychiatric records which reflected that victim "is prone to distort his perception of reality of paranoid and persecutorial ideas" and had "concocted a story about being victimized" and other reports that child acting out sexually and fabricating stories); People v. Foggy, 121 Ill. 2d 337, 349–50, 521 N.E.2d 86, 91 (1988); State v. Judge, 758 So. 2d 313, 317 (La. Ct. App. 2000) ("This proffered evidence did not show the victim's medical history was relevant to show the attack by her uncle was a figment of her imagination. The hallucinations were arguably medically induced and have not occurred since shortly after her release from the hospital, at the latest. There was no evidence that she previously suffered from blackouts or that her bouts with depression could have caused her to imagine this incident. Therefore, we conclude that the trial judge did not err in refusing to allow the Defendant to question the witnesses about the victim's prior medical history." *Id.* at 317); State v. Hutchinson, 597 A.2d 1344, 1346–41 (Me. 1991); Commonwealth v. Tripolone, 425 Mass. 487, 681 N.E.2d 1216 (1997); Commonwealth v. Bishop, 416 Mass. 169, 177–78, 617 N.E.2d 990, 995 (1993) (requiring that a defendant submit in writing theories under which the particular records sought are "likely to be relevant" to an issue in the case. *Id.* at 181, 617 N.E.2d at 997); Commonwealth v. Syrafos, 38 Mass. App. Ct. 211, 646 N.E.2d 429, *review denied*, 420 Mass. 1102, 648 N.E.2d 1285 (1995) (no showing that counseling records of complainant's past abuse were relevant to her confusing two incidents of sexual abuse); People v. Stanaway, 446 Mich. 643, 677–78, 521 N.W.2d 557, 574 (1994); People v. Brown, 24 A.D.3d 884, 806 N.Y.S.2d 262 (2005) ("Precluding cross-examination regarding the victim's counseling sessions was appropriate given the absence of any factual basis that the victim suffered from hallucinations or fantasies or had previously made any false claims of sexual assault" *Id.* at 887, 806 N.Y.S.2d at 265); People v. Duran, 276 A.D.2d 498, 713 N.Y.S.2d 561, *appeal denied*, 95 N.Y.2d 963, 745 N.E.2d 400, 722 N.Y.S.2d 480 (2000) (holding trial court properly declined to review complainant's psychiatric records since there was no showing that there was a "reasonable likelihood" that records contained information bearing on complainant's reliability such as a history of paranoia, hallucinations, delusions, or false claims of sexual attack); People v. Kukon, 275 A.D.2d 478, 711 N.Y.S.2d 870, *appeal denied*, 95 N.Y.2d 936, 744 N.E.2d 148, 721 N.Y.S.2d 612 (2000) (finding trial court properly refused to release victim's psychiatric records since there was no evidence that victim was confused about identity of abuser or suffered from symptoms

Psychiatric records may be confidential but disclosable upon a finding by a court that the interest of justice outweighs the need for confidentiality. The type of issues and facts that overcome the need for confidentiality can be generalized as information, material, or events bearing on the "reliability and accuracy of the witness' testimony."[82]

of child sexual abuse accommodation syndrome as a result of an "unspecified molestation occurring years before the incidents alleged in the indictment"); People v. Fish, 235 A.D.2d 578, 652 N.Y.S.2d 124, *appeal denied*, 89 N.Y.2d 1092, 682 N.E.2d 987, 660 N.Y.S.2d 386 (1997); People v. Arredondo, 226 A.D.2d 322, 642 N.Y.S.2d 630, *appeal denied*, 88 N.Y.2d 964, 670 N.E.2d 1350, 647 N.Y.S.2d 718 (1996); People v. Gutkaiss, 206 A.D.2d 628, 614 N.Y.S.2d 599, *appeal denied*, 84 N.Y.2d 936, 645 N.E.2d 1233, 621 N.Y.S.2d 533 (1994) (defendant's constitutional rights not violated by trial court's *in camera* review of victim's school counseling and medical records); People v. Lussier, 205 A.D.2d 910, 613 N.Y.S.2d 466, *appeal denied*, 83 N.Y.2d 1005, 640 N.E.2d 154, 616 N.Y.S.2d 486 (1994), *cert. denied*, 513 U.S. 1078 (1995) (ruling that trial court had properly precluded a psychological report by the victim's school psychologist when the defense had raised issue only of victim's general credibility and "that defendant failed to sustain his burden of showing a factual predicate that the record could establish the unreliability of the victim or provide a motive to falsify"); People v. Graham, 117 A.D.2d 832, 498 N.Y.S.2d 730 (1986) (upholding trial court's decision to withhold from defense a rape victim's psychiatric records that did not reveal hallucinations or false allegations. The psychiatric records were sealed by the court and made a court exhibit so that they could be reviewed by the appellate court); State v. Rice, 755 A.2d 137, 150–52 (R.I. 2001) (upholding trial judge's decision to seal victim's medical records with respect to her attempted suicide which was irrelevant to her state of mind or credibility); State v. Kholi, 672 A.2d 429, 436–37 (R.I. 1996) ("In the instant case we hold that the trial justice's *in camera* review of the privileged information struck the requisite balance between defendant's constitutional right to effective cross-examination and [complainant's] right to confidentiality." *Id.* at 437); State v. Ball, 2004 SD 9, 675 N.W.2d 192 (2004), *rev'd on other grounds* (holding while complainant's statements in child protective records were relevant, they were not different from her statements in defendant's possession and court was within its discretion in not releasing the confidential social services records); State v. Cates, 632 N.W.2d 28, 35–36 (S.D. 2001); State v. Kalakosky, 121 Wash. 2d 525, 549–50, 852 P.2d 1064, 1077 (1993); State v. McIntosh, 207 W. Va. 561, 534 S.E.2d 757 (2000) (Court noted that party seeking to use evidence of mental disability has burden of establishing that such evidence affects credibility. "Evidence of psychiatric disability may be introduced when it affects the credibility of a material witness' testimony in a criminal case. Before such psychiatric disorder can be shown to impeach a witness' testimony, there must be a further showing that the disorder affects the credibility of the witness and that the expert has had a sufficient opportunity to make the diagnosis of psychiatric disorder." *Id.* at 577, 534 S.E.2d at 773); State v. Richard A. P., 223 Wis. 2d 777, 589 N.W.2d 674 (1998), *review denied*, 225 Wis. 2d 489, 594 N.W.2d 383 (1999) (appellate court upheld trial court's *in camera* review of victim's mental health records which disclosed defense victim's prior sexual abuse, physical and verbal abuse by mother, record of phone call to her mother two weeks prior to alleged offense that she wanted them to suffer and was angry over her parents' behavior; appellate court noted that trial court disclosed information beyond its stated standard of disclosing information which reflects information, a motive to lie, or inability to perceive reality or understand the difference between truth and reality); State v. Shiffra, 175 Wis. 2d 600, 607, 499 N.W.2d 719, 722 (1993); State v. Mainiero, 525 N.W.2d 304 (Wis. Ct. App. 1994) (*in camera* review of victim's psychiatric records appropriately protected defendant's rights. Furthermore, prosecution did not rely on any expert testimony, nor did it rely on or introduce any portion of the complainant's records).

[82] People v. Arnold, 177 A.D.2d 633, 634, 576 N.Y.S.2d 339, 340 (1991), *appeal denied*, 79 N.Y.2d 853, 588 N.E.2d 759, 580 N.Y.S.2d 724 (1992).

When there is an indication that a witness or complainant suffers from a serious mental illness at or about the time period relating to the witness' testimony, the psychiatric records are more likely disclosable.[83]

If a showing can be made that reflects psychological issues relating to cognitive abilities or ability to testify accurately, the records may be relevant. This is particularly true when the records raise an issue of the victim's perception of reality and fabrication of stories on victimization.[84]

A defense theory that a complainant "is a troubled maladjusted child whose past trauma has caused her to make a false accusation" in conjunction with a good faith statement that she suffered previous sexual abuse by a biological father, the non-resolution of which produced a false accusation, represents a sufficient threshold showing of "a reasonable probability that the records contain material information necessary" to the defense requiring an *in camera* inspection.[85]

---

[83] United States v. Lindstrom, 698 F.2d 1154 (11th Cir. 1983); United States v. Partin, 493 F.2d 750 (5th Cir. 1974).

[84] State v. Slimskey, 257 Conn. 842, 779 A.2d 723 (2001) (reversing defendant's conviction due to trial court's failure to disclose to defendant the complainant's school records, including psychological or psychiatric records which reflected that victim "is prone to distort his perception of reality of paranoid and persecutorial ideas" and had "concocted a story about being victimized" and other reports that child acting out sexually and fabricating stories); State v. Webb, 75 Conn. App. 447, 817 A.2d 122, *appeal denied*, 263 Conn. 919, 822 A.2d 244 (2003) (finding trial court should have disclosed confidential records as to victim's visual and auditory hallucinations while smoking cocaine but that error was harmless); Commonwealth v. Barroso, 122 S.W.3d 554 (Ky. 2003); People v. Baranek, 287 A.D.2d 74, 733 N.Y.S.2d 704 (2001):

> Where a primary prosecution witness is shown to suffer from a psychiatric condition, the defense is entitled to show that the witness' capacity to perceive and recall events was impaired by that condition [citation omitted] . . . . The complainant's psychiatric history dated back to 1977, with multiple hospitalizations including involuntary confinement to a psychiatric hospital one year before the incident. Notably, during her most recent hospitalization, the complainant suffered from auditory hallucinations and delusions that people were breaking into her home. The defense should have been permitted to question the complainant about these delusions since he was charged with breaking into her home. The trial court's restriction on the scope of cross-examination was fundamentally unfair, particularly since the People's case was based almost entirely upon the complainant's eyewitness testimony . . . . The trial court also erred in precluding the defense from offering expert testimony regarding the complainant's psychiatric condition [citation omitted] . . . . While the resolution of whether the complainant was competent to testify under oath was the trial court's exclusive responsibility, the determination of the complainant's credibility and the weight to be given her testimony was the province of the jury [citation omitted].

[85] *Stanaway*, 446 Mich. at 682, 521 N.W.2d at 576. *See also* Commonwealth v. Pare, 43 Mass. App. Ct. 566, 686 N.E.2d 1025 (1997), *superseded*, 427 Mass. 427, 693 N.E.2d 1002 (1998) (reversing defendant's conviction due to trial court's failure to disclose "sexual information and trauma team" records of a ten-year-old child who had made false sexual abuse charges, who became suicidal as a result of a "dysfunctional family situation" which records also revealed problems of memory, perception, and recollection, and a "pattern of blaming and accusing those who frustrated or angered complainant").

When there is an indication that the complainant has given inconsistent statements concerning the sexual assault, this may provide a basis for the court to review privileged counseling records.[86] When the counseling records do raise an issue of the child's credibility, it may be reversible error to deny a defendant *in camera* review of the psychiatric or counseling records.[87]

There are ways the privilege may be broken or waived. The prosecution's questioning of a complainant who elicits information provided to a counselor may open the door to the counseling records.[88] Merely testifying about conversations with a therapist[89] or testimony by the therapist[90] does not necessarily waive the confidentiality of counseling records. The disclosure of privileged information to third parties, as with other privileges, opens the door to previously protected communications.[91]

Some courts find that only the complainant can release her counseling records. However, if the complainant does not release the records for review by the court, the complainant's testimony may be precluded.[92] A complainant may waive the applicable privilege for the limited purpose of allowing an *in camera* inspection of her counseling records.[93] A defendant may not waive his daughter's privilege

---

[86] State v. Karlen, 1999 S.D. 12, 589 N.W.2d 594 (1999).

[87] State v. Walther, 240 Wis. 2d 619, 623 N.W.2d 205 (2000)(reversing defendant's conviction due to trial court's failure to conduct an *in camera* review of psychiatric and counseling records, since defendant established more than a "mere possibility" that records may be necessary and fair determination of guilt or innocence).

[88] State v. Karlen, 1999 S.D. 12, 589 N.W.2d 594 (1999) (noting that state may not use the counseling privilege as both a sword and shield).

[89] State v. Kholi, 672 A.2d 429, 436 (R.I. 1996).

[90] Dill v. People, 927 P.2d 1315, 1321 (Colo. 1996) (noting that this depends on whether the therapist's testimony is based on the privileged records or not).

[91] State v. Catch the Bear, 352 N.W.2d 640, 647 (S.D. 1984).

[92] State v. Luna, 122 N.M. 143, 921 P.2d 950 (1996) (complainant refused to comply with court ordered *in camera* review of her counseling records leading to preclusion of her testimony. However, appellate court noted that the prosecution failed to raise the argument that defendant had made an insufficient showing to justify the *in camera* review of the records.). *See also* State v. Francis, 70 Conn. App. 571, 800 A.2d 574 (2002) (appeals court reversed defendant's conviction due to trial court's failure to disclose treatment records of complaining witness, "U").

> After our own thorough review of U's treatment record, we are persuaded by the defendant's argument that the court abused its discretion and improperly refused to disclose the record. Because we are persuaded that the failure to disclose the record impaired both the defendant's rights to present a defense and to impeach a witness, we will address each claim in turn. We note at the outset that we will not divulge specific information or the details of what our *in camera* review has revealed because U may decide to preclude the disclosure of his record at the new trial. [citation omitted]. Consistent with the procedure for disclosing confidential documents, U must consent to the disclosure and waive his privilege so that his treatment record may be disclosed to the defendant. If such waiver is not provided, U's record will not be disclosed and his testimony may be stricken. [citation omitted]

[93] State v. Kelly, 208 Conn. 365, 545 A.2d 1048 (1988), *habeas corpus proceeding, remanded sub nom.* Kelly v. Meachum, 950 F. Supp. 461 (D. Conn. 1996).

to benefit himself.[94] Testifying that one takes prescription medication that alters one's behavior does not necessarily waive a victim's privilege of respect to her psychological records.[95] It may be reversible error when the trial court withholds the complainant's psychiatric records despite a full waiver of confidentiality and such a waiver negates the necessity of an *in camera* review or gate keeping function by the trial court.[96]

When the records do not show any psychosis, mental defect, or deficiency, and do not in any way support a theory that the witness has fabricated charges, there is no reason to release confidential and sensitive information.[97]

For example, a history of blackouts may affect the ability to testify.[98] Past sexual abuse may be part of the counseling history. If the records raise an issue as to whether the complainant is confusing incidents of abuse or the complainant's credibility is affected by prior abuse, the records may be relevant.[99] If the counseling records reflect no such effect upon credibility or ability to perceive and recall, however, the records[100] are likely to be non-disclosable.

---

[94] People v. Buchholz, 23 A.D.3d 1093, 805 N.Y.S.2d 763 (2005).

[95] People v. Higgins, 12 A.D.3d 775, 784 N.Y.S.2d 232 (2004), *appeal denied*, 4 N.Y.3d 764, 825 N.E.2d 139, 792 N.Y.S.2d 7 (2005) ("Contrary to defendant's argument, the victim did not waive the privilege merely by testifying that she was taking prescription medication that would alter her behavior. The victim was not a party to this criminal action and her mental status was not at issue in the case." [citation omitted] *Id.* at 777, 784 N.Y.S.2d at 234).

[96] State v. Palladino, 69 Conn. App. 630, 796 A.2d 577 (2002). *See also*, State v. Sells, 82 Conn. App. 332, 844 A.2d 235 (2004) (since child's guardian consented to release of records, they were no longer confidential and should have been released to defendant, but error was harmless).

[97] United States v. Antone, 981 F.2d 1059, 1061 (9th Cir. Ariz. 1992); United States v. Butt, 955 F.2d 77, 81 (1st Cir. Mass. 1992).

[98] State v. Gonzales, 121 N.M. 421, 912 P.2d 297 (1996) (trial court properly required disclosure of records reflecting complainant's history of blackouts and its effect upon her cognitive difficulties).

[99] Commonwealth v. Baxter, 36 Mass. App. Ct. 45, 627 N.E.2d 487 (1994) (showing made that counseling records of complainant's past abuse affected her ability to perceive and recall events in instant case); People v. Kukon, 275 A.D.2d 478, 711 N.Y.S.2d 870, *appeal denied*, 95 N.Y.2d 936, 744 N.E.2d 148, 721 N.Y.S.2d 612 (2000) (finding trial court properly refused to release victim's psychiatric records since there was no evidence that victim was confused about identity of abuser or suffered from symptoms of child sexual abuse accommodation syndrome as a result of an "unspecified molestation occurring years before the incidents alleged in the indictment."). *See* discussion in § 5.40. Evidence of prior sexual history or prior sexual abuse and allegations to show confusion on witness' part "or qualities as percipient witness."

[100] Commonwealth v. Syrafos, 38 Mass. App. Ct. 211, 646 N.E.2d 429, *review denied*, 420 Mass. 1102, 648 N.E.2d 1285 (1995) (no showing that counseling records of complainant's past abuse were relevant to her confusing two incidents of sexual abuse).

People v. Baranek, 287 A.D.2d 74, 733 N.Y.S.2d 704 (2001):

> Where a primary prosecution witness is shown to suffer from a psychiatric condition, the defense is entitled to show that the witness' capacity to perceive and recall events was impaired by that condition [citation omitted] . . . . The complainant's psychiatric history dated back to 1977, with multiple hospitalizations including

It may make a difference in the discoverability of psychiatric or counseling records if the records are already in the possession of the prosecution. When the prosecution possesses the complainant's psychological records, or has inspected them, they are more likely to be discoverable.[101] When the counseling records are not in the prosecution's possession, a defendant's right of confrontation and compulsory process are more likely not violated by withholding from the defendant privileged counseling records.[102]

In general, the prosecution is "under no duty to investigate the psychiatric history of the victim and obtain her psychiatric records."[103] When the prosecution does not possess the complainant's psychological or counseling records, there is little question of any duty to produce the records as exculpatory evidence.

---

involuntary confinement to a psychiatric hospital one year before the incident. Notably, during her most recent hospitalization, the complainant suffered from auditory hallucinations and delusions that people were breaking into her home. The defense should have been permitted to question the complainant about these delusions since he was charged with breaking into her home. The trial court's restriction on the scope of cross-examination was fundamentally unfair, particularly since the People's case was based almost entirely upon the complainant's eyewitness testimony . . . . The trial court also erred in precluding the defense from offering expert testimony regarding the complainant's psychiatric condition [citation omitted] . . . . While the resolution of whether the complainant was competent to testify under oath was the trial court's exclusive responsibility, the determination of the complainant's credibility and the weight to be given her testimony was the province of the jury [citation omitted].

[101] Commonwealth v. Davis, 437 Pa. Super. 471, 650 A.2d 452 (1994) (holding that any privilege protecting a victim's family therapy counseling records was waived by the victim and his family when they permitted the Commonwealth to have access to the records, which they now sought to shield from the defense); Barker v. Commonwealth, 230 Va. 370, 337 S.E.2d 729 (1985) (making the distinction between psychiatric records not in the possession, custody, or control of the prosecution and those records which are in the prosecution's possession, which would then be disclosable pursuant to *Brady*); State v. Speese, 199 Wis. 2d 597, 545 N.W.2d 510 (1995) (holding any error in failing to provide records to the defendant was harmless).

[102] Commonwealth v. Patosky, 440 Pa. Super. 535, 656 A.2d 499, *appeal denied*, 542 Pa. 664, 668 A.2d 1128 (1995); Commonwealth v. Smith, 414 Pa. Super. 208, 606 A.2d 939 (1992), *appeal denied*, 533 Pa. 624, 620 A.2d 490 (1993); Commonwealth v. Kennedy, 413 Pa. Super. 95, 604 A.2d 1036, *appeal denied*, 531 Pa. 638, 611 A.2d 711 (1992).

[103] People v. Sealey, 239 A.D.2d 864, 659 N.Y.S.2d 639, *appeal denied*, 90 N.Y.2d 910, 686 N.E.2d 234, 663 N.Y.S.2d 522 (1997). *See also* People v. Sakadinsky, 239 A.D.2d 443, 657 N.Y.S.2d 754, *appeal denied*, 90 N.Y.2d 897, 685 N.E.2d 221, 662 N.Y.S.2d 440 (1997) ("[T]he People have no affirmative duty to investigate the psychiatric history of all potential prosecution witnesses." *Id.*, 657 N.Y.S.2d at 755); State v. Chavis, 141 N.C. App. 553, 540 S.E.2d 404 (2000) (holding since defendant presented no evidence that prosecution had complainant's medical or psychiatric records or that such information was favorable to the defendant, prosecution had "no obligation to disclose and obtain" such records); State v. Bacon, 1998 Tenn. Crim. App. LEXIS 31 (Jan. 8, 1998) (noting that with respect to any prior sexual abuse allegations, state has no duty to cast a dragnet investigation into the victim's past conduct without being on some notice that "non-trivial" information existed. *Id.* at 29–30).

§ 1.9   Access to rape crisis counseling records.

Other counseling records that may be involved in a sexual assault case are those of rape crisis centers. Rape crisis counseling records may provide information concerning a complainant's description of the assailant and details of how the sexual assault occurred, as well as details of the victim's life. These details may be quite personal, and defendants' attorneys will argue that they should be able to review such records to determine what information is helpful to their client.

Rape crisis centers do not necessarily enjoy a blanket statutory protection; increasingly, however, states have found some form of privilege or confidentiality for sexual assault victims' communications to rape crisis workers.[104] Many of these statutes are to provide for an *in camera* review of those records rather than making the records available to a defendant's counsel without any showing of necessity and without traditional review. *In camera* review represents the best possible balancing of a defendant's right to a fair trial, and the need to maintain the effectiveness of the counselor-victim relationship and absolute privilege is

---

[104] *See, e.g.,* N.Y. Civ. Prac. L. & R., § 4510 ("A rape crisis counselor shall not be required to disclose a communication made by his or her client to him or her, or advice given thereon, in the course of his or her services. . . nor shall any records made in the course of the services given to the client or recording of any communications made by or to a client be required to be disclosed, nor shall the client be compelled to disclose such communication records"); N.Y. Crim. Proc. Law § 60.76 (When rape crisis records are sought on the ground that privilege has been waived or disclosure is constitutionally required, "the party seeking disclosure must file a written motion supported by an affidavit containing specific factual allegations providing grounds that disclosure is required. Upon the filing of such motion and affidavit, the court shall conduct an *in camera* review of the communication outside the presence of the jury and of counsel for all parties in order to determine whether disclosure of any portion of the communication is required."); 42 PA. Cons. Stat. § 5945.1(b). No sexual assault counselor may, without the written consent of the victim, disclose the victim's confidential oral or written communications to the counselor nor consent to be examined in any court or criminal proceeding. *See, e.g.,* Conn. Gen. Stat. § 52-146(K) After detailed definitions of battered women's center, battered women's counselor, confidential communication, rape crisis center, sexual assault counselor, and victim, this statute states:

> (b) On or after October 1, 1983, a battered women's counselor or a sexual assault counselor shall not disclose any confidential communications made to such counselor at any time by a victim in any civil or criminal case or proceeding or in any legislative or administrative proceeding unless the victim making the confidential communications waives the privilege, provided under no circumstances shall the location of the battered women's center or rape crisis center or the identity of the battered women's counselor or sexual assault counselor be disclosed in any civil or criminal proceeding. Any request made on or after October 1, 1983, by the defendant or the state for such confidential communications shall be subject to the provisions of this subsection . . . .
> (d) A minor may knowingly waive the privilege established by this section. In any instance where the minor is, in the opinion of the court, incapable of knowingly waiving the privilege, the parent or guardian of the minor may waive the privilege on behalf of the minor, provided such parent or guardian is not the defendant and does not have a relationship with the defendant such that he has an interest in the outcome of the proceeding.

more likely to generate a constitutional challenge.[105] Some courts have held that a defendant has an absolute right to rape crisis records in the possession of the prosecution and that a trial judge's *in camera* review is insufficient to protect a defendant's right.[106] Individual statutes must be carefully read to determine the breadth of coverage as well as exceptions to the counseling privilege. For example, there may be no privilege when a sexual assault counselor has knowledge that a complainant has given perjured testimony.[107] As with other records relating to a complainant, a court may require a defendant to make a threshold showing of a need for an *in camera* inspection of rape crisis records.[108] Also, as with other privileges, the privilege is aimed at communications, not necessarily the fact of the relationship. Those portions of rape crisis counseling records which set forth the date, time, and fact of communication between a complainant and counselor may not be considered privileged.[109]

A defendant who establishes that the complainant's conversations with the rape crisis counselor were the "turning point in the case" sets forth a sufficient basis to warrant an *in camera* review of rape crisis counseling records.[110] This is so,

---

[105] *In re* Robert H., 199 Conn. 693, 709, 509 A.2d 475, 485 (1986) (noting that an absolute counselor-victim privilege would violate the defendant's confrontation rights).

[106] Commonwealth v. Miller, 399 Pa. Super. 180, 582 A.2d 4 (1990), *appeal granted*, 530 Pa. 641, 607 A.2d 251 (1992), *citing* Commonwealth v. Lloyd, 523 Pa. 427, 567 A.2d 1357 (1989); (The court in *Miller* agreed with defendant's contention that the rape crisis records "may have contained useful information regarding the motives and mental abilities of the victims." *Id.* at 183, 582 A.2d at 6.).

[107] *See, e.g.,* Conn. Gen. Stat. § 52-146K(e): The privilege established by this section shall not apply: (1) In matters of proof concerning chain of custody of evidence; (2) in matters of proof concerning the physical appearance of the victim at the time of the injury; or (3) where the battered women's counselor or sexual assault counselor has knowledge that the victim has given perjured testimony and the defendant or the state has made an offer of proof that perjury may have been committed.

[108] People v. Thiam, 232 A.D.2d 199, 647 N.Y.S.2d 763, *appeal denied*, 89 N.Y.2d 930, 677 N.E.2d 305, 654 N.Y.S.2d 733 (1996) (holding defendant made insufficient showing of need for an *in camera* inspection of rape crisis center counseling records, *citing* N.Y. Crim. Proc. Law § 60.76).

[109] Commonwealth v. Neumyer, 432 Mass. 23, 28–29, 731 N.E.2d 1053, 1058 (2000) (decision cites cases where this information is not within the scope of other privileges).

[110] *Id.* at 31–33, 731 N.E.2d at 1060–61 (2000):

The key point in the affidavit was that the victim had testified at the probable cause hearing that she only formed the opinion that she was raped after speaking with a rape crisis counselor. The affidavit further stated that the victim testified at the probable cause hearing that she (1) had intercourse with her best friend's boy friend, the defendant, and had not told anyone because she did not want to ruin her friendship with her best friend; (2) vacillated as to whether she "had intercourse" with the defendant or "only oral sex;" (3) was involved in alcohol and drug activity on the night of the alleged incident; (4) lied to her grandmother about the events of that night; (5) continued to socialize with the defendant after the incident, including spending the night of July 3 in his bedroom; (6) was extremely susceptible to

particularly when a "confluence of factors" such as the complainant's emotional state, level of uncertainty about what transpired and the conditions under which she observed events, drug or alcohol use, suggest a real possibility of false allegation.[111]

Information in rape crisis counseling records that a victim had been in conflict with her mother and had undergone therapy with her mother because of physical health problems is "relevant on the issue of the complainant's motives to fabricate a rape accusation in order to avoid parental disapproval of her misconduct."[112]

The privilege may also be breached by testimony of a rape crisis counselor concerning statements made to her by a complainant or if the prosecution obtains access to information of the sexual assault counselor.[113] The privilege is not necessarily breached, however, by signing a consent form permitting disclosure to the police as in the case where the counselor has a statutory duty to report the abuse to the police.[114] It has been suggested that the Victims of Crime Act may provide a shield for the disclosure of rape crisis records in certain situations.[115] This law states:

> Except as otherwise provided by Federal law . . . no recipient of sums under
> this chapter, shall use or reveal any research or statistical information

---

manipulation by peer pressure; and (7) was under treatment for depression and had been prescribed Prozac (apparently at the time of the incident) . . . . The affidavit clearly sets forth sufficient factors to support the judge's conclusion that the conversations of the victim, an 18-year-old young woman, with the counselor were the "turning point" in the case. The victim had been uncertain previously whether she had been raped and she suffered from an impaired memory of the events due to intoxication. Based on the conversations with the counselor, she ultimately concluded that she had been raped and criminal proceedings were instituted. The judge accurately considered the "calls" the "turning point" and concluded that a fact finder could well be influenced by the content of these calls which caused the complainant to become certain of her situation. Further, the exact content of the calls is material that may not be obtained elsewhere; the victim was the only other party to the calls and the accuracy of her memory was questionable. The proffer is clearly sufficient to support the judge's determination that there was a good faith, specific, and reasonable basis for believing that the records would contain exculpatory evidence relevant and material to the defense of the case and that this material could not be obtained from other sources.

[111] *Id.*

[112] Commonwealth v. Fitzgerald, 412 Mass. 516, 525, 590 N.E.2d 1151, 1156 (1992) (noting that review of rape crisis records in Massachusetts is by the defendant's attorney pursuant to Commonwealth v. Stockhammer, 409 Mass. 867, 883–84, 570 N.E.2d 992, 1002 (1991)).

[113] Commonwealth v. Davis, 437 Pa. Super. 471, 486–87, 650 A.2d 452, 460 (1994); Commonwealth v. Gibbs, 434 Pa. Super. 280, 642 A.2d 1132 (1994). *See also* State v. Gonzales, 121 N.M. 421, 912 P.2d 297 (1996) (complainant's release of her medical records to police and prosecutor constituted waiver of her privilege).

[114] Commonwealth v. Askew, 446 Pa. Super. 301, 666 A.2d 1062 (1995), *appeal denied*, 546 Pa. 635, 683 A.2d 876 (1996).

[115] United States v. Alexander, 1996 U.S. App. LEXIS 1662 at * 17–18 (Jan. 18, 1996).

furnished under this chapter by any person and identifiable to any specific private person for any purpose other than the purpose for which such information was obtained in accordance with this chapter. Such information . . . shall be immune from legal process and shall not, without the consent of the person furnishing such information, be admitted as evidence or used for any purpose in any action, suit, or other judicial, legislative, or administrative proceeding.[116]

§ 1.10   Discovery of educational records.

A discovery demand may include: (1) the academic attendance and counseling records of complainant; and (2) records, notes or evaluations of the child from day care, nursery school, or other educational centers. School records can establish dates of attendance, complaints, and behaviors that may or may not be consistent with the allegations of abuse. The relevance of a victim's educational records may depend upon the nature of the charges, the relationship between the accusations, the information sought, and the likelihood of relevant information being found from the records and the specificity of the showing made for the request.[117] If the case involves the issue of identification, ordinarily the contents of a victim's educational records will not be relevant.[118]

As previously noted, the rationale underlying the U.S. Supreme Court's decision in *Pennsylvania v. Ritchie* was the state's compelling interest in insuring confidentiality to those who have information concerning potential child abuse and may be otherwise reluctant to report those suspicions absent a granting of confidentiality by the state. Another area where this issue surfaces is in the discovery of a complainant's or witness' school records. It should also be noted that there may be differences in the law concerning educational versus rape crisis or counseling records. Confidentiality provisions relating to certain child protective, counseling, or rape crisis records may not apply to subpoenaed educational records.

One court has held that when specific information is sought from a victim's educational records, an *in camera* review of the records may be sufficient to determine the existence of such information.[119] On the other hand, when educational records are sought for the broader purpose of challenging the credibility of the victim, the same court found that providing a defense attorney with direct access to those records is essential "to bring the advocate's eye to the review of the records, thus protecting the interest of the defendant in insuring

---

[116] 42 U.S.C. § 10604(d).

[117] Zaal v. State, 326 Md. 54, 82, 602 A.2d 1247, 1260 (1992).

[118] *Id.*

[119] *Id. See also* People v. Gutkaiss, 206 A.D.2d 584, 614 N.Y.S.2d 462, *appeal denied*, 84 N.Y.2d 936, 645 N.E.2d 1233, 621 N.Y.S.2d 533 (1994) (upholding an *in camera* review of victim's school, counseling, and medical records pertaining to the suicide of victim's father, where the records were sought "merely in the hope of discovering material to impeach the victim's credibility").

that relevant, usable exculpatory or impeachment evidence is discovered."[120] The same court states that, when confidential records are reviewed by a defendant's attorney, a school board's counsel, etc., it should be as officers of the court, which will help preclude the unnecessary disclosure of confidential information.[121]

Another argument which has been advanced for the examination of school records is to assist the defense and his expert "in drawing conclusions with respect to whether the victims' learning disabilities rendered them particularly vulnerable to suggestion" in light of the interview techniques utilized.[122] The theory underlying this request is that the school records might contain results of psychological testing which would demonstrate a vulnerability to coercive or repetitive questioning.[123] One appellate court reviewing this argument held that the court properly declined the defense access to the school records after an *in camera* review and that the trial court should balance the public policy favoring confidentiality of school records, especially those of students with special needs, against the defendant's right to cross-examine and confront witnesses against him.[124] Many of the same arguments advanced for and against the disclosure of educational records are the same as those advanced when discovery of psychiatric counseling or rape crisis records are involved. Some courts will require a preliminary showing of cause before requiring that a trial court conduct an *in camera* review of school or educational records.[125] Courts are more likely to entertain a request to review educational counseling or rape crisis records when a basis is set forth explaining why the records may yield relevant information. Care must also be taken when educational records contain material, such as medical and counseling records, which may be protected by privilege or other legal rules. Furthermore, many educational and counseling records may contain information affecting the rights and privileges of third parties. However, a court may require mental health records contained in educational records to be disclosed to the defendant.[126]

---

[120] *Zaal, supra*, note 118, at 87, 602 A.2d 1247 (this approach of allowing a defendant's attorney to determine the relevancy of confidential records is a minority view. *See also* ruling of the Massachusetts Supreme Court in Commonwealth v. Stockhammer, 409 Mass. 867, 570 N.E.2d 992 (1991)).

[121] *Id.* at 86, 602 A.2d 1247.

[122] People v. Boyea, 222 A.D.2d 937, 636 N.Y.S.2d 136 (1995), *appeal denied*, 88 N.Y.2d 934, 670 N.E.2d 451, 647 N.Y.S.2d 167 (1996).

[123] *Id.*

[124] *Id., citing* 20 U.S.C. § 1232g(b).

[125] State v. James, 211 Conn. 555, 578, 560 A.2d 426, 439 (1989).

[126] State v. Slimskey, 257 Conn. 842, 779 A.2d 723 (2001) (reversing defendant's conviction due to trial court's failure to disclose to defendant the complainant's school records, including psychological or psychiatric records which reflected that victim "is prone to distort his perception of reality of paranoid and persecutorial ideas" and had "concocted a story about being victimized" and other reports that child acted out sexually and fabricated stories).

§ 1.11 Overview of issues involved in privileged or confidential records of complainant.

The following is an overview of issues and areas of analysis in dealing with confidential or privileged records. The list summarizes some of the issues raised in the preceding sections.

- Are the records privileged or confidential? If so, what is the nature of the privilege? Is it a qualified privilege? It must first be determined whether the records involved are deemed confidential or covered by a statutory privilege, thus entitling the records to greater protection. Some records may contain information gathered by individuals who are not within the scope of a legal or statutory privilege. Some records will be afforded a qualified privilege. Thus, the records desired may contain a variety of documents which range from non-privileged and non-confidential to privileged.

- Has the privileged or confidential material lost its protection? The privileged or confidential records may lose their protection in a variety of ways. For example, if a witness testifies to the privileged material, the material may be no longer protected. Also, if the prosecution has possession of the records or utilized the potentially confidential or privileged records, they may have lost their protected nature.

- Has the defendant established a sufficient basis that the protected records are material and relevant? Has more than a generalized assertion of the need for the records been set forth in the defendant's request?

- If the defendant has established the basis for an *in camera* review of the confidential or privileged records, do the records contain information which would become material or relevant?

- If the information in the privileged or confidential records is released by the court, the next issue is whether the information in the records is relevant to trial. The probative value of the records must outweigh any potential prejudice or confusion. For example, the information in the records may be relevant because they show an ability to accurately remember events, raise issues of credibility or false reporting, or explain complainant's knowledge of sexual matters. Some of these areas are discussed elsewhere in this text. On the other hand, the court may disclose information in the confidential records pertaining to past sexual abuse. Once the court releases information to the defendant, the prosecution and defense can then make arguments as to the admissibility of such information.

§ 1.12 Discovery from complainant of the complainant's diary, blood, or photographs, or access to the complainant's private residence.

Can discovery be obtained from a complainant? Some attempts have been made to obtain discovery from a complainant of items such as blood, the complainant's diary or personal notes, and photographs, and to obtain access to the complainant's private residence. Some information in a diary may be protected under the Rape Shield Statute. A victim's privacy rights do not necessarily prevent disclosure of the victim's diary. A victim's diary, or portions thereof, may be discoverable as a prior statement of a witness.[127] Other courts take the view that a personal account of a crime written by a rape victim is not discoverable as a prior statement of a witness when it is not in the possession and control of the prosecution and the complainant objects to disclosing it on the grounds of personal privacy.[128] On the theory that a subpoena should not be used to ascertain the existence of evidence, however, one court has ruled that a deceased victim's diary was not available to a defendant where the court had reviewed the diary and found nothing relevant or material to a defendant's case.[129]

A defendant may be entitled to seek a sample of the complainant's blood in a sexual assault case where a showing can be made that the blood and saliva are relevant to the issue of identification and preparation of the defendant's defense,[130] but cannot be furnished without a showing that the complainant's blood may provide probative evidence.[131] Similarly, absent a showing that a photograph of a complainant in a rape case can provide the defense with exculpatory information, a court may not order the taking of the photograph of

---

[127] State v. Enger, 539 N.W.2d 259 (Minn. Ct. App.), *review denied*, 1995 Minn. LEXIS 1068 (Dec. 20, 1995) (holding that trial court properly reviewed complainant's diary and concluded that there was no information in the diary to be disclosed to ensure fairness of the trial); State v. Shaw, 149 Vt. 275, 542 A.2d 1106, (1987) ("Because the diary entries have not been disclosed, it is impossible for defendant to demonstrate or us to find whether or not he was prejudiced. We do know that the entries related to the crucial issue in the trial, the occurrence of the sexual assault." *Id.* at 283, 542 A.2d at 1110).

[128] People v. Reedy, 70 N.Y.2d 826, 517 N.E.2d 1324, 523 N.Y.S.2d 438 (1987) ("Although there was no legally cognizable authority or foundation, the court nevertheless ordered the victim to redact private matters and to turn over to the defense at least a redacted version, instructing her to eliminate only those portions of her three-page writing not related directly to the incident." *Id.* at 827, 517 N.E.2d at 1325, 523 N.Y.S.2d at 439).

[129] People v. Chambers, 134 Misc. 2d 688, 512 N.Y.S.2d 631 (Sup. Ct. 1987) (holding that court should conduct *in camera* review rather than provide defendant's attorney with free access to the diary to determine relevancy).

[130] People v. Trocchio, 107 Misc. 2d 610, 435 N.Y.S.2d 639 (1980).

[131] People v. Manning, 156 A.D.2d 220, 548 N.Y.S.2d 481 (1989), *appeal denied*, 75 N.Y.2d 921, 554 N.E.2d 77, 555 N.Y.S.2d 40 (1990); People v. Nelson, 151 Misc. 2d 951, 574 N.Y.S.2d 144 (Sup. Ct. 1991).

a complainant, and a court does not have the power to compel the prosecution to create a piece of evidence for the defendant.[132]

When a sexual assault occurs in the complainant's private residence, the defense may want to gain access to the residence to ascertain measurements that may not have been taken by the law enforcement investigation or make other observations of the crime scene, such as lighting sources and layout of the rooms. Most courts will not permit such a discovery on the theory that such a proposed inspection is not likely to yield relevant material evidence, and that the police reports and photographs of a scene are likely to provide adequate information to defense counsel.[133]

§ 1.13 Discovery of physical evidence and motion to preserve evidence.

In sexual assault trials, physical evidence plays a key role. This is especially true with the advent of sophisticated serological testing techniques and, in particular, DNA testing. Preservation of physical evidence is also essential to help verify the results of an opposing party's laboratory analysis of the physical evidence. In this regard, it is essential to request the production of all physical evidence, particularly all items that have been tested or can be tested. In the request to preserve, it should be specified that the evidence should not only be physically preserved but also stored under conditions that will minimize any breakdown of the article, particularly of DNA. If physical evidence is destroyed after a request has been made to preserve it, there will be a greater likelihood of establishing a factual predicate necessary for dismissal or other relief.

The motion to preserve evidence need not be directed solely at physical evidence. The motion to preserve evidence can also be used to preserve all notes, tapes, and interviewing aids such as dolls, of a victim's or witnesses' interviews by law enforcement officials, hospital personnel, social service personnel, or child protective workers. In the case of non-prosecutorial agencies, it may be necessary to serve a motion or order to preserve evidence upon the agencies involved.

A defendant is more likely to obtain relief when evidence is lost or not preserved after a specific request to preserve the evidence. For example, if a defendant does not request evidence be preserved for DNA testing, he may forfeit

---

[132] Johnson v. Brandveen, 160 A.D.2d 668, 559 N.Y.S.2d 516 (1990).

[133] Bullen v. Superior Court, 204 Cal. App. 3d 22, 251 Cal. Rptr. 32 (1988) (noting that a defense request to inspect the private residence of a crime victim should be more than speculative and should demonstrate with specificity how the requested examination will assist in the ascertainment of relevant facts); People v. Poole, 123 Ill. App. 3d 375, 462 N.E.2d 810 (1984); People v. Nicholas, 157 Misc. 2d 947, 599 N.Y.S.2d 779 (1993); State ex rel. Beach v. Norblad, 308 Or. 429, 781 P.2d 349 (1989). But see State v. Lee, 461 N.W.2d 245 (Minn. Ct. App. 1990) (approving the defense access to the private residence of a crime victim, but remitting to the trial court for appropriate restrictions on the implementation of the discovery order).

any right to an adverse inference charge that the police failed to store evidence in a manner that would have permitted more effective DNA testing.[134]

§ 1.14 Loss or destruction of evidence or exhibits — Failure to collect or preserve evidence — Evidence consumed in testing.

The issue of the loss or destruction of evidence was addressed by the Supreme Court of the United States in the context of a rape case in *Ariz. v. Youngblood*.[135] *Youngblood* involved a sexual assault trial in which semen samples from the victim's body were not tested in a timely fashion and, therefore, disintegrated. Additionally the victim's clothing was not properly refrigerated and was, therefore, unable to undergo sophisticated serological testing. Prior to *Youngblood*, the Supreme Court had found that preservation of evidence was required only when the exculpatory nature of the physical evidence was clear or was established before the destruction of the evidence and there was no way of duplicating the exculpatory value of the evidence by other means.[136] *Youngblood* set forth a bad-faith requirement in the prosecution's loss or destruction of evidence before there can be a violation of the defendant's rights. The Supreme Court in *Youngblood* held:

> We therefore hold that unless a criminal defendant can show bad faith on the part of the police, failure to preserve potentially useful evidence does not constitute a denial of due process of law.

> In this case, the police collected the rectal swab and clothing on the night of the crime. Respondent was not taken into custody until six weeks later.

---

[134] People v. Mendez, 279 A.D.2d 434, 720 N.Y.S.2d 65, *appeal denied*, 96 N.Y.2d 832, 754 N.E.2d 212, 729 N.Y.S.2d 452 (2001):

> The court properly exercised its discretion in refusing to deliver an adverse inference charge regarding the prosecution's inadvertent failure to store condoms recovered from the crime scene in a manner that would have allegedly permitted more effective DNA testing. Since defendant never requested an analysis of the condoms and never expressed any interest in them until the alleged "degradation" of DNA evidence was revealed during trial, he forfeited any right that he may have had to demand an analysis or to claim that he was prejudiced by the storage methods [citation omitted]. In any event, there is no indication that better DNA testing would have produced any exculpatory evidence.

> *Id.*, 720 N.Y.S.2d at 66.

[135] 488 U.S. 51 (1988).

[136] California v. Trombetta, 467 U.S. 479 (1984) (holding that the test of whether or not the destruction of physical evidence deprives a defendant of a fair trial is "whether it deprives a defendant of *Brady* material." Court noted that *Brady* requires the prosecution to produce evidence material to the defendant's guilt or innocence. "To meet this constitutional standard of materiality, [citation omitted] evidence must possess an exculpatory value that was apparent before the evidence was destroyed and be of such a nature that the defendant would be unable to obtain comparable evidence by other reasonably available means." *Id.* at 489).

The failure of the police to refrigerate the clothing and to perform test on the semen samples can at worst be described as negligent. None of this information was concealed from respondent at trial, and the evidence — such as it was — was made available to respondent's expert who declined to perform any tests on the samples.[137]

Other courts have also found no denial of due process or prejudice in the prosecution's loss or destruction of evidence when no bad faith is established.[138] Some state courts require less than "bad faith" under state constitutional law before imposing sanctions for the loss or destruction of evidence.[139] Absent bad faith, police may return the victim's clothing.[140]

---

[137] *Youngblood*, 488 U.S. at 58. *See also* State v. Walden, 183 Ariz. 595, 905 P.2d 974 (1995), *cert. denied*, 517 U.S. 1146 (1996) (Arizona's Supreme Court declined to revisit *Youngblood* to redefine "bad faith" to include losing or misplacing evidence).

[138] United States v. Deaner, 1 F.3d 192 (3d Cir. 1993) (failing to preserve evidence which may be of use to a defendant is not denial of due process when there is no bad faith on the part of prosecution established); People v. Rodrigues, 8 Cal. 4th 1060, 885 P.2d 1, 36 Cal. Rptr. 2d 235 (1994), *cert. denied*, 516 U.S. 851 (1995) (defendant was not impermissibly prejudiced by the loss of vaginal and rectal swabs and smears and loss of photos used in pretrial identification); State v. Holden, 890 P.2d 341 (Idaho 1995) (As part of an investigation in a rape case, police seized photographs which depicted defendant and complainant nude and in sexually explicit positions. These photographs were returned to the complainant and then lost. However, the photographs were deemed to be not sufficiently probative on the issue of consent to have altered the outcome of the trial, the complainant acknowledged her past consensual relations with the defendant and the nature of the lost evidence was known, thus providing the court the opportunity to assess its significance); State v. Atley, 564 N.W.2d 817, 821, *cert. denied*, 522 U.S. 1004 (Iowa 1997) (failing to present evidence that may be potentially useful does not justify preclusion in absence of bad faith on part of police or prosecutors); State v. Friend, 493 N.W.2d 540, 545 (Minn. 1992) (no prejudice where lost or destroyed fingernail scrapings of victim was not shown to be intentional nor was exculpatory value of evidence apparent and material); People v. Feliciano, 301 A.D.2d 480, 753 N.Y.S.2d 511, *appeal denied*, 100 N.Y.2d 538, 793 N.E.2d 417, 763 N.Y.S.2d 3 (2003) (finding no need to preclude testimony on victim's allegedly bloodstained bathing suit since there was no constitutional duty to produce the bathing suit and its loss was inadvertent); People v. Callendar, 207 A.D.2d 900, 616 N.Y.S.2d 667 (1994), *appeal denied*, 84 N.Y.2d 1029, 647 N.E.2d 457, 623 N.Y.S.2d 185 (1995) (no showing of bad faith in loss of rape kit before testing); State v. Graham, 118 N.C. App. 231, 454 S.E.2d 878, *review denied*, 340 N.C. 262, 456 S.E.2d 834 (1995) (holding that the inadvertent destruction of a rape kit, as a result of a computer printout indicating case had been dismissed, after it had been tested did not require suppression); State v. Pethtel, 2001 Ohio 2445 (2000); Commonwealth v. Moss, 455 Pa. Super. 578, 689 A.2d 259 (1997) (holding destruction of hair sample in rape case which could have been tested for DNA was not prejudicial to defendant since no bad faith established).

[139] State v. Morales, 232 Conn. 707, 657 A.2d 585 (1995); Commonwealth v. Henderson, 411 Mass. 309, 582 N.E.2d 496 (1991); State v. Delisle, 162 Vt. 293, 648 A.2d 632 (1994).

[140] People v. Danielly, 274 Ill. App. 3d 358, 653 N.E.2d 866, *appeal denied*, 163 Ill. 2d 569, 657 N.E.2d 629 (1995) (holding no violation of defendant's due process rights in police conduct in returning complainant's underwear to her following the initial investigation since there was no showing of bad faith, "sinister motive" or "ill will," in returning victim's underwear to her); People v. Escamilla, 244 A.D.2d 805, 666 N.Y.S.2d 278 (1997), *appeal denied*, 91 N.Y.2d 891, 691 N.E.2d 1031, 669 N.Y.S.2d 5, *cert. denied*, 525 U.S. 836 (1998) (holding no adverse inference charge

The police do not have a duty to preserve any physical evidence that might be of conceivable evidentiary significance, especially when the exculpatory value of such evidence is speculative.[141] This would include finding to collect the rape victim's clothing and bed sheets, particularly when the victim initially chooses not to file charges.[142] The *Youngblood* principle has also been applied to the failure by law enforcement authorities to gather potentially exculpatory evidence.[143] This includes dusting for fingerprints or failing to perform DNA testing on seminal fluids.[144] This principle has been specifically applied to the gathering of evidence in the sexual assault field, such as a victim's underpants.[145] There

was required as a result of victim's alleged destruction of her clothing since there was no showing of bad faith on the part of the prosecution or demonstrable prejudice and the defense had the opportunity to cross-examine prosecution witnesses concerning the destroyed evidence).

[141] California v. Trombetta, 467 U.S. 479 (1984); Miller v. Vasquez, 868 F.2d 1116 (9th Cir. 1989), *cert. denied*, 499 U.S. 963 (1991) ("We therefore hold that unless a criminal defendant can show bad faith on the part of the police, failure to preserve potentially useful evidence does not constitute a denial of due process of law." *Id.* at 1120, *citing Youngblood*, 488 U.S. at 58); People v. Scattareggia, 152 A.D.2d 679, 543 N.Y.S.2d 742 (1989) (holding that police did not have the duty to preserve wine glasses from scene of rape and sodomy since "police do not have a duty to preserve all material that might be of conceivable evidentiary significance").

[142] Commonwealth v. Richardson, 49 Mass. App. Ct. 82, 726 N.E.2d 436, *review denied*, 432 Mass. 1108, 737 N.E.2d 468 (2000). In this sexual assault case, the police did not collect the victim's diary, clothes worn by her during the rape, sheets on the bed at the time of the rape, two notes allegedly written by the defendant, and the rape kit prepared by the doctor who examined the victim. The court held:

> Contrary to the defendant's arguments, police officers are under no duty to carry out any particular type of investigation that might lead to the discovery and preservation of exculpatory evidence. Their only obligation is to preserve any evidence actually collected. The basis for this rule is plain; while the defendant is free to pursue leads the police ignore, he is powerless to protect irreplaceable evidence already in the Commonwealth's custody. Consistent with this approach, the government here did not commit a breach of any duty, especially in view of the fact that the victim initially opted not to press charges against the defendant.

Id. at 83, 726 N.E.2d at 438.

[143] *See, e.g.*, Miller v. Vasquez, 868 F.2d 1116 (9th Cir. 1989), *cert. denied*, 499 U.S. 963 (1991) ("Since, in the absence of bad faith, the police's failure *to preserve* evidence that is only potentially exculpatory does not violate due process, then a fortiori neither does the good faith failure to *collect* such evidence violate due process." *Id.* at 1120. However, the court sent the case back for a hearing to determine if there had been bad faith, since there was a colorable claim of bad faith on the part of investigation.).

[144] People v. Smith, 224 A.D.2d 459, 638 N.Y.S.2d 115, *appeal denied*, 88 N.Y.2d 942, 670 N.E.2d 460, 647 N.Y.S.2d 176 (1996) (holding that defendant was not deprived a fair trial by the failure of the police to dust a knife for fingerprints and to perform DNA testing on seminal fluids found on the complainant's clothing).

[145] Colon v. Kuhlmann, 1988 U.S. Dist. LEXIS 5890 (S.D.N.Y. June 1, 1988) (failure to collect a rape victim's underpants does not violate due process since the due process law "does not require that particular evidence be gathered"), *aff'd on other grounds*, 865 F.2d 29 (2d Cir. 1988); State v. Pemental, 434 A.2d 932, 936 (R.I. 1981) (Police's failure to gather a rape victim's bed linen does not violate due process, but suggesting a different result might occur where the bed linen

is not necessarily a duty for law enforcement to compel a sexual assault complainant to undergo a medical examination for the purposes of collecting a sexual assault evidence collection kit.[146]

The fact that a forensic sample is consumed in testing, leaving nothing for the defendant to test, does not necessarily bar the prosecution from utilizing test results of the forensic sample consumed in testing.[147] Sometimes, the forensic test may destroy potentially exculpatory evidence.[148]

Significantly, in *Youngblood* the prosecution did not seek to utilize any test results of the lost evidence. In a situation where the prosecutor does offer test results of evidence lost or destroyed, preclusion of the test results may be appropriate.

An example of the bad faith destruction of potentially exculpatory evidence that amounts to a violation of due process requiring dismissal of the indictment can be seen in *United States v. Bohl*.[149] In *Bohl*, the court noted four areas in analyzing the good or bad faith of the government. First, the defendants had explicitly placed the government on notice that it wished to examine the evidence; second, the defendants established that the lost evidence possessed potentially exculpatory value; third, the government had the ability to control disposition of the evidence when it received notice; and fourth, the destroyed evidence was

---

was "within the reach of the prosecution at the time the request for exculpatory evidence was made." The court went on to hold: "We recognize that police departments in this state, as elsewhere, vary in the degree of sophistication with which they investigate evidence by scientific means. Even the most well-equipped and knowledgeable investigators may overlook or fail to pursue every clue or lead upon which scientific evidence might be predicated. We are reluctant to adopt a rule that would overturn a conviction based upon the required quantum of proof beyond a reasonable doubt solely on the basis that defendant might point out some scientific mode of investigation which was not pursued by the police." *Id.* at 936.).

[146] Johnson v. State, 753 A.2d 438 (Del. 2000).

[147] Lee v. State, 511 P.2d 1076 (Alaska 1973) ("We find that due process of law does not require that the defendant be permitted independent expert examination of evidence in the possession of the prosecution before such evidence is introduced at the trial . . . In those cases where expert analysis exhausts the substance there is clearly no error in the admission of evidence regarding the analysis in the absence of allegations and proof of deliberate destruction, or deliberate attempts to avoid discovery of evidence beneficial to the defense." *Id.* at 1077); State v. Carlson, 267 N.W.2d 170 (Minn. 1978) ("Due process does not require that criminal conduct go unpunished simply because the perpetrator leaves only a small sample of incriminating evidence behind. In this case, the testimony of Strauss clearly indicates that it was absolutely necessary to exhaust the entire bloodstain in order to procure a reliable test result." *Id.* at 175); People v. Allgood, 70 N.Y.2d 812, 517 N.E.2d 1316, 523 N.Y.S.2d 431 (1987); People v. Jones, 236 A.D.2d 846, 654 N.Y.S.2d 495, *appeal denied*, 90 N.Y.2d 859, 683 N.E.2d 1060, 661 N.Y.S.2d 186 (1997). *See also* § 13.14.

[148] People v. Steele, 287 A.D.2d 321, 731 N.Y.S.2d 685, *appeal denied*, 97 N.Y.2d 682, 764 N.E.2d 401, 738 N.Y.S.2d 297 (2001) (finding no sanctions necessary due to destruction of potential exculpatory evidence, i.e., blood evidence on the cardboard box destroyed in tests, which identified defendant's latent prints, since the blood analysis test, which destroyed the evidence, was a reasonable investigative strategy and not the product of bad faith).

[149] 25 F.3d 904 (10th Cir. 1994).

central to the prosecution's case.[150] Finally, the government was unable to offer any "innocent explanation" for the failure to preserve the evidence.[151] Interestingly, the court noted that mere negligence on the government's part in preserving evidence will negate bad faith in the destruction of evidence. Thus, negligently losing evidence or destroying evidence pursuant to a standard procedure may negate any demonstration of bad faith.[152] For example, there is no bad faith in the destruction of a 911 tape recording as part of a routine systematic destruction of 911 tapes. If the People are unable to produce the card on which the defendant allegedly acknowledged his *Miranda* rights, the defendant may be entitled to an adverse inference charge.[153]

Failing to request the preservation of any evidence can waive any claim of prejudice by the defendant.[154] It is also incumbent upon the defense counsel to seek sanctions for the destruction of evidence during the trial to avoid a waiver of a claim of prejudice.[155] Loss of a trial exhibit by the prosecution does not necessarily deprive a defendant effective appellate review. For example, if a victim's taped telephone call to the defendant is lost, whether or not a defendant's right to effective appellate review is jeopardized, depends on whether there is a dispute over its contents and whether the tape is crucial to an appellate issue.[156]

§ 1.15   Lost or destroyed notes or tapes of witness interviews.

Another important area of discovery, especially in child sexual assault cases and sometimes in cases involving adult victims, involves the tape-recorded interviews of the complaining witnesses. The tapes, like the written statements of witnesses, are important for cross-examination. They may also be important to an expert in analyzing the interview process. These tapes are important since the recorded interviews can be analyzed to determine if leading and suggestive

---

[150] *Id.* at 911–12.

[151] *Id.* at 912.

[152] *Id.* People v. Randolph, 261 A.D.2d 154, 690 N.Y.S.2d 195, *appeal denied*, 93 N.Y.2d 1025, 719 N.E.2d 945, 697 N.Y.S.2d 584 (1999). *See also* People v. Wooley, 249 A.D.2d 46, 671 N.Y.S.2d 58, *appeal denied*, 92 N.Y.2d 863, 699 N.E.2d 454, 677 N.Y.S.2d 94 (1998) (holding there was no bad faith in destruction of prison telephone call log book, which related to the sexual assault complainant's testimony about a call to his mother after the assault, since the log book was destroyed either in the ordinary course of business or during a flood in building where the records were stored; therefore, trial court was not required to preclude testimony about the call or provide jury with an adverse inference charge).

[153] People v. Martinez, 276 A.D.2d 645, 714 N.Y.S.2d 129, *appeal denied*, 95 N.Y.2d 966, 745 N.E.2d 404, 722 N.Y.S.2d 484 (2000).

[154] People v. Randolph, 261 A.D.2d 154, 690 N.Y.S.2d 195, *appeal denied*, 93 N.Y.2d 1025, 719 N.E.2d 945, 697 N.Y.S.2d 584 (1999) (defendant's request for 911 tape made one month after it had been destroyed); People v. Perry, 221 A.D.2d 736, 633 N.Y.S.2d 848 (1995).

[155] *Id.*

[156] People v. Yavru-Sakuk, 98 N.Y.2d 56, 772 N.E.2d 1145, 745 N.Y.S.2d 787 (2002) (remitting for consideration of whether the tape was needed for effective appellate review).

techniques were utilized during the interview process. This can be important not only on cross-examination of a complainant or as direct proof in a defendant's case, but also in terms of assessing reliability of hearsay statements admitted under a hearsay exception.

Once tape-recorded interviews are made, it is difficult to justify their destruction. The intentional destruction of a recorded interview can result in the preclusion of a witness' testimony. In one case, an assistant district attorney advised members of a child sexual assault task force investigative team to prepare narrative summaries of tape-recorded interviews with the child victims and then reuse the tapes, which destroyed the recorded interviews. The Tennessee Supreme Court held in this situation "that the state may not use witnesses whose initial interviews were taped and intentionally destroyed by the state investigators."[157]

When a written transcription exists of a destroyed taped interview of the rape complainant, the loss or destruction of the taped interview may not necessarily deny the defendant his right to cross-examine the complainant.[158] Loss or destruction of notes of a child's interview does not necessarily require dismissal of charges, especially if it appears the notes are neither material, exculpatory, nor potentially useful.[159] In cases where it can be shown that the destruction of a taped interview was intentional or due to bad faith, it is possible to request the sanction of striking a complaining witness' testimony. Where a tape of a witness' prior statement cannot be located because it has been lost or destroyed, the testimony of the witness need not be precluded if the court can fashion another appropriate sanction such as an adverse inference instruction.[160] A court is likely to look at the nature of the state's culpability in the loss or destruction of a complainant's statement in determining whether or not to impose a sanction, such as striking the testimony of the complainant, providing an adverse inference instruction, or some other sanction. If there is no claim or proof that the statement was deliberately lost, misplaced, or destroyed, the court is less likely to sanction the prosecution.[161]

---

[157] State v. Ballard, 855 S.W.2d 557, 560 (Tenn. 1993).

[158] Hathcock v. State, 357 Ark. 563 (2004) (finding no error in refusing defendant opportunity to present testimony concerning erasure of tapes of witness statements in rape case); State v. Milum, 197 Conn. 602, 500 A.2d 555 (1985), *rev'd on other grounds.*

[159] State v. Carol, 89 Wash. App. 77, 93, 948 P.2d 837, 846 (1997), *rev'd on other grounds.*

[160] People v. Williams, 223 A.D.2d 491, 637 N.Y.S.2d 379, *appeal denied,* 87 N.Y.2d 1026, 666 N.E.2d 1074, 644 N.Y.S.2d 160 (1996); People v. Gilbo, 214 A.D.2d 771, 624 N.Y.S.2d 659, *appeal denied,* 86 N.Y.2d 735, 655 N.E.2d 713, 631 N.Y.S.2d 616 (1995).

[161] State v. Kelly, 208 Conn. 365, 545 A.2d 1048 (1988), *habeas corpus proceeding, remanded sub. nom.* Kelly v. Meachum, 950 F. Supp. 461 (D. Conn. 1996); Metcalf v. Commonwealth, 158 S.W.3d 740, 746–47 (Ky. 2005) (holding failure to preserve defendant's recorded statement was not a *Brady* violation since investigator attempted in good faith to record interview, but equipment failed; there is no constitutional obligation to create *Brady* material).

§ 1.16 Consequences or sanctions for loss or destruction of evidence — Loss of rape kit.

If evidence has been lost or destroyed, a request may be made for a sanction against the party losing or destroying evidence. Generally, the sanction requested would involve some form of adverse inference charge. Dismissal of charges is rare when there is no bad faith on the part of law enforcement.

To some extent, the nature of the sanction or adverse inference charge may depend on the legal standard a state adopts for dealing with lost or destroyed evidence. Some states do not require bad faith as a prerequisite to an adverse inference charge, new trial, or dismissal when substantial prejudice is demonstrated by a defendant. This standard, articulated in the concurring opinion of *Arizona v. Youngblood*, would suggest a jury instruction as follows: "If you find that the State has . . . allowed to be destroyed or lost any evidence whose content or quality are in issue, you may infer that the true fact is against the State's interest."[162] A more conservative jury charge would add "if no reasonable explanation for that loss or destruction is given."

Reversal of defendant's conviction may be required when a defendant has requested that a particular piece of evidence be preserved, and it is lost or destroyed, and the trial court failed to impose any sanction or provide the jury with an adverse inference instruction.[163] However, when a jurisdiction requires bad faith and there has not been a specific request to preserve evidence until after a piece of evidence is routinely destroyed pursuant to police procedure, there is no bad faith and no requirement of an adverse inference or sanction by the trial court.[164]

A particular issue in sexual assault trials is the loss of a "rape kit" by either medical personnel or law enforcement personnel. A rape kit may contain samples of seminal fluid or other trace evidence, such as hair, fibers, or foreign debris. Most courts dealing with the issue have found no reason to dismiss charges because of a lost rape kit.[165] When a rape kit is lost through the inadvertence

---

[162] Arizona v. Youngblood, 488 U.S. 51, 59–60 (1988) (Stevens, J. *concurring*).

[163] United States v. Bohl, 25 F.3d 904 (10th Cir. 1994) (dismissing the indictment against the defendant for the prosecution's bad faith destruction of potentially exculpatory evidence, discussed in &sect§; 1.14 1.16); People v. Boyne, 174 A.D.2d 103, 579 N.Y.S.2d 338 (1992) (holding that a trial court improperly refused to give an adverse inference instruction or impose another sanction for the destruction of a 911 tape of a witness' telephone call to the police, since the tape had been requested by the defense and the defendant was prejudiced because the witness could not be cross-examined concerning his initial report to the police).

[164] *See* People v. Ortiz, 188 A.D.2d 292, 591 N.Y.S.2d 13 (1992), *appeal denied*, 81 N.Y.2d 890, 613 N.E.2d 984, 597 N.Y.S.2d 952 (1993); People v. Diggs, 185 A.D.2d 990, 587 N.Y.S.2d 406 (1992). Both cases dealt with the prosecution's failure to preserve 911 tapes where there had been no specific request by the defendant for their production.

[165] United States v. Sherlock, 962 F.2d 1349 (9th Cir. 1992), *cert. denied*, 506 U.S. 958 (1992); People v. Allgood, 70 N.Y.2d 812, 517 N.E.2d 1316, 523 N.Y.S.2d 431 (1987) (holding that a

of hospital personnel or the police, dismissal of the charges may not be appropriate, but preclusion of test results or an adverse inference charge may be appropriate. If the loss of the kit was not intentional, however, and no testing had been done on the rape kit, it would be meaningless to preclude testimony concerning the rape kit.[166]

In providing an adverse inference charge, a jury could be instructed that there was a rape kit which was lost and never examined, and that the jury may, if it desires, draw an adverse inference from the prosecution's failure to test, maintain, and preserve the rape kit.[167] However, such an adverse inference charge should be used only when it is relevant to an issue at trial. It may be argued that an instruction on lost or destroyed evidence can confuse a jury and is not necessary.[168] For example, if the defendant admits intercourse with the complainant on the date and time in question, then any evidence from a rape kit or other source to establish intercourse would be immaterial.[169] Likewise, if there is no reason to believe that the lost evidence would be favorable to the defendant, there may be no reason for a sanction or adverse inference against the prosecution.[170]

Preclusion of testimony may be appropriate in a situation where there is "positive evidence to offer." If the prosecution offers evidence tested from the

defendant who had been aware of a rape kit's existence for a period of eight months prior to trial, but did not demand its production until trial, had forfeited whatever right the defendant had to demand its production and thus could not complain of the people's failure to preserve it); People v. Sylar, 21 A.D.3d 1397, 801 N.Y.S.2d 661 (2005) (holding that an adverse inference charge was not required for the discarded rape kit in the absence of bad faith); People v. Scott, 235 A.D.2d 317, 653 N.Y.S.2d 309, *appeal denied*, 90 N.Y.2d 943, 687 N.E.2d 658, 664 N.Y.S.2d 761 (1997) (upholding trial court's decision to deny any sanction for the police's failure to preserve rape kits); People v. Callendar, 207 A.D.2d 900, 616 N.Y.S.2d 667 (1994), *appeal denied*, 84 N.Y.2d 1029, 647 N.E.2d 457, 623 N.Y.S.2d 185 (1995) (no bad faith demonstrated in loss of rape kit before testing and kit's potential value to defendant does not constitute a denial of due process); People v. Bridges, 184 A.D.2d 1042, 584 N.Y.S.2d 360, *appeal denied*, 80 N.Y.2d 973, 605 N.E.2d 878, 591 N.Y.S.2d 142 (1992); State v. Banks, 125 N.C. App. 681, 482 S.E.2d 41 (1997), *cert. denied*, 523 U.S. 1128 (1998) (holding police department's destruction of rape kit did not require dismissal or sanctions since the exculpatory value of possible DNA evidence was "highly speculative"); State v. Graham, 118 N.C. App. 231, 454 S.E.2d 878, *review denied*, 340 N.C. 262, 456 S.E.2d 834 (1995) (In a case where defendant alleged consent as a defense, police destruction of complainant's clothing and rape kit did not violate defendant's rights since evidence was not exculpatory or favorable to defendant and there was no showing of bad faith in the destruction. Defendant also did not request to test evidence which police destroyed until only two months before trial. However, trial court did suppress testimony concerning condition of victim's sweatshirt).

[166] People v. Miller, 156 Misc. 2d 824, 594 N.Y.S.2d 978 (Sup. Ct. 1993).

[167] *Id.* at 829, 594 N.Y.S.2d at 980–81.

[168] *Sherlock, supra* note 166, 962 F.2d at 1355.

[169] *Id.*

[170] State v. Figueroa, 235 Conn. 145, 665 A.2d 63 (1995) (no connection between state's inability to produce rape victim's belt — removed during rape and then recovered near scene but inadvertently destroyed by police — and inference that it would be favorable to defendant and adverse to State).

rape kit, then preclusion of such evidence may be an appropriate remedy when there is destruction of the evidence after a request for its production or other evidence of bad faith. Similarly, preclusion of the testimony of child witnesses where their recorded interviews have been destroyed may also be appropriate.[171]

§ 1.17   Physical and psychological examination of complainant.

A unique area of discovery in sexual assault cases is the defense request for a physical or psychological examination of the complaining witness. These requests are usually predicated upon the defense's need to verify opinions of the state's experts. In other words, if the state's expert has reported in a child victim case that there are certain physical signs of abuse, such as "abnormal" hymen findings, the argument is made that a defense expert should be allowed to examine the child to verify these findings. Similarly, if the prosecution presents psychological evidence concerning certain reactions and behaviors of the child based in part upon an examination or interview with the child, the defense should be entitled the same opportunity so that its expert will have an equal opportunity to comment upon the basis for the state's expert opinion.

Sometimes the requests for a psychological examination of a child are also based upon the need to determine the credibility or competency of a witness. As a general rule, there is no automatic right to a physical or psychological examination of a victim in a sexual assault trial, and the mere demand for such an examination will be insufficient. Courts that have agreed to order such an examination have usually found a well-articulated basis for such an examination.[172]

In establishing the purpose and necessity of a proposed physical and psychological examination of a child, it is important that the purpose not infringe upon an improper area of expert testimony.[173] For example, the examination request could not be supported by a desire to comment on whether the child meets the profile of a victim or for the purpose of determining whether an event took place. A poorly defined or improper purpose could negate any possibility of a physical or psychological examination of a witness.

§ 1.18   Psychological examination of a complainant to determine competency.

In most jurisdictions, the majority of witnesses are presumed competent. The rules of competency are discussed more fully in Chapter 5, §§ 5.2–7. In some situations, a party may move for a psychological examination of a witness to

---

[171] *See* §§ 1.15 and 1.16.

[172] *See generally* Gregory G. Sarno, Annotation, *Necessity or Permissibility of Mental Examination to Determine Competency or Credibility of Complainant in Sexual Offense Prosecution*, 45 A.L.R.4th 310 (1986).

[173] *See* Chapter 11 *generally* on propriety of expert testimony.

determine competency. Competency appears as an issue in sexual assault cases due to the large number of child victims and prosecutions based on the incapacity of a complainant to consent based on mental disease or defect. A prosecution's theory based on the mental disease or defect of a complainant naturally raises the issue of competency if that witness is to testify, although the testimonial competence is not necessarily the same as mental competence to consent to a sexual act.

Courts have traditionally exercised the power to order a psychological examination of a witness for the purpose of determining the competency of that witness. The court may order a psychological examination of a complainant with a mental disability to determine the nature, degree, and effect of such disability. [174] There is no requirement that a trial court order such an examination when there are issues concerning the competency of a witness. A court need not order an investigation of a witness's competency unless the court has reason to doubt the witness's competency. [175] But courts have ruled that failure to order an independent examination for competency may be error when a witness's extreme youth and difficulty in communicating raise a concern regarding competency to testify. [176] The trial court may rely upon other testimony concerning the witness' competency and ability to testify, and the existence of corroborating evidence in establishing the reliability and competency of a witness. [177] Generally, a request for an examination to assess competency must be supported by strong and compelling reasons that will overcome the intrusion of a psychological examination of a complainant. [178] In 1990, Congress passed legislation stating

---

[174] United States v. Benn, 476 F.2d 1127, 1130 (D.C. Cir. 1972); United States v. Frazier, 678 F. Supp. 499 (E.D. Pa.), aff'd, 806 F.2d 255 (3d Cir. 1986) (court relied upon court-appointed psychiatrist to determine a three-year-old was competent to testify).

[175] Commonwealth v. Fulton, 318 Pa. Super. 470, 484, 465 A.2d 650, 657 (1983).

[176] Anderson v. State, 749 P.2d 369, 371 (Alaska Ct. App. 1988) (need for competency examination established by children's age, answers to questions, and state's reliance upon psychological testimony); State v. Stacy, 179 W. Va. 686, 371 S.E.2d 614 (1988) (reversing defendant's conviction for failure to grant defense request for a psychological examination of a five-year-old child, when the complainant had difficulty communicating during competency hearing).

[177] Benn, supra note 175, 476 F.2d at 1131.

[178] Government of Virgin Islands v. A., Leonard, 922 F.2d 1141 (3d Cir. 1991); United States v. Roman, 884 F. Supp. 126 (S.D.N.Y. 1995); People v. Lucero, 724 P.2d 1374 (Colo. Ct. App. 1986) (denying defendant's request for psychological examination of sexual abuse complainant even though she was a patient at a state hospital); State v. Allen, 647 So. 2d 428, 432–33 (La. Ct. App. 1994); Commonwealth v. Trowbridge, 419 Mass. 750, 647 N.E.2d 413 (1995); People v. Herring, 227 A.D.2d 658, 641 N.Y.S.2d 649, appeal denied, 88 N.Y.2d 986, 672 N.E.2d 619, 649 N.Y.S.2d 393 (1996) (noting that a psychological evaluation of complainant to determine competency is not authorized by statute and defendant established no compelling need for such an exam); State v. Bolling, 2005 Ohio App. LEXIS 2402 (May 20, 2005); Commonwealth v. Alston, 2004 Pa. Super. 471, 864 A.2d 539 (2004) (en banc) (finding there was an insufficient basis to compel a psychiatric examination of child complainant to assess competency); State v. Miller, 35 Wis. 2d 454, 471, 151 N.W.2d 157, 165 (1967).

that a court shall not order a psychological or psychiatric examination of a child witness (less than 18 years of age) to assess competency without a showing of compelling need.[179] New Mexico permits the trial court to order a psychological evaluation of sexual assault complainants under the age of 13 when there is "sufficient doubt" as to the complainant's competency.[180] The psychologist or psychiatrist is selected by the court unless the alleged victim has been evaluated by law enforcement during the course of the investigation; if so, then the evaluation "shall be conducted by a psychologist or psychiatrist selected by the court upon the recommendation of the defense."[181]

§ 1.19 Authority supporting pretrial psychological examination of complainant.

The most often-cited reason for courts granting a pretrial psychological examination of a complainant is the need for reciprocity when the prosecution intends to introduce evidence based on a psychological examination of the victim by its experts. Citing due process considerations, the Illinois Supreme Court has held that a defendant's expert should be permitted to examine a victim to determine whether she suffers from "rape trauma syndrome" if the prosecution intends to offer evidence through its expert witness that the complainant suffers from rape trauma syndrome or "post-traumatic stress syndrome."[182] The concern usually cited is that the prosecution's expert will have enhanced credibility if the expert testifies based upon a personal examination of the complainant, and the defense expert has not had such an opportunity. Under the Illinois rule, the prosecution may not introduce testimony of its examining expert that the victim of an alleged sexual assault suffers from post-traumatic stress syndrome or rape trauma syndrome unless the complainant submits to an examination by a defendant's expert who has been qualified by the court.[183] Nonetheless, the

---

[179] 18 U.S.C. § 3509(c)(9).

[180] N.M. Stat. § 30-9-18.

[181] Id.

[182] People v. Wheeler, 151 Ill. 2d 298, 602 N.E.2d 826 (1992) (by statutory authority 725 Ill. Comp. Stat. § 5/115-7.2, Illinois permits the testimony by an expert in sexual assault trials of post-traumatic stress syndrome).

[183] Id. at 312, 602 N.E.2d at 833. See also Anderson v. State, 749 P.2d 369 (Alaska Ct. App. 1988):

> In order to avoid victim harassment, we have adopted a two-prong balancing test to reconcile the defendant's right to gather facts relevant to his defense with the victim's constitutionally protected right to privacy. First, the defendant seeking a psychiatric examination of a prosecuting witness must make a specific showing of need for an evaluation by showing that the prosecuting witness may have specific mental or emotional problems directly related to the issues in the case. Second, we require the defendant to demonstrate that the testimony of the person to be examined is uncorroborated or otherwise untrustworthy . . . [citation omitted]. Given the broad discretion trial courts have in determining the competency of witnesses, we would

prosecution can still offer expert opinion if the prosecution's expert has not examined the complainant. Again, the theory is that the playing field is level if both the prosecution and defense experts are able to testify from the same basis, and there is no undue advantage if neither has examined the complainant.

In *State v. Maday*, Wisconsin also held that when the prosecution expresses an intent to present the testimony of an expert who may have personally examined a complainant, and that the expert will testify whether the victim's behavior is consistent with the behaviors of other victims of sexual assault, the defense may request a psychological examination of the victim.[184] Nonetheless, the defendant must still make a showing of a need or reason for a psychological examination of the complainant. The Wisconsin court, after reviewing the holdings of other state courts, provided a list of criteria, sometimes referred to as *Delaney* factors for the West Virginia cases which articulated them for evaluating a request for a psychological examination:

1. The nature of the examination requested and the intrusiveness inherent in that examination;

2. The victim's age;

3. The resulting physical and/or emotional effects of the examination on the victim;

4. The probative value of the examination to any issue before the court;

5. The remoteness in time of the examination to the alleged criminal act; and

6. The evidence already available for the defendant's use.[185]

To these criteria, the Wisconsin court added a seventh factor for a trial court to consider:

> Whether or not a personal interview with the victim is essential before the expert can form an opinion, to a reasonable degree of psychological or psychiatric certainty, that the victim's behaviors are consistent with the behaviors of other victims of sexual abuse.[186]

South Carolina adopts the approach of Wisconsin and West Virginia:

> not be prepared to say that concerns about competency, standing alone, would warrant psychological evaluations . . . [citation omitted]. Nevertheless, when the very real concerns regarding these witnesses' competency are added to the state's substantial reliance on psychological testimony regarding behavioral patterns as a means of identifying sexually abused children, we believe the right to an independent mental health examination has been established.

Id. at 371.

[184] State v. Maday, 179 Wis. 2d 346, 359–60, 507 N.W.2d 365, 372 (1993).

[185] *Id.,citing* State v. Delaney, 187 W. Va. 212, 417 S.E.2d 903, 907 (1992).

[186] *Maday, supra*, note 185, 179 Wis. 2d at 359–60, 507 N.W.2d at 372.

An absolute bar to the exercise of judicial discretion to consider an order for a psychological evaluation of child complainants ignores the necessary balance which must be sought between a complainant's privacy rights and a defendant's right to a fair trial . . . . Where the complainant and the perpetrator are often the only two witnesses to a sexual assault, fundamental fairness dictates a defendant be entitled to request a psychological evaluation of a child witness where there is *compelling* reason to question the complainant's psychological status. A child complainant who is incompetent to testify may not have the capacity to give an accurate account of the facts. Cases involving child victims present special concerns that weigh in favor of allowing judicial discretion to order psychological evaluations.[187]

Nevada has modified its earlier decision on the psychological examination of a complaint so that a victim may refuse to undergo the examination with the consequence that the prosecutor may not introduce expert evidence to address the victim's behaviors. A defendant may only seek such an examination when the State examines the victim and the defendant establishes a compelling need for its own examination.[188]

These states differ from the Illinois approach in that they do not automatically grant a psychological examination of the complainant when the prosecution is offering testimony of an expert who has interviewed the complainant. Rather, they indicate a lesser showing of necessity before authorizing such an examination and increased likelihood that such an examination should be granted when there will be expert testimony by the prosecution upon an examination or interview of the complainant.

The *Maday* rule has been strictly limited to situations where the prosecution presents expert testimony that the victim's behaviors are consistent with those of a sexual abuse victim or other similar expert testimony.[189] Also, a prosecution expert describing the abilities, limitations, and disabilities of a developmentally disabled complainant does not trigger the defendant's right to examine the complainant.[190]

---

[187] In the Interest of Michael H., 360 S.C. 540, 549, 602 S.E.2d 729, 733–34 (2004).

[188] State v. Eighth Judicial Dist. Court, 97 P.3d 594, 601 (Nev. 2004).

In determining whether a compelling need exists, the trial court must consider: (1) whether little or no corroboration of the offense exists beyond the victim's testimony, and (2) whether there is a reasonable basis "for believing that the victim's mental or emotional state may have affected his or her veracity." Moreover, in the exercise of discretion, we require that trial courts set forth a particularized factual finding that there is reason to believe that a psychological examination is warranted.

Id. at 600–01.

[189] State v. David J.K., 190 Wis. 2d 726, 528 N.W.2d 434 (1994) (denying defendant's request for an examination).

[190] State v. Sasnett, 1995 Wis. App. LEXIS 1046 (Aug. 29, 1995).

Another ground for a psychological examination of the complainant might be where the allegations are brought in the context of divorce proceedings and other evidence either contradicts or does not support the allegations.[191] A defendant's expert opinion that the victim's allegations are consistent with research on false allegations may also support a court order for a psychological examination of the victim.[192]

A court is more likely to order a psychological examination of a complainant when there is little corroborative evidence of the complainant's allegation and if there is specific information in a complainant's psychological history to question the complainant's truthfulness.[193] A child's very young age (four years old at time of alleged crime and six years old at time of trial) and admission of hearing voices telling him to say and do "mean things" to his friends establishes a compelling need for ordering a child to submit to an independent psychiatric examination.[194] Evidence of parental influence in the sexual abuse allegation

---

[191] Jenkins v. State, 668 So. 2d 1003 (Fla. Ct. App.), *review denied*, 675 So. 2d 121 (Fla. 1996).

[192] *Id.*

[193] Ballard v. Superior Court, 64 Cal. 2d 159, 176–77, 49 Cal. Rptr. 302, 313, 410 P.2d 838, 849 (1966) (suggesting that a defendant may obtain a psychological examination of the complainant if a compelling need is shown or undue prejudice established. However, this decision has been overruled by statute. Cal. Penal Code § 1112.); Mack v. Commonwealth, 860 S.W.2d 275 (Ky. 1993) ("We believe that the circumstances in the present case indicate a substantial possibility that a defense or independent expert would provide genuinely relevant beneficial evidence on the questions of concoction or transference resulting from the child's unfortunate past." *Id.* at 277). *But see* Kentucky Supreme Court's decision in Bart v. Commonwealth, 951 S.W.2d 576 (Ky. 1997) (The same court held that a defendant was not entitled to a psychological examination of a complainant who during a competency test stated she heard voices telling her to do wrong things, that some of the voices were demons who had "thick eyebrows that came straight down, ears pointed, with real sharp teeth."); Griego v. State, 111 Nev. 444, 893 P.2d 995 (1995) (defendant's conviction was reversed with respect to certain counts where defendant was denied a psychological evaluation), *citing* Keeney v. State, 109 Nev. 220, 850 P.2d 311 (1993) (Nevada Supreme Court held that the defendant should be permitted an expert psychiatric or psychological exam of the complainant when: (1) the State has employed such an expert; (2) the victim is not shown by compelling reasons to be in need of protection; (3) evidence of the crime has little or no corroboration beyond the testimony of the victim; and (4) there is a reasonable basis for believing that the victim's mental or emotional state may have affected his or her veracity.); State v. Babayan, 106 Nev. 155, 787 P.2d 805 (1990); State v. Jones, 1994 Tenn. Crim. App. LEXIS 587 (Sept. 15, 1994). The Tennessee Court of Criminal Appeals noted as follows:

> Courts of other jurisdictions have listed other relevant factors, including the extreme youth of the victim; a controversy involving the victim's mental state; the lack of an adequate examination of the victim; the state's reliance on psychological testing; a history of fabrication by the victim; persuasive evidence of a deviation from acceptable norms, such as an identifiable or clinical psychiatric disorder or an unusual condition that renders the victim's testimony suspect; and the inability of the victim to be effectively cross-examined in the courtroom.

Id. at *33.

[194] *In Re* Michael H., 360 S.C. 540, 551–52, 602 S.E.2d 729, 735 (2004). [T]he victim's very

may also trigger a right to a psychological examination of the child complainant.[195]

Even when a court has agreed that an examination will be permitted, it must deal with the conditions surrounding the conduct of the examination. Among the conditions to consider is whether the examination will be recorded, the length and place of the interview, the number of interviews, the number of experts that may conduct the interview, the nature of the questions that may be covered during the interview, and who may accompany the victim during the interview.[196]

If the prosecution is not offering any expert testimony at all, a trial court is unlikely to order a psychological examination of a complaining witness. Where the prosecution offers expert testimony based upon an examination of a victim, a request for a psychological examination of a complainant is more likely to be granted. An application for a proposed examination of a victim should set forth those parameters that the movant feels would make the request for a psychological examination a reasonably non-intrusive examination.

Permitting a psychological examination of a complaining witness is the minority view.

§ 1.20   Authority rejecting right to psychological examination of complaining witness.

Clearly the overwhelming majority of jurisdictions that have addressed propriety of a psychological or mental examination of a complainant hold that there is either no authority for such an examination or that such examinations are unjustified. A few jurisdictions hold that a psychological examination of a sexual abuse complainant violates public policy and a victim's privacy rights or unnecessarily traumatizes a victim.[197] It is interesting that some courts have

---

young age (four at the time of the alleged assault and six at trial), the fact that the victim was undergoing counseling, and spoke freely of the incident (indicating he would not be further traumatized by another examination), and the fact that the victim's counselor testified victim was hearing voices during the year when victim alleged the assault occurred, the judge would have been within his discretion to order the victim to submit to an independent psychological examination.

[195] State v. Swoboda, No. C4-99-1455, 2000 Minn. App. LEXIS 182 (Feb. 29, 2000) (given evidence of possible parental influence in sexual abuse allegations and prior allegation of abuse, trial court did not err in granting defendant's request for a psychological evaluation of child, during which child could not be cross-examined about prior statements or evaluations).

[196] *Maday, supra,* note 185, 179 Wis.2d at 361, 507 N.W.2d at 372. The Wisconsin court also suggests that the person accompanying the victim not have a relationship with the prosecution of the defendant. Rather, the person accompanying the victim "should be a parent, spouse, sibling or some other lay person who is a part of the victim's support network." *Id.* n.6. *See also* State v. Cain, 427 N.W.2d 5, 10 (Minn. Ct. App. 1988) (holding that the trial court abused its discretion in failing to place restrictions on adverse psychological examinations of alleged victims of child sexual abuse).

[197] People v. Espinoza, 95 Cal. App. 4th 1287, 116 Cal. Rptr. 2d 700 (2002), *review denied,*

specifically rejected the notion that a defendant should be entitled to a psychological examination of a complainant because a jury may afford greater weight to the testimony of an expert who has actually seen the complainant compared with an expert who has not.[198] Most courts have rejected a psychological examination of a complainant on the ground that there has not been a substantial or compelling need shown for the examination. This burden will not be satisfied by an allegation that the victim's accusations are fabrications,[199] or a general assertion that an examination is necessary to determine whether or not child victims have been traumatized.[200]

Courts have expressed a concern that psychological examinations of a victim may infringe on a witness's right to privacy, may enhance the trauma of a complainant in a sexual assault case, and may be a tool of harassment.[201] Most courts have taken the position that while there may be a situation in which a psychological examination is warranted, and the court may have the power to order such an examination, the defendant in the particular case has failed to establish a compelling need or sufficient basis for an examination in the particular case before the court.[202] Inconsistencies in testimony do not necessarily establish

2002 Cal. LEXIS 3308 (May 15, 2002) (compelling a sexual assault victim to undergo a psychological exam violates victim's right to privacy and traumatizes victim); State v. Horn, 337 N.C. 449, 446 S.E.2d 52 (1994) (finding judge has no discretion to order a psychological examination of the complainant). *See also*, State v. Looney, 294 N.C. 1, 240 S.E.2d 612 (1978) (stating that "the possible benefits to an innocent defendant . . .are outweighed by . . .discouraging victims of crime to report such offenses and other potential witnesses from disclosing their knowledge of them." *Id.* at 29, 240 S.E.2d at 627).

[198] State v. Drab, 546 So. 2d 54, 56 (Fla. Dist. Ct. App.), *appeal denied*, 553 So. 2d 1164 (Fla. 1989).

[199] State v. Redd, 642 A.2d 829, 833 (Del. Super. Ct. 1993).

[200] State v. Michaels, 264 N.J. Super. 579, 610, 625 A.2d 489, 505 (1993) *aff'd*, 136 N.J. 299, 642 A.2d 1372 (1994) (declining to speculate whether a psychological examination might have been granted if, at an evidentiary hearing, the "defendant interlinked the suggestibility of the questioning of the children by the authorities to the ability of the children to testify").

[201] *Redd, supra*, note 200, 642 A.2d at 834.

[202] United States v. Sumner, 119 F.3d 658, 662–63 (8th Cir. 1997); United States v. Rouse, 111 F.3d 561 (8th Cir.) (*en banc*), *cert. denied*, 522 U.S. 905 (1997) (holding that defendant did not establish need for defendant's psychologist to examine complainant given the extensive notes and reports of interviews with children); McCafferty v. Leapley, 944 F.2d 445, 454 (8th Cir. 1991), *cert. denied*, 503 U.S. 911 (1992) (noting that the defendant's access to all materials and reports of the prosecution's experts provided the defendant with sufficient information and that the defendant had failed to make a sufficient showing of necessity to justify a court-appointed psychological examination of the complainant); Gilpin v. McCormick, 921 F.2d 928, 931 (9th Cir. 1990) (holding that defendant's right of confrontation was not violated by the trial court's refusal to order a psychiatric examination of a victim to indicate presence or absence of rape trauma syndrome); United States v. Spotted War Bonnet, 882 F.2d 1360 (8th Cir. 1989), *vacated on other grounds*, 497 U.S. 1021 (1990); United States v. Provost, 875 F.2d 172, 175 (8th Cir.), *cert. denied*, 493 U.S. 859 (1989) (holding the court's refusal to require a second independent examination of a child who had been abused was not an abuse of the court's discretion since the defendant had

(Text continued on page 58)

not made a sufficient showing of need for a second examination); United States v. St. John, 851 F.2d 1096 (8th Cir. 1988) (noting that, not only had defense not made an adequate showing of how a psychological examination of the complainant may assist the defendant, a second examination might substantially harm the complainant); United States v. De Noyer, 811 F.2d 436, 439 (8th Cir. 1987); Joseph v. Government of the Virgin Islands, 226 F. Supp. 2d 726 (D.V.I. 2002), *aff'd*, 2003 U.S. App. LEXIS 11868 (2003) (holding defendant did not establish a "substantial need" for examination of the complainant, such as that she had an identifiable or clinical disorder; prior allegation of sexual abuse does not constitute a psychological or psychiatric disorder); United States v. Roman, 884 F. Supp. 126 (S.D.N.Y. 1995); State v. Eighth Judicial Dist. Court, 97 P.3d 594 (Nev. 2004) (holding that a defendant is entitled to a psychological examination of the complainant only when the state has or is going to do so and there is a compelling psychological need to do so); Pickens v. State, 675 P.2d 665 (Alaska Ct. App. 1984) (holding that the defendant could not obtain a psychological examination of the complainant because the defendant had failed to make a specific showing of need, and it failed to demonstrate that the complainant's testimony was uncorroborated or otherwise untrustworthy); People v. Chard, 808 P.2d 351 (Colo.), *cert. denied*, 502 U.S. 863 (1991); State v. Manini, 38 Conn. App. 100, 659 A.2d 196, *appeal denied*, 234 Conn. 920, 661 A.2d 99 (1995) (holding that trial court properly denied defendant's request for a psychiatric examination and that trial court's "allowing access to the psychiatric records [of complainant] sufficiently protected the defendant's right of confrontation"); Simmons v. State, 683 So. 2d 1101 (Fla. Ct. App. 1996), *review denied*, 697 So. 2d 512 (Fla. 1997) (holding insufficient basis to compel psychological evaluations of developmentally disabled witness to rape-murder); State v. Buch, 83 Haw. 308, 322, 926 P.2d 599, 613 (1996) (holding mere allegation that complainant fabricated story does not establish a "compelling reason" for a mental examination of the complaining witness); Commonwealth v. Trowbridge, 419 Mass. 750, 647 N.E.2d 413 (1995); State v. Elvin, 481 N.W.2d 571 (Minn. Ct. App. 1992) (holding that a court has discretion to order an adverse psychological exam, but that this power should be used judiciously and in a balanced way, and the trial court did not abuse its discretion of denying such an examination in this case); State v. R.W., 104 N.J. 14, 514 A.2d 1287, 1291 (1986) (holding that age alone is an insufficient reason to order a psychological examination of a child victim and that the bald allegation of sensory or mental defects that may affect the witness's credibility is insufficient to order such an examination); Chapman v. State, 16 P.3d 432 (Nev. 2001) (given corroborating evidence, fact that allegations close in context of "ugly divorce" did not establish a compelling reason for psychological examination of child); Koerschner v. State, 116 Nev. 1111, 13 P.3d 451 (2000) (holding defendant must present competent evidence and establish a compelling reason for a psychological evaluation of a complainant, in context of factors such as whether prosecution intends to call an expert in psychology or psychiatry, the level of corroborating, and whether there is a reasonable basis to believe complainant's marked or emotional state may affect his or her truthfulness); State v. Michaels, 264 N.J. Super. 579, 625 A.2d 489 (1993), *aff'd*, 136 N.J. 299, 642 A.2d 1372 (1994); People v. Earel, 89 N.Y.2d 960, 678 N.E.2d 471, 655 N.Y.S.2d 859 (1997) ("We do not reach the question whether a trial court has the power to order a complaining witness to submit to a psychiatric examination. Assuming without deciding that the trial court has such power, the defendant here failed to show record support for his claim that such an examination is compelled to ensure a fair trial" [citations omitted]. *Id.* at 961, 678 N.E.2d at 472, 655 N.Y.S.2d at 860); People v. Brown, 7 A.D.3d 726, 777 N.Y.S.2d 508, *appeal denied*, 3 N.Y.3d 671, 817 N.E.2d 827, 784 N.Y.S.2d 9 (2004) ("While a court may possess the discretion to permit such an examination under appropriate circumstances, the defendant failed to demonstrate that such circumstances were present here." *Id.*, 777 N.Y.S.2d at 509); Brown v. Blumenfeld, 296 A.D.2d 405, 745 N.Y.S.2d 54 (2002); People v. Jones, 287 A.D.2d 339, 731 N.Y.S.2d 180 (2001), *appeal denied*, 98 N.Y.2d 638, 771 N.E.2d 840, 744 N.Y.S.2d 767 (2002); People v. Vozzo, 283 A.D.2d 310, 724 N.Y.S.2d 842, *appeal denied*, 96 N.Y.2d 925, 758 N.E.2d 669, 732 N.Y.S.2d 643 (2001):

(Text continued on page 58)

Since defendant made an unelaborated request for a psychiatric examination of the complainant, unaccompanied by any factual support, his claim that such an examination should have been granted is unpreserved. [citation omitted]. To the extent that defendant is claiming that the examination was compelled by Federal constitutional law, that claim is also unpreserved. We decline to review these claims in the interest of justice. Were we to review these claims, we would find, without deciding whether a trial court has the power to order a complainant in a sexual assault case to undergo a psychiatric examination, that the record does not establish that such an examination was necessary to ensure a fair trial. [citation omitted]. Defendant was provided with a significant portion of the complainant's psychiatric records, which were examined by his expert. The expert was allowed to discuss the diagnosis and give his own opinion as to whether the complainant's behavior fit the pattern of a person with histrionic personality disorder (HPD). Moreover, portions of the complainant's psychiatric records were admitted into evidence for the jury's consideration. Lastly, the complainant was subjected to cross-examination relative to the information contained in her psychiatric records. Thus, the issue of the complainant's diagnosis of HPD was clearly placed before the jury, which was given more than sufficient information to assess the relevance of the disorder to the defense.

Id., 724 N.Y.S.2d at 842.

People v. Kemp, 251 A.D.2d 1072, 674 N.Y.S.2d 525, *appeal denied*, 92 N.Y.2d 900, 702 N.E.2d 849, 680 N.Y.S.2d 64 (1998); People v. Gutkaiss, 206 A.D.2d 628, 614 N.Y.S.2d 599, *appeal denied*, 84 N.Y.2d 936, 645 N.E.2d 1233, 621 N.Y.S.2d 533 (1994) (noting that not only did the criminal procedure law not authorize a psychiatric examination of the victim, but also noting that, "when measured against the traumatic effect this type of examination would have on the victim, there is nothing in the record justifying such an examination in the interest of justice." *Id.* at 630, 614 N.Y.S.2d at 601); People v. Passenger, 175 A.D.2d 944, 572 N.Y.S.2d 972 (1991) ("In the absence of compelling proof of mental or emotional instability, there is no justification for granting defendant's request. And, as for defendant's parallel argument that the failure to order the hearing violated his constitutional right under the Sixth Amendment to confront his accuser, that has been invariably rejected." *Id.* at 945, 572 N.Y.S.2d at 974); State v. Malroit, 2000 Ohio App. LEXIS 5169, *dismissed, discretionary appeal not allowed*, 91 Ohio St. 3d 1460, 743 N.E.2d 400 (2001); State v. Gray, 1995 Ohio App. LEXIS 2818 (June 28, 1995) ("a defendant has no right to examine a state's witness prior to trial unless the mental condition of that individual is a contested, essential element of the crime charged" and noting that such an examination of a victim of alleged sexual abuse "should not be granted lightly." *Id.* at *18); State v. Ramirez, 98 Ohio App. 3d 388, 648 N.E.2d 845 (1994) (holding that psychiatric or psychological testing of a child witness should not be granted without strong showing of necessity); State v. Osgood, 2003 S.D. 87, 667 N.W.2d 687 (2003) (holding defendant has no right "to" duplicate a forensic interview without justification and trauma to victim may be considered in court); State v. Campbell, 904 S.W.2d 608 (Tenn. Crim. App. 1995) ("A trial court should not require a sex abuse victim to undergo a psychological examination unless the 'most compelling reasons' are established by the accused," *citing* Forbes v. State, 599 S.W.2d 318, 321 (Tenn. 1977). *Id.* at 612); State v. Jones, 1994 Tenn. Crim. App. LEXIS 587 (Sept. 15, 1994) (court did not abuse its discretion in denying a psychological examination of the complainant, noting that among the factors to assess in making such a determination are whether or not there is substantial doubt cast upon the victim's sanity, the complainant's prior record of mental disorders or sexual fantasies, credibility of the complainant's story, whether the complainant was examined by other experts who will testify at trial, and corroboration of the charges); State v. Ross, 152 Vt. 462, 568 A.2d 335 (1989) ("We foresee that there will be cases where it is appropriate either to allow examination of a victim by the defense expert or to prohibit the State from providing its expert testimony when the former procedure is

substantial justification to release counseling records.[203]

California has by statute precluded the psychological or psychiatric examination of any witness in a sexual assault prosecution "for the purpose of assessing his or her credibility."[204] This statute has withstood constitutional challenges.[205] Most states, however, have dealt with the issue of psychological examinations of complainants through court decisions.

Establishing substantial need means "there must be a showing of some deviation from acceptable norms, such as an identifiable or clinical psychiatric or similar disorder, beyond the realm of those human conditions that ordinary experience would confirm as normal."[206] The ability to cross-examine the complainant concerning suggestive interviewing techniques may be a sufficient reason to deny a defendant a psychological evaluation of a child on the issue of suggestibility.[207] A defense may concede that an examination is unnecessary, thereby bolstering the claim that the defendant is not entitled to its own examination.[208] There is also some authority that the consent of a child's parents may be necessary to authorize an independent psychological examination of a complainant.[209]

---

inappropriate. But this is not such a case." *Id.* at 466, 568 A.2d at 338); Gale v. State, 792 P.2d 570 (Wyo. 1990) (holding that psychological examination to assist in cross-examination of complainant is not a compelling reason for such an examination).

[203] State v. Cates, 2001 S.D. 99, 632 N.W.2d 28, 35 (2001) (holding inconsistencies in testimony alone do not establish medical delusion nor a "substantial justification" for psychiatric exam of complainant).

[204] Cal. Penal Code at § 1112:

> Psychological examination of witnesses in sexual assault prosecutions. Notwithstanding the provisions of subdivision (d) of § 28 of Article I of the California Constitution, the trial court shall not order any prosecuting witness, complaining witness, or any other witness, or victim in any sexual assault prosecution to submit to a psychiatric or psychological examination for the purpose of assessing his or her credibility.

Other statutes limiting psychological examinations of complainants are: Ariz. Rev. Stat. § 13-4065 (prohibits psychological or psychiatric examination of complainant or witness "except on agreement of the parties"); Idaho Code § 19-3025 (prohibits psychological or psychiatric examination of witness of any offense "except upon agreement of the parties"); Ill. Stat. ch. 725, § 5/115-7.1.

[205] People v. Armbruster, 163 Cal. App. 3d 660, 210 Cal. Rptr. 11 (1985).

[206] State v. R.W., 104 N.J. 14, 21, 514 A.2d 1287, 1291 (1986).

[207] People v. Chilson, 285 A.D.2d 733, 728 N.Y.S.2d 550, *appeal denied*, 97 N.Y.2d 640, 761 N.E.2d 2, 735 N.Y.S.2d 497 (2001).

[208] State v. Rizzo, 267 Wis. 2d 902, 672 N.W.2d 162 (2003) (finding defense expert's statement on cross-examination that he would assess delayed reporting aspects of the case without conducting a personal interview of the child helped to establish that there was no need for a psychological examination of child).

[209] Fitzgerald v. State, 193 Ga. App. 76, 386 S.E.2d 914, 916 (1989).

Even when a complainant testifies at a competency hearing that she hears voices, and that some of the voices were demons with "thick eyebrows that came straight down, ears pointed, with real sharp teeth," and that the demons had animal bodies, a defendant may not have a right to have an independent psychological evaluation of a 15-year-old complainant to determine competency.[210]

§ 1.21 Physical examination of complaining witness.

The defendant may request a second physical examination of a complaining witness to determine if sexual abuse is continuing or to try to verify findings and measurements of an initial examination of a child victim. Some physical findings, such as absence of hymen, should be verifiable upon a second examination. On the other hand, certain tears, abrasions, or redness are likely to heal within a short period of time.

Some courts have held that a trial court does not have the authority to order an unwilling witness to submit to a physical examination.[211] Other courts have held that a court has the power to order a physical examination of a criminal witness only under the most compelling of circumstances, and that such an order must be approached "with utmost judicial restraint and respect for an individual's dignity."[212] Several courts have found that such an examination can be ordered only under "the most compelling of circumstances" and have articulated the following factors for a trial judge to consider in evaluating a request for a physical examination of a complainant.

1) The nature of the examination requested and the intrusiveness associated with such an examination.

2) The victim's age.

3) The resulting physical or emotional effects of the examination upon the victim.

4) The probative value of the examination.

5) The remoteness in time of the examination to the alleged criminal incident.

---

[210] Bart v. Commonwealth, 951 S.W.2d 576 (Ky. 1997).

[211] State v. Joyce, 97 N.C. App. 464, 467, 389 S.E.2d 136, 138–39 (1990); State v. Hewett, 93 N.C. App. 1, 9, 376 S.E.2d 467, 472 (1989); Commonwealth v. Davis, 437 Pa. Super. 471, 650 A.2d 452 (1994), *aff'd*, 543 Pa. 628, 674 A.2d 214 (1996) (holding that court knew of no authority that would enable it to order a complainant to submit to a physical examination, and that it was highly unlikely that any injuries caused during the sexual assaults would still be discernable five years after the assaults).

[212] State v. Delaney, 187 W. Va. 212, 216, 417 S.E.2d 903 (1992).

6)   The evidence already available for the defendant's use.[213]

A majority of courts follow the "compelling need or reason" test as the standard to use in evaluating motions for a second physical examination of a complaining witness.[214] If a physical examination is unlikely to yield helpful finds, a court is unlikely to order a physical examination of the complainant.[215] A "genital or rectal examination has a vastly higher privacy quotient than the examination of the eyes, hair, the throat or the extremities."[216] Such an intrusion into the

---

[213] *Id. See also* State v. Chard, 808 P.2d 351, 355 (Colo. 1991), *cert. denied*, 502 U.S. 863 (1991).

> We therefore adopt the majority view and hold that a trial court may exercise its discretion to order an involuntary physical examination when a defendant demonstrates a "compelling need or reason" for the examination. In exercising this discretion, the trial court must "balance the possible emotional trauma, embarrassment or intimidation to the complainant against the likelihood of the examination producing material as distinguished from speculative evidence."

Id. at 355); State v. Ramos, 553 A.2d 1059, 1061 (R.I. 1989).

[214] Lanton v. State, 456 So. 2d 873, 874 (Ala. Crim. App. 1984), *cert. denied*, 471 U.S. 1095 (1985) (holding that a defendant must demonstrate "extreme necessity" for a physical examination of a sexual assault victim); Fuller v. State, 669 So. 2d 273, 274, *review denied*, 675 So. 2d 929 (Fla. 1996) (in reversing and remanding defendant's conviction for other reasons, appellate court noted there is no *per se* prohibition against an independent physical examination of a sexual assault victim and that the trial court has the authority to compel "an involuntary examination of a · prosecution witness where strong and compelling reasons exist"); State v. Farr, 558 So. 2d 437 (Fla. Dist. Ct. App. 1990); State v. Drab, 546 So. 2d 54, 56 (Fla. Dist. Ct. App.), *review denied*, 553 So. 2d 1164 (Fla. 1989); State v. LaBelle, 887 P.2d 1071 (Idaho 1995) (defendant failed to establish physical examination of victim would likely produce relevant evidence; court reserved ruling on whether Idaho courts have inherent authority to order such an examination); People v. Glover, 49 Ill. 2d 78, 273 N.E.2d 367 (1971); State v. Garrett, 384 N.W.2d 617, 619 (Minn. Ct. App. 1986) (stating that finding of compelling need could be established only in a rare case); State v. D.R.H., 127 N.J. 249, 604 A.2d 89 (1992) ("Consequently, we hold that courts may order the physical examination of a child sex-abuse victim only when satisfied that the defendant has made a sufficient showing that such an examination can produce competent evidence that has substantial probative worth, and if admitted and believed by the trier of fact, that evidence could refute or neutralize incriminating evidence or impugn the credibility of prosecution witnesses. Further, the court must be satisfied that the defendant's need clearly outweighs the possible harmful consequences to the alleged victim." *Id.* at 260-61, 604 A.2d at 95); People v. Beauchamp, 126 Misc. 2d 754, 756, 483 N.Y.S.2d 946, 948 (Sup. Ct. 1985), *modified on other grounds*, 74 N.Y.2d 639, 539 N.E.2d 1105, 541 N.Y.S.2d 977 (1989) (noting that the trial court carefully weighed the rights and needs of victims since "children are not discoverable items"); State v. Barone, 852 S.W.2d 216, 221 (Tenn. 1993).

[215] People v. Melendez, 80 P.3d 883 (Colo. 2003) ("[H]ere, a physical examination of the child revealing no vaginal trauma or evidence of vaginal intercourse would not establish that defendant had not sexually abused her . . . . [T]he results of a physical examination here would have been at best equivocal in regard to defendant's innocence. In these circumstances, it was within the trial court's discretion to deny defendant's motion for a physical examination." *Id.* at 888).

[216] People v. Nokes, 183 Cal. App. 3d 468, 479, 228 Cal. Rptr. 119, 125 (1986) ("We find nothing in the cited cases to suggest that a criminal defendant has the right to compel an intrusion into the body of his or her victim for the purpose of attempting to obtain allegedly exculpatory evidence. In fact, the cases are all to the contrary." *Id.* at 478, 228 Cal. Rptr. at 124.).

body of a child to search for exculpatory evidence in a child molestation trial is too invasive, especially given the effect of an unnecessary rectal examination on a child who may have been abused.[217]

In *Turner v. Commonwealth*, the Kentucky Supreme Court permitted the defendant to compel his four-year-old daughter to submit to a second gynecological exam since the examination may have disclosed evidence to refute the charge and may have been helpful to the defendant at trial because the initial examination revealed tears in the hymenal ring indicative of penile penetration.[218] It was believed that a second examination could challenge the credibility of the physical examination offered by the prosecution and challenge whether such injuries to the hymenal area had actually occurred or, if there were such injuries, whether they were in such a location to indicate a probability of penile penetration.[219] This holding is somewhat difficult to reconcile with other court decisions dealing with compelled physical examinations of a child. The criteria set forth earlier in this section are difficult to meet. The rationale of the Kentucky Court appears to be a much softer standard for permitting a second physical examination of a child than that of other courts. This is an older case, and the wide availability of colposcopy and photography may obviate the need for a second physical examination, since an expert may now view videotape or photographs taken during the initial examination.

Most appellate courts will be unlikely to overturn a trial court's denial of a physical examination of a child because of the compelling-need standard, and because a second exam will not likely offer significantly probative evidence. An intermediate California appellate court has held that, if the second examination would produce, at best, equivocal results on behalf of a defendant, the trial court's decision to deny a second physical examination should not be overturned "unless the exercise of discretion has been so arbitrary and capricious that no reasonable court could have made such a finding."[220] This is indicative of the reluctance of courts to order an intrusive physical examination of a complainant.

If a court does order a physical examination of the complainant, and the complainant refuses to undergo such an examination, the prosecution may be precluded from offering medical testimony based on the original examination.[221] Following its same rule as with a psychological examination of a complainant, Illinois' Supreme Court holds that a trial court cannot order a physical examination of a complaining witness.[222] However, if the prosecution intends to offer

---

[217] *Id.* at 479, 228 Cal. Rptr. at 126.

[218] 767 S.W.2d 557, 559 (Ky. 1988), *cert. denied*, 493 U.S. 901 (1989).

[219] *Id.*

[220] People v. Nokes, 183 Cal. App. 3d 468, 228 Cal. Rptr. 119 (1986); State v. Gersin, 1994 Ohio App. LEXIS 5085 (Nov. 10, 1994).

[221] State v. Diamond, 553 So. 2d 1185 (Fla. Dist. Ct. App. 1988).

[222] People v. Lopez, 207 Ill. 2d 449, 800 N.E.2d 1211 (2003).

evidence from an examining expert of a physical examination and the victim refuses to undergo an examination, the court should determine what, if any, portion of the examination is admissible, i.e., if some portions may be admissible because they are not in dispute.[223]

§ 1.22   Mandated recording of witness or defendant interviews and creation of discovery documents.

Generally, the prosecution will not be required to produce or generate documents as part of the discovery process that do not already exist. Thus, the prosecution cannot be made to make notes of its contacts with witnesses. "There is no requirement that a prosecutor record in any fashion his interviews with a witness."[224]

In some states, a defendant's statement to police in certain situations must be recorded to be admitted into evidence.[225]

One request commonly made in child sexual assault cases is that all further contacts or interviews with child witnesses be recorded. These recordings can then be reviewed by a defendant's expert to provide testimony on the possible suggestiveness of the interview. This can be helpful to the defense in trying to establish the suggestive nature of the interview process or the effect of repeated contact with or questioning by law enforcement authorities; however, such requests may go outside the scope of state provisions regulating discovery. One trial court ordered that all future interviews, conversations, examinations, and meetings with the ten-year-old sexual assault victim "be transcribed, verbatim, by a certified stenographer" and that "the People shall provide defendant with the dates, times and places of all future interviews."[226] The appellate court held that such an order went beyond the court's powers and that discovery must be governed by the state's statutory provisions.[227]

---

[223] People v. Lopez, 207 Ill. 2d 449, 800 N.E.2d 1211 (2003).

[224] People v. Steinberg, 170 A.D.2d 50, 76, 573 N.Y.S.2d 965, 981 (1991), aff'd, 79 N.Y.2d 673, 595 N.E.2d 845, 584 N.Y.S.2d 770 (1992). See also People v. Raibon, 843 P.2d 46 (Colo. Ct. App. 1992) ("Further, while not considered in a constitutional context as such, this court has previously concluded that the prosecution is under no duty to reduce to writing statements made during the course of an interview with a witness." Id. at 49).

[225] The Alaska Supreme Court has taken the position that a failure to record the defendant's interview is a violation of his due process rights under the Alaska Constitution. See Stephan v. State, 711 P.2d 1156 (Alaska 1985). See also Tex. Code Crim. Proc. art. 38.22 § 3.

[226] Catterson v. Rohl, 202 A.D.2d 420, 422, 608 N.Y.S.2d 696, 698, appeal denied, 83 N.Y.2d 755, 635 N.E.2d 296, 613 N.Y.S.2d 127 (1994).

[227] Id. ("Thus, insofar as there is absolutely no authority for the imposition of an affirmative duty on the prosecutor to 'create' Rosario material, we find that, here too, the respondent Justice exceeded his authority." Id. at 423, 608 N.Y.S.2d at 698–99).

Courts have rejected the argument that failure to record a child's interview is suppression of exculpatory evidence[228] or a denial of due process;[229] however, cross-examination and argument to the jury may develop the point that a key witness's interview was not preserved. Another court has stated that investigators should not selectively record interviews with child witnesses, and that in a close case, the failure to record an interview may result in reversal of a defendant's conviction.[230]

§ 1.23 *Brady* Rule and discovery and impeachment evidence and pleas.

In *Brady v. Maryland*,[231] the Supreme Court of the United States established that the prosecution's failure to disclose to a defendant evidence in the prosecution's possession that is both favorable and material to the defense will result in the overturning of a defendant's conviction and the granting of a new trial. In *Brady*, the Court defined the constitutional error as withheld evidence that would "tend to exculpate" the defendant.[232] The United States Supreme Court further refined the *Brady* rule in *Kyles v. Whitley*.[233] Under *Kyles*, the materiality of the failure to disclose is evaluated "collectively" and not item-by-item,[234] and more recently, the Supreme Court emphasized, "When police or prosecutors conceal significant exculpatory or impeaching material in the State's possession, it is ordinarily incumbent on the State to set the record straight."[235] When in doubt about materiality, the "prudent prosecutor will resolve doubtful questions in favor of disclosure."[236]

After enunciating the two-prong approach for determining whether favorable evidence was material,[237] the Supreme Court, in *United States v. Bagley*,[238]

---

[228] State v. Weaver, 290 Mont. 58, 964 P.2d 713 (1998) (holding that police officer's failure to record interviews with child sexual abuse victims did not constitute destruction of material exculpatory evidence); State v. Hanson, 283 Mont. 316, 322–23, 940 P.2d 1166, 1170 (1997).

[229] State v. Carol, 89 Wash. App. 77, 948 P.2d 837 (1997).

[230] United States v. Cabral, 43 M.J. 808, 811 (A.F.C.C.A. 1996), *aff'd*, 47 M.J. 268 (C.A.A.F. 1997).

[231] 373 U.S. 83 (1963).

[232] *Id.* at 88.

[233] 514 U.S. 419 (1995).

[234] *Id.* at 436.

[235] Banks v. Dretke, 540 U.S. 668, 675–76 (2004).

[236] United States v. Agurs, 427 U.S. 97, 108 (1976).

[237] *Id.* at 104 (holding that specifically requested evidence by the defense was material if it might have affected the trial verdict, whereas if there had not been a specific request or only a general request for information, the prosecution's duty to disclose was only if the undisclosed exculpatory evidence would create a reasonable doubt which did not otherwise exist).

[238] 473 U.S. 667, 682 (1985). *See also* Kyles v. Whitley, 514 U.S. 419 (1995) (reiterates the "reasonable probability standard" to determine whether *Brady* violation has occurred); Carroll v.

adopted a single standard that undisclosed evidence is material only if there is a "reasonable probability" that the undisclosed evidence would have altered the outcome of the trial and that a reasonable probability is "a probability sufficient to undermine confidence in the outcome."[239]

Not all courts embrace the reasonable probability standard to measure materiality in the context of the *Brady* rule, but have rather adopted the standard of a "reasonable possibility" that the failure to disclose exculpatory information contributed to the guilty verdict where the prosecution was provided with a specific discovery demand for the information.[240] It is still best that, even under the *Bagley* standard, discovery requests be as specific as possible to enhance the viability of any post-trial arguments concerning the significance of the failure to turn over information.

In *Giles v. Maryland*,[241] the Supreme Court found suppression of favorable evidence to an accused rapist to be a denial of due process. In *Giles*, the complaining witness in a rape case had given inconsistent accounts of the events of the crime. She also suffered from emotional problems, which would tend to discredit her version of the incident.

There are other examples of *Brady* violation in sexual assault cases. In a prosecution based on incapacity to consent based on mental incapacity, the failure to disclose psychological records indicating the complainant knows the difference between "good" and "okay" touches and "uncomfortable" and "not okay" touches, and knows she has the right to say "no" is a *Brady* violation requiring reversal of a defendant's conviction.[242] The materiality of such evidence is all

---

State, 815 So. 2d 601, 619 (Fla. 2002); State v. Harrington, 1994 Minn. App. LEXIS 1105 *4 (Nov. 8, 1994) (In sexual assault prosecution involving discovery obligations, Minnesota follows rule that a new trial should be granted if there is a reasonable probability that had the evidence been disclosed to the defense, the outcome of the trial might have been different.), *citing* State v. Clobes, 422 N.W.2d 252, 255 (Minn. 1988); State v. Johnston, 39 Ohio St. 3d 48, 529 N.E.2d 898 (1988).

[239] Strickland v. Washington, 466 U.S. 668, 694 (1984).

[240] *See, e.g.*, People v. Vilardi, 76 N.Y.2d 67, 555 N.E.2d 915, 556 N.Y.S.2d 518 (1990); State v. Steele, 510 N.W.2d 661 (S.D. 1994) (reversing defendant's conviction due to prosecution's failure to inform the defense that the complainant had contracted chlamydia, a sexually-transmitted venereal disease, from defendant and stating that the standard to be applied in determining whether or not newly discovered evidence required a new trial was the "reasonable possibility that the newly discovered evidence would probably produce a different result on retrial." *Id.* at 665).

[241] 386 U.S. 66 (1967).

[242] Bailey v. Rae, 339 F.3d 1107 (9th Cir. 2003):

Each report contained a professional analysis of not only Winters' general development status and her understanding of physical and moral aspects of physical contact, but also her capacity to consent to improper sexual advances — the linchpin issue presented at trial. The January and March 1994 reports, both of which were prepared after therapy sessions relating to Winters' prior sexual abuse, observed that Winters knew the difference between "good" and "uncomfortable" touches, and that she knew she had the right to say "no" to an "inappropriate" touch. The reports also indicated that, although Winters was "developmentally delayed," she

the more significant when it relates to a significant issue, and the evidence could not be developed from any source available to the defendant.

An example of the *Brady* rule in a child sexual abuse case is *People v. Ramos*,[243] which involved a day-care worker charged with raping a six-year-old girl in a bathroom during nap time. The information withheld by the prosecution which the court ruled was favorable and material to the defense, and which created a "reasonable possibility" that the failure to provide the information contributed to the guilty verdict, was information of the child's prior masturbation and engaging in sexually provocative play with other children, including the use of dolls and "sex play" which would have accounted for the child's ability to describe sexual behavior and undercut the prosecution's argument that the child would not have otherwise been able to discuss sexual matters without having experienced sexual abuse. The withheld information also undercut the significance of the medical testimony which was based not on medical findings but on the child's ability to articulate details of sexual matters. The court also pointed to numerous inconsistent statements in the records which the prosecution failed to disclose, which was of heightened significance when the credibility and reliability of the child witness was the crux of the prosecution case.

Similarly, the prosecution's failing to disclose a letter which contained information contradicting a child's complaint of abuse, when the prosecution had access to the report and knew or should have known of its favorable implications for the defense and its materiality, violates the defendant's right to exculpatory evidence.[244] A complainant's pursuit of a civil lawsuit may be *Brady* material, which should be disclosed to the defendant.[245]

Significant impeachment evidence is exculpatory. "Impeachment evidence . . . as well as exculpatory evidence, falls within the *Brady* rule."[246] To the extent the impeachment has independent exculpatory value, it should be disclosed. For example, the prosecution should disclose a statement by a witness that the defendant did not engage in, or have knowledge of, the acts alleged in the indictment, even if such statement is subsequently contradicted by the witness. This includes a statement that an act never occurred or if it did occur, was without defendant's knowledge or involvement. Impeachment evidence is more likely to be material from a *Brady* perspective when the witness at issue supplied the

---

could easily tell the difference between those touches that are "okay" and those that are not. Given the content of these reports, we find it difficult to conceive how Bailey would not have benefited from this evidence in defending against the State's allegation that Winters was incapable of consent.

Id. at 1114–15.

[243] 201 A.D.2d 78, 614 N.Y.S.2d 977 (1994).

[244] State v. Lewis, 1995 Tenn. Crim. App. LEXIS 33 (Jan. 12, 1995).

[245] *See, e.g.*, People v. Wallert, 98 A.D.2d 47, 469 N.Y.S.2d 722 (1983) and § 5.48.

[246] United States v. Bagley, 473 U.S. 667, 676–77 (1985). *See also Ex parte* Richardson, 70 S.W.3d 865, 871 (Tex. Ct. Crim. App. 2002).

key or only evidence implicating the defendant.[247] When the *Brady* claim consists of changes in testimony by the prosecution's expert in similar cases, the evidence is not material when there is other strong evidence to support the conviction and there is not a reasonable probability that the trial result would have been different.[248] With respect to *Brady*, its applicability to the loss or destruction of evidence[249] or evidence consumed in testing[250] is treated elsewhere in this text.

§ 1.24   Timeliness of *Brady* disclosure and opportunity to use disclosed materials.

There is emerging authority that disclosure of *Brady* material must be in time for its effective use at trial, not just prior to trial. While the concept that a defendant must be given a "meaningful opportunity" to utilize exculpatory evidence has existed for some time,[251] the fact that the defendant is given the information before trial may not defeat sanctions. In *Leka v. Portunondo*,[252] the prosecution provided the defendant nine days before the opening statements and 23 days before the defense began its case with the name of a witness, but failed to disclose that the witness had information helpful to the defense, thereby requiring reversal. The prosecution may not assume that providing the name of a witness who may have important information just prior to trial will be adequate disclosure. The prosecution's *Brady* obligation is not satisfied by providing the name of a witness or knowing that the defense is aware of a witness and believing that the defense might discover the exculpatory evidence if it asks the right questions of the witness.[253] The defendant has no "duty to 'speculate' about what exculpatory evidence a witness or a potential witness might know of and to investigate that possible evidence."[254] In *Leka*, the United States Court of

---

[247] United States v. Petrillo, 821 F.2d 85, 90 (2d Cir. 1987).

[248] People v. Salazar, 35 Cal. 4th 1031, 112 P.3d 14, 29 Cal. Rptr. 3d 16 (2005).

[249] *See* § 1.14.

[250] *See* § 13.14.

[251] *See, e.g.*, State v. White, 229 Conn. 125, 138–39, 640 A.2d 572, 579 (1994) (reversing defendant's conviction because exculpatory information not disclosed in timely manner to permit interview of witnesses); State v. Harris, 272 Wis. 2d 80, 113–14, 680 N.W.2d 737, 755 (2004) (holding exculpatory evidence must be disclosed within a sufficient time for its effective use).

[252] 257 F.3d 89 (2d Cir. 2001).

[253] Keeter v. Texas, 105 S.W.3d 137 (Tex. Ct. App. 2003) (finding *Brady* violation requiring reversal of sexual assault conviction when prosecutor failed to inform defendant that two witnesses, complainant's father and step-mother, told prosecutor that she was not truthful and told prosecutor that her father also did not believe her. On appeal by the State, the Texas Court of Criminal Appeals held the defendant did not preserve his *Brady* claim and affirmed the judgment of conviction, Keeter v. Texas, 105 S.W.3d 137 (Tex. Ct. App. 2003), *rev'd*, 175 S.W.3d 765 (Tex. Crim. App. 2005), *cert. denied*, 126 S. Ct. 114 (2005)).

[254] Keeter v. Texas, 105 S.W.3d 137, 148 (Tex. Ct. App. 2003), *rev'd* 175 S.W.3d 765 (Tex. Crim. App. 2005), *cert. denied*, 126 S. Ct. 114 (2005).

Appeals for the Second Circuit emphasized that disclosure of critical evidence on the eve of trial is a dangerous prosecutorial practice:

. . .

> [O]nce trial comes, the prosecution may not assume that the defense is still in the investigatory mode . . . . For the same reasons, a disclosure made on the eve of trial (or after trial has begun) may be insufficient unless it is fuller and more thorough than may have been required if the disclosure had been made at an earlier stage. [255]

. . .

> The opportunity for use under *Brady* is the opportunity for a responsible lawyer to use the information with some degree of calculation and fore-thought. It is clear enough that the prosecution failed to make sufficient disclosure in sufficient time to afford the defense an opportunity for use. [256]

> When such a disclosure is first made on the eve of trial, or when trial is under way, the opportunity to use it may be impaired. The defense may be unable to divert resources from other initiatives and obligations that are or may seem more pressing, and the defense may be unable to assimilate the information into its case. [257]

Thereafter, in *United States v. Gil*, [258] the same appeals court again reversed a defendant's conviction when an exculpatory piece of information — even though provided to the defense three or four days before trial and in its possession during trial — was not provided in a timely manner so as to allow the defense a meaningful opportunity to use the information at trial. The defendant did not discover the evidence, a memo, until five months after the defendant's conviction. The court noted that in addition to the timing of the disclosure, the "two-page memo was not easily identifiable as a document of significance, located as it was among reams [approximately 2700 pages] of documents." [259] The court remarked that "disclosure of critical information on the eve of trial is unsafe for the prosecution." [260]

Courts will look to the context of the case in evaluating whether or not the "late" disclosure warrants reversal of a conviction. If there is not a "reasonable probability" of a different outcome in light of all the evidence in the case, then late disclosure of exculpatory evidence may be harmless error. [261] If the

---

[255] *Leka, supra* note 253, 257 F.3d at 100–01.

[256] *Id.* at 103.

[257] *Leka, supra*, note 253, 257 F.3d at 106.

[258] 297 F.3d 93 (2d Cir. 2002).

[259] *Id.* at 106.

[260] *Id.*

[261] People v. Elston, 462 Mich. 751, 614 N.W.2d 595 (2000) (holding that emergency room physician's disclosure on the first day of trial of sperm fragments found during his examination of two-year-old was not *Brady* material since it was not favorable to the defense — and the defense did

undisclosed information or statement is cumulative of other evidence used to impeach the complainant, the nondisclosure is less likely to be grounds for a new trial. [262] For example, failing to disclose prior to trial, but revealing during trial, an interview of a child complainant in which she identifies another abuser, which is favorable to the accused, does not necessarily result in a reversal of conviction when there is not a reasonable probability of a different outcome in the verdict had the statement been disclosed prior to trial. [263] Nonetheless, a failure to provide a victim's prior inconsistent statement, in a case based largely on the complainant's testimony, may be a *Brady* violation requiring reversal of a defendant's conviction. [264]

When the prosecution reveals *Brady* information after the close of proof, dismissal of the indictment may be the only effective sanction. [265]

Yet another issue in analyzing the late or trial disclosure of *Brady* information is how the defense responds to the late disclosure. For example, in one child pornography prosecution, the State's failure to disclose that its computer expert failed to wipe clean a target disk, onto which the images forming the basis for the prosecution were copied, was deemed exculpatory evidence. [266] This allowed child pornography images from other cases to remain on the disk, creating the possibility that the images on which the defendant's conviction was based might have been left over from a prior child pornography prosecution.

The court observed:

> Although Taylor provided a statement saying he had at times viewed and downloaded photographs on the internet, he was not convicted of generally viewing or purchasing photographs, whether lewd or otherwise. He was

---

not seek a continuance when the information was disclosed and because there was overwhelming evidence of guilt); Cheek v. State, 119 S.W.3d 475 (Tex. Ct. App. 2003) (upholding a mother's conviction despite tardy disclosure of exculpatory evidence where a trial court delayed the start of voir dire until the next afternoon in order for the mother to procure and view a videotaped interview of the child/victim); Hampton v. State, 106 S.W.3d 846 (Tex. Ct. App. 2003) (holding disclosure on day before it rested its case of report implicating two others in crime did not raise "reasonable probability" of a different result requiring reversal of conviction).

[262] State v. Chalk, 816 A.2d 413 (R.I. 2002) (finding late disclosure of impeaching information contained in residential group home records did not require reversal of conviction, since information previously provided allowed defendant to delve into much of the area covered by the newly discovered files and information would not undermine confidence in jury's verdict — there was also no reason for trial court to have granted defendant's request for a continuance); Lockhart v. Commonwealth, 34 Va. App. 329, 542 S.E.2d 1 (2001).

[263] State v. Baker, 301 Mont. 323, 8 P.3d 817 (2000).

[264] State v. McKinnon, 2001 Ohio App. LEXIS 261 (Jan. 29, 2001); State v. Kearns, 210 W. Va. 167, 556 S.E.2d 812 (2001).

[265] People v. Ariosa, 172 Misc. 2d 312, 660 N.Y.S.2d 255 (Co. Ct. 1997) (after close of proof, prosecution turned over numerous documents provided to prosecution by complainant which would have been material to cross-examination of the complainant).

[266] Taylor v. State, 93 S.W.3d 487 (Tex. Ct. App. 2002).

convicted of possessing nine specific photographs. There is no other evidence to show these photographs were actually contained on his computer. The State's case, therefore, rested on those photographs exclusively and on the credibility of the witness who copied Taylor's computer drive that allegedly contained those photographs. This evidence, which tends both to exculpate Taylor and to impeach the State's witness' testimony, went to the very heart of the State's case and involves the only means used to present that evidence.[267]

However, because the defendant did not ask for a continuance when informed of this evidence, the court held that the defendant waived his *Brady* claim.[268]

On the other hand, an investigator's deletion of e-mail messages and discarding a hard drive, in the absence of bad faith, does not trigger a *Brady* sanction when the information is contained on another drive and the evidence is reasonably available by other means.[269]

§ 1.25 Exceptions to *Brady* rule — Material in defendant's possession or defendant aware of information through reasonable diligence or another source.

There are important exceptions to the *Brady* rule. A court is unlikely to find *Brady* information or evidence when the defendant is already aware of the information,[270] or the information is available to the defendant through the exercise of reasonable diligence.[271] If the *Brady* information can reasonably be obtained from other sources, then it does not fall within *Brady*. For example, when an investigator deleted an e-mail message and discarded a computer hard drive, there is no destruction of exculpatory evidence if the defendant is able to obtain the e-mails from another source.[272]

A court is also unlikely to find a *Brady* violation when a defendant has been given the opportunity during the trial to use the allegedly exculpatory material

---

[267] *Id.* at 501–02.

[268] *Id.* at 502.

[269] United States v. Pearl, 324 F.3d 1210, 1215 (10th Cir. 2003), *cert. denied*, 539 U.S. 934 (2003).

[270] United States v. Stewart, 513 F.2d 957, 960 (2d Cir. 1975).

[271] United States v. Morris, 80 F.3d 1151, 1170 (7th Cir.), *cert. denied*, 519 U.S. 868, 117 S. Ct. 181 (1996); Dalbosco v. State, 978 S.W.2d 236, 238 (Tex. Ct. App. 1998).

[272] United States v. Pearl, 324 F.3d 1210 (10th Cir. 2003):

> All or virtually all of the deleted e-mail messages contained on the damaged and discarded hard drive were contained on another drive [sic], thereby failing to satisfy the "unable to obtain comparable evidence by other reasonably available means" aspect of Trombetta analysis. Furthermore, there was no evidence that the detective acted in bad faith. The loss of e-mail messages and hard drive was, at worst, the product of negligence.

Id. at 1215.

or cross-examine the prosecution's witnesses concerning the alleged exculpatory material. [273]

The *Brady* rule applies only to information in the prosecutor's possession. Thus, while a complainant's counseling records or child welfare records may be accessible under many theories and subject to an *in camera* inspection, a prosecutor is not necessarily obligated to produce records that are not in the prosecution's possession or control. [274]

The *Brady* rule does not create a general right of discovery to all investigative reports and leads. [275]

---

[273] People v. Brown, 67 N.Y.2d 555, 496 N.E.2d 663, 505 N.Y.S.2d 574 (1986), *cert. denied*, 479 U.S. 1093 (1987); People v. Ortiz, 16 A.D.3d 831, 791 N.Y.S.2d 709, *appeal denied*, 4 N.Y.3d 889, 831 N.E.2d 979, 798 N.Y.S.2d 734 (2005):

> The statement that defense counsel claimed should have been turned over earlier, a statement made during an unrelated police investigation indicating that defendant's daughter spent almost every weekend with her father, was not *Brady* material because it was not exculpatory . . . .[citation omitted]. In any event, it was available to counsel days before the witness who made the statement testified, but counsel did not avail himself of the opportunity to review it.

See also People v. Jones, 236 A.D.2d 846, 654 N.Y.S.2d 495, *appeal denied*, 90 N.Y.2d 859, 683 N.E.2d 1060, 661 N.Y.S.2d 186 (1997).

[274] Commonwealth v. Delp, 41 Mass. App. Ct. 435, 672 N.E.2d 114, *review denied*, 423 Mass. 1112, 674 N.E.2d 245 (1996) (holding that complainant's records in possession of Department of Social Services and thus, not *Brady* material or possession of prosecution); People v. Stanaway, 446 Mich. 643, 666–67, 521 N.W.2d 557, 569 (1994), *cert. denied*, 513 U.S. 1121, 115 S. Ct. 923 (1995). *See also* People v. Chilson, 285 A.D.2d 733, 728 N.Y.S.2d 550, *appeal denied*, 97 N.Y.2d 640, 761 N.E.2d 2, 735 N.Y.S.2d 497 (2001) (holding failure of people to disclose caseworker's investigative notes did not violate *Brady* or disclosure rules since notes were not in people's possession); People v. Darling, 276 A.D.2d 922, 714 N.Y.S.2d 393 (2000), *appeal denied*, 96 N.Y.2d 733, 745 N.E.2d 1023, 722 N.Y.S.2d 800 (2001) (noting *Brady* Rule did not apply to medical or mental health records not in people's possession); People v. Sealey, 239 A.D.2d 864, 659 N.Y.S.2d 639, *appeal denied*, 90 N.Y.2d 910, 686 N.E.2d 234, 663 N.Y.S.2d 522 (1997) (holding that prosecution is "under no duty to investigate the psychiatric history of the victim and obtain her psychiatric records," and because the prosecution did not possess the complainant's records, failure to produce them is not a *Brady* violation); People v. Walden, 236 A.D.2d 779, 653 N.Y.S.2d 875, *appeal denied*, 90 N.Y.2d 865, 683 N.E.2d 1066, 661 N.Y.S.2d 192 (1997) (holding that child welfare records are not *Brady* since among other reasons they were not in the possession of the prosecution); Barker v. Commonwealth, 230 Va. 370, 376–77, 337 S.E.2d 729, 734 (1985).

[275] Kyles v. Whitley, 514 U.S. 419 (1995) ("We have never held that the Constitution demands an open file policy (however such a policy might work out in practice), and the rule in *Bagley* (and, hence, in *Brady*) requires less of the prosecution than the ABA Standards for Criminal Justice, which call generally for prosecutorial disclosures of any evidence tending to exculpate or mitigate." *Id.* at 437.); Moore v. Illinois, 434 U.S. 220 (1977); United States v. Roach, 28 F.3d 729, 734 (8th Cir. 1994); State v. Crabtree, 2003 Tenn. Crim. App. LEXIS 81 (Jan. 31, 2003) (holding defendant did not have right to detective's interview notes of child victim and juvenile court records of child and her mother since the documents were neither exculpatory nor relevant and did not qualify as *Brady* material).

Thus, a defendant will not necessarily be entitled to discover the statements or grand jury testimony of a witness whom the defendant may consider calling as a witness.[276]

§ 1.26 *Brady* rights before plea.

The United States Supreme Court in *United States v. Ruiz*[277] has ruled that a defendant may waive the right to exculpatory evidence as part of a plea agreement since the Fifth and Sixth Amendments do not require Federal prosecutors to disclose impeachment information relating to witnesses or informants before entering a binding plea agreement. Because the plea agreement in *Ruiz* proposed providing the defendant with information pertaining to his "factual innocence" (although not *Brady* impeachment information), the court had less of a concern that innocent individuals will plead guilty.[278] One Wisconsin appeals court distinguishes *Ruiz* from a situation in which a defendant makes a written demand for all "exculpatory" evidence prior to plea, in which case the prosecutor must provide *Brady* evidence before the defendant pleads guilty. In *State v. Harris*,[279] the Wisconsin Supreme Court affirmed an order permitting a defendant, accused of sexual contact with a six-year-old, to withdraw his plea after it was disclosed by the child that her grandfather had sexually assaulted her. Because this information provides a possible alternative source for the child's sexual knowledge, the possibility that the child does not wish to disclose the sexual assault by her grandfather and wishes to project it onto the defendant, it may violate the right of confrontation since it impairs the defendant's ability to cross-examine the state's expert on the behaviors of sexual abuse victims; it is exculpatory information which should be disclosed to the defendant prior to his plea in response to his discovery demand for exculpatory evidence.[280] The court, relying on *Ruiz*, did not find that a defendant is automatically entitled under due process to any potentially exculpable information that can form the basis

---

[276] People v. Brooks, 210 A.D.2d 800, 621 N.Y.S.2d 701 (1994), *appeal denied*, 85 N.Y.2d 906, 650 N.E.2d 1331, 627 N.Y.S.2d 329 (1995) (defendant was not entitled to statements of defendant's niece and alibi witness in the prosecution's possession since this was not an exculpatory statement within the *Brady* doctrine); People v. Gardner, 162 A.D.2d 466, 556 N.Y.S.2d 163 (1990).

[277] 536 U.S. 622, 625 (2002) (The plea agreement presented to the defendant specified that evidence pertaining to the factual innocence of the defendant had been supplied the defendant, but that the defendant waived the right to impeachment information pertaining to informants and witnesses. Because the defendant would not agree to such a waiver, the defendant refused the plea agreement, pleaded guilty, and then requested the two-level downward departure he would have received for accepting the "fast-track" plea agreement offered by the government. This is the context of the defendant's appeal to the Supreme Court.). *See also* McCann v. Mangialardi, 337 F.3d 782, 787 (7th Cir. 2003); Gruning v. Dipaolo, 311 F.3d 69, 73 (1st Cir. 2002); People v. Moore, 345 Ill. App. 3d 1043, 804 N.E.2d 595 (2003); *In re* Brennan, 117 Wash. App. 797, 72 P.3d 182 (2003).

[278] *Id.* at 631.

[279] 680 N.W.2d 737 (2004).

[280] *Id.* at 822.

for investigation by the police before his plea. Rather, it relied on the prosecution's violation of the discovery statute, because the defendant had made a demand, pursuant to the discovery statutes, for exculpatory information.[281] The failure to provide the defendant the information after it was authorized by statute, denied the defendant the opportunity to challenge the State's expert witness and the credibility of the victim.[282]

§ 1.27　Motion for severance of multiple counts of sexual assault upon multiple victims.

A strong case of sexual assault can be established against a defendant by multiple allegations. There may be some situations where a defendant feels that a better defense can be made by showing a repeated pattern of mishandling of the investigation, for example, a pattern of poor interviewing techniques. This is likely to be an unusual situation, however. More likely, the prosecution will wish to prosecute multiple acts involving multiple victims together, and the defense will seek to sever allegations involving different victims.

Most courts will permit the joinder of counts when they are based upon the same or similar theory of law or when proof of one charge would be relevant and admissible in the trial of the other charge.[283]

---

[281] *Id.*

[282] *Id.*

[283] Parker v. United States, 751 A.2d 943 (D.C. 2000); State v. Marshall, 197 Ariz. 496, 4 P.3d 1039 (2000) (holding evidence of aberrant acts in some courts were admissible as proof of defendant's propensity to commit other acts and vice versa); State v. Walden, 183 Ariz. 595, 905 P.2d 974 (1995), *cert. denied*, 517 U.S. 1146 (1996) (numerous similarities between defendant's attacks properly permitted joinder of counts); State v. Stevenson, 43 Conn. App. 680, 686 A.2d 500 (1996), *appeal denied*, 240 Conn. 920, 692 A.2d 817 (1997) ("In this case, both crimes were perpetrated in the early morning hours in the same neighborhood. The defendant drove both of his victims, who each separately identified him, to the same area of Fair Haven to commit the crimes. The defendant used the same language with each woman, and threatened each with anal intercourse. Both women were attacked when the perpetrator of the crimes discovered that they were not working as prostitutes." *Id.* at 687, 686 A.2d at 505. Court held probative value of joinder outweighs prejudice); Moore v. State, 1995 Del. LEXIS 69 (Feb. 17, 1995) (court properly permitted joinder of charges involving multiple sexual abuse of adolescent boys which occurred during a roughly two-and-a-half-year period. The charges were properly joined since they were of the same or similar character and which are deemed part of a common scheme or plan.); Griffin v. State, 243 Ga. App. 282, 531 S.E.2d 175, *cert. denied*, 2000 Ga. LEXIS 660 (Sept. 8, 2000); Rocha v. State, 234 Ga. App. 48, 53, 506 S.E.2d 192, 196–97 (1998); Gadson v. State, 223 Ga. App. 342, 477 S.E.2d 598 (1996), *cert. denied*, 1997 Ga. LEXIS 224 (Feb. 14, 1997) (ruling no need to sever multiple sexual assault charges which were committed in a similar way within a five-week period by person matching defendant's description); Stowers v. State, 215 Ga. App. 338, 449 S.E.2d 690 (1994) (upholding joinder of sexual assault convictions involving three of defendant's daughters since charges were related and may have shown an attempt to intimidate the victims into submitting to sexual abuse or to prevent them from reporting it, despite the fact that defendant was acquitted of charges involving two of his daughters); Violett v. Commonwealth, 907 S.W.2d 773, 775–76

(*Text continued on page 75*)

(Ky. 1995) (holding that evidence of one of the offenses would be admissible in a separate trial for the other offense and that there were numerous similarities between the offenses such as the method of gaining access to both children in that each victim was a member of the household at the time the misconduct occurred, the defendant would get each child alone in the bedroom or gain access to the victims by approaching them in the bathroom when they were getting ready or taking a shower, and the defendant warned both victims not to tell anyone about the incidents); State v. Roca, 866 So. 2d 867 (La. Ct. App. 2004) (court permitted joinder of different sexual assaults upon children, since they were under similar circumstances, i.e., under guise of educating his daughter about sex, evidence as to each victim was separate and distinct, and evidence of one assault would have been admissible at trial of the other offense. Also, lapse of 20 years between crimes was not unduly prejudicial); State v. Harris, 765 So. 2d 1230 (La. Ct. App. 2000); State v. Lewis, 736 So. 2d 1004, 1015–16 (La. Ct. App. 1999) (joinder was appropriate in case in which two attacks were similar and proof of one would have been admissible at trial of other where similarities included: (1) attacker broke into homes of both victims; (2) both victims resided in same neighborhood; (3) both attacks occurred at night; (4) both victims were bound; (5) hands of both victims were bound in same manner, i.e., behind their backs; (6) both victims were bound with lingerie, one with stockings and other with her own slip and bra; (7) both victims were penetrated anally and vaginally; and (8) both victims were forced to turn around or over and were then sexually assaulted from behind); State v. Pierce, 2001 Me. 14, 770 A.2d 630 (2001) (joinder was proper due to common plan or scheme that existed in whole or in part in the numerous offenses charged):

> The "common scheme or plan" presented by the State during the hearing on the motion to sever the counts was the following: Sean introduced Pierce, under false name and age, to young girls; Pierce provided drugs and alcohol for the girls; and Pierce requested sexual favors from the girls. Pierce grouped the counts into six incidents and contends that the State's "common scheme or plan" is not present in four of the incidents.

> In Counts 15–18, and likewise, in Counts 6, 13, and 14, Pierce contends that the "common scheme or plan" fails because there was no evidence that Pierce engaged in sexual conduct with any girl. In Counts 1–3, Pierce contends that the "common scheme or plan" was missing because the marijuana was smoked after the sexual conduct; therefore, marijuana was "not used in any way to ply [the girl]." In Count 4, Pierce contends that the "common scheme or plan" did not exist because there were no drugs or liquor.

> That all the parts of the State's "common scheme or plan" were not present in every incident does not mean that the "common scheme or plan" did not exist. The eighteen counts that the court determined were properly joined involved six incidents and ten girls. In each incident, Sean introduced the girls to Pierce, and Pierce used a false identity. In three of the incidents, three different girls were victims of specific sexual crimes. In two of those three incidents, drugs were involved.

> In a fourth incident, liquor was involved and Pierce propositioned the girls to strip dance for money. In a fifth incident, there was liquor and some of the girls' clothing was removed. In a sixth incident, liquor and drugs were present, and one of the girls in this incident was propositioned during a different incident.

These acts were connected in time, purpose, and *modus operandi* and therefore joinable. *Pierce*, 2001 Me. at 14–16, 770 A.2d at 634–35); Commonwealth v. Feijoo, 419 Mass. 486, 646 N.E.2d 118 (1995) (upholding indictment charging sexual abuse with nine victims — there were numerous similarities in the allegations of the abuse, particularly the defendant's *modus operandi* of encouraging his young victims to "overcome his barriers" by submitting to the defendant's sexual wishes, which evidence would have been admissible at all trials if each indictment had been prosecuted independently, as part of an ongoing plan. *Id.* at 494–95, 646 N.E.2d at 124–25.);

(Text continued on page 75)

Commonwealth v. Gagnon, 45 Mass. App. Ct. 584, 590, 699 N.E.2d 1260, 1265 (1998) (upholding joinder of two counts of sexual assault, involving two girls, seven and nine years old, when assaults "were related in terms of the nature of the abuse, the location of the abuse, and the defendant's exploitation of his position as a foster brother and sometime caretaker to perpetrate the abuse"); Commonwealth v. Souza, 39 Mass. App. Ct. 103, 653 N.E.2d 1127, *review denied*, 421 Mass. 1103, 655 N.E.2d 1277 (1995) (sexual abuse allegations of grandchildren of the defendant properly joined since given the "locale, time period, relationship to the accusers and many similarities in the nature of the acts charged," the proof of one child's abuse would have been admissible at trial of the others); Eakes v. State, 665 So. 2d 852 (Miss. 1995); State v. Southern, 1999 Mont. 94, 980 P.2d 3 (1999); State v. Freeman, 253 Neb. 385, 571 N.W.2d 276 (1997) (holding eight sexual assaults properly joined which had similarities, such as blindfolding of victims); State v. Hennessey, 142 N.H. 149, 697 A.2d 930 (1997) (upholding joinder of sexual assault charges involving two brothers, same charges were related and part of common scheme); People v. Cornell, 17 A.D.3d 1010, 794 N.Y.S.2d 226, *appeal denied*, 5 N.Y.3d 805, 836 N.E.2d 1157, 803 N.Y.S.2d 34 (2005); People v. Monte, 302 A.D.2d 687, 756 N.Y.S.2d 293 (2003) (noting charges involving different victims separately presented, uncomplicated, and easily distinguishable and jury acquitted on counts relating to second victim); People v. Kelly, 270 A.D.2d 511, 512–13, 705 N.Y.S.2d 689, 691, *appeal denied*, 95 N.Y.2d 854, 736 N.E.2d 866, 714 N.Y.S.2d 5 (2000) (upholding joinder of sexual assault counts involving two victims where "proof of each crime was separately presented, uncomplicated and easily distinguishable" and "a review of the evidence presented at trial reveal[ed] no substantial difference in the quantum of proof as to each victim"); People v. Johnson, 268 A.D.2d 891, 703 N.Y.S.2d 545, *appeal denied*, 94 N.Y.2d 921, 729 N.E.2d 1160, 708 N.Y.S.2d 361 (2000); People v. Jones, 236 A.D.2d 846, 654 N.Y.S.2d 495, *appeal denied*, 90 N.Y.2d 859, 683 N.E.2d 1060, 661 N.Y.S.2d 186 (1997) (holding joinder of three separate sexual assaults proper because identity of attacker was at issue and assaults sufficiently unique to be of probative value); People v. Grotto, 223 A.D.2d 758, 636 N.Y.S.2d 436, *appeal denied*, 87 N.Y.2d 1020, 666 N.E.2d 1067, 644 N.Y.S.2d 153 (1996) (holding multiple acts involving same victim properly joined); State v. Jarvis, 215 A.D.2d 588, 626 N.Y.S.2d 832, *appeal denied*, 86 N.Y.2d 782, 655 N.E.2d 724, 631 N.Y.S.2d 627 (1995) (no showing by the defendant that he was prejudiced by the court's denial of his motion to sever multiple counts of sexual assault); Griego v. State, 111 Nev. 444, 893 P.2d 995 (1995) (multiple acts of sexual assault involving different individuals are properly joinable since evidence of one count would have been admissible at separate trial of companion charge); State v. Hernandez, 822 A.2d 915 (R.I. 2003) (finding no abuse of discretion in trial court's consolidating three incidents, which were of the "same or similar character" in which defendant was accused of driving up to women on the street and persuading them to enter his vehicle and using either physical force or a weapon to compel the women to engage in sexual activity); State v. Rice, 755 A.2d 137 (R.I. 2000) (joinder of acts proper because they were of a sufficiently similar character, even if some counts involved actual sexual encounters, some involved requests for sexual acts, because all acts occurred within "reasonably condensed time frame of twenty months," "in relative proximity to one another" involving girls who were present on property where he resided); State v. Jones, 325 S.C. 310, 479 S.E.2d 517 (1996) (holding consolidation of charges involving two different victims proper since "offenses charged were of the same general nature involving allegations of a pattern of sexual abuse involving the two minor victims. Evidence was presented at trial that both victims had been taken to the same location and were present in the same motel room on an occasion of abuse. Further, there has been no showing of prejudice resulting from the trial judge's decision." *Id.* at 315, 479 S.E.2d at 520); State v. Russell, 125 Wash. 2d 24, 882 P.2d 747 (1994), *cert. denied*, 514 U.S. 1129 (1995); Simmers v. State, 943 P.2d 1189, 1198 (Wyo. 1997) (upholding joinder of counts involving three young children).

The temporal "continuity" of offenses may also allow their joinder if it appears they occurred as part of a continuous "crime spree."[284] Additionally, some courts find no prejudice not only because proof of the count would be admissible in the trial of the other count, but also when proof involving the different victims is "separate and distinct."[285] Additionally, the testimony presented by the two victims had been simple and distinct. Both victims communicated to the jury the approximate dates, location, and manner in which the sexual abuse had occurred and the jury segregated the evidence it heard regarding the two victims.

However, when charges pertaining to one victim would not be admissible at trial of charges involving another victim, it may be reversible error to not sever the counts.[286] This is particularly so when proof of guilt depends primarily on the victim's testimony.[287] Many of these cases note that proof on one count is admissible as proof on another count. If so, the jury may be instructed to that effect.[288] For example, a defendant's physical assault on a complainant during their relationship may be joined with a sexual assault count.[289] Similar charges permitting joinder may include the offense of possessing child pornography with the offense of transporting a child to engage in sexual activity since both involve the intent to engage in sexual activity with a child.[290]

---

[284] Hutchinson v. State, 731 So. 2d 812 (Fla. Dist. Ct. App. 1999); Beasley v. State, 269 Ga. 620, 502 S.E.2d 235 (1998) (permitting proof of additional crimes committed after murder for which defendant was charged since they were part of "a crime spree"); Moore v. State, 246 Ga. App. 163, 539 S.E.2d 851 (2000), *appeal denied*, 2001 Ga. LEXIS 368 (Apr. 30, 2001) (upholding joinder of two sexual assaults which "occurred mere hours apart, in the same general area, and in the same general manner" on the theory they constituted a single "crime spree").

[285] State v. Cramer, 2000 Ohio App. LEXIS 3623 (Aug. 10, 2000).

Here, joinder of the two indictments is not prejudicial because under Evid. R. 404(B), evidence of the other offenses is admissible in each case to establish Cramer's opportunity, identity, preparation, and plan.

Both indictments allege sexual abuse of young girls who are related to Cramer, most of the incidents occurred in the same location, the offenses themselves are similar in character and manner, and are part of a course of criminal conduct beginning when the girls were five years old and continued over the course of several years.

[286] State v. Moore, 6 S.W.3d 235 (Tenn. 1999) (reversing defendant's conviction because there was no recognized criteria under the common plan or scheme theory, *e.g.*, identity, intent or motive to select a defense of mistake or accident, for joinder of counts); State v. Hambrick, 2000 Tenn. Crim. App. LEXIS 516 (June 27, 2000) (reversing defendant's conviction due to failure to sever counts).

[287] Spicer v. State, 12 S.W.3d 438, 447–49 (Tenn. 2000) (noting also that open-dated charges involving multiple victims are usually, but not inherently, prejudicial because they usually involve testimony of a plethora of acts of abuse).

[288] *See, e.g.*, United States v. Barrow, 42 M.J. 655 (A.F.C.C.A. 1991) (evidence of defendant's sexual activity with adult, which included use of vibrators and sexually explicit magazines, was relevant to charges involving child to establish identity of source of child's sexual knowledge, an issue raised by defendant).

[289] United States v. Chee, No. 98-2038, 1999 U.S. App. LEXIS 8406 (10th Cir. 1999).

[290] United States v. Hersh, 297 F.3d 1233 (11th Cir. 2002), *cert. denied*, 537 U.S. 1217 (2003) (noting the link between pedophile behavior and child pornography).

An example of proper joinder is in a case of sexual assaults committed on seven young boys, all within a four-mile radius of the defendant's home and near a place where the defendant was known to frequent, and all allegedly committed by an assailant in a hooded sweatshirt and a bandana or mask who asked about money before the sexual assault.[291] The similarity and uniqueness of the assaults make them probative on the issue of identity of the assailant.[292] However, if the charges are to be considered separately, i.e., proof of one count cannot be considered in support of another, then the jury should be so instructed.[293]

Nonetheless, there is potential prejudice in the joinder of counts which may require severance. One example of potential prejudice in the joinder of multiple counts of sexual assaults is where a defendant seeks to testify as to one criminal transaction but desires to remain silent as to another transaction or transactions in the indictment. To establish a basis for severance on these grounds, a defendant must make a "convincing showing" by presenting to the court sufficient information "regarding the nature of the testimony he wishes to give on one count and his reasons for not wishing to testify on the other — to satisfy the court that the claim of prejudice is genuine and to enable it intelligently to weigh the considerations of 'economy and expedition in judicial administration' against the defendant's interest in having a free choice with respect to testifying."[294] Setting forth in an affidavit the bare conclusion that a defendant wishes to testify in one count but not another is not a sufficient showing. Facts supporting the conclusion should be set forth and documented in the affidavit. Some states do permit this showing to be made *in camera* to the court.[295] The fact that the defendant may

---

[291] Commonwealth v. Ferraro, 424 Mass. 87, 674 N.E.2d 241 (1997).

[292] *Id.*

[293] State v. Hennessey, 142 N.H. 149, 155, 697 A.2d 930, 934 (1997) (jury properly instructed that sexual abuse counts involving one brother should not influence jury's decision on counts involving other brother).

[294] Baker v. United States, 401 F.2d 958, 977 (D.C. Cir. 1968), *cert. denied*, 400 U.S. 965 (1970).

[295] *See, e.g.,* N.Y. Crim. Proc. Law § 200.20(3): In any case where two or more offenses or groups of offenses charged in an indictment are based upon different criminal transactions, and where their joinability rests solely upon the fact that such offenses, or as the case may be at least one offense of each group, are the same or similar in law, as prescribed in paragraph (c) of subdivision two, the court, in the interest of justice and for good cause shown, may, upon application of either a defendant or the people, in its discretion, order that any such offenses be tried separately from the other or others thereof. Good cause shall include but not be limited to situations where there is: (b) A convincing showing that a defendant has both important testimony to give concerning one count and a genuine need to refrain from testifying on the other, which satisfies the court that the risk of prejudice is substantial. (i) Good cause, under this paragraph (b), may be established in writing or upon oral representation of counsel on the record. Any written or oral representation may be based upon information and belief, provided the sources of such information and the grounds of such belief are set forth. (ii) Upon the request of counsel, any written or recorded showing concerning the defendant's genuine need to refrain from testifying shall be *ex parte* and *in camera*. The *in camera* showing shall be sealed but a court for good cause may order unsealing. Any statements made by counsel in the course of an application under this paragraph (b) may not be offered against the defendant in any criminal action for impeachment purposes or otherwise.

wish to testify with respect to one count of an indictment involving a sexual assault allegation to which he made no statement to the police, but not testify as to another count involving a charge of rape where no statement was provided, by itself is an insufficient showing of a desire or need to testify with respect to only one count and not another.[296]

Another argument against joinder of counts is the increased publicity associated with multiple allegations of sexual abuse; however, the mere possibility of pretrial publicity is an insufficient basis for severance.[297]

A common argument advanced for severance is that the jury will aggregate evidence of the crimes in determining the defendant's guilt. This, however, is a broad allegation, and generally something more must be shown, such as the different levels of proof of the various counts or the significantly prejudicial nature of one charge as opposed to another. The abuse of several children within an institution may also lend itself to joinder of counts involving multiple victims, especially where a common plan or scheme may be involved or there is a common defense, such as there was no intended sexual gratification in the touching of the complainants.[298] In a case involving a ten-year-old male victim and a 13-year-old girl, joinder of the two different crimes was proper where the proof of the identification of the defendant was positive in both cases.[299] The defendant must show how a jury might aggregate the evidence of the different charges and not just allege that there is potential prejudice in the cumulative effect of the charges.[300] The fact that prosecution offers DNA evidence on some counts of sexual assault and DNA evidence is lacking on other counts is not the type of

---

[296] State v. Lewis, 736 So. 2d 1004 (La. Ct. App. 1999); People v. Reome, 309 A.D.2d 1067, 766 N.Y.S.2d 238 (2003), *appeal denied*, 2 N.Y.3d 805, 814 N.E.2d 476, 781 N.Y.S.2d 304 (2004) (In prosecution involving a ten-year-old boy and 16-year-old girl, court upheld denial of defendant's severance motion because "defendant failed to set forth the counts he wished to testify on, the nature of his testimony, or those counts he sought to refrain from testifying on" and the reasons therefore.); People v. Fosmer, 293 A.D.2d 824, 743 N.Y.S.2d 179, *appeal denied*, 98 N.Y.2d 696, 776 N.E.2d 4, 747 N.Y.S.2d 415 (2002) (finding "defendant failed to make a convincing showing that he had important testimony to give concerning the allegations of the older victims, but a genuine need to refrain from testifying concerning the younger ones."); People v. King, 170 A.D.2d 710, 565 N.Y.S.2d 621, *appeal denied*, 77 N.Y.2d 997, 575 N.E.2d 409, 571 N.Y.S.2d 923 (1991); State v. Russell, 125 Wash. 2d 24, 882 P.2d 747 (1994), *cert. denied*, 514 U.S. 1129 (1995) ("Although there has been some recent suggestion that the defendant might elect to testify on one count and not on the others, there has been no offer of proof as to which count the defendant might elect to testify about, no offer of proof as to what he might say, and no showing that he would be prejudiced by any decision he might make regarding his decision to testify on any count or counts and not on another." *Id.* at 661, 882 P.2d at 774).

[297] People v. Boyea, 222 A.D.2d 937, 636 N.Y.S.2d 136 (1995), *appeal denied*, 88 N.Y.2d 934, 670 N.E.2d 451, 647 N.Y.S.2d 167 (1996).

[298] *See, e.g.,* Langham v. State, 494 So. 2d 910 (Ala. Crim. App. 1986) (upholding joinder of counts where defendant utilized similar techniques in exploiting several child victims).

[299] People v. Hoke, 96 A.D.2d 677, 466 N.Y.S.2d 534 (1983).

[300] *King,* 170 A.D.2d at 710, 565 N.Y.S.2d at 622.

difference in proof likely to justify a severance of counts.[301] With appropriate limiting instruction, it is not prejudicial to join an attempted manslaughter charge, based on defendant's HIV status, with a sexual assault charge.[302]

Sometimes the motion to sever may be renewed at the time of trial when there is further factual support for the motion. When it appears in the course of the trial that there are "substantial differences" between multiple sexual assaults, it may be reversible error for a trial court to deny a defendant's request for severance.[303] For example, when one count involves the rape of an adult, and another count involves the rape of a four-year-old, there is no basis to argue that evidence of one crime is admissible in the prosecution of the other, and there

---

[301] State v. Southern, 294 Mont. 225, 980 P.2d 3 (1999).

[302] People v. Dembry, 91 P.3d 431 (Colo. Ct. App. 2003):

> Additionally, the trial court weighed the possible prejudicial effect of defendant's HIV status against the possibility that A.R. would have to testify in two separate proceedings. The jury was instructed not to let its decision on any one count influence its decision on any other and not to let any prejudice dictate its decision.

> Ultimately, the jury did not convict defendant of attempted manslaughter, but of the lesser included offense of reckless endangerment. Thus, defendant has not demonstrated actual prejudice as a result of the trial court's denial of his motion to sever. Therefore, the trial court did not abuse its discretion.

Id. at 436.

[303] Campbell v. State, 1996 Ala. Crim. App. LEXIS 215 (Aug. 23, 1996) (court reversed defendant's conviction because of dissimilarity of joined charges. Some charges were based on force, others based on victim's age and some charges were based on penetration, others were not. Defendant's relationship was also non-familiar with two victims and familiar with another, and noted identity not in issue. Thus, evidence of charges were not properly joined); State v. Ives, 187 Ariz. 102, 927 P.2d 762 (1996) ("Given the narrow definition we have adopted, it is clear that the acts committed with these four girls, separated in time by as much as seven years or more, are not acts of 'a particular plan of which the charged crime is a part.' " [citation omitted]. The type of speculation that the trial court felt was appropriate in this case will, we hope, be minimized in future cases, because the inquiry should hereafter focus on whether the acts are part of an overarching criminal plan, and not on whether the acts are merely similar. Similarity and *modus operandi* may establish identity, but not establish a common scheme or plan. Because the acts in the instant case are merely similar, and because identity and *modus operandi* are not in issue in this case, defendant's motion for severance should have been granted." *Id.* at 108–09, 927 P.2d at 768–69); People v. Willer, 281 Ill. App. 3d 939, 667 N.E.2d 708, *appeal denied*, 168 Ill.2d 622, 671 N.E.2d 742 (1996) (defendant's conviction reversed because of improper joinder of offenses involving two victims in a trial where credibility of victims was a critical issue. Offenses were only peripherally connected in time and place, elements of crime were not the same, there was no common scheme or distinctive pattern.); Reidnauer v. State, 133 Md. App. 311, 755 A.2d 553, *cert. denied*, 361 Md. 233, 760 A.2d 1107 (2000) (defendant's conviction reversed due to impermissible joinder of counts since crimes against one victim would not have been admissible in a separate trial for offenses against the other victim; similarities in crimes are not sufficient for joinder of counts); State v. Jones, 120 N.M. 185, 899 P.2d 1139 (1995); State v. Echols, 128 Ohio App. 3d 677, 716 N.E.2d 728 (1998) (reversing defendant's conviction in robbery-kidnapping trial because trial court did not sever counts which "did not share significant features necessary to establish a *modus operandi* for their use as other acts evidence"); State v. Hoyt, 928 S.W.2d 935 (Tenn. Crim. App. 1995).

is a greater likelihood that a jury will consider each charge separately.[304] Likewise, joining charges which combine issues of identity and consent with less than overwhelming proof of guilt may be prejudicial.[305]

Consolidation of indictments involving different victims may be improper when the state does not present evidence at the time the motion is made — as opposed to proof, which may develop at trial — that the different acts are part of a common scheme or plan.[306]

---

[304] Smith v. State, 249 Ga. App. 39, 547 S.E.2d 598, *cert. denied*, 2001 Ga. LEXIS 720 (2001).

[305] People v. Daniels, 216 A.D.2d 639, 627 N.Y.S.2d 483 (1995) (defendant's conviction was reversed because of improper joinder of sexual assaults over three days. Each was allegedly performed in the front seat of a dark car with bucket seats on a country road. However, the complainant accompanied the defendant without violence during the first two incidents, whereas threats and a sharp object were used on the third. The defendant's identity was disputed as to the third rape. Given the differences in the commission of the crimes and the issue of identification in the third incident, the court found "because the evidence is not overwhelming on any of the charges, and the danger of unfair prejudice arising from the consolidation of the two indictments so profound, defendant's right to a fair trial on each indictment was sorely compromised" and defendant's conviction reversed).

[306] Spicer v. State, 12 S.W.3d 438 (Tenn. 2000):

> Because the State introduced no evidence of a common scheme or plan at the consolidation hearing, we find that the trial court abused its discretion in not holding separate trials on each of the indictments. In all cases in which the state seeks to consolidate multiple offenses by pre-trial motion over the objection of the defendant, the state must bring forth sufficient evidence at the hearing to establish that specific acts constitute parts of a common scheme or plan. When the offenses are alleged in an open-dated indictment, the state may not meet this burden of production with evidence later developed at trial, [footnote omitted] and this Court will not look to such evidence to determine whether consolidation was proper.

Id. at 12 S.W.3d at 447. *See also*, State v. Toliver, 117 S.W.3d 216 (Tenn. 2003). (The court reversed defendant's conviction in part due to the improper joinder of offenses and noted the dissimilarities did not warrant a finding of uniqueness or *modus operandi*):

> While the March 1 and the April 9 incidents share a number of similarities, the method employed in committing the offenses does not constitute a *modus operandi* so unique and distinctive as to be comparable to a signature. According to the evidence offered by the prosecution, the defendant and the victim were alone in the victim's bedroom during the March 1 incident. The defendant struck the victim on the buttocks with a heavy-duty extension cord that was braided with wire and wrapped with duct tape. The incident developed from the victim receiving poor grades on his report card. The April 9 incident developed from the victim failing to bring home his report card, receiving poor grades on his report card, and running away from home after his mother obtained a copy of his report card from his school. While the defendant and the victim were again in the victim's bedroom, on this occasion the victim's mother was standing in the doorway of the room. While the defendant again used a braided extension cord to strike the victim on the buttocks, the extension cord was neither braided with wire nor wrapped with duct tape during the April 9 incident. In addition, during the April 9 incident, the victim was required to lean over a 'barrel' or a 'big plastic tub,' a fact different from the March 1 incident. Furthermore, the prosecution introduced proof to show that during the April 9 incident the defendant wrapped the extension cord around the victim's neck and jerked him around the room, causing the victim to strike

Another ground in support of a motion for severance is the potential confusion that can result from the proof pertaining to the different allegations. Sometimes this confusion results from different legal principles that are applicable to the different counts. An example of the prejudice that can result from the confusion over the different levels of proof or slightly different legal theories involved in various sexually related counts of an indictment is in *People v. Shapiro*.[307] In *Shapiro*, the indictment encompassed 64 counts involving acts over a 17-month period with eight different boys under the age of 17 who received money from the defendant, and then charges involving a more serious crime, not similarly defined by law, of promoting such conduct — allegations that were confined to a single incident of two boys under 17 years of age. The court noted that no one in the first indictment would have any reason to be called as a witness in the trial of the second indictment, that the levels of proof and legal theories were different with respect to these charges, and that there was a real risk that the defendant would be convicted on the more serious promotion charges for reasons other than those relating to the proof of the specific crime of promotion.[308] In refusing to permit these various counts to be tried together, the court emphasized the importance of more than "conclusory generalities" as essential to establish prejudice in severance issues.[309] A defendant's defense of consent as to one sexual assault charge and intoxication as to another are not necessarily logically or practically inconsistent defenses requiring severance;[310] nor does the fact that the defendant asserted his right of self-incrimination with respect to one alleged sexual assault but not the other necessarily require severance.[311] Establishing confusion is easier when there are significantly different theories underlying the different crimes joined. Alleging confusion in the joinder of multiple victims is less likely to be successful when the charges are rape or sodomy, which are similar in legal theory and level of proof. For example, an indictment charging seven counts of various sex crimes involving five women that the defendant dated does not necessarily justify severance when the alleged crimes were "distinct acts with distinct victims so that there was little likelihood of confusion," and the defendant made no particular showing of prejudice.[312] These decisions

---

objects and furniture in the room, to sustain injuries to his abdomen, neck, and face, and to lose consciousness. In short, the evidence relating to the method employed to commit the April 9 offense is markedly different from the proof relating to the method employed to commit the March 1 incident.

Id. at 117 S.W.2d at 229–30.

[307] 50 N.Y.2d 747, 409 N.E.2d 897, 431 N.Y.S.2d 422 (1980).

[308] *Id.*

[309] *Id.* at 757, 431 N.Y.S.2d at 427.

[310] United States v. Duncan, 53 M.J. 494 (C.A.A.F. 2000), *cert. denied*, 531 U.S. 1079 (2001).

[311] United States v. Duncan, 53 M.J. 494 (C.A.A.F. 2000), *cert. denied*, 531 U.S. 1079 (2001).

[312] People v. Johnston, 273 A.D.2d 514, 709 N.Y.S.2d 230, 235, *appeal denied*, 95 N.Y.2d 935, 744 N.E.2d 148, 721 N.Y.S.2d 612 (2000) (holding defendant did not meet burden of establishing prejudice in joinder of counts and noting that jury's acquittal on all counts relating to victim B

emphasize the importance of avoiding form language in a motion for severance and using case-specific analysis and information in the supporting papers. Unfortunately, the advent of the personal computer has made the use of form language too convenient in many areas of motion practice. In many of the motions pertaining to sexual assault crimes, particularly those pertaining to discovery needs, it is important that motions and supporting affidavits set forth case-specific information. New Hampshire now holds that either the prosecutor or defendant has a right to sever unrelated offenses.[313] A related offense is based on the same conduct, upon a single criminal episode or upon a common plan. Under this rule, a sexual assault by a defendant on two brothers may be severed when they are unrelated. Some courts find prejudice is not a factor in deciding whether to consolidate multiple sexual assaults.[314]

§ 1.28 Joinder and severance of defendants.

State and federal law[315] permits the joinder of criminal defendants. It can be seen in sexual assault trials in cases of gang rape, husband-wife abuse of a child, or when several youths are abused by a group of adults. The general principles of joinder apply. Additionally, the age or mental disability of the victim may argue against testifying in multiple trials.[316] In addition to avoiding the inconvenience and trauma of witnesses testifying more than once, joinder avoids "randomly favoring the last trial defendants who have the advantage of knowing the prosecution's case before hand."[317] Judicial economy and avoiding inconsistent verdicts are also cited as reasons for upholding joinder of defendants.[318]

Citing the Supreme Court's decision in *Zafiro v. United States*,[319] federal courts often decline to reverse a trial court's decision on severance of multiple defendants. Typical of the judicial response in cases involving a joinder of defendants can be seen in the rape trial of three defendants charged with attacking a jogger in Central Park in New York City, in which the court cited "the complexity of the evidence," "the number of witnesses," the "duplication of

---

and one count relating to victim A "strongly suggest[ed] that the jury was able to distinguish and discriminate among the victims and the evidence presented"); People v. Smyers, 167 A.D.2d 773, 562 N.Y.S.2d 1017 (1990), *appeal denied*, 77 N.Y.2d 967, 573 N.E.2d 589, 570 N.Y.S.2d 501 (1991). *See also* Simmers v. State, 943 P.2d 1189, 1198 (Wyo. 1997).

[313] State v. Tierney, 150 N.H. 339, 839 A.2d 38 (2003) (applying *Ramos* to case pending on direct appeal and reversing defendant's conviction due to trial court's failure to sever counts involving two brothers); State v. Ramos, 149 N.H. 118, 127–28, 818 A.2d 1228, 1235-36 (2003).

[314] State v. Jones, 184 Or. App. 57, 55 P.3d 495 (2002).

[315] Fed. R. Crim. P. 14.

[316] State v. Cassey, 543 A.2d 670 (R.I. 1988).

[317] Richardson v. Marsh, 481 U.S. 200, 212 (1987).

[318] *Id.*

[319] Zafiro v. United States, 506 U.S. 534 (1993); United States v. Locascio, 6 F.3d 924 (2d Cir. 1993), *cert. denied sub nom.* Gotti v. United States, 511 U.S. 1070 (1994).

testimony" and "the economy of judicial and administrative resources" as justification for the joinder of the defendants.[320]

Severance is not required merely because some evidence may be admissible against one defendant and not another.[321] When there is a great disparity in the quality of evidence against the defendants, however, severance may be required.[322] Severance may be required because the nature of the crimes or evidence is different for each defendant. For example, where a mother and father are charged with significantly different crimes relating to the abuse of the child — such as intimidation of a witness on the part of the mother and indecent liberties with the child against the father — joinder is deemed prejudicial because of the danger of the jury being unable to treat separately the different evidence introduced with respect to each defendant.[323] The problem is significant when charges against each defendant present "separate, distinct and independent allegations and proof of those charges [is] different than the proof required" for the other defendant's charges.[324] Courts will try to determine if the jury can "compartmentalize the evidence as it relates to separate defendants in the light of its volume and limited admissibility."[325] Limiting instructions may help in "compartmentalizing" the evidence.[326]

If the defendant claims that severance is required because of favorable testimony of the co-defendant, the defendant must demonstrate a basis to believe the co-defendant will testify and provide exculpatory evidence, and must balance the benefits and prejudice in joinder and severance, including the benefits of judicial economy.[327]

Courts may order that defendants be severed when their defenses are irreconcilable.[328] Severance is not required just because two defendants have differences

---

[320] People v. Salaam, 187 A.D.2d 363, 364, 590 N.Y.S.2d 195, 196 (1992), *aff'd*, 83 N.Y.2d 51, 629 N.E.2d 371, 607 N.Y.S.2d 899 (1993).

[321] United States v. Reeves, 674 F.2d 739, 746 (8th Cir. 1982).

[322] United States v. Brady, 579 F.2d 1121, 1128 (9th Cir. 1978), *cert. denied*, 439 U.S. 1074 (1979).

[323] State v. Bratt, 250 Kan. 264, 824 P.2d 983 (1992). *See also* State v. Brown, 586 A.2d 1085 (R.I. 1991) (reversing conviction in sexual assault trial where one defendant was prejudiced in ability to defend herself).

[324] *Bratt*, 250 Kan. at 274–75, 824 P.2d at 991.

[325] *Brady*, 579 F.2d at 1128.

[326] *Id.*

[327] United States v. Seifert, 648 F.2d 557, 563–64 (9th Cir. 1980); United States v. Hackett, 638 F.2d 1179 (9th Cir. 1980), *cert. denied*, 450 U.S. 1001 (1981); Hawkins v. State, 538 So. 2d 1204, 1207 (Miss. 1989).

[328] Cruz v. New York, 481 U.S. 186 (1987). *See also* People v. Hurst, 396 Mich. 1, 7, 238 N.W.2d 6, 10 (1976); People v. Mahboubian, 74 N.Y.2d 174, 543 N.E.2d 34, 544 N.Y.S.2d 769 (1989) (holding "that severance is compelled where the core of each defense is in irreconcilable conflict with the other and where there is a significant danger, as both defenses are portrayed to the trial court, that the conflict alone would lead the jury to infer defendant's guilt. In that motions for

on trial strategy, inconsistencies in defenses, or hostilities between them.[329] The Supreme Court has held that mutually antagonistic defenses are not prejudicial *per se*.[330] For example, the joinder must prejudice a specific trial right or prevent the jury from making a reliable decision on guilt or innocence.[331] There must be such an "irreconcilable conflict" between the defendants which would lead to "a significant danger that a jury will unjustifiably infer guilt from the conflict alone."[332] The defenses must be truly antagonistic, irreconcilable, and mutually exclusive.[333] Severance may be required where the jury must choose between believing one defendant's defense of non-involvement in the sexual assault or the co-defendant's position that the defendant was involved.[334]

When both defendants in a sexual assault trial are asserting the same defense, there is no conflict between the defenses and severance will not be required.[335] For example, severance is not required when both defendants claim misidentification,[336] or that each was not present,[337] since the defenses are not irreconcilable nor is one defendant's claim of non-involvement inconsistent with a co-defendant's defense of consent.[338] One court noted that when the proof against

---

severance typically arise at the pretrial stage or in the course of trial, the trial court must apply this standard prospectively, based on its discretionary assessments of the strategies and evidence as forecast by the parties" *Id.* at 184-85, 543 N.E.2d at 39, 544 N.Y.S.2d at 774).

[329] United States v. Matthews, 178 F.3d 295 (5th Cir.), *cert. denied*, 528 U.S. 944 (1999) (holding that even if co-defendants' defenses were mutually antagonistic, court's instructions to consider evidence against each defendant separately and individually cured any prejudice); United States v. Whitehead, 618 F.2d 523 (4th Cir. 1980); McLean v. State, 754 So. 2d 176 (Fla. Dist. Ct. App. 2000) (holding that strategic advantage or hostility among defendants does not by itself require severance and noting that co-defendants in this case neither accused each other nor confessed to crimes); People v. Correa, 188 A.D.2d 542, 591 N.Y.S.2d 447 (1992).

[330] Zafiro v. United States, 506 U.S. 534, 538 (1993). *See also* United States v. Haynes, 16 F.3d 29, 32 (2d Cir. 1994).

[331] *Zafiro*, 506 U.S. at 539.

[332] United States v. Davis, 623 F.2d 188, 194–95 (1st Cir. 1980); People v. Correa, 188 A.D.2d 542, 591 N.Y.S.2d 447 (1992).

[333] United States v. Kopituk, 690 F.2d 1289, 1316 (11th Cir. 1982), *cert. denied*, 461 U.S. 928 (1983); State v. Montes, 28 Kan. App. 2d 768, 776–77, 21 P.3d 592, 598 (2001) (holding defendant was not entitled to severance since he did not present proof of an irreconcilable and mutually exclusive defense).

[334] People v. Figueroa, 193 A.D.2d 452, 597 N.Y.S.2d 685, *appeal denied*, 81 N.Y.2d 1072, 619 N.E.2d 670, 601 N.Y.S.2d 592 (1993).

[335] People v. McDermott, 201 A.D.2d 913, 607 N.Y.S.2d 784, *appeal denied*, 83 N.Y.2d 855, 634 N.E.2d 988, 612 N.Y.S.2d 387 (1994).

[336] People v. Cannon, 236 A.D.2d 294, 654 N.Y.S.2d 129, *appeal denied*, 89 N.Y.2d 1010, 680 N.E.2d 622, 658 N.Y.S.2d 248 (1997).

[337] People v. Reed, 236 A.D.2d 866, 654 N.Y.S.2d 498, *appeal denied*, 89 N.Y.2d 1099, 682 N.E.2d 994, 660 N.Y.S.2d 393 (1997).

[338] People v. Boddie, 226 A.D.2d 120, 640 N.Y.S.2d 47, *appeal denied*, 88 N.Y.2d 980, 674 N.E.2d 341, 651 N.Y.S.2d 411 (1996).

two defendants is virtually identical, "only the most cogent reasons warrant a severance."[339] The severance motion would be considered in light of the evidence before the court at the time the severance motion is made.[340]

§ 1.29   Use of a co-defendant's statements.

A recurring problem in cases involving the joinder of defendants is the violation of the right to cross-examine adverse witnesses when a statement of a non-testifying co-defendant is admitted into evidence, the so-called *Bruton* rule.[341] *Bruton*'s essential holding is that admission of a non-testifying co-defendant's statement which implicates another defendant violates the confrontation clause.[342] An example of the rule can be seen in *United States v. Iron Thunder*.[343] In *Iron Thunder*, both defendants admitted being with the complainant and that certain acts were committed that could form the basis for rape charges, but both defendants denied that any acts were performed without the victim's consent. Since the defendants did not confess to any criminal conduct, it was held that the defendants' convictions must be reversed because of the prejudicial effect of one co-defendant's statement concerning sexual conduct and behavior when there had been no admission by either defendant as to the forcible nature of the contact.[344] In this case, defendant Iron Thunder's co-defendant made statements referring to hearing the bed striking the wall in the room and that the victim was crying, yet Iron Thunder's statement to the police indicated that the victim told him that the co-defendant had raped her.[345] Admission of the co-defendant's statement implicating Iron Thunder violated the *Bruton* rule.

When a non-testifying defendant's statement is admitted into evidence at a joint trial, and the statement is not admissible pursuant to a firmly-rooted hearsay exception such as the co-conspirator exception,[346] a limiting instruction is insufficient to cure the prejudice established by *Bruton*.[347] The Supreme Court

---

[339] People v. Bornholdt, 33 N.Y.2d 75, 305 N.E.2d 461, 350 N.Y.S.2d 369 (1973), *cert. denied*, 416 U.S. 905 (1974) ("But upon a proper showing of need for a co-defendant's testimony, it may be an abuse of discretion to deny severance." *Id.* at 87, 305 N.E.2d at 468, 350 N.Y.S.2d at 378).

[340] State v. Blackman, 201 Ariz. 527, 538, 38 P.3d 1192, 1203 (2002) (finding no abuse of discretion in denying defendant's motion to sever since at the time it was made, the co-defendant's statement implicating defendant was not before him).

[341] Bruton v. United States, 391 U.S. 123 (1968).

[342] *Id.*

[343] 714 F.2d 765 (8th Cir. 1983).

[344] *Id.* at 770–71.

[345] *Id.*

[346] Bourjaily v. United States, 483 U.S. 171 (1987) (permitting use of statements of a co-conspirator, a firmly-rooted hearsay exception foregoing the need to establish reliability of the statements, as long as the prosecution proves the existence of a conspiracy by a preponderance of the evidence. The co-conspirator's statements are admissible without a showing of unavailability.); United States v. Inadi, 475 U.S. 387 (1986).

[347] Cruz v. New York, 481 U.S. 186 (1987).

has expressly overruled the "interlocking confessions" exception to *Bruton*.[348] While it is possible to redact a co-defendant's statement, the redaction must eliminate not only the defendant's name but also any reference to the co-defendant's existence or permitting the jury to infer the co-defendant's existence.[349] Thus, a "blank" or "neutral symbol" in place of the co-defendant's name is precluded by *Bruton* and is reversible error.[350] If the statement does not directly incriminate the co-defendant, the reference may be acceptable.[351] Also, a verbal reference may be acceptable if identification of the defendant is deductible only by reference to evidence other than the redacted statement.[352]

§ 1.30 Use of dual or multiple juries in cases involving multiple defendants.

Another solution to the problem of the joinder of defendants and issues raised by *Bruton* is the use of dual juries or multiple juries to consider the evidence against each defendant separately.[353] It is in effect a modified form of severance. Multiple juries are particularly attractive in sexual assault trials because it avoids a victim's testifying twice. This has been acknowledged as a factor in at least one rape trial tried before multiple juries.[354] This solution is particularly helpful

---

[348] *Id.*

[349] Gray v. Maryland, 523 U.S. 185 (1998).

[350] *Id.* ("[W]e believe that, considered as a class, redactions that replace a proper name with an obvious blank, the word 'delete,' a symbol, or similarly notify the jury that a name has been deleted are similar enough to *Bruton*'s unredacted confessions as to warrant the same legal results." *Id.* at 195). *See also* United States v. Matthews, 178 F. 3d 295 (5th Cir. 1999), *cert. denied*, 528 U.S. 944 (1999) (holding "blank" reference was prejudicial but harmless due to overwhelming evidence of defendant's guilt).

[351] United States v. Lage, 183 F.3d 374 (5th Cir. 1999), *cert. denied*, 528 U.S. 1163 (2000); State v. Blackman, 201 Ariz. 527, 540, 38 P.3d 1192, 1205 (2002) (finding no *Bruton* problems in co-defendant's statements that he and about 30 guys were involved in the sexual assault, and in response to a question whether complainant had sex willingly, co-defendant said things "had gotten out of hand," did not directly point to defendant and defendant could argue that things were still in hand when he had sex with victim).

[352] United States v. Akinkoye, 185 F.3d 192 (4th Cir. 1999), *cert. denied*, 528 U.S. 1177 (2000) (holding reference to "another person" in co-defendant's statement did not "facially implicate" defendant).

[353] *See generally* David Carl Minneman, Annotation, *Propriety of Use of Multiple Juries at Joint Trial with Multiple Defendants in State Criminal Prosecution,* 41 A.L.R.4th 1189 (1985).

[354] People v. Gholston, 124 Ill. App. 3d 873, 889, 464 N.E.2d 1179, 1191 (1984):

Because a substantial portion of the State's testimonial evidence proffered during the course of the proceedings was admissible as against all of the defendants, two simultaneous jury trials were certainly preferable in the interests of judicial economy. Although Kenneth and Danny Gholston adamantly contend that it was improper to allow the victim to testify and make in-court identifications before both juries, our query during oral argument still remains unanswered: How did this particular strategy on the part of the prosecution result in manifest prejudice? As defendants acknowl-

when the proof against each defendant will be virtually identical except for the statements of each defendant. The less similar the proof is with respect to each defendant, or the greater necessity of shuffling the various juries in and out of the courtroom for various testimony, the less beneficial or efficient a procedure. By and large, courts show a willingness to accept this practice and have not found inherent prejudice in the use of multiple juries. [355] Nevada's highest court, while not reversing defendants' convictions obtained by a trial before three juries, has taken a critical view of multiple juries and held that without guidelines from the court system or sanction from the state legislature, a trial court should refrain from conducting trials with multiple juries. [356]

There are several precautions and procedures which should be taken with multiple jury trials. These include: selecting each jury from different panels; insuring that the courtroom can accommodate two juries who can see the witness stand and accommodate adequate numbers of spectators to maintain a public trial;

---

edge, the trial court had a legitimate concern for minimizing the extreme trauma to the youthful victim reliving her ordeal over several court appearances spread out over a number of months. By failing to demonstrate prejudicial error, defendants' mere allegation that such a limitation of courtroom exposure was an 'imprudent solution' is, in our opinion, a legally insufficient basis upon which to predicate an outright reversal of their convictions.

[355] Jackson v. United States, 423 U.S. 949 (1975); United States v. Hayes, 676 F.2d 1359, 1366–67 (11th Cir.), *cert. denied*, 459 U.S. 1040 (1982); United States v. Rimar, 558 F.2d 1271 (6th Cir. 1977), *cert. denied*, 435 U.S. 922 (1978); United States v. Rowan, 518 F.2d 685, 689–90 (6th Cir. 1975), *cert. denied* 423 U.S. 949; United States v. Sidman, 470 F.2d 1158 (9th Cir. 1972), *cert. denied*, 409 U.S. 1127 (1973); People v. Cummings, 4 Cal. 4th 1233, 850 P.2d 1, 18 Cal. Rptr. 2d 796 (1993), *cert. denied*, 511 U.S. 1046 (1994); People v. Wardlow, 118 Cal. App. 3d 375, 382–387, 173 Cal. Rptr. 500, 502–05 (1981); People v. Gholston, 124 Ill. App. 3d 873, 464 N.E.2d 1179 (1984) (upholding multiple bench and jury trials in a rape trial); People v. Kramer, 103 Mich. App. 747, 303 N.W.2d 880 (1981); People v. Brooks, 92 Mich. App. 393, 285 N.W.2d 307 (1979) ("This Court believes that the dual jury procedure used in this case successfully avoided convicting one defendant through the efforts of the other. The Brooks jury heard none of the evidence presented by defendant Martin. Their verdict could only have been based on the evidence presented by the prosecution and in defendant Brooks' defense." *Id.* at 396, 285 N.W.2d at 308); State v. Corsi, 86 N.J. 172, 430 A.2d 210 (1981); People v. Ricardo B., 73 N.Y.2d 228, 535 N.E.2d 1336, 538 N.Y.S.2d 796 (1989); People v. Glover, 4 A.D.3d 852, 771 N.Y.S.2d 619, *appeal denied*, 2 N.Y.3d 740, 810 N.E.2d 919, 778 N.Y.S.2d 466 (2004) (interests of judicial economy and convenience of common sense outweighed risks of error associated with dual jury process); People v. Brockway, 255 A.D.2d 988, 683 N.Y.S.2d 671 (1998); People v. Quinones, 245 A.D.2d 314, 667 N.Y.S.2d 268 (1997), *appeal denied*, 92 N.Y.2d 859, 699 N.E.2d 449, 677 N.Y.S.2d 89 (1998); People v. Brown, 232 A.D.2d 750, 649 N.Y.S.2d 51 (1996), *appeal denied*, 89 N.Y.2d 940, 678 N.E.2d 504, 655 N.Y.S.2d 891 (1997); Brown v. State, 983 P.2d 474 (Okla. 1998) (upholding use of dual or multiple jury process absent a specific showing of prejudice in the procedure).

[356] Ewish v. Nevada, 110 Nev. 221, 871 P.2d 306 (1994), *rev'd on other grounds*, 111 Nev. 1365, 904 P.2d 1038 (1995) (holding that while the court did not approve of multiple juries, "and noting some form of prejudice always exists in joint trials," the error was not of such a dimension to warrant reversal of the defendant's conviction). *See also* State v. Corsi, 86 N.J. 172, 430 A.2d 210 (noting that multiple juries are not recommended); Buff v. State, 114 Nev. 1237, 970 P.2d 564 (1998).

separate openings, closings, and jury charges; and removal of the jury when evidence is not admissible against that jury's defendant. Also, cautionary instructions should direct the juries not to speculate on the reasons for the procedure and not to have any contact with jurors from the other defendant's case. Separate jury rooms are essential throughout the trial. To the extent possible, duplicate exhibits should be prepared. Exhibits that cannot be reproduced, such as a victim's clothing, must be shared and shuttled between juries during deliberations.

While there is some suggestion to the contrary in some decisions, there appears to be no requirement that one jury's verdict be withheld until the second jury reaches a verdict.[357] However, the two juries' verdicts should be announced jointly when there is a concern that a deliberating jury could learn of the other jury's verdict. Some courts expressed reservations with multiple juries, usually over the concern that a party, witness, or court will unintentionally disclose information to the "other" jury.[358]

---

[357] People v. Irizarry, 83 N.Y.2d 557, 634 N.E.2d 179, 611 N.Y.S.2d 807 (1994). The Court of Appeals held:

> The particular error alleged in defendant's case would not require reversal were this a single-jury case. Where complete severance has been granted, one co-defendant generally is convicted prior to the other. That a jury may be aware another person has been convicted of participating in the alleged crime is not deemed inherently prejudicial in that context. Just as sealing of a verdict or a "gag order" is not constitutionally required when severed co-defendants are successively tried, such protections are not invariably necessary to preserve the integrity of a dual jury trial. A trial court may want to impose more restrictive procedures when circumstances, such as extensive publicity, suggest that a failure to seal the first verdict might lead to prejudice, and reversible error. Where the unwieldiness of the procedure (see, e.g., Hedlund v. Sheldon, 173 Ariz. 143, 840 P.2d 1008 (1992)) would outweigh its prophylactic effect, however, a trial court may properly decline to follow such procedures.

Id. at 561, 634 N.E.2d at 182, 611 N.Y.S.2d at 810.

[358] State v. Lambright, 138 Ariz. 63, 673 P.2d 1 (1983), *cert. denied*, 469 U.S. 892 (1984); People v. Williams, 93 Ill. 2d 309, 67 Ill. Dec. 97, 444 N.E.2d 136 (1982), *cert. denied*, 467 U.S. 1218 (1984); People v. Rainge, 112 Ill. App. 3d 396, 419, 445 N.E.2d 535, 550–51 (1983) ("While we have frequently advocated considerations of expense and judicial economy, those factors will in this context usually be outweighed. In addition to the possibility of error, a single trial of multiple defendants before more than one jury creates burdensome administrative problems in caring for the juries and maintaining proper courtroom decorum. Issues and facts before each jury, who testified before which jury, and even which jury is hearing which testimony can all too easily become confused. [citations omitted] Too, some strain is placed on both the prosecution and defense in presenting the case in an orderly, uninterrupted fashion. While we find no reversible error here, the possibility of problems is such that we believe the use of dual juries ought to be viewed with considerable caution." *Id.* at 419, 445 N.E.2d at 550-51); State v. Watson, 397 So. 2d 1337 (La.), *cert. denied*, 454 U.S. 903 (1981) ("[I]t seems apparent that just the physical difficulties of seating and separating two juries in a single courtroom would require tremendous vigilance by the trial court. . . . The possibility of juror speculation as to the justification for such unique procedures could never be completely eliminated.") (The court upheld the defendant's conviction despite the fact that the defendant's jury learned of the co-defendant's statement implicating him.); Scarborough

Some courts have found the use of multiple juries problematic when a multiple jury trial may be longer and there may be many issues which one jury can hear and another cannot and possible prejudice to defendants who have antagonistic defense.[359]

§ 1.31 Motion for more definite statement of time period or to dismiss for vagueness or indefiniteness of time period.

While a defendant has a constitutionally-protected right to be tried on an indictment that provides him with notice of his alleged criminal conduct, many courts in child sexual assault cases permit a broad time period in the indictment.[360] Nonetheless, courts have acknowledged that "[w]here an indictment charges a time interval which is so large that it is virtually impossible for a defendant to answer the charges and to prepare a defense, dismissal should follow even though the People have acted diligently and a shorter period cannot be alleged."[361] Occasionally, a court will hold a time period, such as two years "unreasonable on its face," requiring dismissal of an indictment.[362]

Many complainants cannot remember or specify when a sexual assault took place because cognitively they cannot conceptualize time, or because the events took place in the past, or because of the difficulty of separating numerous acts of sexual contact. The requirement of specificity of a time period in an indictment will vary from crime to crime. Thus, most courts have permitted a broad time period in sexual assault crimes, particularly when children are involved[363]

---

v. State, 50 Md. App. 276, 278–81, 437 A.2d 672, 674–76 (1981) (upholding defendant's conviction, but critical of the potential risks in a multiple-jury proceeding, such as when both juries mingle during the trial, as happened in this case); Ewish v. Nevada, 110 Nev. 221, 871 P.2d 306 (1994), *rev'd on other grounds*, 111 Nev. 1365, 904 P.2d 1038 (1995) ("If not implemented carefully or in the proper circumstances, using multiple juries to administer criminal trials becomes a breeding ground for curious results, tainted justice and issues for appeal." *Id.* at 235, 871 P.2d at 316. However, the trial court refused to reverse the defendants' convictions holding that any problems or errors in the defendants' trial with multiple juries did not warrant reversal.).

[359] People v. Garcia, 194 Misc. 2d 263, 754 N.Y.S.2d 138 (Sup. Ct. 2002).

[360] Russell v. United States, 369 U.S. 749, 763–64 (1962).

[361] People v. Beauchamp, 74 N.Y.2d 639, 641, 539 N.E.2d 1105, 1106, 541 N.Y.S.2d 977, 978 (1989).

[362] People v. Eisemann, 248 A.D.2d 484, 670 N.Y.S.2d 39, *appeal denied*, 92 N.Y.2d 851, 699 N.E.2d 442, 677 N.Y.S.2d 82 (1998).

[363] United States v. Wimberly, 60 F.3d 281 (7th Cir. 1995), *cert. denied*, 516 U.S. 1063 (1996) ("The government presented evidence of molestation in early August 1989, not July. An appellant bears a more difficult burden when the variance involves a date. Such a variance does not require reversal if the date proved is within the statute of limitations and before the indictment date. [citation omitted]. Given this standard and the 'on or about' language used in the indictment, this slight variance does not warrant reversal." *Id.* at 287); State v. Saraceno, 15 Conn. App. 222, 545 A.2d 1116, *cert. denied*, 209 Conn. 823, 824, 552 A.2d 431, 432 (1988) (holding that "in a case involving the sexual abuse of a very young child, that child's capacity to recall specifics, and the state's

(Text continued on page 90)

concomitant ability to provide exactitude in an information, are very limited. The state can only provide what it has. This court will not impose a degree of certitude as to date, time and place that will render prosecutions of those who sexually abuse children impossible. To do so would have us establish, by judicial fiat, a class of crimes committable with impunity." *Id.* at 237); State v. Arceo, 84 Haw. 1, 13, 928 P.2d 843, 855 (1996); State v. Sherman, 70 Haw. 334, 339, 770 P.2d 789, 792 (1989); State v. Roberts, 101 Idaho 199, 610 P.2d 558 (1980); Tapp v. State, 256 Ind. 422, 269 N.E.2d 367, 369 (1971) (noting that alleging that a sexual assault took place in mid-summer of a particular year was proper, since time is not an element of the sexual assault, and there was no showing of how the defendant was prejudiced by the allegation); State v. Johnson, 670 So. 2d 651, 656–57 (La. Ct. App. 1996); Davis v. State, 760 So. 2d 55, 59 (Miss. Ct. App. 2000) (upholding indictment alleging time period " 'on or about and between the 21st day of May, 1998, through the 10th day of August, 1998' and 'on or about and between the 11th day of August, 1998, through the 2nd day of September, 1998' "); State v. Clark, 209 Mont. 473, 482–83, 682 P.2d 1339, 1344–45 (1984); People v. Palmer, 7 A.D.3d 472, 778 N.Y.S.2d 144 (2004) (3-1/2 year period reasonable under all the circumstances); People v. Williams, 280 A.D.2d 563, 721 N.Y.S.2d 366 (2001) (finding two-month period "not so lengthy that it was virtually impossible for the defendant to answer the charges and to prepare an adequate defense"); People v. O'Keefe, 276 A.D.2d 647, 714 N.Y.S.2d 514, *appeal denied*, 96 N.Y.2d 804, 750 N.E.2d 84, 726 N.Y.S.2d 382 (2001) (holding three-month time period for alleged abuse not excessive); People v. Smith, 272 A.D.2d 713, 710 N.Y.S.2d 648, *appeal denied*, 95 N.Y.2d 871, 738 N.E.2d 374, 715 N.Y.S.2d 226 (2000) (upholding indictment alleging abuse occurred in spring and summer of 1997); People v. Keefer, 262 A.D.2d 791, 692 N.Y.S.2d 233, *appeal denied*, 94 N.Y.2d 824, 724 N.E.2d 387, 702 N.Y.S.2d 595 (1999) (upholding indictment alleging abuse occurred in autumn of 1996); People v. Green, 250 A.D.2d 143, 683 N.Y.S.2d 597 (1998), *appeal denied*, 93 N.Y.2d 873, 711 N.E.2d 649, 689 N.Y.S.2d 435 (1999) (upholding five-month time period in sex offense prosecution involving defendant's ten-year-old nephew in view of surrounding circumstances such as the victim's age and the fact that the crimes were not easily discoverable); People v. Melfa, 244 A.D.2d 857, 655 N.Y.S.2d 780 (1997), *appeal denied*, 91 N.Y.2d 895, 691 N.E.2d 1035, 669 N.Y.S.2d 9 (1998) (complainant's age and reluctance to talk about incident justified indictment's three-month period); State v. Gressler, 235 A.D.2d 599, 652 N.Y.S.2d 792, *appeal denied*, 89 N.Y.2d 1036, 681 N.E.2d 1313, 659 N.Y.S.2d 866 (1997) (noting "the tender years of the victim" and surrounding circumstances supported an indictment with courts charging abuse over a period of time); People v. Gargano, 222 A.D.2d 694, 636 N.Y.S.2d 350 (1995), *appeal denied*, 88 N.Y.2d 879, 668 N.E.2d 424, 645 N.Y.S.2d 453 (1996); State v. McBriff, 151 N.C. App. 631, 566 S.E.2d 776 (2002) ("Time variances do not require dismissal if they do not prejudice a defendant's opportunity to present an adequate defense." *Id.* at 637, 566 S.E.2d at 780); State v. Blackmon, 130 N.C. App. 692, 696–97, 507 S.E.2d 42, 45–46, *review denied*, 349 N.C. 531, 526 S.E.2d 470 (1998) (Court upheld eight and one-half month time period commenting that "indeed, in a case such as this, in which the minor child testified at trial that the sexual acts and indecent liberties committed by defendant occurred when she was seven-years-old and that some of those acts happened when it was cold outside and some when it was warm outside, any variance between the indictments brought against the defendant and the proof presented at trial is not fatal to the propriety of the indictments brought by the State." *Id.* at 697, 507 S.E.2d at 45–46); State v. Frazier, 121 N.C. App. 1, 464 S.E.2d 490 (1995), *aff'd*, 344 N.C. 611, 476 S.E.2d 297 (1996) ("We have stated repeatedly that in the interest of justice and recognizing that young children cannot be expected to be exact regarding times and dates, a child's uncertainty as to time or date upon which the offense charged was committed goes to the weight rather than the admissibility of the evidence." *Id.* at 17, 464 S.E.2d at 499, *citing* State v. Everett, 328 N.C. 72, 75, 399 S.E.2d 305, 306 (1991)); State v. Fitch, 2001 Ohio App. LEXIS 392 (Feb. 6, 2001) (reversing trial court's dismissal of an indictment spanning 21 months on the theory that time is not an essential element of crime involving child abuse, and because time is not an essential element in most sexual assault crimes. A court may show latitude with charging a broad time period for a sexual assault which occurred years earlier. [364]

California Supreme Court's view is typical of many courts:

> Does the victim's failure to specify precise date, time, place or circumstance render generic testimony insufficient? Clearly not. As many of the cases make clear, the particular details surrounding a child molestation charge are not elements of the offense and are unnecessary to sustain a conviction.

> The victim, of course, must describe the kind of act or acts committed with sufficient specificity, both to assure that unlawful conduct indeed has occurred and to differentiate between the various types of proscribed conduct (e.g. lewd conduct, intercourse, oral copulation or sodomy). Moreover, the victim must describe the number of acts committed with sufficient certainty to support each of the counts alleged in the information or indictment (e.g., "twice a month" or "every time we went camping"). Finally, the victim must be able

---

defendant failed to demonstrate how time period affected his ability to prepare a defense); State v. Sellards, 17 Ohio St. 3d 169, 478 N.E.2d 781 (1985) (holding precise times and dates are not material elements of an offense); Commonwealth v. Niemetz, 282 Pa. Super. 431, 422 A.2d 1369 (1980) (defendant was charged with sexual assaults beginning in 1972 and continuing until August, 1977. This was proper as long as the time period was within the statute of limitations since the precise date was unknown and the date is not an element of the offense. "Moreover, we do not believe that it would serve the ends of justice to permit a person to rape and otherwise sexually abuse his child with impunity simply because the child has failed to record in a daily diary the unfortunate details of her childhood." *Id.* at 440, 422 A.2d at 1373); State v. Smith, 599 N.W.2d 344 (S.D. 1999) (indictment charging that rape occurred during month of September was neither vague nor lacked specificity since time was not a material element of the offense); State v. Campbell, 904 S.W.2d 608 (Tenn. Crim. App. 1995) ("When the state lacks information to narrow the time frame with descriptive references, an accused's conviction may be affirmed if it appears that the defense was not hampered by the lack of specificity." *Id.* at 612); Harris v. State, No. 05-98-01727-CR, 2000 Tex. App. LEXIS 3072 (May 11, 2000); State v. Ross, 152 Vt. 462, 465, 568 A.2d 335, 337 (1989) (holding that due process of right of notice of time of offense will vary according to the age and circumstance of the victim and how the sexual abuse was carried out); State v. Hayes, 81 Wash. App. 425, 432, 914 P.2d 788, 793, *review denied*, 130 Wash. 2d 1013, 928 P.2d 413 (1996); State v. Miller, 195 W. Va. 656, 466 S.E.2d 507 (1995) ("Because time is not an element of the crime of sexual assault, the alleged variances concerning when the assaults occurred did not alter the substance of the charges against the defendant." *Id.* at 663, 466 S.E.2d at 514).

[364] People v. Latouche, 303 A.D.2d 246, 755 N.Y.S.2d 833 (2003):

> The indictment alleged a proper time frame and was not constitutionally infirm. The count charging rape in the third degree alleged a single incident falling within a specific 37-day period. The victim, defendant's stepdaughter, who was 16 years old at the time of that incident, first reported the crime to her mother several years later, and the specified time frame was the victim's best recollection. The People exercised diligent investigatory efforts and were unable to allege a more specific time period, and the time frame they alleged provided defendant with reasonable notice given all the surrounding circumstances. [citation omitted].

Id.

to describe the general time period in which these acts occurred (e.g., "the summer before my fourth grade," or "during each Sunday morning after he came to live with us") to assure the acts were committed within the applicable limitation period. Additional details regarding the time, place or circumstance of the various assaults may assist in assessing the credibility or substantiality of the victim's testimony, but are not essential to sustain a conviction.[365]

However, it may be reversible error to charge the jury that the prosecution need not establish beyond a reasonable doubt that a crime was committed within the time frame alleged in the indictment, particularly when the charge makes it difficult to differentiate between counts of an indictment.[366]

When the prosecution alleges a time frame in an indictment and the defendant raises the lack of opportunity to commit the sexual assault within that time period, the prosecution must prove the assault occurred within the alleged time period.[367] Simply questioning the complainant's credibility or aspects of her testimony does not raise a time-based defense.[368] Similarly, a general denial is insufficient to raise prejudice from a failure to consider an alibi defense.[369] If the defendant claims he was never alone with the child during a time period, the alibi is not affected by the charging period.[370]

The expression "on or about" in an indictment provides the prosecution with some latitude in proving when an offense took place.[371] The crime must nonetheless be prior to the date of the presentation of the indictment and within the statute of limitations.[372] Even a variance of one year from the date set forth in the indictment has been upheld as proper.[373] However, there is authority that in a child sexual assault prosecution allegation that an assault occurred "on or

---

[365] People v. Jones, 51 Cal. 3d 294, 315–16, 792 P.2d 643, 655–56, 270 Cal. Rptr. 611, 623–24 (1990).

[366] Alicea v. State, 13 P.3d 693, 699–700 (Wyo. 2000).

[367] State v. Williams, 137 N.H. 343, 346, 629 A.2d 83, 85 (1993).

[368] State v. Carter, 140 N.H. 114, 119, 663 A.2d 101, 104 (1995).

[369] Pace v. United States, 705 A.2d 673, 678 (D.C. 1998); State v. Hayes, 81 Wash. App. 425, 441, 914 P.2d 788, 798, *review denied*, 130 Wash. 2d 1013, 928 P.2d 413 (1996).

[370] State v. Baldonado, 124 N.M. 745, 955 P.2d 214, 222 (1998).

[371] Williams v. United States, 756 A.2d 380 (D.C. 2000) (holding variance of approximately two weeks between charged sexual acts and proof "reasonably close" and therefore proof sufficiently conformed to indictment); State v. Hildreth, 267 Mont. 423, 429, 884 P.2d 771, 775 (Mont. 1994); People v. Miller, 226 A.D.2d 833, 640 N.Y.S.2d 904, *appeal denied*, 88 N.Y. 939, 670 N.E.2d 456, N.Y.S.2d 172 (1996) (one day discrepancy between date alleged in the indictment of the sexual assault and date proved at trial did not violate defendant's Sixth Amendment right to "be informed of the nature and cause of the accusation."); State v. McIntosh, 207 W. Va. 561, 578, 534 S.E.2d 757, 774 (2000) (holding variance between proof of sexual abuse and dates in indictment is not prejudicial unless defendant is misled, subjected to an additional burden of proof or otherwise affected by the variance).

[372] Sledge v. State, 953 S.W.2d 253, 256 (Tex. Ct. Crim. App. 1997).

[373] *Id.*

about," without an instruction defining what "on or about" meant, did not authorize a conviction when the crime occurred within a few days of the date in the charging document.[374]

One objection against the charging of multiple acts in one count of the indictment or a broad time period involves due process concerns, including notice of the charges against a defendant and the right to present a defense. Under the Sixth Amendment of the United States Constitution, a defendant has a constitutional right "to be informed of the nature and cause of the accusation."[375] Generally, this requirement is met when the description of the offense in the indictment enables a defendant "to make his defense and to plead the judgment in bar of any further prosecution for the same crime."[376] Another due process argument is that the right to a unanimous jury verdict is violated since jury unanimity may not be achieved when there is testimony concerning repeated identical offenses. This is discussed further in § 1.33.

Another objection raised to a broad time period is that a defendant cannot present an effective alibi defense if the charge covers an extremely broad period of time; however, in cases where an accused child molester lives with the victim or has repeated access to the victim, the defense of alibi or misidentification is not likely to be a reasonable defense.[377] An alibi in a child sexual assault case is likely to require the showing of a lack of opportunity over the whole period of time that the alleged abuse took place and is thus not likely to be effective.[378]

The proof of when the sexual acts occurred may vary from the time period charged. Generally, all that is required is that the proof be reasonably near the specified date.[379] In one case the defendant was charged with sexually abusing a child during the month of April.[380] The nine-year-old child's testimony was that the abuse occurred after Christmas, "in school days, before summertime." This variance did not necessarily mean the defendant was convicted of a factually different offense than the one presented to the grand jury since the proof need establish that the offense was committed on a date reasonably near the date

---

[374] Mireles v. State, 901 S.W.2d 458 (Tex. Crim. App. 1995).

[375] U.S. Const. amend. VI.

[376] Rosen v. United States, 161 U.S. 29, 34 (1896). *See also* Russell v. United States, 369 U.S. 749, 763–64 (1962).

[377] State v. Sloan, 912 S.W.2d 592 (Mo. Ct. App. 1995); State v. Shelton, 851 S.W.2d 134, 137 (Tenn. 1993) (holding that lack of specificity in the period is acceptable as long as defendant is not hampered by ambiguity); State v. Brown, 55 Wash. App. 738, 748–49, 780 P.2d 880, 886 (1989) ("We recognize that more specificity in testimony may be required when alibi or misidentification is raised as a defense." *Id.* at 749, 780 P.2d at 886).

[378] *See, e.g.,* State v. Hildreth, 267 Mont. 423, 884 P.2d 771 (1994); State v. Hensley, 120 N.C. App. 313, 462 S.E.2d 550 (1995); State v. Ross, 152 Vt. 462, 465, 568 A.2d 335, 338 (1989).

[379] United States v. Castillo, 140 F.3d 874 (10th Cir. 1998).

[380] Pace v. United States, 705 A.2d 673 (D.C. 1998).

alleged.[381] The appellate court noted that the defendant did not request a continuance nor did the defendant establish any prejudice.[382]

The Pennsylvania Supreme Court cited the unfairness to a defendant who may wish to present an alibi defense as well as the difficulty a defendant faces in attacking credibility of a victim as a reason to overturn the conviction involving a sexual assault allegation in which a 22-year-old mentally and emotionally-impaired woman alleged that she had been sexually assaulted by the defendant once during a 14-month period.[383] The Court noted that, in addition to the broadly charged period, the defendant was being prejudiced by being unable to attack the credibility of the victim through many usual means, such as questioning the victim's emotional condition after the alleged rape or inquiring as to possible physical evidence or trauma or lack of such evidence or trauma after the alleged rape.[384]

Many states, however, including Pennsylvania, have veered away from requiring more than reasonably broad specificity when there is sufficient justification for the broad time period. There is no mathematical formula by which to gauge whether a time period is too broad. A nine-month period may be too broad in one situation,[385] whereas a ten-month time span involving a four-year-old child has been deemed by another court to be reasonable.[386]

Generally, courts try to balance several factors to assess the reasonableness of the time period set forth in an indictment. Thus, allegations of a sexual assault involving a six-year-old child occurring within a two-year time period were acceptable when there was evidence that the victim was threatened with injury, and that this was a factor in the child's delaying the report of the attack.[387] The court cited the threatened harm, as well as the child's age and lack of support from her family, as factors supporting its approval of an allegation covering a two-year time period.[388] Courts have also cited the fact that a victim's memory

---

[381] *Id.* at 677.

[382] *Id.* at 678.

[383] Commonwealth v. Devlin, 460 Pa. 508, 333 A.2d 888 (1975).

[384] *Id.*

[385] People v. Beauchamp, 74 N.Y.2d 639, 539 N.E.2d 1105, 541 N.Y.S.2d 977, 978 (1989) ("Where an indictment charges a time interval which is so large that it is virtually impossible for a defendant to answer the charges and to prepare a defense, dismissal should follow even though the People have acted diligently and a shorter time period cannot be alleged [citations omitted]. The time period alleged here, even considering the nature of the crime and the ages of the victims, is an excessive interval." *Id.* at 641, 539 N.E.2d at 1106, 541 N.Y.S.2d at 978).

[386] State v. Johnson, 670 So. 2d 651 (La. Ct. App. 1996) (holding that 16-month time frame was not too general for a sexual assault crime involving three-to six-year-old child); State v. D.B.S., 700 P.2d 630, 634 (Mont. 1985).

[387] Commonwealth v. Fanelli, 377 Pa. Super. 555, 547 A.2d 1201 (1988), *appeal denied*, 523 Pa. 641, 565 A.2d 1165 (1989).

[388] *Id.* at 561, 547 A.2d at 1204–05.

may be clouded by the abuse and a desire to forget as a factor in judging the reasonableness of the time frame charged.[389] Older children will more likely be held to a higher standard in providing more specificity as to time that acts of abuse took place. Victims between the ages of eight and 12, for example, should be able to provide a more specific time reference than ten, 12, and 16 months.[390]

One court has summarized the factors to be considered in determining whether a defendant has been adequately informed of the nature of the accusation against him:

1. The length of the time span provided by the prosecution;

2. The knowledge that the prosecution possesses or should acquire with reasonable diligence concerning the exact or approximate date or dates of the crimes;

3. The age of the victim;

4. The intelligence of the victim and other witnesses;

5. The nature of the offense or offenses;

6. Whether the offenses are likely to be discovered immediately;

7. Whether there is a criminal pattern; and

8. All other surrounding circumstances.[391]

Other courts have used similar criteria to define the "reasonably particular" charging requirement and include the nature of offense as a factor to consider in the reasonableness of a broad time period.[392] A trial court's evaluation of

---

[389] State v. Brown, 55 Wash. App. at 747, 780 P.2d at 885 (1989).

[390] People v. Keindl, 68 N.Y.2d 410, 419, 502 N.E.2d 577, 581, 509 N.Y.S.2d 790, 794 (1986).

[391] People v. Watt, 84 N.Y.2d 948, 644 N.E.2d 1373, 620 N.Y.S.2d 817 (1994) (In reviewing lower court's determination on remand, trial court properly upheld the five-month time interval specified in the indictment under the circumstances, which included the number of acts during the period, the continuation of the defendant's unlawful conduct, the time when the indictment was first handed down, the age of the complainant, fact that the abuse occurred in a place where the child went on a daily basis, the serious physical and emotional trauma exhibited by the victim, and the fact that since the defendant lived and worked at the day-care center any potential alibi defense he might have advanced was less meaningful. The court also noted that the defendant had threatened the child to remain silent, thereby making more difficult the prosecution's statutory burden of providing the most precise notice possible.); People v. Boyea, 222 A.D.2d 937, 636 N.Y.S.2d 136 (1995), *appeal denied*, 88 N.Y.2d 934, 670 N.E.2d 451, 647 N.Y.S.2d 167 (1997) ("Given the age and intelligence of the victims, the nature of the crimes charged (which, not infrequently, are neither witnessed by nonparticipants nor reported promptly by the victims), and the fact that the defendant, an authority figure to these children, told them to 'trust me' and not to tell, it is understandable why the people were unable to obtain a more precise estimate of the exact dates the crimes occurred." *Id.* at 938, 636 N.Y.S.2d at 137, *citing* People v. Watt in this footnote.).

[392] State v. Mulkey, 316 Md. 475, 560 A.2d 24 (1989) (decision cites numerous other jurisdic-

these factors and findings will assist appellate review. As noted below, some courts find a hearing helpful or necessary.

As can be seen by these factors, the prosecution does have a duty to obtain as much specific information as possible regarding the date and time of an offense, and if the defense can show that such due diligence and good faith have not been exercised, prejudice may be shown.[393] If the prosecution knows the date on which the offense occurred, it must particularize that date. There must also be "some reliable indicia that the number of acts charged actually occurred."[394]

The prosecution has the opportunity to provide more specific information on the date of an offense in a bill of particulars. This may satisfy the requirements of adequate notice and demonstrate, through further information, a good-faith effort on the part of the prosecution to provide as much specificity as possible. A defendant who fails to timely request a bill of particulars may be precluded from challenging the specificity or time period of an indictment.[395] If a bill of particulars has been served, a defendant may be waiving any issue as to adequate notice in the indictment if the defendant does not renew the motion to dismiss the indictment, unless the alleged error irreparably taints the trial as a matter of law.[396] Otherwise, the error may be reviewed as "an unpreserved allegation

---

tions upholding broad time period in a child sexual assault indictment); State v. Baldonado, 124 N.M. 745, 955 P.2d 214 (1998); State v. Ross, 152 Vt. 462, 465, 568 A.2d 335, 337 (1989) (holding that due process of right of notice of time of offense will vary according to the age and circumstance of the victim and how the sexual abuse was carried out).

[393] *Id. See also* Violett v. Commonwealth, 907 S.W.2d 773, 776 (Ky. 1995) (holding that prosecution need not have provided more specific information on dates since "the record in this case indicates that the prosecution supplied the defendant with all the details of the crime that it had available. . . ." *Id.* at 776); People v. Morris, 61 N.Y.2d 290, 296, 461 N.E.2d 1256, 473 N.Y.S.2d 769, 773 (1984); Eakes v. State, 665 So. 2d 852 (Miss. 1995):

> Eakes' indictment alleges his crimes of sexual penetration against April Myers occurred 'on, about or between' December 1, 1990 and December 24, 1990; February 1, 1991 and April 30, 1991; and 'on or about' May 11 and 12, 1991. At trial April was more specific, claiming Eakes had abused her on December 26, 1990, January 26, 1991, and March 16, 1991. She also provided particular reasons and/or events which caused her to be at Eakes' home on these dates. The dates testified to are close to the dates charged in the indictment. Given that Eakes was fully and fairly advised of the charges against him, the lack of specific dates in the indictment is not fatal.

Id. at 860; State v. Campbell, 904 S.W.2d 608 (Tenn. Crim. App. 1995) (holding that record reflected that prosecution utilized diligent efforts to provide defendant with specificity of allegations); State v. Jones, 1994 Tenn. Crim. App. LEXIS 587 *55–56 (Sept. 15, 1994) (holding that prosecution's description that defendant was wearing Christmas underwear at the time of the assault demonstrated reasonable effort to narrow the time frame of the sexual assault).

[394] LaPierre v. State, 108 Nev. 528, 836 P.2d 56 (1992).

[395] State v. LaMothe, 57 Conn. App. 736, 751 A.2d 831 (2000); State v. Long, 972 S.W.2d 559 (Mo. 1998); State v. Hayes, 81 Wash. App. 425, 440, 914 P.2d 788, 797, *review denied*, 130 Wash. 2d 1013, 928 P.2d 413 (1996).

[396] Lovelace v. State, 241 Ga. App. 774, 527 S.E.2d 878 (2000) (holding defendant failed to

of error as a matter of discretion in the interest of justice,"[397] which represents a much more difficult standard of review. Thus, if there is still a basis for a motion to dismiss the indictment after service of a bill of particulars, it should be renewed.

On a motion to dismiss an indictment for charging an excessive time period, Florida requires a hearing at which the prosecution must establish "clearly and convincingly" that it has exhausted all reasonable means of narrowing the time frames further, and if such a showing is made, the burden shifts to the defendant to demonstrate prejudice from the time period alleged in the indictment.[398] In a child sexual assault indictment covering a 27-month period, the Florida Supreme Court noted that the defense should be permitted to present evidence of how the time period would impair a potential alibi defense, such as when the defendant may have been out of the country on military duty.[399] On the other hand, an alibi of short duration may be insignificant where the defendant had regular access to the victim, such as when both reside in the same household during the time period alleged in the indictment.

New Mexico also mandates a hearing as to whether the prosecution could reasonably have provided greater specificity than a two-year period and whether the failure prejudiced the defendant in a child sexual assault prosecution.[400] The court noted:

> We are particularly concerned about the indications in the record that the State did nothing to try to shorten the charging period to less than two years. It does not appear that there was any attempt to seek specifics from the child or other sources that would have made it possible to correlate the alleged offenses with any events (or even seasons of the year) that would have made possible a shorter charging span.[401]

Another issue to be addressed is when the lengthy time period charged would affect a defendant's ability to defend against an element of the offense — such as the requirement that the defendant or victim be a certain age — but the defendant or victim did not meet that age requirement on at least one or more days during the time period charged.[402] At the hearing to determine prejudice to a defendant, "the trial judge will have discretion to discount the defense's argument regarding prejudice where it appears unreasonable, e.g., where it

---

preserve objection to alleged time variance and defendant should have moved for a continuance, postponement, or recess); People v. Morey, 224 A.D.2d 730, 637 N.Y.S.2d 500, *appeal denied*, 87 N.Y.2d 1022, 666 N.E.2d 1070, 644 N.Y.S.2d 156 (1996); People v. Willette, 109 A.D.2d 112, 113, 490 N.Y.S.2d 290, 292 (1985).

[397] *Id.*

[398] Dell'Orfano v. State, 616 So. 2d 33, 35 (Fla. 1993).

[399] *Id.* at 36.

[400] State v. Baldonado, 124 N.M. 745, 955 P.2d 214 (1998).

[401] *Id.* at _____, 955 P.2d at 221.

[402] *Id.* at _____, 955 P.2d at 221.

appears to be poorly supported or contradicted by other admissible evidence including confessions or admissions."[403]

It also may be necessary to raise the issue of adequate notice at trial or request an adjournment to allow a defendant to investigate and prepare an alibi defense as trial testimony concerning the time period develops at trial.[404] While the indictment may provide adequate notice, due process may require time to develop an alibi defense based on specific and unanticipated or undisclosed aspects of trial testimony. Amending the indictment and changing the time period of the offense at the close of proof may be reversible error, particularly when the defense is based on the original time period provided by the prosecution.[405]

§ 1.32 Duplicity of charges and motion with respect to count of indictment charging multiplicity of acts within a single count or charging that crime may be committed in one of several ways.

Another aspect of an indictment that must be reviewed is whether a single count charges a multiplicity of acts. Generally, one count of an indictment that charges multiple acts is considered duplicitous. Many states have loosened this rule and permitted prosecutors to charge multiple acts in a single count because a child is unable to remember specifically when he or she was abused.[406] Most courts take the view, unless sexual assault is defined as a continuing crime, that each distinct, factually separate knowing act of sexual abuse may be prosecuted.[407] Thus, a defendant may be convicted of four separate counts of sexual assault on a child involving penile penetration, digital penetration, rubbing lotion on the vagina and ejaculation on the stomach.[408] Some states take the view that

---

[403] *Id.*

[404] *Morris*, 61 N.Y.2d at 297, 461 N.E.2d at 1260–61, 473 N.Y.S.2d at 773–74 (1984) ("Defendant argues that unfairness may develop if, at trial, a more precise date for each crime is discovered and he is then precluded from establishing an alibi because he did not provide notice, or if the trial court does not grant an adjournment to allow the defendant to investigate a possible alibi defense. These questions need not be decided at this time. Such determinations, if required at all, should be made in the sound discretion of the trial judge at the time the issues may arise.").

[405] People v. Plaisted, 1 A.D.3d 805, 768 N.Y.S.2d 236 (2003).

[406] State v. Covington, 711 P.2d 1183 (Alaska 1985); State v. Generazio, 691 So. 2d 609 (Fla. Ct. App. 1997) ("We conclude that in a case of ongoing sexual abuse of a child, where the child is unable to remember the specific dates on which he or she was abused, the allegation that the act occurred 'on one or more occasions' is not, *per se*, duplicitous." *Id.* at 611.); Baine v. State, 604 So. 2d 258 (Miss. 1992); State v. Little, 260 Mont. 460, 861 P.2d 154 (1993); State v. Petrich, 101 Wash. 2d 566, 683 P.2d 173 (1984).

[407] *See, e.g.*, Loeblein v. Dormire, 229 F.3d 724 (8th Cir. 2000), *cert. denied*, 532 U.S. 982 (2001); State v. Arceo, 84 Haw. 1, 928 P.2d 843 (1996); Cooksey v. State, 359 Md. 1, 752 A.2d 606 (2000); State v. Sauceda, 168 Wis. 2d 486, 485 N.W.2d 1 (1992).

[408] People v. Woellhaf, 87 P.3d 142 (Colo. App. 2003) (The same court, however, refused to uphold a "pattern of abuse enhancement" under Colorado law because all of the sexual contacts occurred during the same episode.).

with the exception of certain statutes, rape and sodomy is defined as encompassing a single act and not a continuing series of sexual acts.[409] An indictment charging the defendant with a series of acts of sexual molestation upon young children as one crime would be dismissed. For this reason, testimony by a complainant to multiple rapes by a defendant during a specified date and time period renders a rape charge duplicitous.[410] One of the objections to charging multiple acts within a single count is that it makes it "virtually impossible to determine the particular act of sodomy or sexual abuse as to which the jury reached a unanimous verdict."[411] Maryland,[412] Rhode Island,[413] and New Hampshire[414] prohibit as duplicitous charging in a single count a series of sexual offenses committed at different times over an extended period on the same victim.

The prosecution may decide to charge numerous crimes by having several counts, each covering a broad time period. For example, it may allege one act of abuse per month for several months. This would avoid the problem of duplicity.[415] While a state may define rape and sodomy as encompassing a single act, it may also have a crime of endangering the welfare of a child or sexual assault, which, by its nature, may be committed by one act or multiple acts, and which is characterized as a continuing crime.[416] A continuing crime theory also

---

[409] People v. Keindl, 68 N.Y.2d 410, 420–21, 502 N.E.2d 577, 582, 509 N.Y.S.2d 790, 794–95 (1986); People v. Jelinek, 224 A.D.2d 717, 638 N.Y.S.2d 731, *appeal denied*, 88 N.Y.2d 880, 668 N.E.2d 426, 645 N.Y.S.2d 455, *cert. denied*, 519 U.S. 900 (1996) (dismissing counts of indictment because testimony involved selected multiple occasions of abuse during the designated period of time set forth in the counts of the indictment).

[410] Cooksey v. Maryland, 359 Md. 1, 8752 A.2d 606 (2000):

> Finally, we must keep in mind that the prohibition against duplicitous pleading is a broad one; it applies not just to offenses against children but to all criminal and civil pleading. If we were to begin carving out judicial exceptions to the prohibition, on a case-by-case basis, how would we define them, where would we draw the line, and what alternative protective devices would we mandate in each instance?

Id. at 46, 752 A.2d at 620; State v. Patch, 135 N.H. 127, 599 A.2d 1243 (1991); People v. Jiminez, 239 A.D.2d 360, 657 N.Y.S.2d 735, *appeal denied*, 90 N.Y.2d 906, 686 N.E.2d 230, 663 N.Y.S.2d 518 (1997) (dismissing rape charge which encompassed complainant's testimony of multiple rapes but permitting the prosecution to resubmit any appropriate charges arising out of dismissed count); State v. Saluter, 715 A.2d 1250 (R.I. 1998).

[411] *Id.*

[412] Cooksey v. State, 359 Md. 1, 752 A.2d 606 (2000).

[413] State v. Saluter, 715 A.2d 1250 (R.I. 1998).

[414] State v. Patch, 135 N.H. 127, 599 A.2d 1243 (1991).

[415] People v. Cosby, 222 A.D.2d 690, 636 N.Y.S.2d 73, *appeal denied*, 87 N.Y.2d 1018, 666 N.E.2d 1066, 644 N.Y.S.2d 152 (1995) ("The defendant was charged with committing criminal sexual acts from May 1992 to August 1993, and each count of the indictment encompasses a period of one month. Each count is premised upon a single sexual act and not, as the defendant claims, upon multiple acts. Moreover, each sexual act is alleged to have been committed only once within the designated month. Accordingly, the indictment is not duplicitous." *Id.* at 691, 636 N.Y.S.2d at 74).

[416] *Keindl*, supra note 409, 68 N.Y.2d at 421-22, 502 N.E.2d at 582, 509 N.Y.S.2d at 795.

permits a defendant to be guilty of a crime by virtue of committing repeated acts, even though one act in and of itself may be insufficient to constitute the offense.[417]

Some states have defined or redefined crimes involving sexual assault to permit the charging of multiple acts within a single count of an indictment.[418] The statute may permit different types of acts to form the basis for the crime.[419] The prosecution benefits from charging a continuing crime, since many victims are unable to recall exact dates or incidents when there has been chronic sexual abuse. As a continuing offense, the statute of limitations would not ordinarily commence until after the last act of abuse had occurred; however, these statutes also raise the election of offenses issue, discussed in the following section.

The continuing-crime theory does have one potential benefit for a defendant. If convicted, a defendant will face sentencing for only one conviction rather than multiple convictions. Otherwise, the various sexual acts committed over a period of time would subject a person to multiple prosecutions and possible multiple punishments.[420] Even for a continuous course crime, the prosecution must

---

[417] *Id.* For example, a defendant may be guilty of endangering the welfare of a child as a result of the cumulative effect of the alleged act, whereas one act, such as exposing himself to a child, may not constitute the crime in and of itself.

[418] People v. Grant, 20 Cal. 4th 150, 973 P.2d 72, 83 Cal. Rptr. 2d 295 (1999) (continuing sexual abuse of a child statute does not violate prohibitions against *ex post facto* laws in both Federal and California Constitutions.). Cal. Penal Code § 288.5 provides for a crime of continuous sexual abuse of a child:

> (a) Any person who either resides in the same home with the minor child or has recurring access to the child, who over a period of time, not less than three months in duration, engages in three or more acts of substantial sexual conduct with a child under the age of 14 years at the time of the commission of the offense . . . is guilty of the offense of continuous sexual abuse of a child and shall be punished by imprisonment in the state prison for a term of 6, 12, or 16 years. (b) To convict under this section, the trier of fact, if a jury, need unanimously agree only that the requisite number of acts occurred not on which acts constitute the requisite number.

The section's constitutionality has been upheld by intermediate California appellate courts. *See* People v. Avina, 14 Cal. App. 4th 1303, 18 Cal. Rptr. 2d 511 (1993); People v. Higgins, 9 Cal. App. 4th 294, 11 Cal. Rptr. 2d 694 (1992). New York has added the crimes of "Course of Sexual Conduct in the First and Second Degree" to deal with multiple acts of abuse over a period of time when the child is unable to provide specific dates or narrow the time frame within which the acts occurred. *See* N.Y. Penal Law §§ 130.75, 130.80.

[419] People v. Whitham, 38 Cal. App. 4th 1282, 45 Cal. Rptr. 2d 571 (1995); People v. Barron, 34 Cal. App. 4th 1003, 40 Cal. Rptr. 2d 660 (1995) (in construing this statute, the court found that three or more acts did not have to be of the same kind to fall within the statute. The court also noted that the defendant's "right to jury unanimity was satisfied by the jury's unanimous conclusion that a pattern of sexual abuse existed even though they relied on different acts of abuse to establish the pattern").

[420] People v. Valdez, 23 Cal. App. 4th 46, 28 Cal. Rptr. 2d 236 (1994) (holding that defendant was properly convicted of the continuous sex abuse of child and individual acts of child abuse but could not be sentenced to consecutive terms based on the same acts); Dufrene v. State, 853 S.W.2d 86, 89 (Tex. Ct. App. 1993).

document the time period the child was subjected to the sexual abuse.[421] But the usual requirements of specificity do not apply.[422]

A defendant cannot be charged with more than one count of a crime that can be characterized as a continuing offense "unless there has been an interruption in the course of conduct."[423] If a defendant is so charged, the indictment is multiplicitous and the multiplicitous counts dismissed.[424] If the counts are not facially duplicitous, the grand jury minutes may be reviewed to assess duplicity.[425] A victim's language that she was raped "at least once" during a given time can trigger a finding of duplicity.[426] Not all courts find the continuous course of conduct statute constitutional. The Supreme Court of Hawaii found its course of continuous sexual assault statute unconstitutional because "[m]ultiple acts of sexual penetration or sexual contact, committed 'over a period of time,' bespeak 'separate and distinct intents,' which . . .can only occur under circumstances in which the 'defendant intended to commit more than one offense in the course of [the] criminal episode.' "[427]

An indictment which charges multiple acts in one count should not be confused with a count that charges that the crime was committed in one of several ways. For example, consider the following allegation of sexual abuse:

> The defendant . . . subjected a female less than eleven years of age to sexual contact, said contact consisted of the defendant's penis and the victim's mouth, the defendant's mouth and the victim's breast, the defendant's hand and the victim's breast, the defendant's hand and the victim's vagina, the victim's

---

[421] People v. Juara, 279 A.D.2d 479, 719 N.Y.S.2d 102 (2001) (reversing defendant's conviction because there was no evidence of the time period over which the sexual abuse occurred, since the statute requires the abuse occur "over a period of time not less than three months in duration.").

[422] People v. Palmer, 7 A.D.3d 472, 778 N.Y.S.2d 144, *appeal denied*, 3 N.Y.3d 710, 818 N.E.2d 680, 785 N.Y.S.2d 38 (2004).

[423] People v. Quinones, 8 A.D.3d 589, 779 N.Y.S.2d 131, *appeal denied*, 3 N.Y.3d 710, 818 N.E.2d 680, 785 N.Y.S.2d 38 (2004) (Court held the following to be multiplicitous and reversed defendant's conviction:

> The defendant was accused, *inter alia*, of subjecting a child to a course of sexual abuse from September 1, 1998 to May 30, 1999, which was the period of time that the child was in the second grade. In the first count of the indictment, the defendant was charged with the crime of course of sexual conduct against a child in the first degree (*see* Penal Law § 130.75 [1][a]), based on the alleged sexual abuse that took place from September 1, 1998 to December 31, 1998, when the child was in the first 'half' of second grade. In the third count of the indictment, the defendant was charged with another count of the same crime, based on the alleged sexual abuse that took place from January 1, 1999 to May 30, 1999, when the child was in the second 'half' of second grade.

Id., 779 N.Y.S.2d at 132.

[424] People v. Quinones, 8 A.D.3d 589, 779 N.Y.S.2d 131 (2004).

[425] People v. Levandowski, 8 A.D.3d 898, 780 N.Y.S.2d 384 (2004).

[426] People v. Levandowski, 8 A.D.3d 898, 780 N.Y.S.2d 393 (2004).

[427] State v. Rabago, 103 Haw. 236, 252 (2003), *quoting*, State v. Arceo, 84 Haw. 1, 18 (1996).

hand and the defendant's penis, and the defendant's penis and the victim's vagina.[428]

In this charge, the crime of sexual abuse on a particular date and time is alleged to have been committed in one of several ways. This is not duplicitous since the indictment charges only one crime. It is also not necessary for the prosecution to prove that each one of the acts occurred, only that any one of the acts sufficient to constitute the crime of sexual abuse occurred. While a count of an indictment may be valid on its face, if a complainant testifies to sexual abuse on two separate occasions, the charge becomes duplicitous, and a conviction based on such testimony may be reversed.[429]

§ 1.33 Election of offenses.

When multiple acts are alleged in one count of the indictment, there may be a question as to which act or acts a jury finds a defendant guilty, and whether the jury unanimously found that the defendant committed a particular act or acts. In other words, the argument is that all jurors must agree on the acts the defendant committed for there to be a unanimous verdict to ensure that each juror is considering the same occurrence. This raises the issue of jury unanimity and the election of offenses.[430] Thus, the prosecution may be required to elect at the close of its case-in-chief a particular incident for which a conviction is sought.[431]

---

[428] People v. Heinzelman, 170 A.D.2d 841, 567 N.Y.S.2d 180, *appeal denied*, 77 N.Y.2d 995, 575 N.E.2d 407, 571 N.Y.S.2d 921 (1991). *See also* Griffin v. United States, 502 U.S. 46, 50–51 (1991); State v. Chapman, 229 Conn. 529, 643 A.2d 1213 (1994) ("Furthermore, we have held that, where the State charges that a defendant has committed a crime in more than one way, and those ways are charged in the conjunctive, as they must be, and the trial court instructs, as it must, that the State need only prove one of its allegations, and not all, the verdict must be upheld so long as there is sufficient evidence under any of the allegations." *Id.* at 543, 643 A.2d at 1220).

[429] People v. Davila, 198 A.D.2d 371, 603 N.Y.S.2d 185 (1993).

[430] *See generally*, Tim A. Thomas, Annotation, *Requirement of Jury Unanimity as to Mode of Committing Crime Under Statute Setting Forth the Various Modes by Which Offense May Be Committed*, 75 A.L.R.4TH 91 (1990).

[431] Covington v. State, 703 P.2d 436 (Alaska Ct. App. 1985) (reversing defendant's conviction because prosecution failed to elect specific incidents and no clarifying instruction given); State v. Arceo, 84 Haw. 1, 928 P.2d 843 (1996) (Hawaii Supreme Court takes the position of many state courts that sexual assault offense is not a continuing offense. Thus, State is required to elect specific acts upon which prosecution is seeking conviction or court must give the jury a "specific unanimity" instruction); Commonwealth v. Zane Z., 51 Mass. App. Ct. 135, 743 N.E.2d 867 (2001) (reversing defendant's conviction for failure to provide jury with a specific unanimity instruction); State v. Altgilbers, 109 N.M. 453, 465, 786 P.2d 680, 692 (1989), *citing* United States v. Shorter, 608 F. Supp. 871, 876 (D.D.C. 1985), *aff'd*, 809 F.2d 54 (D.C. Cir.), *cert. denied*, 484 U.S. 817 (1987); People v. DeLong, 206 A.D.2d 914, 916, 615 N.Y.S.2d 168, 170 (1994); State v. Walton, 958 S.W.2d 724, 727 (Tenn. 1997) (noting that election of offenses insures that the jury is considering the same occurrence); State v. Rickman, 876 S.W.2d 824, 829 (Tenn. 1994); State v. Shelton, 851 S.W.2d 134 (Tenn. 1993); State v. Hoyt, 928 S.W.2d 935 (Tenn. Crim. App. 1995) ("In this case, it is clear that although the indictment charged the appellant with one distinct sexual offense against each victim, the evidence suggested multiple offenses against each victim. At trial, each

Some jurisdictions hold it plain error to fail to instruct the jury as to the need to reach a unanimous verdict as to at least one specific underlying act of sexual assault on a count involving multiple acts.[432] The unanimity instruction is required if there are separate events or episodes and the jury might disagree concerning which act the defendant committed and yet convict him of the crime charged.[433] In a charge involving sexual contact, a defendant is not necessarily entitled to a specific unanimity instruction regarding the parts of the body he touched.[434] The theory underlying the requirement that the prosecution make such an election is that the defendant will be better able to assert a defense, that the defendant will be protected from double jeopardy by particularization of the crime for which he is being prosecuted, and that a jury's verdict will not be a matter of choice between offenses with some jurors willing to convict on one offense and others willing to convict on another offense. When the prosecution makes an election, but the date or time period encompasses multiple acts or occurrences, this may be tantamount to a non-election of offenses and require a reversal of conviction.[435] The problem may develop when the prosecution does not develop or distinguish through direct examination multiple acts of sexual assault.[436] The election need not reference a specific day. It should be specific enough for a court to evaluate whether there is testimony supporting the elected offense. If the prosecution supplies a date or period, it is sufficient that the complainant's testimony comports with the stated time even if the witness does

---

victim described numerous occasions on which the appellant committed unlawful acts. Under these circumstances, the court should have required the State to elect one of these incidents to rely upon for a conviction. The court's failure to do so abridged the appellant's constitutional right to a unanimous jury verdict, and therefore, also mandates a reversal of the appellant's conviction." *Id.* at 947); Crawford v. State, 696 S.W.2d 903, 905 (Tex. Crim. App. 1985); State v. Root, 95 Wash. App. 333, 975 P.2d 1052 (1999). *But see* State v. Saunders, 893 P.2d 584 (Utah Ct. App. 1995) (Court upheld the following:

> Before the jury arrives at a guilty verdict, the law requires that each of the jurors be satisfied beyond a reasonable doubt that an act alleged in the information occurred. There is no requirement that the jurors be unanimous about precisely which act occurred or when or where the act or acts occurred. The only requirement is that each juror believe, beyond a reasonable doubt, that at least one prohibited act occurred sometime between October of 1991 and May of 1992, . . . involving the victim and the defendant.

Id. at 588.

However, defendant failed to object to the instruction and appellate court reviewed instruction only for plain error.).

[432] State v. Weaver, 290 Mont. 58, 964 P.2d 713 (1998).

[433] Commonwealth v. Conefrey, 37 Mass. App. Ct. 290, 297–98, 640 N.E.2d 116 (1994); Commonwealth v. Ramos, 31 Mass. App. Ct. 362, 366–67, 577 N.E.2d 1012 (1991).

[434] United States v. Miguel, 111 F.3d 666, 673 (9th Cir. 1997); United States v. Gavin, 959 F.2d 788, 792 (9th Cir. 1992).

[435] State v. Walton, 958 S.W.2d 724 (Tenn. 1997).

[436] *Id.*

not state a date. For example, if the prosecution elects a month and year, *e.g.*, August, 1993, and the witness does not recall the date of the abuse but does know it was approximately one month before she was placed in foster care and other testimony establishes that the placement occurred in September, 1993, the combined testimony supports the election.[437] On the other hand, if the evidence does not support the elected offense, even if a specific date is selected, a conviction will likely be reversed.[438] The sufficiency of the evidence supporting the elected offense is reviewed in the same fashion as if the sufficiency of evidence supporting an element of the offense were being reviewed.[439]

When there is ambiguity in the testimony of the complainant about multiple acts, it may be reversible error for a trial judge to fail to require the prosecution to elect upon which act it was seeking a conviction. In the absence of a prosecutor's election, it has also been held that a court's instruction that the jury agrees that the defendant committed the same specific act constituting the crime, and that the act agreed upon need not be stated in the verdict is sufficient to protect the defendant's right to a unanimous jury as long as there is sufficient proof of the act or acts.[440]

Some courts require neither an election by the prosecution nor a jury instruction when there is sufficient proof of "all the elements of all the acts testified to" despite the jury's inability to single out a specific act or offense,[441] or when the victim's testimony is overwhelming on one incident, and little or no details as to other occurrences are available.[442] Other courts have not required an election in statutes permitting the charging of multiple acts of abuse cases or

---

[437] Smith v. State, 745 So. 2d 284, 291 (Ala. Crim. App. 1998).

[438] State v. Hines, No. 01C01-9709-CC-00405, 1999 Tenn. Crim. App. LEXIS 58, at *11–12 (Jan. 27, 1999) (where victim testified that abuse occurred "almost daily" and prosecution elected fifteenth day of each month, but there was no specific testimony supporting abuse occurring on fifteenth, court stated: "Although the jury could have concluded, and obviously did conclude, that the victim was violated one or more times each month, it could not conclude that a violation took place on the fifteenth of any given month as elected by the state.").

[439] *Id.* at *10–11.

[440] People v. Crow, 28 Cal. App. 4th 440, 33 Cal. Rptr. 2d 624 (1994); State v. Petrich, 101 Wash. 2d 566, 688 P.2d 173 (1984) (jury instruction requested that all 12 jurors agree that the same underlying act has been proved beyond a reasonable doubt if prosecution does not elect an act upon which it relies for conviction).

[441] State v. Altgilbers, 109 N.M. 453, 466, 786 P.2d 680, 693 (1989); State v. Ortega-Martinez, 124 Wash. 2d 702, 881 P.2d 231 (1994).

[442] State v. Webb, 1997 Tenn. Crim. App. LEXIS 188 (Feb. 27, 1997) ("Accordingly, in the instant case, we conclude that the State's failure to elect and the trial court's failure to give an augmented instruction, did not constitute reversible constitutional error, because, absent any additional evidence, it can be concluded beyond a reasonable doubt that the verdict was unanimous as to the incident of rape en route to the grocery store in 1982. During its opening statement, the State only alluded to this incident." *Id.* at *32–34.).

when there is no double jeopardy risk or prejudice to the defendant.[443] For example, with a resident child molester, rarely is an alibi or identity defense raised. The unanimity instruction is not required if there is a single charge and "the special and temporal separations between acts are short, that is, where the facts show a continuing course of conduct, rather than a succession of clearly detached incidents."[444] Under California's "resident child molester statute," a

---

[443] People v. Jones, 51 Cal. 3d 294, 299, 270 Cal. Rptr. 611, 792 P.2d 643 (1990); Thomas v. People, 803 P.2d 144 (Colo. 1990); Commonwealth v. Sanchez, 423 Mass. 591, 670 N.E.2d 377 (1996):

> Here, too, as in *Kirkpatrick*, and unlike the situation presented in *Conefrey*, the victim, Alicia, did not identify discrete instances when particular acts took place. She spoke largely in generalities. The critical issue for the jury was whether to believe her testimony that the defendant had raped her repeatedly. As in *Kirkpatrick*, there was no significant likelihood in this case that convictions on the three identical indictments would result from some jurors being satisfied that one or more specific events occurred and other jurors finding the defendant guilty on the basis of different events. The defendant, then, was not entitled to a "specific unanimity" instruction. The judge did not err in that regard, and defense counsel's withdrawal of her request for such an instruction was not ineffective assistance of counsel.

Id. at 600, 670 N.E.2d at 383.; Commonwealth v. Kirkpatrick, 423 Mass. 436, 668 N.E.2d 790, *cert. denied*, 117 S. Ct. 527 (1996):

> The victim's testimony in this case (which the jury found credible) clearly demonstrates the difficulty in requiring the Commonwealth to identify and focus on a particular instance of abuse. The victim did not identify discrete instances when particular acts took place, much less supply a list of dates and times. She provided reasonably detailed descriptions of various distinguishable forms of abuse but otherwise spoke largely in generalities. Her testimony, if believed, established that she had been the victim of a large number of criminal acts by the defendant, but it provided little basis for the prosecution to identify particular acts of abuse on which to focus its prosecution. Clearly, the rule proposed by the defendant, which would have limited or foreclosed prosecution in this case, might effectively insulate the most egregious offenders from prosecution. Following the Supreme Courts of California and Colorado, we also conclude that when the evidence does not create the risk that jurors will 'reach a non-unanimous verdict,' the guarantee of due process does not require that the Commonwealth attempt the artificial task of identifying a specific instance of abuse as a basis for indictment.

Id. at 443–44, 668 N.E.2d at 795.); State v. Hayes, 81 Wash. App. 425, 914 P.2d 788, *review denied*, 130 Wash. 2d 1013, 928 P.2d 413 (1996):

> A defendant charged with multiple counts is adequately protected from any risk of double jeopardy when the evidence is sufficiently specific as to each of the acts charged. The State need not elect specific acts that it will rely upon for each charge so long as the jury is instructed as to the unanimity requirement on each count and different evidence is introduced to support each count. No double jeopardy violation results when the information, instructions, testimony, and argument clearly demonstrate that the State was not seeking to impose multiple punishments for the same offense."

Id. at 440, 914 P.2d at 797.).

[444] Commonwealth v. Thatch, 39 Mass. App. Ct. 904, 653 N.E.2d 1121, *review denied*, 421 Mass. 1105, 656 N.E.2d 1258 (1995).

jury is instructed that it "need unanimously agree only that the requisite number of acts occurred not on which acts constitute the requisite number."[445] This statute is discussed in § 1.31, note 375.

Suggested instructions for unanimity are:

> The defendant is charged with the offense of _____. He may be found guilty if the proof shows beyond a reasonable doubt that he committed any one or more of such acts, but in order to find the defendant guilty, all the jurors must agree that he committed the same act or acts. It is not necessary that the particular act or acts committed so agreed upon be stated in the verdict.

> In order to find the defendant guilty, it is necessary for the prosecution to prove beyond a reasonable doubt the commission of a specific act [or acts] constituting said crime within the period alleged. And, in order to find the defendant guilty, you must unanimously agree upon the commission of the same specific act [or acts] constituting said crime within the period alleged. It is not necessary that the particular act or acts committed so agreed upon be stated in the verdict.[446]

Failing to object to the court's instruction on unanimity may be a waiver of a claimed error in the instruction.[447]

§ 1.34 Motion to restrict further treatment or counseling of a child victim.

Another motion that has been suggested by some experts in the field of psychology is a motion to restrict further treatment or counseling for an alleged victim. The theory behind such a motion is that further counseling or treatment of an individual who has not been determined in fact to be a victim of abuse will further damage the alleged victim and may teach the witness certain victim behaviors. From a due process point of view, it is also suggested that the counseling and treatment of an individual who has not been shown to be a sexual assault victim can provide the witness with highly suggestive information and reinforce the effects of an improperly conducted interview or investigation. The motion is also based on recent studies that indicate that treatment for sexual assault victimization in the absence of real victimization can produce significant emotional *sequelae* in an individual. A sample affidavit supporting such a motion is set forth in Appendix H in this book. This affidavit is by a psychologist who sets forth the basis for the motion to restrict any further counseling or treatment

---

[445] People v. Grant, 20 Cal. 4th 150, 973 P.2d 72, 83 Cal. Rptr. 2d 295 (1999) (noting that under Cal. Penal Code § 288.5(b) jury need not agree precisely when or where the three incidents occurred, only that three acts of abuse occurred in the charged period). CALJIC No. 10.42.6.

[446] State v. Weaver, 290 Mont. 58, 964 P.2d 713 (1998).

[447] State v. Saunders, 893 P.2d 584 (Utah Ct. App. 1995); State v. Speese, 191 Wis. 2d 205, 226, 528 N.W.2d 63, 71 (1995), *rev'd on other grounds*, 199 Wis. 2d 597, 545 N.W.2d 510 (1996).

of an alleged victim until such time that there has been a legal determination of abuse. Since this is a motion of rather recent vintage, there is little authority dealing with it. It is, however, a good example of the dynamic nature of the sexual assault field, which is still generating new research and raising new questions as we learn more about the psychological aspects of sexual abuse, victimization, and the legal system's ability to handle such allegations.

§ 1.35   Motion *in limine.*

Evidence that may have been obtained in violation of a party's constitutional rights is subject to a motion to suppress. When a party seeks to challenge the introduction of evidence on nonconstitutional grounds, the legal avenue is the motion *in limine.*[448] Sexual assault trials lend themselves particularly to the use of motions *in limine.* This motion can be used by both the prosecution and the defense. Among the areas where prosecutors may use motions *in limine* are:

(1)   Restriction of cross-examination of a witness's or complainant's prior sexual history;[449]

(2)   Restriction of cross-examination of the complainant with respect to prior reports of abuse or false allegations;[450]

(3)   Restricting a defendant to particular areas of character proof.

The motion *in limine* also has the advantage of setting forth on the record the basis or documentation in support of the motion. A motion *in limine* can be to restrict the admission of evidence or to argue for the admissibility of evidence. It also provides the trial court with the opportunity to learn more about the facts surrounding the movant's arguments or additional law on the topic. It is especially helpful with novel approaches or novel legal issues where the judge may be considering particular facts or issues for a first time. One author notes, "If you spring the argument on the judge for the first time at trial, the natural inclination of most trial judges will be to uphold the exclusionary rule (the status quo) and reject your 'avant-garde' argument."[451] This same author sets forth also a sample format of a defendant's motion *in limine.*[452]

There are many areas of sexual assault trials in which defendants may want to consider a motion *in limine,* including:

---

[448] The use of the motion *in limine* for this purpose is discussed in Davis v. Alaska, 415 U.S. 308 (1974). *See generally,* Jeffrey F. Ghent, Annotation *Modern Status of Rules as to Use of Motion in Limine or Similar Preliminary Motion to Secure Exclusion of Prejudicial Evidence or Reference to Prejudicial Matters,* 63 A.L.R.3D 311 (1975).

[449] This area of law is discussed more fully in Chapter 5, § 5.29 *et seq.*

[450] This area is discussed more fully in § 5.46.

[451] *See generally,* Edward J Imwinkelried, Exculpatory Evidence. § 15-2, 400 (1990).

[452] *Id.*

(1) Restricting the use of hearsay statements;[453]

(2) Restricting testimony or evidence as to references to defendant's bad acts or references implying defendant's bad character;[454]

(3) Restricting the use of anatomical dolls;[455]

(4) Limiting the scope of expert's testimony;

(5) Restricting the use of closed-circuit television.

§ 1.36 Prosecution discovery, notice of alibi, notice of intent to offer psychological evidence.

Rules governing disclosure of evidence to the prosecution are generally regulated by statute. There is a wide variation from state to state as to the nature and extent of all discovery. For example, some states, such as Indiana, Florida, and Vermont, permit both the prosecution and the defense to depose witnesses. Many states require a defendant to provide the prosecution with copies of statements or notes of interviews of witnesses whom the defense intends to call. Notes that a defendant's attorney or prosecutor makes while interviewing witnesses may be discoverable if the attorney intends to call that person as a witness, even if the notes consist of proposed questions for the witness.[456] Notes made of a defendant's statements by the defendant's attorney or investigator may be protected by the attorney-client privilege, however.[457]

A defendant may be required to disclose medical or scientific tests conducted by the defense.[458] The Supreme Court of the United States has held that statutes requiring a defendant to present a notice of alibi and the names of witnesses in support of an alibi are constitutional and enhance the fairness of the adversary system.[459] "Given the ease with which an alibi can be fabricated, the state's

---

[453] See Chapter 10 for discussion of the legal principles applicable to the admissibility of hearsay statements. To preserve objections to the hearsay evidence, it may be necessary to assert the objections as the evidence is offered. State v. Hester, 114 Idaho 688, 760 P.2d 27 (1988).

[454] See discussion of Character Evidence and Cross-examination of the Defendant in Chapter 6.

[455] The use of anatomical dolls is discussed in §§ 10.6, 11.42 and 14.4. There is also a sample motion to preclude the use of dolls by the prosecution set forth in Appendix G.

[456] United States v. Nobles, 422 U.S. 225 (1975) (upholding as constitutional the defense disclosure of a prior statement of a defendant's witness); People v. Charron, 198 A.D.2d 722, 604 N.Y.S.2d 311 (1993), appeal denied, 83 N.Y.2d 803, 633 N.E.2d 494, 611 N.Y.S.2d 139 (1994) ("We note that County Court redacted the notes to delete the proposed questions which defense counsel intended to ask and thus only required disclosure of those portions that were deemed declarative. We discern no prejudice to defendant in the court's use of this procedure." Id. at 723, 604 N.Y.S.2d at 312); People v. Huhn, 140 A.D.2d 760, 760–62, 527 N.Y.S.2d 643, 643–45 (1988).

[457] People v. Drayton, 198 A.D.2d 770, 605 N.Y.S.2d 723 (1993).

[458] Commonwealth v. Trapp, 423 Mass. 356, 363, 668 N.E.2d 327, 332 (1996).

[459] Wardius v. Oregon, 412 U.S. 470, 473–74 (1973).

interest in protecting itself against an eleventh-hour defense is both obvious and legitimate."[460] The notice of alibi and alibi defense is discussed in Chapter 8.[461] Similar notice provisions can also be seen with respect to a defendant's intent to offer psychiatric evidence. Raising certain mental health issues such as diminished capacity may also trigger disclosure.

The need to supply the prosecution with a notice of psychiatric evidence may apply to situations where the defense offers psychological or psychiatric evidence or syndrome testing.[462] For example, a defendant seeking to present evidence of "battered-wife syndrome,"[463] "torture syndrome"[464] or "low IQ"[465] may be required to file a notice of intent to present such evidence or be precluded from doing so. When a defendant offers expert testimony that he does not meet the psychological characterization of a sex offender and the expert includes testimony about the facts surrounding the crime (in a jurisdiction permitting such testimony), the court may compel the defendant to undergo a psychological examination by the prosecution's expert.[466]

A defendant can be ordered to provide non-testimonial evidence such as blood or saliva or documents. For example, a defendant can be directed to produce documents he may intend to offer in support of an alibi defense.[467]

§ 1.37 Prosecution discovery of non-testimonial evidence.

Significant evidence available to the prosecution from the defendant himself is non-testimonial evidence, such as blood, hair, fingerprints, and handwriting

---

[460] Williams v. Florida, 399 U.S. 78, 81–82 (1970).

[461] *See* §§ 8.37-38.

[462] People v. Almonor, 93 N.Y.2d 571, 715 N.E.2d 1054, 693 N.Y.S.2d 861 (1999) (defendant properly precluded from presenting psychiatric testimony, the nature of which was not properly specified in defendant's notice to offer psychiatric evidence); People v. Berk, 88 N.Y.2d 257, 667 N.E.2d 308, 644 N.Y.S.2d 658, *cert. denied*, 519 U.S. 859 (1996) (holding that the defendant was properly precluded from offering psychological testimony on the relationship between memory loss and traumatic events to support the defendant's position that he could not remember the shooting when defendant failed to file a notice of intention to present such evidence); People v. Rizzo, 267 A.D.2d 1041, 701 N.Y.S.2d 209 (1999), *appeal denied*, 95 N.Y.2d 838, 735 N.E.2d 425, 713 N.Y.S.2d 145 (2000) (holding defendant's notice of intent to offer psychiatric evidence deficient in that it "failed to identify its relationship to a particular defense"); People v. Beecher, 225 A.D.2d 943, 639 N.Y.S.2d 863 (1996) (defendant precluded from introducing evidence of his state of mind or diminished capacity in the absence of appropriate notice to present psychiatric evidence).

[463] People v. Tumerman, 133 A.D.2d 714, 519 N.Y.S.2d 880, *appeal denied*, 70 N.Y.2d 938, 519 N.E.2d 636, 524 N.Y.S.2d 690 (1987), *cert. denied*, 485 U.S. 969 (1988).

[464] People v. Rossakis, 159 Misc. 2d 611, 605 N.Y.S.2d 825 (Sup. Ct. 1993).

[465] People v. Mai, 175 A.D.2d 692, 573 N.Y.S.2d 90, *appeal denied*, 78 N.Y.2d 1081, 583 N.E.2d 956, 577 N.Y.S.2d 244 (1991).

[466] State v. Davis, 254 Wis. 2d 1, 645 N.W.2d 913 (2002) (noting the state's concern that the defendant may offer a denial of the crime through a surrogate).

[467] People v. Sirmons, 242 A.D.2d 883, 662 N.Y.S.2d 645 (1997).

exemplars. The prosecution's right to such non-testimonial evidence from a defendant has been set forth by the Supreme Court of the United States in *Schmerber v. California*.[468] Examples of non-testimonial evidence include examining a rape suspect's body to see if the defendant has been in contact with poison ivy as described by the victim,[469] or for identifying features on the suspect's genitals.[470] A court may order the physical examination of a defendant on the issue of whether the defendant was unable to produce spermatozoa, even if the People improperly acquire a defendant's medical records.[471]

Under the *Schmerber* doctrine, it is not necessary that the defendant be in custody for law enforcement to obtain the defendant's non-testimonial evidence.[472] When a defendant has not been arrested or indicted, a showing of probable cause to believe that the defendant committed the crime for which the evidence is sought may be required.[473] In some situations and jurisdictions investigators may use a subpoena to collect the non-testimonial evidence if there is probable cause to believe a crime occurred and there is a basis to believe a person has evidence tending to prove the crime, not necessarily the suspect. Another requirement under the *Schmerber* doctrine is that obtaining non-testimonial evidence should not impose physical discomfort or risk of harm to a suspect, and that any procedure involving intrusion of the body should be carried out by a qualified physician in accordance with accepted medical standards.[474]

Appendix D provides a sample motion of the prosecution to obtain a defendant's blood sample for purposes of DNA testing. It follows the basic requirements of a court order to obtain blood from a suspect by establishing: (1) probable cause to believe the suspect has committed a crime; (2) a clear indication that probative and relevant evidence will be obtained by the testing and evidence obtained; and (3) that the method used to obtain the evidence from the defendant will be safe and reliable.[475] In the example, the probable cause is established

---

[468] 384 U.S. 757 (1966).

[469] Commonwealth v. Miles, 420 Mass. 67, 648 N.E.2d 719 (1995).

[470] *Ex parte* Jones, 719 So. 2d 256 (Ala. 1998) (Alabama Supreme Court upheld lower court's ruling of decision cited in main text that a trial court could issue a search warrant for the examination photographing of defendant's body to look for distinguishing characteristics on defendant's body and the fact that Alabama's search warrant provisions are limited to "personal property" does not preclude the photographing of a person's body for physical evidence).

[471] People v. Webb, 285 A.D.2d 659, 728 N.Y.S.2d 402, *appeal denied*, 97 N.Y.2d, 764 N.E.2d 409, 738 N.Y.S.2d 305 (2001).

[472] United States v. Chapel, 55 F.3d 1416 (9th Cir. 1995) (arrest not required for taking of suspect's blood; however, probable cause is required); Cupp v. Murphy, 412 U.S. 291, 294 (1973) (holding that the police were entitled to obtain the defendant's fingernail scrapings even though there had not been a formal arrest of the defendant).

[473] *In re* Abe A., 56 N.Y.2d 288, 437 N.E.2d 265, 452 N.Y.S.2d 6 (1982).

[474] *Schmerber*, 384 U.S. at 771–72.

[475] *In re* Lavigne, 418 Mass. 831, 641 N.E.2d 1328 (1994) (upholding use of a search warrant

by virtue of the defendant's indictment. In a situation in which the defendant has not been indicted, the police or prosecution should establish probable cause by witness statements, such as a statement from the complainant. It is the probable cause requirement that is most likely to be challenged in an application to obtain non-testimonial evidence.

Such a motion should set forth the reasons why the non-testimonial evidence is sought, establishing that there is a basis to believe that relevant or valuable evidence can be obtained.

Probable cause may be based on circumstantial evidence such as a defendant's inconclusive alibi and the fact that the defendant and victim were planning to end their relationship.[476] Another example of the type of circumstantial evidence that may be considered by a court in ordering the collecting of body hair and withdrawing of blood is the similarity of past criminal conduct of the defendant with the instant crime for which the warrant is sought in combination with evidence of a relationship to the victim and the matching of a physical description of the person who assaulted the victim.[477] In the view of most jurisdictions, however, the court issuing the warrant can consider only the facts set forth in the warrant and may not base the warrant on sworn yet unrecorded oral testimony submitted with the affidavit.[478] The prosecution need not establish that the test results for which the blood is sought will be admissible at trial since reliability of scientific tests can be determined at a pretrial hearing.[479]

In some jurisdictions if the defendant has been arrested and given counsel, obtaining a search warrant *ex parte* may violate the defendant's constitutional right to counsel resulting in suppression of the blood sample or other evidence.[480]

The motion also should set forth that obtaining the non-testimonial evidence does not place the defendant at any physical risk and is safe and reliable. The extraction of blood has repeatedly been held to be a safe procedure.[481] The issue of safety in seeking discovery from a defendant's body is most often seen in a request for surgical intrusion into a defendant's body to obtain evidence, such

---

to obtain blood for DNA testing when the three criteria cited in text are met, but court must provide the suspect an opportunity to be heard on the requested order); Chaplin v. McGrath, 215 A.D.2d 842, 626 N.Y.S.2d 294 (1995) (noting that "the severity of the crime, the importance of the evidence to the investigation and the unavailability of less intrusive means of obtaining it" are factors to consider in an application for blood samples and dental impressions); *In re* Abe A., 56 N.Y.2d 288, 437 N.E.2d 265, 452 N.Y.S.2d 6 (1982).

[476] Vivanco v. West, 214 A.D.2d 618, 625 N.Y.S.2d 255 (1995).

[477] State v. Dean, 271 Mont. 385, 897 P.2d 1073 (1995).

[478] *See, e.g.*, People v. Sloan, 450 Mich. 160, 538 N.W.2d 380 (1995).

[479] *In re* Lavigne, 418 Mass. 831, 836 n.4, 641 N.E.2d 1328, 1331 n.4 (1994).

[480] People v. Latibeaudierre, 174 Misc. 2d 60, 662 N.Y.S.2d 926 (1997).

[481] *See, e.g.*, Skinner v. Railway Labor Executives' Assoc., 489 U.S. 602, 625 (1989); Winston v. Lee, 470 U.S. 753, 762 (1985) ("blood tests do not constitute an unduly extensive imposition on an individual's privacy and bodily integrity").

as a bullet. The Supreme Court, in *Winston v. Lee*, noted that "[a] compelled surgical intrusion into an individual's body for evidence, however, implicates expectations of privacy and security of such magnitude that the intrusion may be 'unreasonable' even if likely to produce evidence of a crime."[482] Courts loathe to mandate discovery when there is an intrusive procedure involving a defendant's body, especially when there is a risk associated with the procedure. Unlike the taking of blood, it is difficult for the prosecution to establish the necessary safety in requiring a defendant to undergo surgery for the removal of a bullet.[483]

An example of an invasive examination of a defendant in a sexual assault trial can be seen in the test for trichomonas, a sexually-transmitted disease that may be diagnosed in a child victim. This test on a male defendant requires an invasive manual massage of the prostate gland to obtain semen. Requiring such a test for a defendant charged with child molestation is "a very significant invasion of both dignity and privacy" that cannot be justified, especially when there is a question as to the test's reliability and probative value.[484]

§ 1.38   Prosecution's use of blood obtained for one purpose in another case.

Law enforcement may seek to use blood obtained for one purpose for DNA analysis in another case. Probable cause need not necessarily be established for each use of the defendant's blood after it is lawfully taken the first time.[485]

---

[482] 470 U.S. 753, 759 (1985).

[483] People v. Browning, 108 Cal. App. 3d 117, 166 Cal. Rptr. 293 (1980); Bloom on behalf of Davis v. Starkey, 65 A.D.2d 763, 409 N.Y.S.2d 773 (1978) ("In our opinion, the People adduced insufficient evidence upon the evidentiary hearing at Criminal Term to establish that removal of the bullet would not be a major intrusion." *Id.* 763–64, 409 N.Y.S.2d at 774); People v. Richard, 145 Misc. 2d 755, 548 N.Y.S.2d 369 (1989) ("Before the State may surgically search the body of a presumed innocent man, it must show by substantial evidence that the method is safe, with limited risk, will produce relevant evidence which is probative of a material fact, which can be obtained in no other way, and there is not other substantial alternative evidence. This the People failed to do." *Id.* at 759–60, 548 N.Y.S.2d at 372). *See generally* Russell G. Donaldson, Annotation, *Admissibility, in Criminal Case, of Physical Evidence Obtained Without Consent by Surgical Removal from Person's Body*, 41 A.L.R.4th 60 (1985).

[484] People v. Scott, 21 Cal. 3d 284, 294–95, 578 P.2d 123, 145 Cal. Rptr. 876 (1978):

> Factors which must be considered include the reliability of the method to be employed, the seriousness of the underlying criminal offense and society's consequent interest in obtaining a conviction [citations omitted], the strength of law enforcement suspicions that evidence of crime will be revealed, the importance of the evidence sought, and the possibility that the evidence may be recovered by alternative means less violative of Fourth Amendment freedoms. [citation omitted]. These considerations must, in turn, be balanced against the severity of the proposed intrusion. Thus, the more intense, unusual, prolonged, uncomfortable, unsafe, or undignified the procedure contemplated, or the more it intrudes upon essential standards of privacy, the greater must be the showing for the procedure's necessity.

Id. at 293, 578 P.2d at 127, 145 Cal. Rptr. at 880.

[485] People v. Daniels, 62 Cal. App. 4th 1529, 73 Cal. Rptr. 2d 399 (1998) (permitting DNA evi-

As one appellate court held:

> It is also clear that once a person's blood sample has been obtained lawfully, he can no longer assert either privacy claims or unreasonable search and seizure arguments with respect to the use of that sample. Privacy concerns are no longer relevant once the sample has already lawfully been removed from the body, and the scientific analysis of a sample does not involve any further search and seizure of a defendant's person. In this regard we note that the defendant could not plausibly assert any expectation of privacy with respect to the scientific analysis of a lawfully seized item of tangible property, such as a gun or a controlled substance. Although human blood, with its unique genetic properties, may initially be quantitatively different from such evidence, once constitutional concerns have been satisfied, a blood sample is not unlike other tangible property which can be subject to a battery of scientific tests. [486]

A defendant may also consent to providing saliva or blood in lieu of a search warrant. [487] If the blood is obtained by consent of the defendant for a limited purpose or specific investigation, does that limit the blood's use in another criminal investigation? One court has permitted blood obtained by consent in an unrelated case to be used for DNA typing in another case. [488] Another court holds that a defendant's consent to obtain blood for a specified crime scene may not be used for comparison with another crime scene and evidence derived from such use suppressed. [489] Careful drafting of the consent needs to be considered to limit further use of such samples. A defendant's blood sample legally taken in a prior case by search warrant or other legal authority, [490] even if there is

---

dence in rape case compared with defendant's DNA from blood taken in driving under the influence case); People v. King, 232 A.D.2d 111, 663 N.Y.S.2d 610, *appeal denied*, 91 N.Y.2d 875, 691 N.E.2d 646, 668 N.Y.S.2d 574 (1997); State v. Loveland, 2005 S.D. 48, 696 N.W.2d 164 (2005) (holding once defendant's urine properly seized, it is not unreasonable to test it for other than original purpose and the subsequent "search" or testing does not violate the Fourth Amendment).

[486] *Id.* at 117–18, 663 N.Y.S.2d at 614.

[487] *See, e.g.,* Commonwealth v. Blasioli, 454 Pa. Super. 207, 685 A.2d 151 (1996), *aff'd*, 552 Pa. 149, 713 A.2d 1117 (1998).

[488] Washington v. State, 653 So. 2d 362, 364 (Fla. 1994).

[489] *In re* Welfare of J.W.K., 574 N.W.2d 103 (Minn. Ct. App. 1998), *rev'd*, 583 N.W.2d 752 (1998) (court reversed intermediate appellate court on the grounds of inevitable discovery exception to the Fourth Amendment, i.e., "[E]ven if the police exceeded the scope of the suspect's consent in using his blood sample in connection with the investigation of a different crime, the police inevitably would have obtained a blood sample from the suspect for the use in question." *Id.* at 753).

[490] Bickley v. State, 227 Ga. App. 413, 489 S.E.2d 167 (1997)); State v. Hauge, 103 Haw. 38, 79 P.3d 131 (2003); Wilson v. State, 132 Md. App. 510, 550, 752 A.2d 1250, 1272 (2000) (finding no expectation of privacy in blood sample once it is validly seized); State v. Notti, 2003 Mt. 170, 71 P.3d 1233 (2003); People v. King, 232 A.D.2d 111, 117–118, 663 N.Y.S.2d 610, 614–15, *appeal denied*, 91 N.Y.2d 875, 691 N.E.2d 646, 668 N.Y.S.2d 574 (1997); State v. Barkley, 144 N.C. App. 514, 518–21, 551 S.E.2d 131, 134–36, *appeal dismissed*, 354 N.C. 221, 554 S.E.2d 646 (2001)

an acquittal on dismissal,[491] may be used as evidence in a subsequent investigation.

One New York trial level court[492] has ruled that a blood sample taken for DNA can not be disclosed or redisclosed to investigators of an unsolved crime because of defendant's "exclusive property right"[493] to control the dissemination of his genetic makeup, based in part on New York statutory provisions.[494] The trial court granted the defendant's motion for a protective order prohibiting disclosure of any DNA test results resulting from testing of blood obtained by the prosecution's motion.

§ 1.39 Sanctions for a defendant's failure to provide discovery.

The Supreme Court, in *Taylor v. Illinois*,[495] holds that a defendant could be precluded from offering a witness's testimony as a sanction for the defense violation of a discovery rule under the Sixth Amendment's compulsory process clause.[496] In *Taylor*, on the first day of the trial, the defendant's attorney amended his answer to discovery with the names of two eyewitnesses. Those witnesses were not called. On the second day of trial, after the completion of the main part of the prosecution's case, the defendant's attorney again sought to amend his discovery answer to include two additional witnesses. The Supreme Court

---

(holding blood sample obtained in an uncharged crime may be used as evidence in an unrelated crime without violating defendant's constitutional rights; court's finding supported conclusion that defendant's consent was not limited in scope); State v. McCord, 349 S.C. 477, 562 S.E.2d 689 (2002) (upholding use by state authorities of blood sample provided to federal authorities in an unrelated case).

[491] People v. Baylor, 97 Cal. App. 4th 504, 118 Cal. Rptr. 2d 750 (2001) (finding use and retention of DNA sample from dismissed charge proper); Smith v. State, 744 N.E.2d 437 (Ind. 2001) (upholding use of DNA from acquittal charge).

[492] People v. Rodriguez, 196 Misc. 2d 217, 764 N.Y.S.2d 305 (Sup. Ct. 2003).

[493] *Id.* at 225, 764 N.Y.S.2d at 311.

[494] N.Y. Exec. Law § 995-d:

> 1. All records, findings, reports, and results of DNA testing performed on any person shall be confidential and may not be disclosed or redisclosed without the consent of the subject of such DNA testing. Such records, findings, reports, and results shall not be released to insurance companies, employers or potential employers, health providers, employment screening or personnel companies, agencies, or services, private investigation services, and may not be disclosed in response to a subpoena or other compulsory legal process or warrant, or upon request or order of any agency, authority, division, office, corporation, partnership, or any other private or public entity or person, except that nothing contained herein shall prohibit disclosure in response to a subpoena issued on behalf of the subject of such DNA record or on behalf of a party in a civil proceeding where the subject of such DNA record has put such record in issue.

[495] 484 U.S. 400 (1988).

[496] U.S. Const. amend. VI ("In all criminal prosecutions, the accused shall enjoy the right . . . to have compulsory process for obtaining witnesses in his favor. . . .").

found that the Sixth Amendment did not provide a defendant with the right to offer whatever testimony in whatever fashion or at whatever time a defendant may seek. It noted that there are significant limitations upon a defendant's ability to present evidence, including "rules of procedure that govern the orderly presentation of facts and arguments such as not interrupting an opposing party's case or interrupting jury deliberations to prevent newly discovered evidence."[497] The Supreme Court, in the following emphasized statement concerning the Sixth Amendment, held:

> *The Sixth Amendment does not confer the right to present testimony free from the legitimate demands of the adversarial system; one cannot invoke the Sixth Amendment as a justification for presenting what might have been a half-truth.* [498]

The Court noted that one of the purposes of a discovery requirement upon a defendant is to minimize the risk of fabricated testimony, and that defendants who may be willing "to fabricate a defense may also be willing to fabricate excuses for failing to comply with a discovery requirement."[499] In light of the trial judge's finding that the discovery violation by the defendant was both willful and blatant, it was not inappropriate for the trial court to preclude testimony from the defendant's proposed witnesses.

Reciprocal discovery statutes can impose strict requirements upon a defendant to disclose information to a prosecutor or face preclusion of evidence. The rape case of heavyweight boxer Mike Tyson is an example. Most states, including the federal system, do not generally require the prosecution and defense to supply the other party a list of witnesses.[500] Indiana provides not only pretrial depositions of witnesses, but requires both the prosecution and defense to supply the other with a list of witnesses. Tyson was precluded from calling several witnesses whom he learned of during the trial who would have testified that he and the complainant were affectionate toward each other and holding hands as they went to Tyson's hotel room.[501] This preclusion was based on Tyson's failure to comply with the court's discovery order. To promote justice and present unfair surprise, a court can preclude a defendant from offering testimony, since unless there are sanctions, "a party could circumvent disclosure by failing to diligently

---

[497] *Taylor*, 484 U.S. at 411. ("The accused does not have an unfettered right to offer testimony that is incompetent, privileged, or otherwise inadmissible under standard rules of evidence.").

[498] *Id.* at 412–13.

[499] *Id.* at 413.

[500] Fed. R. Crim. P. 16.

[501] Tyson v. State, 619 N.E.2d 276 (Ind. Ct. App. 1993), *cert. denied*, 510 U.S. 1176 (1994) (The court reviewed five factors in its consideration, articulated in Wiseheart v. State, 491 N.E.2d 985 (Ind. 1986): (1) When all the witnesses first became known to the opposing counsel; (2) The nature of the prejudice in disallowing the testimony; (3) The importance of the testimony to the case; (4) The availability of less stringent alternatives; and (5) Will the opponent be unduly surprised and prejudicial by the inclusion of the witnesses?).

discover potential witnesses."[502] There are limits to a court precluding a defendant from presenting testimony based upon the failure to comply with a reciprocal discovery statute. It may be important to determine when the prosecution provided the discovery material triggering the defendant's need to obtain witnesses. For example, where the prosecution did not disclose the results of a rape kit analysis reflecting a positive finding of sperm until ten days before trial, one appellate court held that it was reversible error to preclude a defendant from providing expert medical testimony concerning the defendant's vasectomy and inability to produce sperm to rebut those results.[503] The fact that the defendant notified the prosecution about the expert witness the day before trial did not justify precluding the defendant from presenting this testimony on the ground of the defendant's noncompliance with the reciprocal discovery statute.[504]

---

[502] *Id.* at 282.

[503] Commonwealth v. Dranka, 46 Mass. App. Ct. 38, 702 N.E.2d 1192, *review denied*, 429 Mass. 1101, 709 N.E.2d 1119 (1999).

[504] Commonwealth v. Dranka, 46 Mass. App. Ct. 38, 702 N.E.2d 1192, *review denied*, 429 Mass. 1101, 709 N.E.2d 1119 (1999).

CHAPTER 2

FAIR TRIAL, FREE PRESS, AND DEALING WITH PUBLICITY

§ 2.1   Introduction.

Sexual assault trials, by the nature of the crimes they involve, attract more attention and reporting than other crimes. Publicity about a case will affect its handling from the first contact with the client until the verdict. Even when the publicity surrounding a crime is not significant, news stories concerning sexual assault are more likely to be read than stories of other crimes. The publicity surrounding the crime comes not only from law enforcement sources and prosecutors but from other groups or organizations that may have an interest in speaking out on the issues surrounding the crime. Victim advocacy groups and concerned citizens are more likely to speak out about a crime involving a sexual assault, particularly when children are involved, than in most other reported crimes.

The publicity surrounding sexual assault trials will be magnified when the defendant is a prominent, respected, or well-known individual. The dynamics of sexual assault and pedophilia are such that it is not at all unusual to find individuals who are well-known or well-respected in a community accused of crimes involving children or sexual assault. Despite the fact that many prominent people are involved in allegations of sexual assault, publicity has rarely been a reason for reversal of a defendant's conviction. On the other hand, it is very likely that publicity has played a far greater role in the adjudication process than court decisions have recognized. If one believes that publicity surrounding a crime can have an impact on potential jurors, then it is incumbent to utilize all resources available to eliminate or minimize the effects of such publicity. This chapter will review the tools available both inside and outside the courtroom to counter the potential negative effects of publicity.

The Supreme Court of the United States has repeatedly recognized the importance of the principle that jury decisions be based on the evidence in court and not outside sources of information. Justice Holmes noted that a verdict should be "induced only by the evidence and argument in open court, not by any outside influence, whether of private talk or public print."[1] More recently, the Court has recognized that the principle that a jury's verdict be based upon the trial evidence is fundamental to the concept of trial by jury.[2] Thus, it has realized that modern trial publicity requires regulation by trial courts to insure that it does not invade the fact-finding process.[3]

---

[1] Patterson v. Colorado, 205 U.S. 454, 462 (1907).

[2] Turner v. Louisiana, 379 U.S. 466, 472 (1965).

[3] Sheppard v. Maxwell, 384 U.S. 333, 362–63 (1966).

More important than the nature and extent of publicity can be the trial court's efforts to deal with such publicity. The massive publicity preceding the Watergate trials did not preclude the defendants from receiving a fair trial due to the extensive precautions taken by the trial court, particularly during jury selection.[4] It is the failure to take remedial measures to deal with pretrial or trial publicity that will generate critical appellate review. For counsel's part, it is important to request that the court take steps and provide a basis for the requested action. Otherwise, the issue of pretrial publicity will be lost as an issue for appellate review.

Another aspect of pretrial and trial publicity is its effect upon witnesses, an aspect that has not been widely addressed by courts. Are witnesses more or less reluctant to appear as witnesses when there is publicity surrounding a case? Does publicity affect the reliability of a witness in-court testimony? What is the effect of media remuneration for witness stories? Does the potential publicity for a juror's experience sitting on a trial affect the juror? Little research has been carried out to help courts answer these questions. Pretrial publicity has received some scrutiny in the area of eyewitness identification when a witness observes a defendant's photograph or face on television.[5] In other cases, publicity can shape or reconstruct memories. The use of cameras in the courtroom and court television have diluted the effect of the rule that potential witnesses are to be excluded from the courtroom. Is there any difference between watching a trial on television and reading about trial testimony in a newspaper story?

Publicity surrounding sexual assault litigation involves some special rules. In jurisdictions that broadcast court proceedings, certain restrictions are placed on cases involving rape and sexual abuse, including in many situations, the nondisclosure of the victim's identity. Some jurisdictions also limit the right of court officials and officers to publicly disclose a victim's identity,[6] but these limitations do not exist in others. Most newspapers, radio and television stations, and court TV producers have voluntarily withheld the victim's identity in sexual assault cases. These rules are unique to the area of sexual assault.

Attorneys also have special obligations with respect to fair trials, free press, and publicity in sexual assault cases. Professional rules of conduct in virtually every state restrict an attorney's public comments about a case. Prosecutors may have additional obligations imposed on them by the Code of Professional Responsibility as well as by court decisions. Violation of these rules may not only bring professional disciplinary actions, but can also be the basis for court action. Judges, too, face special problems. While a judge may wish to deal with the dilemma of pretrial or trial publicity by issuing a gag order, there are

---

[4] United States v. Haldeman, 559 F.2d 31 (D.C. Cir. 1976), *cert. denied sub nom.* Ehrlichman v. United States, 431 U.S. 933 (1977).

[5] *See* § 8.22.

[6] *See, e.g.,* N.Y. Civ. Rights Law § 50-b.

significant limitations as to the avenues available to a court in restricting attorneys' comments as well as access to court proceedings and records.

Finally, it should be remembered that the media will almost always be permitted to report on what occurs in a courtroom. Long standing Supreme Court precedent precludes restricting the reporting of courtroom testimony.[7] The Supreme Court has held that the constitution "will not permit a state court to prohibit the publication of widely disseminated information obtained at court proceedings that were in fact open to the public."[8] There are hardly any controls that can be placed by a court on a reporter's story once the reporter has gathered the news, since information obtained through reportorial techniques cannot be restricted by a court.[9] Most legal efforts are aimed at preventing the disclosure of information in the first place and the after effects of the disclosure.

§ 2.2 Closure of courtroom to protect defendant.

The wholesale closure of a courtroom during a trial of a defendant is clearly prohibited. Criminal proceedings are presumptively open to the public. While there is a strong interest in public trials, there is no right of access to a criminal trial on the part of the public; the right to a public trial belongs to the accused.[10] Preliminary hearings are "sufficiently like a trial," whereby public access to them is essential to a fair trial.[11]

A defendant may, however, clearly wish to have a courtroom closed during a pretrial hearing or a preliminary hearing at which testimony presented would, if publicized, be highly prejudicial to the defendant, particularly when the admissibility of such testimony at trial is yet to be determined. This is particularly true of preliminary and suppression hearings when testimony is offered of statements made by a defendant to law enforcement officials. Since statements of the defendant may have been obtained in violation of the defendant's

---

[7] Craig v. Harney, 331 U.S. 367 (1947):

> A trial is a public event. What transpires in the court room is public property . . . . Those who see and hear what transpired can report it with impunity. There is no special perquisite of the judiciary which enables it, as distinguished from other institutions of democratic government, to suppress, edit, or censor events which transpire in proceedings before it.

Id. at 374.

[8] Oklahoma Publ'g Co. v. District Court, 430 U.S. 308, 310 (1977).

[9] Smith v. Daily Mail Publ'g Co., 443 U.S. 97 (1979) (holding that the state cannot criminalize publication of a juvenile delinquent's name when it has been lawfully obtained by a newspaper, regardless of the state's interest in protecting juveniles).

[10] Gannett Co. v. DePasquale, 443 U.S. 368, 379–80 (1979).

[11] Press-Enterprise Co. v. Superior Court, 478 U.S. 1, 12 (1986) (Press Enterprise II). *See also* El Vocero de P.R. v. Puerto Rico, 508 U.S. 147 (1993) (applying same rationale as *Press-Enterprise Co.* to strike down law requiring that preliminary hearing "shall be held privately" unless defendant requests otherwise).

constitutional rights, it would be highly prejudicial to allow potential jurors to receive facts, particularly from a defendant's statement, which would not be admissible at trial.

Preliminary hearings, usually occurring soon after a criminal act or arrest, attract much media attention and can easily breed prejudicial publicity. An additional issue is permitting the reproduction of the visual image of a defendant when identification is an issue in the case. Allowing the defendant's picture to be broadcast or printed may taint the identification of potential witnesses. (*See* discussion in § 8.22.) All of the preceding are reasons for counsel to argue that a preliminary hearing or suppression hearing should be closed; however, it appears that despite the problems of publicity from an open suppression hearing of a defendant's statement or evidence seized, there apparently is no authority that keeping a pretrial proceeding open to the public is reversible error.[12]

While the court has the authority to close a preliminary or suppression hearing, it must do so on notice to all parties affected, including representatives of the media, and afford all interested parties an opportunity to be heard. Closure of a preliminary hearing requires findings on the record by the court that closure is necessary to preserve higher values and is narrowly tailored to serve that interest.[13] If the right to be protected is the defendant's right to a fair trial, there must be a finding of "substantial probability" that the defendant's right would be compromised and reasonable alternatives cannot adequately protect those rights.[14] Similarly, while closure of a suppression hearing may be justified to prevent the jury from learning of unreliable or illegally obtained evidence,[15] it is not justified in every instance, and less restrictive alternatives must be considered, such as jury selection to screen out prejudiced jurors.[16] A defendant who asserts that a proceeding such as a suppression hearing may affect his or her right to a fair trial has the burden of demonstrating not just a possibility of prejudice but a "substantial probability" of prejudice.[17]

---

[12] Mallott v. State, 608 P.2d 737, 744 (Alaska 1980) (affirming defendant's conviction in rape of a three-year-old girl despite failure of trial court to close pretrial hearings as requested by defendant).

[13] Press-Enterprise Co. v. Superior Court, 464 U.S. 501, 510 (1984); State v. Bone-Club, 128 Wash. 2d 254, 258, 906 P.2d 325 (1995).

[14] Press Enterprise Co. v. Superior Court, 478 U.S. 1, 14 (1986).

[15] Gannett Co. v. DePasquale, 443 U.S 368, 378 (1979).

[16] Press Enterprise Co. v. Superious Court, 478 U.S. 1, 15 (1986).

[17] Associated Press v. Bell, 70 N.Y.2d 32, 39, 510 N.E.2d 313, 317, 517 N.Y.S.2d 444, 448 (1987). The Court of Appeals noted:

> While the requirement of "specific findings" cannot be so stringent as to, in effect, divulge that which is sought to be kept confidential, neither defendant in his submission nor the trial court in its findings met the standards required for excluding the public and the press from the courtroom. Defendant himself only hinted at "much information and much detail that has not come out at all." The trial court acknowledged that it did not know what, if any, tainted evidence there might be, and did not know

Washington's Supreme Court sets forth the following five criteria that should be applied on a case-by-case basis in determining whether to use a closed courtroom:

1. The proponent of closure or sealing must make some showing [of a compelling interest], and where that need is based on a right other than an accused's right to a fair trial, the proponent must show a "serious and imminent threat" to that right.

2. Anyone present when the closure motion is made must be given an opportunity to object to the closure.

3. The proposed method for curtailing open access must be the least restrictive means available for protecting the threatened interests.

4. The court must weigh the competing interests of the proponent of closure and the public.

5. The order must be no broader in its application or duration than necessary to serve its purpose.[18]

Closure should be no broader than necessary and should be only of the parts of the proceedings necessary to prevent the substantial danger of prejudice.[19] It can also be temporary, i.e., a transcript of the proceedings may be released when the danger has dissipated.[20]

Failing to close a pretrial hearing may be the basis of an appeal based on prejudicial pretrial publicity emanating from the hearing. However, serial killer Theodore Bundy was unable to prevail on this ground, despite the significant publicity concerning bite-mark evidence developed at pretrial hearings.[21]

§ 2.3   Closure of courtroom for benefit of sexual assault victim.

Prosecutors will often seek closure of the courtroom to minimize the trauma on a sexual abuse victim during testimony. Rejecting the argument that closure

---

whether any such evidence would threaten impaneling an impartial jury, but nonetheless closed the hearing on the "possibility" that there might be such evidence and that it might affect jury selection . . . . There was no specific finding of a substantial probability that the defendant's right to a fair trial would be prejudiced by publicity that closure would prevent, and no finding that reasonable alternatives to closure could not adequately protect defendant's fair trial rights.

Glens Falls Newspapers, Inc. v. Berke, 206 A.D.2d 668, 614 N.Y.S.2d 628 (1994) (holding that closure of a pretrial hearing was improper because the court failed to make specific findings that defendant's rights would be prejudiced by publicity; court should also have given the opportunity to the media representative to appear and be heard in opposition to closure).

[18] State v. Bone-Club, 128 Wash. 2d 254, 258, 906 P.2d 325 (1995).

[19] Waller v. Georgia, 467 U.S. 39 (1984) (holding closure of entire suppression hearing unjustified, especially in light of broad request by state for closure; furthermore, court did not consider alternatives to closure).

[20] See, e.g., Gannett Co., Inc. v. DePasquale, 443 U.S. 368, 393 (1979).

[21] Bundy v. State, 455 So. 2d 330, 337–39 (Fla. 1984), cert. denied, 479 U.S. 894 (1986).

of a courtroom during the testimony of a minor victim of sexual assault is required to encourage child victims to come forward, the Supreme Court of the United States held unconstitutional a Massachusetts law requiring court closure in all cases of child victims without requiring particularized findings of necessity.[22]

A statute that permits closure of a courtroom merely upon request and without a showing of necessity is likely to be unconstitutional.[23]

Federal law permits closure of the courtroom during the testimony of a child abuse victim under provisions of the Child Victim's and Child's Witnesses Rights Law.[24] This law requires that the court determine on the record that the child will suffer "substantial psychological harm" or "would result in the child's inability to effectively communicate" before allowing closure of the courtroom.[25] Such a closure must be "narrowly tailored" and based upon a "compelling interest."[26] Even before passage of this law in 1990, there was authority for the closure of the courtroom during testimony of either a child or adult victim of sexual abuse. It has been called a "frequent and accepted practice where the lurid details of such a crime must be related."[27]

An argument was accepted by one court a half-century ago that the closure of the courtroom denies the defendant his presumption of innocence and is a predecision of his guilt, particularly in cases of alleged consent, and that court closure excludes persons who would create in the victim "the fear of the shame of public exposure of false testimony, a shame to be heightened by the fear of

---

[22] Globe Newspaper Co. v. Superior Court, 457 U.S. 596 (1982).

[23] State ex rel. Stevens v. Circuit Court for Manitowoc County, 141 Wis. 2d 239, 414 N.W.2d 832 (1987) (holding unconstitutional that portion of Wisconsin's statute that permits closure of sexual assault preliminary examinations upon request of complainant without findings of necessity for closure).

[24] 18 U.S.C. § 3509(e):

> Closing the courtroom. When a child testifies, the court may order the exclusion from the courtroom of all persons, including members of the press, who do not have a direct interest in the case. Such an order may be made if the court determines on the record that requiring the child to testify in open court would cause substantial psychological harm to the child or would result in the child's inability to effectively communicate. Such an order shall be narrowly tailored to serve the government's specific compelling interest.

[25] Id.

[26] Id.

[27] Harris v. Stephens, 361 F.2d 888, 891 (8th Cir. 1966), cert. denied, 386 U.S. 964 (1967). See also United States v. Galloway, 963 F.2d 1388, 1390 (10th Cir. 1992), cert. denied, 506 U.S. 957 (1992) (upholding closure of courtroom where court made specific findings that the complainant was 18 years old at time of the offense, she was still living at home and dependent on her parents, the nature of the allegations, and the limited nature of the court's closure); Geise v. United States, 262 F.2d 151, 156 (9th Cir. 1958), cert. denied, 361 U.S. 842 (1959) (upholding the exclusion of spectators during a sexual assault trial during testimony of witnesses aged seven, nine, and 11, one of whom was the complaining witness).

prosecution for perjury."[28] Another unsuccessful argument raised against court closure during a rape victim's testimony is that the closure demonstrated such hostile community sentiment that the defendant could not receive a fair trial without a changed venue.[29] Unless a defendant can articulate clear prejudice in the closure of the courtroom during a sexual assault victim's testimony, a trial court's discretion in closing the courtroom may not be disturbed if limited and sufficiently justified on the record to permit review on appeal.[30] When the closure is unlimited in scope, it is more likely to be held improper.[31]

State statutes also permit the closure of the courtroom during a victim's testimony.[32] Most statutes are specifically applicable to child witnesses, whereas

---

[28] Tanksley v. United States, 145 F.2d 58 (9th Cir. 1944) (noting that complaining witness would be embarrassed in any rape case where defense is consent).

[29] *Harris*, 361 F.2d at 890–91.

[30] United States v. Osborne, 68 F.3d 94 (5th Cir. 1995) (holding partial closure of courtroom reasonable during victim's testimony); United States v. Farmer, 32 F.3d 369 (8th Cir. 1994); United States *ex rel.* Latimore v. Sielaff, 561 F.2d 691 (7th Cir. 1977), *cert. denied*, 434 U.S. 1076 (1978) (upholding the limited closure of the courtroom where the judge closed the courtroom during the victim's testimony, but asked anyone who wished to remain to give his name and reason for staying, permitting members of the press to remain, but excluding all others who had no reason to stay); Aaron v. Capps, 507 F.2d 685 (5th Cir. 1975), *cert. denied*, 423 U.S. 878 (1975) (noting partial closure does not raise same constitutional concerns as total closure).

[31] *See, e.g.*, United States v. Kobli, 172 F.2d 919 (3d Cir. 1949) (deeming exclusion in promoting prostitution case of all young girls in courtroom improper when not limited to those whom the judge had reason to believe should be excluded).

[32] Ala. Code § 12-21-202 ("In all prosecutions for rape and assault with intent to ravish, the court may, in its discretion, exclude from the courtroom all persons, except such as may be necessary in the conduct of the trial; and, in all other cases where the evidence is vulgar, obscene, or relates to the improper acts of the sexes and tends to debauch the morals of the young, the presiding judge shall have the right, by and with the consent and agreement of the defendant, in his discretion and on his own motion, or on the motion of the plaintiffs or defendants, or their attorneys, to hear and try the said case after clearing the courtroom of all or any portion of the audience whose presence is not necessary."); Cal. Penal Code § 868.7(a)(1) (permits closure of courtroom for a minor victim of sex offense "where testimony before the general public would be likely to cause serious psychological harm to the witness and where no alternative procedures, including, but not limited to, taped video deposition or contemporaneous examination in another place communicated to the courtroom by means of closed-circuit television, are available to avoid the perceived harm"); Fla. Stat. § 918.16; GA. Code § 17-8-54; 725 Ill. Comp. Stat. 5/115-11 (where the alleged victim of [a certain specified sex] offense is a minor under 18 years of age, the court may exclude from the proceedings while the victim is testifying, all persons, who, in the opinion of the court, do not have a direct interest in the case, except the media); La. Rev. Stat. § 15:469.1; Mass. Gen. Law ch. 278, § 16A; Minn. Stat. § 631.045; N.Y. Jud. Law § 4 ("Sittings of courts to be public. The sittings of every court within this state shall be public, and every citizen may freely attend the same, except that in all proceedings and trials in cases for divorce, seduction, abortion, rape, assault with intent to commit rape, criminal sexual act, bastardy, or filiation, the court may, in its discretion, exclude therefrom all persons who are not directly interested therein, excepting jurors, witnesses, and officers of the court (statute not limited to child victims.")); N.C. Gen. Stat. § 15-166 ("In the trial of cases for rape or sex offense or attempt to commit rape or attempt to commit a sex offense, the trial judge may, during the taking of the testimony of the prosecutrix, exclude

some also apply to adult complainants. Generally, closure has been upheld when a sufficient showing of necessity and reasonableness in the closure is made under a variety of circumstances.[33]

Some courts make a legal distinction between a total closure of the courtroom where only the actual trial participants remain, and a partial closure when representatives of the media, or the defendant's family are present. In a partial closure, the constitutional impact is not deemed to be as great and only a "substantial" rather than "compelling" reason for the closure need be provided.[34] However, allowing media attendance does not serve as an adequate replacement for the right of the general public to be present at a hearing.[35]

Other courts have not decided whether a less stringent standard applies to partial closure. One circuit court, in declining to decide whether a different test

---

from the courtroom all persons except the officers of the court, the defendant and those engaged in the trial of the case" (statute not limited to child witnesses)); VA. Code Ann. § 19.2-266 ("In the trial of all criminal cases, whether the same be felony or misdemeanor cases, the court may, in its discretion, exclude from the trial any persons whose presence would impair the conduct of a fair trial, provided that the right of the accused to a public trial shall not be violated."). This is the broad statute that was reviewed by the U.S. Supreme Court in *Richmond Newspapers, Inc. v. Virginia*, 448 U.S. 555 (1980).

[33] Nieto v. Sullivan, 879 F.2d 743 (10th Cir. 1989) (upholding closure of courtroom during testimony of victims who expressed fear of two other assailants who had not been apprehended); Lee v. State, 529 So. 2d 181 (Miss. 1988); People v. Glover, 60 N.Y.2d 783, 785, 457 N.E.2d 783, 469 N.Y.S.2d 677 (1983), *cert. denied*, 466 U.S. 975 (1984); People v. Homan, 237 A.D.2d 987, 654 N.Y.S.2d 925, *appeal denied*, 89 N.Y.2d 1094, 682 N.E.2d 989, 660 N.Y.S.2d 388 (1997) (upholding closure of court to public since complainant was nervous and embarrassed to testify about sexual acts performed upon her by her grandfather. "The People advanced an overriding interest that was likely to be prejudiced; the closure was no broader than necessary to protect that interest; the court considered reasonable alternatives to closure; and the court made findings adequate to support its decision partially to close the courtroom to the public." *Id.* at 987–88, 654 N.Y.S.2d at 926); People v. Roberts, 151 A.D.2d 1028, 542 N.Y.S.2d 90, *appeal denied*, 74 N.Y.2d 817, 545 N.E.2d 889, 546 N.Y.S.2d 575 (1989) (court properly closed courtroom during rape victim's testimony based on representation that victim was "tense and would be more comfortable testifying in private," although it would have been preferable for court to conduct hearing); State v. Weaver, 117 N.C. App. 434, 451 S.E.2d 15 (1994) (court properly excluded the mother of victims from the courtroom during their testimony while not excluding social workers and therapists); State v. Zerla, 1994 Ohio App. LEXIS 5864 (Dec. 22, 1994) (court properly excluded a child from the courtroom since the testimony involved "graphic sexual testimony" even though by excluding this child, the child's mother also could not be present); Commonwealth v. Smith, 280 Pa. Super. 222, 225, 421 A.2d 693, 695 (1980) ("Where a rape victim testifies to facts which could prove embarrassing or painful to her, a trial court has authority to exclude spectators from the trial temporarily."); Mosby v. State, 703 S.W.2d 714 (Tex. Ct. App. 1985).

[34] United States v. Brazel, 102 F.3d 1120, 1155 (11th Cir. 1997); United States v. Osborne, 68 F.3d 94, 98–99 (5th Cir. 1995); United States v. Farmer, 32 F.3d 369, 371 (8th Cir. 1994); Douglas v. Wainwright, 739 F.2d 531, 532–33 (11th Cir. 1984) (*per curiam*).

[35] State v. Klem, 438 N.W.2d 798 (N.D. 1989); State *ex rel.* Stevens v. Circuit Court for Manitowoc County, 141 Wis. 2d 239, 414 N.W.2d 832, 837 (1987). *See also* Thompson v. People, 156 Colo. 416, 399 P.2d 776 (1965).

exists for partial closure holds that "the state's interest in protecting minor rape victims is a compelling one."[36] Partial closures have been widely upheld under the "substantial" need, as well as "compelling need."[37]

Partial closure may be in the form of not permitting people to leave or enter during child's testimony.[38]

---

[36] Bell v. Jarvis, 236 F.3d 149, 168 (4th Cir. 2000) (*en banc*), *cert. denied*, 534 U.S. 830 (2001) (upholding closure of court during 12-year-old's testimony to all except defendant's family and media).

[37] United States v. Withorn, 204 F.3d 790, 795 (8th Cir. 2000) (upholding trial court's decision to partially clear courtroom of nanny, victim's mother, and some of defendant's family as justified by "the need to prevent substantial psychological harm to [complainant] and enable her to communicate effectively"); People v. Falaster, 173 Ill. 2d 220, 670 N.E.2d 624 (1996) (upholding trial court's finding that defendant's two nephews and one of their grandfathers did not have a direct interest in the case and could be excluded from the courtroom during victim's testimony; trial court did not exclude the media); People v. Holveck, 141 Ill. 2d 84, 565 N.E.2d 919 (1990) (upholding trial court's closure during child victim's testimony which permitted victim's family members, a psychologist, and members of the media to remain while others were precluded, where the court noted as a basis the large number of people who would otherwise be present in the courtroom during the testimony, the age of the witnesses, the psychological impact upon them, and the interest of the victims' families); State v. Loyden, 899 So. 2d 166 (La. Ct. App. 2005):

> In the present case, prior to the testimony of the minor victims who were seven and eight years old at the time of trial, the trial court cleared the courtroom of anyone other than reporters, social workers, and anyone else who may have been 'exempt[ed].' We find that the trial court did not violate the defendant's constitutional right to a public trial since he did not exclude the media and other essential parties. Our review of the record indicates that the trial court sought to create an atmosphere where the two minor children could testify about their experiences with a minimum amount of embarrassment, in order to facilitate more accurate testimony.

Id. at 179; People v. Mountain, 105 A.D.2d 494, 481 N.Y.S.2d 449 (1984), *aff'd*, 66 N.Y.2d 197, 486 N.E.2d 802, 495 N.Y.S.2d 944 (1985) (upholding the restriction of those who could be present in the courtroom during the victim's testimony to the press, members of the families of the defendant and the victim, friends of the defendant, and a member of a rape crisis organization); State v. Burney, 302 N.C. 529, 276 S.E.2d 693 (1981) (closure of court to all except defendant, defendant's family, defendant's counsel, defendant's witnesses, prosecutor, state's witnesses, and victim's family during testimony of seven-year-old sexual assault victim reasonable and sufficiently limited under circumstances); State v. Fayerweather, 540 A.2d 353–54 (R.I. 1988) (upholding closure of court during six-year-old's testimony to all except defendant's family and media).

[38] People v. Chase, 265 A.D.2d 844, 695 N.Y.S.2d 792 (1999), *appeal denied*, 94 N.Y.2d 902, 728 N.E.2d 985, 707 N.Y.S.2d 386 (2000). The *Chase* court upheld closure of the courtroom during testimony of the infant complainant and noted that the defendant failed to object to closure of the courtroom:

> In any event, the court's limited closure of the courtroom during the testimony of the infant complainant did not constitute a denial of defendant's constitutional right to a public trial. The court, having presided over defendant's previous trial, knew of the embarrassing nature of complainant's testimony, and 'the court's efforts to prevent disruption in the courtroom during complainant's sensitive testimony provides no basis upon which to upset defendant's conviction.' Furthermore, this is not a 'closed courtroom' case. The court merely ordered limited closure to prevent those people

When the trial can be viewed by an alternative means, such as through a televised link, the state need show only a substantial rather than compelling need for the closure.[39] In this situation, the excluded person can see and hear the testimony, and the closure is viewed as a partial closure. Closed-circuit viewing is indeed an alternative to total closure of the courtroom.[40] Utilizing a closed-circuit procedure has strict requirements.[41] Excluding the defendant from the courtroom while a child testifies may violate the defendant's right to be present at every critical stage of a trial.[42]

Statutes permitting closure or limited exclusion of spectators may be strictly construed on behalf of an accused.[43]

Courts are more likely to critically evaluate the closure of a courtroom during a victim's trial testimony in light of recent Supreme Court decisions demanding findings justifying closure of any sort. Closing a courtroom during a sexual assault victim's testimony, while permissible, requires that specific findings of necessity be made by the Court.[44] When a trial court closes a courtroom during

---

in the courtroom from leaving during the infant complainant's testimony and to prevent others from entering during that testimony.

Id. at 844, 695 N.Y.S.2d at 794 [citations omitted].

[39] Lena v. State, 901 So. 2d 227 (Fla. Dist. Ct. App. 2005), *review denied*, 2005 Fla. LEXIS 2591 (Dec. 9, 2005).

[40] *Id.*

[41] *See, e.g.,* §§ 5.23–24.

[42] Price v. Commonwealth, 31 S.W.3d 885 (Ky. 2000) (Trial court invoked closed circuit television scheme to justify procedure without establishing a compelling need for procedure); People v. Krueger, 466 Mich. 50, 643 N.W.2d 223 (2002) (reversing defendant's conviction because he was removed from courtroom during testimony of five-year-old complainant).

[43] People v. Revelo, 286 Ill. App. 3d 258, 676 N.E.2d 263 (1996), *appeal denied*, 172 Ill. 2d 562, 679 N.E.2d 384 (1997) (Defendant's conviction was reversed because trial court excluded defendant's parents and siblings from courtroom. Under Illinois statute, only those who lack a direct interest may be excluded during a minor sexual assault complainant's testimony. Those with a direct interest in the case may not be excluded. Court interpreted defendant's parents and siblings to have a direct interest in the case. Appellate court held that defendant need not prove specific prejudice under the statute; violation of statute presumes prejudice to defendant.).

[44] Globe Newspaper Co. v. Superior Court, 457 U.S. 596, 606 (1982); P.M.M. v. State, 762 So. 2d 384 (Ala. Crim. App. 1999) (reversing defendant's conviction due to closure of courtroom during children's testimony); Renkel v. State, 807 P.2d 1087 (Alaska Ct. App. 1991) (finding reversible error in trial court's closure of courtroom during minor's testimony without particularized finding to support closure); Alonso v. State, 821 So. 2d 423 (Fla. Dist. Ct. App. 2002), *mot. granted*, 837 So. 2d 412 (2003) (reversing defendant's sexual assault conviction in the absence of findings supporting the exclusion of defendant's cousin, defendant's minister, defendant's girlfriend, and several other friends during the testimony of two teenaged witnesses who were not victims); Carter v. State, 356 Md. 207, 233, 738 A.2d 871, 879 (1999) ("To be sure, as we have seen, the State does have an interest, a compelling one, in the physical and psychological well-being of child sex abuse victims. In this case, however, we have concluded that the trial court did not make the requisite case-specific finding necessary to justify the closing of the courtroom to the public. Consequently, it is unnecessary for us to consider or decide whether the court 'narrowly tailored' it's [sic] order.").

the testimony of a sexual assault victim just because the complainant wants the courtroom closed, without establishing the compelling reasons for the closure, a defendant's conviction will be reversed for a violation of the defendant's right to a public trial.[45] Merely reciting the "sensitive nature" of a child's testimony is insufficient justification for closure during a victim's testimony.[46] A general statement that all children who testify suffer trauma is an insufficient reason to clear a courtroom of the defendant's family.[47] An attorney's affidavit is insufficient to justify closure of the courtroom.[48] Without specific justification for closure, closing a courtroom during a rape shield hearing is likely improper.[49] But, expert testimony or affidavits are not essential to establish the need for closure.[50]

Some courts take a less restrictive view of the "findings" required and find that in a case involving long-standing sexual abuse of a minor by a family member, when the trial judge has obviously made a particularized determination

---

[45] Judd v. Haley, 250 F.3d 1308 (11th Cir. 2001) (granting habeas relief due to trial court's failure to make findings to justify total closure of the courtroom: "[t]he court did not take any testimony concerning J.D.J.'s age, psychological maturity, or particular fears or concerns about testifying in open court; nor did the court explain why a total closure, rather than a partial closure was necessary in this case." *Id.* at 1319); State v. McRae, 494 N.W.2d 252 (Minn. 1992); People v. Clemons, 78 N.Y.2d 48, 574 N.E.2d 1039, 571 N.Y.S.2d 433 (1991) ("While the Sixth Amendment does not require a judicial insensitivity to the very real problems that rape victims may face in having to testify in open court . . . it nonetheless does demand a more careful balancing and weighing of the competing interests than that conducted by the trial court here."); People v. Grosso, 281 A.D.2d 986, 722 N.Y.S.2d 846, *appeal denied*, 96 N.Y.2d 800, 750 N.E.2d 80, 726 N.Y.S.2d 378 (2001) (reversing defendant's conviction due to trial court's error to make careful inquiry to insure that there were compelling reasons for closure, specifically: 1) the party seeking closure advised on overriding interest that was likely to be prejudicial; 2) closure was no broader than necessary to protect that interest; 3) the court considered reasonable alternatives to closure; and 4) the court made findings adequate to support closure); State v. Klem, 438 N.W.2d 798 (N.D. 1989) (reversing defendant's conviction due to closure of courtroom to all spectators other than attorneys, parties, court personnel, and media representative without any findings to support closure).

[46] State v. Hightower, 376 N.W.2d 648 (Iowa Ct. App. 1985).

[47] Walker v. State, 121 Md. App. 364, 709 A.2d 177, *cert. denied*, 351 Md. 5, 715 A.2d 964 (1998).

[48] Commonwealth v. Martin, 417 Mass. 187, 194, 629 N.E.2d 297, 303 (1994).

[49] State v. Kelly, 208 Conn. 365, 369–74, 545 A.2d 1048, 1050–53 (1988), *habeas corpus proceeding, remanded sub nom.* Kelly v. Meachum, 950 F. Supp. 461 (D. Conn. 1996).

[50] Lena v. State, 901 So. 2d 227 (Fla. Dist. Ct. App. 2005) *review denied*, 919 So.2d 435 (Fla 2005), *cert. denied,*126 S.Ct. 1884 (2006):

> The trial court ruled that the 11-year-old victim would find the proceedings less traumatic, and speak more freely, in front of a small audience rather than a large one. The trial court's findings on this point are more than sufficient. The trial court correctly rejected the defendant's trial court argument that expert testimony would be needed from a physician or psychologist before the courtroom could be partially closed.

Id. at 231.

that closure is appropriate and has articulated the basic rationale for closing the courtroom, additional "findings" would be little more than a statement of the obvious.[51] These courts also look to the record for the basis for closure.[52]

There is authority that because a violation of the right to a public trial is a structural error in the trial, prejudice need not be shown, only a failure to comply with the procedures to completely remove spectators, and the error is not subject to a harmless error analysis.[53]

Failing to timely assert the right to a public trial in a timely fashion may fail to preserve for the record an objection to the closure of a courtroom during a victim's testimony.[54] Asking for legal authority for closure of the courtroom does not constitute an objection to the courtroom closure.[55]

§ 2.4   Closure of courtroom — excluding defendant's friends, family, and witnesses.

Courts can also restrict a defendant's friends and family to maintain order, decorum, or avoid prejudice. A defendant's child can be restricted from a courtroom in some situations to protect the child's sensibilities and avoid prejudicing the jury by the child's reactions.[56] Closure has been upheld even

---

[51] Bell v. Jarvis, 236 F.3d 149, 172 (4th Cir. 2000), *cert. denied* 534 U.S. 830 (2001).

[52] *Id.* at 172–73, *citing cases*:

> In summary, although the better course would have been for the trial judge to make detailed findings, the findings made, viewed in conjunction with the known circumstances of the case and the record developed, provide a sufficient basis for reviewing courts (the state court, the district court, and this court) to assess the propriety of the closure. Clearly established Supreme Court precedent governing courtroom closures does not require appellate courts to review closure orders in isolation of the record, nor does it mandate a conclusion that Bell's public trial right was violated simply because the trial judge failed to recite exhaustively every fact and inference which justified the obvious.

Id. at 174.

[53] Judd v. Haley, 250 F.3d 1308, 1319 (11th Cir. 2001) ("Judd has successfully demonstrated that the closure of the courtroom in his case was not conducted in conformity with the standards articulated in *Waller*; therefore, he is entitled to habeas relief on his Sixth Amendment claim.").

[54] Hunt v. State, 268 Ga. App. 568, 571, 602 S.E.2d 312 (2004), *cert. denied*, 2004 Ga. LEXIS 901 (Oct. 12, 2004); People v. Chase, 265 A.D.2d 844, 695 N.Y.S.2d 792 (1999), *appeal denied*, 94 N.Y.2d 902, 728 N.E.2d 985, 707 N.Y.S.2d 386 (2000); State v. Tizard, 897 S.W.2d 732 (Tenn. Crim. App. 1994) (Court removed a journalism class of about ten students who entered the courtroom to observe the trial and were present during cross-examination of the victim "when references to masturbation by vulgar vernacular was occurring." Court stated, "I believe all the testimony can be more uninhibited without the presence of the young people and for other reasons, too." However, defendant failed to object to court's action. *Id.* at 749.).

[55] Jones v. State, 883 So. 2d 369 (Fla. Dist. Ct. App. 2004).

[56] Turner v. Commonwealth, 914 S.W.2d 343 (Ky. 1996) (In sexual assault prosecution, trial court properly excluded defendant's three-year-old daughter in light of the nature of the testimony involving her father, and the age of the child made it difficult for her to remain quiet through

when the defendant's wife was excluded from the courtroom during the testimony of the victim, who was the daughter of the defendant's wife.[57] Fear of certain spectators, when supported by findings of fact, may justify excluding these individuals who may so intimidate the witness by their presence that the witness cannot testify. For example, if a witness becomes distraught and expresses fear for himself and family and the court concludes the witness cannot continue to testify in front of the spectators, a court may exclude the individuals who are the source of the witness's fear.[58] This action will require more than an assertion of fear. A court should state the specific reason or observations to support such an exclusion of witnesses.

However, closing a courtroom without any demonstrated need will likely infringe upon a defendant's right to a public trial. In one prosecution for sexual abuse and sodomy, the exclusion of two defense character witnesses after their testimony without any inquiry to establish a need for the exclusion, violates the defendant's right to a public trial.[59] The right to a public trial may be violated if a court prevents a defendant's family members from sitting in the courtroom because there is insufficient seating for them, even if there are no available seats because potential jury members have taken all available seats.[60] Exclusion of the defendant's family, friends, or witnesses to maintain order or security is addressed in the following section.

---

lengthy proceedings); People v. Georgison, 299 A.D.2d 176, 750 N.Y.S.2d 18 (2002), *appeal denied*, 99 N.Y.2d 614, 787 N.E.2d 1171, 757 N.Y.S.2d 825 (2003) (holding "[u]nder the circumstances of this case, the court did not abuse its discretion in excluding defendant's daughter of tender years from the courtroom"); People v. Haley, 195 A.D.2d 873, 600 N.Y.S.2d 842, *appeal denied*, 82 N.Y.2d 896, 632 N.E.2d 473, 610 N.Y.S.2d 163 (1993) (in murder case, after a detailed inquiry, court prohibited defendant's 11-year-old daughter from listening to opening statements to avoid prejudicing fact finders and exposing child to obscenities attributed to her father).

[57] People v. Vredenburg, 200 A.D.2d 797, 606 N.Y.S.2d 453 (1994), *appeal denied*, 83 N.Y.2d 859, 634 N.E.2d 992, 612 N.Y.S.2d 391 (1994).

[58] People v. Ming Li, 91 N.Y.2d 913, 692 N.E.2d 558, 669 N.Y.S.2d 527 (1998) (upholding court's exclusion of individuals at pretrial hearing whom the complainant believed to be members of gang who kidnapped him).

[59] People v. Griffin, 242 A.D.2d 70, 671 N.Y.S.2d 34 (1998).

[60] Williams v. State, 736 So. 2d 699, 703 (Fla. 1999) ("The trial court's total exclusion from the courtroom during voir dire of all members of the public, including Williams' family members, absent a most compelling justification compels reversal of Williams' judgment."). *See also* Metaxotos v. State, 756 So. 2d 199 (Fla. Dist. Ct. App. 2000), *review denied*, 776 So. 2d 277 (2000); State v. Ortiz, 91 Haw. 181, 981 P.2d 1127 (1999) (reversing defendant's conviction because trial court excluded defendant's relatives from courtroom and the exclusion was not a necessary or narrowly tailored remedy); People v. Sbarbaro, 244 A.D.2d 581, 665 N.Y.S.2d 673 (1997), *appeal denied*, 92 N.Y.2d 860, 699 N.E.2d 451, 677 N.Y.S.2d 91 (1998) (exclusion of defendant's brother during jury charge, without demonstration of overriding interest in his exclusion, required reversal of defendant's conviction).

A defendant's request to exclude his witness, and the complainant's grand-mother, is properly denied without sufficient basis.[61]

§ 2.5 Closure of courtroom for other reasons — jury charge, protection or fear of witness, maintaining order or security.

There are other reasons for which a court may justifiably close a courtroom. To ensure that a jury is not distracted during its jury charge, a court may lock the courtroom doors while the jury is being charged without denying a defendant's right to a public trial.[62] For example, a court can be closed prior to the jury charge to prevent children who had been present during the trial from causing a disturbance and distraction by running in and out of the courtroom.[63]

A court can close a courtroom to protect a witness who has a fear of testifying in public.[64] While a court may close a courtroom because a witness does not wish to testify in front of one defendant, it may be improper for a trial court to close the courtroom to all spectators when the witness expresses no objection to testifying before the family members of another co-defendant since there is a reasonable alternative to total closure of the courtroom.[65] A courtroom may be closed during testimony of a five-year-old who, although not a sexual abuse victim, must testify as to potentially embarrassing facts.[66] Another justification for closing a courtroom is to ensure decorum or maintain security. Upon a showing of a threat to the order of a courtroom, a court will be given discretion to close it,[67] and this decision can be based on the trial judge's past experiences

---

[61] People v. Todd, 306 A.D.2d 504, 761 N.Y.S.2d 312 (2003), *appeal denied*, 1 N.Y.3d 581, 807 N.E.2d 910, 775 N.Y.S.2d 797 (2003) (not reversible error to deny defendant's request to exclude the nine-year-old victim's grandmother from the trial, who was a defense witness, because she "had no direct knowledge of the acts testified to by the victim" and therefore, her testimony was merely collateral and not prejudicial to defendant).

[62] People v. Colon, 71 N.Y.2d 410, 418, 521 N.E.2d 1075, 1079–80, 526 N.Y.S.2d 932, 937, *cert. denied*, 487 U.S. 1239 (1988).

[63] Commonwealth v. Jubilee, 403 Pa. Super. 589, 589 A.2d 1112, 1113, *appeal denied*, 529 Pa. 617, 600 A.2d 534 (1991).

[64] United States v. Eisner, 533 F.2d 987, 993–94 (6th Cir.), *cert. denied*, 429 U.S. 919 (1976); People v. Graham, 200 A.D.2d 686, 606 N.Y.S.2d 780, *appeal denied*, 83 N.Y.2d 872, 635 N.E.2d 301, 613 N.Y.S.2d 132 (1994). *But see* Commonwealth v. Smith, 280 Pa. Super. 222, 225, 421 A.2d 693, 694 (1980) (holding that when trial court excluded all spectators in a sexual assault trial and surrounded defendant with guards because he had "exhibited very hostile tendencies while before the Court" and "suffered from certain physical infirmities . . . which could have required immediate attention" there must be an adequate record to support such an action by the court).

[65] English v. Artuz, 164 F.3d 105 (2d Cir. 1998) (emphasizing the importance of seeking alternatives to closure of the courtroom).

[66] Bailey v. State, 729 So. 2d 1255 (Miss. 1999).

[67] United States v. Akers, 542 F.2d 770, 772 (9th Cir. 1976), *cert. denied*, 430 U.S. 908 (1977); United States *ex rel.* Orlando v. Fay, 350 F.2d 967, 971 (2d Cir. 1965), *cert. denied*, 384 U.S.

with the parties at a prior trial.[68] Any closure should be limited to the extent necessary to maintain order. However, there are limits to closing a court even in the face of disruptive behavior. When a witness accosts a defendant, and there is no clear evidence that the defendant's family was involved in the disruption or refused to follow the court's directives to leave the courtroom as the disturbance unfolded, it does not justify barring the defendant's family from attending a suppression hearing and trial.[69] It is important that a court consider less restrictive measures, particularly when it seeks to preclude the defendant's family from attending a trial.[70]

§ 2.6　Disclosure of the identity of a victim of sexual assault.

Many states have statutes precluding the disclosure of the identity of a victim of sexual assault. Federal law[71] and some states, by statute or policy,[72] preclude

---

1008 (1966); People v. Shepard, 243 A.D.2d 290, 663 N.Y.S.2d 31, *appeal denied*, 91 N.Y.2d 868, 691 N.E.2d 650, 668 N.Y.S.2d 578 (1997); State v. Jones, 325 S.C. 310, 479 S.E.2d 517 (1996) (Trial court properly cleared courtroom of spectators after display of emotion by child victim's family. Judge gave curative instruction that no inference was to be drawn from closure and no mistrial was required). *See generally* Thomas M. Fleming, Annotation, *Exclusion of Public from State Criminal Trial in Order to Prevent Disturbance by Spectators or Defendant*, 55 A.L.R.4th 1170 (1987).

[68] People v. Cosentino, 198 A.D.2d 294, 295, 603 N.Y.S.2d 560, 562, *appeal denied*, 82 N.Y.2d 848, 627 N.E.2d 522, 606 N.Y.S.2d 600 (1993):

> Suitably within the trial court's discretion is the power to monitor admittance to the courtroom, as the circumstances require, in order to prevent overcrowding, to accommodate limited seating capacity, to maintain sanitary or health conditions and, generally, to preserve order and decorum in the courtroom [citations omitted]. Accordingly, it has been recognized that spectators can be excluded throughout a trial when they are unruly and disruptive [citation omitted]. Here, the trial court's exclusion of three family members did not constitute an improvident exercise of discretion or a denial of the defendant's right to a public trial. The trial court, having presided over the previous trial on the same charges, witnessed the unruly and disruptive behavior of the friends and family members of the defendant and his codefendant when the verdict was announced. The trial court described their behavior as "unlike any that I've ever seen." In order to prevent a similar disturbance at the second trial, the court barred the three most disruptive family members from the courtroom. Under these circumstances, it cannot be said that the trial court's attempt to preserve order and decorum in the courtroom was improper [citation omitted].

[69] Walker v. State, 125 Md. App. 48, 723 A.2d 922 (1999).

[70] *Id. See also* Vidal v. Williams, 31 F.3d 67, 69 (2d Cir. 1994), *cert. denied*, 513 U.S. 1102 (1995) (cited by court for proposition that there is "special concern for assuring the attendance of family members of the accused").

[71] 18 U.S.C. § 3509(d):

> Privacy Protection. (1) Confidentiality of information. (A) A person acting in a capacity described in subparagraph (B) in connection with a criminal proceeding shall — (i) keep all documents that disclose the name or any other information concerning

(Text continued on page 134)

who does not have reason to know their content has access; and (ii) disclose documents described in clause (i) or the information in them that concerns a child only to persons who, by reason of their participation in the proceeding, have reason to know such information. (B) Subparagraph (A) applies to — (i) all employees of the Government connected with the case, including employees of the Department of Justice, any law enforcement agency involved in the case, and any person hired by the government to provide assistance in the proceeding; (ii) employees of the court; (iii) the defendant and employees of the defendant, including the attorney for the defendant and persons hired by the defendant or the attorney for the defendant to provide assistance in the proceeding; and (iv) members of the jury. (2) Filing under seal. All papers to be filed in court that disclose the name of or any other information concerning a child shall be filed under seal without necessity of obtaining a court order. The person who makes the filing shall submit to the clerk of the court — (A) the complete paper to be kept under seal; and (B) the paper with the portions of it that disclose the name of or other information concerning a child reacted, to be placed in the public record. (3) Protective orders. (A) On motion by any person the court may issue an order protecting a child from public disclosure of the name of or any other information concerning the child in the course of the proceedings, if the court determines that there is a significant possibility that such disclosure would be detrimental to the child. (B) A protective order issued under subparagraph (A) may — (i) provide that the testimony of a child witness, and the testimony of any other witness, when the attorney who calls the witness has reason to anticipate that the name of or any other information concerning a child may be divulged in the testimony, be taken in a closed courtroom; and (ii) provide for any other measures that may be necessary to protect the privacy of the child. (4) Disclosure of information. This subdivision does not prohibit disclosure of the name of or other information concerning a child to the defendant, the attorney for the defendant, a multidisciplinary child abuse team, a guardian ad litem, or an adult attendant, or to anyone to whom, in the opinion of the court, disclosure is necessary to the welfare and well-being of the child.

72 CAL. Penal Code § 293.5 (permits sexual assault victims to be identified by Jane or John Doe in court records and proceedings); CONN. Gen. Stat. § 54-86 e (precludes disclosure of name and address of sexual assault victim except upon order of superior court); 42 PA. Cons. Stat. § 5988 ("Victims of sexual or physical abuse. (A) Release of Name Prohibited — In a prosecution involving a child victim of sexual or physical abuse, unless the court otherwise orders, the name of the child victim shall not be disclosed by officers or employees of the court to the public, and any records revealing the name of the child victim will not be open to public inspection. (B) Penalty — Any person who violates this section commits a misdemeanor."); WASH. Code Rev. § 7.69A.030(4) (Among the rights of child victims and witnesses is the right "to not have the names, addresses, nor photographs of the living child victim or witness disclosed by any law enforcement agency, prosecutor's office, or state agency without the permission of the child victim, child witness, parents, or legal guardians to anyone except another law enforcement agency, prosecutor, defense counsel, or private or governmental agency that provides services to the child victim or witness"); WYO. Stat. § 6-2-310 "((a) Prior to the filing of an information or indictment, neither the names of the alleged actor, or victim of a sexual assault, nor any other information reasonably likely to disclose the identity of the victim shall be released or negligently allowed to be released to the public by any public employee except as authorized by the judge or justice with jurisdiction over the criminal charges. The actor's name may be released to the public to aid or facilitate an arrest. (b) After the filing of an information or indictment and upon the request of a minor victim or another acting on behalf of a minor victim, the trial court may, to the extent necessary to protect the welfare of the minor victim, restrict the disclosure or publication of information reasonably likely to identify the minor victim.). " *See also* State v. Schimpf, 782 S.W.2d 186, 188 (Tenn. Crim. App. 1989) (noting court policy of withholding the identity of child sexual assault victims); Wyo. Stat. § 14-3-106.

the identification in court records of child victims. The federal law restricting the identification of a child victim does not require the closure of a pretrial or trial proceeding to protect the identity of a victim.[73] It has been held not to violate First Amendment principles in its withholding of a complainant's identity.[74] Other states include adult victims with child victims within the scope of individuals whose identity cannot be disclosed.[75] Virtually all these statutes limit nondisclosure to court employees or public officials. They do not apply to the press, to defense counsel, or to courthouse employees (such as janitors) who may come across the name of a victim in an indictment on someone's desk and then disseminate that victim's name. Statutes protecting the identity of a rape victim from being disclosed do not necessarily trigger or justify the sealing of court records pertaining to the crime.[76]

Arguably, certain situations may trigger the need to withhold a sexual assault victim's identity. There may also be situations when it is permissible to withhold the disclosure of the current name and address of a sexual assault complainant if there is some reason to believe that there is a potential danger to the witness

---

[73] United States v. Broussard, 767 F. Supp. 1545 (D. Or. 1991). *See* 18 U.S.C. § 3509(d)(2), note 43 *supra*.

[74] *Id.*

[75] N.Y. Civil Rights Law § 50—b::

Right of privacy; victims of sex offenses. (1) The identity of any victim of a sex offense, as defined in article one hundred thirty or section 255.25 of the penal law, shall be confidential. No report, paper, picture, photograph, court file or other documents, in the custody or possession of any public officer or employee, which identifies such a victim shall be made available for public inspection. No such public officer or employee shall disclose any portion of any police report, court file, or other document, which tends to identify such a victim except as provided in subdivision two of this section. (2) The provisions of subdivision one of this section shall not be construed to prohibit disclosure of information to: (a) Any person charged with the commission of a sex offense, as defined in subdivision one of this section, against the same victim; the counsel or guardian of such person; the public officers and employees charged with the duty of investigating, prosecuting, keeping records relating to the offense, or any other act when done pursuant to the lawful discharge of their duties; and any necessary witnesses for either party; or (b) Any person who, upon application to a court having jurisdiction over the alleged sex offense, demonstrates to the satisfaction of the court that good cause exists for disclosure to that person. Such application shall be made upon notice to the victim or other person legally responsible for the care of the victim, and the public officer or employee charged with the duty of prosecuting the offense; or (c) Any person or agency, upon written consent of the victim or other person legally responsible for the care of the victim, except as may be otherwise required or provided by the order of a court. (3) The court having jurisdiction over the alleged sex offense may order any restrictions upon disclosure authorized in subdivision two of this section, as it deems necessary and proper to preserve the confidentiality of the identity of the victim. (4) Nothing contained in this section shall be construed to require the court to exclude the public from any stage of the criminal proceeding.

[76] People v. Burton, 189 A.D.2d 532, 597 N.Y.S.2d 488 (1993).

that would outweigh a defendant's right to disclosure of her current name and address.[77] In one assault prosecution for exposing another person to the HIV virus, an appeals court upheld referring to the victim as "Jane Doe" since the defendant did not know how he was prevented from presenting evidence or arguing his case.[78]

The restriction on disclosing the identity of a sexual assault victim by radio, television, and newspapers is a voluntary restriction. Attempts to totally restrict the use of a sexual assault victim's name in criminal proceedings by radio, television, or newspapers are likely to fail because such a restriction is a prior restraint and is likely to collide with the First Amendment. Florida's statute that mandated criminal sanctions for anyone who identified a victim of a sexual assault in any instrument of mass communication was held unconstitutional by Florida's Court of Appeals.[79] While this is likely to be the general rule in a criminal proceeding, in a juvenile court proceeding involving physical and sexual abuse, Illinois upheld the preclusion of a reporter from attending an abuse proceeding because the reporter refused to agree not to identify the children who were subject to the proceeding.[80] The court noted the *parens patriae* role of the court in a juvenile proceeding as justification for the restriction on identifying the child abuse victims.[81] This case is a rare example of when a reporter can

---

[77] State v. Vandebogart, 139 N.H. 145, 161–62, 652 A.2d 671, 681 (1994).

[78] State v. Ferguson, No. 21329-0-II, 1999 Wash. App. LEXIS 1905 (Nov. 5, 1999), *aff'd in part*, 142 Wash. 2d 631, 15 P.3d 1271 (2001):

> Without citing any authority, Ferguson claims that the trial court erred by barring him from mentioning, in open court, the real names of the State's Jane Does. He does not claim that the trial court withheld their identities from him, and it is clear that he knew their identities well before trial. He does not claim that he was barred from cross-examining on any relevant matter (e.g., bias). He claims only that he had a right to display their real names to the jury and the community. The trial court recognized that persons associated with HIV have a strong need for privacy and confidentiality. It thought it could accommodate that need without adversely affecting either party's right to present relevant evidence. It stated: 'When an innuendo or inference or a reference to HIV has been [made], in this date and age, [it is] devastating. I believe also that this Court can see to it that all information that is relevant . . . can be obtained by proper direct and cross-examination. I am at this time inclined to maintain the Jane Doe status.' On appeal, Ferguson has not shown that he was prevented from presenting any relevant evidence (e.g., evidence of bias). He has not shown that the trial court's order prejudiced his ability to present or argue his case. He has not shown why the witnesses' names, as opposed to the substance of their testimony, would have been material to the jury. We conclude that the trial court acted within its discretion.

Id. at *18–19 (footnote omitted).

[79] State v. Globe Communications Corp., 622 So. 2d 1066 (Fla. Dist. Ct. App. 1993).

[80] *In re* A Minor, 149 Ill. 2d 247, 595 N.E.2d 1052 (1992).

[81] *Id.* at 255–57, 595 N.E.2d at 1055–56:

> In the case at bar, the State has an interest in the nondisclosure of the minor victims'

gather information yet be prohibited by a court from reporting it.[82]

Even when there is a statute precluding a public official from disseminating a rape victim's name, and a newspaper has a policy of not publishing the names of sex offense victims, a newspaper will not be subject to a civil suit for publishing a rape victim's name obtained from a publicly-released police report.[83] It is significant if the media learns of the name through government dissemination, even if the disclosure is inadvertent. Left to be decided is consequences or punishment for the disclosure of a rape victim's name unlawfully obtained on court documents. A victim's name, like other information that is part of a judicial proceeding, will be available to reporters. This appeals court noted that "at the very least, the *First* and *Fourteenth Amendments* will not allow exposing the press to liability for truthfully publishing information released to the public in official court records."[84] This source of information, namely what takes place in open court, will enjoy special constitutional protection.[85] There may conceivably be a situation where the state may punish the disclosure of a rape victim's name.[86]

---

identities in its role as *parens patriae*. It was in its role as *parens patriae* that the State initiated these juvenile proceedings to provide shelter and care for these abused children. The minor victims reside and will continue to reside in a small community. Public identity could cause continuing emotional trauma to these unfortunate children and impede the lengthy and difficult healing process which they must endure. We find that the danger of public disclosure and the probability of irreparable adverse effects which such disclosure would entail to be a compelling State interest at stake in this case . . . . The minor victims in this case have done nothing to limit or diminish their constitutional right to be free from governmental and nongovernmental invasions of their privacy. They are not juvenile delinquents. They are not participating in the juvenile proceedings begun on their behalf through their own free will. They were victims of abuse by a parent. They were thrust into the juvenile system by actions of third parties, not by their own actions. Under these facts, we find that the minor victims have a compelling interest in their right to be free from invasions of their privacy. Public disclosure of their identities would surely invade their right of privacy in a most egregious manner.

[82] *See also* Carol Schultz Vento, Annotation, *Propriety of Publishing Identity of Sexual Assault Victim,* 40 A.L.R.5th 787 (1996).

[83] *See also* Carol Schultz Vento, Annotation, *Propriety of Publishing Identity of Sexual Assault Victim,* 40 A.L.R.5th 787 (1996). Florida Star v. B. J. F., 491 U.S. 524 (1989) ("But where the government has made certain information publicly available, it is highly anomalous to sanction persons other than the source of its release.").

[84] *Id.* at 496. *See also* Oklahoma Publ'g Co. v. District Court, 430 U.S. 308, 310 (1977) ("The *First* and *Fourteenth Amendments* will not permit a state court to prohibit the publication of widely disseminated information obtained at court proceedings which were in fact open to the public.").

[85] Cox Broad. Corp. v. Cohn, 420 U.S. 469, 492 (1975) (holding unconstitutional a damage award against a television station for broadcasting the name of a rape-murder victim obtained from courthouse records).

[86] *Florida Star,* 491 U.S. at 541 ("We do not hold that truthful publication is automatically constitutionally protected, or that there is no zone of personal privacy within which the State may protect the individual from intrusion by the press, or even that a State may never punish publication of the name of a victim of a sexual offense.").

136

§ 2.7   Cameras in the courtroom and televising of proceedings.

The Supreme Court of the United States, in *Chandler v. Florida*,[87] held that televising or broadcasting of trials is not a *per se* violation of a defendant's fair trial rights, but there is no constitutional right to record or broadcast a trial. The Court noted that a constitutional ban on broadcast coverage of trials cannot be justified on the grounds that there may be situations where publicity generated by such coverage may affect the impartiality of jurors.[88] The Court clarified that *Estes v. Texas*[89] did not create a *per se* constitutional rule barring broadcast coverage under all circumstances, despite the egregious nature of the broadcast coverage in the *Estes* case. No federal appeals court since *Chandler* has found a right to broadcast a trial.[90]

The media has no greater right than the public to attend a trial and the right of access does not translate who has a right to televise court proceedings.[91] While most states permit the photographing or electronic recording of court proceedings, a handful do not.[92]

One argument raised by defendants when electronic coverage of a trial proceeding is permitted is that prejudice arises when there is electronic coverage of only a portion of the proceeding. One defendant contended that a jury is compelled to give greater weight to the testimony of the witnesses who testified when cameras were in place than those who testified when there were no cameras because the presence of cameras reflected a greater importance or weight to be given to those witnesses' testimonies.[93] This argument was rejected.[94] Related to this argument is the one that a defendant's due process rights are violated, not by the presence of cameras in the courtroom, but by the distinctive treatment afforded a victim whose testimony is not televised. This argument has been rejected because the defendant has the burden of showing prejudice on properly ordered limitations on electronic media coverage.[95] A defendant's argument that cameras in the courtroom caused him embarrassment due to the nature of child molestation charges has also been rejected.[96]

---

[87] 449 U.S. 560–69 (1981).

[88] *Id.* at 574–75.

[89] 381 U.S. 532 (1965).

[90] *See, e.g.*, Rice v. Kempker, 374 F.3d 675, 678 (8th Cir. 2004); United States v. Edwards, 785 F.2d 1293, 1295 (1986); United States v. Hastings, 695 F.2d 1278, 1280 (11th Cir. 1983).

[91] Courtroom Television Network LLC v. State, 5 N.Y.3d 222, 231, 833 N.E.2d 1197, 1202, 800 N.Y.S.2d 522, 527 (2005).

[92] *See, e.g.*, N.Y. Civ. Rights Law § 52. The constitutionality of this law was upheld in *Courtroom Television Network v. State of New York, supra.*

[93] People v. Shattell, 179 A.D.2d 896, 578 N.Y.S.2d 694, *appeal denied*, 79 N.Y.2d 1007, 594 N.E.2d 956, 584 N.Y.S.2d 462 (1992).

[94] *Id.*

[95] Commonwealth v. Cordeiro, 401 Mass. 843, 847, 519 N.E.2d 1328, 1331 (1988).

[96] Tijerina v. State, 1998 Tex. App. LEXIS 1384 (Mar. 5, 1998).

The Supreme Court's holding in *Chandler* expressly approves safeguards "to protect certain witnesses — for example . . . victims of sex crimes . . . from the glare of publicity and the tensions of being single 'on camera.' "[97] The Massachusetts Supreme Court also noted that any problems pertaining to the exclusion of cameras during the victim's testimony were adequately dealt with by the court's lengthy and clear instructions on the presumption of innocence, the nature of evidence, and the jury's role of sole finder of credibility.[98] One of the solutions when there is a concern that potential witnesses may be influenced by the publicity or the televising of court proceedings is for the court to issue an order precluding potential witnesses from watching or revealing publicity concerning the court proceedings. One such order is set forth in Appendix C.

One of the oddities of cameras in the courtroom is that it permits potential witnesses to see and hear the testimony of other witnesses even though potential witnesses are ordinarily excluded from the courtroom during the testimony of other witnesses. Is the preclusion of witnesses from a trial becoming an anachronism? Do potential witnesses have to be admonished not to watch television? Is it any different from a potential witness reading a newspaper account of the trial?

Virtually all states permit some form of televised court proceedings. Many states impose restrictions as to how and when the proceedings may be broadcast, particularly in sexual assault trials. The United States Judicial Conference has decided to reinstate its ban on cameras in federal courts after experimenting with cameras in some courts.

§ 2.8   Ethical considerations for attorneys with respect to trial publicity.

The Supreme Court, in *Gentile v. State Bar of Nevada*,[99] held that the extra-judicial statements of an attorney may be regulated by attorney disciplinary rules. Dominick Gentile, a Las Vegas attorney, represented a defendant who was charged with stealing cocaine and traveler's checks from a company's vaults. Several hours after his client was indicted, Gentile held a press conference in which he claimed the proof would show his client to be innocent, and that the culprit was a police officer who had access to the vault. He also commented that many of the prosecution's witnesses were not credible since they were either drug dealers or convicted money launderers. He also implied that the police officer may have been suffering from symptoms of cocaine use.

Gentile was found to have violated Nevada Supreme Court rule 177(1), which prohibits an attorney from making "an extrajudicial statement that a reasonable person would expect to be disseminated by means of public communication if

---

[97] *Chandler*, 449 U.S. at 577.

[98] *Cordeiro*, 401 Mass. at 849, 519 N.E.2d at 1332.

[99] 501 U.S. 1030 (1991).

the lawyer knows or reasonably should know that it will have a substantial likelihood of material prejudicing on adjudicative proceedings."[100] The Court held that the rule's "substantial likelihood of material prejudice" test did not violate the constitution's First Amendment, but that the rule, as interpreted by the Nevada Supreme Court, was void for vagueness. The Court noted that the particular Nevada provision was not necessarily flawed as interpreted and applied, since the phrase "substantial likelihood of material prejudice" "might punish only speech that creates a danger of imminent and substantial harm."[101] In this regard, the Court noted that statements coming to the attention of a jury pool on the eve of trial were more likely to threaten the fairness of a trial. The Court went on to note that much of the information disseminated at the defense attorney's press conference was already available and had been published in one form or another, and that the press conference did not touch upon prejudicial areas and police statements, such as comments on polygraph tests, confessions, or evidence from searches. It also noted there was no further elaboration on the defendant's general theory that witnesses in the case were not credible in that they may have been pressured into making a deal to avoid other legal consequences. Significantly, the Court recognized that "an attorney may take reasonable steps to defend a client's reputation and reduce the adverse consequences of indictment, especially in the face of a prosecution deemed unjust or commenced with improper motives."[102]

The problem in the Nevada proscription was that it also contained, as do most state codes of conduct, a safe-harbor provision, Rule 177(3) which provided that a lawyer "may state without elaboration . . . [the] general nature of the . . . defense," and that statements made under this rule would be protected notwithstanding Rule 177(1). Thus, the rule failed to provide "fair notice to those to whom it is directed."[103] The Court also noted that, given the fairly innocuous statements of the attorney and the safe harbor position of Rule 177(3), this case was "a poor vehicle for defining with precision the outer limits under the constitution of a court's ability to regulate an attorney's statements about ongoing adjudicative proceedings." The Court expressed great reluctance to regulate attorneys' speech despite the fact that attorneys' comments may be relied upon by the press and public more so than other sources of information about a case. The Court expressed optimism that the "constraints of professional responsibility and societal disapproval will act as sufficient safeguards in most cases."[104]

---

[100] *Id.* at 1033.

[101] *Id.* at 1036.

[102] *Id.* at 1043.

[103] *Id.* at 1048 *citing* Grayned v. City of Rockford, 408 U.S. 104, 112 (1972).

[104] *Id.* at 1058.

§ 2.9   Model role of professional responsibility and trial publicity.

The American Bar Association Model Rule of Professional Conduct has been amended in response to the *Gentile* decision and in an attempt to make it more responsive to contemporary criminal litigation. Rule 3.6 now states:[105]

RULE 3.6 TRIAL PUBLICITY

(a) A lawyer who is participating or has participated in the investigation or litigation of a matter shall not make an extrajudicial statement that a reasonable person would expect to be disseminated by means of public communication if the lawyer knows or reasonably should know that it will have a substantial likelihood of materially prejudicing an adjudicative proceeding in the matter.

(b) Notwithstanding paragraph (a), a lawyer may state:

(1) the claim, offense or defense involved and, except when prohibited by law, the identity of the persons involved;

(2) information contained in a public record;

(3) that an investigation of a matter is in progress;

(4) the scheduling or result of any step in litigation;

(5) a request for assistance in obtaining evidence and information necessary thereto;

(6) a warning of danger concerning the behavior of a person involved, when there is reason to believe that there exists the likelihood of substantial harm to an individual or to the public interest; and

(7) in a criminal case, in addition to subparagraphs (1) through (6):

(i) the identity, residence, occupation, and family status of the accused;

(ii) if the accused has not been apprehended, information necessary to aid in apprehension of that person;

(iii) the fact, time, and place of arrest; and

(iv) the identity of investigating and arresting officers or agencies and the length of the investigation.

(c) Notwithstanding paragraph (a), a lawyer may make a statement that a reasonable lawyer would believe is required to protect a client from the substantial undue prejudicial effect of recent publicity not initiated by the lawyer or the lawyer's client. A statement made pursuant to this paragraph shall be limited to such information as is necessary to mitigate the recent adverse publicity.

---

[105] ABA MODEL RULES OF PROFESSIONAL CONDUCT Rule 3.6 (1995). To date, California, Maine, and New York are the only states that do not have professional conduct rules that follow the format of the ABA Model Rules of Professional Conduct. New York follows the predecessor ABA Model Code of Professional Responsibility, and California and Maine developed their own rules.

(d) No lawyer associated in a firm or government agency with a lawyer subject to paragraph (a) shall make a statement prohibited by paragraph (a).

The rule now makes it clear that only attorneys or their associates who are or have been involved in a proceeding are subject to the rule. The former rule and some rules that do not reflect the ABA amendment pertaining to trial publicity proscribe conduct not only by attorneys who represent parties in an action, but also by attorneys who represent related parties or have a nexus to the criminal case, such as a defendant's wife who may be involved in ancillary proceedings where there may be "a spillover effect" in statements made by the nonparty's attorney.[106] Rule 3.6 now authorizes a lawyer to protect a client by responding to what is perceived as prejudicial publicity "not indicated by the lawyer or the lawyer's client." Rather, that all information deemed improper to reveal the Rule sets a standard of statements that will "have a substantial likelihood of materially prejudicing" the proceeding. The former list of proscribed items is now set forth in the comments as "only a guide, not an exhaustive listing":

(1)   the character, credibility, reputation, or criminal record of a party, suspect in a criminal investigation or witness, or the identity of a witness, or the expected testimony of a party or witness;

(2)   in a criminal case or proceeding that could result in incarceration, the possibility of a plea of guilty to the offense or the existence or contents of any confession, admission, or statement given by the defendant or suspect, or that person's refusal or failure to make a statement;

(3)   the performance or results of any examination or test or the refusal or failure of a person to submit to an examination or test, or the identity or nature of physical evidence expected to be presented;

(4)   any opinion as to the guilt or innocence of a defendant or suspect in a criminal case or proceeding that could result in incarceration;

(5)   information that the lawyer knows or reasonably should know is likely to be inadmissible as evidence in a trial and that would, if disclosed, create a substantial risk of prejudicing an impartial trial; or

(6)   the fact that a defendant has been charged with a crime, unless there is included therein a statement explaining that the charge is merely an accusation and that the defendant is presumed innocent until and unless proven guilty.

Another relevant factor in determining prejudice is the nature of the proceeding involved. Criminal jury trials will be most sensitive to extrajudicial speech. Civil

---

[106] People v. Buttafuoco, 158 Misc. 2d 174, 599 N.Y.S.2d 419 (1993) (trial court decision in this highly publicized trial in which Joseph Buttafuoco was charged with rape, sodomy, and endangering the welfare of a child; the court restricted comments by the prosecutor, the defendant's attorney, the defendant's wife, and the attorney for the alleged victim concerning the credibility, reputation, and character of Buttafuoco and the alleged victim).

trials may be less sensitive. Non-jury hearings and arbitration proceedings may be even less affected. The Rule will still place limitations on prejudicial comments in these cases, but the likelihood of prejudice may be different depending on the type of proceeding.

Finally, extrajudicial statements that might otherwise raise a question under this Rule may be permissible when they are made in response to statements made publicly by another party, another party's lawyer, or third persons, where a reasonable lawyer would believe a public response is required in order to avoid prejudice to the lawyer's client. When prejudicial statements have been publicly made by others, responsive statements may have the salutary effect of lessening any resulting adverse impact on the adjudicative proceeding. Such responsive statements should be limited to contain only such information as is necessary to mitigate undue prejudice created by the statements made by others.

California does not have a provision similar to Model Rule 3.6. Many states have adopted variations upon Rule 3.6.[107]

The requirement of material prejudice is significant. It is not enough that there be general statements promoting the position of the party. Televised statements of an attorney that he had not put his client on the stand because the "prosecutor did not prove the case and that there was nothing that would be added" by having his client testify, or commenting on a witness that the jury did not hear such as a psychological expert for the defense and providing a brief summary of what that expert would have testified to, has been held not to be of the type of statement that an attorney should know would have "a substantial likelihood of materially prejudicing the proceeding."[108] In dismissing professional misconduct charges against the attorney, the court noted that the unsequestered jury had been

---

[107] *Delaware* deletes Rule 3.6(b)(6); *District of Columbia:* Rule 3.6 states only: "A lawyer engaged in a case being tried to a judge or jury shall not make an extrajudicial statement that a reasonable person would expect to be disseminated by means of mass public communication if the lawyer knows or reasonably should know that the statement will create a serious and imminent threat to the impartiality of the judge or jury." *Illinois:* Rule 3.6(a) applies to statements that would "pose a serious and imminent threat to the fairness of an adjudicative proceeding." Rule 3.6(b)(1) refers to "the prior criminal record (including arrests, indictments, or other charges of crime)." Illinois omits the requirement in ABA Model Rule 3.6(b)(5) that the inadmissible evidence "would if disclosed create a substantial risk of prejudicing an impartial trial." Illinois completely omits Rule 3.6(b)(6). *Michigan* places Rule 3.6(b) and (c) in its Comment to Rule 3.6. *Minnesota* deletes subparagraphs (b) and (c) of Rule 3.6 in their entirety. *Montana* adds the following language to (b)(4): "or a substantial likelihood of materially prejudicing the outcome of a hearing or trial." *New Jersey* substitutes "reasonable lawyer" for "reasonable person" in Rule 3.6(a). Rule 3.6(b)(1) adds "other than the victim of a crime" after the words "identity of a witness." *Virginia:* DR 7-106(A) prohibits a lawyer "participating in or associated with the investigation or the prosecution or the defense of a criminal matter that may be tried by a jury" from making an extrajudicial statement that "constitutes a clear and present danger of interfering with the fairness of the trial by jury." *See* STEPHEN GILLERS & ROY D. SIMON, JR., REGULATION OF LAWYERS: STATUTES AND STANDARDS, 198–99(1994).

[108] *In re* Sullivan, 185 A.D.2d 440, 443, 586 N.Y.S.2d 322, 324 (1992).

admonished to avoid media accounts of the trial. The court found that these statements were not of the type to materially prejudice the proceedings in this case, particularly when the television interview was a "mere drop in the ocean of publicity surrounding this trial."[109]

§ 2.10   Special responsibilities of prosecutors.

Prosecutors have additional responsibilities imposed by the Model Rules. Model Rule 3.8 states:

RULE 3.8 SPECIAL RESPONSIBILITIES OF A PROSECUTOR.

The prosecutor in a criminal case shall:

(e) exercise reasonable care to prevent investigators, law enforcement personnel, employees, or other persons assisting or associated with the prosecutor in a criminal case from making an extrajudicial statement that the prosecutor would be prohibited from making under Rule 3.6.

If a prosecutor as part of a news conference describes a number of persons arrested during a raid as ex-convicts, but does not necessarily identify a particular defendant as a convict, this is considered an appropriate comment concerning background events of an arrest or the commission of a crime.[110] Inappropriate comments of a prosecutor may be abated by the passage of time and the failure of prospective jurors to remember the prosecutor's comments.[111]

As the Supreme Court noted in *Gentile*, comments made during the pendency of a trial are more likely to have a substantial impact on the trial and will accordingly be scrutinized more carefully. When a prosecutor holds a press conference during a trial expressing his view that white-collar criminals are treated leniently by the presiding judge, a mistrial should be granted or the defendant's conviction reversed even though jurors professed to have seen or heard nothing of the comments.[112] The factors set out for determining whether improper prosecutorial comments will be a basis for reversing a defendant's conviction are "the timing of the statement, the relationship of the prosecutor to the criminal trial, prominence of the public statement, and the relationship of the published views to the issues in the prosecution."[113]

---

[109] *Id.* at 445, 586 N.Y.S.2d at 326.

[110] Wilson v. State, 854 S.W.2d 270, 275 (Tex. Ct. App. 1993). A district attorney may ordinarily issue a press release describing physical evidence seized at the time of arrest but may not state whether such evidence will be presented at trial. New York State Bar Association Committee on Professional Ethics, No. 620 3/21/91 (4/91) No. 620.

[111] *Ex parte* Whisenhant, 555 So. 2d 235, 238 (Ala. 1989), *cert. denied*, 496 U.S. 943 (1990) (no prejudice where prospective jurors did not remember Attorney General's statements that an attorney from his office was joining the Mobile district attorney's office to "make this retrial the last one for Thomas Whisenhant.").

[112] United States v. Coast of Me. Lobster Co., 538 F.2d 899 (1st Cir. 1976).

[113] *Id.* at 902.

Furthermore, a violation of the disciplinary rules or model rules does not necessarily justify the dismissal of an indictment.[114] Misconduct or violation of the rules alone does not justify reversal of a defendant's conviction. It must result in a denial of a fair trial for the defendant because of the prosecutor's actions.[115] For example, disseminating the defendant's criminal history to the media prior to trial does not necessarily entitle defendant to a new trial.[116] However, at least one court has upheld disciplinary action against a prosecutor for making public statements concerning the graphic nature of the injury sustained by a murder victim and using those facts as a basis for asking for the death penalty and for further comments concerning what the prosecutor thought was appropriate punishment for the defendants.[117] Here, the attorney violated a disciplinary rule that prohibited an attorney involved in a criminal case from making statements that relate to "any opinion as to the guilt or innocence of the accused, the evidence or merits of the case."[118] Similarly, New Jersey upheld disciplinary action against a former prosecutor who, after having returned to private practice, made comments concerning a criminal case in which he had previously been associated.[119] Another prosecutor was found to have violated professional ethic standards by making out-of-court statements about a defendant's confession, discussing the plea offer and giving an opinion on the guilt of two other defendants.[120]

§ 2.11   Contracts for sale of rights to client's story.

Another ethical issue raising a potential conflict of interest involves an attorney who enters into a contract for a book or movie pertaining to a client or matters

---

[114] *Wilson* at 275. *See also* United States v. Shorter, 620 F. Supp. 73, 74 (D.D.C. 1985) ("However, when ruling upon a defendant's motion for a mistrial and to vacate the verdicts, this Court's decision does not depend upon the propriety *per se* of the prosecution's conduct under these rules. In contrast to those bodies whose primary function it is to supervise professional conduct, the Court's principal concern is the likely impact of the disputed news coverage upon the fairness of the criminal proceedings before the Court.").

[115] State v. Atwood, 171 Ariz. 576, 607, 832 P.2d 593, 624 (1992).

[116] People v. Tillman, 261 A.D.2d 854, 691 N.Y.S.2d 212, *appeal denied*, 93 N.Y.2d 980, 716 N.E.2d 1111, 695 N.Y.S.2d 66 (1999):

> Defendant is not entitled to a new trial on the ground that the prosecutor provided to the media information concerning defendant's criminal record, allegedly in violation of Code of Professional Responsibility DR 7-107(B)(1) (22 NYCRR 1200.38[b][1]). Although a newspaper story containing the information was printed prior to jury selection, the court eliminated any possible prejudice arising therefrom by asking potential jurors whether they had read the article, and defendant did not seek a change of venue.

261 A.D.2d at 855, 691 N.Y.S.2d at 214.

[117] Zimmerman v. Board of Prof'l Responsibility, 764 S.W.2d 757 (Tenn.), *cert. denied*, 490 U.S. 1107 (1989).

[118] *Id.*

[119] *In re* Rachmiel, 90 N.J. 646, 449 A.2d 505 (1982).

[120] *See also*, Attorney Grievance Comm'n v. Gansler, 377 Md. 656, 835 A.2d 548 (2003).

that he or she is actively handling.[121] Ethical Consideration 5-2 states that a lawyer should not enter accepting employment as an attorney engaged in a contractual relationship that would "tend to make his judgment less protective of the interests of his client." It is supplemented by Ethical Consideration 5-4, which notes that a lawyer who gains an interest in publication rights pertaining to his representation of a client "may be tempted to subordinate the interest of his client to his own anticipated pecuniary gain." There is also the issue of whether entering into the sale of rights to a publisher or production company would violate disciplinary Rule 5-101(a), which prohibits acceptance of employment as attorney if the lawyer's professional judgment will or may be reasonably affected by his own financial, business, property, or personal interest unless there is full disclosure of the relationship to the client.[122]

Furthermore, a lawyer, whether he has made a commercial agreement to write about a case or whether he is merely commenting on the case without any remuneration, is never at liberty to disclose client confidences or secrets or to violate the attorney-client privilege.

§ 2.12   Pretrial publicity.

Pretrial publicity may affect more trials, particularly sexual assault trials, in reality than they do legally. The Supreme Court of the United States reversed a conviction on the ground that pretrial publicity made a fair trial impossible in the case of *Rideau v. Louisiana.*[123] In that case, the defendant was charged with robbery, kidnapping, and murder. Soon after his arrest, the defendant's taped confession was broadcast over a television station. The Supreme Court held that broadcasting of the confession was so prejudicial that it was a denial of the defendant's constitutional rights to deny his motion for a change of venue.[124]

The Supreme Court has held that a defendant has a right to a trial by a jury of impartial and "indifferent jurors,"[125] yet, an indifferent juror need not be an ignorant juror:

> It is not required, however, that the jurors be totally ignorant of the facts and issues involved. In these days of swift, widespread, and diverse methods of communication, an important case can be expected to arouse the interest

---

[121] John Gibeaut, *Defend and Tell,* A.B.A.J., Dec. 1996, at 64–67.

[122] *See, e.g.,* United States v. Hearst, 638 F.2d 1190, 1997–99 (9th Cir. 1980), *cert. denied,* 451 U.S. 938 (1981) (noting that a criminal defendant's lawyer who entered into a contract to write a book about the trial while he still represented the client may have violated Disciplinary Rule 5-101(a)). *Compare* Eberhardt v. O'Malley, 17 F.3d 1023 (7th Cir. 1994) (holding that an assistant prosecutor who was allegedly fired for writing a novel had stated a valid civil rights cause of action for violation of his First Amendment rights unless the prosecutor could establish countervailing public interests for the action).

[123] 373 U.S. 723 (1963).

[124] *Id.* at 726.

[125] Irvin v. Dowd, 366 U.S. 717 (1961).

of the public in the vicinity, and scarcely any of those best qualified to serve as jurors have not formed some impression or opinion as to the merits of the case. This is particularly true in criminal cases. To hold that the mere existence of any preconceived notion as to the guilt or innocence of an accused, without more, is sufficient to rebut the presumption of a prospective juror's impartiality would be to establish an impossible standard. It is sufficient if the juror can lay aside his impression or opinion and render it a verdict based on the evidence presented in court.[126] Many courts have held that there must be a showing of massive pervasive and prejudicial publicity before corrective action need be taken.

The courts considered many factors in assessing the impact of pretrial publicity. These include examining the size and type of the community involved, including the number of news sources within the community and the likelihood that a particular community or the majority of its citizens will have been exposed to only one source of information about a trial. The reputation of the victim within a community is another fact to consider as to whether the publicity has an effect on the jury. Courts also will look at the source of the news stories in assessing prejudice, since stories originating from official sources are more likely to be prejudicial than those based on rumor or unofficial sources. With respect to the news stories themselves, the amount of coverage, the extent of opinions or comments in the reporting, the specificity or nature of facts about the crime, and the manner in which the stories have been presented are other factors the courts will examine. Of particular importance is whether the publicity has included information concerning highly incriminating facts (particularly statements allegedly made by an accused), especially when the incriminating facts or statements will not be admissible at trial. Exposure to inadmissible evidence such as a defendant's criminal history may also be prejudicial. Such exposure does not by itself establish a presumption that the defendant has been deprived a fair trial.[127] The U.S. Supreme Court has also made a distinction between factual and inflammatory reporting of events.[128] Finally, the effect of any publicity is more likely to be of greater impact and perhaps prejudicial the closer it is to the time of trial.[129]

Publicity that misrepresents a defendant's statements as a confession or infers guilt is considered as prejudicial as the broadcasting of a defendant's confession.

---

[126] *Id.* at 722–23. *See also* Cash v. State, 301 Ark. 370, 784 S.W.2d 166 (1990).

[127] People v. Jendrzejewski, 455 Mich. 495, 502, 566 N.W.2d 530, 534 (1997), *cert. denied*, 522 U.S. 1097 (1998).

[128] Murphy v. Florida, 421 U.S. 794, 800 n.4 (1975). *See also* Campbell v. State, 718 So. 2d 123 (Ala. Crim. App. 1997) (noting that most of the publicity of sexual assaults was "straight forward, factual accounts of what was taking place"); State v. Schatz-Sousa, 1998 Wash. App. LEXIS 425 at *12 (Mar. 23, 1998).

[129] For a discussion of some of these criteria and the requirement that a defendant show massive pervasive and prejudicial publicity preceding his trial, see People v. McCrary, 190 Colo. 538, 549 P.2d 1320 (1976).

An example of this type of prejudicial conduct, which can lead to the reversal of a defendant's conviction, occurred in a Colorado case some years ago when law enforcement authorities engaged novelist Erle Stanley Gardner, originator of the Perry Mason series, to assist in solving an actual homicide. Gardner's work, theories, and opinions, which were made available to the press, contained mischaracterizations of the defendant's statements.[130]

§ 2.13 Pretrial publicity — Police invitation of media generating publicity and "perp walks."

Are there legal issues with government facilitated news coverage of a defendant? In *Wilson v. Layne*,[131] the Supreme Court held that a "media ride-along" as police officers executed an arrest warrant in a private home violated the Fourth Amendment. Of particular significance is that the media in *Wilson* actually accompanied the arresting officers inside the suspect's home, and directly observed the confrontation between the suspect and officers in the defendant's living room.[132] The home is a location of particular sanctity and protection under the Fourth Amendment.

In *Lauro v. Charles*, where a detective arranged for the parading of a defendant at the specific request of the media (sometimes colloquially referred to as "perp-walks"), the Second Circuit read *Wilson* as establishing two principles: (i) that the Fourth Amendment regulates both the fact and manner of searches and seizures, dictating that they be reasonable in both of these senses; and (ii) that reasonableness "must be judged, in part, through an assessment of the degree to which [the police's] actions further the legitimate law enforcement purposes behind the search or seizure."[133] Thus, "in staging the perp walk, Detective Charles engaged in conduct that was unrelated to the object of the arrest, that had no legitimate law enforcement justification, and that was an invasion of Lauro's privacy for no purpose. By exacerbating Lauro's seizure in an unreasonable manner, Charles violated the Fourth Amendment."[134] However the court distinguished its holding from most "perp walks," which occur "naturally" in the course of transporting a prisoner:

> It is important . . . to understand the limitations of our holding. First, we do not hold that all, or even most, perp walks are violations of the Fourth Amendment. Thus, we are not talking about cases in which there is a legitimate law enforcement justification for transporting a suspect. Accordingly, we do not address the case — seemingly much more common than the kind of staged perp walk that occurred here — where a suspect is photographed in the normal

---

[130] Walker v. People, 169 Colo. 467, 458 P.2d 238 (1969).

[131] 526 U.S. 603 (1999).

[132] *Id.* at 607–08.

[133] 219 F.3d 202, 211 (2d Cir. 2000).

[134] *Id.* at 213.

course of being moved from one place to another by the police. Nor do we reach the question of whether, in those circumstances, it would be proper for the police to notify the media ahead of time that a suspect is to be transported.[135]

The key is the transporting of the defendant solely to benefit, not which incidentally benefits a defendant. When the video-graphing of the defendant is a by-product of transporting the defendant in the normal course of business, there is no Fourth Amendment violation.

When there is no "fictional recreation" of an arrest, and the events filmed are part of "legitimate law enforcement activities," even the videotaping of arrests and distributing of the tape to the media will not violate the defendant's Fourth Amendment rights.[136] When the "perp walk" is neither fictitious nor staged, and has a legitimate law-enforcement purpose, the Fourth Amendment is not violated.[137]

§ 2.14   Overview of preventative and corrective measures to deal with potentially prejudicial publicity.

Publicity is more likely deemed prejudicial when a court has failed to take the appropriate steps to insure the integrity of the fact-finding process. Prejudice is also more likely to be found when potential corrective measures have been brought to a court's attention, and the court has failed to act on them. It is imperative that the request or motion for a particular corrective action be made. The request should also be supported by factual information. Many steps, such as restraining comments by trial participants and motion for change of venue, can be made before trial.

When jurors are exposed to publicity during trial, the potential for prejudice is more likely. The brunt of the publicity is not attenuated by time, and the effect upon jurors is likely to be greater. When jurors are exposed during trial to

---

135 *Id.* at n.10.

136 Watkins v. City of Highland Park, 232 F. Supp. 2d 744 (E.D. Mich. 2002); Otero v. Town of Southampton, 194 F. Supp. 2d 167, 181 (E.D.N.Y. 2002); Caldarola v. County of Westchester, 142 F. Supp. 2d 431, 433 (S.D.N.Y. 2001) ("Even if the courthouse 'perp walk' could be considered a seizure for purposes of the Fourth Amendment, it did not violate plaintiffs' constitutional rights, because there was a legitimate law-enforcement reason for leaving the police station and bringing plaintiffs into the Mt. Pleasant courthouse — namely, their arraignment. Assuming, *arguendo*, that what the police were doing outside the courthouse was waiting for the press to arrive, I am not persuaded that this action unconstitutionally aggravated the legitimate seizure that occurred when plaintiffs were arrested. The fact is, plaintiffs' arrest was a newsworthy event. The press could not be kept from covering it, and the police are not constitutionally compelled to make their job more difficult." *Id.* at 759–60.).

137 Watkins v. City of Highland Park, 232 F. Supp. 2d 744 (E.D. Mich. 2002); Otero v. Town of Southampton, 194 F. Supp. 2d 167, 181 (E.D.N.Y. 2002).

information such as the defendant's confession or incriminating polygraph results, it can be "inherently prejudicial."[138]

Several avenues are available to deal with prejudicial publicity, and these are discussed in subsequent sections. Jury selection questions and the use of a juror questionnaire to deal with issues of pretrial publicity are discussed in Chapter 3.[139]

§ 2.15 Trial postponement or continuance.

When there has been potentially prejudicial pretrial publicity, particularly on the eve of trial, it is appropriate for a court to grant a continuance in the case until the threat from the publicity abates.[140] Continuance is one of the alternatives recommended by the ABA Standards on Fair Trial and Free Press.[141]

Continuance is often cited by courts as a less drastic alternative than sequestration or change of venue. "[W]here there is reasonable likelihood that prejudicial news prior to trial will prevent a fair trial, the judge should continue the case until the threat abates, or transfer it to another county not so permeated with publicity."[142] A continuance has particular value for a defendant who does not wish to seek a change of venue and prefers to try the case in the district where the indictment was filed. A defendant who believes that the original district still presents a more favorable venire may wish to wait until the pretrial publicity subsides. A defendant can request a continuance without moving for a change of venue and the request can be granted amidst pervasive publicity.[143]

§ 2.16 Motion for change of venue.

The following seven factors are often used in evaluating a motion for a change of venue: (1) nature of pretrial publicity, such as whether it includes highly incriminating facts not admissible at trial and the particular degree to which it has circulated in the community; (2) the connection of government officials with the release of the publicity; (3) the length of time between the dissemination of the publicity and the trial; (4) the severity and notoriety of the offense; (5) the area from which the jury is to be drawn; (6) other events occurring in the community that either affect or reflect the attitude of the community or individual jurors toward the defendant's conviction; and (7) any factors likely to affect the

---

[138] Hughes v. State, 490 A.2d 1034 (Del. 1985). *See also* United States v. Williams, 568 F.2d 464, 469 (5th Cir. 1978).

[139] § 3.6.

[140] Sheppard v. Maxwell, 384 U.S. 333 (1966).

[141] ABA STANDARDS RELATING TO THE ADMINISTRATION OF JUSTICE, FAIR TRIAL AND FREE PRESS § 8-3.2(d) (1968).

[142] *Id.* at 362–63.

[143] United States v. Perez-Casillas, 593 F. Supp. 794 (D.P.R. 1984).

candor and veracity of the prospective jurors on voir dire.[144] This is a good summary of the factors and issues considered by many appellate courts in motions for a change of venue.

Many states require that a party seeking to change the venue of a trial prove actual prejudice — that the dissemination of the prejudicial material would probably result in the party being deprived of a fair trial — unless it can be shown that the influence of the news media has been so outrageous that it can be presumed prejudicial.[145] The fact that a majority of jurors may have knowledge of a sexual assault case does not, standing alone, trigger a change of venue; the exposure to publicity must affect the potential jurors' opinion of the defendant's guilt or innocence.[146] Even if a significant percentage of the array has formed an opinion of the defendant, this will not equate with an unfair trial.[147] The fact

[144] People v. McCrary, 190 Colo. 538, 549 P.2d 1320 (1976); State v. Adams, 394 So. 2d 1204, 1207 (La. 1981) *citing* State v. Bell, 315 So. 2d 307 (La. 1975); State v. Crudup, 11 Wash. App. 583, 524 P.2d 479, *review denied*, 84 Wash. 2d 1012 (1974).

[145] United States v. Grey Bear, 883 F.2d 1382, 1393 (8th Cir. 1989), *cert. denied*, 493 U.S. 1047 (1990); Williams v. State, 489 So. 2d 4 (Ala. Crim. App. 1986) (holding that in an order to prevail on a motion for a change of venue, defendant must show (1) the prejudicial pretrial publicity has so saturated the community as to have a probable impact on the prospective jurors or (2) a connection between the publicity generated . . . and the existence of actual jury prejudice. *Id.* at 6); State v. Smith, 123 Ariz. 231, 599 P.2d 187 (1979), *cert. denied*, 502 U.S. 835 (1991).

[146] Campbell v. State, 718 So. 2d 123 (Ala. Crim. App. 1997) (noting that most of the publicity of the sexual assaults was "straightforward, factual accounts of what was taking place"); Mallott v. State, 608 P.2d 737 (Alaska 1980); Taylor v. State, 515 N.E.2d 1095, 1097 (Ind. 1987); Bowling v. Commonwealth, 942 S.W.2d 293 (Ky. 1997), *cert. denied*, 522 U.S. 986 (1997) ("That prospective jurors merely have heard about the case is not sufficient to sustain a motion for a change of venue. Rather, the test is whether the jurors have heard something that causes a preconception concerning the defendant. Even though a juror may have heard about the case in the past, he is still qualified if the court is assured and satisfied that he will put aside that prior knowledge and decide the case in accordance with the testimony heard in the courtroom and on instructions given by the court." *Id.* at 298–99.); State v. Henderson, 566 So. 2d 1098, 1102–03 (La. Ct. App. 1990); People v. Berry, 235 A.D.2d 571, 652 N.Y.S.2d 785 (1997) ("Here, although there was substantial newspaper coverage of the crime in this rural area, this was most likely due, in no small part, to the gruesome nature of the victim's death and dismemberment. The jurors in this case indicated their belief that they could set aside any preconceived notions and render a fair decision in this case." *Id.* at 573, 652 N.Y.S.2d at 788.); Welch v. State, 993 S.W.2d 690 (Tex. Ct. App. 1999) (while one-half of the jury panel was exposed to media coverage of Southeast Side Rapist story, there was no showing that the pretrial publicity rendered jury impartial since there is no "automatic assumption of prejudice" when jurors are exposed to pretrial publicity and therefore there was no basis for a change of venue); State v. Rice, 120 Wash. 2d 549, 556, 844 P.2d 416, 419 (1993) (holding defendant must show a probability of unfairness or prejudice from the pretrial publicity); State v. Root, 95 Wash. App. 333, 975 P.2d 1052, *review granted in part*, 139 Wash. App. 1001, 989 P.2d 1139 (1999) (upholding trial court's denial of motion for change of venue despite several news accounts describing sexual abuse of the child victims, photographs taken of the children, and interviews of children's parents).

[147] United States v. Moreno Morales, 815 F.2d 725, 735 (1st Cir. 1987); People v. Jendrzejewski, 455 Mich. 495, 513–14, 566 N.W.2d 530, 539–40 (1997), *cert. denied*, 522 U.S. 1097 (1998) (finding his presumptive prejudice in the fact that 15–25% of jurors were excused for lack of impartiality).

that the accused sex offender is well known and the charges receive substantial publicity is insufficient without more to establish a basis for a change of venue.[148] Actual prejudice may be presumed in egregious situations without proof that jurors who sat on the trial were prejudiced by the publicity.[149]

Establishing prejudice usually requires an examination of the effect of the publicity upon the jury members. In fact, in some states a motion for change of venue cannot effectively be made until jury selection has commenced and a showing made that the defendant cannot obtain a fair and impartial jury.[150]

The prejudice can be demonstrated through the voir dire process by showing the number of jurors who have formed opinions concerning the guilt or innocence of the defendant constitutes an unfair or abnormally high percentage of the venire. A juror's comment during voir dire about an unrelated charge against the defendant can support a change of venue.[151]

It has been held, however, that relying on voir dire to establish actual prejudice may be unrealistic.[152]

---

[148] State v. Miller, 1996 Ohio App. LEXIS 1104, *appeal denied*, 76 Ohio St. 3d 1492, 670 N.E.2d 240 (1996) ("Appellant claims that because he is well known in the community, has served in a police department for twenty years, and had a prior rape trial that ended in a conviction, the trial court should have granted his motion for change of venue . . . . Appellee argues that each juror said that he or she could decide the case based only upon the evidence presented at trial. Appellee states that the trial court dismissed one prospective juror for cause due to the prospective juror's inability to decide the case based upon the evidence." *Id.* at 27–28.).

[149] *See, e.g.*, Sheppard v. Maxwell, 384 U.S. 333 (1966) (an example of highly prejudicial media behavior during trial); Rideau v. Louisiana, 373 U.S. 723 (1963) (prejudicial pretrial publicity resulting from televising defendant's confession).

[150] *See, e.g.*, People v. McCrary, 190 Colo. 538, 545, 549 P.2d 1320, 1326 (1976) (. . . "only when the probability is so ubiquitous and vituperative that jurors in a community could not ignore its influence is a change of venue required before voir dire examination"); People v. Parker, 60 N.Y.2d 714, 456 N.E.2d 811, 468 N.Y.S.2d 870 (1983); State *ex rel.* Dayton Newspapers, Inc. v. Phillips, 46 Ohio St. 2d 457, 351 N.E.2d 127 (1976) (holding a motion for a change of venue is premature until it has been shown that a fair trial cannot be had).

[151] Hickson v. State, 707 So. 2d 536 (Miss. 1997) (defendant's conviction reversed in sexual battery case due to failure to change venue). The *Hickson* court held:

> It is, therefore, this Court's conclusion that the trial court abused its discretion in not changing venue in this case as the record evidence indicates that the Jones County community was exposed to pretrial media publicity that was of such a character and content that Hickson could not have received a fair and impartial trial, evidenced in part by the improper question posed by a juror during jury deliberations about another charge against Hickson. Thus, we reverse and remand this matter for a new trial.

707 So. 2d at 544.

[152] *See* Mallott v. State, 608 P.2d 737, 748 (Alaska 1980):

> [T]he voir dire process is not an infallible Geiger counter of juror prejudice, and to rely excessively on its efficacy in uncovering "actual prejudice" places an unrealistic burden on a defendant. Where there has been intensive pretrial publicity, and a substantial number of venire persons appear to have been prejudiced by the publicity, the

Establishing the inability to obtain a fair and impartial jury and the basis of a change of venue motion requires that the jury selection process be stenographically transcribed. Otherwise, a court may not be able to review the propriety of the change of venue motion.[153]

Some courts have found situations where a change of venue motion may be granted before voir dire.[154] For example, the broadcasting of a defendant reenacting the commission of a crime in the presence of law enforcement officials with commentary provided by a reporter is the type of extraordinary factor to justify the granting of a change of venue motion before jury selection.[155]

The exception to having to establish prejudice through voir dire can be summarized as those situations in which the pretrial prejudice can be presumed because (1) the publicity has been sensational, inflammatory, or biased toward conviction "rather than factual and objective"; (2) the publicity discloses a defendant's confession, admission, prior criminal record, or reenactment of the crime; (3) when the publicity has law enforcement as its authoritative source; and (4) when any of these areas of publicity is close in time to the commencement of trial and there has been a brief cooling-off period.[156]

Jurisdictions vary as to the standard of proof required to establish the motion for change of venue. Some courts call it a heavy burden to prove the existence

---

probability that similar prejudices are shared by, but have not been extracted from, impaneled jurors cannot be ignored. We therefore adopt the A.B.A. proposal that a motion for change of venue or continuance shall be granted whenever it is determined that, because of the dissemination of potentially prejudicial material, there is a substantial likelihood that, in the absence of such relief, a fair trial by an impartial jury cannot be had . . . . A showing of actual prejudice shall not be required. (citing ABA STANDARDS RELATING TO THE ADMINISTRATION OF CRIMINAL JUSTICE, FAIR TRIAL AND FREE PRESS, § 8-3.3(c) (1968)).

[153] *See, e.g.*, People v. Parker, 60 N.Y.2d 714, 456 N.E.2d 811, 468 N.Y.S.2d 870 (1983).

[154] People v. Porco, 30 A.D.3d 543, 816 N.Y.S.2d 361 (2006) (finding trial jury selection "may not always successfully root out prejudice"); People v. Boudin, 90 A.D.2d 253, 457 N.Y.S.2d 302 (1982) (citing unabated emotional and prejudicial news coverage of defendant's trial and results of a professional poll of bias in community as basis for granting defendant's change of venue motion before voir dire). *But see* People v. Boudin, 95 A.D.2d 463, 467 N.Y.S.2d 261 (1983) (refusing a second pre-voir dire change of venue motion in the same case because of differences in the circumstances surrounding the publicity in the second county and community reactions, but then the appellate court granted the pretrial venue change to a third county because of publicity when a co-defendant was convicted on the same charges in the second county); People v. Boudin, 97 A.D.2d 84, 469 N.Y.S.2d 89 (1983).

[155] People v. Luedecke, 22 A.D.2d 636, 258 N.Y.S.2d 115 (1965) (noting the similarity with the issues presented in Rideau v. Louisiana, 373 U.S. 723 (1963), wherein defendant's confession was widely broadcast and the U.S. Supreme Court cited this as inherently prejudicial pretrial publicity).

[156] Commonwealth v. Tedford, 523 Pa. 305, 323, 567 A.2d 610, 619 (1989). *See also* Berghahn v. State, 696 S.W.2d 943, 952 (Tex. Crim. App. 1985) (denying change of venue motion where news reporting was "accurate, informative, and objective").

of prejudicial publicity or to get a change of venue.[157] Some courts require showing a substantial likelihood that in the absence of a change of motion, a fair trial by an impartial jury cannot be had.[158] Some states require only a reasonable likelihood that a trial cannot be had in the original county[159] or require only reasonable grounds[160] or reasonable cause,[161] while others require a "will probably result" standard[162] or "apparent probability"[163] whereby the defendant must show pretrial publicity has so saturated the community to have a probable impact on the prospective jurors.

A change of venue in a sexual assault trial of an 11-year-old girl was granted when the pretrial atmosphere had been permeated with statements by law enforcement officials and a prosecutor that "he picked the wrong little girl," which the court construed as an opinion as to the guilt of the defendant, and that the 11-year-old's statement sounded like it was written by a well-educated 29-year-old, and that it was the best statement he had obtained from a rape victim in five years. "Given the problems of credibility associated with a testimony of youthful witnesses, such a comment by the county attorney could only serve to enhance the credibility" of the victim.[164] The court also noted that statements by the prosecutor were outside the scope of the ethical guidelines for trial publicity by attorneys. The motion for a change of venue included letters to the editor of a local newspaper as well as articles detailing the campaign against the judge who had set bail for the defendant and documentation of numerous death threats against the defendant.[165] Change of venue has also been granted where there existed a relationship between many of the prospective jurors and one or more of the parties or witnesses in a case together with prejudicial pretrial publicity.[166]

The results of a professional polling organization can be used to support a change of venue motion to help establish "widespread knowledge and . . . preconceived opinion" about a case.[167] This data is especially persuasive where

[157] Nethery v. State, 692 S.W.2d 686 (Tex. Crim. App. 1985), cert. denied, 474 U.S. 1110 (1986).

[158] Oxereok v. State, 611 P.2d 913, 918 (Alaska 1980).

[159] People v. Coleman, 48 Cal. 3d 112, 768 P.2d 32, 255 Cal. Rptr. 813 (1989).

[160] State v. Link, 194 Mont. 556, 559, 640 P.2d 366, 368 (1981).

[161] N.Y. Crim. Proc. Law § 230.20(2). (Motion of people or defendant to change venue requires "reasonable cause to believe that a fair and impartial trial cannot be had" in county.).

[162] State v. Smith, 123 Ariz. 231, 236, 599 P.2d 187, 192 (1979), cert. denied, 502 U.S. 837 (1991). See also Williams v. State, 489 So. 2d 4, 6 (Ala. Crim. App. 1986); State v. Rice, 120 Wash. 2d 549, 556, 844 P.2d 416, 419 (1993).

[163] State v. Laureano, 101 Wash. 2d 745, 756, 682 P.2d 889 (1984).

[164] State ex rel. Coburn v. Bennett, 202 Mont. 20, 30, 655 P.2d 502, 507 (1992).

[165] Id.

[166] Oxereok, 611 P.2d at 918.

[167] People v. Boss, 261 A.D.2d 1, 6, 701 N.Y.S.2d 342, 346 (1999) (appeals court granted change of venue motion to four police officers accused of murder, relying on poll conducted by defendant's

there is pretrial publicity of a co-defendant's confession implicating the defendant that is inadmissible at trial, and the responses of prospective jurors reflect extensive knowledge of the case.[168] But one court noted that a survey reflecting bias by less than one-half the jury pool does not warrant a change of venue.[169] In some situations, failing to controvert factual allegations in a motion for change of venue may require granting the motion.[170]

§ 2.17　Overview of jury issues concerning pretrial publicity and publicity during trial.

Appellate courts view jury selection as a means of identifying the nature and extent of pretrial publicity as well as a means of effectively neutralizing the effects of prejudicial publicity. There are many techniques that can be used to minimize or eliminate the effect on the jury of pretrial publicity or publicity during trial. The choice of technique will depend on the nature of the problem. The trial court's failure to take corrective action will likely lead to critical appellate review. Voir dire questions dealing with pretrial publicity are set forth in Chapter 5 and in the Juror Questionnaire in Appendix J.

§ 2.18　Motion for additional peremptory challenges.

A tool available for dealing with pretrial publicity is to request the court to provide additional peremptory challenges. This motion can be made before trial, and it can also be made when, during the course of jury selection, it appears that a high percentage of jurors have been exposed to pretrial publicity concerning the case.

A request for additional peremptory challenges can also be based on the sensitive or emotional nature of the sexual assault charges. The Supreme Court of the United States has recognized that the purpose of the peremptory challenge

---

attorneys close in time to projected trial date, which court found demonstrated that "jurors would be under enormous pressure to reach the verdict demanded by public opinion"); People v. Brensic, 136 A.D.2d 169, 526 N.Y.S.2d 968 (1988).

[168] *Id.*

[169] Thorne v. Grubman, 21 A.D.3d 254, 799 N.Y.S.2d 500 (2005).

[170] Taylor v. State, 93 S.W.3d 487, 495–98 (Tex. Ct. App. 2002) (Defendant was a local school teacher charged with possession of child pornography. Appeals court recognized that such a prosecution in a rural community "raises substantial problems that are not present in a large, metropolitan area with a large population and the concomitantly larger and more diverse (and uninformed) jury pool." Court overturned defendant's conviction in part due to trial court's denial of motion for change of venue, which prosecution did not factually dispute.):

> The presentation of an application for change of venue, properly verified, makes it incumbent upon the trial judge to change the venue, unless the application is controverted in the manner prescribed by statute, or unless the controverting affidavit is waived by the accused, and evidence heard justifying the denial of the motion.

93 S.W.3d at 496.

is to allow an attorney to detect possible bias through questions and observations of a potential juror and to remove potentially biased jurors without the fear of incurring a juror's hostility through repeated questioning.[171]

The American Bar Association's Fair Trial Standards provides: "Whenever there is a substantial likelihood that, due to substantial publicity, the regularly allotted number of peremptory challenges is inadequate, the court shall permit additional challenges to the extent necessary for the impaneling of an impartial jury."[172] Several courts have recognized the need to grant a defendant additional peremptory challenges to overcome potentially prejudicial publicity.[173] It is important that a record be made of the reasons the party seeks additional peremptory challenges to allow for appellate review.[174] Without exhausting all his peremptory challenges, a defendant may have no basis for a motion for additional peremptory challenges.[175]

§ 2.19 Sequestered voir dire.

Sequestered voir dire permits an attorney to ask questions of a potential juror without exposing the juror's answers to the entire venire and contaminating potential jurors with the response of one juror. Sequestered voir dire is generally held in the judge's chambers. Sometimes a juror may be asked to explain or respond to the questions at the bench outside the presence of other jurors. Sequestered voir dire is unlikely to be an acceptable procedure for the entire voir dire. More likely, it is requested and granted when there are issues pertaining to trial publicity or issues involving personal questions as to whether jurors have been victims or potential victims of abuse, involved in abusive relationships, or involved in litigation pertaining to abuse. For example, the question of whether a potential juror "will remember if his or her family had been subjected to abuse or whether as an adult or as a child they have had close friends who were abused" is not a question that can be expected to be answered publicly with a full and candid response.

The Supreme Court of the United States, in *Press Enterprise Co. v. Superior Court*, held that the guarantee of open, public proceedings in criminal trials does apply to voir dire proceedings, and that a trial court cannot constitutionally close to the press and public the voir dire process without specific findings that an open jury selection process threatened the right of a defendant to a fair trial or

---

[171] Swain v. Alabama, 380 U.S. 202, 219–20 (1965).

[172] ABA STANDARDS RELATING TO THE ADMINISTRATION OF CRIMINAL JUSTICE, FAIR TRIAL AND FREE PRESS, § 8-3.5(c) (2d ed. 1980).

[173] United States v. Kline, 221 F. Supp. 776 (D. Minn. 1963); Straight v. State, 397 So. 2d 903, 906 (Fla.), *cert. denied*, 454 U.S. 1022 (1981).

[174] *Kline*, 221 F. Supp. at 784.

[175] State v. Root, 95 Wash. App. 333, 975 P.2d 1052, *review granted in part*, 139 Wash. 2d 1001, 989 P.2d 1139 (1999).

the right to privacy of a prospective juror without considering alternatives to closure to protect those interests.[176] The Court did note that a prospective juror might wish to inform the parties that she or a member of her family had been raped and declined to prosecute, and that the embarrassment or emotional trauma from disclosing the incident and the privacy interest of such an individual should be balanced against the needs for openness in the jury selection process.[177] Jurors with privacy concerns can request the opportunity to discuss the matter *in camera* with all parties present and on the record. The Court suggested that a trial judge inform the jury panel of the general nature of the sensitive questions first and then allow those who feel that the matter should be discussed privately do so *in camera*.[178] The affirmative request by the juror helps the trial judge to know that there is in fact a valid reason for believing that the disclosure would infringe upon "a significant interest in privacy" of the potential juror. It is important that the juror should request the *in camera* questioning rather than for the court to close a portion of the voir dire proceeding in anticipation of privacy concerns. Even then, the request for closure should only be for matters "sufficiently sensitive to justify the extraordinary measure of a closed proceeding."[179] This approach has been suggested as the proper one with individuals with past experiences involving abuse.[180] Generally, a trial court has discretion in deciding whether to permit individual voir dire.[181]

One court has stated "that in cases tried hereafter involving sexual offenses against minors, on request, the judge must interrogate individually each prospective juror as to whether the juror has been a victim of a childhood sexual offense."[182] Other courts have found no error in failing to conduct individual voir dire of jurors in sexual assault cases.[183]

---

[176] Press-Enterprise Co. v. Superior Court, 464 U.S. 501 (1984). *See generally* Susan L. Thomas, Annotation, *Exclusion of Public and Media in Voir Dire Examination of Prospective Jurors in State Criminal Case,* 16 A.L.R.5th 152 (1993).

[177] *Press-Enterprise Co.,* 464 U.S. at 512.

[178] *Id.*

[179] *In re* Dallas Morning News Co., 916 F.2d 205 (5th Cir. 1990).

[180] Providence Journal Co. v. Superior Court, 593 A.2d 446 (R.I. 1991).

[181] People v. Britz, 185 Ill. App. 3d 191, 200, 541 N.E.2d 505, 511 (1989), *appeal denied,* 548 N.E.2d 1072, 139 Ill. Dec. 516 (1990) (holding that trial court may, in their discretion, conduct individual voir dire but it is not required).

[182] Commonwealth v. Flebotte, 417 Mass. 348, 353, 630 N.E.2d 265, 268 (1994). *See also* Commonwealth v. Holloway, 44 Mass. App. Ct. 469, 691 N.E.2d 985 (1998) (reversing defendant's conviction because trial court failed to satisfy "the unequivocal requirement of *Flebotte* to examine each juror individually on the issue of sexual assault as requested by the defendant." *Id.* at 473, 691 N.E.2d at 988.).

[183] Geiger v. State, 258 Ga. App. 57, 573 S.E.2d 85 (2002), *cert. denied,* 2003 Ga. LEXIS 154 (Feb. 10, 2003) (Defendant claimed he needed to ask each juror in private what he or she thought about nudism or nudist camps, because jurors may not discuss their feelings in front of a group). The court held:

A party may determine that a juror's answers to questions concerning prior experiences involving abuse may be prejudicial to the rest of the jury panel. [184] Having jurors discuss what they have heard or read in terms of pretrial publicity

> Although a defendant has a right to individualized responses from each member of the panel, he is not entitled to question each juror individually. The granting of sequestered voir dire is within the discretion of the trial court, and a showing of prejudice from denial is necessary to show an abuse of discretion. While the trial court denied Geiger's request to have sequestered individual voir dire before addressing his questions to the entire panel, the court did permit Geiger to individually examine each juror if he believed that additional questions were necessary. Geiger has not shown that any prejudice resulted from the denial of his request.

Id. at 59, 573 S.E.2d at 89; Lewis v. State, 726 N.E.2d 836 (Ind. Ct. App. 2000). In *Lewis*, the defendant's request for a questionnaire about the juror's victimization or relationship with someone who may have been abused and *in camera* voir dire of those who responded affirmatively was denied by the trial court. The appellate court upheld the trial court's denial of the defendant's request and decision to individually question about these areas:

> Each of the questions posed by Lewis were undoubtedly personal in nature. However, personal and sensitive questions are frequently asked during voir dire, and in the case of sex crimes, it would seem that these types of questions would be the rule and not the exception. As Lewis has not shown that the circumstances of his case were highly unusual, we cannot conclude that the trial court abused its discretion by denying Lewis's request for a special voir dire procedure.

Id. at 844–45. State v. Sexton, 256 Kan. 344, 886 P.2d 811 (1994) (holding in rape-murder prosecution involving bondage that individual voir dire concerning jurors' knowledge and attitudes toward sexual bondage was not prejudicial given the apparent ability of jurors to openly discuss the subject); Commonwealth v. Fruchtman, 418 Mass. 8, 633 N.E.2d 369, *cert. denied*, 513 U.S. 951 (1994) (holding that the trial judge was not obliged to provide the defendant with individual voir dire on the questions as to whether any of the prospective jurors had been the victim of a crime or whether the nature of the charges would prevent any of the jurors from being indifferent, when the defendant had an adequate factual basis upon which to formulate a challenge, such as information contained in a juror questionnaire); Eakes v. State, 665 So. 2d 852, 864 (Miss. 1995) (holding that trial court committed no error in denying sequestered voir dire of the venire due to the intimate nature of the questions asked regarding whether any member of the venire had been either victim or perpetrator of sexual abuse; trial judge agreed to individual voir dire if a juror answered in the affirmative to general questions of sensitive nature); State v. Gomes, 690 A.2d 310 (R.I. 1997) (trial judge questioned a group of jurors "whether, either on account of the nature of the charges or a personal experience involving sexual molestation, anyone would be unable to sit and listen to the evidence and render a fair and impartial verdict in the case." Appellate court held that failure to ask these questions in private did not violate defendant's rights nor was there any showing that potential jurors would fail to answer questions truthfully about sexual assault when questioned in a group. Court held: "Moreover, we are not persuaded that individual questioning would have improved on the method employed. Potential jurors were asked as a group a two-part question: did either the subject matter of or personal experience with sexual molestation make it impossible for them to be impartial? Combining these questions, the trial justice ensured that potential jurors need not associate themselves with an upsetting or embarrassing experience in order to be excused from the panel. Asking each juror more pointed questions in private might have actually increased each juror's discomfort over that which they might have encountered under the expedient device utilized by the trial justice.").

[184] *See Gomes, infra.*

during jury selection can be prejudicial to those jurors who either have not seen or heard the same news stories or may have forgotten about them. In this regard, it is important that the jury selection process itself not become a potential source of prejudice, and that the court allow the issue of pretrial publicity to be discussed by a potential juror *in camera* and at the same time allow a defense counsel the opportunity to "explore thoroughly what information each potential juror had previously acquired about the case as well as any preconceived opinions or attitudes about the case or defendant."[185] There is no question that counsel must be concerned about contaminating a jury panel by discussions of media coverage of a trial. This is the type of circumstance that can justify courtroom closure.[186] Such a request must be viewed in the context of the nature of the publicity surrounding the case, since routine, unemotional, and factual reporting is less likely to create a significant risk of prejudice to the defendant. It is not enough that a defendant merely claim a risk of potential prejudice in having jurors discuss pretrial publicity; the risk must be real or significant.[187]

Another reason to request sequestered voir dire is where race or racial prejudices may be involved. The Supreme Court of the United States has recognized that racial considerations in cases of violent crimes can demand expanded voir dire.[188] Racial issues can and do exist in sexual assault trials. When a racial issue exists, or when jury selection introduces racial considerations into the case, it is "incumbent upon the trial court to examine individually the remainder of the juror pool to reveal any bias a juror may harbor."[189] However, the Pennsylvania Supreme Court has noted in a rape case that the mere fact that the defendant and victim were of different races does not automatically trigger sequestered voir dire.[190] Another court has stated that in interracial rape cases, jurors should "be individually questioned."[191]

The Supreme Court of the United States has held that the defendant's right to a fair trial and due process rights do not mandate sequestered voir dire when

---

[185] People v. Pepper, 59 N.Y.2d 353, 452 N.E.2d 1178, 465 N.Y.S.2d 850 (1983), *aff'g* 89 A.D.2d 714, 453 N.Y.S.2d 868 (1982) (discussing issues of pretrial publicity and various steps taken by the trial court to deal with it and juror feelings and opinions involving the trial of a prominent auto dealer charged with child sexual abuse).

[186] State *ex rel.* La Crosse Tribune v. Circuit Court for La Crosse County, 115 Wis. 2d 220, 340 N.W.2d 460 (1983).

[187] Nichols v. Greeley, 1991 U.S. App. LEXIS 29983 (Dec. 10, 1991). ("This disposition is not appropriate for publication and may not be cited to or by the courts of this circuit except as provided by the 9th Cir. R. 36-3.").

[188] Rosales-Lopez v. United States, 451 U.S. 182 (1981).

[189] Commonwealth v. Glaspy, 532 Pa. 572, 579, 616 A.2d 1359, 1372 (1992) (reversing defendant's conviction for failing to conduct sequestered voir dire). *See also* Commonwealth v. Pearce, 427 Mass. 642, 649, 695 N.E.2d 1059, 1065 (1998) (noting in sexual assault case that individual voir dire on case was unnecessary because crime was not clearly interracial).

[190] *Id.*

[191] Commonwealth v. Pearce, 43 Mass. App. Ct. 78, 84, 681 N.E.2d 296, 301 (1997), *superseded*, 427 Mass. 642, 695 N.E.2d 1059 (1998).

there has been substantial pretrial publicity.[192] The Court noted that the American Bar Association's Standards for Criminal Justice require the individual interrogation of each juror with respect to what the prospective juror has read and heard about the case, "[i]f there is a substantial possibility that individual jurors will be ineligible to serve because of exposure to potentially prejudicial material," but that requirement is not constitutionally mandated.[193] Nonetheless, the cumulative effect of failing to conduct sequestered voir dire and inadequate questioning of jurors on the content of pretrial publicity can result in a reversal of a defendant's conviction.[194]

§ 2.20   Exclusion of public or members of public or witnesses from portions of voir dire.

During the jury selection process may the courtroom be closed for reasons other than those pertaining to the discussion of sensitive issues or pretrial publicity? For example, in a child sexual abuse prosecution a court sought to exclude a defendant's ten-year-old son from the courtroom during the jury selection process, even though the defendant's attorney said that the child's presence may be of some assistance to the defendant.[195] It was held that the nature of the case, the allegations, and the substance of the testimony were sufficient reasons for the trial court to rule that the presence of the child might be detrimental to his well-being.[196] But, in the absence of a showing of specific necessity, an attempt to restrict members of the defendant's family is likely to deny the defendant his right to a public trial.[197]

Another issue to consider is whether potential witnesses will be permitted to remain in the courtroom during the jury selection process. Generally, the exclusion of witnesses applies only to the conduct of the trial from the opening statement to the conclusion of proof and does not include the jury selection process or closing statements.

---

[192] Mu'Min v. Virginia, 500 U.S. 415 (1991).

[193] *Id.* at 430, *citing* AMERICAN BAR ASSOCIATION STANDARDS FOR CRIMINAL JUSTICE 8-3.5 (2d ed. 1980) ("The ABA Standards as indicated in our previous discussion of state and federal court decisions, have not commended themselves to a majority of the courts that have considered the question. The fact that a particular rule may be thought to be the 'better' view does not mean that it is incorporated into the Fourteenth Amendment.").

[194] People v. Tyburski, 445 Mich. 606, 518 N.W.2d 441 (1994).

[195] State v. Stafford, 213 Kan. 152, 515 P.2d 769, *modified and reh'g denied*, 213 Kan. 585, 518 P.2d 436 (1973).

[196] *Id.*

[197] Taylor v. State, 284 Ark. 103, 679 S.W.2d 797 (1984) (A court may not prevent the media from attending voir dire conducted in the judge's robing room without specific findings of necessity; generalized fears of prejudging the defendant or that jurors may be unwilling to express their opinions publicly are inadequate justifications); ABC, Inc. v. Steweart, 360 F.3d 90 (2d. Cir. 2004) (noting also that the problem is not cured by providing for the release of the transcripts of the *voir dire* examinations).

§ 2.21 Use of anonymous juries and restricting access to juror identity.

Counsel relies on information pertaining to the backgrounds of jurors, including information about their residence, occupation, and even their name. However, in response to increased press coverage of jury trials and an increased tendency of jurors to publicize their roles in jury trials, an effort has been made in some cases to conceal the identity of jurors. The reason is usually based on possible harassment from the press and protecting the juror's right of privacy. Other reasons include a concern for jury security and prevention of jury tampering.

When juror information is withheld from counsel, it raises the question as to whether a defendant is deprived of the intelligent exercise of peremptory challenges. Another issue is how the court instructs the jury as to the reasons for withholding their names and other identifying information. Failure to object to a court's instruction in this respect or the court's lack of instruction can waive a challenge on these grounds.

When genuinely called for and properly used, an anonymous jury does not infringe on a defendant's constitutional rights.[198] The view upholding the use of an anonymous jury requires that there be a strong reason to believe that the jury needs protection and the taking of reasonable precautions "to minimize the effect of an anonymous jury might have on the jurors' opinions of the defendants."[199] A court cannot seal the transcript of jury selection or withhold jurors' identity after jury selection is conducted in open court without sufficient justification.[200] The right of public access includes not only courtroom

---

[198] United States v. Darden, 70 F.3d 1507 (8th Cir. 1995), *cert. denied*, 517 U.S. 1149 (1996); United States v. Aulicino, 44 F.3d 1102, 1116 (2d Cir. 1995), *cert. denied*, 522 U.S. 1138 (1998) (holding three factors which are relevant in deciding the appropriateness of an anonymous jury: (1) the seriousness of the charges; (2) the potential threat of corruption of the judicial process; and (3) the potential for publicity); United States v. Wong, 40 F.3d 1347 (2d Cir. 1994), *cert. denied*, 516 U.S. 870 (1995) (finding that the government established an adequate basis for an anonymous jury by presenting proof that the defendants, part of a group known as the "Green Dragons," had previously interfered with the judicial process including the intimidation of witnesses); United States v. Paccione, 949 F.2d 1183, 1192 (2d Cir. 1991), *cert. denied sub nom.* Vulpis v. United States, 505 U.S. 1220 (1992); United States v. Vario, 943 F.2d 236, 239 (2d Cir. 1991), *cert. denied*, 502 U.S. 1036 (1992); United States v. Tutino, 883 F.2d 1125 (2d Cir. 1989), *cert. denied*, 493 U.S. 1081 (1990); United States v. Scarfo, 850 F.2d 1015 (3d Cir.), *cert. denied*, 488 U.S. 910 (1988); United States v. Persico, 832 F.2d 705 (2d Cir. 1987), *cert. denied*, 486 U.S. 1022 (1988) (publicity by the news media may be a factor in determining whether to select an anonymous jury); United States v. Thomas, 757 F.2d 1359 (2d Cir.), *cert. denied*, 474 U.S. 819 (1985); United States v. Barnes, 604 F.2d 121 (2d Cir. 1979), *cert. denied*, 446 U.S. 907 (1980); United States v. Muyet, 945 F. Supp. 586 (S.D.N.Y. 1996) (noting that trial court should voir dire jurors to ensure they are not biased against defendant as a result of anonymous jury procedure); State v. Flournoy, 535 N.W.2d 354 (Minn. 1995), *cert. denied*, 516 U.S. 1140 (1996), *aff'd*, 583 N.W.2d 564 (Minn. 1998).

[199] *Thomas*, 757 F.2d at 1363.

[200] United States v. Antar, 38 F.3d 1348 (3d Cir. 1994).

160

proceedings, but also transcripts of court proceedings such as jury selection and "a court may not deny access to a live proceeding solely on the grounds that a transcript may later be made available." [201]

Some state courts have not been as ready to embrace the concept of anonymous juries as have some of the federal circuit courts of appeals. [202] The main argument against the use of an anonymous jury is that it attacks the defendant's presumption of innocence. The Massachusetts Supreme Court has held that the use of an anonymous jury is likely to "trigger due process scrutiny because this practice is likely to taint the jurors' opinion of the defendant, thereby burdening the presumption of innocence." [203] The Massachusetts Court also held that a court must find an anonymous jury "truly necessary" and make written findings on the necessity. [204] Furthermore, if jurors become aware of their anonymity, "the judge must take affirmative measures to protect the due process rights of the accused." [205] This echoes the concern in federal cases that appropriate instructions be given a jury to avoid unfair or prejudicial speculation concerning the need for an anonymous jury.

New Jersey has also reversed a defendant's conviction for the use of an anonymous jury, citing not only the failure to establish adequate cause for the use of an anonymous jury, but also for the effect that an anonymous jury has on "meaningful voir dire." [206] As noted earlier, the court recognized "that information as to the identity and occupation of a prospective juror can lead counsel to request supplemental questions on voir dire as well as the exercise of challenges, peremptory or for cause." [207]

Another barrier to the use of an anonymous jury can be the language of the statutory provisions that establish the parameters of the jury selection process. In New York, "the court shall direct that the names of not less than twelve members of the panel be drawn and *called* as prescribed by the judiciary law." [208]

A federal appeals court holds that a court order prohibiting publication of jurors' names is not only a prior restraint on speech, but also an infringement on the freedom to public information obtained in open court. [209] The same court acknowledged there could be exceptional circumstances justifying restrictions on information acquired in open court, but did not define those circumstances. [210]

---

[201] *Id.* at 1360.

[202] *See generally* William D. Bremer, Annotation, *Propriety of Using Anonymous Juries in State Criminal Trials,* 60 A.L.R.5th 39 (1998).

[203] Commonwealth v. Angiulo, 415 Mass. 502, 527, 615 N.E.2d 155, 171 (1993).

[204] *Id.*

[205] *Id.*

[206] State v. Accetturo, 261 N.J. Super. 487, 492, 619 A.2d 272, 274 (1992).

[207] *Id.*

[208] N.Y. Crim. Proc. Law § 270.15 1-a. (Emphasis added.)

[209] United States v. Quattrone, 402 F.3d 304, 312 (2d Cir. 2005).

[210] *Id.* at 313.

A Michigan intermediate appeals court held the press has a qualified right of access to names and addresses of jurors after a verdict, but that a trial court has discretion to restrict the time and manner of disclosure and even refuse disclosure when there is a demonstrable concern for the safety of the jurors.[211] Any concerns for the jurors' safety should be set forth in the record for appellate review.[212] With respect to the identity of those called to jury duty but not selected as a trial juror, one California appeals court held "[m]embers of the venire who were not sworn as trial jurors are entitled to have their names kept confidential only upon a finding of a compelling interest against disclosure."[213]

By statute in New York, a court for good cause can restrict access to jurors' business or residential addresses by persons other than counsel for either party if the court determines "a likelihood of bribery, jury tampering or of physical injury or harassment."[214] Similarly, Delaware provides that "[t]he names of persons summoned for jury service shall be disclosed to the public and the contents of jury qualification forms completed by them shall be made available to the parties unless the Court determines that any or all of this information should be kept confidential or its use limited in whole or in part in any case or cases."[215] But several states hold that the news media does not necessarily enjoy a constitutional or common-law right to the names and addresses of jurors or to the questionnaire they fill out.[216] It may be significant that the voir dire is open to the public and the press is denied access only to the written questionnaire.[217]

§ 2.22   Gag orders and restraints on publishing of information by the news media.

Another avenue to control prejudicial publicity has been through the use of court orders to restrict the information that can be published by the news media.

---

[211] People v. Mitchell (*In re* Juror Names), 233 Mich. App. 604, 592 N.W.2d 798 (1999).

[212] 233 Mich. App. at 630, 592 N.W.2d at 809.

[213] Bellas v. Superior Court, 85 Cal. App. 4th 636, 639, 102 Cal. Rptr. 2d 380, 382 (2000). *See also* State v. Swart, 1992 Minn. App. LEXIS 1278 (Aug. 20, 1992) (*citing* Minnesota law, "access to records revealing the identities of jurors may be denied only in the interest of justice, 'upon a showing of' exceptional circumstances peculiar to the case.").

[214] N.Y. Crim. Proc. Law § 270.15 1-a.

[215] DEL. Code tit. 10 §4513

[216] Gannett Co. v. State, 571 A.2d 735 (Del. 1990); Newsday, Inc. v. Sise, 71 N.Y.2d 146, 518 N.E.2d 930, 524 N.Y.S.2d 35, *cert. denied*, 486 U.S. 1056 (1988); Commonwealth v. Long, 2005 Pa. Super. 119, 871 A.2d 1262, *appeal granted in part*, 884 A.2d 249 (Pa. 2005) (concluding that *First Amendment* gives a right of access to attend court proceedings; it does not compel a trial court to disclose the names and addresses of empanelled jurors). *But see*, State *ex. rel* Beacon Journal Publ'g Co. v. Bond, 98 Ohio St. 3d 146, 2002 Ohio 7117, 781 N.E.2d 180 (2002) (finding qualified right of access to list of names and addresses of empanelled jurors).

[217] Newsday, Inc. v. Goodman, 159 A.D.2d 667, 552 N.Y.S.2d 965 (1990) (upholding restriction of newspaper's access to a portion of juror questionnaires when voir dire was open to the public and court made findings that jurors' ability to serve without fear of intimidation or harassment was in jeopardy).

Any attempt to restrict information that can be reported by a newspaper, radio, or television station is likely to be met with the argument that it is a prior restraint which can rarely be justified.

In *Nebraska Press Association v. Stuart*,[218] the Supreme Court ruled on an order by a court that restricted the news media from reporting the accounts of confessions or admissions made by the accused to law enforcement officers or third parties or other facts "strongly implicative" of the accused. The Court noted that there is a heavy burden to meet in upholding any prior restraint on the news media, and that while the court had a legitimate concern for the effect of publicity on prospective jurors, the potential impact of such publicity was speculative in that the court made no findings that alternative protections were not available to protect the defendant's fair trial rights.[219]

The Supreme Court also noted that there were significant practical problems in using a prior restraint to effectively protect an accused's right, such as the limited territorial jurisdiction of the trial court issuing the restraining order, the difficulty in determining exactly what information will affect jury impartiality, and the problem of drafting an order that would effectively keep prejudicial information from jurors.[220]

As a general rule, a trial court cannot limit the reporting of what takes place in open court.[221]

Similarly, an order limiting the press from printing only matters that transpired in the courtroom and directing that they not print any information concerning the background of the defendant would be considered a prior restraint, absent specific findings on the record establishing that the drastic measures of such restrictions were justified.[222]

Attempts to control the news media from using certain pieces of information are also likely to fail. For example, a court order that the media was to refrain from using the words "sugar house rapist" in reporting on a trial would not be upheld.[223] In refusing to uphold such a prior restraint, the Utah Supreme Court noted that the expression may be "sensational and unsavory," but that the "epithet is still an instrument used to communicate information or ideas."[224] If prior

---

[218] 427 U.S. 539 (1976).

[219] *Id.* at 562–65.

[220] *Id.* at 566–68.

[221] *See, e.g.,* Oklahoma Publ'g Co. v. District Court, 430 U.S. 308, 310 (1977). *See also* § 2.1, notes 7 and 8.

[222] New York Times Co. v. Starkey, 51 A.D.2d 60, 380 N.Y.S.2d 239 (1976).

[223] KUTV, Inc. v. Conder, 668 P.2d 513, 525 (Utah 1983). *See also* Arkansas Gazette Co. v. Lofton, 269 Ark. 109, 598 S.W.2d 745 (1980) (holding that court could not forbid media from referring to a defendant as "Qua Paw Corner Rapist" in news stories published prior to the empanelling of a jury).

[224] *KUTV, Inc.,* 668 P.2d at 525.

restraint cannot be used to withhold information and ideas, neither can it be used to censor the vocabulary through which they are communicated.[225]

§ 2.23   Gag orders and restraint on communication of information by trial participants.

Rather than restrain the media in the reporting of information concerning trials, a court is more likely to restrict the parties involved in a criminal trial from commenting about a case or providing information. A court may restrict trial participants' comments on its own or on motion of either the prosecution or defense. Often the defense will object to a prosecution request to restrict commentary on the ground that the prosecution has already significantly influenced the public through its disclosures, either publicly or through leaks or other sources, and that a restriction on commentary denies the defense the opportunity to "level the playing field." Ironically, the same Supreme Court decision that recognizes the right to restrict pretrial statements by an attorney also recognizes the role of an attorney who is stopping "a wave" of potentially prejudiced publicity that may affect a defendant's reputation, or health, or potential trial jurors.[226] Courts may be loath to issue an order restricting comments to allow a party to issue prejudicial statements as a response to another party's prejudicial statements.

There is a significantly diminished constitutional barrier to overcome in a restraining order directed at trial participants as opposed to the press.[227] "When

---

[225] *Id.*

[226] Gentile v. State Bar of Nev., 501 U.S. 1030, 1043 (1991):

> An attorney's duties do not begin inside the courtroom door. He or she cannot ignore the practical implications of a legal proceeding for the client. Just as an attorney may recommend a plea bargain or civil settlement to avoid the adverse consequences of a possible loss after trial, so too an attorney may take reasonable steps to defend a client's reputation and reduce the adverse consequences of indictment, especially in the face of a prosecution deemed unjust or commenced with improper motives. A defense attorney may pursue lawful strategies to obtain dismissal of an indictment or reduction of charges, including an attempt to demonstrate in the court of public opinion that the client does not deserve to be tried.

[227] *In re* Application of Dow Jones & Co., 842 F.2d 603 (2d Cir. 1988). In this case, the Second Circuit Court of Appeals upheld the following order restricting the communications of trial participants:

> ORDERED, that the United States Attorney and the District Attorney for Bronx County, their representatives and agents, defendants SHALL NOT MAKE ANY extrajudicial statement concerning this case (1) to any person associated with a public communications media, or (2) that a reasonable person would expect to be communicated to a public communications media, except that nothing in the Order shall prohibit any individual from:
>
> (A) Stating, without elaboration or characterization—
>
>   (1) the general nature of an allegation or defense;
>
>   (2) information contained in the public record;

restricting parties, witnesses and attorneys from discussing a pending case, the test is whether there is a 'reasonable likelihood of prejudice' that a defendant will be prejudiced."[228] A defendant can also be prevented from conducting press interviews while an inmate pursuant to a correction facility's legitimate disciplinary regulations and institutional needs.[229]

Nonetheless, there must be a showing of necessity before restricting extrajudicial comments.[230]

Restrictions on comments by witnesses will be justified when there is a showing that when balancing the relative ineffectiveness of alternatives, there is a necessity of suppressing the speech of potential witnesses in order to insure a fair trial for the defendant.[231] In *Russell*, the court issued the following order:

> Any person who is a potential witness in this case, as defined in subparagraph (a) below, SHALL NOT make any extrajudicial statement that relates to, concerns, or discusses the testimony such potential witnesses may give in this case, *or* any of the parties or issues such potential witness expects or reasonably should expect to be involved in this case, *or* the events leading up to and culminating in the shooting incident at Everitt and Carver Streets in Greensboro, North Carolina, on November 3, 1979, *if* such statement is intended for dissemination by means of public communication.
>
> (a) A "potential witness" is a person who has been notified by the government or by defendants that he or she may be called to testify in this case, or any person who has actually testified in this case.
>
> (b) Potential witnesses SHALL NOT conduct any interviews with the print or electronic media during which such potential witness makes any statement, orally or in writing, that is proscribed by this paragraph of this Order.
>
> (c) An extrajudicial statement proscribed by this paragraph of this Order SHALL NOT be made by any potential witness if such potential witness *intends* such statement to be disseminated by means of public communication.

---

(3) the scheduling or result of any step in the proceedings; or

(B) Explaining, without characterization, the contents or substance of any motion or step in the proceedings, to the extent such motion or step is a matter of public record.

[228] *In re* Russell, 726 F.2d 1007, 1010 (4th Cir. 1984), *cert. denied*, Russell v. Flannery, 469 U.S. 837 (1984). *See also* Central S.C. Chapter, Soc'y of Prof'l Journalists, etc. v. Martin, 431 F. Supp. 1182 (D.S.C.), *aff'd*, 556 F.2d 706, 708 (4th Cir. 1977).

[229] Pell v. Procunier, 417 U.S. 817 (1974); Saxbe v. Washington Post Co., 417 U.S. 843 (1974).

[230] Lowinger v. Lowinger, 264 A.D.2d 763, 695 N.Y.S.2d 127, 128 (1999) ("The relief was not warranted under the circumstances presented. Orders restraining extrajudicial comments by the parties or their attorneys are not generally permitted unless there is a reasonable likelihood of the existence of serious threat to the right to a fair trial (*see*, Matter of National Broadcasting Co. v. Cooperman, 116 A.D.2d 287, 292 (1986); Sheppard v. Maxwell, 384 U.S. 333 (1966)). The defendant's moving papers did not satisfy this standard.").

[231] *In re* Russell, 726 F.2d 1007, 1010 (4th Cir. 1984), *cert. denied*, Russell v. Flannery, 469 U.S. 837 (1984).

> This includes any proscribed statement by a potential witness to any third party whom such potential witness authorizes, intends, or expects to disseminate such statement by means of public communication.

Trial courts may also attempt to control or restrict the communications of trial attorneys. Courts can use the ethical standards and guidelines for attorney conduct to issue an order restricting trial attorneys from commenting on cases in which they are involved. [232] One of the leading appellate decisions on this issue was the case of New York attorney Bruce Cutler concerning statements he made while representing John Gotti. [233] Among the statements that Cutler made that were found to violate the trial court's order were:

> The government will stop at nothing in their quest to convict Mr. Gotti . . . .

> They tell everyone and anyone that the key to open their cell door is giving false information against Mr. Gotti . . . . The tapes do not say what [the prosecutor] says they say, and the conversations that he put forth are totally and deliberately taken out of context by the government . . . . They [the prosecutors] claim they want a fair fight, but that's a lie . . . . They would like a rigged deck . . . . They are afraid of a fair and good fight . . . . [The prosecutors are] a sick and demented lot.

In response to Cutler's claim that the order was vague, the court noted that Cutler should have requested clarification or guidance from the court as to the acceptable parameters of the extrajudicial speech or he should have objected to the order by means of the appeals process rather than by testing it by making public statements. [234] The court found that the defendant's attorney knew that there was "a reasonable likelihood that such dissemination [would] interfere with a fair trial or otherwise prejudice the due administration of justice" and that he knew the statements would probably be publicized and seen, heard, and read by prospective jurors, and may have made them for this purpose, and that the attorney himself had made public admissions that he intentionally sought to influence "prospective venire men out there" prior to trial with statements that will "help my client." [235]

But the same court that upheld the contempt proceeding against Bruce Cutler has also noted that an order restricting comment by participants is invalid if too broad, such as an order barring "no more statements" that "have anything to do with this case" or that even "may have something to do with the case." [236] Such an order is invalid because the court did not consider less restrictive alternatives

---

[232] Use of a state disciplinary authority to discipline an attorney for comments made about a pending criminal indictment has been discussed earlier. *See* § 2.8.

[233] United States v. Cutler, 840 F. Supp. 959 (E.D.N.Y. 1994), *aff'd*, 58 F.3d 825 (2d Cir. 1995) (upholding contempt order against defense attorney discussed in text).

[234] *Id.*

[235] *Id.*

[236] United States v. Salameh, 992 F.2d 445 (2d Cir. 1993).

and discouraged the affected parties from the proffering of alternatives while failing to make a record in support of the blanket order.[237] This decision stresses the importance of a showing of necessity in any restriction on the flow of information from a trial or its participants.

A party may wish to seek an order from the court limiting comments or release of information by parties. The order restricting extrajudicial communications with the media by counsel and police in the Florida trial of William Kennedy Smith is set forth in Appendix B. That order sets forth specific findings in light of the requirements of court decisions requiring such findings. It also specifically delineates who and what is restricted. The order is narrowly tailored and bars only certain types of extrajudicial commentary. The news media is specifically exempted from the order. This order should be helpful in guiding parties to some of the issues that should be addressed in such an order.

§ 2.24   Restrictions on and access to information from court records.

Courts also may seek to restrict access to court records and filings in an attempt to prevent the flow of prejudicial publicity. This is another motion that can be made by counsel. Orders sealing documents, motions, or records in a criminal trial may be ordered only when there is a "substantial probability" that the defendant's right to a fair trial will be prejudiced by public access of records, there is a "substantial probability" that the sealing will prevent prejudice, and there are not reasonably less restrictive alternatives to the sealing. This is the standard for closure of pretrial proceedings, which has been adopted to the sealing of records during pretrial and trial proceedings.[238] This standard is higher than the reasonable likelihood standard required for restricting the comments of parties to a criminal trial. Thus, because there is a presumption that the public and press have a right of access to criminal proceedings and documents, it is improper for a court to restrict the release of pretrial detention documents and financial affidavits for court-appointed counsel where a defendant cannot show a substantial probability of irreparable damage to a defendant's right of a fair trial.[239] The American Bar Association Standards for criminal justice suggest that court documents and exhibits should be available to the public.[240]

---

[237] *Id.* at 447.

[238] Press-Enterprise Co. v. Superior Court, 478 U.S. 1, 12–13 (1986) (Press Enterprise II). *See also* Washington Post v. Robinson, 935 F.2d 282, 289–90 (D.C. Cir. 1991); *In re* State-Record Co., 917 F.2d 124 (4th Cir. 1990).

[239] Seattle Times Co. v. United States Dist. Court for W. Dist., 845 F.2d 1513 (9th Cir. 1988).

[240] AMERICAN BAR ASSOCIATION STANDARDS FOR CRIMINAL JUSTICE 8-3.2:

Public Access to Judicial Proceedings and Related Documents and Exhibits. (a) In any criminal case, all judicial proceedings and related documents and exhibits, and any record made thereof, not otherwise required to remain confidential, should be accessible to the public, except as provided in section (b). (b)(1) A court may issue

In a rape trial, release of the DNA results from court records linking the defendant with semen found on the victim may be prejudicial, but it is insufficient to assert the possibility of prejudice. The "substantial probability" of prejudice must be established. The argument of prejudice can easily be undercut by a previously open hearing regarding the admissibility of the DNA identification evidence. [241]

Search warrant applications are of interest to the media. Before or after trial, they confirm not only factual assertions, but also opinions and conclusions often inadmissible at trial, and highly speculative. Sealed search warrant applications, unless part of testimony and exhibits admitted in open court, may remain sealed to insure a defendant's right to a fair trial, particularly where the crime involves a publicized rape and murder of a child. [242]

Another issue is the availability of court documents to the press both before and during trial. There is a common-law right to inspect and copy judicial records, and this right extends to those records that are not in written form, such as audio and video tapes. [243] The tradition of access to court records is also tempered by the supervisory power of the court over its own records and files, and access to records can be denied when there is a basis to believe that the disclosure of the records could be a vehicle for "improper purposes," such as promoting "public scandal" in a divorce case, or when the court records may be reservoirs of "libelist statements for press consumption" or sources of "business information that might harm a litigant's competitive standing." [244]

Even though a court has discretion as to whether to release records, it is generally an abuse of such discretion to deny access unless there is a clear

---

a closure order to deny access to the public to specified portions of a judicial proceeding or related document or exhibit only after reasonable notice of and an opportunity to be heard on such proposed order has been provided to the parties and the public and the court thereafter enters findings that: (A) unrestricted access would pose a substantial probability of harm to the fairness of the trial or other overriding interest which substantially outweighs the defendant's right to a public trial; (B) the proposed order will effectively prevent the aforesaid harm; and (C) there is no less restrictive alternative reasonably available to prevent the aforesaid harm . . . .

[241] People v. Burton, 189 A.D.2d 532, 536–37, 597 N.Y.S.2d 488, 492 (1993) ("There is no demonstration whatsoever in County Court's decision that publication of the DNA reports that are in the court file will prejudice defendant more than the disclosure of the same materials and information during the hearing to be held in closer proximity to the trial."); People v. Sullivan, 168 Misc. 2d 803, 640 N.Y.S.2d 714 (1996) (holding that reporter may examine alleged statements of defendant filed with prosecution papers since defendant did not demonstrate such access would jeopardize her right to a fair trial).

[242] Westerfield v. Superior Court, 98 Cal. App. 4th 145, 119 Cal. Rptr. 2d 588 (2002) (noting that public does not have right to pretrial disclosure of questionable evidence).

[243] See United States v. Myers, 635 F.2d 942, 949–50 (2d Cir. 1980); United States v. Mitchell, 551 F.2d 1252, 1258 (D.C. Cir. 1976), rev'd on other grounds sub nom. Nixon v. Warner Communications, Inc., 435 U.S. 589 (1978).

[244] Nixon, 435 U.S. at 598 (1978).

showing that justice requires sealing of the records after considering all relevant facts and circumstances, weighing the interests of all parties, and balancing this with the public interest and duty of open courts. Video and audio tapes of a defendant's conduct are available to the public, including during a trial, since the alleged risk of possible prejudice at a hypothetical second trial is an insufficient reason to deny the access, although innocent third persons mentioned on the tapes may be entitled to file objections to the release of those portions on the tape that might affect them.[245] Documents and evidence in tape recordings can also be released even when the tapes involve defendants who are awaiting trial.[246]

The prosecution, defense, or both, may wish to seal the plea minutes of a potential witness in a forthcoming trial. A sealing of plea minutes will require the showing of a compelling interest to justify sealing the plea agreement and findings made by the court in support of the decision. Furthermore, the government must file a written motion to seal the plea agreement, notice of which must be entered in the public docket, and the trial court must allow interested persons an opportunity to be heard before ruling on the motion and entering the sealing order.[247] The sealing order must be placed on the docket, and the government may seek leave of the court to file under seal its written motion to seal pending disposition of the motion, provided it is entered on the docket with notice to interested individuals.[248] There is some authority that when an individual's safety or life is at risk, there may be a delay in the docketing of sealing motions.[249] There is also authority for the sealing of plea minutes that may involve "matters occurring before a grand jury."[250]

Another obstacle in sealing plea minutes and court records is the argument that sealing is not proper if most of the information is already public knowledge or on the public record.[251] This argument is somewhat specious, since it allows prejudicial, improper, or unnecessary publicity to serve as a basis for permitting further disclosures that may affect the venire. The argument allows the flow of publicity based on unsanctioned disclosures from whatever source. Exactly what are the "proceedings" to which the media has access? Not every meeting of the parties is open to the press. Discussions concerning plea offers, or scheduling,

---

[245] *In re* Application of Nat'l Broad. Co., 653 F.2d 609 (D.C. Cir. 1981).

[246] United States v. Martin, 746 F.2d 964 (3d Cir. 1984).

[247] Washington Post v. Robinson, 935 F.2d 282, 289 (D.C. Cir. 1991).

[248] *Id.*

[249] United States v. Haller, 837 F.2d 84, 87 (2d Cir. 1988).

[250] *Id.* at 88.

[251] *See, e.g.,* CBS, Inc. v. United States Dist. Court for Cent. Dist., 765 F.2d 823, 825–26 (9th Cir. 1985).

or jury questionnaires are likely not available to the public, whereas plea minutes and hearings on a motion to quash are available to the public.[252]

When sexual assault trials are involved, the interest of third parties or innocent individuals is an important factor to consider in the release of the statements and documents.[253] The rights of third parties are particularly important in evaluating the release of information in sexual assault trials. Certain documents may expose a victim to humiliation or degradation, and the release of court records may also involve the rights of third parties. A court is more likely to find justification denying the release of photographs and videotape involving a recorded rape or act of abuse because of the effect upon a victim and public sensibilities.[254]

Nonetheless, there are limits to the access to information contained in government records. For example, neither reporters nor the public is entitled to examine photocopied police reports in an active, ongoing criminal prosecution because of countervailing interest of due process, confidentiality, and privacy.[255] Also, the reports of probation officers used by a court in setting bail or determining a sentence are not public, even when the bail or sentencing proceeding is a matter of public record.[256]

§ 2.25   Jury admonitions and instructions to negate effects of prejudicial publicity.

Another tool available to deal with the effects of prejudicial publicity, particularly publicity occurring during trial, is to ensure that the court provides adequate instructions to the jury concerning the publicity. The publicity may deal with the trial itself or the subject matter of the trial. A crucial assumption is that jurors will follow a court's admonitions.[257] This assumption is often cited by

---

[252] Herald Co. v. Burke, 261 A.D.2d 92, 699 N.Y.S.2d 247 (1999) (Newspaper entitled to transcript of "proceedings" up to time court refused to accept guilty plea, as well as arguments on disqualification of district attorney and hearing on motion to quash a subpoena issued to social worker. Newspaper not entitled to discussions concerning trial schedule and questionnaires and plea offers).

[253] Commonwealth v. Tedford, 523 Pa. 305, 323, 567 A.2d 610, 619 (1989).

[254] See, e.g., In re Application of KSTP Television, 504 F. Supp. 360 (D. Minn. 1980) (court refused to release to television station color videotapes made by a defendant of his blindfolded victim on a blanket on the floor with her hands and feet bound as part of the kidnapping and rape; release of the tapes was opposed by the victim, the government, and the defendant).

[255] Cox Ariz. Publ'ns, Inc. v. Collins, 169 Ariz. 189, 201–02, 818 P.2d 174, 186–87 (1991).

[256] 18 U.S.C. § 3153(c)(1); FED. R. CRIM. P. 32(c)(3).

[257] Delli Paoli v. United States, 352 U.S. 232, 242 (1957) ("It is a basic premise of our jury system that the court states the law to the jury and that the jury applies that law to the facts as the jury finds them. Unless we proceed on the basis that the jury will follow the court's instructions where those instructions are clear and the circumstances are such that the jury can reasonably be expected to follow them, the jury system makes little sense. Based on faith that the jury will endeavor to follow the court's instructions, our system of jury trial has produced one of the most

courts in denying post-verdict relief in many areas, especially trial publicity. It also is one of the reasons that appellate courts will uphold a trial court's failure to undertake other remedial measures, such as sequestration.[258] There is little empirical data to support or rebut the assumption. Depending on circumstances, the admonition should be tailored to specific issues of publicity concerning the particular case and repeated with frequency depending on the prevalence of publicity. An example of a simple and general admonition is the following instruction:

> Further, members of the jury, the court orders and directs that you are not, under any circumstance, to read anything about this case in any newspaper, magazine, or in any other publication. You are not to watch or listen to TV news programs concerning this case, nor are you to listen to any radio broadcasts concerning the same.[259]

A standard admonition to merely disregard everything not heard in court may be insufficient to obviate problems caused by publicity occurring during the trial.[260] Thus, when specific reports of problems develop at trial, specific instructions are required. Failing to object to the content of the court's admonition or frequency of the admonition can be considered a waiver of the right to raise the issue on appeal.[261]

It is also helpful if jury instructions and admonitions in a highly-publicized trial are made even before questioning the jury panel members. For example, the following jury admonition concerning pretrial publicity, which was repeated every day during trial just prior to the evening recess, and usually prior to the noon recess, and at any time counsel requested the court to do so, was considered by the reviewing court to be sufficient to deal with the daily news reporting and inaccuracies in press coverage of the defendant's trial.

> Now, I think you can understand better the importance of that instruction and the need for you to follow it religiously if I tell you the reason for it. In a court of law, a person is found guilty or not guilty of a crime by a jury on the basis of the evidence that is presented in the courtroom, by documents that are presented and by the testimony of witnesses who take the stand.

---

valuable and practical mechanisms in human experience for dispensing substantial justice."); Johnson v. State, 666 So. 2d 784, 794 (Miss. 1995) (appellate court held that trial jurors would be presumed to follow judge's instructions concerning televised story concerning child sexual abuse trial). *But see* Parker v. Randolph, 442 U.S. 62, 70 (1979) (questioning whether jurors will or can always follow a judge's instructions and noting the limited value of a judge's instruction in some situations).

[258] United States v. De Peri, 778 F.2d 963, 972–73 (3d Cir. 1985), *cert. denied sub nom.* Pecic v. United States, 475 U.S. 1110 (1986).

[259] N.Y. Crim. Jury Instructions 3.38.

[260] Williams v. Griswald, 743 F.2d 1533, 1539 (11th Cir. 1984).

[261] United States v. Porcaro, 648 F.2d 753, 757 (1st Cir. 1981).

[The] point of it is that the things you hear in this room are regulated under court supervision, the things that you may properly hear that will not be prejudicial to these defendants. Of course, newspaper accounts and radio and television accounts sometimes are not always accurate and they may contain material which is not a correct reflection of what is actually going on in the courtroom. Sometimes newspaper accounts are headed by headlines which probably are not always reflective of the true story . . . .

After the 12 jurors and four alternates had been sworn, the Court said:

I wish to emphasize to you all a point which you have heard me talk about two or three times already today, and I can't emphasize it too much, and that is the importance of your not talking with anybody about this case at any time that you are serving as jurors — you are permitted to go home, of course, at night — or permit anybody to talk to you about the case; that you do not read any newspaper accounts about this trial or about this whole matter; listen to any radio programs about it or observe and listen to any television programs about it.

Now, I am afraid I'm going to have to repeat that admonition time and time again, so much so that you will maybe get tired of hearing it, but the fact that I do repeat it and will repeat it probably indicates its importance to you, importance far more reaching than you can maybe understand at this time.

So I enjoin you to be very particular about following that admonition. [262]

The admonition to avoid news stories about a specific case applies also to programs or articles on the *subject matter* of the trial. This has particular relevance to a sexual assault trial that receives repeated coverage. A judge should pay special attention to upcoming broadcasts and instruct the jury not to watch programs that concern sexual abuse. A judge's failure to instruct a jury not to watch "Something About Amelia," a television movie about child sexual abuse, was one of the reasons for reversing a defendant's conviction, because the movie "showed a positive result from a determination that there had been sexual abuse of a child by a father" similar to the facts of the case. [263]

The court explained its concern over the court's lack of admonitions as follows:

The vice of allowing the jurors to see the show was the possibility that one or more of them may have thought the outcome could have been similar to that in the movie if defendant was convicted. We, of course, have no way of knowing whether the show in fact had any impact on the verdict but we do know that the jurors were not sequestered during the trial and thus had the opportunity to see the movie. We are satisfied that the judge abused his discretion in refusing to instruct the jury not to watch the movie. The small

---

[262] United States v. Kline, 221 F. Supp. 776, 785 (D. Minn. 1963).

[263] State v. R.W., 200 N.J. Super. 560, 571, 491 A.2d 1304, 1310 (1985), *modified*, 104 N.J. 14, 514 A.2d 1287 (1986).

imposition on the jurors of such an instruction pales in significance to the outcome of this case on defendant. We emphasize that ordinarily we would not reach this conclusion but the unusual circumstances of this case compel it.[264]

§ 2.26 Access to testimony and documents of representatives of news media.

A party to a criminal case may wish to obtain information in the possession of news reporters. For example, sometimes television stations or news photographers will record images of crime scenes that will provide information not available through law enforcement records or photos. Also, sometimes information contained in news stories and articles can be used to support a motion for change of venue or continuance, or even support a charge of prosecutorial misconduct. Reporters also conduct interviews of witnesses, including police officers, whose statements can be impeachment material or can lead to other witnesses.

A subpoena for the production of photographs or records of a news reporter is likely to be challenged. There is the inevitable challenge based on the first amendment to any subpoena for notes of a news reporter. The Supreme Court of the United States has provided only vague assistance in determining when such a subpoena is proper. In a sharply divided opinion, it has held that the first amendment does not offer total protection from a subpoena and that a reporter can be required to appear or testify as to information obtained, provided the documents or testimony are necessary.[265] The problem has been defining what is necessary. Generally, reporters have the same obligation to appear before a grand jury and answer questions as other citizens.[266] Generally, a reporter will have to testify about events personally witnessed. For example, a newspaper photographer who witnesses criminal activity does not have a qualified privilege to refuse to testify and disclose unpublished photographs.[267] Courts have recognized a limited news-gathering privilege within the penumbra of the first amendment.[268] Protection for news gatherers and reporters has been afforded

---

[264] *Id.* at 571–72, 491 A.2d at 1310.

[265] Branzburg v. Hayes, 408 U.S. 665 (1972). *See also* New York Times Co. v. Jascalevich, 439 U.S. 1317, 1322 (1978) ("There is no present authority in this Court either that newsmen are constitutionally privileged to withhold duly subpoenaed documents material to the prosecution or defense of a criminal case or that a defendant seeking the subpoena must show extraordinary circumstances before enforcement against newsmen will be had.").

[266] *Branzburg,* 408 U.S. at 685.

[267] State v. Turner, 550 N.W.2d 622, 628 (Minn. 1996) (noting that reporters do not have protection beyond the First Amendment).

[268] United States v. La Rouche Campaign, 841 F.2d 1176, 1182 (1st Cir. 1988); United States v. Burke, 700 F.2d 70, 77 (2d Cir. 1983), *cert. denied,* 464 U.S. 816 (1983); United States v. Cuthbertson, 630 F.2d 139, 147 (3d Cir. 1980), *cert. denied,* 449 U.S. 1126 (1981).

by statute in New York State [269] and by constitution and statute in California. [270] The requirement of a threshold showing that a litigant needs information outweighs the burden imposed upon a media representative. [271] A defendant's

---

[269] N.Y. Civ. Rights Law § 79-h. This statute provides an absolute protection for confidential news and a qualified protection for nonconfidential news:

> (b) Exemption of professional journalists and newscasters from contempt: *Absolute protection for confidential news.* Notwithstanding the provisions of any general or specific law to the contrary, no professional journalist or newscaster . . . shall be adjudged in contempt by any court in *connection with any civil or criminal proceeding, or by* the legislature or other body having contempt powers, nor shall a grand jury seek to have a journalist or newscaster held in contempt by any court, legislature or other body having contempt powers for refusing or failing to disclose any news *obtained or received in confidence* or the *identity of the* source of any such news coming into *such person's* possession in the course of gathering or obtaining news . . . notwithstanding that the material or identity of a source of such material or related material gathered by a person described above performing a function described above is or is not highly relevant to a particular inquiry of government and notwithstanding that the information was not solicited by the journalist or newscaster prior to disclosure to *such person.*

> (c) Exemption of professional journalists and newscasters from contempt: *Qualified protection for nonconfidential news.* Notwithstanding the provisions of any general or specific law to the contrary, no professional journalist or newscaster shall be adjudged in contempt by any court in connection with any civil or criminal proceeding, or by the legislature or other body having contempt powers, nor shall a grand jury seek to have a journalist or newscaster held in contempt by any court, legislature, or other body having contempt powers for refusing or failing to disclose any unpublished news obtained or prepared by a journalist or newscaster in the course of gathering or obtaining news as provided in subdivision (b) of this section, or the source of any such news, where such news was not obtained or received in confidence, unless the party seeking such news has made a clear and specific showing that the news: (i) is highly material and relevant; (ii) is critical or necessary to the maintenance of a party's claim, defense or proof of an issue material thereto; and (iii) is not obtainable from any alternative source. A court shall order disclosure only of such portion, or portions, of the news sought as to which the above-described showing has been made and shall support such order with clear and specific findings made after a hearing.

[270] CAL. Const. art. 1, § 2(b) (A newsperson "shall not be adjudged in contempt . . . for refusing to disclose the source of any information procured while so connected or employed [as a newsperson] . . . or for refusing to disclose any unpublished information obtained or prepared in gathering, receiving, or processing of information for communications to the public." *See also* CAL. EVID. CODE § 1070.

[271] State v. Turner, 550 N.W.2d 622 (Minn. 1996) ("We recognize, however, that some courts have required a threshold showing of relevance, need and unavailability before a reporter will be forced to disclose nontestimonial, unpublished information (i.e., written notes and photographs) [citation omitted]. We believe that concerns of overburdening the news media justify the implementation of an *in camera* procedure for reviewing unpublished information, including photographs, before forcing a news organization to disclose information in its possession to a litigant. If a litigant asserts that unpublished information or photographs possessed by a newspaper may be relevant to his or her case, *in camera* review by the district court is an appropriate means of balancing the defendant's need for evidence to support his or her claims against the public's interest in a free and independent press." *Id.* at 629.).

subpoena of a reporter who wrote an article about the defendant's sexual relationship with his daughter, the complainant in the charges, was quashed because the defendant did not show the information was relevant to the defendant's motion to change venue and the subpoena would also require the reporter to reveal confidential sources.[272] However, many courts have held that a reporter's protection under a shield statute must give way to a defendant's Sixth Amendment right to compulsory process.[273]

There are many situations in which a criminal defendant will be able to subpoena information gathered by a reporter to assist in his defense, despite the qualified privilege afforded by a state shield statute or by courts where such a privilege has been found under the state or federal constitution. For example, California, despite the language of its constitution and statute concerning legal protection for reporters, has held that a defendant may be entitled to subpoena a newsperson's testimony in certain circumstances.[274] While its shield law "is not restricted to information obtained in confidence by a newsperson," the shield law's protection can be overcome in a criminal proceeding by a defendant's showing that nondisclosure would deprive him of his right to a fair trial.[275] This reasoning is also grounded in a defendant's right to compulsory process under the Sixth Amendment.

The standard required for a defendant to make such a showing is a "reasonable possibility the information will materially assist his defense," and a defendant need not show that the information will go to the heart of his case.[276] The California Supreme Court articulated four factors in determining whether there is a reasonable possibility the information will assist in his defense:

(1)   Whether the information is confidential or sensitive;

(2)   The interests sought to be protected by the shield law;

(3)   The importance of the information to the defendant; and

(4)   Whether there is an alternative source to the information sought.[277]

---

[272] Gohring v. State, 967 S.W.2d 459 (Tex. Ct. App. 1998).

[273] *See, e.g., In re* Farber, 78 N.J. 259, 268–69, 394 A.2d 330, 334, *cert. denied*, 439 U.S. 997 (1978) (referring to the Supreme Court holding in Branzburg v. Hayes, 408 U.S. 665 (1972) that a reporter may be required to appear before a grand jury; "[T]he obligation to appear at a criminal trial on behalf of a defendant who is enforcing his Sixth Amendment rights is at least as compelling as the duty to appear before a grand jury.").

[274] Delaney v. Superior Court, 50 Cal. 3d 785, 789 P.2d 934, 268 Cal. Rptr. 753 (1990).

[275] *Id.* at 799, 805, 789 P.2d at 942, 268 Cal. Rptr. at 761, 765.

[276] *Id.* at 808, 789 P.2d at 948, 268 Cal. Rptr. at 767.

[277] *Id.* at 810–12, 789 P.2d at 949–51, 268 Cal. Rptr. at 768–69. *See also* State v. Siel, 122 N.H. 254, 444 A.2d 499 (1982) (New Hampshire Supreme Court affirmed the Superior Court ruling of Judge Souter that denied the defendant the right to depose reporters concerning stories they had written about the victim in the case. The trial court found the defendant did not exhaust reasonable alternatives to develop the information sought and that the defendant did not establish with sufficient certainty to overcome the qualified reporters' privilege that the news sources had

Some courts have not engaged in a balancing of factors in denying a reporter's privilege for information gathered through observations, such as through witnessing a defendant's arrest. This can be seen in numerous state and federal decisions.

A request or subpoena for materials that have already been broadcast is much less likely to meet with resistance. Since there is no confidentiality involved with such materials, there is not the same degree of concern as with a subpoena for reporter's notes or videotape or film yet to be shown. Quite often these materials will be provided voluntarily. Some news sources will also make available for court use material that has been broadcast and will honor a request to view it as actually broadcast or hold it so that it is not destroyed. It is imperative that a request be made as soon as it becomes apparent that the material may be of evidentiary value so that it is not lost or destroyed.

One court has noted that a TV station's unedited footage is not *Brady* material since the TV station does not have the same obligations as a prosecutor.[278] In some situations, television videotape that has not been broadcast may be available if a proper showing of necessity and importance is made, for example, a videotape of a defendant's arrest, especially when the government was involved in permitting the news gathering.[279] In a case in which a defendant sought television footage, never broadcast, of a search conducted of the defendant's premises to obtain information that might be relevant to the defendant's motion to dismiss the indictment and to suppress certain evidence,[280] and after conducting an *in camera* review of the subpoenaed videotape, the federal trial court held that the following must be established to overcome the "news-gathering privilege". The information requested must be (1) highly material and relevant; (2) necessary or critical to the maintenance of the party's claim; and (3) not obtainable from other sources.[281] In this case, the reporters accompanied federal agents on an

---

significantly helpful information on the issue of whether the defendant committed the crime in question. The three-prong standard of the trial judge adopted by the court was that "a defendant may overcome a press privilege to withhold a confidential source of news only when he shows: (1) that he has attempted unsuccessfully to obtain the information by all reasonable alternatives; (2) that the information would not be irrelevant to his defense; and (3) that, by a balance of the probabilities, there is a reasonable possibility that the information sought as evidence would affect the verdict in his case." *Id.* at 259, 444 A.2d at 503.) *But see* Miami Herald Publ'g Co. v. Morejon, 561 So. 2d 577, 578 (Fla. 1990) (holding that a qualified news-gathering privilege "has utterly no application" to information received by reporters through eye-witness observation).

[278] WTHR-TV v. Milam, 690 N.E.2d 1174 (Ind. 1998).

[279] CBS, Inc. v. Jackson, 578 So. 2d 698 (Fla. 1991).

[280] United States v. Sanusi, 813 F. Supp. 149 (E.D.N.Y. 1992).

[281] *Id.* at 154. *Compare* Krase v. Graco Children Prods. (*In re* Nat'l Broad. Co.), 79 F.3d 346 (2d Cir. 1996) (refusing to provide television outtakes and notes because of insufficient showing that information was critical and necessary to party seeking material). *See also* Gonzales v. National Broad. Co., 194 F.3d 29 (2d Cir. 1999). In *Gonzalez*, the court recognized a qualified privilege for non-confidential press information, but found that the privilege may be overcome in some situations:

execution of a search warrant. There was no authority under the search warrant for anyone other than law enforcement officials to enter the premises of the citizen accused. The television network crew trespassed at the defendant's home, and with the acquiescence of law enforcement engaged in conduct contrary to the Fourth Amendment. The court relied on this fact — that the television network had engaged in illegal conduct in gathering their information — in making the nonbroadcast videotapes available to the defendant.[282]

It has been noted that "the press may not use [the news-gatherers' privilege] to justify otherwise illegal actions."[283] In applying a three-part test, the *Sanusi* court found that the potentially exculpatory evidence on the videotape showed that an exhaustive search of the defendant's apartment failed to uncover any evidence of the crime for which the search warrant was issued. Even though the defendant was free to make this argument without use of the videotape, the court felt that the videotape significantly enhanced the defendant's argument. The court also noted that the tape could not be obtained from any other source, although, arguably, the same information could be. Whether the evidence was necessary to the defense was a matter that the court felt should be determined by the defense.

Where a defense attorney sought testimony and published notes of reporters concerning his statements as well as those of government officials and sought the production of out-takes of various news media to assist in defending himself against charges of engaging in prejudicial pretrial publicity and violation of a court order,[284] the appellate court ruled that the media need not turn over statements of the government officials concerning the case. However, it should be required to turn over the reporter's testimony and unpublished notes concerning statements made by the attorney to the reporters in connection with the articles that were the subject of the disciplinary proceeding.[285]

> Where a civil litigant seeks nonconfidential materials from a nonparty press entity, the litigant is entitled to the requested discovery notwithstanding a valid assertion of the journalists' privilege if he can show that the materials at issue are of likely relevance to a significant issue in the case, and are not reasonably obtainable from other available sources.

194 F.3d at 36.

[282] The television network's conduct in this case eventually led to a civil lawsuit against the television network and federal agents. *See* Joseph P. Fried, *CBS Reaches a Settlement on Videotaped Search,* NEW YORK TIMES, Mar. 20, 1994, § 1, at 44.

[283] *Sanusi,* 813 F. Supp. at 155. *See also* Galella v. Onassis, 487 F.2d 986, 994–96 (2d Cir. 1973) (ruling that injunctive relief was available to Jacqueline Kennedy Onassis against a photographer who had committed tortuous acts while attempting to photograph her and her family and had engaged in conduct that interfered with Secret Service efforts to protect the Onassis family; the court observed that "crimes and torts committed in news gatherings are not protected").

[284] *See* § 2.30.

[285] United States v. Cutler, 6 F.3d 67 (2d Cir. 1993). *Compare* Krase v. Graco Children Prods. (*In re* Nat'l Broad. Co.), 79 F.3d 346 (2d Cir. 1996) (refusing to compel disclosure of outtakes because information not necessary or critical to party and no clear and specific showing that material unavailable from other sources).

§ 2.27   Polling a jury concerning trial publicity.

More serious issues are raised by publicity during trial than by publicity prior to trial. Remedial measures in these cases are essential because information reported during a trial is more likely to remain in the mind of a juror, since jurors are likely to be attentive to information about the case they are asked to decide. An important tool in dealing with issues concerning trial publicity is the request that the jury be polled with respect to what, if any, information it has received, as well as to the effect of that information.

In general, trial courts are vested with broad discretion in determining whether to grant a request to poll a jury. [286] A court may require a showing of necessity before polling a jury. This necessity can be shown by evidence of a juror having read or been influenced by an article, or by the inherently prejudicial nature of the publicity. Factual reporting, however extensive, does not mandate polling the jury.

Failure to request that a jury be polled concerning alleged prejudicial midtrial publicity will probably result in a waiver of the right to raise such a failure to poll the jury on appeal. [287] When a dramatic event occurs during trial that receives extensive publicity, polling of the jury or even a mistrial may be necessary. Take for example a criminal defendant's escape during a trial. The court should make a record, question the jury, and make sure that the event and publicity surrounding it will not preclude a juror from rendering a fair and objective verdict based on the evidence. When a court fails to question the jury about a significant event like a defendant's escape, or poll the jury about its effect upon them, a defendant's eventual conviction may be reversed. [288]

It may not be necessary to present independent evidence that jurors have been exposed to the prejudicial publicity during the trial. Rather than requiring the party to establish such exposure, some courts have established a three-step process to evaluate the possibility of prejudice from midtrial media reports and to determine what steps, if any, the court should take with respect to the trial publicity. The three-step process entails: (1) determining whether the publicity or coverage has the potential for unfair prejudice; (2) canvassing the jury to find

---

[286] United States v. Goodman, 605 F.2d 870 (5th Cir. 1979); United States v. Gigax, 605 F.2d 507 (10th Cir. 1979); United States v. Williams, 604 F.2d 1102 (8th Cir. 1979); United States v. Armocida, 515 F.2d 29 (3d Cir. 1975), *cert. denied,* 423 U.S. 858 (1975); State v. Hobbs, 168 W. Va. 13, 42–43, 282 S.E.2d 258, 274–75 (1981).

[287] Prince v. State, 623 So. 2d 355 (Ala. Crim. App. 1992).

[288] *See, e.g.,* United States v. Aragon, 962 F.2d 439 (5th Cir. 1992); People v. Swan, 130 A.D.2d 6, 519 N.Y.S.2d 581, *appeal denied,* 70 N.Y.2d 804, 516 N.E.2d 1235, 522 N.Y.S.2d 122 (1987) (Following the defendant's capture, the defendant's attorney argued to the judge that after the defendant's escape a juror was "visibly upset" and had asked whether "it was safe for her to leave courthouse." The defendant's counsel also pointed out that another juror was afraid to go downstairs by herself because she was afraid the defendant was hiding in the stairwell. The court refused the request to voir dire the jury or declare a mistrial.).

out if they have learned of the potentially prejudicial publicity; and (3) examining, individually, exposed jurors outside the presence of other jurors to learn the nature and extent of their knowledge of the publicity and the effect, if any, on their ability to decide the case.[289] If the trial court determines that jurors are not aware of the details of the publicity or the contents of an article, it is not necessarily required that the judge take the third step of ascertaining whether the jurors can remain impartial.[290]

There can be differences of opinion as to what constitutes prejudicial publicity during trial. During a child molestation trial, a newspaper article referred to pedophiliacs as "among the sickest" people, but interrogation of the jury was deemed unnecessary because "the article itself was not factually similar to the present case"; the story did not refer to the appellant or his case specifically, but only a general class of persons. Since the article was not demonstrably prejudicial, the trial court had no reason to poll the jury.[291] Exposure to inadmissible evidence or publicity during a trial is insufficient to presume prejudice, and there is no need to poll a jury when adequate jury admonitions are given concerning pretrial publicity.[292]

Failing to take any steps to deal with potentially prejudicial publicity may be reversible error.[293] For example, trial publicity demonstrating that the defendant is undergoing counseling and had previous sexual assault convictions is prejudicial and requires judicial intervention to make sure that the information has not prejudiced the jury when there is a realistic possibility that the information reached the jury.[294]

The trial court should inquire if the jury has been exposed to prejudicial extraneous information.[295]

---

[289] United States v. Thompson, 908 F.2d 648 (10th Cir. 1990); United States v. Gaggi, 811 F.2d 47, 51 (2d Cir. 1987), *cert. denied*, 482 U.S. 929 (1987); United States v. Halbert, 712 F.2d 388, 389 (9th Cir. 1983), *cert. denied*, 465 U.S. 1005 (1984); People v. Barrow, 133 Ill. 2d 226, 549 N.E.2d 240, 256–67 (1989), *cert. denied*, 497 U.S. 1011 (1990); State v. Bey, 112 N.J. 45, 548 A.2d 846, 866–67 (1988).

[290] United States v. McDonough, 56 F.3d 381, 386–87 (2d Cir. 1995).

[291] Bauwens v. State, 657 P.2d 176, 179 (Okla. Crim. App. 1983).

[292] State v. Smart, 136 N.H. 639, 649–50, 622 A.2d 1197, 1204–05, *cert. denied*, 510 U.S. 917 (1993) ("Not only was the bulk of the publicity merely factual reporting, analysis of the material submitted by the defendant for our review indicates that most of the items appeared after the jury had been selected and had been continually instructed by the trial court not to read or watch anything connected to the case.").

[293] State v. Howe, 1997 Wash. App. LEXIS 1584 (Sept. 22, 1997).

[294] *Id.*

[295] James v. State, 777 So. 2d 682 (Miss. Ct. App. 2000), *appeal after remand*, 912 So. 2d 982 (Miss. Ct. App. 2004) (remanding case of defendant charged with killing child to trial court for hearing on whether jury learned during deliberations of death of another child under defendant's care).

Some courts have taken the position that the jury is presumed to follow a court's instructions and that a defendant must show that a jury has violated the court's admonition.[296] However, this is generally going to be difficult, if not impossible, to do, especially given the ethical rule that prohibits attorneys from communicating with jurors during a trial.

A court may deem a juror's denial of influence from the trial publicity, coupled with the court's instructions, to be sufficient to insure that no prejudice has occurred.[297] Even if a juror follows the court's instructions or admonitions, a juror can inadvertently be exposed to the prejudicial publicity without having intentionally read or listened to news reports. Jurors' promises or assurances to not consider news reports they were exposed to may be insufficient in some cases.[298]

In one sexual assault trial, a defendant's conviction was reversed because the trial court did not, upon the defense's request, poll the jury concerning a newspaper article published during the trial that discussed the defendant's prior conviction for sexual assault on a child, the same type of crime for which the defendant was being tried.[299] The reviewing court, noting the highly prejudicial nature of publicity concerning the defendant's prior conviction and the strong

---

[296] United States v. Metzger, 778 F.2d 1195, 1209 (6th Cir. 1985), *cert. denied*, 477 U.S. 906 (1986) (requiring party to demonstrate or prove a jury's exposure to the outside information as a prerequisite to polling of jury). *See also* State v. Novosel, 120 N.H. 176, 186, 412 A.2d 739, 746 (1980) (refusing to poll jury regarding prejudicial publicity permissible when adequate jury instructions were given to jury to avoid media accounts of trial); United States v. McDonough, 56 F.3d 381 (2d Cir. 1995); Johnson v. State, 666 So. 2d 784, 794 (Miss. 1995) (Jurors indicated they would not be affected by what they saw on television concerning child sexual assault trial and would accept judge's instructions to follow the law).

[297] State v. Banks, 692 So. 2d 1051 (La. 1997) (during sexual assault trial, publicity concerning defendant's pending similar charges was read by two jurors). Court declared:

> Given the emphatic and unequivocal assurances of continuing impartiality by both jurors, obvious even on a cold appellate record, the content of the newspaper article, which referred to accusations of other similar crimes but not to convictions [citations omitted] and the absence of any evidence that information in the news account infected the entire jury panel and became a matter of general discussion, we find no abuse of discretion by the trial court in concluding that the jurors had not been so impressed by the article that they were incapable of following its final instructions and of rendering a fair and impartial verdict based solely on the evidence presented at trial.

Id. at 1053–54.

[298] Wright v. State, 131 Md. App. 243, 748 A.2d 1050, *cert. denied*, 359 Md. 335, 753 A.2d 1032 (2000) (appellate court reversed defendant's murder-sexual assault conviction because trial court denied defendant's motion for mistrial after jury read two newspaper articles about defendant containing information about similar offenses committed in past by defendant; court rejected jurors' promises to decide case solely on basis of evidence presented and not consider information in news articles).

[299] Harper v. People, 817 P.2d 77 (Colo. 1991).

likelihood that this could influence a jury verdict, held that the highly prejudicial news story demanded a direct inquiry of the jury.[300]

When a jury is exposed to outside information, the court must hold a hearing to determine its impact in the view of some courts. For example, a judge should hold a hearing where there is an indication that defendant's mother-in-law held up pictures of defendant's wife's bruised face in view of the jury.[301]

Because a trial judge has broad discretion in dealing with the issue of juror prejudice, individual polling of the jury concerning their exposure to publicity is not always required.[302]

Establishing the nature of the publicity during the trial for appellate review is essential. The trend is that courts should initially conduct an inquiry of the jury collectively to determine if there has been exposure to the potentially prejudicial publicity.[303] If there is a significant possibility that a juror has been exposed to publicity or other information outside the courtroom during a trial, it is best to conduct *in camera* questioning of the juror.[304] This format helps prevent transmitting the effect of the prejudicial publicity. A record should always be made of any *in camera* court inquiries.

§ 2.28   Sequestration of jury.

Probably the ultimate preventive measure in dealing with prejudicial publicity during a trial is to sequester the jury. The purpose of sequestration is to protect jurors from outside influence during the course of trial that might affect their verdict. If sequestration is not requested, the failure to grant it cannot be reviewed upon appeal. Generally, courts are reluctant to grant sequestration because of the hardship imposed upon jurors as well as the cost to the government,

---

[300] *Id.* at 84–86. *See also* United States v. Attell, 655 F.2d 703, 705 (5th Cir. 1981) (failing to poll jury about exposure to potentially prejudicial publicity was reversible error).

[301] State v. Henderson, 2000 Ohio App. LEXIS 4579 (Sept. 29, 2000):

> Here, the trial court, being confronted with allegations of juror tampering, was obligated to hold a hearing to investigate the possibility that a biased attitude within the jury might prevent a just determination of appellant's guilt. Nevertheless, the trial court refused to hold a hearing or even question the person whom allegedly held up the pictures before the jury. While the trial court may be in the best position to determine the nature and extent of the proceeding surrounding claims of juror tampering, doing nothing is surely unacceptable and constitutes an abuse of discretion.

Id. at *6.

[302] People v. Velez, 222 A.D.2d 539, 634 N.Y.S.2d 758 (1995), *appeal denied*, 87 N.Y.2d 978, 664 N.E.2d 1270, 642 N.Y.S.2d 207 (1996) (upholding trial judge's general question to jury panel concerning whether they had been exposed to an article in local newspaper on previous day concerning defendant's prior conviction as a sex offender).

[303] *Harper*, 817 P.2d at 84–86. *See also* United States v. Gaggi, 881 F.2d 47, 51 (2d Cir. 1987), *cert. denied*, 482 U.S. 929(1987).

[304] Virgin Islands v. Dowling, 814 F.2d 134, 137 (3d Cir. 1987).

particularly for trials of long duration. A refusal to sequester a jury is a matter of discretion and will generally be upheld on appeal absent a showing of actual prejudice.[305] This may be difficult to do without polling the jury and showing that it has been exposed to significantly prejudicial information. Sequestration is viewed as an extreme measure and one of the most cumbersome and costly measures to ensure a fair trial.[306]

A motion for sequestration should not be simply a request for sequestration; a record should be made that jurors were exposed to prejudicial publicity during the trial or before the trial began and are likely to continue to be so exposed or that the publicity during the trial is of such a sensational or prejudicial nature that even the *risk* of exposure to the publicity creates a likelihood of prejudice.[307]

For example, when improper or prejudicial stories appear in the course of the jury selection, the trial court can order the immediate sequestration of jurors as they are accepted to eliminate any further contact with the press.[308]

§ 2.29   Should a defendant make public statements?

Defendants are likely to be confronted with a spate of publicity in sexual assault cases from law enforcement or other sources. Unlike other crimes, the nature and details of the charges are likely to be reported and commented upon. A defendant may wish to speak out about the case or his defense, since information about the case is likely to be exclusively from law enforcement or prosecutional sources. There is nothing that prohibits a defendant from making statements concerning his case to the media, although such a step should be carefully considered and any statements carefully limited. Some attorneys believe that having a defendant come forward and make statements in his or her defense is helpful in controlling the flow of information about a case as well as placing the client in the most favorable light. An interview of an accused while under investigation or soon after an arrest may help defuse the negative publicity associated with the alleged crime and help focus on those issues that the defendant's attorney wants to spotlight in a trial. Naturally, this presupposes that there has been an evaluation of the case by the defendant's attorney and that he or she is armed with adequate information so that the client can be properly advised. Without such advice, based upon counsel's adequate evaluation and understanding of the case, the defendant's statements are not likely to be helpful. A free-flowing interview offers less control over a client, but offers him the

---

[305] Burke v. State, 484 A.2d 490, 500 (Del. 1984); State v. Smart, 136 N.H. 639, 657–58, 622 A.2d 1197, 1209–10, *cert denied*, 510 U.S. 917 (1993).

[306] United States v. Porcaro, 648 F.2d 753, 755 (1st Cir. 1981) (court agreed to reconsider sequestration motion if publicity problems arose during trial, but defendant did not renew motion after commencement of trial; trial court also cited shortage of hotel rooms in Boston, where trial was held, and inconvenience of transporting jurors from another location).

[307] State v. Ng, 104 Wash. 2d 763, 776, 713 P.2d 63 (1985).

[308] State v. Van Duyne, 43 N.J. 369, 204 A.2d 841 (1964), *cert. denied*, 380 U.S. 987 (1965).

chance to appear more credible. Although it does not make for the most effective presentation, a defendant can decline to answer certain questions. If the defendant has been properly advised, and the circumstances of the case are such that making public statements is advisable, the defendant should appear alone, thus demonstrating self-confidence in the face of the allegations. An attorney may appear alongside a defendant, but a defendant is likely to make a better impression without such a crutch.

A defendant making a public statement, but accepting no questions, offers more control over the information communicated and can offer some counterbalance to potentially prejudicial material, but it is not as likely to be well-received by the media and public. A public statement with no questions may be quite simple and need not address any details of the case. There is no difficulty in having the defendant make a statement professing his innocence, noting that the grand jury has heard only one side of the story, that his friends and family continue to have faith in him, and that he has faith in the justice system. In any event, regardless of whether a defendant will answer questions when making a public statement, an attorney should carefully review with a client the scope and content of the statement before it is made.

Another consideration is the timing of the statement. Any statement of a defendant in a sexual assault case is more likely to be well-received if given at a time when the interest in the case is high. Some sexual assault cases will maintain a high level of public interest for a long period of time, while others will incite interest only at the time of arrest, indictment, or some other noteworthy development in the case. The adage of "primary and recency" has relevance. Since the first impression can be significant, the best opportunity is when the case is initially publicized.

There are risks to making public statements by a defendant. A defendant's statements may touch upon an inculpatory area or an area for which a defendant or his attorney is not prepared. Inevitably, if questions are permitted, they will involve details of the case, creating the risk that the defendant's answers could be used against him or her later. It is not unusual for a defendant's public statements to reporters to be used against him or her at the trial. Statements made by a defendant to a newspaper or television reporter can be admitted as admissions or as consciousness of guilt.[309] Statements that are not made to law enforcement officials are not the subject of suppression hearings and may not be within the scope of state discovery provisions.

Another risk is that a defendant may lose control during an interview. Loss of control may yield not only damaging statements but an unfavorable impression

---

[309] People v. Cain, 10 Cal. 4th 1, 40 Cal. Rptr. 2d 481, 489, 892 P.2d 1224 (1995), *cert. denied*, 516 U.S. 1077 (1996) (defendant's statement to television reporter denying any knowledge of crimes properly admitted as a false statement inconsistent with defendant's statement to police and prosecution's proof and thus was evidence of consciousness of guilt); People v. Craver, 191 A.D.2d 817, 594 N.Y.S.2d 848, *appeal denied*, 81 N.Y.2d 1012, 616 N.E.2d 857, 600 N.Y.S.2d 200 (1993).

of a defendant. Even if a defendant is not going to make a public statement or grant an interview, he or she should be counseled concerning the nature of his public appearances and the possibility of press coverage. The defendant should be prepared to be asked questions at such times and be prepared to answer them, politely decline to answer them, or refer them to his or her attorney.

Any defendant facing a publicized proceeding should be advised concerning his or her visual image and also be advised to give the appropriate respect due officials and others. At any time, the defendant may be photographed or filmed, thus generating a public image. Defendants should be warned that intemperate behavior, such as striking out at TV cameras or press photographers, or yelling or name calling, is likely to create a negative impression, thereby compounding the effects of unfavorable pretrial publicity.

The defendant's attorney will likely be asked questions by the media in a publicized sexual assault case. Counsel should be prepared to respond to a TV reporter's questions on camera without appearing to be evasive, flustered, or defensive. Rather than avoid the media, counsel should respond politely to general statements and explain why detailed comments are not appropriate. One criminal defense lawyer suggests the following guidelines.[310]

(1) Appear helpful and do not resist the reporter. Demonstrate this with responses such as, "I'm limited in what I'm allowed to say about these allegations," or "that is still under investigation," or "I'd like to invite you to my office so I can answer your questions more completely," or "I can't answer that question until the trial is over." Repeat your willingness to cooperate and why you feel restricted.

(2) Answer questions that can be answered.

(3) Answer in "sound bites," that is, short phrases that can easily be used to tell a story. Repeat your theme or sound bite often, but use only short answers. Remember that most television news stories are less than a minute and one-half, which does not permit long, rambling comments. (On the other hand, the visual image of an attorney or defendant running from a camera is easily included in a news story and presents a powerful negative image.)

(4) Avoid legalese or phrases that are not likely to be understood or likely to be considered "technicalities" by a lay person. Counsel may also wish to obtain the assistance of an advisor in the area of public relations. More and more professionals in the field of public relations are advising lawyers and law firms in many aspects of public appearances and presentations by attorneys and clients. Since this is not an area of expertise for most attorneys, they should consult with experts who may be able to provide them with valuable guidance and assistance. Such

---

[310] Bruce Lyons, *Unique Problems in Representing People Accused of Sex Abuse*, B-10, 11, May 21, 1993, Las Vegas, NV, National Association of Criminal Defense Attorneys.

advisors can also assist the drafting of press releases. However, any advisor should have limited or no contact with a defendant, since communications between them are not privileged.

There is another risk for attorneys who make statements or who allow their clients to make statements that generate pretrial publicity. Such statements can be cited by a court in denying a motion for change of venue or other requested relief on the grounds that the defendant is responsible in large part for the pretrial publicity of which he or she complains.

Attorneys should also be wary of any "off the record" comments. The attorney should be prepared for the possibility that such comments will be reported as well as for the possibility that the attorney will be identified directly or indirectly as the source. *All* comments to a reporter should be carefully weighed for propriety as well as impact. Attorneys should always remember that their statements and conduct are governed by ethical considerations and court decisions governing pretrial publicity and attorney conduct, which are discussed earlier in this chapter.

§ 2.30   Role of defendant's attorney in making public statements as a means of dealing with prejudicial publicity.

As noted in the previous section, an attorney representing the defendant in a sexual assault case should advise the client on whether or how to make public statements about the case. The attorney also must make sure that his or her own statements do not damage the case. Public statements of a defendant's attorney that the defendant was home at the time of a crime followed by the assertion of an inconsistent defense, such as an insanity defense, can create serious problems for the defendant and his attorney. A public misstatement by a defendant or attorney about the case, especially about the theory of the case or defense, can boomerang when the theory or defense changes or becomes insupportable.

The attorney should take time to establish a role in providing helpful and accurate information about a case or topic in a manner consistent with the ethical guidelines and court decisions pertaining to trial publicity. This role may be a very active one in providing information about a case, yet still be within the legal parameters and rules governing trial publicity.

One of the problems with the publicity surrounding sexual assault cases is that sexual assault and the criminal charges emanating therefrom are emotionally charged and multidimensional matters in terms of the dynamics of crime as well as the legal issues surrounding the case. The reporting process does not always deal with these complexities. A reporter does not always have time to learn about the crime and the area of law governing it or to prepare a report on what has been learned. An attorney should understand the constraints of the reporting process and be prepared to provide helpful and accurate information in a timely and succinct manner to reporters.

Failing to cooperate with reporters is more likely to increase mistakes and inaccuracies in the reporting of complex matters, since reporters will lack the benefit of necessary information. Even if an attorney does not wish to discuss details of a case, he or she may still be in a position to educate the public about the dynamics of the crime involved, the scheduling of the court proceedings involving the case, or the legal process generally.

If there is a concern over prejudicial pretrial publicity, its effect can be magnified if an attorney does not attempt to appropriately balance the news coverage of the attorney's client. No comment equals no balance. An attorney can request equal time to respond to reports representing one view of a case. While equal time is not legally required, most news outlets will attempt to provide an opposing viewpoint on an issue if the request is timely and appropriately made. Providing prerecorded interviews of members of a defendant's family may not qualify as an appropriate response; making the defendant's family available soon after the arrest is announced may be more suitable. Also, an attorney can and should request corrections of inaccuracies in the reporting of major facts surrounding a case.

A defendant through his or her attorney can issue a press release denying the charges. At a minimum, a public denial is expected and is acceptable as a public comment. An advantage of a press release is that there is no opportunity to question the defendant or his or her attorney.

Another technique is to aggressively deal with the issue of pretrial publicity in motions. Motions can deal with issues that a defendant wishes to focus on, including the possible bias and motives of the prosecution. For example, one defense attorney suggests calling a grand jury investigation "an inquisition" or "an exercise in retribution" in the brief accompanying a motion and then allowing these comments to be used to shape public opinion and counterbalance the effects of publicity prejudicial to the defendant.[311]

Some defense attorneys include polygraph results or expert reports as part of the factual basis in support of motion to dismiss, for discovery, or for other relief. These motions are part of the public record and available for the media to report on.

§ 2.31 Summary of legal remedies available to deal with prejudicial publicity.

There are many different approaches and remedies available to deal with issues of pretrial or during-trial publicity. While not all remedies will be necessary in

---

[311] Stanley E. Preiser and C. Crady Swisher III, *Representing the White-Collar Defendant,* TRIAL, Oct. 1988 at 72–78.

every situation, virtually every avenue requires that it be requested of the trial court to assure a review of its denial on appeal. The use of jury selection as a means to deal with publicity is set forth in Chapter 5.

Following are the various motions that can be made.

The use of jury selection as a means to deal with publicity is set forth in Chapter 5.

(1) Motion for Additional Peremptory Challenges

(2) Motion for Sequestered Voir Dire

(3) Motion for Change of Venue

(4) Motion for Continuance

(5) Motion for Order Restraining Comments by Parties, Law Enforcement Officials, or Witnesses

(6) Motion Sealing Records in Case

(7) Motion for Repeated Jury Admonitions Concerning Trial Publicity

(8) Motion to Poll the Jurors During Trial

(9) Motion to Sequester Jury

(10) Motion to Dismiss in the Interest of Justice Based on Prejudicial Publicity, Prosecutorial, or Law Enforcement Misconduct

(11) Motion for Mistrial Based on Juror Exposure to Prejudicial Publicity

(12) Motion to Exclude Cameras from the Courtroom or During Testimony of Certain Witness

(13) Post-trial Motion for *In Camera* Examination of the Jury for Possible Failure of the Jury to Follow Court Instructions with Respect to Reading or Watching News Accounts of the Trial[312]

---

[312] *See, e.g.*, United States v. Simone, 14 F.3d 833 (3d Cir. 1994).

CHAPTER 3

JURY SELECTION

189

§ 3.1 Introduction.

Jury selection is crucial in most cases. It is the part of a trial over which the attorney has the least control. It is not a science, and although certain principles may apply, tremendous judgment must be exercised. Most jurors will make decisions based upon feelings, emotions, and previously held beliefs, and not just upon the rational analysis of the facts. Beliefs and attitudes can change and have changed about sexual assault, which are reflected in significant changes in the laws that apply to sexual assault. These beliefs and attitudes must be assessed.

The "beliefs-and-attitudes" approach is now a leading strategy in jury selection. Assessing jurors on beliefs and attitudes through questioning is probably the most popular approach to jury selection today. Social science research conducted on juries supports the validity of that approach, and in those jurisdictions where the judge does the entire questioning of prospective jurors, this is the only approach that is readily applicable.[1]

While this chapter sets forth areas of possible questioning, general rules as to who makes an ideal juror will be broken in practice because of the wide variables in human beings. Understanding individuals' feelings and instincts, as developed through practice, are crucial to this part of the trial. Questions can only help jurors express themselves. Listening, observing, and processing responses and demeanor are more difficult.

Questions involving a jurors' specific attitude toward sexual assault and child abuse are probably the most instructive and helpful in predicting his or her reaction in a case. This is set forth more fully in § 3.15 of this book, which discusses some of the research conducted in this area.

Because the principles of *Batson v. Kentucky* (discussed in §§ 3.24–30) represent a substantial area of appellate review of jury selection procedures, these principles, which are still evolving, receive attention in this chapter. A considerable discussion of *Batson* and its progeny is presented because of the decision's importance not just on the issue of racially-based challenges, but also because the principles of *Batson* presumably apply to the application of *J.E.B. vs. Alabama*,[2] the decision precluding gender-based challenges. For some, gender (discussed in § 3.30) has been considered an important factor in jury selection; however, it is no longer permissible as a basis of a peremptory challenge.

[1] Thomas A. Mauet, *Fundamentals of Trial Techniques* 26 (3d ed. 1992).

[2] J.E.B. v. Alabama, 511 U.S. 127 (1994).

Improper challenges based on race or gender, unlike other errors during jury selection, are not subject to the harmless error doctrine and thus deserve the particular attention of trial attorneys in the field of sexual assault.

§ 3.2 Research and studies of jurors in sexual assault and child abuse cases.

There has been some research on jury selection and jurors in rape cases. The authors of the classic and frequently cited *The American Jury*,[3] which was published over 40 years ago, studied 106 forcible rape cases involving adult victims and found that juror feelings about a victim's behavior were crucial in determining whether to convict or acquit a defendant. These were the authors' conclusions:

> The law recognizes only one issue in rape cases other than the fact of intercourse: Whether there was consent at the moment of intercourse. The jury, as we came to see it, does not limit itself to this one issue; it goes on to weigh the woman's conduct in the prior history of the affair. It closely, and often harshly scrutinizes the female complainant and is moved to be lenient with the defendant whenever there are suggestions of contributory behavior on her part . . . [or] assumption of risk. When it perceives an assumption of risk, the jury, if given the option of finding the defendant guilty of a lesser crime, will frequently do so. It is thus saying not that the defendant has done nothing, but rather that what he has done does not deserve the distinctive opprobrium of rape. If forced to choose in these cases between total acquittal and finding the defendant guilty of rape, the jury will usually choose acquittal as the lesser evil.[4]

More recently, the National Center for Prevention and Control of Rape, a division of the National Institute of Mental Health, reviewed 37 sexual assault trials in Indianapolis from July 1978 through July 1980. Despite changes in attitudes about "proper behavior" for women in cases of adult rape, the authors of the study found:

> If the case does come to court, the jurors are as likely to be influenced by the behavior of the victim as by the factors of the assault. They treat more seriously the rape of a woman who appears chaste or is traditional in her life style. They are more likely to exonerate men charged with raping women who reputedly are sexually active outside of marriage or women who knew the assailant.[5]

As for defendants, the study found:

> If they came across as losers, scruffy, held no job and were unmarried, they tended to be biased against him [sic]. But if they were attractive, had evidence

---

[3] Harry Kalvin & Hans Zeisel, *The American Jury* (1966).

[4] Harry Kalvin & Hans Zeisel, *The American Jury* 249, 254 (1966).

[5] Nadine Brozan, *Jurors in Rape Trials Studied*, N.Y. TIMES, June 13, 1985, at C13.

of having a girlfriend or were married and thus had access to a woman, the jurors could not believe that they would commit rape. More often than any other statement, we heard, "But he doesn't look like a rapist."[6]

Some of the findings of a 1980 study of jurors and sexual assaults found that of those surveyed:

(1) Two-thirds (66%) agreed with the statement, "women provoke rape by their appearance and behavior."

(2) Forty-one percent thought "a charge of rape two days after the act has occurred is probably not rape."

(3) One-third (34%) stated "in order to protect the male, it should be difficult to prove that rape has occurred."

(4) One-third (34%) reported that "a woman should be responsible for preventing her own rape."

(5) Nearly one-third (32%) felt "the degree of a woman's resistance should be the major factor in determining if a rape has occurred."

(6) Nearly one-third (29%) felt "most charges of rape are unfounded" and that rape of a woman by a man she knows can be defined as a "woman who changed her mind afterward."[7]

The study looked at several other factors in jurors' backgrounds that might affect their decisions, but there was, as might be expected, a significant amount of unpredictability. There does appear to be gradual movement away from the stereotypes and beliefs reflected in the earlier studies, but these stereotypes are resilient and still present in the jury pool.

A 1992 study surveyed 50 child abuse experts and 150 jurors using a 40-item questionnaire.[8] Jurors differed from the experts on 22 of 28 questions. Over one-half of the jurors believed that children are easily manipulated into false reports, and over half of the jurors expected physical damage.[9] (See Chapter 12 for a review of literature concerning the likelihood of physical damage in sexual assault cases.) More than one-third of the jurors believed that allegations frequently prove false, and that more than one-third of victims resist, run, and tell after being sexually abused.[10] There was a high level of agreement between jurors and experts that children do not invite abuse (86%), and that moral and legal responsibility rests with the adult (88%). Jurors between 53–83 years of age were

---

[6] Nadine Brozan, *Jurors in Rape Trials Studied,* N.Y. TIMES, June 13, 1985, at C13.

[7] Hubert S. Fields & Leigh B. Bienen, *Jurors and Rape* 50–53 (1980).

[8] Susan Morison and Edith Greene, *Juror and Expert Knowledge of Child Abuse,* 16 Child Abuse and Neglect 595–613 (1992).

[9] Susan Morison and Edith Greene, *Juror and Expert Knowledge of Child Abuse,* 16 Child Abuse and Neglect 595–613 (1992).

[10] Susan Morison and Edith Greene, *Juror and Expert Knowledge of Child Abuse,* 16 Child Abuse and Neglect 595–613 (1992).

less knowledgeable about the dynamics of child sexual abuse than younger jurors.[11] Jurors 18–31 believed that allegations of child sexual abuse are usually not false, that allegations are often retracted, and that children do not invite abuse. The study also indicated that higher-educated jurors scored better on knowing that most abuse is not intercourse; violence, resistance, and crying are atypical, and lack of physical injury is common in these cases.

A 1993 study by the Illinois State Attorney General of jurors in 23 sexual assault trials found that jurors' attitudes regarding victims were better predictors of the trial outcome than strength of the case.[12] This is a significant finding and likely true in adult and child sexual assault cases. A survey of actual jurors studied concluded 80% of jurors found children credible, and 88% had empathy for the victims.[13] Interestingly, the survey of jurors found negative juror attitude toward a case which utilized special child hearsay statutes.[14] This study, too, found that more educated jurors were more receptive to abuse allegations.[15]

Another study of child sexual assault victims found that corroborating testimony of a child victim increased the credibility of a child victim and that exposure to a defendant's criminal acts or other negative defendant character evidence heightened perceived victim's credibility and a defendant's guilt.[16]

§ 3.3 Importance of establishing the theme of the case.

Before selecting the jury, it is important to have a theme of the case. Research indicates that jurors process testimony, facts, and pieces of information by composing a story that allows them to make sense of what they are hearing.[17] Jurors need a story or theme to explain events and behavior of parties and witnesses that helps them put together what may appear to be disconnected evidence. As might be expected, jurors also bring certain assumptions with them, depending on the story they create. The theme or story line of the trial also helps the juror to fill in gaps in the evidence and provides the motives or reasons for behavior.

---

[11] Susan Morison and Edith Greene, *Juror and Expert Knowledge of Child Abuse*, 16 Child Abuse and Neglect 595–613 (1992).

[12] Nick Maroules & Charles Reynard, *Voir Dire in Child-Victim Sex Trials: A Strategic Guide for Prosecutors*, Illinois State's Attorney Appellate Prosecuter Child Witness Project (1993).

[13] Nick Maroules & Charles Reynard, *Voir Dire in Child-Victim Sex Trials: A Strategic Guide for Prosecutors*, Illinois State's Attorney Appellate Prosecuter Child Witness Project (1993).

[14] Nick Maroules & Charles Reynard, *Voir Dire in Child-Victim Sex Trials: A Strategic Guide for Prosecutors*, Illinois State's Attorney Appellate Prosecuter Child Witness Project (1993).

[15] Nick Maroules & Charles Reynard, *Voir Dire in Child-Victim Sex Trials: A Strategic Guide for Prosecutors*, Illinois State's Attorney Appellate Prosecuter Child Witness Project (1993).

[16] Bette L. Bottoms & Gail S. Goodman, *Perceptions of Children's Credibility in Sexual Assault Cases*, 24 Journal of Applied Social Psychology 702–732, n.8 (1994).

[17] Nancy Pennington & Reid Hastie, *A Cognitive Theory of Juror Decision Making: The Story Model*, 13 Cardozo L. Rev. 519–57 (1991).

Research has identified what constitutes a good theme. The three most important components to a good story are consistency, plausibility, and completeness.[18] Pennington and Hastie write:

> A story is consistent to the extent that it does not contain internal contradictions either with evidence believed to be true or with other parts of the explanation. A story is plausible to the extent that it corresponds to the decision maker's knowledge about what typically happens in the world and does not contradict that knowledge. A story is complete when the expected structure of the story 'has all of its parts.' . . . Missing information, or lack of plausible inferences about one or more major components of the story structure, would decrease confidence in the explanation.[19]

The authors note that once jurors determine what happened, or establish a story, it is difficult for them to change their opinions.[20] This supports the proposition that a convincing theory of the case should be presented as early as possible in the opening statement and a foundation laid for that theme in voir dire.

Establishing a theme of the case will help guide the jury selection, opening statement, and examination of witnesses. Themes are not found in law books; they are developed from life experiences and, more importantly, the facts of the case and interactions between attorney and witnesses. A theme should be short and simple; it should explain the testimony and tie diverse pieces of testimony together. A good theme should deal with both constraints and weaknesses.

To establish a theme, write down the important points in your case, the negative factors in your case, and any response to the weaknesses in your case. The lists should then be synthesized. Then think about unifying traits or characteristics or expressions that tie various thoughts together.

A common theme for prosecutors in child sexual assault cases is the "betrayal of trust." This theme can explain how the abuse began, how it continued, why the victim did not complain at first, and why the victim may have recanted her allegations. For a defendant, a theme may be the "return to discipline" or "bad judgment." Such a theme can explain the motive for a victim to come forward with allegations of abuse and explain foolish decisions the defendant may have made in terms of contact with the victim, denials of certain facts to law enforcement authorities, and placing himself in vulnerable situations. Themes can be tested on friends, family, and office staff for effectiveness and for suggestions for improvement or modification.

---

[18] Nancy Pennington & Reid Hastie, *A Cognitive Theory of Juror Decision Making: The Story Model,* 13 Cardozo L. Rev. 519, 528 (1991).

[19] Nancy Pennington & Reid Hastie, *A Cognitive Theory of Juror Decision Making: The Story Model,* 13 Cardozo L. Rev. 519, 528 (1991).

[20] Nancy Pennington & Reid Hastie, *A Cognitive Theory of Juror Decision Making: The Story Model,* 13 Cardozo L. Rev. 519, 556 (1991).

Use the theme statements made to a jury during jury selection. The theme can help identify issues, characteristics, and traits of preferred jurors. Determine who best understands your theme. To whom does the theme's message make the most sense? Establishing a theme helps identify those jurors who will be most sympathetic with your case. If the theme involves "lost innocence" of a child victim, ask yourself what type of juror is most likely to identify with the child's innocence and who would be least sympathetic to that claim. Themes are also discussed in Chapter 4.

§ 3.4   Establish an ideal juror profile.

Given the inherent weaknesses and uncertainties in the jury selection process, it is helpful to have as many guidelines as possible before the process begins. Identifying the most important desirable traits in a juror before jury selection begins allows an attorney to make decisions more quickly, which is important in view of the usually limited time for jury questioning and the usually limited information available on prospective jurors.

Before undertaking jury selection, have a sense of who the ideal juror would be in your case. The establishment of a theme (*see* § 3.3) helps develop the "ideal juror profile." Who will most likely understand and accept the theme? Try to identify as many characteristics as possible in the ideal juror. The more characteristics you can identify, the more likely you are to identify key issues in your case that will affect potential jurors. Just as important as the ideal juror profile is the "most negative juror profile." Establish those traits and characteristics that are least desirable. After writing down the positive and negative characteristics and the ideal juror profile, try to prioritize the characteristics. The profile is only a guide, however, and should yield to the attorney's judgment as more specific information about a juror is learned.

The ideal juror will identify with your client in the case. The fact that a juror will identify with a defendant, witness, or victim is based on the theory that people will like, trust, and believe those most like themselves, either through a shared experience or similar background. A juror, for example, who is a parent with a pre-school child may identify with a four-year-old complainant.

Who will identify with a defendant schoolteacher charged with sexually abusing a child? Perhaps another schoolteacher, a boy scout leader, or an individual who also works with children and may feel particularly vulnerable to allegations of abuse. Who will identify most with the biographical characteristics of the defendant? A married, middle-aged juror with two children may feel sympathy for a married, middle-aged defendant with two children. For prosecutors, who will identify with a young, single woman who complains that she was sexually assaulted by an individual she met in a bar after work? A substantially older woman may not identify with the younger woman who works, is independent, and socializes at bars. In fact, an older woman who answers on jury selection

195

that she has been married since she was 20 years of age may never have had a period of socialization as a single woman. On the other hand, a younger, single female may identify with the victim because she may have been in a similar situation herself.

In finding the juror who will identify most with a client, it is important to identify the most important issues in the case and characteristics of the party. Once again, theme development helps an attorney find those areas that will be most important in jury selection.

§ 3.5 Obtaining juror information — Use of consultants and discovery of prosecution information about past jury service.

The more detailed information counsel can obtain about a specific potential juror and his or her background, values, and ideals, the more likely an intelligent decision can be made regarding that person as a juror.

These judgments, of course, are subject to variables, and there are many ways in which a juror can identify with both a defendant or a victim at the same time. A jury consultant may be of value here. Professional jury consultants have a variety of backgrounds and training, including psychology, sociology, marketing, social work, public relations, and communications. Such a consultant can help identify community attitudes or issues. More importantly, a consultant can help identify the ideal juror profile by determining what demographic groups are most accepting of or hostile to a party. The consultant can also help formulate questions for voir dire. Furthermore, their work may form the basis for a change of venue.

Pollsters also can provide information concerning the makeup of the jurisdiction in which the case is being tried and the attitude of various people toward a party or witness. This type of polling data provides information on how specific groups and a community react to issues of a case. It can also help to identify themes for a case. While the use of such consultants may appear to be costly, this is not necessarily so. Many universities have professors with experience conducting telephone polls and related research who are willing to provide these services at a reasonable cost or enlist the assistance of graduate students. Political campaigns often use such telephone surveys. There are also many books available that can assist a trial attorney in undertaking surveys. While these techniques may not provide precise information, they can be used as a tool to identify the characteristics of ideal jurors and issues to address in jury selection.

Another source of information about jurors is to file a motion to discover information about past jury service that may be contained in a prosecutor's office files. This information may indicate how a juror voted in a particular case and what the verdict was.

Generally, a trial court has broad discretion in denying a defendant access to the prosecution's records of a potential juror's prior service or background as long as the defendant is given a fair and impartial jury and no prejudice is shown in withholding the information. The prosecutor's research and records are usually viewed as work product.[21] This approach is particularly true when the information in the prosecution's possession is from public records, or sources, equally accessible to the defendant.[22] A court may also find that a defendant's request for information is outside the scope of a state's statutory discovery provisions.[23]

However, courts have also held that a court does have discretion to order release of jury records and reports in the prosecution's possession,[24] particularly when the information is developed from law enforcement sources.[25]

For example, if law enforcement has questioned potential jurors, the information disclosed from such questioning should be available to the defendant.[26] One court has noted that while a defendant has no absolute right to inspect a prosecutor's dossier on potential jurors, a prosecutor is under a duty to disclose information within his knowledge that would show that a prospective juror holds a fixed prejudice or bias against an accused that would support a challenge for cause.[27]

§ 3.6   Use of juror questionnaires.

One technique to obtain information about juror experiences, feelings, or bias based on pretrial publicity or past experience involving sexual abuse is the juror questionnaire. In some jurisdictions potential jurors fill out questionnaires prior to jury selection. Attorneys can often review the questionnaire before the jury selection process begins. In some situations, an application to the court may be

---

[21] United States v. Falange, 426 F.2d 930 (2d Cir.), *cert. denied*, 400 U.S. 906 (1970); People v. Morris, 53 Cal.3d 152, 180, 807 P.2d 949, 962, 279 Cal. Rptr. 720, 733 (1991); State v. Wright, 344 So. 2d 1014 (La. 1977); Commonwealth v. Von Smith, 457 Pa. 638, 326 A.2d 60 (1974); State v. Grega, 168 Vt. 363, 721 A.2d 445 (1998) (finding no showing of prejudice in prosecution's failure to provide defense with criminal history checks of potential jurors); State v. Farmer, 116 Wash. 2d 414, 805 P.2d 200 (1991) (denying a defendant's request for information about past juror service in the prosecutor's possession).

[22] People v. Stinson, 58 Mich. App. 243, 227 N.W.2d 303 (1975).

[23] Sacket v. Bartlett, 241 A.D.2d 97, 671 N.Y.S.2d 156, *appeal denied*, 92 N.Y.2d 806 (1998) (denying defendant's discovery request for all information in prosecution's possession of "the name, gender, and race of each and every juror who was excused by a peremptory challenge or who sat on the jury, together with the name of the defendant, the docket number, and whether the juror was challenged by the prosecution or the defense").

[24] People v. Murtishaw, 29 Cal. 3d 733, 765–67, 631 P.2d 446, 175 Cal. Rptr. 738 (1981).

[25] Losavio v. Mayber, 496 P.2d 1032 (Colo. 1972) (requiring disclosure to defense of public records of potential jurors obtained by prosecution); People v. Aldridge, 47 Mich. App. 639, 209 N.W.2d 796 (1973) (requiring disclosure of prosecution's juror dossier which listed adverse contacts of jurors with law enforcement).

[26] Commonwealth v. Smith, 350 Mass. 600, 215 N.E.2d 897 (1966).

[27] Couser v. State, 282 Md. 125, 140, 383 A.2d 389, 398, *cert. denied*, 439 U.S. 852 (1978).

required to obtain this information. The information obtained through these questionnaires is usually well worth the effort.

Attorney-prepared juror questionnaires allow an attorney to gain a better understanding of the demographic makeup of the venire as well the occupations of the potential jurors. The questionnaire can expedite the questioning process. Summarizing each individual's response will help the attorney during voir dire. From such a summary, an overview of the panel can be developed which can be helpful in making jury selection decisions. For example, if counsel seeks young single jurors, it would be important to know that only a handful of such jurors exist on the panel. The decision to challenge a young single potential juror who presents concerns based on other factors would have to be evaluated in light of the fact that there are few other young, single jurors on the panel.

The residence of jurors is an important piece of information that can be learned through juror questionnaires. It is important for counsel to know the demographics of the various geographical areas in the community in evaluating a jury panel.

Instead of yes/no answers, the questionnaire can provide more insight if the juror can answer along a scale such as agree strongly, agree/disagree, disagree strongly, no opinion. This helps particularly with questions likely to generate either a yes or no.

The use of a juror questionnaire is not constitutionally required and is usually a matter of a trial court's discretion. [28] When there is extensive pretrial publicity, the court must find a way to address the potential prejudice from the publicity and the questionnaire is one such tool. An appellate court can look to the use of a questionnaire to determine the efficiency of the trial court's handling of pretrial publicity. [29] When there has been a failure by a trial court to adequately address pretrial publicity by other means, a court's failure to use a questionnaire can result in the reversal of a defendant's conviction. [30]

In some jurisdictions, juror questionnaires are used routinely. In others, questionnaires are used to expedite the jury selection process when large numbers of jurors will be called for a case. A juror questionnaire, in general, will provide more information or at least answers to more questions for more potential jurors in a given period of time than the traditional jury selection process. The juror questionnaire may also help gain more information about sources of pretrial publicity received by a potential juror. The questionnaire can also address potential areas of prejudice arising out of pretrial publicity, such as factors in the defendant's or victim's background, or political, or religious issues.

When a juror questionnaire is used, the attorneys are unable to observe the demeanor of the potential jurors in responding to the questions. The demeanor

---

[28] Burgess v. State, 723 So. 2d 742, 762 (1997)..

[29] People v. Jendrzejewski, 455 Mich. 495, 509, 566 N.W.2d 530, 538 (1997).

[30] People v. Tyburski, 445 Mich. 606, 518 N.W.2d 441 (1994).

of, and interaction with, jurors concerning questions can be particularly important in assessing the jurors' qualifications. The questionnaire may also be used by the attorney or court when questioning potential jurors.

There is no guarantee that a juror will be any more truthful in writing than when questioned directly, but some jurors feel that it is easier to communicate information concerning certain areas, such as prior victimization on a juror questionnaire. Generally, individuals do not want to discuss personal or sensitive matters at all, but are less likely to do so in front of others. The questioning can be asked without relating the questions to a particular party.

It is important that questions on a juror questionnaire, just like questions on polling surveys, be carefully written and selected. This may require the use of outside consultants.

Juror questionnaires are becoming more prevalent not only in highly publicized trials but also routine criminal cases as well since questionnaires can save time. Most questionnaires must be approved by the court. By providing counsel with more information about a juror's background, counsel is more likely to be able to use a challenge for cause rather than a peremptory challenge.

The same areas of questions can be used in a juror questionnaire as in jury selection; however, in sexual assault cases, particular emphasis should be placed on sensitive topics, such as prior involvement in sexual assault, prior accusations of abuse, whether the juror has ever been the victim of abuse, and questions concerning opinions or feelings about the topic of sexual assault or child abuse generally.

Counsel should be prepared to argue the propriety of proposed questions by submitting a legal memorandum in support of questions that may be contested by the opposing side. Juror questionnaires offer a better opportunity to make arguments in support of particular questions. Many voir dires are not recorded. Even when a voir dire is stenographically transcribed, it is more difficult for a court to make an immediate decision on a disputed question, and it is more difficult for counsel to argue the authority supporting a question during the give and take of voir dire.

With jury questionnaires, there is the question of whether a court will make the responses available for public review and identify the respondents. In sexual assault trials, however, judges consider the sensitive nature of many of the questions and recognize that the answers might unduly infringe on jurors' concerns for privacy.

A sample juror questionnaire is set forth in Appendix J of the book. This questionnaire, used in the Florida trial of William Kennedy Smith, contains a good example of the questions frequently asked of potential jurors in a sexual assault case.

One California appeals court has ruled that a trial court can not order a defendant to return juror questionnaires to the court.[31] The court held:

> The First Amendment of the United States Constitution guaranteeing public access to judicial proceedings overwhelms any countervailing privacy interests of prospective jurors as to the content of questionnaires they complete. Where trial courts wish to protect their content from public observation, the constitutionally permitted procedure mandates that the judge advise members of the venire at the time the questionnaires are distributed that, upon completion, they will become public records accessible to anyone, and as an alternative to writing in sensitive personal data, jurors can answer those questions on the record in chambers with counsel present. Even in that event, trial judges should take care that the individual prospective juror is not given either explicit or implicit assurances that the transcript of *in camera* questioning will be protected from public disclosure in all instances.

> Moreover, any expectation of privacy prospective jurors may have in the content of their questionnaires completed during jury selection does not extend to a criminal defendant and counsel. As we explain, because the raison d'etre of juror questionnaires is to assist both sides and counsel in the selection of a fair and impartial jury, juror privacy is not advanced by harvesting them from the confidential files of the Public Defender's office when their content was purposefully divulged to defense counsel.[32]

§ 3.7   Barriers to obtaining juror information.

Potential jurors, for a variety of reasons, will not always provide essential information. This is due in part to the jury selection process which does not always allow for the free flow of information. This is particularly true with judge-controlled voir dire as well as in many lawyer-conducted voir dire proceedings in which counsel tend to ask leading and suggestive questions or questions that clearly ask for only one answer. An example of such a question is: "Is there anyone here who feels, because of the facts of this case, that he or she cannot be a fair and impartial juror in this case?" It is obvious to most jurors that one should be fair and impartial and that a negative response to such a question is inappropriate. Few people want to describe themselves as unfair, especially publicly.

Many questions on voir dire are close-ended and do not allow a juror to discuss past experiences. For example, the question "Is there anything that you saw or read about this case that will affect your ability to be fair and impartial?" will yield little beneficial information. If a juror is not permitted to discuss the content of news stories he or she has read or seen about the case, it is difficult to assess

---

[31] Bellas v. Superior Court, 85 Cal. App. 4th 636, 102 Cal. Rptr. 2d 380 (2000).

[32] Bellas v. Superior Court, 85 Cal. App. 4th 636, 638–639, 102 Cal. Rptr. 2d 380, 381–382 (2000).

what it was that a juror read, how important the information was in the context of the case, and the true effect of that information upon the juror.

Potential jurors also engage in self-censorship. They may not wish to disclose personal information, particularly when it appears that the person asking the questions does not really care about the answers. Some potential jurors actually may have more nefarious reasons for a lack of complete honesty; for example, they may want to get on a jury to right some past "wrong" or perhaps "get back" at the criminal justice system.

§ 3.8 Right to, and scope of, voir dire.

The right to a fair trial only entitles a defendant to a fair and impartial jury — the attorney's vision of an ideal jury. There is also no constitutional right to exercise peremptory challenges.[33] Recent decisions regarding discriminating use of peremptory challenges have suggested that perhaps the peremptory challenge should be abolished.[34] There is, however, acknowledgment that adequate voir dire is necessary for intelligent peremptory challenges.[35] This may include the right to question a potential juror about his or her expressed bias.[36] For example, if a juror states that he or she may be biased because their son had a similar sexual assault charge made against him, precluding the defendant's attorney from further questioning and possibly rehabilitating the juror is an abuse of discretion.[37] In Federal court, questioning of jurors is a matter within the trial judge's discretion.[38] Many states will grant a trial judge discretion in permitting

---

[33] Frazier v. United States, 335 U.S. 497, 505 n.11 (1948); United States v. Wood, 299 U.S. 123, 145 (1936); Stilson v. United States, 250 U.S. 583, 586 (1919).

[34] See § 3.24, n.165.

[35] United States v. Whitt, 718 F.2d 1494, 1497 (10th Cir. 1983).

[36] Melendez v. State, 700 So. 2d 791 (Fla. Dist. Ct. App. 1997).

[37] Melendez v. State, 700 So. 2d 791 (Fla. Dist. Ct. App. 1997). The appellate court noted that the defendant's attorney was improperly precluded from questioning another juror during the following exchange:

> State: Do you agree with the premises [sic] that some people do some things to put themselves in risk of harm?
>
> Juror: They do things.
>
> State: Like the example I used before walking around with money.
>
> Juror: Well, that's life. You do what you got to do.
>
> State: And would you agree just because I would do something like that doesn't mean I want to get robbed?
>
> Juror: I would think you're an asshole but I mean I won't hold that — excuse me.
>
> State: Go ahead.
>
> The Court: Excuse me, thank you, Mr. (Juror). You may go on back down to the jury room.
>
> Defense Counsel: For the record I would ask the Court to note my objection.

[38] See, e.g., Yarborough v. United States, 230 F.2d 56, 63 (4th Cir.), cert. denied, 351 U.S. 969 (1956), aff'g 16 F.R.D. 212 (D. Md. 1954).

questions on voir dire that allow attorneys to seek information that will assist their exercising peremptory challenges. Other courts limit questioning to areas "reasonably likely to disclose cause for disqualification," and other inquiries are at the discretion of the court. [39] The trial court often has the power to limit the length of voir dire. [40] Questioning potential jurors about the effects of stress on perception, for example, does not go to a juror's qualification. [41]

Many courts take the view that there is not necessarily a right to question jurors about areas of law such as the presumption of innocence, burden of proof, reasonable doubt, or the meaning or purpose of an indictment. [42] Since a juror is bound to follow the court's instructions on the law, the juror's knowledge or ignorance of principles of law is not a proper subject of inquiry, only whether the juror will follow the court's instructions. [43] A juror who states she will hold the defendant's failure to testify against him and is equivocal on whether she would follow an instruction to the contrary should be disqualified for cause. [44] For this reason, a trial judge "has broad discretion to control and restrict the scope of the voir dire examination." [45] A judge may, for example, limit questioning

---

[39] Davis v. State, 333 Md. 27, 39, 633 A.2d 867, 873 (1993) (but also noting there may be inquiry of certain areas reasonably related to the case); Cal. Code Civ. Proc. § 223:

> In a criminal case, the court shall conduct the examination of prospective jurors. However, the court may permit the parties, upon a showing of good cause, to supplement the examination by such further inquiry as it deems proper, or shall itself submit to the prospective jurors upon such a showing, such additional questions by the parties as it deems proper. . . . Examination of prospective jurors shall be conducted only in the aid of the exercise of challenges for cause.

See also People v. Boulerice, 5 Cal. App. 4th 463, 474–76, 7 Cal. Rptr. 2d 279, 285–86 (1992).

[40] People v. Koury, 268 A.D.2d 896, 701 N.Y.S.2d 749, appeal denied, 94 N.Y.2d 949, 731 N.E.2d 623, 710 N.Y.S.2d 6 (2000) (upholding 15-minute time limit in sexual assault trial, particularly since defendant did not object at outset to "guideline" and never requested additional time to inquire further).

[41] People v. Sanders, 51 Cal. 3d 471, 506, 797 P.2d 561, 580, 273 Cal. Rptr. 537 (1990), cert. denied, 500 U.S. 948 (1991) (counsel argued that these questions would provide evidentiary support for his motion to introduce expert testimony on eyewitness testimony; the California Supreme Court held that they were an improper use of voir dire).

[42] State v. Stacy, 680 So. 2d 1175 (La. 1996) (defendant's attorney was not denied the opportunity to examine the jurors' competency and impartiality concerning the principle of accessory after-the-fact, and there was no undermining of a crucial aspect of voir dire examination); People v. Boulware, 29 N.Y.2d 135, 272 N.E.2d 538, 324 N.Y.S.2d 30 (1971) (citing the decisions of several other states taking the same position).

[43] People v. Boulware, 29 N.Y.2d 135, 272 N.E.2d 538, 324 N.Y.S.2d 30 (1971).

[44] People v. Kenner, 8 A.D.3d 296, 777 N.Y.S.2d 669 (2004).

[45] People v. Boulware, 29 N.Y.2d 135, 140, 272 N.E.2d 538, 540, 324 N.Y.S.2d 30, 32 (1971). See also People v. Byrd, 214 A.D.2d 581, appeal denied, 86 N.Y.2d 733, 655 N.E.2d 710, 631 N.Y.S.2d 613 (1995) (holding that "trial court did not improvidently exercise its discretion in questioning a juror who expressed doubts as to her ability to remain fair and told the court that she felt sympathy for the defendant").

on issues relating to sexual abuse.[46]

If the jury selection process is not transcribed, it will be difficult to raise legal challenges to the conduct of jury selection without a record, as in raising or defending against *Batson* challenges. (*See* §§ 3.24–29.) Request that the jury selection process be transcribed; it is helpful in many situations. A stenographically transcribed jury selection is particularly important in establishing the prejudicial effect of pretrial publicity. Without such a record, a party may not be able to establish the prejudicial effect of publicity or establish the basis for a change of venue motion.[47]

A juror who states she does "not understand what was going on" and "didn't understand the lawyers and she didn't understand the judge" may be grossly unqualified to serve as a juror and requires an inquiry by the court.[48]

When a challenge for cause is denied, it may be necessary to exhaust all peremptory challenges in order to appeal the denial of a challenge to a juror.[49] If a defendant uses a peremptory challenge when a juror should have been removed for cause, the defendant's right to exercise is not necessarily impaired or denied.[50] A transcript will also help in challenging or defending a judge's "for cause" determination on a juror.

---

[46] Brown v. State, 686 So. 2d 385 (Ala. Crim. App. 1995), *aff'd*, 686 So. 2d 409 (Ala. 1996), *cert. denied*, 520 U.S. 1199 (1997) (trial court exercised appropriate discretion in refusing to ask questions about potential jurors' reactions to child victim's sexual abuse before killing).

[47] *See, e.g.*, People v. Parker, 60 N.Y.2d 714, 456 N.E.2d 811, 468 N.Y.S.2d 870 (1983).

[48] People v. Sanchez, 99 N.Y.2d 622, 790 N.E.2d 766, 760 N.Y.S.2d 391 (2003).

[49] Williams v. State, 338 Ark. 97, 112, 991 S.W.2d 565, 573 (1999); Wilson v. State, 753 So. 2d 683 (Fla. Dist. Ct. App. 2000), *review denied*, 773 So. 2d 59 (Fla. 2000) (defendant in sexual assault case did not preserve challenge to trial court's refusal to excuse several jurors for cause because defendant did not exhaust all peremptory challenges, forcing an objectionable juror to be seated); Hammond v. State, 727 So. 2d 979 (Fla. Dist. Ct. App. 1999) (noting that to preserve an error for failure to strike a juror for cause, the "defendant must use all his peremptory challenges, request an additional challenge, and identify the objectionable juror he would strike"); State v. Hart, 691 So. 2d 651 (La. 1997); People v. Jendrzejewski, 455 Mich. 495, 514, 566 N.W.2d 530, 540 (1997), *cert. denied*, 522 U.S. 1097 (1998); Chisolm v. State, 529 So. 2d 635, 639 (Miss. 1988); People v. Torpey, 63 N.Y.2d 361, 365, 472 N.E.2d 298, 482 N.Y.S.2d 448, 450 (1984); People v. Libardi, 12 A.D.3d 534, 784 N.Y.S.2d 636 (2004), *appeal denied*, 4 N.Y.3d 765, 825 N.E.2d 141, 792 N.Y.S.2d 9 (2005); State v. Watson, 61 Ohio St. 3d 1, 16, 572 N.E.2d 97, 110 (1991); State v. Key, 1995 Tenn. Crim. App. LEXIS 490 at *10; State v. Howell, 868 S.W.2d 238, 248 (Tenn. 1993), *cert. denied*, 510 U.S. 1215 (1994).

[50] Watley v. Williams, 218 F.3d 1156 (10th Cir. 2000), *cert. denied*, 531 U.S. 1089 (2001) (*citing* United States v. Martinez-Salazar, 528 U.S. 304 (2000)) (finding no constitutional denial of defendant's right to an impartial jury in a sexual assault trial where defendant was forced to use a peremptory challenge when trial court erroneously denied his challenge for cause to a juror whose home was burglarized and mother-in-law and close friend had been raped and where daughter was in a Bible study group of one of the victims).

§ 3.9   Basic areas of voir dire.

In most trials, there is certain basic information that should be gathered on voir dire.

  (1)   Age (may be estimated on circumstantial factors or from the juror questionnaire data available through the court, or asked directly);

  (2)   Education;

  (3)   Family status and household makeup;

  (4)   Past and present employment of self, spouse, and children; supervisory responsibility; what does juror like or dislike about job;

  (5)   Location of past and present residences;

  (6)   Ownership of home or other property;

  (7)   Prior jury (civil and criminal) or grand jury service;

  (8)   Military service;

  (9)   Hobbies, organizations, leisure activities;

 (10)   Any knowledge of the parties, attorneys, or witnesses involved in case;

 (11)   Jurors' awareness of publicity surrounding the case and its source;

 (12)   Physical problems that will prevent that person from sitting on the jury;

 (13)   Does the juror have a preference not to serve on this case;

 (14)   Does the juror know any other jurors on the panel;

 (15)   Interest in the legal system, or law-related organizations, or legal employment;

 (16)   Prior accusations of criminal conduct by or against juror;

 (17)   Prior victimization;

 (18)   Law enforcement relationships;

 (19)   Relationship with individuals accused of crime.

This list offers some basic criteria to evaluate in formulating a model of the ideal juror (*see* § 3.4) in a particular case. More detailed discussion of some of these areas is set forth below. Some areas may require extensive probing or questioning depending on the juror's initial response. Dishonesty in answering these areas of questioning may result in dismissal of the juror even after the jury has been empanelled.[51]

---

[51] State v. Lemker, 2001 Ohio App. LEXIS 1389 (Mar. 23, 2001) (holding trial court properly dismissed a juror, after jury empanelled, who had falsely declared in jury selection that he had never been convicted of a crime).

§ 3.10 Questions about family.

Questions concerning family composition and relationships provide information about a juror's life experiences. Experiences with and attitudes about family can especially play a role in a juror's evaluation of child sexual assault allegations. Does the juror have children who are adults? Are these children individuals who may have shared experiences similar to those of the victim or defendant? Has the family relationship been marked by discord or problems? What is the attitude of the juror toward his or her children or spouse? How does the juror describe the current activities of family members? Has the family experience been limited to one geographical area or has there been substantial movement? Are those moves unexplained or are they the product of career advancement?

Typically, jurors will express concern about hearing evidence in a case involving a child victim when the juror has minor children or grandchildren. This will not necessarily justify a challenge for cause. Such a juror may ultimately declare, "I would still want to be fair. There is still emotion, but I want to be fair. And I want to hear the whole story."[52]

§ 3.11 Questions concerning juror's experience with children.

Jurors who have experience with children on a personal or professional level will bring stronger opinions to a case involving child victims. For example, someone who works with children, such as a teacher, may fear the allegation of sexual abuse. Past work or social experiences with children may be strong factors in an individual's view of children. Experience with children in a family may be important if arguments are presented as to how children would behave in a particular situation. Experience with children may also provide a juror with different insight on either physical or emotional child development. At least one court in a child sexual assault trial has found no abuse of discretion in a trial court's failure to ask a juror questions about child care, child development, child custody, or medical or nursing training.[53] It may be reversible error to preclude questioning concerning venirepersons' attitudes and feelings about victims' ages.[54]

Consider the following questions individually or to the group:

(1) Have you had any job that involved working with infants or young children?

(2) Does anyone or a close family member baby-sit for children?

---

[52] People v. Robinson, 874 P.2d 453, 457 (Colo. App. 1993).

[53] United States v. Payne, 944 F.2d 1458, 1475 (9th Cir. 1991) ("Those questions do not fall within one of the three recognized classes raising a real possibility of bias and are only speculatively related to bias.").

[54] State v. Clark, 981 S.W.2d 143 (Mo. 1998).

(3)   Does anyone or a close friend or family member have an occupation that brings him or her in regular contact with children, such as school teacher, day care worker, or little league coach?

(4)   Does anyone have children? Tell me about your children.

(5)   Who has a child, or is close to a child who is about the age of the complainant in this case?[55]

(6)   Has your contact with children ever involved discussing sexual matters or allegations of sexual abuse?

(7)   Has child development been an area of interest to you?

(8)   Have you taken courses in child development?

(9)   Have you read any books, watched, or attended programs on the subject? Describe them, please.

The follow-up to many questions is crucial. If the potential juror has had contact with a particular area of concern, allow the juror to honestly express feelings rather than inhibiting disclosure by asking, "Could you still be fair and impartial?" For example, consider the following questions:

Q.   Tell us about your experiences working with children in foster care.

A.   Well, it's challenging, frustrating.

Q.   Were any abused?

A.   Yes, many of the children I work with in foster care have been.

Q.   And how might that affect you?

A.   I'm not sure.

Q.   You are somewhat uncertain how those experiences might affect you in this case?

A.   It's hard to say.

Q.   And because it's hard to say, this may not be the case for you?

A.   Perhaps not.

Q.   And because of that uncertainty, you feel it's best that you not sit on this case?

A.   Yes, I'd rather not sit on this case.

Had the juror been confronted immediately with "Can you be fair and impartial because of that association?" or something to that effect, the juror probably would not have expressed her reluctance to sitting on this case. There may be many such issues in a trial that touch emotional experiences or deeply held feelings. Rather than guess about the juror's reactions to those experiences, it is best to

---

[55] The court's failure to ask this question is not necessarily an abuse of discretion. *See, e.g.,* United States v. Joe, 831 F.2d 218, 221 (10th Cir. 1987), *cert. denied,* 484 U.S. 1072 (1988).

let the juror express them as much as possible so that peremptory challenge and challenges for cause can be wisely used.

§ 3.12 Questions about relationship with law enforcement officers, or prosecutors, or defense attorney.

Generally, courts permit voir dire regarding juror's attitudes toward the testimony of police officers, but the failure to permit such questions does not necessarily constitute reversible error. The significance of the refusal to permit such questions and whether a conviction will be reversed depends on the importance of the officer's testimony, the extent of a credibility issue surrounding the officer's testimony, and the sufficiency of other voir dire inquiries on the topic of law enforcement or government agents.[56]

Courts with an expansive view of voir dire will permit inquiry concerning a juror's relationship with individuals employed in law enforcement. A state taking the view that law enforcement employment or association does not provide the basis of a challenge for cause, even when the case involves credibility of a police officer, will restrict questioning about law enforcement employment or association.[57] However, it may be reversible error to deny a challenge for cause to a juror who expresses a bias toward police testimony who alters that opinion in the face of "adversarial" questioning by the court.[58] Courts vary widely on whether such a relationship will constitute a basis of challenge for cause. A typical view is that when the potential juror is a police officer or law enforcement person, challenge for cause will generally be granted only when the potential juror has a "real relationship" with the case, such as a member of the same police force as witnesses in the case or some other relationship to police officers in the case.[59] In some jurisdictions, a court must grant a challenge for cause to

---

[56] United States v. Payne, 944 F.2d 1458, 1475 (9th Cir. 1991) *citing* United States v. Powell, 932 F.2d 1337, 1340 (9th Cir. 1991); United States v. Contreras-Castro, 825 F.2d 185, 187 (9th Cir. 1987) (reversing defendant's conviction where court limited this line of questioning and credibility of government agent's testimony was crucial to case); United States v. Baldwin, 607 F.2d 1295, 1298 (9th Cir. 1979).

[57] Davis v. State, 333 Md. 27, 36–37, 633 A.2d 867, 872 (1993):

Davis's proposed voir dire inquiry does not relate to cause for disqualification. Davis merely sought to discover whether any prospective juror was either a law enforcement officer or was related to or associated with any law enforcement officers. Assuming that the court would have allowed such an inquiry, an affirmative answer would not have established cause for disqualification. First, the fact that a prospective juror is or was a member of a law enforcement body does not automatically disqualify that venire person. [citations omitted] . . . In general, the professional, vocational, or social status of a prospective juror is not a dispositive factor establishing cause to disqualify. Rather, the proper focus is on the venire person's state of mind. . . .

[58] Davis v. State, 333 Md. 27, 36–37, 633 A.2d 867, 872 (1993); People v. White, 275 A.D.2d 913, 714 N.Y.S.2d 179 (2000).

[59] People v. Cassidy, 16 A.D.3d 1079, 791 N.Y.S.2d 259, *appeal denied*, 5 N.Y.3d 760, 834

a prospective juror who is a compensated employee of a public law enforcement agency.[60] This includes a military police reservist.[61] A court's adversarial questioning of a juror who expresses bias toward police testimony and alters that opinion in the face of such questioning can be reversible error. A former probation officer is not necessarily disqualified to sit in a criminal case.[62] For example, a corrections officer is not *per se* disqualified from sitting on a case involving an assault upon a correctional officer.[63] Typically, an acquaintance with police officers, without more, is not grounds for disqualification from jury service.[64] The fact that a potential juror has relatives in the same profession as a prosecution witness usually does not, in and of itself, make a juror unqualified to serve.[65] Being acquainted with a police officer who testifies does not usually disqualify a juror,[66] and some courts will even find that being related to a police officer who testifies at trial is not a basis for a challenge to cause.[67] Sometimes a juror's relationship to an officer involved in the case will justify a challenge for cause,[68]

N.E.2d 1264, 801 N.Y.S.2d 254 (2005) (While two of the prospective jurors were retired police officers who had some familiarity with witnesses who testified at trial, and one of those two prospective jurors had known a witness for many years, the witnesses did not fall within the class of persons that would have required those prospective jurors to be disqualified [N.Y. Statute]. The fact that either prospective juror was "a former police officer who had 'nodding acquaintance[s]' with several of the prospective witnesses did not render him inherently biased so as to justify disqualification for cause."); People v. Lopez, 7 A.D.3d 350, 775 N.Y.S.2d 861, *appeal denied*, 3 N.Y.3d 708, 818 N.E.2d 678, 785 N.Y.S.2d 36 (2004) (holding mere fact that a prospective juror is a police officer is not a ground for challenge for cause); People v. Willard, 226 A.D.2d 1014, 641 N.Y.S.2d 896, *appeal denied*, 88 N.Y.2d 943, 670 N.E.2d 461, 647 N.Y.S.2d 177 (1996) (court properly denied challenge for cause in a rape case of a corrections officer who stated he would render a verdict based on the evidence even though he wore a shirt that said "Support Your Local Corrections Officers. Reinstate Capital Punishment"); Commonwealth v. Lee, 401 Pa. Super. 591, 585 A.2d 1084 (1991) (holding proper the trial court's refusal where the officer had been retired 17 years and the case did not hinge upon the credibility of police officers); Zakkizadeh v. State, 920 S.W.2d 337 (Tex. App. 1995).

60 Colo. Rev. Stat. 16-10-103(1)(k): (1) The court shall sustain a challenge for cause on one or more of the following grounds: (k) The juror is a compensated employee of a public law enforcement agency or a public defender's office.

61 Hung Ma v. People, 121 P.3d 205 (Colo. 2005).

62 Strickler v. Commonwealth, 241 Va. 482, 492, 404 S.E.2d 227, 233–34 (1991).

63 Williams v. Commonwealth, 21 Va. App. 616, 466 S.E.2d 754 (1996).

64 State v. Bahn, 218 Wis. 2d 164, 578 N.W.2d 208 (1998).

65 State v. Henderson, 566 So. 2d 1098, 1103 (La. Ct. App. 1990); People v. Colon, 71 N.Y.2d 410, 418, 521 N.E.2d 1075, 1080, 526 N.Y.S.2d 932, 937 (1988), *cert. denied*, 487 U.S. 1239 (1988); Commonwealth v. Jones, 477 Pa. 164, 383 A.2d 874 (1978) (holding that one's status as a law enforcement officer in and of itself is insufficient to require disqualification as a juror in a criminal case).

66 State v. Landers, 969 S.W.2d 808 (Mo. Ct. App. 1998).

67 State v. Chapman, 410 So. 2d 689 (La. 1981).

68 Commonwealth v. Dye, 2000 Pa. Super. 382, 765 A.2d 1123 (2000), *appeal denied*, 566 Pa. 677, 784 A.2d 114 (2001) (reversing defendant's conviction due to trial court's failure to excuse for cause a juror who was married to a trooper who was the immediate supervisor of the arresting officer in the case; court noted that defendant had exercised all of his peremptory challenges).

as will a juror's equivocal assurance about whether the relationship will affect her ability to render a fair and impartial verdict, [69] and the failure to grant it will warrant a new trial.

A potential juror's relationship with a law enforcement person should be carefully explored to determine the nature and extent of his or her contacts with that person and the effects of those contacts as the juror's decision-making process. The specific area of work or specialty of the law enforcement person also should be explored. Does the police officer have experience with internal affairs investigations and, perhaps be more likely to view police officer misconduct differently? What kind of experience does that law enforcement person have? Is it administrative? Furthermore, many jurors will not understand what law enforcement encompasses. A question should clearly indicate that law enforcement may be more than just uniformed police; it encompasses many investigative arms of government, including, for example, Internal Revenue Service and military investigators. Sometimes, the question can be broadened to include relationships with individuals who have investigative or prosecutorial-like duties, such as are commonly found in administrative agencies.

In a sexual assault trial, if a potential juror has had a relationship with a law enforcement official or worked for a law enforcement agency, counsel should explore the situation as follows:

(1)   Does that officer work cases involving sexual assault or rape?

(2)   How often do you see him or her?

(3)   How many years did you work with that agency?

(4)   As a result of those contacts, did you become friendly or develop a bond with some of the officers?

Many other questions can be asked about jurors' attitudes and opinions concerning police officers, especially when their conduct is material to the trial. Two well-known jury consultants suggest the following questions concerning police officers. [70]

(1)   When you think about the police department in your city, what's the first thing that comes to your mind?

---

[69] People v. Williams, 302 A.D.2d 412, 754 N.Y.S.2d 563, *appeal denied,* 100 N.Y.2d 544, 793 N.E.2d 424, 763 N.Y.S.2d 10 (2003):

> Here, one of the prospective jurors gave equivocal responses when questioned by counsel as to whether the fact that her husband was a postal inspector would prevent her from being fair and impartial. The trial court failed to obtain a personal, unequivocal declaration or assurance of impartiality from that prospective juror. Because of the possible predisposition of that prospective juror against the defendant, which raised a serious doubt regarding her ability to render an impartial verdict, the defendant was not assured of his right to a trial before an unbiased fact-finder. [citations omitted]

[70] Cathy E. Bennett & Robert B. Hirschhorn, *Voir Dire in Criminal Cases,* Trial, October 1992, at 68, 74–75.

(2) How reliable do you think a police officer's testimony is? Why?

(3) How reliable do you think the testimony of an accused or of an accused's witness is? Why?

In sexual assault cases, questions about law enforcement may not make that much difference unless the law enforcement testimony is more vital to the case than the complainant's, such as when a victim is unable to identify the defendant, and the sole evidence connecting the defendant to the crime is a police officer's testimony regarding the defendant's admissions.[71] In sexual assault trials, attitudes about the victim and defendant are more likely to play a greater role than attitudes about police or law enforcement.

Juror relationships with the prosecution or defense can be an area of concern. If the juror is a prosecutor or employee in the same office as the case prosecutor, the juror should be disqualified under the appearance of impropriety test even if the potential juror states he or she can be impartial.[72] Some states, by statute, may preclude jurors who have a working relationship with the prosecution.[73] While a relationship with a prosecutor may not rise to a *per se* implied bias, relatives of a prosecutor might in some situations be subject to challenge for cause.[74] A juror's past professional relationship with the prosecutor can be the basis of a challenge for cause.[75] Sometimes, a past relationship with the elected district attorney can be grounds to challenge a juror for cause, even if the juror claims that the relationship would not influence her verdict.[76] A prejudicial relationship with a district attorney can exist through a juror's deceased husband, as where a juror and her husband had socialized with a district attorney, and

---

[71] Commonwealth v. Colon, 223 Pa. Super. 202, 299 A.2d 326 (1972) (an officer on the same police force as officers in the case whose testimony is being challenged on the involuntary nature of the defendant's confession bears a real relationship to the case). *See generally* Annotation, *Law Enforcement Officers as Qualified Jurors in Criminal Cases,* 72 A.L.R.3d 895 (1976).

[72] State v. Kauhi, 86 Haw. 195, 948 P.2d 1036 (1997) ("Where a prospective juror is a prosecutor currently employed by the same office as the prosecutor trying the defendant, the court shall imply bias as a matter of law and dismiss the prospective juror for cause."); State v. Kauhi, 86 Haw. 195, 200, 948 P.2d 1036, 1041 (1997). *See also* Beam v. State, 260 Ga. 784, 400 S.E.2d 327 (1991) (holding it was reversible error to permit employee of district attorney's office to be trial juror).

[73] Idaho Code § 19-2020; Minn. R. Crim. Proc. Law § 26.02(5); N.Y. Crim. Proc. Law § 270.20(1); N.D. Cent. Code § 29-17-36; Okla. Stat. tit. 22 § 660; Or. Rev. Stat.§ 136.220; S.D. Codified Laws § 23A-20-13.

[74] United States v. Colombo, 869 F.2d 149 (2d Cir. 1989); People v. Walters, 12 A.D.3d 953. 785 N.Y.S.2d 192 (2004) (reversing defendant's conviction because under New York law a juror who is related within the sixth degree of consanguinity or affinity to counsel for the People is automatically disqualified as a juror and prosecuting attorney's first cousin who was selected as juror falls within this definition).

[75] Fugate v. Commonwealth, 993 S.W.2d 931 (Ky. 1999) (reversing defendant's conviction because of juror's past professional relationship with prosecutor and holding that a trial court is required to excuse for cause a juror who has had a prior professional relationship with the prosecutor even if the juror professes not to seek such a professional relationship in the future).

[76] People v. Clark, 125 A.D.2d 868, 510 N.Y.S.2d 223 (1986).

several years earlier had been on a cruise with him (sponsored by a veteran's organization to which they all belonged), and the juror's deceased husband had been on a firstname basis with him.[77]

A potential juror's relationship with a prosecutor does not necessarily justify a challenge for cause.[78] The fact that a juror did not disclose attending school with the trial prosecutor does not necessarily warrant a reversal of a defendant's conviction when a presumption of bias has been sufficiently rebutted and there is no showing that the relationship affected the outcome of the proceedings.[79] Likewise, concealing a relationship with an Assistant District Attorney in the prosecutor's office, but not involved in the prosecution, does not entitle a defendant to a new trial in the absence of a showing of prejudice to a defendant's substantial right.[80] A relationship with a member of the prosecutor's family will not automatically justify a challenge for cause if there is no showing that the relationship affects the juror's decision-making process.[81] A potential juror who

---

[77] People v. Clark, 125 A.D.2d 868, 510 N.Y.S.2d 223 (1986).

[78] Sholler v. Commonwealth, 969 S.W.2d 706, 709 (Ky. 1998) (holding that mere social acquaintance with prosecutor by itself does not indicate a probability of partiality); Harman v. Commonwealth, 898 S.W.2d 486 (Ky. 1995) (juror's past representation by Commonwealth's attorney did not justify challenge for cause, although juror was challenged peremptorily); State v. Harris, 765 So. 2d 1230 (La. Ct. App. 2000), writ. denied, 795 So. 2d 322 (2001) (Trial court refused to grant challenge for cause for juror who knew one of testifying police officers in sexual assault trial, which was upheld on appeal. "The mere fact that a prospective juror is somehow related to a law enforcement officer is not sufficient to grant a challenge for cause. Such should be granted only if that relationship influences the juror in his ability to make a decision in the case." State v. Harris, 765 So. 2d 1230, 1237 (La. Ct. App. 2000), writ. denied, 795 So. 2d 322 (2001)); People v. Whittington, 267 A.D.2d 486, 699 N.Y.S.2d 733, 733–34 (1999), appeal denied, 94 N.Y.2d 926, 729 N.E.2d 1165, 708 N.Y.S.2d 366 (2000) ("The defendant unsuccessfully challenged for cause a prospective juror whose spouse was a supervising Assistant District Attorney in the office of the District Attorney which was prosecuting him. The record reveals that the juror was unacquainted with the trial prosecutor and that her spouse had no interaction with him. As the prospective juror unequivocally stated that she had no predisposition and would base her verdict upon the evidence, the court properly denied the defendant's challenge for cause.").

[79] State v. Bolton, No. 03C01-9707-CR-00255, 1999 Tenn. Crim. App. LEXIS 173 (Feb. 25, 1999).

[80] People v. Rodriguez, 100 N.Y.2d 30, 790 N.E.2d 247, 760 N.Y.S.2d 74 (2003). Juror withheld information concerning his friendship with prosecutor because:

> [H]e wanted to be selected for defendant's jury because the judge predicted that the trial would be relatively short. He believed that if he divulged his friendship with [prosecutor], he might have been returned to the jury pool for another, possibly longer, case. [Juror] had no contact with [prosecutor] during the trial and unequivocally stated that his relationship with [prosecutor] did not influence his deliberations in the slightest. Based on this testimony, the trial court determined that although [juror's] failure to disclose the friendship constituted misconduct, it was "harmless" and did not result in substantial prejudice to defendant.

People v. Rodriguez, 100 N.Y.2d 30, 36, 790 N.E.2d 247, 251, 760 N.Y.S.2d 74, 78 (2003).

[81] Commonwealth v. Blasioli, 454 Pa. Super. 207, 685 A.2d 151 (1996), aff'd, 713 A.2d 1117

previously appeared as a prosecution witness in an unrelated robbery case is not necessarily precluded from sitting in a sexual assault prosecution.[82] A juror's relationship with the defendant's attorney may also be cause for concern. For example, if the prospective juror has a relationship with a victim whose attacker was represented by the defense attorney or some public defender's officer, it may be reversible error to refuse to strike the juror for cause.[83]

§ 3.13 Questions concerning litigation experience and law.

Past experiences with the legal system are very informative because most individuals who have come in contact with the legal system are likely to develop opinions as a result of their experiences. Find out why a potential juror has had an experience with the legal system, whether strong feelings have developed as a result of that experience, and whether those feelings will color the juror's decision-making process in the case. If a potential juror has had an experience as a witness in a legal proceeding, he or she may have developed an impression of cross-examination. Of particular importance is past litigation experience in the family court system. In any litigation experience, a potential juror can develop attitudes and feelings concerning attorneys and judges that can also affect the decision-making process.

The following questions can be asked concerning litigation experience:

(1) Have you, or a close friend, or family member been involved as a litigant or a witness in a civil or criminal proceeding?

(2) Could you describe your involvement with the case?

(3) Did the proceeding involve any of the issues similar to this case or domestic violence?

(4) Did the proceeding involve doctors or professional experts?

(1998) (holding no need to grant challenge for cause to juror who worked at hospital with prosecutor's wife, had seen her socially at hospital fund raisers, and was her patient, and who affirmed she would not let her physician-patient relationship with prosecutor's wife affect her decision, and the relationship "did not rise to the level where the trial court could have presumed the likelihood of prejudice").

[82] People v. Dehler, 216 A.D.2d 643, 628 N.Y.S.2d 413, *appeal denied*, 86 N.Y.2d 734, 655 N.E.2d 712, 631 N.Y.S.2d 615 (1995).

[83] Medici v. Commonwealth, 260 Va. 223, 532 S.E.2d 28 (2000):

Here, the prospective juror's husband had been murdered and the accused murderer was represented by a lawyer in the same Public Defender's Office that also served as counsel for Medici. While we have no reason to question Bennett's honesty and sincerity, we think that permitting her to sit as a juror, in the circumstances of this case, would weaken public confidence in the integrity of criminal trials. Accordingly, we hold that the trial court abused its discretion in failing to strike Bennett as a juror and that the ruling constitutes reversible error.

Medici v. Commonwealth, 260 Va. 223, 227, 532 S.E.2d 28, 31 (2000).

(5) Have you, or a close friend, or family member had experience with family court proceedings, divorce proceedings? What was the nature of the proceeding?

(6) Were you a witness or a party?

(7) What was the case about?

(8) Was the case resolved?

(9) In what ways, if any, do you think that experience could influence or affect you here?

Family court experiences are particularly important since they may touch upon a person's victimization or experience with accusations involving family problems, or even abuse. When those experiences involve domestic violence, custody disputes, marital discord, or problems with children, they are likely to be strong, emotional experiences and may well affect a juror's feelings about men, women, children, police, or the legal system. If the potential juror has had prior involvement in a family court proceeding, a marital dispute, or litigation involving issues pertaining to child abuse or domestic violence, and counsel would prefer not to have that person on the jury, consider questions that would provide him or her with a reason to be excused, e.g., "As a result of that experience, do you feel that sitting on this case may trigger some difficult or painful memories?" or "And as a result, perhaps this may not be the case for you?"

Note that these two questions allow a juror to express his or her feelings without being confronted with the question, "Do you feel that as a result of that experience you could be fair or impartial?" When phrased in terms of being fair and impartial, the juror is more likely to answer that the experience would not affect his or her ability to be fair and impartial. The way the above questions are phrased, however, permits a juror to state that he or she may be an acceptable juror generally, but perhaps not on this case.

It may also be relevant to ask about a potential juror's relationship with lawyers; for example:

(1) Do you know any lawyers or judges?

(2) What kind of law does he or she practice?

(3) How often do you see him or her?

(4) Do you get a chance to discuss his or her work?

(5) Has he or she ever expressed an opinion about his or her work? Or criminal justice issues? Or the lawyers or judges in this case?

(6) How does that relationship affect you?

(7) Have you taken any courses relating to law or legal issues, or criminal justice issues?

§ 3.14 Questions concerning publicity about the case and sexual assault in general.

Questions concerning publicity about the case may best be handled through sequestered voir dire, which is discussed more fully in Chapter 2.[84] "In a case of *substantial* pretrial publicity, the voir dire must not simply call for the jurors' objective assessment of their own impartiality, and it must not be so general at it does not adequately probe the possibility of prejudice."[85] Of course, if potential jurors say they have not heard about the case, no more than broad questions about pretrial publicity will be required.

The basic test for determining the impartiality of a juror who has been exposed to publicity about a case is whether the juror can lay aside any impression or opinion and render a verdict based upon the evidence presented in court. Extensive knowledge in the community concerning the crime or the defendant is, in itself, not a basis for striking a juror for cause or for reversal for being denied a fair trial.[86] As noted previously, the Supreme Court holds that the indifferent juror required for a fair trial need not be ignorant of all the facts or ignorant about the case, but must be able to "lay aside his impression or opinion and render a verdict based on the evidence presented in court."[87] The fact that the juror cannot meet the test of impartiality must be demonstrated and not be a matter of speculation.[88]

To ascertain juror feelings based on publicity, ask jurors about their sources of news and information. Determine what newspapers or magazines the jurors read and with what degree of regularity. Ask about the television programs they watch concerning the topic of sexual assault or rape and what news programs they saw when the media covered the particular case. Did the juror discuss the case or news programs or articles and form any opinions based on the information

---

[84] *See* § 2.19.

[85] United States v. Polizzi, 500 F.2d 856, 879 (1974), *cert. denied*, 419 U.S. 1120 (1975).

[86] Dobbert v. Florida, 432 U.S. 282, 303 (1977):

> Petitioner's argument that the extensive coverage by the media denied him a fair trial rests almost entirely upon the quantum of publicity which the events received. He has directed us to no specific portions of the record, in particular the voir dire examination of the jurors, which would require a finding of constitutional unfairness as to the method of jury selection or as to the character of the jurors actually selected. But under *Murphy* [Murphy v. Florida, 421 U.S. 794, 798 (1975)], extensive knowledge in the community of either the crimes or the punitive criminal is not sufficient by itself to render a trial constitutionally unfair. Petitioner in this case has simply shown that the community was made well aware of the charges against him and asks us on that basis to presume unfairness of constitutional magnitude at his trial. This we will not do in the absence of a trial atmosphere . . . utterly corrupted by press coverage.

[87] Irvin v. Dowd, 366 U.S. 717, 723 (1961).

[88] United States v. Haldeman, 559 F.2d 31, 60 (D.C. Cir. 1976), *cert. denied sub nom.* Ehrlichman v. United States, 431 U.S. 933 (1977).

he or she acquired? If an opinion has been formed, determine whether it is firmly held. From a defendant's perspective, it is more helpful to develop this avenue rather than asking the ultimate question of whether an opinion has been formed. Allow the juror to discuss more realistically the information he or she has been exposed to and reactions to that information. Sometimes open-ended questions will be effective, such as:

(1) What has been your source of information concerning this case?

(2) What do you remember seeing, reading, or hearing about this case? How did you feel when you saw, read, or heard it?

(3) What did you think about the defendant after seeing, reading, or hearing that? About the victim?

(4) What, if anything, do you remember about this defendant?

(5) When was the last time you saw or heard anything about this case?

(6) Do you necessarily believe everything that you read in newspapers concerning an alleged crime?

(7) What role, if any, do you think such publicity plays in a defendant obtaining a fair trial?

(8) Have you received information from, or had discussion with, anyone about this case?

(9) With whom have you discussed that article or news story?

(10) As a result of that news story or article what, if any, opinions did you form about this case?

(11) Has anyone expressed an opinion to you about this case?

(12) Have you discussed this case with anyone?

The above questions will not always be permitted by a court; there is tremendous variation and discretion in the conduct of voir dire. Place any proposed questions on the record. If a court then refuses to permit their use, an appellate argument can be made.

The failure to ask specific questions about the contents of the news reports to which the jurors have been exposed does not necessarily violate a defendant's right to an impartial jury or right to due process.[89] According to the Supreme Court's holding in *Mu'Min v. Virginia*, it is only when the failure to ask such questions renders a trial "fundamentally unfair" that content-based questions must

---

[89] State v. Barton, 998 S.W.2d 19 (Mo. 1999), *cert. denied sub nom.* Mu'Min v. Virginia, 500 U.S. 415 (1991). *See also* Gacey v. Welborn, 994 F.2d 305, 314–15 (7th Cir. 1993), *cert. denied*, 510 U.S. 899 (1993); Barton v. Missouri, 528 U.S. 1121 (2000) (holding trial court did not abuse its discretion in precluding questions about source of venirepersons' pretrial information about case and limiting questioning to whether potential juror formed opinion of guilt or innocence and whether venirepersons could determine guilt or innocence based on evidence adduced at trial).

be asked.[90] Despite this holding, at least one appellate court has reversed a defendant's conviction when voir dire regarding media exposure was restricted in a manner that prevented the development of "a factual basis for the exercise of challenges for cause and peremptory challenges."[91]

Ask questions about highly publicized events that may affect jurors' opinions in the case for which they have been called. In particular, ask questions about highly publicized trials that attracted widespread commentary. Be concerned that a juror may transfer feelings or opinions about the publicized trial to the trial for which he or she has been summoned.

Also, consider asking questions concerning sources of information about the topic of sexual assault generally:

(1) I imagine it is difficult to not have heard about the problem of sexual assault. What, if any, programs have you seen or articles have you read recently concerning this topic?

(2) From what magazines, newsletters, or TV programs have you received any news or stories about the topic of sexual assault or child abuse?

(3) What is your reaction to those types of stories or television programs?

(4) What is your feeling about newspaper or television coverage of sexual assault?

(5) What kind of effect do you think this type of reporting has had on public attitudes or children?

(6) Do you think stories in this area are always helpful to a better understanding of the problem of sexual assault?

(7) How easily will you be able to put out of your mind whatever you may have seen, or heard, or read about the topic of sexual assault? Realistically, how easily do you think you will be able to do this?

(8) What, if any, role or effect do you think stories you have read or programs you have seen should have on this trial?

The last question can be particularly important in driving home the point that a juror's decision should be based on the facts of the case and not on preconceived notions that may have been articulated in press accounts.

When concerned about pretrial publicity, stress that the public and jurors have heard no proof in the case and that the jurors would agree that their verdict should be based only on the proof heard in court. Stress that the public does not know this proof, and only they, the sworn jurors, will know and hear this proof.

A juror may form an opinion about the guilt or innocence of the defendant based on pretrial publicity or some other factor. Jurors often will admit to having

---

[90] Mu'Min v. Virginia, 500 U.S. 415, 425–426 (1991).

[91] People v. Tyburski, 445 Mich. 606, 518 N.W.2d 441 (1994).

formed an opinion as to a defendant's guilt or innocence as a result of publicity surrounding the case. When a juror has heard or read about a case and formed an opinion about a defendant's guilt, the juror may make an "expurgatory oath," which is a declaration that the juror could be fair and impartial and base a verdict on the evidence addressed at trial despite the prior opinion.[92] However, this declaration will be strictly construed, and the juror must unequivocally state that the opinion or impression will not influence his or her verdict, and that the juror can render an impartial verdict according to the evidence. According to one view, if the juror's oath does not include these two elements, the juror must be disqualified.[93] It is insufficient if the juror states the commitment in the form of an acknowledgment, a duty to decide the case with impartiality; it must be expressed as a belief of the juror.[94] The juror's promise is also nullified by impeaching statements or equivocation by the juror after the expurgatory oath is made.[95]

§ 3.15   Questions concerning opinions on rape, child abuse, or sexual assault.

In sexual assault trials, it is important on voir dire to know a juror's attitude, feelings, and opinions about rape and sexual assault. Unlike other background information on jurors, jury research shows that individuals' attitudes about crime in general and rape in particular are an important element of juror bias.[96] To the extent permitted by the court, attitudes and feelings about sexual assault crimes should be explored.

Many individuals feel uncomfortable listening to testimony involving sexual assault and discussing matters of a sexual nature with 11 strangers. The same can be true when asked to view graphic images or listen to explicit language in child pornography prosecutions. Many potential jurors will readily ask to be excused if given the opportunity. When given the opportunity to forgo sitting on a sexual assault case, a "jury walkout" may result, which sometimes necessitates calling multiple panels for jury service.

---

[92] Commonwealth v. Impellizzeri, 443 Pa. Super. 296, 661 A.2d 422 (1995), *appeal denied*, 543 Pa. 725, 673 A.2d 332 (1996) (while two jurors stated they had read newspaper accounts of the sexual assault and were uncertain whether they could be fair about the case, further questioning by the court developed jurors' declarations that they could put aside their emotions and follow the law as given by the judge and render a verdict based on the facts presented in court).

[93] People v. Culhane, 33 N.Y.2d 90, 305 N.E.2d 469, 350 N.Y.S.2d 381 (1973).

[94] People v. Culhane, 33 N.Y.2d 90, 305 N.E.2d 469, 350 N.Y.S.2d 381 (1973).

[95] People v. Culhane, 33 N.Y.2d 90, 305 N.E.2d 469, 350 N.Y.S.2d 381 (1973).

[96] Reid Hastie, Steven D. Penrod & Nancy Pennington, *Inside the Jury* 127, 128 (1983) ("In effect, no research has provided evidence that social scientific methods can be a powerful aid to attorneys in the task of detecting juror bias. However, attitudes, particularly case-relevant attitudes, such as toward the death penalty or rape, appear to be the most powerful individual difference predictors of verdict preference that have been studied to date.").

As a general rule, a court need not excuse for cause a juror who voices misgivings about sitting on a sexual assault case, unless the juror expresses a preconceived notion of the defendant's guilt.[97] A juror need not necessarily be disqualified because she may have difficulty being a fair juror, because she has two young granddaughters and the case involves the sexual abuse of a young girl, if the juror states that she will be fair.[98] A juror who feels sympathy toward children and commits to follow the law "to the extent humanly possible" is not subject to a challenge for cause since a court is not required to discharge any juror who cannot claim a total absence of bias or prejudice.[99] Generally, sympathy toward sexual abuse victims does not disqualify a juror who does not have a preconceived notion of guilt and professes to be fair and impartial.[100] Misgivings about convicting a person of sexual assault is also relevant to whether potential juror is qualified to serve. A potential juror's reluctance to convict a person of a sexual assault charge that carries a particular sentence may be grounds to challenge the potential juror for cause.[101] However, when a juror has difficulty with, or opinions about, particular aspects of a case, the juror is more likely to be excused for cause. When a juror expresses a strong attitude about an issue in a case and cannot state "with conviction" that such bias will not influence his or her verdict, the juror should be excused for cause.[102] In considering

---

[97] *See, e.g.,* People v. Zurak, 168 A.D.2d 196, 571 N.Y.S.2d 577, *appeal denied,* 79 N.Y.2d 834, 588 N.E.2d 112, 580 N.Y.S.2d 214 (1991), *cert. denied,* 504 U.S. 941 (1992).

[98] Noltie v. Peterson, 9 F.3d 802 (9th Cir. 1993).

[99] People v. Harris, 247 A.D.2d 630, 669 N.Y.S.2d 355 (1998). *See also* State v. Blackman, 201 Ariz. 527, 535, 38 P.3d 1192, 1200 (2002) (In a case involving capacity to consent of a mild to moderately retarded person, the following response of a juror was deemed to demonstrate juror had an open mind and could follow court's instructions:

> I believe sex is an important decision, because it can be, it can have serious conse-quences and potentially fatal consequences, and I don't believe that a mentally impaired person could necessarily make the distinction and foresee the events that might come to pass after that . . . And you can't consent to something that you can't fully conceive.

People v. Hagenbuch, 267 A.D.2d 948, 701 N.Y.S.2d 213 (1999), *appeal denied,* 95 N.Y.2d 797, 733 N.E.2d 237, 711 N.Y.S.2d 165 (2000) (holding it was proper to deny defendant's challenges for cause to jurors who expressed sympathy toward children but did not have preconceived notion of defendant's guilt).

[100] State v. Verhoef, 2001 S.D. 58, 627 N.W.2d 437 (2001) (holding no need to disqualify juror who had strong feelings about child sexual abuse but stated she could be fair and impartial).

[101] State v. Johnson, 759 So. 2d 1052 (La. Ct. App. 2000), *cert. denied,* 797 So. 2d 60 (La. 2001) (holding trial judge properly dismissed a juror for cause who stated he could not send someone to prison for life, especially on a rape charge, since drug dealers are not sent to prison for life).

[102] People v. Harris, 14 A.D.3d 622, 789 N.Y.S.2d 210 (2005):

> This matter involves the alleged statutory rape of a 13-year-old girl where the only direct evidence of the sexual act was her testimony. Here, during the course of voir dire, one prospective juror made a statement that cast doubt upon her ability to render a fair verdict under the proper legal standards when she indicated that, in her opinion, a child who testified would have 'nothing to gain by fabricating.' Additionally, another

whether the juror's promise is unequivocal, the entire responses of the juror must be considered and not just one answer that the juror can be fair and impartial.[103]

Striking for cause, a juror who may have difficulty accepting particular facts of an abuse case can present a different situation. For example, a defendant's conviction was reversed where the trial court granted a challenge for cause of a prospective juror who first said he would have difficulty believing a child who did not promptly complain of sexual assault, but later indicated he could be fair and impartial.[104] This was error because the court dismissed a juror who expressed a legitimate question as to a potential weakness in the prosecution's case; the court's action may have had a prejudicial effect on the jury members that sat in defendant's trial.[105] If the juror's opinion is fixed, a challenge for cause would be appropriate.[106]

The following are some of the questions to consider in exploring this area:

(1) Does anyone feel that the presumption of innocence or burden of proof should be higher or lower because this is a case involving child sexual abuse (or rape)?

(2) What does rape (or sexual abuse) mean to you?

(3) Could you accept a different definition if the court told you there was a different definition you had to use in evaluating the issues in this case?

---

prospective juror failed to provide an unequivocal assurance that she would be able to render a verdict based solely upon the evidence adduced at trial. In both of these instances, the court should have granted the defendant's challenges for cause. Since the defendant exhausted his peremptory challenges prior to the completion of jury selection, this constituted reversible error. [citation omitted].

People v. Webster, 177 A.D.2d 1026, 578 N.Y.S.2d 43 (1991) (holding that the juror's statements that she "thought" or "hoped" that she could put aside her attitudes about gun control and the senseless, "unnecessary" killing of a child were equivocal and uncertain declarations of impartiality on the juror's part).

[103] Bryant v. State, 765 So. 2d 68, 69 (Fla. Dist. Ct. App. 2000) (defendant's conviction reversed because trial court refused to excuse for cause a prospective juror who expressed revulsion toward accusations of child sexual abuse, even though the juror later vowed to be fair; among the juror's comments were "right off the bat I've got him guilty" and "This is a kid. I feel like, you know, they could go find somebody else to do it, not molest a kid. It's a child, you're damaging that child for the rest it [sic] of its life."); People v. Blyden, 55 N.Y.2d 73, 78, 432 N.E.2d 758, 447 N.Y.S.2d 886, 888–89 (1982).

[104] Commonwealth v. Lane, 521 Pa. 390, 555 A.2d 1246 (1989) ("A review of this record only reflects that this prospective juror might well place great weight upon the belated accusations against the accused than another serving in that capacity. The record also indicates that the same venire person indicated he would assess that fact with all the other evidence presented . . . . Moreover, it is well established in this Commonwealth that the lack of a prompt complaint is a factor to be considered by a juror in cases involving sexual offenses." Commonwealth v. Lane, 521 Pa. 390, 396, 555 A.2d 1246, 1249 (1989)).

[105] Commonwealth v. Lane, 521 Pa. 390, 394–395, 555 A.2d 1246, 1249 (1989).

[106] Commonwealth v. Lane, 521 Pa. 390, 396, 555 A.2d 1246, 1249 (1989).

(4)   Does anyone have experience through courses or work with sexual abnormalities?

(5)   Will anyone here have any difficulty in sitting and listening to testimony from a young child or young woman concerning matters of a graphic sexual nature?

(6)   Does the emotional component of these charges give you feelings about sitting on this case?

(7)   What do you think should happen to people accused of molesting children?

(8)   Will anyone here have difficulty sitting and listening to testimony of a graphic and sexual nature and discussing it with 11 strangers?

(9)   Does anyone here have any difficulty with my asking questions concerning graphic sexual acts to the complaining witness or other witnesses?

(10)   Is there anyone who feels because there may be testimony of a graphic and sexual nature that you might be inclined to turn off and not listen to the questions or answers concerning such testimony?

(11)   What is it about the topic of this sexual assault case that you feel might make it difficult for you to listen to the testimony?

(12)   Do you feel that difficulty might make it a problem for you to discuss some of the issues in this case?

(13)   Do you feel because of that difficulty this might not be the case for you?

§ 3.16   Questions about juror's victimization, relationship with crime victim in general, or sexual assault in particular.

Questions about a potential juror's victimization or relationship with a crime victim are basic voir dire questions in criminal trials. So are questions about relationships with alleged offenders. It is important to explore the nature and extent of these relationships as well as the attitudes and feelings developed as a result of the other person's experiences, since a relationship with a crime victim does not necessarily justify a challenge for cause.[107]

---

[107] Lattany v. State, 193 Ga. App. 438, 388 S.E.2d 23 (1989) (trial court properly denied a challenge for cause in assault case with respect to juror who stated that her father had been assaulted "and for that reason I think I am somewhat biased," but then stated she could set aside any prejudices or preconceived notions and determine defendant's guilt solely on basis of evidence); Sanders v. Commonwealth, 801 S.W.2d 665 (Ky. 1990) (holding fact that juror has been victim of a similar crime is insufficient basis to challenge a juror for cause); State v. Walker, 577 So. 2d 770 (La. Ct. App. 1991) (trial court in murder case properly denied defendant's challenge for cause to prospective juror whose brother had been murdered); People v. Bartell, 234 A.D.2d 956, 652 N.Y.S.2d 172 (1996) appeal denied, 89 N.Y.2d 983, 678 N.E.2d 1358, 656 N.Y.S.2d 742 (1997) (holding that trial court did not abuse discretion in denying defendant's challenge for cause of a prospective juror whose mother had been a crime victim). See generally Annotation, Fact That Juror in Criminal Case, or Juror's Relative or Friend, Has Previously Been Victim of Criminal Incident as Ground of Disqualification, 65 A.L.R. 4th 743 (1988).

It is not necessarily improper for a court to restrict the areas of inquiry concerning personal experiences with child abuse.[108] Another court noted that a defense attorney is not ineffective in failing to make specific inquiry of prospective jurors as to whether they or their friends had been sexually abused. "While voir dire related to the discovery of grounds for challenges for cause will certainly aid counsel in exercising peremptory challenges, counsel is not entitled under Pennsylvania law to ask questions intended solely to aid the exercise of peremptory challenges."[109] Nonetheless, a defendant's conviction will be reversed where voir dire does not adequately address jurors' past experiences in an area of crime victimization or religious beliefs that may relate to issues of the case that can prejudice a juror against a defendant.[110] At least one court has deemed it reversible error to prohibit the defense from asking the following question: "Have you or any member of your family been involved previously with a rape or proceeding involving a sexual crime?"[111] Of course, counsel should consider inquiring, if the court does not, about prior victimization, i.e., "Has anyone here been the victim of sexual abuse or have a close friend or family member who has?" A juror who is a prior crime victim who cannot unequivocally state that her experience will not affect her should be disqualified for cause.[112] However, a sexual assault victim is not necessarily disqualified from sitting on a sexual assault case.[113] This is particularly true if the juror's

---

[108] United States v. Payne, 944 F.2d 1458, 1474–75 (9th Cir. 1991):

> The proposed voir dire questions concerning sexual molestation, including whether the venire members had been victims of child sexual abuse, whether they had ever been accused of child molestation, whether they were associated with any group supporting child sexual abuse victims, and whether they had read, heard, or seen anything about child sexual abuse, clearly relate to an area about which the community harbors strong feelings. In such a case we review the trial court's refusal to ask the proffered questions for abuse of discretion.

United States v. Payne, 944 F.2d 1458, 1474 (9th Cir. 1991).

See also United States v. Boise, 916 F.2d 497, 504 (9th Cir. 1990).

[109] Commonwealth v. Slocum, 384 Pa. Super. 428, 435, 559 A.2d 50, 53 (1989).

[110] United States v. Shavers, 615 F.2d 266–68 (5th Cir. 1980).

[111] Commonwealth v. Fulton, 271 Pa. Super. 430, 413 A.2d 742 (1979).

[112] People v. Jackson, 265 A.D.2d 342, 697 N.Y.S.2d 288 (1999) ("The prospective juror at issue, who had been a crime victim, could only declare that she 'hope[d]' her experience would not affect her. Where there remains any doubt in the wake of such statements, when considered in the context of the prospective juror's overall responses, the prospective juror should be discharged for cause." People v. Jackson, 265 A.D.2d 342, 343, 697 N.Y.S.2d 288, 289 (1999)); Brown v. Commonwealth, 33 Va. App. 296, 533 S.E.2d 4 (2000) (reversing defendant's conviction because trial court did not excuse for cause a juror who stated that her sexual victimization might "possibly" affect her ability to decide case impartially).

[113] United States v. Miguel, 111 F.3d 666, 673 (9th Cir. 1997); Gonzales v. Thomas, 99 F.3d 978 (10th Cir. 1996), *cert. denied*, 520 U.S. 1159 (1997) (noting that rape victims are not as a matter of law incapable of being impartial in a sexual assault trial); Richardson v. Commonwealth, 161 S.W.3d 327 (Ky. 2005) ("The fact that a prospective juror has been a victim of a similar crime is insufficient, in and of itself, to warrant removal for cause . . . . Other than admitting

sexual assault is not recent and the juror is not in the process of recovery from the sexual assault experience or is otherwise actively influenced by it,[114] or declares that he or she can be fair and impartial and not tainted by the experience.[115] If the juror is still affected by the sexual assault and has not fully recovered from it, it may be reversible error to decline a challenge to a juror who is a sexual assault victim.[116] If there are significant differences between the juror's sexual assault experiences and the case being tried, this may allow

---

she had been a victim of a sex crime fourteen years earlier, Juror 6 made no statements indicating that she had any bias or preconceived opinions of Appellant's case. She unequivocally confirmed that she could fairly and impartially decide the case." Richardson v. Commonwealth, 161 S.W.3d 327, 330–331 (Ky. 2005)); Whalen v. Commonwealth, 891 S.W.2d 86 (Ky. Ct. App. 1995) (holding trial court did not abuse its discretion in a sexual assault trial in refusing to strike a juror who had been raped by her stepfather and who also stated she could be objective); People v. Nowlin, 297 A.D.2d 554, 747 N.Y.S.2d 92, appeal denied, 98 N.Y.2d 770, 781 N.E.2d 923, 752 N.Y.S.2d 11 (2002) ("The court properly exercised its discretion in denying defendant's challenge for cause. In this case involving the sexual abuse of two boys, the record supports the court's determination that the prospective juror, who herself had been abused as a child, gave the requisite unequivocal assurance of impartiality." People v. Nowlin, 297 A.D.2d 554, 555, 747 N.Y.S.2d 92, 93, appeal denied, 98 N.Y.2d 770, 781 N.E.2d 923, 752 N.Y.S.2d 11 (2002)); People v. Kimbro, 237 A.D.2d 211, 655 N.Y.S.2d 481, appeal denied, 89 N.Y.2d 1037, 681 N.E.2d 1315, 659 N.Y.S.2d 868 (1997) ("The trial court properly denied defendant's challenge for cause to a venireperson who was questioned extensively regarding her experience as a victim of a sexual assault similar in some aspects to the crime charged herein, and who maintained consistently that she would be able to put aside this experience, which had occurred more than 15 years prior to the time of trial herein, and to determine this case fairly and impartially, based on the evidence adduced at trial." People v. Kimbro, 237 A.D.2d 211, 212, 655 N.Y.S.2d 481, appeal denied, 89 N.Y.2d 1037, 681 N.E.2d 1315, 659 N.Y.S.2d 868 (1997)); Webb v. Commonwealth, 11 Va. App. 220, 397 S.E.2d 539 (1990).

[114] State v. Mundy, 99 Ohio App. 3d 275, 298–99, 650 N.E.2d 502, 516–17 (1994), appeal denied, 72 Ohio St. 3d 1420, 648 N.E.2d 513 (1995); State v. Erickson, 227 Wis. 2d 758, 596 N.W.2d 749 (1999), cert. denied, 528 U.S. 1140 (2000) (while prospective juror was a victim of sexual abuse, the assault was under different circumstances, the juror spoke of the assault without emotion, and the juror's sexual assault was remote in time, lessening the chance it would impair her judgment and thus the juror was not objectively biased).

[115] People v. Woellhaf, 87 P.3d 142 (Colo. Ct. App. 2003), rev'd on other grounds, 105 P.3d 209 (Colo. 2005) (upholding trial court's denial of challenge for cause of juror who had worked with child sexual assault victims, but who indicated she would try to put her biases aside and that she thought she could be fair); Green v. State, 249 Ga. App. 546, 552–53, 547 S.E.2d 569, 576, cert. denied, 2001 Ga. LEXIS 817 (Oct. 1, 2001), cert. denied, 535 U.S. 1080 (2002) (upholding trial court's refusal to strike for cause a juror who was a victim of rape, since she stated she could be impartial); Rocha v. State, 248 Ga. App. 53, 545 S.E.2d 173 (2001) (holding no per se exclusion of jurors as sexual victims or their family members; focus is whether prospective juror declares ability to decide case fairly and based on the evidence); State v. Hopkins, 908 So. 2d 1265 (La. Ct. App. 2005) (noting that juror who was a prior rape victim indicated she could separate her experience from a fair review of proof in defendant's case); State v. Robinson, 833 So. 2d 1207 (La. Ct. App. 2002) (upholding denial of challenge for cause of a juror who was rape victim and whose aunt was a rape murder victim, since she stated she could be fair and there was no indication of her bias or partiality due to her victimization).

[116] State v. Zerla, 1992 Ohio App. LEXIS 1280 (Mar. 17, 1992).

a court to accept the juror's declaration of impartiality. In upholding one trial court's denial of a defendant's challenge for cause of a prospective juror who had been sexually abused a few years earlier, an appellate court explained:

> [W]e hold that no error was committed because the prospective juror's comments did not create an inference of partiality or prejudice against defendant. The juror was not the victim of a crime sufficiently similar to raise such an inference. The juror indicated her boyfriend sexually abused her after she reached adulthood. In contrast, the State charged defendant with multiple incidents of incestuous child sexual abuse. Moreover, subsequent questioning by both the trial court and defense counsel sufficiently dispelled any inference of bias that may have been raised by the juror's initial response. She unequivocally stated that she would be fair and impartial and believed defendant to be innocent until proven guilty. Her candid admission that she felt uncomfortable with the topic of sexual abuse does not automatically preclude her from objectively evaluating testimony that defendant might offer in opposition to the charges of sexual abuse.[117]

However, careful questioning about the sexual assault experience and its consequences might develop opinions and attitudes inconsistent with the ability to sit fairly and impartially on a case. Should it develop that a rape victim deliberated on a case without disclosing that fact, a court may seek to determine what role the victimization played in deliberation and whether the juror harbored actual fear as a result.[118] Similarly, a juror's failing to disclose a relationship with a sexual abuse victim which surfaces during deliberations will not necessarily result in a reversal of conviction if the relationship does not appear to have affected the juror's impartiality.[119] If a juror conceals information about his or her

---

[117] State v. Saunders, 893 P.2d 584, 587–88 (Utah Ct. App. 1995).

[118] Gonzales v. Thomas, 99 F.3d 978 (10th Cir. 1996), *cert. denied*, 520 U.S. 1159 (1997) (holding the fact that a juror who convicted defendant was a prior rape victim — a fact she failed to disclose — did not require a finding of actual bias on her part and there was no showing that she drew upon this experience to bolster her opinions in deliberation); State v. Jackson, 81 Haw. 39, 49–50, 912 P.2d 71, 81–82 (1996), *rev'd on other grounds* (holding that juror's childhood sexual assault — not disclosed during jury selection — did not affect or infringe on defendant's right to a fair trial by impartial jury since juror did not "communicate her recollection" or utilize it in support of the victim's credibility); State v. Parsons, 1997 Tenn. Crim. App. LEXIS 1262 (Dec. 12, 1997) (juror disclosed during jury deliberations, but not jury selection, that her father had sexually abused her. While court stated she should have disclosed this information, there was no evidence she was biased against the defendant or exposed the jury to prejudicial information). *Compare* State v. Larue, 68 Haw. 575, 722 P.2d 1039, 1042 (Haw. 1986) (holding that juror who was a sexual assault victim "was vouching for, and attempting to secure the acceptance by the jury of the reliability of the statements of the minor [child molestation victims] as to their sexual molestation by appellant, based not upon evidence in the record, or their appearance on the stand, but upon her own similar personal experience and recollection thereof").

[119] Fitzgerald v. Greene, 150 F.3d 357 (4th Cir. 1998) (finding no new trial warranted even though juror stated he had no sympathy for a rapist because his granddaughter had been molested as a child, but juror's impartiality not shown to have been affected).

victimization and the non-disclosure was not caused by the defendant's lack of diligence, the defendant may be entitled to a new trial.[120] If a juror forgets to mention his or her knowledge of the victim, it may be reversible error to allow the juror to continue sitting in the case.[121]

One must carefully pose questions seeking to ascertain prior victimization. For example, in one case, the judge asked, "Have you or has any member of your immediate family ever been involved in a similar type of incident?" A rape victim answered no. She explained later that there were different circumstances in her case.[122]

A trial court has based discretion in limiting questions[123] concerning a juror's relationship with a sex abuse victim.

Courts generally do not find a relationship with a sexual assault victim to be sufficient by itself to challenge a juror for cause. Courts have upheld the selection of jurors whose daughter,[124] granddaughter,[125] sister,[126] niece,[127] cousin, or other relatives[128] were sexual assault victims. Some courts suggest excusing

---

[120] Young v. State, 720 So. 2d 1101 (Fla. Dist. Ct. App. 1998) (remanding to trial court for determination of whether one juror withheld information of her own experience of sexual abuse and holding that if juror did withhold such information, defendant is entitled to a new trial).

[121] Franklin v. State, 138 S.W.3d 351 (Tex. Crim. App. 2004) (after seeing victim testify, juror informed court that girl was in her daughter's Girl Scout troop and that she did not recognize her until she saw her; juror's failure to reveal this information during jury selection was material, since defendant's counsel was unable, through no fault of his own, to intelligently exercise his peremptory strikes or to request a strike for cause on this juror and actual bias need not be shown).

[122] Gonzales v. Thomas, 99 F.3d 978 (10th Cir. 1996), *cert. denied*, 520 U.S. 1159 (1997).

[123] State v. Reed, 2000 UT 68, 8 P.3d 1025 (2000) (Court found no error in trial judge's refusal to follow up question to jurors who had personally known a victim of sexual abuse. Appellate court felt questioning jurors on whether they would automatically believe a child witness over an adult or vice versa and evaluate credibility without regard to employment, age, or circumstances was an adequate exercise of court's discretion in conducting voir dire.).

[124] Jamison v. State, 164 Ga. App. 63, 295 S.E.2d 203 (1982) (juror's daughter was a rape victim); State v. Percy, 156 Vt. 468, 477, 595 A.2d 248, 253 (1990), *cert. denied*, 502 U.S. 927 (1991) (juror's daughter was a rape victim).

[125] Commonwealth v. Henderson, 275 Pa. Super. 350, 357, 418 A.2d 757, 761 (1980) (holding trial court properly denied challenge to a juror whose granddaughter was a rape victim).

[126] People v. Arredondo, 226 A.D.2d 322, 642 N.Y.S.2d 630, *appeal denied*, 88 N.Y.2d 964, 670 N.E.2d 1350, 647 N.Y.S.2d 718 (1996).

[127] People v. Smyers, 167 A.D.2d 773, 562 N.Y.S.2d 1017 (1990), *appeal denied*, 77 N.Y.2d 967, 573 N.E.2d 589, 570 N.Y.S.2d 501 (1991).

[128] United States v. Miguel, 111 F.3d 666, 673 (9th Cir. 1997); United States v. Barrow, 42 M.J. 655 (A.F.C.C.A. 1995), *aff'd*, 45 M.J. 478 (C.A.A.F. 1997). In *Barrow*, two jurors stated they had close family members who had been sexually abused as children. Trial judge rejected challenges for cause. Air Force Court of Criminal Appeals noted:

> Likewise, an individual is not disqualified from serving as a court member solely because the individual, or a family member, has been the victim of a crime similar to the one charged against the accused. [citation omitted]. Instead, the military judge must determine whether an actual or implied bias exists which disqualifies the member.

jurors whose immediate family members, such as a spouse or a child, have been crime victims.[129]

A court need not necessarily excuse for cause a prospective juror whose friend has been the victim of sexual abuse.[130]

Some courts have even held that a relationship with the complainant in the case does not necessarily disqualify the juror.[131] In many states a juror will be disqualified for cause if related by certain degree of consanguinity to the complainant. However, such a challenge may be waived if not made prior to the swearing of the juror. Having met the complainant may be an insufficient basis to challenge a juror for cause.[132] The fact that a juror's children go to school with the complainant without more, is likely an insufficient challenge for cause.[133] Thus, voir dire questioning should include not only "Do you know the complainant?", but also "Do your children attend the same school as the complainant?". Knowing a prosecution witness, coupled with an opinion on the witness' credibility, may require excusing the juror for cause even if the prospective juror feels he or she will be unbiased.[134] Recognizing the victim's family and "leaning toward the defendant," justifies a court's dismissing a potential juror for cause.[135]

Some questions to consider with respect to exposure to sexual assault are:

(1)   Has anyone here been the victim of sexual abuse or have a close friend or family member who has?

(2)   Do you know anyone accused of sexual abuse allegations either officially or informally?

(3)   Do you know anyone who has ever made a false allegation of sexual or physical abuse?

---

[129] People v. Smyers, 167 A.D.2d 773, 562 N.Y.S.2d 1017 (1990), *appeal denied*, 77 N.Y.2d 967, 573 N.E.2d 589, 570 N.Y.S.2d 501 (1991).

[130] People v. Belle, 277 A.D.2d 143, 715 N.Y.S.2d 701 (2000), *appeal denied*, 96 N.Y.2d 780, 749 N.E.2d 213, 725 N.Y.S.2d 644 (2001) (noting prospective juror indicated that relationship would not affect ability to be fair and impartial).

[131] George v. Commonwealth, 885 S.W.2d 938, 941 (Ky. 1994), *rev'd on other grounds*, (fact that trial juror was sexual assault victim's third-cousin did not create a presumption of prejudice where the juror stated that he could be fair and impartial and that the relationship would not affect his judgment); State v. Verhoef, 627 N.W.2d 437 (S.D. 2001) (juror's acquaintance with rape victim and her mother did not require challenge for cause since juror said she could be fair and impartial).

[132] State v. Bubeck, 1997 Wash. App. LEXIS 367 (Mar. 20, 1997) (being related to a witness or having met the complainant are not grounds for a challenge on implied bias).

[133] Herrington v. State, 690 So. 2d 1132, 1139 (Miss. 1997) (noting that in voir dire the juror did not know complainant went to school with her children, a fact she only learned later).

[134] State v. Faucher, 227 Wis. 2d 700, 596 N.W.2d 770 (1999) (holding a prospective juror who knew a potential witness and knew the witness to be a "person of integrity" who "wouldn't lie" should be stricken for cause even though he later stated he could put aside those beliefs).

[135] Pendleton v. Commonwealth, 83 S.W.3d 522, 527 (Ky. 2002).

(4)   Has anyone here ever reported a case of possible sexual abuse?

The handling or results of any past sexual abuse allegations should also be discussed for potential impact upon the juror. Questioning of jurors concerning victimization may be handled in an individual and sequestered fashion. This is discussed in greater detail in § 2.19 (sequestered voir dire).

§ 3.17   Questions about experts — General questions, mental health experts, medical experts.

Expert testimony plays a significant role in many sexual assault trials. If the testimony is significant, a potential juror's contact and experience with that area of expertise should be explored, since it may reveal a bias or prejudice. It also may reveal a knowledge level of the juror that would suggest that the juror has preconceived opinions on topics in that field.

Question the potential jurors about their view of the role of the expert trial witness. The questions utilized and approach taken may depend on whether the other party is also calling an expert witness and how critical a view of the expert testimony counsel wants the jury to take.

Some general questions to consider on expert testimony are:

(1)   Have you ever listened to the testimony of an expert witness?

(2)   Are you ever intimidated by persons who have a higher level of education than you have?

(3)   Would you tend to believe the testimony of an expert witness just because that person is called an "expert" witness?

(4)   Do you think that "expert" witnesses are capable of being incorrect or untruthful?

(5)   If you are instructed to evaluate the testimony of an expert witness as you would the testimony of all other witnesses, do you think that you would be able to follow that instruction?

(6)   Do you think you would be capable of rejecting the testimony of an "expert" witness if the testimony of that witness did not appear to be reliable or consistent with common sense?

(7)   How do you feel about evaluating the testimony of an expert witness and deciding whether to accept it or reject it?

(8)   Could you reject the testimony of an expert?

(9)   Are you going to accept testimony just because someone with a degree says so?

(10) Do you think an expert witness should be treated differently by you?

(11) Do you agree that an expert can have a bias or motive just like other witnesses?

(12) Do you think experts are always right?

(13) Do you think that you would have to like a witness in order to believe his or her testimony?

Many child sexual abuse cases involve mental health or psychological expert testimony. Explore potential jurors' backgrounds and experiences in this area with the following questions:

(1) Do you have any special training in the area of social work, psychology, or psychiatry?

(2) Do you have any close friends or relatives who have training in the area of psychology or psychiatry?

(3) Have you or a close friend or relative ever gone to any sort of counseling?

(4) Has anyone here or a close friend or family member ever had contact with a social worker, psychologist, or psychiatrist?

(5) Does anyone have a friend or family member who works in the field of mental health, social work, psychiatry, or psychology?

(6) Do you or a close friend or family member work with individuals who have alleged abuse?

While some questions overlap, certain questions may elicit positive responses where others do not.

If the case involves medical opinion testimony, there should be questions about the juror's background and his or her contact with medicine in general, medical issues, and medical institutions.

(1) Do you or a close friend or family member work in the field of pediatrics or emergency medicine?

(2) Do you or a close friend or family member have a background or training in nursing, medicine, child care, or emergency medicine?

(3) Have you had medical care or contact with the institution where a testifying expert works?

(4) What kind of experience did you have there?

(5) Have you ever had a dispute with a physician?

(6) Do you have a pediatrician?

(7) Has he or she ever discussed sexual issues or sexual abuse with you or your child?

(8) Have you ever disagreed with an opinion of your pediatrician?

§ 3.18 Questions about intent, mental state, and charges.

Certain sexual assault charges, such as attempted rape or sexual abuse, may have a specific intent requirement. In other words, it may be necessary for the prosecution to establish that the defendant intended to accomplish a certain act or that the defendant intended to engage in sexual contact for sexual gratification. Question jurors about their understanding of "intent" when this element of the offense is likely to be part of the defendant's theme. There may also be instances in which a prosecutor may wish to focus on whether a juror may have difficulty understanding or accepting the law with respect to the mental state required for the particular charge.

The following are questions that may assist in this area:

(1) Do you have any difficulty with the fact that the law requires that there be more than just touching of another individual to be guilty of a crime, and that there has to be a certain intent when the touching is done?

(2) Do you think you would convict simply because there has been an act of touching in this case without examining what was meant or intended at the time of the touching?

(3) Does the fact that there was an act of touching end all your thoughts or discussions about this case or will you be willing to look at the issue of what the defendant meant or intended at the time?

The prosecutor may wish to emphasize that certain charges do not require a particular mental state. Many sexual assault crimes are "strict liability" crimes, in that the prosecution must simply prove that the act was performed with someone under the age of consent. The following questions may help in this area:

(1) Do you understand that these charges do not require the prosecution to demonstrate that the defendant forced the child to have sexual contact?

(2) Do you understand that, regardless of what the defendant may have thought, the law simply requires that the People prove that this defendant had sexual contact with this 15-year-old?

Mental state questions may be important when intoxication is an issue. In some states and situations, intoxication is relevant to the intent element of sexual assault trials. If a defendant breaks into an apartment and engages in sexual contact while intoxicated, the defendant's intent may be crucial to an evaluation of the charges.

§ 3.19   Memberships in groups and organizations involving rape crisis work.

Participation in groups and organizations can be particularly revealing as to a juror's feelings and preferences. Participation is more significant than mere membership. The fact that an individual takes the time to engage in the activities of an organization represents, in most situations, a significant commitment. Persons active in organizations often have strong feelings about certain criminal justice issues, particularly organizations that have legislative or political agendas. Memberships in organizations that deal with any of the issues that might arise in a sexual assault trial, such as rape crisis or victim counseling, are particularly significant. The following are some questions dealing with this area:

(1) What social, neighborhood, professional, political, or religious groups do you or your spouse belong to?

(2) Do you hold a leadership position in any of these groups or organizations?

(3) Is there anyone here who is a member in any group or organization that advocates on behalf of crime victims?

(4) Is there anyone here who is a member of any group or organization that advocates on behalf of domestic violence or sexual abuse victims, or is a member of a rape crisis organization or victim counseling program?

(5) Do any of you belong to any groups or organizations that are active in civic or political matters or legal issues such as Mothers Against Drunk Driving, ACLU, or Common Cause?

(6) Is there anyone here who is a member of any group or organization that advocates on behalf of those accused of crimes or those in our correctional system (such as prisoner rights, legal services, ACLU)?

(7) Is there anyone who is a member of a group or organization that has as its goal or purpose or as part of its agenda changing the laws of our criminal justice system or the laws in the area of sexual assault, the law of the age of consent, or the operation of our correctional system?

Also find out if potential jurors belong to any organizations that advocate positions on government and the family, corporal punishment, unwed mothers, public assistance, family values, or similar issues that might come up during testimony and trigger a reaction in a particular juror who has strong feelings about those areas.

The failure of a court to permit questions about a potential juror's association with rape crisis or alcohol victim centers is not necessarily an abuse of discretion.[136] For example, one court concludes that a prospective juror may not be challenged for cause because of membership in a rape advocacy program since opposition to rape is a widely shared sentiment and that expressing that opinion by "[joining] an organized group of persons who share the same sentiment does not necessarily render a person incapable of weighing evidence impartially to determine whether a rape has occurred in fact or whether the person accused is in fact the person who committed the act."[137] The same court held that a trial court need not permit an attorney to ask about membership in a rape advocacy organization.[138] A court need not necessarily question a rape crisis worker

---

[136] United States v. Joe, 831 F.2d 218, 221 (10th Cir. 1987).

[137] Commonwealth v. Myers, 376 Pa. Super. 41, 48, 545 A.2d 309, 312–13 (1988), *appeal denied*, 522 Pa. 588, 561 A.2d 741 (1989).

[138] Commonwealth v. Myers, 376 Pa. Super. 41, 48, 545 A.2d 309, 312–13 (1988), *appeal denied*, 522 Pa. 588, 561 A.2d 741 (1989).

whether that experience would make her treat a rape victim the same as any other witness, as long as the court inquires whether her experience as a rape crisis volunteer would affect her ability to be impartial.[139] More detailed questioning may be requested when a rape crisis center is involved in the case, or where testimony is expected from a rape crisis center employee who is a fact witness or expert witness. Any proposed questions that the court forbids should be recorded for appellate review.

§ 3.20   Questions about leisure activity.

A juror's leisure activities can speak volumes about his or her feelings and preferences — how we spend the little free time we have indicates what is truly important to us. An individual's activities can give one insight into his or her beliefs and attitudes. Are the leisure activities of a potential juror associated with family? Are they group activities or are they done alone? Do they involve children? Do they involve compassionate activities such as volunteering time to help the homeless or the elderly in nursing homes?

Questions about leisure activity are likely to elicit honest responses from potential jurors, since they allow them to discuss something they feel comfortable about and enjoy doing. Among the questions that may be asked are:

    (1)   How do you spend your free time or leisure time?

    (2)   Do you ever get a chance to spend any time watching TV or reading?

    (3)   What type of shows do you like to watch?

    (4)   What is your favorite TV show?

    (5)   What kind of books or magazines do you enjoy reading?

    (6)   How often do you get a chance to do that?

§ 3.21   Questions concerning witness credibility of witnesses.

Many sexual assault trials pit the word of the victim against that of the defendant. Certainly the motives and credibility of the victim are fundamental issues in these trials. This may be extremely important in child abuse cases. In questioning a potential juror, explore preconceived opinions on children and the truthfulness and motivations of witnesses. Among the questions to consider are:

    (1)   How many of you believe children always tell the truth?

    (2)   Has anyone here ever had occasion to evaluate the truthfulness of someone's story?

    (3)   Do you believe children are more or less honest than adults?

---

[139] State v. Walden, 183 Ariz. 595, 608, 905 P.2d 974, 987 (1995), *cert. denied*, 517 U.S. 1146 (1996).

(4) Would you automatically believe an adult over a child or a child over an adult who testifies?

(5) Do you have any difficulty being asked to judge the credibility and honesty of a witness? How about a witness who may be very emotional in providing that testimony?

(6) Do you feel just because a child or adult testifies about a sexual assault that it must necessarily be true or untrue?

(7) Do you believe that a witness is more or less honest because that witness may be emotional when providing his or her testimony?

Some prosecutors ask potential jurors whether they could convict based on the testimony of a single witness, if the juror believes the witness establishes all elements of the crime beyond a reasonable doubt. If a juror indicates that more than a single witness would be required under these circumstances, this may establish a challenge for cause on the grounds that the juror is holding the prosecution to a standard higher than beyond a reasonable doubt.[140] However, this argument has not been accepted by all courts.[141] Some courts permit questions about whether veniremembers would have a problem believing a child witness and about the lack of medical evidence on the theory that such questions relate to a bias or prejudice against a child's testimony.[142] The trial judge has broad discretion in permitting questioning about the facts of a case or hypothetical questions about the juror's reaction to certain facts. Some courts permit questioning by the prosecutor to determine whether jurors will consider all the evidence and not acquit solely on the victim's denial of rape or the lack of eyewitnesses.[143]

---

[140] Jones v. State, 1996 Tex. App. LEXIS 4305 (Sept. 19, 1996) ("A venire member who states he cannot convict based upon the testimony of only one witness, even though he believes that witness beyond a reasonable doubt, may be properly challenged for cause." Jones v. State, 1996 Tex. App. LEXIS 4305, *3–4 (Sept. 19, 1996)); Decker v. State, 894 S.W.2d 475 (Tex. Ct. App. 1995) (juror who stated during voir dire that he could not find a person guilty of sexually abusing a child unless the child's testimony was corroborated by medical evidence was properly excluded for cause since he would have held the state to a higher burden of proof than required by law. "The state is entitled to a jury composed of persons who will objectively consider the available evidence." Decker v. State, 894 S.W.2d 475, 478 (Tex. Ct. App. 1995)).

[141] Castillo v. State, 913 S.W.2d 529 (Tex. Crim. App. 1995) ("We now hold that a venireman who categorically refuses to render a guilty verdict on the basis of only one eyewitness is not challengeable for cause on that account so long as his refusal is predicated on his reasonable understanding of what constitutes proof beyond a reasonable doubt." Castillo v. State, 913 S.W.2d 529, 533 (Tex. Crim. App. 1995)). See also Zinger v. State, 932 S.W.2d 511 (Tex. Crim. App. 1996); Leonard v. State, 923 S.W.2d 770 (Tex. Crim. App. 1996).

[142] Garza v. State, 18 S.W.3d 813, 820 (Tex. Ct. App. 2000) (noting that "a potential juror who could not believe a witness simply for the fact of being a child would properly be excused for cause").

[143] State v. Harris, No. 02C01-9807-CR-00209, 1999 Tenn. Crim. App. LEXIS 1177 (Nov. 23, 1999). The Harris court upheld the following questions asked during voir dire:

STATE: Could you take that evidence if you were told and you found beyond a reasonable doubt and to a moral certainty the presence of sperm in a 12 year old's vagina, could you take that, Ms. Barker, as that being rape?

A prosecutor should not inquire about a particular vulnerability of a victim, but may inquire why a victim may deny the sexual abuse. However, "there is a fine line between arguing the facts of a case and exploring possible prejudices among the venire."[144]

Another major concern is the vulnerability of witnesses, particularly child witnesses, to suggestive or leading questions. This may have to be explored in some detail in questioning potential jurors:

(1) Does anyone have feelings about how a child should be interviewed or questioned about sexual abuse?

(2) Has anyone here ever had experience with children who have been influenced by adults?

(3) Is there anyone here who believes that a child could not be influenced by an adult to say or act in a particular way?

(4) What role, if any, do you think adults play in children's reporting of events?

A trial court's refusing to allow an attorney to ask about children lying in a sexual assault case is not necessarily reversible error.[145]

A defense attorney who discusses a child's potential to be manipulated by adults does not necessarily open the door to a defendant's prior acts.[146] Yet, care must be taken to avoid questions which may open the door to a defendant's prior acts by questions which suggest a complainant's fantasizing or hallucinating.[147]

. . .

STATE: But could you consider, Mr. Harrison, the fact that if semen is found in the vagina, that even if it's just bodily fluids that penetrated the, let's say the imaginary lining of the vagina, that would be penetration?

. . .

STATE: Can you all agree, too, and understand, or consider the fact that in a rape case that normally you have two people involved only and that it's not done at the footsteps of the United Methodist Church in Bartlett?

State v. Harris, No. 02C01-9807-CR-00209, 1999 Tenn. Crim. App. LEXIS 1177, *14–15 (Nov. 23, 1999).

[144] Beartusk v. State, 6 P.3d 138, 144 (Wyo. 2000).

[145] Skipper v. Commonwealth, 23 Va. App. 420, 477 S.E.2d 754 (1996) (holding defendant's attorney's question, "For those with children, have you ever caught them in a lie to excuse what they were not permitted to do?" did not relate to qualifications or bias of jurors).

[146] Sundling v. State, 679 N.E.2d 988, 993 (Ind. Ct. App. 1997) (suggesting that had defendant's attorney claimed that the complainant had fantasized this abuse, the defendant's prior acts may have been admissible; in this case, the admission of prior acts was reversible error).

[147] Sundling v. State, 679 N.E.2d 988, 993 (Ind. Ct. App. 1997).

§ 3.22   Questions concerning particular issues in victim's or defendant's background.

There may be issues involving a victim's or defendant's background that must be explored in questioning prospective jurors. They may involve socioeconomic issues. For example, is the defendant or victim on public assistance? If so, does the potential juror have any particular opinion about persons receiving public assistance? Does the juror have friends or family who now receive or have received public assistance? If so, perhaps the factors that led the victim or defendant to be on public assistance should be explored.

Ethnic and racial issues can also be significant. Is the victim or defendant part of an interracial relationship? Will this fact have an effect on jurors? Inquiry into possible racial bias should be permitted if reasonably related to the issues of the case.[148]

While perhaps it is unrealistic to expect all potential jurors to answer honestly and forthrightly questions involving sensitive issues, the issues must be explored. If there is any hope of uncovering the bias or prejudice of a potential juror, the attorney must encourage him or her to examine those areas that may cause difficulty in being fair or impartial and make every effort to be objective. Questions concerning the gender of a party may also be appropriate. One court upheld the propriety of a prosecutor questioning prospective jurors by asking them, "Would the fact that the defendant is a female in any way affect your deliberations with regard to the death penalty" in a prosecution involving felonious child abuse.[149]

§ 3.23   Questions concerning juror's reaction to particular facts.

Questions concerning a victim's or defendant's background are part of the "red flag" issues that occur in many cases. Bring out potential problems during jury selection and try to neutralize any possible negative effects. A judge, however, has wide latitude on controlling such questioning. Consider the following questions in an adult sexual assault case:

(1)   If you were to hear evidence about a person having used drugs, would you be more inclined to give his testimony less weight than any other witness that you did hear?

(2)   If you were to hear testimony concerning drug addiction or use of drugs, do you think, deep down inside of you, that you would be inclined to reject any evidence offered by parties indicating that they have used drugs?

However, one appellate court found the above questions improper because they sought jurors' possible responses to isolated pieces of evidence.[150]

---

[148] Bowie v. State, 324 Md. 1, 15, 595 A.2d 448, 455 (1991).

[149] State v. Anderson, 350 N.C. 152, 513 S.E.2d 296, *cert. denied*, 528 U.S. 973 (1999).

[150] Commonwealth v. Werts, 483 Pa. 222, 224, 395 A.2d 1316 (1978).

Many trial courts refuse to permit hypothetical questions about a juror's opinion on certain facts that may be developed at trial, for example, that the use of drugs was involved in the case. If this occurs, approach the issue indirectly. While the following questions may not elicit direct answers, they may provide some insight about possible juror reactions.

(1) Do you or a close friend or family member work with or have experience with individuals who have a substance dependency?

(2) Do you belong to a group or organization advocating change or reform of our nation's drug laws?

An attorney may form voir dire questions to address potentially troubling facts in the case. For example, a prosecutor might ask:

(1) Have you ever hitchhiked? Or gone to a bar alone?

(2) Do you know anyone in your family who hitchhikes? (Or has gone alone to a bar?)

(3) Do you feel that by hitchhiking (or going alone to a bar) a woman gives up any rights?

(4) Do you feel a person who hitchhikes (or goes alone to a bar) invites or contributes to a rape? How about a robbery?

Many courts preclude detailed questioning of jurors' attitudes about issues in a case, preferring to limit the inquiry to a general question, e.g., whether a fact or issue will preclude a fair and impartial verdict. A potential area of inquiry in a sexual assault trial may involve jurors' attitudes about homosexuality or homosexual acts. In the highly publicized sexual assault and homicide trial of John Wayne Gacey, counsel was not permitted to ask potential jurors the specifics of what they had read or their thoughts about homosexuality beyond general questions such as: "Does the fact that the defendant is charged with homosexual conduct prevent you from being fair to either side?" and "Could you put aside any feeling that you might have regarding homosexuality in rendering your verdict in this case?"[151] The reviewing court supported this position on the theory that further questioning would be counter-productive.[152] To sum up, on voir dire consider broad inquiries when specific questions are precluded by the court.

---

[151] Gacey v. Welborn, 994 F.2d 305, 314–15 (7th Cir.), *cert. denied,* 510 U.S. 899 (1993).

[152] Gacey v. Welborn, 994 F.2d 305, 315 (7th Cir.), *cert. denied,* 510 U.S. 899 (1993) ("To do more would have extended the jury-selection process considerably and left many jurors flustered and resentful, which in the end may have worked against the defendant. Defendants' safety lies in the size of the jury and in cautions from the court, not in extra questions posed in advance of trial. A long series of probing questions can anesthetize or offend the panel rather than enlighten judge and counsel. Experienced judges accordingly prune the list, omitting some that may look appropriate in isolation.").

§ 3.24 *Batson* rules and procedures and peremptory challenges based on race.

The Supreme Court of the United States, in *Batson v. Kentucky*,[153] ruled that a prosecutor's exercise of peremptory challenges against blacks can be challenged under certain situations. The prosecutor's peremptory challenge can be contested when the facts and circumstances of the case raise an inference that the challenge was based on race. When there has been such a prima facie showing, the prosecutor must provide a race-neutral explanation for the removal of the juror. A prosecutor may not challenge a juror simply because the defendant is of the same race as the potential juror and therefore the potential juror may be biased toward the defendant. The fact that other jurors of the same race have been accepted will not, in itself, defeat a *Batson* claim.

The *Batson* rule has been applied to Hispanics,[154] Native Americans,[155] and Caucasians.[156] The Supreme Court has also held that a "criminal defendant may object to race-based exclusions of jurors affected through peremptory challenges whether or not the defendant and the excluded juror share the same race."[157] Sometimes, however, a court will consider the fact that the defendant and challenged juror are of a different race as part of the surrounding circumstances to evaluate the motive of the strike.[158] A white defendant has standing to object to the improper exclusion of black potential jurors.[159] The *Batson* decision has also been applied to defense attorneys; prosecutors have the right to object to the use of race-based peremptory challenges by defense lawyers.[160]

The *Batson* challenge should be raised before the jury has been sworn.[161] Analyze the pattern of strikes made during voir dire. Compare characteristics of individuals excluded with those selected. When jurors of the same race share

---

[153] 476 U.S. 79 (1986).

[154] Hernandez v. New York, 500 U.S. 352 (1991).

[155] United States v. Chalan, 812 F.2d 1302 (10th Cir. 1987); State v. Locklear, 349 N.C. 118, 505 S.E.2d 277 (1998), *cert. denied*, 526 U.S. 1075 (1999).

[156] Roman v. Abrams, 822 F.2d 214 (2d Cir. 1987), *cert. denied*, 489 U.S. 1052 (1989).

[157] Powers v. Ohio, 499 U.S. 400 (1991) (holding Caucasians may object to prosecutor's peremptory challenges against African-American jurors).

[158] Commonwealth v. Serrano, 48 Mass. App. Ct. 163, 166, 718 N.E.2d 863, 867 (1999), *review denied*, 430 Mass. 1114, 723 N.E.2d 33 (2000) (in upholding a prosecutor's challenge of an African-American venire in a case of a Hispanic defendant, court noted the charges, in this case, drug charges, were not the type to execute racial bias and that "it is significant, although certainly not dispositive, that the defendants, all Hispanics, were members of a different group than the challenged juror, who was African-American." The court did note that "the issue of jury composition requires the greatest scrutiny where defendant and victim belong to different racial groups — particularly where the crimes in question are violent or sexual in nature.").

[159] Campbell v. Louisiana, 523 U.S. 392 (1998).

[160] Georgia v. McCollum, 505 U.S. 42 (1992).

[161] Lewis v. Commonwealth, 25 Va. App. 745, 492 S.E.2d 492 (1997).

the same characteristic and one is struck, this may give rise to an inference of pretext.[162] However, there is authority that *Batson* is not violated when two jurors of different races provide the same response and one is excused and the other is not.[163] In racially motivated crimes, a party may inquire about race related bias, and if there is a specific reason to believe the juror is incapable of confronting or suppressing an attitude of racism; but there is no exception for "race-related issues."[164] Maryland allows questioning about racial biases regardless of defendant's race and regardless of whether the crime has racial overtones.

The *Batson* decision has generated numerous court decisions as to what a race-neutral explanation is for the challenge of a particular juror. It has also sparked a debate as to the role of peremptory challenges, whether the *Batson* ruling means the end of peremptory challenges and to what extent should discrimination be forbidden during jury selection.[165] Justice Marshall's concurring opinion in

---

[162] Ford v. Norris, 67 F.3d 162, 169 (8th Cir. 1995).

[163] Howard v. Moore, 131 F.3d 399, 408 (4th Cir. 1997), *citing* Matthews v. Evatt, 105 F.3d 907, 918 (4th Cir. 1997), *cert. denied*, 522 U.S. 833 (1997).

[164] United States v. Pospisil, 186 F.3d 1023, 1028 (8th Cir. 1999), *cert. denied*, 529 U.S. 1089 (2000); Hernandez v. State, 357 Md. 204, 742 A.2d 952 (1999).

[165] Gilchrist v. State, 97 Md. App. 55, 78–79, 627 A.2d 44, 55, *cert. granted*, 332 Md. 741, 633 A.2d 102 (1993) (Wilner, C.J. concurring) ("[O]ccasionally, the Supreme Court starts a march that, years later, it realizes has led it into a swamp, and it reverses course. It may be too early yet to know whether that will happen here, but I suspect that it will not. . . . A whole new area of appellate review will blossom; indeed, the buds are already growing. I recognize that the abolition of peremptory challenges would mark a dramatic change in the way our jury system has traditionally operated, and, if we were to do that, we would need to be more liberal in allowing challenges for cause and in permitting voir dire examination for the purpose of making those challenges. The question is whether that would be more, or less, efficient and whether it would produce a more fair, or less fair, result than the hoops we need to jump through now under *Batson* and its children. I don't know the answer to that, but I think it is a question we urgently need to address." Gilchrist v. State, 97 Md. App. 55, 78–79, 627 A.2d 44, 55–56, *cert. granted*, 332 Md. 741, 633 A.2d 102 (1993)); People v. Bolling, 79 N.Y.2d 317, 325–31, 591 N.E.2d 1136, 1142–43, 582 N.Y.S.2d 950, 956–60 (1992) (Bellacosa, J. concurring) ("The rationale of *Bolling*, however, along with the eight-year experience in this State with the effectiveness — or lack of same — of the *Batson* remedy, and the proliferation and permutation of problems in the appellate pipeline, point inexorably to the need for a broader remedy: the elimination of the peremptory challenge process. If the purpose, quoted above, is to be honored and achieved, then the euphemisms and the rationalizations should be ended. Peremptories have outlived their usefulness and, ironically, appear to be disguising discrimination — not minimizing it, and clearly not eliminating it. The time and circumstances warrant the Legislature addressing these important issues. The process that requires courts to sift through counsel's words for patterns or pretexts of discrimination has not served the goal of cutting the discriminatory weeds out of the jury selection process. . . . Analytically, peremptories and race-neutral articulations present a quintessential and untenable dualism. A peremptory challenge by its nature should not have to be explained. . . . It has become virtually impossible for appellate courts or trial courts to discern proper gradations and variations and to provide meaningful procedural guidance guaranteeing some measure of consistent application. . . . It is time for the Legislature to come to terms with the undisputed fact that peremptory challenges constitute a jury selection practice that permits 'those to discriminate who are of a mind to discriminate,' and that the *Batson* effort has failed to fulfill its stated goal of eradicating invidious discrimination from

Batson invited the Supreme Court to ban peremptory challenges.[166]

A proposed extension of *Batson* beyond race to race and gender has been rejected by at least one court. A defendant argued that a prosecutor exercised peremptory challenges to eliminate black males from a jury (the selected jury had five black females), reinforcing the stereotype that black men have been made "obsolete as a social member of the family."[167] This was rejected as beyond the scope *of Batson*, and the court noted:

> If we apply the *Batson* principles at the prima facie stage of the analysis to subcategories of race and gender, not only will we have created new hybrid suspect groups, but we will have effectively destroyed both the peremptory challenge and the *Batson* decision. It would become a thing of the past for defendants to claim only general race discrimination or even gender discrimination, because all challenged jurors could easily fit into some subcategory. Numerous *Batson* hearings would have to be held because every challenged juror would belong to several general categories and, of course, hybrid subcategories would grow exponentially. Establishing a prima facie case of discrimination would always be easier when a challenged juror belongs to a subcategory rather than a general category. In theory, if the categories are narrowed down enough, there would be some potential jurors with certain characteristics who could never be challenged without making a full blown *Batson* hearing necessary.[168]

Most courts recognize a three-part process for reviewing *Batson* challenges. First, the party raising the challenge has the burden of establishing sufficient facts to support an inference of intentional discrimination.[169] A broad assertion of discriminatory challenges by a party is insufficient to support a prima facie

---

the jury selection process." People v. Bolling, 79 N.Y.2d 317, 326, 591 N.E.2d 1136, 1142–43, 582 N.Y.S.2d 950, 956–60 (1992)). *But see* J.E.B. v. Alabama *ex rel.* T.B., 511 U.S. 127 (1994), discussed in § 3.30.

[166] Batson v. Kentucky, 476 U.S. 79, 107 (1986) (Marshall, J. concurring) (inherent potential of peremptory challenges to distort the jury process by permitting the exclusion of jurors on racial grounds should ideally lead the Court to ban them entirely from the criminal justice system).

[167] People v. Washington, 257 Ill. App. 3d 26, 33, 628 N.E.2d 351, 356 (1993).

[168] People v. Washington, 257 Ill. App. 3d 26, 34, 628 N.E.2d 351, 356 (1993). *But see* People v. Garcia, 217 A.D.2d 119, 636 N.Y.S.2d 370 (1995) (remanding to trial court for a hearing on the issue of whether or not prosecutor exercised peremptory challenges for non-discriminatory reasons since trial court's ruling that black females do not have protection as a class of jurors precluded a full inquiry as to whether the *Batson* test should be applied and that by holding that black females do not have such protection, their equal protection was violated).

[169] *Ex parte* Brooks, 695 So. 2d 184 (Ala.), *cert. denied*, 522 U.S. 893 (1997); People v. Arias, 13 Cal. 4th 92, 134–35, 51 Cal. Rptr. 2d 770, 797–98, 913 P.2d 980, 1007 (1996); Melbourne v. State, 679 So. 2d 759 (Fla. 1996); Commonwealth v. Burnett, 418 Mass. 769, 642 N.E.2d 294 (1994); Stewart v. State, 662 So. 2d 552 (Miss. 1995); People v. Payne, 88 N.Y.2d 172, 666 N.E.2d 542, 643 N.Y.S.2d 949 (1996); Satterwhite v. State, 858 S.W.2d 412, 423 (Tex. Crim. App. 1993), *cert. denied*, 510 U.S. 970 (1993).

claim.[170] A single peremptory challenge against a racial or ethnic group is generally insufficient to establish a *Batson* violation,[171] nor will disproportionate challenges against a racial or ethnic group establish a *Batson* violation.

If the first step is met, the burden shifts to the other party to establish a race-neutral reason which need not rise to the level of a challenge for cause. Failing to require the striking party to present a race-neutral reason for striking an African-American juror when a *Batson* challenge is raised may require remanding a case to determine whether there was a basis for striking the challenged juror.[172] A party may attempt to challenge the race-neutral reason by demonstrating that similar claims can be made about non-excluded jurors.[173] In a decision which the dissenting opinion states a major retreat from its decision in *Batson*, the United States Supreme Court has held that a reason for the strike need not be "persuasive or even plausible" as long as it does not deny equal protection.[174] The "ultimate burden of persuasion regarding racial motivation rests with, and never shifts from, the opponent of the strike."[175] The Supreme Court held that a prosecutor's explanation that he did not like a juror's looks "because he had long, unkempt hair, a mustache, and a beard" may be a race-neutral reason and articulates a nondiscriminatory reason for the strike.[176]

As noted by the Supreme Court, the step-two explanation need not be "persuasive or even plausible, but only factually neutral."[177] Thus, excusing all jurors of high educational background defeats an allegation of intentional discrimination.[178] At the third stage, the party challenging the peremptory has the burden of convincing the trial court that the party exercising the peremptory challenge has utilized pretextual reasons. The court's focus during step 3 is not the reasonableness but rather the genuineness of the strike.[179] After race-neutral

---

[170] People v. Scott, 197 A.D.2d 644, 602 N.Y.S.2d 681, *appeal denied*, 82 N.Y.2d 903, 632 N.E.2d 480, 610 N.Y.S.2d 170 (1993) (holding in both cases that a "perfunctory statement that ten excluded prospective jurors were black did not establish the existence of facts and other relevant circumstances sufficient to raise an inference" that peremptory challenges were exercised to exclude individuals because of their race); People v. Copeland, 197 A.D.2d 629, 602 N.Y.S.2d 683, *appeal denied*, 82 N.Y.2d 848, 627 N.E.2d 522, 606 N.Y.S.2d 600 (1993).

[171] Commonwealth v. Simmons, 541 Pa. 211, 232, 662 A.2d 621, 631–32 (1995), *cert. denied*, 516 U.S. 1128 (1996).

[172] State v. Bolton, 271 Kan. 538, 23 P.3d 824 (2001).

[173] United States v. Bentley-Smith, 2 F.3d 1368, 1373–74 (5th Cir. 1993).

[174] Purkett v. Elem, 514 U.S. 765, 768–89, 115 S. Ct. 1769 (1995). *See also* Matthews v. Evatt, 105 F.3d 907, 917 (4th Cir. 1997), *cert. denied sub nom.* Matthews v. Moore, 522 U.S. 833, 118 S. Ct. 102 (1997).

[175] Purkett v. Elem, 514 U.S. 765, 768–89 (1995).

[176] Purkett v. Elem, 514 U.S. 765, 768–89, 115 S. Ct. 1769 (1995). *See also* Matthews v. Evatt, 105 F.3d 907, 917 (4th Cir. 1997), *cert. denied sub nom.* Matthews v. Moore, 522 U.S. 833, 118 S. Ct. 102 (1997).

[177] People v. Starks, 238 A.D.2d 621, 656 N.Y.S.2d 399 (1997).

[178] People v. Starks, 238 A.D.2d 621, 656 N.Y.S.2d 399 (1997).

[179] Melbourne v. State, 679 So. 2d 759, 764 (Fla. 1996).

reasons are provided by the non-movant, the moving party, who has the burden of making a record, should argue why the reasons are pretextual prior to the judge's fact finding determination.[180]

Some appellate courts are urging trial courts to clearly articulate the bases of factual findings pertaining to *Batson* challenges.[181] Generally, a court's findings are accorded great deference.[182] This includes a finding as to whether the prima facie showing of impropriety has been made.[183] To avoid a waiver, *Batson* challenges should be raised before the conclusion of jury selection.[184]

A challenging party may be required to make a specific objection to any juror still claimed to have been the object of discrimination, including individuals struck in a previous round.[185]

A defendant's conviction may be reversed if the trial court improperly applies *Batson* in disallowing a defendant's peremptory challenge.[186] Some courts hold that a *Batson* challenge is untimely if raised for the first time on appeal or after the jury is sworn.[187] If a court finds there has been a *Batson* violation, the judge may declare a mistrial. Some states take the position that the entire panel must be discharged.[188] A mistrial may actually reward the offending party by providing it with another jury panel.

Another approach reinstates the stricken juror on the panel.[189] To establish a pattern of discriminatory challenges may require the retroactive seating of previously challenged jurors, provided they have been retained during future rounds of jury selection.[190] Such an approach is conservative and allows a trial

---

[180] People v. Smocum, 99 N.Y.2d 418, 786 N.E.2d 1275, 757 N.Y.S.2d 239 (2003) ("It is therefore the moving party's burden to make a record that would support a finding of pretext.").

[181] United States v. Perez, 35 F.3d 632 (1st Cir. 1994); People v. Payne, 88 N.Y.2d 172, 666 N.E.2d 542, 643 N.Y.S.2d 949 (1996).

[182] United States v. Roebke, 333 F.3d 911, 912 (8th Cir. 2003).

[183] Commonwealth v. Burnett, 418 Mass. 769, 642 N.E.2d 294 (1994).

[184] McCrory v. Henderson, 82 F.3d 1243 (2d Cir. 1996).

[185] People v. James, 99 N.Y.2d 264, 784 N.E.2d 1152, 755 N.Y.S.2d 43 (2002).

[186] Cudjoe v. Commonwealth, 23 Va. App. 193, 475 S.E.2d 821 (1996) (reversing defendant's conviction because trial court disallowed defendant's challenge of a white juror because he read *Wall Street Journal* and his activities indicated juror may not "relate" to defendant).

[187] Mooney v. State, 105 P.3d 149 (Alaska Ct. App. 2005).

[188] People v. Wheeler, 22 Cal. 3d 258, 583 P.2d 748, 765, 148 Cal. Rptr. 890 (1978); State v. McCollum, 334 N.C. 208, 433 S.E.2d 144, 159 (1993); State v. Franklin, 318 S.C. 47, 456 S.E.2d 357, 360 (1995).

[189] State v. Grim, 854 S.W.2d 403, 416 (Mo. 1993) *(en banc)*.

[190] People v. Moten, 159 Misc. 2d 269, 603 N.Y.S.2d 940 (Sup. Ct. 1993) (holding that propriety of challenges can best be evaluated as jury selection proceeds; court announced that black jurors challenged by defendant would be seated if pattern of discrimination were established in future rounds). *See also* People v. Irizarry, 165 A.D.2d 715, 718, 560 N.Y.S.2d 279, 281 (1990), *aff'd*, 83 N.Y.2d 557, 634 N.E.2d 179, 611 N.Y.S.2d 807 (1994).

judge the benefit of more information in evaluating a jury challenge. It also raises numerous problems, including the position the retroactive seated juror will occupy and what to do if there are insufficient seats for the improperly challenged jurors.

Most jurisdictions give the trial court latitude in fashioning the remedy for a *Batson* violation.[191] If the juror is reseated, some courts have held that once the discriminating motivation is established, the striking party cannot then use a peremptory challenge.[192] For the same reason, a peremptory strike will not be upheld if supported by one acceptable and one constitutionally infirm reason.

§ 3.25 Application to *Batson* to challenges based on exclusion of ethnicity or religion.

An emerging area of analysis under the *Batson* principle is the use of peremptory challenges based upon the religion or religious beliefs of a juror. Courts appear willing to scrutinize challenges based on religion more carefully. In fact, some courts have extended the *Batson* principle to the issues of religion and ethnicity.[193] It has been applied to the challenge by an Irish Catholic defendant to the exercise of peremptory challenges to exclude jurors of a distinct ethnic group, Irish Americans, where ethnicity is characterized by "Irish-sounding" surnames.[194]

However, many other courts have not extended *Batson* to religion and have held that religion or expressions of religious belief may form the basis of a race-neutral reason for a *Batson* challenge.[195] For example, a prosecutor's explanation

---

[191] Jefferson v. State, 595 So. 2d 38, 41 (Fla. 1992); Jones v. State, 343 Md. 584, 683 A.2d 520 (1996) (holding that jurors dismissed as a result of race-based peremptory challenges may be reseated if the trial court finds that there is little likelihood that jurors will hold prejudice toward the party who excused them; decision cites many cases from other jurisdictions on the different approaches on what action should be taken by a trial court when a *Batson* violation has occurred such as striking the entire panel or reseating the improperly stricken juror); Stewart v. State, 662 So. 2d 552, 558 (Miss. 1995); Coleman v. Hogan, 254 Va. 64, 486 S.E.2d 548 (1997) ("We agree with the majority of states that the choice of remedy should be within the discretion of the trial court. A number of factors, such as the point at which the challenge to the strike is sustained and the knowledge of the jurors regarding the improper strike, affect the determination of which remedy to choose. The trial court is uniquely positioned to evaluate the circumstances in each case and to exercise its discretion in selecting the appropriate remedy." Coleman v. Hogan, 254 Va. 64, 67, 486 S.E.2d 548, 549–550 (1997)).

[192] United States v. Bentley-Smith, 2 F.3d 1368, 1372 (5th Cir. 1993); State v. Franklin, 318 S.C. 47, 456 S.E.2d 357 (1995); Coleman v. Hogan, 254 Va. 64, 486 S.E.2d 548 (1997).

[193] People v. Snow, 44 Cal. 3d 216, 242 Cal. Rptr. 477, 746 P.2d 452 (1987); State v. Alen, 616 So. 2d 452 (Fla. 1993); State v. Gilmore, 103 N.J. 508, 511 A.2d 1150 (1986).

[194] Commonwealth v. Carleton, 418 Mass. 773, 641 N.E.2d 1057 (1994).

[195] United States v. Clemmons, 892 F.2d 1153, 1157 (3d Cir. 1989), *cert. denied*, 496 U.S. 927 (1990); People v. Malone, 211 Ill. App. 3d 628, 570 N.E.2d 584, 588–89, *appeal denied*, 142 Ill. 2d 660, 584 N.E.2d 135 (1991); State v. Gowdy, 88 Ohio St. 3d 387, 727 N.E.2d 579 (2000)

that a prospective juror's Jehovah Witness faith meant that the juror's religious beliefs meant that a "higher power will take care of all things necessary" and that in her experience "Jehovah Witnesses are reluctant to exercise authority over their fellow human beings" when sitting on juries constituted a race-neutral explanation.[196] Clergy may be excluded from juries on the ground that religion-based professionals, such as pastors, ministers, and rabbis may be more sympathetic to criminal defendants.[197] Likewise, challenging a juror because he or she is a Mason and believing the accused is a Mason is a sufficient race-neutral explanation for a peremptory challenge.[198] But merely identifying a juror's religion may be insufficient. The attorneys should provide an explanation of how that juror's belief forms the basis of the attorney's challenge.[199]

While a strike based on religious affiliation may be unconstitutional, some courts hold that a strike based on particular *religious beliefs* may be proper.[200] Several courts hold the strike based on religious affiliation or membership may be unconstitutional, but that possible inferences from a juror's beliefs may be permissible.[201] While Connecticut's highest court holds that religion-based

---

(holding in sexual assault trial that prospective juror's wearing of cross, his strongly held religious beliefs, and his vagueness in answering questions were race-neutral reasons for exercising peremptory challenge); Caserez v. State, 913 S.W.2d 468 (Tex. Crim. App. 1994).

[196] State v. Davis, 504 N.W.2d 767, 768 (Minn. 1993). *See also* Davis v. Minnesota, 511 U.S. 1115, 114 S. Ct. 2120 (1994) (Supreme Court denied certiorari; Justices Scalia and Thomas dissented stating: (1) the Minnesota court's judgment should be vacated because the Minnesota court improperly viewed *Batson* as limited to racial discrimination, and (2) the utilization of a "heightened equal protection scrutiny" in *J.E.B.* permits a broader application of equal protection than race or gender discrimination. Davis v. Minnesota, 511 U.S. 1115, 114 S. Ct. 2120, 2121–2122 (1994)); James v. Commonwealth, 247 Va. 459, 463, 442 S.E.2d 396, 398 (1994) (prosecutor provided race-neutral explanation that the commonwealth was "concern[ed] over jurors perceived to be sympathetic to persons facing possible incarceration" and this concern was reinforced by a juror's "visible display of a religious symbol").

[197] Rodriguez v. State, 826 So. 2d 494 (Fla. Dist. Ct. App. 2002).

[198] United States v. Williams, 44 M.J. 482, 485 (C.A.A.F. 1996).

[199] State v. Davis, 504 N.W.2d 767, 772 (Minn. 1993).

[200] United States v. DeJesus, 347 F.3d 500, 510 (3d Cir. 2003), *cert. denied*, 541 U.S. 1086 (2004) (In this case, one juror, with several religious degrees expressed forgiveness for his cousin's killers; prosecutor argued this indicated reluctance to pass judgment. The prosecutor expressed similar concern with another juror who only reads the Bible and holds office in church. However, defense did not raise before trial court its appellate court argument that strong religious beliefs has a disparate impact upon African–Americans.) *See also* United States v. Friesel, 224 F.3d 107 (2d Cir. 2000) (electing to refrain on ruling whether to extend *Batson* to strikes based on religion because the prosecutor gave a non-discriminatory explanation for the strike); United States v. Stafford, 136 F.3d 1109 (7th Cir. 1998) (noting "[I]t would be improper and perhaps unconstitutional to strike a juror on the basis of his being a Catholic, a Jew, a Muslim, etc.," but holding it was not plain error to strike a potential juror on the basis of religion).

[201] State v. Purcell, 199 Ariz. 319, 326, 18 P.3d 113, 120 (2001) (strike proper because it was based on juror's beliefs rather than affiliation); Thorson v. State, 721 So. 2d 590, 594 (Miss. 1998); State v. Fuller, 356 N.J. Super. 266, 279, 812 A.2d 389, 397 (2002) (permitting strike based on inference from juror's traditional Muslim clothing).

peremptory challenges are unconstitutional, it permitted striking of a juror, who indicated that if there were a conflict between the court's instruction and his religious beliefs, he would seek guidance from his religious leader, since this declaration suggested he could not follow the court's instruction or discuss the case with anyone during its pendency.[202]

§ 3.26   Applicability of *Batson* to peremptory challenges — sexual preference or sexual orientation.

There is some authority that sexual orientation, or sexual preference, is a protected class, as is race, for jury selection purposes.[203] However, one federal appeals court rejects the idea that sexual orientation is a *Batson* classification.[204]

§ 3.27   Race-neutral explanations analyzed, including criminal background, neighborhood.

Once an attorney provides a prime facie showing of *Batson* violations, courts must analyze whether a race-neutral explanation has been provided for the exercise of a peremptory challenge. More than other issues in jury selection, this issue has generated substantial appellate review. A race-neutral explanation for exclusion of a potential juror need not rise to the level required to challenge a juror for cause.[205] The reason should be "articulable,"[206] but need not be "quantifiable."[207] The reason should be more than the juror's "background."[208] In a rape case, however, the fact that a juror may not be sympathetic to a rape complainant due to differences in background may be a race-neutral reason.[209] The facts of a case may dictate what is an acceptable race-neutral reason for a challenge. For instance, when the prosecution expresses a concern over the

---

[202] State v. Hodge, 248 Conn. 207, 726 A.2d 531, *cert. denied*, 528 U.S. 969 (1999).

[203] People v. Garcia, 77 Cal. App. 4th 1269, 1281, 92 Cal. Rptr. 2d 339, 347–48 (2000), *reh'g denied*, 2000 Cal. App. LEXIS 112 (Feb. 22, 2000).

[204] United States v. Ehrmann, 421 F.3d 774, 782 (8th Cir. 2005), *cert. denied*, 126 S. Ct. 1099 (2006) (finding the prosecutor's proffered reasons for striking a panel member were not pretextual and further noting "we seriously doubt *Batson* and its progeny extend federal constitutional protection to a venire panel member's sexual orientation.").

[205] *Batson*, 476 U.S. at 97–98. *See also* People v. Hernandez, 75 N.Y.2d 350, 552 N.E.2d 621, 553 N.Y.S.2d 85 (1990), *aff'd*, 500 U.S. 352 (1991).

[206] United States v. Horsley, 864 F.2d 1543, 1544–46 (11th Cir. 1989).

[207] United States v. Clemons, 941 F.2d 321, 325 (5th Cir. 1991).

[208] People v. Van Hoesen, 307 A.D.2d 376, 761 N.Y.S.2d 404 (2003) (reversing defendant's conviction due to trial court's failure to grant his *Batson* challenge in a case where prosecutor struck four of six African-Americans in the venire and prosecutor's only stated reason was that juror's background would lead her to favor the defendant; prosecutor's statement was a stereotypical assumption that an African-American is biased against the prosecution).

[209] People v. King, 195 Cal. App. 3d 923, 241 Cal. Rptr. 189 (1987) (upholding prosecutor's explanation that juror's traditional values may make juror less sympathetic to the complainant).

ability of Latinos to accept the court testimony of translation of tape-recorded conversations offered in evidence, a prosecutor's dismissal of several Latino jurors has a race-neutral basis.[210]

The following dialogue from a sexual assault and murder trial illustrates an example of a race-neutral explanation for challenging a potential juror.[211] Based on the following questions and answers, the appellate court found it proper for the prosecutor to strike a potential juror who had not heard anything about a highly publicized case either because the juror was not being candid or because the prosecutor found such "obliviousness" strange.

THE COURT: This case involves, allegedly, burglary, rape, and murder. The victim's name is Debbie D. Davis. It happened in the Southside of Richmond, September, last. The defendant's name is Timothy Spencer. The press has . . . has given [the murderer] the name of the Southside Strangler.

Have you heard anything about these cases?

MS. SHELTON: No.

THE COURT: You haven't read or heard anything about the cases at all?

MS. SHELTON: No.

THE COURT: Then you could sit impartially?

MS. SHELTON: Yes.

. . .

MR. EVERHART: Have you read any articles or heard any reports about a scientific process called DNA fingerprinting, or DNA printing?

MS. SHELTON: No.

The prosecutor stated as his race-neutral explanation the following:

Next, we had Chrita Shelton, who hadn't heard anything about the case. Quite frankly, I am concerned about the literacy and the educational level of someone who has not heard anything about either DNA, or anything about the Southside Strangler, or Timothy Spencer by now in this jurisdiction. The publicity has been extensive, and I am afraid if you heard nothing, as she indicated, she is not an informed citizen. So I did not want that type of individual on the jury.

This case represents an example of the type of analysis that courts must routinely engage in as a result of the *Batson* decision. The number of black jurors accepted or challenged is not dispositive of the *Batson* issue. In one child sexual assault trial, the prosecutor exhausted all seven of her peremptory challenges to

---

[210] Pemberthy v. Beyer, 19 F.3d 857 (3d Cir. 1994).

[211] Spencer v. Murray, 5 F.3d 758, 763 (4th Cir. 1993), *cert. denied*, 510 U.S. 1171 (1994). *See also* United States v. Bentley-Smith, 2 F.3d 1368, 1376 n.9 (5th Cir. 1993) (noting that a prospective juror's inability to comprehend evidence can be a race-neutral reason).

exclude black venire persons.[212] The appellate court accepted the prosecutor's race-neutral reason for all seven challenges. One race-neutral explanation accepted by the court was that three potential jurors were security guards or related to security guards.[213] Other reasons that the court accepted included a potential juror's lack of experience with young children, since "[i]n a case involving child sexual abuse, knowledge and familiarity with children may be a relevant quality," and past involvement with the criminal justice system such as a black venireman's friendship with a person accused of rape or whose son had been incarcerated.[214] Many cases hold that a relationship with someone accused of a crime is a race-neutral reason for striking a juror.[215]

---

[212] Commonwealth v. Smulsky, 415 Pa. Super. 461, 609 A.2d 843, *appeal denied*, 532 Pa. 663, 616 A.2d 984 (1992).

[213] Commonwealth v. Smulsky, 415 Pa. Super. 461, 465, 609 A.2d 843, 845, *appeal denied*, 532 Pa. 663, 616 A.2d 984 (1992) (The prosecutor stated, "Your Honor, I struck him because he had been a security guard, I mean, in his past. It is my feeling, based on experience that I have had with juries, that security guards are often individuals who were turned down at one time for being not qualified to be police officers and often have some checkered pasts. Also, security guards tend to have seen a great deal of crime and have kind of, I think a jaundiced view and that is why I struck Mr. Simmons.").

[214] Commonwealth v. Smulsky, 415 Pa. Super. 461, 468–469, 609 A.2d 843, 846–847, *appeal denied*, 532 Pa. 663, 616 A.2d 984 (1992).

[215] State v. Williams, 182 Ariz. 548, 555–56, 898 P.2d 497, 504 (1995) (potential juror's relative who had been convicted of a criminal offense was a legitimate race-neutral reason for exercise of peremptory challenge); Cunningham v. State, 838 So. 2d 627 (Fla. Dist. Ct. App. 2003) (holding juror's sister's imprisonment for theft a race-neutral reason, even though white jurors with negative police experiences were not excused, the court noted: "There is a palpable difference between having close relatives prosecuted and imprisoned and merely having a negative police experience. Thus, we cannot say that the trial judge was clearly erroneous in its determination that the State had a race-neutral reason for striking the African-American juror." Cunningham v. State, 838 So. 2d 627, 631 (Fla. Dist. Ct. App. 2003)); Smith v. State, 799 So. 2d 421 (Fla. Dist. Ct. App. 2001) (having a relative who was prosecuted and incarcerated is a race-neutral reason, even if the same challenge was not made to a white juror who was convicted and not incarcerated); Glass v. State, 255 Ga. App. 390, 395–96, 565 S.E.2d 500, 508–09, *cert. denied*, 2002 Ga. LEXIS 757 (Sept. 6, 2002) (finding that "familial involvement with the criminal justice system constitutes a race-neutral reason for striking a potential juror," even if prosecution accepts Caucasian jurors with such involvement and can articulate differences in the Caucasian jurors' criminal justice involvement); Redding v. State, 219 Ga. App. 182, 464 S.E.2d 824 (1995) (in sexual assault trial, prosecutor offered race-neutral reasons that juror's sister had been charged with a felony, another sister left police department with possible bad feelings toward department and was friendly with another juror charged with child molestation and sexual assault); State v. Ashley, 940 S.W.2d 927 (Mo. Ct. App. 1997) (fact that juror's stepson prosecuted by prosecutor's office a race-neutral reason); State v. Johnson, 930 S.W.2d 456 (Mo. Ct. App. 1996); People v. Morgan, 24 A.D.3d 950, 806 N.Y.S.2d 742 (2005), *appeal denied*, 6 N.Y.3d 815, 845 N.E.2d 1286, 812 N.Y.S.2d 455 (2006) (finding as race-neutral, prosecutor's explanation that "juror had a son who had been successfully prosecuted by the District Attorney's office"); People v. Garayua, 268 A.D.2d 283, 701 N.Y.S.2d 379, *appeal denied*, 95 N.Y.2d 796, 733 N.E.2d 236, 711 N.Y.S.2d 164 (2000).

This may include the prosecutor's belief or personal knowledge that a juror may be related to someone with a criminal history or conviction.[216]

Attitudes toward law enforcement[217] or the fairness of the legal system[218] may also be race-neutral reasons.

A juror's prior service on a jury return on acquittal[219] or lesser offenses[220] may also be a race-neutral reason. Even a juror's having served on a jury rendering a prior conviction may be a race-neutral reason if the prosecutor states that the potential juror may be expecting the same type of evidence as was produced in the prior rape trial.[221] In addition, a veniremember's view on the death penalty has been upheld as non-pretextual.[222]

A prosecutor may raise a challenge on personal knowledge or acquaintance of the defendant.[223] In one rape case in which the prosecutor challenged all three black prospective jurors, the appellate court found satisfactory race-neutral explanations for each of the challenges. One prospective juror's husband was

---

[216] Curry v. State, 238 Ga. App. 511, 516–17, 519 S.E.2d 269, 275–76 (1999) (upholding as race-neutral an African-American juror who had same last name and came from town of a defendant prosecutor tried for murder; fear that juror may be related to murder defendant a race-neutral reason even though prosecutor did not question juror about possible relationship); State v. Coleman, 85 Ohio St. 3d 129, 139, 142–43, 707 N.E.2d 476, *cert. denied*, 528 U.S. 954 (1999) (Prosecutor's challenge of juror whose son was in prison for drug trafficking, who was also known by prosecutor to have "an attitude" about her son doing no wrong and that everybody was lying about her son at the time of his prosecution, provided sufficient race-neutral reason for peremptory challenge.); Wilson v. State, 854 S.W.2d 270, 274 (Tex. Crim. App. 1993) (another example of a prosecutor's personal knowledge of a potential juror's relatives' involvement in the criminal justice system as an acceptable race-neutral challenge); James v. Commonwealth, 247 Va. 459, 462–63, 442 S.E.2d 396, 398 (1994) (prosecutor's belief that a prospective juror may have been "related to persons with serious criminal convictions or charges pending against them," based on the similarity between the name of the defendant and prospective juror, was a sufficient race-neutral explanation after defendant raised a *Batson* challenge).

[217] People v. Showers, 300 A.D.2d 151, 752 N.Y.S.2d 53 (2002) (upholding as race-neutral prosecutor's statement that he overheard panelist utter a hostile comment about police officers).

[218] Medlock v. State, 79 Ark. App. 447, 464, 89 S.W.3d 357, 368–69 (2002) (finding juror's previous arrest for failure to answer a summons, pending case before Arkansas Supreme Court, and his statement that he struggled with the fact that system was not fair, provided race-neutral challenge).

[219] United States v. Roan Eagle, 867 F.2d 436, 441–42 (8th Cir. 1989), *cert. denied*, 490 U.S. 1028 (1989).

[220] State v. Griffin, 564 N.W.2d 370, 376 (Iowa 1997).

[221] People v. Garayua, 268 A.D.2d 283, 701 N.Y.S.2d 379, *appeal denied*, 95 N.Y.2d 796, 733 N.E.2d 236, 711 N.Y.S.2d 164 (2000).

[222] *Ex parte* Travis, 776 So. 2d 874 (Ala. 2000), *cert. denied*, 531 U.S. 1081 (2001) (explaining the prosecutor's use of 11 out of 12 peremptory strikes to exclude black members was not pretextual because of those struck, ten expressed opposition to the death penalty and the prosecutor also had struck a white veniremember due to his ambivalence toward the death penalty).

[223] Patterson v. State, 729 N.E.2d 1035 (Ind. Ct. App. 2000) (knowing defendant or acquaintance with defendant is race-neutral reason justifying peremptory challenge).

a multiple-felony offender who was currently serving a sentence for assault. This same juror was also employed by a social services agency and expressed dissatisfaction with the police investigation of a crime involving her. A second prospective juror had a first cousin serving a lengthy sentence for rape. This same juror had failed to disclose a relative's prior convictions, a fact known only because the assistant district attorney had previously prosecuted him. [224] The third prospective black juror had a son who had committed a juvenile offense and had violated his probation. Also, this juror's son's age and circumstances of his crime were similar to the defendant's, which was considered sufficient justification for the prosecutor's assertion that the juror might "tend to identify or empathize with defendant." [225] These exclusions were upheld even though the prosecutor had excluded two Caucasian venire persons who had been convicted of misdemeanor and felony drunk driving crimes, since the prosecution had not excluded the black prospective jurors solely on the basis of criminal convictions. [226]

It has also been held in a sexual assault trial that a potential juror living in a neighborhood in which the prosecutor had investigated a multiple homicide, [227] or that a potential juror knew six other venire members and who might be overly influenced by them, [228] or that other relatives of the juror "had been involved in similar cases or experiences of a sexual nature" are legitimate race-neutral reasons for the exercise of the peremptory challenge. The association of a juror's neighborhood with members of a particular race or ethnicity is not *per se* a race-related factor but may be weighed in the court's determination. [229] A relationship or acquaintance with a defendant's family is another recognized race-neutral reason for exercising a peremptory challenge. [230]

Many courts have found age to be a race-neutral reason in sexual assault [231] as well as other cases. [232] There is some authority that age may be a suspect

---

[224] People v. Richardson, 193 A.D.2d 969, 598 N.Y.S.2d 341, *appeal denied*, 82 N.Y.2d 725, 622 N.E.2d 323, 602 N.Y.S.2d 822 (1993).

[225] People v. Richardson, 193 A.D.2d 969, 598 N.Y.S.2d 341, *appeal denied*, 82 N.Y.2d 725, 622 N.E.2d 323, 602 N.Y.S.2d 822 (1993).

[226] People v. Richardson, 193 A.D.2d 969, 598 N.Y.S.2d 341, *appeal denied*, 82 N.Y.2d 725, 622 N.E.2d 323, 602 N.Y.S.2d 822 (1993).

[227] Commonwealth v. Caldwell, 418 Mass. 777, 781, 641 N.E.2d 1054, 1057(1994).

[228] State v. Williams, 182 Ariz. 548, 555–56, 898 P.2d 497, 504 (1995).

[229] People v. Payne, 88 N.Y.2d 172, 666 N.E.2d 542, 643 N.Y.S.2d 949 (1996).

[230] Wilson v. State, 854 S.W.2d 270, 273 (Tex. Ct. App. 1993).

[231] State v. Degree, 114 N.C. App. 385, 442 S.E.2d 323 (1994) (In a prosecution for a rape of an acquaintance, court accepted as race-neutral prosecution's challenges based upon age (less than 21) and marital status, although prosecutor did not challenge a third juror who was 28.); Reilly v. Commonwealth, 21 Va. App. 330, 464 S.E.2d 508 (1995) (holding that age is a permissible basis upon which to exercise a peremptory strike, but reversing conviction because peremptory challenges were applied to women, albeit older women, from the jury panel).

[232] People v. Mays, 254 Ill. App. 3d 752, 626 N.E.2d 1154, 1163 (1993); Bridges v. State, 116

factor,[233] and authority that age is a race-neutral reason.[234] Marital status can also be a race-neutral reason,[235] as well as familiarity with a crime scene[236] and victimization status, as long as not appearing to be an "afterthought."[237]

§ 3.28 Challenges based on education and employment.

A juror's educational level[238] or the inability of a juror to follow "complicated issues" of a trial may be a race-neutral reason[239] or belief by the prosecutor that the juror did not seem capable of understanding scientific or complex evidence, such as DNA evidence,[240] may be a "race-neutral" explanation. The concern over the ability to follow testimony may be based on the juror's command of the English language.[241] A juror's statement of requiring more than DNA evidence to convict and that the juror was in favor of the O.J. Simpson verdict may also be a race-neutral reason.[242]

Challenges based on employment may or may not be race-neutral reason. Often employment is accepted as a race-neutral reason.[243] However, court holdings

---

Md. App. 113, 695 A.2d 609 (1997) ("*Batson* does not apply to age-based peremptories." Bridges v. State, 116 Md. App. 113, 695 A.2d 609, 619 (1997)); State v. Barnett, 980 S.W.2d 297, 302 (Mo. 1998), *cert. denied*, 525 U.S. 1161 (1999); State v. Winters, 949 S.W.2d 264 (Mo. Ct. App. 1997).

[233] *Ex parte* Bird, 594 So. 2d 676, 683 (Ala. 1991).

[234] Howard v. Moore, 131 F.3d 399, 408 (4th Cir. 1997).

[235] State v. Barnett, 980 S.W.2d 297, 302 (Mo. 1998), *cert. denied*, 525 U.S. 1161 (1999); State v. Degree, 114 N.C. App. 385, 442 S.E.2d 323 (1994).

[236] People v. Simmons, 79 N.Y.2d 1013, 594 N.E.2d 917, 584 N.Y.S.2d 423 (1992).

[237] People v. Meyers, 217 A.D.2d 639, 629 N.Y.S.2d 794, *appeal denied*, 86 N.Y.2d 844, 658 N.E.2d 232, 634 N.Y.S.2d 454 (1995) (prospective juror's status as crime victim is not pretextual on its face, but was applied in a discriminatory manner when only white juror crime victim was challenged by defendant and six non-white jurors who were crime victims were not challenged by defendant); People v. Jupiter, 210 A.D.2d 431, 434, 620 N.Y.S.2d 426, 428 (1994), *appeal denied*, 85 N.Y.2d 911, 650 N.E.2d 1335, 627 N.Y.S.2d 333 (1995) (explaining that while victimization status is not pretextual on its face, in this case "the references to victimization were mere afterthoughts").

[238] Commonwealth v. Caldwell, 418 Mass. 777, 781, 641 N.E.2d 1054, 1057 (1994).

[239] United States v. Grimmond, 137 F.3d 823, 834 (4th Cir. 1998).

[240] Williams v. State, 338 Ark. 97, 991 S.W.2d 565 (1999) (upholding in rape homicide prosecution, prosecution's statement of race-neutral challenge based on need to obtain a jury capable of understanding complex evidence, particularly DNA evidence, and prosecution's challenge of one of the jurors due to her relatively low education level and that she did not seem "bright").

[241] State v. Bowman, 945 P.2d 153, 154 (Utah Ct. App. 1997).

[242] Harris v. State, 996 S.W.2d 232 (Tex. Ct. App. 1999).

[243] United States v. Perez, 35 F.3d 632 (1st Cir. 1994) (holding that prosecutor's reason for striking a black juror was that her employment as a receptionist at the local housing authority may have exposed her to drugs was a race-neutral reason since the explanation was based on "something other" than the race of the juror); United States v. Miller, 939 F.2d 605, 607 (8th Cir. 1991) (potential juror's employment as a legal services' employee and her possible sympathy toward

in this area may not appear consistent. For example, a prosecutor's argument that a potential juror's background as a social worker and involvement with a soup kitchen would adversely affect her attitude toward the justice system was deemed a race-neutral explanation for the exercise of a peremptory challenge, [244] while in another case, an argument that a black juror's role as an affirmative action officer gave her a bias in giving minorities a fair shake was not a sufficiently race-neutral explanation. [245]

The fact that a prospective juror is an attorney is a race and gender neutral reason, but the reason that southerners take a negative view of pregnant women who work is a non-neutral, gender-based reason for striking an African-American. [246]

Challenges based on type of employment may be pretextual if exercised as to one race of potential jurors but ignored as to jurors of another race. [247]

---

defendant held to be a race-neutral reason). *See also* State v. Simmons, 955 S.W.2d 729 (Mo. 1997) (prosecutor's reason that potential juror was a postal worker, an occupation with whom the prosecutor had poor results during past jury trials, was a race-neutral reason); State v. Johnson, 930 S.W.2d 456 (Mo. Ct. App. 1996) (juror's employment as a county jail correctional officer held to be a race-neutral reason); State v. McGuire, 892 S.W.2d 381 (Mo. Ct. App. 1995) (court upheld defendant's attempted rape conviction, rejecting defendant's claim that prosecution had failed to set forth race-neutral reasons for exclusion of two jurors. Court found that prosecutor's explanation that one juror's work in the military record department could cause problems "because of his familiarity with records and record keeping" in a case where the prosecution anticipated some difficulties with records it would be offering through two custodians of records was a race-neutral explanation. It also accepted as race-neutral with respect to another juror that his background as a HUD inspector was reasonably related to prosecutor's belief that his job may unduly influence and predetermine his perceptions of the victim and her family who lived in low-income housing); State v. Easterling, 119 N.C. App. 22, 457 S.E.2d 913, *review denied*, 341 N.C. 422, 461 S.E.2d 762 (1995) (In this sexual assault case, appellate court held that it was race-neutral to challenge jurors who did not meet profile of being in the mainstream of the community, employed and with a family.).

244 People v. Craig, 194 A.D.2d 687, 599 N.Y.S.2d 110, *appeal denied*, 82 N.Y.2d 716, 622 N.E.2d 314, 602 N.Y.S.2d 813 (1993).

245 People v. Dabbs, 192 A.D.2d 932, 596 N.Y.S.2d 893, *appeal denied*, 82 N.Y.2d 707, 619 N.E.2d 682, 601 N.Y.S.2d 604 (1993).

246 State v. Lucas, 199 Ariz. 366, 18 P.3d 160, *cert. denied*, 534 U.S. 1014 (2001).

247 People v. Morales, 308 Ill. App. 3d 162, 171, 719 N.E.2d 261, 269 (1999), *appeal denied*, 187 Ill. 2d 584, 724 N.E.2d 1273 (2000) (reversing defendant's conviction based on prosecutor's pretext contention that length of trial would affect juror's job, but did not apply standard to a white college student in last semester of college). *Compare* United States v. Jones, 245 F.3d 990 (8th Cir. 2001) (court upheld as race-neutral the prosecution's reasons of a juror's profession and familiarity of the area of crime:

> The prosecutor struck similarly situated veniremembers—one who was familiar with the vicinity and another who shared the defendant's profession. These factors were relevant because, as the prosecutor explained, he wanted jurors to whom he could provide a fresh conceptualization of the scene and, also, because those who shared the defendant's line of work might be sympathetic to him for reasons other than his culpability. The defense rebutted neither explanation, nor developed the record to

However, a court may require the party offering employment as a race-neutral reason to explain how that employment relates to the juror's ability to serve in the instant case.[248]

Unemployment may also be considered a race-neutral reason for striking a juror.[249]

§ 3.29   Challenges based on prospective juror's demeanor or appearance.

Courts have recognized that demeanor is part of the intuitive component in attorney decision making. However, challenges based on a juror's demeanor deserve "careful scrutiny." Challenges based on "gut reaction" or "hunch" have been criticized.[250] This includes the explanation that a juror seemed more

---

address the assertions that the veniremember appeared tired and was inappropriately dressed.

United States v. Jones, 245 F.3d 990, 993–994 (8th Cir. 2001).

[248] People v. Smith, 266 A.D.2d 570, 699 N.Y.S.2d 104 (1999):

> After the first round of jury selection, the prosecutor peremptorily challenged four prospective jurors. The court noted that "[t]hey are all black," and the defense counsel asked for race-neutral reason for challenging the prospective jurors. The prosecutor was unable to recall a race-neutral reason for challenging one of those prospective jurors, and the court ordered that prospective juror seated. She proffered race-neutral reasons for challenging two of the other prospective jurors. With respect to the fourth prospective juror, the prosecutor noted "he's a postal worker . . . I had experience with them on juries before and based upon my past experience I don't . . . relate to them well when they're on a jury." The defense counsel objected, arguing that the prosecutor's challenge based on her dislike of postal workers was not race-neutral. However, the court accepted the prosecutor's reason.
>
> . . . .
>
> Where a peremptory challenge is based upon a prospective juror's employment, the concerns regarding the employment must be related to the factual circumstances of the case, and the qualifications of the juror to serve on that case [citations omitted]. Here, the prosecutor made no effort to explain how a prospective juror's employment as a postal worker related to the facts of the case, or to the juror's qualifications. No relationship between the prospective juror's employment as a postal worker and the instant case is apparent from the record.

People v. Smith, 266 A.D.2d 570, 571, 699 N.Y.S.2d 104, 105 (1999).

[249] Commonwealth v. Johnson, 542 Pa. 384, 396, 668 A.2d 97, 102 (1995), *cert. denied*, 519 U.S. 827 (1996); State v. Green, 306 S.C. 94, 409 S.E.2d 785 (1991), *cert. denied*, 503 U.S. 962 (1992).

[250] Brown v. Kelly, 973 F.2d 116, 121 (2d Cir. 1992), *cert. denied*, 506 U.S. 1084 (1993) ("Yet, because such after-the-fact rationalizations are susceptible to abuse, a prosecutor's reason for discharge bottomed on demeanor evidence deserves particularly careful scrutiny. Prosecutors would be well advised — when contemplating striking a juror for reasons of demeanor — to make contemporaneous notes as to the specific behavior on the prospective juror's part that renders such person unsuitable for service on a particular case."); *Ex parte* Bird, 594 So. 2d 676, 684 (Ala. 1991).

"receptive" to the opposing counsel[251] is an insufficient race-neutral reason that an attorney "just got a feeling" about the juror.[252]

The attorney's impression of the conduct and demeanor of a prospective juror during voir dire may provide a legitimate basis for the exercise of a peremptory challenge.[253] This can include a juror's hand mannerisms and body language,

[251] People v. Grier, 261 A.D.2d 555, 690 N.Y.S.2d 648, *appeal denied*, 93 N.Y.2d 1019, 719 N.E.2d 939, 697 N.Y.S.2d 578 (1999):

> Contrary to the defendant's contention, the Supreme Court did not err in disallowing his peremptory challenges of two Asian prospective jurors on the basis that defense counsel's facially race-neutral explanations were pretextual. Defense counsel stated that the prospective jurors appeared to be "very conservative" and more "receptive" to the prosecutor, as indicated by their eye contact and body language, and further, had nothing in their backgrounds that would "make them favorable to the defense." The Supreme Court observed that the challenged jurors had responded to all questioning uniformly and were completely neutral in their demeanor, and concluded that the two jurors "could not have been excluded for any reason other than their race." Bearing in mind the advantage trial courts have in making determinations of this nature, [citations omitted] and that defense counsel's explanations were purely intuitive and based on counsel's subjective impression rather than upon facts adduced at voir dire, [citations omitted] we agree with the finding of pretext.

[252] United States v. Horsley, 864 F.2d 1543, 1546 (11th Cir. 1989).

[253] *See, e.g.*, Brown v. Kelly, 973 F.2d 116, 121 (2d Cir. 1992), *cert. denied*, 506 U.S. 1084 (1993). *See also* United States v. Bentley-Smith, 2 F.3d 1368, 1375 (5th Cir. 1993):

> In erroneously stating that intuition is not a sufficient ground, standing alone, on which to base a peremptory challenge, the district court simply may have been expressing the understandable concern that counsel's claim to an intuitive reaction is not susceptible to the ordinary methods of proof and thus may be suspect as a proxy for a race-based challenge. But the ultimate inquiry for the judge is not whether counsel's reason is suspect, or weak, or irrational, but whether counsel is telling the truth in his or her assertion that the challenge is not race-based. This is no different from the credibility choices that finders of fact — whether judges or juries — are called upon constantly to make. An attorney who claims that he or she struck a potential juror because of intuition alone, without articulating a specific factual basis such as occupation, family background, or even eye contact or attentiveness, is more vulnerable to the inference that the reason proffered is a proxy for race. That is not to say, however, that the reason should be rejected out of hand; that is a call for the judge to make, based upon his or her evaluation of such things as the demeanor of counsel, the reasonableness of the justifications given, and even the court's personal observation of the venireman.

This decision found that a belief that a juror was a follower was insufficient basis. State v. Caldwell, 418 Mass. 777, 641 N.E.2d 1054 (1994); State v. McRae, 494 N.W.2d 252 (Minn. 1992); People v. Morgan, 24 A.D.3d 950, 806 N.Y.S.2d 742 (2005), *appeal denied*, 6 N.Y.3d 815, 845 N.E.2d 1286, 812 N.Y.S.2d 455 (2006) (accepting as a race-neutral explanation juror's "demeanor, his evasive answers to the prosecutor's questions and a perceived antagonism between him and the prosecutor"); State v. Locklear, 349 N.C. 118, 505 S.E.2d 277 (1998), *cert. denied*, 526 U.S. 1075 (1999) (upholding as race-neutral prosecution's challenge of juror based in part on her demeanor and based in part on her prior conviction for possession of marijuana despite the fact that the prosecutor did not challenge white jurors with drug and DUI convictions).

such as covering his mouth and appearing disingenuous.[254] It can also include timidity, weakness, or nervousness of the prospective juror, or the flippancy of the prospective juror in responding to questions.[255] It can be failing to make eye contact and not appearing assertive.[256] The juror may appear "indecisive and easily led by other jurors."[257] The juror may appear to have reservations and apprehensions about serving.[258] Juror inattentiveness or boredom during voir dire can be another race-neutral reason for excluding a prospective juror.[259] A challenge based on a juror's demeanor has more basis if the attorney can articulate an objective, such as that a juror was slow in answering questions or had to have questions repeated,[260] and the attorney can identify specific questions and answers.

---

[254] People v. Sprague, 280 A.D.2d 954, 721 N.Y.S.2d 205 (2001) (reversing defendant's sodomy conviction because trial court rejected his attorney's explanation to *Batson* challenge that juror's folding her arms across the chest indicated hostility to the defendant); Commonwealth v. Smulsky, 415 Pa. Super. 461, 466–67, 609 A.2d 843, 846, *appeal denied*, 532 Pa. 663, 616 A.2d 984 (1992) (juror's demeanor was cited along with the fact that he had been retired a long time and appeared detached from the outside world).

[255] Brown v. Kelly, 973 F.2d 116, 120–121 (2d Cir. 1992), *cert. denied*, 506 U.S. 1084 (1993).

[256] United States v. Sherrills, 929 F.2d 393, 395 (8th Cir. 1991); United States v. Garrison, 849 F.2d 103, 106 (4th Cir.), *cert. denied*, 488 U.S. 996 (1988); State v. Ashley, 940 S.W.2d 927 (Mo. Ct. App. 1997) (failing to respond to questions during voir dire held a race-neutral reason); State v. Malone, 1997 Tenn. Crim. App. LEXIS 278 (Mar. 20, 1997) (holding potential juror's seeming bored and inattentive sufficient race-neutral reason for challenging black juror); Brewer v. State, 932 S.W.2d 161, 164–65 (Tex. Crim. App. 1996) (prospective juror's appearing "slow" during responses and prosecutor wanting accelerated jurors is a race-neutral reason).

[257] People v. Borkowski, 247 A.D.2d 828, 668 N.Y.S.2d 835, *appeal denied*, 91 N.Y.2d 970, 695 N.E.2d 718, 672 N.Y.S.2d 849 (1998). *See also* United States v. Bentley-Smith, 2 F.3d 1368, 1376 (5th Cir. 1993) (race-neutral reason was that juror appeared to be a follower); State v. Jones, 123 N.M. 73, 934 P.2d 267 (1997).

[258] Bryant v. Speckard, 131 F.3d 1076, 1077 (2d Cir. 1997), *cert. denied*, 524 U.S. 907 (1998).

[259] United States v. Marrowbone, 211 F.3d 452 (8th Cir. 2000) (holding juror's inattentiveness and demeanor may be race-neutral reasons); United States v. Sherrills, 929 F.2d 393, 395 (8th Cir. 1991); United States v. Garrison, 849 F.2d 103, 106 (4th Cir. 1988), *cert. denied*, 488 U.S. 996 (1988); Farmer v. State, 764 So. 2d 448 (Miss. Ct. App. 2000); People v. Artis, 262 A.D.2d 215, 694 N.Y.S.2d 5, 6 (1999), *aff'd sub nom.* People v. Jeanty, 94 N.Y.2d 507, 727 N.E.2d 1237, 706 N.Y.S.2d 683 (2000) ("The record supports the court's conclusion that the reasons proffered by the prosecutor for exercising a peremptory challenge against the prospective juror in question, that she seemed bored and disinterested in the proceedings, were race-neutral and non-pretextual." [citations omitted])

[260] Bousquet v. State, 59 Ark. App. 54, 953 S.W.2d 894 (1997) (holding that challenges to one juror's inattentiveness during questioning and another juror's unresponsive answer on questionnaire, coupled with not looking at prosecutor when responding to questions, were both race-neutral reasons for challenging each juror); Commonwealth v. Caldwell, 418 Mass. 777, 641 N.E.2d 1054 (1994) (holding that in sexual assault trial, potential juror's equivocation in her responses, reaction, and hesitation to several questions about police officers is a legitimate race-neutral explanation for exercise of peremptory challenge since the prosecutor's reasons are related to her personal reactions to specific questions as observed by the judge); State v. Barnett, 980 S.W.2d 297, 302 (Mo. 1998), *cert. denied*, 525 U.S. 1161 (1999) (holding a prospective juror's silence is a permissible race-neutral explanation for a peremptory strike).

Vagueness in answering questions may also be race-neutral when there are specific answers to which the attorney can point.[261]

Knowledge of the juror's demeanor may be from outside the record. For example, the striking of a juror whom the lead detective knew to be a "high-strung, critical person" who would likely polarize the jury has been deemed a race-neutral reason.[262] Appearance, e.g., facial hair or failing to remove a hat, may form the basis of a race-neutral challenge.[263]

§ 3.30 Applicability of *Batson* to peremptory challenges based on gender.

Some attorneys feel that gender is an important factor to consider in selecting jurors in sexual assault trials. Gender, together with age, may be a significant variable in a potential juror's identification with a victim or defendant. There is some research to support the proposition that women jurors are more likely to convict in sexual assault trials and that male jurors are more likely to believe that a rape victim's conduct contributed to the rape.[264] There is other research suggesting that women do not differ markedly from men in their attitudes on rape.[265]

---

[261] State v. Gowdy, 88 Ohio St. 3d 387, 727 N.E.2d 579 (2000):

> The third and final reason advanced by the prosecutor as a basis for challenging Smith was his alleged vagueness in answering questions about his religion. Again, the defendant points to Smith's final answer where he identified his church and even pinpointed an address. However, the record shows that before he ultimately volunteered the information, he generically identified himself as "just a Christian," and "nondemoninational."

State v. Gowdy, 88 Ohio St. 3d 387, 394, 727 N.E.2d 579, 586 (2000).

[262] State v. Haigler, 334 S.C. 623, 515 S.E.2d 88 (1999).

[263] People v. Morales, 308 Ill. App. 3d 162, 178, 719 N.E.2d 261, 279 (1999), *appeal denied,* 187 Ill. 2d 584, 724 N.E.2d 1273 (2000).

[264]

> Neither student nor citizen judgments for typical criminal case materials have revealed differences between male and female verdict preferences. [citation omitted]. The picture differs for rape cases, where female jurors appear to be somewhat more conviction-prone than male jurors. [citation omitted]. For example, male students were more inclined to think that a rape victim made a causal contribution to the rape, attributed more fault to the victim, and characterized her more negatively than did female students. [citation omitted]. Male student jurors gave more lenient sentences in rape and robbery cases when victims did not resist, while females gave harsher sentences under the same conditions. [citation omitted]. In a rape case female students favored conviction more often than males before and after deliberation. [citation omitted]

Reid Hastie, Steven D. Penrod & Nancy Pennington, *Inside the Jury* 140–141 (1983).

[265] Nadine Brozan, *Jurors in Rape Trials Studied,* N.Y. Times, June 13, 1985, at C13 (citing study by a University of Michigan sociology professor for the National Center for Prevention and Control of Rape, a Division of National Institute of Health, of 37 sexual assault trials in Indianapolis between July 1978 and September 1980).

Gender has probably played a role in many jury profiles established by attorneys. However, social and generational differences may well supersede gender as a factor in understanding a defendant or victim's lifestyle, such as a young, single woman's socializing in a bar or inviting a date back to her apartment. Gender, like many other demographic criteria, is a crude tool for jury selection and a crude indicator of a juror's experiences, feelings, and opinions.

The Supreme Court of the United States has ruled that gender, like race, cannot form the basis for a peremptory challenge. Women, however, unlike African-Americans, are not a numerical minority. "[G]ender, like race, is an unconstitutional proxy for juror competence and impartiality," the Supreme Court held in a case in which a prosecutor had excluded all men from the jury in a child support and paternity case, and the defendant had excluded all women. [266] Since the jury panel contained twice as many women, the prosecution was able to obtain an all-women jury. Justice O'Connor's concurring opinion notes that this decision may, even more so than *Batson,* generate time-consuming hearings and litigation involving jury selection. [267] Her concurring opinion also notes that one of the effects of the Court's holding may be to preclude a defendant who asserts a battered-wife defense from using her peremptory challenges to select a jury with as many women as possible.

Batson and *J.E.B.* represent the most significant legal developments in the area of jury selection. Since gender is a possible issue that can be raised with virtually any juror, it will spawn many objections to the exercise of peremptory challenges and appellate decisions on what constitutes gender-neutral challenges. Both decisions encourage counsel to analyze jurors' race and gender, raise objections, and request hearings based on the exclusion of jurors for race and gender reasons. *J.E.B.* may foreshadow the elimination of peremptory challenges, although Justice Blackmun's opinion stated that, "[o]ur conclusion that litigants may not strike potential jurors solely on the basis of gender does not imply the elimination of all peremptory challenges." [268]

The Court tried to breathe some life into peremptory challenges by noting that other group characteristics, such as occupation, may be appropriate. Even if the occupation is disproportionately associated with one gender, such as the military or nursing, the court noted that these characteristics are not gender or race-based. [269]

Striking a female juror in a sexual assault case based on the belief that "the fewer women you have on a rape case, . . . the better" is precisely the type of gender-based reason prohibited by the Supreme Court in *J.E.B.* [270]

---

[266] J.E.B. v. Alabama *ex rel.* T.B., 511 U.S. 127 (1994).

[267] J.E.B. v. Alabama *ex rel.* T.B., 511 U.S. 127, 129 (1994).

[268] J.E.B. v. Alabama *ex rel.* T.B., 511 U.S. 127, 143 (1994).

[269] J.E.B. v. Alabama *ex rel.* T.B., 511 U.S. 127, 142 n.14, 145 n.18 (1994).

[270] Maddox v. State, 708 So. 2d 220, 228 (Ala. Crim. App. 1997).

One appellate court reviewed a defendant's sexual assault conviction when the prosecution systematically struck "older women" from the jury panel.[271] Other situations where a prosecutor excludes jurors based on gender can also lead to reversal.[272] For example, it is error for a trial court to fail to consider whether the prosecution excluded male jurors in a domestic violence case solely on the basis of a presumed group bias.[273]

A defendant also can be precluded from exercising challenges based on gender.[274] For example, a defense counsel's assertion that he did not like spinsters or young and attractive women on a sexual assault jury was found by the court to be improper gender-based peremptory challenges.[275] Yet, a defendant's conviction can also be reversed for improperly precluding a defendant's exercise of peremptory challenges which do have a gender-neutral basis.[276] An attorney may not provide as a race-neutral reason gender-based stereotypes of females to counteract the perceived exclusions of males.[277] Even if the defendant does not raise the gender bias issue at trial, it could be raised on appeal because it affects a constitutional right.[278]

---

[271] Riley v. Commonwealth, 21 Va. App. 330, 464 S.E.2d 508 (1995).

[272] Drawdy v. State, 644 So. 2d 593 (Fla. Dist. Ct. App. 1994) (defendant's conviction for capital sexual battery reversed based upon prosecutor's systematic exclusion of all men from the jury).

[273] People v. Williams, 78 Cal. App. 4th 1118, 93 Cal. Rptr. 356 (2000), *review denied*, No. S087330, 2000 Cal. LEXIS 4916 (June 14, 2000).

[274] McGlohon v. State, 228 Ga. App. 726, 492 S.E.2d 715 (1997) (holding that defendant, charged with aggravated battery against a woman, improperly utilized gender to excuse two female jurors since reasons articulated were equally applicable to male jurors who were not struck).

[275] Koo v. State, 640 N.E.2d 95 (Ind. Ct. App. 1994), *aff'd*, Young Soo Koo v. McBride, 124 F.3d 869 (7th Cir. 1997) (trial court refused to allow defense counsel to exclude two prospective jurors. Defense counsel's explanation for attempting to exclude one juror was that she was young and attractive, counsel felt there was an attraction between her and the male prosecutor, she left a male doctor for a female doctor, she had previous experiences with Valium and codeine that he felt may be relevant to issues at trial, and because he did not think it wise in his years of practice to place attractive females on the jury. With respect to the other female juror, the defense counsel stated that he exercised a peremptory challenge because she never had children, and that based on his experience, he did not like "spinsters" on the jury. Appellate court held that these "explanations were a mixture of neutral reasons as well as reasons that can be only described as gender biased." Koo v. State, 640 N.E.2d 95, 99 (Ind. Ct. App. 1994), *aff'd*, Young Soo Koo v. McBride, 124 F.3d 869 (7th Cir. 1997)).

[276] People v. Dixon, 202 A.D.2d 12, 615 N.Y.S.2d 904 (1994) (holding that defendant was improperly denied his right to exercise peremptory challenges since defense counsel's challenge of ten female jurors was supported by the gender-neutral basis of their victimization and that status was uniformly applied to all prospective jurors).

[277] State v. Beliz, 104 Wash. App. 206, 213–14, 15 P.3d 683, 687–88 (2001) (Court reversed defendant's conviction. Prosecutor admitted it was looking for a predominantly older male jury in response to an inquiry about the race-neutral reason for the prosecutor's challenge.).

[278] State v. Beliz, 104 Wash. App. 206, 214, 15 P.3d 683, 687–88 (2001).

§ 3.31 Improper comments during voir dire.

There are many areas that cannot be addressed in voir dire. Many improper areas are the same areas that would be off-limits during other phases of the trial. While improper comments will often be overlooked, an understanding of the most common abuses allows counsel to lodge a prompt objection and seek remedial measures. Remedial measures may include terminating the line of questioning, curative instructions, dismissing a jury panel, or mistrial.

A potentially prejudicial infraction in jury selection is referring to inadmissible evidence or suggesting that there is more evidence in support of a party's position than the party will be able to produce. However, if the reference is brief and may have a valid purpose, the error is harmless.[279] Comments on possible punishment are impermissible at any stage of a trial. During voir dire it is impermissible for a prosecutor to ask: "Does everyone understand that upon conviction that probation is always an option?"[280] A related error is improperly discussing law during jury selection. The law is the province of the court, although many trial judges will allow some latitude in this regard.

A party should also avoid characterizing facts or evidence in the case. Comments on the evidence should be objected to. For example, characterizing an act of abuse as "brutal" should probably be avoided.[281]

During voir dire, the prosecutor must avoid improperly defining legal principles to the jury. For example, a prosecutor should not suggest that "the lapse of time in child rape cases lessen[s] the need for physical evidence" or that "child molestation trials require less evidence for a conviction than trials for other crimes."[282] This could be done by implying that "mere presence of an adult" establishes force when a child is the complainant.[283]

If the prosecution makes a misstatement during voir dire, such as the defendant only admitted to intercourse after DNA test results, it is insufficient for defendant's counsel to simply object.[284] The attorney should ask the court to admonish the jury to disregard the statement or take other curative action.[285]

---

[279] People v. Mincey, 2 Cal. 4th 408, 6 Cal. Rptr. 2d 822, 827 P.2d 388, 412–13 (1992) (prosecutor's reference to selecting photographs to introduce evidence of tortured child and suggesting there were worse photographs of the child was a brief remark, and the trial court also helped to ascertain "whether the gruesome nature of the evidence might have an adverse effect on the prospective juror's ability to sit as a fair and impartial juror.").

[280] Prince v. State, 623 So. 2d 355, 357 (Ala. Crim. App. 1992).

[281] See, e.g., Strickland v. State, 247 Ga. 219, 275 S.E.2d 29 (1981).

[282] State v. Henderson, 2000 Ohio App. LEXIS 4579 at *16–18 (reversing defendant's conviction because of numerous improper comments by prosecutor).

[283] State v. Henderson, 2000 Ohio App. LEXIS 4579 at *19.

[284] Hayes v. Commonwealth, 58 S.W.3d 879 (Ky. 2001).

[285] Hayes v. Commonwealth, 58 S.W.3d 879 (Ky. 2001).

CHAPTER 4

OPENING STATEMENT

§ 4.1 Introduction.

The importance of opening statements is often overlooked. The opening statement creates a critical first impression. "Studies have shown that jury verdicts are, in the substantial majority of cases, consistent with the critical impressions made by the jury during the opening statements . . . and initial impressions become lasting impressions."[1] Given the nature of individuals to form an opinion and then seek evidence to justify an opinion, it is important to try to win over jurors early on in a case. The party's position should be clear and stated with certainty. If it appears that a party, particularly a defendant, has not decided on his position, a juror may dismiss the party's point of view. If a defense is going to be asserted, it must be stated early. For example, if the issue in the case is the identification of the defendant, it should be clearly stated that there is no question that the victim was raped and brutalized, but that the case is one of identification. Similarly, the defendant's denial of guilt should be clear.

It is very important that the opening statement be accurate, and that the attorney must not promise to produce evidence that cannot be produced. Do not try to predict the unpredictable. A favorable impression can be created by facts woven into a compelling story. Facts presented as part of a story will be more memorable and convincing and are an essential part of jury persuasion.[2] From the presentation of a story an effective theme can be developed.

The opening statement should leave something to the imagination. Providing too much detail can eliminate suspense and interest in the party's case. There is another consideration in providing details of a defense in the opening. As a general rule, one should deny guilt and establish the basis of a defense during the opening statement. Raising a defense in opening, however, can open the door to the introduction of evidence by the prosecution that contradicts that defense. For example, if the defendant raises the defense of entrapment in the opening statement of a child pornography case, the prosecutor need not wait until rebuttal to present evidence of the defendant's predisposition.[3] Allowing the proof to be presented as part of the prosecution's direct case does allow the defendant to preview it before presenting the defense, which may be an advantage. What is important is to understand the ramifications of presenting details in opening.

---

[1] Thomas A. Mauet, *Fundamentals of Trial Techniques* 41 (3d ed. 1992).

[2] *See* Nancy Pennington and Reid Hastie, *A Cognitive Theory of Juror Decision Making: The Story Model,* 13 Cardozo L. Rev. 519–57 (1991). *See also* § 3.3 herein.

[3] *See, e.g.,* People v. Mann, 31 N.Y.2d 253, 288 N.E.2d 595, 336 N.Y.S.2d 633 (1972).

The opening should simplify the case for the jury. If the jury cannot understand your case and arguments, it opens the door for your adversary to convince the jury. If you have complex medical evidence to present, simplify it in opening. If the relevant anatomy is not well known, explain it in opening.

The opening can make the case stand for a principle larger than the case. This larger principle can be weaved into the theme. An example of such a larger principle is "a woman's right to say no." This approach also applies to the closing argument.

Argument and unnecessary or irrelevant appeals to emotion should be avoided in the opening statement. Going outside the facts and involving other issues should be objected to and, when necessary, bring a motion for mistrial to preserve the issue. When a prosecutor goes outside the bounds of legitimate argument, such as talking about police officers "doing their jobs protecting the community that has been plagued by violence, senseless violence, shootings and killings," the trial judge should provide a prompt curative instruction.[4]

§ 4.2 Law governing opening statements and preliminary instruction by court on elements of crime.

An opening statement is designed primarily to alert jurors to what counsel anticipates the evidence will show. An attorney may refer to admissible evidence expected to be presented at trial.[5] The American Bar Association's Standards for Criminal Justice exhorts that both prosecutors and defense attorneys confine themselves in opening statements "to a statement of issues in the case . . . [that the attorney] believes in good faith will be available and admissible."[6] There

---

[4] United States v. Moreno, 991 F.2d 943, 947 (1st Cir. 1993), *cert. denied*, 510 U.S. 971 (1993). The judge cautioned the jury:

> I must give you some instructions to disregard some of the things that were said in the opening statement. There were references to violence in the area, to other incidents in the area than those that are the subject matter of this trial. I will instruct you to disregard all of those references. Some were made very early in the opening statement, others were made in the course of it and toward the end of the opening statement. We are here to try on the evidence with respect to the charges against these defendants, only the charges against these defendants. It is not your function or the function of the court or anyone else to be concerned about anything other than the charges against these defendants and the evidence bearing upon that. You will erase from your mind the arguments about other violence, and the phrase "senseless killings" that was used. Those are not matters to be considered by you as you weigh and evaluate the evidence that relates to this case.

United States v. Moreno, 991 F.2d 943, 948 (1st Cir. 1993), *cert. denied*, 510 U.S. 971 (1993).

[5] State v. Piche, 71 Wash. 2d 583, 585, 430 P.2d 522, 524 (1967), *cert. denied*, 390 U.S. 912 (1968).

[6] American Bar Association Standards for Criminal Justice, The Prosecution Function Standard 3-5.5. The Defense Function Standard 4-7.4 (1992).

should be no reference to evidence "unless there is a good faith and reasonable basis for believing that such evidence will be tendered and admitted in evidence."[7] The law of the opening statement has been summarized by former Chief Justice Burger as follows:

> An opening statement has a narrow purpose and scope. It is to state what evidence will be presented, to make it easier for the jurors to understand what is to follow, and to relate parts of the evidence and testimony to the whole; it is not an occasion for argument. To make statements which will not or cannot be supported by proof is, if it relates to significant elements of the case, professional misconduct. Moreover, it is fundamentally unfair to an opposing party to allow an attorney, with the standing and prestige inherent in being an officer of the court, to present to the jury statements not susceptible of proof but intended to influence the jury in reaching a verdict.[8]

A prosecutor has a duty to make an opening statement and cannot waive the opening statement. The opening statement should set forth the nature of the charges against the accused and state briefly facts and evidence in support of those charges. In some jurisdictions, failing to delineate the particular offenses against an accused and how the charges are to be proven will result in granting a defendant's motion for a mistrial to dismiss the charges, although the prosecutor may be afforded an opportunity to correct the defective opening statement.[9] Because an opening statement is not evidence, a jury may not rely on statements made in opening as evidence.[10] The defendant, too, can be restricted in an opening. A defendant may be precluded in opening from arguing that the police "planted evidence."[11] Failing to object to the prosecutor's opening and depriving

---

[7] American Bar Association Standards for Criminal Justice, The Prosecution Function Standard 3-5.5. The Defense Function Standard 4-7.4 (1992).

[8] United States v. Dinitz, 424 U.S. 600, 612 (1976) (Burger, C.J. concurring) (holding trial court did not erroneously exclude one of defendant's attorneys from trying the case because of the attorney's improper comments during his opening statement).

[9] People v. Kurtz, 51 N.Y.2d 380, 414 N.E.2d 699, 434 N.Y.S.2d 200 (1980), *cert. denied*, 451 U.S. 911 (1981). *See also* People v. Thomas, 21 A.D.3d 643, 799 N.Y.S.2d 653 (2005) (holding trial court should have dismissed sodomy charge because prosecutor failed to sufficiently outline the charge, but that there was no prejudice from the failure to dismiss since defendant was acquitted of charge).

[10] State v. Frazier, 73 Ohio St. 3d 323, 338, 652 N.E.2d 1000, 1013 (1995).

[11] People v. Green, 268 A.D.2d 443, 702 N.Y.S.2d 317, *appeal denied*, 95 N.Y.2d 797, 733 N.E.2d 237, 711 N.Y.S.2d 165 (2000), *cert. denied*, 536 U.S. 926 (2002):

> The trial court properly sustained the prosecutor's objections to those portions of defense counsel's opening statement in which he attacked the reliability of the complainant's identification of the defendant and suggested that the police planted evidence on the defendant to bolster a weak case. The remarks exceeded the bounds of an appropriate opening statement.

People v. Green, 268 A.D.2d 443, 702 N.Y.S.2d 317, 318, *appeal denied*, 95 N.Y.2d 797, 733 N.E.2d 237, 711 N.Y.S.2d 165 (2000), *cert. denied*, 536 U.S. 926 (2002).

the prosecutor of the opportunity to correct any deficiency in the opening may waive the ability to raise the issue on appeal.[12]

The court must be careful in its preliminary instructions to the jury. Providing the jury with the elements of the indicted crime creates the possibility of a juror's premature analysis of evidence and may in some jurisdictions be improper.[13]

§ 4.3 Improper comments on what opposing party will produce.

It is generally considered improper for a prosecutor to comment on what the defendant will produce as testimony. For example, stating that a defendant "will testify but we don't know which version of facts he will testify to" is an improper comment on the defendant's right to remain silent and on his credibility before he introduces any evidence.[14] However, another court held that a prosecutor's reference to two people who knew what happened in the course of the sexual assault and that the victim was going to testify, while inappropriate, is not reversible where the defendant elected to testify and the record indicated that his testimony was planned before the prosecution's opening.[15] A prosecutor cannot express a comment concerning the plausibility or credibility of the anticipated testimony of a defendant, even when the defendant does testify at trial.[16] A prosecutor cannot ask the jurors "what's he [the defendant] going to say after all this evidence is presented?"[17] Nor may a prosecutor turn to the defendant during a murder trial and, in referring to the gun used in the crime, ask: "Where did you get it?"[18] Some courts will allow a certain amount of preening by the prosecutor; for example, consider the following opening statement:

> Ladies and gentlemen, the evidence in this case will be compelling. It will be convincing. It will be overwhelming. I have the burden of proof. I welcome that burden of proof, particularly in this case.
>
> The defendant does not have to present any evidence, but, I will tell you now, if he does — and, remember, he has a constitutional right not to — but, if he does, we will expose whatever defense they attempt to put on, if they do, and we will expose it for what it will really be.[19]

The court found that the prosecutor's comments were not comments on the defendant's silence, but "anticipatory remarks that the evidence would support

---

[12] People v. Shannon, 269 A.D.2d 839, 703 N.Y.S.2d 764 (2000).

[13] People v. Townsend, 67 N.Y.2d 815, 492 N.E.2d 766, 501 N.Y.S.2d 638 (1986). *See also* People v. Davis, 12 A.D.3d 456, 783 N.Y.S.2d 850 (2004).

[14] State v. Pierce, 231 Neb. 966, 439 N.W.2d 435, 443–45 (1989).

[15] State v. Miller, 195 W. Va. 656, 466 S.E.2d 507 (1995).

[16] State v. Miller, 195 W. Va. 656, 466 S.E.2d 507 (1995).

[17] Meadows v. State, 291 Ark. 105, 111, 722 S.W.2d 584, 587 (1987).

[18] Bird v. State, 527 S.W.2d 891, 93 (Tex. Crim. App. 1975).

[19] Commonwealth v. Meadows, 534 Pa. 450, 633 A.2d 1081 (1993).

the charges," and that the remarks exuded a "confidence" of the prosecutor, but were not inherently prejudicial.[20] Other courts may view such comments more critically.

In contrast with situations where a prosecutor comments or suggests that the defendant should testify or has an obligation to present proof is a prosecutor commenting upon omissions in the defendant's statement or commenting upon the defendant's initial denial of involvement with the rape victim when initially questioned.[21] An isolated reference to the defendant's post-arrest silence, while improper, is not necessarily reversible error.[22]

§ 4.4 Comments by a prosecutor on facts or evidence not produced.

Another pitfall in opening statements for prosecutors is to refer to facts that are not produced in the course of trial. Courts vary widely on whether such comments will result in a mistrial or reversal of conviction. Many courts take the position that a reference by a prosecutor to testimony that is not forthcoming is acceptable, absent a showing of bad faith or significant prejudice to the defendant.[23] Some courts find that prejudice to the defendant is the overriding factor and that such prejudice overrides the good faith or bad faith of the prosecutor.[24] When a showing can be made that there is a reasonable possibility that the reference to inadmissible evidence contributed to the defendant's conviction, there is more likely to be a reversal or a mistrial.[25] For example,

---

[20] Commonwealth v. Meadows, 534 Pa. 450, 633 A.2d 1081 (1993).

[21] People v. Otero, 217 A.D.2d 796, 629 N.Y.S.2d 825, *appeal denied*, 87 N.Y.2d 849, 661 N.E.2d 1390, 638 N.Y.S.2d 608 (1995). *See also* § 6.27.

[22] State v. Olivieri, 860 So. 2d 207 (La. Ct. App. 2003):

> Specifically, the State stated, 'And then when Agent Riker asked him about the rapes, the Defendant decided he didn't want to talk any more.' While such a remark appears impermissible, it does not warrant reversal.

> The prosecutor's reference to defendant's post-arrest silence during opening statement was brief. The record shows the State's opening statement was approximately 18 pages and only one sentence out of the 18 pages referenced defendant's post-arrest silence. There is no indication that the brief reference by the prosecutor was a deliberate attempt to inject or exploit the issue. The remark was made at the beginning of a three-day trial and there is no indication the State attempted to stress or make continued references to defendant's post-arrest silence. Additionally, the evidence against defendant was overwhelming.

State v. Olivieri, 860 So. 2d 207, 214–215 (La. Ct. App. 2003).

[23] United States v. Tolman, 826 F.2d 971 (10th Cir. 1987); State v. Rainey, 580 A.2d 682, 686–87 (Me. 1990); Commonwealth v. Johnson, 287 Pa. Super. 58, 429 A.2d 718 (1981). *See generally* Michael G. Walsh, Annotation, *Prosecutor's Reference in Opening Statement to Matters Not Provable or Which He Does Not Attempt to Prove as Ground For Relief*, 16 A.L.R.4th 810 (1982).

[24] People v. Mariani, 203 A.D.2d 717, 610 N.Y.S.2d 967, *appeal denied*, 84 N.Y.2d 869, 642 N.E.2d 334, 618 N.Y.S.2d 15 (1994); People v. Cruz, 100 A.D.2d 882, 474 N.Y.S.2d 142 (1984).

[25] State v. West, 190 Mont. 38, 42, 617 P.2d 1298, 1300 (1980); State v. W.L., 292 N.J. Super.

a reference in opening to numerous sexual assault charges that cannot be proven at trial can be so prejudicial as to result in reversal of a defendant's conviction on another charge.[26] When the prosecutor refers to a particularly crucial event, for example, that a witness will testify that the defendant had the stolen necklace, and that witness is not produced, the defendant is denied a fair trial on the theory that the prosecutor has presented his own unsworn testimony in lieu of competent evidence.[27]

Suggesting testimony that the victim's mother will give, after removing her from the witness list before opening when there is "no good faith basis for believing the mother would testify as represented to the jury" is also improper.[28]

It is grossly improper for a prosecutor to convey to a jury that there is information linking a defendant to a crime that is outside the scope of the evidence a jury has a right to consider. An example of this is the following opening statement, which suggests that there is other evidence linking the defendant to the crime charged.

> Now, you're going to hear from Jeffrey McQuilla, you're going to hear him tell you what happened to him. But, what's also important here, too, is the fact that you're going to hear from an officer, Pablo Rosa, who arrests, based upon an investigation — now, an investigation is composed of hearsay, so you can't hear that, but based upon an investigation Anthony Hamilton was arrested and he was taken to the precinct.[29]

One California appeals court, in reversing a defendant's conviction for the prosecutor's reference to evidence that was not produced, noted that the prosecution does have some discretion in referring to evidence that it reasonably believes will be produced, but offers a three-part test for determining prejudice when there is a variance between the opening statement and the proof produced.[30] First, was there a motion made *in limine* or an objection lodged to the opening statement? Second, was the jury informed by the court or by the prosecutor that

---

100, 678 A.2d 312 (1996) (holding that reference in a prosecutor's opening statement to sexual abuse, defendant's telling victim to pour roach spray down his mother's mouth or to stab his cousin's eyes, were improper since no such evidence was introduced, together with other prejudicial comments on opening, was part of reason for reversal of defendant's conviction).

[26] People v. Camacho, 209 A.D.2d 534, 618 N.Y.S.2d 842 (1994) (complete failure on the part of prosecution to present proof of 34 sex crime counts, as forecast in opening statement, improperly influenced jury's consideration of endangering welfare of child charge for which defendant was convicted).

[27] People v. Weinger, 101 Ill. App. 3d 857, 866, 428 N.E.2d 924, 938 (1981).

[28] People v. Gorghan, 13 A.D.3d 908, 787 N.Y.S.2d 178 (2004), *appeal denied*, 4 N.Y.3d 798, 828 N.E.2d 90, 795 N.Y.S.2d 174 (2005) (reversing defendant's conviction for this, as well as other improper comments in opening).

[29] People v. Hamilton, 121 A.D.2d 176, 178, 502 N.Y.S.2d 747, 748 (1986).

[30] People v. Barajas, 145 Cal. App. 3d 804, 193 Cal. Rptr. 750 (1983).

the opening statement is not evidence? Third, did the opening statement result in a violation of the defendant's Sixth Amendment right to confrontation?[31]

§ 4.5   Appeals for sympathy and attacks on defendant's character.

A prosecutor in a sexual assault case must be careful not to make highly inflammatory comments or generate undue sympathy for the victim or anger and hatred for the defendant. A court may reverse a defendant's conviction when such comments are more than isolated references and become a "flagrant appeal for sympathy for the victim and an equally flagrant attack on the defendant's character and credibility"[32] as in the following example:

> Now, a lot of people you know they think about well pressures of life, of my life get so much to me, geez wouldn't it be nice to go back be a kid again, have those things. I didn't have any worries, I didn't have a job I had to be to, didn't have to pay bills, worry about this or that. That's one part of it.

> When you think about it, when you're a kid, you also have something that an adult doesn't, you lack something an adult has which is freedom. The ability to protect yourself. When you're older if things get too much, if you want that private little moment you can do whatever it is you want to do. If you like to jog, go to a museum, go fishing, whatever it is you can do it, jump in a car, take a drive be by yourself. When you're a kid, you don't have that. You just can't say that's it, I've had enough, I want to be by myself, go off by myself, especially if you're a young child like the children in this case were, one of them still is.

> When you're a child, when you think about it you have maybe three things that should be your own and that should be unique to a child which should never, ever be tampered with or damaged by anybody. You should be safe in your home. When you talk to a kid, don't go out talk to strangers, watch when you cross the street, don't talk to this guy in the playground or that guy on the corner. But when you're home, it's supposed to end, I'm home now let's just relax.

> You know when you're a kid you should also have your own body, your own body should be yours, we call our private parts our private parts for a reason, because you know they're not exposed to everybody, we don't have to have like — we have our face exposed, our hair, whatever, everybody can look at. Your private parts are obviously covered up. To a kid it's one of the few things I have, my privacy, some kids call it my private part, mine, they're mine.

---

[31] People v. Barajas, 145 Cal. App. 3d 804, 809, 193 Cal. Rptr. 750, 753 (1983).

[32] State v. W.L., 292 N.J. Super. 100, 105–08, 678 A.2d 312, 314–17 (1996).

You also have when you're a kid, you're supposed to have innocence, you know, you're supposed to be a kid, you're supposed to worry about whether or not I'm going to get that candy bar or whether or not I'm going to make the little league team, you're not supposed to worry about or know about sex. I mean it's just not right.

Now, those three things, the sanctity of the home, the sanctity of one's own body, the sanctity of that child like innocence, all of those things were shattered and taken away in this case on two boys, two boys. One of them by their father, the other by their stepfather, it's the same man, it's this man right here, this defendant. He took these things away from little [W.L.] who's now seven, who was then about four and a half, five years old and [L.C.] his stepson who's about 15 now, was about 10, 11, 12. He terrorized these children, terrorized their mother and destroyed the family, destroyed them.

Now when they went down there the defendant also spoke about what happened with [W.L.] and what he said, well, it's for you to decide. But what he said when you hear it is so perverse in it — in that it's so ridiculous that to expect anybody to believe it is really offensive. He said that he was asked [sic] your son was screaming, your wife ran into the bathroom, saw this, what do you have to say about that? Well yeah he was screaming, this is him talking now. He would scream every time we went into the bathroom because see I was trying to get into this habit after he would go to the bathroom, I would put him up there on the sink and I would take soap and water, as he said I would wipe his little butt out then because I believe that it was necessary to maintain these delicate tissues in the body. I would take cold water, slash it up there into his butt. That's why he was screaming.

And the reason why his penis was up, I don't think it was up, but the reason why his penis was up well see he wasn't circumcised like I wanted him to be and the pediatrician said he should look like his brother. I didn't have the nerve to take the skin off his penis myself so I just couldn't stand it. She was supposed to look after it and she never did and it just it was, it wasn't right that should happen. That was it.

Like that, that this happened and this boy, this little boy is saying his father did these horrible things to him and the mother says she saw it and he's saying that well he was teaching him hygiene. The thing about and I don't quite understand what the explanation about the penis and the circumcision is all about, but that's what he said.

So she said enough was enough, the reign of terror which is what it was and these boys are living with it till today and I hope not much longer, but who knows, is over, is over. Because this guy here, the defendant destroyed these people and that's just not right, that's why we come here to you, to the community to hear the case and you decide what happened, you decide if he's guilty or if he's innocent. You listen to the evidence and if you feel the State has not proven this case beyond a reasonable doubt, then you find him not guilty. But if you do, you have an equally strong duty to find him guilty. I'm going to tell you here that I submit to you that after you hear it you will find the man guilty because he is. You know the little boy [W.L.] who you're going to see, he's just a little thing. About April of this year he had to be taken to the hospital because he said that he was going to put roach spray into his own body and kill himself, he's seven years old. Like I said you know when a seven-year-old child wanted to kill himself, well that says a lot about the truth.

Now, about the roach spray. That's an odd thing for a seven-year-old to think up on his own. Well, you'll also hear from [W.L.] one of the other things his father did to terrorize the family, to just distort this child was he would say when your mother is sleeping take the roach spray, go pour it down her mouth. Or when your cousins are over, staying over, when they're sleeping, take the knife, stab out their eyes. He's five years old for God's sake. He remembers this when he's seven and this is all too much.

Now, that's why we're here on account of all that, on account as I said a seven-year-old kid, he should be out today in school, when he comes home he should go out, play ball, trade baseball cards or whatever, but he's not. He's in here testifying about how his father, his father did this to him, touched his own body like that. And he suffers the way he does and the 15-year-old will come in here [L.C.], five years or so after, he still lives with it.

Here he is, he's a young man coming into manhood, 15 years old. What does he have as his legacy from his childhood? That he was violated, that he was violated by not his father but somebody his mother took in and was supposed to protect him as well, like he was his own son. We're here on account of that.

Also the mother went through hell, went through hell, her life was terrorized to the point that her own son from another marriage, [L.C.], her own flesh and blood who was violated by this guy that she brought in, that she brought in and that happened to him. The son they had together, it happened to him too after she already knew about the first kid, she lives with that. She lives with how petrified she was of this man that she couldn't even protect her own.

We're here on account of all that. I tell you that this all happened, all this destruction happened because of one person, that one person is guilty.

While a prosecutor's reference to a defendant in a sexual assault trial as "despicable,"[33] "pedophile," or "sick"[34] is improper in opening, an appropriate

---

[33] State v. J.A., 337 N.J. Super. 114, 121, 766 A.2d 782, 786 (2001) (holding error was not prejudicial in context of this case although such a comment is impermissible).

[34] People v. Carney, 222 A.D.2d 1006, 636 N.Y.S.2d 524 (1995), *appeal denied*, 88 N.Y.2d 877, 668 N.E.2d 422, 645 N.Y.S.2d 451 (1996). References to a defendant's sexual orientation or characterizing the defendant's sexual interests are also discussed in §§ 6.48 and 15.11.

curative instruction by the court will negate the prejudicial impact of such a comment on the defendant's character.[35] Also, an isolated reference in opening to convict the defendant so that this would be the "final time . . . [complainant] has to . . . relive this experience," while improper, is not necessarily reversible error.[36] One court, however, permitted a reference to "sexual predator" as an isolated reference.[37]

§ 4.6 Expression of personal knowledge or opinion.

In opening, an attorney should not express personal knowledge or opinion. However, this does not preclude a comment on what the evidence will show and including the proof that will lead to a particular conclusion. For example, the following statement in a sexual assault case was not deemed to be a personal assertion of testimony, but rather an inference that the elements of proof will be met by the prosecution: "I think our evidence is strong and . . . you will be convinced and I will ask you to convict."[38]

§ 4.7 References to inadmissible prior act or other inadmissible evidence or mischaracterizing evidence.

If the prosecution refers to evidence which is later deemed to be inadmissible, how the evidence is presented in opening may be relevant in assessing the impact of such evidence. If, for example, the prosecution suggests that inadmissible prior

---

[35] Commonwealth v. Riberio, 49 Mass. App. Ct. 7, 725 N.E.2d 568, *review denied*, 432 Mass. 1102, 733 N.E.2d 1065 (2000). (The appeals court commented that in child sexual abuse cases that care should be taken to avoid emphasizing sympathy for victims over proof of the alleged crimes. In this case, "[a]ny sympathy was overcome by the judge's strong and repeated instructions that the jurors base their verdict on the evidence." The trial judge also struck the prosecutor's reference to the defendant as "sick.").

[36] People v. Stephens, 2 A.D.3d 888, 767 N.Y.S.2d 514 (2003), *appeal denied*, 2 N.Y.3d 739, 810 N.E.2d 918, 778 N.Y.S.2d 465 (2004).

[37] State v. Smith, 2004 Ohio App. LEXIS 646 (2004):

> A review of the transcript does reveal that the prosecutor did make these references at least sixteen times during his opening statement. However, given the nature of this case, we find no fault in this type of statement. Given that the State charged Smith with [sexual assault] of five different child victims, from three different families, we cannot say that the prosecutor acted improperly in characterizing Smith as a sexual predator. There is nothing in the record of the opening statements to suggest that the prosecutor was using the term 'sexual predator' as a legal term of art, and a lay juror would most likely agree to a characterization of the acts with which Smith was charged as the acts of a sexual predator.

State v. Smith, 2004 Ohio App. LEXIS 646 at *12 (2004).

[38] State v. Larsen, 2005 Ut. App. 201, 113 P.3d 998 (2005) (noting also that "in this context, the term 'I think' does not operate as an assertion of testimony, and to the contrary, expresses a degree of uncertainty about the result that emphasizes the jury's discretion to reach another conclusion.").

act evidence demonstrates a propensity to commit a sexual offense, this may compound the error in the admission of such testimony. [39]

A prejudicial opening is often the result of multiple improper comments. In addition to referencing prior bad acts of the defendant, which were not admissible, an opening should not spend "more time . . . discussing and detailing uncharged crimes and bad acts than the crimes for which defendant is on trial." [40] It is also improper to draw an inference "devoid of tactical support" from prior act evidence. Thus, it is improper to argue in a sexual assault charge involving force that the defendant possessed a gun on the day of assault, when the other act evidence of gun possession occurred in another year, and suggests that the defendant's gun possession was relevant to the element of force of the crime charged. [41] As in many other areas of improper conduct, failing to object may waive all but plain error. [42]

§ 4.8   Opening the door to the introduction of otherwise inadmissible evidence.

An argument in opening may open the door to evidence which might otherwise be precluded. "Door-opening" is an issue on direct and cross-examination of a complainant and defendant. [43] By arguing that charges against a defendant was not the result of criminal behavior but were instead the product of a woman scorned, opens the door to a previously undisclosed witness whose testimony rebuts the defendant's theory. [44] But, not every reference to positive traits of a defendant opens the door to the defendant's character. [45] For example, a defense attorney in opening, who describes the defendant as a veteran and father of three as part of a general description of the defendant, does not open the door to other acts of evidence. [46]

---

[39] Rosky v. State, 111 P.3d 690, 699 (Nev. 2005), *aff'd in part, rev'd in part* (finding that prosecution's opening helped to place defendant's character at issue).

[40] People v. Gorghan, 13 A.D.3d 908, 787 N.Y.S.2d 178 (2004), *appeal denied*, 4 N.Y.3d 798, 828 N.E.2d 90, 795 N.Y.S.2d 174 (2005) (reversing defendant's conviction for this and other improper comments).

[41] People v. Gorghan, 13 A.D.3d 908, 787 N.Y.S.2d 178 (2004), *appeal denied*, 4 N.Y.3d 798, 828 N.E.2d 90, 795 N.Y.S.2d 174 (2005).

[42] State v. Wilson, 2005 Ohio 6666.

[43] *See* §§ 5.27 and 6.15.

[44] Lowry v. State, 2005 Ark. LEXIS 625, __ Ark. __, __ S.E.2d __ (Oct. 20, 2005).

[45] *See, e.g.*, Terry v. State, 332 Md. 329, 338–39, 631 A.2d 424 (1993) (holding that admission of prior conviction for same or similar crime to counter defense counsel's improper opening statement was prejudicial and "tantamount to killing an ant with a pile driver").

[46] People v. Stanbridge, 348 Ill. App. 3d 351, 810 N.E.2d 88 (2004):

> Contrary to the State's assertions, defense counsel did not "cross the line" to create an impression of a blemish-free life. In addition, given that the State's own opening statement had already alluded several times to defendant's children, the fact that

§ 4.9   Establishing goals for the opening statement.

Establish goals for the opening. These goals will depend on the type of case as well as its strengths and weaknesses. Your goals may include preparing jurors for sexual language and direct or cross-examination of your witnesses. For the defendant, perhaps a goal will be to establish a minimal opening statement, deny the charges, and create a favorable atmosphere based on the presumption of innocence and burden of proof. What impression do you want to create? Where do you want the jury to focus its attention?

Jurors will form an impression of the attorney presenting an opening. The person delivering a message can make a difference in how it is received. Do you seem too uptight? Do you seem as if you are withholding something? Do you project aloofness? Do you reassure your audience? These are factors to consider in establishing your goals.

For a defendant there is usually the issue of motive to address. Why is the child or adult saying this if it is not true? Additionally, in the case of a child, how could the child know about these sexual matters if they did not occur?

§ 4.10   Using a theme and telling a story.

The opening statement should contain a theme. The theme is the emotional context of the reason to convict or acquit. The theory of the case is the legal basis for prosecution or defense. In some situations, they may be the same. For example, in a prosecution based on the age of consent, a theme of 40-14 = guilty is based on the legal theory of the case where the defendant is 40 and the complainant 14. This theme should be simple and clear and explain the positive aspects as well as the negative aspects of the case. (*See also* § 3.3.)

The theme should explain how the charges happened or came about. It should simplify the case. A good theme reads like a newspaper headline. If a defense theme is one of "a case with two victims," of "overzealous investigators," or that "the complainant is not credible," evidence can be tied in by pointing out how the child was interviewed and subjected to leading or suggestive questions. This type of theme also provides a motive for the allegations. A defense theme in a case of mistaken identification can be "a young man in the wrong place at the wrong time." For a defendant accused of sexual assault who has prior similar convictions a fitting theme might be, "This case is about a troubled teenager trapped by her lies, and an innocent man hounded by his past."

In the O.J. Simpson criminal case the defense dealt with the prosecution's DNA evidence with an effective theme that the physical evidence had been "corrupted,

---

defense counsel described defendant as a father is unremarkable. Nor should counsel's comment that defendant was a veteran have been used to allow the State to introduce inadmissible evidence. Court found the use of prior act evidence in this case to be reversible error.

People v. Stanbridge, 348 Ill. App. 3d 351, 357, 810 N.E.2d 88, 95 (2004).

contaminated and compromised." This simple message was in contrast to the complicated and perhaps confusing prosecution presentation of DNA testimony. It is easier to understand and makes sense (plausibility of a theme), better accounts for the major aspects of the opponent's case (completeness of a theme), and fits better with evidence believed to be true, such as bias of a witness who handled evidence or incompetence of witnesses handling the evidence (consistency of the theme) than the evidence presented by the prosecution. Significantly, the prosecution did not have a message for the jury, only lots of information that was similar to unconnected pieces of a puzzle.

Related to the theme is the importance of telling a story. A good story helps to simplify the case. A story will make facts interesting. Develop your story and practice telling it to different people. A story should be clear and easy to follow and compelling. Often it will have a "good guy and bad guy."

As noted in § 3.3 of this book, a story will help the jury evaluate evidence and fill in gaps in the evidence. It provides a structure for processing evidence. If you do not provide a story, the jury will likely develop its own story, which may not be as favorable. Is the case about an exploited child or naive defendant? Is the complainant or defendant a victim of circumstances? Whoever tells the most convincing story first has a better chance to move the jury's attention to their point of view.

A careful choice of words can help create impact. Here is a sample theme that explains both the strengths and weaknesses of the prosecution's case.

> Thank you, Judge Sheridan. Ladies and gentlemen of the jury, this is a case about Charles Bailey sexually and physically exploiting a physically and mentally weaker 33-year-old woman by the name of Priscilla Cadberry.

In the above case the victim lived with the defendant, had consensual relations with him, and came back to live with the defendant when she had no place else to live, at which time the victim alleged the defendant raped her. The theme emphasizes the physical strength of the defendant (there had been assaultive behavior by the defendant toward the victim prior to the rape) and the physical and mental weakness of the victim, who is learning-impaired. This helps explain the victim's behavior in returning to the defendant as well as how she could find herself in the relationship in the first place. The verb "exploiting" also highlights an unfairness in the defendant's relationship with the victim.

Here is a beginning of an opening statement that effectively summarizes the prosecution's theme in a case involving allegations of sexual assault by five different women who had dated the defendant.

> Throughout this week we'll be going back in time to between October 1992, and July 1993. You'll hear testimony about a scheming, plotting, planning, overpowering, manipulative, and deceptive defendant. We will see that there are five different situations, five different dates, five different times, five

different places, and five different victims. Common to this is one six-foot three, 210-pounder, the defendant.

This simple opening statement actually covers many issues in the case. There are "different" victims who behaved "differently," which helps to explain issues that the prosecution must deal with, such as victims' maintaining contact with the defendant, socializing with the defendant after the sexual assault, sending a rose to the defendant after one of the assaults, and failing to timely report the assaults. The statement sends a message that different people will behave differently, which is developed further in the opening (*see* Section 4.13 and 4.14 on educating the jury). The different cases and women are united by one person, the defendant. The picture of him as "scheming, plotting, planning, overpowering, manipulative, and deceptive" not only defines the defendant, but also helps to explain the weaknesses in the prosecution's case with regard to the victims' behaviors and reactions. The opening statement simplifies these issues for the jury.

§ 4.11   Opening involving teenager, adult, alcohol and drugs.

The following opening develops the age differential and physical differences between the parties — two common differences that often can form the basis for a theme. It also develops the defendant's use of alcohol and drugs to lure the complainant.

On June 4th, 1995, a 27-year-old man invited 14-year-old Gina Lynn into his car at the intersection of Michigan Avenue and California in the City of Schenectady. Fourteen-year-old Gina Lynn went in that car and went for a ride and a journey. Not only did he meet Gina at that intersection, it was also the intersection of opportunity and vulnerability — of young and old, of weak and strong. And that journey in that car would take Gina to the Community Hospital where she would be examined by a physician who would observe that she had lacerations and abrasions to her genital area, a tear, tenderness on her wrists, tenderness on her thighs to the extent that she would curl up as the doctor attempted to examine her; the product of injuries inflicted by this defendant.

This case will be about what happened between the time this 27-year-old man invited this 14-year-old to come with him and Gina Lynn arrived at the Community Hospital. It will be about what happened to this child, who weighs 80 pounds at the time, trying to do physical struggle and mental struggle with an adult.

It began as Gina Lynn had been out with her mother shopping and seeing some friends and she was walking in the neighborhood, and a man she had seen but did not know driving around in a car approached her. He asked some questions about a restaurant and began to probe her: "How are things at home? What's going on? Would you like to smoke some marijuana?" And she said

271

no to the marijuana. "Would you like to have some beer?" And to this 14-year-old child, that was bait. She took it.

And she will describe to you how she got in that car, learned some very tough lessons. She went in that car and she will describe the route they took, which involved going to a Stewart's store, getting some beer, drinking some beer in the car. Driving around, and this man who told her that he was in Schenectady to sell drugs also said, "Well, let's go to a motel." And he said, "No, don't worry, nothing's going to happen. We will have a little more privacy."

She had some beer, she winds up in a room where the drinking and smoking continues. A 14-year-old who weighs 80 pounds in a room and 180 pound man is on top of her now. And this begins a struggle, not only mental struggle, a physical struggle. She has had to decide, she has been in a situation now where she has to decide how she's going to survive. She tries different things. She tries saying no; that doesn't work. She tries physical struggle, she does resist, she does fight. She tries.

But you know what? When she is 80 pounds, she's not able to get off that bed, and at some point she's still struggling as the defendant tries to remove her clothes, as the defendant is holding her hands down, holding her wrists, and holding her legs down. That's what she did.

He tries to put his penis in her mouth. There is enough struggling going on that he is not able to place his penis in her mouth and that's why one of the counts of this indictment is only an attempted sodomy. She was able to stop that.

She tries talking her way out of this. She tries saying things to him about her state of mind. "I can't, I don't want to, please don't. This brings back bad memories." She tries talking her way out. She's crying. He doesn't listen. And he wins the fight. He sports a hundred pound weight advantage in this. And he places his penis in her vagina while he holds her down. And it hurts.

§ 4.12 Opening with theme taken from defendant's statement.

Sometimes an effective opening or theme can be found in the statement of a witness. Look for statements and references in the proof that may produce an effective beginning to the opening or theme. In the following example, the theme is taken from a defendant's statement.

"I have had a problem being around young girls for 15 years." That's what this defendant tells Sergeant Tim Cummings when questioned about one set of child molestation allegations. It is this defendant's problems with young girls and children that unite three young girls in this trial — Laura, Tammy, and Diane.

There are three girls, three beginnings. And, hopefully, there will be one ending — this trial.

§ 4.13 Educating the jury.

Another goal in opening statement is to educate the jury, i.e., define terms, and explain events. The opening statement is the second step after voir dire in the process of explaining a difficult issue. If there are complex issues, the opening is a good time to state what the evidence will be on those issues. If you expect testimony on a medical issue, discuss that evidence briefly in your opening statement. When the expert witness then testifies, the jury will have heard the evidence already and will be better able to follow and comprehend the expert's testimony. This can be particularly true in interpreting genital findings in sexual abuse cases.

A prosecutor may also choose to explain typical behaviors of abused children to pave the way for expert testimony on recantation[47] or why the complainant returned to the defendant. This is an area that most jurors will not readily understand. See the sample opening statement of a prosecutor in § 4.27 dealing with the recantation of sexual abuse allegations by a child's mother. A defendant may wish to discuss anticipated proof on the suggestiveness of the child victim's interview process.

§ 4.14 Example: .

In the following example, the prosecution uses the opening to educate the jury about "acquaintance rape." The case involves five women who worked with the defendant and either socialized, dated, or engaged in consensual relations with him. The prosecutor must explain certain aspects of the victims' behaviors and reactions that may not be readily understood by the jury. For example, in the opening of the case the prosecutor points out that, since the defendant was the women's supervisor, the complainants were vulnerable. The prosecutor also develops an opening theme that makes different people react differently in situations, which should help the jury understand the complainants. The prosecutor also explains why the complainants went back to the defendant, because they needed to make a living, a fact with which many of the jurors may be able to identify.

Acquaintance Rape. They all knew the defendant; they all worked with him at Pedro's Restaurant. Katrina, Lauren, Patricia, and Tammy were all waitresses; Maria was the hostess. The defendant was the waitresses' kitchen supervisor. Maria had to rely on the defendant for access to the office. In short, they were all subordinate to him at work. We will see that these girls were his victims. We didn't choose the facts and circumstances of this case; we did not choose the facts and circumstances of the sexual assaults.

As individuals, each victim reacted during each incident, and after each incident, in a different manner. The girls, hard workers, come to you from all

---

[47] *See* Chapter 11 for a discussion on when expert testimony is admissible on this topic.

walks of life. One thing they do have in common is the need to earn money, whether to support a child or to put themselves through school. They needed their jobs. Now, they worked and they socialized with other co-workers, as co-workers will do. There's some social drinking and drug use, as we indicated during jury selection. Now, as we hear the testimony, we'll be able to separate those uses from the specific incidents of each sexual assault. We may not approve of the alcohol or drug use, but they are not at issue in this trial; this is not a D.W.I. or a narcotics case. What is at issue and what we all should focus on are sexual assaults on five women at the sole hands of this defendant.

Now, six of the seven counts in the indictment involve the use of physical force by this six-foot three, 200-pound man; he literally overpowered them. Lauren, Patricia, Tammy, and Maria will testify to that. Each situation was different. The other counts involve a sodomy of Katrina, who was unable to register a protest because she was asleep and, by the law, physically helpless. Please listen carefully to these young women. You will hear common threads throughout the testimony. One is that the defendant used them for rides. He doesn't drive. It's common knowledge at Pedro's that he used people for rides every day. Now, in the driver's seat of the car the women were in control. Once they left that driver's seat, the defendant dominated them. We will hear, too, that these girls didn't report the sexual assaults to the authorities until sometime after Maria reported her assault. The assaults took place over a nine-month period of time. Maria reported it about three weeks after she was raped. Katrina, Lauren, Patricia, and Tammy will tell you why they did not report immediately; they will also share with you why they ultimately did report. Again, as they testify as to what happened to them, you'll hear varying responses to the varying situations. And because we all react in different ways, so did they. We are human and we are all individuals — we bring with us different characteristics.

§ 4.15   Example: Child witness suggestibility.

Educating the jury involves taking facts or issues of a case and explaining them from the perspective of the party. Throughout this book, many of these issues are identified in terms of their legal analysis — eyewitness identification, motive for the allegations, delay in reporting, or credibility of the witness — just to name a few. Every case has issues or human behavior that needs to be explained. Identify the important areas and begin teaching the jury about them in opening.

In the following example, the fact that the witness is young and suggestible is explained in the opening statement by reference to the trial judge's admonition to the jurors that they are not to be exposed to outside influences during the trial and are not to read about or discuss the case.

You will notice that the Judge will instruct you that you are not to talk about this case with anyone, discuss it with one another, or read about it in the paper, or watch news reports about it. Why? Because the law knows and recognizes that you, like anyone, are suggestible. If you're exposed to outside influence, you won't be able to do your job, reach a fair and impartial decision. If that's true, how much more true is it with this five-year-old child?

§ 4.16 Defense's response to prosecutor's opening.

Address important legal principles brought out in a prosecutor's opening, such as the rule on reasonable doubt, by tying it to a colorful expression that the jury is likely to remember. Here is an example:

> You have all heard where there is smoke there is frequently but not always fire, so there is a natural tendency to conclude where there's smoke there's fire. Each of you have given Mr. Jensen your oath that you will resist that natural human tendency and he accepts that.

> But the question here is going to be not whether there is smoke, but whether you are convinced beyond a reasonable doubt that there is fire, whether you are convinced beyond a reasonable doubt of the cause of that fire.

The response need not be point-by-point; it may be a broad response.

In response to the prosecutors' opening statement about a "terrible" rape, the defense in the following example magnifies the rape and then follows it with the contradictory behavior of the victim. At the same time, the defense points out facts that have been omitted by the prosecutor in her opening, which is an effective way to convince a jury that all the facts have not been presented and that they might have to await the defense's cross-examination.

> Tammy will freely admit to you that she had sex with him voluntarily. She says that two days after that, he came to her apartment and raped her. And she says that she's horrified by this; this was a terrible, terrible thing. It was an awful thing. Here's a man that she voluntarily had sex with, and then two nights later she said no, and "no" means "no." And I think she's going to tell you, because she told the District Attorney, who took notes of her conversation with her, that she thought of counseling; she's had headaches and nightmares, and this has been an awful thing for her. And who can blame her? To be raped as she described is a terrible thing. How does she live with it? One year later she writes a card to Keith with a flower and says, "Happy Anniversary" — one year after she says she's raped. Now, you haven't heard about that, have you? And wait until she gets on the stand to tell you, "Well, I guess I don't know what I did." She sent him a card, almost a year to the day after she claims this man raped her, and says, "Hey, Keith, have a nice anniversary." She also works at Pedro's. And she's also saying nothing afterwards to anybody at the restaurant. Now, she may have a story now as to why she doesn't say anything, but this woman, who's been horribly abused, will come in and tell you — "Did you tell anyone that?" "No." "Did you continue to work with Keith?" "Yes."

275

§ 4.17   Dealing with problems in the opening statement.

Each criminal trial presents a party with its own problems. There is usually some piece of evidence or some testimony that is going to be unfavorable to your side. Often, it involves certain characteristics of the victim or the defendant. Address such problems during jury selection and the opening statement.

An explanation must be provided. If the problem involves unwanted characteristics of the victim or the defendant, find ways to personalize her or him. Talk about the human side of the person's life, which will allow a juror to empathize or identify with the person. For instance, the fact that a party or witness receives public assistance, is unemployed, or appears to provide little to the community can be neutralized by explaining the hardships that led him or her to such unfortunate circumstances.

Alcohol or drug abuse issues must be dealt with in the opening statement. Another problem area that surfaces in many sexual assault cases is the sexual lifestyle of the victim or defendant. Sexual preferences or activities may be an area of potential prejudice; many jurors may not be able to understand certain sexual activities that differ from their own.

Another problem that attorneys should anticipate is the difficulty a witness may have in providing testimony, especially children or a defendant who may not articulate well or have difficulty recalling events. In the opening statement, alert the jurors to those difficulties. With child witnesses, one must carefully outline what the expected testimony will be. An attorney who thinks he or she can predict the testimony of a child will often be surprised — "Kids say the darnedest things."

§ 4.18   Example: Emotional nature of complainant's testimony.

Sexual assault trials often involve emotional testimony. In jury selection and in the opening statement, alert the jury that the witness's testimony may be emotional and tearful, but remind them that emotions do not affect the reality of the evidence. Here is a way of addressing the issue of the emotional nature of a sexual assault victim's testimony.

> You promised us, all of us, that the nature of the charge itself and the emotion that it carries with it would not obscure your objectivity, would not make it difficult for you to evaluate this case upon the evidence, upon the facts. I will remind you of that because I'm sure that Jennifer's testimony is going to be dramatic.

§ 4.19   Example: The intoxicated victim and witnesses with problems in their backgrounds.

In the following example, a young woman's intoxication is used by the prosecutor as a basis for her victimization.

> She left intoxicated and got lost, was vulnerable, and within a matter of hours was sexually exploited. She was lost in a part of Albany where she had never been before in her life. She was a stranger on the streets she was walking. She was a 21-year-old trusting, innocent, intoxicated woman. No match for a man and a woman more savvy in the ways of the streets than Cheryl ever was.

Note that the intoxicated condition of the victim is tied to the innocence of her conduct. Also, a dichotomy is presented between a naive and innocent young victim and clever and cunning defendants.

Many witnesses will have different backgrounds from most jurors. Those differences may make it difficult for the jury to accept the witnesses' testimony. Differences in a victim's or defendant's background, criminal history, drug use, or alternative lifestyles must all be addressed in the opening statement if the jury is going to hear those details during the proof. Be direct and to the point. For example:

> You're going to hear about the world they live in. It may be different from the world you live in. But we don't choose our witnesses. They were the witnesses who were there. We take them as we find them, and you are going to hear about these witnesses, warts and all.

Another phrase that can be used in many situations is a request for empathy:

> Sometimes you may have to walk out of your shoes and step in the shoes of someone else.

If there is something that places a negative fact in context, state it; for example, the person who has a criminal record but has led a productive life since that conviction.

The following portion of an opening statement deals with a complainant who alleges that a man whom she met at a bar raped her as he was taking her home. The complainant has a history of drug use, has spent time in jail, and also has a venereal disease, which the defendant will raise as part of his defense. It is best that factors such as these be announced early and by the party calling the witness; they can be presented for the first time as the party wants them portrayed, and they will be less shocking to the jury when they hear them later. In the following example, the potential negatives are contrasted with the principle that "a woman has a right to say no whoever she is."

> Before I go further into what happened that night, I should tell you about Annie because she is going to tell you about herself. She is who she is. She is a citizen of this state. She is on parole for a drug conviction and assaulting a police officer. She has been out of jail approximately a year and a half. She has worked regularly, as has testified her parole officer, and she is doing well now. She has been convicted of a drug charge and she has been convicted of a misdemeanor in New York City which she will tell you about.

277

She is of Hispanic background. She does not speak or understand English well, as you will hear and witnesses will describe. She also had syphilis when she was examined at the hospital after the rape.

You listen and you determine what relevance her background is to what happened to her that night, and what relevance it is to her credibility, or what relevance it is to her right not to be molested, because as you will see, whoever she is, whatever her background, she had no right to be harmed that night and had every right to say no.

§ 4.20   Example: Dealing with a child's knowledge of sexual acts and findings of seminal fluid.

Deal directly with a strong piece of evidence such as a preschool victim's ability to describe sexual acts and the finding of seminal fluid in her genital area. This may entail discussing personal aspects of the defendant's lifestyle, but this may be necessary. In the following example, the implication is that the child's mother engaged in an active sex life, not just with the defendant, but other men also, who may be the source of the traces of seminal fluid found on the child. There is also the beginning of the suggestion that the child's mother may have been upset with the defendant on the day in question.

> Tammy [the child's mother] and John [defendant] were not just friends, they were sexual playmates, and we will show you that. You are going to hear that John would go over and he would have sex with Tammy numerous times in the month before the date in the indictment; that he would come over, and you are going to hear that they would have sex and sometimes stay in bed all day long. And they would have sex, fall asleep, and when he was charged up again, he would do it all over again.

> Now, right or wrong, this is the proof in the case. And you are going to hear that this child — and you are going to see her — was present during this. At times she actually observed the act and at other times she came in immediately afterwards.

> So, you are going to hear that Tammy and John had sex a lot; you are going to hear what it was like. That's what this case is about. And you will hear, and I will tell you now, the way they performed sex, because it will have a bearing on this case.

> Now, we are also going to show you that on the day in question, in the morning, John came to the house early in the morning. And he will tell you that usually when he came in this house, Tammy couldn't get her clothes off fast enough and neither could he. But that morning he was upset about something and tired, and they started talking and finally he retired and he fell asleep. And then he woke up and Tammy was leaving. And Tammy was going out with another man that day who John saw come over to the apartment.

We will show you also that other men at other times had opportunity and were at that apartment with Tammy. Tammy did not stay with one man. She had other men at other times, many times. You are going to hear that.

§ 4.21 Dealing with motive for allegations.

An important issue in sexual abuse cases is the complainant's reasons for the allegations and the circumstances surrounding the disclosure of abuse. When there is no motive to bring the allegations, the prosecutor will stress that fact in support of the victim's credibility and argue in summation: "Why would this woman come in and testify the defendant raped her if he didn't?" "What does she have to gain?" If a defendant has a response to these questions, it should be made in the opening statement.

If the motive issue is not addressed, the jury is likely to believe there is no reason why, and that belief will solidify the longer it is unaddressed. Here is a common explanation provided in the opening statement by the defense where the defendant and victim have had a prior consensual relationship.

> The evidence in this case will make you want to ask the question "Why?" Why would someone declare what was otherwise mutually consensual sexual activity to be criminal? The reason is simple. She loved Rich. She wanted Rich. She wanted to live with him. But there came a point in time that she realized for the first time that the same love and respect that she had for Richard was not shared by him, in that he no longer wanted a part of the relationship. As a matter of fact, Rich told her one night that the relationship was over. And he told her on the night these so-called acts occurred, she says against her will, that "this is the last time that we will have sex together." "You have to get out." When she realized that she could not have what she wanted, she couldn't have Rich, then she wanted him to suffer along with her.

§ 4.22 Opening based on complainant's consent — Motive to provide explanation for her activities.

The following two-word theme — Mary's hickey — provides an explanation for the allegations as well as what happened between them. It implies consent. Thus it provides a motive — a key element to a defendant's opening.

> This case is about Mary's hickey — how she got it, and because she had to tell her mother where she got it, is why we are here.

> Mary ended up on the other couch with Steve making out, and they were kissing and they were doing what kids do, and during the course of the kissing that took place with Mary and Steve, she ended up with a hickey on her neck.

> And what you're going to hear, ladies and gentlemen, is that there came a point in time when Mary was confronted by her mother who asks, "How'd

you get that hickey on your neck?" And the explanation is going to come here in this courtroom because she's gone too far with it, and you're going to see how it was that this case developed into why we're here today.

We're not here to pass moral judgment on what happened between Mary and Steve. We're not going to ask you to pin a medal on him for being with this 17-year-old. But, he never forced her — the only force was when Mary's mother demanded an explanation that landed Steve here today.

§ 4.23 Painting a picture.

Unlike most of the trial, the opening statement lets an attorney control the use of words. Use words to paint a picture for the jury. Here is an example.

> A strange dark basement apartment. It was like a dungeon. Stripped naked. She was cold. She was crying. She was hysterical. She feared for her life. Suddenly a knife flashed before her face.

This is much more effective than: "The evidence will show she was crying and upset when she was in the defendant's apartment." On the other hand, do not engage in hyperbole or exaggerate a situation. Jurors will be quick to penalize a party who overstates the facts.

Consider opening with a gripping fact that captures interest and allows a story to develop. Also, the present tense will have more impact in telling a story and give a greater sense of action:

> On June 3, 1993, Tom Quill is driving on Jefferson Avenue when he hears and sees a naked woman trying to stop cars. He stops his car and allows her to approach him. She bangs on the window, begs him to let her in. Lip bleeding, naked, and screaming, "Take me home, I've been raped." This case will be about why that woman screamed, "Take me home, I've been raped."

§ 4.24 Using demonstrative evidence in the opening statement.

Attorneys may use demonstrative evidence in opening statements if that evidence will be presented at trial. If the exhibit is powerful, it may be best to use it on opening.

Courts vary in their acceptance of demonstrative evidence in opening statements, but there is legal authority permitting the use of a visual aid in an opening statement.[48] The demonstrative evidence may be a chart or diagram explaining a complex set of facts or events.[49] When the rules call for pre-admission of exhibits, there should be no problem, because the exhibit is already in evidence. In other situations, raise the issue with the court and your adversary before

---

[48] United States v. De Peri, 778 F.2d 963, 979 (3d Cir. 1985), *cert. denied sub nom.* Pecic v. United States, 475 U.S. 1110 (1986).

[49] United States v. De Peri, 778 F.2d 963, 979 (3d Cir. 1985), *cert. denied sub nom.* Pecic v. United States, 475 U.S. 1110 (1986).

beginning your opening, then move to permit the use of the exhibit, and be prepared to show the foundation for the exhibit since your opponent will probably object.

Demonstrative evidence can be particularly helpful in a sexual abuse case where the abuse continued over a long period of time with many important triggering events. A drawing of a complex crime scene or a photograph or illustration of a significant injury, or medical finding may be helpful in the opening.

Some courts will permit the use of a blackboard or flip charts in an opening. This, too, can help a jury remember an important phrase, element of a crime, or date. As with demonstrative evidence generally, there should be a careful selection of quantity and quality. It is easy to overdo exhibits or visual aids to the point that their effectiveness is lost.

§ 4.25 Dealing with witness credibility.

If there are questions about the credibility of an opponent's witness, this information should be presented in your opening statement. Convince the jury in advance that the facts will discredit important testimony. Hearing this in your opening will make a juror question more carefully the witness's credibility when the testimony is heard. If any "deals" have been made with a witness, attack them in opening. If an important witness had given inconsistent statements, zero in on them. For example:

> To believe these charges, you have to believe the witness. We are going to show you that this star witness can't tell the truth. He has given not one, not two, not three, but four different stories of what happened. He told stories concocted to fit the occasion. We are going to show you this.

When a key witness has a particular problem that could affect his credibility, utilize understatement to emphasize the issue:

> You are going to hear from the witness's own mouth that at the time, in December, he used to take drugs a little bit — like every day — and he used to drink a little bit — like a couple of six-packs and a fifth of whiskey every day — and he used to drink, and he used to use crack, and he used to take drugs, and by his own admission he was antisocial, and he had lost jobs.

§ 4.26 Use language of case.

In an opening, use language that is expected from a witness testimony, which is particularly effective, or language from the expected jury charge. For example, a defense attorney might open:

> You will hear allegations that my client touched Eva. Perhaps he did brush against her. But, whatever happened was not with any "intent of sexual gratification."

281

This language mirrors the jury instruction that the sexual contact component of a sexual abuse charge requires a touching of the sexual or intimate parts for purposes of sexual gratification. Such an opening statement alerts the jury to this crucial issue, which can be the theory of the defense.

The following is an example of using the words or facts in the case to paint a picture for the jury in the opening. The prosecutor carefully constructs an effective ending to his opening by using the defendant's own words from his statement to the police. It is a message that strikes a responsive chord, namely "to care."

> The proof will come from the defendant's mouth through Investigator Apple. He told Investigator Apple explicitly what he did. He had no difficulty remembering what he did to Priscilla, no difficulty saying, "I raped her," and no difficulty saying, "She said stop, but I didn't care." He didn't care about Priscilla. We're going to ask you to care about the proof in this case. We're going to ask you to listen to the proof in this case, to listen to the testimony of Priscilla. If you care about the proof in this case and listen to the testimony in this case, I have every reason to have faith in what your verdict will be in this case, the only verdict consistent with all the proof in this case, guilty of all counts. Thank you.

§ 4.27   Sample opening statement of prosecutor.

The following is an opening statement by the prosecutor in a child sexual assault case. The case involves recantation of the allegations by a mother who reported the abuse of her daughter. The mother, who has a minimal education, is expected to now testify that the allegations did in fact occur consistent with her original report to the police. There is some equivocal medical evidence. The testimony of the mother, who is an eyewitness to the abuse, is crucial to the case since the child is too young to testify.

PROSECUTOR:

> Thank you, your Honor. Ladies and gentlemen of the jury: The opening statement is an opportunity to go into some of the unusual facts, the bizarre twists, that there are in a case involving sexual abuse of a child.
>
> I think there are a few facts we can agree on right from the beginning. Jennifer was born in August of 1983. She was three years old at the time of the incident alleged in the first count and approximately four years old at the time of the incident alleged in the second count.
>
> There will be no dispute of that according to the birth certificate, which we intend to offer in evidence, and according to the testimony of Jennifer's mother, who will testify that this defendant was the father of the child.
>
> The father, while not married to this woman, is accused of attempting to have sexual intercourse with Jennifer on two occasions. The first count alleges

November 9, 1986, at Osborne Street in the City of Albany, and the second count alleges an attempt to engage in intercourse at their residence at Quinton Street on September 20, 1987.

I think there will be no dispute that at those two time periods the defendant, the victim, and the mother were all living together at those residences.

After that rather brief, somewhat clinical, hygienic explanation of those two counts, I think there's something that we have to lay out right now. This is a different world. The allegations here dealing with sexual abuse of children are another world and your expectations before you walked into this case should be put to one side.

(Author's Note: The prosecutor is developing the theme of "another world" to help explain behaviors and conduct that would not be readily apparent to the jury. This theme deals with the negatives of the case and also offers an explanation as to why the abuse occurred in the first place.)

We are going to attempt, through the witnesses in this case, to explain to you the dynamics of what happens. There's another world, just like in the forest at night. There's another world out there of critters and creatures.

What happens sometimes when you go out there at night and shine the light on those critters? They start to run away under the rocks. And that's what happened in this case. It's a world that doesn't like the spotlight, the scrutiny of someone else. We'll explain what happens in this case and why mother did and didn't do certain things.

There will also be no dispute that this child has been examined several times at the Albany Medical Center for various reasons — suspicion of child abuse and other reasons. But perhaps one of the most significant episodes was on November 10, 1986 when Dr. Robert Samuelson — at that time senior pediatric resident, he is now the chief pediatric resident of Albany Medical Center Hospital — was called in to examine this child. It was significant because the mother brought the child there not for suspicions of abuse but for abdominal pain.

He will testify that that was the chief complaint at that time. But there were some things that took place that in retrospect were very significant. One was a changing of history on the part of the mother. He will tell you that his suspicions were raised when the mother said, "I want the child examined for the possibility of abuse but I don't think anything took place."

Now, in reality what was happening was the day before this defendant had been seen by Barbara attempting to place his penis in the three-year-old's vagina. But the mother didn't tell the doctor this. That's the way it is. That's the proof of this crime — the fact that the mother didn't report it.

(Author's Note: The seemingly inexplicable conduct of the mother in not reporting the abuse of her child is explained as a positive fact, i.e., that such conduct is affirmative proof of a crime.)

Dr. Samuelson will tell you that he saw sperm in the child's urine and that's when they started to ask some questions. "What happened?" "Why?"

He decided to conduct some further tests. As part of those tests he utilized a rape kit. He explained to the mother why he had to do this. The mother indicated that an individual next door, a young boy, a teenager perhaps, abused the child.

Once again, I bring to your attention the changing of the history of what happened to her child on the mother's part.

When Dr. Samuelson utilized the rape kit, he did a test called the acid-phosphate test. He took some slides. He will explain that sperm decomposes. Rarely do you find it after 24 hours. It's very susceptible to destruction. In fact there's a greater decomposition rate of sperm as opposed to seminal fluid. You're more likely to find seminal fluid than sperm as time passes. Seminal fluid is what carries the sperm.

(Author's Note: The prosecutor is explaining some of the anticipated scientific and medical testimony with which the jury probably will be unfamiliar. This will help the jury to better understand this testimony when it is presented by the experts.)

He will tell you that this test, called the acid phosphate test, which is a chemical in the seminal fluid, is done simply by wiping the suspected area of contact for seminal fluid, and that he did that in this case and a small portion of the tab turned purple right away, which indicates the presence of seminal fluid.

In light of what happened the night before, when this defendant tried to place his penis in the vagina of this young girl, the fact that there was seminal fluid on the genital area of this child is not at all unusual and is consistent proof and additional proof of what happened on November 9, 1986 in Osborne Street.

The doctor will also testify that, after four years of pediatric residency, he is used to dealing with three-and four-year-old children, and that this child, more than most children, was uncooperative at the time of the genital examination when he attempted to examine that area which, from the behavioral point of view, was an indicator that this child felt uncomfortable.

(Author's Note: The prosecutor is reinforcing the information he has provided the jury on the credentials of the expert witness physician. Discussing the credentials of an expert in the opening statement is helpful in the later direct examination of that expert.)[50]

So what happened? The mother saw this and didn't report it. Is that possible? That's the way that world works.

---

[50] *See* § 11.44 on the direct examination of experts.

In fact, mother will come in and tell you that she knew this happened again. Specifically, on September 20, 1987, while she was living with this person he again tried to have sexual intercourse with their child.

At this point it's important to talk about the mother and who she is. Certain things never show up on printed records. You will have a chance to see witnesses, and I think one of the things you will observe is that this mother is not the most intelligent person in the world. I don't say this to be mean, but so that you can understand her a little bit better.

She is a special education graduate. Minimal education. I think it is important that you look at the context of her testimony and actions.

(Author's Note: The prosecutor has alerted the jury that the witness's mother suffers from limitations, and that this may affect her testimony and ability to express herself, as well as provide for a better understanding of her conduct and behavior in this case.)

The mother finally told Tim Crane, an Albany police officer, in September of 1987, about these two specific incidents, that: Yes, she saw it; yes, she covered it up; and that yes, she, too, had sexually abused the child.

(Author's Note: At this point, after explanations of the unusual and bizarre behavior of this mother and the unusual dynamics of sexual abuse, the prosecutor has alerted the jury, after preparing them as much as possible, for the highly explosive fact that this mother has also sexually abused the child. He then tries to provide an explanation for this seemingly inexplicable behavior by the chief witness in the case.)

Barbara will admit before you that she, too, had engaged in sexual contact with her own child. Normal? Of course not. But it's an abnormal world we're dealing with here. The usual reactions that you might expect are not going to be the ones you're going to see in this case. You're going to have to look at it differently in the context of the proof of this case.

In September of 1987, the child's mother, for the first time, admitted not only what she had seen this defendant do on two occasions, but what she herself had done to that child, for which she pled guilty and for which she stands convicted when she comes in here and testifies. Sexual abuse of her own child.

The mother's reactions, what she saw, what she didn't report, her covering up, are explained by a myriad of factors. She'll testify that among those factors was a strong dependency upon this defendant — financially and emotionally. She was wrapped up, tied up, in a web of his world. That dependency continued for a long time. As well as the financial and emotional dependency, there was another real, concrete dependency — a physical security issue — because for Barbara, her years of association with this defendant had been marked with repeated instances of violence and physical beatings. She will testify to those, but not just those — not just the direct physical beatings

285

which took place before September 1987 — but numerous attempts since the time she brought these allegations, to make her recant, to make her change her testimony, to attempt to influence her testimony, to attempt to make her sign statements which do not reflect the truth, through an associate of this defendant. I believe that's what the proof will show.

(Author's Note: In the above, the prosecutor has outlined the facts explaining why the mother recanted her allegations of abuse and why such a recantation should be expected as normal by the jury.)

To help tie this together we anticipate calling Miles Parker, an expert in the field of child sexual abuse, who will explain to you the behaviors that may be difficult to understand, such as the failing to report this immediately and the withdrawal of the report. The actions that took place in this case are credible, and form part of the proof of the abuse charges of this case.

He will testify as to the mother's background. He has been involved in the treatment and counseling of dozens of victims and offenders, having testified before the courts of this state and other states, and having testified before legislative committees in this state. I submit to you there is no one in this community more qualified to discuss the dynamics of sexual abuse of children than Miles Parker.

(Author's Note: Once again, the prosecutor provides the credentials of an expert witness, who, in this case, will be used to explain the seemingly inconsistent and inexplicable events.)

He will tie together for you the various events that took place in this case; how the mother's revealing the abuse in September of 1987 and the doctor's examination in November of 1986 fit in. November 9 — which was her sister's birthday by the way, another reason she can recall that date — as well as the fact she told the police that "it was the day before I took the child to the hospital." It makes sense now why she told the doctor, "I don't think my child has been abused, but please check it." It makes sense why that child reacted the way she did when Dr. Samuelson examined her.

We have the benefit of hindsight, and in hindsight we say, "Why didn't you do this? Why didn't this happen?" But it's a different world out there. Part of our job in this case is going to be to try to keep the light shining — shining on the people in this case so that you can see what is going on. If you do, I have every reason to believe that your verdict will be guilty in this case.

Thank you.

§ 4.28 Opening statement of defendant based on presumption of innocence and burden of proof.

Many times a defendant's attorney will be unsure of what approach to take in an opening statement. This may be because of uncertainties over what the prosecution will establish or what proof may be available to the defendant. Regardless of this uncertainty, an opening statement should still be made. Counsel should assert the defendant's innocence and provide a basic framework for the jury to acquit.

The following opening is very basic, but it does assert the defendant's denial of guilt and addresses the important issues of reasonable doubt and credibility of the witnesses. It also subtly asks the jury to focus on the sexual relationship between the defendant and the child's mother.

> May it please your Honor, Mrs. Forelady, ladies and gentlemen of this jury: At this time, every defendant's lawyer has the right, as did the Assistant District Attorney, to come before you and briefly tell you what he expects the proof to be. I represent Kevin Skillman in this case. And I have the privilege, as the prosecutor stated to you, I have the privilege to represent Mr. Skillman or any defendant in any case.

> The believable proof that will come from the mouths of these witnesses, which I expect to show you people, is that any sex in this case — the only sex in this case — was sex between my client and the girl's mother. On the believable proof, the believable testimony in this case, that's it. I think what you will have to believe is that the only sex was as I have just outlined it to you. I am not going to make any speeches now or go into any of the details. That will be brought before you by the witnesses on their direct and cross-examination. But I'm asking each of you again now, as you have promised me before, not to believe what the prosecutor said as gospel truth. And I would ask you to keep a clear and open mind until the last gun is fired before you start to make up your mind in this case. Did the People prove my client guilty beyond a reasonable doubt? And after all the proof is in, I again will have the opportunity to come before you and to discuss with you the proof that, by that time, we all will have had an opportunity to listen to. And I'm sure that, at that time, I can come before you and in good conscience, based on the proof in this case, argue that the People failed to prove beyond a reasonable doubt that Kevin Skillman sodomized or had sexual contact with any young woman. Thank you very much.

§ 4.29 Expanded opening statement of defendant.

The following is an example of an expanded opening statement of the defendant in a case of a defendant charged with sexually molesting a teenage girl.[51]

> May it please the Court, Miss Prosecutor, ladies and gentlemen: Sam Miles is 69 years of age. As we mark the most serious moment of his 69-year life, it is my privilege to represent him, my privilege because I represent an innocent man. Mr. Miles has entered a plea of not guilty to all of these

---

[51] Based on the opening statement of E. Stewart Jones, Esq., Troy, New York.

charges. Mr. Miles will take the stand and justify for you that plea of not guilty.

(Author's Note: Counsel asserts immediately the defendant's innocence. If a defendant is going to take the stand, this should be stated forcefully in the opening to maximize the benefit of his willingness to face cross-examination.)

As this case begins, there is but one presumed fact, that of Mr. Miles' innocence. This is a case where you have to maintain an open mind. You have to listen to the examination of the witness, which will develop the improbabilities of the testimony, the vagueness of the testimony, the indefiniteness of the testimony, and the lack of any specific time. For the first time today, the prosecutor tells you in her opening statement that an act of intercourse occurred in another county. The indictment that was prepared by her and is before this Court alleges an act of intercourse in Berkshire County. For the first time today, a year later, it's alleged that an act of intercourse took place some place else. That is the kind of confusion that you are going to hear from the prosecution's principal witness.

(Author's Note: The defendant's attorney has laid the foundation for arguing reasonable doubt and brings out the prosecutor's difficulties in establishing jurisdiction for the crime because of inconsistent statements of the victim.)

When Mr. Miles was arrested, he told the police officers that this was a frameup. He told the investigators on two separate occasions that he was innocent. He had no lawyer there. When he did that, he was unrepresented by counsel. He told those officers it was a frameup, and it was a frameup because the young woman's daughter owed him money and she was not going to pay him the money and he was therefore going to close down her restaurant, a place of business that he had invested in and that he had started.

(Author's Note: The defendant's attorney makes good use of the defendant's statement to the police. While the prosecution intends to offer some admissions in these statements, the defendant's attorney uses them to assert the core of a defense. This approach also deals with one of the key negatives in the case — the defendant's admission to the police. The defendant is also providing a motive for the allegation.)

Sam Miles is guilty of stupidity, of getting associated with this young woman's mother, but nothing else. Now, he will take the stand and he will tell you that what the police officers say about incriminating statements was not so. What he told them was that he was innocent. And they will admit that what he told them was that he committed no act of intercourse and they will admit that. What he told them is that he was framed and they will admit that. The afterthought of the police officers that the statement should be incriminating will be denied by Sam Miles. He will take the stand and he will tell you about his relationship with this young woman's mother, about the investment that he made and about the problem that developed in the fall of 1988, and how shortly after those problems developed and after he threatened to close this restaurant down, all of a sudden Samuel Miles was implicated in this scandal. This is an unfortunate case. I don't mean to diminish the unfortunate things that have happened to the young girl who is going to testify here. But the greater tragedy is that she has seen fit to incriminate Samuel Miles.

(Author's Note: The defendant's attorney seeks to provide some compassion for the victim, balancing it with compassion for the defendant.)

I beg you to listen to all of the proof in this case, all the way through the Court's charge on the law. Keep an open mind. This trial is going to be like a jigsaw puzzle. You can't tell where the pieces fit. But there will be too many pieces or too few pieces until you have heard it all. That includes argument of counsel at the conclusion of this case and the Judge's instructions on the law. Please, please, keep your minds open. There Sam sits, the loneliest place in the world.

(Author's Note: Here the prosecutor objected and was sustained by the court.)

That is why you sit here in partnership with the Court to enforce the rules of law that the Court will instruct you about. If you do that, Mr. Miles and I have no reason to fear your verdict, for your verdict will be not guilty.

Thank you very much.

CHAPTER 5

DIRECT AND CROSS-EXAMINATION OF COMPLAINING WITNESS

291

§ 5.1   Competency to testify.

Federal Rule of Evidence 601 states the general rule of competency followed by most jurisdictions: "Every person is competent to be a witness except as otherwise provided in these rules."[1] Generally, a witness's competency is presumed and the party objecting to a witness's competence has the burden of so establishing.[2] The seminal case on competency to testify is *Wheeler v. United States*,[3] an 1890s murder case involving testimony by a boy approximately 5 1/2 years old. The crime took place when the child was five. The decision set forth what has now become the standard litany for determining whether a witness is competent to testify, i.e., that the witness knew the difference between the truth and a lie, knew that if he told a lie he would be put in jail, and knew as a general proposition that it was wrong to lie and that he was to tell the truth.[4] There were also questions with concern to the boy's background and whether he had ever been to school, to which he responded in the negative. The key language of the Court's decision is as follows:

> That the boy was not by reason of his youth, as a matter of law, absolutely disqualified as a witness, is clear. While no one would think of calling as a witness an infant only two or three years old, there is no precise age which determines the question of competency. This depends on the capacity and intelligence of the child, his appreciation of the difference between truth and falsehood, as well as of his duty to tell the former. The decision of this question rests primarily with the trial judge, who sees the proposed witness, notices his manner, his apparent possession or lack of intelligence, and may resort to any examination which will tend to disclose his capacity and intelligence as well as his understanding of the obligation of an oath. As many of these matters cannot be photographed into the record, the decision of the trial judge will not be disturbed on review unless from that which is preserved it is clear that it was erroneous.[5]

The principles articulated in this Supreme Court decision nearly one hundred years ago form the basis for most legal determinations of witness competency, particularly child competency. In 1990, Congress elaborated on Federal Rule 601 by clarifying the procedures to be used in the federal courts for a determination of competency.[6] This legislation, part of the Child Victims' and Child Witnesses'

---

[1] Fed. R. Evid. 601.

[2] Commonwealth v. Harvey, 571 Pa. 533, 548, 812 A.2d 1190, 1199 (2002); Commonwealth v. D.J.A., 2002 Pa. Super. 176, 800 A.2d 965, 969 (2002), *appeal denied*, 579 Pa. 700, 857 A.2d 677 (2004) ("Competency of a witness is presumed, and the burden falls on the objecting party to demonstrate incompetency." *Id.* at P.7, 857 A.2d at 969).

[3] 159 U.S. 523 (1895).

[4] *Id.* at 524.

[5] *Id.* at 524–25.

[6] 18 U.S.C. § 3509(c).

Rights Act, states that "a child is presumed to be competent" and that "a competency examination of a child witness may be conducted by the Court only upon written motion to offer proof of incompetency by a party."[7] This statute has been cited as creating a presumption of child witness competency and that a competency hearing is only required for "compelling reasons."[8]

Apart from Child Victims' and Child Witnesses' Rights Act, many federal courts hold that a court has an obligation to determine that a witness has met a minimum standard of competency before calling a witness to testify.[9] A few federal courts have treated Rule 601 as limiting the inquiry into witness competence.[10] Some states have clearly indicated that children should be competent to testify. A Connecticut statute states that "no witness shall be automatically adjudged incompetent to testify because of age and any child who is a victim of assault, sexual assault or abuse shall be competent to testify without prior qualification."[11] The constitutionality of this statute has been upheld.[12] New York's rule is that a person may be a witness unless the Court finds "by reason of infancy or mental disease or defect, he does not possess sufficient intelligence or capacity to justify the reception of his evidence."[13] At nine years of age and above, a person is presumed to be able to testify under oath unless otherwise shown.[14] Other states, as does New York, require a trial judge to assess

---

[7] *Id.* § 3509(c)(2)(3).

[8] United States v. Boyles, 57 F.3d 535 (7th Cir. 1995) (noting in its determination to admit videotape deposition of child that 18 U.S.C. § 3509(c)(2) states that "a child is presumed competent" and "a trial judge need not pronounce any litany of magic words in making a finding of competency . . . and the court need only conduct a competency hearing if there are 'compelling reasons' on the record, other than the child's age alone to suggest that the child is incompetent to testify." *Id.* at 546, n.15).

[9] *See, e.g.,* United States v. Odom, 736 F.2d 104 (4th Cir. 1984) (noting that a trial judge may preclude a witness from testifying if the witness does not understand the duty to testify truthfully).

[10] *See, e.g.,* United States v. Ramirez, 871 F.2d 582, 584 (6th Cir. 1989), *cert. denied,* 493 U.S. 841 (1989) (noting that while competency inquiry may be precluded by Rule 601, competency may be reviewed under Rules 403 and 603); United States v. Roach, 590 F.2d 181 (5th Cir. 1979) ("under the . . . Federal Rules of Evidence it is doubtful that mental incompetence would even be grounds for disqualification of a prospective witness. . . . Nowhere is mental competence mentioned as a possible exception [to Rule 601]. . . . There seems no longer to be any occasion for judicially-ordered psychiatric examinations or competency hearings of witnesses. . . ." *Id.* at 185–86.).

[11] Conn. Gen. Stat. § 54-86h. *See also* Idaho Code § 9-202 (a child under 10 is not automatically rendered incompetent to testify); Ill. Comp. Stat. ch. 725, § 5/115-14 ("Every person, irrespective of age, is qualified to be a witness. . . ."); Minn. Stat. § 595.02 subd. 1(m) ("A child under ten years of age is a competent witness unless the court finds that the child lacks the capacity to remember or to relate truthfully facts respecting which the child is examined. A child describing any act or event may use language appropriate for a child of that age.").

[12] State v. James, 211 Conn. 555, 560 A.2d 426 (1989).

[13] N.Y. Crim. Proc. Law § 60.20(1).

[14] N.Y. Crim. Proc. Law § 60.20(2).

a child's competency, usually by following the *Wheeler* standard that the child has sufficient intelligence, is capable of making accurate observations by facts to which he or she may testify, and is capable of understanding the duty to tell the truth.[15] Some states require a judicial determination of child witness competency even under a statute comparable to Federal Rule 601.[16]

A major area in which the competency requirement has been relaxed is the area of hearsay declarations. Previously, a hearsay statement would not be admissible unless the declarant was competent at the time the declaration was made. Now, by virtue of court decisions and legislation, some jurisdictions admit a child's hearsay statements regardless of competency.

§ 5.2   Procedure for determining witness competency.

A witness's competency is usually determined by the trial judge out of the presence of the jury. While a determination of competency in the presence of the jury is not advisable, it has been deemed a permissible exercise of the court's discretion.[17]

A defendant may be excluded from a competency hearing of a child witness. The Supreme Court of the United States, in *Kentucky v. Stincer*,[18] held that the exclusion of a defendant from a competency hearing does not violate the defendant's right of confrontation or his due process rights. The Court requires that the opportunity to cross-examine the witness must be available during the trial and that any significant answers developed through the competency hearing can be repeated by counsel at trial. "Thus, the critical tool of cross-examination was available to counsel as a means of establishing that the witnesses were not

---

[15] Ariz. Rev. Stat. § 12-2202; Ga. Code § 24-9-5; Idaho Code § 9-202; Mich. Comp. Laws § 600.2163; Minn. Stat. § 595.02 subd. 1(f); Ohio Rev. Code § 2317.01.

[16] Newsome v. State, 686 N.E.2d 868 (Ind. Ct. App. 1997) ("In light of the majority position of the federal courts and the purposes behind Federal Evidence Rule 601 — and by implication Ind. Evidence Rule 601 — we think the better reading of Ind. Evidence Rule 601 is to require the trial court to continue to conduct an inquiry into witness competency to ensure that minimum standards of competency are met. Thus, we hold that Ind. Evidence Rule 601 does not affect previous Indiana decisions regarding the competence of children to testify. A trial court will still be required to [determine]. . .whether the child (1) understands the difference between telling a lie and telling the truth, (2) knows she is under a compulsion to tell the truth, and (3) knows what a true statement actually is." *Id.* at 872).

[17] State v. Tuffree, 35 Wash. App. 243, 246, 666 P.2d 912, 914, *review denied*, 100 Wash. 2d 1015 (1983) ("At times, appellate courts have observed that it is more prudent, more orderly, or a better practice to conduct a child's voir dire examination as to competency out of the presence of the jury if for no other reason than that such procedure obviates any risk that the jury may hear testimony which the court ultimately determines inadmissible." The court also noted that, at a competency hearing, the judge is not bound by the rules of evidence, and thus the jury may hear improper or inadmissible evidence since the court is not following the rules of evidence. *Id.* at 246–47, 666 P.2d at 914–15.).

[18] Kentucky v. Stincer, 482 U.S. 730 (1987).

competent to testify, as well as a means of undermining the credibility of their testimony."[19] Thus, a defendant has no right to be present at a competency hearing.[20] At trial, a child witness can be impeached with his answers from a competency hearing just as any witness can be impeached with prior testimony or statements. The Court also noted that the defendant was unable to show that his presence at the competency hearing would have insured a "more reliable determination as to whether the witnesses were competent to testify."[21]

The Child Victims' and Witnesses' Rights Act further defines the competency hearing by noting that the hearing may be conducted only if the court determines, on the record, that "compelling reasons" exist for the competency hearing and states that a child's age alone is not a compelling reason.[22] Under federal law, the only persons who can attend the competency hearing are the Judge, the attorney for the government, the attorney for the defendant, court reporter, and support persons whom the court deems necessary for the well-being of the child.[23] The competency examination, according to federal statute, "shall be conducted out of the sight and hearing of a jury."[24] This is the usual procedure and the better practice. If a defendant does not object, it is not necessarily error to conduct the hearing before the jury.[25] As to the direct examination of the child, the statute delineates the parameters of direct examination of the child witness during the competency colloquy:

> Examination of a child related to competency shall normally be conducted by the court on the basis of questions submitted by the attorney for the government and the attorney for the defendant including a party acting as an attorney *pro se*. Court may permit an attorney but not a party acting as an attorney *pro se* to examine a child directly on competency if a court is satisfied that the child will not suffer emotional trauma as a result of the examination.

---

[19] *Id.* at 744.

[20] People v. Morales, 80 N.Y.2d 450, 606 N.E.2d 953, 591 N.Y.S.2d 825 (1992); People v. Lora, 298 A.D.2d 328, 749 N.Y.S.2d 236, *appeal denied*, 99 N.Y.2d 537, 782 N.E.2d 576, 752 N.Y.S.2d 598 (2002) ("Defendant had no right to be present at the preliminary examination of the child victim to determine whether he understood the nature of an oath.").

[21] Stincer, *supra* note 18, 482 U.S. at 747:

> He has presented no evidence that his relationship with the children, or his knowledge of facts regarding their background, could have assisted either his counsel or the judge in asking questions that would have resulted in a more assured determination of competency. On the record of this case, therefore, we cannot say that respondent's rights under the Due Process Clause of the Fourteenth Amendment were violated by the exclusion from the competency hearing.

[22] 18 U.S.C. § 3509(c)(4).

[23] *Id.* at § 3509(c)(5).

[24] *Id.* at § 3509(c)(6).

[25] State v. Hensley, 120 N.C. App. 313, 462 S.E.2d 550 (1995), *rev'd on other grounds* (holding that conducting competency examination before a jury not error when defendant interposed no objection).

The questions asked at the competency examination of a child shall be appropriate to the age and developmental level of the child, shall not be related to the issues at trial, and shall focus on determining the child's ability to understand and answer simple questions. [26]

Much in this legislation sets forth a typical format for a competency hearing. It is generally felt that, while the trial court has broad discretion as to the type of questions that may be asked at a competency examination, it need not follow the rules of evidence. Some have argued that the trial court should not use questions pertaining to the subject matter of the offense or anticipated testimony because of the suggestibility of young children. [27] However, it is not unusual to find trial courts that do conduct competency examinations with questions involving the substantive charges. On the other hand, many trial courts are willing to accept proposed questions or areas of examination from counsel in formulating the content of competency questions. It is advisable to use questions appropriate to the age and developmental level of the child. Certainly, asking children questions such as "What is the difference between truth and falsehood?" — a question that adults would have difficulty answering — will not provide much insight into the potential witness's competency. Demonstrating that the child understands a true statement as opposed to a false one is more constructive. A simple child competency hearing is set forth in Appendix K.

While a trial court will make an initial determination of competency based on its preliminary examination, the judge may change his mind concerning a witness's competency, remove the child from the stand, and instruct the jury to disregard his or her testimony. [28] Competency determinations are within a trial court's discretion. [29] An appellate court will review not only the competency hearing responses of the witness to determine competency, but will search the entire record to determine whether the witness was competent to testify. [30]

A trial court does not have unlimited discretion in establishing the procedure to determine a child's competency. For example, allowing a five-year-old

---

[26] 18 U.S.C. § 3509(c)(7)(8).

[27] Moll v. State, 351 N.W.2d 639, 643 (Minn. Ct. App. 1984).

[28] See, e.g., Litzkuhn v. Clark, 85 Ariz. 355, 360, 339 P.2d 389, 392 (1959); Davis v. Weber, 93 Ariz. 312, 317, 380 P.2d 608, 611 (1963).

[29] See, e.g., In re R.R., 79 N.J. 97, 113, 398 A.2d 76, 84 (1979); People v. Parks, 41 N.Y.2d 36, 46, 359 N.E.2d 358, 390 N.Y.S.2d 848 (1976) (trial court's determination as to the testimonial capacity of a witness will not be disturbed "unless it is plain from the record that the determination was an abusive discretion"); State v. Frazier, 61 Ohio St. 3d 247, 251, 574 N.E.2d 483, 486–87 (1991), cert. denied, 503 U.S. 941 (1992).

[30] People v. Joval, 212 A.D.2d 547, 622 N.Y.S.2d 528, appeal denied, 85 N.Y.2d 975, 653 N.E.2d 631, 629 N.Y.S.2d 735 (1995); Commonwealth v. Hunzer, 2005 Pa. Super. 13, 868 A.2d 498 (2005), appeal denied, 880 A.2d 1237 (2005); Commonwealth v. Trimble, 419 Pa. Super. 108, 615 A.2d 48 (1992) ("Our review is not limited to the trial court's questioning of the child prior to the child's testimony. It is appropriate for an appellate court to look not only to the trial court's questioning of the child prior to the child testifying, but also to the child's actual testimony." Id. at 114, 615 A.2d at 51).

complainant to testify without first conducting a preliminary examination to determine whether she understood the nature of an oath or had sufficient intelligence capacity to justify the reception of her testimony may be reversible error.[31] Similarly, allowing a child to state that she knows the difference between a truth and lie, without other testimony or examples, is an abuse of a trial court's discretion to determine competency.[32]

§ 5.3 Psychiatric or psychological examinations to determine competency.

In certain situations a judge may permit a psychiatric or psychological examination of a witness to assist in the competency determination. Such an examination is rarely deemed necessary; however, there may be situations where a court will order such an examination. The law pertaining to such examinations is discussed in §§ 1.17–1.20.

§ 5.4 Competency requirements and determination.

Traditionally, there are generally four criteria to meet in establishing a witness's competency.[33] First, the witness should have a capacity to communicate and give expression to events as demonstrated by his or her understanding of the questions and ability to provide meaningful answers. Second, the witness should possess an ability to observe the event. Third, there should be a capacity to remember the event. Finally, the witness should be able to understand an oath, or the need to tell the truth. The focus is on the ability to understand the duty to tell the truth, not the likelihood that the witness will tell the truth.

Capacity to remember an event becomes an issue when a child testifies to an event that occurred years earlier. Can a nine-or ten-year-old really remember an event that occurred at age three? Is it truly remembering or is it the product of teaching or suggestion? Some courts have held children competent to testify to events occurring many years earlier.[34] But a court may also find a child

---

[31] People v. Rose, 223 A.D.2d 607, 637 N.Y.S.2d 172 (1996), *appeal dismissed sub nom.* Rose v. Golia, 89 N.Y.2d 1085, 659 N.Y.S.2d 858 (1997).

[32] Newsome v. State, 686 N.E.2d 868 (Ind. Ct. App. 1997).

[33] Commonwealth v. Washington, 554 Pa. 559, 563, 722 A.2d 643, 646 (1998); Seabra v. Trafford-Seabra, 655 A.2d 250, 252 (R.I. 1995). *See, e.g.*, Commonwealth v. Brusgulis, 398 Mass. 325, 329, 496 N.E.2d 652 (1986); Rosche v. McCoy, 397 Pa. 615, 620, 156 A.2d 307, 310 (1959).

[34] Commonwealth v. Hunzer, 2005 Pa. Super. 13, 868 A.2d 498, *appeal denied*, 880 A.2d 1237 (2005) (holding approximately six-year-old child was competent to testify to alleged abuse when she was three years old since she recalled "events surrounding the alleged incident with extreme detail, including the layout of her bedroom and the style of pajamas she was wearing on the day in question." *Id.* at P16, 868 A.2d at 508; Commonwealth v. McMaster, 446 Pa. Super. 261, 666 A.2d 724 (1995) (trial court found eight-year-old complainant had sufficient mental capacity to observe and recall events over three years earlier); De Lio v. Hamilton, 227 Pa. Super. 581, 308 A.2d 607 (1973) (holding ten-year-old may testify to events when the child was four).

incompetent who testifies many years later about an event occurring during pre-school years,[35] and require that the child have "mental capacity at the time of the occurrence concerning which he is to testify to receive an accurate impression of it."[36]

The "inability to place events in a temporal framework does not render a child incompetent," since it is well recognized that young children have difficulty with the concept of time and still may be truthful.[37] A child's difficulty in recalling his last birthday is not critical to competency.[38] A six-year-old's inability to remember the location of his school does not necessarily render a child witness incompetent.[39] An eight-year-old child, five at the time of the sexual abuse, is not necessarily incompetent to testify because of an inability to stay focused on any one topic for an extended period of time, especially when the subject matter deals with unpleasant topics.[40] Similarly, inconsistency and hesitancy in a child's answers is a matter of credibility, not of competency, and should be left for consideration by the trier of fact.[41]

The child should possess a basic comprehension of the oath, which can be defined as a consciousness of the duty to speak the truth or possessing a

---

[35] State v. Rippy, 626 A.2d 334 (Me. 1993) (defendant's conviction reversed because child, 11 at time of trial, could remember nothing about her life at the time of the sexual abuse and thus should have been found incompetent to testify).

[36] Simmers v. State, 943 P.2d 1189, 1199 (Wyo. 1997).

[37] Commonwealth v. Gamache, 35 Mass. App. Ct. 805, 808–09, 626 N.E.2d 616, 620 (1994) citing State v. Struss, 404 N.W.2d 811, 815 (Minn. Ct. App. 1987) (child was five years old at the time of trial and 22–33 months old when the alleged crimes occurred); State v. Eiler, 234 Mont. 38, 43, 762 P.2d 210 (1988); State v. D.B.S., 216 Mont. 234, 240, 700 P.2d 630 (1985); State v. Lairby, 699 P.2d 1187, 1196 (Utah 1984).

[38] State v. Olah, 146 Ohio App. 3d 586, 767 N.E.2d 755 (2001), appeal denied, 94 Ohio St. 3d 1485, 763 N.E.2d 1184 (2002) (holding fact that child could not correctly respond to questions about his last birthday did not establish incompetency to testify).

[39] State v. Johnston, 979 S.W.2d 461, 464 (Mo. Ct. App. 1998).

[40] Commonwealth v. D.J.A., 2002 Pa. Super. 176, 800 A.2d 965 (2002), appeal denied, 579 Pa. 700, 857 A.2d 677 (2004) (finding eight-year-old witness, five years old at the time of the abuse, competent to testify at trial).

[41] Walters v. McCormick, 122 F.3d 1172 (9th Cir. 1997) (holding that Montana trial court's determination of four-year-old's competency supported by record despite numerous inconsistencies and difficulties in her testimony); State v. Allen, 647 So. 2d 428, 433–34 (La. Ct. App. 1994), cert. denied, 654 So. 2d 1352 (La. 1995) (trial court properly found an eight-year-old witness competent even though she was unresponsive when asked if she knew what it meant to tell the truth, responded "no" when asked if she knew what it meant to tell a lie, and stated that she did not understand the consequences of telling a lie. However, the child appeared to be somewhat intimidated by the courtroom. She was also able to demonstrate that she knew when something was true or not true by specific examples, and knew that children would get punished for not telling the truth. The court noted that "hesitant or unresponsive answers do not necessarily indicate incompetency. Instead they may be part of an overall demeanor in the unfamiliar, which favorably reflects testimony only as to what is clear to the child."); Eakes v. State, 665 So. 2d 852, 869 (Miss. 1995) (holding that seven-year-old was competent to testify despite inconsistencies between earlier accusations and subsequent retractions of allegations).

compulsion to tell the truth.[42] While traditionally some courts looked for a child to go to church or have a religious background as part of understanding the oath, today, such a requirement may be considered an abuse of discretion.[43] It is not necessary that a child understand why one raises a hand and places the other on the Bible, or to understand who wrote the Bible.[44] Nor is it necessary that the child understand or define oath.[45] This comprehension can be expressed in terms of an understanding that a six-year-old would "go to the devil"[46] if he lied, or a child would "go to jail" if he or she lied,[47] or it is wrong for the witness to lie.[48] A sufficient understanding of an oath can be expressed by a child who knows the difference between the truth and a story and who knows that she would get a spanking if she told a story.[49] It is sufficient if the child states she will tell the truth and that telling lies is bad.[50] When there is no expressed

---

[42] Butler v. State, 178 Ga. App. 110, 342 S.E.2d 338 (1986); Baxter v. State, 522 N.E.2d 362, 369 (Ind. 1988) (child must understand the compulsion to tell the truth); Commonwealth v. Gamache, 35 Mass. App. Ct. 805, 806, 626 N.E.2d 616, 618 (1994) (requiring child to possess "belief that failure to perform the obligation [to tell the truth] will result in punishment"); People v. Robrigado, 254 A.D.2d 438, 680 N.Y.S.2d 109, appeal denied, 92 N.Y.2d 1037, 707 N.E.2d 457, 684 N.Y.S.2d 502 (1998) (upholding court's determination that seven-year-old complainant could be sworn given the child's understanding of an oath including that giving false testimony could result in punishment by God); Commonwealth v. Trimble, 419 Pa. Super. 108, 615 A.2d 48 (1992); Commonwealth v. Penn, 497 Pa. 232, 439 A.2d 1154 (1982); Rogers v. Commonwealth, 132 Va. 771, 773, 111 S.E. 231–32 (1922).

[43] See, e.g., People v. Cordero, 257 A.D.2d 372, 684 N.Y.S.2d 192, appeal denied, 93 N.Y.2d 968, 716 N.E.2d 1099, 695 N.Y.S.2d 54 (1999).

[44] State v. Weaver, 117 N.C. App. 434, 451 S.E.2d 15 (1994).

[45] People v. Guerrero, 250 A.D.2d 703, 672 N.Y.S.2d 763, appeal denied, 92 N.Y.2d 879, 700 N.E.2d 564, 678 N.Y.S.2d 26 (1998) (upholding court's determination to allow seven-year-old complainant to testify under oath since "the child indicated that he knew the difference between the truth and a lie and knew that he would be punished if he did not tell the truth"); People v. Cintron, 214 A.D.2d 349, 625 N.Y.S.2d 148, appeal denied, 86 N.Y.2d 733, 655 N.E.2d 711, 631 N.Y.S.2d 614 (1995) (holding that seven-year-old was competent to testify even though the child was unable to define terms such as "oath").

[46] Commonwealth v. Riley, 458 Pa. 390, 326 A.2d 384 (1974).

[47] Commonwealth v. Mangello, 250 Pa. Super. 202, 378 A.2d 897 (1977).

[48] People v. Guerrero, 250 A.D.2d 703, 672 N.Y.S.2d 763, appeal denied, 92 N.Y.2d 879, 700 N.E.2d 564, 678 N.Y.S.2d 26 (1998) (upholding court's determination to allow seven-year-old complainant to testify under oath since "the child indicated that he knew the difference between the truth and a lie and knew that he would be punished if he did not tell the truth"); Rhea v. State, 705 S.W.2d 165, 169 (Tex. Ct. App. 1985) (summarizing Texas' standards, including a child's indicating that he or she would go to jail or the devil will get the child).

[49] Dufrene v. State, 853 S.W.2d 86, 88 (Tex. Ct. App. 1993) (noting that a child no longer needs to understand the obligation of the oath, but only the duty of being truthful).

[50] Commonwealth v. Lamontagne, 42 Mass. App. Ct. 213, 675 N.E.2d 1169, review denied, 424 Mass. 1106, 678 N.E.2d 1333 (1997) (four-year-old deemed competent to testify when she disputed she did not go to school because she attended "day care" and testified she was going to tell the truth and that telling lies is bad).

understanding of the need to tell the truth, the witness should not be found competent.[51] A child's developmental disability may affect the child's competency.[52]

If a witness knows the meaning of an oath and has the ability to observe, recollect, and relive facts, a witness may be "competent even if she hears voices telling her to do 'wrong things,' sees things that are not real, and hears demons who have 'thick eyebrows' and 'ears pointed with real sharp teeth.' "[53]

Competency determinations of preschool-age children are much more likely to be challenged and evaluated carefully by an appellate court. It is rare to see decisions upholding the competency of a child less than four years of age, and it would seem doubtful that a child of two or three would have sufficient intelligence to justify receiving his or her testimony; however, using the foregoing standards, courts have found a three-year-old competent to testify[54] and have upheld the testimony of four-year-olds.[55] It is not uncommon for children five years old and above to be found competent.[56] Competency determinations are

---

[51] Jones v. State, 68 Md. App. 162, 510 A.2d 1091 (1986) (five-year-old did not demonstrate the obligation to tell the truth and had a "total inability to understand basic questions"); Rhea v. State, 705 S.W.2d 165, 170 (Tex. Ct. App. 1985).

[52] People v. Pullman, 234 A.D.2d 955, 652 N.Y.S.2d 433 (1996), *appeal denied*, 89 N.Y.2d 1099, 682 N.E.2d 994, 660 N.Y.S.2d 393 (1997) ("It was an abuse of discretion, however, for the court to permit the victim to be sworn because she did not demonstrate the necessary comprehension and appreciation of the nature of an oath. Nevertheless, reversal is not warranted because there is sufficient evidence, including defendant's confession, to corroborate the victim's testimony [citation omitted]." *Id.*, 652 N.Y.S.2d at 434).

[53] Bart v. Commonwealth, 951 S.W.2d 576 (Ky. 1997).

[54] United States v. Frazier, 678 F. Supp. 499 (E.D. Pa. 1986), *aff'd*, 806 F.2d 255 (3d Cir. 1986) (three-year-old); Commonwealth v. McEachin, 371 Pa. Super. 188, 537 A.2d 883 (1988) (three-and-one-half-year-olds).

[55] State v. Brotherton, 384 N.W.2d 375 (Iowa 1986); Barnett v. State, 757 So. 2d 323 (Miss. Ct. App. 2000) (holding four-year-old competent to testify); People v. Scott, 86 N.Y.2d 864, 658 N.E.2d 1040, 635 N.Y.S.2d 167 (1995) (holding that trial court did not abuse discretion in permitting four-year-old witness to give unsworn testimony after determining the child understood the difference between a truth and a lie); People v. Groff, 71 N.Y.2d 101, 518 N.E.2d 908, 524 N.Y.S.2d 13 (1987) (involving competency determination by prosecutor before a grand jury of a four-year-old sexual assault victim); People v. Lowe, 289 A.D.2d 705, 733 N.Y.S.2d 555 (2001) (finding four-year-old, three years old at the time of sexual assault, competent to testify); People v. Johnston, 273 A.D.2d 514, 709 N.Y.S.2d 230 (2000) (finding two children less than six years old at time of trial, and four and five years old at the time of the incident were able to recall or relate prior events and properly permitted to testify as sworn witnesses); People v. Jacobs, 148 A.D.2d 811, 538 N.Y.S.2d 647, *rev'd on reh'g on other grounds*, 149 A.D.2d 112, 544 N.Y.S.2d 1011, *appeal denied*, 74 N.Y.2d 949, 549 N.E.2d 486, 550 N.Y.S.2d 284 (1989) (case involved testimony of a four-year-old concerning sexual abuse that occurred when the child was three). (Note: New York law has provision for unsworn testimony; *see* § 5.5); Commonwealth v. Pankraz, 382 Pa. Super. 116, 554 A.2d 974, *appeal denied*, 522 Pa. 618, 563 A.2d 887 (1989); Commonwealth v. Stohr, 361 Pa. Super. 293, 522 A.2d 589 (1987) (four-and-one-half-year-old); Dufrene v. State, 853 S.W.2d 86 (Tex. Crim. App. 1993).

[56] State v. Ellis, 669 A.2d 752 (Me. 1996) (upholding competency of five-and seven-year-old

a matter of a trial court's discretion and are not overturned absent abuse of discretion or misapplication of some legal principle.

§ 5.5   New York rule on competency.

New York has a unique rule that permits the unsworn testimony of a witness. A witness's testimony will be unsworn if the witness has competency to testify but does not understand the nature of an oath.[57] New York criminal law presumes a child nine years old or above may testify under oath, while those less than nine years of age require a hearing to determine the witness's ability to understand the oath.[58] Thus, a child may have sufficient intelligence to justify a court's receipt of his or her testimony but be unable to understand the significance of swearing to tell the truth and, therefore, be unable to take the oath. The jury is instructed that the testimony is unsworn and subject to less weight.

In these situations, New York requires that there be corroboration of the unsworn witness's testimony. This corroborating evidence must satisfy two requirements: it must tend to (1) establish the crime and (2) connect the defendant with the commission of the crime. In establishing this corroboration requirement, it is not necessary that there be evidence of the actual crime itself. For example, if the allegation is one of intercourse, there need not be scientific or medical evidence of intercourse, and a defendant's statement that there was touching of the complainant's genitals would be deemed corroboration, as would evidence of genital irritation. The corroborating evidence can also consist of circumstantial evidence. The corroborating testimony may be that of a mother observing a defendant zipping his pants as he left the child's bedroom, and a forensic chemist's testimony that examination of the defendant's clothing revealed "fecal

---

witnesses); People v. Dorsey, 265 A.D.2d 567, 697 N.Y.S.2d 305, *appeal denied*, 94 N.Y.2d 862, 725 N.E.2d 1099, 704 N.Y.S.2d 537 (1999) (court found seven-year-old able to give sworn testimony: "The voir dire examination of the victim revealed that she understood the difference between telling a lie and telling the truth, and the meaning of a promise to tell the truth, that she would be punished if she did not keep a promise to God, and that she would have to tell the truth in court." *Id.* at 568, 697 N.Y.S.2d at 306); People v. Shavers, 205 A.D.2d 395, 613 N.Y.S.2d 393, *appeal denied*, 84 N.Y.2d 939, 645 N.E.2d 1236, 621 N.Y.S.2d 536 (1994) (Trial court properly allowed a seven-year-old to testify under oath when she testified that she knew the difference between the truth and a lie and that the word "swear" means "that you will always tell the truth." Child's testimony that "she would lie to protect her mother from being hurt does not, standing alone, require a contrary finding."); Ryan v. State, 988 P.2d 46 (Wyo. 1999) (court held that child who was five years old at time of occurrence was competent to testify given not only her understanding that oath was a promise to God, but also her ability to recall details about the night her mother was killed).

[57] N.Y. Crim. Proc. Law § 60.20; People v. Groff, 71 N.Y.2d 101, 109, 518 N.E.2d 908, 524 N.Y.S.2d 13 (1987); People v. Tomczak, 189 A.D.2d 926, 592 N.Y.S.2d 486, *appeal denied*, 81 N.Y.2d 977, 615 N.E.2d 236, 598 N.Y.S.2d 779 (1993); People v. McGuire, 152 A.D.2d 945, 543 N.Y.S.2d 822, *appeal denied*, 74 N.Y.2d 849, 546 N.E.2d 197, 546 N.Y.S.2d 1014 (1989).

[58] N.Y. Crim. Proc. Law § 60.20.

matter on the bottom portion of defendant's shirt and the fly area of defendant's pants."[59]

New York law does not permit corroboration of unsworn witness's testimony by another unsworn witness. The rule is that when corroboration is required of two witnesses's testimony by the same statute, the witnesses may not corroborate each other.[60] Thus, an unsworn child witness may not corroborate the unsworn testimony of another child witness.[61] However, if the other testimony being offered as corroboration requires corroboration under a different New York statute (such as accomplice testimony[62] or a defendant's confession),[63] the testimony requiring corroboration under a different statute is permissible corroboration of the unsworn child witness.[64]

§ 5.6 Limits on competency of child witnesses.

Except as noted above, if a child has no understanding of an oath, he or she will be unable to testify. One method of challenging a child witness is to challenge his or her ability to effectively respond to questions. If a child cannot respond effectively, the defendant is denied the right of confrontation. Another approach, which has redefined the competency criteria, is to raise the issue of suggestiveness and challenge the reliability of the child's testimony.

Nevada's Supreme Court has taken a strict approach to the competency of child witnesses and expanded the traditional criteria for competency. In a decision reversing the competency determination of a trial court, the Nevada Supreme Court listed the following factors for a court to consider in evaluating a child's competency:

(1) The child's ability to receive and communicate information;

(2) The spontaneity of the child's statements;

(3) Indications of "coaching" and "rehearsing";

(4) The child's ability to remember;

(5) The child's ability to distinguish between truth and falsehood; and

(6) The likelihood that the child will give inherently improbable or incoherent testimony.[65]

---

[59] People v. Lykes, 178 A.D.2d 927, 578 N.Y.S.2d 794 (1991), aff'd, 81 N.Y.2d 767, 609 N.E.2d 132, 593 N.Y.S.2d 779 (1993).

[60] People v. Coleman, 42 N.Y.2d 500, 369 N.E.2d 742, 399 N.Y.S.2d 185 (1977).

[61] People v. St. John, 74 A.D.2d 85, 426 N.Y.S.2d 863 (1980) (dismissing child victim's testimony that was corroborated only by an unsworn child witness and sustaining those counts corroborated by admission of the defendant).

[62] N.Y. Crim. Proc. Law § 60.22.

[63] Id. at § 60.50.

[64] Coleman, 42 N.Y.2d at 500.

[65] Felix v. State, 109 Nev. 151, 173, 849 P.2d 220, 235 (1993).

These criteria add the elements of "coaching," "rehearsing," "spontaneity," and "probability" to the traditional requirements. It is a significant departure from the liberal approach of most courts. In the Nevada case, a child was three and one-half years of age at the time she attended a day-care center at which the acts allegedly occurred and approximately eight years old when she testified at trial. Some of her allegations involved the killing of people and animals at the day-care center and being forced to eat dog feces and drink dog urine, which the court considered incredible. The court held that there was a serious question about the child's ability to "recollect and relate truthfully what. . . she observed," that the testimony was "inherently improbable," and that the witness "could not differentiate between fact and fantasy," and for these reasons she should not have been found competent to testify.[66] The court also noted that interviewing techniques and coaching on the part of individuals involved in the investigation of the day-care center were also grounds on which to challenge the competency of the witness.[67] This decision represents a challenge to the fairly liberal, traditional approach toward child competency.

A child's competency can also be challenged by the inability to respond to cross-examination. A child witness may become confused or distracted during questioning and refuse to answer questions. Depending on the extent of this problem and at what point it occurs during cross-examination, the child's inability to respond on cross-examination may constitute a violation of the confrontation clause. Additionally, the testimony might be excluded because it is so unreliable that its potential for prejudice substantially outweighs its probative value.[68]

A child may be precluded from testifying on direct because the trial judge is concerned that he or she will not be willing to respond to cross-examination, thus rendering the child incompetent.[69] "When a victim will testify only about the fact of abuse by a defendant, and will not effectively respond to cross-examination attempting to elicit more detail of the incident or evidence relevant to impeachment, a constitutional question of defendant's right to confront the witness against him may be raised."[70] Even if a child is capable of narrating information, the child's difficulty in observing and recollecting facts may render

---

[66] Id., 849 P.2d at 236.

[67] Id.

[68] Government of Virgin Islands v. Riley, 750 F. Supp. 727 (D.V.I. 1990), aff'd, 973 F.2d 224 (3d Cir. 1992) (holding that child's deposition satisfied confrontation clause, even though child had difficulty responding on cross-examination, but court precluded the child's trial testimony); State v. Eldredge, 773 P.2d 29 (Utah 1989) (noting that lapses in a child's memory are within the scope of Rule 403 and involve a weighing of prejudice versus probative value of the testimony).

[69] Riley, 750 F. Supp. at 729.

[70] State v. Stacy, 179 W. Va. 686, 690–91, 371 S.E.2d 614, 618–19 (1988).

the child incompetent, especially when the prosecution's case is completely dependent on the child's ability to observe and recollect facts.[71]

Failing to object to the child's testimony on the grounds that its prejudicial outweighs its probative value.[72]

§ 5.7   Competency determinations for individuals with developmental disabilities.

The issue of competency also exists when victims suffer from developmental disabilities. The fact that an individual suffers from a developmental disability or is mildly mentally disabled does not disqualify the person as a witness, even when he or she has difficulty communicating or testifying. Several courts have upheld the testimony of complainants of sexual abuse who suffer from developmental disabilities.[73] In the course of determining competency of an individual suffering from developmental disability, the court may, if it chooses, accept testimony from an individual, such as a teacher, who knows the witness and can provide information on the witness's academic or intellectual abilities, and such testimony may be presented to the jury.[74] But, a child's developmental abilities

---

[71] Fuller v. State, 669 So. 2d 273, *review denied*, 675 So. 2d 929 (Fla. 1996) (reversing defendant's conviction because competency examination of the child demonstrated insufficient ability to observe and recollect facts when prosecution's case was "completely dependent" on the child's testimony; even though child knew the importance of telling the truth, the child stated that he has trouble paying attention and that when this happens he begins to "guess" and that this might happen during his trial testimony).

[72] *Eldredge*, 773 P.2d at 33. *See also* Royal v. Commonwealth, 2 Va. App. 59, 62, 341 S.E.2d 660, 662 (1986), *rev'd on other grounds*, 234 Va. 403, 362 S.E.2d 323 (1987).

[73] Logan v. Lockhart, 994 F.2d 1324, 1327 (8th Cir. 1993) *cert. denied*, 510 U.S. 1057 (1994) (concerning testimony of a 17-year-old mildly retarded victim, the court noted that he was able "to provide accurate testimony about himself, his family, his employment history, and his former school. [The complainant] was also able to describe the sexual attacks by Logan in considerable detail."); People v. Lawler, 181 Ill. App. 3d 464, 536 N.E.2d 1283 (1989); People v. Berardicurti, 167 A.D.2d 840, 561 N.Y.S.2d 949 (1990) (upholding sworn testimony from a 13-year-old complainant with a stated mental age of 8 1/2 years); State v. Sweet, 1993 Ohio App. LEXIS 492 (Jan. 26, 1993) (upholding competency determination of a 28-year-old witness who had the I.Q. of a six-year-old child); State v. Lynch, 854 A.2d 1022 (R.I. 2004) (finding developmentally disabled girl competent to testify given her ability to point to body parts when asked, identifying defendant, describing her living arrangement, and testifying to details of sexual assault); State v. Zukowski, 2003 Tenn. Crim. App. LEXIS 62 (Jan. 31, 2003) (finding competent a mildly mentally retarded 14-year-old appellant who knew the difference between truth and lie, promised to tell the truth and acknowledged that when people lie in school, to parents, or in court, they get "in trouble").

[74] People v. Parks, 41 N.Y.2d 36, 359 N.E.2d 358, 390 N.Y.S.2d 848 (1976):

Moreover we believe that where a particular witness's testimony may be crucial to the case and it is established that the witness's testimonial ability is impaired, independent evidence respecting the nature of the impairment may be presented to the jury prior to the actual testimony of the impaired witness. The advantage to admitting to the preliminary testimony of physicians, teachers, or others with

may factor in determining that a child is incompetent.[75]

A physical condition affecting mental ability may be such as to render a witness incompetent.[76] The court also should not rely on an interpreter's interpretation of a witness's answers.[77]

§ 5.8   Preparation and approach to direct examination.

As with jury selection and the opening statement, the direct testimony of a complaining witness should support the theme. It should help tell a logical and compelling story and present some understanding of the goals of the case. If the theme of the case is "betrayal of a trust," then it is important to establish on direct examination the trust that existed between the victim and the offender, how that trust was developed, and why it was so important to the complainant. If the theme is a day in the life of the victim that she will never forget, develop from the victim's memory details surrounding the event in question, which will supposedly underscore the witness's ability to identify the defendant.

An attorney should spend adequate time with a witness to develop an understanding of the system and the court process. Adequate time will depend on the individual. Individuals differ in their background, their general understanding, and their ability to grasp the dynamics of the legal system.

An effective direct examination requires that the complainant have self-confidence. This can be developed to some extent through the complainant's general understanding of the process but, more importantly, it should be gained through discussion of what is expected of her, how she will be treated by the court and opposing counsel, and appropriate dress and demeanor. Also, in answering questions, it is important that the witness avoid hedging and be positive and confident of answers to all important areas of inquiry.

> knowledge of the alleged incompetent's state is that both the court and the jury may
> be alerted to the nature of the witness's condition and may be provided with a
> framework in which the testimony and behavior of the witness may be considered.

Id. at 48, 359 N.E.2d at 368.

[75] People v. Pullman, 234 A.D.2d 955, 652 N.Y.S.2d 433 (1996), *appeal denied*, 89 N.Y.2d 1099, 682 N.E.2d 944, 660 N.Y.S.2d 393 (1997).

[76] State v. Dunning, 2000 Ohio App. LEXIS 5774 (Dec. 11, 2000), *dismissed*, 91 Ohio St. 3d 1508, 746 N.E.2d 611 (2001) court held 60-year-old complainant's Huntington's Chorea disease was such that court abused discretion in allowing her to testify, although error was harmless:

> This conclusion is based upon the fact that Loretta's testimony at the competency
> hearing cannot be said to demonstrate any coherence or ability to truly relate impres-
> sions. Loretta's lack of competence to testify was confirmed at trial by Dr. Avecilla,
> who testified that Loretta was suffering from the mental degeneration associated with
> Huntington's such that he could treat her only with the aid of a family member. It
> was also confirmed by Loretta's trial testimony, which again demonstrated the extent
> to which Huntington's was affecting her.

Id. at *10–11.

[77] *Id.* at *19.

Some jurisdictions maintain a formal support system for complainants and victims, usually known as victim advocacy programs. However, other individuals — relatives, close friends, a spouse, a teacher — can be vital in providing necessary support for complainants. These individuals should be integrated as part of the pretrial preparation. The victim should be given a choice as to whom she wishes to be present in the courtroom during her direct examination. Victims vary widely in making this decision and may need help in deciding. The best answer will come from a thorough discussion with the victim of her feelings in this area.

It is important that there be trust and understanding between a complainant and the prosecutor. The victim's needs should be addressed, and she should be allowed the time necessary to prepare for direct examination.

The complainant should be prepared for the use of "legalese" and other magical phrases employed during direct examination. For example, most attorneys are used to using the phrase "is this a fair and accurate representation" of a photograph shown a witness. Such foundation questions may seem strange to the complainant. The witness also may not understand why leading questions cannot be used on direct examination and why there will be objections to those questions. The witness needs to understand exactly what an objection is and that it is an expected and normal part of the questioning process.

Among the most difficult areas for witnesses to understand is the hearsay rule. While a legal education on the hearsay rule is not possible, at least some explanation may help the complainant understand why, at times, there may be strenuous objections from opposing counsel when she begins to recount what an individual said, while at other times the opponent will offer no objection at all. Many witnesses also do not understand that on direct examination they may tell the examiner that they do not understand the question and have the right to ask that it be rephrased. Too often, on both direct and cross-examination, witnesses feel compelled to answer questions even if they do not understand them.

Often overlooked by attorneys on direct examination, particularly in the examination of complainants, is how the witness's testimony can be shortened. This is where it helps to have a clear understanding of the themes and goals of the presentation. The examiner on direct should focus on what is really essential to the case. Certain areas may be best left to cross-examination. Any witness may tire under lengthy and boring questioning, particularly children, who may have difficulty sitting for long periods of time. If the witness needs a break or does not feel well, this should be addressed to the court. Most judges will consider the emotional element in testifying in sexual assault trials and provide a witness with necessary breaks. (*See* § 5.19.)

Another helpful way to prepare a complainant for direct examination is to meet with her at the scene of the crime (or the route traveled prior to the crime). However, consideration should be given to the traumatic effect this could have upon the complainant. It is always wise for the attorney to visit the scene of the crime to gain a better understanding of the relationships of objects, buildings, etc., especially from the complainant's perspective. Also, it allows the complainant to reacquaint herself with basic information that can be developed on direct examination and, of course, may refresh her recollection of important events. To a lesser extent, photographs of the scene or route traveled can be helpful. This can be particularly important in sexual assault cases where, because of the traumatic effect of the events, the complainant may repress certain details.

The complainant also should be informed of the purpose and parameters of the redirect examination. Often there are issues that need not or cannot be addressed on direct examination. The complainant must be made to understand that usually the goal in redirect is to explain testimony or issues that she was not given an opportunity to explain on cross-examination, and that often redirect can be as important as, if not more important than, direct examination.

§ 5.9   Areas of direct examination in sexual assault trial.

Many areas of direct examination of the complainant in a sexual assault trial are similar to those in any trial. Any direct examination of the complainant should include adequate *background information* to enable the jury to understand essential details, including the relationship of the parties and the role of other individuals whom the jury will hear about through the complainant or other witnesses. Background information also would include testimony as to the education, work experience, and physical abilities and disabilities of the complainant. Sometimes, information concerning the physical layout of a scene of the assault or the relationship between rooms of an apartment or house must be developed on direct examination of the complainant.

Often certain background information is not essential to the prosecution's case, but would likely be of interest to the jury. For example, while not essential to the case, a jury may wonder where the complainant was coming from when she encountered the defendant. Had she been drinking or taking any drugs? Had she been working all day? However, good judgment must be used here; if it appears that the questions are not relevant, and that time is being wasted, it can have an adverse effect on the jury.

Demonstrative evidence also may be utilized on direct examination of the complainant to simplify the questioning. If there is important information to explain concerning the crime scene or route traveled by the complainant, it is often best to do it through demonstrative evidence.[78] Lengthy verbal descriptions by the complainant may be confusing to the jurors and they may become bored. Sometimes this can be avoided by a short video, which, with the help of counsel, can be used by the complainant to explain her testimony. A child may use illustrations or drawings to explain what happened.[79]

---

[78] *See* discussion of this area of direct examination in §§ 14.11, 14.23–24, and 14.29.

[79] *See* § 14.23.

A major area to develop on direct examination is the complainant's *vulnerability*. It is this vulnerability that often forms the basis of lack of consent, an essential element in sexual assault crimes. If the complainant is a child, there should be questions not only as to her actual age, but also questions that reflect the child's development. For example, develop during direct examination of a six-year-old girl that on the day she was assaulted she was playing in a sandbox and carried a little toy. While a six-year-old may be able to read, allow her to explain that she reads Dr. Seuss, and that other books are read to her by her mommy or daddy. This emphasizes not only the age and abilities of the child, but also her dependency on adults and her vulnerability.

Vulnerability can be developed in other ways. It may be the superior strength of the defendant. In establishing the use of force, it may be important for the complainant to testify as to the defendant's height, weight, and strength compared to that of the complainant. (*See* § 7.18.) If this information is not developed on the record, it will not be available for an appellate court to review. If a threat was made, that, too, must be developed. A threat may be direct and expressed or it may be implied, such as by the defendant's tone of voice or gestures. This must be explained in words the jury understands and also in such a way that an effective record is made for appellate review.

Vulnerability may also be established because of the complainant's low intelligence or mental problems. If the complainant has developmental disabilities or mental health problems, have the complainant explain their effect on her daily life and her ability to handle threatening or difficult situations.

With many complainants, particularly children, vulnerability can be shown through their need for affection and attention. If the defendant and complainant were acquainted, have the complainant explain any good things the defendant did for her and how these good things were important to her. If the defendant provided for the complainant's material needs, this is appropriate for the complainant to explain on direct examination. In some cases, the victim is financially dependent upon the perpetrator or works for the defendant.

There is a *context* within which a sexual assault takes place. It can be simple: a woman walking to her car on a lonely street, a scene that jurors will understand. However, there may have been a complex series of events, perhaps a trust and bond that existed between the accused and the complainant over a period of time. Such a relationship may have resulted in the defendant's exploitation of the complainant, but it also may explain why the complainant delayed in reporting the crime, or perhaps why she later recanted her allegations. Explaining these events through the direct examination of the complainant early on is often more effective than through the testimony of an expert later in the trial.

Sometimes it is necessary, especially in cases of sexual abuse of children, to address the complainant's *reason* for coming forward and reporting the incident. Was the disclosure accidental or intentional? Was the abusive conduct discovered by someone else? Perhaps the complainant heard something in class about sexual abuse that led her to report the events. Perhaps an adult victim read a story in the newspaper about "date rape" that prompted her to report an experience years later. The reason for reporting can be very important to jurors, partially because, without a reason, coming forward and telling the story may not seem logical. Direct examination should provide logic to the case and to the prosecution's theme and presentation.

The complainant should describe on direct examination *what she had to endure* in reporting the crime and bringing her case to court. (This also can be described by the individuals involved: police officers, physicians, hospital personnel, rape crisis counselors, etc.) The complainant should describe the medical examination — what she had to endure and how she felt about it.[80] Sometimes it is important to review the medical history in the medical records with the complainant, particularly if there appears to be inconsistencies or omissions. What was the complainant's mental state? Was he or she fatigued? Did the complainant understand all vocabulary used in questions, such as "penetration," "sodomy," or "ejaculation?"

A most important area to discuss on direct examination of the complainant is the *act of sexual assault*. If the complainant has extreme difficulty testifying about the sexual act, the court may find the evidence insufficient to support the charge. The complainant's testimony must clearly establish the sexual conduct alleged in the indictment or information. If necessary, as in the case of a child victim, it may be established by marking an anatomically correct diagram,[81] or the use of anatomically correct dolls.[82] Vague testimony that a defendant touched a child complainant's "behind" has been held insufficient to establish contact between the penis and anus.[83] Testimony that the defendant's "peter" touched the child's "butt," which is properly defended by the child, may be sufficient.[84] If the testimony has not established what the complainant means by "butt" or

---

[80] *See* § 7.21.

[81] United States v. Eagle, 137 F.3d 1011, 1014 (8th Cir. 1998) (complainant's testimony that defendant touched her on her "Ch'na" and then circling the female genital area on a drawing to point out where she had been touched sufficient to establish a sexual act); United States v. St. John, 851 F.2d 1096, 1099 (8th Cir. 1988).

[82] State v. Estes, 99 N.C. App. 312, 393 S.E.2d 158 (1990) (child's testimony that defendant "stuck his thing" in the "back and front," together with demonstration with doll, established requisite elements of sexual contact).

[83] United States v. Plenty Arrows, 946 F.2d 62, 65 (8th Cir. 1991) ("The government made no further effort to elicit what the victim meant by this — whether he was referring to his buttocks, anus, or to some other part of his anatomy. While it is indeed likely, as the government argues, that a young child would not be familiar with or use the word 'anus,' the testimony here is too vague to support the inference that contact involving penetration occurred between the penis and anus. The statute is anatomically specific, and the testimony lacks the necessary specificity." *Id.* at 65).

[84] Riehle v. State, 823 N.E.2d 287 (Ind. Ct. App. 2005).

"behind," or similar term, the element of contact with the areas may not be met.[85] Clarity in the complainant's testimony may be crucial to the legal sufficiency of the proof. For example, a defendant's contact with the complainant's "buttocks" may not be criminal, whereas contact with the complainant's anus is actionable.[86] Testimony of touching is insufficient to establish intercourse.[87]

In a case involving vaginal and anal intercourse, a complainant's testimony that "we had intercourse a couple times" has been held insufficient to establish that the defendant had either vaginal or anal intercourse with the victim.[88] A child's testimony that she vaguely recalled feeling "pressure between [her] legs and inside [her] vagina," or no recollection of the pressure or other details about the incidents, and no reference to an "instrumentality of penetration" will not establish the element of penetration.[89] A child's testimony that the defendant "put his 'peter' . . . 'in his butt' " or "private"[90] or "placed his penis in my butt and it hurt"[91] may establish anal intercourse. One court held that when the prosecution relies solely on the complainant's testimony to establish penetration and the testimony is entirely inconsistent on direct examination, e.g., testifying both that the defendant placed his penis "in" and "on" her vagina, there may be insufficient proof to establish the essential element of penetration.[92] It implied that this problem does not exist if the inconsistencies are developed on cross-examination or if there is other evidence to support a finding of penetration.[93] "Circumstantial testimony" may, however, be sufficient to establish the requisite

---

[85] State v. Strughold, 973 S.W.2d 876 (Mo. Ct. App. 1998); State v. O'Neill, 134 N.H. 182, 589 A.2d 999 (1991) (holding complainant's use of words "bum" while pointing to a general area of the body was insufficient to establish anal penetration).

[86] State v. Harrison, 996 S.W.2d 704 (Mo. Ct. App. 1999). *See also* Downey v. State, 726 N.E.2d 794 (Ind. Ct. App. 2000) (defendant's conviction reversed due to insufficient proof of deviate sexual intercourse. "In this case, there was evidence of contact only with the buttocks—not with the anus. To hold that a person could commit deviate sexual conduct without contact with the anus would yield a result surely not intended by the legislature." *Id.* at 798).

[87] People v. Dunn, 204 A.D.2d 919, 612 N.Y.S.2d 266, *appeal denied*, 84 N.Y.2d 907, 645 N.E.2d 1224, 621 N.Y.S.2d 524 (1994) (testimony by child established only "touching" and not penetration and thus was insufficient to establish element of sexual intercourse).

[88] State v. Ferguson, 5 Ohio St. 3d 160, 450 N.E.2d 265 (1983). *See also* People v. Cammarere, 204 A.D.2d 762, 611 N.Y.S.2d 682, *appeal denied*, 83 N.Y.2d 965, 639 N.E.2d 757, 616 N.Y.S.2d 17 (1995) (insufficient testimony of complainant to support element of sexual contact).

[89] People v. Carroll, 95 N.Y.2d 375, 740 N.E.2d 1084, 718 N.Y.S.2d 10 (2000) (reversing defendant's conviction due to insufficient evidence to establish element of penetration).

[90] State v. Hlavsa, No. 76221, 2000 Ohio App. LEXIS 2106, *discretionary appeal allowed*, 90 Ohio St. 3d 1430, 736 N.E.2d 26 (2000).

[91] Wisneskey v. State, 736 N.E.2d 763, 765 (Ind. Ct. App. 2000).

[92] Moore v. Commonwealth, 254 Va. 184, 491 S.E.2d 739 (1997).

[93] *Id.* at 189, 491 S.E.2d at 742.

element of sexual contact. Testimony that a defendant's penis was between the victim's legs and it hurt can establish penetration.[94]

Testimony that the defendant stuck his penis "in my vagina area" may also establish vaginal penetration.[95] Testimony that defendant touched her "privates"[96] or in the place where she goes to the bathroom can establish the element of sexual contact.[97] Testimony of the defendant's "licking" can establish oral intercourse.[98] Also, a complainant's testimony of "oral intercourse" has been held sufficient to establish oral sodomy.[99]

Thus, the complainant must understand the question and the importance of clearly identifying and explaining the sexual contact constituting the crime. Avoid appellate issues by making the record of complainant's testimony clear. While the court may permit some leading questions in this regard, it is important that

---

[94] Swain v. State, 629 So. 2d 699, 700 (Ala. 1993) (testimony of complainant that defendant's penis was between her legs and "[a]ll I know it was hurting" sufficient to establish penetration); Wilson v. State, 132 Md. App. 510, 752 A.2d 1250 (2000). In *Wilson*, the complainant testified she had been raped "back and front many times," explaining that "Well, I mean the front part of me, my vagina, and the back, the rectum." The court stated:

> The victim's description of what occurred to her was sufficient to establish, prima facie, that penetration occurred. As we said in *Simms v. State*, 52 Md. App. 448, 453, 449 A.2d 1196 (1982), it is clear that the victim need not go into sordid detail to effectively establish that penetration occurred during the course of a sexual assault. Where the key to the prosecutor's case rests with the victim's testimony, the courts are normally satisfied with descriptions which, in light of all the surrounding facts, provide a reasonable basis from which to infer that penetration has occurred.

Id. at 521, 752 A.2d at 1256. *See* State v. King, 151 N.H. 59, 855 A.2d 510 (2004) (use of words "privates," "crotch," and "pee-pee," with testimony that defendant touched her and placed fingers inside her was sufficient to establish digital penetration); People v. Hayes, 261 A.D.2d 872, 690 N.Y.S.2d 358, *appeal denied*, 93 N.Y.2d 1019, 719 N.E.2d 939, 697 N.Y.S.2d 578 (1999) (holding that elderly victim's testimony that defendant's penis "penetrate[d] her vagina '[a] little bit' and very slightly" was sufficient to establish penetration under definition of sexual intercourse).

[95] People v. Carpenter, 268 A.D.2d 798, 702 N.Y.S.2d 228, *appeal denied*, 94 N.Y.2d 945, 731 N.E.2d 619, 710 N.Y.S.2d 2 (2000).

[96] State v. Lansberry, 2001 Ohio App. LEXIS 51 (Jan. 10, 2001) (holding child's testimony that defendant would "rub up and down . . . on [his] private" sufficient to establish sexual contact); Murphy v. State, 4 S.W.3d 926, 929 (Tex. Ct. App. 1999) (finding child's testimony that defendant touched her "privates," in conjunction with testimony about "first hole" and "second hole" sufficient to prove sexual contact); Hill v. State, 3 S.W.3d 249 (Tex. Ct. App. 1999).

[97] *Hill*, 3 S.W.3d 249.

[98] People v. Otero, 217 A.D.2d 796, 629 N.Y.S.2d 825, *appeal denied*, 87 N.Y.2d 849, 661 N.E.2d 1390, 638 N.Y.S.2d 608 (1995) (complainant's testimony that defendant "started to lick [her]" in context of follow-up question "when you say he licked [you], did he lick your skin, your actual skin, with his tongue?," to which victim responded in the affirmative was sufficient to establish act of sodomy); State v. Vestal, 1999 Tenn. Crim. App. LEXIS 1182 (Nov. 22, 1999) (holding child's testimony that her pants were down and defendant "was licking my privates" sufficient to establish cunnilingus).

[99] United States v. Barrow, 45 M.J. 478 (C.A.A.F. 1997).

the testimony come from the complainant. The law in this area parallels the law relating to jury instructions and the element of sexual contact which is discussed in § 16.18.

In describing the sexual acts, it is very important that the complainant express her feelings at the time of the act. Did the victim feel helpless? Threatened? Fear for her life? Did a child feel that he was complying with a duty? If there is any doubt that the complainant's reactions or feelings at the time of the act would not be readily understood by the jury, the complainant must explain them as clearly as possible. The complainant may have felt so helpless that, not only was she unable to defend herself, but she was also unable to immediately report the attack. Perhaps the complainant was concerned about siblings or other family members. When material to an issue in a case, a complainant may testify as to intention, motive, or "other physically unexpressed mental state."[100] This is particularly relevant where there is the element of forcible compulsion, where the assault placed the complainant in fear of serious physical injury or death. The "proper focus is on the state of mind produced in the victim by the defendant's conduct" ruled New York's highest court.[101]

It is better that a complainant not testify to the conclusion that she "was raped." The complainant's testimony should focus on the conduct, actions and threats involved, and not the conclusion of force or rape. However, while testimony by a victim that she was "raped" is probably objectionable as invading the province of the jury, some courts will accept such testimony as a short-hand statement of fact.[102]

Direct examination should utilize the principles of primacy and recency, which states that we remember best what we hear first and last. Important areas should be developed at the beginning and end of the complainant's direct examination, when jurors will be most likely to remember the testimony. A direct examination of any witness should end strong. If the victim's identification of the defendant is an important issue, the prosecution should have the complainant identify the defendant at the end of the direct examination, which highlights the significance of the identification. The complainant can be asked to stand and look around the courtroom to see if the individual whom she says assaulted her is present in the courtroom. Another technique is to ask the complainant to step down from the stand and tap the defendant on the shoulder.

---

[100] Starr v. Starr, 293 Ala. 204, 301 So. 2d 78 (1974).

[101] People v. Thompson, 72 N.Y.2d 410, 416, 530 N.E.2d 839, 842, 534 N.Y.S.2d 132 (1988) (This case involved a 16-year-old male jail inmate who accused a 35-year-old fellow-inmate of sodomy. Through bars separating a catwalk from the rest of a tier, the defendant stated to the complainant that he could "put the word out," that he "could have anybody kick [the complainant's] ass," and that he would make sure the victim had "a rough time" while in jail. Following these threats the defendant engaged in sexual acts with the complainant. The threats, although not capable of being immediately carried out, were sufficient to establish forceful compulsion because of their effect on a victim's state of mind.).

[102] State v. See, 301 N.C. 388, 391, 271 S.E.2d 282, 284 (1980).

When identification is at issue, it is also important to ask the complainant for the description of her assailant that she gave to the police. Such testimony is probative in that it assists the jury in evaluating the complainant's opportunity to observe at the time of the crime, the reliability of her memory, and the accuracy of her identification. [103] It will help the jury determine whether the complainant's later description of the assailant was "the product of intervening memory failure or suggestion." [104]

Direct examination should include the complainant's report — when, how, and the circumstances of the disclosure of the sexual assault. What did the complainant go through? How difficult was it to go through the interviews and investigative process? What were the circumstances of the interview? Was the witness tired? Did the witness understand everything asked? Was the vocabulary clear? If the report was delayed or recanted, what were the reasons for the delay or recantation? A witness may, for example, testify that nothing happened after she had reported previous sexual assaults to explain why she delayed reporting the instant offense. [105]

Rather than simply providing answers to leading questions, narrative responses are most effective in projecting credibility on direct examination. However, a narrative response should not be too long, because long answers sometimes are difficult to follow.

In a case in which the defense is consent, it may be important to establish the physical force involved in the attack. The strongest evidence of this will likely be the injuries suffered by the complainant. Thus, a direct examination could end by having the plaintiff describe the injuries she received and the pain she endured, and then identify photos of her injuries.

§ 5.10 References in complainant's direct testimony to defendant's statements of past criminal conduct or bad acts.

A complainant's testimony may include statements about past criminal behavior or misconduct, which may be relevant to the complainant's state of mind and fear. There are a variety of theories under which a complainant may testify to uncharged acts of abuse or a defendant's statements of other criminal behavior or bad acts.

Quite often, as in the following example the testimony is admissible to show the fear experienced by the complainant.

Q. OK, now after he had oral sex with you again, what happened next?

---

[103] People v. Huertas, 75 N.Y.2d 487, 553 N.E.2d 992, 554 N.Y.S.2d 444 (1990).

[104] *Id.* at 493, 553 N.E.2d at 995, 554 N.Y.S.2d at 447.

[105] State v. Daniels, 42 Conn. App. 445, 681 A.2d 337, *appeal denied*, 239 Conn. 928, 683 A.2d 397 (1996).

A. He pushed me or he pulled me forward.

Q. How did he do that?

A. He grabbed my ankles.

Q. OK. Did he say anything to you at this point?

A. He said that he had done this twice before. Once to a young girl in Bellefonte.

Q. OK. At that point what happened?

A. He stuck his penis in my vagina.[106]

The statements of the defendant, whether or not the defendant actually engaged in the acts, are relevant to the claimant's state of mind or fear of the complainant and the element of force.[107] Similarly, statements by a defendant to a

---

[106] Commonwealth v. Corley, 932 Pa. Super. 371, 638 A.2d 985, *appeal denied*, 538 Pa. 641, 647 A.2d 896 (1994).

[107] Summerour v. State, 242 Ga. App. 599, 530 S.E.2d 494 (2000) (permitting child's testimony that she heard defendant tell her 12-year-old brother that defendant would kill him if he ever hurt the victim since this was relevant to victim's fear of defendant); State v. Martinez, 910 P.2d 776 (Idaho Ct. App. 1995) (upholding admissibility of testimony from complainant that defendant told him that he had just been released from prison on the theory that such a statement was probative on the issue of force, namely "that the victim was prevented from resistance by threats of immediate and great bodily harm, accompanied by the apparent power of execution . . . [the defendant's] statement to [the complainant] that he had just been released from prison had the likely effect of intimidating and threatening [the complainant] so that he would not resist." *Id.* at 780); Berry v. Commonwealth, 84 S.W.3d 82 (Ky. 2001) (holding victim's reference to defendant's homosexuality not introduced for truth but to establish his state of mind in not reporting offense); People v. Gainey, 4 A.D.3d 851, 771 N.Y.S.2d 404, *appeal denied*, 2 N.Y.3d 799, 814 N.E.2d 470, 781 N.Y.S.2d 298 (2004) (holding trial court properly allowed child to testify to sexual acts predating those in indictment, and defendant's threats to use his service revolver to obtain her compliance, since such evidence went to element of forcible compulsion); People v. Kerruish, 288 A.D.2d 921, 732 N.Y.S.2d 526 (2001), *appeal denied*, 97 N.Y.2d 756, 769 N.E.2d 362, 742 N.Y.S.2d 616 (2002) (holding in sexual assault prosecution that complainant was properly permitted to testify regarding her belief that defendant had previously beaten his wife. The statement was relevant to the victim's state of mind with respect to the element of forcible compulsion. (citation omitted)); People v. Kirkey, 248 A.D.2d 979, 670 N.Y.S.2d 946, *appeal denied*, 92 N.Y.2d 900, 702 N.E.2d 849, 680 N.Y.S.2d 64 (1998) (holding that victim's testimony concerning defendant's possession of a gun and threats to kill her and others was relevant to and probative of the element of forcible compulsion); People v. Van Nostrand, 217 A.D.2d 800, 630 N.Y.S.2d 101, *appeal denied*, 87 N.Y.2d 851, 661 N.E.2d 1393, 638 N.Y.S.2d 610 (1995) (defendant's statement to complainant that he would kill everyone admissible as to her state of mind). *See also* Commonwealth v. Claypool, 508 Pa. 198, 495 A.2d 176 (1985):

> In a case such as this, in which the defendant himself has made his prior criminal activity or conviction — whether or not the defendant actually did engage in such criminal activity or did have such a conviction — an element of the crime with which he is now charged, our failure to allow this evidence to be admitted would grant to a whole class of criminals' immunity from their crimes. If such evidence were not admissible, a criminal would only need to make sure that the fear needed for the commission of his crime emanated from a threat which only embodied a class of

complainant that he had raped a girl before and that he would kill the victim if she did not shut up and stop screaming,[108] or that the defendant stated during the course of the attack that he was a rapist and a murderer and that he had been incarcerated for 12 years for raping another woman, and that he would kill her unless she followed his instructions,[109] as well as defendant's reference to "connections to the Maffia"[110] are all relevant to the element of force and a complainant's state of mind. Testimony about a defendant's statement connecting himself to the mob may also be relevant to the defendant's intent to provide a false identity.[111]

Prior acts of the defendant may be admissible when seen or observed by the complainant.[112] A complainant's testimony of past violence against the complainant and her family may be admissible to explain complainant's submission to sexual acts and her response to the abuse.[113]

> prior criminal activity to be 'excused' for his activity. If there are other threats, or fear accompanying the defendant's claim that he engaged in prior criminal activity, the exclusion of evidence of defendant's statement would present a much weaker case.

Id. at 202, 495 A.2d at 179.

[108] State v. Martin, 138 N.H. 508, 643 A.2d 946 (1994) (upholding admission of defendant's statements to victim that he had killed her pets and that she would suffer a similar fate if she did not submit to sexual relations with him or if she reported the assault); People v. De Leon, 135 A.D.2d 555, 521 N.Y.S.2d 777 (1987), *appeal denied*, 71 N.Y.2d 895, 523 N.E.2d 311, 527 N.Y.S.2d 1004 (1988).

[109] People v. King, 162 A.D.2d 473, 556 N.Y.S.2d 166, *appeal denied*, 76 N.Y.2d 859, 561 N.E.2d 899, 560 N.Y.S.2d 999 (1990).

[110] State v. Pellerin, 164 Vt. 376, 381–82, 670 A.2d 255, 259 (1995) (upholding admission of testimony by child sexual assault complainant that defendant "had warned her of his connections to the mafia and threatened to have her or her family members killed" even though coercion was not an element of the sexual assault on the minor since utilization of force during a sexual assault on a minor would nonetheless be relevant).

[111] State v. Pierce, 770 A.2d 630 (Me. 2001):

> There is no indication that this testimony pertaining to Pierce's purported mob connections moved the trier of fact to decide the counts on an improper basis. The State presented the testimony to prove Pierce used a false identity when he was around the girls, which was part of the "common scheme or plan" the State presented throughout the trial. Other witnesses testified that Pierce used a false name and age, and the "mob connection" testimony was another incident during which Pierce falsely identified his identity. In addition, only one witness testified about Pierce's "mob" connection, and the testimony did not indicate that she or the State actually believed that Pierce was connected with the mob. Therefore, we find that the court did not abuse its discretion by allowing the witness to testify about Pierce's statements because the probative value was not, substantially outweighed by the danger of unfair prejudice.

Id. at 638.

[112] *See generally* § 6.43.

[113] United States v. Powers, 59 F.3d 1460 (4th Cir. 1995), *cert. denied*, 516 U.S. 1077 (1996) ("We have approved bad acts evidence to show the context of the crime in many circumstances,

Sometimes the defendant's statements or threats are necessary to present a "complete and coherent story" or "complete the narrative."[114] For example, the prosecution may be permitted to ask a complainant about defendant's threat to rape her on the day she revealed the rape as intertwined with the charged crime

often simply to complete the story of the offense." *Id.* at 1466); State v. McPhee, 58 Conn. App. 501, 755 A.2d 893, *appeal denied*, 254 Conn. 920, 759 A.2d 1026 (2000) (upholding child's testimony concerning defendant's prior acts of discipline, including striking with a belt, as relevant to element of forcible compulsion and fear of retribution if child complained of abuse); State v. Campbell, 143 S.W.3d 695 (Mo. Ct. App. 2004) (upholding evidence of uncharged acts of physical abuse in defendant's household as relevant to element of forcible compulsion as the evidence was probative of:

> [w]hether violence or threats preceded the sexual acts; the atmosphere in the home where the acts occurred; the extent to which the accused was in a position of authority, domination, and control over the victim; and whether the victim was under duress . . . [and] to explain why [complainant] did not consistently resist the sexual abuse and why she failed to report it to her mother or anyone else until after she had moved out of the family home.

Id. at 701. People v. Arce, 309 A.D.2d 1191, 764 N.Y.S.2d 758, *appeal denied*, 1 N.Y.3d 567, 807 N.E.2d 897, 775 N.Y.S.2d 794 (2003) ("We further conclude that the court properly permitted the People to present proof on their case-in-chief concerning an uncharged incident in which defendant, while brandishing a knife, chased one of his sons outside the house. The probative value of that evidence on the issue of forcible compulsion outweighed its prejudicial tendency to establish that defendant had a criminal propensity." *Id.* at 1192, 764 N.Y.S.2d at 759); People v. Crandall, 306 A.D.2d 748, 763 N.Y.S.2d 847, *appeal denied*, 100 N.Y.2d 619, 799 N.E.2d 625, 767 N.Y.S.2d 402 (2003), *rev'd. on other grounds*:

> Inasmuch as there must be a new trial as to the sexual abuse count in the first indictment, we note that we find no error in Supreme Court's decision to permit evidence of defendant's prior assaultive conduct with regard to the victim. Defendant attempted to prove, through cross-examination, that the victim did not resist defendant's advances, thus inviting the jury to erroneously conclude that the episode was consensual. In order to controvert such claim, the People were permitted to prove that the victim was afraid to resist based upon defendant's prior violent conduct toward her [citation omitted].

Id. at 751, 763 N.Y.S.2d at 850. Commonwealth v. Barger, 1999 Pa. Super. 306, 743 A.2d 477 (1999) (holding prior assaults by defendant upon child and mother relevant to reasons why victim offered no physical resistance and delayed reporting crime).

[114] People v. Poquee, 9 A.D.3d 781, 780 N.Y.S.2d 247, *appeal denied*, 3 N.Y.3d 741, 820 N.E.2d 300, 786 N.Y.S.2d 821 (2004) (permitting uncharged acts of violence against domestic violence rape victim because they were inextricably interwoven with the charged crimes, provided background and helped to complete the witnesses narrative; other acts of violence were sparred by defendant's jealousy of what he perceived to be her relationship with other men; such evidence was relevant to defendant's intent and motive); People v. Gilley, 4 A.D.3d 127, 770 N.Y.S.2d 868, *appeal denied*, 2 N.Y.3d 799, 814 N.E.2d 471, 781 N.Y.S.2d 299 (2004) (holding in sexual assault of child, proof of uncharged acts "completed her narrative and assisted the jury in its comprehension of the crimes charged, providing necessary background material to explain her relationship with defendant while they lived together in the homeless shelters, and to place the events in a believable context.").

being prosecuted.[115] A defendant's statements about prior bad acts has also been admitted under a "consciousness of guilt" theory.[116]

Sometimes the acts testified to may be upon relatives outside the immediate family or third parties. A defendant's killing of his son-in-law who was several years older than him may be relevant to the complainant's state of mind for the purpose of establishing forceful compulsion.[117] Evidence of advances toward a complainant's friend while the two were together earlier in the evening is admissible when there is basis to believe that the defendant became angry and frustrated by the friend's rejection of the defendant. Such evidence is admissible to detail "the overall sequence of events leading up to the crime."[118]

A defendant may open the door to a complainant's reference to other acts of the defendant. For example, if a defendant challenges the complainant's failure to report the abuse, the complainant may testify she came forward only after a friend had told her she had been raped by the defendant.[119] In such a situation, as in other references to possible past criminal conduct or association, a limiting instruction should be provided.[120]

Nonetheless, some courts will restrict references in a complainant's direct testimony to a defendant's statements of past criminal conduct or limit the admissibility of such statements. Idaho's Supreme Court has held that a defendant's statement to a sexual assault complainant, "If you ever decide to tell somebody, tell me first because I don't want to go back to prison" is too prejudicial when the threat of violence or force is not an element of the crime.[121] The court suggested that the "reference to prison could have been severed from the statement and replaced by something less inflammatory . . . [that the defendant] told her to tell him first before she told anyone else about his conduct because he did not want to get into trouble."[122] The court noted that the statement of the defendant may be relevant to a complainant's failure to report should the failure to report be raised.[123] If a defendant shows a newspaper clipping to the

---

[115] Levy v. State, 724 So. 2d 405 (Miss. Ct. App. 1998).

[116] Jackson v. State, 132 Md. App. 467, 752 A.2d 1227, *appeal denied*, 360 Md. 487, 759 A.2d 231 (2000) (upholding victim's testifying that defendant told her he had been arrested before and also said, "have you figured out what I have been arrested for" as consciousness of guilt and an exception to the admission of prior bad acts).

[117] People v. Brown, 261 A.D.2d 410, 691 N.Y.S.2d 532, *appeal denied*, 93 N.Y.2d 967, 716 N.E.2d 1098, 695 N.Y.S.2d 53 (1999).

[118] Commonwealth v. Montgomery, 455 Pa. Super. 202, 687 A.2d 1131 (1996) (defendant's "mood, demeanor and intent in approaching the victim are all connected to his earlier behavior with [complainant's friend]").

[119] Commonwealth v. Richardson, 38 Mass. App. Ct. 384, 391–92, 648 N.E.2d 445, 450 (1995), *aff'd*, 423 Mass. 180, 667 N.E.2d 257 (1996).

[120] *Id.*

[121] State v. Bingham, 124 Idaho 698, 864 P.2d 144 (1993).

[122] *Id.* at 701, 864 P.2d at 147.

[123] *Id.*

complainant that refers to past crimes, the newspaper articles should not be admitted if there is no testimony that the victim read or was aware of the content of the clippings.[124] Furthermore, even though the references in complainant's testimony may be relevant to an element of the sexual assault, the references to the defendant's statements may be precluded on the theory that the probative value of the defendant's statement is outweighed by its prejudicial effect when there is other evidence to establish the element.[125]

While testimony concerning a defendant's past criminal behavior or other activities may be admissible, it may be reversible if the admission of such testimony is not accompanied by a limiting instruction.[126] For example, a defendant's statement to a sexual assault complainant that he has AIDS may be prejudicial, although relevant to the complainant's state of mind so that its admission without limiting instructions is reversible error.[127] The court suggested the following as a possible limiting instruction:

> [I]f the jury believes that the defendant made the statement to the complainant, they shall consider the statement only on the issue of the complainant's state of mind at the time of the alleged assaults and rapes but they are not to allow themselves to become prejudiced against the defendant because they believe he has AIDS.[128]

On the other hand, where a complainant testified that a defendant stated that he had been in jail for about seven years, it was improper to preclude the defendant from testifying on direct examination that he had not previously been convicted of a crime, when such testimony was relevant to the defense of identification.[129] Not only does precluding a defendant from offering such testimony undermine the defendant's right to present a meaningful defense, but it also can give "a distorted view of defendant's character."[130]

---

[124] State v. Winkler, 112 Idaho 917, 736 P.2d 1371 (1987).

[125] People v. Johnson, 280 A.D.2d 683, 721 N.Y.S.2d 108 (2001) ("[During the sexual assault, the defendant] told the complainant that he had served time in jail for manslaughter. Under the circumstances of this case, the trial court should have precluded evidence of this uncharged crime. While it was probative of the forcible compulsion elements of the crimes charged, there was sufficient other evidence to prove that element. Therefore, the probative value of the defendant's statement was outweighed by the potential for prejudice." [citation omitted] *Id.* at 684, 721 N.Y.S.2d at 109).

[126] Commonwealth v. Richardson, 38 Mass. App. Ct. 384, 391–92, 648 N.E.2d 445, 450 (1995), *aff'd*, 423 Mass. 180, 667 N.E.2d 257 (1996).

[127] Commonwealth v. Martin, 39 Mass. App. Ct. 658, 660 N.E.2d 670, *review granted*, 422 Mass. 1105, 663 N.E.2d 575 (1996).

[128] *Id.* at 664, 660 N.E.2d at 675.

[129] People v. Rosa, 153 A.D.2d 257, 550 N.Y.S.2d 886, *appeal denied*, 75 N.Y.2d 969, 555 N.E.2d 626, 556 N.Y.S.2d 254 (1990).

[130] *Id.* at 261, 550 N.Y.S.2d at 888.

§ 5.11 Accommodating the sexual abuse victim in the courtroom — Gifts to child witness, comments of trial judge, supportive statements and actions toward complainant by court and prosecutor.

A trial judge has wide discretion in setting the parameters in the examination of a witness. The Federal Rules of Evidence state:

> The court shall exercise reasonable control over the mode and order of interrogating witnesses and presenting evidence so as to (1) make the interrogation and presentation effective for the ascertainment of the truth, (2) avoid needless consumption of time, and (3) protect witnesses from harassment or undue embarrassment.[131]

This rule gives broad, but not unlimited, power to reduce the witness's anxiety and stress and to assist witnesses who have difficulty testifying. A trial court's procedures in eliciting testimony are reviewed under an abuse of discretion standard.[132] The Child Victims' and Witnesses' Act further broadens and defines these powers. The problems created by the courtroom environment and the ability of the legal system to find solutions to accommodating child victims were addressed by Judge Charles Schudson and Billie Wright Dziech.

> Courtrooms were designed for the large numbers of adults who become participants and spectators in trials. Their furniture, lighting, acoustics, and uniformed personnel assure a serious and, in some ways, intimidating atmosphere. The theory is that in such an environment, witnesses and jurors will be more likely to take their responsibilities seriously. For children, however, the courtroom can do more than encourage civic responsibility — it can terrify and silence. . . . At the first hint that their wardrobe or their position in the courtroom should ever change, many judges react with anger or amusement. Claiming dignity, law, and tradition, they reveal their weakness as legal historians. Fixed in neither law nor tradition, robes, courtroom arrangements, and judicial symbols evolved from shifting philosophies, none of which has any absolute legal hold on contemporary judges. . . . When judges consider the traditions that guide trial procedures and even their own appearances and positioning in courtrooms, they must do so with an accurate view of legal history. They may thus be more likely to honor the true tradition of flexibility to facilitate the search for truth.[133]

Attempts have been made to accommodate victims of sexual assault to testify. Some of these efforts, such as the use of leading questions, have always existed, whereas others, such as use of closed-circuit TV, are recent innovations unique to child sexual abuse cases. It is important to remember that certain courtroom

---

[131] Fed. R. Evid. 611 (a).

[132] State v. Johnson, 38 Ohio App. 3d 152, 154, 528 N.E.2d 567 (1986).

[133] Billie Wright Dziech & Charles Schudson, On Trial 170–71 (1989).

traditions are not required by law or court rules. The courtroom environment itself can be changed to accommodate individual and public needs. In fact, judges at one time rode the circuit and went to various communities and sat wherever space could be found, sometimes holding court outdoors.[134] This is but an example of the historical precedent of the court system adapting to the needs of the public.

In virtually no jurisdiction is there a requirement that a judge wear a black robe. A black robe can be intimidating to a child, and judges are free to remove it for a child witness or, for that matter, at any point during a proceeding.

Trial courts have broad discretion in allowing special measures to assist or comfort children and traumatized witnesses.[135] "The protection of children from undue trauma when testifying is an important public policy goal."[136] However, measures that may affect the right of confrontation should be undertaken only on a showing of necessity.[137] The Supreme Court of the United States, in *Coy v. Iowa*,[138] held that the right of confrontation cannot be limited by a statute that restricts a face-to-face confrontation by allowing a screen to be placed between a child sexual assault victim and the defendant without specific findings of necessity on a case-by-case basis. A statute cannot create necessity by a legislatively imposed presumption of trauma for sexual assault complainants who must testify before their alleged assailants.[139] However, when there is a showing that child witnesses are fearful of testifying in the defendant's presence, it may be acceptable for them to testify out of the line of sight of the defendant.[140]

The requirement of case-specific necessity for a special procedure is set forth in many of the statutes that provide measures for accommodating child witnesses, such as the use of closed-circuit testimony. California has enacted legislation for child molestation victims that provides reasonable breaks for the child, permits the trial judge to remove his robe, permits rearranging the configurations and seating of the courtroom, and limits testimony to the child's normal school hours.[141]

---

[134] *Id.*

[135] State v. Suka, 70 Haw. 472, 477 n.2, 777 P.2d 240, 243 n.2 (1989); Baxter v. State, 522 N.E.2d 362 (Ind. 1988) (permitting a mother to hold a child's hand while she testified). *See also* Justus v. Commonwealth, 222 Va. 667, 676, 283 S.E.2d 905, 910 (1981), *cert. denied*, 455 U.S. 983 (1982).

[136] State v. T.E., 342 N.J. Super. 14, 30, 775 A.2d 686, *cert. denied*, 170 N.J. 86, 784 A.2d 719 (2001).

[137] State v. Rulona, 71 Haw. 127, 130, 785 P.2d 615, 617 (1990).

[138] 487 U.S. 1012, 1020–21 (1988).

[139] *Id.* at 1021.

[140] State v. Lopez, 306 S.C. 362, 412 S.E.2d 390 (1991) (involving testimony of five-and seven-year-old children testifying against defendant charged with murdering their three-year-old brother). *Cf.* Coy v. Iowa, 487 U.S. 1012, 1019 (1988); State v. Wright, 61 Wash. App. 819, 829, 810 P.2d 935, 940, *appeal denied*, 117 Wash. 2d 1012, 816 P.2d 1225 (1991) (recognizing the importance of visual contact between witness and accused).

[141] Cal. Penal Code § 868.8.

Not all accommodations are proper. Some attempts to accommodate child victims have resulted in reversal of convictions on the grounds that the accommodation has denied the defendant a right of confrontation or denied defendant a fair trial. For example, a trial judge rewarding a child witness with lollipop, cookies, and ice cream in front of the jury for providing real as opposed to pretend testimony is improper.[142]

These actions are improper because they suggest that the judge has given his opinion as to the accuracy of the child's testimony.[143] Similarly, a prosecutor giving gifts to a child prior to testifying may be reversible error since gift giving may impact the victim's suggestibility.[144]

A trial court, too, cannot, by its comments in attempting to comfort a child victim, improperly vouch for the credibility of a child witness.[145]

A prosecutor must use care in accommodating a child witness. Not all attempts at compassion or empathy are improper, but they may still raise an objection of creating undue sympathy for the child.[146]

---

[142] State v. R.W., 200 N.J. Super. 560, 569–70, 491 A.2d 1304, 1309 (1985), *modified*, 104 N.J. 14, 514 A.2d 1287(1986).

[143] *Id.*

[144] State v. Aponte, 249 Conn. 735, 738 A.2d 117 (1999). The court noted the impropriety was compounded by the trial court's failure to permit questioning of the child about contacts with the prosecutor:

> We conclude that the actions of the prosecutor in giving the victim a Barney doll prior to her testifying, along with the trial court's limitations on the defendant's ability to expose to the jury the impact that such conduct may have had on her testimony, harmfully deprived the defendant of due process in connection with one of the assault convictions.

Id. at 737, 738 A.2d at 120.

[145] People v. Rush, 250 Ill. App. 3d 530, 620 N.E.2d 1262, *appeal denied*, 153 Ill. 2d 567, 624 N.E.2d 815 (1993) (defendant's conviction for child sexual assault reversed due to trial court's comment during its questioning of child witness as follows:

The court: Are you sure he put his finger in your butt?

The witness: Yes.

The court: Any doubt in your mind he did that?

The witness: No.

The court: Very important that you tell the truth now.

The witness: Yes.

The court: I know you are telling the truth. Are you sure he put his finger in your butt?

The witness: Yes.

But see State v. Alidani, 2000 SD 52, 609 N.W.2d 152 (2000) (holding judge's comment to child in front of jury that "I know you are going to tell the truth," while not recommended, was not unduly prejudicial, and court's instructions about comments helped cure any prejudice).

[146] State v. Thomason, C.C.A. No.02C01-9903-CC-00086, 2000 Tenn. Crim. App. LEXIS 229 at *39 (Mar. 7, 2000) (finding no prejudice on prosecutor's putting child on shoulders, brushing hair from her eyes and telling her, "It's almost over now, Honey").

§ 5.12   Reference to complaining witness as "victim" by prosecutor or court.

Should a prosecutor be allowed to refer to the complainant as a "victim," particularly when a defendant alleges consent as a defense or that no crime took place? Does the term not presuppose a crime was committed? The argument is that the term "victim" violates the presumption of innocence since the complaining witness is not a victim unless the defendant is proven guilty. Some courts find such a reference improper, since whether a complaining witness is a "victim" is for the jury to decide, and the description favors the prosecution by bolstering the position of the witness that a crime was committed.[147] For similar reasons, it may be reversible error for a court to refer to the complainant as victim in its charge.

> We agree with the defendant that given the particular circumstances of this case, as well as the fact that the complainant's credibility was a critical issue, the better practice would have been for the court to refer to the complainant by some term other than "victim." We conclude that the court's instructions constituted reversible error. Although the defendant did not ask the court to deliver a curative instruction after the court delivered its charge, the court made it clear that it would not deliver such an instruction when the defendant raised his objection to the charge. . . .
>
> We also ask whether any prejudicial effect of the court's use of the term "victim" was negated by the court's other instructions to the jury. [citation omitted]. We are confident that the court's other instructions could not have negated such effect under these circumstances, in which the jury faced two conflicting versions of events and had to credit one witness's word over that of another witness.[148]

§ 5.13   Use of leading questions.

The Federal Rules of Evidence state: "Leading questions should not be used on the direct examination of a witness except as may be necessary to develop the witness's testimony."[149] While leading questions are generally not acceptable

---

[147] Allen v. State, 644 A.2d 982 n.1 (Del. 1994) (holding that when consent is the defense in a rape case, it is improper to refer to complainant as victim). *See also* Veteto v. State, 8 S.W.3d 805, 816–17 (Tex. Ct. App. 2000); State v. Wigg, 2005 Vt. 91, 889 A.2d 233 (2005) (While the court found the error harmless, it ruled the term "victim" lacked probative value, and held "that there was a danger of unfair prejudice because the detective's choice of language implied that he and the prosecution believed the complainant's testimony, adding weight to the State's case." *Id.* at *P10, 889 A.2d at 237).

[148] State v. Cortes, 84 Conn. App. 70, 86–87, 851 A.2d 1230, 1241 (2004), *aff'd*, 276 Conn. 241, 885 A.2d 153 (2005); State v. Wright, 2003 Ohio App. LEXIS 3208 (July 2, 2003) (finding defendant's rights were not substantially affected by court's, prosecutor's, and defendant's attorneys' reference to "victim").

[149] Fed. R. Evid. § 611(C).

on direct examination, there is a long-standing exception for witnesses who have difficulty communicating, such as children and witnesses with mental disabilities or communication impairments. Leading questions are a common tool to assist children in direct examination.

Many courts accept the use of leading questions with children who are reluctant to testify about, or have difficulty communicating the details of, sexual abuse.[150]

---

[150] United States v. Goodlow, 105 F.3d 1203, 1207–08 (8th Cir. 1997); United States v. Butler, 56 F.3d 941, 943 (8th Cir.), *cert. denied*, 516 U.S. 924 (1995) (upholding leading questions posed to nine-year-old victim because the victim had "such a limited ability to communicate verbally that only his mother can understand him"); United States v. Boyles, 57 F.3d 535, 547 (7th Cir. 1995) (leading questions of four-year-old permitted); United States v. Tome, 3 F.3d 342, 252 (10th Cir. 1993), *rev'd on other grounds*, 513 U.S. 150 (1995); United States v. Castro-Romero, 964 F.2d 942 (9th Cir. 1992) (eight-year-old witness); United States v. Demarrias, 876 F.2d 674, 678 (8th Cir. 1989); R.D. v. State, 706 So. 2d 770 (1997) (leading questions permitted for victims under age of 16 pursuant to Ala. Code § 15-25-1); McCurley v. State, 455 So. 2d 1014 (Ala. Crim. App. 1984); Clark v. State, 315 Ark. 602, 870 S.W.2d 372 (1994) (four-year-old); Johnson v. State, 71 Ark. App. 58, 25 S.W.3d 445 (2000) ("We hold that the trial court did not abuse its discretion in allowing the State to use leading questions in this case. The victim was as young as six years when the abuse occurred, and was nine years old at the time of the trial. She was understandably reluctant to answer embarrassing questions regarding specific acts of sexual abuse by James. The record shows a repeated pattern of the victim stating that she could not remember when asked what happened in general terms, but then providing detailed responses to specific questions. Moreover, she appeared unfamiliar with the proper terminology needed to describe James' actions to the jury." *Id.* at 76, 25 S.W.3d at 456); State v. Hydock, 51 Conn. App. 753, 765, 725 A.2d 379, 386–87, *appeal denied*, 248 Conn. 921, 733 A.2d 846 (1999) (upholding leading questioning of six-year-old who demonstrated fear and hesitancy in testifying); Begley v. State, 483 So. 2d 70 (Fla. Dist. Ct. App. 1986) (five-year-old witness); State v. Roman, 622 A.2d 96, 101 (Me. 1993) ("the State is accorded much latitude in attempting to elicit relevant testimony from a child witness"); Gandy v. State, 788 So. 2d 812 (Miss. Ct. App. 2001) (leading questions of 12-year-old to clarify sexual terminology was acceptable); Eakes v. State, 665 So. 2d 852, 869–70 (Miss. 1995) (while upholding leading questions to a seven-year-old witness, court warned against the continued use of leading questions particularly if the trial judge follows up with questioning after cross-examination that tends to reconstitute the witness's testimony); Jones v. State, 606 So. 2d 1051 (Miss. 1992) ("The classic example for allowing the use of leading questions is where a child is a witness, [citation omitted]. A trial court, in its discretion, may allow leading questions, unless there has been an abuse of discretion to the prejudice of a complaining party, it is not reversible error." *Id.* at 1059); People v. Cuttler, 270 A.D.2d 654, 705 N.Y.S.2d 416, *appeal denied*, 95 N.Y.2d 795, 733 N.E.2d 235, 711 N.Y.S.2d 163 (2000); People v. Wasley, 249 A.D.2d 625, 626, 671 N.Y.S.2d 767, 768, *appeal denied*, 91 N.Y.2d 1014, 698 N.E.2d 971, 676 N.Y.S.2d 142 (1998) (noting that "a prosecutor will be given considerable latitude in his or her questioning of a child victim of a sex crime who is apparently unwilling to testify freely"); People v. Tyrrell, 101 A.D.2d 946, 475 N.Y.S.2d 937–39 (1984) (leading questions are acceptable to develop testimony of a child victim of a sex crime who may be unwilling to testify); People v. Greenhagen, 78 A.D.2d 964, 433 N.Y.S.2d 683 (1980) ("The only other point requiring comment is the prosecutor's use of leading questions to examine the two victims. Both children had difficulty in relating the facts of the incident and in view of their age and the intimate and embarrassing nature of the crimes, the court did not abuse its discretion in permitting the prosecutor to use leading questions to examine them." *Id.* at 966, 433 N.Y.S.2d at 685–86); State v. Madden, 15 Ohio App. 3d 130, 472 N.E.2d 1126 (1984); State v. Holt, 17 Ohio St. 2d 81, 246 N.E.2d 365 (1969); State

A court has recognized the difficulty of a young child talking to strangers in a strange surrounding about sexual acts performed by the child's father.[151] According to one court, the leading questions may even be in the form of reading the contents of a complainant's prior statement.[152]

The reasons justifying the use of leading questions with child witnesses have been summarized by the Supreme Court of Arkansas as:

> (1) the seriousness of the crime, (2) the natural embarrassment of the witness about the incident, (3) the child's fear of being in a courtroom full of people, (4) the necessity of testimony from a victim, (5) threats toward victims from those perpetrators, and (6) avoiding the possibility that an accused might escape punishment for a serious offense merely because of the victim's reluctance to testify.[153]

Unlike many accommodations to sexual assault victim cases, specific findings are not necessary before allowing leading questions.[154]

The use of leading questions has also been approved with older complainants who have difficulty testifying, such as a 67-year-old rape victim.[155]

Leading questions may also be appropriate with individuals who have physical impairments[156] or developmental disabilities[157] which affect their ability to

---

v. Johnson, 1994 Tenn. Crim. App. LEXIS 239 at 5 (Apr. 20, 1994); State v. Pearson, 238 Wis. 2d 95, 617 N.W.2d 677, *review denied*, 239 Wis. 2d 773, 621 N.W.2d 629 (2000). The *Pearson* court held questioning of eight-year-old not unduly leading, stating:

> Here, we have reviewed the prosecutor's questions. They did not directly suggest the answers sought. For example, the prosecutor prefaced the questions with words like "what happened," "what did you do," "did anything happen," and "what did he do." These questions were neutral in substantive content. They were designed to overcome Chelsea's natural inhibitions due to her youth and the embarrassing subject matter. To the extent some of the questions may have suggested the desired answer, trial courts may permit such neutral, nonparticular leading questions under these circumstances.

Id. at *3; Rhodes v. State, 462 P.2d 722 (Wyo. 1969).

[151] State v. Johnson, 1994 Tenn. Crim. App. LEXIS 239 at 5 (Apr. 20, 1994).

[152] Demarrias, 876 F.2d at 678.

[153] Clark v. State, 315 Ark. 602, 870 S.W.2d 372 (1994).

[154] United States v. Wright, 119 F.3d 630, 635 (8th Cir. 1997).

[155] State v. Delarosa-Flores, 59 Wash. App. 514, 799 P.2d 736, *review denied*, 116 Wash. 2d 1010, 805 P.2d 814 (1990).

[156] Commonwealth v. Smolko, 446 Pa. Super. 156, 666 A.2d 672 (1995) (holding that leading questions were particularly appropriate in light of the limited ability of the complainant to communicate verbally; witness suffered from Pelizaeus Merzbacher Syndrome, a disease that affects the central nervous system and causes the victim to have the inability to speak, control motor movements and leaves the person with little strength; the victim had "such a limited ability to communicate verbally that only his mother can understand him," 446 Pa. Super, at 446, 666 A.2d at 678).

[157] United States v. Goodla, 105 F.3d 1203, 1207 (8th Cir. 1997) (complainant's mental retardation permitted use of leading questions).

communicate. Leading questions may be permissible with 12-year-old[158] teenage witnesses who are hesitant to answer questions.[159] Leading questions, even to an older teenager, which direct the victim to the charged time span is not necessarily an abuse of discretion by a trial judge.[160]

It may not always be advisable to use leading questions on direct examination even if it is permissible. A child's credibility will be enhanced to the extent that the witness can freely discuss or talk about the incident. While leading questions should be avoided if possible, there is no question that they are sometimes necessary not only with children but also adult complainants who have difficulty in testifying about a traumatic event. If defense counsel feels that leading questions are unnecessary or the practice is being abused, an objection should be lodged, since failure to object will constitute a waiver.[161] A defendant may wish to use leading questions of a reluctant adult witness. However, the trial court will have wide latitude in limiting defendant's use of leading questions.[162] As with many evidentiary issues, failing to object specifically to a question as leading may result in an appellate review limited to plain error.[163]

§ 5.14 Positioning child witness off witness stand, or closer to jury, or to minimize view of defendant.

While some judges want a child to sit in the same chair as other witnesses, this is not a requirement. Wheelchair-bound individuals are generally permitted to testify from their wheelchair. Seating a child so that he or she can be heard or seen better by the jury is not only permissible, it may be necessary to ensure that the jury has the opportunity to evaluate the demeanor of the witness. Allowing a child witness to testify from a chair closer to the jury than to the witness stand is part of a trial judge's discretion in regulating courtroom conduct.[164]

---

[158] United States v. Archdale, 229 F.3d 861 (9th Cir. 2000) (upholding leading questions of a 12-year-old complainant since her "failure to respond coupled with the prosecutor's reaction to her silence demonstrates that J.K. was having difficulty testifying about this very personal matter. Moreover, the district judge had the opportunity to witness J.K.'s demeanor on the witness stand." *Id.* at 866).

[159] United States v. Rossbach, 701 F.2d 713, 718 (8th Cir. 1983), *cert. denied*, 498 U.S. 827 (1990) (permitting leading questions with 15-and 17-year-old); Altmeyer v. State, 519 N.E.2d 138 (Ind. 1988) (14-year-old witness); State v. Brown, 574 A.2d 745 (R.I. 1990) (16-year-old complainant allowed to be led on issue of defendant's penetration when she was upset and crying during her testimony).

[160] State v. Young, 2001 Ohio App. LEXIS 119 (Jan. 19, 2001) (while discussion is unclear, victim was at least 16 years old when questioned at trial).

[161] State v. Timperio, 38 Ohio App. 3d 156, 158, 528 N.E.2d 594, 596 (1987).

[162] State v. Wiggins, 136 N.C. App. 735, 526 S.E.2d 207 (2000).

[163] United States v. Archdale, 229 F.3d 861, 866 (9th Cir. 2000); State v. Jones, 2000 Ohio App. LEXIS 3268 (July 21, 2000).

[164] People v. Woellhaf, 87 P.3d 142, 152–53 (Colo. Ct. App. 2003), *rev'd on other grounds*, 105 P.3d 209 (Colo. 2005).

To minimize trauma to a child sexual assault witness, some prosecutors seek to shield the child from the defendant while testifying. As long as the defendant is able to have some view of the child witness and the child witness is able to view the defendant, positioning the child witness so that the witness is looking away from the defense table will most likely provide adequate right to face-to-face confrontation.[165] A child witness may be able to testify from a table rather than an elevated witness stand while the defendant is about 20 feet away.[166] The fact that the child's attention may not be naturally focused in the direction of the defendant does not render such a procedure unconstitutional.[167] It is not necessary that the witness constantly look at the defendant as long as the witness is able but chooses not to look at the defendant.[168] A defendant cannot "coin a right to a particular seating arrangement in the courtroom."[169] Such an arrangement can be justified by the United States Supreme Court holding in *Maryland v. Craig*, which held that something less than literal face-to-face confrontations are required between an adult defendant and child victim.[170] Similarly, a child witness may be allowed to testify from a miniature chair and

[165] People v. Sharp, 29 Cal. App. 4th 1772, 36 Cal. Rptr. 2d 117 (1994), *cert. denied*, 514 U.S. 1130 (1995). *See also* Stanger v. State, 545 N.E.2d 1105 (Ind. Ct. App. 1989).

[166] Commonwealth v. Sanchez, 423 Mass. 591, 670 N.E.2d 377 (1996).

[167] *Id.* (The special seating arrangement should be justified by case-specific findings of necessity. Ordinarily, if there is such justification, special seating arrangements or courtroom reconfigurations are permissible as long as a physical or opaque barrier is not utilized.); Ellis v. United States, 313 F.3d 636, 646–653 (1st Cir. 2002), *cert. denied*, 504 U.S. 839 (2003) (child witness sat in a chair facing jurors, but facing away from defendant. Trial court found that defendant's threats of harm if she told about the abuse, coupled with defendant's menacing gestures during pretrial proceedings, striking her in the past and repeatedly violating a "no contest" order after his arrest justified a special seating arrangement. "[A] defendant does not have a constitutional right to force eye contact with his accuser, *id.*, and we refuse to fashion a bright-line rule that the lack of such an opportunity, in and of itself, automatically translates into a constitutional violation." *Id.* at 652); Smith v. State, 340 Ark. 116, 8 S.W.3d 534 (2000):

> Where, as here, the method of eliciting testimony permits jury, witness, and defendant all to see and hear each other and possesses the added virtue of actually facilitating the truthfinding function at the trial, positioning the witness away from the defendant is but a reasonable limitation on the defendant's interest in physical confrontation. As the Court noted with respect to cross-examination, confrontation does not mean in whatever way and to whatever extent a defendant might wish.

Id. at 122, 8 S.W.3d at 538; Richardson v. State, 276 Ga. 639, 581 S.E.2d 528 (2003) ("The *Confrontation Clause* does not compel the witness to fix his eyes upon the defendant; he may studiously look elsewhere. However, that constitutional provision does guarantee the defendant a face-to-face meeting with witnesses appearing before the trier of fact." [citations omitted]. *Id.* at 641–42, 581 S.E.2d at 530; State v. Brockel, 733 So. 2d 640, 644–46 (La. Ct. App. 1999); Commonwealth v. Sanchez, 423 Mass. 591, 670 N.E.2d 377 (1996); State v. Miller, 2001 ND 132, 631 N.W.2d 587, 594 (2001).

[168] Sharp, 29 Cal. App. 4th at 1781–82, 36 Cal. Rptr. 2d at 123.

[169] *Id.* at 1782, 36 Cal. Rptr. 2d at 123.

[170] 497 U.S. 836, 849–50 (1990).

table rather than from the usual witness chair.[171] The Massachusetts Supreme Court has stated that regardless of its earlier decisions, it "unequivocally" holds that the trial court should "refrain from designing seating configurations which comfortably shield a witness from a face-to-face meeting."[172] The court noted the importance of particularized findings to justify any infringement upon the constitutional right to confront witnesses. However, the court noted that a trial court has more discretion in undertaking special arrangements which may make the courtroom more intimate or less intimidating such as the judge not wearing robes, or utilizing special child-sized chairs and tables, or allowing the child to have a parent or toy near the witness.[173]

There are limits to the blocking of the view between a child witness and defendant. If the view is totally blocked and a defendant is unable to see the face of a child witness, the procedure is likely to violate the right of confrontation since precluding eye contact between a witness and defendant is different from compelling a witness to maintain eye contact with the defendant or placing a witness in the courtroom so that the witness is not required to observe the defendant.[174] Thus an angle of 45 degrees may be acceptable since the defendant can observe the complainant's profile and demeanor, whereas an angle between the child witness and defendant of between 112 and 145 degrees would make it impossible for the defendant to see the profiles or lip movements of a child and thus be unconstitutional.[175] As with many procedures to accommodate the child witness in the courtroom, a finding of compelling need for the protection of the complainant should be made before the technique is utilized.[176]

A prosecutor shielding a child victim with his body during direct examination so that the witness cannot see the defendant, without any showing of the necessity for such a procedure, violates a defendant's right to a face-to-face confrontation and interferes with the defendant's ability to properly cross-examine the witness.[177] Using podiums which prevent a child witness and a defendant from

---

[171] Brandon v. State, 839 P.2d 400 (Alaska Ct. App. 1992).

[172] Commonwealth v. Amirault, 424 Mass. 618, 632, 677 N.E.2d 652, 663 (1997).

[173] Id. at 635, 677 N.E.2d at 664.

[174] Commonwealth v. Johnson, 417 Mass. 498, 631 N.E.2d 1002 (1994); Commonwealth v. Spear, 43 Mass. App. Ct. 583, 686 N.E.2d 1037, review denied, 426 Mass. 1105 (1997) (appellate court reversed defendant's conviction, stating: "During her testimony, the child sat in a chair in front of the jury box facing the jury, and was not required to face the defendant. It is also undisputed that the defendant, acting pro se, was required to remain standing behind counsel table during his cross-examination." Id. at 590, 686 N.E.2d at 1043); State v. Lipka, 174 Vt. 377, 817 A.2d 27 (2002) (reversing defendant's conviction because seating arrangement precluded defendant from seeing his daughter while testifying and there were inadequate findings on the necessity of such an arrangement).

[175] Commonwealth v. Conefrey, 410 Mass. 1, 14, 570 N.E.2d 1384, 1391 (1991).

[176] Commonwealth v. Johnson, 417 Mass. 498, 631 N.E.2d 1002 (1994).

[177] Smith v. State, 111 Nev. 499, 894 P.2d 974 (1995).

seeing one another will violate the constitutional right to confrontation.[178] Such a procedure is not justified by closed-circuit television processes which require specific findings of necessity.[179]

Providing the defendant the opportunity to hear the child's testimony, discuss it with his counsel and cross-examine the child is insufficient to overcome the due process right to be heard on the issue of a child witness testifying outside the defendant's presence.[180]

Shielding adult victims of sex crimes from a defendant requires an even higher level of scrutiny. Placing a one-way glass between the defendant and adult witness is likely to violate a defendant's constitutional right to confrontation and due process, particularly when there is no "case-specific finding of necessity."[181]

§ 5.15   Use of court school.

One approach in preparing children as witnesses is known as "court school." Court school is a program run by witness advocates or a prosecutor's office to teach children about court procedures. Some programs are called "court school," while others have adopted some of the procedures developed in court school. Court schools do vary in the length, format, and intensity of the preparation. It may include providing the child witness with written materials or a visit to a real or mock courtroom.

Court school programs have been held to be appropriate as long as they are designed primarily with educating a witness about courtroom protocol and

---

[178] People v. Lofton, 194 Ill. 2d 40, 740 N.E.2d 782 (2000).

[179] People v. Lofton, 194 Ill. 2d 40, 740 N.E.2d 782 (2000).

[180] South Carolina Dep't of Soc. Servs. v. Wilson, 352 S.C. 445, 574 S.E.2d 730 (2002) (holding that family court proceeding, like criminal proceeding, requires case-specific reasons for denying a defendant a face-to-face confrontation).

[181] People v. Murphy, 107 Cal. App. 4th 1150, 132 Cal. Rptr. 2d 688 (2003). The court noted that the People presented no authority showing the state has a "transcendent" or "compelling" interest in protecting adult victims of sex crimes from further psychological trauma from a face-to-face confrontation with the defendant in court. The court noted:

> In any event, the court in this case consented to the prosecution's request to use the one-way glass without holding an evidentiary hearing to determine whether, and to what degree, the testifying victim's apparent anxiety was due to the defendant's presence rather than, for instance, the witness's general emotional fragility or the trauma of testifying in court or revisiting a past experience the witness would rather not recall. Even assuming that, in an appropriate case, the court might allow a testifying adult victim, who would otherwise be traumatized, to use a one-way screen to avoid seeing a defendant without violating the right of confrontation, we do not think a court may do so without making the necessary factual findings based upon evidence. In other words, a court may not, as the court did in this case, dispense with complete face-to-face confrontation merely upon a prosecutor's unsworn representation that defendant's presence was part of a distraught adult witness's problem.

Id. at 1157–58, 132 Cal. Rprtr. 2d at 694.

procedure and do not engage in coaching with respect to issues of the case in which the witness is a complainant.[182] Further authority for court school and similar programs can be found in state statutes or court rules designed to accommodate child witnesses and minimize their trauma related to testifying.[183] Nonetheless, it is entirely appropriate to question witnesses concerning the utilization of a court school and the nature and extent of the witness's preparation.

§ 5.16   Use of dolls and drawings in direct examination.

An innovation used to assist complaining witnesses, particularly child witnesses, in sexual assault trials is the anatomical doll. Generally, the use of a demonstrative aid during the examination of a witness is at the trial judge's discretion. Nevertheless, many states have enacted legislation permitting the use of anatomical dolls to assist a witness in testifying. These devices are not without controversy, however. Some feel that the use of dolls with children is fraught with problems, with the primary objection being that they may be unduly suggestive. The use of anatomical dolls and the legal issues surrounding their use is discussed elsewhere in this book.[184]

§ 5.17   Closing the courtroom.

It is possible to assist a victim of sexual assault in testifying by closing the courtroom. Under federal law, the courtroom can be closed to certain individuals, such as those who do not have a direct interest in the case.[185] Closure of a courtroom is governed by state and federal statutes as well as court decisions, including the Supreme Court of the United States. In certain situations it is clearly permissible, but must generally be narrowly tailored to serve a specific need in a case. Findings of necessity should be set forth on the record. Closure of a courtroom during a sexual assault victim's testimony is discussed in detail in Chapter 2.[186]

§ 5.18   Advocate, friend, family member, or prosecutor sitting with victim or assisting with questions.

A recent innovation in assisting child victims in providing testimony is to have a support person, sometimes a family member, sit with or near the witness, and in some cases, hold a child's hand. An objection to this practice is that it bolsters the child's credibility. Another danger is that the support person might suggest answers or communicate nonverbally with the witness.

---

[182] People v. McNeill, 204 A.D.2d 975, 613 N.Y.S.2d 302, *appeal denied*, 84 N.Y.2d 829, 614 N.E.2d 170, 617 N.Y.S.2d 149 (1994).

[183] *Id.*

[184] *See* Chapters 10, 11, 14, and Appendix G.

[185] 18 U.S.C. § 3509(e).

[186] *See* § 2.3.

The Child Victims' and Child Witnesses' Rights Act makes specific provisions for a child witness (person who is under the age of 18) "to be accompanied by an adult attendant to provide emotional support to the child."[187] The court has discretion to allow the adult attendant to be "in close physical proximity to or in contact with the child while the child testifies" or to hold the child's hand or allow the child to sit on the adult attendant's lap throughout the course of the proceeding.[188] The adult attendant, however, may not provide a child witness with any answer "or otherwise prompt a child."[189] The use of an adult attendant under the federal statute has been upheld by at least one federal appeals court, which permitted a teacher and Brownie troop leader of three nine-year-old girls to serve as the attendant.[190]

Several states provide in some fashion for a family member or advocate to sit with or otherwise assist a child witness while testifying.[191] Some courts may require a showing of necessity before allowing a support person to assist the child witness.

One court has required a showing of a "compelling necessity" for a child to testify in the lap of a sexual abuse counselor where the record reflected that the child had previously testified unaided before the grand jury, and where there was no special showing made that the child was unable to testify without sitting on

---

[187] 18 U.S.C. § 3509(i).

[188] *Id.*

[189] *Id.*

[190] United States v. Grooms, 978 F.2d 425, 429 (8th Cir. 1992). (The defendant's contention that the attendant's presence prompted the girls' testimonies was unsupported, where the girls testified in open court and the record was void of anything to suggest that the attendant prompted them in any way. The court also noted that the failure to videotape the adult attendant, as required by statute, was not reversible error.).

[191] Ark. Code § 16-42-102; Cal. Penal Code § 868.5; Conn. Gen. Stat. § 54-86g(b)(2) ("[A]n adult who is known to the child and with whom the child feels comfortable shall be permitted to sit in close proximity to the child during the child's testimony, provided such person shall not obscure the child from the view of the defendant or the trier of fact."); Del. Code § 11-5134(b); Haw. Rev. Stat. § 621–28; Idaho Code § 19-3023; Mich. Stat. 27A.2163(a)(4) ("A witness who is called upon to testify shall be permitted to have a support person sit with, accompany, or be in close proximity to the witness during his or her testimony. A notice of intent to use a support person shall name the support person, identify the relationship the support person has with the witness, and shall give notice to all parties to the proceeding that the witness may request that the named support person sit with the witness when the witness is called upon to testify during any stage of the proceeding. The notice of intent to use a named support person shall be filed with the court and shall be served upon all parties to the proceeding. The court shall rule on any motion objecting to the use of a named support person prior to the date at which the witness desires to use the support person."); Minn. Stat. § 631.046 (requires a written notice if support person is a prosecution witness and "evidence that the person's attendance is both desired by the prosecuting witness for support and will be helpful to the prosecuting witness."); N.Y. Eeec. Law § 642-a(6); R.I. Gen. Laws § 12-28-9(2); Wash. Rev. Code § 7.69A.030(8) (allows an advocate to be present in court while the child testifies in order to provide emotional support to the child).

the counselor's lap. [192] A counselor sitting with a witness without a showing of necessity may be deemed to unfairly bolster a child's credibility and deny the defendant a fair trial. [193]

Other courts have not required a finding of necessity [194] and have shown a broad willingness to permit an adult family member or friend to sit near or with

---

[192] State v. Rulona, 71 Haw. 127, 130, 785 P.2d 615, 617 (1990).

[193] State v. Suka, 70 Haw. 472, 476, 777 P.2d 240, 242 (1989).

[194] People v. Lord, 30 Cal. App. 4th 1718, 36 Cal. Rptr. 2d 453 (1994), *review denied*, No. S039733, 1995 Cal. LEXIS 2203 (Mar. 30, 1995); People v. Adams, 19 Cal. App. 4th 412, 23 Cal. Rptr. 2d 512 (1993), *appeal denied*, 1994 Cal. LEXIS 78 (Jan. 12, 1994) (upholding constitutionality of Cal. Penal Code § 868.5, which permits a support person to accompany a child at the stand); State v. Gollaher, 905 S.W.2d 542, 547–48 (Mo. Ct. App. 1995) (declining to require such a threshold finding but noting no objection or request for such a finding was made by defendant at trial); People v. Oatman, 12 A.D.3d 790, 787 N.Y.S.2d 128, *appeal denied*, 4 N.Y.3d 747, 824 N.E.2d 60, 790 N.Y.S.2d 659 (2004) (finding no error in counselor sitting beside a court attendant, behind the victim and out of direct line of sight); State v. Alidani, 2000 SD 52, 609 N.W.2d 152 (2000). The court permitted a victim-witness assistant to accompany eight-year-old to stand, stating:

> Here, the court balanced the defendant's objections against the court's desire to make testifying "the least frightening situation" for the minor victim. In overruling Alidani's objection that Ms. Scott's presence would appear to be a "stamp of approval" by the State on the victim's testimony, the trial court reminded Alidani that the jury understands the State endorses its witnesses; otherwise it would not have brought the charges and called these witnesses. The trial court ruled Alidani's reasons were not sufficient to overcome the court's desire to make the victim's courtroom experience less frightening.
>
> In the present case, the record reveals (and Alidani admits), that victim testified in a straightforward manner; neither exhibiting fear of the court proceedings nor of him. Alidani argues this shows the accompanying third party was not required and only served to bolster the victim's testimony with the jury. However, it may also show that the trial court was successful in making the courtroom as comfortable an environment as possible for the minor victim so that she could testify freely. Moreover, there is no evidence in the record of any influence on victim's testimony attributable to Ms. Scott's presence. Alidani does not claim any hesitation by victim or glances at Ms. Scott for confirmation during her testimony. It appears from this record that Ms. Scott acted properly in solely being present in the courtroom as support for the victim and did not act or speak in a suggestive manner in any way. [citation omitted]

Id. at P18–19; 609 N.W.2d at 157–58; People v. Adams, 19 Cal. App. 4th 412, 23 Cal. Rptr.2d 512 (1993), *review denied*, 1994 Cal. LEXIS 178 (1994) (The court noted):

> The presence of a support person at the stand does not necessarily rob an accused of dignity or brand him or her with an unmistakable mark of guilt. The presence of a second person at the stand does not require the jury to infer that the support person believes and endorses the witness's testimony, so it does not *necessarily* bolster the witness's testimony. Finally, the presence of a support person does not interfere with the decorum of the judicial proceedings. Consequently, in the absence of an articulable deleterious effect on the presumption of innocence, we must reject the contention that use of a support person at the stand deprives the defendant of a fair trial.

Id. at 437, 23 Cal. Rptr. at 526.); Hall v. State, 634 N.E.2d 837 (Ind. Ct. App. 1994); Commonwealth v. Amirault, 404 Mass. 221, 535 N.E.2d 193 (1989); People v. Hyland, 212 Mich. App. 701, 708–09,

a child witness,[195] or hold a child's hand while testifying,[196] or for a counselor to comfort a deaf witness who was confused by the proceedings.[197]

Sometimes just having a parent or family member in the courtroom will help a child and permit the child to testify more easily. If this person is a prospective witness, a court's sequestration order does not necessarily preclude him or her from sitting in the courtroom during the child's testimony.[198] There is also authority that the person sitting with the complainant should be excluded from the courtroom so as not to hear the complainant's testimony.[199] Sequestration is a matter of a trial court's discretion.[200] Such discretion does have limits. For

538 N.W.2d 465, 468–69 (1995) (upholding trial court's decision to allow eight-year-old's aunt to sit as support person in jury box as if child were testifying to her — decision based in part on defendant's failure to object to the procedure); State v. Brockman, 184 Neb. 435, 168 N.W.2d 367 (1969); State v. Reeves, 337 N.C. 700, 727, 448 S.E.2d 802, 814 (1994) (permitting a five-year-old to sit in stepmother's lap while testifying); Commonwealth v. Pankraz, 382 Pa. Super. 116, 554 A.2d 974, *appeal denied*, 522 Pa. 618, 563 A.2d 887 (1989) (four-year-old permitted to sit on grandmother's lap while testifying); State v. Keeley, 8 Utah 2d 70, 328 P.2d 724 (1958); State v. Jones, 178 W. Va. 519, 362 S.E.2d 330 (1987).

195 Baxter v. State, 522 N.E.2d 362 (Ind. 1988); State v. Gollaher, 905 S.W.2d 542, 546–47 (Mo. Ct. App. 1995) (allowing complainant's eight-year-old sister, who witnessed abuse, to testify while her grandfather held her hand); Soap v. State, 562 P.2d 889 (Okla. Crim. App. 1977).

196 *Baxter*, 522 N.E.2d 362; Soap v. State, 562 P.2d 889 (Okla. Crim. App. 1977).

197 Commonwealth v. Meadows, 381 Pa. Super. 354, 365, 553 A.2d 1006, 1012, *appeal denied*, 524 Pa. 618, 571 A.2d 381 (1989) (holding that a rape crisis counselor could comfort a deaf rape victim while she was on the stand after the judge and attorneys left courtroom for a conference, and the witness "was confused and concerned by the sudden departure of the attorneys and [judge] and was looking to the people with whom she was familiar for some advice").

198 State v. McGraw, 137 N.C. App. 726, 529 S.E.2d 493 (2000), *review denied*, 352 N.C. 360 (2000) (holding no violation of sequestration order in child complainant's looking at her mother while testifying); Commonwealth v. Berry, 355 Pa. Super. 243, 513 A.2d 410 (1986):

> A sequestration order is designed to preclude prospective witnesses from conforming their testimony to that of witnesses preceding them; witnesses shall attest entirely to their own observations and perceptions [citation omitted]. Where, however, there is minimal risk that subsequent witnesses will merely echo preceding witnesses, the court may allow those witnesses to remain, with good cause, despite a sequestration order. [citation omitted] The victim's mother, Mary Jo Berry, testified as to her children's relationship with appellant and the altercation her other daughter had with him which prompted the victim to report the rapes. She corroborated the victim's testimony on collateral issues, but she could not testify concerning the actual crimes as she was not home. Therefore, the mother's testimony was unlikely to echo that of her daughter, for in the main, they testified about different topics and events. Furthermore, Mary Jo could provide more support for her daughter than the counselors could. The victim and her mother had a relationship of mutual respect and love, presumably greater than the victim had with the counselors. For these reasons, we find no error in not sequestering the victim's mother.

Id. at 253–54, 513 A.2d at 415.

199 Clark v. State, 323 Ark. 211, 216, 913 S.W.2d 297, 299–300 (1996) (holding breach of preclusion order was harmless in this case).

200 Yorke v. Commonwealth, 212 Va. 776, 188 S.E.2d 77 (1972) (noting that the better practice is for the trial court to grant a motion for sequestration).

example, refusing to allow the defendant to present a key witness who was in the courtroom during part of the testimony of a prosecution witness should not be precluded from testifying when there is an insufficient basis to conclude the defendant was at fault for violation of the sequestration order. Preclusion of a defense witness may violate the defendant's constitutional right to call a witness. [201] Some states have special statutory provisions which permit a victim or a member of the victim's immediate family to be present during the trial as part of recent legislative efforts to enhance the rights of crime victims. [202]

There is some authority that a child's mother can repeat the child's answers, which the child whispered in the mother's ear, where the child was reluctant to speak aloud in front of others in the courtroom. [203] The mother had the same authority as an interpreter. This procedure was held not to violate the defendant's right of confrontation given the judge's finding of necessity by the judge. [204] On the other hand, a prosecutor's relinquishing of the questioning of a four-year-old to the child's therapist went beyond having a support person in the courtroom and was reversible error, since actual questioning must be done by members of the bar. [205] Nevertheless, Wisconsin permits as part of its videotape deposition procedure for children, a "questioner to have an adviser to assist the questioner, and upon permission of the judge, to conduct the questioning." [206]

While having a victim advocate, counselor, friend, or family member sitting with a witness during testimony is likely to generate an objection and may result in appellate scrutiny of the procedure, a prosecutor sitting with a witness is more likely to be scrutinized. One court has held that it is "generally improper for the prosecutor to sit with a witness during her testimony"; if the witness needs assistance because of "age, timidity or frailty," it should be rendered by someone other than the prosecuting attorney. [207]

---

[201] People v. Melendez, 80 P.3d 883 (Colo. 2003), *aff'd*, 102 P.3d 315 (2004) (reversing defendant's sexual assault conviction because "it was an abuse of discretion to impose the extreme sanction of witness exclusion without an inquiry into the factors governing the imposition of such a sanction, and, in particular, without evidence that the defense was at fault for the violation").

[202] *See, e.g.*, Cal. Penal Code § 1102.6; N.C. General Statute § 15A-1225 (upon motion of a party, the judge may order all or some of the witnesses, other than the defendant, to remain outside the courtroom until called to testify, except that when a minor child is called as a witness, the parent or guardian may be present while the child is testifying, even though his parent or guardian is to be called subsequently).

[203] United States v. Romey, 32 M.J. 180, 183, *cert. denied*, 502 U.S. 924 (1991) (suggesting that a more neutral party should have been used for this procedure).

[204] *Id.* at 182–83.

[205] State v. Warford, 389 N.W.2d 575, 582 (Neb. 1986).

[206] Wis. Stat. § 967.04(b)(6).

[207] Sexton v. Howard, 55 F.3d 1557 (11th Cir. 1995), *cert. denied*, 516 U.S. 1124 (1996); Sexton v. State, 529 So. 2d 1041, 1044 (Ala. Crim. App. 1988) (While not condoning the prosecutor's actions in this case and cautioning prosecutors to refrain from similar conduct in the future, the reviewing court declined to reverse the defendant's conviction under the circumstances.).

Any person sitting with a child should be instructed not to prompt or lead the child in providing responses to questions. A defendant's conviction was reversed when a friend of the victim's family made signals and gestures to the child witness, including mouthing "You're doing fine" and making "approving gestures by winking and a thumbs-up sign."[208] The court held that such approval and comfort at a time when the child's credibility was being assessed may have unfairly strengthened her ability to withstand cross-examination.[209] There are also limits as to the age at which a witness is eligible to receive assistance from a support person.[210] The jury should be instructed to draw no inferences from the person's presence.

§ 5.19   Recess, break, or time limits on questioning to assist sexual assault victims.

Courts have the discretion to allow a recess to be taken to allow a complainant to regain composure. During this recess, courts have allowed the witness to consult with the prosecuting attorney. Typical of most appellate courts' view on such a practice is the following:

> The record reflects that the victim became emotionally upset when testifying about the crimes committed against her. The circumstances under which the recess was taken do not appear to have promoted an opportunity for the state to coach the victim's testimony. Rather it is clear from the record that the purpose of the recess was to allow the victim to regain her composure. The trial court was well within its discretion to allow communications between the State and the victim if it determines such communications would help console the victim. Furthermore, defense counsel had the opportunity on cross-examination to explore any unfair coaching he suspected took place during the brief recess.[211]

Young children are usually granted recesses.[212] By statute, California gives

---

[208] Sharp v. Commonwealth, 849 S.W.2d 542, 546–47 (Ky. 1993).

[209] *Id.* at 547 ("It would be impossible to say that the witness did not derive confidence and assurance from this positive reinforcement which influenced the jury to believe her.").

[210] State v. Alexander, 875 S.W.2d 924 (Mo. Ct. App. 1994) (suggesting, but not holding, that a child sitting on a great-aunt's lap would not be appropriate upon retrial when the child will be 11 years old).

[211] Frierson v. State, 543 N.E.2d 669, 673 (Ind. Ct. App. 1989). *See also* State v. Delarosa-Flores, 59 Wash. App. 514, 517, 799 P.2d 736, 738, *appeal denied*, 116 Wash. 2d 1010, 805 P.2d 814 (1990) (permitting a 67-year-old rape victim to confer with the prosecutor after becoming anxious over an answer on direct examination that contradicted her pretrial statements, and holding that if any improper coaching by the prosecutor occurred, the appropriate remedy was "skillful cross-examination").

[212] People v. Nayyar, 3 A.D.3d 387, 772 N.Y.S.2d 1, *appeal denied*, 2 N.Y.3d 764, 811 N.E.2d 44, 778 N.Y.S.2d 782 (2004) ("The court properly exercised its discretion in permitting the prosecutor and the five-year-old victim's foster mother to have a private conversation with the victim in the middle of her testimony [citation omitted]. This conference was for the sole purpose

the trial court the power to provide recesses to a child witness.[213] A court in its inherent power to control the examination of witnesses may limit, in appropriate circumstances, the length of examination of a witness. It may also be a power granted by statute. Iowa, upon motion of a party or upon the court's motion, permits the court testimony of a child "to be limited in duration in accordance with the developmental maturity of the child" and limits the child's "uninterrupted testimony to one hour" before allowing the child a recess.[214]

It is permissible for a prosecutor and a witness to meet privately during a recess or between direct and cross-examination, as long as the defense, the court, and the jury are informed of the meeting and its circumstances, and defense counsel has adequate opportunity to question the witness about any discussions or the nature of the contact during the recess.[215]

§ 5.20   Use of teddy bear or other prop by witness.

Part of accommodating a child witness can be improving the child's comfort level. One way to achieve this is to allow the child to hold a teddy bear or doll for comfort. Several courts have upheld this procedure, usually finding a necessity for the procedure in that it assists the child in testifying by calming the child and thereby producing more coherent testimony.[216] These decisions find these benefits outweigh any potential prejudice to the defendant.

of comforting the child and it could not have caused any prejudice to defendant." *Id.* at 388; 772 N.Y.S.2d at 1–2); State v. Higginbottom, 312 N.C. 760, 769–70, 324 S.E.2d 834, 841 (1985); State v. Hewett, 93 N.C. App. 1, 14, 376 S.E.2d 467, 475 (1989) (nine-year-old victim permitted to interrupt testimony and leave courtroom to regain composure accompanied by rape crisis counselor and prosecuting attorney); State v. Lewis, 1995 Tenn. Crim. App. LEXIS 33 (Jan. 12, 1995) (holding that trial court had the authority to grant a recess during testimony of child complainant under the court's authority to supervise the testimony of the witness, and noting that the defendant did not establish any improper influence upon the child during the recess); Will v. Commonwealth, 31 Va. App. 571, 525 S.E.2d 37 (2000) (Trial judge granted recess after child had difficulty testifying and being heard, stating: "We hold that the decision to grant a recess and allow a conference between a lawyer and a testifying witness, while narrow in scope, falls within the broad discretion of a trial court and will not be reversed absent an abuse of discretion."). *See also* United States v. Castro-Romero, 964 F.2d 942 (9th Cir. 1992).

[213] Cal. Penal Code § 868.8.

[214] Iowa Code § 910A.14(4). The statute also permits expert testimony to be received to determine the appropriate limit on a child's testimony. For an example of a court using its inherent power to limit the length of the cross-examination of a witness, *see* People v. Broom, 200 A.D.2d 515, 606 N.Y.S.2d 687 (1994) (holding in a robbery case that trial judge properly exercised its discretion in placing a half-hour time limit on further cross-examination when the complainant's 20-minute direct examination was followed by 3½ hours of repetitive cross-examination over two days).

[215] United States v. De Jongh, 937 F.2d 1 (1st Cir. 1991).

[216] State v. McPhee, 58 Conn. App. 501, 755 A.2d 893, *appeal denied*, 254 Conn. 920, 759 A.2d 1026 (2000) (permitting 12-year-old to hold stuffed gorilla which she brought with her to court); State v. Cliff, 116 Idaho 921, 921–24, 782 P.2d 44, 44–47 (1989); State v. Marquez, 124

Part of the authority for a trial court's permitting a child to hold a doll is the trial court's traditional discretion and control over the manner of interrogating witnesses.[217] The Federal Rules of Evidence also give a court broad discretion in controlling the mode and order of interrogating witnesses. Authority may also be found in statutes seeking to assist child witnesses. For example, a court may properly permit a child to hold a teddy bear while testifying under a state statute governing fair treatment of child victims as witnesses, which states that a trial judge "should be sensitive to the psychological and emotional stress a child witness may undergo when testifying."[218] If the record demonstrates no basis or necessity for the use of a teddy bear or doll, there may be appellate issues.

One court found that a child's holding of a teddy bear while testifying was error where the record did not show any "compelling necessity" for the procedure.[219] In this case the defense attorney had argued that the teddy bear was a "blatant prosecutorial ploy to make the child even more appealing and attractive than she already is."[220] There is some authority that a prosecutor's giving a child

---

N.M. 409, 951 P.2d 1070 (1997), *cert. denied*, 124 N.M. 311, 950 P.2d 284 (1998); People v. Gutkaiss, 206 A.D.2d 628, 614 N.Y.S.2d 599, *appeal denied*, 84 N.Y.2d 936, 645 N.E.2d 1233, 621 N.Y.S.2d 533 (1994); State v. Presley, 2003 Ohio 6069, 2003 Ohio App. LEXIS 5401 (Nov. 13, 2003):

> A review of the record reveals that the trial court's decision to permit Josie to hold a stuffed teddy bear during cross-examination neither diminished defendant's constitutional right to confront his accuser nor prejudiced his right to a fair trial. Although Josie was 13 years old at the time of trial, she was described as being 'mildly developmentally delayed.' The court's control over the mode of interrogation appeared to have struck a balance between ascertaining the truth and protecting Josie from undue embarrassment. Defendant makes much of the fact that Josie did not hold the teddy bear while she testified on direct examination. However, it is understandable that Josie might feel more embarrassed and vulnerable answering questions posed by defense counsel with whom she was unfamiliar than she would be in answering questions posed by the prosecutor whom she had already met . . . . Furthermore, allowing Josie to hold a stuffed teddy bear while she testified did not deny defendant his right to a face-to-face confrontation with his accuser. The record indicates that defendant was given a full and fair opportunity to explore and expose any infirmities in Josie's testimony through cross-examination.

Id. at *P45. Sperling v. State, 924 S.W.2d 722 (Tex. Ct. App. 1996) (child's holding of teddy bear during testimony not unduly prejudicial).

217 *Marquez, supra* note 216, 124 N.M. at 411, 951 P.2d at 1072.

218 *Gutkaiss, supra* note 216, 206 A.D.2d at 631, 614 N.Y.S.2d at 602 (Appellate Court held that child's holding of a teddy bear while testifying was not prejudicial to defendant when the trial judge informed the jury that the teddy bear had nothing to do with the truth or falsity of the child's testimony and cited N.Y. Exec. Law § 642-a(4)).

219 State v. Palabay, 9 Haw. App. 414, 423, 844 P.2d 1, 7 (1992), *appeal denied*, 74 Haw. 652, 849 P.2d 81 (1993).

220 *Id.* at 421, 844 P.2d at 5. *See also* State v. Gevrez, 61 Ariz. 296, 148 P.2d 829 (1944) (noting that the defendant in a murder case was denied a fair trial when a young child called by the prosecution took the stand carrying a doll, which the defense claimed had been pre-arranged by the prosecution to arouse the sympathy of the jury).

witness a doll to hold while testifying might impact the child's suggestibility and is improper.[221]

§ 5.21   Use of interpreter or speech therapist.

Sometimes a complainant will have difficulty communicating because of a language problem, a developmental disability, a speech impairment, or some other communication disorder. Florida, by statute, permits use of a translator or interpreter to assist any person, "such as a child or a person who is mentally or developmentally disabled, who cannot be reasonably understood, or who cannot understand questioning without the aid of an interpreter."[222] There is little law on who is qualified to be an interpreter for a person with communication disorders. An interpreter should not be allowed for any individual unless a showing of necessity is made.

Because there are no standards governing the qualifications of interpreters and translators, there is a wide variation in the skills and abilities of those who provide these services. An acquaintance of the victim may serve as an interpreter as long as the translation is accurate and there is no prejudice to the defendant.[223] A victim's grandson may translate, particularly if the witness speaks an unusual dialect.[224] In a case involving a 33-year-old adult male sodomy victim with a mental age of a six-year-old child who had suffered polio when he was six years old, which had paralyzed his throat and palette and severely impaired his speech, the victim's father was allowed to interpret for him.[225] While familiarity with the witness and the witness's impairment may assist an interpreter, a disinterested interpreter helps avoid a claim of prejudice.[226] Using a victim's mother as an interpreter can be improper where the trial judge does not determine if a less interested interpreter is available, particularly when the victim's mother is a primary witness in the proceeding.[227] At least one court has noted an advantage in using a professional speech therapist instead of a victim's sister to provide interpreter services at a criminal trial.[228]

---

[221] State v. Aponte, 249 Conn. 735, 738 A.2d 117 (1999); cf. State v. McPhee, 58 Conn. App. 501, 755 A.2d 893, appeal denied, 254 Conn. 920, 759 A.2d 1026 (2000) (upholding child's use of a stuffed animal which she brought with her to court).

[222] Fla. Stat. § 90.606(1)(b).

[223] Commonwealth v. Riley, 354 Pa. Super. 422, 512 A.2d 22 (1986).

[224] State v. Heck Van Tran, 864 S.W.2d 465 (Tenn. 1993), cert. denied, 511 U.S. 1046 (1994).

[225] Fairbanks v. Cowan, 551 F.2d 97 (6th Cir. 1977).

[226] State v. McLellan, 56 N.C. App. 101, 286 S.E.2d 873 (1982) (court held that the trial judge in a robbery case did not improperly permit the victim's sister to interpret for him, since there was no showing of any specific prejudice, but it noted that a disinterested interpreter might be better in certain situations).

[227] In re R.R., 79 N.J. 97, 398 A.2d 76 (1979).

[228] People v. Thompson, 34 A.D.2d 561, 309 N.Y.S.2d 861 (1970), aff'd, 28 N.Y.2d 616, 268 N.E.2d 804, 320 N.Y.S.2d 77 (1971).

The interpreter should translate and not interpret a witness's response. For example, a court may not rely on an "interpretation" of a complainant with a physical disability (Huntington's Chorea Disease) in determining competency.[229]

§ 5.22   Facilitated communication.

More controversial than traditional speech therapist services or sign language interpretation is "facilitated communication." Facilitated communication professes to allow individuals who cannot speak or use sign language to communicate through the use of a device with a keyboard and a "facilitator," a person who supports the arm, wrist, and hand of the disabled individual, who, with such assistance, points to or touches pictures, words, or letters. Facilitated communication is used with individuals who have disabilities such as Down's syndrome and autism. The main criticism of facilitated communication is that the facilitator influences the witness's answers. Cases of sexual abuse have been reported by individuals using facilitated communication.

One article in the medical journal *Pediatrics*[230] reviewed the controlled studies of facilitated communication and concluded:

> The optimistic side of FC, that nonspeaking children could miraculously become competent communicators, is unfortunately a myth. The dark side of the phenomenon of FC includes false hope, false communication, family disruption, losses of job and reputation, and inappropriate use of scarce resources. Unwitting pediatricians have accepted transcripts of FC that described sexual abuse by family members. The result was removal of the child from the family and prosecution of the alleged perpetrator even though the evidence suggested that the communication came from the facilitator and not from the child.[231]

Much case law on scientific reliability or admissibility of facilitated communication arises from sexual abuse cases in the family court setting. One issue is

---

[229] State v. Dunning, 2000 Ohio App. LEXIS 5774 (Dec. 11, 2000), *dismissed, discretionary appeal not allowed*, 91 Ohio St. 3d 1508, 746 N.E.2d 611 (2001):

> At the competency hearing, the trial court relied upon the "interpretation" of Loretta's answers by Caudill, or Caudill's answers themselves, in making its judgment that Loretta was competent to testify. This was error. It is the witness's answers and demeanor that should be considered, not those of an interpreter. This is not a case where the witness spoke a foreign language which would make an interpreter an essential participant in the proceedings. That Loretta could only communicate with the aid of someone else "interpreting" her response, or occasional lack of response, should have been an indication of Loretta's incompetence to testify. In fact, at the competency hearing, Loretta was incorrect as to with whom she lives and the proceedings for which she was present. She confused her children and siblings. Many of her answers were given after prompting or "clarification" from Caudill.

Id. at *19–26.

[230] Sharon V. Hostler, *Facilitated Communication*, 97 Pediatrics 584 (1996).

[231] *Id.* at 585.

whether the *Frye* test or some other threshold of scientific reliability is required for the use of facilitated communication. One court has held that the *Frye* test is not the standard for this procedure, that the facilitator is qualified and reliable "since the ability of an interpreter, translator, 'signer' or anyone else who transmits the testimony of a witness is not based on a scientific theory."[232] Other courts have taken a much more critical view of facilitated communication and the possibility that the facilitator may influence the testimony of the witness. These courts have taken a position that facilitated communication is not accepted as a reliable method of communication by the relevant scientific community.[233]

Kansas' Supreme Court is the highest level appellate court to consider the use of facilitated communication in a criminal trial. In *State v. Warden*[234] the defendant, who worked at a facility for the developmentally disabled, provided residential care, taught independent living skills, recreational skills, and behavior management for a 12-year-old diagnosed with autism and severe or profound mental retardation, was charged with allegedly sexually abusing the 12-year-old. The decision discusses the studies that conclude that the technique of facilitated communication has not been validated, but holds that the use of facilitated communication does not fall within the realm of *Frye* as scientific testimony, although the decision notes *Frye* does apply to testimony involving a psychiatric diagnosis such as rape trauma syndrome.[235] As a method of communication, general acceptance of facilitated communication need not be established in the court's view.[236] It did, however, develop requirements for the future use of facilitated communication, including an oath by the facilitator that he or she will repeat the witness's responses in spoken English to the best of his or her skill and judgment, and an oath not to influence the witness's responses while assisting the witness in typing.[237] When possible, the witness should be allowed to sign "yes" and "no," use drawings, or otherwise provide independent responses without involvement of the facilitator.[238] It was also noted that the validity of

---

[232] *In re* Luz P., 189 A.D.2d 274, 595 N.Y.S.2d 541 (1993) (proceeding in family court involving allegations of sexual abuse of an 11-year-old autistic and mentally retarded girl by her parents).

[233] *In re* Department of Soc. Servs. *ex rel.* Jenny S. v. Mark S., 156 Misc. 2d 393, 593 N.Y.S.2d 142 (Fam. Ct. 1992); *In re* M.Z., 155 Misc. 2d 564, 578, 590 N.Y.S.2d 390 (Fam. Ct. 1992) ("[T]aking the record to date as a whole, the court concludes that petitioner has not made a prima facie case as to the admissibility of testimony based on facilitated communication with the child diagnosed as having Down's syndrome. The experts presented by petitioner did not present any coherent theory as to the underlying principle. They did indicate that the technique itself is subject to manipulation, and produces variable results with different children and different facilitators; that there is no established procedure for training, monitoring or evaluating practitioners; and that they were not aware of any empirical studies relating to the technique or to its results." 155 Misc. 2d at 578, 590 N.Y.S.2d at 398).

[234] 257 Kan. 94, 891 P.2d 1074 (Kan. 1995).

[235] *Id.* at 108–09, 891 P.2d at 1085.

[236] *Id.* at 113, 891 P.2d at 1088.

[237] *Id.* at 117, 891 P.2d at 1090.

[238] *Id.* at 122, 891 P.2d at 1093.

facilitated communication for a witness should be established by the trial judge on a case by case basis.[239] Other procedural requirements implemented by the Kansas court are as follows:

> The facilitator should listen to "noise" or music through headphones while the witness is being questioned. Fact-specific questions should be asked to insure the answers are not subject to facilitator influence or cuing. Tests should be conducted sufficient to convince the trial judge that the witness can communicate and is free of any influence of the facilitator. Moreover, the trial court may also consider other evidence bearing on the validity of the witness's ability to communicate through facilitation, including evidence of any research which has been conducted as to the validity of the witness's facilitation. If the trial court is satisfied that the witness's ability to communicate through facilitation is validated, the court may permit the witness to testify. This is a matter for the discretion of the trial judge.[240]

Significantly, the American Psychological Association (APA) in its Resolution on Facilitated Communication noted that "use of facilitated communication in otherwise unsubstantiated allegations of abuse has led to psychological distress, alienation, or financial hardship of family members and caregivers" and concluded:

> Studies have repeatedly demonstrated that facilitated communication is not a scientifically valid technique for individuals with autism or mental retardation. In particular, information obtained via facilitated communication should not be used to confirm or deny allegations of abuse or to make diagnostic or treatment decisions.

> THEREFORE, BE IT RESOLVED that APA adopts the position that facilitated communication is a controversial and unproved communicative procedure with no scientifically demonstrated support for its efficacy.[241]

§ 5.23   Closed-circuit TV testimony — Constitutionality.

Another innovation used to assist children in providing testimony in sexual assault cases is closed-circuit television. This permits a child to testify in a room outside the presence of the defendant or vice versa. The defendant and complainant can see each other on television monitors. Most statutes that provide for closed-circuit television testimony exclude the defendant from the room where the complainant is testifying, and in those states that permit the defendant to remain in the room, there is a provision allowing the judge to exclude the defendant. The Supreme Court of the United States, in *Maryland v. Craig*,[242]

---

[239] *Id.* at 123, 891 P.2d at 103.

[240] *Id.*

[241] American Psychological Association, *Resolution on Facilitated Communication*, Aug. 14, 1994.

[242] 497 U.S. 836(1990).

upheld the constitutionality of closed-circuit television testimony by children in sexual assault cases, but only when the trial court makes a finding of necessity in that particular case. The Supreme Court held that "the state interest in protecting child witnesses from the trauma of testifying in a child abuse case is sufficiently important to justify the use of a special procedure that permits a child witness in such cases to testify at trial against a defendant in the absence of face-to-face confrontation with the defendant."[243] The Court noted that the right of confrontation under the Sixth Amendment does not contain an absolute right to confront witnesses physically, an observation made in several decisions admitting the hearsay testimony of child witnesses who do not testify.[244] The crux of the Supreme Court's decision is that there be a case-specific determination that a specialized procedure such as closed-circuit television is necessary for the best interest of the child. The need to testify by closed-circuit TV should be to protect the welfare of a particular child because the child will be traumatized, not just because the child must appear in court, and there needs to be a showing that testifying before the defendant will result in significant emotional trauma, which must be more than "mere nervousness or excitement or some reluctance to testify."[245] The child's distress from testifying in open court before the defendant must be more than *de minimis*. Closed-circuit TV is not justified by the general trauma experienced in retelling events or by the intimidating atmosphere in a courtroom.[246]

Most state courts that have reviewed the constitutionality of closed-circuit television statutes have upheld their constitutionality.[247] However, the highest courts of Illinois, Massachusetts, and Pennsylvania have interpreted their own state constitutions to require a face-to-face confrontation of the defendant and witness, and have held that the use of closed-circuit television violates this right.[248] Some of the state courts that have upheld the constitutionality of their

---

[243] *Id.* at 855.

[244] *Id.* at 849.

[245] *Id.* at 855–56 [citations omitted].

[246] *Craig*, 497 U.S. at 856.

[247] Reutter v. State, 886 P.2d 1298 (Alaska Ct. App. 1994), *cert. denied*, 522 U.S. 851 (1997) (in upholding constitutionality of Alaska's closed-circuit TV provision, court noted that despite the fact that the statute did not explicitly address certain *Craig* requirements concerning the child witness's emotional distress caused by testifying in the presence of the defendant, such a requirement would be deemed an implicit part of the statutory provision and would be in keeping with the traditional preference for interpreting statutes in a manner that avoids constitutional problems); State v. Vess, 157 Ariz. 236, 756 P.2d 333 (1988); People v. Van Brocklin, 293 Ill. App. 3d 156, 687 N.E.2d 1119 (1997), *appeal denied*, 178 Ill.2d 594, 669 N.E.2d 1037 (1998); Brady v. State, 575 N.E.2d 981 (Ind. 1991); State v. Chisholm, 245 Kan. 145, 777 P.2d 753 (1989); Commonwealth v. Willis, 716 S.W.2d 224 (Ky. 1986); State v. Schaal, 806 S.W.2d 659 (Mo. 1991); State v. Crandall, 120 N.J. 649, 577 A.2d 483 (1990); People v. Cintron, 75 N.Y.2d 249, 551 N.E.2d 561, 552 N.Y.S.2d 68 (1990); State v. Self, 56 Ohio St. 3d 73, 564 N.E.2d 446 (1990); State v. Foster, 135 Wash. 2d 441, 957 P.2d 712 (1998).

[248] People v. Fitzpatrick, 158 Ill. 2d 360, 633 N.E.2d 685 (1994) ("Unlike it's Federal counter-

state's closed-circuit television provisions have not addressed the face-to-face constitutional issue.

The constitutionality of statutes permitting closed-circuit television testimony must be reviewed in light of the requirements of *Craig*. This can be seen in the federal statute providing for closed-circuit television testimony. The federal statute requires the prosecution, the child's attorney, or a guardian *ad litem* to apply for two-way, closed-circuit television testimony at least five days before trial unless there is a finding on the record that the need for such an order was not reasonably foreseeable.[249] According to the statute, the court may order that the testimony be provided via closed-circuit television for the following reasons:

(i)   The child is unable to testify because of fear

(ii) There is a substantial likelihood, established by expert testimony, that the child would suffer emotional trauma from testifying

(iii) The child suffers a mental or other infirmity

(iv) Conduct by defendant or defense counsel causes the child to be unable to continue testifying.[250]

The issue has been raised that the federal statute's requirements may be less than those set forth in *Craig*, in that the statute would permit closed-circuit testimony upon a showing of a general fear of the courtroom rather than fear caused by the presence of the defendant in a particular case, which would justify taking the child's testimony in another less threatening location, yet in the defendant's presence.[251]

§ 5.24   Application of closed-circuit TV — Legal and practical issues.

Using closed-circuit television presents practical and legal considerations for both the prosecution and the defense. First, using closed-circuit television requires substantial equipment and space that may not be readily available. The equipment and transmission should be of good quality so that the witness's testimony can be adequately seen and heard by all those involved.

---

part, however, Article I, Sect. 8, of the Illinois constitution clearly, emphatically and unambiguously requires a 'face-to-face' confrontation. Based upon this distinction, the United States Supreme Court's reasoning in *Craig* should not be applied to the instant case." *Id.* at 367, 633 N.E.2d at 688); Commonwealth v. Bergstrom, 402 Mass. 534, 524 N.E.2d 366, 371 (1988); Commonwealth v. Louden, 536 Pa. 180, 638 A.2d 953 (1994); Commonwealth v. Ludwig, 527 Pa. 472, 594 A.2d 281 (1991) (Pennsylvania's highest court has found the amendments made to its provisions for videotaped depositions and closed-circuit television testimony to still be in violation of the Pennsylvania constitution).

[249] 18 U.S.C. § 3509(b)(1)(A).

[250] *Id.* at § 3509(b)(1)(B).

[251] United States v. Carrier, 9 F.3d 867, 870 (10th Cir. 1993), *cert. denied*, 511 U.S. 1044 (1994) (declining to decide whether 18 U.S.C. § 3509(b)(1)(B) falls short of the constitutional requirements of *Craig*, since the district court's finding in this case satisfied the *Craig* requirements).

Monitors must be placed to insure the witness and defendant and jurors have an adequate view. Given the multiple participants in a criminal trial, a truth-inducing two-way system can be difficult to establish. Testimony that cannot be clearly seen or heard is of little value to the prosecution, and from the defendant's perspective, if the transmission is inadequate, it may violate the defendant's constitutional rights. [252]

One federal appeals court finds that the confrontation afforded by a two-way closed circuit television system does not satisfy the Confrontation Clause because of crucial differences in the electronic confrontation, which results in a virtual rather than face-to-face confrontation, which does not produce the same "truth-inducing" process. [253]

Second, the prosecution must decide whether the testimony of the child witness will be less effective via closed-circuit television testimony. The demeanor of a witness testifying on television is generally not the same as when the witness testifies in court.

It is important that specific findings of vulnerability be clearly established to justify the use of closed-circuit television procedures. These findings should establish that the child involved will suffer trauma as a result of testifying in the presence of the defendant. [254] One court expresses this requirement that the

---

[252] People v. Henderson, 156 A.D.2d 92, 101–02, 554 N.Y.S.2d 924, 927, *appeal denied*, 76 N.Y.2d 736, 557 N.E.2d 1194, 558 N.Y.S.2d 898 (1990) (holding that defendant's right of confrontation was violated through use of two-way closed-circuit television partially as a result of the poor quality of the equipment).

[253] United States v. Bordeaux, 400 F.3d 548, 554–55 (8th Cir. 2005).

> Given the ubiquity of television, even children are keenly aware that a television image of a person (including a defendant in the case of a two-way system) is not the person — something is lost in the translation. Thus, a defendant watching a witness through a monitor will not have the same truth-inducing effect as an unmediated gaze across the courtroom.

Id. at 554.

[254] United States v. Weekley, 130 F.3d 747 (6th Cir. 1997) ("The district court, after hearing expert testimony and talking with Adan *in camera*, concluded that Adan would be unable to testify in open court due to Weekley's presence. The record supports the district court's decision. Dr. DeYoung testified that Adan was fearful of Weekley and that he would be traumatized if he was required to testify in open court in Weekley's presence. Dr. DeYoung's opinion was made based on her meeting with Adan and his father, her familiarity with research studies in the area, and her years of experience as a clinical consultant to child sexual abuse treatment programs. The district court, after meeting with Adan *in camera*, agreed with Dr. De Young." *Id.* at 753); United States v. Carrier, 9 F.3d 867 (10th Cir. 1993), *cert. denied*, 511 U.S. 1044 (1994); United States v. Farley, 992 F.2d 1122 (10th Cir. 1993); State v. Jarzbek, 210 Conn. 396, 554 A.2d 1094 (1989); Hopkins v. State, 632 So. 2d 1372, 1376 (Fla. 1994) (holding that a trial court should cite the facts supporting its ruling); State v. Smith, 158 N.J. 376, 730 A.2d 311 (1999) (New Jersey Supreme Court found the child in this case was properly permitted to testify by closed-circuit television given her fear of the defendant and the courtroom and that the child's video-taped statement to the police made several days after the crime was sufficiently reliable to be admissible); People v. Guce, 164 A.D.2d

fear of the defendant should be the dominant reason why the child can not testify in open court.[255] For example, testimony that a child began to wet and soil his pants and engage in other behaviors in response to the possibility of testifying before the defendant is concrete evidence that a child witness is vulnerable to testifying before the defendant.[256] The child's parents or child advocate may help establish the child's fear of facing the defendant in the courtroom and the substantial likelihood that the child will suffer traumatic and emotional distress if forced to face the defendant in the courtroom.[257] Testimony by a child protection investigator that if the child were to testify in front of the defendant the child would feel that he was betraying "secrets" with the offender and that if forced to testify in open court the child could "suffer such emotional distress that he would be unable to reasonably communicate" provides a specific basis beyond a general fear of the courtroom to justify use of closed-circuit television.[258] In addition to the emotional harm from testifying, the decision to use

---

946, 560 N.Y.S.2d 53 (1990) (upholding use of closed-circuit TV testimony where prosecution presented testimony of social worker describing severe mental or emotional harm child witnesses had already sustained and would again suffer if required to testify in open court); State v. Sibert, 98 Ohio App. 3d 412, 648 N.E.2d 861 (1994); State v. Taylor, 562 A.2d 445 (R.I. 1989) (sufficient findings made when seven-year-old victim froze on the witness stand and was unable to testify because she believed that defendant, when he got out of prison, would kidnap and kill her); Hightower v. State, 822 S.W.2d 48, 51 (Tex. Crim. App. 1991); Gonzales v. State, 818 S.W.2d 756, 762 (Tex. Crim. App. 1991).

[255] Bordeaux, supra, note 253, 400 F.3d at 555.

[256] LaBayre v. Iowa, 97 F.3d 1061 (8th Cir. 1996), cert. denied, 519 U.S. 1136 (1997) (court found following reasons justified eight-year-old's closed-circuit testimony:

> The boy's guardian ad litem said the boy expressed fear of being in the same room as LaBayre during the trial. The boy's counselor testified the boy had said that if LaBayre was in the courtroom when the boy went there to testify, the boy would probably not be able to tell a jury and full courtroom about the sexual abuse, and would probably not say anything. The counselor also testified the boy had asked whether LaBayre would be handcuffed to his chair, and was afraid LaBayre would be able to touch him. Although the counselor told the boy that LaBayre would not be able to touch him and there would be people to protect him in the courtroom, the boy's behavior was regressing as the trial was approaching. The boy's foster mother testified the boy began to wet and soil his pants, would not sleep without a light, and would check all the windows and doors to make sure they were locked. As the trial drew closer, the boy slept on the couch rather than in his bedroom. The boy said LaBayre was going to get him, and reasoned that when LaBayre came to the house, he would go to the boy's bed and the boy wouldn't be there. The boy also told his foster mother he was afraid of testifying and of being in the same room with LaBayre. When asked whether the boy was afraid of the courtroom in general, the foster mother stated the boy connects LaBayre with a courtroom.

Id. at 1062.)

[257] Bradley v. State, 921 So.2d 385 (2005) ("These witnesses established that both children were frightened of Bradley, more than just nervousness, and that the use of closed circuit television for their testimony was necessary for their welfare." Id. at 388).

[258] People v. Van Brocklin, 293 Ill. App. 3d 156, 170, 687 N.E.2d 1119, 1127 (1997), appeal denied, 178 Ill.2d 594, 669 N.E.2d 1037 (1998).

closed circuit television may be based on the nature of the crime, the defendant's position of authority toward the child and statements made by defendant to the child about the consequences of testifying. [259]

The following testimony from a Texas trial is an example of evidence justifying the use of closed-circuit television. [260]

Prosecutor:	Dr. Malone, assume with me that the child was brought in a courtroom as we are, today, and the defendant, Rick Dufrene, was physically present in that courtroom. Do you have an opinion as to what the physical presence of the defendant, Rick Dufrene, in [the child's] presence would do or not do to [the child]?
Doctor:	It very likely would traumatize her further. Prosecutor: Have you been able, from your conversations with [the child], to identify the source of her trauma?
Doctor:	The treatment of her by her parent figures, Rick and Paula Dufrene.
Prosecutor:	What effect, if any, do you think it would have on the child . . . for her to testify in the physical presence of Rick Dufrene?
Doctor:	I think she's at greater risk for further traumatization. . . . If she's now exposed, with work having been done to get distance between her and her parent figures . . . it will likely traumatize her. . . . There's going to be the traumatic experience from being exposed to Rick Dufrene.

---

[259] People v. Pierce, 266 A.D.2d 721, 698 N.Y.S.2d 753 (1999), *appeal denied*, 94 N.Y.2d 951, 731 N.E.2d 625, 710 N.Y.S.2d 8 (2000):

> Factually, this case presents several of the extraordinary circumstances which, if established by clear and convincing evidence, will support a finding that the child would suffer severe emotional harm if required to testify with defendant present: notably, (1) the manner of the commission of the offense defendant was accused of committing was particularly heinous . . . it was alleged he inserted his penis as well as a grease gun filled with water into the victims' rectums; (2) at the time, defendant occupied a position of authority with respect to the child witness . . . as the boyfriend of the victims' grandmother he was viewed as a grandfather figure; and (3) defendant admonished the victims that he would go to prison if they divulged what had occurred.

> Additionally, County Court credited testimony of an experienced social worker who counseled the female victim and opined that if she were to testify in court with defendant present, she would suffer severe mental or emotional harm. Not insignificantly, this opinion was buttressed by the court's personal observation (made of the victim when she was initially examined regarding the incident) that she was "extremely frightened, extremely upset."

Id. at 721, 698 N.Y.S.2d at 754.

[260] Dufrene v. State, 853 S.W.2d 86, 91 (Tex. Ct. App. 1993).

The above testimony describes the counter-therapeutic effect of testifying before the defendant in light of the treatment the child is receiving.

A general fear of the courtroom is insufficient justification for the use of closed-circuit television testimony.[261] Failing to set forth case specific findings requiring the use of closed circuit television may be reversible error.[262]

A court should also consider an alternative to closed-circuit testimony that allows the victim to testify outside the defendant's presence but before the jury if the defendant waives his presence in the courtroom during the child's testimony. When dealing with multiple child victims, the court should find the procedure necessary for each child and not make an "all or nothing ruling."[263]

---

[261] United States v. Rouse, 111 F.3d 561, 568 (8th Cir. 1997) (*en banc*), *cert. denied*, 522 U.S. 905 (1997); United States v. Quintero, 21 F.3d 885, 892 (9th Cir. 1994); United States v. Carrier, 9 F.3d 867, 870–71 (10th Cir. 1993), *cert. denied*, 511 U.S. 1044 (1994); United States v. Garcia, 7 F.3d 885, 887 (9th Cir. 1993); United States v. Farley, 992 F.2d 1122, 1125 (10th Cir. 1993); Cumbie v. Singletary, 991 F.2d 715, 722 (11th Cir.), *cert. denied*, 510 U.S. 1031 (1993):

> Several portions of the transcript and the record lead us to agree with the district court that the state trial court failed to make findings sufficient to defeat Cumbie's right to a face-to-face encounter as it was understood after Coy. No one at trial even appears to have considered Cumbie's Confrontation Clause rights. The state's 'Motion for Use of Closed-Circuit Television' did not mention the necessity, nor even request, that Cathy testify outside the presence of the defendant. There was no discussion whatsoever during the brief hearing on the state's motion about whether there would be a danger of significant traumatization to Cathy if Cumbie stayed in the courtroom during her testimony.

Id. at 722; State v. Vincent, 159 Ariz. 418, 768 P.2d 150 (1989); People v. Van Brocklin, 293 Ill. App. 3d 156, 170, 687 N.E.2d 1119, 1127 (1997), *appeal denied*, 178 Ill.2d 594, 669 N.E.2d 1037 (1998); Price v. Commonwealth, 31 S.W.3d 885 (Ky. 2000) (Court reversed defendant's sexual assault conviction — but not homicide conviction about which child did not testify — on grounds that the defendant was excluded from courtroom under Kentucky's closed-circuit television provisions without any findings of "compelling need." The fact that testifying may be stressful is an insufficient basis to remove defendant from courtroom or involve closed-circuit television scheme.); State v. Wright, 690 So. 2d 850 (La. Ct. App.), *cert. denied*, 701 So. 2d 978 (1997) (reversing defendant's conviction for failure to show compelling need for video testimony since a general fear of the courtroom setting is insufficient); Wildermuth v. State, 310 Md. 496, 530 A.2d 275 (1987).

[262] United States v. Turning Bear, 357 F.3d 730 (8th Cir. 2004) (reversing defendant's conviction for, among other reasons, trial court's failure to make adequate case specific findings of necessity of closed circuit testimony; court noted genealogical traumatic experience from testifying in open court is insufficient, and if there is a problem with the physical setting, i.e., a large courtroom, a different physical setting can be used to satisfy the face-to-face confrontation requirement); State v. Bray, 342 S.C. 23, 535 S.E.2d 636 (2000).

[263] State v. Lewis, 324 S.C. 539, 478 S.E.2d 861 (1996):

> Lewis argues that the trial court's final ruling does not reflect a case-specific finding of necessity, but instead was based on an "all or nothing" rule for the sake of consistency. In its final ruling, the trial court did not specifically find that Cory Schmidt in particular, or any other individual child, would be traumatized by testifying in Lewis' presence. Though the court specifically named the six individual victims when

Some courts require expert testimony by someone who has experience with children's mental health.[264] There is some authority that a trial court can find necessity for the closed-circuit procedure from its own observations without any expert testimony.[265] There is other authority that finding of harm based on a trial court's own observation also may be insufficient.[266]

On the other hand, a New Jersey court criticized the trial judge for failing to interview child witnesses as part of its specific findings with respect to each child.[267] The need for closed-circuit testimony is belied by the child witness's having testified without problem before a grand jury in a room comparable to the trial courtroom, by the failure of the child to manifest "reticence" or "emotion" when speaking of the abuse or defendant, and by the ability of the child to have stood "repeated, intense investigative interviews without outward consequences being reported."[268] It was also insufficient justification where a mental health expert simply testified that all child witnesses in sexual abuse cases suffer harm by testifying in the presence of a perpetrator and failed to establish why the particular children involved in a case would suffer emotional harm.[269]

It is also important to determine if the statute providing for closed-circuit testimony applies to a particular witness. For example, the statute may only apply to a child victim and not any child witness. Utilizing closed-circuit television

---

> it ruled that each would testify via CCTV, it merely referred to the children collectively when it discussed the harm and trauma of testifying in open court in Lewis' presence. While there is no requirement that a trial court's finding contain magic words in order to satisfy the Confrontation Clause, at a minimum, under *Craig*, a trial court should at least convey that the alternative procedure is necessary to protect a particular child from being traumatized by testifying in the defendant's presence. Thus, the better practice is for trial courts to be more specific in indicating the evidentiary basis supporting a ruling on necessity as to each particular child.

Id. at 546, 478 S.E.2d at 864–65.).

[264] United States v. Moses, 137 F.3d 894 (6th Cir. 1998); United States v. Weekley, 130 F.3d 747 (6th Cir. 1997).

[265] United States v. Rouse, 111 F.3d 561 (8th Cir.) (*en banc*), *cert. denied*, 522 U.S. 905 (1997) (holding that justification for closed-circuit procedure of 18 U.S.C. § 3509 does not require an expert to support the "because of fear" factor; "finding . . . may be based on court's own observations and questioning of a severely frightened child").

[266] United States v. Moses, 137 F.3d 894 (6th Cir. 1998) (holding federal act requires expert testimony to establish trauma); People v. Cintron, 75 N.Y.2d 249, 263, 551 N.E.2d 561, 570, 552 N.Y.S.2d 68, 77 (1990) (holding the court's findings should "be based on something more than the disputed subjective impressions of the trial judge, no matter how sincere. There must be sufficient record evidence for a reviewing court to determine that the evidence was clear and convincing").

[267] State v. Michaels, 264 N.J. Super. 579, 614, 625 A.2d 489, 507 (1993), *aff'd*, 136 N.J. 299, 642 A.2d 1372 (1994).

[268] *Id.* ("Having been visited by the prosecutor's staff the night before their testimony in almost every instance, their testimony appeared well-prepared, rote and detached.").

[269] People v. Henderson, 156 A.D.2d 92, 99–100, 554 N.Y.S.2d 924, 928 (1990).

for a child witness, when the statute is specifically limited to child victims, may be reversible error.[270]

The closed-circuit proceeding must be properly conducted. There should be no favoritism shown by the judge, and in the case of child witnesses, the judge should not play with them, hold them on his or her lap, compliment them, or take over the questioning of them.[271] If the closed-circuit proceeding is conducted "in a manner so far removed from proper standards of impartiality," a defendant can be denied a fair and impartial trial.[272]

A cautionary instruction may be prudent. The following is an example:

> The testimony of _____ is going to be taken by two-way closed-circuit television. The law allows for this type of testimony in a proceeding involving an alleged offense against a child. I am instructing you that the fact that the law allows testimony in this manner cannot be considered by you in any way. Do not even discuss it during your deliberations.[273]

§ 5.25   Use of videotape testimony.

As with closed-circuit television, videotape testimony may be constitutionally permissible in certain situations. While permissible under the federal constitution, a state may find testimony by videotape to be violative of its own state constitution.[274] It may be unconstitutional to admit a child's videotaped statement when the victim is available for cross-examination.[275] The Child Victims' and Child Witnesses' Rights statute provides for the use of videotaped deposition of children for the same reasons that justify closed-circuit television testimony.[276] However, it is important that the requirements of the statute be carefully followed. The statute requires, for example, contemporary communication between a defendant and his counsel during a deposition.[277]

As with closed-circuit television testimony, statutes that permit the use of a child's videotape testimony taken outside the physical presence of the defendant

---

[270] *See, e.g.*, George v. Commonwealth, 885 S.W.2d 938 (Ky. 1994).

[271] State v. Michaels, 264 N.J. Super. 579, 615, 625 A.2d 489, 508 (1993), *aff'd*, 136 N.J. 299, 642 A.2d 1372 (1994).

[272] *Id.* at 615, 625 A.2d at 507.

[273] United States v. Weekley, 130 F.3d 747, 753 (6th Cir. 1997).

[274] Commonwealth v. Louden, 536 Pa. 180, 638 A.2d 953 (1994).

[275] People v. Bastien, 129 Ill. 2d 64, 541 N.E.2d 670 (1989).

[276] 18 U.S.C. § 3509(b)(2); United States v. Boyles, 57 F.3d 535 (7th Cir. 1995) (upholding admission of videotape testimony of child victim since expert provided foundation that the child "would suffer emotional trauma by testifying about the alleged rape in open court, and testified that the potential trauma that [the child] would suffer would be reduced if he were not required to testify in the presence of [the defendant]." *Id.* at 546).

[277] United States v. Miguel, 111 F.3d 666, 669–670 (9th Cir. 1997) (holding that statute is constitutional and that while the trial court did not provide for contemporaneous communication the error was harmless in this case).

requires specific and individualized findings of the need to abridge the defendant's right of confrontation.[278] For example, expert testimony that a child will suffer from trauma if testifying in open court provides an adequate basis for use of videotaped testimony. These requirements of specific findings of a necessity apply not only to the trial phase but also to the taking and using of preliminary hearing videotape testimony of children that the prosecution intends to offer at trial.[279] If these requirements are met, a child's videotape testimony is likely to be admissible.[280]

Videotape depositions may be available for adult witnesses. Statutes permitting such depositions are usually more restricted in their availability and still require case-specific findings by the trial court. Being "old and frail" is insufficient to establish a "mental incapacity" or "physical incapacity" to justify use of a 94-year-old's videotape deposition, particularly since she had gone to the courthouse only a few days earlier to make the videotape.[281]

An additional issue with videotaped testimony is its quality and playback equipment. Any videotape statement must also be of sufficient quality to be admissible, as set forth in § 14.27, n. 197. The playback equipment should also be adequate for jurors and the parties to see and hear the testimony.

Once videotaped testimony is admitted, questions have arisen as to whether it can be played back for the jury during deliberations. Many courts refuse to permit the jury unrestricted access to the videotaped testimony on the theory it is the "equivalent to allowing a live witness to testify a second time in the jury room."[282] One court has noted that, "[b]ecause videotaped interviews with child victims, when introduced to prove allegations of sexual abuse, are self-serving, testimonial, and deny an accused the right of cross-examination, they are not permitted in jury rooms during deliberations."[283] If the jury requests a replay

---

[278] State v. Apilando, 79 Haw. 128, 900 P.2d 135 (1995) (Defendant's conviction reversed due to prosecution's introduction of child's videotaped interview when there was no showing of unavailability due to her age, inability to communicate, lack of memory, or insufficient recollection. The Hawaii statute involved, which did not require a showing of necessity, violated the defendant's right of confrontation); People v. Peck, 285 Ill. App. 3d 14, 674 N.E.2d 440 (1996); Rickey v. State, 661 N.E.2d 18 (Ind. Ct. App. 1996); State v. Castaneda, 621 N.W.2d 435 (Iowa Ct. App. 2001) (reversing defendant's conviction in part because defendant's Sixth Amendment right to confrontation violated by admitting 10-year-old's video taped interview without determining whether videotape was trustworthy); State v. Peterson, 530 N.W.2d 843 (Minn. Ct. App. 1995) (12-year-old's videotaped testimony violated defendant's right of confrontation); State v. Tafoya, 108 N.M. 1, 765 P.2d 1183 (1988); State v. Murrell, 302 S.C. 77, 393 S.E.2d 919 (1990).

[279] Felix v. State, 109 Nev. 151, 171–79, 849 P.2d 220, 238–39 (1993).

[280] State v. Hydock, 51 Conn. App. 753, 725 A.2d 379, *appeal denied*, 248 Conn. 921, 733 A.2d 846 (1999); State v. Marshall, 45 Conn. App. 66, 694 A.2d 816 (1997) (prosecution established compelling need by clear and convincing evidence).

[281] State v. Benitez, 360 N.J. Super. 101, 821 A.2d 547 (2003).

[282] United States v. Binder, 769 F.2d 595, 601 n.1 (9th Cir. 1985).

[283] Jassan v. State, 749 So. 2d 511, 512 (Fla. Dist. Ct. App. 1999) (*citing* Young v. State, 645

of the videotape, it has been suggested that the trial court instead provide for the reading of a transcript of the testimony;[284] the argument being that the videotape is testimony and not an exhibit. With respect to a child's videotaped testimony, one court held:

> There is an important distinction between having parts of testimony dispassionately read to a jury and allowing the jury to hear, and see, the entire testimony of an empathetic witness, such as a child describing a painful experience in his young life. The possibility for abuse is, we believe, substantially increased with video technology. This being so, a trial judge should carefully consider the alternatives before placing the video in the unrestrained hands of the jury during deliberation. We believe that the risk of prejudice is great in this situation.[285]

This does not mean that the videotape can never be replayed for the jury, just that discretion should be exercised. If the jury's request appears "reasonably necessary to its deliberations," and reading the transcript cannot satisfy the jury's request, then the court may replay the videotape.[286]

§ 5.26   Cross-examination of a sexual assault complainant.

The cross-examination of a sexual assault complainant should be carefully prepared in advance. Certain legal parameters will define the nature and extent of the cross-examination, most notably the rape shield statute. (*See* § 5.29 *et seq.*)

The emotional and traumatic nature of many sexual assaults can require great skill on the part of the cross-examiner to insure that cross-examination does not become ineffective or counter-productive. An effective theme helps develop the focus of the outcome.

An excellent source on cross-examination in general is Pozner & Dodd's *Cross-Examination: Science and Technique*[287] In one portion of the book, they describe, for example, how to deal with the crying witness. They give the example of cross-examining about the location of a sexual assault. This may trigger an emotional response. They provide a typical cross-examination and compare it with another approach that removes the victim mentally from the physical surroundings by referencing locations that are not "emotionally laden."[288]

So. 2d 965 (Fla. 1994)) (while noting that the submission of the child's videotaped statement to the jury was improper, there was no contemporaneous objection; therefore the issue was not preserved for appellate review).

[284] *Jassan. See also* State v. Michaels, 264 N.J. Super. 579, 644, 625 A.2d 489, 524 (1993), *aff'd*, 136 N.J. 299, 642 A.2d 1372 (1994).

[285] Martin v. State, 747 P.2d 316, 319–20 (Okla. Crim. App. 1987).

[286] *Michaels*, 264 N.J. Super. at 644, 625 A.2d at 524.

[287] Larry J. Pozner, Roger J. Dodd, Cross-Examination: Science and Technique (1993).

[288] *Pozner* at § 28.15.

A poor example:

Q. You say it was behind the lockers?

A. Yes.

Q. It was dark?

A. Yes.

Q. There was only one light bulb at the very end?

A. Yes.

Q. It is a small area?

A. Yes.

Q. Old benches and chairs were stored back there?

A. Yes. (The witness is glazed with tears streaming down her face.)

Compare this with the following series of questions that require the witness to make multiple comparisons of a description of the same area:

Q. You say that it was behind the lockers?

A. Yes.

Q. Not out in front of the bleachers?

A. No.

Q. It was dark?

A. Yes.

Q. Darker than at the other end of the gym?

A. Yes.

Q. There was only one light bulb?

A. Yes.

Q. The light was not as bright as the bulb at the top of the steps of the gym?

A. True.

Q. It is a small area?

A. Yes.

Q. The area in front of the lockers was larger?

A. Yes.

Q. Old benches and chairs were stored back there?

A. Yes.

Q. Old benches and chairs were also stored at the other end of the gym?

A. Yes.

Their book can be consulted for numerous other techniques of cross-examination that can be explored only in a text on cross-examination.

Sometimes the defense cannot cross-examine all areas of potential weakness in the prosecution's direct examination, since it may be difficult to keep the complainant on the stand for a long period of time. Also, a lengthy cross-examination of a complainant in a sexual assault case usually will not be effective unless there is a reason for it. Cross-examination may engender more sympathy for an already sympathetic witness. However, focusing on key areas that relate to the defense's theme is extremely important.

Aspects of cross-examination in identification cases and consent cases are set forth in the chapters dealing with these topics.

§ 5.27   Cross-examination of the child complainant.

There is no set way to cross-examine a child complainant. Judgment must be exercised depending on many variables. Given the atmosphere created by a child's testimony of sexual assault, it is important that the cross-examination begin in a fashion that will reduce the stress and tension of the courtroom for all those involved. Unlike the cross-examination of an adult witness, usually it is not beneficial to "start strong."

Children vary tremendously in their ability to communicate and articulate. Initially, a child's ability to communicate and articulate should be assessed. This can help develop an approach for cross-examination. It is important to make this assessment also to gauge the length of the cross-examination. A lengthy cross-examination of an inarticulate complainant, a complainant who has difficulty communicating, or a young child ready for nap time, can backfire when a cross-examiner appears to be overbearing or unfairly pressuring. One of the best ways this assessment can be made is through observation at a competency hearing. The questions and answers from the competency hearing may also be areas of impeachment (*See* § 5.2). In those situations where counsel does not have the benefit of a competency hearing, this assessment should be made through investigation conducted by the defense, an interview of the defendant, or through a review of discovery materials that contain either direct references to the functioning level of the child or through a review of records of the interview of the child.

Initial questions on cross-examination can also attempt to assess the ability of the child to communicate by questioning the child about certain events in his or her life, school subjects, or childhood stories with which the child may be familiar. Such an assessment is important since there is little to be gained by emphasizing that a child does not know when an event took place if the prosecution can demonstrate that the complainant would not be expected to know because of developmental factors. But, if the child did state a time period, questions about the ability to recall time periods may be appropriate.

Given the tension and stress under which most cross-examination of youthful witnesses are conducted, it is important that areas of cross-examination be carefully chosen so as not to waste time, be counter-productive, or develop further sympathy for the witness. It is not necessarily wrong to conduct a lengthy cross-examination of a child as long as goals are being met in the process. However, juries are more likely to be less receptive to a nonproductive, lengthy cross-examination of a child than an adult.

Another basic area that can be explored on cross-examination is the complainant's relationship with the offender. This may include collateral details of the relationship — whether there were problems between them or whether their relationship was very good — depending on the theme of the defense. Certainly, if the defense is alleging that the child complainant had reason to be upset at the defendant and this is a possible motive for the allegations, then probing problem areas in the relationship or discipline imposed by the defendant would be an avenue of examination. This area of cross-examination can be relatively safe, since the cross-examiner should have a good idea what the answers to the question should be through investigation and discovery.

An extremely risky area of cross-examination involves questions about the alleged sexual acts. For a variety of reasons a child may deny the acts under questioning. Such questions may also open the door to expert testimony to explain the child's behavior in the courtroom or recantation.[289] On the other hand, many child witnesses will not only reaffirm their direct testimony, but provide stronger and more detailed testimony concerning the acts. The fact that such detailed information is developed on cross-examination can have even greater weight than when the testimony is developed on direct-examination. It may also fill in gaps in the direct testimony of the child. However, cross-examination of the acts surrounding the abuse may be helpful when the allegations involve particularly bizarre or so-called ritualistic allegations, such as animal abuse or the drinking of blood. When such allegations are part of the prosecution's case, those details may be emphasized and repeated, since they may add to the incredibility of the allegations.

If the defense theory is that the child has been the victim of leading and suggestive questioning by family, friends, or professionals involved in the case, questioning the child concerning the act is less helpful to the theme, since the defense theory would be that the child has been programmed for the court testimony, and it is expected the child will provide details of the act. If the defense is one of suggestive and leading pretrial interviews of the child, then the nature and extent of those contacts can be explored with the child. This can include asking the child about the different people the child spoke to about the allegations, the number of meetings, location of the meetings, and especially any rewards that the child received as part of the interview process. This may include asking the child what the interviewers may have said about the defendant, particularly comments that disparaged or demonized the defendant. The relationship between

---

[289] *See* § 11.19.

the child and interviewer should also be explored as to whether the interviewer was a trusted authority figure. This, too, can influence the child. Sometimes the problems of suggestive and leading interviews are compounded by discussions the child has with friends, parents, or other family members — other possible relationships to explore.

One way of addressing the issue of suggestibility of a child in cross-examination is to discuss with the child a well-known story or fairytale. The child may be asked, "Do you remember the part where . . .?", and then insert both correct and incorrect details to see whether the child will accept changes in the story or additional details in the story. Or was the child taught by someone that the story could only be told one way? A story provides a vehicle for developing many areas of a party's theme with a child.

In certain situations, it may be helpful to discuss with the child other events and activities in the child's life that could be the source of knowledge of sexual behaviors observed by the child or sexual matters that the child reported. This is explained in greater detail in § 5.39.

There are alternatives to cross-examining the child about particular facts. A cross-examiner may decide that it is best to impeach the child through the testimony of third parties because of the difficulties in cross-examination of that particular child. Expert testimony can be helpful in developing the role of improper interview techniques and suggestibility in leading to the charges.[290] (See § 11.40–41.) Experts can also help develop areas of cross-examination.

Some of the issues that may be encountered in the cross-examination of a child complainant are discussed in the commentaries included in the sample testimony in Appendix L of this book.

§ 5.28 Limiting cross-examination of complainant by *pro se* defendant.

A *pro se* defendant questioning a complainant may be quite traumatic for the witness. In an effort to minimize this trauma some have suggested limiting the *pro se* defendant's right to personally cross-examine a complainant, and as an alternative have substituted the defendant's written questions asked by an attorney.

While a defendant has a right to self-representation, one federal appeals court has held that the defendant did not necessarily have a right to personally cross-examine 11-year-old through 13-year-old girls.[291] It upheld the trial court's determination that it was necessary to prevent the defendant from cross-examining the girls to protect the girls from emotional trauma.[292] A basis for

---

[290] *See, e.g.*, Felix v. State, 109 Nev. 151, 849 P.2d 220 (1993); State v. Michaels, 136 N.J. 299, 642 A.2d 1372 (1994).

[291] Fields v. Murray, 49 F.3d 1024 (4th Cir. 1995).

[292] *Fields* at 1036.

the court's upholding of this restriction of cross-examination was the U.S. Supreme Court's restriction of the Confrontation Clause in cases involving child sex abuse victim testimony.[293]

As an alternative, the defendant was offered the opportunity to write out questions that he wished to ask the girls and have the question read by a lawyer, a procedure upheld by the appellate court.

Some state courts have also noted that a defendant's Sixth Amendment rights are not absolute and that a defendant's confrontation rights may give way to society's interest in protecting child witnesses.[294] Citing the trial court's power to control witness interrogation, the Washington Court of Appeals upheld the restriction of a *pro se* defendant's cross-examination of child witnesses under the facts of the case because:

> First, it appears that Estabrook was permitted to maintain "actual control over the case he [chose] to present to the jury." He prepared the questions asked of J.H. He had the opportunity to ask follow-up questions. Furthermore, the judge was persistent in asking Estabrook's questions, rephrasing questions and obtaining answers when J.H. initially did not understand certain questions. Secondly, the procedure followed did not "destroy the jury's perception that [Estabrook was] representing himself." The court carefully explained to the jury several times that Estabrook was representing himself, and indeed, that that was the reason why the judge was asking the questions prepared by the defendant. After reviewing the entire record before this court, we are satisfied that Estabrook had a fair chance to present his case in his own way and to make his voice heard.[295]

---

[293] *Id.* at 1035 ("If a defendant's Confrontation Clause right can be limited in the manner provided in *Craig*, we have little doubt that a defendant's self-representation right can be similarly limited.").

[294] Partin v. Commonwealth, 168 S.W.3d 23 (Ky. 2005) (Appeals court upheld decision to deny defendant's right to personally examine child complainant and that defendant had to use stand-by counsel for questioning:

> Cross-examination can be used to attack the human components of the prosecution's case-in-chief through intimidation. In certain cases, the intimidation of the witness during cross-examination and the tactical advantage gained by it may exceed what the Constitution and fundamental fairness in the adversarial process require.

. . . .

> Appellant participated in the cross-examination of the victims by preparing questions to be asked, and he does not claim that counsel's cross-examination was deficient in any respect. The trial court's decision to require counsel to actually pose the questions to the victims was not an abuse of discretion and did not violate Appellant's right of self-representation.

Id. at 29; State v. Taylor, 562 A.2d 445, 454 (R.I. 1989) (however, this statement was in the context of a decision dealing with the use of videotaped testimony); State v. Estabrook, 68 Wash. App. 309, 842 P.2d 1001, 1006, *review denied*, 121 Wash.2d 1024, 854 P.2d 1084 (1993).

[295] *Estabrook*, 68 Wash. App. at 318, 842 P.2d at 1006.

Massachusetts, however, has held that restricting *a pro se* defendant's cross-examination of a complainant infringes the constitutional right to conduct one's own defense.[296] It also noted that:

> [the] record contains nothing to show that the defendant intended to exploit or manipulate the right of self-representation for ulterior purposes. There is also no indication that the defendant's questioning of the complainant would harm her, that it would violate the rules of evidence and protocol which normally apply in this sort of trial, or that the complainant would not respond truthfully to his questions. The judge's determination, that the defendant had made a valid constitutional choice to represent himself, necessarily assumed that the defendant would cooperate in good faith with rulings and directions of the judge throughout the trial, and that he would engage in a properly conducted examination of all witnesses.[297]

It may also be unconstitutional to restrict a *pro se* defendant's view of the complainant by requiring him to stand behind counsel table while a child sits in a chair in front of the jury so as not to face the defendant.[298]

§ 5.29   Rape shield statutes and applicability to deceased victims, and effect of evidence improperly admitted in violation of rape shield statutes.

One of the most important developments in sexual assault cases in the past generation has been the enactment of rape shield statutes. Such statutes limit the extent to which the complainant's prior sexual history can be presented to a jury. The constitutionality of rape shield statutes has been upheld, since "the right to present relevant testimony is not without limitation. The right 'may, in appropriate cases, bow to accommodate other legitimate interests in the criminal trial process.' "[299] Also, the Supreme Court of the United States has held that the trial judge has "wide latitude" to limit cross-examination of a witness based on concerns of "harassment, prejudice, confusion of the issues, the witness's safety or interrogation that is repetitive or only marginally relevant."[300] However, the rape shield statute does not permit a trial court to curtail cross-examination of a complainant concerning nonsexual matters on the theory that sex crime victims deserve special protection with respect to cross-examination.[301]

---

[296] Commonwealth v. Conefrey, 410 Mass. 1, 570 N.E.2d 1384 (1991).

[297] *Commonwealth* at 17, 570 N.E.2d at 1390.

[298] Commonwealth v. Spear, 43 Mass. App. Ct. 583, 686 N.E.2d 1037, *review denied*, 426 Mass. 1105 (1997).

[299] Rock v. Arkansas, 483 U.S. 44, 55 (1987) (*quoting* Chambers v. Mississippi, 410 U.S. 284, 295 (1973)).

[300] Delaware v. Van Arsdall, 475 U.S. 673, 679 (1986).

[301] People v. Griffin, 242 A.D.2d 70, 671 N.Y.S.2d 34 (1998).

A complainant's history of "picking up" males at bars is inadmissible when there are differences in the circumstances of the complainant's encounter with the defendant.[302] This is one reason that prior sexual history is often deemed irrelevant or not probative of consent. Even if the crimes for which the defendant are charged do not fall within the rape shield statute, the complainant's prior sexual history may be inadmissible on the grounds of relevancy, such as when there is a defense of alibi.[303]

Rape shield statutes are usually limited in applicability to sexual assault crimes. Some statutes have been enacted to apply the protection of rape shield statutes to deceased victims.[304] Sometimes the protection to deceased rape victims has been extended by case law.[305] In state statutes where certain crimes, such as incest, are not specifically enumerated as falling within the rape shield statute, evidence of prior sexual history must still pass the test of relevancy.[306] If non-sexual assault crimes are part of the charges, the rape-shield provisions still apply.[307]

While the constitutionality of rape shield statutes in general has been upheld, there are certainly limitations as to how far these statutes may limit cross-examination of a complainant. For example, some statutes require that the defense give notice of the intent to use prior sexual history of a complainant. If the defendant does not comply with this notice requirement, evidence of prior sexual history can be precluded. The court must review the specific facts of a case to determine whether preclusion violates the defendant's Sixth Amendment rights.[308] (*See* § 5.32.) The Supreme Court also has noted that preclusion of

---

[302] State v. Peite, 122 Idaho 809, 815–16, 839 P.2d 1223, 1229–30 (1992).

[303] Mobley v. State, 212 Ga. App. 293, 441 S.E.2d 780 (1994).

[304] *See, e.g.*, N.Y. Crim. Proc. Law § 60.43; People v. Tenace, 232 A.D.2d 896, 649 N.Y.2d 218 (1996), *appeal denied*, 89 N.Y.2d 889, 678 N.E.2d 1364, 656 N.Y.S.2d 748 (1997) (holding that defendant must make specific, not general, offer of proof with respect to deceased's prior sexual conduct).

[305] *See, e.g.*, Jenkins v. State, 627 N.E.2d 789 (Ind. 1993); State v. Friend, 493 N.W.2d 540 (Minn. 1992); State v. Clowney, 299 N.J. Super. 1, 690 A.2d 612 (1997) (all cases applying rape shield statute to victim killed after rape).

[306] Evans v. State, 317 Ark. 532, 538–39, 878 S.W.2d 750, 754 (1994) ("Since consent is never an issue in the crime of incest, whether this victim had subsequent sexual relations with another, and whether she initially admitted or denied such conduct to investigating authorities is entirely collateral. Nothing in her direct testimony at trial was contradictory to her initial statement. Even if we could say there was relevance to this subsequent conduct, giving due deference to the trial court, as we are pledged to do, we cannot say that the probative value of such evidence was not substantially outweighed by the danger of unfair prejudice." *Id.* at 539, 878 S.W.2d at 754).

[307] Osterhout v. State, 266 Ga. App. 319, 596 S.E.2d 766 (2004).

[308] Michigan v. Lucas, 500 U.S. 145 (1991) (remanding to the Michigan Court of Appeals for further proceedings and assessment of whether Michigan's Rape Shield Statute authorized preclusion and whether on the facts of the case presented the preclusion violated the defendant's rights under the Sixth Amendment).

testimony concerning a victim's sexual relationship with a key witness against a defendant amounts to an unconstitutional abridgement of the Sixth Amendment right to confrontation when that sexual relationship goes to the heart of the defense that the victim had concocted the rape allegations to protect her relationship with the witness.[309]

The Federal Rape Shield statute was revised in 1994 to include civil proceedings as well as all criminal proceedings, regardless of the charges. Previously, as in many rape shield statutes, preclusion of sexual history was limited to sexual assault crimes and did not apply to other charges, such as kidnapping. Now Rule 412 proscribes not only evidence of sexual "behavior" but also evidence of sexual "predisposition." This latter term may include "mode-of-dress, speech, or life-style" according to the notes of the Advisory Committee.

The federal statutes, as do many state statutes, require that a pretrial motion be made if the defendant seeks to introduce other sexual behavior or predisposition, although a later motion may be made for good cause, such as newly discovered information or a newly arisen issue in the case. The rule also requires the sealing of motion papers to protect the victim's privacy. The revised Rule 412 reads as follows:[310]

(a) EVIDENCE GENERALLY INADMISSIBLE. The following evidence is not admissible in any civil or criminal proceeding involving alleged sexual misconduct except as provided in subdivisions (b) and (c):

(1) Evidence offered to prove that any alleged victim engaged in other sexual behavior.

(2) Evidence offered to prove any alleged victim's sexual predisposition.

(b) EXCEPTIONS.

(1) In a criminal case, the following evidence is admissible, if otherwise admissible under these rules:

(A) evidence of specific instances of sexual behavior by the alleged victim offered to prove that a person other than the accused was the source of semen, injury or other physical evidence;

(B) evidence of specific instances of sexual behavior by the alleged victim with respect to the person accused of the sexual misconduct offered by the accused to prove consent or by the prosecution; and

(C) evidence the exclusion of which would violate the constitutional rights of the defendant.

(2) In a civil case, evidence offered to prove the sexual behavior or sexual predisposition of any alleged victim is admissible if it is otherwise admissible

---

[309] Olden v. Kentucky, 488 U.S. 227 (1988) (noting also that the defense wished to provide testimony that the complainant and key witness were living together at the time of trial and that the "impartiality" of the key witness would have been "impugned by revelation of his relationship" with the complainant. *Id.* at 230, 233.).

[310] Fed. R. Evid. 412.

under these rules and its probative value substantially outweighs the danger of harm to any victim and of unfair prejudice to any party. Evidence of an alleged victim's reputation is admissible only if it has been placed in controversy by the alleged victim.

(c) PROCEDURE TO DETERMINE ADMISSIBILITY.

(1) A party intending to offer evidence under subdivision (b) must—

(A) file a written motion at least 14 days before trial specifically describing the evidence and stating the purpose for which it is offered unless the court, for good cause requires a different time for filing or permits filing during the trial; and

(B) serve the motion on all parties and notify the alleged victim or, when appropriate, the alleged victim's guardian or representative.

(2) Before admitting evidence under this rule the court must conduct a hearing *in camera* and afford the victim and parties a right to attend and be heard. The motion, related papers, and the record of the hearing must be sealed and remain under seal unless the court orders otherwise.

Some courts consider in evaluating admissibility of a victim's prior sexual activity whether the evidence would be prejudicial to the prosecution because it was "raised for the first time during the trial, thus not giving the prosecution a chance to investigate the allegation."[311]

When a defendant introduces evidence in violation of a rape shield statute, a trial court may find "manifest necessity" to declare a mistrial.[312] The trial court's discretion is not "boundless" and the court should consider if there are reasonable alternatives to a mistrial.[313]

§ 5.30   Notice requirement.

The federal rule and many state statutes require the defense to give notice of the intent to offer the prior sexual history of a complainant. This provides an opportunity for the court to review the basis for the allegations as well as determine whether there is a valid reason for accepting this testimony. As noted in the preceding section, the Supreme Court of the United States has upheld the notice requirement, although it questioned the *per se* exclusion of evidence because of failure to comply with the notice provision.[314]

Failure to comply with the notice requirement, as with any discovery rule violation, can be cited as a basis for denying the defendant the opportunity to

---

[311] State v. Hammer, 236 Wis. 2d 686, 613 N.W.2d 629, 642 (2000).

[312] Banks v. State, 230 Ga. App. 258, 495 S.E.2d 877 (1998); People v. Savinon, 293 A.D.2d 413, 740 N.Y.S.2d 853 (2002), *aff'd*, 100 N.Y.2d 192, 791 N.E.2d 401, 761 N.Y.S.2d 144 (2003); Maynard v. Wait, 246 A.D.2d 853, 668 N.Y.S.2d 263 (1998).

[313] *Maynard*, 246 A.D.2d at 854, 668 N.Y.S.2d at 265.

[314] Michigan v. Lucas, 500 U.S. 145 (1991).

present evidence.[315] Before precluding evidence due to a notice violation, a court should consider whether it was a tactical or willful decision, the prejudice to the prosecution and the alternative to preclusion, such as a continuance or prosecutional comment on the discovery violation.[316] Some statutes require an offer of proof by the defendant at an *in camera* hearing.[317]

Some state statutes do not require notice, but clearly state that prior sexual conduct evidence should not be admitted unless there is a determination by the court outside the hearing of the jury that such evidence is relevant and admissible, and that the court, as New York statute requires, makes a statement of its findings of fact.[318] As to the offer of proof, a hearing can be satisfied by the defense being given the opportunity to summarize the evidence and explain its relevance.[319] The failure of the defense at such a hearing to explain how the evidence of prior sexual history is probative will result in its preclusion since "the burden of making a threshold showing of relevance [rests] on the defense as moving party."[320] No doubt it is essential that a showing of relevance and materiality be made not only to assist the trial judge, but also for appellate review. The hearing to determine whether prior sexual acts are precluded by a rape shield statute may be closed in the discretion of the court to protect a rape victim's privacy[321] or by the statute[322] where an *in-camera* hearing or offer of proof by the defendant is not required. A prosecutor can file a motion *in limine* to avoid having the issue addressed before the jury. This also allows a ruling before the witness testifies.

Prosecutors and defense counsel should determine if there is evidence of a complainant's prior sexual assault and determine the relevancy of such evidence to the case. Prosecutors must determine whether such evidence may be exculpatory or should be submitted to the court for an *in-camera* determination.

---

[315] United States v. Eagle Thunder, 893 F.2d 950 (8th Cir. 1990); United States v. Provost, 875 F.2d 172, 177 (8th Cir.), *cert. denied*, 493 U.S. 859 (1989); Sherman v. State, 778 So. 2d 859 (Ala. 2000); State v. Cuni, 159 N.J. 584, 733 A.2d 414 (1999); State v. Scherzer, 301 N.J. Super. 363, 417, 694 A.2d 196, 222, *cert. denied*, 151 N.J. 466, 700 A.2d 898 (1997); State v. Jensen, 200 N.D. 28, 606 N.W.2d 507 (2000).

[316] *Scherzer*, 301 N.J. Super. at 418, 694 A.2d at 222.

[317] 725 Ill. Comp. Stat. ch. 725, § 5/115-7(b). ("Such offer of proof shall include reasonably specific information as to the date, time and place of the past sexual conduct between the alleged victim and the defendant.")

[318] N.Y. Crim. Proc. Law § 60.42(5).

[319] People v. Williams, 81 N.Y.2d 303, 614 N.E.2d 730, 598 N.Y.S.2d 167 (1993).

[320] *Williams*, 81 N.Y.2d at 314–15, 614 N.E.2d at 735, 598 N.Y.S.2d at 172. *See also* Byrum v. State, 318 Ark. 87, 97, 884 S.W.2d 248, 254 (1994); People v. Hackett, 421 Mich. 338, 365 N.W.2d 120 (1984).

[321] State v. Howard, 121 N.H. 53, 426 A.2d 457 (1981). For a discussion of courtroom closure during the testimony of a rape complainant, *see* § 2.3.

[322] MD. Code art. 27, § 461A(b) (court must hold "*in camera* hearing to determine the admissibility of the evidence" of prior sexual history).

Prosecutors can refer to law enforcement and prosecutorial files, review complainant's psychological or medical records in the prosecutor's possession, and question the complainant about prior assaults. It is best to seek this information well in advance of trial.

§ 5.31   General applicability of rape shield statute and situations where prior sexual history is precluded or admissible to establish state of mind, motive, and applicability to sexual history after sexual assault.

Evidence of a complainant's prior sexual history will be precluded if it is offered to attack the general credibility of the complainant. Prior sexual history or conduct is inadmissible when it is offered to show that the victim would be willing to engage in sexual activities. A key issue is to what extent sexual activity and conduct is covered by a rape shield statute. Posing in *Penthouse Magazine* has been held to fall within the rape shield statute.[323] "Swinger" photographs, which exhibit the complainant sexually or provocatively, are generally not admissible on the theory that such evidence would only confuse the jury and, except in certain limited situations, would not be probative on the question of the complainant's consent.[324] Other oblique references to sexual history may likewise be precluded. For example, a court may preclude references to the fact that the complainant has a child on the theory that this introduces evidence that she has had prior sexual experiences.[325]

A typical application of the rape shield statute involves testimony of the victim's appetite for "risky sex" by making reference to the complainant's sexual activity[326] or testimony of the complainant's one-night stands.[327] Another

---

[323] Wood v. Alaska, 957 F.2d 1544 (9th Cir. 1992) (complainant having posed in *Penthouse Magazine* not relevant to issue of consent).

[324] People v. Mandel, 48 N.Y.2d 952, 401 N.E.2d 185, 425 N.Y.S.2d 63 (1979), *cert. denied*, 446 U.S. 949 (1980); People v. Willard, 226 A.D.2d 1014, 641 N.Y.S.2d 896, *appeal denied*, 88 N.Y.2d 943, 670 N.E.2d 461, 647 N.Y.S.2d 177 (1996) (court properly precluded a photograph offered by defendant of complainant posing for the camera holding her boyfriend's penis).

[325] Johnson v. State, 245 Ga. App. 690, 538 S.E.2d 766 (2000):

> The trial court correctly excluded all references to the fact that 16-year-old S.S. had a child of approximately 21 months of age. The only possible desired inference arising from the victim's motherhood is that, because she had had prior sexual experience with someone other than defendant, she consented to his indecent liberties on this occasion. Such inference is clearly prohibited under Georgia's Rape Shield Statute
> . . . .

Id. at 692, 538 S.E.2d at 768.

[326] Commonwealth v. Widmer, 446 Pa. Super. 408, 667 A.2d 215 (1995), *rev'd on other grounds*, 547 Pa. 137, 689 A.2d 211 (1997) (defendant's offer of proof concerning complainant's sexual encounter with her boyfriend 11 hours before alleged rape, to demonstrate "victim's appetite for 'risky' sex" is the type of conduct precluded by the rape shield statute as irrelevant).

[327] United States v. Sanchez, 44 M.J. 174 (C.A.A.F. 1996) (evidence of complainant's five to ten one-night stands were not so close to crime charged to warrant admission).

typical application of the rape shield statute is to redact references to pregnancies and sexual history contained in medical records offered into evidence.[328] The rape shield statute has also precluded testimony of a complainant's sexual relationship with a prosecutor which led to his office's removal from the case.[329] However, it is reversible error to preclude questioning of a complainant's involvement with the detective investigating her case when it is hours after the alleged assault and may be relevant in considering her behavior so soon after an alleged sexual assault.[330]

A defendant may be limited in testifying to his conversation with a complainant when it refers to specific sexual exploits while allowed to testify to the complainant's generally flirtatious conversation.[331] However, a complainant's provocative statements may be outside the rape shield statute and relevant to motive or state of mind. For example, a complainant's statements to a third person after a sexual assault may be relevant to establish her state of mind.[332] A

---

[328] Smith v. State, 669 A.2d 1 (Del. 1995):

> The trial judge questioned whether the examining physician would need to know about Anderson's prior pregnancies in order to properly evaluate her physical condition on July 22, 1993. The prosecutor was unable to answer the judge's question, and was given permission to consult with the doctor on that point. The prosecutor then advised the trial judge that, according to the doctor, Anderson's prior pregnancies would have no bearing upon the medical examination. In light of that response, which was not disputed at trial or on appeal, the motion to redact the medical records was granted. That ruling was well within the sound discretion of the trial judge.

Id. at 4. *See also* Banks v. State, 230 Ga. App. 258, 495 S.E.2d 877 (1998).

[329] Griffin v. State, 224 Ga. App. 225, 480 S.E.2d 608 (1997), *cert. denied*, 1997 Ga. LEXIS 398 (Apr. 24, 1997).

[330] State v. Horrocks, 57 Conn. App. 32, 747 A.2d 25, *appeal denied*, 253 Conn. 908, 753 A.2d 941 (2000).

[331] State v. Hale, 917 S.W.2d 219 (Mo. Ct. App. 1996) (defendant was permitted to testify "that the victim initiated a conversation about sex which lasted approximately two hours, that the victim's conversation had been 'raunchy' and embarrassing, that the victim encouraged her friend to relate specific instances of past sexual behavior, that the victim gave Hale condoms without his asking for them. Further, Hale was allowed to testify that he thought the victim was making 'a pass' at him and that the victim was drunk and flirtatious. The only thing the circuit court did not allow Hale to testify about was specific aspects of the conversations relating to specific instances of the victim's past sexual conduct." *Id.* at 221).

[332] Commonwealth v. Killen, 545 Pa. 127, 680 A.2d 851 (1996) (The court held the statements precluded by the trial, requiring reversal of defendant's conviction, did not reference past sexual conduct. The statement to a fireman who treated the complainant after the assault, "she asked him in a 'very forward' and 'aggressive tone':

> 'Is it true, you know, what I hear about black men,' and that she began laughing afterwards saying she apologized if she embarrassed him. [He] would have also testified that the complainant further asked him, 'Can you tell me why the hair on a white woman's vagina is the same as the hair on a black man's head?' and again started to laugh afterwards. With respect to her demeanor in the ambulance, he would testify that she was very 'friendly' toward him, and that she was smiling at him,

complainant's statements are not protected by the rape shield statute because they are not necessarily evidence of sexual conduct. The statements may be admissible, not necessarily for their truth, but to demonstrate a state of mind,[333] and a defendant is not necessarily precluded from questioning a complainant about a relationship with an ex-boyfriend and whether the desire to re-establish the relationship was a motive for a false claim.[334]

Past sexual conduct may refer to sexual conduct after a sexual assault. For example, that at some time after a rape the victim was found to be "hanging all over a gentleman friend"[335] may be admissible and within the rape shield statute. "Past" is an ambiguous term — it may refer only to the acts before the alleged sexual assault or before the complainant testifies. Michigan's Supreme Court in analyzing the relevance of subsequent consensual relations between a defendant and victim has held that many factors should be considered in determining whether to admit evidence of a complainant's sexual activities with a defendant after a sexual assault, including the circumstances and nature of the relationship between the complainant and the defendant.[336] The court felt that evidence of sexual history after the sexual assault should be admitted in certain situations where the evidence is truly probative.[337] The proximity in time between the alleged crime and other sexual activity by a complainant may be relevant in determining admissibility of the other sexual activity.[338] In one case, however, testimony of a complainant's sexual relations with a former boyfriend to support the theory that it would be unusual for a rape victim to engage in sexual relations so soon after an attack was found inadmissible because the inference was too uncertain.[339]

> 'looking in his eyes,' and pulling her body toward him throughout the ambulance ride. [He] would also allegedly have testified that the complainant acted in a flirtatious manner toward the emergency physician at the hospital."

Id. at 131, 680 A.2d at 852.).

[333] People v. Jovanovic, 263 A.D.2d 182, 700 N.Y.S.2d 156 (1999):

> For instance, here, the complainant's statements to Jovanovic regarding sadomasochism were not necessarily offered to prove the truth of what she said, i.e., that she actually was a sadomasochist. Rather, much of their importance lay in the fact that she chose to say these things to Jovanovic in the context of her electronic, on-line conversation with him, so as to convey to him another message, namely, her interest in exploring the subject of such activities with him.

Id. at 193–94, 700 N.Y.S.2d at 166.

[334] Richardson v. State, 276 Ga. 639–41, 581 S.E.2d 528, 529 (2003) (reversing defendant's conviction for trial court's preclusion of such testimony based on the rape shield statute).

[335] Sandoval v. Acevedo, 996 F.2d 145 (7th Cir. 1993).

[336] People v. Adair, 452 Mich. 473, 550 N.W.2d 505 (1996).

[337] *Id.*

[338] State v. Perez, 26 Kan. App. 2d 777, 995 P.2d 372 (1999), *review denied*, 269 Kan. 939 (2000) (noting that victim had not returned home for two nights and complainant's activities provided motive for allegation). *See also* discussion in § 5.32 of "past" sexual conduct.

[339] State v. Beeler, 166 Or. App. 275, 999 P.2d 497 (2000).

The rape-shield statute includes sexual assaults perpetrated by the victim.[340] Testimony that the complainant was seen touching herself in the genital area may be inadmissible under the theory underlying rape shield statutes.[341]

§ 5.32 Admissibility of complainant's prior sexual conduct with the defendant and sexual statements by complainant to defendant.

Every rape shield statute provides that the defense can offer evidence of prior sexual activity between the complainant and the defendant. However, the testimony between the defendant and victim must not be speculative. If the witness has no actual knowledge of the relationship, or has just seen the two go into a bedroom but no more, the evidence's probative value is outweighed by its prejudicial effect.[342] Some courts go further and require additional evidence, beyond the defendant's, to connect the prior acts to the consent alleged in the current charge.[343] Other courts find it improper for the trial court to weigh the defendant's credibility in determining whether to admit evidence of defendant's allegations of prior sexual relations with the complainant.[344] A state statute's language may determine whether the trial court is to make factual findings. (Federal Rule of Evidence 412 was amended in 1994 to preclude a trial court's fact finding role.) The exception may also be inapplicable where the defendant denies any sexual contact with the complainant at the time of the incident alleged in the indictment, since consent is not in issue, and past sexual

---

[340] People v. Gholston, 26 P.3d 1 (Colo Ct. App. 2000).

[341] People v. Miller, 295 A.D.2d 746, 746 N.Y.S.2d 50 (2002).

[342] Hall v. Commonwealth, 956 S.W.2d 224 (Ky. 1997).

[343] Graydon v. State, 329 Ark. 596, 953 S.W.2d 45 (1997):

> [T]he only evidence presented that supports appellant's version of events was his own self-serving testimony. There was no corroborating evidence that even linked appellant with the victim prior to the date of the offense, let alone evidence of their having carried on a clandestine affair for several months. The primary purposes of the rape-shield statute are to protect the victim and encourage rape victims to participate in the prosecution of their attackers. [citation omitted]. Such worthy purposes would surely be thwarted if every defendant in a rape case was allowed to present uncorroborated 'evidence' that he and the victim had previously engaged in sexual intercourse over the victim's denial that she had ever known her assailant before the incident. Particularly in this case, where the victim was badly beaten and injured, the minute probative value of allegations of prior consensual intercourse between the victim and the attacker are clearly outweighed by the inflammatory nature of the alleged evidence. Furthermore, appellant failed to offer any additional evidence connecting the alleged prior acts to the consent alleged in the present incident.

Id. at 602, 953 S.W.2d at 48.

[344] State v. Sanchez-Lahora, 261 Neb. 192, 622 N.W.2d 612 (2001) (upholding reversal of defendant's conviction due to trial court's preclusion of defendant's evidence of previous relations with complainant, based on court's assessment of defendant's credibility; trial court could only determine relevancy of the prior relations).

conduct between the complainant and the defendant is not relevant.[345] The exception may also be inapplicable when the previous consensual sexual relations were not the same as those alleged in the indictment (*e.g.*, sadomasochistic sexual conduct)[346] or when the prior relations involved single partner as opposed to multi-participant rape.[347]

Where the complainant denies having had prior consensual sexual relations with the defendant, the defendant will be permitted to testify as to such alleged activities, but there is a question as to the extent the defendant can present other evidence of the victim's sexual activity to bolster his claim that he and the complainant had prior sexual relations. For example, in one case the complainant denied any prior sexual activity with the defendant who claimed he had had intercourse with her approximately one month prior to the date of the rape.[348] While there was an entry in the hospital emergency room records that "alluded" to a prior act of intercourse by the complainant, the complainant denied any prior intercourse with anyone, and, although the author of the entry could not be identified, one of the nurses who took the complainant's history testified that the complainant stated that she had never had intercourse before.[349] In this context, the court properly limited the defense's cross-examination of the complainant to questions as to whether she had prior intercourse with the defendant and precluded further inquiry into the matter, which allowed the defendant to present his defense of a prior relationship and protected his right of cross-examination without allowing "an aimless fishing expedition for evidence of prior sexuality."[350] When the complainant denies any romantic involvement with the defendant, it may be reversible error to preclude testimony from a third party attesting to physical contact between them.[351]

When the complainant denies relations with the defendant during a hearing, the court may preclude cross-examination of the complainant about the alleged relationship with the defendant until the defendant presents proof of the relationship, such as through the defendant's testimony.[352] The term "past" is ambiguous

---

[345] State v. Williams, 128 Ariz. 453, 626 P.2d 617 (1981); People v. Westfall, 95 A.D.2d 581, 469 N.Y.S.2d 162 (1983).

[346] People v. Schuldt, 217 Ill. App. 3d 534, 577 N.E.2d 870 (1991).

[347] People v. Williams, 416 Mich. 25, 330 N.W.2d 823 (1982).

[348] People v. Tortorice, 142 A.D.2d 916, 531 N.Y.S.2d 414 (1988).

[349] *Id.* at 919, 531 N.Y.S.2d at 417.

[350] *Id.*

[351] People v. Loja, 305 A.D.2d 189, 761 N.Y.S.2d 7, *appeal denied*, 100 N.Y.2d 584, 796 N.E.2d 486, 764 N.Y.S.2d 394 (2003):

> The goal, as we have previously characterized evidence regarding prior intimacy between a sexual abuse complainant and a defendant, is not to impute unchastity to the complainant, but rather to examine state of mind evidence and defendant's intent as related to the disputed issue of consent [citation omitted], so that this evidence was not properly barred by the rape shield law.

[352] State v. Graham, 118 N.C. App. 231, 454 S.E.2d 878, *review denied*, 340 N.C. 262, 456

when referring to "past" sexual conduct with the defendant. The restrictive view takes the position that "past" refers to the time period before the crime charged, and does not refer to sexual acts between the defendant and the victim occurring subsequent to the crime charged when the defendant is taking the position that the incident charged never took place. Michigan's Supreme Court has held that the rape shield statute does not automatically foreclose inquiry of sexual activities after the sexual assault, but that a trial court should carefully consider the probative value of such evidence before admitting it. [353] The court held:

> The rape shield statute provides that the trial court should balance these considerations in determining whether the proposed evidence is material and whether its probative value is outweighed by its prejudicial nature. On a common-sense level, a trial court could find that the closer in time to the alleged sexual assault that the complainant engaged in subsequent consensual sexual relations with her alleged assailant, the stronger the argument would be that if indeed she had been sexually assaulted, she would not have consented to sexual relations with him in the immediate aftermath of sexual assault. Accordingly, the evidence may be probative. Conversely, the greater the time interval, the less probative force the evidence may have, depending on the circumstances.

> Even so, time should not be the only factor. The trial court should also carefully consider the circumstances and nature of the relationship between the complainant and the defendant. If the two did not have a personal relationship before the alleged sexual assault, then any consensual sexual relations after the alleged sexual assault would likely be more probative than if the two had been living together in a long-term marital relationship. Additionally, the trial court could find that there may be other human emotions intertwined with the relationship that may have interceded, leading to consensual sexual relations in spite of an earlier sexual assault. Depending on the circumstances, the trial court may find that these other considerations have intensified the inflammatory and prejudicial nature of subsequent consensual sexual conduct evidence and properly conclude that it should be precluded or limited. [354]

Other courts have held that "past" refers to all sexual conduct before trial. [355]

S.E.2d 834 (1995) (court properly precluded cross-examination of complainant concerning her pregnancy and whether she told the defendant he was the father of her child where complainant denied any relationship with defendant during voir dire. Once defendant testified in his case-in-chief, court allowed testimony of pregnancy from emergency room physicians and permitted defendant the right to recall victim to cross-examine her on this issue).

[353] People v. Adair, 452 Mich. 473, 550 N.W.2d 505 (1996).

[354] Id. at 486, 487, 550 N.W.2d at 512.

[355] United States v. Torres, 937 F.2d 1469, 1472 (9th Cir. 1991); Flurry v. State, 290 Ark. 417, 419, 720 S.W.2d 699, 700 (1986); Commonwealth v. Jones, 2003 Pa. Super. 220, 826 A.2d 900 (2003) (rape shield statute applies to sexual activity before and after the alleged crime); Cuyler v. State, 841 S.W.2d 933, 936 (Tex. App. 1992); State v. Gulrud, 140 Wis. 2d 721, 412 N.W.2d 139 (1987).

Statements made by a victim to a defendant may be considered the equivalent of sexual conduct distinguished from prior sexual history. For example, a complainant's e-mails to the defendant describing her sexual interests and fantasies would be relevant on the issue of consent. [356] Statements made by a victim about her past sexual conduct may be viewed differently when they are contained in a defendant's statement to law enforcement in which he attributes statements to the complainant of past sexual conduct. [357] When relevant, it is reversible error to preclude evidence of past sexual relations between a defendant and victim. [358]

The condition for the admission of evidence of prior sexual conduct may violate constitutional rights. Requiring that the evidence of prior contact be "highly material" and "the probative value of the evidence offered substantially outweighs its collateral nature or the probability that its admission will create undue prejudice, confusion of the issues, or unwarranted invasion of the privacy of the victim" and that "in the absence of clear and convincing proof to the contrary," such evidence "occurring more than one year before the date of the offense charged is presumed to be inadmissible" precludes evidence admissible under the Confrontation and Compulsory Process Clauses. [359] Thus, precluding evidence from several of a complainant's flirtatious behavior, consisting of physical attention, obsessive attention, sexual innuendos, fussing and banter about an affair toward the defendant over many years because it fails to overcome these

---

[356] People v. Jovanovic, 263 A.D.2d 182, 700 N.Y.S.2d 156 (1999) (reversing defendant's conviction for redacting victim's e-mails to defendant since they were part of the history of intimacies relevant to arrest).

[357] People v. Curry, 11 A.D.3d 150, 782 N.Y.S.2d 66, *appeal denied*, 4 N.Y.3d 743, 824 N.E.2d 56, 790 N.Y.S.2d 655 (2004) (Here, the statement in contention is not one made by complainant but by defendant. Defendant did not seek to introduce a statement complainant had made for its evidentiary value; defendant merely sought to use her alleged statement as a means to elicit testimony from complainant as evidence-in-chief, which defendant presumes would have rebutted the People's evidence that he caused complainant's injuries. This would appear to be precisely the sort of speculative foray into a victim's sexual history that the Rape Shield Law was designed to prevent. *Id.* at 158–59, 782 N.Y.S.2d at 72–73.).

[358] Napoka v. State, 996 P.2d 106 (Alaska Ct. App. 2000) (reversing defendant's conviction due to trial court's failure to admit evidence of prior consensual sexual relations between defendant and victim, which court deemed relevant to element of consent); State v. Cortes, 84 Conn. App. 70, 851 A.2d 1230, *affirmed*, 276 Conn. 241, 885 A.2d 153 (2005) ("holding evidence of a sexual relationship between the complainant and his brother was relevant to undermining the complainant's version of events and, specifically, her testimony that the defendant had forced her to accompany him and that she was unable to seek help during the drive to Lawrence"); Ivey v. State, 264 Ga. App. 377, 590 S.E.2d 781 (2003) (reversing defendant's conviction because defendant was precluded from testifying about his sexual relationship with the complainant); State v. Atkinson, 276 Kan. 920, 80 P.3d 1143 (2003) (reversing defendant's convictions due to failure of trial court to permit evidence of complainant's prior sexual relations with defendant the night before the alleged rape, which would explain presence of DNA matching his on DNA found during medical examination).

[359] State v. Garron, 177 N.J. 147, 827 A.2d 243 (2003), *cert. denied*, 540 U.S. 1160 (2004).

requirements of a rape shield statute violates a defendant's constitutional rights.[360]

§ 5.33   Prior sexual conduct to explain source of semen.

Another exception to the preclusion of evidence found in most rape shield statutes deals with testimony that would provide evidence of an alternative source for semen found on or in the complainant. The use of this exception is contingent on the facts surrounding the prior sexual activity as well as on the medical or scientific evidence concerning the semen. In a case of a defense of mistaken identity, where there was testimony that nonmotile sperm in the complainant's vagina exists for up to five days, a defendant who had a vasectomy should have been permitted to inquire if the complainant had sexual relations on the night of the alleged rape with someone other than the defendant, even though the defendant was unable to identify any such person.[361] It may be reversible error to preclude testimony which would explain the presence of DNA offered in support of the sexual assault claim.[362]

It may also be reversible error to preclude evidence of a DNA, which shows that the defendant's DNA is excluded as a source of seminal fluid found in the

---

[360] State v. Garron, 177 N.J. 147, 827 A.2d 243 (2003), *cert. denied*, 540 U.S. 1160 (2004)

In this case, the information withheld from the jury did not concern the victim's intimate relations with persons other than this defendant. The withheld evidence did not paint the victim as a woman with a sordid past, making her allegations unworthy of belief. The withheld evidence, however, did shed light on the victim's relationship with defendant. However unflattering or embarrassing the details, the evidence was offered for a legitimate objective, to support defendant's consent defense. The story left untold by defendant was of a woman infatuated with him and who pursued him aggressively, even in the presence of her fellow office workers and his wife. The defendant needed to explain why he was at the victim's house in the early morning of September 28, why he followed her into the laundry room of her home, and why he reasonably believed she consented to have sexual relations with him. The untidy details of defendant's relationship with J.S. were essential to understanding his side of the story. Selectively editing those details, as the trial court did here, did not advance the truth-seeking function of the trial. . . . We need not parse the record to itemize which remarks and conducts were flirtatious or which were sexual because we conclude that the prior relationship evidence, whatever the characterization, was relevant to and necessary for a fair determination of the issues.

Id. at 176, 827 A.2d at 260.

[361] Commonwealth v. Fitzgerald, 412 Mass. 516, 590 N.E.2d 1151 (1992). *See also* Heflin v. State, 643 So. 2d 512 (Miss. 1994) (reversing defendant's conviction for the failure to admit complainant's prior sexual history to rebut inference that the defendant was the source of semen found during the medical examination).

[362] State v. Atkinson, 276 Kan. 920, 80 P.3d 1143 (2003) (reversing defendant's convictions due to failure of trial court to permit evidence of complainant's prior sexual relations with defendant the night before the alleged rape, which would explain presence of DNA matching his on DNA found during medical examination).

complainant after a sexual assault[363] to establish the defense of misidentification. The prosecution's willingness to stipulate that the defendant's semen was not found on the complainant, but refusal to allow the jury to hear evidence that other persons' semen was found on her, is an inadequate alternative.[364]

On the other hand, if a defendant admits to sexual relations with the complainant, and identification is therefore not an issue, the defendant cannot present testimony concerning the complainant's sexual encounter with another person to establish a possible source for the semen or sperm recovered from the complainant or her clothing.[365] In such a situation, the source of the semen or sperm is not relevant to any material issue and introducing evidence of the complainant's sexual relationship with a third person would be evidence ordinarily precluded by a rape shield statute.

The prior sexual behavior must have occurred within a reasonable time of the alleged rape to be relevant to the source of semen or sperm found on the complainant.[366] For example, if the medical testimony is that sperm in the vagina will be present for up to five days after intercourse, evidence of a complainant's sexual relations two weeks before the incident is inadmissible to explain the source of semen.[367] When the prosecution offers evidence of pregnancy as proof of sexual conduct between the complainant and defendant, the defendant may introduce evidence of the complainant's sexual conduct within the conception period, but not outside the conception period.[368]

---

[363] State v. Smith, 85 Conn. App. 96, 856 A.2d 466, *appeal granted*, 271 Conn. 945, 861 A.2d 1178 (2004):

> In the present case, the evidence the defendant sought to have admitted would not exonerate him unequivocally, but it would be relevant and central to his claim that he was misidentified as the complainant's attacker. The exclusion of the evidence would interfere with his right to use a defense of misidentification and, therefore, could not be harmless. When the excluded evidence is relevant to the primary issue at trial, namely, the identity of the attacker, and central to the defendant's plea of not guilty and is the most compelling evidence available to the defendant, it is crucial to his defense, and the elimination of such evidence conflicts with the defendant's right to present a defense.

Id. at 110–11, 856 A.2d at 475.

[364] *Id.*

[365] People v. Mathis, 8 A.D.3d 966, 778 N.Y.S.2d 613, *appeal denied*, 3 N.Y.3d 709, 818 N.E.2d 679, 785 N.Y.S.2d 37 (2004); People v. Rasmussen, 275 A.D.2d 926, 713 N.Y.S.2d 427, *appeal denied*, 95 N.Y.2d 968, 745 N.E.2d 406, 722 N.Y.S.2d 485 (2000); People v. Kalaj, 247 A.D.2d 633, 669 N.Y.S.2d 358, *appeal denied*, 92 N.Y.2d 880, 700 N.E.2d 565, 678 N.Y.S.2d 27 (1998).

[366] United States v. Torres, 937 F.2d 1469 (9th Cir. 1991), *cert. denied*, 502 U.S. 1037 (1992) (holding that evidence of an incident of prior relations of a 17-year-old female with a male other than the defendant was not relevant to the source of semen found on the complainant's panties, since this sexual activity occurred many months after the allegations of abuse against the defendant, and the panties had been in police custody).

[367] Commonwealth v. Whitman, 29 Mass. App. Ct. 972, 561 N.E.2d 525 (1990).

[368] State v. Weeks, 891 P.2d 477 (Mont. 1995).

Generally, the fact that semen or seminal fluid was found on an article of clothing or on a vaginal swab does not trigger the exception unless the evidence is introduced by the prosecution. The defense cannot bootstrap the evidence of prior sexual history by offering the evidence of semen or laboratory results indicating sexual contact before introducing evidence of prior sexual history.[369] Thus, the victim cannot be cross-examined concerning her prior sexual conduct if she is called as a witness before testimony is introduced concerning the discovery of semen or sperm. It has also been held that a defendant cannot offer an earlier denial of intercourse, such as to a hospital doctor, and then introduce the laboratory test results to impeach the complainant's credibility.[370] However, the complainant can be recalled as a witness for purposes of cross-examination about prior sexual conduct or history if such scientific testimony is later offered by the prosecution.

§ 5.34   Evidence of prior sexual conduct to refute evidence of physical injury.

A common exception advanced under the rape shield statutes involves the introduction of past sexual conduct to rebut the inference of the prosecution's evidence that the defendant was the source of physical injury suffered by the complainant. A classic example is a third party's intercourse with a child to explain why the condition of an eight-year-old's hymen could have been caused by someone or something other than the defendant.[371] Another example is a

---

[369] United States v. Richards, 118 F.3d 622 (8th Cir. 1997) ("We believe, however, that the rule does not allow for the admission of such evidence when it was the defendant's decision, and not the prosecution's, to introduce the existence of the semen into evidence in the first instance. Were we to hold otherwise, a defendant could bootstrap himself into the exceptions contained in Fed. R. Evid. 412(b)(1)." *Id.* at 623–24.); People v. Mitchell, 10 A.D.3d 554, 782 N.Y.S.2d 45, *appeal denied*, 3 N.Y.3d 759, 821 N.E.2d 980, 788 N.Y.S.2d 675 (2004) (since DNA established, and defendant admitted that semen found on deceased belonged to him, evidence concerning a second semen stain was speculative and irrelevant); People v. Rendon, 301 A.D.2d 665, 756 N.Y.S.2d 229, *appeal denied*, 100 N.Y.2d 542, 793 N.E.2d 421, 763 N.Y.S.2d 7 (2003) (trial court properly excluded under rape shield statute evidence of second semen stain found on piece of clothing); People v. Mount, 285 A.D.2d 899, 727 N.Y.S.2d 819, *appeal denied*, 97 N.Y.2d 642, 761 N.E.2d 4, 735 N.Y.S.2d 499 (2001); People v. Mountain, 105 A.D.2d 494, 496, 481 N.Y.S.2d 449 (1984), *aff'd*, 66 N.Y.2d 197, 486 N.E.2d 802, 495 N.Y.S.2d 944 (1985); State v. Calloway, 207 W. Va. 43, 528 S.E.2d 490 (1999) (upholding trial court's preclusion of DNA results found on victim's mattress, which was not that of defendant, since there was no showing the semen was directly related to the assault).

[370] United States v. White Buffalo, 84 F.3d 1052 (8th Cir. 1996) ("Because the victim's statement about unrelated consensual sexual intercourse was of little or no probative value on the question of whether she falsely accused Ernest of rape, the exclusion of the test results did not deprive Ernest of a constitutional right. *See* United States v. Bartlett, 856 F.2d 1071, 1088–89 (8th Cir. 1988). Thus, we conclude the district court did not abuse its discretion when it prohibited impeachment of the victim with her past sexual behavior." *Id.* at 1054.)

[371] People v. Haley, 153 Mich. App. 400, 405, 395 N.W.2d 60, 62–63 (1986).

defendant offering testimony that a child had intercourse with another person to explain the prosecution's testimony that the victim had two genital lacerations resulting from forced penetration.[372]

Courts have varied widely in interpreting this exception beginning with "what is a physical injury?" One federal appeals court has ruled that a widened vaginal opening or nonintact hymen is not an injury in the absence of tears to the hymen, cuts, scratches, bruises, blood, injury to the vaginal canal, healing tears, or scars.[373] "The absence of all these indicia, however, strongly suggests that while the condition of [the complainant's] vaginal area may have changed, she was not injured."[374] Holding that all "physical consequences" do not trigger the exceptions under the rape shield statute, the court refused to allow evidence of an 11-year-old's prior relations with seven young boys.[375]

A defendant cannot present evidence of physical signs of sexual abuse and then rebut that evidence with proof of the complainant's prior sexual history to establish the source of those injuries.[376] To trigger the physical injury exception to the rape shield statute, the prior sexual history should be in response to the prosecution's introduction of physical evidence of sexual assault, as with semen, discussed in the previous section.

Where there was medical evidence of injury to the vaginal canal consistent with multiple episodes of sexual intercourse, evidence that the complainant had been found in a trailer "in a state of partial undress engaged in heavy petting with a boy" would not account for the physical injury where no one, including the defendant, alleged that the complainant had engaged in sexual intercourse in the trailer, and the extent of the complainant's activities in the trailer were speculative.[377]

The relevancy of past sexual conduct may depend on medical testimony. Where a physician testifies that the physical condition of the victim's vaginal opening is not caused by "one person's jabbing at another," the defense is properly precluded from presenting testimony that the four-year-old's younger brother had touched her, since such testimony would fall within the scope of the rape shield statute.[378] Similarly, the existence of a nonrecent tear and its possible source was not relevant to the source of tears in the victim's hymenal ring that were only hours old.[379] Where the medical testimony was that the victim's vaginal

---

[372] Herrington v. State, 690 So. 2d 1132 (Miss. 1997) (reversing defendant's conviction for trial court's failure to admit evidence that 12-year-old had relations with another male).

[373] United States v. Shaw, 824 F.2d 601, 605 (8th Cir. 1987), *cert. denied*, 484 U.S. 1068 (1988).

[374] *Id.*

[375] *Id.* at 607.

[376] People v. Gagnon, 75 N.Y.2d 736, 550 N.E.2d 448, 551 N.Y.S.2d 195 (1989).

[377] United States v. Payne, 944 F.2d 1458, 1468–70 (9th Cir. 1991), *cert. denied*, 503 U.S. 975 (1992).

[378] King v. State, 574 So. 2d 921, 926 (Ala. Crim. App. 1990).

[379] United States v. Eagle Thunder, 893 F.2d 950 (8th Cir. 1990). *See also* State v. Knox, 634

laceration would be painful and an indication of force, prior testimony of consensual relations was irrelevant.[380] If the defendant alleges a consensual intercourse caused the injury and medical testimony includes that the physical finding is consistent with consensual relations, then evidence of prior relations may be irrelevant. Relevance must still be established for the admission of the prior relations.[381] Similarly, a complainant's sexual activities after the act set forth in an indictment cannot provide a reasonable alternative explanation for physical findings.[382] If the prosecution's medical expert explains the physical change in the victim's hymen may not have been caused by sexual abuse, the

---

A.2d 952, 953 (Me. 1993) (court properly precluded evidence of a 10-year-old boy's sexual activity with nearly 15-year-old male complainant four or five years before the alleged assault on theory it would rebut medical evidence of injuries to his rectum when, although the doctor could not say how old the scar or tissue was, it was unlikely the scar would have left the victim with an open wound after several years).

[380] United States v. Azure, 845 F.2d 1503 (8th Cir. 1988).

[381] People v. Harris, 43 P.3d 221 (Colo. 2002) Prosecution presented evidence of victim's vaginal abrasion. Victim had sexual relations with another. Court noted:

> Evidence of P.A.'s prior sexual encounter proved nothing. It was not logically relevant to the question of whether Harris committed sexual assault and the trial court properly excluded it under the rape shield statute's presumption of irrelevance. Such prior sexual relations evidence would have shown only that Harris may not have caused the abrasion. It would not, and logically could not, have shown whether P.A. consented to her sexual encounter with Harris. As we will discuss, this is the only logical conclusion that can be reached in light of Harris's consent defense and the facts of this case.

> If the jury accepted Harris's theory that consensual intercourse could have caused the abrasion, then the question of who caused the abrasion was irrelevant to whether Harris used force. Alternately, if the jury believed that only nonconsensual intercourse could have caused the abrasion, then evidence of P.A.'s consensual intercourse with her boyfriend was irrelevant to whether Harris used force. Thus, in light of Harris's defense of consent and Nurse Larkin's testimony that consensual intercourse could have caused the abrasion, evidence that P.A. had consensual intercourse with her boyfriend four days before her encounter with Harris is not logically relevant to whether Harris committed sexual assault.

Id. at 226. *See also* Commonwealth v. Beltz, 2003 Pa. Super. 234, 829 A.2d 680 (2003):

Defendant claimed relations between complainant and boyfriend earlier in day was relevant because it tended to negate not the fact that sex took place between the two, which Mr. Beltz freely admitted, but rather its coercive nature, that it was not against her will. And the evidence was highly probative and not prejudicial inasmuch as it undermined her credibility with regard to the source of the spermatozoa and slight bruises.

We fail to understand, however, how the fact that the victim had sex earlier that day could be in any way determinative of whether she consented to the intercourse she subsequently had with Appellant. We are also unconvinced that the source of spermatozoa is of any import, since Appellant admitted that he had sex with the victim, and a prosecution witness credibly testified that use of a condom does not eliminate the presence of some spermatozoa.

[382] United States v. Powers, 59 F.3d 1460, 1470 (4th Cir. 1995), *cert. denied*, 516 U.S. 1077 (1996).

complainant's prior sexual activities are not necessary to rebut the prosecution's testimony.[383]

The nature of proof offered in support of the alleged prior relations may affect admissibility. For example, evidence of a prior sexual encounter to rebut the evidence of a complainant's physical injury may be inadmissible if based on the hearsay testimony of a third party, rather than the testimony of the defendant or the person with whom the sexual encounter allegedly occurred.[384] Sometimes, there may be limitations on how the proof is used. While a defendant's videotaped statement may refer to a complainant's statement that one of her tricks beat her, the rape shield statute precludes cross-examining her that her injuries were sustained by one of her "tricks."[385]

In many situations, the failure to permit the introduction of the victim's prior sexual conduct will result in reversible error if it prevents the defendant from presenting evidence that reflects the source of physical injury found on the complainant or physical evidence offered by the prosecution.[386] When physical

---

[383] Commonwealth v. Fink, 2002 Pa. Super. 32, 791 A.2d 1235 (2002).

[384] *Ex parte* Dennis, 730 So. 2d 138 (Ala. 1999).

[385] People v. Curry, 11 A.D.3d 150, 782 N.Y.S.2d 66, *appeal denied*, 4 N.Y.3d 743, 824 N.E.2d 56, 790 N.Y.S.2d 655 (2004).

[386] United States v. Bear Stops, 997 F.2d 451, 457–58 (8th Cir. 1993) (reversing defendant's conviction (on one count of the indictment) because trial court precluded evidence of child's other uncontroverted sexual assaults at about the same time, which offered an alternative explanation for bloody underwear offered by the prosecution, which was the only physical evidence of a sexual assault upon the child); Rancourt v. State, 766 So. 2d 1071 (Fla. Ct. App. 2000) (holding trial court should have permitted, after doctor's testimony that genital tenderness finding is possible after consensual intercourse, that complainant gave history of no sexual intercourse in over a year, to permit inference that the complainant's vaginal tenderness was due to prolonged abstinence rather than a non-consensual encounter; however, defendant's attorney did not preserve issue for appellate review); Audano v. State, 641 So. 2d 1356 (Fla. Dist. Ct. App. 1994) ("If the state introduces evidence that upon physical examination of a victim a physician has determined that a child has engaged in sexual intercourse, then the defendant is entitled to introduce evidence that the child had previously engaged in sexual intercourse with persons other than the defendant." *Id.* at 1360); Lemacks v. State, 207 Ga. App. 160, 427 S.E.2d 536 (1993) (reversing defendant's conviction when prosecution offered evidence of sexual abuse and trial court refused to permit defendant to introduce proof of past sexual behavior of the complaining witness, which would have accounted for her injuries); People v. Mason, 219 Ill. App. 3d 76, 578 N.E.2d 1351 (1991) (holding that the rape shield statute does not preclude evidence that child victim had previously inserted jumbo crayons in her vagina when such evidence would explain that an injury offered as relating to an alleged rape may have been otherwise caused); Anderson v. Commonwealth, 63 S.W.3d 135 (Ky. 2001) (holding physician's testimony of "loose vaginal opening" in child opened door to child's statement to nurse that she had sex with another boy and the failure to admit this evidence of prior sexual history to rebut the medical testimony was reversible error); Herrington v. State, 690 So. 2d 1132 (Miss. 1997) (reversing defendant's conviction for failure to receive evidence from victim's friend that someone other than defendant had sexual relations with complainant which would have been an alternative source of two genital lacerations testified to by prosecution's physician); Amacker v. State, 676 So. 2d 909 (Miss. 1996) (reversing defendant's conviction because of trial court's exclusion of evidence offered by defendant which provided conflicting

findings would be consistent with the complainant's sexual intercourse with another individual several months before the incident with the defendant, such evidence of prior sexual conduct must be admitted, particularly when the prosecution is relying on the evidence of an enlarged hymen as evidence of molestation.[387]

Where the prosecutor offers testimony of an enlarged hymenal ring of the eight-year-old victim to support its case, evidence that the victim had been abused by her father at about two years of age was relevant since the medical testimony supported the relevancy of earlier penetration to the child's hymen.[388] Evidence of prior sexual encounters is admissible when it is impossible to determine on the basis of the physical examination, if a complainant's symptoms and findings reflected "one violent sexual penetration or repeated penetrations over a period of time."[389]

---

source of injury); State v. Harris, 166 N.C. App. 386, 602 S.E.2d 697 (2004) (reversing defendant's conviction due to failure to permit evidence of complainant's sexual relations with another on evening of day in question given prosecution's evidence of vaginal and rectal trauma); State v. Kilgore, 107 Wash. App. 160, 26 P.3d 308 (2001), aff'd, 147 Wash. 2d 288, 53 P.3d 974 (2002) (reversing two counts of defendant's sexual abuse conviction because trial court refused to allow evidence of victim's prior abuse to explain physical findings).

[387] United States v. Begay, 937 F.2d 515 (10th Cir. 1991); People v. Anthony Roy W., 324 Ill. App. 3d 181, 186–87, 754 N.E.2d 866, 869–70, appeal denied, 197 Ill. 2d 566, 763 N.E.2d 772 (2001) (complainant's sexual activity a month before alleged assault relevant to explain physical evidence of a cleft hymen); Goodson v. State, 566 So. 2d 1142, 1152 (Miss. 1990) (holding that evidence that child's hymen was not intact justifies admission of prior sexual history to show that the defendant is not the cause of this physical finding.); State v. Brown, 29 S.W.3d 427 (Tenn. 2000), cert. denied, 531 U.S. 916 (2000):

> Applying this test to the facts of this case, we are of the opinion that the hearsay testimony Brown sought to introduce—that the complainant admitted to two friends that she had sexual intercourse with an adolescent male during the same time period the defendant allegedly committed aggravated rape—should have been admitted. As previously stated herein, the testimony Brown sought to introduce was clearly relevant to rebut the State's medical proof of the complainant's physical condition and met the threshold admissibility standard of Tennessee Rule of Evidence 412. Moreover, courts considering similar issues have explained that when proof of hymenal injury is offered in a sexual assault or abuse case involving a child complainant, rebuttal proof of prior sexual experience is particularly critical to the defense since it offers the jury an alternative explanation for the hymenal injury. In the absence of such rebuttal proof, most jurors will presume that the child is sexually innocent and attribute the hymenal damage to the alleged criminal act.

Id. at 434.

[388] Jones v. State, 600 So. 2d 1138–39 (Fla. Ct. App. 1992).

[389] Id. at 519. See also Tague v. Richards, 3 F.3d 1133 (7th Cir. 1993) (holding that an Indiana trial court's application of the rape shield statute to exclude evidence indicating another possible source of hymenal damage to the complainant was improper but harmless error).

The prosecution may also be required to provide the defense with information in their possession of an alternative explanation for the complainant's genital injuries.[390]

§ 5.35   Evidence of prior sexual conduct and sexually-transmitted disease.

Another situation where the physical injury or interest of justice exception can be triggered is when there is evidence that the complainant suffered from a sexually-transmitted disease. If the prosecution presents evidence that a complainant had a sexually-transmitted disease that neither the defendant nor his wife contracted, the defendant may be given permission to explore the complainant's past sexual behavior, since such evidence could give rise to an unfair inference that the defendant had been the source of the victim's disease.[391]

If the complainant testifies that the defendant gave her gonorrhea through unprotected sex, the complainant's medical records and history of sexually-transmitted disease is not protected by the rape shield statute, because it involves the sexual act for which the defendant is on trial. However, the admissibility of such evidence, even when the witness testifies the defendant gave her a sexually-transmitted disease, may be restricted by the rule of relevance. For example, if the complainant's records state only that her unidentified "partner" had gonorrhea, then the medical records of the victim are not relevant since they do not contradict or impeach the witness's testimony.[392] However, when evidence of sexually-transmitted disease is not offered by the prosecution, the trial court's decision as to whether to admit evidence of prior sexual conduct will be difficult without a showing of relevance. If the defense is one of consent, admission of testimony concerning the sexually-transmitted disease would arguably be less relevant than in the situation where the defense is one of identification. Then, too, the admissibility of the sexually-transmitted disease may depend upon the disease itself, the likelihood of transmission, and the offer of proof made by a party offering such evidence. In a defense of mistaken identification, the defendant may wish to argue that the defendant did not engage in the act of intercourse with the complainant as evidenced by the fact that he did not contract the sexually-transmitted disease. While transmission of the disease is not inevitable, the defendant could argue that the medical testimony

---

[390] People v. Ramos, 201 A.D.2d 78, 614 N.Y.S.2d 977 (1994) (reversing defendant's conviction for, among other reasons, the prosecution's failure to provide the defense with information in its possession which provided "an extremely compelling alternative explanation for the medical evidence that the child's genital area had been subjected to inappropriate contact in that numerous witnesses reported that, long prior to the date of the alleged rape, the child masturbated with disturbing frequency and engaged in sexually provocative behavior with other children." *Id.* at 87, 614 N.Y.S.2d at 982).

[391] Chambers v. State, 205 Ga. App. 78, 421 S.E.2d 326 (1992).

[392] State v. Thompson, 139 N.C. App. 299, 533 S.E.2d 834 (2000).

would indicate more than a possibility of transmission, and such facts should be considered by a jury.

The prosecution may present evidence of a complainant's sexually-transmitted disease to establish sexual abuse or contact. The probativeness of such testimony and issues surrounding such evidence, are discussed in § 12.14.

The prosecution may be required to disclose to the defendant information that the complainant has a sexually-transmitted disease.[393] Some courts feel the information must be probative on the case, otherwise it need not be disclosed.[394]

What if there is evidence that the complainant has a sexually-transmitted disease, evidence which neither the prosecution nor the defendant presents? Can the complainant's positive test results be introduced by the defendant implicitly raising past sexual conduct? The answer is that usually, but not always, such evidence is excludable given the likelihood of transmission of the particular disease, the possibility of such sexual transmission, or the possibility that the defendant's negative test results are not probative. A defendant's offer of proof may be crucial to the determination of admissibility. For example, consider the following court's analysis in which it held as irrelevant evidence that the defendant sought to introduce that the four-year-old victim had trichomoniasis and the defendant did not have the disease:

> From what little information is included in the record, it appears that trichomoniasis is a relatively innocuous form of venereal disease that can be cured by a single seven-day treatment. Hence, the fact that the victim was infected with trichomoniasis on a certain date, but co-defendant Starrett (the only person identified in the record from whom the child could have contracted the disease) was not infected two months later is, simply, immaterial. It fails to establish that Starrett was not infected two months earlier, since he might have been treated and cured in the meantime. Moreover, even if Starrett could prove that he had never had trichomoniasis, this fact would not necessarily establish that he did not sexually abuse the victim. At most, it would tend to prove that someone else had also abused her. As for the petitioner in this case, Cecilia Garrett, information about her status as a carrier of trichomoniasis would have had even less probative value, since there is no plausible set of facts in the record under which the infection could have been transmitted directly from the petitioner to the victim. Indeed, Garrett could have been altogether free of infection at the time Starrett sexually

---

[393] *Ex parte* Geeslin, 505 So. 2d 1246 (Ala. 1986); State v. Steele, 510 N.W.2d 661 (S.D. 1994) (Prosecution committed reversible error by failing to inform defendant that complainant had contracted Chlamydia, despite the fact that the defendant's theory was consent. The South Dakota Supreme Court specifically ruled that the rape shield statute was inapplicable to the evidence of complainant's contraction of Chlamydia).

[394] State v. Warren, 661 A.2d 1108 (Me. 1995) (Prosecution's failure to disclose to defendant that victim tested negative for HIV was not exculpatory. HIV test had no predictive value on whether intercourse occurred.).

abused the child if Starrett himself had contracted the disease from a third party and had transmitted it to the victim but had not transmitted it to Garrett. Finally, there is some indication in the record that trichomoniasis can be contracted from sources other than by sexual transmission, such as a contaminated toilet seat or a wet towel. Obviously, further litigation of this issue would have entangled the trial court in a dispute over a largely — if not wholly — collateral matter. [395]

Iowa's Supreme Court has held:

Evidence of the defendant's freedom from a sexually-transmitted disease has some relevance on whether there was sexual contact but not much. It has low probative value because it can't be established with reasonable clarity that the victim had the sexually-transmitted disease at the time of the alleged contact. Most importantly, even if she had a sexually-transmitted disease, it is probable and likely that the defendant would not catch it from her during intercourse. Thus, the absence of a sexually-transmitted disease is very weak proof that no abuse occurred. Balanced against the low probative value is the highly inflammatory aspect of the inquiry into venereal disease. Such questions would have a high potential to harass, annoy and humiliate the witness. Finally, allowing such questions would certainly be time-consuming and distract the inquiry by focusing on the victim's conduct rather than the defendant's. In light of the low probative value and high potential for prejudice, such evidence is not admissible. [396]

Other courts have employed similar rationale for precluding evidence of a complainant's sexually-transmitted disease and defendant's negative test results. [397] In addition to the lack of probative value of defendant's negative test

---

[395] Garrett v. Money, 1994 U.S. App. LEXIS 30609 at *17–18 (Oct. 28, 1994).

[396] People v. Redman, 135 Ill. App. 3d 534, 542–43, 481 N.E.2d 1272, 1278–79 (1985) (upholding preclusion of victim's positive gonorrhea results six days after rape and defendant's negative gonorrhea results 30 days after assault given the time lag between the assault and the defendant's negative results); State v. Knox, 536 N.W.2d 735 (Iowa 1995) (defendant sought to offer evidence that complainant had Chlamydia when examined at a hospital shortly after the alleged sexual assault and that the defendant did not have the disease when he was tested three months later. The appellate court held that his evidence of sexual history was of little probative value since the chance of the defendant contracting Chlamydia was slight and there was evidence that Chlamydia is easily treatable with widely available antibiotics and the defendant could have been infected at the time of the alleged incident but be cured when tested three months later. Evidence of complainant's Chlamydia was held to fall within the rape shield statute); State v. Carmichael, 240 Kan. 149, 727 P.2d 918 (1986) (holding that the fact that the defendant did not have gonorrhea and the complainant did have the disease would not necessarily mean that the defendant did not have sexual contact with the complainant, since gonorrhea is not necessarily transmitted during intercourse, and evidence that the victim had gonorrhea was not relevant since this would only show that she had intercourse with someone prior to the rape, which conduct falls within the rape shield statute).

[397] Van Ricks v. State, 249 Ga. App. 80, 546 S.E.2d 919 (2001) (finding that trial court properly precluded evidence of complainant's trichomoniasis one year after the alleged crime, since there was no evidence that she had it closer to the time of the crime, and "[m]ore importantly, there

results, the defendant's test results may also be rejected for lack of proper chain of custody in the defendant's testing of his samples.[398] A recurring issue is the scientific or medical proof offered of the likelihood of transmission of the disease.

If the prosecution offers evidence of the complainant's sexually-transmitted disease, testimony that the complainant had relations with a third person may be precluded if the defendant does not have proof that the third party also had the disease.[399]

---

was no assertion or offer of proof to show that Ricks had been tested for the disease at any time. Thus, there was no indication that he did, or did not, have the disease. Thus, the evidence was irrelevant and was properly excluded." *Id.* at 81, 546 S.E.2d at 920); Green v. State, 242 Ga. App. 868, 870, 532 S.E.2d 111 (2000); State v. Ervin, 723 S.W.2d 412, 415 (Mo. Ct. App. 1986) (defendant's negative gonorrhea test, six weeks after the alleged rape, was of little probative value); State v. Marsh, No. E1998-00057-CCA-R3-CD, 2000 Tenn. Crim. App. LEXIS 365 (May 8, 2000):

> In this appeal, the defendant, who never contracted gonorrhea, maintains that evidence that the victim had the disease was a circumstance suggesting that no sexual encounter had taken place. In other words, the defendant argues that he would have contracted gonorrhea if he had had sex with the victim. The only proof in the record is that the victim had the disease in November of 1995, when she moved into the defendant's residence. There is no evidence with regard to how long the victim had the disease or when she was treated for it. That is, there is no direct proof that the victim actually had gonorrhea at the time of the sexual encounter with the defendant. Nor is there any evidence as to the strain of gonorrhea the victim had, how gonorrhea is transmitted, or the rate at which gonorrhea is transmitted from women to men. As such, evidence of the victim's gonorrhea would have been properly excluded as irrelevant.

Id. at *18–19. State v. Jarry, 161 Vt. 629, 641 A.2d 364, 365–66 (1994) (upholding trial court's preclusion of sexual assault victim's Chlamydia where defendant did not test negatively for Chlamydia until four months after the alleged rape).

[398] White v. State, 330 Ark. 813, 958 S.W.2d 519 (1997):

> We conclude that there was no abuse of discretion in the trial court's finding that the testimony presented to establish a foundation for White's independent test was inadequate. Both of the witnesses called by the defense testified that the procedures at the lab were reliable. Yet, neither of the witnesses could testify as to who collected the samples from White and if that person actually followed an established protocol. The sum and substance of the testimony was the trial court could not be assured of how the samples were collected, when they were collected, or even if they were taken from White. Something more must be done to establish the legitimacy of the tests than was done in this case. We have often stated that proof of the chain of custody for interchangeable items like blood must be more conclusive. . . . Dr. Denman, the State's expert in pathology, testified that antibiotics could cure Chlamydia in as little as two to three days. White's independent test was conducted on July 21, 1994, four days after purchasing an antibiotic that could cure Chlamydia. The fact that he did not have Chlamydia on that particular date shed no light on whether he had Chlamydia on July 12, 1994.

Id. at 820–21, 958 S.W.2d at 522.

[399] Rouse v. State, 204 Ga. App. 845, 420 S.E.2d 779, *appeal denied*, 204 Ga. App. 922, 420 S.E.2d 779 (1992) (Prosecution offered evidence that child complainant contracted gonorrhea, which defendant sought to rebut by testimony that the victim's stepfather had sexually molested the complainant. This evidence was offered as an explanation for the source of the nine-year-old's

There is some authority that a defendant should be permitted to present evidence of his negative test results if the prosecution presents evidence of a sexually-transmitted disease. [400] The defendant should also be permitted to show he volunteered to submit to testing if the prosecution presents evidence of the complainant's sexually-transmitted disease. [401] Even when the prosecution offers evidence of a sexually-transmitted disease, it does not necessarily open the door to all of the complainant's prior sexual activity. There must still be some reasonable connection between the sexual activity and the disease. For example, the defendant may not ask the complainant about past sexual encounters when the prosecution presents evidence of the HIV virus when there is no evidence to connect the past sexual encounters with the victim's contracting of the virus. [402]

§ 5.36 Prior sexual conduct to rebut references to positive character of victim or to her statements or indication that she is a virgin or lack of sexual relations and evidence of complainant's sexual preference.

Do efforts by a prosecutor to portray a complainant as "a paragon of innocence and virtue . . . culminating in a suggestion . . . that [she] had been a virgin" [403]

---

venereal disease. "However, defendant failed to offer proof that the victim's stepfather was also infected with gonorrhea. Consequently, any evidence of the victim's sexual activity with her stepfather would have shed no light on the origin of the victim's sexually-transmitted disease. Under these circumstances, the trial court did not err in refusing to allow the offered testimony regarding other sexual assaults upon the victim." *Id.* at 846, 420 S.E.2d at 780); State v. McGuire, 892 S.W.2d 381 (Mo. Ct. App. 1995) (In a case in which a child contracted gonorrhea, and where physician testified the gonorrhea "must be transmitted by direct mucosa to mucosa contact," and that the disease is only sexually-transmitted, even though some medical authorities left open the possibility of non-sexual transmission of the disease, the expert's opinion that non-sexual transmission of the disease was not possible in children was a sufficient basis for precluding defense testimony concerning the alleged hygiene of members of the child's household since "defendant did not present evidence that any member of [child complainant's] household had gonorrhea. All the male members tested negative. The female members were not tested. Without evidence that anyone in the household was infected with the disease, and that it could be indirectly transmitted, it would not be possible for [child complainant] to have contracted it in any manner from one of them." *Id.* at 385.).

[400] Reece v. State, 192 Ga. App. 14, 383 S.E.2d 572 (1989) (reversing defendant's conviction and holding that defendant should have been permitted to show that the defendant's wife's medical records and his own showed no sign of trichomoniasis after complainant testified that she had not had sexual relations with anyone else, and the prosecution introduced testimony concerning the complainant's contraction of the disease).

[401] People v. Bull, 218 A.D.2d 663, 630 N.Y.S.2d 354, *appeal denied*, 87 N.Y.2d 899, 663 N.E.2d 1258, 641 N.Y.S.2d 228 (1995) (reversing defendant's conviction because while children's gonorrhea and Chlamydia results were relevant to sexual assault charges, "defendant should have been permitted to testify that he voluntarily submitted to testing after learning that he was under investigation for raping and abusing the complainants").

[402] Weaver v. State, 56 Ark. App. 104, 939 S.W.2d 316 (1997).

[403] Tyson v. State, 619 N.E.2d 276, 289–90 (Ind. Ct. App. 1993), *cert. denied*, 510 U.S. 1176 (1994).

open the door to a complainant's prior sexual conduct? Heavyweight boxer Michael Tyson's attorneys made this argument in attempting to introduce evidence of the complainant's prior sexual conduct. The prosecution, they contended, created an impression of innocence by evidence of her church activities, good deeds, and academic accomplishments. The Indiana appellate court rejected this argument and held the rape shield statute "squarely" precludes evidence of prior sexual conduct in these circumstances.[404]

What happens when a complainant makes an affirmative statement that she had no sexual experience prior to the alleged crime and the defendant seeks to introduce evidence of prior sexual conduct on her part? This will open the door, but it may depend on exactly what was said on direct examination and the context of the case. When a prosecutor asked a 17-year-old developmentally disabled witness if the defendant was "the only one that's ever done those bad things to you," the victim's affirmative response was deemed not to open the door to two prior sexual experiences, since they were not similar to the forcible rape by the adult defendant and thus were not relevant.[405] A prosecutor may elicit a response that the complainant never had sexual relations with anyone other than her common-law husband when this testimony is on redirect examination and offered "as an explanation as to why she did not inform her husband of the rape immediately," and in response to the defendant's contention that there was a consensual sexual encounter in exchange for employment.[406] The rape shield statute does not preclude this type of testimony. An eight-year-old's statement that she never had sexual intercourse before does not necessarily open the door to a prior forcible sexual assault upon the child since in the context of a child a prior forced sexual act would "not count" as prior sexual intercourse in the view of one court.[407] Most courts find that the prosecution should not present testimony that a complainant is a "virgin" since this fact is not relevant or probative.[408]

---

[404] *Id.* at 290.

[405] Logan v. Lockhart, 994 F.2d 1324, 1330–31 (8th Cir. 1993) (upholding a decision of the Arkansas Supreme Court in a habeas petition).

[406] People v. Wigfall, 253 A.D.2d 80, 690 N.Y.S.2d 2, *appeal denied*, 93 N.Y.2d 981, 716 N.E.2d 1112, 695 N.Y.S.2d 67 (1999).

[407] Commonwealth v. Pearce, 427 Mass. 642, 695 N.E.2d 1059 (1998).

[408] Herndon v. State, 232 Ga. App. 129, 499 S.E.2d 918 (1998) (finding evidence of complainant's virginity were precluded by the rape shield law); People v. Bone, 230 Mich. App. 699, 584 N.W.2d 760, *appeal denied*, 459 Mich. 922, 589 N.W.2d 776 (1998) (holding prosecution's introduction of evidence of complainant's virginity violated rule on use of character evidence); State v. Burke, 354 N.J. Super. 97, 804 A.2d 617 (2002) (Appeals court upheld trial court's decision to preclude prosecution from presenting evidence that victim was a virgin before engaging in intercourse with defendant. This decision was based in part that New Jersey traditionally excludes character evidence to prove or disprove an act that did or did not occur on a particular day. The court noted:

One of the inherent dangers with the introduction of character evidence is its suscepti-

Some jurisdictions, however, hold the introduction of a victim's virginity is relevant and outside the scope of the rape shield statute.[409]

Statements in another proceeding do not necessarily open the door to the introduction of prior sexual history during the criminal trial.[410]

At some point in time a complainant may tell someone that she is a virgin. The statement may be made to the defendant prior to or in the course of the assault. The argument has been made that such a statement opens the door to the introduction of proof that the complainant is not a virgin. However, this impeaches the complainant on a collateral matter. If a young girl claims she was sexually abused by her father and had told him that she was a virgin, proof of her prior sexual activity would be inadmissible, since whether she was a virgin would be irrelevant to whether she was raped, particularly if the victim later testified that she really was not a virgin, but that under relentless pressure from the defendant, she told him that she was.[411]

A similar situation is a complainant's statement that she was a virgin during the course of the sexual assault. In this situation, the rape shield statute does not apply; the statement would be irrelevant and have little probative value, whether or not it is true.[412]

Thus, courts will find the complainant's statement during a sexual assault that she was a virgin relevant to the issue of consent, but not necessarily an argument by the prosecutor as to the truth of the statement.[413] This would apply to any

---

bility to convert a trial of the issue to a judgment of the person. If it is fair to infer that evidence of prior chastity is relevant to establish a lack of consent on the part of an alleged victim, then is not the converse also true? Is it not equally probative that a person with a history of prior sexual conduct would be more likely to consent than one who has none?

Id. at 109, 804 A.2d at 624.

[409] State v. Preston, 121 N.H. 147, 427 A.2d 32 (1981) (holding evidence of virginity relevant to element of consent); State v. Pugh, 2002 SD 16, 640 N.W.2d 79 (2002).

[410] Commonwealth v. Frey, 390 Mass. 245, 454 N.E.2d 478 (1983) (testimony by a complainant in a related civil proceeding that she had been a virgin prior to intercourse with the defendant did not open the door for defendant to introduce evidence of complainant's prior sexual activity where the complainant did not testify affirmatively at trial that she was a virgin before sexual relations with the defendant); State v. Ferguson, 5 Ohio St. 3d 160, 450 N.E.2d 265 (1983) (complainant's prior testimony on a preliminary matter that she had not had sexual relations ten days prior to assault does not open the door to evidence that complainant engaged in relations two days earlier, particularly where the issue at trial is whether complainant consented to relations with the defendant and thus evidence of prior sexual conduct is not material to an issue in the case).

[411] Heflin v. State, 643 So. 2d 512 (Miss. 1994) ("This was done at a time and under circumstances . . . when she had reason to be afraid to give any other answer . . . . The victim's virginity is not relevant." *Id.* at 518).

[412] People v. Kellar, 174 A.D.2d 848, 571 N.Y.S.2d 144, *appeal denied*, 78 N.Y.2d 1128, 586 N.E.2d 68, 578 N.Y.S.2d 885 (1991).

[413] People v. Harris, 297 Ill. App. 3d 1073, 697 N.E.2d 850 (1998), *appeal denied*, 179 Ill. 2d

statement made by a complainant during a sexual assault. If a victim were to assert to an attacker that he would be beat up by a particular gang if he did not stop his advances, it would be improper to permit rebuttal testimony as to whether such a statement was true or false.

Nor can a defendant present evidence of a complainant's out-of-court statement of virginity in an attempt to rebut it. If a complainant states to a physician in the course of a medical examination that she was a virgin at the time of the rape, a defendant cannot offer that statement and then present testimony to rebut the statement.[414] Nor can a defendant question a complainant in a voir dire hearing about whether or not she had sexual relations with any other person and then present testimony to rebut the complainant's statement.[415] However, a complainant's statements to an investigator, "I've only been with [my boyfriend]" should be admissible to rebut her trial testimony accusing the defendant of previous sexual assault.[416]

600, 705 N.E.2d 443 (1998) (upholding complainant's testimony that she told defendant she was a virgin, but finding harmless error a prosecution's argument to jury as to truth of her statements); State v. Singleton, 102 N.M. 66, 691 P.2d 67 (1984) (upholding admission of complainant's pleas to defendant during assault not to rape her because she was a virgin as relevant to element of consent).

[414] Jones v. Goodwin, 982 F.2d 464, 469–70 (11th Cir. 1993); Hathcock v. State, 357 Ark. 563 (2004); Turner v. State, 355 Ark. 541, 141 S.W.3d 352 (2004) (prejudicial value of evidence of complainant's sexual history outweighed probative value to permit impeachment of her statements to police about her virginity); People v. Santos, 211 Ill. 2d 395, 813 N.E.2d 159 (2004), 543 U.S. 1091 (2005) (defense was not entitled to introduce complainant's statements admitting that she incorrectly told medical personnel that she had not engaged in sexual relations in the 72 hours previous to the examination, since this was a collateral matter and it was not relevant to the DNA analysis, which excluded the defendant); Thompson v. Commonwealth, 28 Va. App. 543, 507 S.E.2d 110 (1998) (where complainant stated to police in the presence of her mother that she had never before engaged in any type of sexual intercourse, complainant's false denial of earlier intercourse did not open the door to evidence of complainant's prior sexual activity); State v. Guthrie, 205 W. Va. 326, 518 S.E.2d 83 (1999) (sexual assault complainant's statement at hospital that last time she engaged in sexual intercourse was approximately two months earlier did not permit defendant to offer evidence of test results conducted at hospital which showed presence of sperm since complainant did not make her previous sexual conduct an issue at trial and did not testify about prior sexual conduct; such evidence may be admissible had complainant made her sexual history an issue or if the test results were offered as "substantive exculpatory evidence of [the defendant's] innocence").

[415] Commonwealth v. McGee, 42 Mass. App. Ct. 740, 679 N.E.2d 609, *review denied*, 425 Mass. 1107, 684 N.E.2d 1198 (1997). *Jones, supra* note 414.

[416] Mooney v. State, 266 Ga. App. 587, 597 S.E.2d 589, *cert. denied*, 2004 Ga. LEXIS 750 (Sept. 7, 2004), *cert. denied*, 125 S. Ct. 1974 (2005):

> [T]he defense sought to use the statement to show that the victim's 'past sexual behavior' did not include him and that the victim's trial testimony concerning her sexual experiences with Mooney was a fabrication. As one of the purposes of the *Rape Shield Statute* is to assist the truth-seeking process, we believe that it should not provide 'justification for letting the witness affirmatively resort to perjurious testimony in reliance on [Mooney's] disability to challenge her credibility.' Under the circumstances presented by this case, the trial court erred in restricting Mooney from cross-examining the victim concerning her prior statement.

Somewhat related to this area is the issue of the admissibility of a complainant's sexual preference. There may be situations where the sexual preference of the complainant may be deemed relevant and admissible. For example, in a sexual assault charge involving two adult males, evidence may be admissible to establish the sexual preference and orientation of a complainant on the issue of consent and the victim's credibility where the prosecution sought to establish that the victim was heterosexual and would not consent to a homosexual experience.[417]

Ordinarily, the complainant's sexual preference is irrelevant.[418] The prosecution, by referencing the complainant's sexual preference to create an inference that complainant would not consent to a sexual act, may open the door to sexual history.[419]

§ 5.37   Testimony concerning a complainant's previous abortion or birth control practices.

Testimony concerning a complainant's previous abortion is evidence of prior sexual conduct and, accordingly, falls within the scope of a rape shield statute. Claiming that a complainant's prior abortions may have provided a victim with a motive to fabricate is a "purely speculative" assertion, and it is not in the interest of justice to admit such inflammatory evidence without a further showing of relevance to the case.[420]

A victim's fear that her defendant father would beat her in reaction to her planned abortion is not relevant as to bias and motive to fabricate when the defendant denies the use of corporal punishment as a form of discipline and claims a close relationship with his victim-daughter and that she did not fear him.[421] Had there been a history of physical abuse or evidence that the victim

---

However, we conclude that the error was harmless.

Id. at 594, 597 S.E.2d at 597.

[417] People v. Murphy, 899 P.2d 294 (Colo. Ct. App. 1994) (also noting that expert testimony should have been admitted concerning the reactions and behavior of individuals in conflict with their sexual identity who engage in homosexual contact).

[418] People v. Dembry, 91 P.3d 431 (Colo. Ct. App. 2003), *cert. denied*, 2004 Col. LEXIS 466 (June 1, 2004) (trial court properly excluded evidence that complainant was predisposed to having homosexual pedophilic experiences, since complainant's sexuality is irrelevant to whether defendant sexually assaulted him). *See also* § 14.29.

[419] State v. Lessley, 257 Neb. 903, 601 N.W.2d 521 (1999) (prosecution opened the door to complainant's sexual history with men when it elicited testimony that complainant is lesbian and had never previously engaged in act which she accused defendant of committing, creating an inference that she would not consent to anal intercourse).

[420] People v. Perryman, 178 A.D.2d 916–17, 578 N.Y.S.2d 785, 787 (1991), *appeal denied*, 79 N.Y.2d 1005, 594 N.E.2d 954, 44 N.Y.S.2d 460 (1992). *See also* People v. Davis, 238 A.D.2d 517, 657 N.Y.S.2d 924, *appeal denied*, 90 N.Y.2d 903, 686 N.E.2d 227, 663 N.Y.S.2d 515 (1997) (holding that relevance of complainant's abortion weeks before the charged offense too speculative to be admissible).

[421] Commonwealth v. Weber, 549 Pa. 430, 438, 701 A.2d 531, 535 (1997).

had an unfounded fear that the defendant would physically abuse her, testimony concerning the abortion would have been relevant.[422]

There are situations, however, where evidence of a prior abortion or the victim's desire to have an abortion may become relevant. Where the prosecution presents evidence on direct examination of the complainant's pregnancy which she allegedly discovered shortly after the rape, this clearly opens the door to cross-examination concerning the complainant's desire to have an abortion and wanting the defendant to pay for it.[423]

Evidence of a complainant's birth control practices also implicates sexual conduct and will be precluded without a showing of necessity and relevance. For example, testimony of a complainant's possession or use of birth control pills is considered an unwarranted intrusion into the private life of the victim.[424] California now provides that in sexual assault prosecutions in which consent is at issue "evidence that the victim suggested, requested, or otherwise communicated to the defendant that the defendant use a condom or other birth control device, without additional evidence of consent, is not sufficient to constitute consent."[425]

There are situations where a complainant's birth control practices are relevant to knowledge of sexual matters. For example, in prosecution based on a theory that the complainant has an incapacity to consent based on a mental disability and lack of appreciation or understanding of sexual intercourse, a court may permit inquiry on birth control practices to explore the complainant's understanding of sexual activity.[426]

§ 5.38   Evidence of complainant's prostitution or exchanging sex for drugs.

Some rape shield statutes specifically permit the introduction of testimony concerning a complainant's history of prostitution. In those situations there is

---

[422] *Id.*

[423] Commonwealth v. Riley, 434 Pa. Super. 414, 643 A.2d 1090 (1994) (noting that had the prosecution not opened the door on this issue the defendant would have been required to file a proper motion in order to discuss this aspect of the complainant's history; by placing the matter in issue, the prosecution nullified the rape shield law's requirement of a prior written motion and hearing on the issue).

[424] United States v. Galloway, 963 F.2d 1388, 1390 (10th Cir. 1992), *cert. denied*, 506 U.S. 957, 418 (1992); Jackson v. State, 375 So. 2d 1271 (Ala. Crim. App. 1979), *cert. denied*, 375 So. 2d 1274 (1979).

[425] Cal. Penal Code § 261.7.

[426] *In the Interest of* Doe, 81 Haw. 447, 918 P.2d 254 (1996) (reversing defendant's conviction due to trial court's failure, in a prosecution based on complainant's marital status, to allow defendant to cross-examine state's expert psychologist about complainant's use of birth control pills and past sexual behavior); State v. Scherzer, 301 N.J. Super. 363, 418, 694 A.2d 196, 222, *appeal denied*, 151 N.J. 466, 700 A.2d 878 (1997).

a presumption of admissibility. Unless set forth as an exception in the rape shield statute, evidence of prostitution is evidence of prior sexual conduct and evidence of character, and therefore subject to the same proscriptions of the state's rape shield statute.[427] One view is that while a motive to fabricate will generally justify admissibility of evidence ordinarily precluded by the rape shield statute, acts of prostitution alone do not demonstrate a motive to fabricate in the eyes of some courts.[428] Many courts require clearly similar behavior between the alleged acts of prostitution and the charged sexual assault.[429] Acts of prostitution, in these courts' view, do not show a motive to fabricate.[430]

On the other hand, some courts take the position that even if the rape shield statute does not specifically provide for the admission of the complainant's prior acts of prostitution, they are relevant to the complainant's credibility. Nevada's Supreme Court explains the rationale behind admissibility:

> When dealing with illegal acts of prostitution, however, the policies behind the rape shield laws largely disappear. Illegal acts of prostitution are not intimate details of private life. They are criminal acts of sexual conduct engaged in, for the most part, with complete strangers. The legislature could not have intended to afford special protection, beyond that afforded to other criminal conduct, to acts of illegal prostitution just because those acts happen to involve sexual conduct. . . . This is not to say that a victim's prior arrest record for prostitution must always be admitted in a sexual assault case. By this opinion, we merely place a prior arrest record for prostitution on an equal footing with other evidence of misconduct. Like other kinds of evidence, a prior arrest record for prostitution is subject to considerations of, for example, confusion and prejudice.[431] The facts of the case may determine the relevance of the complainant's prostitution. If the victim claims that she accepted money from the defendant to hasten her departure from the defendant's apartment, it may be reversible error to preclude the complainant's testimony of prior prostitution.[432] It may also provide a motive to fabricate the allegations.[433]

---

[427] State v. Graber, 1994 Ohio App. LEXIS 4818 (Sept. 30, 1994).

[428] State v. Johnson, 123 N.M. 640, 944 P.2d 869 (1997) (holding that if defendant seeks to offer alleged acts of prostitution, defendant needs to specify how the acts are probative beyond a "yes-yes" inference since acts of prostitution do not inherently provide a motive to fabricate).

[429] Jeffries v. Nix, 912 F.2d 982, 985, 987–88 (8th Cir. 1990), cert. denied, 499 U.S. 927 (1991); People v. Tennin, 162 Ill. App. 3d 520, 525, 515 N.E.2d 1056, 1059 (1987); Commonwealth v. Houston, 430 Mass. 616, 722 N.E.2d 942 (2000); State v. Crims, 540 N.W.2d 860 (Minn. Ct. App. 1995).

[430] Bryant v. Adams, 859 A.2d 1093 (D.C. 2004) (complainant's prostitution activities after alleged rape properly excluded); State v. Johnson, 123 N.M. 640, 944 P.2d 869 (1997).

[431] Drake v. State, 108 Nev. 523, 527, 836 P.2d 52, 55 (1992).

[432] State v. DeJesus, 270 Conn. 826, 856 A.2d 345 (2004).

[433] Id.

Evidence of a complainant's work activities at a nightclub, apparently designed to suggest that the complainant was a prostitute or an extremely "loose" woman, must also meet the test of relevance as well as not violate the rape shield statute.[434] Trying to denominate such evidence as relevant to defendant's state of mind to support a mistake of fact offense is likely to run afoul of the same principles.[435] When relevant to credibility and the circumstances of the case, the prosecution may be required to disclose evidence in its possession of a complainant's prior prostitution.[436] A defendant may introduce evidence that a complainant had previously engaged in exchanging sexual favors for drugs as evidence of her motive for accusing the defendant of rape, where there is a "close" factual connection between the past conduct and the fact pattern of defendant's charges,[437] but not when there is insufficient evidence of a pattern of distinctive sexual behavior, and then there is "no logical connection" or a sufficient similarity between any alleged past trading of sex for drugs and any motive to accuse the defendant[438] or the defense is no intercourse at all in which case the evidence

---

[434] United States v. Greaves, 40 M.J. 432 (C.M.A. 1994), *cert. denied*, 513 U.S. 1114 (1994) ("Evidence of the prosecutrix's previous employment as a hostess at a Japanese bar added nothing legitimate to the defense." *Id.* at 439).

[435] *Id.* at 439. Mistake of fact is discussed in § § 16.16 and 16.17.

[436] Demers v. State, 209 Conn. 143, 547 A.2d 28 (1988).

[437] Jackson v. State, 254 Ga. App. 562, 564–65, 562 S.E.2d 847, 849–50, *aff'd in part, rev'd in part*, 275 Ga. 576, 571 S.E.2d 376 (2002) (defendant properly permitted to testify about his history of exchanging drugs for sex with complainant, although based on defendant's offer of proof, only his testimony was admissible on the relationship); Johnson v. State, 332 Md. 456, 474–75, 632 A.2d 152, 153 (1993); Commonwealth v. McGregor, 39 Mass. App. Ct. 919, 655 N.E.2d 1278 (1995) (reversible error to preclude evidence of complainant's past homosexual behaviors with street pimps for shelter and drugs which were relevant to defense of a consensual relationship and exchange of drugs for sex); State v. Sheline, 1996 Tenn. Crim. App. LEXIS 360 (June 14, 1996) (reversible error to preclude complainant's past sexual conduct which was "evidence of a distinctive pattern, so resembling the defendant's version of the story that it tends to prove that the victim consented to sexual relations with the defendant").

[438] United States v. Saunders, 943 F.2d 388 (4th Cir. 1991), *cert. denied*, 502 U.S. 1105 (1992); State v. Montes, 28 Kan. App. 2d 768, 773–75, 21 P.3d 592, 596–97 (2001) (requiring more than factual similarity of exchanging sex for drugs to admit into evidence prior sexual encounter of complainant); State v. Crims, 540 N.W.2d 860 (Minn. Ct. App. 1995) ("Crims asserts he gave T.K. $20, after which she purchased drugs, and then led him to the side of the building with the intention of 'compensating' him. This sort of behavior is dissimilar from T.K.'s history of agreeing to prostitute herself for a specific quantity of drugs, performing her end, and then receiving her bargained-for earnings." *Id.* at 868.); State v. Ginyard, 122 N.C. App. 25, 468 S.E.2d 525 (1996), *rev'd on other grounds* (holding that evidence that complainant exchanged sex for drugs on one prior occasion, did not establish a pattern of such conduct to warrant its admission) — court requires more than one or a "few isolated mistakes" of consensual activities to establish a pattern); State v. Thompson, 131 Or. App. 230, 884 P.2d 574 (1994); Commonwealth v. Guy, 454 Pa. Super. 582, 686 A.2d 397 (1996) ("To allow such evidence to be introduced at trial would have the immediate and direct effect of shifting the focal point of the trial away from a determination of the events of the night in question to a determination of whether the victim had, in the past, acted in a manner that was less than virtuous. This result is unacceptable. Regardless of whether appellant's proffer is accurate, the victim must not be made to suffer such prejudice, ridicule and humiliation in payment for past indiscretions." *Id.* at 591, 686 A.2d at 402).

is irrelevant.[439] Strong evidence of physical force may support a trial court's conclusion that the act could not reasonably be viewed as consensual, thereby permitting the trial court to preclude evidence of any prior exchanging of drugs for sex.[440] If there is no evidence that the complainant offered to trade sex for drugs at the time of the incident charged, it may be irrelevant to the offer to trade the drugs for sex two weeks earlier.[441]

Generally, a victim's use of drugs other than at the time of a sexual assault is collateral.[442]

§ 5.39   Evidence of prior sexual history and conduct to explain sexual awareness, common knowledge, or terminology.

Another reason proffered for delving into a complainant's sexual history is to explain the source of a complainant's knowledge or awareness of sexual matters. This is particularly an issue in child sexual assault prosecutions when it is argued that the child would not have known of the sexual acts described unless exposed to them by the defendant. Sometimes this argument is also made with older individuals. A starting point in this analysis of admissibility is relevance. The first issue is whether the witness is demonstrating awareness of sexual matters or terminology that is unusual or beyond his or her years. If it is not that "unusual" for the complainant to have knowledge of sexual matters, there is no reason to bring in evidence of the complainant's other sexual activities. Simply describing touching of "privates" and "private area" is not likely to be "extraordinary sexual knowledge," triggering the right to present evidence of a child's prior sexual activity.[443]

Knowledge of the body is not knowledge of why someone would want to engage in sexual contact.[444]

---

[439] White v. State, 324 Md. 626, 598 A.2d 187 (1991).

[440] Davis v. State, 235 Ga. App. 362, 509 S.E.2d 655 (1998).

[441] Shand v. State, 341 Md. 661, 672 A.2d 630 (1996) ("Petitioners' argument is analogous to a hypothetical motor tort trial in which the plaintiff, who has no proof that the defendant motorist was driving while drunk at the time of the accident, offers to prove that fact by evidence that the defendant was driving while drunk two weeks prior to the accident." *Id.* at 673, 672 A.2d at 636).

[442] State v. Jackson, 800 So. 2d 854 (La. 2001).

[443] United States v. Torres, 937 F.2d 1469, 1474 (9th Cir. 1991), *cert. denied*, 502 U.S. 1037 (1992) ("We need not decide whether such evidence might be admissible in a proper case. Here, the victim's testimony did not demonstrate any unusual knowledge of sexual techniques or nomenclature. Rather her testimony was replete with simple references to 'private spot' and 'private parts' and 'private places.' " *Id.* at 1474); State v. Hoffstadt, 652 A.2d 93, 95 (Me. 1995).

[444] Chapman v. State, 117 Nev. 1, 16 P.3d 432 (2001) (holding "incidents of supposed sexual conduct and familiarity with the male anatomy were neither specific nor indicative of any ability on the part of the victim to contrive charges against Chapman."); State v. St. George, 252 Wis. 2d 499, 643 N.W.2d 777 (2002):

If a defendant wishes to reference a complainant's sexual behaviors, the sexual conduct must relate to the allegations against the defendant. The prior sexual activity must somehow support an inference that the prior activity is the source of the current complaint. [445]

For example, a child's exposing herself to a neighbor boy may not relate in any way to the accused adult's sexual assault of the child. [446] It is insufficient to simply allege that the complainant's knowledge of or access to sexual activity

> Kayla's sexual knowledge fails to satisfy the relevancy requirement of factor three. There is nothing precocious about Kayla's statements that someone touched her body. Kayla's accusation that the defendant touched her vagina and "wiggled and jiggled" is not a description of age-inappropriate knowledge. Kayla's description is neither graphic nor precise enough that a jury would infer that a child Kayla's age would be able to make this description only if the conduct charged actually occurred. The sexual knowledge Kayla possessed was mere knowledge of her body. Such knowledge is not so unusual as to raise an inference that some sexual contact with the defendant must have taken place.
>
> The defendant asserts that the jury inference comes not from Kayla's knowledge of her body, but from the knowledge that someone would have a desire to fondle the private parts of another. Kayla has not expressed knowledge that someone would want to touch her body for sexual gratification, which arguably would be evidence of sexual precociousness or knowledge beyond her years. Kayla expressed knowledge about the part of her body touched, not knowledge about why someone would desire to touch her.
>
> We conclude that the testimony that Kayla claimed to have been touched on the vagina does not show such precocious sexual knowledge that a jury would believe that some sexual contact with the defendant must necessarily have occurred.

Id. at 517–58, 643 N.W.2d at 784.

[445] State v. Wellington, 150 N.H. 782, 787–88, 846 A.2d 1171, 1175–76 (2004) (12-year-old's masturbation not admissible to show sexual knowledge, since it was not probative of the sexual activity with which the defendant was charged); State v. Ellsworth, 142 N.H. 710, 709 A.2d 768 (1998):

> Here, the defendant conceded that prior abuse was not the only source of sexual knowledge, because 'while [the victim] was at Spaulding Youth Center, he was engaged in constant therapy about sexual abuse.' Accordingly, we cannot disturb the trial court's ruling that the 'defendant failed to prove his theory that it was the experience at age three, as opposed to any other, that gave complainant the information to support the present allegations,' and therefore the prior sexual abuse was irrelevant and inadmissible. Moreover, the probative value of this information is almost negligible, while 'the potential prejudice . . . is manifest, as an inquiry into the prior allegation would likely compromise the victim's privacy and mislead the jury.'

Id. at 721; 709 A.2d at 775, 709 A.2d at 775, *citing* State v. Berrocales, 140 N.H. 647, 649, 670 A.2d 1045, 1047 (1996).

[446] State v. Sharp, 180 Wis. 2d 640, 511 N.W.2d 316 (1993) (upholding trial court's decision refusing to allow evidence of child's prior sexual conduct of exposing herself to a neighbor boy since it was not 'apparent' that one child's display of genitalia to another child closely resembles or relates in any way to an adult's sexual assault of a child." *Id.* at 648, 511 N.W.2d at 320).

at home,[447] prostitution by a parent's friend,[448] school,[449] or pornography,[450] is relevant to the accusation.

[447] State v. Sloan, 912 S.W.2d 592, 598 (Mo. Ct. App. 1995) (holding that trial court properly precluded testimony from child's grandmother that one night she opened the door of the child's room and saw her on top of her aunt simulating sexual intercourse and that child then told her grandmother that she saw her mother and another man having sexual relations); Commonwealth v. Fink, 2002 Pa. Super. 32, 791 A.2d 1235 (2002) (holding defendant neither entertained sexual conduct between complainant and babysitter, nor that babysitter was source of victim's sexual knowledge; other similar evidence proffered by defendant was also conjectural and not exonerating of charged conduct).

[448] State v. Hydock, 51 Conn. App. 753, 767–69, 725 A.2d 379, 388, *appeal denied*, 248 Conn. 921 (1999) (finding neither good faith basis nor relevance to questions about child's mother's friend about prostituting herself to support a heroin habit which allegedly exposed child witness to adult sexual behavior).

[449] Clanton v. State, 271 Ga. App. 444, 609 S.E.2d 761 (2005) (defendant claimed court should have permitted testimony that six-year-old observed mother having intercourse, which was source of her sexual knowledge. Court rejected this noting:

> Even assuming that J.C. noticed the sexual activity, the proffered testimony did not show that the young child, then three-and-a-half or four years old, retained any memory of it for approximately the next three years. Nothing in the record showed that J.C. ever mentioned seeing her mother engaged in any sexual activity or related in any way that one episode to what she later described as someone 'put[ting] his thing that he pees with where she pees and jump[ing] up and down.' Rather, the evidence showed that when J.C. saw similar behavior after her encounter with Clanton, she volunteered, 'that's just like [Clanton] did.' We conclude that, under these circumstances and pretermitting whether the incident was part of the child's sexual history, the evidence sought to be admitted did not logically tend to prove Clanton's claim or any material fact at issue in this case.

Id. at 445–46, 609 S.E.2d at 763. State v. Steffes, 887 P.2d 1196 (Mont. 1994):

> We have previously rejected the argument that a defendant may introduce evidence of how a victim obtained his or her knowledge of sexual matters. . . . We held that this type of attack upon the victim's credibility is impermissible under the rape shield statute. . . . In this case, one of the victims testified that he had acquired some knowledge of sexual matters at school. In so testifying, the victim was not claiming that all of his knowledge concerning sexual matters was gained through his contact with Steffes and, therefore, Steffes had no reason to rebut this testimony.

Id. at 1207.

[450] United States v. Johns, 15 F.3d 740, 744 (8th Cir. 1994). *See also* United States v. St. Pierre, 812 F.2d 417, 419 (8th Cir. 1987) (upholding trial court's preclusion of evidence that a complainant's knowledge of sexual matters may have come from sexually-explicit magazines); United States v. Frazier, 678 F. Supp. 499 (E.D. Pa. 1986), *aff'd*, 806 F.2d 255 (3d Cir. 1986); State v. Brossette, 634 So. 2d 1309 (La. Ct. App. 1994), *cert. denied*, 640 So. 2d 1344 (1994) (upholding trial court's decision to permit introduction of three sexually-explicit publications found either out of place in the victim's house or on one occasion under the victim's bed, but precluding the defense attorney from highlighting to the jury specific sexual information in the publications since there was no showing that the complainant had ever actually read the material, especially the portions that defense counsel wanted to read to the jury); State v. Sexton, 929 S.W.2d 909 (Mo. Ct. App. 1996) (holding trial court properly excluded evidence concerning child victim's knowledge of sexual matters gained from pornographic magazines since this was a collateral issue and outside scope of direct, cross, and redirect).

The complainant's age is a factor to consider in whether prior sexual abuse or conduct is relevant to the child's sexual knowledge. To find an exception to a rape shield statute, the child's sexual knowledge must be truly extraordinary for his or her age.[451] A teenager by virtue of age, sexual counseling, and sex education likely has knowledge of sexual acts apart from what the defendant may have.[452] In such a situation, "evidence of the victim's prior abuse is marginally relevant and is more prejudicial than probative."[453]

Without showing a connection to the instant charge, prior sexual abuse will not be admissible to explain sexual knowledge.[454] If a victim can not remember the prior sexual abuse, it is difficult to conclude a child developed sexual knowledge from the prior sexual abuse.[455]

Similarly, a child victim's parent's sexual abuse experiences may not be admissible unless those experiences relate to the complaining child's experience or testimony.[456]

---

[451] State v. Knox, 634 A.2d 952, 953 (Me. 1993) (finding ten-year-old boy's knowledge of sexual matters not beyond his age).

[452] Frederic v. State, 770 So. 2d 719 (Fla. Ct. App. 2000):

> The Defendant relies upon cases in which the courts held that due to the victim's age or mental capacity, the jury might perceive the victim as naive and thus should have been allowed to consider evidence that might help them evaluate the victim's testimony of sexually-explicit matters [citations omitted]. . . To contrast, here, the trial evidence showed the victim was 13 at the time of the abuse. She became pregnant as a result of the abuse, so she had already reached puberty. Further, defense counsel elicited testimony from her that she had had sex education classes in school and knew enough about sex to understand what semen was and that a pre-pubescent boy could not have caused her pregnancy. The Defendant cannot now argue that the only explanation for the victim's knowledge of sex was some previous instance of sexual abuse. The trial court did not abuse its discretion in excluding this testimony.

Id. at 720. State v. Jones, 490 N.W.2d 787 (Iowa 1992); Commonwealth v. Allburn, 721 A.2d 363, 366 (1998), appeal denied, 559 Pa. 662, 739 A.2d 163 (1999) (holding that teenager could have learned about sex from many sources other than her previous sexual activity and thus her prior sexual activity was not relevant).

[453] State v. Jones, 490 N.W.2d at 791.

[454] United States v. Bordeaux, 400 F.3d 548, 557–59 (8th Cir. 2005) (holding evidence of complainant's statement that her "brother's friend placed his penis in her mouth" was properly precluded to prevent harassment or embarrassment of complainant and because it was not shown to be probative of her sexual knowledge); State v. Butts, 938 S.W.2d 924 (Mo. Ct. App. 1997) (defendant not permitted to introduce evidence of forcible rape 38 years earlier to explain her "mental disorder" when there is no showing that any mental disability affects her ability to recall); Commonwealth v. Appenzeller, 388 Pa. Super. 172, 565 A.2d 170 (1989) (evidence of a child's prior sexual assault not relevant to show child's knowledge of sexual matters).

[455] People v. Garayua, 268 A.D.2d 283, 701 N.Y.S.2d 379, appeal denied, 95 N.Y.2d 796, 733 N.E.2d 236, 711 N.Y.S.2d 164 (2000) ("The court properly exercised its discretion by precluding defendant from introducing evidence of a prior incident of sexual abuse against the victim, since she had little or no memory of the prior incident and since there was no indication that her 'sexual knowledge' was gleaned from that incident." Id. at 284, 701 N.Y.S.2d at 381).

[456] Commonwealth v. Souza, 39 Mass. App. Ct. 103, 653 N.E.2d 1127, review denied, 421 Mass. 1103, 655 N.E.2d 1277 (1995).

Other courts find that a victim's access to information on sexual acts or witnessing of sexual acts is relevant to charges against a defendant, given the implication that a child would not know of the sexual acts testified to when the defendant allegedly committed the acts with the complainant.

Unlike some courts, New Hampshire's Supreme Court has taken the view that the average 12-year-old victim would be considered sexually innocent and that a jury would likely believe that her testimony of sexual experience must have occurred.[457] Thus, the following evidence, according to the New Hampshire court, was necessary for a defendant to show that the complainant has "the experience and ability to contrive a statutory rape charge against him."[458]

> [The 12-year-old complainant] was seen "masturbating a bull"; that the alleged victim's stepmother is her stepsister; that the prosecutrix undressed young boys to expose them and play with them while babysitting; that the prosecutrix had sex with her father and grandfather, the latter in exchange for money; that the prosecutrix lived with a man not her husband in an apartment; that the defendant "was the only man who had befriended the complainant in a non-sexual way"; that a Nashua police report contains allegations of sexual contact between the prosecutrix and the Edwards brothers; that the prosecutrix would engage in sexual activities with others while being shown on closed circuit television; that at a probable cause hearing for the Edwards brothers, the prosecutrix refused to appear and press charges; and that the prosecutrix has undergone psychiatric counseling.[459]

The court found that the complainant's prior sexual history could be relevant to demonstrate that, due to her "decadent sexual environment, . . . she suffered certain psychiatric trauma," had "never been truly assimilated into normal society," and consequently there were questions "whether she places any value on the telling of the truth or other values one would normally expect of a 12-year-old child when placed in the impressive surroundings of a courtroom."[460] The latter portion of the court's rationale is a particularly broad approach to the relevancy of a complainant's prior sexual history and that a sexual history has a bearing on credibility in the courtroom.

One court reasoned that a jury "would perceive the average 12-year-old girl as a sexual innocent" and that jurors would believe that the sexual experience she describes must have occurred in connection with the incident being prosecuted; otherwise, she could not have described it. However, if statutory rape victims have had other sexual experiences, it would be possible for them to provide detailed, realistic testimony concerning an incident that may never have

---

[457] State v. Howard, 121 N.H. 53, 426 A.2d 457 (1981).

[458] Id. at 61, 426 A.2d at 462.

[459] Id. at 55, 426 A.2d at 458–59.

[460] Id. at 61, 426 A.2d at 462.

happened. To preclude a defendant from presenting such evidence to the jury if it is otherwise admissible may be error.[461]

Many other courts have followed this line of reasoning in holding that a defendant should be permitted to present evidence of a child's sexual experiences or exposure to sexual matters.[462]

---

[461] State v. Budis, 243 N.J. Super. 498, 510, 580 A.2d 283, 290 (1990), *aff'd*, 125 N.J. 519, 593 A.2d 784 (1991).

[462] People v. Salas, 30 Cal. App. 4th 417, 36 Cal. Rptr. 2d 374 (1994) (defendant's conviction reversed due to the erroneous exclusion of child's prior accusations of sexual abuse against others, which were relevant to child's sexual knowledge, as well as motive for fabrication of the charges against defendant, namely that the child knew that an accusation of molestation would have the effect of removing defendant from her life); People v. Mason, 219 Ill. App. 3d 76, 578 N.E.2d 1351 (1991) (holding rape shield statute does not apply to evidence of a seven-year-old's viewing of pornographic videotapes to explain her knowledge of sexual activities); State v. Jacques, 558 A.2d 706, 708 (Me. 1989) (in prosecution involving five-and ten-year-old victims, court held, "A defendant therefore must be permitted to rebut the inference a jury might otherwise draw that the victim was so naive sexually that she could not have fabricated the charge."); Commonwealth v. Ruffen, 399 Mass. 811, 507 N.E.2d 684 (1987) (holding defendant should have been permitted to determine whether there was evidence of previous sexual abuse of the victim similar to the abuse alleged in the case to determine victim's knowledge of sexual matters); Commonwealth v. Rathburn, 26 Mass. App. Ct. 699, 706–07, 532 N.E.2d 691, 696, (1988), *review denied*, 404 Mass. 1104, 537 N.E.2d 1248 (1989); State v. Benedict, 397 N.W.2d 337, 341 (Minn. 1986) (holding that, despite the rape shield statute, "a trial court has discretion to admit evidence tending to establish a source of knowledge of or familiarity with sexual matters in circumstances where the jury would likely infer that the defendant was the source of the knowledge"); People v. Ramos, 201 A.D.2d 78, 614 N.Y.S.2d 977 (1994) (defendant's conviction was reversed for, among other reasons, prosecution's failure to provide the defense with information in its possession that the "child's ability to accurately describe sexual behavior long pre-dated the date of the alleged incident, and that she had extensive knowledge of sexuality derived from obviously inappropriate exposure to sexual information at home. This was particularly crucial in light of the inconclusive nature of the medical evidence and Dr. Vasquez's testimony that her conclusion that the child had been sexually abused was primarily based on this young child's ability to describe what had happened. . . . The undisclosed documents demonstrating the child's prior knowledge of sexual matters and her prior conduct with regard to the use of the anatomically correct dolls that have sharply undercut the basis of both the doctor's opinion and the argument made on summation [that a five-year-old child was not capable of making up testimony concerning sexual abuse]." *Id.* at 87, 614 N.Y.S.2d at 982–83; State v. Ungerer, 1996 Ohio App. LEXIS 2947 (June 5, 1996) (defendant's conviction reversed because trial court precluded evidence of prior abuse. "[T]he State's witnesses testified regarding behaviors they observed which contributed to their suspicions the child had been abused. We find the defendant should have been permitted to cross-examine the witnesses regarding those behaviors, and what reason the witnesses had to conclude those behaviors were indicative of abuse. For this purpose, the evidence of prior sexual abuse is addressed not to the child's credibility, but rather, to the credibility of the witness testifying regarding how the child behaved and what the behavior implied." *Id.* at * 13–14.); State v. Grovenstein, 340 S.C. 210, 530 S.E.2d 406 (2000) (holding trial court erred in precluding evidence of child victim's prior sexual experience to demonstrate source of victim's ability to testify about sexual matters); State v. Carver, 37 Wash. App. 122, 678 P.2d 842, *review denied*, 102 Wash. 2d 1019 (1984) ("Merely because the evidence pertains to a sexual experience does not mean we must strain to fit it into the special confines of the rape shield statute. Rather, we must apply general evidentiary principles of relevance,

As noted earlier, not all courts follow this reasoning. It has been suggested that to present evidence of a complainant's prior sexual history to show an alternative source of sexual knowledge, a defendant should establish before trial (1) proof the acts occurred, (2) that the acts were similar to those of the present case, (3) that the prior acts of abuse are relevant to a material issue at trial, (4) that the evidence is necessary for the defense, and (5) that the probative value of evidence of prior sexual abuse outweighs its prejudice.[463] A limiting instruction might also be provided to the jury to explain the purpose of the evidence to minimize its prejudicial effect.[464] Washington's Court of Appeals suggests the following analysis to determine the probative value of a victim's prior abuse to explain sexual awareness:

> When determining the probative value, courts should consider (1) the age of the victim: the older the child, the less likely the jury will give significant weight to the fact that the child can describe sexual acts; (2) how explicit was the child's testimony: the more explicit, the more likely the Carver influence will arise; (3) whether the evidence suggests other sources for the child's knowledge — such as learning it from other children — that are independent of the alleged abuse by the defendant and the other abuser; (4) whether the evidence suggests any bias or motive falsely to accuse the defendant: if one exists, the prior abuse will be more relevant; and (5) the remoteness in time of the prior abuse: the longer ago it occurred, the less relevant it will be.[465]

§ 5.40　Prior sexual conduct to rebut prosecution's behavioral expert or testimony concerning child sexual abuse accommodation syndrome.

Often the prosecution will present expert testimony to explain the behavior, conduct, or reactions of a sexual assault victim.[466] The argument has been made that prosecution testimony that the complainant exhibits symptoms of the Child Sexual Abuse Accommodation Syndrome (CSAAS)[467] is evidence of a disease within the meaning of the rape shield statute and can be rebutted by evidence of prior sexual conduct.[468] This argument may have merit if the behavioral

---

probative value and prejudice. Using this approach, our first inquiry is whether the evidence of prior sexual abuse was relevant. Defendant offered the evidence, not to attack the character of the little girls, but rather to rebut the inference they would not know about such sexual acts unless they had experienced them with defendant." *Id.* at 124, 678 P.2d at 843–44).

[463] State v. Pulizzano, 155 Wis. 2d 633, 656, 456 N.W.2d 325, 335 (1990) (holding that evidence of prior sexual assault of preschool child should have been admitted to establish possible basis for child's sexual knowledge).

[464] *Id.* at 653, 456 N.W.2d at 333.

[465] State v. Kilgore, 107 Wash. App. 160, 180, 26 P.3d 308, 318 (2001).

[466] *See* Chapter 11.

[467] *See* § 11.14 *et seq.*

[468] State v. Christiano, 228 Conn. 456, 464, 637 A.2d 382, 386 (1994) (court declined to address

symptoms or opinion of the expert suggests that, or are based on the assumption, that the defendant is the person who abused the complainant. Once the prosecution introduces evidence of a child's behavioral symptoms, it may be reversible error to preclude a defendant from introducing evidence of prior sexual conduct by the child to explain those behaviors.[469] This is analogous to the rule that evidence of semen can be rebutted with prior sexual conduct if the prosecution has offered such evidence, but not if the defense seeks to offer it, because the prosecution must open the door. But if the expert explains a delay in reporting abuse inflicted by a parent or authority figure (i.e., because it is difficult for victims to confront an abuser when the abuser is a parent or a trusted adult), then sexual conduct with brothers and foster brothers would not be "analogous to the situation."[470] Nonetheless, the argument that the prosecution has opened the door to rebuttal testimony of prior sexual conduct may be accepted in other situations or when supported by testimony of a defense expert.

There must be enough similarity between the past behavior and current behavior to be admissible. Also, there must be a connection between the behaviors

---

this issue directly because defendant failed to preserve this objection; court did address issue of whether prior evidence of sexual conduct could be used to provide an alternate explanation to prosecution's expert's testimony explaining victim's delay in reporting crime); Rocha v. State, 248 Ga. App. 53, 56, 545 S.E.2d 173, 175–76 (2001).

[469] United States v. Bear Stops, 997 F.2d 451, 454–55 (8th Cir. 1993) (holding that evidence of child's prior sexual encounters should have been admitted as an alternative explanation to the testimony of the prosecution's expert concerning the child's behavioral manifestations of a sexually-abused child); Hall v. State, 196 Ga. App. 523, 396 S.E.2d 271 (1990) (court reversed defendant's conviction due to trial court's refusal to allow evidence of six-year-old's prior sexual assault to explain prosecution's expert's behavioral testimony reasoning as follows):

> Testimony regarding the syndrome and all the child's symptoms and injuries having been properly admitted, the evidence regarding other possible causes of her behavior and injuries was necessary to prevent the jury from reaching the unwarranted conclusion that the only possible explanation for the medical findings and the existence of behavior consistent with the child sexual abuse accommodation syndrome was that the victim had been molested by appellant. Moreover, a jury's awareness that the victim had been molested previously could affect its judgment of the victim's credibility, as the credibility of a young child's report of an improper touching must necessarily be greater if the child has had no occasion to learn about such behavior from prior incidents.

Id. at 525, 396 S.E.2d at 273; State v. W.L., 278 N.J. Super. 295, 650 A.2d 1035 (1995) (reversing defendant's convictions for, among other reasons, trial court's failure to admit into evidence complainant's diaries that showed sexual activity with another person and resulting feelings about that relationship which prosecution tried to attribute to complainant's sexual encounters with defendant); State v. Fussell, No. 73713, 1999 Ohio App. LEXIS 2296 (May 20, 1999) (noting that trial court's initial ruling excluding all evidence of complainant's prior sexual abuse to explain her behavioral problems may have been an abuse of discretion, but that evidence of past sexual abuse developed through cross-examination of child's mother cured any possible error by the trial court).

[470] Christiano, 228 Conn. at 474–75, 637 A.2d at 391.

and the alleged prior abuse.[471]

§ 5.41   Evidence of prior sexual history or prior sexual abuse and allegations to show confusion on witness's part "or qualities as percipient witness."

Another theory occasionally offered in support of admitting proof or testimony of prior allegations of abuse is that the complainant is confusing separate and distinct sexual experiences, experiencing a flashback, and thereby misidentifying perpetrators or mistakenly attributing the assaults of others to the defendant. Many of the same areas of analysis discussed in the preceding sections also apply to this theory. Past abuse may also be relevant when there is evidence, such as from a psychiatrist, that the complainant suffers from "flashbacks" of the prior abuse that affects the witness's ability to distinguish the events in question with the past event and to perceive and recall events. In *Commonwealth v. Baxter*,[472] a Massachusetts court held that evidence of the prior rape should have been admitted under the defense theory (supported by expert testimony and the complainant's psychological records), that because of the prior rape "she was experiencing psychiatric problems which left her unable to distinguish between the two incidents." When such a theory is not supported by the defendant, the prior sexual assault conduct is likely to be inadmissible.[473]

---

[471] State v. Dunlap, 250 Wis. 2d 466, 640 N.W.2d 112 (2002) (noting defendant could not rule out the possibility that the child learned the behavior from exposure to pornography or from having viewed sexual activity).

[472] 36 Mass. App. Ct. 45, 627 N.E.2d 487 (1994) (The court noted it viewed rape shield statute as precluding evidence of sexual promiscuity, not necessarily past rapes. Other statutes, such as Federal Rule of Evidence 412, and courts may view rape shield statute more broadly. However, in this case the defendant exhibited a strong factual and expert testimony predicate linking the past rape and current charge to support the theory that the complainant could not distinguish between the two events.).

[473] State v. Beliveau, 237 Conn. 576, 678 A.2d 924 (1996) (holding that defendant's theory of "transference of any beefs or any problems" from prior sexual assault not substantiated and therefore prior allegations inadmissible — defendant needed to establish with proof relevance of his theory); People v. Walker, 223 A.D.2d 414, 636 N.Y.S.2d 765, *appeal denied*, 88 N.Y.2d 887, 668 N.E.2d 433, 645 N.Y.S.2d 462 (1996):

> The trial court appropriately exercised its discretion in precluding cross-examination of the complainant regarding alleged prior sexual abuse, as defendant made no showing that the circumstances of these unrelated allegations bore a significant probative relation to the instant charges [citation omitted]. The trial court's denial of defendant's application to call an expert witness who would testify regarding the possibility that the complainant's accusations against defendant were the result of post-traumatic stress disorder was also an appropriate exercise of discretion [citation omitted]. As noted by the trial court, the complainant's medical records did not even suggest that the complainant had exhibited any of the symptoms suggested by defendant as the cause of her accusations against defendant, the proposed expert psychiatric witness had not personally examined the complainant and concededly was not familiar with all of the facts of the case, and the unrelated sexual abuse which

It is probably insufficient to allege that the victim is confusing the two sexual experiences, and the bare allegation of such confusion is insufficient to overcome the preclusion of prior sexual history as mandated by most rape shield statutes. There must be some showing that the prior sexual conduct or reported abuse casts substantial doubt on the testimony or allegations in the instant case.[474] There may be situations where a complainant's prior sexual intercourse is relevant to the complainant's ability to perceive and recall. Thus, a complainant's prior consensual relations that occurred 30 minutes before the charged rape, but not remembered by the complainant, may be relevant to the "state of her sobriety at the time of the charged rape" and her "qualities as a percipient witness."[475]

§ 5.42   Evidence of complainant's prior sexual conduct to explain defendant's reasonable mistake of fact.

In seeking to establish a defendant's reasonable mistake as to a fact such as the complainant's age or consent, a defendant may seek to offer evidence of the

---

defendant argued could possibly trigger later imagined sexual abuse, actually commenced after the initial incident alleged herein, rendering the proposed testimony of no utility to the jury in determining the issues before it [citation omitted]. *Id.* at 415; 636 N.Y.S.2d at 766.

[474] United States v. Pagel, 45 M.J. 64 (C.A.A.F. 1996); State v. Kulmac, 230 Conn. 43, 50–56, 644 A.2d 887, 892–94 (1994) (holding that whether or not a victim is confused so as to permit cross-examination into other instances of abuse is best left to the discretion of the trial court, and in this case, the past instances of abuse were too remote to cause confusion); Croy v. State, 247 Ga. App. 654, 545 S.E.2d 80 (2001) (upholding trial court's decision to preclude evidence of child's abuse by someone else since there was insufficient showing child was confusing incidents); State v. Jones, 490 N.W.2d 787 (Iowa 1992) (no showing that abuse five years earlier was in any way related to the current allegations of abuse); Commonwealth v. Syrafos, 38 Mass. App. Ct. 211, 646 N.E.2d 429, *appeal denied*, 420 Mass. 1102, 648 N.E.2d 1285 (1995) ("In this case, the rape for which the defendant was being tried was not 'remarkabl[y] similar' to the two rapes that had occurred over seven years before. Further, as we have previously stated, the clinic records did not show that the victim suffered 'flashbacks' or 'auditory hallucinations.' " *Id.* at 218, 646 N.E.2d at 434); People v. Fields, 279 A.D.2d 405, 720 N.Y.S.2d 63, *appeal denied*, 96 N.Y.2d 828, 754 N.E.2d 208, 729 N.Y.S.2d 448 (2001) ("The court correctly applied the Rape Shield Law . . . . to preclude evidence of the victim's sexual conduct with a man other than defendant earlier on the night of the crime, at a different location. Defendant's contention that the intoxicated victim could have confused defendant's conduct with what went on in the earlier incident was nothing more than speculation."); People v. Rogowski, 228 A.D.2d 728, 644 N.Y.S.2d 334 (1996) ("Defendant's contention that the victim was confused between the abuse she suffered at the hands of her father and that which she contended occurred at the hands of her uncle is unavailing. Testimony revealed that she specifically described the separate incidents to both the medical doctor and her counselor. Accordingly, we find that the court properly limited the scope of cross-examination" [citation omitted]. *Id.* at 729, 644 N.Y.S.2d at 335-36); People v. Day, 215 A.D.2d 894, 626 N.Y.S.2d 888, *appeal denied*, 86 N.Y.2d 793, 656 N.E.2d 605, 632 N.Y.S.2d 506 (1995); People v. Charlton, 192 A.D.2d 757, 596 N.Y.S.2d 210, *appeal denied*, 81 N.Y.2d 1071, 619 N.E.2d 668, 601 N.Y.S.2d 590 (1993) (upholding trial court's decision to preclude testimony of the victim's prior abuse by another man, which the defense offered in support of its theory that the victim was confusing the two incidents).

[475] United States v. Tiller, 41 M.J. 823 (N.M.C.C.A. 1995).

complainant's prior history. This would emasculate the general premise of some shield statutes; i.e., that past sexual history is not relevant to consent. The admission of prior sexual history to establish the defense of mistake has been rejected by at least one appeals court.[476] This is also discussed in §§ 16.16–16.17 with respect to jury instructions.

§ 5.43 Evidence of prior sexual history relating to motive to fabricate — The ulterior motive exception.

A complainant's prior sexual history may be offered on the theory that such evidence tends to provide a motive for a complainant to fabricate the charges. This may qualify as an "ulterior motive exception" under the rape shield statute.[477] The decisions in this area are inconsistent and vary widely with regard to the interpretation of a relevant motive to fabricate and what constitutes evidence of a motive to fabricate. If the area of cross-examination is not related to sexual history, the collateral matter still may be admissible on the issue of motive to fabricate.[478] A common situation is where a defendant alleges that the complainant's sexual relations with another are a motive for the complainant to make allegations against the defendant. This assertion has been made by a defendant wanting to show that the reason a teenager left the defendant's home was to continue a relationship with a boyfriend and not because the defendant had made advances toward her.[479] When phrased in terms of a general reason to fabricate a story or evidence of unreliability, such testimony is likely to be prohibited under the rape shield statutes.[480]

---

[476] Little v. State, 650 N.E.2d 343 (Ind. Ct. App. 1995); State v. Perez, 26 Kan. App. 2d 777, 995 P.2d 372 (1999), *review denied*, 269 Kan. 939 (2000) (complainant's sexual activities so close in time to charged crime relevant in determining whether defendant believed complainant was consenting to his sexual advances).

[477] *See, e.g.*, MD. CODE art. § 461A(a)(3).

[478] People v. Rosovich, 209 A.D.2d 554, 619 N.Y.S.2d 85 (1994) (reversing defendant's conviction because trial court precluded: (1) questions concerning the infant's discipline and school problems, which tended to prove a motive in accusing the defendant of sodomy, and (2) cross-examination concerning the infant's prior untrue statements made to her mother concerning her school and after school activities which were relevant to impeach the infant's credibility).

[479] People v. Halbert, 175 A.D.2d 88, 572 N.Y.S.2d 331 (1991), *aff'd*, 80 N.Y.2d 865, 600 N.E.2d 618, 587 N.Y.S.2d 891 (1992), *cert. denied*, 507 U.S. 922 (1993). *See also* State v. Jalo, 27 Or. App. 845, 557 P.2d 1359 (1976) (holding that 41-year-old defendant should have been permitted to introduce evidence that defendant told victim he had discovered and would inform her parents that the ten-year-old complainant was having relations with defendant's 13-year-old son and another young boy, and that this series of events plus complainant's fear of getting in trouble was her motive for accusing him of rape).

[480] *See, e.g.*, United States v. Azure, 845 F.2d 1503, 1506 (8th Cir. 1988) (holding that the trial court properly excluded testimony of a 13-year-old that he had sexual intercourse with the ten-year-old complainant despite the defense's assertion that it would demonstrate the complainant's capability to fabricate a story); Hathcock v. State, 357 Ark. 563, 183 S.W.3d 152 (2004) (trial court properly precluded evidence of complainant's sexual history offered on theory that her false

Another scenario often encountered is where the defendant alleges that the complainant claims that he raped her to avoid the wrath of a jealous boyfriend and compel him to forgive past acts of infidelity. Pennsylvania's Supreme Court held that testimony concerning an argument between a complainant and her boyfriend over infidelity is so closely tied to her prior sexual conduct that they are "one and the same" for purposes of the rape shield law and "precisely the type of allegation regarding past sexual conduct" from which the law is designed to protect victims.[481] It may be sufficient to permit a defendant to explore the relationship with the complainant's other partner without allowing testimony concerning the sexual component of the relationship.[482] Similarly, the rape shield statute may preclude evidence of a complainant's being caught naked in bed with a boy as part of the defense theory that she falsely accused the defendant in retaliation for the defendant's mother's strict disciplinary rules as long as the court permits exploration of the relationship between defendant's mother and the complainant, including the complainant's dislike of the disciplinary rules.[483]

One court permitted evidence of a victim's incestuous relationship with her brother on the theory that this was relevant to her motive in alleging that her father had raped her and that her father was attempting to stop the incestuous relationship.[484]

---

accusation of rape was based on defendant's restrictions of her social life because of her sexual activity); State v. Adderly, 803 So. 2d 760 (Fla. Ct. App. 2001):

> The defendant in this case contends that S.D. made up the charge against the defendant so that S.D. could disclose to her mother that she had previously had sexual intercourse with her boyfriend, without the mother being angry at S.D. The logic, according to the defendant, is that if S.D. falsely charged the defendant with sexual assault, the mother would be angry with the defendant, not S.D. The defense relies on the Lewis decision, but that reliance is misplaced.

Id. at 762. Violett v. Commonwealth, 907 S.W.2d 773, 776 (Ky. 1995) (upholding preclusion of evidence of relationship between complainant and her boyfriend that was offered on theory that the criminal charge against the stepfather was made in order to get complainant's boyfriend out of the way; court held evidence of relationship did not relate directly to charge); Commonwealth v. Frey, 390 Mass. 245, 454 N.E.2d 478 (1983) (precluding testimony of complainant's prior sexual allegations to support defense theory that such activity accounted for complainant's upset mental condition); Commonwealth v. Herrick, 39 Mass. App. Ct. 291, 655 N.E.2d 637 (1995) (defendant sought to present evidence of complainant's fear of a physical examination and evidence that she was romantically involved with another young man to show (1) that the victim feared her mother would subject her to a physical examination to determine whether she was a virgin and invented the rape story to hide the fact that she had been intimate with her boyfriend and (2) she feared that her boyfriend was going to end their relationship and accused the defendant to forestall the termination; this evidence was properly precluded because of insufficient basis to support defendant's theories).

[481] Commonwealth v. Berkowitz, 537 Pa. 143, 151, 641 A.2d 1161, 1165 (1994), *rev'd on other grounds.*

[482] *Halbert,* 175 A.2d at 89, 572 N.Y.S.2d at 332.

[483] Commonwealth v. Gagnon, 45 Mass. App. Ct. 584, 699 N.E.2d 1260 (1998).

[484] Commonwealth v. Black, 337 Pa. Super. 548, 487 A.2d 396 (1985). *But see* Commonwealth v. Poindexter, 372 Pa. Super. 566, 572, 539 A.2d 1341, 1344, *appeal denied,* 520 Pa. 573, 549 A.2d 134 (1988).

Another court permitted evidence that the child had an ulterior motive of avoiding charges involving a half-sister.[485]

In other cases, courts have permitted evidence of past sexual assaults to show the child's understanding of the consequences of a sexual abuse claim to establish why the complainant might fabricate a claim.[486] A defendant's past discipline of a complainant over sexual matters may raise a sufficient basis for evidence of the complainant's past sexual behaviors.[487] It is also possible that a defendant can testify that a complainant falsely accused him out of anger and fear that the defendant would publicly disclose her sexual activities.[488]

A victim's reporting of the defendant's sexual abuse when questioned about his own improprieties may open the door to cross-examination above the victim's sexual activities as the ulterior motive for the complaint.[489] Also, the child's

---

[485] Commonwealth v. Fernsler, 1998 Pa. Super. LEXIS 862, 715 A.2d 435 (1998) (upholding trial court's decision to allow defendant to introduce evidence that child victim had ulterior motive to fabricate the current charges against defendant, *i.e.*, to escape possibility of future refiling of sexual assault charges against him as result of his actions toward his half-sister).

[486] People v. Salas, 30 Cal. App. 4th 417, 36 Cal. Rptr. 2d 374 (1994) (reversing defendant's conviction for the failure to admit evidence of the complainant's prior allegations of sexual abuse that would have shown not only sexual awareness, but also provided a motive for fabrication of charges against the defendant, namely that the child knew that the accusation of molestation would have the effect of removing defendant from her life); Commonwealth v. Wall, 413 Pa. Super. 599, 606 A.2d 449, *appeal denied*, 532 Pa. 645, 614 A.2d 1142 (1992).

[487] Keene v. United States, 661 A.2d 1073 (D.C. App. 1995) (reversing defendant's conviction for trial court's failure to admit testimony about two occasions when the defendant, a counselor at complainant's group home, allegedly had disciplined her for engaging in improper sexual behavior together with evidence of a tape in which the complainant allegedly fantasized about oral sex, since such evidence would have been probative of complainant's motive to fabricate); Gonzalez v. State, 471 So. 2d 214 (Fla. Dist. Ct. App. 1985) ("We believe the trial court erred in excluding evidence of the prosecutrix's prior forgery of a note dealing with sexual explicit conduct and of alleged play acting or fantasizing of sexual activity prior to the incident involving sexual molestation of which the appellant is charged. In our view such evidence was relevant to the defense's claim that the prosecutrix fabricated the charges in question.").

[488] State v. Finley, 300 S.C. 196, 387 S.E.2d 88 (1989).

[489] Hannon v. State, 84 P.3d 320 (Wyo. 2004):

[T]he witness Mr. Hannon sought to cross-examine was the state's material witness. TB was the only witness to the alleged crime. There was no physical evidence tying Mr. Hannon to the alleged assault nor were there any eyewitnesses. TB did not report the allegations of sexual assault by Mr. Hannon until three months after the fact when he was brought in for questioning about his own sexual improprieties with another boy. Had defense counsel been allowed to explore this issue with TB during cross-examination, the jury reasonably might have inferred TB was fearful about what would happen to him as a result of his own acts and concocted the allegations against Mr. Hannon to shift the focus of the police inquiry away from him. At the least, this line of questioning could have cast doubt on his credibility by exposing a motive for him to accuse Mr. Hannon. We conclude the prohibited cross-examination was sufficiently probative of a possible ulterior motive to warrant allowing it and the trial court's ruling denied Mr. Hannon the opportunity to fully explore this before the jury thereby depriving him of his Sixth Amendment right of confrontation.

Id. at 332.

past sexual activity may explain her advances toward the defendant.[490]

§ 5.44 Evidence of prior sexual conduct through defendant's direct testimony.

Another situation in which an aspect of sexual history may be raised is through the testimony of a defendant. When a defendant testifies as to statements made by a complainant, either in the course of a relationship or, particularly, during the course of an assault, such testimony may be admissible. Consider this example:

A. And we were proceeding to have sex, when I heard her weeping.

Q. You heard her what?

A. Weeping.

Q. All right. Tell us.

A. I had my eyes closed at the time, so I opened my eyes up and I noticed she was crying. So I stopped making love to her. I was still on top of her and I asked her what was wrong. She mentioned to me that she was raped once before and had to get an abortion because of it. At that time I got off her, but I was still laying next to her on my side. I put my hands underneath her head and around on her head and I was pushing her hair off her face, and I was talking to her. I asked her if she reported it to the police, she told me no, she didn't.

Testimony concerning a complainant's fear of pregnancy, however, may not always be admitted, even during the defendant's testimony. When such evidence has nothing to do with a defendant's defense, as in when the defendant denies committing the acts with the complainant, the complainant's sexual history and her fear of pregnancy become a collateral matter, and the court may limit the defendant to simply asking the complainant whether she made the statement and prohibit testimony from the defendant or others on that point.[491]

While a defendant's statement introduced into evidence may refer to statements the complainant allegedly made about her sexual history, this does not necessarily permit cross-examination of the complainant about her sexual history.[492]

---

[490] United States v. Gray, 40 M.J. 77, 80 (1994) (holding it was error to preclude evidence of nine-year-old's previous sexual activity since this would explain her advances toward the defendant).

[491] People v. Todd, 241 Ill. App. 3d 542, 547–53, 608 N.E.2d 933, 936–40 (1993).

[492] People v. Curry, 11 A.D.3d 150, 782 N.Y.S.2d 66, *appeal denied*, 4 N.Y.3d 743, 824 N.E.2d 56, 790 N.Y.S.2d 655 (2004) (defendant sought to cross-examine victim about references in his statement to police that she allegedly made to him that the injuries she sustained were inflicted by one of her "tricks." The court found such cross-examination was covered by the rape shield statute. Court held:

Here, the statement in contention is not one made by complainant but by defendant. Defendant

The trial court may also limit the nature and extent of the defendant's testimony. For example, where a defendant attempted to testify that he and the complainant were "doing it doggy fashion," and he asked her, "Don't you like it like this? . . . Tim Hall said you did," the trial court limited the defendant's testimony to a statement that he said something that angered the complainant that caused her to fabricate the charges.[493]

§ 5.45   Cross-examination regarding complainant's attire.

Another area of cross-examination in sexual assault cases deals with the dress or attire of the complainant, particularly in adult assault cases. Questioning a complainant concerning her dress is designed to suggest that perhaps she is promiscuous or desired sexual relations with individuals, including the defendant. Many individuals, especially victim advocates, stress that there is little relationship between a complainant's dress and whether or not she was raped. Certainly, it is difficult to find recent appellate decisions supporting the proposition that a complainant's dress or apparel demonstrates consent to being sexually attacked. In fact, there is appellate authority to the contrary.[494]

Some states have statutes that deal specifically with the admissibility of evidence of a victim's manner of dress.[495] Louisiana's code states "the manner

---

did not seek to introduce a statement complainant had made for its evidentiary value; defendant merely sought to use her alleged statement as a means to elicit testimony from complainant as evidence in chief, which defendant presumes would have rebutted the People's evidence that he caused complainant's injuries. This would appear to be precisely the sort of speculative foray into a victim's sexual history that the *Rape Shield Law* was designed to prevent.

Notably, defendant does not contend that any statement was withheld from the factfinder. Defendant's videotaped statement was played for the jurors, who heard him assert that complainant alleged that she had been beaten by one of her tricks.

Id. at 158–59, 782 N.Y.S.2d at 72.

[493] Stephens v. Miller, 13 F.3d 998 (7th Cir. 1994), *cert. denied*, 513 U.S. 808 (1994).

The Indiana Rape Shield Statute was enacted to prevent just this kind of generalized inquiry into the reputation or past sexual conduct of the victim in order to avoid embarrassing her and subjecting her to possible public denigration. [citation omitted]. Its application to exclude references here to 'doggy fashion' sexual intercourse and partner switching effectuate its purpose. The Indiana trial court properly balanced Stephens' right to testify with Indiana's interest because it allowed him to testify about what happened and that he said something that upset [the complainant]. The Constitution requires no more than this. The interests served by the Indiana Rape Shield Statute justify this very minor imposition on Stephens' right to testify.

Id. at 1002. The court also rejected the argument that the victim's statements were part of the *res gestae*, since this could "gut" the purpose of rape shield statutes. *Id.* at 1003.

[494] People v. Stengel, 211 Ill. App. 3d 337, 570 N.E.2d 391, *cert. denied*, 141 Ill. 2d 556, 580 N.E.2d 130 (1991); People v. Leonhardt, 173 Ill. App. 3d 314, 527 N.E.2d 562 (1988).

[495] *See, e.g.*, La. Code Evid. 412.1; N.D. Cent. Code § 12.1-20-15.1; N.Y. Crim. Proc. Law § 60.48 (precludes testimony of manner in which a victim was dressed at time of offense unless the court finds this information relevant and admissible in the interests of justice after a hearing).

and style of the victim's attire should not be admissible as evidence that the victim encouraged or consented to the offense."[496] Other states incorporate restrictions on the cross-examination of a complainant's dress in their rape shield statutes.[497] Illinois's statute deals with the issue by stating that "the manner of dress of the victim at the time of the offense shall not constitute consent."[498] One court has held that if a defendant raises the issue of a complainant's dress in questioning a witness, a trial court has "manifest necessity" to declare a mistrial.[499]

Where the issue is not governed by statute, it is up to the prosecution to argue that evidence concerning a complainant's dress or attire is irrelevant. While this may be true, many courts are inclined to allow questioning in this area. It is not within the scope of most states' rape shield laws. However, given the changing attitudes, such questioning should be carefully evaluated for its effectiveness. Certainly, a younger jury may be less receptive to an argument concerning "immodest dress" that may have been better received 30 or 40 years ago.

§ 5.46   Prior allegations of sexual abuse, true or false.

Prior allegations of sexual abuse or rape do not involve sexual conduct of a complainant, and thus do not fall within the scope of a rape shield statute.[500] Usually, a threshold issue is establishing that a prior act occurred, even before addressing the truth or falsity of the allegation. Proof from a defendant and his mother, who are biased, may be insufficient to establish the act occurred.[501]

---

[496] La. Code Evid. 412.1.

[497] Fla. Stat. § 794.022(3); Ga. Code § 24-2-3(a).

[498] Ill. Comp. Stat. ch. 720, 5/12-17.

[499] Maynard v. Wait, 246 A.D.2d 853, 668 N.Y.S.2d 263 (1998).

[500] United States v. Stamper, 766 F. Supp. 1396, 1399–1400 (W.D.N.C. 1991), aff'd, 959 F.2d 231 (4th Cir. 1992); Ex parte Loyd, 580 So. 2d 1374 (Ala. 1991); People v. Burrell-Hart, 192 Cal. App. 3d 593, 237 Cal. Rptr. 654, 656 (1987); People v. Wall, 95 Cal. App. 3d 978, 157 Cal. Rptr. 587, 590 (1979); People v. Grano, 286 Ill. App. 3d 278, 676 N.E.2d 248 (1996); Fugett v. State, 812 N.E.2d 846 (Ind. 2004); State v. Walton, 715 N.E.2d 824, 827 (Ind. 1999); State v. Baker, 679 N.W.2d 7, 10 (Iowa 2004) ("Because a false allegation of sexual activity is not sexual behavior, such statements fall outside both the letter and spirit of the rape shield law."); State v. Barber, 13 Kan. App. 2d 224, 766 P.2d 1288 (1989); State v. Smith, 743 So. 2d 199 (La. 1999); Cox v. State, 51 Md. App. 271, 281–82, 443 A.2d 607, 613–14 (1982), aff'd, 298 Md. 173, 468 A.2d 319 (1983); People v. Garvie, 148 Mich. App. 444, 384 N.W.2d 796, 798, appeal denied, 426 Mich. 851 (1986); People v. Gibson, 2 A.D.3d 969, 768 N.Y.S.2d 511 (2003), appeal denied, 1 N.Y.3d 627, 808 N.E.2d 1285, 777 N.Y.S.2d 26 (2004) (victim's complaint of unrelated sex crime falls outside scope of rape shield statute); People v. Lippert, 138 A.D.2d 770, 525 N.Y.S.2d 390 (1988); People v. Mandel, 61 A.D.2d 563, 569–71, 403 N.Y.S.2d 63, 68 (1978), rev'd on other grounds, 48 N.Y.2d 952, 401 N.E.2d 185, 425 N.Y.S.2d 63 (1979), cert. denied, 446 U.S. 949 (1980); State v. Baron, 58 N.C. App. 150, 153, 292 S.E.2d 741, 743 (1982); State v. Le Clair, 83 Or. App. 121, 730 P.2d 609 (1986).

[501] State v. Hammer, 236 Wis. 2d 686, 714, 613 N.W.2d 629, 642 (2000).

The prior allegations may be accusations made subsequent to the complaint against the defendant.[502]

Prior accusations by a complainant, in and of themselves, may not be admissible for the mere fact that the complainant has previously been victimized or previously alleged abuse. Generally, to be admissible, it must be shown that a prior accusation in some way relates to the present accusation, or that the prior accusation was false, not merely "unfounded," or constitutes a pattern of deceit by the complainant in sexual abuse allegations. When presented as a general attack on the victim's credibility with no showing of falsity, such evidence is inadmissible.

An overwhelming number of courts have upheld the preclusion of prior allegations of sexual abuse when there is no showing that the prior allegation is false.[503] There is no clear, consistent standard for determining falsity of an

---

[502] Humphrey v. State, 207 Ga. App. 472, 428 S.E.2d 362, *cert. denied*, 1993 Ga. LEXIS 601 (May 13, 1993); Commonwealth v. Nichols, 37 Mass. App. Ct. 332, 639 N.E.2d 1088 (1994) (reversing defendant's conviction when there was independent evidence of the falsity of the allegations made subsequent to the complaints against the defendant and trial judge's distinction between a prior and subsequent false allegation was irrelevant. "Indeed, a lie subsequent to the primary event, if closer in time, may be more probative of a proclivity to lie and fabricate than a prior false allegation." *Id.* at 335–36, 639 N.E.2d at 1090.).

[503] United States v. Withorn, 204 F.3d 790 (8th Cir. 2000) (noting that trial court properly precluded testimony about a prior rape allegation since it would be "sheer speculation" that it was untrue); United States v. Bartlett, 856 F.2d 1071 (8th Cir. 1988); United States v. Cardinal, 782 F.2d 34 (6th Cir. 1986), *cert. denied*, 476 U.S. 1161 (1986); West v. State, 290 Ark. 329, 722 S.W.2d 284 (1997); State v. Stevenson, 43 Conn. App. 680, 686 A.2d 500 (1996), *appeal denied*, 240 Conn. 920, 692 A.2d 817 (1997) ("In this case, the defense attorney had no information that J's prior sexual assault claims were false. The defendant claims that although he had no evidence that the prior claims were false, he was prejudiced by not being permitted to question the victim about them because she has a history of delusional behavior. There was, however, no evidence that, if the victim had delusions, they were of a sexual nature." *Id.* at 695, 686 A.2d at 508); Candler v. State, 837 N.E.2d 1100, 1103 (Ind. Ct. App. 2005) (holding that to be admissible and outside the rape shield statute, prior allegation must be "false" or demonstrably false); Fugett v. State, 812 N.E.2d 846 (Ind. 2004) (holding defendant's evidence was "too tenuous" to establish prior allegation was demonstrably false); Koo v. State, 640 N.E.2d 95 (Ind. Ct. App. 1994) (complainant's prior report of a "forced sexual encounter" that complainant testified was not rape in her mind, did not constitute a prior false allegation of sexual misconduct); State v. Decuir, 364 So. 2d 946 (La. 1978) (in a forcible rape prosecution, there was no showing of a correlation between a prior allegation of statutory rape and the current charge and no showing of falsity in the earlier allegation); State v. Kirsch, 836 So. 2d 390 (La. Ct. App. 2002) (The defendant failed to produce sufficient admissible evidence such that reasonable jurors could find that the victim had made a prior false accusation. *Id.* at 394); State v. Richard, 812 So. 2d 737 (La. Ct. App. 2002) ("Two requirements, therefore, exist before evidence of prior sexual activity can be admitted for impeachment purposes, assuming this evidence is otherwise admissible. First, the activity must be of a sexual nature. Second, there must be evidence the statement is false." *Id.* at 740.); State v. Judge, 758 So. 2d 313 (La. Ct. App. 2000); Commonwealth v. Wise, 39 Mass. App. Ct. 922, 655 N.E.2d 643 (1995) ("To open the gate to cross-examination, the evidence of falsity of an accusation must be solid, as when the accusing witness has recanted the other allegation. . . . When, as here, the victim

(Text continued on page 406)

witness has not recanted, the circumstance that charges were not pressed is an insufficient basis for inferring that they were false." *Id.* at 922–23, 655 N.E.2d at 645); State v. Steffes, 887 P.2d 1196, 1206 (Mont. 1994); Miller v. State, 105 Nev. 497, 502–03, 779 P.2d 87, 90 (1989); People v. Hill, 17 A.D.3d 1081, 793 N.Y.S.2d 800 (2005), *appeal denied*, 5 N.Y.3d 806, 836 N.E.2d 1158, 803 N.Y.S.2d 35 (2005) (holding evidence of complainant's prior accusations of sexual molestation against family members properly excluded absent a showing they were false or suggest a pattern that casts doubt on validity of charges or bore some probative value to instant charge); People v. Byrd, 309 A.D.2d 593, 765 N.Y.S.2d 354 (2003), *appeal denied*, 1 N.Y.3d 625, 808 N.E.2d 1283, 777 N.Y.S.2d 24 (2004) ("The court properly exercised its discretion in precluding inquiry into an allegation of prior sexual assault involving the victim's younger sister. There was no basis to conclude that the allegation was false or unfounded, that there was a pattern casting doubt on the validity of the instant charge, or that the prior allegation was otherwise material." *Id.* at 593–94, 765 N.Y.S.2d at 355); People v. Brown, 303 A.D.2d 175, 755 N.Y.S.2d 237, *appeal denied*, 100 N.Y.2d 579, 796 N.E.2d 481, 764 N.Y.S.2d 389 (2003) (The court properly exercised its discretion in precluding cross-examination of the victim regarding alleged prior sexual abuse by persons other than defendant, since there was a lack of proof that any of these incidents constituted false allegations and since defendant made no showing that the circumstances of these unrelated allegations bears a "significant probative relation" to the charges in question. [citation omitted]); People v. O'Malley, 282 A.D.2d 884, 723 N.Y.S.2d 270, *appeal denied*, 96 N.Y.2d 866, 754 N.E.2d 1123, 730 N.Y.S.2d 40 (2001); People v. Breheny, 270 A.D.2d 926, 705 N.Y.S.2d 160, *appeal denied*, 95 N.Y.2d 851, 736 N.E.2d 863, 714 N.Y.S.2d 2 (2000); People v. Duggan, 229 A.D.2d 688, 645 N.Y.S.2d 158, *appeal denied*, 88 N.Y.2d 984, 672 N.E.2d 616, 649 N.Y.S.2d 390 (1996) (holding court properly denied cross-examination of complainant's prior complaints since "the basis of his assertions as to the victim's false accusations were based upon numerous inadmissible hearsay statements"); People v. Colon, 213 A.D.2d 490, 623 N.Y.S.2d 633, *appeal denied*, 86 N.Y.2d 733, 655 N.E.2d 711, 631 N.Y.S.2d 614 (1995); People v. Sprague, 200 A.D.2d 867–68, 606 N.Y.S.2d 813, 815–16, *appeal denied*, 83 N.Y.2d 877, 635 N.E.2d 306, 613 N.Y.S.2d 137 (1994) (evidence of prior claims of abuse properly precluded in a case where defendant did not establish the falsity of the prior claims or that they were "suggestive or a pattern that cast doubt on the validity of, or bore a significant probative relation to, the instant charges"); People v. Passenger, 175 A.D.2d 944, 572 N.Y.S.2d 972 (1991):

> [O]ther than defense counsel's suggestion that the child had a proclivity to make sexual charges, there was no proof that these earlier complaints were false or suggested a pattern or deceit [citations omitted]. . . . Here, the sexual abuse accusations that the child purportedly leveled at her former foster parents in Maryland, which predated the events giving rise to defendant's indictment, were never reduced to formal complaints. As for the sex violation charges she allegedly made against her foster father, with whom she had been placed after being removed from defendant's home, that was resolved with an *Alford* plea. Accordingly, exclusion was proper. In addition, as the victim's asserted morbid sexual interest and exposure to promiscuity would not, as defendant claims, have necessarily tended to prove that she had fabricated the charges against him, county court did not err in excluding this evidence. [citation omitted]

Id. at 946, 572 N.Y.S.2d at 974; People v. Moore, 159 A.D.2d 521, 552 N.Y.S.2d 389 (1990) ("The trial court properly exercised its discretion in excluding from evidence any mention of the fact that the complainant had been the victim of a rape some two years previously on the ground that it was irrelevant to the case at bar." [citation omitted] *Id.* at 523, 552 N.Y.S.2d at 391); Commonwealth v. L.N., 2001 Pa. Super. 352, 787 A.2d 1064 (2001), *appeal denied*, 800 A.2d 931 (2002); State v. Leggett, 164 Vt. 599, 664 A.2d 271 (1995) ("As a threshold matter, defendant

allegation. Some courts hold the offering party must show the previous allegations to be "demonstrably false"; others articulate a "reasonable probability" of falsity[504] standard or "substantial proof" of falsity.[505] Some courts articulate a clear and convincing standard[506] or a preponderance of evidence standard.[507]

---

failed to make a sufficient showing that the victim's prior allegations were, in fact, false. Defendant's only offer of proof was the police report, but without more, the mere fact that the allegation was not prosecuted does not show that the allegation was false." *Id.* at 600, 664 A.2d at 272.

[504] Williams v. State, 266 Ga. App. 578, 597 S.E.2d 621 (2004); Wagner v. State, 253 Ga. App. 874, 560 S.E.2d 754 (2002); Fugett v. State, 812 N.E.2d 846 (Ind. 2004) (holding false complaint is demonstrably false "where the victim has admitted the falsity of the charges or they have been disproved"); State v. Walton, 715 N.E.2d 824 (Ind. 1999); Little v. State, 413 N.E.2d 639, 643 (Ind. Ct. App. 1980); Berry v. Commonwealth, 84 S.W.3d 82, 91 (Ky. Ct. App. 2001); Hall v. Commonwealth, 956 S.W.2d 224 (Ky. Ct. App. 1996) ("It appears the general rule which has emerged in cases involving sexual offenses, is that the admissibility of evidence of similar accusations made by the victim depends on whether they have been proven to be demonstrably false." *Id.* at 227.); State v. Chamley, 1997 SD 107, 568 N.W.2d 607, 616 (1997) (utilizing a "demonstrably false" foundational standard); Richardson v. Commonwealth, 42 Va. App. 236, 590 S.E.2d 618 (2004).

[505] United States v. Stamper, 766 F. Supp. 1396, 1403 (W.D.N.C. 1991), *aff'd, In re* One Female Juvenile Victim, 959 F.2d 231 (4th Cir. 1992); Allen v. State, 210 Ga. App. 447, 436 S.E.2d 559 (1993) (upholding trial court's decision to preclude defendant from offering prior allegations of abuse by the child complainant since the defendant failed to "make a threshold determination outside the presence of the jury that a reasonable probability of falsity exists"); State v. Barber, 13 Kan. App. 2d 224, 766 P.2d 1288 (1989) (stating the standard is one of "reasonable probability of falsity"); State v. Gordon, 146 N.H. 258, 770 A.2d 702 (2001):

> The only evidence of the prior false allegation in this case was the defendant's uncorroborated assertion to that effect. The defendant failed to proffer any independent evidence to substantiate his assertion. Despite the fact that the defendant claimed to have informed school administrators of the allegations, school records contained no documentation of the incident. Moreover, while the defendant claimed that the victim made the false allegation one year prior to trial while enrolled at the Hillside School, she had not attended that school for four years. Finally, the victim denied that she made the false allegation and believed the defendant may have been referring to an incident that had occurred seven or eight years earlier after she had been pushed by a schoolmate, but not sexually assaulted.

> Based upon this evidence, we hold that no reasonable fact finder could conclude that the defendant met his burden of showing, clearly and convincingly, that the victim made a prior accusation of sexual assault.

Id. at 262, 770 A.2d at 705); Clinebell v. Commonwealth, 235 Va. 319, 324–25, 368 S.E.2d 263, 265–66 (1988) (evidence of a prior false allegation of abuse by the complainant is admissible to impeach the complainant's credibility or as substantive evidence that the instant offense did not occur "only if court makes a threshold determination that a reasonable probability of falsity exists").

[506] State v. Gilfillan, 196 Ariz. 396, 404–05, 998 P.2d 1069, 1077–78 (2000); State v. Gordon, 146 N.H. 258, 770 A.2d 702 (2001); State v. White, 145 N.H. 544, 547–48, 765 A.2d 156, 159 (2000).

[507] Morgan v. State, 54 P.3d 332 (Alaska Ct. App. 2002):

> We note that "preponderance of the evidence" is the foundational standard commonly

New Jersey permits evidence of a prior false allegation after the defendant establishes it by a preponderance of evidence at an admissibility hearing considering the following factors: 1) whether the credibility of the victim-witness is the central issue in the case; 2) the similarity of the prior false criminal accusation to the crime charged; 3) the proximity of the prior false accusation to the allegation that is the basis of the crime charged; 4) the number of witnesses, the items of extrinsic evidence, and the amount of time required for presentation of the issue at trial; and 5) whether the probative value of the false accusation evidence will be outweighed by undue prejudice, confusion of the issues, and waste of time.[508] The Louisiana Supreme Court holds that admissibility is determined by whether "reasonable jurors could find, based on the evidence presented by the defendant, that the victim made prior false accusations."[509] In addition, a defendant would have to establish that allegedly false complaint was "suggestive of a pattern that cast doubt on the validity of, or bore a significant probative relation to, the instant charges."[510] A few jurisdictions require only some evidence of falsity to permit the defendant to raise the issue.[511] The prior false report may be too remote or too speculative to justify its admissibility.[512] The fact that an accusation is not prosecuted does not necessarily establish falsity.[513]

---

used in Alaska to determine similar questions of admissibility or exclusion n36. We also note that if we adopted the "clear and convincing evidence" standard, we would require trial judges to exclude evidence of a complaining witness's prior accusations of sexual assault even after the judge had concluded that those prior accusations were probably false. For these reasons, we conclude that "preponderance of the evidence" is the proper standard of proof.

Id. at 339; State v. West, 95 Haw. 452, 459–60, 24 P.3d 648, 655–56 (2001); State v. Long, 140 S.W.3d 27, 32 (Mo. 2004) (*en banc*) (holding defendant must establish by a preponderance of the evidence that the "prosecuting witness previously made knowingly false allegations.").

[508] State v. Guenther, 181 N.J. 129, 157, 854 A.2d 308, 324 (2004) (noting that trial judge should "ensure that testimony on the subject does not become a second trial, eclipsing the trial of the crimes charged.").

[509] State v. Smith, 743 So. 2d 199, 203 (La. 1999); State v. DeSantis, 155 Wis. 2d 774, 456 N.W.2d 600, 606–07 (1990).

[510] People v. Sprague, 200 A.D.2d 867, 888, 606 N.Y.S.2d 813, *appeal denied*, 83 N.Y.2d 877, 635 N.E.2d 306, 613 N.Y.S.2d 137 (1994).

[511] Williams v. State, 266 Ga. App. 578, 597 S.E.2d 621, *cert. denied*, 2004 Ga. LEXIS 751 (Sept. 7, 2004) (noting that non-prosecution reflects insufficient evidence and does not address truth or falsity).

[512] People v. Wronski, 277 A.D.2d 999, 716 N.Y.S.2d 512 (2000) (holding trial court did not abuse its discretion in precluding questioning of a 14-year-old victim in sodomy trial of his statements during trial court's voir dire of him, in an assault trial, when he was four years old that he had burned himself on a toaster and his mother had instructed him to falsely accuse the defendant).

[513] Williams v. State, 266 Ga. App. 578, 597 S.E.2d 621, *cert. denied*, 2004 Ga. LEXIS 751 (Sept. 7, 2004) (noting that non-prosecution reflects insufficient evidence and does not address truth or falsity).

Child abuse reports may be "unfounded," usually meaning there is no credible evidence to support an allegation of abuse. An "unfounded" report does not necessarily mean it is false and therefore is likely to be inadmissible without further evidence of falsity.[514]

If there is an indication that the prior allegations of abuse were false, the evidence may be utilized. In *United States v. Stamper*,[515] the defendant argued that the complainant had previously made false accusations for the purposes of "manipulating her custodians, avoiding therapy, [and] keeping her younger sister at home." The court listed several factors that led to its conclusion that the prior allegations were false and relevant to the current charges. The present allegations were close in time to the prior allegations, and all the allegations were made against "older men who either dwelt in or frequented the custodial parent's home."[516] The court also noted that the complainant had moved back in with her mother and another accused offender after the present allegations were filed, even though she had moved out a year earlier, presumably to get away from that male custodian, which supported the defendant's claim that the allegations were made in an attempt to manipulate her living arrangements. The court noted that to preclude this area of cross-examination "would be to block out an area of possible truth constituting the very context in which the charges arose."[517]

---

[514] State v. Smith, 85 Conn. App. 96, 856 A.2d 466 (2004), *rev'd. on other grounds* (after viewing social services file, court found no reason to believe prior recanted allegation was false); People v. Mason, 219 Ill. App. 3d 76, 82, 578 N.E.2d 1351, 1356 (1991) (holding that a child welfare agency's determination to not pursue an abuse allegation was not a final determination that the accusation was false; defendant should demonstrate that the prior allegation "more likely than not" was false); State v. Gaal, 800 So. 2d 938 (La. Ct. App. 2001) ("The evidence of the victim's prior accusations against this defendant could have been relevant and admissible to impeach the credibility of the victim if the defendant had established that the victim made prior false statements of sexual abuse. . . . However, no such showing was made in this case. The fact that the defendant was accused of sexual abuse and then the State entered a *nolle prosequi* to the charges . . . does not establish that the accusations were false." *Id.* at 950); Lopez v. State, 86 S.W.3d 228 (Tex. Crim. App. 2002):

> [T]he prior accusation was never shown to be false. The record reflects that the Texas Department of Human Services "closed" the case and "ruled out" the abuse. But their file also indicates that the "likelihood of maltreatment is moderate" and that the case was closed because the mother was seeking counseling. This could simply indicate a lack of evidence to prove the allegation at that time, or an administrative decision that, despite the allegation's validity, the parties would best be served by closing the case.

> Because the defendant could not demonstrate the previous allegation was false, the defendant could not introduce the prior report as a prior inconsistent statement to his trial testimony that he has never "lied about big things."

[515] 766 F. Supp. 1396, 1401 (W.D.N.C. 1991), *aff'd, In re* One Female Juvenile Victim, 959 F.2d 231 (4th Cir. 1992).

[516] *Id.* at 1402.

[517] *Id.* at 1401.

The circumstances surrounding prior unsubstantial allegations of abuse may trigger their relevance and admissibility. For example, when the complainant and her sister told a child protective worker that they did not want to see their father and knew that if the charges had been sustained, they would not see him again, and then made the instant allegations without ever reporting the allegations to the worker who was handling their case during the time period of the abuse, the prior allegations "demonstrated both a relevant pattern of behavior by the mother and the subjection of the children to repeated situations in which they were their father's accusers."[518]

The pattern or circumstances of the prior complaints and the complainant's conflicting statements may trigger a right to raise past complaints of abuse.[519]

There must be more than an allegation that the prior charges were false. *Stamper* indicates there must be a "substantial proof of falsity" of the prior allegation,[520] although no clear standard has evolved in this respect. There is some authority that prior allegations, even if withdrawn and no further showing is made as to falsity, can be utilized for cross-examination,[521] but most courts will require some showing of falsity. However, a recantation of an allegation does not necessarily equate with a false allegation.[522] Producing "denial

---

[518] State v. E.B., 348 N.J. Super. 336, 344, 791 A.2d 1124, 1129, *cert. denied*, 174 N.J. 192, 803 A.2d 1163 (2002) (noting that error was compounded by admission of multiple hearsay statements of child).

[519] People v. Bridgeland, 19 A.D.3d 1122, 796 N.Y.S.2d 768 (2005) (noting also that complainant's privileged statements to psychologist yielded to defendant's constitutional Right of Confrontation).

[520] United States v. Stamper, 766 F. Supp. 1396, 1403 (W.D.N.C. 1991), *aff'd, In re* One Female Juvenile Victim, 959 F.2d 231 (4th Cir. 1992). *See also* State v. Barber, 13 Kan. App. 2d 224, 766 P.2d 1288 (1989) (stating the standard is one of "reasonable probability of falsity").

[521] State v. Oliveira, 576 A.2d 111 (R.I. 1990).

[522] State v. MacDonald, 131 Idaho 367, 956 P.2d 1314 (1998) (At a Rule 412 hearing, the complainant "recanted her recantation" of a sexual assault by her father when she was eight years old. The appellate court noted the complainant's

> prior allegation involved conduct which occurred when she was a minor and was incapable of consent while her consent was the only disputed issue in the instant case; that the allegation involved conduct remote and dissimilar to that which was here alleged; and that even if the prior allegation was relevant, it would still be inadmissible because it was "so highly prejudicial that it would not be helpful to the jury, but would rather be confusing and would . . . have a tendency to ignite them, to make them do things they would not normally do because of its high prejudice." We hold that the district court did not abuse its discretion under a Rule 403 analysis. Permitting the admission of evidence regarding J.L.'s prior recanted allegation would be opening a Pandora's box of unfairly prejudicial, confusing and time-consuming issues. The highly intimate nature of the prior allegation was compounded by J.L.'s history of victimization. In addition to her prior allegation of sexual abuse by her father and her subsequent impregnation by her foster father, she was involved in a sexual relationship with a man who was 21 when she was 15, which also resulted in a conviction of statutory rape for the man. In order to explain the reason for her recanta-

testimony" by individuals previously accused of sexual abuse by the complainant does not necessarily justify questioning the complainant about her prior complaints.[523] However, while the defendant may be precluded from questioning the victim about specifics of prior allegations, the defendant may be able to present testimony concerning the complainant's reputation for untruthfulness.[524] Even if the prior allegation is false, it may be inadmissible because the prior accusation was the result of "coercion and duress from the alleged abuser."[525]

The principle is clear that when there is a reliable indication that prior sexual abuse allegations were false, the fact of the prior allegations may be inquired into,[526] and the defendant must be given the opportunity to demonstrate that

tion of the allegation against her father, J.L. would have had to testify regarding her impregnation by her foster father and her desire not to be placed in another foster home. The admission of this testimony would be necessary to rehabilitate J.L.'s credibility following her mother's testimony that she falsely accused her father of raping her. In addition, MacDonald has conceded, for purposes of rebuttal, the admissibility of J.L.'s prior truthful allegations of sexual abuse resulting in these convictions. As the district court noted, permitting inquiry into these areas would have created a 'trial within a trial' where the jury would be required to determine whether J.L. was being truthful with respect to her prior allegation of sexual abuse against her father. In addition, the jury may have been ignited to evaluate the instant offense on the basis of J.L.'s prior history rather than on the basis of the facts before them. Given this history and under these circumstances, the district court did not abuse its discretion in determining that the probative value of the prior allegation was substantially outweighed by its prejudicial effect under Rule 403.

Id. at § § 370–71, 956 P.2d at 1317–18.).

[523] Quinn v. Haynes, 234 F.3d 837 (4th Cir. 2000), *cert. denied*, 532 U.S. 1024 (2001) (Court noted that defendant does not have an unlimited right to cross-examine a complainant about other uncorroborated sexual assault allegations. Court also noted defendant could establish falsity by medical evidence that contradicts the allegation, an admission of falsity or proof that the accused was not physically present at the time of the alleged incident.). *See also* State v. Pettrey, 2000 Ohio App. LEXIS 4931 (Oct. 23, 2000); Richardson v. Commonwealth, 42 Va. App. 236, 590 S.E.2d 618 (2004).

[524] *Haynes*, 234 F.3d at 848.

[525] Eley v. State, 266 Ga. App. 45, 47, 596 S.E.2d 660, 662–63 (2004).

[526] Covington v. State, 703 P.2d 436, 442 (Alaska Ct. App. 1985); State v. Oliver, 158 Ariz. 22, 29, 760 P.2d 1071, 1078 n.4 (1988); People v. Makela, 147 Mich. App. 674, 383 N.W.2d 270, 276 (1985); People v. Mikula, 84 Mich. App. 108, 269 N.W.2d 195 (1978); State v. Goldenstein, 505 N.W.2d 332, 340 (Minn. Ct. App. 1993), *review denied*, 1993 Minn. LEXIS 728 (Oct. 19, 1993) (holding that once the trial court makes a threshold determination that there is a "reasonable probability of falsity" in the prior allegation, it is reversible to exclude the evidence, which should be received both to "attack the credibility of the complainant and as substantive evidence tending to prove that the instant offense did not occur"); People v. Badine, 301 A.D.2d 178, 752 N.Y.S.2d 679 (2002) (reversing defendant's conviction in part because of trial court's failure to permit complainant to be cross-examined about a prior charge she made against her cousin's brother, since the charges were essentially rebutted by hospital records indicating her "hymen was intact and no bruises or lesions were present"); State v. McGill, 141 N.C. App. 98, 539 S.E.2d 351 (2000) (reversing defendant's conviction due to trial court's failure to provide defendant with information contained in child welfare files that child had previously made false accusations against the defendant); State v. Le Clair, 83 Or. App. 121, 730 P.2d 609 (1986); State v. Padilla, 110 Wis. 2d 414, 329 N.W.2d 263 (1982).

a victim's prior claims were false. The failure to do so is a violation of a defendant's right to present a defense.[527] Where there was an indication that a complainant had alleged being raped six different times by a relative of her foster parents and that handcuffs were used in each of those rapes, just as they were allegedly used by the defendant-stepfather in the current case, and there were indications of accusations of rape against two other relatives, a trial court's failure to conduct "any inquiry into the underlying facts of the allegedly false rape charges by the victim" required a reversal of the defendant's conviction.[528]

Courts vary in the procedures for determining the falsity of a prior accusation. Some courts require the filing of a written notice by the proponent followed by a hearing outside the presence of the jury that the prior charge was made, is false, and that the evidence is more probative than prejudicial.[529] As a threshold matter, it should be established that the allegation was in fact made,[530] although this does not require a formal filing of charges.[531]

The opportunity to establish that a complainant's past accusations were false does not necessarily include the opportunity to question the complainant at a hearing in the hope that the defendant may establish the falsity of a prior allegation.[532]

---

[527] Phillips v. State, 545 So. 2d 221 (Ala. Crim. App. 1989); State v. Manini, 38 Conn. App. 100, 659 A.2d 196, *appeal denied*, 234 Conn. 920, 661 A.2d 99 (1995) (defendant heard evidence of complainant's prior delusions and hallucinations of a highly sexualized nature and wished to utilize such information with respect to cross-examination pertaining to prior claims of rape. Defendant's offer of proof "satisfied the requirement of demonstrating a sufficient basis for the court to exercise its discretion to allow the defendant to present the victim's testimony in an evidentiary hearing. . . . In this case, the trial court abused its discretion when it concluded that the defendant was not entitled to an evidentiary hearing to determine the admissibility of evidence of the victim's prior sexual conduct." For this reason the defendant's conviction was reversed.); State v. Baker, 679 N.W.2d 7 (Iowa 2004) (reversing defendant's conviction because trial court erred in excluding evidence of complainant's prior false claim of sexual behavior); State v. Goldenstein, 505 N.W.2d 332, 340 (Minn. Ct. App. 1993); People v. Stein, 10 A.D.3d 406, 781 N.Y.S.2d 654 (2004), *appeal denied*, 4 N.Y.3d 768, 825 N.E.2d 144, 792 N.Y.S.2d 12 (2005) (reversing defendant's conviction in part due to trial court's restriction on cross-examination of one complainant concerning a false report and due to prosecution's failure to turn over information concerning complainants' notices of intention to file civil lawsuits); People v. Harris, 132 A.D.2d 940, 518 N.Y.S.2d 269 (1987).

[528] People v. Becraft, 198 A.D.2d 868–69, 604 N.Y.S.2d 436, 437–38 (1993).

[529] State v. Baker, 679 N.W.2d 7, 11 (Iowa 2004); State *ex rel* Mazurek v. District Court of the Mont. Fourth Judicial Dist., 277 Mont. 349, 358, 922 P.2d 474, 480 (1996); Miller v. State, 105 Nev. 497, 502–03, 779 P.2d 87, 90 (1989); State v. Boggs, 63 Ohio St. 3d 418, 588 N.E.2d 813 (1992) (holding that court should conduct an *in camera* hearing to determine whether or not prior accusations are "totally unfounded" before permitting inquiry into prior allegations of abuse).

[530] Merzbacher v. State, 346 Md. 391, 445, 697 A.2d 432, 445 (1997).

[531] State *ex rel* Mazurek v. District Court of the Mont. Fourth Judicial Dist., 277 Mont. 349, 357, 922 P.2d 474, 479 (1996).

[532] Berry v. State, 210 Ga. App. 789, 437 S.E.2d 630 (1993), *appeal denied*, 1994 Ga. LEXIS 166 (Jan. 21, 1994).

After a trial court makes a determination to admit testimony concerning prior allegations of sexual abuse, it must then determine the scope of the examination. The cross-examination may be limited in developing the details of the prior allegations.[533]

Related to prior allegations of sexual assault are a victim's prior statements to others that he or she might bring a sexual assault charge at some time. These may be admissible as evidence of motive or prior inconsistent statements, depending on the circumstances. The fact that a rape victim at one time made statements "that she could go into a bar with no money, get drunk and leave with money and that if anyone messed with her or did not do what she wanted, she would cry rape" may be admissible on cross-examination for impeachment purposes even if direct testimony concerning the statements is inadmissible.[534]

The prosecution may open the door to testimony or questioning concerning prior allegations. When a prosecution's medical expert testifies that her opinion of abuse was based on the fact the "children her age usually don't make up things like that," the basis of this opinion can be tested on cross-examination by inquiring into the prior allegations, particularly where the victim did not testify at trial and was therefore not subject to cross-examination.[535]

§ 5.47 Presenting extrinsic evidence of prior allegations.

Traditionally, a cross-examiner is bound by the answer of a witness on cross-examination of a collateral matter. Thus, if a witness denies a prior untruthful act, extrinsic evidence of the untruthful act is not permitted. Some areas of impeachment are deemed not collateral, so that extrinsic evidence is allowed. For example, evidence of a witness's bias, prejudice, or impairment of senses, such as eyesight, at the time is not collateral. While a sexual assault complainant may be impeached by evidence that she has a bad reputation for truthfulness, the defendant may not present testimony concerning specific acts of misconduct.[536] Federal Rule of Evidence 608(b) does not allow proof of specific acts of misconduct (other than a prior criminal conviction),[537] in the court's discretion

---

[533] People v. Wilson, 678 P.2d 1024, 1027 (Colo. Ct. App. 1983), *cert. denied*, 469 U.S. 843 (1984).

[534] Moore v. State, 1994 Minn. App. LEXIS 292 (Apr. 5, 1994) (discussing this testimony in the context of the defendant's claim for post-verdict relief on the ground that his trial attorney failed to cross-examine the victim concerning these statements).

[535] State v. Leyman, 1994 Ohio App. LEXIS 4788 (Oct. 17, 1994).

[536] *See, e.g.*, Mooney v. State, 105 P.3d 149 (Alaska Ct. App. 2005) (holding witness may certify to victim's reputation for stealing, but not to specific acts of stealing tip money); People v. Santos, 211 Ill. 2d 395, 813 N.E.2d 159 (2004); People v. Robert P., 354 Ill. App. 3d 1051, 821 N.E.2d 1259 (2005).

[537] Davis v. Alaska, 415 U.S. 308 (1974) (A court may restrict use of prior juvenile adjudications. *See, e.g.*, 2005 UT 72, 125 P.3d 878 (2005). However, the United States Supreme Court has ruled juvenile adjudication should be permitted when relevant to prejudice, motive to lie or bias.).

cross-examination concerning the witness, or another witness's character for truthfulness or untruthfulness. Many states have codified a similar rule.

As to a sexual assault complainant's prior false allegation, courts differ on whether the prior untruthful act is collateral. Thus, even if falsity is established under one of the standards identified in the preceding section, many courts have traditionally held a prior false allegation is "an entirely collateral matter which may not be proved by extrinsic evidence"[538] that the allegations were false.[539] Some courts find no confrontation clause violation in such an approach.[540]

Other courts hold that once a defendant establishes that a complaining witness has made a false allegation of sexual assault, the defendant can both cross-examine and present extrinsic evidence concerning the prior false allegation when a witness denies having made the prior allegation.[541] These courts feel that a prior false allegation is a central issue in a sexual assault case. Because a sexual assault case often turns on whether or not to believe the complainant, the credibility of the complainant is particularly crucial. (Yet, some courts take the position that "[c]redibility of the witnesses is no more important in sex offenses than in any other case.")[542] Some courts find that extrinsic evidence of a false complaint should be admitted under the confrontation clause or a similar state constitution provision.[543]

---

[538] State v. Boggs, 63 Ohio St. 418, 422, 588 N.E.2d 813, 817 (1992); State v. Driver, 192 Or. App. 395, 86 P.3d 53, *review denied*, 337 Or. 248, 95 P.3d 729 (2004), *cert. denied*, 543 U.S. 1126 (2005) (holding extrinsic evidence of prior false allegations of sexual abuse inadmissible under Oregon evidence code and confrontation clause of Oregon constitution); State v. Wyrick, 62 S.W.3d 751, 780–82 (Tenn. Crim. App. 2001).

[539] State v. Almurshidy, 1999 ME 97, 732 A.2d 280 (1999).

[540] Boggs v. Collins, 226 F.3d 728, 736–40 (6th Cir. 2000), *cert. denied*, 532 U.S. 913 (2001) (finding no Sixth Amendment right to confrontation violation in restrictions on use of extrinsic evidence to establish false allegations of sexual assault).

[541] Morgan v. State, 54 P.3d 332 (Alas. Ct. App. 2002); Smith v. State, 259 Ga. 135, 377 S.E.2d 158, 160 (1989); Little v. State, 413 N.E.2d 639, 643 (Ind. Ct. App. 1980); State v. Smith, 743 So. 2d 199, 202 (La. 1999) (suggesting that defendant can present extrinsic evidence of the false allegation); State v. Cox, 298 Md. 173, 181–83, 468 A.2d 319, 323–24 (1983); State v. Long, 140 S.W.3d 27 (Mo. 2004) (*en banc*) ("An issue is not collateral if it is a 'crucial issue directly in controversy.' Where, as in this case, a witness's credibility is a key factor in determining guilt or acquittal, excluding extrinsic evidence of the witnesses' prior false allegations deprives the fact-finder of evidence that is highly relevant to a crucial issue directly in controversy; the credibility of the witness." [citations omitted] *Id.* at 30–31. Courts permitted testimony of these witnesses concerning false allegations made by complainant.); Miller v. State, 105 Nev. 497, 500–01, 779 P.2d 87, 89–90 (1989); State v. Gordon, 146 N.H. 258, 770 A.2d 702 (2001); State v. Scott, 113 N.M. 525, 529–30, 828 P.2d 958, 963 (1991).

[542] Lopez v. State, 18 S.W.3d 220, 224 (Tex. Crim. App. 2000), *rev'd*, 86 S.W.3d 228 (Tex. Crim. App. 2002).

[543] *Morgan*, 54 P.3d at 333; State v. Baker, 679 N.W.2d 7, 12 (Iowa 2004) (holding any potential embarrassment concerning previous sexual experience is outweighed by probative value of clearly relevant evidence, especially when the "countervailing right of a defendant to present a defense to a criminal charge is at stake.").

If the prior false accusation is not of a sexual assault, it may be precluded as an offer of impeachment based on a specific act.[544]

§ 5.48   Cross-examination of complainant concerning pending or contemplated civil lawsuit.

The increase in sexual assault prosecutions is mirrored by an increase in the number of civil actions by sexual assault complainants. In addition to a legal and social environment encouraging the reporting of sexual assaults, expansion of civil laws such as liberalizing of statutes of limitations on behalf of crime victims, has aided those seeking monetary damages as a result of sexual assault. The lawsuit may, for example, be against the individual defendant who committed the assault, an employer who is accused of negligently hiring an employee, a municipality in its proprietary capacity or for failing to fulfill a duty toward an injured plaintiff, or against a landowner for failing to provide adequate security.

A pending lawsuit relating to the subject matter of the criminal prosecution relates to the bias, motive, or interest of the witness. Thus, a sexual assault complainant or witness can be cross-examined about a pending lawsuit arising out of the sexual assault, and the failure to do so may be reversible error,[545] unless there is sufficient evidence to support a harmless error finding.[546] The existence of a civil lawsuit may be considered *Brady* information, especially when the prosecutor argues there is no motive for the complainant to accuse the defendant of sexual assault.[547] The prosecution's failure to disclose that two complainants had filed notices of claim with the defendant's employer (a school district) based on the sexual abuse for which he is on trial is a violation of the *Brady* rule.[548] A complainant's lawsuit gives the complainant a financial interest

---

[544] People v. Robert P., 354 Ill. App. 3d 1051, 821 N.E.2d 1259, *appeal denied*, 214 Ill. 2d 547, 830 N.E.2d 7 (2005) (holding that court properly precluded evidence that complainant had previously falsely accused defendant of biting her).

[545] State v. Milum, 197 Conn. 602, 500 A.2d 555 (1985); State v. Whitman, 429 A.2d 203 (Me. 1981); Commonwealth v. Elliot, 393 Mass. 824, 473 N.E.2d 1121 (1985); State v. Ferguson, 5 Ohio St. 3d 160, 450 N.E.2d 265 (1983); State v. Vanek, 2003 Ohio 6957, 2003 Ohio App. LEXIS 6343 (2003) (holding that because complainant's credibility was crucial to case, her pending civil suit reflected a pecuniary interest in the outcome of the case affecting her credibility, and the failure to permit her to be cross-examined on her civil lawsuit was reversible error); Barker v. Commonwealth, 230 Va. 370, 337 S.E.2d 729 (1985); State v. Smits, 58 Wash. App. 333, 339, 792 P.2d 565, 568 (1990). *See generally* Wayne F. Foster, Annotation, *Right to Cross-Examine Prosecuting Witness As To His Pending Or Contemplated Civil Action Against Accused For Damages Arising Out Of Same Transaction*, 98 A.L.R. 3d 1060 (1980).

[546] People v. Crosser, 117 Ill. App. 3d 24, 30, 452 N.E.2d 857, 863 (1983); State v. Rammel, 721 P.2d 498 (Utah 1986).

[547] People v. Wallert, 98 A.D.2d 47, 469 N.Y.S.2d 722 (1983).

[548] People v. Stein, 10 A.D.3d 406, 781 N.Y.S.2d 654 (2004), *appeal denied*, 4 N.Y.3d 768, 825 N.E.2d 44, 792 N.Y.S.2d 12 (2005) (noting the failure to turn over this evidence was aggravated by the prosecution's arguing on summation that there was no evidence that the complainants were bringing a civil lawsuit and that complainant's attorney took steps to keep the notices confidential).

in the outcome of the prosecution. This is especially true when the suit is against the same defendant, since a criminal conviction against the defendant may be *res judicata* against the defendant in a civil proceeding. On the other hand, evidence that a rape complainant is not intending to sue the defendant cannot be offered to discount any motive to testify falsely since such testimony is bolstering.[549] While generally agreeing that a complainant may be cross-examined about the fact of a pending lawsuit, courts diverge on whether the cross-examination may include the amount sought as damages. Many courts feel that the amount sought as damage is not probative since the amount is generally not determined by the complainant nor is it likely to correlate with the amount actually received by a plaintiff in a civil action.[550] The complaint itself and details of the lawsuit are likely to be irrelevant.[551]

Another issue over which courts may differ is whether a contemplated lawsuit is a proper area of cross-examination. The contemplation of a lawsuit may be reflected in the filing of a notice of claim against a municipality, consulting an attorney, or engaging in settlement negotiations with the defendant or a representative of the defendant. The policy of protecting offers of compromise in civil cases does not generally apply to offers to terminate criminal proceedings for monetary compensation,[552] and courts have held that a rape victim's or witness's contemplated civil action is a proper area of cross-examination.[553]

It may not be necessary to question the victim about a financial motivation before introducing evidence that the witness was looking for financial compensation from the defendant since evidence of a victim's financial motive to fabricate is not a matter of collateral impeachment.[554]

---

[549] State v. Johnson, 149 Wis. 2d 418, 428, 439 N.W.2d 122, 126 (1989).

[550] People v. Jones, 70 Ill. App. 3d 338, 345–46, 387 N.E.2d 1010, 1015 (1979); Koo v. State, 640 N.E.2d 95, 102 (Ind. Ct. App. 1994); Merzbacher v. State, 346 Md. 391, 697 A.2d 432 (1997) ("As the trial court pointed out, however, figures contained in ad damnum clauses often mean very little. We think it sufficient and protective of Merzbacher's right of cross-examination that he was able to establish that Murphy had a significant financial stake in the outcome of the criminal proceedings. Under these circumstances, the exact dollar figure was irrelevant and would have added little to information already possessed by the jury." *Id.* at 414, 697 A.2d at 444); State v. Roden, 674 S.W.2d 50, 57 (Mo. Ct. App. 1984); People v. Savastano, 280 A.D.2d 498, 719 N.Y.S.2d 896, *appeal denied*, 96 N.Y.2d 867, 754 N.E.2d 1125, 73 N.Y.S.2d 42 (2001) (upholding trial court properly exercised its discretion in limiting defense counsel's cross-examination to fact that civil lawsuit was filed and that damages were sought); People v. Abranko, 162 Misc. 2d 739, 621 N.Y.S.2d 433 (App. Term 1994).

[551] State v. Quatrevingt, 670 So. 2d 197 (La. 1996), *cert. denied*, 519 U.S. 927 (1996).

[552] State v. Milum, 197 Conn. 602, 613, 500 A.2d 555, 561 (1985).

[553] State v. Whitman, 429 A.2d 203, 206 (Me. 1981); Commonwealth v. Elliot, 393 Mass. 824, 473 N.E.2d 1121 (1985); State v. Smits, 58 Wash. App. 333, 339, 792 P.2d 565, 568 (1990); State v. Whyde, 30 Wash. App. 162, 632 P.2d 913 (1981).

[554] People v. Mink, 267 A.D.2d 501, 699 N.Y.S.2d 742 (1999), *appeal denied*, 94 N.Y.2d 950, 731 N.E.2d 624, 725 N.Y.S.2d 735 (2001).

The contents of a sexual assault victim's complaint and bill of particulars in the civil proceeding need not necessarily be disclosed as a prior statement where they are based upon interview notes previously provided to the defendant.[555]

The trial judge must be careful to properly instruct the jury on the issue of the lawsuit. For example, instructing the jury that "it is not unusual for an alleged wrongful act to give rise to both a criminal prosecution and a related civil lawsuit" may improperly imply that the lawsuit has no bearing on credibility and makes an improper finding of fact.[556]

§ 5.49 Impeachment through witnesses and character witnesses of complainant's reputation for truth and veracity.

A defendant may call character witnesses on his behalf.[557] A defendant also may testify to a witness's bad reputation for truthfulness and veracity to impeach the witness's credibility,[558] and this includes a complainant in a sexual assault trial.[559] The failure to allow testimony that a key prosecution witness has a bad reputation in the community for truth and veracity may be reversible error.[560] Without a sufficient foundation in terms of the basis for the opinion of a witness about a complainant, veracity, the nature of the community, and the extent of the witness's conduct with the community, the court may preclude the character testimony.[561] However, a defendant may not call a witness to testify as to specific instances of untruthfulness by a complainant.[562] Specific acts of untruthfulness, however, may be used on cross-examination as impeachment of the witness's credibility.

§ 5.50 Cross-examination of complainant to establish bias — Gang membership.

Establishing bias is a fundamental area of cross-examination. A complainant's gang membership may well be probative of her bias.[563]

---

[555] People v. Anderson, 160 A.D.2d 806, 553 N.Y.S.2d 845 (1990).

[556] State v. Ross, 141 N.H. 397, 685 A.2d 1234 (1996).

[557] See § 6.49.

[558] People v. Pavao, 59 N.Y.2d 282, 451 N.E.2d 216, 464 N.Y.S.2d 458 (1983).

[559] Commonwealth v. Butler, 423 Pa. Super. 472, 621 A.2d 630, *appeal denied*, 535 Pa. 613, 629 A.2d 1376 (1993).

[560] People v. Hanley, 5 N.Y.3d 108, 833 N.E.2d 248, 800 N.Y.S.2d 105 (2005).

[561] Bowles v. State, 737 N.E.2d 1150, 1153 (Ind. 2000).

[562] Mooney v. State, 105 P.3d 149 (Alaska Ct. App. 2005) (holding witness may certify to victim's reputation for stealing, but not to specific acts of stealing tip money); People v. Santos, 211 Ill. 2d 395, 813 N.E.2d 159 (2004); State v. Hewett, 93 N.C. App. 1, 16, 376 S.E.2d 467, 476 (1989); State v. Graber, 1994 Ohio App. LEXIS 4818 (Sept. 30, 1994).

[563] State v. Magdaleno, 28 Kan. App. 2d 429, 17 P.3d 974, *review denied*, 2001 Kan. LEXIS 354 (May 1, 2001) (reversing defendant's conviction due to trial court's failure to allow cross-examination as to complainant's gang membership).

§ 5.51   Cross-examination of complainant by omission.

A frequent issue in cross-examination of any witness, and particularly sexual assault complainants, is the omission by the witness of certain information from previous statements. The theory justifying questioning about the omission is that the earlier omission is a prior inconsistent statement. For example, a defendant may in certain circumstances be questioned about omissions in his prior statements. (*See* § 6.28.) Under the traditional rule of cross-examination, the cross-examiner should establish that the complainant was specifically asked about the information or facts omitted in a statement. Similarly, a witness cannot be impeached concerning omissions in her direct or cross-examination if the subject areas were not developed in questioning.[564] Without a proper foundation, a complainant may not be impeached with questions that he or she omitted certain facts in a previous statement.[565] Thus, a complainant's incident report is not necessarily a prior inconsistent statement when the evidence reflects that any omissions from the incident report were "attributable to the officer and not the victim."[566]

Under another view, omission is a proper impeachment when it is reasonable to assume that it would be "unnatural" to omit certain facts in the statement. For example, a police officer could be cross-examined about his failure to document evidence of sneaker prints observed at a crime scene.[567] On the other hand, some areas or details may not be raised during the taking of a witness's statement and "may naturally crop up for the first time at trial, and it is not appropriate to consider the omission of such details to be 'inconsistencies'."[568]

---

[564] People v. Suarez, 289 A.D.2d 154, 735 N.Y.S.2d 508 (2001), *appeal denied*, 97 N.Y.2d 762, 769 N.E.2d 369, 742 N.Y.S.2d 623 (2002) (holding police officer could not be impeached with omission in his grand jury testimony if he had not been specifically questioned about that area); People v. Velez, 242 A.D.2d 473, 662 N.Y.S.2d 479, *appeal denied*, 91 N.Y.2d 882, 691 N.E.2d 653, 668 N.Y.S.2d 581 (1997); People v. Brown, 235 A.D.2d 303, 653 N.Y.S.2d 301, *appeal denied*, 89 N.Y.2d 1032, 681 N.E.2d 1310, 659 N.Y.S.2d 863 (1997) (upholding limitation upon defense counsel's cross-examination of complainant regarding omission of certain "non-critical facts" since the witness could not be impeached solely because a fact had been omitted or not more fully stated and counsel must establish that witness's attention had been called to the matter in question and specifically asked questions about the facts allegedly omitted).

[565] People v. Bornholdt, 33 N.Y.2d 75, 305 N.E.2d 461, 350 N.Y.S.2d 369 (1973), *cert. denied*, 94 S. Ct. 1609 (1974); People v. Singh, 249 A.D.2d 338, 670 N.Y.S.2d 346, *appeal denied*, 92 N.Y.2d 861, 699 N.E.2d 451, 677 N.Y.S.2d 91 (1998).

[566] People v. Brown, 254 A.D.2d 57, 679 N.Y.S.2d 278, *appeal denied*, 92 N.Y.2d 980, 706 N.E.2d 749, 683 N.Y.S.2d 761 (1998).

[567] People v. Bishop, 206 A.D.2d 884, 615 N.Y.S.2d 163, *appeal denied*, 84 N.Y.2d 932, 645 N.E.2d 1230, 621 N.Y.S.2d 530 (1994) (reversing defendant's conviction for failure to permit cross-examination on witness's omission in report). See also Cisneros v. State, 692 S.W.2d 78, 83 (Tex. Crim. App. 1985) (permitting impeachment on cross-examination by use of witness's prior silence "when such silence occurred under circumstances in which she would be expected to speak out").

[568] State v. Hartford, 21 Ohio App. 3d 29, 31, 486 N.E.2d 131 (1984). See also People v. Byrd, 284 A.D.2d 201, 728 N.Y.S.2d 134, *appeal denied*, 97 N.Y.2d 679, 764 N.E.2d 398, 738 N.Y.S.2d

Practically, cross-examination of a complainant concerning omissions is generally utilized in many situations such as omissions in a description of a defendant. (*See* § 8.16.) Whether or not an omission in an earlier statement may be utilized in cross-examination is largely a matter of a trial court's discretion.

§ 5.52   Redirect examination.

The scope of redirect examination is largely a matter of the trial court's discretion; however, there are some situations that will naturally lead to redirect. For example, sometimes issues are raised on cross-examination that require explanation or clarification by the witness. Sometimes this involves prior inconsistent statements that may have to be explained to demonstrate that the testimony was not the product of a recent fabrication.[569] Sometimes this involves a witness's failure to report in a timely fashion. By cross-examining a child about the timing of the disclosure of sexual abuse, and referring to a letter written to the defendant's girlfriend, the prosecution can introduce into evidence the letter, which complained of defendant's sexual molestation of her and asked for advice about this problem.[570] Sometimes the door has been opened on cross-examination to entirely new matters, such as other instances of abuse by the defendant.[571] Another common use for redirect examination would be for the witness to explain an entire conversation of which only a portion was elicited on cross-examination. If a complainant is cross-examined as to part of the details of a complaint, the prosecutor may elicit further details of the complainant in response to issues raised on cross-examination.[572]

A good example of the use of redirect examination in a sexual abuse case occurred in *People v. Greenhagen*[573] in which defense counsel's cross-examination of a 15-year-old sibling who reported abuse of younger family members attempted to discredit her by showing that she was vindictive because of restrictions placed upon her dating and that the defendant was actually a "good" father trying to control her. This line of questioning was deemed to open the

---

294 (2001) (holding trial court properly precluded impeachment of police officers on omissions in the grand jury testimony since defendant did not lay a foundation for such testimony and there was no showing they were "unnatural" omissions).

[569] *See, e.g.*, Commonwealth v. Graves, 35 Mass. App. Ct. 76, 616 N.E.2d 817 (1993) (permitting rape victim on redirect examination to read entire five-page handwritten statement in response to defendant's suggestion that victim's mention of knife was a recent contrivance.) *See also* discussion in § 10.49.

[570] People v. Baker, 287 A.D.2d 879, 731 N.Y.S.2d 555 (2001), *appeal denied*, 97 N.Y.2d 727, 767 N.E.2d 156, 740 N.Y.S.2d 699 (2002).

[571] People v. Greene, 13 A.D.3d 991, 787 N.Y.S.2d 466 (2004), *appeal denied*, 5 N.Y.3d 789, 835 N.E.2d 670, 801 N.Y.S.2d 810 (2005) (holding redirect of other acts precluded by trial court's ruling was proper since defendant in cross-examination implied sexual abuse charged was an isolated incident).

[572] R.D. v. State, 706 So. 2d 770, 782 (Ala. Crim. App. 1997).

[573] 78 A.D.2d 964–66, 433 N.Y.S.2d 683, 685 (1980).

door on redirect examination for the witness to testify that the defendant had tried to rape her also because:

> Defense counsel attempted to show that the witness was not credible because of her dislike of defendant for a reason that may fairly be characterized as frivolous or illegitimate in that she was a problem child and that defendant was a responsible father. Thus, defense counsel opened the door on the subject, and in view of his trial strategy as revealed in his opening statement, in the sweeping nature of his cross-examination, the prosecution was entitled to examine further as to the basis for [the witness's] animosity toward her stepfather and to show that it had a legitimate basis. [citations omitted].[574]

Similarly, cross-examining a complainant about uncharged acts and attempting to establish a motive to fabricate, opens the door on redirect examination to details of the prior uncharged acts.[575]

Nevertheless, there are limits to redirect examination, and if testimony is elicited that goes well beyond the scope of cross-examination, it may result in a reversal of a conviction.[576] In general, a trial court has "great discretion in controlling the redirect examination of witnesses."[577] For example, if the prosecutor questions a victim's mother about a previous meeting between them, this does not permit redirect examination on whether the meeting included a discussion about her and her husband's medical condition and whether either ever had a sexually transmitted disease.[578]

---

[574] *Id. See also* State v. Parkinson, 128 Idaho 29, 909 P.2d 647 (1996) (Rape complainant permitted on redirect to explain after cross-examination suggested her dislike of the defendant, that defendant had beaten his wife and that was the basis of her dislike of the defendant); People v. Pierre, 215 A.D.2d 599, 627 N.Y.S.2d 66, *appeal denied*, 86 N.Y.2d 800, 656 N.E.2d 612, 632 N.Y.S.2d 513 (1995).

[575] People v. Carey, 244 A.D.2d 952, 665 N.Y.S.2d 175 (1997), *appeal denied*, 92 N.Y.2d 849, 699 N.E.2d 439, 677 N.Y.S.2d 79 (1998).

[576] People v. Melendez, 55 N.Y.2d 445, 434 N.E.2d 1324, 449 N.Y.S.2d 946 (1982) (redirect examination elicited highly prejudicial hearsay evidence resulting in reversal of defendant's conviction). This case contains a good discussion on the nature, scope, and extent of redirect examination.

[577] State v. Chapman, 410 So. 2d 689, 703 (La. 1981).

[578] State v. Bolden, 852 So. 2d 1050 (La. Ct. App. 2003), *remanded*, 901 So. 2d 445 (2005).

CHAPTER 6

DIRECT AND CROSS-EXAMINATION OF DEFENDANT

§ 6.1   Introduction.

One of the major decisions for the defense is whether the defendant should testify. While it is not absolutely necessary that this decision be made before trial commences, it is helpful to know so that the fact can be addressed in jury selection and opening statement. If a defendant is going to testify, the jury should be told early on to give added weight to the argument that the jury should not make a decision in the case until they have heard all the evidence, particularly the defendant's testimony. Knowing that the defendant will testify will also make a jury anticipate the defendant's testimony.

There will be situations in which defense counsel is not sure whether to allow the defendant to testify; however, by the time trial begins, counsel should have a fairly good idea of the prosecution's case. Defense counsel, by requesting a pretrial ruling concerning the defendant's prior acts or convictions, should be able to gauge if the defendant must be concerned about this area on cross-examination.

Defense counsel should also know prior to the beginning of trial to what extent he or she may have other witnesses to establish factual elements of the defense. Counsel may also be aware that prosecution witnesses, on cross-examination, will be in a position to establish key points for the defense. If other witnesses can establish facts for the defense, there may be less need to call the defendant.

The decision to allow the defendant to testify should be made on the basis of an adequate investigation. Such an investigation entails determining what information the prosecution may be able to develop on cross-examination of the defendant. Sometimes, this information can be gathered from a frank discussion with the defendant or his friends or family. Potential areas of the prosecution's cross-examination of the defendant may also be developed through an independent investigation, which should be separate and apart from interviews with the defendant.

Defense counsel should assess a defendant's possible impact upon the jury, which includes the defendant's demeanor, appearance, and ability to articulate. Will the defendant snap back on cross-examination? Does the defendant project sincerity on being questioned? Will the defendant follow the advice of counsel with respect to direct and cross-examination? Not all defendants equally benefit from the recommendations of counsel; there is no correlation between level of intelligence, guilt, or innocence and ability to follow advice.

It is important that a defendant is willing to make a commitment to testify. Such a commitment entails preparation, time, and a belief in his testimony.

Whether the defendant is going to be called as a witness is, of course, ultimately the defendant's decision. To avoid misunderstandings, it may be advisable to have the defendant sign a statement that he understands his rights with respect to testifying and not testifying (particularly when a defendant chooses not to testify). Some defense attorneys place such a statement on the record.

§ 6.2   Order of defendant's testimony.

The defendant is an important witness for the defense — most likely the most important. The usual rule of calling the defendant as the defense's last witness applies in sexual assault cases. By testifying last, the defendant has had an opportunity to hear all witnesses in the case, answer any of the case's unanswered questions, and assist his attorney in weaving together the threads of his defense. Also, by testifying last, the defendant's testimony will be relatively fresh in the juror's minds when they leave the courtroom to deliberate.

There may be situations, however, when it would make sense to begin the defense case with the defendant. The defendant can set the stage for other witnesses and provide a good introduction and overview of the case. In some situations, the defendant's testimony may be a necessary predicate for other defense witnesses' testimony, especially expert testimony. If the defendant might not be a strong witness, it might be better to place him first.

§ 6.3   Preparing the defendant to testify.

Preparation for direct examination of the defendant should begin well in advance of the trial. It is crucial for a defendant to share with his attorney as much information as possible about a case. The defendant should be given the opportunity in pretrial meetings to answer open-ended questions about what areas of information may be available in his defense. (*See* § 1.1.) Does the defendant have any evidence that can be used on direct examination relevant to the issue of the complainant's consent, such as evidence of the purchase of a gift by the complainant or a photograph documenting a shared evening after the complainant alleges the relationship ended?

Preparation also entails determining all of the defendant's statements made to law enforcement officials or other parties that may be in the possession of the prosecution. Also, reviewing the statements of witnesses and police reports should help a defendant's attorney develop areas of direct examination.

All photographs and exhibits should be reviewed by the defendant to assist counsel in preparing for direct examination. Again, this questioning process should be open-ended: the defendant should be shown the photograph or exhibit and asked what he sees that may assist his defense. In all likelihood, by the time the defendant testifies, photographs and important items of physical evidence will already have been introduced by the prosecution. Knowing that there are favorable areas to develop concerning a particular photograph or exhibit will assist the defense in determining whether to object to the admission of a particular exhibit.

§ 6.4   Beginning the direct examination with a denial of guilt.

Research indicates that individuals best remember things that they hear first and last. This is called the principle of primacy and recency. Accordingly, direct and cross-examinations of key witnesses should start strong and end strong. The beginning of the defendant's direct examination is a good place to begin with a clear and unequivocal denial of guilt. Consider the following:

Q. You are David Henzel?

A. Yes.

Q. You are the defendant in this case?

A. Yes.

Q. How old are you David?

A. 26.

Q. What do you presently do?

A. I'm currently a mechanic at Grayson's Garage.

Q. Are you married?

A. Yes.

Q. To whom?

A. Elizabeth Henzel.

Q. David, directing your attention to the evening of September 25th, 2005, can you tell us whether or not between 11:00 and 11:30 on that evening you were on Jefferson Avenue in the City of Brewster?

A. I was not.

Q. Can you tell us whether or not at that same time, date, and place you had any contact with Christie Collins?

A. I did not.

Q. Have you had occasion to give thought to your activities during the week surrounding September 25, 2005?

A. I have.

Q. Can you tell us, David, where you were on the evening of September 25, 2005.

A. Yes. I was home with my wife and children.

It is advisable later during direct examination of the defendant, particularly at the end, to have the defendant deny once again the allegations against him. In a case where the defendant is denying any sexual contact whatsoever, the question should be asked, "Can you tell us whether or not you have ever had sexual intercourse with Christie Collins?" or "Have you ever sexually abused Christie Collins?" The outright denial of guilt at the beginning of a direct examination when the jury's attention is freshest is a good way to start a direct examination.

The introductory questions concerning denial of guilt should also tie into the theme of the defense. The introductory questions on direct examination of the defendant should be simple, as above, and not require the defendant to hesitate or think about the answers. Introductory questions can also help humanize the defendant by discussing the defendant's work or family. More involved questions and answers can be used later in the direct examination, but simple questions and answers are easy for the jury and witness to follow. This approach to introductory questions also precludes objections.

§ 6.5 Denying material facts.

After a general denial of guilt, it might be appropriate to deny material aspects of the prosecution's proof. This may be a statement offered by the prosecution purportedly made to law enforcement officials. This may be done as follows:

Q. Following your arrest, did you speak about the allegations with investigators?

A. I did.

Q. Tell us in words or substance what you told the investigators.

A. They asked me if I wanted to give them a statement, and I said I would, and when they said "Well, what do you have to say," I told them, "I didn't do anything to the young girl and that I wasn't guilty of any crimes."

Q. Did you say anything else to them?

A. That's pretty much all I said, but they wouldn't write it down, and they didn't write it down.

During the prosecution's presentation of its case, outline the key areas of the prosecution's proof that the defendant is in a position to refute. This list will help you decide whether to call the defendant as a witness and, if you do decide to call him, it will help you to evaluate the efficacy of his testimony. If possible, combine some of these areas of the prosecution's proof into one or two questions to streamline the defendant's direct testimony.

§ 6.6 Dealing with motive.

In cases other than mistaken identity, it is important to adress the motive for the complainant to accuse the defendant of a sexual assault. A complainant's credibility is significantly bolstered by the fact that he or she has no motive to accuse the defendant. If the defense can offer proof as to a possible motive on the part of the complainant, it may be addressed through the direct examination of the defendant. This might be established through statements that were made by the complainant to the defendant, or through evidence of a component of the relationship between the two of them. For example, perhaps the defendant and a relative of the complainant had a business or personal relationship that was unsuccessful or conflict-ridden. Perhaps the defendant can explain a reason for the complainant being jealous of his relationship with a third party. Whether or not the defendant has information to offer concerning a motive on the part of the complainant is another factor to consider in determining whether to call the defendant as a witness. If the defendant has nothing to offer in this regard, there may be little to gain by calling the defendant, particularly if he will be a weak witness. On the other hand, even if he is a weak witness, if only he can establish a motive, then it may be crucial to call him.

In the following example, a defendant accused of child sexual abuse addresses the motive issue by testifying to what he told investigators and referring to the complainant's unwillingness to perform chores.

Q. Did the investigator ask you, Tim, why you thought your stepdaughter would make such a charge? Did he ever ask you that?

A. Yes, sir, he did.

Q. Do you recall if you answered him as to what possible motive you thought she might have?

A. Yes. I said because the family unit was breaking up and she was — her grandmother was going to live with my sister.

Q. Did you assign a lot of chores for Cindy to do?

A. She had chores to do, yes.

Q. Did she do them all the time?

A. No.

Q. Did you talk to her about that?

A. Yes.

Q. What was her response?

A. She would get quite upset and told me no one, especially someone who is not her father, was going to tell her what to do.

Related to motive is the nature and extent of a relationship between a defendant and a complainant. The relationship may have been troubled or it may have been fine, or it may have been both at times, but whatever it was, the complainant's charges will be evaluated within its context. While not every aspect of the relationship can be developed on direct examination, examples of the *defendant's* definition of the relationship can be provided. In this regard, the pretrial preparation is essential to determine what aspects should be presented. For example, if a defendant and complainant met at a bar and engaged in sexual relations hours later, probably not every word that was exchanged between them need be repeated, but there may be certain bits of conversation that will be important, and the defense attorney must direct the defendant to, and draw out from him, these important areas.

§ 6.7   Explaining changes in a complainant's behaviors after certain events.

In cases in which a defendant has had a relationship with a complainant, the defendant may want to testify as to changes in the complainant's behavior or attitude toward the defendant that may throw some light on a possible motive for the complainant to bring charges. This change in behavior or attitude may be the result of factors outside of the relationship. A defense may be that the complainant's allegations came about as a result of a third party entering the picture.

An example of a case in which the involvement of a third-party was the cause of a complainant's charges occurred in Oregon. The defendant, 41 years old, claimed he had discovered a ten-year-old having relations with his 13-year-old son, another boy, and her uncle, and that he was going to report this to her parents, but before he could, she accused him of rape.[1]

The psychological basis of the behavior of some complainants in sexual assault litigation is a complex matter, and expert witnesses are often necessary to provide explanations. This is discussed in Chapter 11's discussion of expert testimony. The defendant's testimony can be a foundation for the expert's testimony.

§ 6.8   Testimony concerning the opportunity to commit the crime.

In some cases, it is important for a defendant in a sexual assault case to testify on the issue of the opportunity to commit the crime. In an identification defense, this is an alibi. As to lack of opportunity, perhaps a defendant in a child abuse case can testify that he was at work at the times the complainant said the acts took place. If the defendant was in a caretaker role, such as a teacher or bus driver, then the opportunity to commit the crime may have been limited by the fact that the defendant was rarely, if ever, alone with the child, or had insufficient time while alone, to engage in the sexual acts described by the complainant.

Sometimes the opportunity to commit the crime can be challenged because of physical limitations of the defendant, such as the inability to engage in particular sexual acts.

§ 6.9   Direct testimony concerning prior bad acts or convictions.

Counsel for a defendant who has elected to testify and knows that the prosecution will be cross-examining with respect to the defendant's prior convictions or bad acts should begin an explanation of this issue during jury selection and opening statement. For the defense, it is bad enough for the jury to hear for the first time from the defendant about prior bad acts or convictions, but it is worse yet to hear about them for the first time on cross-examination

---

[1] State v. Jalo, 27 Or. App. 845, 557 P.2d 1359 (1976).

of the defendant. Mitigating circumstances should be mentioned, but not over-stated. These include the passage of time from the date of the prior conviction or bad act, the age of the defendant at such time, substance abuse problems at the time, and any restitution made.

By introducing the issue of a defendant's convictions or bad acts during jury selection and opening, and then through the defendant's direct examination, it allows the defendant's history to be presented as the defense wishes. The defendant's attorney can point out in his or her opening statement that while the defendant has no obligation to testify, the defendant has made the decision to testify despite the fact that the prosecutor will question the defendant about his record.

§ 6.10 Form of answers on direct examination.

Long and rambling answers on direct examination are difficult for a jury to follow. Questions should not be phrased so as to require long answers, and the defendant should be cautioned not to provide long answers.

Research reveals that the most credible answers are those that are set forth in narrative fashion. Leading questions do not lend themselves to a narrative response and are less likely to project credibility. A defense attorney should avoid the temptation to use leading questions as a substitute for effective pretrial preparation. If the defendant gives an answer that needs further explanation, let the witness expand on the answer if possible. This can be done by simple questions such as, "Could you explain that?" or "What do you mean by that answer?"

§ 6.11 Anticipating cross-examination.

An important part of direct examination is anticipating cross-examination. Undesirable issues may be diffused on direct examination. This does not mean that the direct examination of the defendant should simply become a response to the prosecutor's argument, which can negate the effect of the defense theme. It does mean that certain areas may be better addressed on direct examination than allowed to be introduced for the first time on the prosecution's cross-examination. A common example is a defendant's statement to the police. Another example, in an acquaintance assault case, might be writings sent by the defendant to the complainant. The prosecution may not have introduced such writings as part of its direct case, but the defendant, having told his counsel about such correspondence, might explain that he did have occasion to write the complainant and the circumstances surrounding the writings. Thus, before the defendant is cross-examined by the prosecution with a particular statement from a letter — which probably will be incriminating — the *context* of the statement has been explained. This approach of dealing with issues that might be raised by the prosecution for the first time on cross-examination of the defendant is particularly effective with exhibits.

§ 6.12 Demonstrating by the defendant.

There may be situations where it will be helpful on direct examination to have the defendant demonstrate how an act took place, particularly if there is evidence of a struggle. There are also situations where the defendant may wish to exhibit certain personal characteristics, such as eye color or a scar. The use of a defendant for such demonstrations is set forth more fully in the chapter on demonstrative evidence.[2]

§ 6.13 Use of defendant's statement to the police or prior consistent statement in lieu of or in addition to direct examination.

Sometimes the decision not to testify is based on the fact that the defendant's defense can be put forth in statements made by the defendant to the police. Exculpatory statements given by a defendant to the police are not unusual and are often introduced by the prosecution as part of its direct case. Such statements may be helpful to the defendant in establishing his case without having to undergo direct or cross-examination. If the statement is not included in the prosecution's evidence, however, the defendant who does not testify himself will lose the opportunity to assert whatever is contained therein unless it can be elicited through other witnesses.

The defendant who seeks to offer an exculpatory statement as an exhibit can be precluded from doing so, because an exculpatory statement given to the police is not a statement against interest and "it is not the intent of the law to permit the defendant to avoid taking the stand and being subject to cross-examination by allowing his story to be presented through . . . hearsay testimony. . . ."[3] For example, a defendant does not have a right to introduce a tape recording between the defendant and victim, surreptitiously made by the victim several days after the alleged assault in which the defendant repeatedly denies the assaults.[4] Such "prior consistent statements do not fall within any of the recognized exceptions to the general rule barring the use of out-of-court utterances to prove the truth of the matters asserted therein."[5]

---

[2] See §§ 14.34–35.

[3] People v. Richardson, 193 A.D.2d 969, 972, 598 N.Y.S.2d 341, 344 (1993) (citing People v. Dvoroznak, 127 A.D.2d 785, 512 N.Y.S.2d 180 (1987)). See also People v. Hughes, 228 A.D.2d 618, 645 N.Y.S.2d 493, appeal denied, 88 N.Y.2d 987, 672 N.E.2d 619, 649 N.Y.S.2d 393 (1996).

[4] People v. Harris, 247 A.D.2d 630, 669 N.Y.S.2d 355, appeal denied, 91 N.Y.2d 1008, 698 N.E.2d 965, 676 N.Y.S.2d 136 (1998).

[5] People v. Harris, 247 A.D.2d 630, 669 N.Y.S.2d 355, appeal denied, 91 N.Y.2d 1008, 698 N.E.2d 965, 676 N.Y.S.2d 136 (1998).

It should also be noted that if a defendant is impeached with a portion of a statement he gave the police, he may not be permitted to introduce the entire statement on the theory of relevancy if the other matters in the statement are unrelated to the matters upon which he was impeached.[6] If the prosecution offers the inculpatory portions of a defendant's grand jury testimony, the defendant has no right to present the remainder of the testimony in an attempt to "bolster his own trial testimony" with "self-serving denials of culpability."[7] However, when only a portion of a defendant's statement is used by the prosecution, and there are remaining portions that are important to an explanation of the context of the statement used by the prosecution, or that in some way rehabilitate the defendant's statement, the remaining portions of the statement may be offered into evidence by the defendant.[8]

A defendant's prior statement may qualify under the excited utterance or present sense impression exceptions to the hearsay rule.[9] These exceptions are discussed in Chapter 10. Ordinarily, a defendant's statements to law enforcement officials are not made without reflection, thereby not qualifying under these hearsay exceptions. A defendant's excited utterance, however, may be admitted even if self-serving and the declarant is available to testify at trial.[10] Just as a defendant cannot refer to his prior consistent statements, a defendant cannot refer to his cooperation with the police under a consciousness of innocence theory. (*See* § 10.12.)

§ 6.14 Limitations on defendant's direct examination — references to complainant.

A trial court may limit a defendant's testimony with respect to attacks on a complainant's credibility. For example, a defendant may be limited in his testimony about a collateral issue of the victim's credibility, such as a rape victim's alleged drug use.[11] Rules concerning testimony by a defendant to

---

[6] People v. Ramos, 70 N.Y.2d 639, 512 N.E.2d 304, 518 N.Y.S.2d 783 (1987) ("Relevance alone is an insufficient basis for admitting a prior consistent statement and the mere fact that a portion of a statement is raised by the prosecutor to impeach defendant on a particular issue does not entitle defendant to bolster his own credibility by introducing other portions containing prior consistent statements on unrelated matters." 70 N.Y.S.2d at 640–41, 512 N.E.2d at 305, 518 N.Y.S.2d at 784); People v. Williams, 217 A.D.2d 713, 630 N.Y.S.2d 91 (1995), *appeal denied*, 87 N.Y.2d 1026, 666 N.E.2d 1074, 644 N.Y.S.2d 160 (1996).

[7] *Harris*, 672 N.Y.S.2d at 155.

[8] Husseain v. State, 805 So. 2d 1066 (Fla. Ct. App. 2002) (reversing defendant's conviction, because defendant was not permitted to offer initial statements made to police, which should have been permitted under "rule of completeness").

[9] People v. Cannon, 228 A.D.2d 513, 644 N.Y.S.2d 311 (1996) (reversing defendant's conviction due to trial court's failure to admit defendant's hearsay statement heard by witness).

[10] *Id.*

[11] People v. Weaver, 302 A.D.2d 872, 753 N.Y.S.2d 781, *appeal denied*, 99 N.Y.2d 633, 790 N.E.2d 289, 760 N.Y.S.2d 115 (2003).

statements made to him by a complainant, such as those concerning sexual history, are discussed in Chapter 5.[12]

§ 6.15 Caution: Opening the door on direct examination and cross-examination to character, prior bad acts and other acts of abuse, and defendant's right to remain silent.

Direct examination should be structured for impact and to avoid self-destruction. Careless questions and responses can have a devastating effect. The United States Supreme Court in *Walder v. United States* recognized that a defendant who goes beyond a mere denial of the charged crime in his direct testimony can open the door to questions and evidence of matters either suppressed or otherwise precluded.[13] For example, a defendant's assertions on direct examination may open the door to cross-examination on a pending unrelated criminal charge, which would otherwise be precluded.[14] A defendant testifying on direct examination that he has never been "in trouble"[15] or is not a violent person[16] opens the doors to past conduct. Similarly, testimony by the defendant that he "never put a knife to anyone's throat"[17] or would "never do

---

[12] *See* § 5.32.

[13] Walder v. United States, 347 U.S. 62, 74 S. Ct. 354, 98 L. Ed.2d 503 (1954):

> Take the present situation, of his own accord, the defendant went beyond a mere denial of complicity in the crimes of which he was charged and made the sweeping claim that he had never dealt in or possessed any narcotics. Of course, the Constitution guarantees a defendant the fullest opportunity to meet the accusation against him. He must be free to deny all the elements of the case against him without thereby giving leave to the Government to introduce by way of rebuttal evidence illegally secured by it, and therefore not available for its case in chief. Beyond that, however, there is hardly justification for letting the defendant affirmatively resort to perjurious testimony in reliance on the Government's disability to challenge his credibility.

Id. at 65.

[14] People v. Williams, 299 A.D.2d 568, 750 N.Y.S.2d 504 (2002), *appeal denied*, 99 N.Y.2d 621, 787 N.E.2d 1178, 757 N.Y.S.2d 832 (2003).

[15] Rubio v. State, 939 P.2d 238, 244 (Wyo. 1997).

[16] People v. Santmyer, 231 A.D.2d 956, 648 N.Y.S.2d 69 (1996) (defendant opened door to previous assault conviction by testifying that he was not a violent person).

[17] People v. Gordon, 202 A.D.2d 166, 608 N.Y.S.2d 192, *appeal denied*, 83 N.Y.2d 911, 637 N.E.2d 284, 614 N.Y.S.2d 393 (1994) (Defendant's testimony that he "never put a knife to anyone's throat" in response to cross-examination question directed solely at the use of knife in the case for which defendant was on trial opened the door to the prosecution's questioning, previously excluded by the trial court, regarding the defendant's use of a knife on two prior occasions, although the prosecution was not permitted to inquire into the fact that the prior uses of the knife were related to sexual assaults). State v. Eldridge, 2003 Ohio App. LEXIS 6411 (Dec. 22, 2003) (holding defendant's testimony during direct examination that "I would never have done nothing [sic] like that. I've never done nothing [sic] like that" opened door to defendant's prior assault conviction, even though meaning of "like that" was ambiguous).

anything to hurt that woman,"[18] or "nothing like that,"[19] or that his personal standards and attitudes toward women prevented him from doing the charged acts[20] will open the door to prior bad acts. Implying a peaceable relationship with the complainant during the defendant's direct examination may open the door to cross-examination about whether the defendant even struck the complainant.[21] A defendant can open the door to cross-examination of prior bad acts if he is asked on direct examination a question such as, "Did you use any force or any threats at the time that you did that?" and he answers, "I have never used any force or threats."[22] By this answer, the defendant raises his credibility as the key issue of whether he ever threatened the complainant in connection with molesting her.[23]

Even denying a material element of the offense, such as not receiving sexual gratification from a particular act, can open the door to other testimony about the defendant's sexual activities.[24]

A typical pitfall in this regard is a defendant who blurts out that, not only did he not abuse the complainant, he has never had any sexual contact with any child. Such testimony on direct examination opens the door for possible testimony of prosecution witnesses who claim to have had prior sexual contact with the defendant, since the defendant has introduced the issue of his prior sexual activities.[25]

---

[18] People v. Wynn, 208 A.D.2d 576, 617 N.Y.S.2d 62 (1994) (testimony by defendant on direct examination that he "would never do anything to hurt that woman" opened door to cross-examination of defendant about acts against the complainant).

[19] Eldridge, 2003 Ohio App. LEXIS 6411 (Dec. 22, 2003) (holding defendant's testimony during direct examination that "I would never have done nothing [sic] like that. I've never done nothing [sic] like that" opened door to defendant's prior assault conviction, even though meaning of "like that" was ambiguous).

[20] People v. Mays, 187 A.D.2d 535, 589 N.Y.S.2d 922 (1992), appeal denied, 81 N.Y.2d 843, 611 N.E.2d 781, 595 N.Y.S.2d 742 (1993) (testimony by defendant that his personal standards and attitudes toward women precluded him from conduct alleged at trial opened door to questioning of defendant about prior sexual misconduct).

[21] People v. Gillis, 279 A.D.2d 260, 719 N.Y.S.2d 28, appeal denied, 96 N.Y.2d 800, 750 N.E.2d 79, 726 N.Y.S.2d 377 (2001).

[22] People v. Senior, 3 Cal. App. 4th 765, 777, 5 Cal. Rptr. 2d 14, 22 (1992).

[23] Id. at 3 Cal. App. 4th at 778–79, 5 Cal. Rptr. 2d at 23.

[24] People v. Rossman, 95 A.D.2d 873, 463 N.Y.S.2d 891 (1983) (where defendant testified on direct examination that he did not receive sexual gratification from touching or cutting a female's hair, this testimony opened the door to rebuttal evidence of the defendant's act of masturbation after giving police an envelope containing hair, scissors, and a knife while the police were searching his apartment).

[25] State v. Banks, 71 Ohio App. 3d 214, 593 N.E.2d 346 (1991). See also Acuna v. State, 332 Md. 65, 629 A.2d 1233 (1993) (defendant's "universal denial" on direct examination that he had "never licked" the complainant was held to open the door to prior uncharged conduct of similar oral sexual contact with the same four-year-old, which had originally been held inadmissible by the judge).

A defendant's comments on direct examination volunteering that he never had any complaints concerning his conduct toward children or never touched an underage person opens the door to other uncharged acts of the defendant.[26] By testifying on direct examination that he was not the family's sole disciplinarian and that he never conditioned the complainant's privileges on the performance of sexual acts, the defendant allows the prosecutor to present evidence of an uncharged sexual assault.[27] Direct examination of a defense witness about defendant's conduct around her and the infant victim can also open the door to character evidence.[28] On the other hand, a defendant's testimony that he is not the type of person to have sexual relations with young people, and cross-examination of a detective that pedophiles usually collect child pornography and defendant did not, may not open the door to questions about specific instances of sexual contact with children.[29]

While it has been suggested a defendant deal with his prior criminal history on direct examination if there will be cross-examination in this area, a defendant must be careful in answering these questions. Sometimes careless testimony on direct examination in an attempt to explain prior convictions into which the prosecution has been permitted to inquire on cross-examination will open the door for the prosecution to develop details of additional bad acts committed by the defendant that might otherwise have been precluded.[30] Trying to explain past

---

[26] United States v. Stroh, 46 M.J. 643, 647–48 (A.F.C.C.A. 1997); Thornton v. State, 653 N.E.2d 493 (Ind. Ct. App. 1995) (defendant voluntarily claiming on cross-examination that he never touched any of his daughter's friends in a sexual manner opened the door to prosecution presenting proof of prior acts of sexual misconduct directed by the defendant at them); State v. Barling, 779 So. 2d 1035 (La. Ct. App. 2001) (holding defendant's testimony that he never conducted himself in a sexual manner with any teenage member of his family opened the door to other crimes evidence, even if those crimes were not in state's notice); People v. Katt, 248 Mich. App. 282, 639 N.W.2d 815 (2001) (holding defendant's answer on direct examination "I did not do this. It's not . . . it's not my nature to go around and have sex with children," opened the door to rebuttal testimony of other acts of abuse); People v. Fosmer, 293 A.D.2d 824, 743 N.Y.S.2d 179, *appeal denied*, 98 N.Y.2d 696, 776 N.E.2d 4, 747 N.Y.S.2d 415 (2002) ("However, it was defense counsel who twice asked defendant on direct examination whether he had ever been accused of molesting children before, to which he responded in the negative. Thus, the door was open for the prosecutor, who then demonstrated a good faith basis for the inquiry, to question defendant about such a prior accusation.").

[27] State v. Kholi, 672 A.2d 429, 433–34 (R.I. 1996).

[28] Hill v. State, 243 Ga. App. 124, 128, 532 S.E.2d 491, 495 (2000) ("[D]uring direct examination of Hill's sister, defense counsel asked her, 'How was Pete around the baby?' and she responded, 'He was a great father.' This amounts to evidence of good character that may be rebutted by a prior conviction." (citation omitted)). *See also* State v. Smiley, 2004 SD LEXIS 190, 689 N.W.2d 427 (2004) (noting that when defendant called a former supervisor who testified that the defendant had good work skills and good "people-type relationships with individuals," this brought defendant's character into question and opened the door to defendant's prior forgery conviction).

[29] State v. Hobson, 2003 Tenn. Crim. App. LEXIS 1050 (Dec. 18, 2003) (noting defendant waived any objection to this rule, suggesting defendant could not be cross-examined about specific instances of sexual contact with children).

[30] Taylor v. State, 264 Ga. App. 665, 592 S.E.2d 148 (2003), *cert. denied*, 2004 Ga. LEXIS 372

bad acts or convictions can open the door. Asserting that one plead guilty in past cases because he was guilty on those cases but not the instant offense can open the door to otherwise precluded bad acts.[31] Also, a defendant who answers his attorney's question as to why he went to prison and responds "attempted murder, attempted rape, kidnap and that's it" and omits his rape conviction, opens the door to questioning concerning the facts of his earlier conviction.[32] Volunteering that an earlier charge was dismissed opens the door to the reasons for dismissal.[33]

A defendant can also open the door to questioning on his right to remain silent by testifying that no one ever interviewed him about complainant's allegations.[34]

Another area concerns personal achievements or other statements which place character in issue. A defendant's testimony concerning medals and awards he won in the military has placed a defendant's character in issue and opened the door for the prosecution to inquire if the defendant had ever been convicted of a crime, even after a pretrial ruling that the prosecution could not inquire of the defendant concerning prior convictions.[35] A defendant's explanation of certain behaviors or certain actions of a complainant may also open the door to damaging rebuttal expert testimony.

(Apr. 27, 2004) (defendant's referencing interview with detective and discussion of his being "locked up" opened door to cross-examination about other crimes he committed); Sweeney v. State, 233 Ga. App. 862, 506 S.E.2d 150 (1998) (holding defendant's testimony concerning problems he had before leaving his position as a police officer opened the door to testimony by chief of police about defendant having once tried to pressure a woman into having sex with him).

[31] People v. Cooper, 92 N.Y.2d 968, 706 N.E.2d 745, 683 N.Y.S.2d 757 (1998) (defendant opened door on cross-examination to otherwise precluded evidence of bad acts by seeking "to elicit an incorrect jury inference that he had pleaded guilty and served prison terms in prior cases, but that he would not plead guilty in this case because he was in fact innocent"); People v. Ferguson, 190 A.D.2d 610, 593 N.Y.S.2d 817, *appeal denied*, 81 N.Y.2d 970, 615 N.E.2d 228, 598 N.Y.S.2d 771 (1993).

[32] People v. Shea, 39 Cal. App. 4th 1257, 46 Cal. Rptr. 2d 388 (1995).

[33] People v. Gordon, 202 A.D.2d 166, 608 N.Y.S.2d 192, *appeal denied*, 83 N.Y.2d 911, 637 N.E.2d 284, 614 N.Y.S.2d 393 (1994) ("Similarly, defendant opened the door to cross-examination regarding the reasons for dismissal of the criminal charges in connection with the two prior incidents in question, because defendant volunteered that the charges had been dismissed, again in an obvious attempt to mislead the jury into believing that there was no substance to the prior charges.").

[34] State v. Winward, 941 P.2d 627 (Utah Ct. App. 1997) ("On cross-examination, the prosecutor did not overstep his bounds in clarifying appellant's statement on direct that no one had ever interviewed him. It was proper for the prosecutor to attempt to counter the implication from appellant's testimony that he had never been interviewed in spite of his eagerness to tell his story." *Id.* at 634.).

[35] People v. Morehouse, 5 A.D.3d 925, 928–29, 774 N.Y.S.2d 100, *appeal denied*, 3 N.Y.3d 644, 816 N.E.2d 206, 782 N.Y.S.2d 416 (2004) ("During defendant's testimony, he attested to his good character by submitting his military service record. Therefore, he opened the door to questioning concerning the prior bad act."); People v. Jones, 121 A.D.2d 398, 503 N.Y.S.2d 109 (1986).

A defendant is entitled to rebut allegations of abuse outside the indictment presented by the prosecution without opening the door to character evidence.[36]

§ 6.16   Cross-examination of the defendant.

The prosecutor needs to have fingertip control of all facts of the case, especially statements made by the defendant about the case to any person, not just law enforcement officials. This information is essential so that the defendant who strays from the facts can be challenged on cross-examination or at a later time. Failure of the prosecution to marshal the facts before cross-examination will allow the defendant considerable leeway in his testimony.

In cross-examination, the prosecution should have clear goals in mind and tie the testimony into the theme of the prosecution's case. Testimony on irrelevant issues dilutes the cross-examination and wastes time. The length of a cross-examination is not a measure of effectiveness, and ineffective lengthy cross-examination can be counterproductive. Research indicates that jurors tend to empathize with witnesses the longer they are on the stand.

One of the basic elements of cross-examination that is often overlooked is the need to listen carefully to the defendant's testimony on direct examination to determine what the defendant is saying and not saying. The defendant's statement may not only be vulnerable to contradiction by other witnesses, but also may be inconsistent or illogical. Such inconsistency or illogic does not always appear at first hearing. Concentration is essential while listening to the defendant. Similarly, it is necessary to listen carefully to the defendant's answers on cross-examination. Often these answers will suggest a rich area of further cross-examination that was never anticipated. Also, as noted in the preceding section the defendant may open the door to otherwise precluded areas of examination.

§ 6.17   Cross-examination of defendant by having him characterize complainant or a witness as a liar.

A common cross-examination technique is to ask the defendant if a witness or the complainant is a liar. While some jurisdictions may permit this technique, it has also been criticized as prejudicial to the defendant since the defendant has no burden to prove that a witness is lying. Its efficacy is also subject to question.

Some jurisdictions have a clear cut prohibition against cross-examining a defendant by asking if another witness has lied[37] or placing the witness in a

---

[36] State v. Saunders, 1999 UT 59, 992 P.2d 951 (1999).

[37] United States v. Weiss, 930 F.2d 185, 195 (2d Cir. 1991) (noting credibility is a jury issue); United States v. Richter, 826 F.2d 206 (2d Cir. 1987) (holding improper to ask defendant if FBI agent was lying); Allen v. United States, 837 A.2d 917 (D.C. 2003) (noting jurisdiction firmly established rule against this type of cross-examination and that "it plays unfairly upon jurors' natural reluctance to attribute perjury to law enforcement officers"); State v. Singh, 259 Conn. 693, 706-

position to challenge the prosecutor's credibility,[38] or stating during cross-examination of a witness that the witness lied.[39]

The following is an example of such a cross-examination that resulted in a reversal of a defendant's conviction in a sexual assault case:

Q. Mr. Kim, it is your testimony that you never touched Miss A's [true name deleted] breast, you never put her [sic] hand down her pants, you never groped around her crotch, and you never tried to kiss her [sic], is that your testimony?

A. All four, no, I didn't do it.

Q. Everything she said is not true?

A. It's all lies.

Q. Lies, everything she said is a lie?

A. That is right. I didn't do anything.

Q. You are calling her a liar?

A. Yes, she is a liar.[40]

Similarly, asking a sexual assault defendant's wife whether she believed her children were telling the truth is improper.[41] Court will reverse convictions based on a prosecutor's questioning a defendant about whether other witnesses were lying.[42]

711, 793 A.2d 226, 236–39 (2002); State v. Graves, 668 N.W.2d 860 (Iowa 2003) (noting that there may be many reasons people have different perceptions and recollections of an event, and that the technique unfairly questions the defendant to make the defendant look bad in front of the jury, regardless of the response and declining to recognize any exceptions to this rule); Fisher v. State, 128 Md. App. 79, 110, 736 A.2d 1125, 1163 (1999); Commonwealth v. Long, 17 Mass. App. Ct. 707, 462 N.E.2d 330 (1984); Daniel v. State, 78 P.3d 890 (2003), *cert. denied*, 541 U.S. 1045 Nev. (2004):

We adopt a rule prohibiting prosecutors from asking a defendant whether other witnesses have lied or from goading a defendant to accuse other witnesses of lying, except where the defendant during direct examination has directly challenged the truthfulness of those witnesses. . . . Because it can be difficult to say whether lying is the only possible explanation for inconsistent testimony, we reject an exception to the rule on that ground.

Id. at 904. *See also* State v. Castenada-Perez, 61 Wash. App. 354, 810 P.2d 74 (1991)

[38] United States v. Henry, 47 F.3d 17, 21 (2d Cir. 1995) (holding it was improper for prosecutor to ask defendant witness if a prosecution witness "pulled the wool over . . . the prosecutor's eyes").

[39] Commonwealth v. Bricker, 506 Pa. 571, 487 A.2d 346 (1985).

[40] People v. Kim, 209 A.D.2d 167, 167–70, 617 N.Y.S.2d 748, 750 (1994).

[41] State v. Jerrels, 83 Wash. App. 503, 925 P.2d 209 (1996).

[42] United States v. Akitoye, 923 F.2d 221 (1st Cir. 1991); Scott v. United States, 619 A.2d 917, 924–25 (D.C. 1993); People v. Berrios, 298 A.D.2d 597, 750 N.Y.S.2d 302 (2002) (finding reversible error in sexual assault trial for prosecution to repeatedly ask defendant in cross-examination whether prosecution witnesses, including complainant and detectives, lied); People v. Leuthner, 216 A.D.2d 327, 627 N.Y.S.2d 776 (1995); People v. Ortiz, 207 A.D.2d 279, 615 N.Y.S.2d 387, *appeal denied*, 84 N.Y.2d 909, 645 N.E.2d 1226, 621 N.Y.S.2d 526 (1994).

Sometimes, courts will find the technique improper but not reversible when there is overwhelming evidence of guilt[43] or the instances of such questioning were isolated,[44] or if the defendant failed to object, thereby requiring review under the plain error standard.[45]

However, some courts permit forcing the defendant to characterize a witness as a liar when the defendant testifies in a way that leaves no possibility that the prosecution's witness is mistaken and impugns the truthfulness of the witness or witnesses. The rationale for permitting this line of questioning is explained by one appellate court as follows:

> More to the point though, a distinction has to be made between a defendant's testimony that conflicts with that of the People's witnesses and yet is susceptible to the suggestion that the witnesses spoke out of mistake or hazy recollection and the situation where, as here, the defendant's testimony leaves open only the suggestion that the People's witnesses have lied. In the latter circumstances, the prosecution has the right to ask whether the witnesses are liars. Here, defendant testified that Santana and the other officers attacked him. The prosecution witnesses testified to defendant's assault of Santana and the other officers. The contradictory accounts cannot be based on mistake or hazy recollection. Indeed, defendant himself volunteered that both Officers Santana and Delgado were liars. In such circumstances, the prosecutor was well within his rights in asking defendant whether those witnesses had lied. Of course, in any case of direct conflict between a defendant's testimony and that of a People's witness, the prosecutor is entitled to ask the defendant whether the witness had been mistaken in his testimony [citation omitted] and, for that matter, whether the witness's testimony was not true. Thus, the prosecutor quite properly asked defendant whether Officer Fuentes had not told 'the whole truth.'[46]

---

[43] State v. Roper, 136 S.W.3d 891, 899–903 (Mo. Ct. App. 2004) (condemning the practice in this sodomy prosecution but noting the defendant's failure to object and the substantial evidence of guilt); Gaxiola v. State, 2005 Nev. LEXIS 79, 119 P.3d 1225 (2005) (holding that cross-examination was improper but that prosecutor had no "wrongful intent" and error was not prejudicial).

[44] People v. Roman, 13 A.D.3d 1115, 787 N.Y.S.2d 568 (2004), *appeal denied*, 4 N.Y.3d 802, 828 N.E.2d 94, 795 N.Y.S.2d 178 (2005).

[45] People v. Lawrence, 4 A.D.3d 436, 771 N.Y.S.2d 362, *appeal denied*, 2 N.Y.3d 802, 814 N.E.2d 473, 781 N.Y.S.2d 301 (2004) (finding "any error committed by the prosecutor in pursuing this line of questioning was harmless in light of the overwhelming evidence of the defendant's guilt"); Jensen v. State, 2005 Wyo. 85, 116 P.3d 1088 (2005); Beaugureau v. State, 2002 Wyo. 160, 56 P.3d 626, 633–34 (2002) (holding cross-examination of defendant as to whether or not defendant believed other witnesses were lying if they contradicted her was improper but not reversible error in light of overwhelming evidence of guilt).

[46] People v. Overlee, 236 A.D.2d 133, 139, 666 N.Y.S.2d 572, 576–77 (1997), *appeal denied*, 91 N.Y.2d 976, 695 N.E.2d 724, 672 N.Y.S.2d 855 (1998).

Many courts permit the defendant to be asked if a witness is lying when the reasonable conclusion is that a victim or prosecution witnesses have lied and are not mistaken.[47]

Cross-examination of a defendant about his statement to the police and his discussion of why the complainant accused him as follows is not the equivalent of having a witness comment on the testimony of another witness:

Q. "Why would [the victim] accuse you of sexually abusing her?"

A. "I came up with two conclusions. Maybe she's mad at me. She's kind of evil and she lies a lot. The other is maybe somebody else did it."[48]

Similarly, by testifying on direct examination that a complainant's decision to smoke crack and have intercourse with the defendant was consensual, the prosecution may ask the defendant "whether a disagreement had arisen between him and complainant that would have motivated her to falsely accuse him of forcibly engaging in sex and stealing her belongings."[49]

In the following example, the prosecutor's question challenging the defendant to explain why the DNA evidence is deemed analogous to legitimate prosecutorial comment on the evidence rather than impermissible burden shifting.

Q. When you earlier testified that you don't think or you don't believe it was your blood in that hotel room and in the Ordway suitcases, that does not comport with what the D.N.A. expert testified early today. You heard her testify, isn't that true?

A. Yes.

---

[47] Green v. State, 242 Ga. App. 868, 532 S.E.2d 111 (2000) (permitting defendant charged with sexual abuse to be cross-examined if state's witnesses were lying); State v. Pilot, 595 N.W.2d 511 (Minn. 1999) (holding because "the focus of the defense was that the State's witnesses were lying and that the evidence against him was fabricated as part of a vast conspiracy to convict him of a crime he did not commit" the prosecution was justified in posing, "Were they lying?" questions to the defendant on cross-examination); State v. Hart, 303 Mont. 71, 15 P.3d 917 (2000) (noting this type of questioning may be acceptable when defendant says everyone else is lying); People v. Allen, 13 A.D.3d 892, 787 N.Y.S.2d 417 (2004), *appeal denied*, 4 N.Y.3d 883, 831 N.E.2d 973, 798 N.Y.S.2d 728 (2005) ("Since defendant's testimony was that the victim's account was entirely false, we discern no error in asking defendant why the victim would so fabricate this incident, and if she was lying, which were relevant, nonrhetorical questions which were not phrased in such a way as to shift the burden of proof to defendant to provide an explanation or motive for her fabrication." *Id.* at 897, 792 N.Y.S.2d at 420); People v. Marcos, 249 A.D.2d 105, 670 N.Y.S.2d 110, *appeal denied*, 92 N.Y.2d 901, 702 N.E.2d 850, 680 N.Y.S.2d 65 (1998) (holding "cross-examination of defense witnesses concerning truthfulness of prosecution witnesses was permissible given the nature of the defense testimony"); State v. Johnson, 2004 WI 94, 681 N.W.2d 901 (2004) (permitting cross-examination of defendant on whether other witnesses were lying as appropriate challenge to witness's credibility to highlight inconsistencies and to provide opportunity to explain inconsistencies).

[48] Commonwealth v. Colon, 64 Mass. App. Ct. 303, 832 N.E.2d 1154 (2005).

[49] People v. Haywood, 212 A.D.2d 386, 622 N.Y.S.2d 170, 270–71, *appeal denied*, 85 N.Y.2d 939, 651 N.E.2d 926, 627 N.Y.S.2d 1001 (1995).

Q. She testified that your D.N.A. was a perfect match. Your blood D.N.A. was a perfect match to the evidence recovered from inside the Ordway suitcases and inside Room 714, right? You heard that?

A. Yes.[50]

A defendant's attempt to explain away much of the prosecution's evidence is also deemed to open the door to the prosecution's questions and comments.[51]

§ 6.18   Areas of agreement.

It is possible for the prosecution to develop areas of agreement with a defendant. This is a good way to begin a cross-examination before delving into contested or unknown areas. One area of agreement may be the defendant's physical description. Perhaps the complainant's description of the defendant matched the defendant's height, weight, hair color, glasses, body weight, build, or clothing. The defendant may be safely asked whether he would agree that, on the date in question, he possessed each and every one of these features.

Areas of agreement also can be established as to the time, place, and opportunity to commit the crime. Perhaps the defendant will agree that he was with the complainant on numerous occasions, that he was alone with the complainant on numerous occasions, or that he was alone with her at his or her residence for substantial periods of time. Where the complainant is a child, the defendant might agree that there was no problem in their relationship, that they did many things together, that he got along well with the child, that the child never threatened him, and that he never threatened the child. Potential areas of agreement are an effective way to begin the cross-examination and help chart the rest of the cross-examination.

§ 6.19   Cross-examination about opportunities to commit the crime.

If the defendant has admitted on direct examination to an opportunity to commit the crime, the prosecution should develop on cross-examination not only what happened, but also collateral details concerning the event. If the opportunity to commit the crime is based on the fact that the defendant was living, working or socializing in the area at the time of the crime, or if the defendant claims mistaken identity, questions concerning collateral events would be extremely important in probing the veracity of such testimony. If the defendant had no opportunity to be alone with the complainant during the time period in question, establish this on direct examination.

---

[50] State v. Hauge, 103 Haw. 38, 79 P.3d 131 (2003).

[51] *Id.* at 57, 79 P.3d at 150.

§ 6.20 Questions concerning sexual discussions or activities with child complainant.

If the defendant takes the position that there were sexual discussions or contact with the complainant, but not those alleged in the indictment, it is important for the prosecution to explore such admissions in detail. If the case involves a child complainant, were there any problems as a result of these discussions? Exactly what was said or done in terms of touching or other sexual activity? The cross-examiner should be explicit and have the defendant clearly articulate as to what activities or discussions took place and how often they occurred. Is the defendant's story probable? Did the victim molest the defendant? How did these discussions end? Did the defendant talk to anyone about these activities?

In the following example, the defendant, charged with sexually abusing a child, is questioned about playing a version of "doctor" and the child's apparent attraction to the defendant.

Q. You told the police about playing doctor, right?

A. Yes.

Q. And did you tell the police about this coroner's game that you would play, coroner with the kids?

A. Yes.

Q. Now, you also played the coroner's game as part of the doctor game, right?

A. Yes.

Q. In the coroner's game somebody plays medical examiner; is that the idea?

A. Yes.

Q. Somebody plays dead? Is this a well-known game with the children?

A. No. It was an evasive tactic to end —

Q. What tactic?

A. Evasive. I was trying to avoid continuing the game.

Q. Which game?

A. Doctor.

Q. You didn't want to play doctor anymore?

A. No.

Q. Is this a game that you play with other 24-year-olds?

A. No.

Q. No. You just play it with 12-year-olds and seven-year-olds?

A. No. I don't just play it with 12-year-olds. I play it with her to keep her happy.

Q. Okay. To keep her happy, right?

A. Because she wanted to be with me.

Q. You couldn't keep her away from you, could you?

A. Yes, I could have.

Q. She couldn't resist you, could she? Right?

A. I have no way of knowing that.

Q. She would pat you on your butt all the time, right?

A. Not all the time, but on many occasions, yes.

Q. She would tell you you were cute, right?

A. Yes.

Q. And how do you feel about that?

A. I am embarrassed.

Q. You didn't like being called cute?

A. Not by her, no.

Q. You didn't think it was odd that a ten-year-old or 12-year-old was calling you cute and attractive?

A. Yes, I did.

Q. You didn't think it odd that somebody's hand was on your crotch area when she was ten years old?

A. Yes, I did.

Q. It bothered you?

A. Yes, it did.

The questioning then focuses on what the defendant did in response to this sexually provocative child, and whether the defendant's response makes sense.

Q. No. Who did you tell?

A. I didn't.

Q. Did you go to Jill's parents and say "I think we have got a problem here"?

A. No, I didn't.

Q. A ten-year-old putting her hands on my crotch; did you do that?

A. No, I didn't.

Q. Do you go to her church?

A. Yes, I have.

Q. Well, did you go to somebody at the church and say there is a problem here?

A. No, I did not.

Q. Did you call Child Abuse Hotline?

A. No, I didn't.

Q. Did you do anything about this behavior that Bill said wasn't right and that you said, I think on direct, you weren't comfortable with?

Q. Did you ever do anything?

A. I ignored it.

Q. Did you go to your parents and say there is this ten or 11-year-old girl and she can't keep her hands off me?

A. Not right at that particular moment, no.

Q. Did you ever, until April 25, 2005, go to anybody, your parents, your friends, the police and say this girl is molesting me?

A. No, I didn't.

Q. You wanted to help Jill learn about sex, right?

A. I wanted to help her understand about it.

Q. Sure. This was your job to help this 12-year-old understand sex, right?

A. It wasn't my job, but nobody else was doing it.

Q. Well, what about Janie? Was it your job to give an opinion as to her sexual activities?

A. No.

Q. I mean, it was your opinion that Janie was definitely too young for sex, right, at seven years old?

A. Yes. That was in response to a note that Janie wrote to me.

Q. And this was important for you as a 24-year-old to tell Jill and Janie that seven years old is too young for sex, right?

A. Yes. I didn't see anything wrong with telling them a fact.

Q. So that if you look at People's four, you start by giving your opinion that Janie at seven is too young for sex, right?

A. Yes.

Q. And this was something that you had to tell them, right?

A. Yes.

Q. What was the question that was asked of you by Janie or Jill about a seven-year-old having sex that you were answering?

A. Her exact words in the note were, "I want to have sex with you."

Q. Who wanted to have sex with you?

A. Janie.

Q. So that this seven-year-old wanted to have sex with you, right?

A. That's what the note said.

Q. And your answer was too young, right?

A. I was completely shocked.

Q. No. Your statement in that note is definitely too young for sex, right?

A. Yes.

Q. And that's because Janie, you say, wanted to have sex with you, right?

A. That was in response to that note, yes.

Q. And so, you send this note, being the 24-year-old that you are, to these children, right?

A. Yes.

Q. Now, do you tell Jill or Janie's parents that there is this seven-year-old that wants to have sex with me? Did you do that?

A. No, I didn't.

Q. You didn't?

A. No, I didn't.

Q. Whose job did you think it was to make sure that this seven-year-old didn't have sex?

A. The mother and the father.

Q. Did you tell them that?

A. No.

§ 6.21   Questions on complainant's lack of motive.

The motive for a sexual assault complaint is an issue on direct examination. (*See* § 6.6.) On cross-examination, a prosecutor can develop the lack of motive on the complainant's part as in the following cross-examination of a defendant in a child sexual assault case.

Q. Now, throughout the years that you have known Jill, you never had problems with her where she ever complained to you or threatened you; is that fair to say?

A. That's fair to say.

Q. As far as you can tell, it's been a good relationship, right?

A. Yes.

Q. The same thing with Janie's parents, right? As long as you have known them you haven't had problems with them, correct?

A. Correct.

Q. No reason for Jill to come here and say something that isn't true as far as you know, correct?

A. As far as I know.

Q. And the same thing with Janie, correct? You can't think of any reason why Janie would come in here and say something that isn't true, correct?

A. Correct.

Q. Same thing with Jill and Janie's parents, right?

A. True.

Note that the motive of third parties, such as a parent, may also be important as in the latter part of the example.

A well-prepared defendant may be ready to provide a motive in the form of a non-responsive answer. Consider the following questions and answers of William Kennedy Smith at his rape trial.

Q. Didn't you carry through with your threat, Mr. Smith, and do everything you could to make sure nobody would believe her?

A. Miss Lash, I don't, I've searched myself every night since March 29th to try to find out why Patty would make an allegation against me that's not true, that's going to destroy my family, destroy my career, possibly send me to jail for 15 years. I understand Patty Bowman had a lot of problems, and she talked about her neck, she talked about her child, she talked about her relationship with her family, all of those things make me feel very sorry for Patty Bowman. But, that's not the issue here. The issue here is I'm innocent, and how do you defend yourself from somebody who says the word "rape" over and over again?

Of course, the problem in this situation is an open-ended question that allows the witness tremendous leeway in responding.

§ 6.22 Questions concerning consent.

In cases involving adult complainants in which the defendant claims the act was consensual, the prosecution should explore precisely the alleged consensual act and the surrounding circumstances, especially statements or conduct on the part of the complainant that led to the defendant's conclusion that the act was consensual. This area of cross-examination can be difficult and requires careful attention to the defendant's answers. This is definitely an area where control must be exercised by the examiner; the defendant should not be asked broad questions, such as, "What made you believe that the complainant wanted to have sexual relations with you?" This invites a broad and self-serving response. Rather, especially when the defendant has not made a prior statement, the defendant's testimony should be evaluated for inconsistency and improbability and then developed through further cross-examination.

For example, in questioning a defendant on consent, an open-ended question is an invitation to disaster. Consider the following question on the issue of consent posed to William Kennedy Smith at his trial by the prosecutor.

Q. How did she consent? What did she do that led you to believe she consented?

A. Well, uh, I would have to say that it was a lot of different things. Um, I can tell you that she, uh, put me inside of her when we were on the lawn. Um, I can tell you that I was not quite ready, and that she helped me inside of her.

In some situations, non-leading questions may be appropriate on the issue of consent. In the following example a defendant who allegedly raped a woman at gunpoint is cross-examined about his claim of an ongoing sexual relationship with the complainant. The non-leading questions allow the defendant to portray an unlikely scenario as well as his personality.

Q. Now, did Jane ever tell you whether she enjoyed having sexual relations with you?

A. She seemed to like it. She didn't have any problem with it. I mean we had . . . we didn't discuss it.

Q. Did she ever say anything though?

A. Like dirty sex or —

Q. Sure.

A. Do I have to say what she said?

Q. If she said something tell us what it is.

A. Okay. She was saying, "Spank me daddy. Spank me daddy." Things like that.

Q. Anything else?

A. No. She seemed to like it.

Q. Okay. There were no problems with you and her sexually from day one until June 25?

A. That's correct.

Q. And did you enjoy it?

A. With Jane?

Q. Yes.

A. Yeah.

Q. Did you love her?

A. Love is a relative concept. I cared about her a lot, but I don't know if I loved her.

Q. And did you care about her on June 25, 2005?

A. Yes, I did.

Q. And as part of your caring relationship did you ever give her any gifts?

A. Not on June 25.

Q. Did Jane love you?

A. I don't think that Jane — I can't tell you if she loved me or not. With me it was more like just a casual relationship. With her she seemed kind of distant all the time.

Q. Well, did she say anything to you that she cared for you?

A. She indicated she cared about me a lot.

Q. Did she say she loved you?

A. She said that I remind her of her father. She really cared about me.

Q. And she said she enjoyed you sexually?

A. She never said that. She never said, "I enjoy you sexually," but during sex she seemed happy.

Q. How did you know that?

A. Because like I said she was into it; her body movements, the things that we did, the stuff that she would instigate.

Q. What would she instigate?

A. There would be times she would instigate the entire sexual act. When I was in the bathroom on the 25th she came in and started grabbing on me, pushed me up against the wall.

Q. She pushed you up against the wall?

A. Yeah.

Q. Did you want to be pushed up against the wall?

A. Didn't matter.

Q. So she forced you against the wall and then what did she do?

A. She didn't force me. Just pushed me up against the wall.

Q. She pushed you up against the wall in the bathroom. Then what did she do?

A. We started kissing.

Q. Then what happened?

A. I picked her up by her legs, put her on the sink.

Q. You said this was a wooden sink?

A. Well, it's a ceramic top with a big wooden base to it.

Q. And there was intercourse?

A. After she undressed, yeah.

Q. And through from May until June 25 did she ever, you know, send you a card?

A. No. She never sent me a card.

Q. Did she ever give you a gift?

A. She wrote me a couple of notes.

Q. What kind of notes?

A. Just little cute notes, you know.

Q. Like what?

A. Like common notes like smiles from me to you, things like that, little smiley face stuff like that.

Q. A smiley face note?

A. Yeah.

Q. What did it say?

A. Just smiles from me to you, things like that.

Q. Smiles from me to you?

A. Yeah.

Q. Anything else?

A. Not really.

Q. That's all she would write you?

A. That's it.

§ 6.23 "Shaped" testimony by the defendant.

If it appears that the defendant's testimony is being "shaped," the prosecution should review the testimony of witnesses whom the defendant had the opportunity to hear or review before he himself testified. The defendant may have met with individuals and discussed the manner in which testimony would be presented, the charges or issues about which the witness offered testimony.

Consider the following example of a prosecutor's cross-examination of a defendant's preparations for testimony:

Q. Prior to testifying today, you had the opportunity to review the grand jury testimony of several witnesses, correct?

A. Correct.

Q. Prior to testifying here today, you have had the opportunity to review police reports made by the state police with respect to this case, correct?

A. Correct.

Q. Prior to testifying here today, you have had the opportunity to listen to taped calls that were made by the state police, correct?

A. Correct.

Q. And prior to testifying here today, you have had the opportunity to sit through pretrial hearings in this case, correct?

A. Correct.

Q. And you have had the opportunity to hear all the witnesses testify in this trial, correct?

A. Correct.

Q. And you have had the opportunity to listen to seven-year-old Robert testify, correct?

A. Correct.

Q. Prior to coming here today, have you discussed with anyone the manner in which you would conduct yourself as a witness?

A. Yes.

Q. And would it be fair to say that you have spent hours preparing for your testimony here today?

A. Well, several hours.

The argument against such a cross-examination is that by exercising the defendant's constitutional right to confront witnesses and testify on his behalf, it permits an inference that the defendant is untruthful. That argument was made on an appeal involving the following cross-examination in a sexual assault trial.

Q. Mr. Walker, you've been in this courtroom the whole proceeding, right?

A. Yes.

Q. You've heard — all the testimony in the case.

A. Yes, sir.

Q. You've had an opportunity to look over all the State's exhibits and statements of all the witnesses, haven't you?

A. Yes.

Q. In order to be able to form what your testimony would be right now.

A. Yes.

Q. Right. These other ones didn't have that opportunity, did they?

A. No.

Q. You have been able to listen to everybody's testimony, right?

A. Have I been here and listened to it?

Q. Yes.

A. Yes.

Q. All right. And you could form whatever you would like to say today, based upon the evidence that was presented by your defense or in the cross-examination of the witness.

A. So, could you repeat that question again?

Q. Let me back up. You have heard everything in the courtroom here today.

A. Yes.

Q. You've heard all the witnesses in here today.

A. Yes.

Q. You've had an opportunity to, if necessary, to adjust your testimony to what the evidence is in this trial?

A. Yes.

Q. Correct. No one else has that opportunity to do that.

A. Well —

Q. Yes or no, sir?

A. Well, I guess everybody has got the opportunity to do that.

Q. Well, you know there's exclusion of witnesses and they're not in the courtroom.

A. Well, when —

Q. You've heard all the testimony of the witnesses today.

A. Right.

Q. Right.[52]

In this case, the appeals court found no "plain error" in the cross-examination, especially since the defendant was asked on direct examination whether he "had heard the testimony up to this part in the trial," thereby opening the door to the line of cross-examination.[53] Other courts have taken the position that the line of questioning is a legitimate attack on credibility.[54] Failing to object to the line of questioning may waive review of the issue.[55]

§ 6.24 Defendant's contact with other witnesses.

In many cases, a defendant has had contact with defense witnesses prior to their testimony. Of course this is expected in the case of family members or close friends. Whether expected or not, this provides the defendant with the opportunity to discuss testimony that will be provided at trial. This is crucial with alibi witnesses and witnesses whose testimony may be on events that involve the defendant directly.

---

[52] State v. Walker, 972 S.W.2d 623 (Mo. Ct. App. 1998).

[53] *Id.* at 627.

[54] Davis v. State, 221 Ga. App. 131, 470 S.E.2d 520 (1996); State v. Martin, 101 N.M. 595, 686 P.2d 937 (1984); People v. King, 293 A.D.2d 815, 740 N.Y.S.2d 500, *appeal denied*, 98 N.Y.2d 698, 776 N.E.2d 6, 747 N.Y.S.2d 417 (2002).

[55] Sherrod v. United States, 478 A.2d 644 (D.C. 1984); State v. Grilli, 369 N.W.2d 35 (Minn. Ct. App. 1985).

With which witnesses did the defendant have contact? What was the nature of those contacts? Did anyone discuss the case? Who initiated the conversation? What documents or exhibits were reviewed? How many times were there such contacts? Where did these meetings take place? Do jail records reflect the defendant meeting with witnesses? Did anyone make any notes, records, or tape recordings at these meetings? What did the defendant say to the witness? What did the witness say to the defendant? Were any third parties present? What relationship did the third party have with the defendant or witness? Did the defendant utilize any third party to communicate messages or information to a witness? Were any notes, records or tape recordings made at any of the meetings which discussed the case? If so, where are they or what happened to them?

The answers to these questions may indicate that the witness's testimony was shaped in some fashion. This may make their testimony, as well as the defendant's, less credible.

§ 6.25 Develop significant areas of defendant's background.

A defendant's past may reveal important information that may be helpful in developing the prosecution's case. For example, if the defendant is a police officer or attorney, his or her training should have included courses on topics relevant to the case: substantive law, such as what constitutes rape or the age of consent, or procedural matters, such as *Miranda* rights.

For defendants who have made statements to investigators, it may be important to develop the level of education of the defendant. Has the witness had the chance to review documents before signing in other situations? Has the witness had the opportunity to utilize the services of an attorney? Has the witness worked with children before? A defendant's background with children may be important in evaluating the defendant's conduct toward a child in some cases. Did the defendant behave in a way consistent or inconsistent with this experience?

When force is an issue, the defendant's fitness or past experience with physical force may be helpful in developing the defendant's physical and mental superiority over the complainant. A defendant's military training or martial arts background may help to develop the element of physical force.

§ 6.26 Cross-examination of defendant concerning prior statements.

Where the defendant made statements to witnesses who have testified at trial — law enforcement officials, physicians, or other parties — these statements should be reviewed with the defendant on cross-examination. When those statements involve admissions or inconsistencies, this may require a line-by-line or sentence-by-sentence review with the defendant on cross-examination. If the defendant admits making the statements, then their validity is established.

To the extent that the defendant denies making a statement, this will pit the defendant's credibility against that of the witness. Even when the defendant denies making certain inculpatory statements, his admission to having made other statements and the fact that he has provided information that only he was in a position to provide will enhance the credibility of the other party's testimony. If the defendant has made statements that have been recorded, the defendant still should be asked about them, so that his admission will be before the jury. To the extent that the defendant omitted significant details or facts in his statement to the police, this should be stressed. In this regard, establish that he had the opportunity to communicate this information or read the statement before signing it, but failed to provide this crucial information.

A defendant may also be cross-examined on inconsistencies between his trial testimony and statements made to a non-testifying defense expert. For example, if the prosecution learns through pretrial discussions with defendant's attorney of an expert who determined that defendant did not match the profile of a child molester, the prosecutor can use statements made to that expert, even though the prosecutor learned of the statements from a report provided as part of pretrial discussions with defendant's attorney.[56]

§ 6.27 Cross-examination of defendant concerning prior statement to police.

Cross-examination of a defendant concerning statements to police should be carefully developed. The prosecution should determine if the defendant provided information that only he would know. If necessary, the defendant should be cross-examined as to his statements on a line-by-line basis to establish exactly what defendant did say, since the defense may have touched upon this lightly on direct examination. Consider the following sample testimony:

Q. And you started to talk to the police after that, you say?

A. I was talking to the police the whole time, telling them to stop it.

Q. Did you talk about what had happened that day at all?

A. I told them I wanted to speak to an attorney.

Q. Did you talk to them about what had happened that day at any time?

A. Yes.

Q. And you gave them certain pieces of factual information, correct?

A. Correct.

Q. You told them that you were 20 years old?

A. Correct.

---

[56] People v. Crow, 28 Cal. App. 4th 440, 33 Cal. Rptr. 2d 624 (1994).

Q. They didn't tell you that?

A. That's correct, even though they had my ID there. I don't know why they asked me.

Q. You told the investigator you were single, correct?

A. Correct.

Q. You told him that you lived at Swanson Street, correct?

A. Yes.

Q. And that you lived in Troy, New York, with your brother?

A. Correct.

Q. And that you lived with a roommate named John, but that you didn't know his last name, correct?

A. Correct.

Q. The investigator didn't tell you that your roommate's name was John, did he?

A. That's correct.

Q. Did you tell the investigator that you got to your girlfriend's house at about 7 a.m.?

A. I believe so, yes.

Q. The investigator didn't tell you that, did he?

A. No, the investigator didn't tell me that.

Q. You told him where your girlfriend lived, correct?

A. Correct.

Q. You told him what her name was?

A. Correct.

Q. And you told the investigator you didn't know her last name, correct?

A. Correct.

Q. You told the investigator that you had been seeing her occasionally, didn't you?

A. Correct.

Q. You told him that you went to her house on this day to visit her, correct?

A. Correct.

Q. Did you tell the investigator that you thought you took a cab to get there?

A. Yes, I believe I did.

Q. And that was true, wasn't it?

A. I did take a cab.

Q. And you told the investigator that in the afternoon, early in the afternoon, Toni went out, correct?

A. Correct.

Q. And you told the investigator that she had told you she had a doctor's appointment, correct?

A. Correct.

Q. And that you told the investigator that she asked you to mind her daughter, correct?

A. Yes.

Q. Did you tell the investigator, "I told her to take her with her, but she left her with me"?

A. I don't know if I told him that, but that's what happened.

Q. Well, did the investigator tell you that's what happened?

A. No.

Q. Did you tell the investigator, "I am not sure of the little girl's name. It is Lisa or something like that"?

A. Yes.

At this point the cross-examination begins to focus on admissions of sexual contact in the statement. Note the difficulty the defendant has in maintaining his position. While the defendant does not admit to everything in the statement, substantial concessions are elicited that challenge his credibility.

Q. Did you tell the investigator, "The whole thing started on the waterbed"?

A. What whole thing?

Q. Did you use that phrase with him?

A. I didn't use that phrase with him. He put that in. I didn't tell him anything happened. Nothing happened. At that point he was pressuring me.

Q. Did you tell him something in substance, though, the whole thing started on the waterbed?

A. Yes.

Q. Did you tell the investigator, "Me and the little girl were laying on the bed playing, jumping around." Did you tell the investigator that?

A. No.

Q. Did he tell you that you were on the bed playing around with the girl?

A. Yes.

Q. Did you tell the investigator, "I fell asleep for awhile and she was in the room right next to the waterbed"?

A. Yes and no.

Q. Did you tell Jefferson, "I was jerking off and got cum all over the front of me"?

A. I said that because he wanted me to say that. I put in some of those words. You know, before, he wanted — he wanted penetration. He said, "You better say something that says penetration on here. I don't want to hear you were jerking off."

Q. You said the words that you were jerking off and got cum over you, correct?

A. Yeah.

Q. And did you tell the investigator, "She started playing with the cum, using it like Playdough"?

A. Did I tell him that?

Q. Q. Yes.

A. I was forced to tell him something in the effect that would place me with that girl, that something had been done. I told him a lie. Right there on that piece of paper is a big lie, fabricated so he would let me go.

Q. But did you use words to that effect in speaking to the investigator?

A. I used all the words on that confession. All right? He used them, too. I didn't put all those words in, and he forced me to put the ones in that I did put in.

Q. So, you did say something, though, to the effect that the girl was playing with the cum, using it like Playdough?

A. Yes.

Q. And you told the investigator that you didn't actually penetrate her, correct?

A. That was an answer to a question of, "How many times did you fuck her? How many times did you go in and out?"

Q. And you said something to the effect, "I didn't actually penetrate her," correct?

A. That's correct.

Q. And did you tell the investigator, "She started fooling around with my penis"?

A. Yes.

Q. And did you tell the investigator she got the cum near her genitals?

A. That was the reply to "We have a doctor's statement saying that she has been penetrated and has semen in the vagina." He wanted me to link something — how the cum got there.

Q. Did you say something to the effect to the investigator that she got cum near her genitals?

A. I don't remember.

Q. Did you say to the investigator something to the effect, "She got cum near her genitals"?

A. Correct. Yes.

Q. Did you tell the investigator, "The only thing I did was touch her leg with my penis"?

A. That was another reply to — after I told him about the fingers, he said, "That's not good enough. We want penetration. How many times did you stick your dick inside of her?" And that's where I said that, because I was — the whole time I was hard pressed to say that, because it's not true.

Q. You did say something to the effect, "The only thing I did was touch her leg with my penis," correct?

A. I guess so, that's correct.

Q. Did you tell the investigator she had her overalls down?

A. I don't know if I said that.

Q. Did you tell the investigator she was exposed?

A. I don't know if I said that.

Q. Did you say to the investigator, "I don't remember penetrating her"?

A. Yes.

Q. Did you say to the investigator, "That's all I can remember"?

A. Yes.

Q. Did the investigator ask you if you can read and write?

A. Yes.

Q. You can read and write, can't you?

A. Yes, I can.

Q. Take a look at People's Exhibit 3, the statement. That's your signature on there, isn't it?

A. This is my signature.

Q. Yes?

A. It was my signature at the time, yes.

Q. Did you read it before you signed it?

A. They told me to. I don't believe I read it thoroughly. I knew what they were trying to do.

Q. My question is: Did you read the statement before you signed it?

A. Yes.

The following questions utilize the defendant's own answer to emphasize the illogic of his testimony.

Q. And you say you knew what they were trying to do?

A. Yes.

Q. Did you initial certain changes there?

A. Yes.

Q. So you initialed changes and signed the statement after you read the statement, correct?

A. Yes.

§ 6.28 Cross-examination of defendant concerning omissions in prior statements.

One of the benefits of an investigation that obtains the defendant's version of events is that the defendant will be committed to a particular set of facts. If the defendant claims he did not commit the crime, he should be asked where he was. If the defendant did not provide an alibi at the time of the interview and later asserts an alibi, this is significant information. If the defendant asserts at trial that the act of intercourse was consensual and the defendant had engaged in sexual relations previously, it is important to establish whether the defendant made this assertion in his initial statement to the police. A defendant may be cross-examined about his failure to provide certain information in a statement to the police that he later asserts at trial.[57] The defendant's failure to mention certain facts to the police was, in effect, a prior inconsistent statement and cross-examination on this point was not an unfair abuse of the defendant's right to remain silent because a defendant who voluntarily speaks after receiving *Miranda* warnings has not been induced to remain silent.[58] A defendant can be cross-examined on omissions in his statements to police, particularly those "exculpatory circumstances he could reasonably have been expected to mention."[59] When a defendant admits to the police that he committed a crime, for example a shooting, and then he adds at trial that the shooting was in self-defense or accidental, the prosecutor may establish through cross-examination that the exculpatory version of the event testified to by the defendant was not provided by him to the police.[60]

---

[57] Anderson v. Charles, 447 U.S. 404, 100 S. Ct. 2180, 65 L. Ed. 2d 222 (1980).

[58] *Id.*

[59] People v. Struss, 228 A.D.2d 711, 644 N.Y.S.2d 340, *appeal denied*, 89 N.Y.2d 867, 675 N.E.2d 1243, 653 N.Y.S.2d 290 (1996).

[60] *See, e.g.*, People v. Savage, 50 N.Y.2d 673, 409 N.E.2d 858, 431 N.Y.S.2d 382, *cert. denied*, 449 U.S. 1016 (1980); People v. Cole, 5 A.D.3d 177, 772 N.Y.S.2d 518, *appeal denied*, 2 N.Y.3d

Equivocal statements by a defendant will not trigger Fifth Amendment protection.[61]

The following testimony of colloquy between defendant and investigator permits comment by the prosecution on the defendant's statements or omissions:

Q. Did you tell him why you asked him to come in to speak to you?

A. Yes, I contacted him and had him come into the office, that I was investigating a sexual assault case wherein he was the alleged perpetrator.

Q. In the course of your conversation with him, did you ask him if he had had intercourse with [the complainant]?

A. Yes, I did.

Q. And what did he say?

A. He denied to answer that and further stated that he felt that that was up to her to prove that.

Q. Now, were you present when the defendant testified [at the first trial]?

A. Yes.

Q. And what did he say about that having intercourse with [the complainant] that day?

A. If I remember correctly, he indicated that they did have but it was consensual.

Q. But he didn't say that to you when you interviewed him, is that correct?

A. No, he did not.

Q. Did you ask him about other events on that evening of what occurred?

A. After — as far as he indicated that he would talk with me in reference to the relationship, as far as other incidents that evening that we got into that later.

Q. What did he say about what they did during the time that they were alone together?

A. He indicated that there was some contact between the two of them. There was some kissing and hugging. And I believe he used the term — there was intimacy between them.

Q. Did he ever say that they had intercourse?

797, 814 N.E.2d 468, 781 N.Y.S.2d 296 (2004) (noting cross-examination was proper because defendant had acknowledged that his written exculpatory statement was a complete account of the incident, so that his failure to mention the omitted exculpatory information at that time was an unnatural omission).

[61] People v. Stark, 4 Cal. App. 4th 1407, 6 Cal. Rptr. 2d 408 (1992) (rape defendant's equivocal statements "I am not saying one way or the other" and "I am not going to answer that" were more of an attempt to limit course and scope of his response than to invoke Fifth Amendment).

A. No, he did not.

Q. His only statement regarding intercourse was that she had to prove that, is that correct?

A. Correct[62]

Michigan's Supreme Court upheld this form of cross-examination since:

> [W]hen an individual has not opted to remain silent, but has made affirmative responses to questions about the same subject matter testified to at trial, omissions from the statements do not constitute silence. The omission is nonverbal conduct that is to be considered an assertion of the nonexistence of the fact testified to at trial if a rational juror could draw an inference of inconsistency. To be sure, the witness may explain the omission by a desire not to implicate himself or because of a lapse of memory. Such explanations, however, do not remove the relevance of the inconsistency.[63]

Even a brief statement or denial by a defendant can open the door to cross-examination about the defendant's failure to provide the police with information, such as an alibi, which is part of the defendant's trial testimony.[64]

The following is another example of a cross-examination of a defendant in a rape trial that may appear to be a comment on the defendant's postarrest silence.[65]

Q. Sir, when you were asked by the police whether you had sex with Becky [M.], you said no; correct?

A. That's true.

Q. That was a lie; correct?

A. Yes, it was.
DEFENSE: Objection, Your Honor. He already went through this.
COURT: The objection is overruled.

Q. Sir, when you found out your pubic hairs had been matched to the underwear in front of you, that Jimmy Lansidal's hadn't, that's the first time you said you had sex, correct, with Becky [M.]?

A. That's the first that I had said? That's the — I'd imagine that's about the time.

---

[62] People v. Sholl, 453 Mich. 730, 733–34, 556 N.W.2d 851, 853 (1996).

[63] *Id.* at 736, 556 N.W.2d at 854.

[64] State v. Bowler, 892 S.W.2d 717 (Mo. Ct. App. 1994) (even defendant's brief oral statement to police officer, "I did not do anything like that and I want a lawyer" held to be sufficient statement to question the defendant about his failure to provide alibi to police officer, and an example of the principle that if a defendant "answers a question or makes a statement while in custody, the right to remain silent and to not have the State comment on that silence is waived on the subject matter of those statements").

[65] Commonwealth v. Meadows, 381 Pa. Super. 354, 361–62, 553 A.2d 1006, 1009–10, *appeal denied*, 524 Pa. 618, 571 A.2d 381 (1989).

Q. That's about the time you started telling people about this, correct?

A. I don't remember when I said it.

Q. You didn't tell the police officers the sex was consensual, right?

A. No, I didn't.

Q. You didn't tell the District Attorney's Office or any investigative body the sex was consensual, right?
DEFENSE: Your Honor, objection. We have been over this ground already.
PROSECUTION: I never asked this question before.
COURT: I am going to permit you to go a little longer, Mr. Carmody, but I think you have been over this ground.
PROSECUTION: This will be final. I will wind it up here, Your Honor.

Q. You didn't tell the District Attorney's Office or anybody else about this, did you?

A. No, I didn't.

Q. You lied, sir, when you thought it could help you, correct?

A. No, that's not true.

Q. It was only when you were trapped by the physical evidence in front of you is when you told us, this jury, that the sex was consensual?

A. No, sir, that is not true.

The above is appropriate cross-examination because it highlights the defendant's contradictory statements as evidence of guilt.[66] Commenting on an accused's failure to give a tape-recorded statement after speaking with a detective is not an improper comment on the defendant's right to remain silent.[67]

There are important limits to the use of silence as a method of impeachment. If the defendant has not made a statement to the police and has asserted the right to remain silent, there may be no cross-examination whatsoever concerning the defendant's silence. It is only when the defendant has given a version of events and made statements to the police that silence may be used against him.

Use of a defendant's silence or non-verbal responses to "other" statements is also problematic. For example, in a sexual assault prosecution where the prosecution seeks to use a theory of adoptive admission when a defendant nods his head or remains silent in the face of an accusation, the trial court should

---

[66] *Id.* at 362, 553 A.2d at 1110 ("It is well established in Pennsylvania law that 'false or contradictory statements by the accused are admissible since the jury may infer therefrom that they were made with an intent to divert suspicion or to mislead the police or other authorities, or to establish an alibi or innocence, and hence are indicatory of [consciousness of] guilt.' ") *citing* Commonwealth v. Bolish, 381 Pa. 500, 524, 113 A.2d 464, 476 (1955).

[67] Rancourt v. State, 766 So. 2d 1071 (Fla. Dist. Ct. App. 2d Dist. 2000).

make an adequate preliminary determination whether the defendant has adopted the statements.[68]

Another problematic area is the use of a defendant's pre-arrest silence for impeachment purposes. While a defendant in custody who is given his *Miranda* warning and chooses not to speak is protected from the use of his silence, a defendant's pre-arrest silence is not necessarily protected under the United States Constitution. In *Jenkins v. Anderson,*[69] the Supreme Court of the United States held that the use of a defendant's pre-arrest silence to impeach a defendant does not necessarily violate the fundamental fairness of the Fourteenth Amendment, but noted that each jurisdiction is free to establish rules limiting the use of impeachment through the use of pre-arrest silence. Because of the strong effect that a defendant's pretrial silence may have on a jury, some state courts conclude that it is too prejudicial to be used.[70] Because of the limitation on the use of pre-arrest silence by state courts, this area should only be used on cross-examination when it is absolutely clear that it is permitted under state law.

§ 6.29 Use of defendant's prior convictions and bad acts.

One of the more complex areas of criminal trials is the rule pertaining to the use of prior convictions and bad acts. The complexities of these rules as articulated by state and federal courts are not always consistent, even within a particular jurisdiction. These complexities are magnified when issues concerning the use of prior acts of sexual abuse or activities by a defendant are involved. The Federal Rules of Evidence state the general rule:

> Evidence of other crimes, wrongs or acts is not admissible to prove the character of a person in order to show action in conformity therewith. It may, however, be admissible for other purposes, such as proof of motive, opportunity, intent, preparation, plan, knowledge, identity, or absence of mistake or accident.[71]

Courts that have admitted prior misconduct evidence of a defendant charged with a sexual assault have done so by finding that the prior sexual acts in some way fall within the traditional exceptions of motive, intent, common plan, or scheme, or the non-traditional "lustful inclination" or amorous design exception. Some courts have found a willingness to find a common plan or scheme in a

---

[68] State v. Gano, 92 Haw. 161, 988 P.2d 1153 (1999) (reversing defendant's conviction because defendant's non-verbal reactions were too ambiguous to establish defendant adopted others' statements as his own and therefore admission of the statements was erroneous hearsay); People v. Augustine, 6 A.D.3d 543, 774 N.Y.S.2d 397 (2004) (reversing defendant's conviction due to prosecutor's questions on whether the defendant made an outcry or filed a police report after his arrest as violating his right to remain silent).

[69] 447 U.S. 231, 100 S. Ct. 2124, 65 L.Ed. 2d 86 (1980). *See also* State v. Martinez, 128 Idaho 104, 910 P.2d 776 (1995) (accused rapist's silence prior to *Miranda* warning permissible).

[70] *See, e.g.,* People v. Conyers, 52 N.Y.2d 454, 420 N.E.2d 933, 438 N.Y.S.2d 741 (1981).

[71] FED. R. EVID. 404(b).

defendant's prior and current sexual abuse. What constitutes a prior bad act and whether it is probative is not always easily defined, and it is certainly not defined in the same way by each jurisdiction. Evidence of a defendant's bad acts can weave itself into a trial through the direct testimony of a witness or cross-examination of a witness without warning or notice. By charging the prior conduct, a prosecutor can avoid many objections to the use of prior uncharged evidence. But the other acts may not be indictable because they are barred by the statute of limitations, because they occurred outside the indicting jurisdiction, or because competent proof is not available to sustain the charges.

While the following sections do not intend to offer the complete state and federal law concerning the use of prior bad acts and convictions, they do identify certain areas of analysis to be applied in evaluating admissibility.

§ 6.30   What is a bad act?

Defining a bad act is not always a simple matter. Not every unflattering reference to or description of a defendant qualifies as a bad act or character evidence. If the act is "innocent," it should not be viewed as a bad act. Rather, its admission will be determined by its relevance and probative value.

For example, references to a defendant's lack of employment may be relevant to show that a defendant stayed at home with the child victim and thus had access and opportunity to commit the crime.[72] A defendant's drinking habits may be probative of the defendant's deteriorating relationship with a child.[73]

Testimony concerning defendant's participation in a residential alcohol and drug treatment program and receipt of food stamps does not qualify as bad acts.[74]

A defendant's words and phrases such as interest in "family fun" or the defendant's collection of "nude studies" may be analyzed within the framework of *modus operandi* or signature aspect of a crime.[75] Prior actions of a defendant which are sexually oriented, such as toe sucking, but not a crime or bad act may be admissible on the issue of identity.[76] Also, some courts hold that possessing

---

[72] State v. McAbee, 120 N.C. App. 674, 463 S.E.2d 281 (1995), *review denied*, 342 N.C. 662, 467 S.E.2d 730 (1996).

[73] *Id.*

[74] People v. Gonsa, 220 A.D.2d 27, 644 N.Y.S.2d 346 (1996).

[75] *See* §§ 6.39, 6.44 and 11.33.

[76] State v. Gaines, 260 Kan. 752, 926 P.2d 641 (1996) (In a rape case in which defendant was charged with rape and sodomy and sucking the victim's toe similar to a thumb, the prosecution was properly allowed to present defendant's ex-wife's testimony that he did the same type of toe sucking on five occasions during their one-year marriage because this was relevant to the defense of identity. The Court noted that toe sucking is not a character trait or character evidence. The Kansas Supreme Court ruled that the toe sucking of defendant was relevant to the identity of the perpetrator). *See also* United States v. Ellis, 935 F.2d 385 (1st Cir.), *cert. denied*, 502 U.S. 869 (1991) (defendant's toe sucking with adult partners admissible in child sexual abuse trial involving similar activity).

reading material or pornography which is lawful "is simply not the type of conduct" which qualifies as a bad act.[77]

A defendant's statements as to what he is feeling or plans to do, such as a threat, is not a bad act.[78]

A defendant's statement to young girls "I can't help it if I like pretty 13-year-old girls" is neither a crime, a wrong or bad act, and may be relevant to the "defendant's lewd disposition toward and motive for molesting" the young girl victims.[79] Not all courts, however, will accept evidence of a defendant's lewd disposition. (*See* § 6.40.) Because a defendant's use of an alias does not carry an inference of criminal propensity, alias evidence does not necessarily require a pretrial hearing or pretrial disclosure unlike most "bad act" evidence.[80]

§ 6.31   Federal Rules of Evidence 413 and 414 and state statutes admitting prior acts for any reason, including propensity.

Flying in the face of traditional evidentiary principles that propensity evidence should be viewed skeptically and unduly prejudicial, the United States Congress in 1994 adopted Federal Rules of Evidence 413 and 414 to allow past conduct specifically to establish propensity.

Rule 413 states, in part:

> (a) In a criminal case in which the defendant is accused of an offense of sexual assault, evidence of the defendant's commission of another offense or offenses of sexual assault is admissible, and may be considered for its bearing on any matter to which it is relevant.

Rule 414, dealing with evidence of similar crimes in child molestation cases, states, in part:

> (a) In a criminal case in which the defendant is accused of an offense of child molestation, evidence of the defendant's commission of another offense

---

[77] Guam v. Shymanovitz, 157 F.3d 1154, 1159 (9th Cir. 1998) ("Here there is simply no doubt that a wide gulf separates the act of possessing written descriptions or stories about criminal conduct from the act of committing the offenses described.").

[78] *See, e.g.,* Hicks v. State, 690 N.E.2d 215, 221 n.11 (Ind. 1997) (involving defendant's statement that he wanted or wished victim dead).

[79] State v. Rice, 755 A.2d 137 (R.I. 2000). *See also* State v. Covell, 157 N.J. 554, 725 A.2d 675 (1999) (holding defendant's statement that he has a "problem with girls" and "never was interested in older women, just young girls and teenage girls" was not an improper reference to sexual predisposition, but necessary to explain the defendant's luring of the child and relevant to the defendant's motive and intent).

[80] People v. Brazeau, 304 A.D.2d 254, 759 N.Y.S.2d 268, *appeal denied,* 100 N.Y.2d 579, 796 N.E.2d 481, 764 N.Y.S.2d 389 (2003). *See also* People v. Thomas, 11 A.D.3d 569, 782 N.Y.S.2d 798, *appeal denied,* 4 N.Y.3d 742, 824 N.E.2d 56, 790 N.Y.S.2d 655 (2004) (noting there is no *per se* rule prohibiting cross-examination of a defendant concerning his or her past use of aliases).

or offenses of child molestation is admissible, and may be considered for its bearing on any matter to which it is relevant.

Several states have adopted rules of evidence similar to Federal Rules 413 and 414. These statutes make it much easier to obtain convictions in sexual assault prosecutions.[81]

West Virginia has adopted the Federal Rules of Evidence, including Rules 413 and 414.

Courts have consistently rejected constitutional challenges under the Due Process and Equal Protection clauses to Federal Rules 413 and 414 and other similar state statutes.[82]

---

[81] Alaska R. Evid. 404(b); Ariz. Rev. Stat. 13-1420 ("If the defendant is charged with a violation of a sexual offense, the court may admit evidence that the defendant committed past acts which would constitute a sexual offense and may consider the bearing this evidence has on any matter to which it is relevant."); Cal. Evid. Code § 1108; Fla. Stat. ch. 90.404. *See* 725 Ill. Comp. Stat. 5/115-7.3: In most sexual assault cases, evidences of other offenses "may be considered for its hearsay on any matter to which it is relevant (c) In weighing the probative value of the evidence against undue prejudice to the defendant, the court may consider: (1) the proximity in time to the charged or predicate offense; (2) the degree of factual similarity to the charged or predicate offense; or (3) other relevant facts and circumstances."; La. Code Evid. Ann. Art. 412.2(A) ("When an accused is charged with a crime involving sexually assaultive behavior, or with acts that constitute a sex offense involving a victim who was under the age of 17 at the time of the offense, evidence of the accused's commission of another crime, wrong, or act involving sexually assaultive behavior or acts which indicate a lustful disposition toward children may be admissible and may be considered for its bearing on any matter to which it is relevant subject to the balancing test provided in Article 403"); Mo. Rev. Stat. § 566.025 (In prosecutions under Chapters 566 or 568 involving a victim under 14 years of age, whether or not age is an element of the crime for which the defendant is on trial, evidence that the defendant has committed other charged or uncharged crimes involving victims under 14 years of age shall be admissible for the purpose of showing the propensity of the defendant to commit the crime or crimes with which he is charged, provided that such evidence involves acts that occurred within ten years before or after the act or acts for which the defendant is being tried).

[82] United States v. Julian, 427 F.3d 471, 487 (7th Cir. 2005) (rejecting Due Process challenge to Rule 413 since it is tempered by Rule 403); United States v. Drewry, 365 F.3d 957 (10th Cir. 2004), *vacated and remanded on other grounds*, 543 U.S. 1103 (2005); United States v. LeMay, 260 F.3d 1018, 1026 (9th Cir. 2001), *cert. denied*, 534 U.S. 1166 (2002) (concluding nothing fundamentally unfair in Rule 414 as long as protection of Rule 403 remains in place); United States v. McHorse, 179 F.3d 889 (10th Cir.), *cert. denied*, 528 U.S. 944 (1999) (admission of uncharged acts of child molestation pursuant to Fed. R. Evid. 414 did not violate defendant's right to due process or right to equal protection of the laws under Fifth Amendment or his right to confront witnesses under Sixth Amendment Confrontation Clause, and evidence was not inadmissible under Fed. R. Evid. 414(a); United States v. Mound, 149 F.3d 799, 800–02 (8th Cir. 1998), *cert. denied*, 525 U.S. 1089 (1999); United States v. Castillo, 140 F.3d 874, 883 (10th Cir. 1998), *cert. denied*, 529 U.S. 1005 (2000); United States v. Wright, 53 M.J. 476, 482 (C.A.A.F. 2000) (holding Military Rule of Evidence 413 does not violate Due Process or Equal Protection Clauses); McGill v. State, 18 P.3d 77, 81 (Alaska Ct. App. 2001); People v. Falsetta, 21 Cal. 4th 903, 89 Cal. Rptr. 2d 847, 986 P.2d 182 (1999), *cert. denied*, 529 U.S. 1089 (2000) (California Supreme Court upheld constitutionality of Cal. Evid. Code § 1108 and found no due process violation); People v. Davis, 71 Cal. App. 4th 1492, 84 Cal. Rptr. 2d 628 (1999) (finding no due process violation in California's Section

While there is a long history of disallowing evidence of prior acts to establish propensity, one court noted that the fact that "the practice is ancient does not mean it is embodied in the Constitution."[83] The United States Supreme Court has not ruled on these statutes and in another case involving evidence of prior acts of child abuse, wrote: "We express no opinion on whether a state law would violate the Due Process Clause if it permitted the use of 'prior crimes' evidence to show propensity to commit a charged crime."[84]

A defendant's prior acts must still be balanced by Rule 403 to exclude evidence that is either unreliable or prejudicial. Since Rules 413 and 414 hold propensity evidence to be relevant to a jury's determination of guilt, courts have not found much reason in Rule 403 to preclude evidence of prior sexual acts. Propensity is no longer an unfair prejudice. Rather, it is a permissible inference from the past acts. Courts have routinely found that the unfair prejudice of evidence admitted under Rules 413 and 414 does not substantially outweigh its probative value.[85]

1108); People v. Soto, 64 Cal. App. 4th 966, 991–92, 75 Cal. Rptr. 2d 605, 621 (1998) (upholding admission into evidence of defendant's prior sexual assault involving victims within same age range as complainant in current case as "extremely probative of appellant's sexual misconduct when left alone with young female relatives, and is exactly the type of evidence contemplated by the enactment of § 1108 and the parallel Federal Rules").

[83] United States v. Enjady, 134 F.3d 1427, 1432 (10th Cir.), *cert. denied,* 525 U.S. 887 (1998).

[84] Estelle v. McGuire, 502 U.S. 62, 75 n.5 (1991).

[85] United States v. Carter, 410 F.3d 1017 (8th Cir. 2005) (noting that trial court limited number of witnesses that prosecution could call concerning prior acts); United States v. Drewry, 365 F.3d 957 (10th Cir. 2004), *vacated and remanded on other grounds,* 543 U.S. 1103 (2005) (finding trial court properly weighed prejudicial effect of admitting defendant's acts of child molestation 25 years earlier with clear similarities in the present case: "[s]ufficient factual similarity can rehabilitate evidence of prior uncharged offenses that might otherwise be inadmissible due to staleness"); United States v. Gabe, 237 F.3d 954, 959–60 (8th Cir. 2001) ("Rule 403 is concerned only with 'unfair prejudice, that is, an undue tendency to suggest decision on an improper basis' [citation omitted]. Holly Thompson's testimony is prejudicial to Gabe for the same reason it is probative—it tends to prove his propensity to molest young children in his family when presented with an opportunity to do so undetected. Because propensity evidence is admissible under Rule 414, this is not unfair prejudice."); Id. at 960; United States v. Sumner, 204 F.3d 1182 (8th Cir. 2000)(upholding trial court's findings that defendant's prior acts of molestation properly admitted under Rule 414 since they were relatively recent and substantially similar to crimes charged and without any undue prejudice); United States v. Withorn, 204 F.3d 790 (8th Cir. 2000) (finding defendant's prior sexual abuse admitted as Rule 413 propensity evidence presented no unfair prejudice); United States v. McHorse, 179 F.3d 889 (10th Cir.), *cert. denied,* 528 U.S. 944 (1999); United States v. Mound, 149 F.3d 799 (8th Cir. 1998), *cert. denied,* 525 U.S. 1089 (1999) (holding trial court properly balanced possible prejudice in admitting into evidence a 1987 conviction for defendant's sexual assault of a 12-year-old girl by forced intercourse since that conduct was similar to the charges for which he was on trial); United States v. Eagle, 137 F.3d 1011 (8th Cir. 1998) (upholding trial court's admission into evidence after conducting a balancing test on defendant's prior sexual abuse conviction ten years earlier); United States v. Guardia, 135 F.3d 1326, 1330–31 (10th Cir. 1998); United States v. Enjady, 134 F.3d 1427 (10th Cir.), *cert. denied,* 525 U.S. 887 (1998); United States v. Sumner, 119 F.3d 658, 661–62 (8th Cir. 1997); United States v. Meacham, 115 F.3d 1488, 1495 (10th Cir. 1997); United States v. Larson, 112 F.3d 600, 604–05 (2d Cir. 1997).

Rules 413 and 414 still require a trial court to weigh the probative value of the prior acts against their substantial prejudice and make a clear record of its findings.

Many of the same standards used in admitting prior acts under other exceptions will apply to Rules 413 and 414, such as the similarity of the acts, their closeness in time to the charged acts, the frequency of the prior acts, the presence or lack of intervening events, and the need for evidence beyond the testimony of the defendant and alleged victim.

One California appeals court holds that it is error to preclude evidence that the defendant was acquitted of the prior act offered into evidence.[86] The defendant may be able to present witnesses to dispute the prior act evidence.[87] It should be remembered that statutes providing for the admissibility of a defendant's prior sexual assaults do not supersede other rules of evidence such as hearsay restrictions, as well as rules designed to prevent the presentation of evidence which may be unduly prejudicial. Even when a statute specifically provides for prior act evidence in prosecution for a particular case, the evidence must still be relevant and not outweighed by its prejudicial effect.[88] Among the factors suggested by one court to consider are: 1) How strong is the government's evidence that the defendant actually committed the other acts? 2) What character trait do the other acts tend to prove? 3) Is this character trait relevant to any material issue in the case? How relevant? And how strongly do the defendant's other acts tend to prove this trait? 4) Assuming that the offered character evidence is relevant to a material issue, how seriously disputed is this material issue? Does the government need to offer more evidence on this issue? And is there less prejudicial evidence that could be offered on this point? In other words, how great is the government's need to offer evidence of the defendant's other acts? Or, if evidence of one or more other acts has already been admitted, how great is the government's need to offer *additional* evidence of the defendant's other acts? 5) How likely is it that litigation of the defendant's other acts will require

---

[86] People v. Mullens, 119 Cal. App. 4th 648, 14 Cal. Rptr. 3d 534 (2004).

[87] State v. Hughes, 841 So. 2d 718 (La. 2003).

[88] Bingaman v. State, 76 P.3d 398 (Alaska Ct. App. 2003) (reversing defendant's conviction for failure of trial court to assess prejudicial effect and relevancy of other acts of domestic violence, even though such evidence is "admissible" under Alaska's rules of evidence in domestic violence cases and finding same principles apply to Alaskan rules permitting evidence of prior sex acts); McGill v. State, 18 P.3d 77 (Alaska Ct. App. 2001); Wardlow v. State, 2 P.3d 1238, 1246 (Alaska Ct. App. 2000) (stating that Alaska R. Evid. 404(b)(3) "was enacted by the legislature in direct response to decisions of this court that limited the State's ability to introduce evidence of a defendant's prior sexual crimes when, in a prosecution for sexual assault or attempted sexual assault, the defendant asserted that the sexual activity was consensual." Court noted that admission of prior acts must still be balanced with unfair prejudice, but this no longer includes the fact that evidence tends to prove defendant's propensity); People v. Soto, 64 Cal. App. 4th 966, 984, 75 Cal. Rptr. 2d 605, 616 (1998); People v. Stanbridge, 348 Ill. App. 3d 351, 810 N.E.2d 88 (2004) (holding where Illinois' statute in permitting evidence of other acts evidence, prior acts were too remote and dissimilar to charged offense); State v. Olivieri, 860 So. 2d 207 (La. Ct. App. 2003).

an inordinate amount of time? 6) And finally, how likely is it that evidence of the defendant's other acts will lead the jury to decide the case on improper grounds, or will it distract the jury from the main issues in the case?[89]

The similarity of the sexual acts and their closeness in time to the charge may bolster the prior acts' relevance because they suggest "a pattern of criminal behavior."[90]

The *corpus delicti* rule does not apply to the admission of evidence under Rules 413 and 414, and thus a defendant's statements of prior abuse are admissible without any other proof of the prior acts.[91] Yet, courts rarely find that prior sexual acts have substantial prejudice outweighing their probative value. In one case where a defendant's conviction was reversed on this ground, the prior act was a particularly vicious and perverse act compared with the indicted charges, remote in that it had occurred 23 years earlier, and was confusing because it gave the impression that the defendant was unpunished for the prior act, necessitated lengthy instructions and, because of its dissimilarity, was not probative.[92]

In another case, a court found that even under Rule 413, testimony of four other women who claimed they were touched inappropriately by the defendant gynecologist was confusing and dissimilar.[93] However, such prejudice has rarely been found by courts applying Rules 413 and 414.[94]

---

[89] *Bingaman*, 76 P.3d at 415–16.

[90] Mooney v. State, 105 P.3d 149 (Alaska Ct. App. 2005) (The defendant's prior sexual assault conviction was admissible because the facts in the case were similar to the facts of the current charges against Mooney. Although he considered the age of the conviction, he concluded that the evidence was probative because Mooney was an adult at the time he committed the offense. *Id.* at 154); People v. Yovanov, 69 Cal. App. 4th 392, 81 Cal. Rptr. 2d 586, *review denied*, 1999 Cal. LEXIS 2358 (Apr. 14, 1999).

[91] United States v. Norris, 428 F.3d 907, 913–14 (9th Cir. 2005).

[92] People v. Harris, 60 Cal. App. 4th 727, 70 Cal. Rptr. 2d 689, *review denied*, 1998 Cal. LEXIS 2350 (Apr. 15, 1998).

[93] While Rules 413 and 414 and parallel state statutes are designed to open the door to a defendant's prior sexual assaults, a prior sexual assault can still be improperly admitted under such a statute. If the prior act is so remote or so inflammatory and lacks any similarity or other probative purpose, admission of the act can be so prejudicial as to require reversal of a defendant's convictions. United States v. Guardia, 135 F.3d 1326 (10th Cir. 1998).

[94] United States v. Guardia, 135 F.3d 1326, 1329–32 (10th Cir. 1998) ("Admission of the testimony would transform the trial of two incidents into the trial of six incidents, each requiring description by lay witnesses and explanation by expert witnesses. The subtle factual distinctions among these incidents would make it difficult for the jury to separate the evidence of the uncharged conduct from the charged conduct." *Id.* at 1332). *See also* United States v. Bird, 372 F.3d 989 (8th Cir. 2004); United States v. Meacham, 115 F.3d 1488 (10th Cir. 1997); United States v. Berry, 61 M.J. 91 (C.A.A.F. 2005) (reversing defendant's conviction because court found defendant's conviction as a 13-year-old failed Rule 403 balancing test because of its age, interviewing circumstances, and confusion).

§ 6.32   Need for trial court to balance factors in admitting prior act evidence.

It is important for a court that admits evidence of the defendant's prior bad acts to place on the record the balancing process that it undertakes in deciding to admit such evidence and not make findings and conclusions which are generic in nature, clearly indicating the specific exception under which the bad act evidence is being admitted and how the exception applies to the particular facts and nature of the cause at hand. "Evidence of the uncharged crimes and bad acts should be closely controlled so that those acts do not again eclipse the reason for the trial, i.e., the crimes with which defendant is charged."[95] The standard for review of Rule 403 determinations is generally abuse of discretion.[96] A trial court's failure to make such specific findings may result in reversal of a defendant's conviction.[97]

For example, a trial court's ruling "...if I have to make a finding under 403, then I find it's relevant and the probative value is not substantially outweighed by any prejudice," does not meet the standard of specific findings.[98] A court's failure to set forth on the record the factors in its decision to introduce other acts evidence does not preclude an appellate court from independently reviewing the record to determine a reasonable basis for the trial court's decision.[99] When the defendant is the only person who can dispute the complainant's testimony,

---

[95] People v. Gorghan, 13 A.D.3d 908, 787 N.Y.S.2d 178 (2004), *appeal denied*, 4 N.Y.3d 798, 828 N.E.2d 90, 795 N.Y.S.2d 174 (2005) (reversing defendant's conviction for prosecutorial misconduct but noting on retrial court should conduct "a more detailed analysis of the probative value versus potential for prejudice of the uncharged crimes and bad acts.").

[96] United States v. Withorn, 204 F.3d 790, 794 (8th Cir. 2000). *But see* United States v. Bird, 372 F.3d 989, 991 (8th Cir. 2004) (applying a *de novo* standard on reviewing court's interpretation of sexual propensity rule, but abuse of discretion in its applications).

[97] Hickson v. State, 697 So. 2d 391, 396 (Miss. 1997) (In reversing defendant's sexual assault conviction, appellate court noted that trial court did not find that probative value of defendant's prior sexual assault conviction outweighed its prejudicial effect. "No on-the-record determination was made by the trial judge in the case *sub judice* that the probative value of admitting the prior conviction outweighed the prejudicial effect. The judge's ruling that evidence of the prior conviction could be admitted had a chilling effect on Hickson's testifying, and he did not testify. This omission by the trial judge constitutes reversible error." *Id.* at 397.); Commonwealth v. Ardinger, 2003 Pa. Super. 506, 839 A.2d 1143 (2003) (remanding to trial court for determination of whether admission of prior acts evidence, sufficient to satisfy 404(b) requirements, would be outweighed by its potential for prejudice; State v. Steele, 510 N.W.2d 661 (S.D. 1994) (in reversing defendant's conviction on other grounds, court noted that upon retrial, the trial judge should make more than generic findings and conclusions as to why prior bad act evidence was admissible, and should perform an analysis of the facts and nature of the prior bad acts); State v. Sullivan, 216 Wis. 2d 768, 576 N.W.2d 30 (1998).

[98] United States v. Castillo, 140 F.3d 874, 884 (10th Cir. 1998).

[99] State v. Root, 95 Wash. App. 333 (1999) (*citing* State v. Binkin, 79 Wash. App. 284, 291, 902 P.2d 673 (1995), *review denied*, 128 Wash. 2d 1015, 911 P.2d 1343 (1996)); State v. Hunt, 263 Wis. 2d 1, 666 N.W.2d 771 (2003).

it may be more prejudicial to permit cross-examination concerning a prior similar sexual assault crime.

In reversing a defendant's sexual assault conviction for use of defendant's prior sexual assaults, Wyoming's Supreme Court has articulated a five-prong test for determining the admissibility of prior act evidence that summarizes many of the issues surrounding the use of such evidence. The five factors are:

1. The extent to which the prosecution plainly, clearly, and convincingly can prove the other similar crimes;

2. The remoteness in time of those crimes from the charged offense;

3. The extent to which the evidence of other crimes is introduced for a valid purpose such as proof of motive, opportunity, intent, preparation, plan, knowledge, identity, or absence of mistake or accident;

4. The extent to which the element of the charged offense, that the evidence is introduced to prove, is actually at issue;

5. The extent to which the prosecution has a substantial need for the probative value of the evidence of the other crimes.[100]

The need to balance probative value of a defendant's prior acts against their prejudice or unreliability applies to Federal Rules 413 and 414, which favor admission of prior uncharged acts of the defendant, discussed in the preceding section.

§ 6.33 Use of defendant's prior acts to prove fact or element conceded by defendant.

The United States Supreme Court has ruled that the prosecution's refusal to stipulate to an element of proof as to a prior qualifying conviction conceded by the defendant may constitute unfair prejudice.[101] However, the court also noted that a defendant's offer to stipulate or concede an element of an offense does not deprive it of relevance.[102] More importantly, it distinguished between conceding a qualifying crime and bad acts, which are admitted under 404(b), which a jury should be able to hear so that there are no gaps in the story or proof which would lead to nullification or unjustified acquittal.[103] Thus, an appeals court has ruled that when a defendant offers to concede elements of a

---

[100] Sorensen v. State, 895 P.2d 454, 456 (Wyo. 1995) (defendant's conviction reversed because trial court admitted evidence of prior sexual acts of defendant without addressing each prong of a five-part test for admissibility of such evidence under Wyoming law). *See also* Rigler v. State, 941 P.2d 734 (Wyo. 1997).

[101] Old Chief v. United States, 519 U.S. 172, 117 S Ct. 644, 136 L.Ed. 2d 574 (1997) (involving prosecution's failure to accept defendant's stipulation to a qualifying conviction for the offense being prosecuted).

[102] *Id.*, 519 U.S. at 186-89.

[103] *Id.*, 519 U.S. at 190-92.

crime, such as intent and knowledge, prior bad acts evidence offered to prove those elements is admissible since the prior bad acts then do not relate to the status of the crime but other elements such as motive and intent. [104]

§ 6.34 Substantiation required for use of prior bad acts; use of acquitted conduct.

There must be a good faith basis for the use of any evidence of a defendant's prior bad acts. The U.S. Supreme Court has held that there must be sufficient evidence for a jury to "reasonably conclude that the act occurred and that the defendant was the actor." [105] It also held that there need not be a finding by the trial judge, that the Government has established the prior acts by a preponderance of the evidence. [106] The trial court need only assess the conditional fact to determine if the jury could find the conditional fact by a preponderance of the evidence. [107] It may await the trial proof to determine if there is sufficient evidence to allow the jury to consider the evidence. [108] The Supreme Court has also held that a prior acquittal on the proffered bad act does not necessarily preclude its use since the preponderance of evidence standard is lower than the beyond a reasonable doubt standard. [109] Several courts have upheld the use of prior acquitted conduct or dismissed acts of sexual assault. [110] If a defendant wishes to challenge an appeal on the lack of basis for a prior act, a record is important. For example, failing to include in the record evidence that the prior conviction was expunged may preclude review of the issue of admissibility. [111]

---

[104] United States v. Crowder, 141 F.3d 1202 (D.C. Cir. 1998), *cert. denied*, 525 U.S. 1149 (1999).

[105] Huddleston v. United States, 485 U.S. 681, 689, 108 S. Ct. 1496, 99 L.Ed. 2d 771(1988).

[106] *Id.*

[107] *Id.* at 690.

[108] *Id.*

[109] Dowling v. United States, 493 U.S. 342, 348–49, 110 S. Ct. 668, 107 L. Ed. 2d 708 (1990) (noting that trial court instructed the jury as to defendant's acquittal and the limited purpose of the testimony).

[110] Hess v. State, 20 P.3d 1121 (Alaska 2001) (upholding use of prior acquitted sexual assaults); People v. Wallen, 996 P.2d 182 (Colo. Ct. App. 1999), *cert. denied*, 2000 Colo. LEXIS 483 (Mar. 27, 2000) (holding that defendant's prior acquittal of sexual assault charge did not bar admission of that act in subsequent sexual assault trial); Cartwright v. State, 242 Ga. App. 825, 531 S.E.2d 399 (2000) (court upheld use of prior sexual assault for which defendant was acquitted because statutory rape was issue at defendant's past trial, not this time, and age of consent had increased from 14 to 16 in interim, and thus although consensual intercourse was not criminal at time of past act, it was at time of this trial, and court found prior act was relevant to defendant's *modus operandi*); State v. Dean, 589 A.2d 929, 932 (Me. 1991); State v. Sanchez, 257 Neb. 291, 597 N.W.2d 361 (1999); People v. Morales, 273 A.D.2d 102, 709 N.Y.S.2d 544, 545 (2000) ("The court properly permitted the People to inquire about the underlying facts of a dismissed rape charge because it was relevant to defendant's willingness to place advancement of his individual self-interest ahead of the interests of society, and thus to his credibility because the dismissal was not a disposition on the merits." [citations omitted]).

[111] Davidson v. State, 2005 Ark. LEXIS 416 (June 23, 2005).

Even though it may be permissible to utilize evidence of a prior crime for which the defendant was acquitted, the prosecution must still establish the relevance of the prior crime.[112] Other courts have found charges for which a defendant is acquitted may not be used against him on a subsequent retrial of remaining counts due to the prejudicial impact of such evidence.[113] A defendant may also be cross-examined about a conviction based on an *Alford* plea (a plea of guilty where the defendant does not admit the facts underlying the case) since it is still a conviction.[114]

Many states require by statute[115] or case law[116] that a defendant's prior acts be established by clear and convincing evidence. Admitting into evidence collateral accusations which are not established by clear and convincing can be reversible error.[117] Other jurisdictions that follow the Federal Rules of Evidence have adopted the *Huddleston* standard of preponderance of the evidence instead of a clear and convincing standard.[118] Texas is unique in requiring that prior bad acts be established beyond a reasonable doubt by the prosecution.[119] The failure to instruct the jury of the reasonable doubt standard may be error.[120]

Evidence admitted under a special statute permitting evidence of similar conduct against a victim of domestic violence or against family or household

---

[112] State v. Cotton, 778 So. 2d 569 (La. 2001).

[113] People v. Carroll, 300 A.D.2d 911, 913, 753 N.Y.S.2d 148 (2002), *appeal denied*, 99 N.Y.2d 626, 790 N.E.2d 281, 760 N.Y.S.2d 107 (2003).

[114] People v. Miller, 91 N.Y.2d 372, 694 N.E.2d 61, 670 N.Y.S.2d 978 (1998).

[115] Ariz. R. Evid. 404; NEB. REV. STAT. § 27-404(3) (prosecution must establish by clear and convincing evidence that defendant committed any prior bad act or crime); Tenn. R. Evid. 404(b).

[116] State v. Terrazas, 189 Ariz. 580, 944 P.2d 1194, 1198 (1997); Streater v. State, 352 Md. 800, 807, 724 A.2d 111, 114 (1999); State v. Spaeth, 552 N.W.2d 187, 193 (Minn. 1996); State v. Filippi, 335 N.W.2d 739, 743 (Minn. 1983); State v. Sanchez, 257 Neb. 291, 597 N.W.2d 361 (1999) (defining the "clear and convincing" standard as sufficient evidence that the other act was committed by the defendant so as to warrant submission of the other act to the jury as if the other act or crime had been charged); State v. Moorman, 286 N.J. Super. 648, 670 A.2d 81 (1996) ("clear and convincing" evidence established that defendant committed prior acts of physical abuse upon child); People v. Robinson, 68 N.Y.2d 541, 503 N.E.2d 485, 510 N.Y.S.2d 837 (1986) (for other crime evidence to be admissible on the issue of identity, the identity of defendant as the perpetrator of the other crime, if not conceded or previously adjudicated, must be established by clear and convincing evidence); State v. Dubose, 953 S.W.2d 649, 654 (Tenn. 1997); State v. McCary, 922 S.W.2d 511, 514 (Tenn. 1996).

[117] Audano v. State, 641 So. 2d 1356 (Fla. Dist. Ct. App. 1994).

[118] People v. Garner, 806 P.2d 366, 372 (Colo. 1991). *See, e.g.*, State v. Crawford, 672 So. 2d 197, *cert. denied*, 679 So. 2d 1379 (La. 1996) (*citing* LA. CODE EVID. ANN. art. 1104 requiring the burden of proof at a bad acts hearing to be identical to that required by the Federal Rules of Evidence); State v. Norlin, 134 Wash. 2d 570, 951 P.2d 1131 (1998); State v. McDaniel, 211 W. Va. 9, 560 S.E.2d 484, 487 (2001); State v. Gray, 225 Wis. 2d 39, 590 N.W.2d 918 (1999).

[119] TEX. CODE CRIM. PROC. ANN. art. 37.07; George v. State, 890 S.W.2d 73, 76 (Tex. Crim. App. 1994); Harrell v. State, 884 S.W.2d 154, 157 (Tex. Crim. App. 1994).

[120] *See* Poole v. State, 974 S.W.2d 892 (Tex. App. Austin 1998) (while holding failure of court to provide reasonable doubt standard was error, error was harmless in this case).

members need not be established by clear and convincing evidence.[121] The theory is that the evidence is offered as direct evidence to prove an element of the charged offense.[122]

Testimony by prior victims of abuse and the testimony of a psychologist can be a sufficient basis for a jury to determine that the defendant committed the prior acts.[123] Testimony by the complainant may also be sufficient to establish the prior bad acts.[124] If sexual assault charges are dismissed against a defendant at the close of the state's case, permitting the jury to receive evidence of those acts may be prejudicial.[125]

§ 6.35   Similarity of prior act to pending charge as a basis to preclude cross-examination as to defendant's credibility.

Apart from their admissibility as direct proof, a defendant's prior bad acts may be used on cross-examination to impeach the defendant's credibility. Impeaching a defendant on cross-examination with a past conviction that is similar to the charged crime is prejudicial in the view of many courts when considering the propriety on cross-examination of a prior sex abuse conviction in a sexual assault trial.[126]

Some courts decline to adopt an absolute prohibition on a prior crime simply because it is similar to the charged offense.[127]

But courts have also permitted a prior sexual assault conviction in a rape trial on the theory that "[a]lthough it was similar to the crime charged, it was a crime of calculated violence which demonstrated the defendant's determination to further his own self-interest at the expense of society."[128] Other courts, too, have

---

[121] (Interpreting MINN. STAT. § 634.20 "We believe that the interests of justice are best served by allowing the introduction of evidence of similar acts by the accused against the alleged victim of domestic abuse without requiring that they first be established by clear and convincing evidence.").

[122] State v. McCoy, 682 N.W.2d 153 (Minn. 2004)682 N.W.2d at 160.

[123] United States v. Yellow, 18 F.3d 1438, 1441 (8th Cir. 1994).

[124] United States v. Tsinnijinnie, 91 F.3d 1285 (9th Cir. 1996); State v. Haley, 141 N.H. 541, 689 A.2d 671 (1997).

[125] State v. Conley, 938 S.W.2d 614 (Mo. Ct. App. 1997).

[126] See, e.g., Hopkins v. State, 639 So. 2d 1247 (Miss. 1993); State v. Ford, 1995 Tenn. Crim. App. LEXIS 753 (Sept. 14, 1995) (defendant's prior sexual battery conviction too similar to the instant rape charge to be admitted into evidence).

[127] People v. Hayes, 97 N.Y.2d 203, 764 N.E.2d 963, 738 N.Y.S.2d 663 (2002).

[128] People v. Johnson, 283 A.D.2d 331, 724 N.Y.S.2d 857, appeal denied, 96 N.Y.2d 920, 758 N.E.2d 663, 732 N.Y.S.2d 637 (2001) (holding defendant's prior rape conviction relevant to credibility and prejudice minimized by precluding reference to underlying facts). People v. Watson, 57 A.D.2d 143, 393 N.Y.S.2d 735 (1977), rev'd on other grounds, 45 N.Y.2d 867, 382 N.E.2d 1352, 410 N.Y.S.2d 577 (1978). See also People v. Cherry, 106 A.D.2d 458, 482 N.Y.S.2d 551 (1984), appeal denied, 64 N.Y.2d 888 (1985).

permitted the use of prior sexual assault convictions or bad acts on cross-examination of the defendant.[129]

§ 6.36   Use of pending charges or indictment as areas of cross-examination.

Courts are divided on the propriety of using pending charges or indictments against a defendant. Pending rape charges may be deemed a proper area of cross-examination when they are offered for a purpose reasonably related to a material issue raised in a defendant's testimony on direct examination.[130]

Consider a rape case where the defendant, a state trooper, was charged with raping a young woman whom he had stopped for a traffic violation on an interstate highway. There was a pending indictment against the defendant for official misconduct for attempting to use Department of Motor Vehicle records improperly to obtain information concerning a complainant through misrepresentations and false statements, including statements to a DMV clerk that he was an active police officer. The appeals court ruled that permitting the defendant to be cross-examined concerning a pending indictment for an attempt to obtain further information about the rape victim by improperly obtaining information about her and misrepresenting his official position was not sufficiently connected to the crime for which the defendant was charged, nor was it admissible under

[129] People v. Williams, 24 A.D.3d 882;, 806 N.Y.S.2d 266 (2005) *appeal denied*, 6 N.Y., 3d 854, 816 NYS 2d 760 (2006) (permitting inquiry of a defendant accused of rape of eight-year-old, sodomy conviction, and two four-year-old child endangerment convictions which were sexual in nature); People v. Kelly, 270 A.D.2d 511, 705 N.Y.S.2d 689, *on recons., appeal denied*, 95 N.Y.2d 854, 736 N.E.2d 866, 714 N.Y.S.2d 5 (2000); People v. Sager, 251 A.D.2d 433, 673 N.Y.S.2d 325, *appeal denied*, 92 N.Y.2d 905, 702 N.E.2d 854, 680 N.Y.S.2d 69 (1998) (upholding use of similar past sexual assaults since similarity of past crimes to the one charged "does not automatically preclude the prosecutor from using evidence of such crimes for impeachment purposes"); People v. Conway, 241 A.D.2d 752, 660 N.Y.S.2d 749, *appeal denied*, 91 N.Y.2d 871, 691 N.E.2d 641, 668 N.Y.S.2d 569 (1997) (in child homicide prosecution defendant's prior statutory "rape conviction demonstrated that defendant was predisposed to placing his own self-interest and personal gratification above the interests of society, [and therefore] the conviction was relevant on the issue of defendant's credibility"); People v. Laraby, 219 A.D.2d 817, 632 N.Y.S.2d 355 (1995), *appeal denied*, 88 N.Y.2d 849, 667 N.E.2d 346, 644 N.Y.S.2d 696 (1996) ("The fact that the prior convictions of defendant for sexual abuse and rape are similar to the crimes presently charged does not preclude their use on cross-examination."); People v. Prise, 151 A.D.2d 787, 543 N.Y.S.2d 117, *appeal denied*, 74 N.Y.2d 850, 546 N.E.2d 198, 546 N.Y.S.2d 1015 (1989) (permitting in a sodomy prosecution cross-examination into defendant's prior public lewdness conviction involving defendant's exposing his penis to a 13-year-old girl).

[130] Rhoden v. Rowland, 10 F.3d 1457, 1461 (9th Cir. 1993) (holding that two pending rape charges were relevant to whether or not the defendant had a "reasonable good faith belief that the victim consented"). *See also* United States v. Cuozzo, 962 F.2d 945 (9th Cir.), *cert. denied*, 506 U.S. 978 (1992); People v. Sanchez, 289 A.D.2d 265, 734 N.Y.S.2d 850 (2001), *appeal denied*, 97 N.Y.S.2d 733, 767 N.E.2d 163, 740 N.Y.S.2d 706 (2002) (noting that a defendant may open door to cross-examination on pending charge).

a theory of consciousness of guilt.[131] The legal theory underpinning this decision is that "a defendant-witness does not generally and automatically waive the privilege against self-incrimination as to pending criminal charges."[132] This is certainly a cogent legal argument to make with respect to the use of pending criminal charges on cross-examination.

Likewise, it is improper to permit cross-examination on a pending assault charge involving a different person, when the prosecution argues that victim did not come forward until learning that defendant had committed a subsequent assault.[133] However, had the defendant raised the issue of the first victim's delay in reporting the assault, then the defendant would have opened the door to the subsequent assault.[134]

§ 6.37   Age and remoteness of prior convictions or bad acts as a factor in admissibility.

Another factor to consider in determining the admissibility of a prior conviction or bad act is remoteness. While many courts have adopted a ten-year rule as a cutoff, some have declared there is no arbitrary time period to determine remoteness of a conviction. A defendant's sexual abuse more than ten years prior to the sexual acts for which the defendant was charged is not necessarily too remote to be admissible as prior bad act evidence.[135] In this view, age is but

[131] People v. Bennett, 79 N.Y.2d 464, 593 N.E.2d 279, 583 N.Y.S.2d 825 (1992).

[132] People v. Betts, 70 N.Y.2d 289, 294–95, 514 N.E.2d 865, 867–68, 520 N.Y.S.2d 370, 373 (1987) (reversing defendant's rape conviction because of trial court's ruling that if defendant took the stand he could be cross-examined about a pending burglary charge).

[133] People v. Park, 12 A.D.3d 942, 785 N.Y.S.2d 180 (2004) (noting the subsequent assault was not necessary to complete the narrative nor was it "inextricably interwoven" with the original assault).

[134] Id. at 943, 785 N.Y.S.2d at 182.

[135] United States v. Hadley, 918 F.2d 848 (9th Cir. 1990), cert. dismissed, 506 U.S. 19 (1992); Harmon v. State, 908 P.2d 434, 438 (Alaska Ct. App. 1995) (defendant's 12-year-old sexual assault convictions not too remote to be admitted into evidence); Sewell v. State, 244 Ga. App. 449, 452, 536 S.E.2d 173, 177 (2000) (holding evidence of defendant's prior acts of fondling and attempted anal sodomy on his cousins 20 years earlier neither too remote nor "impermissibly stale" to establish defendant's state of mind toward young victim); Vehaun v. State, 244 Ga. App. 136, 534 S.E.2d 873 (2000) (upholding use of defendant's prior child molestation conviction, which was over 20 years old, a factor which goes to weight to be accorded similar crime evidence and not its admissibility); Swift v. State, 229 Ga. App. 772, 774, 495 S.E.2d 109, 112 (1997) (holding that defendant's prior sexual assaults more than ten years earlier not inadmissible); State v. Sebasky, 547 N.W.2d 93 (Minn. 1996) ("while ten or 12 years elapsed between the Spreigl acts and the charged crimes, a close temporal relationship is not necessary if the evidence is otherwise relevant." Id. at 98); State v. Penland, 343 N.C. 634, 653–54, 472 S.E.2d 734, 745 (1996), cert. denied, 519 U.S. 1098 (1997) (holding that ten-year period did not render prior instances of sexual misbehavior too remote to be part of a common scheme); State v. Harris, 140 N.C. App. 208, 535 S.E.2d 614 (2000) (holding trial court in sexual assault case properly found defendant's 14-year-old conviction probative value to assess defendant's credibility outweighed its prejudicial effect); State v. Hopkins, 698 A.2d 183,

one factor in admissibility. Other courts have held that convictions seven to ten years old may be relevant to credibility determinations,[136] while some courts have held the age of a seven-year-old conviction for touching a child is a factor weighing against admissibility.[137]

Another factor to consider is whether the defendant was incarcerated for any appreciable period between the date of the past conviction and the date of the current charge. Thus, convictions entered 12, 14, or 18 years ago may be relevant to a credibility determination when the defendant was incarcerated for approximately 13 years.[138] Other courts also consider a defendant's incarceration in weighing the admissibility of a defendant's prior bad act.[139] In the view of one

---

186 (R.I. 1997) (upholding use of prior abuse ten years before alleged molestation and 14 to18 years before trial); Turner v. Commonwealth, 259 Va. 645, 529 S.E.2d 787 (2000) (permitting use of 13-year-old other crimes evidence); State v. McIntosh, 207 W. Va. 561, 572, 534 S.E.2d 757, 768 (2000) (finding "[t]he probative value of other bad act evidence is not completely nullified by the fact that the other sexual assaults occurred within four, seven, and 13 years of the crimes charged" and the decision on remoteness is generally a matter of the trial court's discretion). *See generally* W.A. Harrington, Annotation, *Remoteness in Time of Other Similar Offenses Committed by Accused as Affecting Admissibility of Evidence Thereof in Prosecution for Sex Offenses,* 88 A.L.R.3d 8 (1978).

[136] State v. Kulmac, 230 Conn. 43, 644 A.2d 887, 897 (1994) (defendant's prior acts of abuse, seven years earlier were not too remote to possess probative value); State v. Hassett, 124 Idaho 357, 859 P.2d 955 (1993) (permitting the use in a physical child abuse prosecution of bad acts that were seven to nine years old); People v. Alhadi, 151 A.D.2d 873, 543 N.Y.S.2d 175, *appeal denied,* 74 N.Y.2d 804, 545 N.E.2d 876, 546 N.Y.S.2d 562 (1989) (in a prosecution for rape in the third degree, appeals court held the fact that "the convictions were some ten years old does not make their use *per se* improper." *Id.* 151 A.D.2d at 874, 543 N.Y.S.2d at 177); People v. Benson, 123 A.D.2d 470, 506 N.Y.S.2d 480 (1986) (ten-year-old assault conviction admissible in cross-examination in rape trial).

[137] *See, e.g.,* Hopkins v. State, 639 So. 2d 1247 (Miss. 1993).

[138] People v. Zillinger, 179 A.D.2d 382, 578 N.Y.S.2d 153, *appeal denied,* 79 N.Y.2d 955, 592 N.E.2d 817, 583 N.Y.S.2d 209 (1992).

[139] United States v. Eagle, 137 F.3d 1011, 1016 (8th Cir. 1998) (holding defendant's claim that prior conviction had little probative value because it occurred ten years earlier was "seriously weakened by the fact that he had spent six of those years incarcerated for that crime"); United States v. Cuch, 842 F.2d 1173, 1178 (10th Cir. 1988) (seven and one-half-year-old prior assault must be considered in light of defendant's 30-month assault sentence); People v. Davis, 71 Cal. App. 4th 1492, 1498, 84 Cal. Rptr. 2d 628, 632 (1999) (holding defendant's prior offenses—13 to 19 years prior to trial—were not too remote given that defendant had spent many years in prison); State v. Massengill, 133 N.M. 263, 62 P.3d 354 (2002) (citing New Mexico rule permitting consideration of defendant's incarceration); People v. Smalls, 16 A.D.3d 1154, 792 N.Y.S.2d 748, *appeal denied,* 5 N.Y.3d 769, 834 N.E.2d 1274, 801 N.Y.S.2d 264 (2005) (holding in rape prosecution that "[a]lthough defendant's prior convictions were between 12 and 17 years old, defendant had spent ten of those years in prison"); People v. Johnson, 283 A.D.2d 331, 724 N.Y.S.2d 857 (2001) (defendant's incarceration relevant on issue of remoteness of defendant's prior conviction); People v. McCullough, 254 A.D.2d 750, 751, 679 N.Y.S.2d 227, 229, *appeal denied,* 92 N.Y.2d 1035, 707 N.E.2d 455, 684 N.Y.S.2d 500 (1998) (holding that defendant's "convictions were not too remote in light of the fact that defendant was incarcerated for ten of the 11 intervening years"); State v. Chavis, 141 N.C. App. 553, 540 S.E.2d 404 (2000) (holding

court "[t]here is no precise point at which a prior act is considered too remote, and remoteness must be considered on a case by case basis."[140]

Under the Federal Rules of Evidence 413 and 414, there are no time limits." Thus, admission of a defendant's molestation of his stepdaughters 30 years earlier has been upheld.[141] The federal appeals court in that case noted in reviewing the Rules' legislative history:

> No time limit is imposed on the uncharged offenses for which evidence may be admitted; as a practical matter, evidence of other sex offenses by the defendant is often probative and properly admitted, notwithstanding very substantial lapses of time in relation to the charged offense or offenses.[142]

Another appeals court noted there is no time limit for the admission of prior sex offenses and upheld admission of prior acts of the defendant committed 16 to 20 years prior to trial.[143] It reasoned:

> Those events closely paralleled the events complained of by Furs, taking place in the same geographic locations, with Larson using the same enticements for both boys, plying both with alcohol, and engaging both in similar progressions of sexual acts. The similarity of the events clearly demonstrated the Stevens testimony's relevance. The court was entitled to view both the traumatic nature of the events and their repetition over a span of four years as strong indicators of the reliability of the witness's memory. We see no abuse of discretion in the admission of this testimony.[144]

Other states have permitted prior acts more than ten years old under "propensity" statutes.[145] Some states have a limit on the age of the prior acts in their propensity statutes.[146] But, if the proponent does not establish probative value, it may be an abuse of discretion to admit prior acts more than ten years old.[147] Evidence of prior sexual acts, which may be too "stale" or "old" to be admissible may still be admissible by virtue of its similarity to the charged crime.[148]

---

defendant's incarceration should be considered in determining remoteness); State v. Davis, 101 N.C. App. 12, 18–19, 398 S.E.2d 645, 649–50 (1990), *review denied*, 328 N.C. 574, 403 S.E.2d 516 (1991).

[140] State v. Hammer, 236 Wis. 2d 686, 707, 613 N.W.2d 629, 639 (2000).

[141] United States v. Meacham, 115 F.3d 1488 (10th Cir. 1997).

[142] *Id.* at 1492.

[143] United States v. Larson, 112 F.3d 600, 605 (2d Cir. 1997).

[144] *Id.*

[145] United States v. Drewry, 365 F.3d 957, 959–60 (10th Cir. Okla. 2004), *vacated on other grounds*, 125 S. Ct. 987 (2005) (permitting use of 25-year-old prior acts of sexual assault); United States v. Gabe, 237 F.3d 954 (8th Cir. S.D. 2001) (upholding admission under Rule 414 of acts occurring 20 years earlier).

[146] *See, e.g.*, Alaska R. Evid. 404(b) provides for a ten-year limit.

[147] State v. Green, 200 Ariz. 496, 29 P.3d 271 (2001).

[148] United States v. Drewry, 365 F.3d at 960 (upholding admission under Rule 414(a) of defendant's child molestation 25 years earlier). *See also* United States v. Gabe, 237 F.3d 954, 959 (8th Cir. 2001); United States v. Meacham, 115 F.3d 1488, 1495 (10th Cir. 1997).

§ 6.38 Admitting evidence of defendant's prior uncharged conduct as part of a common plan or scheme.

The most often encountered exception used for the admission of a defendant's prior uncharged sexual conduct is that it constitutes evidence of a common plan or scheme. (The common plan or scheme theory is also a basis for the joinder of multiple counts of sexual abuse, as discussed in § 1.27.) The common plan or scheme requires a great degree of similarity between the charged act and past conduct to prove its existence, but, unlike uncharged acts to establish identity, the plan or scheme need not be unusual or distinctive. [149] The common plan or scheme theory is used to establish that the defendant committed the act charged, whereas the identity exception assumes the act was committed. [150]

After determining that there is a common plan or scheme, the evidence's probative value must be evaluated by considering factors such as the independent nature of the acts, the degree of proof or substantiation, similarity between the charged crime and past acts, the inflammatory nature of the prior uncharged conduct, and the time period between the uncharged and charged acts. [151] In a Louisiana case, evidence of previous sexual assaults against the defendant's daughter at a period of time analogous to the time period in the case for which the defendant was on trial and under circumstances similar to the case at trial — such as being intoxicated and alone with the complainant while others were away or asleep — demonstrated a "motive and a plan to systematically engage in non-consensual relations with his daughters as they matured physically." [152] In another Louisiana case, the use of alcohol prior to sexual assaults upon individuals with whom the defendant had some contact was deemed part of a system or plan. [153] The common plan or scheme permits testimony that indicates the defendant previously sexually abused a child approximately the same age under similar circumstances. [154] Some courts permit introduction of prior sexual

---

[149] People v. Ewoldt, 7 Cal. 4th 380, 867 P.2d 757, 27 Cal. Rptr. 2d 646 (1994) (The definition of what is common varies widely from court to court. For some courts, basic similarity in the acts is sufficient. For others, an "overarching" pattern must connect the acts.).

[150] Id.

[151] Id.

[152] State v. Howard, 520 So. 2d 1150 (La. Ct. App. 1987), cert. denied, 526 So. 2d 790 (La. 1988). See also State v. Tyler, 619 So. 2d 807 (La. Ct. App. 1993).

[153] State v. Crawford, 672 So. 2d 197, 209 (La. Ct. App.), cert. denied, 679 So. 2d 1379 (La. 1996).

[154] State v. Roscoe, 184 Ariz. 484, 486, 910 P.2d 635, 642 (1996) (noting Arizona's liberal admissibility of other crime evidence in child sexual abuse cases); State v. Crane, 166 Ariz. 3, 799 P.2d 1380 (1990); People v. Rath, 44 P.3d 1033 (Colo. 2002) (upholding admission of four other witnesses who were taken to secluded areas by defendant as evidence of a common plan or scheme and to refute defendant's contention that victim's claim of sexual intercourse was a fabrication); State v. Kulmac, 230 Conn. 43, 62–63, 644 A.2d 887, 897–98 (1994) (defendant's prior acts of abuse with young girls similar in age to the complainant, and to all of whom defendant had access

(Text continued on page 479)

because of a relationship with the victim's family, evidenced a common scheme to abuse young girls sexually); Phelps v. State, 158 Ga. App. 219, 279 S.E.2d 513 (1981); State v. LaBelle, 887 P.2d 1071 (Idaho 1995) (upholding admissibility of prior molestation of two girls under ten years old, available to the defendant by virtue of defendant's connection to a parent of the victim, since such evidence was relevant as part of the defendant's general plan to exploit and sexually abuse an identifiable group of young female victims) (*citing* State v. Moore, 120 Idaho 743, 819 P.2d 1143 (1991)); State v. Zornes, 774 So. 2d 1062, *on remand*, 814 So. 2d 113 (La. 2002) (testimony concerning abuse of defendant's half-sister "carried out in the same manner, place and time period as the charged offense" was relevant to defendant's "motive or system" in committing the instant offense and probative value outweighed prejudicial effect); State v. Johnson, 670 So. 2d 651 (La. Ct. App. 1996) ("In the instant case, the evidence of previous sexual assaults against a daughter at a period of time analogous to the current victim (pre-teen years) and under similar circumstances (appellant intoxicated and alone with the victim in that others are either away or asleep) demonstrated motive and a plan to systematically engage in nonconsensual relations with his daughters as they matured physically." *Id.* at 654); State v. Sebasky, 547 N.W.2d 93, 97–98 (Minn. Ct. App. 1996) (finding similarities in that both boys worked for defendant and would live with him for a few days at a time, the defendant waited until the boys were spending the night in his bed before engaging in sexual conduct, and he gave them gifts and repeatedly abused the boys over a period of time); State v. Harrison, 1995 Minn. App. LEXIS 1031 (Aug. 9, 1995) (holding abuse of three other persons beginning at age eight was admissible as part of common scheme plan); State v. Kerr, 767 S.W.2d 344, 346 (Mo. Ct. App. 1989), *habeas corpus proceeding*, 956 F.2d 788 (1992); State v. Curry, 153 N.C. App. 260, 569 S.E.2d 691 (2002) (holding ages of victims in defendant's prior offenses and manner in which he pursued them were similar enough to be probative of his intent and common plan or scheme); State v. Frazier, 344 N.C. 611, 476 S.E.2d 297 (1996) (holding testimony of three other female members of defendant's household who alleged sexual abuse as children by the defendant were part of a common scheme or plan by the defendant even though committed seven to 27 years prior to trial); State v. Starner, 152 N.C. App. 150, 566 S.E.2d 814 (2002) (holding evidence of defendant's sexual assault against his daughter reflected a common plan or scheme to abuse young family members); State v. Williamson, 146 N.C. App. 325, 553 S.E.2d 54 (2001); State v. Chavis, 141 N.C. App. 553, 540 S.E.2d 404 (2000) ("In this case, the 1990 assault and the current charges are similar in nature. In both instances, the victims, similar in age, visited various residences or places in which they were unfamiliar and then were taken by automobile to isolated areas at night. During both instances, defendant told the victims something was wrong with the automobile, asked the victims to get out of the automobile, and then proceeded to sexually assault them."); State v. Thompson, 139 N.C. App. 299, 533 S.E.2d 834 (2000) ("[T]he evidence at trial demonstrated an ongoing pattern whereby defendant would wait until N's mother was gone, send N's siblings upstairs, and then proceed to perform sexual acts on N, or force her to perform sexual acts upon him." Court noted that five-year break in activity did not defeat admission of evidence since defendant did not have opportunity to be alone with child during this period.); Commonwealth v. O'Brien, 2003 Pa. Super. 425, 836 A.2d 966 (2003), *appeal denied*, 577 Pa. 695, 845 A.2d 817 (2004) (upholding admission of prior crime involving sexual assault of child to show a common scheme, plan, or design); State v. Rice, 755 A.2d 137, 145 (R.I. 2000) (recognizing that a defendant's sexual misconduct with persons other than the victim who are under defendant's control may in certain circumstances be admissible as part of a common scheme or plan); State v. Davidson, 263 Wis. 2d 537, 613 N.W.2d 606 (2000). (Court found defendant's other acts were admissible as part of a common plan and scheme and noted the "greater latitude rule" in sexual assault cases:

> In both assaults, the victim was particularly vulnerable. Tina H., a 13-year-old girl, had been drinking wine given to her by the defendant; Cindy P., a six-year-old girl, had ventured alone to the basement of the church to get a drink of water. Also, both

assaults when there are simply similarities between the sexual assaults without any overarching plan or connection between them.[155] The similarities may be driving to low-income areas, calling women over to his car and pretending to know them, and portraying himself as charming, helpful, and trustworthy before sexually assaulting them.[156]

The common design or plan theory permitted the introduction of a defendant's prior uncharged conduct upon the complainant and her older sister where there were sufficient common features with the charged offenses to support the inference that both the uncharged misconduct and the charged offenses were manifestations of a common design or plan, such as the fact that both young girls were the defendant's stepdaughters and were of a similar age at the time of the abuse.[157] The common plan could be that all acts involved male boys between the ages of seven or eight and 13 when they were either living with or working for the defendant.[158] Federal court rulings have also permitted testimony between a victim and defendant that are related to opportunity, intent, preparation, or plan, or between the defendant and other children in the same house or under similar circumstances.[159]

---

offenses took place in unlikely locations, in which the defendant could easily have been apprehended during the commission of the offense. Tina H. was assaulted in a camper while family members slept nearby; Cindy P. was assaulted in the basement of the church, next to the men's room and near to an occupied nursery, which church services took place on the main floor. Finally, both assaults involved touching the girls between the legs.

Id. at 568, 613 N.W.2d at 606).

[155] Sims v. State, 275 Ga. App. 836, 621 S.E.2d 869 (2005) (similarities were that person approached a woman in same area of city, told her he had a gun, demanded jewelry, and then ordering her to a secluded area and raped her); State v. Harris, 140 N.C. App. 208, 535 S.E.2d 614, *review denied*, 353 N.C. 271, 546 S.E.2d 122 (2000) ("Specifically, in each situation, defendant befriended the women, took them to a secluded place, pinned the women down, became aggressive with them, sexually assaulted and raped them and afterwards acted like nothing happened.").

[156] Fells v. State, 2005 Ark. LEXIS 246 (April 21, 2005).

[157] People v. Ewoldt, 7 Cal. 4th 380, 867 P.2d 757, 27 Cal. Rptr. 2d 646 (1994).

[158] State v. Hopkins, 698 A.2d 183 (R.I. 1997).

[159] United States v. Peden, 961 F.2d 517, 520–21 (5th Cir.), *cert. denied*, 506 U.S. 945 (1992) (admitting defendant's prior sexual assault conviction to establish defendant's intent to take advantage of one incapable of resisting or unable to appreciate a sexual act as well as his knowledge that young children are easily victimized); United States v. St. Pierre, 812 F.2d 417, 420 (8th Cir. 1987); United States v. Azure, 801 F.2d 336, 341 (8th Cir. 1986); United States v. Weisbeck, 48 M.J. 570 (A.C.C.A. 1998):

The similarities between the charged offenses and the testimony of the P brothers overwhelmingly suggest a common plan. We specifically make the following findings of fact, under Article 66(c), UCMJ: (1) Both sets of victims were brothers from broken homes who lived with their respective mothers and stepfathers; (2) Both sets of brothers were approximately 12 and 15 years old when appellant molested them; (3) Before sexually molesting his victims, appellant befriended these boys by playing basketball with them, giving them gifts and money, and taking them on trips to such

The bad act may also be after the charged offense. For example, evidence that soon after a rape and robbery a defendant committed a similar rape and robbery in another jurisdiction is admissible as part of a common plan or scheme that is relevant to demonstrate that the defendant "either employed or developed that plan in committing the charged offenses."[160] The probative value of the out-of-state rape was enhanced because it was reported independently of, and occurred close in time to, the charged offense.[161]

Another example of the application of the common plan or *modus operandi* exception was seen in the case of a deputy sheriff accused of raping a female motorist whom he had stopped along a highway for a motor vehicle violation.[162] The court permitted the prosecution to present testimony of another woman who claimed she was stopped two days later and instructed by the defendant to raise her brassiere and pull down her pants while she sat in his patrol car. The appellate court, in upholding the admission of this testimony, found that this was part of the deputy sheriff's plan to pull over women traveling alone, accuse them of crossing the center line, and then ordering them into his patrol car.[163] Using a "blue light" to pull over woman traveling alone at night and using a ski mask and forcing the victim to cover her face with a shirt are examples of acts falling within the *modus operandi* exception.[164]

This theory was applied in the case of a coach and teacher's aide charged with sexually abusing five juvenile boys. Evidence of prior sexual acts with young children were admissible "because the state sought to use it to prove defendant's motive or plan, i.e., molesting juvenile males, not to prove any system for the commission of the charged crimes against the five victims."[165] Prior acts of abuse against the same children have been admitted under the common scheme or plan rationale because the crimes were so related to one another that proof of one more or less tended to prove the others.[166]

---

places as shopping malls, movies, restaurants, and the beach; (4) With each victim, appellant would initiate the acts of sexual abuse by asking the victim about puberty, what the victim knew about sex, and whether the victim had any pubic hair. Appellant then coached each victim into showing him the victim's penis, which appellant would then touch or stroke in a similar fashion; and (5) After molesting his victims, appellant told them not to tell anyone.

Id. at * 10–11.

[160] People v. Balcom, 7 Cal. 4th 414, 418, 867 P.2d 777, 779, 27 Cal. Rptr. 2d 666, 668 (1994).

[161] *Id.*

[162] Dillon v. State, 311 Ark. 529, 844 S.W.2d 944 (1993).

[163] *Id.* at 541–42, 844 S.W.2d at 950 (but reversing the defendant's conviction because of the prosecution's insinuations during cross-examination about other acts of misconduct for which there was no substantiation); Pendleton v. Commonwealth, 685 S.W.2d 549, 552 (Ky. 1985) ("Evidence of other crimes of sexual misconduct is also admissible for the purpose of showing motive, a common pattern, scheme or plan.").

[164] Burmingham v. State, 342 Ark. 95, 27 S.W.3d 351 (2000).

[165] State v. DeRoche, 629 So. 2d 1267, 1272 (La. Ct. App. 1993).

[166] State v. Hewett, 93 N.C. App. 1, 10, 376 S.E.2d 467, 473 (1989) ("[I]t is the practice in this state 'liberally' to admit evidence of similar sex crimes under this exception.").

The introduction of common plan evidence can be defeated on several grounds. One is that the prejudicial value of the evidence outweighs its probative value. A second is the remoteness of the prior uncharged conduct. For instance, evidence of prior conduct involving an older daughter that occurred eight or more years earlier was prejudicial to a defendant due to its remoteness to the current charges.[167] A third ground is the lack of sufficient similarity between the uncharged and charged acts. The nature of the sexual abuse may be different, therefore establishing a non-common element. The common plan can be challenged if the only similarity is the abuse of a child, which is not unique. Some courts emphasize and stress that the common plan or scheme requires that the sexual assaults be part of an overarching plan of the defendant, and that the crimes should not be independent of one another.[168]

One court has criticized the common plan or scheme exception in sexual assault cases as having become "a series of crimes theory" and more evidence of propensity than a common scheme or plan that connects the misconduct with the present crime, with the effect being that "[t]he exception, in effect, engulfs the rule."[169] With this in mind, a defendant's conviction was reversed because the defendant's prior acts, which were admitted, were not that unusual and distinctive.[170] The court concluded, "It may be sad commentary of society in 1993, but the luring of young boys into a barn with the promises of working on machinery and looking at dirty pictures with the purpose of sodomizing them cannot . . . be held that unusual or distinctive to support corroborative testimony."[171]

---

[167] United States v. Fawbush, 900 F.2d 150 (8th Cir. 1990).

[168] Rosky v. State, 2005 Nev. LEXIS 18, 111 P.3d 690 (Nev. 2005):

> We cannot conclude that the instant offense and the prior bad acts were part of a single preconceived overarching plan that resulted in improper sexual contact with CJW. These crimes were independent of one another, and neither could be planned until each victim came within reach. Finally, the prior bad act took place some eight years before the instant event. We therefore conclude that the district court abused its discretion in admitting evidence of Rosky's prior bad acts as evidence of a common scheme or plan.

[169] State v. Bernard, 849 S.W.2d 10, 16 (Mo. 1993).

[170] State v. Bird, 854 S.W.2d 807, 810 (Mo. Ct. App. 1993).

[171] Id. at 810. See also Kulling v. State, 827 So. 2d 311 (Fla. Ct. App. 2002):

> The State argues that Kulling's acts share unique characteristics in that Kulling 'Makes eye contact with female victims, gets sexually aroused and pleasures himself in front of them. The women are nearby neighbors who can identify him.' While there are similarities between the cases, the acts described by the State contain no characteristics that are so unusual as to point to Kulling or constitute 'fingerprint' evidence. In fact, the State describes actions typical of any perpetrator who masturbates in public. Similar crime evidence is not admissible simply because it involves the same type of offense.

827 So. 2d at 314; Farrill v. State, 759 So. 2d 696 (Fla. Dist. Ct. App. 2000) (engaging in oral and vaginal sex with young girls between the ages of six and nine not so unique in determining

Other courts, too, have rejected the common plan or scheme exception because there is little unique or distinctive similarity in the prior and current abuse.

Improperly admitting prior acts as part of a common plan or scheme are likely to be prejudicial and result in reversal of a conviction.[172]

§ 6.39　Admitting evidence of defendant's prior conduct to establish defendant's identity on *modus operandi*.

When the identity of a perpetrator is in issue, but not so much the occurrence of the act, evidence of a defendant's prior acts is admissible to establish identity. To trigger this exception, identity should be at issue. When there is no issue that the defendant is the person who had sexual contact with the complainant, the prejudicial effect of such evidence outweighs its probative value.[173] Unlike the common plan or design theory, the prior acts and the charged crime should possess unique, unusual, and distinctive characteristics to permit the logical inference that the same person committed the acts. The unique elements may be the way the crime is committed, the location of the crime, the characteristics of the victim, the voice of the defendant, and words articulated or conduct of the defendant during the crime.

For example, uniqueness between a prior crime and pending crime is established when the prior burglary and sexual assault took place within three or four blocks of the crime for which the defendant is on trial, both crimes took place less than three blocks of the defendant's home, the earlier incident involved a seven-year-old girl and the present incident involved an eight-year-old girl, the earlier incident involved the cutting of the child's nightgown and the present incident involved pulling down the child's underpants while she lay in bed, and in both instances the defendant used a flashlight.[174] Evidence of a similarity

---

similarity of criminal acts); State v. Sweeney, 999 P.2d 296 (Mont. 2000); State v. Rogers, 992 P.2d 229, 236 (Mont. 1999) (court found that there was nothing particularly distinctive in meeting women at a bar, driving them to a secluded area, and having sexual relations with them to bring those acts within exception for other acts evidence: "Indeed, the other acts evidence in this case . . . suggests only that Rogers will spontaneously take advantage of opportunities that present themselves for sexual encounters with women. In other words, Rogers' acts of sexual aggression are dictated by his character and the situation at hand; they do not reflect a systematic plan . . . .").

172 United States v. Has No Horse, 11 F.3d 104, 106 (8th Cir. 1993) (holding that defendant's prior sexual advances toward two teenage girls was not part of a common plan or scheme and represented inadmissible propensity evidence); Prickett v. State, 220 Ga. App. 244, 245, 469 S.E.2d 371, 373 (1996) (fact that defendant previously drove by two girls on a tractor, "grabbed his groin, flicked his tongue, and gestured with the middle finger of his hand" not sufficiently similar to charge of raping 15-year-old babysitter and impermissibly placed his character in issue); State v. Burress, 1995 Neb. App. LEXIS 141 (Apr. 18, 1995) (evidence of defendant's prior digital penetration of a 19-year-old woman is not probative of defendant's guilt involving allegations of digital penetration of a four or five-year-old child; court noted that acts which violate the same statute have a higher probative value than acts that do not).

173 Rosky v. State, 2005 Nev. LEXIS 18, 111 P.3d 690 (Nev. 2005).

174 Commonwealth v. Vosburg, 393 Pa. Super. 416, 574 A.2d 679 (1990), *appeal denied*, 529 Pa. 648, 602 A.2d 859 (1991).

in the injuries inflicted upon a prior victim, and the injuries sustained by the complainant in the pending charge, such as bite marks or genital injuries, may permit the introduction of the defendant's past conduct to establish identity.[175] The unique activity may consist of having sexual relations with the victim after killing her and posing the body.[176]

Common physical characteristics of victims and how they are approached may establish identifying elements, even if the prior approaches did not result in a consummated crime. Thus, in a murder prosecution, a defendant's prior approach to teenage, blond-haired girls walking on sparsely populated roads was relevant as the issue of identity in his murder prosecution of a similarly approached female who physically resembled the other girls.[177] While the prior acts may only "be suspicious or distasteful, it is only in retrospect that they take on a more sinister visage" and therefore have probative value.[178]

The location and timing of the sexual assaults may provide them a "signature quality."[179] The instrument used, such as an electrical cord, during a sexual assault may also be sufficiently unique to connect sexual assaults.[180]

---

[175] People v. Smith, 63 N.Y.2d 41, 468 N.E.2d 879, 479 N.Y.S.2d 706 (1984), *cert. denied*, 469 U.S. 1227 (1985) (upholding the admission of a bite mark inflicted by the defendant upon an unrelated victim, which the defendant admitted inflicting several years earlier, which was compared to a bite mark in the present case, in which the defendant was alleged to have bitten off the victim's nipples); State v. Moseley, 338 N.C. 1, 39, 449 S.E.2d 412, 436, *cert. denied*, 514 U.S. 1091 (1994) (slides of genital injuries sustained by defendant's previous victim admissible to establish similarities of attacks on the two victims and the identity of perpetrator).

[176] State v. Russell, 125 Wash. 2d 24, 66–68, 882 P.2d 747, 774–75 (1994), *cert. denied*, 514 U.S. 1129 (1995) (uniqueness included, among other factors, sexually assaulting victims after killing them and then posing victims with the aid of props).

[177] Smithart v. State, 946 P.2d 1264 (Alaska Ct. App. 1997).

[178] *Id.* at 1273.

[179] United States v. Bailey, 111 F.3d 1229 (5th Cir.), *cert. denied*, 522 U.S. 927 (1997):

> The Government maintains that the evidence shows that there were substantial similarities among the three incidents. All three took place uninvited in the homes of single women living on Fort Hood; all occurred during pre-dawn hours; and each victim was physically touched in some way without consent, two of whom were touched while they were sleeping. Bailey correctly points out that the facts that the women were all single and were physically touched in some way while they were sleeping is not compelling because these are characteristics shared by a number of sexual assaults. However, the location and timing of each intrusion — Fort Hood during pre-dawn hours — is of signature quality.

Id. at 1234.

[180] Harmon v. State, 908 P.2d 434 (Alaska Ct. App. 1995) (in each rape, attacker was armed with a knife and used an electrical cord to tie up his victims); State v. Hudgins, 810 S.W.2d 664, 666 (Mo. Ct. App. 1991) (Evidence of prior abuse that involved an electric extension cord was admissible to help identify the defendant: "In the instant action, the evidence showed that there was no mistake in the witness's identification of the electric cord as belonging to defendant. The evidence was relevant because it linked defendant to the cord allegedly used to strangle the child. The testimony also established why the witness was familiar with that particular cord and why she was able to connect the cord with defendant.").

Another example of uniqueness between a defendant's prior acts and pending charges involved six rapes allegedly committed by the defendant during the five months preceding the crime for which the defendant was on trial. The defendant followed his victims to an apartment, used force or a ruse to enter the apartment, grabbed each victim by the throat, threatened to strangle the victim if she did not comply, rummaged through the victim's lingerie, directed the victim to wear a slip if he found one, and in several of the cases used pantyhose to bind the victim. His mention to the victims of his wife or fiancée, or stories about them, and four of the six women being able to describe a similar pattern in the assailant's voice — that it was low or deep — and that he articulated words well and spoke in a calm, steady tone,[181] utilizing the pretext of looking for an apartment,[182] or approaching victims and asking for help in finding his dog,[183] may be a sufficiently distinctive aspect of a sexual assault to establish identity. In general, courts will permit evidence of prior acts to establish identity when any fact or combination of facts creates an inference that one person committed all acts.[184] If some of the victims did not see the perpetrator, or the

---

[181] People v. Allweiss, 48 N.Y.2d 40, 396 N.E.2d 735, 421 N.Y.S.2d 341 (1979).

[182] State v. Brown, 41 Conn. App. 317, 675 A.2d 1369 (1996), *rev'd on other grounds*, 242 Conn. 445, 700 A.2d 1089 (1997) (in prosecution where defendant was accused of sexually assaulting a woman under pretext of looking for an apartment for his sister, evidence that he had previously approached another apartment under similar circumstances was admissible on the issue of identity).

[183] State v. Vince, 305 So. 2d 916 (La. 1974) (upholding the use of two prior rapes, similar to the current charge, in that the defendant approached a victim asking for help in finding his dog and stole jewelry as part of the rape).

[184] Harmon v. State, 908 P.2d 434, 436–38 (Alaska Ct. App. 1995) (evidence of defendant's prior sexual assaults was sufficiently distinctive to be relevant to establishing identity — defendant's meeting victim socially, being rejected, consuming alcohol, physically assaulting victim, using knife and using an electrical cord during the assault); State v. Van Adams, 194 Ariz. 408, 984 P.2d 16 (1999), *cert. denied*, 528 U.S. 1172 (2000) (court upheld trial court's admission into evidence of defendant's prior sexual assaults on young sales agents in residential real estate sales office, all occurring during day, and similar attacks to help establish defendant's identity as well as defendant's opportunity and intent); State v. Figueroa, 235 Conn. 145, 665 A.2d 63, 76 (1995) (Following similarities of rape defendant's crime held relevant to issue of identity: "(1) both offenses occurred at night, to lone women; (2) in each instance, the assailant kidnapped the victim and held a knife to her throat; (3) both victims were forced into the passenger seat of their own cars and were warned not to look at the assailant; (4) the assailant drove both of the victims' cars for a considerable period of time; (5) both assaults occurred near a particular barn at the Culbro tobacco field, where the defendant had previously worked; (6) in each instance the assailant attempted to remove the victim's clothes; (7) both assaults involved a demand for oral sex; (8) in each instance, the assailant abandoned an attempt to perform or request a specific sex act when the victim resisted; (9) each victim described her assailant as an Hispanic male with similar features; and (10) both assaults occurred within weeks of each other"); State v. Champ, 2001 Neb. App. LEXIS 61 (Mar. 20, 2001) (Court found that how victims were located, approached, positioned, spoken to, and assaulted were sufficiently similar to be probative of defendant's identity:

> In both sexual assaults, the evidence established that the assaults occurred in the evening in deserted rooms on college campuses. In each case, the assailant grabbed the victim from behind, demanded money, covered the victim's head, turned off the

defendant denies being in the room where the assault occurred, this may raise a sufficient basis for the introduction of the defendant's prior acts of abuse committed in a similar manner.[185]

To qualify under the identity exception there must be more than one or two similarities pertaining to the manner in which the crime was committed, how and what type of force was used, the time of the crime, the location of the crime, or the characteristics of the victim. General similarities or just one or two similar aspects will not be sufficient to establish true *modus operandi* in the view of many, but not all, courts.[186] For example, an attacker in a dark jacket approaching

lights in the room, and made the victim lie face down. The assailant performed digital anal penetration of H.H. and attempted penile anal penetration of L.G., and in both cases the assailant used saliva or another lubricant. Ultimately, both victims were required to roll over onto their backs, at which point they were penetrated vaginally until the assailant ejaculated. Sexual questions were posed to both victims, including how they had lost their virginity, and both described their assailant as having good usage of the English language and sounding intelligent and educated. In summary, the two assailants are remarkably similar.

Id. at *11. State v. Carter, 246 Neb. 953, 964–65, 524 N.W.2d 763, 773 (1994) (In murder prosecution involving child victim, court permitted evidence of prior sexual assaults of the half-sister and daughters of the defendant in the present case where similarities included that all were young girls, all were subjected to multiple assaults, all assaults occurred at the defendant's residence, his mother's residence, or the victim's residence, all the victims had a familial or family-like relationship to the defendant, all the sexual assaults occurred while the defendant had exclusive control or custody of the girls, and all girls were incapable of giving consent. Court ruled that absolute identity in every detail was not required, but that a qualitative evaluation demonstrated there were enough similarities for purpose of identity (as well as for purposes of showing the defendant's motive)); Bolin v. State, 114 Nev. 503, 521, 960 P.2d 784, 796 (1998), *cert. denied*, 525 U.S. 1179 (1999) (two crimes were probative of identity of attacker where, "[i]n both, young white women of similar age, complexion and build were abducted in their vehicles late at night, their wedding rings and other valuables taken, and their vehicles used to secrete them to remote locations where they were subjected to brutal sexual assaults"); People v. Rossman, 95 A.D.2d 873, 463 N.Y.S.2d 891 (1983) (admitting on the issue of identity the defendant's prior cutting of a young woman's hair in a subsequent prosecution of which defendant was accused of robbery in cutting and taking the complainant's hair—given the issue of identity and the lack of identification by the victim).

[185] State v. Hammer, 236 Wis. 2d 686, 704–06, 613 N.W.2d 629, 637–38 (2000).

[186] Hayes v. State, 660 So. 2d 257 (Fla. 1995) (insufficient similarity between past sexual assault where victim had voluntarily gone out with the defendant before returning with defendant to her room and resulting charge was only simple assault and no sexual assault and instant offense which involved a forcible sexual assault even though both females were grooms working with the defendant at a racetrack); Peek v. State, 488 So. 2d 52, 55 (Fla. 1986); State v. Sweeney, 999 P.2d 296 (Mont. 2000):

In this case, there is some similarity between the age and gender of the victim and the sexual behavior involved in the 1988–89 sexual assault and the 1996 sexual assault, however, there are also a number of differences. The sexual behavior involved in 1988–89 included Sweeney getting on top of his five-year-old stepdaughter, licking her genitalia, and placing her hands on his penis. With regard to the 1996 assault, Sweeney's nine-year-old niece testified that Sweeney had licked her genitalia and

an elderly woman in a neighborhood is too general a characteristic to be a common plan in the opinion of one court.[187] Evidence that a defendant

> had on another occasion unbuttoned her shirt and pants and touched her chest. In addition, Sweeney's niece testified that on the occasion where he had unbuttoned her clothing, Sweeney had put his hand over her mouth to stop her from screaming and told her to shut up.
>
> As repulsive as Sweeney's alleged conduct may be on both occasions, it is not necessarily distinctive in the context of sexual assaults. Sweeney allegedly performed acts, involving different victims, of a nature that unfortunately give rise to many sexual assault cases. There is nothing in Sweeney's alleged conduct that was sufficiently distinctive to warrant an inference that since he committed the prior sexual assault he must have committed the sexual assault in 1996. For prior sexual conduct or convictions to be admissible in order to establish identity in a subsequent prosecution, there must be something distinctive about the conduct, not just the fact that the defendant committed a prior sexual assault, which points to the defendant as the perpetrator. There was nothing particularly distinctive here. As such, we conclude that the evidence of Sweeney's prior sexual assault conviction was improperly admitted for the purpose of proving Sweeney's identity as the perpetrator of the 1996 sexual assault.

Id. at 302. *See* Avila v. State, 18 S.W.3d 736 (Tex. App. 2000) (reversing defendant's conviction due to admission of prior sexual assault, involving other women in a particular city, since similar cities were common to type of crime in general, not peculiar to the offenses); State v. McDaniel, 211 W. Va. 9, 560 S.E.2d 484 (2001) Court reversed defendant's conviction because similarities between rape 12 years earlier involving rape of woman whose apartment was broken into by defendant were too general with too many dissimilarities. Court observed:

> The two alleged incidents are similar because in both instances, the attacker broke into a victim's home at night. However, the incident against Ms. D. allegedly involved a forcible beating and rape, where the attacker forced his way to complete sexual assault, despite the victim's strenuous and lengthy efforts to fight off her attacker. In contrast, Ms. O. did not make any allegation of a beating or an attempt to rape. Further, Ms. O. testified that she woke up to a touching, and ordered her attacker out of her bedroom, whereupon Mr. McDaniel left. Ms. D. testified that she was physically attacked by a single individual. Ms. O., in contrast, testified that two people were present in her home during her attack. Ms. D. testified that she had no further contact with her attacker, while Ms. O. testified that the defendant attempted to contact her several times soon after the incident.

Id. at 14, 560 S.E.2d at 489.

[187] Commonwealth v. Bryant, 515 Pa. 473, 530 A.2d 83, 86 (1987) defendant's conviction reversed due to the introduction of a prior crime, where the only similarities were that the crimes were committed by someone with a dark jacket against elderly women in the same neighborhood. The court held:

> In short, there is not evidence of a 'common scheme' or 'such a logical connection between the two crimes' that one would naturally conclude that the same individual was responsible for both crimes. . . . There may be some similarities to be perceived between the crimes, but those similarities are confined to relatively insignificant details that would likely be common elements regardless of who had committed the crimes. . . . A number of differences between the two crimes could also be noted, such as the fact that the perpetrator of the earlier crime defecated on the floor in the victim's house whereas nothing comparable occurred in connection with the instant

subsequently engaged in a "peeping tom" incident is not "uniquely similar to entering a locked home through a window and touching a woman's vagina while masturbating."[188]

Evidence of a defendant's prior sexual abuse of the complainant's siblings may be admissible in a situation where the defendant seeks to portray someone else as the offender.[189]

The theory of identity has also been cited as a reason to admit prior abuse between a defendant and complainant.[190] However, this would not conform with the majority definition of this exception.

Prior actions of a defendant that are sexually oriented, but not a crime or bad act, may be admissible on the issue of identity.[191]

§ 6.40 Admitting evidence of defendant's prior conduct under the "lustful inclination," "depraved sexual instinct," or "amorous design" theory.

In cases involving child sexual assault, several jurisdictions have admitted evidence of a defendant's prior conduct to demonstrate that a defendant had a "lustful inclination" or "amorous design" toward the victim or toward children generally, where the prior acts were fairly close in time to the incident giving rise to the charges for which the defendant was being tried.[192] Rarely has the

---

crime, but, inasmuch as features which the two crimes had in common were lacking, it is not necessary to further address such differences.

[188] People v. Reilly, 19 A.D.3d 736, 796 N.Y.S.2d 726 (2005).

[189] United States v. Yellow, 18 F.3d 1438, 1441 (8th Cir. 1994).

[190] United States v. Butler, 56 F.3d 941, 944 (8th Cir.), cert. denied, 516 U.S. 924 (1995) (defendant denied ever being alone with complainant in a room and court held evidence of prior sexual abuse was relevant to identity).

[191] State v. Gaines, 260 Kan. 752, 926 P.2d 641 (1996) (In a rape case in which defendant was charged with rape and sodomy and sucking the victim's toe similar to a thumb, the prosecution was properly allowed to present defendant's ex-wife's testimony that he did the same type of toe-sucking on five occasions during their one-year marriage because this was relevant to the defense of identity. The Court noted that toe sucking is not a character trait or character evidence. The Kansas Supreme Court ruled that the toe sucking of defendant was relevant to the identity of the perpetrator.).

[192] State v. Roscoe, 184 Ariz. 484, 910 P.2d 635 (Ariz.) (en banc), cert. denied, 519 U.S. 854 (1996); State v. Phillips, 102 Ariz. 377, 379, 430 P.2d 139, 141 (1967); Thompson v. State, 322 Ark. 586, 910 S.W.2d 694 (1995); State v. James, 211 Conn. 555, 578, 560 A.2d 426, 439 (1989); Parker v. United States, 751 A.2d 943 (D.C. 2000); Saffor v. State, 660 So. 2d 668, 672 (Fla. 1995) ("The additional showing of similarity will vary depending on the facts of the case and must be determined on a case-by-case basis. Thus, we do not eliminate the requirement of similarity . . . . However, the strict similarity in the nature of the offenses and the circumstances surrounding their commission which would be required in cases occurring outside the familial context is relaxed by virtue of the evidence proving that both crimes were committed in the familial context.");

(Text continued on page 489)

Gutherez v. State, 809 So. 2d 16 (Fla. Ct. App. 2002) (applying exception, even though defendant and victim's mother were roommates and technically not in a familial relationship); Pastor v. State, 792 So. 2d 627 (Fla. Ct. App. 2001) (reversing defendant's conviction, *citing Saffor*, because state failed to establish enough similarities: "The victim and the brother were not the same age or gender, the duration of the abuse differed, the location where the abuse occurred differed, the time of the abuse differed, and the manner of abuse differed."); Eggleston v. State, 247 Ga. App. 540, 544 S.E.2d 722 (2001); Swift v. State, 229 Ga. App. 772, 774, 495 S.E.2d 109, 112 (1997) (holding defendant's prior sexual acts with siblings ten years earlier admissible to show defendant's "bent of mind"); Morgan v. State, 226 Ga. App. 327, 328, 486 S.E.2d 632, 634 (1997) ("In crimes involving sexual offenses, evidence of similar transactions is admissible to show the lustful disposition of the defendant and to corroborate the victim's testimony. There need only be evidence that the defendant was the perpetrator of both acts and sufficient similarity or connection between the independent transaction and the offenses charged.") (*citing* Hathcock v. State, 214 Ga. App. 188, 192, 447 S.E.2d 104 (1994)); Fitzgerald v. State, 193 Ga. App. 76, 77, 386 S.E.2d 914, 917 (1989) (stating that in sexually oriented crimes, evidence of prior acts is admissible to show lustful disposition and to corroborate the testimony of a victim as to acts charged); People v. Failor, 271 Ill. App. 3d 968, 649 N.E.2d 1342, *appeal denied*, 163 Ill. 2d 570, 657 N.E.2d 629 (1995), *cert. denied*, 516 U.S. 1134 (1996) ("In sex offense cases involving child victims, evidence of prior sexual acts between the defendant and the child victim is admissible to show intent, design, course of conduct, the intimate relationship between the parties, or to corroborate the victim's testimony regarding the charged offense." *Id.* at 971, 649 N.E.2d at 1344); People v. Jahn, 246 Ill. App. 3d 689, 705–06, 615 N.E.2d 1270, 1281, *appeal denied*, 152 Ill.2d 569, 622 N.E.2d 1217 (1993) (holding defendant's prior conduct with some child admissible to prove a course of conduct and corroborate the victim's testimony); People v. Wilson, 246 Ill. App. 3d 311, 320, 615 N.E.2d 1283, 1288, *appeal denied*, 152 Ill. 2d 578, 622 N.E.2d 1225 (1993); State v. Maestas, 224 N.W.2d 248, 251 (Iowa 1974); State v. Malvoisin, 779 So. 2d 73 (La. Ct. App. 2001); State v. Johnson, 670 So. 2d 651 (La. Ct. App. 1996) ("In a prosecution for the commission of rape of a female under the age of consent, the evidence of prior sex offenses committed by the defendant with the same prosecutrix is generally admissible. Such evidence has been admitted for various reasons, such as corroboration of the offense charged, to show intimate relations between the parties, the lustful disposition of the defendant and the probability of his having committed the offense charged, or to rebut the defense of alibi."). *Id.* at 658, *citing* State v. Morgan, 296 So. 2d 286, 288 (La. 1974)); State v. Allen, 647 So. 2d 428, 434–35 (La. Ct. App. 1994) (holding that defendant's prior abuse of two young female relatives who had been molested by the defendant was "admissible to show the defendant's 'lustful disposition' toward young female relatives and his motivation by an unnatural interest in prepubescent females"); Mitchell v. State, 539 So. 2d 1366 (Miss. 1989); Findley v. State, 94 Nev. 212, 214, 577 P.2d 867, 868 (1978); State v. Reeder, 105 N.C. App. 343, 413 S.E.2d 580, *review denied*, 331 N.C. 290, 417 S.E.2d 68 (1992); State v. Shively, 172 Ohio St. 128, 131, 174 N.E.2d 104, 107 (1961); State v. Sexton, 1998 Ohio App. LEXIS 1302 (Mar. 9, 1998) ("Therefore, evidence of physical, emotional, and verbal abuse which transpires in a home between the defendant and his children, may be relevant and probative of a method of control used to force sex upon his son, thus being inextricably related to the charge of rape." *Id.* at *10–11.); State v. Greene, 823 A.2d 1129 (R.I. 2003); State v. Kilgore, 147 Wash. 2d 288, 53 P.3d 974 (2002); State v. Schut, 71 Wash. 2d 400, 402, 429 P.2d 126 (1967); State v. McIntosh, 207 W. Va. 561, 534 S.E.2d 757 (2000) (upholding the lustful disposition exception in a case involving defendant teacher and his teenage students); State v. Edward Charles L., 183 W. Va. 641, 651, 398 S.E.2d 123, 133 (1990); State v. Hunt, 263 Wis. 2d 1, 46, 666 N.W.2d 771, 793 (2003), *citing* State v. Davidson, 236 Wis. 2d 537, 613 N.W.2d 606 (2000) (noting Wisconsin's greater latitude test in reviewing admissibility of other acts evidence in sexual assault cases); State v. Tarrell, 74 Wis. 2d 647, 648, 247 N.W.2d 696, 703 (1976).

"lustful disposition" been applied to sexual assaults upon adult victims.[193]

By statute, some states, such as Texas, permit in certain child abuse cases evidence of defendant's prior bad acts to establish the previous and subsequent relationship between the defendant and child as well as state of mind of the defendant and child.[194]

Kentucky and Louisiana both hold that the "lustful disposition" theory is not limited to intrafamilial situations.[195] However, other courts continue to limit the lustful disposition exception to prior acts between the defendant and the victim of the charged offense.[196] In Louisiana, the lustful disposition exception to prior acts is not applicable unless the other acts are to prove a specific element of the crime charged, "unless the State is able to demonstrate that the other crimes evidence is independently relevant under either a statutory or judicially-recognized exception to this general exclusionary rule."[197] This decision was overruled by a statute permitting evidence of other prior sexual offenses, subject to a weighing of prejudicial effect, in sex crimes involving a victim less than 17 at the time of the offense.[198] Federal Rules of Evidence 413 and 414, as well as states with similar statutes admitting evidence of prior sexual acts for any relevant purpose, including propensity are discussed in § 6.31.

One court has also spoken of a pedophile exception to show sexual proclivity toward a class of persons.[199] Another court referred to a defendant's "unnatural

---

[193] State v. Crawford, 672 So. 2d 197 (La. Ct. App.), *cert. denied*, 679 So. 2d 1379 (La. 1996) ("While the details of the various attacks were not so similar so as to produce a distinct *modus operandi*, we find the trial judge properly admitted the testimonies because they . . . show a pattern and intent or "lustful disposition" on defendant's part to force women, with either a knife or through strangulation and brute force, to engage in nonconsensual sex. . . . However, we see no reason to deviate from those holdings [in cases establishing the lustful disposition] simply because the victims in the incidents involving Crawford were neither minors nor relatives." *Id.* at 210.).

[194] TEX. CODE CRIM. PROC. ANN. art. 38.37.

[195] Pendleton v. Commonwealth, 83 S.W.3d 522 (Ky. 2002) (victim permitted to testify to multiple acts of abuse by defendant and fact that some incidents were not charged was not improper in light of KY. RULE EVID. 404(b)(1)); State v. Miller, 718 So. 2d 960, 966 (La. 1998) (holding prosecution's evidence that "defendant's statement to his neighbor's child that he had seen her naked in his bedroom with her arms and legs open was admissible to show his intent to molest the victim of the charged offense and to show that the molestation was not an accident").

[196] Lambert v. State, 724 So. 2d 392, 394 (Miss. 1998) ("The state would have this Court expand [the lustful disposition exception] to include testimony that shows a defendant's character of lustful behavior toward children in general . . . . Such an expansion would not be consistent with the purposes of M.R.E. 404(b), not consistent with the notion that a defendant is on trial for a specific crime and not for generally being a bad person.").

[197] State v. Kennedy, 803 So. 2d 916, 920 (La. 2001). *See also* State v. Morgan, 830 So. 2d 304 (La. Ct. App. 2002); State v. Smith, 815 So. 2d 412 (La. Ct. App. 2002).

[198] LA. CODE EVID. 412.2.

[199] Hathcock v. State, 357 Ark. 563 (2004) (In a case involving defendant's uncharged conduct of playing a game called "Texas Titty Twister" in which he twisted the nipples of members of his family, such evidence was admissible under Arkansas pedophile exception, which permits

lust for female students under his authority" as justification for admitting other sexual acts with students.[200]

While noting that the lewd disposition exception should be sparingly used, Rhode Island's court has permitted it to demonstrate the special relationship between a defendant and victim in a child sexual assault case.[201] The same court reversed a conviction where the lewd disposition was not deemed necessary to establish material elements or facts of the crime.[202]

Part of the rationale for the amorous design exception is that it provides a fair opportunity for the jury to assess the credibility of the witnesses. The lustful inclination or amorous design exception is, in effect, a rule that permits the use of a defendant's prior uncharged acts to establish predisposition on the part of the defendant. One court, in admitting such evidence in an incest case, noted that permitting evidence of other intercourse or acts between a victim and the defendant either before or after the time period set forth in an indictment was "admissible for the purpose of throwing light upon the relations of the parties and the incestuous disposition of the defendant toward the other party, and to corroborate the proof of the act relied upon for conviction."[203]

A defendant's statement about his predisposition toward a child may be admissible on a theory other than lustful disposition. For example, a defendant's statement to police that he has "a problem with girls" and "never was interested in older women, just young girls and teenage girls" may be relevant to explain the defendant's luring of a young child victim as well as to explain the defendant's motive and intent if at issue in a trial.[204]

---

evidence of similar acts with same or other children in the same house in cases of child abuse or incest); Clark v. State, 323 Ark. 211, 215, 913 S.W.2d 297, 299 (1996) (evidence of similar acts with the same child or other children admissible under "pedophile exception" to show a proclivity toward a specific act with a person or class of persons with whom the defendant has an intimate relationship); Hyatt v. State, 63 Ark. App. 114, 975 S.W.2d 443 (1998) (reiterating Arkansas's "pedophile exception," permitting proof of similar acts with same child or other children in same household when helpful to show proclivity toward a specific act with a person or class of persons with whom an accused has an intimate relationship).

[200] Campbell v. State, 1997 Ala. Crim. App. LEXIS 385 *22 (Aug. 22, 1997).

[201] State v. Gomes, 690 A.2d 310 (R.I. 1997) (Rhode Island's Supreme Court noted that the lewd disposition exception should be sparingly used and excluded when merely cumulative. The Court noted that the other acts should be related to a particular reason — such as common scheme or special relationship — and that the trial court should designate the appropriate reasons and provide the jury with limiting instructions. In this case, the court held the uncharged acts demonstrated the special relationship with her grandfather, a common scheme, and the special relationship between the defendant and victim.).

[202] State v. Quattrocchi, 681 A.2d 879 (R.I. 1996).

[203] Brown v. Commonwealth, 208 Va. 512, 516–17, 158 S.E.2d 663, 667 (1968).

[204] State v. Covell, 157 N.J. 554, 725 A.2d 675 (1999).

The constitutionality of the "lustful disposition" exception has been upheld on the theory that it must still pass a balancing test where its probative value is weighed against its danger of unfair prejudice.[205]

Other jurisdictions reject the amorous design exception. Holding that corroboration of a victim's testimony was not necessary and that no specific intent was required for the crime, New York's Court of Appeals held that inadmissible testimony concerning uncharged acts of intercourse between a defendant and the victim was improperly received and abrogated the amorous design rule:

> [The victim's] allegation concerning defendant's prior actions did not render her testimony pertaining to the crime more trustworthy because a witness cannot buttress her own testimony by making further unsubstantiated accusations. The victim's statements regarding the prior uncharged crimes, therefore, carried no probative weight. [citation omitted] Apparently the evidence was offered to explain why [the victim] did not resist her father's advances, but the presence or absence of resistance was irrelevant to whether defendant committed [the crime]. It could do no more than permit the jury to speculate that if defendant committed [the crime] before, he must have done so again.[206]

In rejecting the "depraved sexual instinct" exception, the Supreme Court of Missouri held:

> A blanket rule allowing evidence of any recent misconduct by the defendant with a child of the same sex as the victim may encourage the jury to convict the defendant because of his propensity to commit such crimes without regard to whether he is actually guilty of the crime charged.[207]

Other states have also rejected the "lustful disposition" exception as being unduly prejudicial.[208] A complainant's testimony of other offenses in no way

---

[205] Kerr v. Caspari, 956 F.2d 788, 790 (8th Cir. 1992).

[206] People v. Lewis, 69 N.Y.2d 321, 328, 506 N.E.2d 915, 918–19, 514 N.Y.S.2d 205, 209 (1987). *See also* Lantrip v. Commonwealth, 713 S.W.2d 816, 817 (Ky. 1986) ("Prior acts are no longer admissible for the purpose of showing lustful inclination.").

[207] State v. Bernard, 849 S.W.2d 10, 16 (Mo. 1993) (but finding that certain prior sexual acts that are sufficiently unusual and distinctive may be admissible such as the defendant directing children to run naked in front of, or sit naked upon, slow-moving vehicle; however, testimony that the defendant had in the past possessed and displayed nude photographs of children to other children was similar to behavior alleged in the present case, but not so unusual and distinctive as to be a signature of the defendant's *modus operandi*). *See also* Bell v. Commonwealth, 875 S.W.2d 882, 890 (Ky. 1994) (As for the prejudice side, there exists universal agreement that evidence of this sort is inherently and highly prejudicial to a defendant. It is very difficult for jurors to sift and separate such damaging information to avoid the natural inclination to view it as evidence of a defendant's criminal disposition, especially in child sexual abuse cases. For this reason, a trial judge must consider whether a clear instruction limiting the jury's use to its *proper* purpose is likely to be effective.).

[208] Lannan v. State, 600 N.E.2d 1334 (Ind. 1992); State v. Nelson, 331 S.C. 1, 501 S.E.2d 716 (1998); State v. Tizard, 897 S.W.2d 732, 744 (Tenn. Crim. App. 1994).

strengthens the witness's testimony as to the offenses charged, unless the probative value of such evidence is outweighed by its prejudicial effect.[209]

An example of the argument that prior unsubstantiated allegations do not provide probative evidence is *People v. Hudy*,[210] which involved a teacher charged with sexual abuse of eight students. The prosecution offered testimony concerning a student who had previously made allegations against the teacher on the theory that, since this accusation was made before those of the current victims, the current allegations were more credible. However, this evidence was deemed prejudicial because the defendant's prior misconduct toward another student had "no legitimate, legally cognizable bearing on the truthfulness of the other children's allegations."[211] This approach holds that the use of such prior misconduct evidence is yet another way of saying that if the defendant did it to another child, he did it again. The court also noted that the admission of this evidence was highly prejudicial because the alleged prior victim's testimony was "qualitatively different from the testimony of the other boys, in that it was not subject to impeachment on the defense's 'rumor theory.'"[212]

Evidence of prior uncharged acts was not available to rebut the allegation that the victim and her mother fabricated charges of sexual abuse since there was not necessarily a logical relevance between other acts involving the victim's sibling and the credibility of the current charges.[213] Once again, the reason for this exclusion is simply that the probative value is outweighed by unfair prejudice and is also only minimally relevant.

---

[209] People v. Stanley, 67 Cal. 2d 812, 433 P.2d 913, 63 Cal. Rptr. 825 (1967); Braunstein v. State, 40 P.3d 413, 118 Nev. 68 (2002):

> We specifically overrule the legal proposition enunciated in Findley that evidence of other acts offered to prove a specific emotional propensity for sexual aberration is admissible and that, when offered, it outweighs prejudice. In so doing we ensure that the trial courts will always properly weigh the probative value of the evidence against the risk that the defendant will be unfairly prejudiced by its admission.

Id. at 418. *See generally* Timothy E. Travers, Annotation, *Admissibility, in Rape Case, of Evidence That Accused Raped or Attempted to Rape Person Other Than Prosecutrix,* 2 A.L.R.4th 330 (1980).

[210] 73 N.Y.2d 40, 535 N.E.2d 250, 538 N.Y.S.2d 197 (1988).

[211] *Id.*, 73 N.Y.2d at 55, 535 N.E.2d at 259, 538 N.Y.S.2d at 206.

[212] *Id. See also* People v. Peters, 187 A.D.2d 883, 884, 590 N.Y.S.2d 916, 916–18 (1992), *appeal denied,* 81 N.Y.2d 891, 613 N.E.2d 984, 597 N.Y.S.2d 952 (1993) (trial court committed reversible error when it admitted testimony about a school teacher's prior consensual sexual relationship with a 17-year-old female student, since this testimony was not relevant to any issue in the case other than showing the defendant's propensity to commit the crime charged.).

[213] State v. Mayfield, 302 Or. 631, 733 P.2d 438 (1987).

§ 6.41 Admitting evidence of defendant's prior conduct to establish defendant's intent.

When a defendant raises the defense that he engaged in certain conduct, but not with the intent to engage in a sexual act or crime, it is likely to open the door to prior conduct that helps reveal the defendant's intent.[214]

Many courts find it permissible to admit prior similar but disconnected crimes to prove that a defendant had the intention of arousing or gratifying the sexual desires of either himself or the victim when intent is an essential element of the charged crime.[215] Also, if a defendant claims he touched the complainant, but

---

[214] United States v. Cuch, 842 F.2d 1173 (10th Cir. 1988) (admitting defendant's prior sexual assault of a probation officer to rebut defendant's claim that he did not intend to sexually assault a woman whom he accosted at gunpoint); Glass v. State, 255 Ga. App. 390, 565 S.E.2d 500 (2002), *cert. denied*, 2002 Ga. LEXIS 757 (Sept. 6, 2002) (defendant's being acquainted with two different women, taking them to his residence, overpowering them, and instructing them to relax, digitally penetrating and then raping them were sufficiently similar incidents to prove bent of mind and intent to overcome current defense); Johnson v. State, 722 N.E.2d 382 (Ind. Ct. App. 2000) (permitting introduction of defendant's prior attempted rape to counter defendant's claim of consensual relations with complainant).

[215] United States v. Butler, 56 F.3d 941, 944–45 (8th Cir.), *cert. denied*, 516 U.S. 924 (1995); United States v. Tanksley, 54 M.J. 169 (C.A.A.F. 2000) (holding defendant's prior fondling of defendant's daughter 30 years earlier, under "strikingly similar" circumstances, relevant to element of defendant's intent in current charge); Bohanan v. State, 992 P.2d 596 (Alaska Ct. App. 1999) (holding defendant's prior acts relevant to establishing whether he intended to engage in sexual penetration with complainant); People v. Wilson, 343 Ill. App. 3d 742, 798 N.E.2d 772 (2003) (holding prior acts were part of a similar *modus operandi*, which was relevant to defendant's sexual intent); State v. Jackson, 625 So. 2d 146 (La. 1993); People v. Nowlin, 297 A.D.2d 554, 747 N.Y.S.2d 92, *appeal denied*, 98 N.Y.2d 770, 781 N.E.2d 923, 752 N.Y.S.2d 11 (2002) ("The court properly exercised its discretion in admitting testimony by two previous victims of defendant. In light of the defense raised by defendant at trial, this evidence was admissible on the sexual abuse counts to prove defendant's intent and was relevant to rebut the suggestion of mistake or accident."); State v. Miesse, 2000 Ohio App. LEXIS 3719 (Aug. 18, 2000):

> [T]he State was entitled to introduce evidence regarding Miesse's admissions to others that he was sexually aroused by touching, kissing, and blowing on children's stomachs, and that he had engaged in this activity in the past on a number of occasions. The evidence demonstrated Miesse's motive, intent, or purpose in engaging in this seemingly innocuous activity and demonstrated the absence of accident or mistake on his part. Without it, Miesse may well have been able to persuade the jury that his contact with the children's stomachs was innocuous.

Id. at *14; State v. Wilhelm, 168 Or. App. 489, 492–93, 3 P.3d 715, 717 (2000) (finding defendant's "romantic" and "very intimate" albeit not "explicitly sexual" letters to juvenile complainant were admissible as being probative of whether the defendant's actions were for a sexual purpose and were "relevant to demonstrate his sexual predisposition for this particular victim"); State v. Veach, 246 Wis. 2d 395 (Wis. Ct. App.), *review granted*, 634 N.W.2d 318 (Wis. 2001) (holding defendant's prior abuse of his daughter 11 years earlier relevant to defendant's intent on touching victim in interest case was for sexual gratification, but reversing defendant's conviction because his counsel was ineffective for failing to stipulate that acts, if committed, were for sexual gratification to avoid introduction of other acts evidence).

not in her intimate parts, prior abuse may be relevant to establish "intentional conduct" with the motive of sexual gratification.[216] This can be seen where a defendant admits having physical contact with the complainant, but claims there was no intent of sexual gratification. In an assault prosecution, testimony by a family member concerning a victim's assaultive behavior toward the victim may not only explain the relationship with the victim, but also establish intent and absence of mistake or accident.[217]

The Michigan Supreme Court, in *People v. Vandervliet*,[218] suggests that the prosecution should be entitled to establish the element of intent, but that the probative value of such evidence must be evaluated in a case-by-case basis for the potential prejudicial effect of the evidence weighed against its probative value. *Vandervliet* is a comprehensive look at the use of prior uncharged acts on a sexual assault trial. In *Vandervliet*, the defendant was a case manager working with developmentally disabled young men. At trial, the prosecution sought to introduce evidence of uncharged sexual acts toward other clients with whom the defendant had worked. The court noted that the rule concerning prior acts was not a rule of exclusion, but a rule of inclusion, and it defined four factors to evaluate in admitting evidence of prior acts. First, there must be a basis for believing that the prior acts had occurred; second, there must be a relationship between the charged and uncharged offenses that supplies a link between them or assures that the evidence of the prior act is probative of some fact other than the defendant's character; third, the proffered evidence must be relevant to some matter in issue; and, fourth, the general rule that the probative value of the evidence must not be outweighed by its prejudicial effect.[219] In this case, the court found that, by using its four-prong test, the evidence of the defendant's prior contact with other clients helped to demonstrate that the defendant's physical contact with the complainants was with intent of sexual gratification and not inadvertent or accidental. This evaluation may be made as the proof unfolds in a case; cross-examination of witnesses in the case-in-chief may make clear, for example, that intent with which an act was committed may be a significant issue.[220] Part of the theoretical underpinning of this decision is that the prosecution must prove all elements of a crime, and even if a defendant makes a decision not to contest an essential element of an offense, the prosecution must still prove all elements, and proof establishing those elements is relevant and admissible.

---

[216] State v. Veach, 255 Wis. 2d 390, 648 N.W.2d 447 (2002) (Defendant's prior abuse of his daughters 11 years previously was properly admitted to rebut defendant's "innocent" explanation of sexual conduct.).

[217] People v. De Fayette, 16 A.D.3d 708, 790 N.Y.S.2d 301, *appeal denied*, 4 N.Y.3d 885, 831 N.E.2d 975, 798 N.Y.S.2d 730; (2005).

[218] 444 Mich. 52, 508 N.W.2d 114 (1993).

[219] *Id.* ("The relationship of the elements of the charge, the theories of admissibility, and the defenses asserted govern what is relevant and material." *Id.* at 75, 508 N.W.2d at 126.).

[220] *Id.* at 90, 508 N.W.2d at 114.

Issues also may be created by cross-examination and the proof as it unfolds even if a defense is not formally put forth.[221] This position has not been accepted by all courts, but is the crucial factor in other decisions to accept evidence of a defendant's prior acts of sexual abuse on the theory that it establishes motive or intent. This analysis can be seen in cases admitting prior acts of sexual abuse by a defendant. For example, in *United States v. Hadley*,[222] the Court of Appeals held:

> Hadley cannot preclude the government from proving intent simply by focusing his defense on other elements of his crime. Hadley's choice of defense did not relieve the government of its burden of proof and should not prevent the government from meeting this burden by an otherwise acceptable means. Rule 404(b) permits the government to prove intent by evidence of prior bad acts. . . .

Courts are divided on whether the prosecution can introduce such evidence where the defendant does not raise the issue of lack of intent. Some courts take the position that the prosecution is required to establish all elements of a crime and cannot be precluded from establishing an element by the failure of a defendant to contest an element.

The Supreme Court, in a decision concerning the admissibility of the battered child syndrome and prior acts of physical abuse of a child, held that "the prosecution's burden to prove every element of the crime is not relieved by a defendant's tactical decision not to contest an essential element of the offense."[223]

A different view is "that defendant's plea [of not guilty] does put the elements of the crime in issue for the purpose of deciding the admissibility of evidence [of uncharged misconduct], unless the defendant has taken some action to narrow the prosecution's burden of proof."[224] Other courts have required an issue of intent before the prior conduct can be admitted[225] and find a denial of charges does not necessarily open the door to the introduction of other acts evidence to establish the defendant's intent.[226]

The Michigan Supreme Court, in *Vandervliet*, noted that in taking this approach it was adopting a modification to its Rule 404(b) that requires the prosecution

---

[221] *Id.* at 79, 508 N.W.2d at 128.

[222] 918 F.2d 848, 852 (9th Cir. 1990), *cert. dismissed*, 506 U.S. 19 (1992) ("We must also investigate, however, whether prior bad acts should have been excluded because their probative value was substantially outweighed by the danger of unfair prejudice."). *See also* United States v. Yellow, 18 F.3d 1438, 1441 (8th Cir. 1994); State v. Plymesser, 172 Wis. 2d 583, 594, 493 N.W.2d 367, 372 (1992).

[223] Estelle v. McGuire, 502 U.S. 62, 69, 112 S. Ct. 475, 481, 116 L. Ed. 2d 385, 397 (1991).

[224] People v. Daniels, 52 Cal. 3d 815, 857–58, 802 P.2d 906, 925 (1991).

[225] State v. Ives, 187 Ariz. 102, 111, 927 P.2d 762, 771 (1996); State v. G.V., 162 N.J. 252, 259–60, 744 A.2d 137, 142 (2000); State v. Lipka, 174 Vt. 377, 817 A.2d 27 (2002).

[226] State v. Kennedy, 803 So. 2d 916 (La. Ct. App. 2001).

to give pretrial notice of intent to introduce other acts by authorizing the trial judge (which it noted was a power that trial judges in other states possessed) to require the defendant to articulate a theory or theories of his defense in order to assist the judge in making a determination as to the probative value of prior-act evidence, and that the court may also, if it desires, delay ruling on proffered bad-act evidence until after the examination and cross-examination of prosecution witnesses, and in some situations, even permit this testimony to be offered after presentation of the defense's case.[227]

A defendant's prior conviction may be admissible to demonstrate that the defendant intended to take advantage of a child who was incapable of resisting or unable to appreciate the nature of the act "as well as his knowledge that young children are easily victimized."[228] Evidence that is put forth in the name of intent, but that shows primarily the defendant's propensity, is an improper admission of prior acts evidence and may result in reversal of a defendant's conviction.[229] The fact that a defendant is suffering from a life-threatening disease, i.e., he is HIV positive, does not open the door to questioning about the defendant's HIV status on the theory that this is evidence that the defendant intended to commit the crimes for which he was charged because he had nothing to lose by committing them in the absence of any evidence to support that theory.[230] Since intent is not an element of statutory rape, a defendant's prior assault should not be admitted to establish intent for either statutory or attempted statutory rape.[231] A defendant's possession of sexually-explicit homosexual literature, K-Y Jelly, children's underwear, and dildos is not necessarily relevant to a defendant's intent to sexually abuse a child.[232]

---

[227] People v. Vandervliet, 444 Mich. 52, 89–90, 508 N.W.2d 114, 133 (1993).

[228] United States v. Peden, 961 F.2d 517, 520–21 (5th Cir.), *cert. denied*, 506 U.S. 945 (1992).

[229] United States v. Has No Horse, 11 F.3d 104, 106 (8th Cir. 1993) (holding that trial court's admission into evidence that defendant had previously made sexual advances toward two other teenage girls was more in the nature of propensity evidence and was not relevant to defendant's intent); People v. Vargas, 88 N.Y.2d 856, 666 N.E.2d 1357, 644 N.Y.S.2d 484 (1996); People v. Sparer, 293 A.D.2d 630, 740 N.Y.S.2d 246, *appeal denied*, 98 N.Y.2d 681, 774 N.E.2d 236, 746 N.Y.S.2d 471 (2002); Guill v. Commonwealth, 255 Va. 134, 141, 495 S.E.2d 489, 493 (1998) (reversing defendant's conviction because of admission of evidence of a prior crime, allegedly to show defendant's intent, which appellate court found "lacked a logical relationship to the offense charged and, thus, was irrelevant and showed only the defendant's propensity to commit the crime charged").

[230] People v. Felix-Torres, 281 A.D.2d 649, 721 N.Y.S.2d 415 (2001), *appeal denied*, 97 N.Y.2d 681, 764 N.E.2d 400, 738 N.Y.S. 2d 296 (2001) (Trial court allowed prosecution to question defendant whether he had a life-threatening disease. If defendant replied "no," prosecution was to be allowed to ask the defendant if he is HIV positive. While error, it was harmless in this case, but remand was necessary to resolve an issue relating to the failure to disclose certain reports.)

[231] State v. Chavis, 141 N.C. App. 553, 540 S.E.2d 404 (2000) (finding error was harmless since prior acts were relevant for another purpose).

[232] Guam v. Shymanovitz, 157 F.3d 1154, 1159 (9th Cir. 1998) (the possession of sexually-explicit materials is not ordinarily "distinctive or remarkable in the universe of sexual offenses against minors.").

There may be situations where the defendant's sexual intent or motivation is either related to the crime or raised by the defendant. For example, a defendant who claims he was not sexually stimulated by touching a female's hair permits testimony of the defendant's act of masturbation while the police were searching his apartment.[233] When a defendant asserts that photographing his child naked is not sexually motivated, it opens the door to his showering naked with the child.[234] In a prosecution for meeting an undercover police officer whom the defendant met online and believed to be a 14-year-old girl, evidence of undated photographs and logs of computer chats are relevant to establish defendant's intent in meeting with the undercover officer, i.e., whether the intent was non-criminal or to engage in sexual relations with a child.[235]

In some situations, a defendant's prior acts toward a victim may be relevant and probative of the defendant's motive and intent and lack of mistake in committing a crime.[236] For example, a defendant's previous rape of his wife might be admissible in his murder trial as probative of his intent to kill his wife.[237]

§ 6.42 Admitting evidence of defendant's prior conduct to establish lack of consent.

The traditional argument against the use of prior acts of a defendant to rebut the defense of consent is that sexual assaults committed by a defendant upon other women are inadmissible because they are not relevant to any material fact on the pending charge other than to show the predisposition of the defendant

---

[233] People v. Rossman, 95 A.D.2d 873, 463 N.Y.S.2d 891 (1983).

[234] State v. Query, 594 N.W.2d 438 (Iowa Ct. App. 1999).

[235] People v. Harris, 2004 Mich. App. LEXIS 2642 (Oct. 12, 2004) (but noting that "[t]he closer question is whether the probative value of the evidence was substantially outweighed by its prejudicial effect").

[236] State v. Collier, 1997 Tenn. Crim. App. LEXIS 14 at *27 (Jan. 13, 1997); State v. Hunt, 263 Wis. 2d 1, 37, 666 N.W.2d 771, 788 (2003) (holding prior acts of abuse admissible in part to establish that defendant intentionally touched victim, and not by accident or mistake); State v. Hammer, 236 Wis. 2d 686, 705, 613 N.W.2d 629, 638 (2000) (holding prior acts relevant to show touching not accidental and done with interest of sexual gratification).

[237] United States v. Joe, 8 F.3d 1488, 1495–96 (10th Cir. 1993), cert. denied, 510 U.S. 1184 (1994). See also State v. Long, 173 N.J. 138, 801 A.2d 221 (2002) (permitting prosecution to utilize defendant's out-of-court statements to prove defendant's motive for killing his wife where the declarations imply the defendant was involved in another death not classified as a homicide); People v. Bierenbaum, 301 A.D.2d 119, 748 N.Y.S.2d 563 (2002), appeal denied, 99 N.Y.2d 626, 790 N.E.2d 281, 760 N.Y.S.2d 107 (2003) (holding in a domestic violence homicide prosecution's evidence of defendant's prior threats and aggressive behavior admissible as evidence of motive and intent).

because "[t]he issue of consent is unique to an individual, and the lack of consent of one person is not proof of the lack of consent of another."[238]

However, when sufficient similarity is shown between the charged and uncharged acts, the prior acts may be admissible on the issue of consent. The similarity must be more than the use of force or the abuse of an acquaintance relationship. The similarities should extend to unique statements used to deceive or lure the victims, unique conduct before or during the sexual assault such as smoking marijuana and discussing interracial dating[239] or hiding in a vehicle to find a victim and claiming he had mistaken the car for his brother's,[240] or engaging women in a conversation about sex and drugs and then, in a secluded spot, grabbing them from behind.[241] The similarities may revolve around the use of alcohol to overpower the defendant's victims.[242]

The defendant's prior acts may be admissible on the issue of consent if a defendant claims he reasonably believed that the complainant consented to his advances. This places a defendant's state of mind in issue and the prior misconduct evidence can "disprove that the defendant had that state of mind."[243] This defense is also discussed in § 16.16.

---

[238] Hodges v. State, 403 So. 2d 1375, 1378 (Fla. Dist. Ct. App. 1981). *See also* Velez v. State, 762 P.2d 1297 (Alaska App. 1988); Jenkins v. State, 474 N.E.2d 84 (Ind. 1985); State v. Harris, 140 N.C. App. 208, 535 S.E.2d 614, *review denied, appeal dismissed*, 353 N.C. 271, 546 S.E.2d 122 (2000) (holding defendant's prior rapes were inadmissible to establish lack of consent, especially since they involved different victims, but that error was harmless); State v. Beaulieu, 116 R.I. 575, 359 A.2d 689 (1976); Caldwell v. State, 477 S.W.2d 877 (Tex. Crim. App. 1972); Foster v. Commonwealth, 5 Va. App. 316, 362 S.E.2d 745 (1987).

[239] People v. Oliphant, 399 Mich. 472, 250 N.W.2d 443 (1976).

[240] Williams v. State, 110 So. 2d 654, 657–58 (Fla.), *cert. denied*, 361 U.S. 847 (1959).

[241] Williams v. State, 621 So. 2d 413, 414 (Fla. 1993). *See also* State v. Hill, 104 Ariz. 238, 450 P.2d 696 (1969); State v. Willis, 370 N.W.2d 193, 198 (S.D. 1985) (admitting prior acts of abuse by authority figure to establish lack of consent by demonstrating that defendant exploited his "official position of dominance and superior intelligence, coupled with his superior size and strength, [to ravish] the physically mature, yet vulnerable, females").

[242] Howard v. State, 220 Ga. App. 267, 469 S.E.2d 396 (1996) (Similarities between defendant's prior and current charge included use of alcohol by defendant and providing alcohol to victims, acquaintance with victim, making sexual advances which were rebuffed and overpowering but not striking the women. The court held "[t]he connecting thread pervading the two offenses is a corresponding course or conduct and intent or bent of mind which is sufficient to justify the admission of the similar transaction evidence." *Id.* at 269, 469 S.E.2d at 396).

[243] State v. Oliver, 133 N.J. 141, 155, 627 A.2d 144, 152 (1993) ("Determination of [the defendant's state of mind] becomes especially significant in those situations in which the evidence suggests that the defendant could reasonably have believed that permission had been given." *Id.* at 156, 627 A.2d, at 152).

§ 6.43 Evidence of defendant's prior uncharged acts with complainant or others to establish the complainant's state of mind.

The reasonableness of a complainant's fear of the defendant or failure to report the sexual assault is another theory upon which a defendant's prior acts of abuse have been admitted. These prior acts may be abuse upon the same victim, abuse upon another person witnessed by the complainant, or statements by the defendant that he has abused someone else. This evidence may be developed through direct examination of the complainant as part of the proof of lack of consent and is discussed in the sections dealing with these topics. [244]

This theory can be applied to many different fact patterns. A prisoner's testimony that he witnessed the defendant assault another inmate is relevant to the inmate victim's state of mind and reasonable fear of the defendant and can establish the forcible nature of the sexual assault upon the prisoner victim. [245] A victim's testimony of prior uncharged abuse at the hands of her husband was probative as to the victim's state of mind and the consent issue, and provides an explanation of her failure to immediately report the burglary and sexual abuse she alleged was committed by the defendant. [246] These prior acts can explain a victim's delay in reporting. [247] Many courts have allowed evidence of prior

---

[244] *See* §§ 5.10 and 7.15.

[245] People v. Tas, 51 N.Y.2d 915, 415 N.E.2d 967, 434 N.Y.S.2d 978 (1980) ("In establishing lack of consent, the People properly could introduce evidence which was probative of the victim's state of mind at the time of the attack.").

[246] People v. Naylor, 196 A.D.2d 320, 323, 609 N.Y.S.2d 954, 956 (1994).

[247] United States v. Robles, 53 M.J. 783 (A.F.C.C.A. 2000) (upholding admission of defendant's abuse against his wife and former wife since those acts helped explain the victims' delay in reporting, an issue raised in the defendant's opening statement). *See also* People v. Medunjanin, 276 A.D.2d 719, 716 N.Y.S.2d 314, *appeal denied*, 95 N.Y.2d 966, 745 N.E.2d 404, 722 N.Y.S.2d 484 (2000) (holding evidence of defendant's prior misconduct toward the victim's mother properly introduced on issue of victim's state of mind and delayed report; defendant never requested limiting instructions); State v. Thompson, 139 N.C. App. 299, 533 S.E.2d 834 (2000):

> We next consider whether the trial court improperly admitted the evidence of defendant's prior physical abuse of N's siblings and his physical violence against the cat. . . . At trial, defendant relied heavily on N's failure to report the sexual abuse in suggesting that such abuse never in fact occurred. By bringing forth this defense, defendant thereby specifically made N's state of mind relevant. The State could therefore introduce any evidence tending to explain N's state of mind. The evidence of physical abuse and animal abuse here did just that: it tended to explain N's fear of defendant and why she never reported all the incidents of sexual abuse. N even specifically testified that she never reported the sexual abuse because, in light of all the other abuse that she witnessed, she knew he would beat her if she did report it. We do express caution with a trial court admitting evidence of animal abuse and/or physical abuse in cases only involving sex abuse. Such evidence must be relevant, and being lewd and despicable does not necessarily make it relevant. Furthermore, such evidence has the potential of being highly prejudicial to a defendant and thus

abuse between a defendant and victim or others known by the victim to explain the victim's state of mind, fear of the defendant, submission to the defendant, or lack of consent[248] or recantation.[249]

> should be scrutinized carefully by the trial judge. We emphasize that the only reason the evidence is admissible here is because the physical and animal abuse was done in N's presence and because defendant specifically made N's state of mind relevant. To the extent evidence of physical and/or animal abuse not done in N's presence was admitted, such admission was error, but would not have changed the outcome so as to require a new trial.

[248] United States v. Tsinnijinnie, 91 F.3d 1285 (9th Cir. 1996) (evidence of defendant's prior physical abuse of victim relevant to explain child's submission to sexual acts and not tell her mother); Russell v. State, 934 P.2d 1335 (Alaska Ct. App. 1997) (holding defendant's prior assaults on complainant relevant to issue of lack of consent); State v. Ali, 233 Conn. 403, 660 A.2d 337 (1995) (the defendant's prior misconduct, including the use of a machete toward the complainant, tended to explain why she was afraid of the defendant "and why she feared for her safety and that of her children. It also showed, at the very least, that the defendant had used a knife to engage in forceful conduct toward the victim and therefore was evidence that the parties' subsequent activities were not consensual." Id. at 428, 660 A.2d at 349); Smith v. State, 1995 Del. LEXIS 216 (June 14, 1995) (acts of prior abuse between defendant and his wife properly admitted on the question of whether during one of the couple's domestic disputes the complainant consented to sexual intercourse); Johnson v. State, 238 Ga. App. 677, 679, 520 S.E.2d 221, 224 (1999) (complainant's testimony that defendant "had previously 'stuck a dude in the neck with a screwdriver' " relevant to element of force and complainant's state of mind); People v. Cook, 93 N.Y.2d 840, 710 N.E.2d 654, 688 N.Y.S.2d 89 (1999) (upholding admission into evidence of defendant's prior uncharged act of violence toward the complainant as admissible evidence to prove the element of forcible compulsion in rape case); People v. Laviolette, 307 A.D.2d 541, 762 N.Y.S.2d 168, appeal denied, 100 N.Y.2d 643, 801 N.E.2d 430, 769 N.Y.S.2d 209 (2003) (court upheld evidence of defendant's prior physical abuse to explain defendant's relationship with the victim, explain the victim's behavior, complete the narrative and depict the controlling setting:

> The evidence permitted related largely to defendant's excessive use of corporal punishment, threats of violence and psychological control over the victims and included testimony regarding the prior involvement of child protective services with the family.

People v. Smith, 283 A.D.2d 175, 724 N.Y.S.2d 590 (2001) (finding uncharged acts between defendant and victim probative of element of forcible compulsion and as well as victim's behavior during the charged crimes); People v. Chase, 277 A.D.2d 1045, 716 N.Y.S.2d 486 (2000), appeal denied, 96 N.Y.2d 733, 745 N.E.2d 1022, 722 N.Y.S.2d 799 (2001) (holding defendant's threats of violence against victim or argument with others in presence of victim was directly relevant to show defendant's sexual acts perpetrated against the victim by forcible compulsion and to negate defense of consent); People v. Sturdivant, 277 A.D.2d 607, 714 N.Y.S.2d 839, appeal denied, 95 N.Y.2d 970, 745 N.E.2d 408, 722 N.Y.S.2d 488 (2000) ("Defendant also takes issue with Supreme Court's pretrial Molineux ruling which permitted the People to present evidence that for several days prior to the rape, defendant repeatedly contacted the victim both at work and at home after being told to cease such conduct. Evidence of defendant's prior abusive behavior toward her was relevant to the element of forcible compulsion.); People v. Rogner, 265 A.D.2d 688, 689, 697 N.Y.S.2d 363, 365 (1999) ("Defendant also takes issue with County Court's pretrial Molineux ruling permitting the People to present evidence during their case-in-chief of alleged prior acts of sexual and/or physical abuse perpetrated by defendant on both the victim and her mother. Since this evidence is relevant to the element of forcible compulsion and since its probative value outweighed its prejudicial effect, we discern no error in the ruling." [citations omitted]); People v. Brown, 261 A.D.2d 410, 691 N.Y.S.2d 532, appeal denied, 93 N.Y.2d 967, 716 N.E.2d 1098, 695 N.Y.S.2d

A good example of defendant's prior uncharged acts against his family were admitted into evidence to explain the context of a crime.[250] In *United States v. Powers*, the court permitted testimony that the defendant would hit his wife and children with a belt, a hickory stick, or his hands, and that he had threatened "to burn the house up" with the children and his wife inside. This evidence was admissible to explain the child's "submission to the acts and her delay in reporting the sexual abuse."[251] The appeals court noted that this testimony helped explain her failure to report the sexual abuse and her fear of retribution and that bad acts evidence can be admitted "to show the context of the crime."[252]

Evidence that a defendant struck his wife with a baseball bat one year earlier is relevant not only to the defense of consent, but also to explain the inconsistencies in the complainant's testimony and denial of certain events.[253]

Uncharged acts from nonsexual contact to sexual contact to allegations of rape by the defendant of the complainant may be admissible to establish the trust between the parties and to establish the progressive desensitization of the victim.[254] The prior acts may be "needed to understand how the sexual relationship between the complainant and the defendant originated and developed."[255]

---

53 (1999) (permitting complainant's testimony that defendant had killed his son-in-law several years before he raped and sodomized complainant as relevant to complainant's state of mind and the element of forcible compulsion); People v. McClain, 250 A.D.2d 871, 672 N.Y.S.2d 503, *appeal denied*, 92 N.Y.2d 901, 702 N.E.2d 850, 680 N.Y.S.2d 65 (1998) (defendant's prior abuse of complainant relevant to the victim's lack of consent and element of forcible compulsion in rape case); People v. Negrette, 218 A.D.2d 751, 630 N.Y.S.2d 780, *appeal denied*, 87 N.Y.2d 905, 663 N.E.2d 1265, 641 N.Y.S.2d 235 (1995) (evidence of defendant's prior abuse of complainant relevant to her state of mind and lack of consent); People v. Lanier, 163 A.D.2d 902, 558 N.Y.S.2d 424 (1990) (evidence of prior beatings of infant victims by the defendant were relevant to show victim's continuing fear of defendant and was relevant to element of forcible compulsion); People v. Thompson, 158 A.D.2d 563, 551 N.Y.S.2d 332, *appeal denied*, 76 N.Y.2d 797, 559 N.E.2d 696, 559 N.Y.S.2d 1002 (1990) (holding that evidence of prior sexual assaults of victim by defendant were relevant to element of forcible compulsion); Commonwealth v. Richter, 551 Pa. 507, 711 A.2d 464 (1998) (holding that evidence of the defendant's past physical and verbal intimidation of the victim were admissible to prove the element of forcible compulsion and that "failure to allow the admission of such evidence would, in essence, grant immunity to criminals for their deliberate intimidation, whether it be by statement to the victim of their criminal past or whether it be by physically abusive behavior with which the victim is all too familiar." *Id.* at *9.).

[249] State v. Clark, 83 Haw. 289, 926 P.2d 194 (1996) (evidence of defendant's prior violence toward victim relevant to explain complainant's recantation).

[250] 59 F.3d 1460 (4th Cir. 1995), *cert. denied*, 516 U.S. 1077 (1996).

[251] *Id.* at 1464.

[252] *Id.* at 1465–66.

[253] Arcoren v. United States, 929 F.2d 1235 (8th Cir. 1991). *See* § 11.35.

[254] State v. Haley, 141 N.H. 541, 689 A.2d 671 (1997).

[255] Commonwealth v. Sosnowski, 43 Mass. App. Ct. 367, 372, 682 N.E.2d 944, 948 (1997); People v. Williams, 241 A.D.2d 911, 663 N.Y.S.2d 1023, *appeal denied*, 91 N.Y.2d 837, 690 N.E.2d 500, 667 N.Y.S.2d 691 (1997) (upholding admission into evidence of four prior domestic incidents involving defendant and his former girlfriend "to show the nature of their relationship up to the time of the incident and defendant's motive and intent with respect to the crimes charged").

The acts between the defendant and victim may also be admissible on the theory that they are related to and intertwined with the charged offense.[256] Prior conduct of tickling, kissing, and using a vibrator may be "probative" of the defendant's preparation to commit the charged acts.[257] By statute, Texas permits evidence of a defendant's prior bad acts in certain child abuse prosecutions to establish the state of mind of the defendant and the child.[258] A defendant's wife may be cross-examined about alleged acts of physical abuse against her to show her bias.[259] However, once she denies the allegations, the state may not offer evidence to refute her denial.[260]

However, introducing evidence of a defendant's past sexual assault upon his wife at a second sexual assault trial may be reversible where the prosecution does not show that the prior conviction was related to the complainant's conduct, such as intimidating her or preventing her from reporting his subsequent crimes, or related to any motive such as assaulting his wife to retaliate for his earlier arrest and conviction.[261] When there is a substantial time gap between the prior

---

[256] State v. Malvoisin, 779 So. 2d 73 (La. Ct. App. 2001).

[257] *Haley*, 141 N.H. at 546, 689 A.2d at 675.

[258] TEX. CODE CRIM. PROC. ANN. art. 38.37. *See, e.g.*, McCulloch v. State, 39 S.W.3d 678 (Tex. Ct. App. 2001):

> Court upheld child's testimony concerning sexual assaults both before and after the charged offense, *citing* TEX. CODE CRIM. PROC. art. 38.37, which permits other acts between a defendant and victim in certain sexual assault prosecutions when relevant to: (1) the state of mind of the defendant and the child, and (2) the previous and subsequent relationship between the defendant and the child. "The testimony concerning the prior and subsequent 'acts' is relevant to T.R.'s and McCulloch's state of mind. T.R.'s account of the 'acts' reveals McCulloch's dominance over her and her fear of him. The evidence also shows McCulloch's 'necessary intent and ability' to commit the offense and further demonstrates that T.R. was 'compelled to acquiesce.' . . . [citation omitted]. The prior and subsequent 'acts' reveal the nature of their relationship both before and after the charged offense. . . [citation omitted]. In the absence of evidence of how the step-father misused his position of authority as the disciplinarian in the family to create an unnatural relationship, the jury may have been led to believe it 'illogical and implausible' that the charged act could have occurred. [citation omitted]." The evidence not only explained how the step-father was able to commit the assault without being apprehended for nine years, an issue in dispute at trial, but it also explained to the jury that the single charged offense simply did not occur in an otherwise healthy relationship. If the jurors were not told of the pattern of sexual assault, they may well have been persuaded that the absence of such evidence was proof that the one assault did not occur in this step-father and child relationship. Whether the jury believed the evidence we do not know; but we cannot say the evidence was irrelevant under article 38.37 to the charged offense.

Id. at 681.

[259] State v. Ward, 31 Kan. App. 2d 284, 64 P.3d 972, *review denied*, 276 Kan. 974 (2003).

[260] 276 Kan. 974 (2003).

[261] State v. Bassett, 139 N.H. 493, 659 A.2d 891 (1995).

assault on this victim and the current charge, "a clear logical connection is necessary to overcome the lack of temporal proximity."[262]

Many cases upholding the use of a defendant's past abusive acts toward the complainant note that such evidence, like other bad act evidence, should be accompanied by a limiting instruction so that a jury understands the proper role of the evidence. (*See* § 6.47.)

§ 6.44   Evidence of defendant's prior acts when defendant's predisposition at issue, or use of entrapment defense.

If a defendant raises an entrapment defense, this places his predisposition to commit the offense at issue. For example, if a defendant claims he was entrapped to possess, buy, give, receive mail, or provide child pornography to an undercover police officer, the defendant opens doors to past conduct that shows a sexual interest in children. Numerous decisions hold that a defendant's previous sexual abuse of children or acts indicating a sexual preference for children are admissible to show predisposition in child pornography prosecuting when predisposition is at issue.[263] The same rule applies to a defendant's prior activities with child pornography.[264]

The prosecution can also present evidence of the defendant's collection of nude photographs of children or other apparent legal pictures or displays of children when there is proof to support the conclusion they evidence a sexual interest in children.[265] A postal inspector may testify to a defendant's use of photos of "miniature erotica," "Lolita," and "Wonderboy" as terms of the child pornographic subculture.[266] This is discussed further in § 11.33. However, child pornography legally obtained may be inadmissible to show predisposition.[267]

§ 6.45   Admission of defendant's prior acts to explain complainant's behavior, reactions, or rebut defendant's suggestions.

A defendant's prior acts may be relevant to explain a victim's behaviors or reactions. Past abuse upon others may also be relevant to explain a complainant's

---

[262] *Id.* at 500, 659 A.2d at 897 (time period of approximately a year and a half deemed evidence of lack of temporal proximity).

[263] United States v. Byrd, 31 F.3d 1329, 1339 (5th Cir. 1994), *cert. denied*, 514 U.S. 1052 (1995); United States v. Moore, 916 F.2d 1131, 1137 (6th Cir. 1990); United States v. Thomas, 893 F.2d 1066, 1071 (9th Cir. 1990) (prior act of child sexual abuse relevant to show defendant knew pornography involved a minor).

[264] United States v. Layne, 43 F.3d 127, 133 (5th Cir.), *cert. denied*, 514 U.S. 1077 (1995); United States v. Gifford, 17 F.3d 462, 469 (1st Cir. 1994).

[265] United States v. Cross, 928 F.2d 1030 (11th Cir. 1991), *cert. denied*, 502 U.S. 985 (1991); United States v. Moore, 916 F.2d 1131, 1137 (6th Cir. 1990).

[266] United States v. Byrd, 31 F.3d 1329 (5th Cir. 1994), *cert. denied*, 514 U.S. 1052 (1995).

[267] United States v. LaChapelle, 969 F.2d 632, 638 (8th Cir. 1992).

delay in reporting or to rebut the suggestion that the charges are the response to the defendant's efforts at discipline. A sex abuse victim may testify about physical abuse of her mother to explain the delay in reporting. The door to prior bad acts can be opened by suggesting the complainant does not like the defendant and is therefore biased against the defendant. In such a case, a complainant could then explain on redirect why she did not like the defendant and what he had done.[268] This topic is discussed in further detail in § 5.52.

§ 6.46   Evidence of defendant's prior bad acts introduced as a result of defendant opening door.

Evidence of a defendant's prior bad acts can be developed on cross-examination or through direct testimony as a result of a defendant opening the door to such testimony through questions of the defendant's attorney or responses of the defendant. Sometimes this unwittingly occurs through careless questioning of, or answers by, the defendant on direct or cross-examination of the defendant or complainant. (*See* §§ 5.52, 6.15, and 6.50.) It can also occur by the introduction of testimony of other witnesses, such as character witnesses or expert witnesses.

The door is not opened simply by questioning the victim's account or claiming that the child was influenced by an adult in making the allegation.[269] Suggesting that a complainant accused the defendant of rape because of a relationship with another teenager does not open the door to testimony on redirect of the complainant that the defendant impregnated the other teenager.[270]

To determine whether the defendant has opened the door on direct examination, the testimony must be carefully evaluated to determine precisely what the defendant has asserted. For example, a defendant's denial on direct examination that he had never physically abused his ex-wife does not open the door to a prior conviction for malicious destruction of property which involved only physical damage and not personal injury.[271] Very general answers by a defendant, such as it would have been "disrespectful" for the defendant to do an act, does not open the door to a prior conviction.[272]

---

[268] *See, e.g.*, State v. Parkinson, 128 Idaho 29, 909 P.2d 647 (1996). *See also* §§ 5.52 and 6.15.

[269] Sundling v. State, 679 N.E.2d 988, 993 (Ind. Ct. App. 1997).

[270] Commonwealth v. Blackwell, 44 Mass. App. Ct. 804, 695 N.E.2d 208, *review denied*, 427 Mass. 1107 (1998) (holding the error was harmless due to strength of prosecution's case).

[271] Heidelberg v. State, 36 S.W.3d 668, 673–74 (Tex. Ct. App. 2001) (defense counsel's questioning of child protective worker about what defendant said during her interview did not open the door to references about other uncharged crimes, but defense counsel failed to ask that response be stricken, thereby not preserving error).

[272] Commonwealth v. Lavoie, 47 Mass. App. Ct. 1, 710 N.E.2d 1011, *review denied*, 430 Mass. 1106, 717 N.E.2d 1015 (1999).

Failing to object or ask that an answer be stricken may preclude raising the argument that the door was not opened to uncharged acts.[273]

§ 6.47 Necessity of limiting instructions when evidence of prior sexual acts is admitted.

Evidence that is admitted for a limited purpose, such as prior bad act evidence, should be subject to cautionary instructions to the jury. The charge may be that the testimony "may be considered by you only to the extent that it bears upon the defendant's opportunity, intent, preparation, or plan to commit the acts charged in the indictment."[274] But such an instruction does not precisely address the limited purpose of the prior bad act evidence.

Limiting instructions should be provided pursuant to Federal Rule of Evidence 105, which has a parallel statute or principle in most jurisdictions. Furthermore, many jurisdictions now require that limiting instructions as to uncharged acts be specific in identifying the limited purpose for which the prior evidence is being offered so that the probative value of the evidence can be evaluated for that purpose.[275]

---

[273] State v. Lewis, 27 Kan. App. 2d 380, 5 P.3d 531 (2000):

> There is no evidence to support a conclusion that the defendant tried to characterize his past life as blemish free or make other assertions of his good character. While it is true that the defendant's answers were very expansive and not always responsive, they do not as a matter of law put the defendant's good character at issue. As a result, the trial court committed reversible error in admitting the evidence of his prior convictions.

Id. at 385, 5 P.3d at 534–35 [citation omitted].

[274] United States v. Azure, 801 F.2d 336, 342 (8th Cir. 1986). *See also* United States v. St. Pierre, 812 F.2d 417 (8th Cir. 1987); State v. Mayfield, 302 Or. 631, 647, 733 P.2d 438, 448 (1987); State v. Catsam, 148 Vt. 366, 534 A.2d 184 (1987).

[275] United States v. Tanksley, 54 M.J. 169 (C.A.A.F. 2000) (noting importance of limiting instruction to insure jury not use other acts evidence other than purpose for which admitted); People v. Ewoldt, 7 Cal. 4th 380, 867 P.2d 757, 27 Cal. Rptr. 2d 646 (1994); State v. Miller, 718 So. 2d 960, 962 (La. 1998); People v. Katt, 248 Mich. App. 282, 639 N.W.2d 815 (2001) (noting limiting instruction helped insure trial jury did not misuse evidence of defendant's prior sexual assaults); State v. McManus, 257 Neb. 1, 594 N.W.2d 623 (1999); State v. Oliver, 133 N.J. 141, 157–59, 627 A.2d 144, 153–54 (1993); Commonwealth v. Richter, 551 Pa. 507, 711 A.2d 464 (1998); State v. McIntosh, 207 W. Va. 561, 534 S.E.2d 757 (2000):

> When offering evidence under Rule 404(b) of the West Virginia Rules of Evidence, the prosecution is required to identify the specific purpose for which the evidence is being offered and the jury must be instructed to limit its consideration of the evidence to only that purpose. It is not sufficient for the prosecution or the trial court merely to cite or mention the litany of possible uses listed in Rule 404(b). The specific and precise purpose for which the evidence is offered must clearly be shown from the record and that purpose alone must be told to the jury in the trial court's instruction . . . . A limiting instruction should be given at the time the evidence is offered, and we recommend that it be repeated in the trial court's general charge to the jury at the conclusion of the evidence.

Under this view, the limiting instructions should not just generally explain the use of other crimes or bad acts in abstract terms, but should detail and illustrate for the jury the issues and facts upon which the other crime evidence may be considered. The specific limiting instructions not only give greater guidance to the jury in evaluating the evidence of uncharged acts, but they also allow an appellate court to review more precisely the basis for the admission of the uncharged acts. The limiting instructions should be given both at the time of the admission of the evidence and during the court's final charge.[276]

It is not unusual for a court to find that any prejudice in the admission of prior act evidence is cured by a limiting instruction.[277] On the other hand, some courts acknowledge that the prejudice arising from evidence of a prior sexual assault can not be cured with a limiting instruction.[278]

Failure to request the limiting instructions may waive the issue on appeal.[279] If the limiting instruction would be ineffective, there is authority that the evidence should not be admitted.[280] There are situations, however, when an appellate court will deem the failure to provide a limiting instruction plain error even though defendant did not request such an instruction.[281] In reversing one defendant's conviction for the failure to provide limiting instructions upon the admission of similar transaction evidence, one court noted that "although a trial judge is not

---

Id. at 569–70, 534 S.E.2d at 765–66; State v. Hammer, 236 Wis. 2d 686, 709–10, 613 N.W.2d 629, 639–40 (2000).

[276] United States v. Cuch, 842 F.2d 1173 (10th Cir. 1988); United States v. St. Pierre, 812 F.2d 417 (8th Cir. 1987); State v. Hammer, 236 Wis. 2d 686, 709–10, 613 N.W.2d 629, 639–40 (2000).

[277] *See, e.g.,* People v. Frazier, 89 Cal. App. 4th 30, 42, 107 Cal. Rptr. 2d 100, 109, *review denied,* 2001 Cal. LEXIS 5512 (Aug. 15, 2001).

[278] *See, e.g.,* Government of Virgin Islands v. Pinney, 967 F.2d 912, 918 (3d Cir. 1992).

[279] United States v. Powers, 59 F.3d 1460, 1468 (4th Cir. 1995), *cert. denied,* 516 U.S. 1077 (1996) (noting that a failure to object to the specific wording of a limiting instruction will only be reviewed for plain error and that it is rare to reverse a conviction for an improper jury instruction when no objection has been made to the trial court); People v. De Fayette, 16 A.D.3d 708, 790 N.Y.S.2d 301, *appeal denied,* 4 N.Y.3d 885, 831 N.E.2d 975, 798 N.Y.S.2d 730 (2005); People v. Castro, 281 A.D.2d 935, 722 N.Y.S.2d 854, *appeal denied,* 96 N.Y.2d 860, 754 N.E.2d 1117, 730 N.Y.S.2d 34 (2001).

[280] Bell v. Commonwealth, 875 S.W.2d 882 (Ky. 1994); State v. McIntosh, 207 W. Va. 561, 571, 534 S.E.2d 757, 767 (2000).

[281] *Ex parte* Minor, 780 So. 2d 796 (Alaska 2000) (holding it was plain error for trial court to fail to give a limiting instruction that jury could consider prior to convictions introduced by defendant on client testimony, only for impeachment, and not substantive purposes); Prickett v. State, 220 Ga. App. 244, 245–46, 469 S.E.2d 371, 373 (1996); Robinson v. State, 735 So. 2d 208 (Miss. 1999) (holding trial court has duty to instruct a jury *sua sponte* when prior conviction is for the same offense as charged offense); Commonwealth v. Billa, 521 Pa. 168, 555 A.2d 835 (1989) (reversing defendant's conviction even though defendant's prior sexual assault was relevant to the defendant's motive and intent and was relevant to negate his claim of accident, and even though defendant's counsel did not request limiting instruction, since the trial court's failure to give a limiting instruction as to its limited purpose resulted in the prior sexual assault evidence becoming inflammatory and prejudicial).

required in the absence of a request to give a limiting instruction when similar transaction evidence is admitted, it would be better for the trial judge to do so."[282]

§ 6.48 Prejudicial introduction of evidence pertaining to defendant's sexual tendencies.

A common event in sexual assault trials is for the prosecution to introduce evidence that the defendant possessed certain sexual materials or engaged in other activities of a sexual nature. When such evidence is part of the crime for which the defendant is on trial, this is not likely to be a problem.[283] For example, if a defendant displays photographs of nude children to his victim or shows the victim sexually explicit photographs of nude children to lower the sexual inhibitions of the child, it is reasonable to introduce such evidence as part of the crime.[284] A photograph of a person masturbating in a particular way may be admissible to prove *modus operandi* when it is identical to the complainant's testimony concerning defendant's behavior.[285] Testimony that the defendant masturbated while giving his statements to the police may be relevant to an assessment of the confession's reliability and voluntariness.[286] The sexually explicit evidence may be appropriate as demonstrative evidence.[287] On the other hand, if the reason investigators approached a suspect involved the videotaping of another child and inducing that child to watch a pornographic movie, that background is not inextricably interwoven with a charged offense, and is unnecessary and prejudicial if elicited at trial.[288]

---

[282] State v. Belt, 269 Ga. 763, 765, 505 S.E.2d 1, 2 (1998).

[283] Simpson v. State, 271 Ga. 772, 523 S.E.2d 320 (1999):

In a prosecution for a sexual offense, evidence of sexual paraphernalia found in defendant's possession is inadmissible unless it shows defendant's lustful disposition toward the sexual activity with which he is charged or his bent of mind to engage in that activity. Under this rule, sexually explicit material cannot be introduced merely to show a defendant's interest in sexual activity. It can only be admitted if it can be linked to the crime charged.

Id. at 774, 523 S.E.2d at 321–22. *See also* Mooney v. State, 266 Ga. App. 587, 597 S.E.2d 589 (2004) (upholding prosecution's use of a videotape of defendant's engaging in oral sex, offering drugs to women in exchange for oral sex, as he had offered to the complainant in present cases; "[t]he link between the videotape and the crimes charged in this case was Mooney's course of conduct — exchanging drugs for oral sex."); Commonwealth v. Holloway, 44 Mass. App. Ct. 469, 691 N.E.2d 985 (1998), *rev'd on other grounds* ("Thus, the complainant's testimony that the defendant had shown her pornographic videos on several occasions was admissible as evidence of a pattern or course of conduct engaged in by the defendant to exploit the complainant's trust, and also as evidence of the defendant's motive or intent to engage the complainant in a sexual relationship." *Id.* at 476, 691 N.E.2d at 990.).

[284] State v. Nolan, 717 S.W.2d 573, 577 (Mo. Ct. App. 1986).

[285] United States v. Todd, 964 F.2d 925, 932 (9th Cir. 1992).

[286] Pierce v. State, 761 N.E.2d 826, 829 (Ind. 2002).

[287] *See* § 14.29.

[288] Metcalf v. Commonwealth, 158 S.W.3d 740 (Ky. 2005).

Sometimes a defendant may make a statement reflecting sexual preferences or prior acts. When the statements may be deemed admissions, they are admissible irrespective of their reference to past acts or preferences. For example, if a defendant tells an investigator that he "fingered" his daughter after reading pornographic materials and because he remembers doing things with his sisters when he was 12 or 14 years old, this is an admission because it reflects that the physical act was done with an intent of sexual gratification, a necessary element of the crime.[289] This creates a connection between defendant's prior acts and the charged crime which would otherwise not exist. A defendant's statement to police that he has a "problem with girls" and "never was interested in older women, just young girls and teenage girls" is not necessarily an improper reference to a defendant's sexual predisposition, but may be relevant to explain the defendant's luring of the child and relevant to the defendant's motive and intent if in dispute, especially if there is no other evidence to establish the defendant's motive and intent.[290]

In some situations, evidence of a defendant's sexual orientation or sexual preferences may be admissible on the issue of the defendant's motive for the crime. (*See* § 14.29.) A defendant's statement that he uses petroleum jelly to "get into tight places" and evidence of his homosexuality may be relevant when connected to a particular fact pattern.[291] Such evidence must always be carefully balanced with the potential for prejudice and limited to minimize the inflammatory nature of such testimony. When the defendant's sexual orientation may be inferred from the circumstances of the sexual assault, a prosecutor's questioning about the defendant's sexual orientation is not necessarily unduly prejudicial as long as improper inferences are not drawn from the defendant's sexual orientation, *e.g.*, that the defendant is more likely to commit the crime because of his sexual orientation.[292] Sometimes, a witness may refer to the defendant in a way

---

[289] State v. Eves, 163 Or. App. 588, 989 P.2d 46 (1999).

[290] State v. Covell, 157 N.J. 554, 725 A.2d 675 (1999). *See also* State v. Rice, 755 A.2d 137 (R.I. 2000) (defendant's statement to young girls "I can't help it if I like pretty 13-year-old girls" neither a crime, a wrong, nor a bad act and was relevant to establish "defendant's lewd disposition toward and motive for molesting these young girls").

[291] Green v. State, 242 Ga. App. 868, 532 S.E.2d 111 (2000):

> The trial court did not err in admitting into evidence proof that, two years before, defendant had been discovered kissing then six-year-old J. A. G. or in admitting proof of defendant's statement that he used petroleum jelly to "get into tight places." Evidence of homosexuality or pederasty and indications of such sexual preferences are admissible in a trial for aggravated sodomy. While evidence of homosexuality unrelated to the offenses charged is inadmissible, both the prior act and statement in question have a logical connection to the offenses charged in that they illustrate defendant's preference for a particular victim or type of victim, plus reveal defendant's bent of mind, or his *modus operandi*.

Id. at 871, 532 S.E.2d at 114 [citations omitted].

[292] Commonwealth v. Capone, 39 Mass. App. Ct. 606, 659 N.E.2d 1196, *review denied*, 422

that has a sexual connotation. For example, a prosecutor's reference to "Mr. Dick" may be proper if the record clearly establishes the child knew the defendant and referred to the defendant as "Mr. Dick."[293]

But where evidence of a defendant's possession of pornography, or trip to a nudist camp, or evidence of nudity in the household, is introduced without demonstrating a relationship between that evidence and the crime for which the defendant is charged, such evidence is prejudicial and falls within the prohibition of propensity or character evidence.[294] For this reason, in a prosecution for child

Mass. 1106, 663 N.E.2d 576 (1996) (noting, however, that prosecution should avoid insinuations about a defendant's sexual orientation which are likely to prejudice a defendant and citing cases in support of this proposition).

[293] People v. Wasley, 249 A.D.2d 625, 671 N.Y.S.2d 767, *appeal denied*, 91 N.Y.2d 1014, 698 N.E.2d 971, 676 N.Y.S.2d 142 (1998).

[294] Guam v. Shymanovitz, 157 F.3d 1154, 1161 (9th Cir. 1998) ("The government's conduct indicates that it used the evidence of the 'Stroke' magazines in order to convince the jury that Shymanovitz was a perverted person who was prone to do bad things and to exploit its prejudices and fears as to his character. The introduction of evidence for such purposes is, of course, 'precisely the type of abuse that Rule 404 was designed to prevent.' " (*citing* United States v. Vizcarra-Martinez, 66 F.3d 1006, 1015 (9th Cir. 1995)); Simpson v. State, 271 Ga. 772, 523 S.E.2d 320 (1999) (holding that in a sexual assault prosecution, defendant's possession of sexual paraphernalia is inadmissible unless it shows defendant's lustful disposition toward the sexual activity with which he is charged on his bent of mind to engage in that activity; it can not be introduced merely to show a defendant's interest in sexual activity); State v. Castaneda, 621 N.W.2d 435 (Iowa Ct. App. 2001) (reversing defendant's conviction in a child sexual assault case in part because of prejudicial testimony by defendant's ex-wife of sex acts she allegedly performed on defendant in presence of children); People v. Mercado, 188 A.D.2d 941, 943–44, 592 N.Y.S.2d 75, 77 (1992). *See also* Sharp v. Commonwealth, 849 S.W.2d 542, 548 (Ky. 1993); State v. Alexander, 875 S.W.2d 924 (Mo. Ct. App. 1994) (Prosecution failed to demonstrate that pornographic material was displayed to the victim or that the pornographic material was placed under the victim's bed where it was found. Proof that the pornographic material was in the defendant's house, even if under the complainant's bed, "does not by itself logically tend to show that the defendant had deviate sexual intercourse with the victim. Neither does such evidence legitimately tend to prove a material fact in the case by corroborating the testimony of the victim as to the sodomy." Such pornographic evidence was, therefore, irrelevant and inadmissible. *Id.* at 929); State v. Smith, 241 Neb. 311, 488 N.W.2d 33 (1992) (holding that questioning a defendant concerning whether a phone call he made to his wife was placed from a topless go-go bar was improper, irrelevant, and highly prejudicial); People v. Seaman, 239 A.D.2d 681, 657 N.Y.S.2d 242 (1997), *appeal dismissed*, 91 N.Y.2d 954, 694 N.E.2d 881, 671 N.Y.S.2d 712 (1998) ("Here, the People introduced *inter alia*, evidence of nudity at defendant's cabin, the availability of a *Playboy* magazine, which defendant's son and his friends were permitted to view, the presence of the books *Joy of Sex* and *Freedom of Women's Pleasure* at defendant's residence, as well as the fact that defendant's son and his friends were permitted to go 'skinny dipping' in defendant's swimming pool. Such evidence bore no relationship whatsoever to the crime charged and could only have been aimed at convincing the jury of defendant's sexual proclivity. Such testimony was clearly prejudicial and can hardly be considered harmless inasmuch as the determination of guilt or innocence rested primarily on a determination of the respective credibility of defendant and the victim." [citation omitted]); People v. Singh, 186 A.D.2d 285, 288–89, 588 N.Y.S.2d 573–74 (1992) (holding that cross-examination of a defendant concerning his viewing of a pornographic videotape that was unconnected to the victim's testimony was not relevant to the defendant's credibility nor "necessary to explain, clarify or fully elicit any issue in the case" and was therefore prejudicial to the defendant).

molestation, it was reversible error to offer evidence that the defendant possessed 30-year-old pictures of his nude wife.[295]

Other references to a defendant's sexual activities or preferences, when not connected to any particular fact or issue in a case, are also improper. This can be seen in sexual assault trials where the prosecution offers testimony or makes reference to a defendant's interest in anal sex[296] or homosexuality. Such evidence is highly prejudicial, particularly given the biases and stereotypes that a jury may bring to the issue of homosexuality.[297] Presenting evidence that a defendant is a pedophile, i.e., someone with a sexual preference for children, also is a prejudicial reference to defendant's character.[298] Unduly dwelling on a defendant's homosexuality may compound the impropriety of improperly arguing defendant's homosexuality.[299]

---

[295] Tyson v. State, 232 Ga. App. 732, 503 S.E.2d 640 (1998).

[296] State v. Williams, 117 N.M. 551, 557–59, 874 P.2d 12, 18–20 (1994) (holding that defendant's interest in consensual anal sex with adult partner not relevant, not suggestive of defendant forcing himself on victim, nor so distinctive to be a "signature" act, although error was harmless).

[297] Guam v. Shymanovitz, 157 F.3d 1154 (9th Cir. 1998). In *Guam*, the court reversed the defendant's conviction due to the prosecution's introduction into evidence of condoms, surgical gloves, K-Y Jelly, children's underwear, a calendar, sexually explicit magazines, including "Stroke" and "After Midnight," together with descriptions of content of the sexually explicit materials, including men masturbating, performing auto-fellatio, ejaculating, using sex toys, wearing "leather equipment," paddling, and descriptions of the use of dildos, since such evidence was not relevant to the defendant's intent in engaging in sexual contact for the purpose of sexual gratification, and the defendant's possession of such pornography reflected only an interest in gay male pornography or gay male erotica and was not probative of the defendant actually engaging in sexual conduct of any kind. The court analogized that such information was just as irrelevant as a murder defendant's possession of Agatha Christie mysteries or James Bond novels. The court concluded that: "Evidence implicating Shymanovitz's sexual orientation was particularly prejudicial because he was being tried on numerous sex offense charges: the jury's inference that Shymanovitz was gay could in all likelihood have caused it also to infer that he deviated from traditional sexual norms in other ways, specifically that he engaged in illegal sexual conduct with minors." 157 F.3d at 1160; United States v. Gillespie, 852 F.2d 475 (9th Cir. 1988); Stevens v. State, 748 P.2d 771, 774 (Alaska Ct. App. 1988) (holding trial court erred in admitting portions of defendant's statements concerning his homosexual fantasies since such evidence had no relevant or probative value and was more in the nature of propensity evidence); People v. Mercado, 188 A.D.2d 941, 943–44, 592 N.Y.S.2d 75, 75–76 (1992) (evidence of "defendant's expulsion from military school many years earlier because of an allegedly homosexual encounter, [was] aimed at convincing the jury (and may well have done so) that defendant had a propensity for child abuse. The enormous prejudice generated by this sort of testimony outweighs any slight probative value that it may have." [citations omitted]).

[298] Turtle v. State, 600 So. 2d 1214, 1221 (Fla. Ct. App. 1992) (reversing defendant's conviction because of references to defendant meeting a "pedophile profile"); State v. Hester, 114 Idaho 688, 760 P.2d 27 (1988); State v. Nelson, 331 S.C. 1, 501 S.E.2d 716 (1998) (reversing defendant's conviction due to introduction of physical evidence seized from defendant which reflected on defendant's pedophilia); Brewington v. State, 802 S.W.2d 691, 692 (Tex. Crim. App. 1991).

[299] People v. De Vito, 21 A.D.3d 696, 800 N.Y.S.2d 250 (2005):

While defense counsel did raise the issue of defendant's homosexuality during jury

510

Similarly, evidence that a defendant is a member of the North American Man-Boy Love Association (NAMBLA), which advocates sexual relations between adults and children, has been held improper and inadmissible on the issue of the defendant's intent at the time he engaged in alleged sexual acts with underage youths, where the defendant denied any sexual contact with the victims and the defendant's intent was not at issue.[300] The court ruled that a defendant's membership in such an organization is "powerful evidence of his sexual tendencies and desires," but the prosecutor attempted to utilize the evidence of membership as "proof of his misdeeds," and it thus became predisposition evidence.[301] The prosecutor compounded the problem by not only bringing out evidence of the defendant's homosexuality, but by presenting testimony that the defendant was a known pedophile to the police, evidence that:

> [P]laced before the jury a wealth of prejudicial information about defendant's deviate lifestyle and associations. As the prosecutor's summation graphically makes clear, the true purpose behind the introduction of this evidence was to expose defendant's sexual preferences and attitudes in order to demonstrate a propensity to commit the crimes charged. The use of this evidence for such a purpose was a clear violation of well-settled legal principles.[302]

NAMBLA membership or possession of NAMBLA materials or other pornographic materials are not admissible to corroborate a complainant's testimony when the complainant does not know their contents.[303]

In the context of a possession of child pornography charge, it is prejudicial to admit into evidence explicit narratives in the defendant's possession depicting

---

selection in an attempt to ensure an impartial venire, he did not open the door to the degree of exploitation and denigration undertaken by the prosecutor during trial. Examples of the prosecutor's malevolence and impropriety abound on cross-examination and, most notably, during summation. During defendant's cross-examination, the prosecutor improperly probed defendant's sexual conduct with his past and present homosexual partners, clearly attempting to divert the jury's attention away from the evidence relating to the charged crimes. While questions concerning the content of photographs contained on defendant's computer were relevant to impeach defendant's direct testimony regarding how and when his wife learned of his homosexuality, we find that the prosecutor's prolonged inquiry was excessive and highly inflammatory.

[300] People v. Bagarozy, 132 A.D.2d 225, 522 N.Y.S.2d 848 (1987) ("As a review of the record makes clear, the court and the prosecutor mistakenly equated 'intent' with 'inclination' or 'proclivity,' subjects expressly proscribed by [the rule concerning introduction of prior uncharged conduct]." Id. at 132 A.D.2d at 236).

[301] Id. at 236–37, 522 N.Y.S.2d at 854–55.

[302] Id. at 235, 522 N.Y.S.2d at 853. See also United States v. Harvey, 991 F.2d 981 (2d Cir. 1993) (overturning child pornography conviction because of the introduction of highly prejudicial references to the defendant's ownership of legal X-rated movies and other pornography, which the government failed to show was relevant to the prosecution).

[303] See, e.g., State v. Sebasky, 547 N.W.2d 93, 98–99 (Minn. Ct. App. 1996) (but holding no reasonable likelihood of prejudice by presentation of NAMBLA's statement of purpose, read from NAMBLA bulletins).

violent sexual contact between adults and children, even though such evidence is relevant to the charge, since the narratives were of a different sexual nature than the photographs.[304] Also, in a child pornography case, it may be an improper use of character evidence to cross-examine the defendant on the "xxxteens.com" web site, even if the defendant affirmatively rebuts the charge of possession of child pornography on his computer.[305]

There have been cases in which the state has attempted to offer evidence of the defendant's involvement with Satanism. This evidence is not necessarily excludable, but presents serious issues if it is not connected with the charges or has a strong prejudicial impact. Presenting a book to a jury entitled *Satanism: Is Your Family Safe?*, with the cover of a man in a priestly robe holding a dagger and stating, "So long as jurors shy away from convicting people with alleged satanic connections, such atrocities will occur," has a potential for prejudice.[306] Such materials must be carefully reviewed for their content and possible prejudicial effect.[307]

§ 6.49   Character evidence on behalf of the defendant.

A defendant may present character testimony on his behalf. With regard to a defendant's "reputation in the community," the community need not be limited to the defendant's residential neighborhood, and the defendant may use his business contacts and occupation of many years as a predicate for a defense character witness in a sexual assault trial.[308] The general rule is that a defendant can present evidence about his general character or about a specific character trait that is relevant to the trial.[309] Generally, evidence of a defendant's sexual propriety is pertinent to whether a defendant acted in a sexually improper manner.[310] There is some authority that evidence of a defendant's sexual morality is not pertinent to a charge involving sexual conduct.[311] There is also some authority that a defendant's reputation for truthfulness is not relevant in cases

---

[304] United States v. Grimes, 244 F.3d 375 (5th Cir. 2001).

[305] State v. Atkin, 2003 UT App. 359, 80 P.3d 157 (2003), *cert. denied*, 90 P.3d 1041 (Utah 2004) (however, given other proof of defendant's possession of child pornography, and prosecutor's agreement to not reference the web site in summation, the error was harmless).

[306] State v. Naylor, 474 N.W.2d 314, 319 (Minn. 1991) (while finding the admission of such evidence improper, such error was harmless).

[307] *See generally* George L. Blum, Annotation, *Admissibility and Prejudicial Effect of Evidence, In Criminal Prosecution, of Defendant's Involvement with Witchcraft, Satanism, or the Like,* 18 A.L.R.5th 804 (1994).

[308] People v. Bouton, 50 N.Y.2d 130, 405 N.E.2d 699, 428 N.Y.S.2d 218 (1980).

[309] Edward J. Imwinkelried et al., Courtroom Criminal Evidence § 804 (3d ed. 1998).

[310] State v. Enakiev, 175 Or. App. 589, 29 P.3d 1160 (2001) (holding preclusion of such testimony was reversible error because case turned on credibility).

[311] State v. Jackson, 46 Wash. App. 360, 365, 730 P.2d 1361, 1364 (1986).

involving child sexual abuse, since traits such as honesty and truthfulness do not make it less likely that a defendant committed such a crime.[312]

Character evidence in a sexual assault trial cannot be phrased in terms of "Do you believe the defendant is capable of raping anyone?" since such opinion evidence "may not be phrased using a legal term of art carrying a specific legal meaning not readily apparent to the witness."[313] The character witness also cannot testify as to whether he or she believes that the defendant committed the particular crime in question. A character witness cannot be asked about the defendant's behavior around children, since a character witness cannot be asked about particular traits based upon personal knowledge.[314]

Opinion evidence that the defendant had never been arrested does not amount to character evidence warranting a jury instruction on the defendant's character, particularly where the witness demonstrates no knowledge of the defendant's reputation in the community.[315] The opinion of the character witness should also be formulated on opinions developed at a time relevant to the pending charge and not on opinions remote from the event for which the defendant is on trial.[316]

Some jurisdictions will permit a defendant to offer expert testimony that he does not possess the characteristics of a child molester or abuser as evidence relating to defendant's good character.[317] This is discussed further in § 11.30 dealing with expert testimony on profile evidence. However, most jurisdictions will not permit such expert testimony concerning a defendant's character.

Another issue is the effect of character evidence and the appropriate charge that would be given a jury. While character evidence may give rise to reasonable doubt, it is not necessarily proper to charge a jury that character evidence in and of itself, or standing alone, may create a reasonable doubt, since the jury must consider character evidence in light of all the evidence in the case.[318]

---

[312] State v. Blake, 157 Conn. 99, 249 A.2d 232 (1968); Daly v. State, 99 Nev. 564, 571, 665 P.2d 798, 803 (1983); State v. Robinson, 44 Wash. App. 611, 623, 722 P.2d 1379, 1386–87 (1986); State v. Harper, 35 Wash. App. 855, 670 P.2d 296 (1983).

[313] State v. Najewicz, 112 N.C. App. 280, 292–93, 436 S.E.2d 132, 139–40 (1993).

[314] State v. Graham, 906 S.W.2d 771, 780 (Mo. Ct. App. 1995), *vacated in part, cause remanded,* 969 S.W.2d 759 (Mo. Ct. App. 1998) (defendant's offer of character testimony concerning defendant's interaction with children at church of character witness was not reputation evidence but rather evidence of specific acts); People v. McGuinness, 245 A.D.2d 701, 665 N.Y.S.2d 752 (1997).

[315] Commonwealth v. Rue, 362 Pa. Super. 470, 474, 524 A.2d 973, 975 (1987).

[316] Imwinkelried, *supra* note 307, at § 804.

[317] People v. Stoll, 49 Cal. 3d 1136, 265 Cal. Rptr. 111, 783 P.2d 698 (1989); State v. Jones, 1994 Tenn. Crim. App. LEXIS 587 (Sept. 15, 1994).

[318] *See* § 16.8 for a discussion of the "standing alone" instruction.

§ 6.50 Unwitting character evidence and opening the door to defendant's prior bad acts.

The defendant must be careful not to raise the issue of character unwittingly, thereby opening the door to the prosecution's introduction of unwanted character evidence. For example, a defendant has placed his character at issue by direct testimony that he once received medals and awards for good conduct.[319] Opening the door by a defendant on direct and cross-examination by character references is discussed in § 6.15. However, in a child sexual abuse prosecution, it has been held that the defendant's testimony that he could not have molested the child is not a statement by the defendant placing his character in issue.[320] General background testimony, such as that the defendant was well off, came from a privileged background, and had no need to enter into an illegal business, does not necessarily open the door to character.[321] Ambiguous testimony by a defendant does not open the door to previously precluded bad acts. For example, a defendant testifying that he does not know about the "dangerousness" of a particular neighborhood does not open the door to defendant's past criminal activities in that geographical area.[322] Providing a jury background information on the defendant during opening arguments, such as that he is a veteran and father of three, does not imply the defendant is heterosexual and opens the door to his sexual misconduct, as long as the implication is not that the defendant led a blemish-free life.[323]

It is important that character testimony be strictly limited. A defendant who offers character witnesses to show that the defendant is of "good character for sexual morality, decency, respect for women, those topics" and then calls two adult witnesses who testified that the defendant gave them full body massages while they were almost totally unclothed without improper sexual advances opens the door to the issue of the defendant's sexual morality in general.[324] Cross-examining a complainant with respect to a failure to call out to a family member while she was being raped or introducing a prior statement which refers to the defendant's prior bad acts may also open the door to prior uncharged crimes which would otherwise be precluded.[325] A defense witness's comment that the defendant never showed signs of being a child molester opened the door to the character trait of defendant's propensity to molest children.[326]

---

[319] People v. Jones, 121 A.D.2d 398, 503 N.Y.S.2d 109 (1986).

[320] United States v. Gillespie, 852 F.2d 475 (9th Cir. 1988).

[321] United States v. McLister, 608 F.2d 785, 790 (9th Cir. 1979).

[322] People v. Moore, 92 N.Y.2d 823, 699 N.E.2d 415, 677 N.Y.S.2d 56 (1998).

[323] People v. Stanbridge, 348 Ill. App. 3d 351, 357, 810 N.E.2d 88, 94–95 (2004).

[324] State v. Mainiero, 525 N.W.2d 304, 311, 312, 189 Wis. 2d 80, 98 (1994).

[325] People v. Houston, 250 A.D.2d 535, 673 N.Y.S.2d 425, *appeal denied*, 92 N.Y.2d 983, 706 N.E.2d 752, 683 N.Y.S.2d 764 (1998).

[326] State v. Writer, 2003 Tenn. Crim. App. LEXIS 519 (June 10, 2003).

§ 6.51 Cross-examination of character witnesses.

Just as the direct testimony of a character witness cannot contain references to specific instances or acts of good character, some jurisdictions do not permit a prosecution witness to refer to specific acts of misconduct to rebut a character witness.[327] However, when a defendant chooses to offer evidence of reputation or character, he opens the door to cross-examination of the witness's knowledge of specific acts of prior misconduct or crimes. For example, a defendant charged with statutory rape could subject his character witness to cross-examination as to whether the witness's opinion would change if he had known that the defendant was once accused of molesting a child in another country.[328] However, this does not mean that the prosecution can present proof of the specific acts. The prosecutor is bound by the character witness response. Even when a jurisdiction permits cross-examination of a character witness with specific acts, extrinsic evidence of the specific acts may be buried.[329] The prosecution can also call its own character witnesses to rebut the defendant's character witnesses.

Cross-examination must also be geared toward the particular trait placed in issue by the defendant's character witnesses. If a defendant introduces testimony of his reputation for truth and veracity, this does not necessarily place his general character in issue. A physician charged with statutory rape could not be impeached with rebuttal reputation testimony that "the doctor was fresh, and he had wandering hands. They didn't trust him."[330] Cross-examination of defense

[327] People v. Mancini, 213 A.D.2d 1038, 627 N.Y.S.2d 488, *appeal denied*, 85 N.Y.2d 976, 653 N.E.2d 632, 629 N.Y.S.2d 736 (1995) (defendant's conviction reversed because trial court allowed "people's character witness to testify on rebuttal about specific acts committed by defendant against her when she was a foster child in defendant's home during the 1960's"); Commonwealth v. Scott, 496 Pa. 188, 436 A.2d 607 (1981); Weimer v. Commonwealth, 5 Va. App. 47, 53, 360 S.E.2d 381, 384 (1987).

[328] Porter v. State, 243 Ga. App. 498, 532 S.E.2d 407 (2000) (holding that in child abuse case defendant had opened the door to questioning of her character witness about specific acts of defendant to "test" the basis and foundation of character witness's testimony); State v. Fitzgerald, 39 Wash. App. 652, 663, 694 P.2d 1117, 1124 (1985). *See also* Brady v. State, 540 N.E.2d 59, 68 (Ind. Ct. App. 1989); State v. Wall, 87 N.C. App. 621, 361 S.E.2d 900, *review denied*, 321 N.C. 479, 363 S.E.2d 72 (1987) (holding that, in an incest prosecution, the prosecutor did not improperly cross-examine two of defendant's character witnesses as to whether they had heard rumors that defendant had had an affair with an 18-year-old girl and that defendant's wife had made a statement that she had "expected something was going on" between defendant and their daughter).

[329] State v. Hobson, 2003 Tenn. Crim. App. LEXIS 1050 (Dec. 18, 2003) (reversing defendant's conviction in part due to extrinsic evidence submitted of defendant's past sexual relationships with child offered to rebut character testimony).

[330] People v. Viloria, 160 A.D.2d 499, 554 N.Y.S.2d 163 (1990). *See also* Bombailey v. State, 580 So. 2d 41, 48–49 (Ala. Crim. App. 1990) ("Here, the character witness only testified that [the defendant] had a good reputation for truth and veracity. Whether [the defendant] had hit a child is not relevant to the trait of truth and veracity, and thus, the prosecutor's question was improper.").

character witnesses concerning whether the witnesses would have the same opinion of the defendant if the charged crimes were proven receives scrutiny, since it is a "guilt-assuming hypothetical question which creates a great risk of impairing the presumption of innocence."[331] However, when a defendant raises an entrapment defense, thereby conceding the alleged acts, it may be proper to cross-examine the character witness by assuming the acts occurred since this does not implicate the entrapment defense.[332]

Matters resulting in acquittal may be improper for cross-examination of a character witness.[333] It may be necessary for the cross-examiner to have not only a good faith basis for a specific act, but also a good faith basis that the witness or community should have known about it.[334]

§ 6.52 Sample direct examination of a character witness in a sexual assault trial.

In the following example, the defendant, a teenage boy, was accused of walking into a dormitory room and raping a young woman who was asleep and intoxicated. He called a character witness because he had no criminal record and no prior involvement with the law. After introducing the witness, defense counsel establishes the foundation for the character testimony.

Q. Do you know Bruce Wayne?

A. Yes.

Q. The gentleman that's seated here with me at counsel table?

A. Yes.

Q. Is that also his address?

A. Yes.

Q. You're a resident of the same apartment building?

A. Yes.

---

[331] United States v. Oshatz, 912 F.2d 534, 539 (2d Cir. 1990). *See also* United States v. Russo, 110 F.3d 948, 952 (2d Cir. 1997); United States v. Smith-Bowman, 76 F.3d 634 (5th Cir.), *cert. denied*, 518 U.S. 1011 (1996); United States v. Barta, 888 F.2d 1220, 1224–25 (8th Cir. 1989); United States v. Siers, 873 F.2d 747, 749–50 (4th Cir. 1989); United States v. Page, 808 F.2d 723, 731–32 (10th Cir. 1987), *cert. denied*, 482 U.S. 918 (1987); United States v. Williams, 738 F.2d 172, 176–77 (7th Cir. 1984); People v. Lowery, 214 A.D.2d 684, 626 N.Y.S.2d 205 (1995), *modified, remanded sub nom.* People v. Payne, 88 N.Y.2d 172, 666 N.E.2d 542, 643 N.Y.S.2d 949 (1996).

[332] United States v. Damblu, 134 F.3d 490, 494–95 (2d Cir. 1998).

[333] People v. Bouton, 50 N.Y.2d 130, 140, 405 N.E.2d 699, 704, 428 N.Y.S.2d 218, 223 (1980).

[334] United States v. Monteleone, 77 F.3d 1086 (8th Cir. 1996) (defendant's prior act of lying before a grand jury 25 years earlier would not probably be known by community, due to secrecy of grand jury proceedings).

Q. Just for our benefit up here, roughly how many families would constitute that apartment building, roughly?

A. There are 12 apartments, 12 families in this building, but there are seven connected buildings which share facilities in the courtyard. All together in this building complex there are 105 apartments.

Q. And how long have you been a neighbor of the Waynes'?

A. We lived in this complex, my wife and I, since November of 2001. We moved into this particular building in January of 2003, and the Waynes moved in, I believe, a few months after we did.

Q. So for some nine or ten years had you been neighbors down there?

A. Yes.

Q. In that area. What is your occupation, Mr. Gerhardt?

A. I'm a member of the Board of Directors and the Treasurer of the Levine Paper Company.

Without foundation, a character witness cannot provide character testimony. This can be developed further if counsel believes that it would be helpful.

Q. Now, with respect to that neighborhood community within which you live, that apartment house community, I'm going to ask you whether or not from the neighbors you have heard the reputation with respect to truthfulness, veracity, and lawfulness discussed as it would pertain to Bruce Wayne?

A. The answer is yes.

Following the foundation questions, the basic area of direct examination involves the character traits in question.

THE COURT: Sir, now let's make it clear. That's not what you think, but from the speech of the people in that community that you live in. Do you understand that?

THE WITNESS: Yes, your Honor, I understand that.

In the above, the court makes an important point that the witness cannot give his opinion, but only tell what he has heard in the community. If the witness responds with her opinion of the defendant, then the answer will be stricken. This should be discussed with the witness in advance, since most lay witnesses will believe they are being asked their opinion of the defendant, rather than the opinion of others in the community.

Q. And what is his reputation in the community for lawfulness?

A. The opinion is that he's a law-abiding young citizen.

Q. And what would his reputation be for truthfulness?

A. Fine, excellent.

Q. And for lawfulness?

A. Excellent.

The witness should answer these questions clearly and directly and not equivocally such as, "To the best of my knowledge, it's always been favorable." The witness should be prepared for counsel questions and the unusual rules of character testimony.

§ 6.53   Cross-examination of the character witness.

The first area of cross-examination of a defendant's character witness might probe of the basis of the testimony. The cross-examiner might suggest that the testimony is based upon an inadequate foundation or that the witness, if a neighbor, is not part of the community where defendant engages in the majority of his activities, which may be different from what he does at home.

Q. It's your testimony that in this apartment complex you sit around and discuss people's traits for truthfulness, is that correct?

A. We are neighbors, sir, and we sit around and talk about the neighborhood and about our building and about our neighbors. The answer is yes.

Q. And as part of those discussions you would include whether or not a certain neighbor is truthful?

A. From time to time, yes, especially when it comes to children.

Q. And, specifically, you can think of times when you have discussed the truthfulness of this defendant?

A. Absolutely. Not only with neighbors, but also with the superintendent of the building.

Q. And your community, is that just where you live, or does that include the school the defendant goes to, when he does attend, where he goes out at night?

A. The area where he lives, that's all.

As noted earlier, jurisdictions vary on the extent to which character witnesses can be cross-examined regarding specific acts of misconduct by the defendant. The witness can be asked if he or she heard about the defendant's less than truthful behavior or his less than favorable conduct and, if so, whether it would change his or her opinion of the defendant. Note that the questions are phrased in terms of "Have you heard?" In this case, there was proof that defendant was carrying false identification on the night in question. Otherwise, questioning about other acts of the defendant must have a good-faith basis.

Q. And had you heard in your community that this defendant used fake or false identification cards?

A. Never.

Q. In his life. You never heard that?

A. Never.

Q. In your mind does that have anything to do with truthfulness?

A. If I were to hear that he used a fake identification card, it might have something to do with that.

Q. Would that change your opinion on his truthfulness or veracity if you knew that?

A. Perhaps.

Even if there is little about which to question a character witness, unless the witness absolutely raised no issues, the cross-examiner should at least try to make a few points. When in doubt as to what to ask, a safe area of questioning is that the witness does not really know what happened at the time of the alleged assault. Such questioning emphasizes the point that the jury should focus on the *proof* of whether the defendant committed the crime for which he is charged.

Q. You have not heard the proof in this case have you?

A. No.

Q. You were not present on March 10th at Hadley Hall?

A. No.

Q. And you have no knowledge, do you, of what happened in Hadley Hall on the morning of March 10th, 1997, do you?

A. No.

CHAPTER 7

CONSENT

§ 7.1   Introduction.

For a conviction, there are three elements required in a sexual assault case: sexual contact, lack of consent, and identification. The investigation of a sexual assault should focus on developing proof in each of these three areas; conversely, the defense in a sexual assault crime will virtually always focus on showing that one of these three elements has not been established. With adult victims, the great majority of defenses will be based on either consent or failure of identification. With child victims, identification may be an issue, but the nonoccurrence of the act or lack of sexual contact usually will be asserted as a defense.

Lack of consent is defined in one of several ways. All states have an age of consent under which an individual is deemed incapable of consent. In crimes based upon the age of consent, the prosecution will attempt to establish that the act occurred and that the complainant was under the age of consent. Lack of consent can also be based upon the incapacity of an adult to consent to sexual contact. Incapacity to consent can be based upon a mental disability of a complainant or upon a form of physical helplessness, which would include the case in which a victim was asleep. This incapacity of consent can also be based upon the administration of an intoxicating liquor or a drug that renders a complainant incapable of understanding what he or she was doing and thus was unable to consent. Force can also overcome the capacity of consent. Force is usually based upon either physical force, a threat (express or implied), or some form of intimidation. As will be seen in this section, there is wide variation in the courts' interpretation as to what constitutes appropriate physical force or threats sufficient to sustain the lack of consent element in a sexual assault prosecution.

At one time, the marital relationship was deemed to provide implicit consent to sexual relations. This so-called marital exemption for rape statutes has been superseded by legislation or overruled by court decisions.

Some states deem certain relationships subject to special definitions concerning the capacity of consent. For example, some states criminalize sexual conduct between a psychotherapist and patient, or corrections officer and inmate. Under these statutes, the consent of the patient to such conduct is no defense to the crime.

§ 7.2 Age, consent, and proof of age.

In most states, a person is deemed incapable of consent under a particular age. The level of crime for statutes based upon age is usually inversely related to the age of the child. The age of consent varies widely from state to state. In one state it may be permissible for a 17-year-old to consent to sexual relations but not drink alcoholic beverages. It may be legal for an adolescent to marry in some states while at the same time that same adolescent cannot engage in consensual sexual relations with an unmarried adult.

In a prosecution based upon age as the reason for the incapacity to consent, it is essential for the prosecution to establish the age of the complainant, and in some crimes, it is also essential to establish the age of the defendant. As noted elsewhere in this text, in child pornography prosecution, there is a body of law that permits a jury to determine by its observation the age of a person in an image.[1] If a child who is an unsworn witness testifies to his or her age, observation by the jury may corroborate the ordinarily unsworn child's testimony concerning age.[2] Where age of the defendant or the victim is an element of the crime, mere observation of the parties during the trial may be insufficient to establish their age.[3] Usually, in addition to observation, the prosecution will rely

---

[1] *See* § 12.23.

[2] People v. Petrie, 3 A.D.3d 665, 668, 771 N.Y.S.2d 242, 245 (2004). *See also* Oliver v. United States, 711 A.2d 70 (D.C. App. 1998) (permitting jury to find defendant was four years older than victims, as requested by statute, by virtue of jury's observations and defendant's taking children on camping trips for 20 years).

[3] Hawkins v. State, 549 So. 2d 552 (Ala. Crim. App. 1989):

While the jury, observing the appellant, could estimate his probable age, the statutory requirement demands more. There must be something in the transcript which permits a legal inference of the age of the appellant at the time of the alleged sexual abuse. Where the language of a statute is plain and unambiguous, and its meaning is obvious, this court must give effect to the legislature's manifestation of its intent, as there is no room for construction of that statute. [citation omitted] The plain language of this statute makes it clear that the age of the accused is a material element of first degree sexual abuse. In cases involving similarly worded statutes, we have been required

upon evidence such as a birth certificate, direct testimony of the party, a statement during an interview with a police officer,[4] or pedigree statements to establish age.[5] The pedigree exception to the *Miranda rule* permits the use of information, such as the defendant's birth date, provided at the time of a defendant's booking.[6] Some courts will permit circumstantial evidence in addition to observation to establish age. Such circumstantial evidence may be testimony that the defendant engaged in adult activities or purchased beer or cigarettes.[7]

States also vary as to whether a defendant's failure to know the age of a complainant is a valid defense to a sexual assault crime based upon the age of the victim. California does permit a good faith reasonable mistake as to a victim's

---

by the clear statutory language to hold that the age of the accused was an element of the offense which must be proven by the State in order to establish a prima facie case against the accused.

Hawkins v. State, 549 So. 2d 552, 555–556 (Ala. Crim. App. 1989); State v. Lauritsen, 199 Neb. 816, 261 N.W.2d 755, 757 (1978) ("It is uniformly the rule that a defendant's physical appearance may be considered by the jury in determining his or her age. It has been held, however, that the jury may not fix the age of the defendant by merely observing him during the trial; and that there must be some other evidence in conjunction with the appearance of the defendant."); People v. Perryman, 178 A.D.2d 916, 578 N.Y.S.2d 785 (1991), *appeal denied*, 79 N.Y.2d 1005, 594 N.E.2d 954, 584 N.Y.S.2d 460 (1992) (circumstantial evidence of defendant's age was testimony by 14-and 20-year-old witnesses that defendant was their father); People v. Blodgett, 160 A.D.2d 1105, 553 N.Y.S.2d 897, *appeal denied*, 76 N.Y.2d 731, 557 N.E.2d 1188, 558 N.Y.S.2d 892 (1990) (reversing defendant's conviction due to prosecution's failure to establish defendant's age). *See generally*, Annotation, John D. Perovich, *Burden of Proof of Defendant's Age, In Prosecution Where Attainment of Particular Age is Statutory Requisite of Guilt*, 49 A.L.R.3d 526 (1973).

[4] People v. Kittles, 23 A.D.3d 775, 803 N.Y.S.2d 771 (2005) ("Here, the victim testified that she had known defendant for approximately five years and knew that he was over the age of 18. That testimony, coupled with the jury's observation of defendant, provided a legally sufficient basis for the jury to find that defendant was at least 18 years old at the time of the offense. [citations omitted]"); People v. Ford, 233 A.D.2d 946, 649 N.Y.S.2d 883 (1996).

[5] State v. Locklear, 138 N.C. App. 549, 531 S.E.2d 853, *review denied*, 352 N.C. 359, 544 S.E.2d 553 (2000) (holding defendant's age properly proven through defendant's statement as to his date of birth during the booking process since *Miranda* warnings are not required for gathering of data, which is part of booking process).

[6] Pennsylvania v. Muniz, 496 U.S. 582, 601 (1990) (holding that routine booking questions, such as name, address, height, weight, eye color, and date of birth are exempt from *Miranda's* requirements); State v. Montes, 1997 Wash. App. LEXIS 521 (Apr. 11, 1997) (defendant's statement as to his date of birth was non-custodial. However, decision raises issue of whether sibling's testimony of victim's birth date is double hearsay).

[7] *See, e.g.*, Barnett v. State, 488 So. 2d 24 (Ala. Crim. App. 1986) (fact that defendant had been married for eight years and testimony about former marriage, together with jurors' observation, provided circumstantial evidence to establish defendant was at least 16); Flynn v. State, 847 P.2d 1073, 1076–77 (Alaska Ct. App. 1993); State v. Thompson, 365 N.W.2d 40, 43 (Iowa Ct. App. 1985); People v. Rosio, 220 A.D.2d 851, 632 N.Y.S.2d 255, *appeal denied*, 86 N.Y.2d 875, 659 N.E.2d 779, 635 N.Y.S.2d 956 (1995) (testimony that defendant's children were 18-and 12-years-old was sufficient circumstantial evidence to establish that defendant was more than 21-years of age). *See* § 14.34, discussing observation of a complainant or defendant as demonstrative evidence to establish age.

age as a defense to a statutory rape charge,[8] but not as to a lewd or lascivious conduct charge with a child under 14 years of age.[9] Illinois permits as a defense to its statutory sexual assaults that "the accused reasonably believed the person to be 17 years of age or over."[10] Under this approach, if there is an issue as to the defendant's reasonable belief of the victim's age, the prosecution has the burden of proving that the defendant did not believe that the victim was the age of consent.[11] The laws of many states are similar to the New York law, which states that the defendant's lack of knowledge of the age of the child is not a defense to a crime unless expressly so stated in the statute defining a crime.[12] Usually, lack of knowledge of age is not a defense to a sexual assault crime based upon age.[13] When there is a defense of reasonable mistake as to age, it may be reversible error to exclude testimony of lay witnesses that the minor appeared to be a particular age.[14]

The use of the word "knowingly" in a criminal statute involving a child victim does not necessarily trigger a requirement that the defendant must know the age of the victim. For example, a child abuse statute which criminalizes "knowingly or willingly" battering a child does not require that the accused know the age of the child abused, as well as the fact of abuse.[15] The U.S. Supreme Court made a distinction between requiring a defendant to know a performer's age in a videotape, where "[t]he opportunity for reasonable mistake as to age increases significantly once the victim is reduced to visual depiction" and sexual assault crimes where the defendant "confronts" the victim and may be reasonably required to ascertain the victim's age."[16]

Another issue that occasionally arises is whether a child who may be incapable of consenting to sexual activity can be prosecuted for the criminal offense even

---

[8] People v. Hernandez, 61 Cal. 2d 529, 393 P.2d 673, 39 Cal. Rptr. 361 (1964).

[9] People v. Olsen, 36 Cal. 3d 638, 205 Cal. Rptr. 492, 685 P.2d 52 (1984).

[10] Ill. Comp. Stat. ch. 720 5/12-17.

[11] People v. Lemons, 229 Ill. App. 3d 645, 593 N.E.2d 1040, *appeal denied*, 146 Ill. 2d 641, 602 N.E.2d 466 (1992) (noting, however, that the defendant failed to raise sufficient evidence to assert the issue of his reasonable belief that the victim's age was above the age of consent).

[12] N.Y. Penal Law § 15.20 subd. (3). *See also* § 16.17.

[13] Hodge v. State, 866 So. 2d 1270, 1273 (Fla. Ct. App. 2004) (holding ignorance or mistake as to age is no defense to a statutory rape prosecution); Grady v. State, 701 So. 2d 1181 (Fla. Dist. Ct. App. 1997), *review denied*, 717 So. 2d 531 (Fla. 1998) (holding defendant's knowledge of person procured for prostitution not an element of crime); State v. Buch, 83 Haw. 308, 926 P.2d 599 (1996) ("To further its policy of protecting children from sexual exploitation by adults, the legislature expressly deleted knowledge of the child's age as an element of sexual assault offenses in which the child's age is an attendant circumstance."); State v. Stiffler, 117 Idaho 405, 788 P.2d 220 (1990); *See generally*, Colin Campbell, Annotation, *Mistake or Lack of Information as to Victim's Age as Defense to Statutory Rape*, 46 A.L.R.5TH 499 (1997).

[14] United States v. Yazzie, 976 F.2d 1252 (9th Cir. 1992).

[15] Witt v. State, 780 So. 2d 946 (Fla. Dist. Ct. App. 2001), *review denied*, 799 So. 2d 220 (Fla. 2001).

[16] United States v. X-Citement Video, Inc., 513 U.S. 64, 72 n.2 (1994).

though he or she is within the protected age group of the criminal statute. This issue can also be seen in delinquency proceedings. [17]

If the statute for which the defendant is prosecuted utilizes a victim's age as an aggravating factor in sentencing, it may not be necessary to present proof of the complainant's age at trial, since in such a case it is not considered an element of the crime. [18]

§ 7.3 Consent and mental disability.

There is a wide range of mental disabilities that form the basis for lack of consent, and state courts take different approaches in defining the level of understanding required for an adult to consent to sexual acts. These prosecutions usually involve complainants who have mental diseases or suffer from developmental disabilities. [19]

An initial question that must be answered in prosecutions based upon a complainant's mental disease or defect is whether the complainant has sufficient capacity to testify as a witness. In situations where the complainant lacks the capacity to testify, he or she may lack the capacity to consent. Capacity to testify is a different standard than capacity to consent. However, often in such situations where the incapacity to consent issue is the clearest, the prosecution is deprived of an essential witness. In such situations, the prosecution may have to dismiss because of the seriousness of the complainant's mental condition. This is sometimes seen in situations where, as a result of the sexual assault, the complainant deteriorates psychologically to such an extent that he or she is incapable of testifying. Another dilemma for the prosecution is that it may be arguing that the complainant has the capacity to testify as a witness but not the capacity to consent to sexual conduct. While this argument is not necessarily mutually exclusive with certain witnesses, a prosecutor who takes both positions can appear inconsistent to a jury.

Many states have defined the capacity to consent in terms of a person's ability not only to understand the nature and consequences of sexual intercourse, but also the societal aspects or implications of the sexual act. [20] The understanding of the sexual act may include:

---

[17] *See generally* Susan M. Kole, Annotation, *Statute Protecting Minors in a Specified Age Range From Rape or Other Sexual Activity as Applicable to Defendant Minor within Protected Age Group,* 18 A.L.R.5th 856 (1994).

[18] State v. Baker, 301 Mont. 323, 8 P.3d 817 (2000).

[19] *See generally* K.H. Larsen, Annotation, *Rape or Similar Offense Based on Intercourse with Woman Who Is Allegedly Mentally Deficient,* 31 A.L.R.3d 1227 (1970).

[20] Brooks v. State, 555 So. 2d 1134, 1136–37 (Ala. Crim. App. 1989); Jackson v. State, 890 P.2d 587 (Alaska Ct. App. 1995); People v. Gross, 670 P.2d 799, 801 (Colo. 1983); State v. Gonsalves, 5 Haw. App. 659, 706 P.2d 1333, 1337 (1985); People v. McMullen, 91 Ill. App. 3d 184, 414 N.E.2d 214 (1980); People v. Easley, 42 N.Y.2d 50, 364 N.E.2d 1328, 396 N.Y.S.2d 635 (1977); State v. Callender, 181 Or. App. 636, 47 P.3d 514, 520, *review denied,* 334 Or. 632,

The development of emotional intimacy between sexual partners; it may under some circumstances result in a disruption of one's established relationships; and, it is associated with the possibility of pregnancy with its accompanying decisions and consequences as well as the specter of disease and even death. While the law does not require an alleged victim to understand any or all of these particulars . . . [all] are elements of a meaningful understanding of the nature and consequences of sexual intercourse and are important for a trier-of-fact to bear in mind when it is evaluating whether a person had a condition which prevented him or her from having a meaningful understanding of the nature or consequences of the act of sexual intercourse. They are especially important to acknowledge in prosecutions involving the mentally disabled because such individuals may have a condition which permits them to have a knowledge of the basic mechanics of sexual intercourse, but no real understanding of either the encompassing nature of sexual intercourse or the consequences which may follow.[21]

The moral applications of the sexual act include the understanding of how society views the sexual act and the consequences of the sexual act. It would be insufficient that an individual understands that intercourse can lead to children. (Of course not knowing that sexual intercourse can lead to pregnancy would be strong evidence of lacking the ability to consent to sexual relations.)[22] It would be essential that the person understand the consequences of bearing children and the societal view of children born out of wedlock. This might be called the moral quality surrounding the sexual act. The problem with such an approach is the use of the word moral. The moral quality of the sexual act is a variable yardstick by which to measure an individual's understanding of sexuality. This definition has been criticized as allowing a jury to evaluate the capacity to consent based on the jury's view of morality rather than the specific facts of the case.[23] Other courts have spoken in terms of an individual understanding the consequences as well as the nature of sexual acts; this is still a broad approach, but it focuses less on the moral quality of the individual's understanding.[24] The consequences

---

54 P.3d 1042 (2002) ("[B]eing capable of appraising the nature of a person's conduct requires more than a mere understanding of the physical aspects of the conduct. Instead, it includes an ability to contemplate and assess the 'right or wrong' and the 'moral quality' of the conduct."); State v. Ortega-Martinez, 124 Wash. 2d 702, 881 P.2d 231 (1994).

[21] Metzger v. State, 565 So. 2d 291 (Ala. Crim. App. 1990).

[22] State v. Ortega-Martinez, 124 Wash. 2d 702, 712, 881 P.2d 231, 237 (1994).

[23] State v. Sullivan, 298 N.W.2d 267, 272 (Iowa 1980).

[24] State v. Johnson, 155 Ariz. 23, 745 P.2d 81, 84 (1987); People v. Whitten, 269 Ill. App. 3d 1037, 647 N.E.2d 1062, appeal denied, 162 Ill. 2d 579, 652 N.E.2d 348 (1995) (Complainant's mental disability, her lack of sex education, statements that she had sex with defendant against her will, mild mental retardation, the fact that she had never lived alone, and defendant's use of his position of authority met the prosecution's burden of establishing that the victim "had insufficient intelligence to understand the act, its nature, and possible consequences." With respect to the defendant's use of a position of authority, the court noted that "courts have devoted little

usually spoken of in these decisions are pregnancy or disease, financial obligations pertaining to children, or responsibilities relating to pregnancy. An ability to understand where babies come from would appear to be the type of understanding concerning sexual matters that would be quite relevant to the capacity to consent.[25] The New Jersey Supreme Court has criticized the various views on capacity and consent and has formulated its own approach. In *State v. Olivio*,[26] the New Jersey court eliminated awareness of consequences of sexual activity or the moral quality component as factors in the capacity to consent to sexual activity. According to the New Jersey court, an individual is mentally defective and incapable of consenting to a sexual act:

> If, at the time of the sexual activity, the mental defect rendered him or her unable to comprehend the distinctively sexual nature of the conduct, or incapable of understanding or exercising the right to refuse to engage in such conduct with another . . . in the context of this criminal statute, that knowledge extends only to the physical or physiological aspects of sex; it does not extend to an awareness that sexual acts have probable serious consequences such as pregnancy in birth, disease, infirmities, adverse psychological or emotional disorders, or possible adverse moral or social effects.[27]

An important part of this definition is that the individual understands that the conduct is sexual and understands that he or she has the right to refuse to engage in the sexual act and has the ability to assert that right.[28] This means that a person should have some understanding that his or her body is private and that he or she has a right to be free from the advances of others and to refuse sexual activity that entails a certain level of social maturity.[29] It should be noted that the New Jersey statute, like some statutes, imposes criminal liability only if the defendant "knew or should have known" that the complainant was mentally defective, which

---

attention to the state of mind or intent of the perpetrator in relation to the victim's ability to give knowing consent. Perhaps it is time for the courts to broaden the inquiry." People v. Whitten, 269 Ill. App. 3d 1037, 1042, 647 N.E.2d 1062, 1066, *appeal denied*, 162 Ill. 2d 579, 652 N.E.2d 348 (1995)); People v. Washington, 167 Ill. App. 3d 73, 520 N.E.2d 1160, 1162, *appeal denied*, 121 Ill. 2d 584, 526 N.E.2d 838 (1988); Stafford v. State, 455 N.E.2d 402, 406 (Ind. Ct. App. 1983); State v. Sullivan, 298 N.W.2d 267 (Iowa 1980); Keim v. State, 13 Kan. App. 2d 604, 777 P.2d 278, 280 (1989); State v. McDowell, 427 So. 2d 1346, 1350 (La. Ct. App. 1983); State v. Zeh, 31 Ohio St. 3d 99, 103–04, 509 N.E.2d 414, 418 (1987) (Ohio Supreme Court held a person's incapacity to consent is "established by demonstrating a present reduction, diminution, or decrease in the victim's ability, either to appraise the nature of [her] conduct or to control [her] conduct.").

[25] People v. Whitten, 269 Ill. App. 3d 1037, 647 N.E.2d 1062, *appeal denied*, 162 Ill. 2d 579, 652 N.E.2d 348 (1995); People v. Velasco, 216 Ill. App. 3d 578, 575 N.E.2d 954, *appeal denied*, 142 Ill. 2d 663, 584 N.E.2d 138 (1991).

[26] State v. Olivio, 123 N.J. 550, 589 A.2d 597 (1991).

[27] State v. Olivio, 123 N.J. 550, 564, 589 A.2d 597, 605 (1991).

[28] State v. Olivio, 123 N.J. 550, 567, 589 A.2d 597, 606 (1991).

[29] State v. Olivio, 123 N.J. 550, 567, 589 A.2d 597, 606 (1991).

means that there is a subjective element of whether the defendant knew, and an objective element of whether the defendant should have known the mental condition of the complainant.[30] The New Jersey court also states that in prosecutions based upon a complainant's incapacity to consent, the jury should be given not just the language of the statute but sufficient guidance as to what constitutes capacity to consent in order to avoid "speculation, misunderstanding or confusion" in determining the issue of capacity to consent.[31]

In applying this principle in a case involving multiple individuals who had sexual relations with a sexually active, mentally impaired individual, a New Jersey appellate court emphasized that not only did the victim not understand she had the right to refuse to consent to sexual relations, but also she generally could not decline any request.[32]

Failing to develop the extent to which a complainant does or does not understand and appreciate sexual activity may lead to a reversal of conviction. The fact finder may not infer the complainant's inability to understand the nature and consequences of her sexual activity.[33]

The argument that juries should be given expanded instructions on the issue of consent is comparable to the belief that jurors should be given expanded instructions when evidence of prior uncharged acts is presented to them.[34] The court notes that instructions in this regard "should inform the jury that the alleged victim's capacity to understand and consent to the proffered sexual conduct must be considered in the context of all the surrounding circumstances in which it occurred."[35]

Understanding the context of the complainant's capacity to consent requires investigation. This means collecting all information concerning the complainant's psychological, educational, and medical history. It is important to understand the activities in which the individual has engaged in society, especially work and independent living skills. School records may shed some light on the level of an individual's understanding and provide one of the more common areas of

---

[30] N.J. Stat. § 2C:14-2C(2). *See also* Ohio Rev. Code § 2907.02(A)(1)(c).

[31] State v. Olivio, 123 N.J. 550, 568, 589 A.2d 597, 606 (1991).

[32] State v. Scherzer, 301 N.J. Super. 363, 405–06, 694 A.2d 196, 216, *appeal denied*, 151 N.J. 466, 700 A.2d 878 (1997) ("The State presented ample evidence that all three defendants were aware of M.G.'s acquiescent nature in sexual and other matters and that they had taken advantage of that aspect of her personality in the past. Even if they could not be expected to have labeled her as "mentally defective", they, as reasonable young persons were shown under the circumstances presented to have known that M.G. did not understand that she could say no to a request." State v. Scherzer, 301 N.J. Super. 363, 406, 694 A.2d 196, 216, *appeal denied*, 151 N.J. 466, 700 A.2d 878 (1997)).

[33] Adkins v. Commonwealth, 20 Va. App. 332, 457 S.E.2d 382 (1995). *See* § 7.4, nn.38–39.

[34] *See* § 6.47.

[35] State v. Olivio, 123 N.J. 550, 568, 589 A.2d 597, 606 (1991).

social interaction for most individuals. This analysis also may trigger the issue of a complainant's prior sexual history.[36]

§ 7.4   Mental incapacity and the need for expert testimony to establish mental disability.

Many courts have held that expert testimony is not a prerequisite to establishing the developmental limitations and incapacity to consent of a complainant.[37] "A person's capacity to understand . . . is a factual issue for the jury and, like other facts, may properly be established by circumstantial evidence"[38] or the surrounding facts or circumstances.[39]

A statute which refers to a person's incapacity to consent "because of mental disorder or developmental or physical disability" does not necessarily require that a victim be diagnosed as "developmentally disabled" for the issue of consent to be given to a jury.[40] A complainant's limitations can be established through circumstantial evidence, such as a victim's inability to spell her last name, to correctly state her age, and other statements of the complainant which indicate a lack of understanding of sexual conduct.[41] Additional evidence of a victim's comprehension can be supplied by a victim's parents or a person such as a program manager or counselor who has knowledge of the complainant's activities and background.[42]

---

[36] *See* § 7.5.

[37] Jackson v. State, 890 P.2d 587 (Alaska Ct. App. 1995); State v. Soura, 118 Idaho 232, 237–38, 796 P.2d 109, 114–15 (1990); People v. Novak, 212 A.D.2d 740, 622 N.Y.S.2d 783, *appeal denied*, 85 N.Y.2d 941, 651 N.E.2d 928, 627 N.Y.S.2d 1003 (1995); State v. Tate, 2000 Ohio App. LEXIS 4960 (Oct. 26, 2000); Wootton v. State, 799 S.W.2d 499, 501 (Tex. App. 1990).

[38] Jackson v. State, 890 P.2d 587, 592 (Alaska Ct. App. 1995).

[39] State v. Callender, 181 Or. App. 636, 47 P.3d 514, *review denied*, 334 Or. 632, 54 P.3d 1042 (2002):

> [T]he inquiry into whether the victim was incapable of appraising the nature of the sexual conduct at issue was not confined to the victim's understanding of the mechanics of that conduct. Accordingly, in instructing the jury regarding its assessment of whether the victim was 'incapable of appraising the nature of' her conduct . . . the trial court did not err in instructing it to consider the victim's understanding of the consequences of the sexual acts by considering surrounding facts and circumstances.

State v. Callender, 181 Or. App. 636, 648, 47 P.3d 514, 520, *review denied*, 334 Or. 632, 54 P.3d 1042 (2002).

[40] People v. Mobley, 72 Cal. App. 4th 761, 85 Cal. Rptr. 2d 474 (1999), *review denied*, 1999 Cal. LEXIS 6181 (Cal. Sept. 1, 1999).

[41] People v. Cratsley, 206 A.D.2d 691, 615 N.Y.S.2d 463 (1994), *aff'd*, 86 N.Y.2d 81, 653 N.E.2d 1162, 629 N.Y.S.2d 992 (1995).

[42] People v. Mobley, 72 Cal. App. 4th 761, 85 Cal. Rptr. 2d 474 (1999), *review denied*, 1999 Cal. LEXIS 6181 (Cal. Sept. 1, 1999) (complainant's incapacity to consent because of mental disorder or developmental disability established not only by prosecution's experts but also by

Testimony of the complainant's parents or family members, together with jurors' observations of the complainant's testimony, may support a finding that the complainant lacked sufficient understanding of sexual activity to connect to sexual relations.[43] Expert testimony may, of course, be utilized and may open the door to other opinions and information on cross-examination.[44]

In the view of other courts, failing to establish through medical or expert testimony a complainant's mental incapacity and its effect upon knowing and understanding sexual relations may be fatal to a prosecution under a theory of mental disability. Where there is no direct testimony from any witnesses concerning a complainant's capacity to appraise the nature of sexual conduct, and the conviction is based on assumptions deriving from the victim's testimony, conviction based on incapacity to consent due to mental illness or mental defect will be reversed.[45] Under this view merely presenting proof of a complainant's developmental disabilities may be insufficient to sustain a conviction. A defendant's conviction may be dismissed on the grounds of sufficiency when no proof is presented to establish that the complainant does not know or understand the nature and consequences of the sexual act, and expert testimony should relate any mental incapacity to this standard. In reversing a defendant's conviction based on the insufficiency of evidence, the Virginia Court of Appeals held:

> The fact finder cannot infer from proof of general mental incapacity or retardation or an IQ range or mental age that a victim is prevented or unable to understand the nature and consequences of a sexual act, unless the evidence proves that the victim lacks the ability to comprehend or appreciate either the distinguishing characteristics or physical qualities of the sexual act or the

victim's brother and mother); State v. Tate, 2000 Ohio App. LEXIS 4960 (Oct. 26, 2000) (holding complainant's incapacity established through her own and her mother's testimony); State v. Kelley, 1 P.3d 546 (Utah 2000) (complainant's incapacity to and consent to or understand consequences of a sexual act established by her special education teacher who worked with professionals, such as psychologists, psychiatrists, and doctors to determine individuals' intellectual and physical abilities, and he could also utilize psychological testing as part of that assessment, since such testimony is "reasonably relied on by experts in that particular field." State v. Kelley, 1 P.3d 546, 551 (Utah 2000)).

[43] Jackson v. State, 890 P.2d 587 (Alaska Ct. App. 1995) (Jury could rely on testimony of complainant's mother concerning her abilities as well as jury's observations of complainant when she testified; expert testimony was not required to support charge based upon victim's mental incapacity.); People v. Beasley, 314 Ill. App. 3d 840, 732 N.E.2d 1122, *appeal denied*, 191 Ill. 2d 537, 738 N.E.2d 929 (2000) (trial court sitting as finder of fact could rely on its own observations and testimony of complainant and her aunt to find her incapable of consent).

[44] People v. Brown, 7 A.D.3d 726, 777 N.Y.S.2d 508 (2004) (upholding expert testimony to explain complainant's intellectual limitations in aftermath of the crime; when the expert was challenged as to complainant's truthfulness on cross-examination, this opened the door to prosecutor's redirect examination and the question of whether the complainant was capable of fabricating such an elaborate lie and maintaining it over a period of time and his opinion that the victim was intellectually incapable of doing so).

[45] State v. Tunis, 1994 Del. Super. LEXIS 588 (Nov. 18, 1994).

future natural behavior or societal results or effects which may flow from the sexual act.[46]

§ 7.5   Complainant's sexual history in prosecution based on mental incapacity.

Medical records or rape-crisis counseling records that would reflect whether a complainant has engaged in other sexual activities may be relevant in exploring whether the individual possesses the appropriate level of understanding of the sexual act as defined by law. Prior sexual history may not be relevant in such a scenario if it is shown that the individual's mental status has changed significantly. An individual may have been capable of consent five or seven years earlier, but because of a deteriorating mental condition, he or she may now be incapable of consent. Furthermore, a court may also take the position that a complainant may knowingly consent to relations with one person, yet be unable to knowingly consent to relations with another.[47] A mentally defective victim's prior sexual experiences may also be precluded because they lack relevance and materiality, and would be misleading because of their age as well as unduly confusing to the jury.[48] There may also be a "heightened" protection of the rape shield laws for "particularly vulnerable" mentally incapacitated victims.[49]

A trial court may allow a defendant to show that the complainant is "sexually knowledgeable and aggressive in her school and neighborhood, as well as with defendants, from which the jury could infer that she might have consented . . . and that defendants thought she understood sex and her right to say no."[50] Nonetheless, the inquiry may be limited.[51]

A defendant should be permitted to cross-examine an expert who testifies to a complainant's incapacity to consent about the complainant's use of birth control pills and past sexual behavior since this is relevant to her understanding of the

---

[46] Adkins v. Commonwealth, 20 Va. App. 332, 346, 457 S.E.2d 382, 389 (1995). *See also* White v. Commonwealth, 23 Va. App. 593, 478 S.E.2d 713 (1996).

[47] People v. Whitten, 269 Ill. App. 3d 1037, 1044, 647 N.E.2d 1062, 1067 (1995). *But see* State v. Anderson, 137 Or. App. 36, 902 P.2d 1206, *review denied*, 322 Or. 362, 907 P.2d 249 (1995) (noting that prosecutor's statement at a hearing that mentally incapacitated complainant may in some circumstances have been able to engage in consensual sexual relationships may be a judicial admission regarding the complainant's capacity to consent. However, the court did not need to reach this issue in the facts of the case.).

[48] State v. Cuni, 159 N.J. 584, 733 A.2d 414 (1999) (noting that the passage of time—11 years— and the fact that earlier consensual activities by the mentally defective victim involved friends rather than a stranger rendered them too dissimilar to current charged crime to be admissible).

[49] State v. Cuni, 159 N.J. 584, 733 A.2d 414 (1999).

[50] State v. Scherzer, 301 N.J. Super. 363, 414, 694 A.2d 196, 220, *appeal denied*, 151 N.J. 466, 700 A.2d 878 (1997).

[51] State v. Scherzer, 301 N.J. Super. 363, 414, 694 A.2d 196, 220, *appeal denied*, 151 N.J. 466, 700 A.2d 878 (1997).

physiological, medical, and societal aspects of sexual relations.[52] The complainant's sexual activity with another may not necessarily be relevant in a prosecution based on incapacity to consent based on mental defect,[53] and a mentally retarded victim's reputation for promiscuous sexual activity is most likely immaterial as to whether the defendant was aware of the victim's mental retardation.[54]

It may be impossible to assess issues concerning a complainant's sexual history and ability to consent to sexual activity without a review of a complainant's medical and psychological records. While in some situations such a review of records may be conducted by the court, there may well be other situations where the issue of mental status or ability to engage in sexual relations is debatable or subject to interpretation. In such situations, it may be helpful for an expert to review such records for evidence of the complainant's capacity to understand and consent at the time of the sexual act.

§ 7.6 Physical helplessness or physical inability to consent.

Typical of many statutes defining consent is California's Penal Code, which states that rape can be committed:

> (3) Where a person is prevented from resisting by any intoxicating or anaesthetic substance, or any controlled substance, administered by or with the privity of the accused. (4) Where a person is at the time unconscious of the nature of the act and this is known to the accused. As used in this paragraph, "unconscious of the nature of the act" means incapable of resisting because the victim meets one of the following conditions: (A) Was unconscious or asleep, (B) Was not aware, knowing, perceiving, or cognizant that the act occurred, (C) Was not aware, knowing, perceiving, or cognizant of the essential characteristics of the act due to the perpetrator's fraud in fact.[55]

---

[52] *In re* Doe, 81 Haw. 447, 918 P.2d 254 (1996):

> In the instant case, defendant's purpose in seeking to probe into complaining witness's past sexual behavior was not to attack complaining witness's character but to explore whether complaining witness had a basic understanding of the physiological elements and medical consequences of sexual activity, as well as an understanding of the moral and societal implications of pregnancy and sexual intercourse outside of marriage. Since the jury needed this information to determine whether complaining witness was mentally defective and whether defendant knew that complaining witness was mentally defective, defendant was entitled, under the due process and confrontation clauses, to elicit such evidence.

In re Doe, 81 Haw. 447, 918 P.2d 254, 263 (1996).

[53] Commonwealth v. Thomson, 449 Pa. Super. 159, 673 A.2d 357, *appeal denied*, 546 Pa. 679, 686 A.2d 1310 (1996) ("The fact that the victim had sexual intercourse with another individual does not render her capable of giving consent during that encounter nor during the encounter with [the defendant].").

[54] State v. Anderson, 137 Or. App. 36, 902 P.2d 1206, *review denied*, 322 Or. 362, 907 P.2d 249 (1995).

[55] Cal. Penal Code § 261(3)(4).

The California statute states that the intoxicating substance need not be administered by the accused, but need only be administered by someone in privity with him. The implication is that the intoxicating or other substance that affected the complainant's ability to resist came from someone in privity with the defendant. Not all statutes or courts, however, will require the prosecution to establish who administered the intoxicant or to identify the substance used.[56] Related to this is whether a victim's voluntary intoxication can render her incapable of providing or knowing consent. Voluntary intoxication has been accepted as a basis for a complainant's incapacity to consent.[57] The evidence of key is evidence of the intoxicated complainant's lack of awareness or inability to communicate.[58] The evidence of unconsciousness supports the theory that an intoxicated complainant is unable to give knowing consent.

---

[56] Rapetti v. James, 784 F.2d 85 (2d Cir. 1986), *cert. denied*, 471 U.S. 1022.

[57] United States v. Barrett, 937 F.2d 1346 (8th Cir.), *cert. denied*, 502 U.S. 916 (1991) (complainant testified that she had eight beers and smoked marijuana and was not freely awake at the time the defendant penetrated her, which was sufficient to establish her physical helplessness under the federal statute); People v. Fisher, 281 Ill. App. 3d 395, 667 N.E.2d 142, *appeal denied*, 168 Ill. 2d 606, 671 N.E.2d 736 (1996),

> The jury had before it testimony from the complainant as well as from Heather that S.G. was unconscious immediately prior to and during at least part of the sex act. A reasonable fact finder could conclude that the amount of alcohol ingested by the 125-pound complainant could have left her incapable of being sufficiently roused to have knowingly given or refused consent to the defendant's advances. The fact that the complainant was able to move herself into the kitchen and that she eventually roused enough to realize what was happening do not necessarily undermine her contention that she was unconscious, or in a pronounced stupor, during the sex act.

People v. Fisher, 281 Ill. App. 3d 395, 403, 667 N.E.2d 142, 147, *appeal denied*, 168 Ill. 2d 606, 671 N.E.2d 736 (1996).

[58] People v. Thomas, 21 A.D.3d 643, 799 N.Y.S.2d 653 (2005) ("Here, defendant admitted that sexual intercourse occurred, the People proffered evidence of the victim's state of inebriation, which was such that her friends were unable to awaken her upon their departure leaving her alone with defendant, and the victim testified that she did not have any recollection of engaging in sexual relations with defendant." People v. Thomas, 21 A.D.3d 643, 645, 799 N.Y.S.2d 653, 656 (2005)); People v. Morrow, 304 A.D.2d 1040, 758 N.Y.S.2d 215, *appeal denied*, 100 N.Y.2d 564, 795 N.E.2d 47, 763 N.Y.S.2d 821 (2003) (holding that "[p]hysical helplessness can include a victim unable to communicate or unwillingness to act because of sleep induced by alcohol"; victim had a blood alcohol content of .29% and a paramedic testified that victim was unable to communicate regarding her condition); People v. Himmel, 252 A.D.2d 273, 686 N.Y.S.2d 504, *appeal denied*, 93 N.Y.2d 899, 711 N.E.2d 987, 689 N.Y.S.2d 711 (1999) (holding Boy Scout's testimony that he was very intoxicated and unable to speak supported finding of physical helplessness); People v. Ferrer, 250 A.D.2d 860, 672 N.Y.S.2d 795, *appeal denied*, 92 N.Y.2d 879, 700 N.E.2d 564, 678 N.Y.S.2d 26 (1998) (finding "substantial testimony" that complainant was so intoxicated that she lacked the capacity to consent); People v. Cole, 212 A.D.2d 822, 622 N.Y.S.2d 354, *appeal denied*, 86 N.Y.2d 733, 655 N.E.2d 711, 631 N.Y.S.2d 614 (1995) (complainant's voluntary drinking of beer and whiskey and smoking of marijuana, which included the consumption of eight "shots" and six beers, was sufficient credible evidence for the jury to find that the victim was "physically helpless" and the defendant guilty); People v. Cirina, 143 A.D.2d 763, 764, 533 N.Y.S.2d 305, 306 (1988) (complainant's voluntary intoxication was sufficient for a jury to find

However, there is also authority that if the proof fails to show that the substance, such as crack cocaine, was ingested by the victim without her consent and that she was incapable of controlling her conduct because of the ingested substance, the victim may not be mentally incapacitated.[59]

A person can be physically helpless and incapable of consent by virtue of being asleep, even if a statute does not define sleep as being physically helpless.[60]

---

that she lacked capacity to consent due to her general weakened condition); State v. Martin, 2000 Ohio App. LEXIS 3649 (Aug. 14, 2000) while holding voluntary intoxication is a basis for physical helplessness and mobility to consent, the court noted:

> [a] person's conduct becomes criminal under this section only when engaging in sexual conduct with an intoxicated victim when the individual knows or has reasonable cause to believe that the victim's ability to resist or consent is substantially impaired because of voluntary intoxication.

State v. Martin, 2000 Ohio App. LEXIS 3649, *16 (Aug. 14, 2000); Commonwealth v. Erney, 548 Pa. 467, 698 A.2d 56 (1997),

> When the assault began, she displayed no awareness of external events. As the crime progressed, she believed that she was shouting for appellant to stop, but was completely unable to perceive how she was communicating — i.e., that she was merely mumbling. She offered no response when Beck questioned her during the assault. Additionally, although Beck made several statements in J.R.'s presence which were audible to appellant in an effort to convince appellant to stop the assault, J.R., who had no knowledge of what ultimately brought an end to appellant's actions, was unaware of those statements. Her complete lack of awareness of the duration of the assault further indicates that she was not conscious throughout its entirety. Thus, despite her ability to perceive some aspects of the incident, her lack of knowledge of much of what occurred supports the finding that she was unconscious during portions of the assault and was, therefore, unable to consent to sexual intercourse. Because there was ample evidence from which the jury could properly find that the victim, during at least portions of the assault, lacked knowledge or awareness of both her own sensations and external events, and was not in the normal waking state, the evidence was sufficient to support the finding that she was unconscious within the meaning of the statute.

Commonwealth v. Erney, 548 Pa. 467, 473, 698 A.2d 56, 59 (1997).

[59] Boone v. Commonwealth, 155 S.W.3d 727 (Ky. Ct. App. 2004) (holding that whether sleep is induced by a drug or normal process, "the state of sleep renders one unable of making a conscious choice"); State v. Stevens, 311 Mont. 52, 53 P.3d 356 (2002); People v. Thomas, 210 A.D.2d 992, 620 N.Y.S.2d 693 (1994).

[60] King v. State, 978 P.2d 1278, 1279–80 (Alaska Ct. App. 1999); People v. Smith, 16 A.D.3d 1033, 790 N.Y.S.2d 805 (2005) (noting "unequivocal" testimony of victim that she was asleep when she found defendant on top of her having intercourse); People v. Greene, 13 A.D.3d 991, 787 N.Y.S.2d 466 (2004), appeal denied, 5 N.Y.3d 789, 835 N.E.2d 670, 801 N.Y.S.2d 810 (2005); People v. Krzykowski, 293 A.D.2d 877, 742 N.Y.S.2d 138 (2002), appeal denied, 100 N.Y.2d 643, 801 N.E.2d 430, 769 N.Y.S.2d 209 (2003); People v. Sensourichanh, 290 A.D.2d 886, 737 N.Y.S.2d 670 (2002) (noting evidence that victim's sleep was drug and alcohol induced); People v. Beecher, 225 A.D.2d 943, 639 N.Y.S.2d 863 (1996) ("physical helplessness" established by testimony that 13-year-old legally blind child drove home from restaurant with defendant, fell asleep, and awoke to find defendant's hands on his genitals); People v. Irving, 151 A.D.2d 605, 606, 542 N.Y.S.2d 693 (1989); State v. Moorman, 320 N.C. 387, 358 S.E.2d 502 (1987); Woodward

Victim's prior consent does not negate consent when the victim is unconscious.[61]

The ability to communicate "no" or in some other fashion communicate unwillingness to let defendant engage in sexual acts does not necessarily negate the theory of physical helplessness.[62]

A state of physical helplessness would include a 62-year-old female patient who was suddenly penetrated sexually by her physical therapist.[63] Also, a person can be physically helpless from a severe broken nose that renders the victim incapable of communicating an unwillingness to engage in sexual relations.[64]

There should, however, be a physical inability to communicate the unwillingness to engage in the sexual act under this theory. A complainant because of a developmental disability may have a difficult time determining what she would or would not be willing to do. If the complainant is able to communicate an unwillingness to engage in a sexual act, even if nonverbally, this may invalidate a prosecution based on lack of consent due to physical helplessness.[65]

---

v. Commonwealth, 12 Va. App. 118, 402 S.E.2d 244 (1991) (concluding that even if sleeping victim had some sensory perception, she could be physically helpless); State v. Puapuaga, 54 Wash. App. 857, 776 P.2d 170 (1989) (holding "[t]he state of sleep appears to be universally understood as unconsciousness or physical inability to communicate unwillingness).

[61] People v. Dancy, 102 Cal. App. 4th 21, 124 Cal. Rptr. 2d 898 (2002), *review denied*, 2002 Cal. LEXIS 8124 (Nov. 26, 2002) (finding defendant guilty of rape when he engaged in sexual intercourse with a woman he knew to be unconscious, regardless of defendant's belief that she had consented prior to sexual act).

[62] State v. Chaney, 269 Kan. 10, 5 P.3d 492 (2000) (court found sufficient evidence that victim was unable to consent because of effects of alcohol, noting that victim's ability to protect defendant's actions did not equate with sobriety). *See also* People v. Teicher, 52 N.Y.2d 638, 422 N.E.2d 506, 439 N.Y.S.2d 846 (1981).

[63] State v. Sedia, 614 So. 2d 533 (Fla. Dist. Ct. App. 1993).

[64] Perez v. State, 479 So. 2d 266 (Fla. Dist. Ct. App. 1985).

[65] People v. Huurre, 84 N.Y.2d 930, 645 N.E.2d 1210, 621 N.Y.S.2d 511 (1994), *aff'g* 193 A.D.2d 305, 603 N.Y.S.2d 179 (1993) (A 35-year-old woman with an IQ of 16 to 20, with cerebral palsy and epilepsy, was still able to physically communicate an unwillingness to engage in sexual assault. This was held insufficient to support prosecution's theory that she was "physically helpless."); People v. Conto, 218 A.D.2d 665, 630 N.Y.S.2d 542, *appeal denied*, 87 N.Y.2d 845, 661 N.E.2d 1384, 638 N.Y.S.2d 603 (1995); People v. Clyburn, 212 A.D.2d 1030, 623 N.Y.S.2d 448, 449 (1995) (holding that the fact that the complainant suffered from Huntington's Chorea was insufficient in itself to establish that she was physically helpless and unable to communicate an unwillingness to engage in sexual relations); State v. Dunning, 2000 Ohio App. LEXIS 5774 (Dec. 11, 2000), *dismissed, discretionary appeal not allowed*, 91 Ohio St. 3d 1508, 746 N.E.2d 611 (2001) (Court upheld defendant's conviction for sexual assault based on theory of victim's incapacity to consent based on fact of her Huntington's Chorea disease. Prosecution presented both expert and lay testimony. Appeals court held:

> The state overwhelmingly demonstrated that Loretta's ability to consent was impaired by her condition. Dr. Avecilla testified extensively about the effects of Huntington's upon its sufferers and how Loretta was affected by the disease. He testified that she could not engage in complex thought processes, or even basic processes such as simple math. She could only communicate through the aid of someone "interpreting" her

§ 7.7   Marital exemption.

For centuries the assumption was made that by entering a marriage contract, a woman gave her consent to sexual relations with her husband, and such consent could not be retracted. This belief was codified in many rape statutes by defining a female as any person "not married to the actor." Nevertheless, the marital exemption has been successfully challenged as violating the equal protection laws of the Constitution on the ground that there is no rational basis for distinguishing between marital rape and nonmarital rape, and that if a statute makes a distinction for a marital partner, the distinction must be reasonable and based upon "some ground of difference that rationally explains the different treatment."[66] Most states have rejected the marital exemption as unconstitutional.[67]

With abrogation of the marital exemption, "foundation for any supposed immunity against prosecution for the separate crime of attempt disappeared."[68] Many states have redefined their rape statutes to eliminate the marital exemption. California has defined a crime of "spousal rape" to eliminate the marital exemption, which, in effect, parallels the definition of "rape."[69]

§ 7.8   Gender distinction in sexual assault statutes.

Similar to the issue of the marital exemption is the gender distinction in many rape statutes. Traditionally, most statutes defining rape have applied only to male

---

replies, but only after the questions were made very simple, and only if the "interpreter" was a person who extensively interacted with Loretta. Dr. Avecilla's diagnosis of the severity of Loretta's condition was confirmed by the lay testimony of Caudill, Roberts, and Landock. Although Roberts, who is Dunning's girlfriend, testified that Loretta could communicate under limited circumstances, the testimony at trial conclusively established that she was incapable of consenting to sexual conduct.

State v. Dunning, 2000 Ohio App. LEXIS 5774, *22 (Dec. 11, 2000), *dismissed, discretionary appeal not allowed*, 91 Ohio St. 3d 1508, 746 N.E.2d 611 (2001); State v. Clark, 2000 Tenn. Crim. App. LEXIS 653 (Aug. 25, 2000) (complainant was groggy from medication, awakened, and thought person on top of her was her boyfriend, said his name until she realized it was the defendant after which she "jumped up" and left the room. Since she was able to verbalize her "unwillingness" to have sexual intercourse, evidence was insufficient to support a charge of rape due to physical helplessness, but there was evidence to support a conviction for a count of rape by force).

[66] Eisenstadt v. Baird, 405 U.S. 438, 447 (1972).

[67] Merton v. State, 500 So. 2d 1301 (Ala. Crim. App. 1986); State v. Smith, 401 So. 2d 1126 (Fla. Dist. Ct. App. 1981); Warren v. State, 255 Ga. 151, 336 S.E.2d 221 (1985); People v. M.D., 231 Ill. App. 3d 176, 595 N.E.2d 702, *appeal denied*, 146 Ill. 2d 643, 602 N.E.2d 467 (1992); Commonwealth v. Chretien, 383 Mass. 123, 417 N.E.2d 1203 (1981); State v. Smith, 85 N.J. 193, 426 A.2d 38 (1981); People v. Liberta, 64 N.Y.2d 152, 474 N.E.2d 567, 485 N.Y.S.2d 207 (1984); Weishaupt v. Commonwealth, 227 Va. 389, 315 S.E.2d 847 (1984); Shunn v. State, 742 P.2d 775 (Wyo. 1987). *See generally*, Michael G. Walsh, Annotation, *Criminal Responsibility of Husband for a Rape or Assault to Commit Rape on Wife*, 24 A.L.R.4th 105 (1983).

[68] Lane v. State, 348 Md. 272, 292, 703 A.2d 180, 191 (1997).

[69] Cal. Penal Code § 262 (statute also provides that court may require defendant, as part of his sentence, to make a payment of up to $1,000 to a battered woman's shelter).

offenders. The constitutionality of so-called statutory rape laws that discriminate on the basis of gender (men alone can be criminally liable under most statutory rape laws) has been upheld on the ground that there is a legitimate state interest in statutory rape laws in that they have as a goal the prevention of illegitimate teenage pregnancies.[70] The Supreme Court of the United States has determined that the statutory rape laws protect women from sexual intercourse and pregnancy and the consequences of pregnancy when they are most vulnerable to the physical, emotional, and psychological consequences of illegitimate teenage pregnancies.[71] However, gender discrimination is not permitted with respect to statutes defining forcible rape.[72]

§ 7.9   Lack of consent based upon relationship of parties — Position of trust, therapeutic relationships and jail inmates.

Some states criminalize sexual relations based on the relationship of the parties. Just as individuals under a certain age or with a certain level of mental incapacity cannot consent to relations, neither can certain persons in certain relationships.

A typical example is statutes involving "therapeutic deception" that deal with therapists who engage in sexual relations with patients. These statutes forbid a psychotherapist to represent to a patient that sexual relations are a part of or consistent with the client's treatment.[73] The statute may forbid sexual conduct between a client or patient and health care provider or mental health professional "during a treatment session, consultation, interview or examination." Such statutes seemingly permit sexual relations outside the clinical relationships and have been held constitutional.[74] Under the Minnesota statute, criminal sexual conduct in the third degree occurs when a psychotherapist and patient have sexual relations either during or outside the psychotherapy session and, in some situations, where the complainant is a former patient who is emotionally dependent upon the psychotherapist or where there is "therapeutic deception."[75] Consent by the patient-complainant is not a defense.

[70] Michael M. v. Superior Court of Sonoma County, 450 U.S. 464 (1981).

[71] Michael M. v. Superior Court of Sonoma County, 450 U.S. 464, 470–473 (1981).

[72] People v. Liberta, 64 N.Y.2d 152, 169, 474 N.E.2d 567, 576–577, 485 N.Y.S.2d 207, 216–217 (1984). *See also* Thomas R. Trenkner, Annotation, *Constitutionality of Rape Laws Limited to Protection of Females Only,* 99 A.L.R.3d 129 (1980).

[73] Colo. Rev. Stat. § 18-3-405.5; Fla. Stat. 491.0112; Minn. Stat. § 609.341(16–20), § 609.344, § 609.345. *See generally* Jay M. Zitter, Annotation, *Conviction of Rape or Related Sexual Offenses on Basis of Intercourse Accomplished Under the Pretext of, or in the Course of, Medical Treatment,* 65 A.L.R.4th 1064 (1988); N.Y. Penal Law 130.05(h).

[74] Ferguson v. People, 824 P.2d 803 (Colo. 1992) *(en banc)*; Shapiro v. State, 696 So. 2d 1321 (Fla. Dist. Ct. App. 1997).

[75] Minn. Stat. § 609.344(h), (i), (j), (k).

The crime can also occur between members of the clergy and a complainant who engaged in sexual relations with a clergyman during a time when the complainant was seeking or receiving spiritual advice, aid, or comfort.[76] Under the statute, a complainant will be deemed incapable of consent.[77]

Prosecutions of individuals in therapeutic relationships with patient-complainants may also occur under statutes defining incapacity to consent to include incapacity caused by a mental or physical inability to provide a meaningful consent.[78] A representative case is *McNair v. State*, where the Supreme Court of Nevada upheld the conviction of a gynecologist who sexually abused several of his patients. The conviction was based upon a Nevada statute that defines sexual assault not just in terms of force but "under conditions in which the perpetrator knows or should know that the victim is mentally or physically incapable of resisting or understanding the nature of his conduct."[79]

In a case involving sexual abuse by physician during a medical examination, expert testimony concerning proper medical procedure can be relevant to show that the sexual contact was not accomplished for medical purposes.[80]

A defendant's prior actions or conduct with other clients may be relevant under a common plan or scheme theory.[81] Some statutes have a broad definition of those in a position of authority who may not engage in sexual relations in conjunction with a particular age category. For example, Mississippi's definition of sexual battery encompasses many groups:

> A person is guilty of sexual battery if he or she engages in sexual penetration
> with a child of fourteen (14) but less than eighteen (18) years of age if the

---

[76] Minn. Stat. § 609.344(k)(1)(i)–(ii).

[77] *See, e.g.*, State v. Dutton, 450 N.W.2d 189 (Minn. Ct. App. 1990) (upholding conviction of pastor for violating psychotherapist-patient criminal sexual conduct statute).

[78] McNair v. State, 108 Nev. 53, 825 P.2d 571 (1992).

[79] Nev. Rev. Stat. § 200.366(1). *See also* State v. Sedia, 614 So. 2d 533 (Fla. Dist. Ct. App. 1993) (upholding prosecution's legal theory that a 62-year-old woman was physically helpless and thus incapable of consenting to relations with her physical therapist); People v. Burpo, 164 Ill. 2d 261, 647 N.E.2d 996 (1995) (gynecologist convicted of sexually abusing several patients — by tricking women into submitting to sexual penetration on the ruse that it was part of an appropriate medical exam — under a statute based on a complainant's inability to give knowing consent, even though women were not asleep, unconscious, or suffering from a mental impairment).

[80] State v. Tizard, 897 S.W.2d 732, 748 (Tenn. Crim. App. 1994).

[81] Shapiro v. State, 696 So. 2d 1321 (Fla. Dist. Ct. App. 1997), *review denied*, 701 So. 2d 868 (Fla. 1997) ("Here, the witness's testimony reveals appellant's common scheme, plan, or design to sexually exploit his patients while purporting to help them improve self-esteem and feel good about themselves. Similar fact evidence of collateral crimes may be admitted as relevant even if it is not uniquely similar. [citation omitted] In both instances the victims were married but separated from their husbands. Neither victim sought sexual counseling from appellant, but rather he initiated their conversations about sex. Both victims were complimented and then digitally penetrated by appellant in the office during a therapy session." Shapiro v. State, 696 So. 2d 1321, 1324 (Fla. Dist. Ct. App. 1997), *review denied*, 701 So. 2d 868 (Fla. 1997)) *See generally* § 6.38.

person is in a position of trust or authority over the child including without limitation the child's teacher, counselor, physician, psychiatrist, psychologist, minister, priest, physical therapist, chiropractor, legal guardian, parent, stepparent, aunt, uncle, scout leader, or coach.[82]

Some states render corrections officers personnel incapable of having relations with inmates.[83]

§ 7.10 Force and rape.

A complainant's incapacity to consent to an act of sexual intercourse because of the assailant's use of force has been a long-standing basis for the crime of rape. This force is usually defined in terms of physical force or threats, either express or implied, that place the complainant in fear of harm or physical injury.

Some statutes include duress and deception as part of force. It is possible for a person to consent to one sexual act and not another. Since sexual intercourse and sodomy are two separate occurrences, they are two separate crimes, and a jury may find a defendant guilty of forcing a complainant into one act and not another.[84]

Reforms over the past several decades have gradually eliminated resistance, in most jurisdictions, by the victim as an element of forcible rape. Nonetheless, the requirement that forcible compulsion overcomes earnest resistance can still be found if earnest resistance is required, and courts will look to a "totality of the circumstances" test, in determining whether the force used is sufficient to overcome reasonable resistance.[85] Those factors considered include: "whether violence or threats precede the sexual act; the relative ages of the victim and accused; the atmosphere and setting of the incident; the extent to which the accused was in a position of authority, domination, and control over the victim; and whether the victim was under duress."[86] Some states also required at one

---

[82] Miss. Code § 97-3-95(2).

[83] *See, e.g.,* Haw. Rev. Stat. § 707–731; N.Y. Penal Law § 130.05(e)(f).

[84] Padilla v. State, 601 P.2d 189 (Wyo. 1979).

[85] State v. Niederstadt, 66 S.W.3d 12, 15 (Mo. 2002) (noting that prior beatings, age of victim, and location — home where victim was sent by her parents — were factors establishing forcible compulsion overcoming earnest resistance).

[86] State v. Niederstadt, 66 S.W.3d 12, 15 (Mo. 2002). *See also,* State v. Vandevere, 175 S.W.3d 107 (Mo. 2005) (noting defendant used age and position as a participant in a national child's competition to overcome the victim's earnest resistance); State v. Campbell, 143 S.W.3d 695 (Mo. Ct. App. 2004) (considering the "totality of the circumstances," the court found it reasonable to find defendant guilty of forcible sodomy, where the defendant had previously used physical force to compel victim to have sexual intercourse with him; a considerable age difference existed between victim and defendant; the abuse occurred at home where the defendant often used physical violence and threatened the victim; the defendant was the father to the victim; and, victim was clearly under duress); State v. Spencer, 50 S.W.3d 869 (Mo. Ct. App. 2001) (noting that forcible compulsion overcoming earnest resistance under Missouri law is determined by "totality of circumstances").

time the corroboration of an adult rape victim's testimony, even in cases of forcible rape. This requirement has also been eliminated.[87]

The definition of force varies from state to state, which has resulted in some significant differences in the interpretation of the same set of facts. As a general rule, physical force will constitute sufficient forcible compulsion. The element of force can be established by proof that the defendant used his superior age, size, or strength to prevent a victim from exercising free will.[88] Generally, the physical force element of a forcible rape charge is met by proof of force greater than that required to commit the sexual act, and should be more than the physical interaction accompanying the sexual act and be such that the sexual act would not have occurred without the force.[89]

---

[87] *See §* 16.2.

[88] Howell v. State, 636 So. 2d 1260 (Ala. 1993) (holding that ages of the victim and the accused, mental and physical conditions of victim and the accused, atmosphere and physical setting, and defendant's position of authority are all factors to consider on issue of duress); People v. Bolander, 23 Cal. App. 4th 155, 28 Cal. Rptr. 2d 365 (1994), *review denied,* 1994 Cal. LEXIS 3242 (June 15, 1994) ("[D]efendant's acts of overcoming the victim's resistance to having her pants pulled down, bending the victim over, and pulling the victim's waist towards him constitute[s] force."); State v. Kulmac, 230 Conn. 43, 74–75, 644 A.2d 887, 903 (1994) (force established by complainant's testimony that she did not wish to have intercourse with the defendant, and that she tried unsuccessfully to push defendant away but defendant was too big and strong for her to succeed in pushing him away); People v. Smith, 302 A.D.2d 677, 756 N.Y.S.2d 290, *appeal denied,* 100 N.Y.2d 543, 793 N.E.2d 422, 763 N.Y.S.2d 8 (2003) (noting that significant size discrepancy between defendant and complainant is significant in establishing forcible compulsion); People v. Ayala, 236 A.D.2d 802, 654 N.Y.S.2d 59, *appeal denied,* 90 N.Y.S.2d 855, 683 N.E.2d 1055, 661 N.Y.S.2d 181 (1997) (holding that complainant's testimony that she complied with defendant's demands because of "the look in his eyes and the fact that he raised his hand in a threatening manner [and] she feared that he would harm her" established forcible compulsion); People v. Webster, 205 A.D.2d 312, 613 N.Y.S.2d 12, *appeal denied,* 84 N.Y.2d 834, 641 N.E.2d 176, 617 N.Y.S.2d 155 (1994) (forcible compulsion established by proof that the defendant, "who was considerably older, larger and stronger than his 12-year-old daughter, threatened that he was going to show [her] how to 'tongue kiss', followed her into the kitchen where she was alone, came up behind her, pushed his body up against her, then 'wiggl[ed] his penis in [her] lower back', right above her buttocks while she pleaded for him to 'move' away."); People v. Cook, 186 A.D.2d 879, 588 N.Y.S.2d 919 (1992), *appeal denied,* 81 N.Y.2d 761, 610 N.E.2d 396, 594 N.Y.S.2d 723 (1992); People v. Roman, 179 A.D.2d 352, 578 N.Y.S.2d 544, *appeal denied,* 79 N.Y.2d 952, 592 N.E.2d 814, 583 N.Y.S.2d 206 (1992); Commonwealth v. Rhodes, 510 Pa. 537, 556, 510 A.2d 1217, 1226 (1986); Commonwealth v. Garaffa, 440 Pa. Super. 484, 656 A.2d 133, *appeal denied,* 666 A.2d 1051 (1995) (complainant's testimony that she was pushed back on the bed and frightened established element of force).

[89] People v. Carlson, 466 Mich. 130, 644 N.W.2d 704 (2002):

> Force does not mean 'force' as a matter of mere physics, i.e., the physical interaction that would be inherent in an act of sexual penetration, nor, as we have observed, does it follow that the force must be so great as to overcome the complainant. It must be force to allow the accomplishment of sexual penetration when absent that force the penetration would not have occurred. In other words, the requisite 'force'. . . does not encompass nonviolent physical interaction in a mechanical sense that is merely incidental to an act of sexual penetration. Rather, the prohibited 'force'

However, "even conduct which might normally attend sexual intercourse, when engaged in with force sufficient to overcome the victim's will, can support a forcible rape conviction."[90]

It may be reasonable for a previous threat to form the basis of the element of force when there is testimony about the lasting effects of the threats on a child.[91] Georgia's Supreme Court makes clear there is no presumption of force because a victim is underage.[92] However, the amount of evidence necessary to prove force with a child is less than an adult and a function of the age of the victim.[93] It has been described as minimal.

In addition to these factors, the subservient relationship of the victim to the defendant or the defendant's position of authority over the victim are factors to consider in assessing the element of forcible compulsion.[94]

---

encompasses the use of force against a victim to either induce the victim to submit to sexual penetration or to seize control of the victim in a manner to facilitate the accomplishment of sexual penetration without regard to the victim's wishes.
People v. Carlson, 466 Mich. 130, 140, 644 N.W.2d 704, 709 (2002).

[90] People v. Griffin, 33 Cal. 4th 1015, 94 P.3d 1089, 16 Cal. Rptr. 3d 891 (2004) holding "force" under California law has a common usage meaning rather than a specialized legal definition and finding sufficient evidence of force in the following testimony by a ten-year-old:

Q. Let me ask you, specifically. You are sitting on the floor and what did he do, specifically?

A. Lay down. He told me to lay down and I laid down and he started putting his mouth on my vagina and then he got on top of me and I was . . . .

Q. . . . Was he holding your wrists with his hands?

A. Yes.

Q. And were your arms on the floor:

A. On my back on the floor, yes.

Q. He was on top of you?

A. (Nods.)

Q. Were you able to move your arms?

A. No, they were like that.

Q. Was what he did without your consent?

A. Yes.

Q. Against your will?

A. Yes.

Q. And he held your arms down while he put his penis inside you?

A. Yes.

[91] People v. Nailor, 268 A.D.2d 695, 701 N.Y.S.2d 476 (2000).

[92] Brewer v. State, 271 Ga. 605, 523 S.E.2d 18 (1999).

[93] Chancey v. State, 258 Ga. App. 716, 574 S.E.2d 904 (2002); Patterson v. State, 242 Ga. App. 885, 531 S.E.2d 759 (2000).

[94] People v. Bott, 234 A.D.2d 625, 651 N.Y.S.2d 207 (1996), *appeal denied*, 89 N.Y.2d 1009,

This means, for example, considering whether a child was alone with a care-giver or in a position to complain.[95] Many cases permit an inference of force when statements are made and sexual contact occurs in a parent-child or familial relationship.[96]

---

680 N.E.2d 621, 658 N.Y.S.2d 247 (1997) ("In our view, the evidence that defendant placed his hand on the victim's thigh and genitalia despite the victim's protestations and physical resistance, coupled with defendant's dominance over the victim by reason of his age, status as a trusted friend, the victim's physical disability and isolation from familiar surroundings provide legally sufficient evidence establishing [forcible compulsion]"); People v. Archer, 232 A.D.2d 820, 649 N.Y.S.2d 204 (1996), *appeal denied*, 89 N.Y.2d 1087, 682 N.E.2d 982, 660 N.Y.S.2d 381 (1997) (noting that forcible compulsion was established in part by victim's young age and defendant's relationship with complainant's aunt); People v. Beecher, 225 A.D.2d 943, 639 N.Y.S.2d 863 (1996) (holding defendant's age, status, and position as trusted friend and victim's physical disability of being legally blind were all factors in sustaining element of forcible compulsion); People v. Dehler, 216 A.D.2d 643, 628 N.Y.S.2d 413, *appeal denied*, 86 N.Y.2d 734, 655 N.E.2d 712, 631 N.Y.S.2d 615 (1995) ("Defendant was clearly a figure of authority to the children, and considering the substantial discrepancy in age, size, and strength between defendant and the children, together with the isolated nature of the acts, we find the evidence sufficient to establish that defendant used his domination of the young victims to have sexual contact with them."); State v. Eskridge, 38 Ohio St. 3d 56, 526 N.E.2d 304 (1988) ("The force and violence necessary to commit the crime of rape depends upon the age, size and strength of the parties and their relation to each other. With the filial obligation of obedience to a parent, the same degree of force and violence may not be required upon a person of tender years, as would be required were the parties more nearly equal in age, size and strength." State v. Eskridge, 38 Ohio St. 3d 56, 59, 526 N.E.2d 304, 306 (1988), *citing* State v. Labus, 102 Ohio St. 26, 38–39, 130 N.E. 161, 164 (1921)).

[95] Commonwealth v. Moniz, 43 Mass. App. Ct. 913, 683 N.E.2d 703, *review denied*, 426 Mass. 1103, 687 N.E.2d 642 (1997).

[96] Powe v. State, 597 So. 2d 721, 729 (Ala. 1991) finding defendant guilty of having sexual intercourse with his daughter by forcible compulsion, because of the unique relationship between child and defendant — "a position of domination and control over them may be taken into consideration in determining whether the element of forcible compulsion has been established":

> At this point, however, we note that our holding in this case is limited to cases concerning the sexual assault of children by adults with whom the children are in a relationship of trust. The reason for the distinction between cases involving children as victims and those involving adults as victims is the great influence and control that an adult who plays a dominant role in a child's life may exert over the child. When a defendant who plays an authoritative role in a child's world instructs the child to submit to certain acts, an implied threat of some sort of disciplinary action accompanies the instruction. If the victim is young, inexperienced, and perhaps ignorant of the 'wrongness' of the conduct, the child may submit to the acts because the child assumes the conduct is acceptable or because the child does not have the capacity to refuse. Moreover, fear of the parent resulting from love or respect may play a role as great as or greater than that played by fear of threats of serious bodily harm in coercing a child to submit to a sexual act.
>
> . . .
>
> Our holding in this case establishes a mechanism by which the unique relationship between children and the adults who exercise a position of domination and control over them may be taken into consideration in determining whether the element of forcible compulsion has been established.

One federal court noted that in defining the element of fear in child molestation "there is always a substantial risk that physical force will be used to ensure the child's compliance" and that "a jury may infer that a male parent sexually abusing a child would place them in fear of bodily harm."[97] It is sufficient if the defendant's actions, under this analysis implicitly place the victim in fear of some bodily harm.[98]

Force may be established by a defendant's threat to harm a third party close to the child, such as a mother or sister.[99]

Other factors to consider on the issue of force or fear include the complainant's medical condition[100] This principle is set forth in some states' statutes.[101]

Powe v. State, 597 So. 2d 721, 728–729 (Ala. 1991). Subsequently, the same court distinguished the situation of a juvenile offender in *Ex parte* J.A.P., 853 So. 2d 280 (Ala. 2002) (reversing judgment against 14-year-old defendant for using forcible compulsion in an attempt to engage in sexual intercourse with his half-sister, because the lower court improperly extended Powe's forcible compulsion analysis to minors); State v. Straughter, 727 So. 2d 1283, 1287, *writ denied*, 747 So. 2d 14 (La. 1999) (fact that child was only four at the time of the alleged rape and that offender was her father, and child's testimony that when her father penetrated her it felt "bad," permitted an inference that the victim was "forced" to submit to an act of sexual intercourse even though she was unable "to express it directly"); State v. Presley, 2003 Ohio App. LEXIS 5401 (Nov. 13, 2003) (upholding and citing other Ohio authority upholding jury instruction defining force in sexual assault case as follows:

> When the relationship between the victim and the Defendant is one of child and parents, the element of force need not be openly displayed or physically brutal. It can be subtle or slight and psychologically or emotionally powerful.); State v. Hudson, 2003 Ohio App. LEXIS 6444 (Dec. 23, 2003) (The compulsion constituting force is determined by the surrounding circumstances and whether they lead the victim to fear the use or threat of force. Here, defendant's statements to victim, his sister, about her parents disowning her, telling her something bad would happen if she told, stated "cruelly and manipulatively" and that she knew that if she did not perform willingly, he would "do it the hard way.").

[97] United States v. Castillo, 140 F.3d 874 (10th Cir. 1998).

[98] United States v. Cherry, 938 F.2d 748 (7th Cir. 1991).

[99] Parks v. State, 587 So. 2d 1015 (Ala. Crim. App. 1991) ("Clearly, the appellant's threat of serious physical injury to the victim's mother constituted forcible compulsion, and the State presented sufficient evidence to sustain the appellant's conviction." Parks v. State, 587 So. 2d 1015, 1016 (Ala. Crim. App. 1991)); Bright v. State, 244 Ga. App. 23, 535 S.E.2d 14 (2000); People v. Samuel, 239 A.D.2d 527, 658 N.Y.S.2d 959 (1997), *appeal denied*, 91 N.Y.2d 1012, 698 N.E.2d 970 (1998) (holding defendant's threat to complainant's sister constitutes evidence of force).

[100] State v. Gray, 1995 Ohio App. LEXIS 2818 (June 28, 1995) (Complainant suffering from a defense mechanism known as "conversion hysteria," which caused her to go into a trance-like state when certain words, including sexually explicit words, were spoken in her presence. This is relevant to her inability to resist because of her unique mental disability); People v. Beecher, 225 A.D.2d 943, 639 N.Y.S.2d 863 (1996) (holding defendant's age, status, and position as trusted friend and victim's physical disability of being legally blind were all factors in sustaining element of forcible compulsion); Commonwealth v. Smolko, 446 Pa. Super. 156, 666 A.2d 672 (1995) (Complainant suffering of Pelizaeus-Merzbacher Syndrome, a totally and permanently debilitating disease of the central nervous system that left him with very little strength is a most relevant factor in evaluating whether the element of force has been established).

A defendant need not threaten a victim with immediate physical harm to be guilty of using force. The complainant's fear may be supported by knowledge of the defendant's HIV status.[102] An adult male who drove a 15-year-old girl to a remote location and then told her that she was "going to do something for him or get out and walk" threatened the victim, even though he did not display a weapon or threaten her with physical harm, when she testified that "she was afraid that if she resisted the appellant he would hurt her."[103] In a similar case, the defendant offered to take a 17-year-old female home, which was approximately a 20-mile drive, and during the trip he requested that she perform a sexual act. When she declined, the defendant stated, "well, you have a problem." He then stopped the vehicle on a rural back road and said, "Don't move. Stay there or you are going to be in trouble."[104] In this context, the defendant's statements were sufficient to constitute implied threats of physical injury when she testified that "I didn't know what was going to happen to me. I didn't know if I was going to live to the next day."[105] This testimony was sufficient to demonstrate that the defendant had implicitly placed the victim in fear of some bodily harm.

The threats need not be capable of being immediately carried out since the focus is on the state of mind produced in the victim by the defendant's conduct.[106] Thus, threats by an inmate to a 16-year-old prisoner that "he could

---

[101] Or. Rev. Stat. § 2907.02(c) ("The other person's ability to resist or consent is substantially impaired because of a mental or physical condition or because of advanced age, and the offender knows or has reasonable cause to believe that the other person's ability to resist or consent is substantially impaired because of a mental or physical condition or because of advanced age.").

[102] State v. Deal, 319 S.C. 49, 459 S.E.2d 93 (1995).

[103] Myers v. Commonwealth, 11 Va. App. 634, 636, 400 S.E.2d 803, 804–05 (1991) ("When told to submit or walk, she was frightened at the prospect of being alone and on foot in a deserted area and was fearful of whom she might meet and what might be done to her. She explained this and explained her reason, based on a book that she had read, for considering non-resistance to be the wiser course." Myers v. Commonwealth, 11 Va. App. 634, 637, 400 S.E.2d 803, 805 (1991)). *See also* United States v. Cherry, 938 F.2d 748, 754–55 (7th Cir. 1991) (Under federal sexual assault statute, complainant was placed in fear of the defendant by the fact that the defendant had prevented her from leaving home and her fear that she "didn't know what he would do to me . . . he was bitter and violent.").

[104] People v. Di Gioia, 168 A.D.2d 865, 564 N.Y.S.2d 533 (1990), *appeal denied*, 77 N.Y.2d 994, 575 N.E.2d 406, 571 N.Y.S.2d 920 (1991).

[105] People v. Di Gioia, 168 A.D.2d 865, 564 N.Y.S.2d 533 (1990), *appeal denied*, 77 N.Y.2d 994, 575 N.E.2d 406, 571 N.Y.S.2d 920 (1991). *See also* People v. Sweezey, 215 A.D.2d 910, 626 N.Y.S.2d 584, *appeal denied*, 85 N.Y.2d 980, 653 N.E.2d 637, 629 N.Y.S.2d 741 (1995) (defendant driving complainant to a "sparsely populated dirt road," stopping, and stating that the truck "died" for a reason, and that he was going "to get something out of this" establishes element of force).

[106] Blansit v. State, 248 Ga. App. 323, 324, 546 S.E.2d 81, 83 (2001) (defendant argued that there was no evidence that defendant's threats induced child to engage in sexual activity. Appellate court held that force was established by her testimony that defendant would touch her after she said "no," on one occasion rubbed a knife on her breasts and across her chest, and that defendant threatened her if she ever told anyone); People v. Black, 304 A.D.2d 905, 908, 757 N.Y.S.2d 635

have people kick [his] ass," that "anything could happen . . . to the victim, that he could "put the word out" on the victim, and that "he would make sure [the victim] would have a rough time" while he was an inmate at the jail, while not capable of being carried out immediately, were sufficient for the jury to believe that the victim reasonably feared physical injury if he did not comply with the defendant's request to engage in sexual activity.[107] This view of forcible compulsion looks at all the attendant circumstances surrounding the sexual contact. In the jail situation, the defendant had to gain access to the juvenile tier even though this was off-limits by jail policy. The fact that the defendant could make his way onto the juvenile tier without interference from officials was a fact to be considered not only by the victim but also by the jury in assessing whether the defendant had the ability to "get" the victim elsewhere in the jail. Other inmates viewed the assault without offering any assistance. As the court noted:

> The victim was only sixteen years old and a novice to the world of incarceration. The defendant was more than twice his age, powerfully built, and had made it clear to the victim that he held a position of power in the oppressive and unfamiliar environment the victim had recently entered. Indeed, defendant's mere presence in the restricted juvenile tier was evidence of the influence at his disposal. That the defendant was not specific about when the threats might be carried out is of little consequence. The breadth of his threats encompass the possibility that the harm could be delivered by anyone, including those with immediate access to the victim, and at any time, including the present.[108]

If there is an implicit threat of harm by a third person, but the victim does not hear the remarks or feel threatened by the defendant, the element of force may not be established.[109]

In cases that establish forceful compulsion based on the implicit threats of a defendant, it is important that testimony by the complainant establish the actual effect of the defendant's conduct upon the complainant, as well as support the complainant in the context of the defendant's statements and actions. If there is no proof that the difference in size between a defendant and his victim creates an implied threat of force, or that threats were made by the defendant after a sexual act, there may be insufficient evidence of force.[110] A 15-year-old niece

---

(2003) (observing that forcible compulsion is measured by what victim fears defendant might do if she does not comply and that prior abusive behavior toward victim by defendant is relevant to this determination).

[107] People v. Thompson, 72 N.Y.2d 410, 530 N.E.2d 839, 534 N.Y.S.2d 132 (1988). *See also* §§ 5.10 and 6.43.

[108] People v. Thompson, 72 N.Y.2d 410, 417, 530 N.E.2d 839, 843, 534 N.Y.S.2d 132, 135 (1988).

[109] State v. Ferguson, No. 99AP-819, 2000 Ohio App. LEXIS 2208 (May 25, 2000).

[110] Commonwealth v. Feijoo, 419 Mass. 486, 646 N.E.2d 118 (1995) (Defendant's conviction involving a young male victim was reversed. Although the defendant was "physically imposing

of a defendant was deemed to be forced into an act of sexual intercourse when she was continually importuned to engage in sexual relations and told that she would be returned to the home of an abusive relative if she did not agree to engage in sexual relations, and where she also was told by the defendant and his wife that since they had custody of her, they could punish her for anything she did of which they disapproved.[111] Part of the equation in analyzing whether a sexual act is a product of force is whether the accused is a person whom the victim is accustomed to obeying and therefore more likely to fear the defendant.[112] These cases can be summarized by the statement "submission through fear to sexual intercourse is not consent."[113]

Forcible rape may include rape by duress; however, duress does not necessarily require physical force. Some courts will distinguish rape by force from rape by duress. Duress may be the result of an authority relationship between the parties and a warning by the defendant that reporting the sexual abuse could jeopardize the family unit.[114] "A simple warning to a child not to report a molestation reasonably implies the child should not otherwise protest or resist the sexual imposition."[115] The court may find such conduct, as well as the complainant's pulling away from the defendant, insufficient proof of force.[116] Other courts have taken a contrary view and found that physical force can be broadly defined.[117]

---

and trained and experienced in violence," there was no evidence that the complainant "submitted to the conduct with which the defendant was charged because of fear of physical harm if he refused." Prosecution did not establish any nexus between defendant's physical prowess and experience in violence and the complainant's submission to sexual acts. Commonwealth v. Feijoo, 419 Mass. 486, 490, 646 N.E.2d 118, 122 (1995). Another of the defendant's convictions involving a young male was also reversed since the defendant's telling a young male "about several instances in which the defendant had resorted to violence and threats of violence" was insufficient by itself to establish that the complainant submitted to the defendant because of intimidation as opposed to benefits the victim hoped to obtain from the defendant. Commonwealth v. Feijoo, 419 Mass. 486, 491–492, 646 N.E.2d 118, 123 (1995)); People v. Reckart, 163 A.D.2d 846, 558 N.Y.S.2d 375 (1990).

[111] Sutton v. Commonwealth, 228 Va. 654, 660, 324 S.E.2d 665, 668 (1985).

[112] Sutton v. Commonwealth, 228 Va. 654, 664, 324 S.E.2d 665, 670 (1985).

[113] Sutton v. Commonwealth, 228 Va. 654, 664, 324 S.E.2d 665, 670 (1985).

[114] People v. Senior, 3 Cal. App. 4th 765, 775, 5 Cal. Rptr. 2d 14, 20 (1992) (Section 262(2) of the California Penal Code states that rape may be accomplished "by means of force, violence, duress, menace, or fear of immediate and unlawful bodily injury on the person or another").

[115] People v. Senior, 3 Cal. App. 4th 765, 775, 5 Cal. Rptr. 2d 14, 20 (1992).

[116] People v. Senior, 3 Cal. App. 4th 765, 774, 5 Cal. Rptr. 2d 14, 20 (1992).

[117] People v. Babcock, 14 Cal. App. 4th 383, 17 Cal. Rptr. 2d 688 (1993), review denied, 1993 Cal. LEXIS 3758 (July 15, 1993) (complainant's pulling her hand away from defendant's crotch and saying "no" followed by defendant's putting her hand back is sufficient to establish force); People v. Bergschneider, 211 Cal. App. 3d 144, 259 Cal. Rptr. 219 (1989) (physical force established by complainant trying to push defendant's head away while attempting oral intercourse); People v. Mendibles, 199 Cal. App. 3d 1277, 245 Cal. Rptr. 553 (1988) (defendant's pulling complainants' necks as they tried to leave and pulling their heads forward to engage in oral intercourse is sufficient to establish physical force).

§ 7.11 Does "No" mean "No"?

As appellate decisions have broadened the definition of what constitutes an implicit threat sufficient to constitute force in sexual assault cases, courts have struggled to define the level of conduct on the part of the defendant sufficient to justify branding a sexual act as "forcible." This can be seen in some of the decisions cited in the previous section on whether sufficient physical force or threat has been established. Is it sufficient if a complainant says "No," or must there be some physical force or threat that overcomes the statement that the complainant does not wish to engage in a sexual act?

The issue surfaced in a Pennsylvania Supreme Court case, which held that under the then existing definition of forcible compulsion:

> [E]ven though the complainant stated "No" throughout the encounter, and that such a fact is relevant to the issue of consent, it is not relevant to the issue of forcible compulsion. The court noted that, not only must there be a force or threat, there must also be an element of compulsion, which, in the court's view, is supported by the legislature's decision to define a separate crime, a misdemeanor, which is based simply on lack of consent of the complainant. Since the complainant did not testify to the use of any force or threat against her, because the defendant's hands were not restraining her in any manner during the actual penetration, there were no verbal threats, and the complainant was able to leave the room but never attempted to go out or unlock the door, there was no forcible compulsion. The complainant's statement of "No" was insufficient to support any conclusion of forcible compulsion and thus does not mean "No." The complainant's testimony in this case did not set forth a fear of the defendant or fear of consequences if she did not comply with the defendant's request to engage in sexual relations.[118]

Under a statute defining forcible compulsion or physical force which compels a person to engage in a sexual act, one court reversed a sodomy conviction based solely on the complainant's testimony that she did not want to engage in sexual intercourse and that she was "forced" but gave no facts to support the conclusory assertion.[119]

Subsequently, Pennsylvania modified its definition of forcible compulsion to include the "use of physical, intellectual, moral, emotional or psychological force, either express or implied. The term includes, but is not limited to compulsion resulting in another person's death, whether the death occurred before, during or after sexual intercourse."[120] Thus, saying "no" throughout a sexual encounter would establish lack of consent.

---

[118] Commonwealth v. Berkowitz, 537 Pa. 143, 641 A.2d 1161 (1994).

[119] People v. Mirabal, 278 A.D.2d 526, 717 N.Y.S.2d 404 (2000).

[120] 18 Pa. Code § 3101.

In the view of New Jersey's Supreme Court:

> [A]ny act of sexual penetration engaged in by the defendant without the affirmative and freely given permission of the victim to the specific act of penetration constitutes the offense of sexual assault. Therefore, physical force in excess of that inherent in the act of sexual penetration is not required for such penetration to be unlawful. The definition of physical force is satisfied . . . if the defendant applies any amount of force against another person in the absence of what a reasonable person would believe to be affirmative and freely-given permission to the act of sexual penetration.[121]

The view that only the force required for sexual penetration is sufficient for the element of physical force has also been accepted by a Florida appellate court.[122] California's statutory definition of consent is defined as "positive cooperation in act or attitude pursuant to an exercise of free will. The person must act freely and voluntarily and have knowledge of the nature of the act or transaction."[123] California's Supreme Court broadly defines the threat necessary to constitute force. For example, it holds that a defendant who approaches a young woman in her apartment, pulls down her pants, fondles her buttocks, and inserts his penis inside her, can be deemed to have forced the complainant to engage in sexual relations when she testifies that she was afraid that if she said or did anything, his reaction could be of a violent nature.[124] The complainant's testimony of her fear of the defendant in this situation was supported by a psychologist who testified on rape trauma syndrome and how some victims of rape are paralyzed by fear in a response termed "frozen flight," which supported the victim's testimony that she froze in response to the defendant's sudden appearance because she was afraid.[125] These cases take the view that the

---

[121] State in Interest of M.T.S., 129 N.J. 422, 444, 609 A.2d 1266, 1277 (1992).

[122] State v. Sedia, 614 So. 2d 533, 535 (Fla. Dist. Ct. App. 1993) (noting the broad definition of Fla. Stat. § 794.011(5)).

[123] Cal. Penal Code § 261.6. *See* People v. Gonzalez, 33 Cal. App. 4th 1440, 39 Cal. Rptr. 2d 778 (1995) (Approving the following construction, CALJIC 1.23.1: "[T]he word 'consent' means positive cooperation in an act or attitude as an exercise of free will. The person must act freely and voluntarily and must have knowledge of the nature of the act or transaction involved. The fact, if established, that the defendant and [complainant] engaged in a current or previous dating relationship does not by itself constitute consent.").

[124] People v. Iniguez, 7 Cal. 4th 847, 872 P.2d 1183, 30 Cal. Rptr. 2d 258 (1994). *See also* People v. Cardenas, 21 Cal. App. 4th 927, 26 Cal. Rptr. 2d 567 (1994), *review denied*, 1995 Cal. LEXIS 4370 (Apr. 20, 1994) (Defendant, a faith healer, provided treatment to various women whom he allegedly abused. The defendant's psychological and physical coercion and one woman saying "no" during sexual act, constituted sufficient forcible compulsion even if the women submitted to his "treatment." "Even unreasonable fear of immediate bodily injury may suffice if the accused takes advantage of that fear in order [to] accomplish a sexual offense.").

[125] People v. Iniguez, 7 Cal. 4th 847, 872 P.2d 1183, 30 Cal. Rptr. 2d 258 (1994) (The prosecution also established that the defendant weighed 205 pounds and the complainant 105 pounds. The California Supreme Court, in interpreting California Penal Code § 261, held:

complainant's unwillingness to engage in sexual relations is sufficient to support a charge of forcible rape. It does not require that the defendant use physical force or threats to "compel" the victim to engage in sexual relations.

The statutory definition of force is pivotal in determining whether a victim stating "no" is sufficient to constitute legal force. Some states' statutes define lack of consent not just in terms of forcible compulsion, but also circumstances in which it is reasonable to conclude that the victim clearly did not want to engage in sexual relations.[126] The Kansas statute states that rape is sexual intercourse with a person who does not consent to the sexual intercourse "when the victim is overcome by force or fear."[127] Thus, telling a defendant to stop, even if no force is applied, or threats made by the defendant, may constitute rape if a jury finds the victim is overcome by fear.[128]

A sexual assault statute may also be based on fraud (i.e., "deceit, trickery, misrepresentation and subterfuge")[129] or "duress and deception,"[130] thereby eliminating the requirement of force or threats by a defendant. Thus, engaging

---

Thus, the element of fear of immediate and unlawful bodily injury has two components, one subjective and one objective. The subjective component asks whether a victim genuinely entertained a fear of immediate and unlawful bodily injury sufficient to induce her to submit to sexual intercourse against her will. In order to satisfy this component, the extent or seriousness of the injury fears is immaterial. . . . In addition, the prosecution must satisfy the objective component, which asks whether the victim's fear was reasonable under the circumstances, or if unreasonable, whether the perpetrator knew of the victim's subjective fear and took advantage of it.

People v. Iniguez, 7 Cal. 4th 847, 856–857, 872 P.2d 1183, 1188, 30 Cal. Rptr. 2d 258 (1994).

[126] N.Y. Penal Law § 130.5 subd.2(d): Defining lack of consent to include "circumstances under which the victim clearly expressed that he or she did not consent to engage in such act, and a reasonable person in the actor's situation would have understood such person's words and acts as an expression of lack of consent to such act under all the circumstances."

[127] Kan. Stat. § 21-3502(1).

[128] State v. Borthwick, 255 Kan. 899, 880 P.2d 1261 (1994) (In *Borthwick*, the complainant was a student of the defendant's wife's learning disabilities class. She was incapable of walking without assistance and moved about her house by crawling. Her testimony was that she told the defendant to stop and that the defendant did not force her in any fashion and that he did not threaten her. She also testified that she did not give him any indication, verbal or otherwise, that she was afraid, other than through attempts to keep her legs together. Under the Kansas definition of rape it is not necessary that the defendant utilize physical force or threats. The court upheld the defendant's conviction since the complainant testified she was afraid, did not consent to the sexual intercourse, felt powerless to do anything to stop the assault, and told the defendant to stop but he nevertheless continued. "Under the circumstances of this case, a reasonable fact finder could have found [the complainant] was overcome by fear." State v. Borthwick, 255 Kan. 899, 912, 880 P.2d 1261, 1270 (1994)).

[129] Tenn. Code § 39-13-503(a)(3); Tenn. Code § 39-13-505(a); and Tenn. Code § 39-11-106(a)(13).

[130] Haw. Rev. Stat. § 702-235(4).

in sexual contact under false pretenses can support a sexual assault conviction under such a definition.[131]

§ 7.12 Force and reasonable belief of consent.

While a threat need not be capable of being immediately carried out, the consent to an act of intercourse must precede the sexual act and not be speculative. Sometimes a defendant will claim that he honestly and reasonably believed that the complainant would consent to sexual conduct in the future. This argument was advanced by boxer Michael Tyson in his rape case. The Indiana appellate court held that the trial court "exercised sound discretion when it determined that the proffered testimony that Tyson and D.W. were 'hugging and kissing' in the limousine and that they walked into the hotel hand-in-hand or arm-in-arm was not vital."[132]

The reasonable belief of consent charge is discussed in Chapter 16, Jury Instruction, § 16.16.

§ 7.13 Revocation of consent after initiation of sexual contact.

There is authority that consent to a sexual act may also be withdrawn after the initiation of sexual intercourse.[133] The California Supreme Court has ruled that a victim's objections need not be raised before intercourse begins and that consent may be withdrawn during intercourse.[134] Illinois by statute specifically provides, "a person who initially consents to sexual penetration or sexual conduct is not deemed to have consented to any sexual penetration or sexual conduct that occurs after he or she withdraws consent during the course of that sexual penetration or sexual conduct."[135] A few courts have held to the contrary.[136] One court notes this is an area of law, which "is subject to reasonable dispute, such that competent judges and attorneys might reasonably disagree concerning

---

[131] State v. Tizard, 897 S.W.2d 732 (Tenn. Crim. App. 1994) (case involved a defendant physician who touched victim's genitals for sexual purposes under the guise of a medical examination and treatment and court held that victim reasonably believed that the touching was for medical purposes, thus the physician perpetrated a fraud upon the patient, although court reversed defendant's conviction on other grounds).

[132] Tyson v. State, 619 N.E.2d 276, 286 (Ind. Ct. App. 1993), *cert. denied*, 510 U.S. 1176 (1994).

[133] McGill v. State, 18 P.3d 77 (Alaska Ct. App. 2001); State v. Siering, 35 Conn. App. 173, 182–83, 644 A.2d 958, 963 (1994); State v. Robinson, 496 A.2d 1067, 1070–71 (Me. 1985); State v. Crims, 540 N.W.2d 860, 865 (Minn. Ct. App. 1995).

[134] *In re* John Z., 29 Cal. 4th 756, 60 P.3d 183, 128 Cal. Rptr. 2d 783 (2003).

[135] 720 Ill. Comp. Stat. Ann. 5/12-17(c) (2004). *See also* Hugo v. State, 2001 Alas. App. LEXIS 78 (2001) (rejecting defendant's argument that he should not be found guilty of a first-degree sexual assault, because at the time the defendant sexually penetrated the victim, she was asleep and her expression of non-consent after she woke is irrelevant).

[136] Battle v. State, 287 Md. 675, 414 A.2d 1266 (1980); State v. Way, 297 N.C. 293, 254 S.E.2d 760 (1979).

the answer."[137] Yet, few courts to date accept the principle that consent to intercourse can not be revoked by a person.

§ 7.14   Prior abusive conduct of the defendant toward victim and others as proof of force.

In determining whether a defendant forced a complainant to engage in sexual intercourse and whether the complainant's fear of the defendant was reasonable under the circumstances, some courts permit the introduction of testimony that the defendant abused or assaulted the complainant or others on previous occasions. Evidence of these prior acts of abuse is deemed relevant to the victim's state of mind and the element of forceful compulsion.[138] The use of testimony concerning a defendant's prior bad acts or assaultive behavior is discussed in the chapter on the direct and cross-examination of the defendant.[139]

§ 7.15   Complainant's prior sexual history as relevant to the issue of consent.

Rape shield statutes have been enacted to preclude the introduction of evidence concerning a complainant's prior sexual history. The theory of these statutes is that a complainant's prior sexual history is generally not relevant to the issue of the complainant's consent in the case being tried. However, there are many exceptions to the rape shield statute, including when prior sexual history may be relevant to the issue of consent. The principles of the rape shield statute and the exceptions permitting introduction of a complainant's prior sexual history are set forth in detail in the chapter on direct and cross-examination of a complainant.[140]

§ 7.16   Investigation and development of proof of force or consent.

Equally as important as the principles defining forcible compulsion is the factual development of evidence of a complainant's consent or a defendant's force. Neighbors can be canvassed as possible witnesses to the presence or absence of sounds of struggle, screams, complaints of pain, or statements heard

---

[137] Hugo v. State, 2001 Alas. App. LEXIS 78 (2001).

[138] *See, e.g.,* People v. Lanier, 163 A.D.2d 902, 558 N.Y.S.2d 424 (1990) ("The testimony of the infant victims that defendant, their mother's boyfriend, had previously disciplined them by beating them with an extension cord, belts, or switches, was properly admitted to show the victims' continuing fear of defendant as evidence of forcible compulsion."); Sutton v. Commonwealth, 228 Va. 654, 660, 324 S.E.2d 665, 668 (1985) (*citing* as evidence of the complainant's reasonable fear of the defendant that she had seen the defendant strike his stepson in the face, causing him to bleed).

[139] *See* §§ 5.10 and 6.42.

[140] *See* §§ 5.29–5.44.

at a particular time in question. The scene itself should be reviewed, particularly the initial photos, for any evidence of a struggle: objects thrown about, a grassy field matted down, etc. Overturned furniture and broken objects at a scene can be significant. The clothing of a complainant and defendant worn at the time in question can be examined for rips, tears, dirt, stains, and, especially, missing buttons — evidence that would be consistent or inconsistent with the version of events described by the parties and witnesses. Any items at the scene that were allegedly used, or could have been used, as weapons — including improvised weapons, such as pens, letter openers, articles of furniture — should also be examined for any role they may have played in the course of the assault.

A complainant's prompt outcry (discussed in the chapter on hearsay)[141] and prompt report of a sexual assault can be important evidence. Equally important, however, is the emotional condition of the complainant as observed by the "prompt outcry witness" or other witnesses who see the complainant soon after the assault. In describing a complainant, witnesses may testify to "confused or dazed behavior," "bewilderment or disorientation," "apparent hysteria or crying," "fear or remorse," "incoherent or jumbled speech," or "sobriety or insobriety". These same witnesses can also provide testimony concerning the condition of the complainant's clothing.

Medical witnesses and law enforcement investigators may also testify to the victim's appearance and behavior, including facial discoloration, disarrayed clothing, smeared makeup, and bruises or other physical marks. However, since some bruises and marks may develop several days after an injury is inflicted, these injuries may not be reflected in the medical records of the initial examination of the complainant. Investigators should be aware of this fact in their search for physical evidence. Laboratory examination for torn hair or bite marks may also provide evidence of a forcible sexual assault.[142]

If possible, the defendant also should be examined by investigators or physicians, or investigated through statements of witnesses, for dishevelment, physical injuries, or any indications of a struggle at the time in question. A photo of the defendant taken as part of the arrest process may reflect the presence or absence of such evidence. Jail booking records may also establish injuries to a defendant.

Apart from the legal definitions of force and the investigation for evidence of force, the direct and cross-examination of the complainant and the defendant on the issue of consent presents many opportunities for counsel to develop proof in this area. This aspect of consent is discussed in the following sections.

---

[141] *See* §§ 10.13–10.19.

[142] *See* §§ 13.26–13.32.

§ 7.17   Direct examination of complainant on the issue of force — General.

Direct examination of the complainant in a case involving force must describe fully the conduct of the defendant and the effect of that conduct on the complainant. How did the offender approach the complainant? When physical force is alleged, it is important that it be detailed, not just phrased in terms of the defendant "forced me." The word "forced" does not describe for a jury what a defendant actually did. It is a conclusion. If the defendant grabbed the complainant, then the witness must describe exactly how she was grabbed, describe where she was grabbed, and describe the strength the defendant used in grabbing her.

If there were threats, what was a defendant's tone of voice? In what manner did he verbalize the threats? Did he make demands? What were they? As to the words used by the defendant, the complainant should be encouraged to describe them exactly as he said them and not censor them in any way.

Any strength, height, and weight differences between the parties should also be described by the complainant to show physical intimidation by the defendant. It should be remembered that a record on appeal does not reflect the physical description or characteristics of a defendant or a complainant unless these are verbalized by a witness.

How did the complainant feel as the defendant approached her, spoke to her, or commanded her? What was her state of mind? The complainant should be able to articulate why she feared the defendant. (If this fear was based on prior conduct of the defendant, this should have been discussed with the prosecutor well in advance of trial so that the appropriate pretrial rulings could be obtained on the admissibility of such testimony.)

Did the complainant resist in any fashion? Was there so-called passive resistance, where the victim simply did not comply with the offender's demands? Was there active, physical resistance? Was there screaming? Was there pleading? Did the complainant attempt to delay or negotiate with the offender? What were the offender's reactions to the response of the complainant? Did the offender change his demands, compromise, or negotiate?

It is helpful to view the direct examination of a complainant as a scene in a movie that must be verbalized. If the assault were on film, it would be clear to all that the complainant was frightened, intimidated, and threatened. But much of this impression would be the result of nonverbal conduct.

§ 7.18   Example of direct examination of complainant on issue of force — General.

The following testimony demonstrates some of the basic techniques on direct examination of a rape complainant. The complainant met the defendant, an acquaintance, in a bar and was being driven home when she alleges he sexually assaulted her. The complainant herself was on parole for a drug sale and for assaulting a police officer. Note that the witness provides narrative responses to the prosecutor's questions, but they are not so long that they cannot be comprehended by the jury. The witness does not testify merely that the defendant forced her. The force is detailed. Likewise, when she testified that she was grabbed, she states how and where on her body she was grabbed by the defendant.

Although this complaining witness does not speak English as her native language, she is able to effectively and graphically describe the physical force and threats of the defendant. The approach as set forth above in this section is followed, in that the threats and physical force are described, as is her resistance and the defendant's reaction to such resistance. When the complainant testifies that the defendant "banged her on the floor," the prosecutor immediately clarifies that she was thrown against the ground and that the ground had grass and rocks and was near a concrete walk. This verbalizes the picture that would be seen had the assault been filmed.

Q. Did you get hit anyplace else beside your mouth?

A. No, he just punched me in my mouth.

Q. Did he say anything else while you were in the car before you got out of the car?

A. Yeah, he said he was going to rape me. He was telling me all kind of stuff, what he was going to do to me, saying he was going to rape me and that if I start screaming or anything he is going to kill me. At that point I was scared.

Q. Well, this is in the car, right?

A. Yeah.

Q. Did he say why he was going to do that to you?

A. No. He just said it.

Q. There was no other discussion or conversation in the car before that about asking you or anything like that about sex or anything, is that right?

A. He just said that he was going to rape me.

Q. And at some point you got out of that car?

A. Right.

Q. And do you know where that was?

A. No, I am not too sure where it was. I know he dragged me somewhere, in an alley. I am not too sure.

Q. Do you know if you were on Barrington Avenue at some time before that?

A. I remember I was on Barrington, he was driving before he punched me.

555

Q. Do you know how you got from Barrington Avenue to wherever you wound up?

A. No, I don't.

Q. And I think you said you were still —

A. In a daze.

Q. You still had your clothes on?

A. Yeah, at the time I did.

Q. From the car where did you go?

A. He dragged me in some alley.

Q. Do you know where that was?

A. No.

Q. What happened when you got in the alley?

A. Well, when we got in the alley he throw me down on the floor and that's when he raped me.

Q. How did you get down on the floor?

A. He throw me down on the floor.

A. THE COURT: All right, just relax.

Q. So he threw you down?

A. Yeah.

Q. Did that hurt?

A. Yes, it did.

Q. What did he say or do then?

A. That's when he took off all my clothes.

Q. When you say, "all your clothes," what were you wearing?

A. I was wearing a shirt with a pair of shorts.

Q. And what did he say to you?

A. He said that if I screamed that he was going to kill me.

Q. And what did you do?

A. I started screaming and then that's when he put his hand over my mouth.

Q. Was there any other struggling going on?

A. Yeah, I was trying to fight him and he grabbed me by my neck and started banging on the floor.

Q. When you say, "banging on the floor," where did he grab you?

A. By the neck.

Q. And what did he bang you against?

A. The ground.

Q. What kind of ground was it?

A. It had grass and it was, like, rocks on the floor and all that.

Q. Were you near any walk or sidewalk or concrete?

A. Yeah, there was concrete there and I seen a bench.

Q. Like a park bench?

A. Yeah.

Q. And you continued to scream?

A. Yeah.

Q. Do you know what you were screaming?

A. I was yelling for help, somebody help me.

Q. Did you see anybody?

A. No, I did not.

Q. Did you keep screaming?

A. Yes.

Q. At some point what did he do to you?

A. He took out — he unzippered his pants, I am not too sure if he unzippered them or took his pants down, he took out his penis and put it in my vagina.

Q. Where were you when this happened?

A. I was still on the ground.

Q. Was he saying anything else to you?

A. No, he just said he was going to kill me if I keep on screaming and all that.

Q. So at some point he put his penis in you, is that right?

A. Yes.

Q. What else happened between you and him while you were there in terms of the struggle or any fighting?

A. We started struggling. I don't know how, God must have helped me, but I got up and I started running.

Q. What was your state of mind while you were there on the ground in this area?

A. I was hysterical and scared for my life. I thought he was going to kill me.

Q. Did you get out of there somehow?

557

A. Yes, I did.

Q. Do you know how?

A. No, I don't. I just got up and started running.

Q. When you started to run how were you dressed?

A. I was undressed. I didn't have no clothes on but a pair of sneakers and socks.

Q. Did you have any underpants on?

A. Nothing on.

§ 7.19 Direct examination developing defendant's superior strength and complainant's state of mind and fear.

The record will not reflect the physical appearance or differences of the parties. This is relevant to the element of force.

Q. Do you know how tall you are now?

A. I'm between five-foot and five-foot-one.

Q. Is that pretty much what you were back on that day?

A. Yes.

Q. And how much do you weigh now?

A. Between 100 and 105 pounds.

Q. And is that about what you weighed when this assault occurred?

A. Yes.

Q. So, who was bigger and heavier?

A. He was.

Q. How tall was he?

A. About five-foot-ten to six-feet.

Q. How much did he weigh?

A. I'd say about 180 to 190 pounds.

Q. Was he stronger than you?

A. Yes.

Q. Could you get up when he was on top of you?

A. No.

Then, the complainant's state of mind can be developed based not only on the foregoing facts, but on other circumstances.

Q. How did you feel at that point?

A. At that point I felt scared.

Q. Why?

A. Because I didn't know what the result was going to be and I was in a strange place.

Q. Were you expressing yourself emotionally in any way?

A. I was crying and I was telling him to stop repeatedly.

Q. Did he stop?

A. No.

Q. And did you feel anything as he was doing that?

A. Pain, force, pressure.

Q. What were you thinking about?

A. A few weeks before this happened, there was a girl found not too far away who was raped and dead. I didn't know if that was going to be me.

Q. So you were scared, right?

A. Yes.

While the next to last response may be objectionable, the complainant's state of mind is relevant.[143] If there is a question on the admissibility of such testimony, it should be presented to the court prior to the complainant's testimony. A limiting instruction may be appropriate. Section 5.10 deals with the complainant's references to bad acts of the defendant in establishing the element of force and the complainant's state of mind.

§ 7.20 Direct examination developing targeting of victim.

On direct examination it may be helpful to develop dialogue between a defendant and victim as to the defendant's probing of the complainant's problems and weaknesses. These same problems which may be used against the witness also help to explain why the witness was victimized. It also shows the defendant to be targeting an individual for exploitation.

In the following example, a teenage complainant discusses her initial contact with a much older defendant.

Q. What did he ask you about?

A. He asked me about my family life, who I lived with, if I had problems with my mother.

Q. What did he want to know about your family life?

A. Who I lived with.

Q. What did you tell him?

---

[143] *See* § 10.10.

A.   I told him my two brothers and I lived with my mother and my father had left us.

Q.   What did you tell him about any problems?

A.   Just that I didn't get along with my mother, she didn't like my going out and had caught me smoking marijuana.

In this context, the defendant's questions appear motivated not by concern, but by a search for a vulnerable person.

§ 7.21   Direct examination developing what complainant went through — The medical exam.

It is important to develop on direct examination what the victim went through in reporting the sexual assault. In the following testimony, the prosecutor helps paint a picture of a terrified teenager going through a difficult medical examination — testimony that helps paint the context of a forcible sexual encounter.

Q.   And, who drove you to the doctor?

A.   My Mom.

Q.   Did you leave the house before that?

A.   I couldn't leave the house. I was too afraid to leave the house.

Q.   As of this point, did you even know where the defendant lived?

A.   No.

Q.   Which doctor did you see?

A.   A woman gynecologist, Dr. Joyce.

Q.   And, why didn't you go to the hospital?

A.   I wouldn't go.

Q.   Why not?

A.   I was afraid. I didn't want people touching me. I didn't want people looking at me.

Q.   Was there any particular reason why you went to a female doctor?

A.   Because I was afraid to have a male look at me or touch me.

Q.   And, what do you remember about going to the doctor?

A.   I remember driving in the car. I remember crouching down in my seat.

Q.   I am sorry, I didn't —

A.   Crouching down in my seat so nobody would see me.

Q.   And, did you get to the doctor's office?

A.   Yes.

Q.   Was your Mom with you?

A. Yes.

Q. And, what happened at Dr. Joyce's office?

A. We went into her office and she was sitting at her desk and she said she was going to ask me some questions. She asked me a couple questions about what happened the night before. I told her. And she asked me if I was in pain and she asked me about some of the things that he did to me.

Q. And, did you respond to her questions?

A. Yes.

Q. Who else was present while these questions were going on?

A. My mother.

Q. And, what was your mother doing while you were answering these questions?

A. Holding my hand.

Q. What happened next?

A. The doctor said she wanted to take a look.

Q. And, did you know what she meant by that?

A. I figured it out.

Q. And, what happened next?

A. She showed me the room and said that I need to go into this other room and my Mom can't go in with me.

Q. And, what happened next?

A. I started crying. I didn't want to be alone. I was afraid.

Q. What then?

A. The doctor told me that she wouldn't hurt me, that she would stop if I asked her to and that I was going to be all right. I went into the room and my Mom stayed outside.

Q. What did the examining room look like?

A. It looked like a doctor's office, a regular examination room.

Q. And, was there an examining table there?

A. Yes.

Q. Tell the Jury, please, what the examining table looked like.

A. A white examining table with two steel things sticking out of it.

Q. Two steel things, did you know what they were?

A. No.

Q. Do you know now what they are?

A. Yes.

Q. What are they?

A. They are called stirrups.

Q. And, what is the purpose of a stirrup?

A. To put your feet in so you can spread your legs.

Q. So, did you get undressed?

A. Um-uh, yes.

Q. And, what happened after you got undressed?

A. I got on the table. She touched me, looked at me and then told me to lay down.

Q. What do you remember happening next?

A. She was looking inside me and then she told me that she was going to do an internal exam.

Q. An internal exam of what?

A. I guess my cervix, inside my vagina.

Q. And, what happened next?

A. She pulled out this big steel thing and told me she was going to put it inside me to open me up.

Q. And, what happened next?

A. It started hurting.

Q. What happened next?

A. I sat up and told her to stop, it hurt too much.

Q. So, did she continue?

A. No.

Q. Was that the end of the physical examination?

A. Yes.

Q. And, did you get dressed?

A. Yes.

Q. What happened after that?

A. She was talking to my Mom. I was sitting in the waiting room. There was nobody there. I was freezing. I was shaking.

Q. And, what happened after that?

A. We got into the car and my Mom asked me how I was and she said you don't have to do this if you don't want to.

Q. What did she mean by that; did you know?

A. Tell the police about the rape.

Notice how this direct testimony does more than establish a medical examination took place. It develops the complainant's state of mind, anxiety, and fear. These are all circumstantial facts in developing the context of a non-consensual encounter.

§ 7.22 Cross-examination of complainant on issues of consent and motive.

Cross-examination of a complainant on the issue of consent may be directed toward a lack of physical evidence that would suggest force or struggle, the lack of physical injury, the lack of screaming on the part of the complainant, or, if the complainant did claim that she screamed, the fact that other individuals would have been in a position to hear such screams. Cross-examination in many of these areas should be in conjunction with testimony developed through other witnesses.

Knowing that the medical testimony will reveal no evidence of injury to the complainant would allow a relatively safe cross-examination on the issue of lack of physical force. Likewise, knowing that booking photos reveal no injury to the defendant soon after the crime, and that the defendant is prepared to testify that he had no injury, would allow a risk-free cross-examination of the complainant on this issue. However, if counsel is not sure whether witnesses in the area heard the complainant cry out, this would be a hazardous area in which to cross-examine. The answers to such questions should be known beforehand from the complainant's statements and testimony, police reports, statements of other witnesses, or the defense investigation generally.

A review of statements, police reports, and testimony at trial will reveal those areas upon which there may be agreement as well as those that will be difficult for the witness to dispute. It is important that the cross-examination of the complainant be controlled either through leading questions or through the ability to contradict the complainant's answers by means of rebuttal testimony or common sense.

In a defense of consent it is impartial to develop a motive for the charges.

§ 7.23 Cross-examination suggesting motive on part of complainant to avoid getting in trouble with parent.

The following cross-examination seeks to develop a motive for the complainant's accusation in that the victim had to account for her whereabouts or activities and feared getting in trouble for either staying out late, being somewhere she was not permitted to be, drinking, or substance abuse. In short, it suggests the charges arose from the complainant's breaking the rules.

Q. And prior to the date you say this happened to you, how was your relationship with your mother?

A. We had our arguments, but it wasn't nothing bad.

Q. You've had occasion before that to come in after you were drinking, did you not?

A. Yes.

Q. And you got in trouble with your mother for doing that, did you not?

A. Yes.

Q. And your mother is a single parent trying to do the best she can, right?

A. Yes.

Q. And one of your mother's rules was that you should call home when you weren't back by a certain time, correct?

A. Yes.

Q. And at times you weren't really paying attention to her rules, were you?

A. No.

Q. And, in fact, you were in trouble on a number of occasions with your mother, were you not?

A. Yes.

Q. And you knew that when you went home that day, after you had not called home while you were directed to do so, you were going to get in trouble; you knew that, didn't you?

A. Yes.

Q. And you knew you were going to be in deep trouble, did you not?

A. Yes.

Q. And especially since you were drinking, right?

A. Yes.

§ 7.24   Cross-examination suggesting motive on part of complainant to avoid problems with family as result of complainant's drinking.

One motive often developed on cross-examination is the complainant's fear of problems or discipline as a result of engaging in some illicit or banned activity, often drugs or alcohol use. In the following example, the teenage complainant is cross-examined about her drinking prior to the alleged rape which she reported to her family after she arrived home late. The defendant drove the complainant home from a party after she told her father not to pick her up.

Q. Well, how frequently would you go to a party?

A. Not too frequently.

Q. And, how frequently is not too frequently?

A.   Well, what is frequently?

Q.   How often, in a 12-month period, how often would you go to a party?

A.   At what age?

Q.   Age 15 all the way up to this incident.

A.   Probably once every month or two.

Q.   So, where would those parties be held?

A.   All over.

Q.   Was this party that night the first party that you had ever been to in Palm Beach, with people around your age and drinking was going on?

A.   No.

Q.   Well, when had you gone to other parties where there had been drinking going on?

A.   Prior to that night.

Q.   And, how frequently had you gone to other parties prior to that night when drinking had been going on?

A.   I really don't remember.

Q.   And, I assume that you were drinking at these other parties where drinking was going on; isn't that correct?

A.   I really don't remember.

Q.   Was this the first time you ever drank at a party in Palm Beach, as far as you can recall?

A.   No.

Q.   Nevertheless, you will agree with me that you were an inexperienced drinker; isn't that correct?

A.   Yes.

Q.   And, you will agree with me that there was no parental supervision at this party, right?

A.   Not that I saw, no.

Q.   And, as a matter of fact, drinking was something right or wrong your parents didn't want you to do; isn't that correct?

A.   Right.

Q.   And, you had strict rules or stern rules in your family about drinking; isn't that correct?

A.   We just weren't allowed to drink.

Q.   Now, would it be fair to say that you had a concern about your parents learning about the fact that you were drinking at this party?

565

A. Yes.

Q. And, isn't it a fact that about the last thing you would want to have happen is for your father to pick you up at this party and see that there was drinking going on?

A. No.

Q. Isn't it a fact that about the last thing you would want to happen is for your father to see you in a condition where you were a little bit tipsy, so to speak?

A. I wasn't in that condition.

Q. So, when you told your father not to pick you up, although he said he would, you weren't concerned about the drinking that was going on at the party and you weren't concerned about your condition. Is that your testimony?

A. Yes.

§ 7.25 Cross-examination of complainant on motive — Concern for pregnancy.

Another possible motive is a complainant's concern about the consequences of pregnancy. In the following example, the complainant reported a rape after she returned to her parents' home. The cross-examiner suggests that the complainant's fear of pregnancy and concern over the defendant's lack of use of a condom motivated the rape report.

Q. And, do you remember any discussion with him about the wearing of a condom?

A. Yes.

Q. Tell us what the discussion was on that subject.

A. He told me he was going to wear one.

Q. And, did he tell you that in response to a question that you may have had?

A. No.

Q. And, you asked him if he had used any protection on that evening; is that right?

A. After he raped me, I asked him.

Q. Well, did you ask him any questions before the event took place?

A. No.

Q. And, so, when did the subject of this condom come up?

A. When he brought it up.

Q. How did he bring it up?

A. He told me he was going to use a condom.

Q. And, when did he tell you he was going to use a condom?

A. When his fingers were in my vagina.

Q. He told you he was going to wear a condom at that point?

A. Yes.

Q. And, you remember that very clearly?

A. Yes.

Q. And, did you see him put on a condom?

A. No.

Q. Was he holding your neck at the time?

A. I don't remember.

Q. And, when did this subject come up again?

A. After he was done raping me.

Q. He then had another conversation about the condom; is that right?

A. I asked him if he used one.

Q. And, you asked him not once but you asked him several times; isn't that correct?

A. I asked him once.

Q. Well, you talked about whether or not you would become pregnant with him that evening; isn't that correct?

A. He told me I wasn't going to be pregnant three times.

Q. And, how many times did you ask him if you were going to be pregnant?

A. None.

Q. So, he volunteered to you several times that you weren't going to become pregnant?

A. Yes.

Q. But, as a matter of fact, you were never sure that he wore a condom?

A. No.

Q. And, as a matter of fact when you went home that evening, you didn't know whether or not you might become pregnant because you didn't know whether or not he wore a condom; isn't that correct?

A. No.

Q. And, as a matter of fact, you were concerned about becoming pregnant; isn't that correct?

567

A. He was concerned about me becoming pregnant.

Q. And, you were concerned about being pregnant as well; isn't that correct?

A. No.

Q. Well, you testified previously that you were concerned about becoming pregnant.

A. I testified that I was concerned about being pregnant and I was concerned about getting a disease.

Q. But, you did testify previously that you were concerned about being pregnant?

A. Yes.

Q. No question about that?

A. No.

Q. Well, you said you were concerned about becoming pregnant; isn't that correct?

A. You asked me if I was concerned. I answered yes.

§ 7.26   Cross-examination of complainant on circumstances of unintentional disclosure.

Sometimes the complainant reports a sexual assault because of actions of a third person. The circumstances may raise a question of whether the complainant's report was made to legitimize otherwise proscribed conduct.

Q. When you went to school the following day, did you tell a friend that you had intercourse with Tom?

A. Yes.

Q. And you told more than one friend, correct?

A. Yes.

Q. And when you got home one day that week, your mother's boyfriend knew what you told your friends, correct?

A. Yes.

Q. He told your mom, correct?

A. Yes.

Q. Then you went to the police, correct?

A. Yes.

The effectiveness of this cross-examination is its simplicity and the juxtaposition of events — the mother's learning of the daughter's sexual activity and the report to the police.

§ 7.27 Cross-examination on issue of voluntary conduct and lack of objection prior to sexual act.

An important area of cross-examination in cases where consent is an issue is the nature of the contact between the complainant and the defendant prior to any act of alleged sexual assault. Questioning will concern the level of interaction between the parties and the complainant's failure to object to advances made by the defendant.

In the following cross-examination, the mutuality of conduct is developed through careful cross-examination that focuses on the use of alcohol and marijuana by the parties while sitting on a couch watching television. This is established through the use of leading questions, rather than by allowing the witness to provide narrative responses that may detract from the focus of the cross-examination. The words used in cross-examination can also be important. Note in the following testimony that, when the TV was turned off by the defendant, the cross-examiner asks the question, "Did you make any objection to that?" and then again a few questions later, after the defendant kisses the complainant for the first time, the cross-examiner once again asks, "You didn't object to that?" Note how the cross-examiner also skillfully develops the voluntary actions on the part of the complainant after the kiss, in removing her clothing despite her claim that she was frightened at that time. While the defendant was pulling out the sofa bed, the complainant neither attempted to leave nor scream.

Q. You were both watching TV?

A. Yes, sir.

Q. This would be about 12:15?

A. Yes, sir.

Q. David Letterman was on?

A. Yes, sir.

Q. Is that correct? And both of you were having a beer?

A. Yes, sir.

Q. There were both of you sitting on the couch?

A. Yes, sir.

Q. Did there come a time when some marijuana was produced by John?

A. Yes, sir.

Q. And did both you and he smoke the marijuana?

A. Yes, sir.

Q. And I believe you smoked it for how many minutes?

A. I smoked it — I had two drags, he smoked it for a couple of minutes.

569

Q. All right. You had two drags, but he smoked it for a couple of minutes?

A. Yes, sir.

Q. Now, you were also having your bottle of Rolling Rock?

A. Yes, sir.

Q. Now, during this time were you both sitting on the couch?

A. Yes, sir.

Q. Before David Letterman was turned off, or went off the air, was there any kissing between the two of you?

A. No, sir.

Q. Now then, there came a time when David Letterman went off the air?

A. Yes, sir.

Q. At this time both you and John were still on the couch?

A. Yes, sir.

Q. Then he turned on the radio, was it?

A. Yes, sir.

Q. Now, I would take it in order for him to do that, he would have to — well, you tell me — did he have to get up off the couch?

A. He got up, turned off the TV and turned on the radio.

Q. Some music?

A. Yes, sir.

Q. Did you make any objection to that?

A. No, sir.

Q. Now then, after he put the radio on, then did he come back down and sit on the couch with you at this time?

A. Yes, sir.

Q. Now, was the radio on for the rest of the evening?

A. I believe so.

Q. Now then, there came a time you say that John kissed you?

A. Yes, sir.

Q. You didn't object to that?

A. Not right away, sir.

Q. When he kissed you, did you object to it?

A. No.

Q. As a matter of fact, you told these ladies and gentlemen that when he kissed you, you kissed him back?

A. Yes, sir.

Q. Now, you were 20 or 21 years of age; is that correct?

A. Yes, sir.

Q. You had latched your apartment door?

A. Yes, sir.

Q. And this was a young man that you had met for the first time at the Black Hole; is that correct?

A. Yes, sir.

Q. Now then, after he kissed you and you returned the kiss, then you say you became scared?

A. Yes, sir.

Q. Is that correct?

A. Yes, sir.

Q. Up until this time, after he kissed you and you returned his kiss, you had no reason to be scared at all; is that correct?

A. Not at that time.

Q. Not at any time before he kissed you or you returned his kiss, you had no reason to be scared?

A. No, sir.

Q. And then there came a time when he asked you to take your clothes off?

A. Yes, sir.

Q. You took your clothes off?

A. Yes, sir.

Q. Did you have to stand up to remove your clothes?

A. Yes, sir.

Q. And was he also standing, removing his clothes?

A. I believe so, sir.

Q. Did there come a time when you were both completely naked?

A. Yes, sir.

Q. Then he pulled out the couch?

A. Yes, sir.

Q. Now, could you tell us just what type of a couch-bed or couch-sofa this was and how it pulled out?

A. You grab it by a handle and pull it out, and then you have to pull it again.

Q. And at any time while he was pulling that couch out to make it into a bed, did you attempt to leave that apartment?

A. No, sir.

Q. At any time while he was pulling that couch out to make it a bed, did you scream?

A. No, sir.

Q. Now then, when he had the couch out making it into a bed, then both of you were on the bed?

A. Yes, sir.

By use of leading questions and by stringing together a series of voluntary acts, the cross-examiner suggests the theme of two individuals engaged in mutual conduct.

§ 7.28 Cross-examination concerning act by use of common sense.

Another area that is basic to the factual development of a consent defense is the testimony of the defendant and complainant concerning the act itself. This may include having the complainant demonstrate an aspect of the sexual assault.[144] A trial judge does, however, have discretion in controlling questions concerning the manner in which the assailant performed sexual acts.[145] In the following cross-examination of the complainant in the case described in the previous section, the cross-examiner once again uses leading questions to establish the failure of the complainant to object and the implausibility of a forcible sexual act occurring in the manner described by the witness. The cross-examiner also brings out that the first attempt by the complainant to leave is *after* the sexual act. The use of leading questions clearly paints a picture and allows the cross-examiner to control the complainant's testimony.

Q. And then there came a time when you were both naked, you both had disrobed, and he had intercourse with you; is that correct?

A. Yes, sir.

Q. Now, as I understand it, your testimony is that during and while he was having intercourse, he had his hands on both your knees?

A. Yes, sir.

Q. So when he had both of his hands on both of your knees, both of your arms were free, were they not?

A. Yes, sir.

Q. And the only restraint that he had on you at this time was both of his hands on your knees; is that correct?

---

[144] *See* § 14.32 and example therein.

[145] State v. Mason, 315 N.C. 724, 729, 340 S.E.2d 430, 434 (1986).

A. Yes, sir.

Q. And you're saying to these ladies and gentlemen that from his hands being on your knees, both knees, these marks resulted from both hands on your knees; is that correct?

A. Yes, sir.

Q. Now then, he had intercourse, sexual intercourse?

A. Yes, sir.

Q. All right. Then there came a time when you say he rolled you over?

A. Yes, sir.

Q. And he attempted to have anal intercourse?

A. Yes, sir.

Q. Is that correct? And I believe you told the jury that when he was attempting this, he had both his hands again on your knees?

A. Yes, sir.

Q. And, again, at this time both of your arms were free?

A. Yes, sir.

Q. Now then, after this attempt at anal intercourse, you say he rolled over or got off the bed?

A. Yes, sir.

Q. Before he had vaginal intercourse with you, how many times did you scream?

A. Once.

Q. How many times did you scream before or during the attempted anal intercourse?

A. None.

Q. And at no time did you strike John?

A. No, sir.

Q. At any time did you attempt to knee him?

A. No, sir.

Q. Now then, after the attempt at anal intercourse, as I understand it, he got off the bed some way?

A. Yes, sir.

Q. And he — and I quote your description — "walked into the bathroom."

A. Yes, sir.

Q. He walked into the bathroom?

573

A. Yes, sir.

Q. Isn't it a fact that when John got off the bed and walked into the bathroom, that was the first time this evening that you attempted to leave your apartment?

A. Yes, sir.

Q. And I take it that in order to get out of the apartment, you had to remove the latch?

A. Yes, sir.

Q. He didn't grab you at that time, did he?

A. No.

Q. And after removing the latch, you had to open the door?

A. Yes, sir.

Q. He wasn't grabbing you at that time?

A. No, sir.

§ 7.29 Cross-examination concerning post-incident conduct and behavior inconsistent with rape.

Where there has been a relationship between the parties involved in a sexual assault case in which consent is the issue, there may have been contact between them after the incident that would appear to be inconsistent with the assault testified to by the complainant. Caution should be exercised in exploring this area, however, since it may open the door to expert rebuttal testimony.[146]

The cross-examination on the complainant's post-incident behavior should begin by establishing the seriousness of the assault and its consequences, followed by questions concerning the inconsistent behavior. In the first part of the following cross-examination, the defendant's attorney emphasizes the alleged emotional trauma of the rape to highlight the complainant's behavior in seeing the defendant socially after the rape — which included dancing with him, driving alone with him, and even sending him a card and rose. In the example, the cross-examiner's technique of expansive questioning concerning the conduct is appropriate when the complainant's behavior seems inexplicable; however, this technique is not recommended where a complainant's conduct would appear reasonable or an isolated inconsistent act.

Q. And as a result of that rape you say you have suffered some emotional consequences; is that correct?

A. Yes.

Q. You have had terrible nightmares?

---

[146] *See* §§ 11.8, 11.12, 11.17, and 11.19.

A. Uh huh.

Q. Is that correct?

A. Yes.

Q. And would you describe to the jury how many times you have had these nightmares?

A. Over two dozen times. They still occur, I had one the night before last.

Q. And these nightmares are associated with that rape; are they not?

A. Yes, they are.

Q. You never had them before; did you?

A. No.

Q. And I suppose these nightmares are something that would scare you?

A. Very much.

Q. And they frighten you?

A. Yeah.

Q. And those are things that have occurred on at least two dozen occasions; is that right?

A. Yes, sir.

Q. And they are awful; aren't they?

A. Yes.

Q. And they are terrible; right?

A. Correct.

Q. And as you sit here today, you don't have any reason to believe that you might not have one tonight, tomorrow night, and maybe all next week; do you?

A. I never know when they're going to happen.

Q. And there's no question that Keith is the person that caused these nightmares; right?

A. There's no question in my mind.

Q. Well, you shudder when you think of Keith holding you; don't you? I mean, just the thought of this man even holding you makes you shudder; doesn't it?

A. I shake when I think about having sex with him.

Q. Don't you even shake when you think of him holding you?

A. No.

Q. And when you shake and you think about him having sex with you, it doesn't bother you to have him hold you; is that correct?

A. I guess it does bother me a little, but —

At this point, having established the emotional upset produced by the crime, the defendant points out the complainant's conduct of dancing with him, driving alone with the defendant to a secluded area, and giving him a card and rose, all after the alleged assault.

Q. And you told the grand jury that you wouldn't get in a car with Keith at night; correct?

A. It was my feeling at the time.

Q. You told the grand jury that you didn't want to get in a car with him at night; isn't that right?

A. I'm allowed to change my feelings.

Q. When did they change?

A. After the grand jury, after the grand jury testimony I sought counseling.

Q. And after that counseling you were no longer afraid to get in the car with Keith at night; do I understand that correctly?

A. I was resolving some feelings. I guess you could say yes, I felt more control in the situation.

Q. You're now more in control to get in the car with a rapist; that's about it, isn't it?

A. Yes.

Q. And not only did you get in the car with him once at night, but you went to a very secluded place that night; didn't you?

A. Yes, we did.

Q. More secluded than your apartment where you say you were raped; isn't that right?

A. Yes.

Q. I'd like to show you Defendant's Exhibit B.

A. Yes.

Q. Would you tell us what that is?

A. I'm sorry, what it is?

Q. What is it?

A. It's the card I gave to Keith the morning that I dropped off the flower.

Note in the following questioning that the cross-examiner listens carefully to the answer and uses the complaining witness's own language to further dramatize her post-incident behavior.

Q. The card you gave to him a year from when he had slept with you?

A. That we had slept together willingly.

Q. Not a year that you had slept together willingly?

A. Exactly.

Q. But, of course, when you slept together unwillingly, that was only two days after, or one day after you slept together willingly; right?

A. Two.

Q. Well, you slept together what, Saturday night?

A. Yes. I'm sorry, there were two nights we slept together. The night I'm referring to on the card was the first night we were together, so it was two days after the first night we were together that it was an unwilling situation.

DEFENDANT'S ATTORNEY: I would like to offer this, Judge.

PROSECUTOR: No objection.

THE COURT: Received.

Q. Did you ever go dancing with Keith?

A. I danced with him the first night I went out with him and had sex with him, and I danced with him a night at Fantasies.

Q. The time at Fantasies was after the rape?

A. Yes.

Q. And after the rape you also sent him flowers and a letter in which you expressed your love to him.

A. Well, yes, it's hard to explain.

After establishing the emotional trauma of the rape and the complainant's inconsistent conduct, they should be contrasted. Part of the inconsistency is that the behavior occurred after the complainant testified to the grand jury, presumably at which point she would be unwilling to have contact with a person she has identified as a rapist.

Q. And yet you wrote Keith a letter or a card, in which you may have signed it love, to the man who has caused you these nightmares that are still recurring; isn't that right?

A. Yes.

Q. And this is the man who raped you; isn't it?

A. He knows about the nightmares.

Q. This is a man that raped you; isn't it?

A. Sure, yes.

Q. And this is a man who caused you to lose weight?

A. Uh huh.

Q. And the man who caused you to have depression; correct?

577

A. Yes, sir.

Q. A man who has caused you to think about counseling; correct?

A. Yes.

Q. A man who because of his actions, according to you, prevented you from seeing other men; right?

A. Yes.

Q. A man who violated your very body; correct?

A. Correct.

Q. And this is the man you went dancing with; isn't it, afterwards? Right?

A. Yes.

Q. And he held you; right?

A. Yes.

Q. And this is after the nightmares; right?

A. Yes.

Q. And so all the world could see you and this rapist were on the floor, on the dance floor in a public place, you were holding him; weren't you?

A. Yes.

Q. And he wasn't forcing you that night; was he?

A. No.

Q. He didn't drag you out on the floor; did he?

A. No.

Q. He said, "Come on, let's dance"; didn't he?

A. Yes.

Q. This is after your grand jury testimony; right?

A. Yes.

Q. After you went in the grand jury and said that this man is a rapist, you went out on the floor at Fantasies and danced with him; right?

A. Yes.

Q. You didn't tell Keith to get away from you; did you?

A. No.

Q. You didn't slap him in the face; did you?

A. No, never slapped him.

Q. You didn't tell him you thought he was repulsive; did you?

A. No.

Q. In fact, you never told him that; have you?

A. No.

Q. You indicated you saw Keith on Valentine's Day; is that correct?

A. Yes.

Q. You took a cab with him back to your apartment that night; didn't you?

A. That's correct.

Q. And he came in and you showed him your apartment; right?

A. Yes.

Q. I'm going to show you Defendant's Exhibit C. Does that look familiar to you?

A. Yes, and it's very nicely preserved. This is the flower I gave Keith, along with that card; I put it on his door, I slipped the card underneath this.

Q. By the way, when you left Valentines — when he left your apartment Valentine's Day that night, did you jump on his back when he left?

A. Oh, yeah, yes.

Q. And the dancing with Keith and flower and card you gave him was all after you say Keith raped you?

A. Yes.

There are many forms of behavior that may or may not be consistent with consent and inconsistent with a forcible sexual act. If the conduct appears favorable to the defendant, it should be carefully developed and emphasized through cross-examination as set forth above. Remember that such an approach invites a response from the complainant or the prosecutor that may or may not answer the questions asked. It may also invite testimony by an expert concerning post-incident behavior or rape trauma syndrome.[147]

§ 7.30 Cross-examination of complainant alleging sexual assault after prior consent to relations.

In the following example, the complainant alleges a sexual assault the day after she agreed to relations with the defendant, although she did not appear at the agreed-upon date and time.

A key point by the cross-examiner is when and where the complainant changed her mind and whether she communicated her change of heart. The complainant not only admits she did not communicate her withdrawal of consent, but also that she lied to the defendant about why she did not appear for the relations.

Q. You were supposed to see Dave the day before?

---

[147] *See* §§ 11.12 and 11.19.

A. Yes.

Q. And where were you supposed to see him?

A. In my apartment.

Q. You invited him to your apartment?

A. When we decided on a place, I said he could come to my room.

Q. A place for what?

A. To — I mean he just — when he was going to see me.

Q. Come on. You had decided to have sexual intercourse with Dave, correct?

A. Yes.

Q. And you didn't have this sexual intercourse the day before as you had planned. Did you?

A. Right.

Q. That's because your roommate was there. Wasn't it?

A. No. That's not true.

Q. What do you say is the reason you didn't have sexual intercourse with Dave the day before?

A. Because I made it my business not to be in the room at that time.

Q. This was after you agreed you would have sex with Dave. Correct?

A. Yes.

Q. And is it your testimony now, Ms. Roberts, you changed your mind?

A. Yes.

Q. OK. When and where was it you changed your mind?

A. That day I changed my mind.

Q. What did you tell him was the reason you didn't show up?

A. I told him I had a last minute appointment.

Q. Was that true?

A. No.

Q. OK. You lied to him about what had happened the day before. Correct?

A. Yes.

Q. OK. You did not say to Dave, "I do not want to have sex with you." Correct?

A. Correct.

Q. You made up a false story about having a last minute appointment?

A. Yes.

Q. And on the day in question, when Dave asked you to do it now, you knew that meant sexual relations. Correct?

A. Yes.

Q. And how did you answer Dave?

A. I said I had people working on my apartment.

Q. You didn't say to Dave, "I don't want to have sex with you." Did you?

A. No.

The cross-examination establishes the earlier consent and the complainant's failure to clearly withdraw consent, helping establish a reasonable doubt as to the crime. It also establishes the witness as lying to the defendant, rather than the defendant lying or deceiving the complainant.

§ 7.31 Cross-examination of complainant on lack of damage to clothing.

A cross-examination on the issue of consent may examine the lack of physical evidence by examining the complainant's clothing during the assault. In the following example, the cross-examiner starts by establishing that the clothing introduced by the prosecution was worn during the assault. The cross-examination highlights for the jury the lack of tears or other damage to the clothing. It is a safe approach since the cross-examiner knows there is no damage to the clothing, yet allows the cross-examiner to repeatedly emphasize the lack of evidence of force.

Q. Is Exhibit 7 the shirt you were wearing that night?

A. Yes.

Q. All right. And is this the condition of the shirt when you gave it to the police with the exception of the cut marks that have been taken out of it for laboratory analyses?

A. Yes.

Q. Can we agree the two top buttons are still buttoned?

A. Yes.

Q. Is that the way you turned it over to the police at the hospital?

A. Yes.

Q. Can we agree that there are no rip marks on the shirt?

A. Yes.

Q. Were you also wearing pants?

A. Yes.

Q. These pants, Exhibit 12, in evidence?

A. Yes.

Q. Can we agree that your pants were not torn in any way, shape, or fashion?

A. Yes.

Q. And can we agree that the button and zipper of the jeans was not broken?

A. Yes.

Q. The zipper is still working fine?

A. Yes.

Q. Exhibit 10, your underwear, can we agree they are not ripped or torn either?

A. Yes.

§ 7.32 Cross-examination concerning information provided at trial and omitted in previous testimony and statements.

Sometimes at trial a complainant will add significant details on the issue of consent that she previously omitted. The cross-examiner may want to suggest that the witness is forgetful or unreliable, or was trying to embellish her testimony or the prosecution's case, as in the following example.

Q. Now, you were called before the grand jury; weren't you?

A. Yes, I was.

Q. And the prosecutor questioned you at that time?

A. Yes, she did.

Q. And she asked you to tell the truth as accurately as you could; correct?

A. Of course.

Q. And you did; didn't you?

A. Yes, of course I did.

Q. And you wanted to cooperate with the prosecutor and grand jury; didn't you?

A. Yes.

Q. You never told the grand jury about that conversation with the defendant, "Look what you have done to me"; did you?

A. No, but there's a reason for that.

Q. I'm sure there is, but you didn't tell them that; did you?

A. No, I didn't.

Q. And you were told or asked to tell the grand jury what happened; isn't that right?

A. Yes.

Q. Today is the first time you mentioned that; isn't it?

A. Uh huh.

Q. You're not adding that to kind of help the story along a little, are you?

A. I'm only telling the truth.

Q. All right. So the answer to that would be no?

A. Exactly.

Q. Did you forget about that in the grand jury?

A. Yes.

Q. And you told the grand jury that you had sex with him once before this occasion; didn't you?

A. That's correct.

Q. Actually you had sex with him twice; didn't you?

A. Yes.

Q. Voluntarily?

A. Yes.

Q. Well, now what happened there, did you forget about that also?

A. Yes.

Q. Did you ever come back to the prosecutor and tell her you would like to correct what you said in front of the grand jury?

A. No.

§ 7.33   Cross-examination of defendant where consent is asserted as defense.

The defendant also can be cross-examined concerning developments in the course of the investigation that have produced evidence on the issue of force or on the issue of the complainant's consent. Particularly helpful is any physical evidence, such as torn clothing or injuries of the complainant or defendant, that can be connected to the incident.

Many important facts are likely to be left unanswered in the course of the investigation. In cases where there has been an ongoing relationship between a complainant and defendant, it is important to know what has transpired between the parties. If the defendant made a statement to a complainant at some point in a relationship that could be threatening or intimidating, this may be developed on cross-examination of the defendant. Statements by the defendant to the complainant or to third parties reflecting a demeaning opinion of the complainant or an attitude of hostility are helpful if the defense is claiming consent.

Another issue the prosecutor may want to bring out on cross-examination of the defendant is the lack of an ulterior motive on the complainant in asserting the charges. Assuming the defendant has not mentioned a motive on direct examination, the prosecutor may want to develop this area. This does not mean asking the defendant directly if he knows of any motive, since such an open-ended question invites a surprise answer and potentially devastating consequences. What must be developed are the circumstances surrounding the relationship that would indicate no such motive, and unless the cross-examiner is certain from prior statements of the defendant that the motive area can be safely pursued — with only one possible response from the defendant — should the subject be explored.

§ 7.34 Cross-examination concerning intentions on the day in question.

Another subject to develop on cross-examination of the defendant, if appropriate, is the intentions of the defendant on the day or evening in question. These questions can be helpful where the defendant has met the complainant for the first time and proceeds to have sexual relations that the defense claims were with the complainant's consent.

Q. Did you go out that evening with the intention of obtaining sex?

A. That was something on my mind, yes.

Q. So having sexual relations was on your mind when you left that evening to go to the Black Hole?

A. Sure.

Q. When you met her that night at the Black Hole, you were interested in her?

A. Yes.

Q. Found her attractive?

A. Yes.

Q. Found her pleasant?

A. Yes, sir.

Q. Found her charming?

A. Yes, sir.

Q. And you were having a friendly conversation with her at that point?

A. Yes, sir.

Q. And at that time was it still your intention to have sexual relations that evening with someone?

A. Yes, sir.

Q. Did you want to go to the apartment to have sex with her?

A. At that time it never crossed my mind.

Q. Had you thought of sex at all up until that point with her?

A. No.

The above cross-examination suggests to the jury that the defendant is less than credible and is providing inconsistent responses. This approach allows the witness to impeach himself, and it begins the prosecution's portrayal of the defendant as deceptive and manipulative in his relationship with the complainant.

§ 7.35 Questions concerning contraception or protection from disease.

In cases of sexual acts that are claimed to be consensual, the participants should be questioned about the use of condoms or other birth control measures. The use of such protection may suggest an element of consent, although this is not necessarily so — some rapists have used condoms in a sexual assault in an attempt to suggest consent or prevent the detection of DNA evidence. Nonetheless, concern about venereal disease, AIDS, and pregnancy might be expected on the part of a woman.

Q. And was there ever any discussion when you were with her in the apartment about the use of condoms or other protection?

A. No, sir.

Q. Did she have any means of protection?

A. Not that I know of, sir.

Q. Did you have any condoms?

A. No, sir.

Q. Was there any time that anyone expressed any concern about contraception or protection from disease?

A. No, sir.

Cross-examination on this issue should end at this point and not be pursued with any type of argumentative questions. If this area is to be argued, it should be done in summation. The necessary facts for the argument will have been established here, and there is no need to lose control of this area by further questions.

§ 7.36 Cross-examination on facts inconsistent with consensual relationship.

Given that a defendant could not be expected on cross-examination to admit that an act of intercourse was not consensual, the cross-examiner must develop facts or circumstances that are inconsistent with the assertion of a consensual relationship. The defendant's story should be reviewed to see if his testimony makes sense and is internally consistent and logical. Inconsistencies in a

585

defendant's own story are among the best targets on cross-examination. In the following example, the defendant claims that he had consensual relations with the complainant, whom he first met that night, and that there were no problems between them.

Q. How did you feel after your sexual relations?

A. I felt relaxed.

Q. And was she still your friend?

A. I thought so, yes.

Q. And as you left that apartment, you had nothing to hide; did you?

A. As I left that apartment I had nothing to hide?

Q. Right.

A. No, sir.

Q. You weren't afraid of the police?

A. No, sir.

Q. You knew she knew who you were?

A. Yes, sir.

Q. You were still interested in her when you left the apartment?

A. Yes, sir.

Q. You were still interested in her feelings?

A. Yes, sir.

Q. You left some of your belongings, including marijuana, behind in her apartment?

A. Yes, sir.

Q. Did you ever attempt to get them back?

A. No, sir.

Q. And after your sexual relations with her, you felt there were no problems between the two of you?

A. Correct.

Q. Did you call her the next day?

A. No, sir.

Q. Did you visit her at work?

A. No, sir.

Q. Did you visit her at school?

A. No, sir.

Q. Were you still concerned about her in the days following your intercourse with her?

A. Yes, sir.

Q. Did you ever contact her again after that evening?

A. No, sir.

Q. Did you still like her?

A. I don't know.

The defendant's story that there were no problems between him and the complainant, which also suggests there would be no motive on the part of the complainant to accuse him of rape, is belied by the fact that he left belongings in her apartment that he never attempted to recover, and that he never again tried to get in touch with this woman that he was so interested in and concerned about. By his last answer on cross-examination, the defendant suggests that he is confused as to exactly what his relationship was with the complainant. If the defendant has doubts at this point in his story, then the jury also should have doubts about his story.

§ 7.37 Example of failing to control defendant during cross-examination in a defense of consent.

The following cross-examination of the defendant, William Kennedy Smith, is an example of questions that not only fail to have a clear goal but also allow the defendant to develop and expand his defense. It is not only ineffective but also counter-productive.

Q. Would you consider the story that you've told to the jury today to describe an act of love?

A. It is not a story, it's the truth.

Q. Didn't you carry through with your threat, Mr. Smith, and do everything you could to make sure nobody would believe her?

A. Ms. Lash, I don't, I've searched myself every night since March 29th to try to find out why Patty would make an allegation against me that's not true; that's going to destroy my family, destroy my career, possibly send me to jail for 15 years. I understand Patty Bowman has a lot of problems, and she talked about her neck, she talked about her child, she talked about her relationship with her family. All of those things make me feel very sorry for Patty Bowman, but that's not the issue here. The issue here is I'm innocent and how do you defend yourself from somebody who says the word "rape" over and over again?

Author's Note: What is the goal of these two questions? What answers can be expected?

Q. How did she consent to such, what did she do that led you to believe that she consented?

A. Well, I would have to say that it was a lot of different things. I can tell you that she put me inside of her when we were on the lawn. I can tell you that I was not quite ready and that she helped me inside of her.

Author's Note: This is a totally open-ended question that allows the defendant a "free shot" at his defense.

Q. Now she not only rubbed against you and asked if she could take you home, now she's actually a person who put your penis in her vagina?

A. That's correct.

Q. What are you saying, that she raped you, Mr. Smith?

A. Absolutely not.

Author's Note: The cross-examination reinforces the defendant's story and places the defendant in control.

Q. When Ms. Bowman turned to leave and go up the stairs and leave the Kennedy estate, your ego couldn't take that rejection, could it?

A. That is absolutely not true.

Note how in the course of cross-examining the defendant, the prosecutor has allowed the defendant to provide a motive for the allegation and to portray the victim as troubled, unbalanced, and vengeful.

The above cross-examination will only help the defendant establish his case.

CHAPTER 8

IDENTIFICATION AND IDENTIFICATION DEFENSE

§ 8.1   Introduction.

In cases involving adult victims in which consent is not alleged as the defense, the defense usually is one of mistaken identity. From a psychological standpoint, identification involves perception, retention, and retrieval. These areas form the basis of direct and cross-examination of an eyewitness.

The defense of mistaken identity in a sexual assault case is similar to the defense of mistaken identity in other criminal cases, except that the emotional trauma experienced by complainant may play a role in identification, and the complainant's opportunity to observe the defendant may be greater or less than in other crimes, depending on the circumstances surrounding the attack.

Cross-examining the victim of sexual assault requires skill, because a careless cross-examination may bring back the victim's memories of the assault and lead to an emotional reaction and, in rare cases, even cause the victim to recall the face of the attacker whose image her mind has suppressed.

The extent of a witness's identification of the offender will be based upon factors that affect his or her opportunity to observe that individual. It is that opportunity that must be evaluated. Lighting, the duration of an assault, distance, and time are all typical variables that surround the event. Witness factors also include the age and physical condition of the witness, the effect of drugs or alcohol, and the stress of a traumatic event. These are the usual areas of cross-examination and sometimes the subject of expert testimony. Third-party witnesses may testify to factors such as lighting. The opportunity to observe can also be assessed by comparing the description originally provided by a witness with the actual description of the defendant. Assuming a witness initially perceives and observes accurately, the person can later forget certain perceptions and observations.

The next step to evaluate is how information concerning the eyewitness perception was retrieved. Suggestiveness in interviewing and identification procedures may play a role here. The second observation that a witness makes is usually a law enforcement-initiated encounter of the defendant, which must be evaluated for its potential suggestiveness and reliability, particularly when there has been a long period of time between the incident and the second encounter with the defendant. Finally, the courtroom identification of the defendant must be evaluated in light of possible earlier contacts with the assailant.

Alleging a case of mistaken identification is closely associated with an alibi defense. If the defendant is not the person who committed the crime, the defendant had to be someplace else. The identification defense is greatly strengthened with the presentation of alibi witnesses; however, as will be seen, the alibi defense may contain legal and tactical pitfalls. The risks involved in an alibi should be carefully understood and evaluated before selecting it as a means of defense.

For the prosecution, identification involves the same issues as for the defense — the opportunity for the witnesses to observe the offender, the original description of the offender, and all the other areas the defense attorney will be evaluating — however, the prosecutor must investigate and develop proof as to the identification of the defendant in advance of trial.

Cases based solely upon the identification of one witness are difficult to prove, although certainly not impossible. Every detail in the complainant's identification should be corroborated if possible, whether such details relate to the description of the defendant or the opportunity to observe. A careful investigation will include use of available scientific resources, such as DNA testing. Even if a scientific test is not likely to yield beneficial results, it should be considered to establish the thoroughness of the investigation. Innovative techniques should also be considered when appropriate, such as voice identification and the procedure whereby the complainant has the opportunity to observe the defendant in a large group of people, such as a bar, as opposed to a lineup. A thorough understanding of the issues of identification will allow a prosecutor to effectively present the testimony of a complainant.

An excellent book on identification, *Eyewitness Testimony*,[1] makes several points germane to sexual assault cases. One is that victims are not necessarily more accurate eyewitnesses and may be less accurate at times than witnesses

---

[1] ELIZABETH F. LOFTUS & JAMES M. DOYLE, EYEWITNESS TESTIMONY: CIVIL AND CRIMINAL (3d ed. 1997).

who are not victims.[2] Another observation is that the victim of an assault may well be sincerely convinced of the accuracy of his or her testimony and that aggressive cross-examination may yield a credible and sincere witness rather than a pausing, hesitating, and fidgeting witness.[3] This means that greater caution is required in cross-examining a victim who is sincerely convinced that the defendant is the assailant.

There is reason to believe that the more aggressively the defendant's attorney cross-examines the sincere victim, the more the witness will appear to be truthful and accurate, thereby reinforcing the jury's confidence in the testimony.[4] Given the sympathy that a victim is likely to engender in a case of a conceded brutal sexual assault, many traditional aggressive cross-examination techniques of a rape victim will lack efficacy when identification is an issue. Most of the approaches to cross-examination of complainants in this chapter are limited to high-safety questions based on known information regarding witness's descriptions and statements and take into consideration the dynamics of sexual assault, such as stress and distraction on the part of complainants.

A theory used in some of these approaches involves *separation* of the witness from the identification. "The eyewitness is ordinarily a consumer (even a victim) of an identification procedure designed and operated by others."[5] These questions attack the process rather than the witness, with questions such as "The police took you to the scene?" rather than "So, you went to the scene?"[6] Possible defects in the process include suggestiveness in the identification procedure, delaying or failing to pursue leads, and delaying or failing to gather and investigate all likely sources of evidence.

§ 8.2 Defense that someone other than defendant committed alleged crime.

The defense may wish to suggest that someone other than the defendant committed, or had the motive, intent, or opportunity to commit the alleged crime. The evidence of another person's possible involvement should be more than the opportunity to commit the crime[7] and must raise more than a suspicion that the

---

[2] *Id.* at 90–91.

[3] *Id.* at 227.

[4] *Id.*

[5] *Id.* at 230.

[6] *Id.*

[7] People v. Kaurish, 52 Cal. 3d 648, 802 P.2d 278, 276 Cal. Rptr. 788 (1990), *cert. denied*, Kaurish v. California, 502 U.S. 837 (1991) (holding evidence of a third party's commission of crime should be more than "mere motive or opportunity" and that there must be direct or circumstantial evidence linking the third person to the crime; People v. Perez, 972 P.2d 1072, 1074 (Colo. Ct. App. 1998), *cert. denied*, Perez v. People, No. 98SC752, 1999 Colo. LEXIS 200 (Mar. 1, 1999) (defendant sought to introduce evidence that son of woman who reported sexual assaults, who was living in house at time of assault and was on probation for misdemeanor sexual assault, was alternate

person committed the crime.[8] The evidence offered by a defendant must tend to connect the other person to the crime.[9]

Evidence of another person's motive or threats alone is inadmissible without other evidence tending to connect the other person with the commission of the crime charged.[10] The combination of motive and opportunity may provide the necessary circumstantial evidence to require admission of the evidence of another possible perpetrator.[11] Even if there are similarities in the crimes, the prejudice,

suspect, but appellate court upheld trial court's decision to preclude such evidence, since defendant must offer direct proof that other person committed crime and "evidence that another person had an opportunity to commit the crime for which defendant was being tried is not sufficient."

[8] Karvonen v. State, 205 Ga. App. 852, 853–54, 424 S.E.2d 47, 49 (1992) (holding trial court properly precluded evidence that babysitter had opportunity to commit abuse); People v. Bradley, 8 A.D.3d 169, 778 N.Y.S.2d 687, appeal denied, 3 N.Y.3d 704, 818 N.E.2d 674, 785 N.Y.S.2d 32 (2004) (finding trial court properly precluded accused rapist's offer of third party culpability, since "[t]he possible connection of another person to the crimes was too speculative to have any probative value."); People v. Wade, 236 A.D.2d 777, 653 N.Y.S.2d 773, appeal denied, 89 N.Y.2d 1016, 680 N.E.2d 629, 658 N.Y.S.2d 255 (1997) (noting that defendant has right to show someone else committed crime, but the evidence must "do more than raise a mere suspicion" and "show a clear link between the third party and the crime"); People v. Brown, 133 A.D.2d 773, 520 N.Y.S.2d 166 (1987), appeal denied, 70 N.Y.2d 953, 520 N.E.2d 555, 525 N.Y.S.2d 837 (1988) ("While the defendant has the right to introduce evidence that a person other than himself was the perpetrator of the crime charged, such evidence must do more than raise a mere suspicion that another person committed the crime: there must be a clear link between the third party and the crime in question." [citations omitted] 133 A.D.2d at 774).

[9] Smithart v. State, 946 P.2d 1264 (Alaska Ct. App.1997); State v. Walden, 183 Ariz. 595, 905 P.2d 974 (1995), cert. denied, 517 U.S. 1146 (1996); Burmingham v. State, 342 Ark. 95, 108–10, 27 S.W.3d 351, 359–60 (2000), subsequent appeal, 346 Ark. 78, 57 S.W.3d 118 (2001) (court held evidence of other similar "blue light" rapes, without evidence pointing to a third party's guilt, should not be admitted); People v. Bradley, 8 A.D.3d 169, 778 N.Y.S.2d 687, appeal denied, 3 N.Y.3d 704, 818 N.E.2d 674, 785 N.Y.S.2d 32 (2004) (holding possible evidence of third-party culpability was too speculative to justify its admission); Garza v. State, 18 S.W.3d 813, 822 (Tex. Ct. App. 2000) (upholding trial court's restriction on questioning detective about other suspects in sexual assault case since connection between other suspect and crime was speculative).

[10] Shields v. State, 357 Ark. 283, 166 S.W.3d 28 (2004) (upholding the trial court's prohibition on the admission of evidence that a third party had a motive for the murder because of the lack of direct and circumstantial evidence linking the third person to the actual perpetration of the murder); Walker v. State, 353 Ark. 12, 110 S.W.3d 752 (2003) (ruling it is "highly speculative and conjectural to admit evidence of a third person who 'may' have had a motive for revenge against one of the murder victims); State v. Cerreta, 260 Conn. 251, 796 A.2d 1176 (2002):

We have recognized consistently that a defendant has a right to introduce evidence that indicates that someone other than the defendant committed the crime with which the defendant has been charged . . . . The defendant must, however, present evidence that directly connects a third party to the crime . . . . It is not enough to show that another had the motive to commit the crime . . .nor is it enough to raise a bare suspicion that some other person may have committed the crime of which the defendant is accused. [citations omitted]

Id. at 262–63, 796 A.2d at 1183; State v. Clark, 78 Wash. App. 471, 478, 898 P.2d 854, 858, review denied, 128 Wash. 2d 1004 (1995).

[11] United States v. Blum, 62 F.3d 63, 68 (2d. Cir. 1995).

confusion, and delay from introduction of such evidence may preclude its admission.[12] Even if evidence of third-party culpability is relevant, its admissibility is reviewed under the rules governing admission of all evidence, i.e., such as weighing its probative value against the prospect of trial delay, undue prejudice to the opposing party, confusing the issues, or misleading the jury.[13] But if the prosecution's case is largely circumstantial, the defendant may use evidence of the same character to point to a third person as the perpetrator.[14] New York's highest court defines the "clear link" or "direct connection" standard as no more than an "abbreviation" for the conventional balancing test.[15] It notes that the "clear link" or "direct connection" standard may be misleading to the extent it implies that third-party evidence "occupies a special category of proof."[16] The evidence of another person's motive or threats is inadmissible unless "coupled with other evidence tending to connect such other person with the actual commission of the crime charged." An offer of proof can be made outside the presence of the jury.[17] Testimony offered to connect the third person must still meet the rules of admissibility. For example, a third party's statements are hearsay unless qualifying under a recognized hearsay exception.[18]

Thus, while the evidence should clearly connect the defendant, a defendant can meet this requirement with substantial circumstantial evidence that is

---

[12] State v. Tankersley, 191 Ariz. 359, 956 P.2d 486 (1998); People v. Schulz, 4 N.Y.3d 521, 529, 829 N.E.2d 1192, 1197, 797 N.Y.S.2d 24, 29 (2005) (upholding trial court's preclusion of a photograph of a third-party whom the defendant claimed had committed the crime and whom committed robberies in the area and matched the victim's description, when there was no proof to connect the third-party to the crime, since such evidence "would have caused undue delay, prejudice and confusion."); People v. Wade, 236 A.D.2d 777, 653 N.Y.S.2d 773, *appeal denied*, 89 N.Y.2d 1016, 680 N.E.2d 629, 658 N.Y.S.2d 255 (1997) (noting that defendant has right to show someone else committed crime, but the evidence must "do more than raise a mere suspicion" and "show a clear link between the third party and the crime").

[13] State v. Tankersley, 191 Ariz. 359, 956 P.2d 486 (1998).

[14] State v. Tankersley, 191 Ariz. at 478–79, 898 P.2d at 858; People v. Primo, 96 N.Y.2d 351, 753 N.E.2d 164, 728 N.Y.S.2d 735 (2001) (reversing defendant's conviction due to trial court's failure to admit ballistics report linking a third person to gun used to shoot victim where the ballistics report matched a gun of a person who was at scene of crime and defendant said committed the crime).

[15] *Primo*, 96 N.Y.2d at 356, 753 N.E.2d at 168, 728 N.Y.S.2d at 739.

[16] *Primo*, 96 N.Y.2d at 356, 753 N.E.2d at 168, 728 N.Y.S.2d at 739.

[17] *Id. See also* Shields v. State, 357 Ark. 283 (2004) (upholding the trial court's prohibition on the admission of evidence that a third party had a motive for the murder because of the lack of direct and circumstantial evidence linking the third person to the actual perpetration of the murder); Walker v. State, 353 Ark. 12, 110 S.W.3d 752 (2003) (ruling it is highly speculative and conjectural to admit evidence of a third person who "may" have had a motive for revenge against one of the murder victims); State v. Clark, 78 Wash. App. 471, 478, 898 P.2d 854, 858, *review denied*, 128 Wash. 2d 1004, 907 P.2d 296 (1995).

[18] State v. Grega, 168 Vt. 363, 721 A.2d 445 (1998) (noting there was no direct evidence to connect third party to crime and that third party's statements were not declarations against interest because he was available as a witness).

evaluated in the context of the prosecution's case.[19] A defendant, of course, can argue any inference from the evidence, including that another person committed the crime.[20] The defendant may possibly inquire of investigators about other suspects[21] or fingerprints depending on the context. For example, evidence of an unidentified palm print or fingerprint found at the scene of a crime, without any other information to suggest another perpetrator is too speculative to admit into evidence.[22] However, evidence of unidentified hair and fingerprints recovered from victim's body and ligatures used to bind the victim's hands and feet, and the victim's personal effects, may be relevant to establishing someone other than the defendant who committed the crime.[23]

A defendant cannot necessarily raise his exculpation on another charge, even if his argument is that the perpetrator is the same in the pending case.[24]

In sexual assault cases, while a defendant has a right to show that someone else other than him committed the crime, there must be a link between the third party or the other crimes and the crime for which the defendant is charged.[25] Evidence that the complainant's father[26] had previously been convicted of sexual abuse, or that complainant's grandfather abused the complainant's mother,[27] or

---

[19] Smithart v. State, 946 P.2d 1264, 1278 (Alaska Ct. App. 1997) ("Thus, circumstantial evidence of another person's guilt can properly be excluded when, viewed in light of the other evidence in the case, it does no more than raise speculative possibilities. When, however, the evidence as a whole discloses a substantial possibility that the defendant has been wrongly charged, a trial judge would abuse his or her discretion to exclude the offered evidence of third-party guilt." *Id.*); State v. Bellaphant, 535 N.W.2d 667 (Minn. Ct. App. 1995), *review denied*, No. C4-94-2232, 1995 Minn. LEXIS 849 (Sept. 28, 1995) (defendant's conviction for shaking her child to death reversed. Prosecution based their use on circumstantial evidence of defendant being primary caretaker and defendant's equivocal statements. Given the prosecution's proof, the defendant should have been able to present evidence that a third party — deceased father — may have killed child.).

[20] *Id.* at 1279.

[21] Commonwealth v. Miles, 420 Mass. 67, 648 N.E.2d 719 (1995) (holding that trial court should have permitted defendant to inquire of police investigators about other suspects; however, error was harmless in light of substantial evidence of defendant's guilt).

[22] State v. West, 274 Conn. 605, 624–27, 877 A.2d 787, 802–03 (2005).

[23] State v. Cerreta, 260 Conn. 251, 263, 796 A.2d 1176, 1184 (2002).

[24] State v. Hummert, 188 Ariz. 119, 126, 933 P.2d 1187, 1194 (1997) (noting that defendant's acquittal on another sexual assault charge was not relevant to instant case, given the differences between the two, even though defendant wished to argue the perpetrator of other sexual assault was the perpetrator in this case).

[25] State v. Russell, 125 Wash. 2d 24, 75–77, 882 P.2d 747, 779–80 (1994), *cert. denied*, 514 U.S. 1129 (1995) (holding that before proof is introduced of other crimes or other suspects, there should be proof of a connection or circumstances "clearly" pointing to another person as the offender).

[26] People v. Sparman, 202 A.D.2d 452, 608 N.Y.S.2d 672, *appeal denied*, 84 N.Y.2d 833, 641 N.E.2d 174, 617 N.Y.S.2d 153 (1994).

[27] Walters v. McCormick, 122 F.3d 1172, 1177 (9th Cir. 1997), *cert. denied*, 523 U.S. 1060 (1998) (holding that trial court properly precluded defendant from cross-examining victim's mother about her allegations of abuse against her own father since the theory that her father rather than defendant was the perpetrator was not supported by "substantial evidence").

that victim's then boyfriend committed suicide,[28] or that the victim's aunt's boyfriend was arrested for sexual molestation,[29] without more, would be insufficient to suggest that the third person was the true perpetrator.

When a defendant seeks to portray someone else as the offender, it may open the door to the defendant's prior sexual abuse to rebut this defense.[30]

§ 8.3 Discovery in identification cases.

The circumstances surrounding the identification of the assailant as well as law enforcement identification procedures generally should be sought by the defense through discovery. These details may be helpful to explore at a pretrial identification suppression hearing. The following are some suggested discovery demands when identification is an issue. The information obtained can be used to develop the areas of cross-examination set forth later in this chapter.

 (1) The number of, date and time of, location of, and persons present at each "identification procedure" participated in or witnessed by the complainant or any witnesses in this case.

 (2) State whether any photos, drawings, or composites of the defendant were shown the complainant and, if so, state when, at what time, where, in whose presence, under what circumstances, and the results thereof.

 (3) All photos, drawings, or composites of the accused shown to the complainant.

 (4) All photos, drawings, or composites of any other individual or individuals shown to the complainant in conjunction with the photos of the accused.

 (5) All photos, drawings, or composites of any lineup witnessed by the complainant whether this accused was in such lineup or not, and all records relating to any such lineup.

 (6) State whether or not the accused was inadvertently, or otherwise observed by, or shown to the complainant or any other witness prior, during, or after arrest. If so, state the date, time, and location of such procedure, the purpose and results of such showing.

Sometimes a defendant may wish to request the names of the other individuals exhibited to the complainant through photographs or by lineup. This may be helpful for a variety of reasons, including establishing that the complainant may have previously seen or known another member of the lineup or photo array.

---

[28] Territory of Guam v. Ignacio, 10 F.3d 608, 615 (9th Cir. 1993) (holding that trial court properly excluded evidence concerning the suicide of the victim's mother's boyfriend that was offered in an attempt to link the boyfriend to the crime since there was not "substantial evidence" linking him to the indicted crime).

[29] People v. Neal, 248 A.D.2d 406, 670 N.Y.S.2d 860, *appeal denied*, 91 N.Y.2d 1011, 698 N.E.2d 968, 676 N.Y.S.2d 139 (1998).

[30] United States v. Yellow, 18 F.3d 1438, 1441 (8th Cir. 1994).

The following demands relate to descriptive information concerning the assailant, including summaries compiled by police agencies and provided through teletypes.

(1) All statements, notes, records, reports, memoranda, descriptive data, information, statements, or any other documents or data relating to:

   (a) Any description furnished by the complainant;

   (b) The viewing of the accused by the complainant;

   (c) The viewing of a photograph of the accused by the complainant;

   (d) The viewing of a lineup or lineups by the complainant;

   (e) The identification of the accused by the complainant;

   (f) The identification of any other person by the accused in connection with the transactions that are the subject of this indictment.

(2) All testimonial, or written, or oral, or recorded descriptions given that purportedly relate to the accused, which in any shape, way, manner, or form, or respect are inconsistent with the physical appearance of the accused or any physical feature of the accused.

(3) Any composite, drawing, or sketches prepared or compiled in connection with the transactions set forth in the indictment by any person or witness, including, but not limited to, any composite, drawing, or sketch to which the complainant contributed descriptive information or identifying information or physical features.

(4) All police bulletins, teletypes, log book entries, investigative reports, statements, memoranda, writings, or any other documents or data reflecting, incorporating by reference, or summarizing any descriptive or identifying information related by any person or alleged witness to any of the acts or circumstances involved in, leading to, following, or surrounding the transactions set forth in the indictment.

(5) All photographs, composites, sketches, drawings, or any other descriptive data furnished to the news media.

The following demands relate to identification errors or failure to identify the defendant, followed by a catch-all demand for evidence favorable to the accused or on the issue of identification.

(1) A specification and statement as to whether or not the complainant failed to identify the accused or identified another individual as the assailant, and, if so, state when, where, in whose presence, and under what circumstances, and describe the identification procedure being used and provide any records relating to such failure to identify.

(2) All notes, records, memoranda, documents, or other data relating to any identification errors or mistakes or any misidentification relating to the transactions described in the indictment.

(3) All other "identification errors" of this complainant, whether relating to the accused or to anything owned, used, or possessed by the accused or owned, used, or possessed by the person who was actually physically present with the complainant at the time and place of the alleged crime.

(4) Any and all information, evidence, documents, statements, transcripts, descriptions, photographs, reports, sketches, composites, memoranda, notes, records, logs, or any other data or portions of data which is, or may be helpful to the accused, or is or may be favorable to the accused, or exonerates or may tend to exonerate the accused, or may be of material importance or relevant to the defense on either the question of culpability, or the question of punishment, or which does or may tend to impeach or impair the credibility of the prosecution's witnesses with respect to the identification of the accused, or otherwise undermine or impair the credibility of the prosecutions' identification witnesses.

§ 8.4 The opportunity to observe the assailant.

The opportunity to observe the assailant during a sexual assault involves such factors as: the distance between the assailant and the witness; the witness's perspective, such as whether they were face-to-face; the period of time the witness had to observe; and the lighting conditions under which the observations were made. Each of these factors should be established by the prosecution on direct examination and viewed by the defense attorney as potential areas of cross-examination.

While many encounters between victims and assailants are brief, rapes usually provide the victim with a greater opportunity to observe the offender; however, during the course of the assault the assailant may block the victim's view, or the assailant's face may not be completely exposed. Also, many rapes occur at night in unlighted areas.

§ 8.5 Observation affected by trauma of event.

One of the differences between sexual assaults and other crimes is that sexual assaults will generally be more traumatic for the complainant. The effect of stress upon the ability to observe and recall one's observations has been discussed in the literature. This issue may be developed in the following matter:

Q. You were startled when approached by this man?

A. Yes.

Q. You were at this time very anxious, were you not?

A. I'm not sure I understand your question, sir.

Q. Well, were you afraid?

A. Yes, sir.

Q. Were you concerned for your own safety and well-being?

A. Yes, sir.

Q. You have told us that you were screaming.

A. Yes, sir.

Q. Were you crying?

A. Yes.

Q. Would it be fair to say that your primary concern at that time was for your own safety and well-being?

A. Yes, sir.

Q. At that point you feared for your life, correct?

A. Yes, sir.

Q. Were you hysterical?

A. Somewhat, yes.

The role of stress may be the subject of expert testimony on the effect of stress or other factors on eyewitness identification. However, as discussed in § 8.31, such testimony is subject to many objections.[31]

§ 8.6 Was there a reason to observe the assailant before the assault?

In many situations in which there was contact between the complainant and the assailant prior to the assault, if nothing was amiss and there was no suspicion of a problem, there may not have been a reason for the complainant (or any other witness) to observe the assailant. When examining the complainant on the witness stand, this can be handled with the following question: "And you had not anticipated anything occurring until the moment that you felt someone grab you, correct?"

§ 8.7 Was the opportunity to observe affected by distractions?

Just prior to a sexual assault, not only may there have been no reason for the witness to observe the assailant, there may have been distractions that would interfere with the ability of the witness to make observations. This is particularly true in encounters that take place outdoors. Such distractions often include other people in the area, automobile, or bicycle traffic, or music.

---

[31] *See, e.g.,* Commonwealth v. Spence, 534 Pa. 233, 245, 627 A.2d 1176, 1182 (1993) (excluding such testimony under Pennsylvania's narrow acceptance of expert testimony to explain witness behaviors).

§ 8.8 Was the opportunity to observe affected by problems of the complainant, such as alcohol, drugs, or poor vision?

The ability to observe may be affected by a witness's use of alcohol or drugs. If a complainant or other witness has been drinking or taking drugs, the prosecutor should bring this out on direct examination — there is nothing to be gained by allowing the defense to raise the issue for the first time and make it appear as though this information was being withheld. The next question is whether the extent of the alcohol or drug use and, therefore, the witness's intoxication, can be corroborated in any extrinsic matter. Were blood tests taken? Were there police officers or other individuals who interviewed the witness who can verify the level of intoxication? Were there friends or family members who had contact with the witness who can testify concerning his or her use of alcohol or drugs?

A witness's vision may be affected by alcohol or drugs, or because that person's vision is generally poor. Expert testimony concerning the effect of the ingestion of cocaine upon a complainant, and whether or not the cocaine was a factor in a victim's "fantasizing" about her rape may be admissible in the discretion of the court when a sufficient foundation is made. However, a court has discretion with respect to such testimony and expert testimony concerning the effects of cocaine use which is merely speculative, will be precluded particularly where there is no proof that the victim has "ingested a particular amount of either crack cocaine or alcohol, or, if she had, at what time she had done so."[32] This should be determined by the police in the course of their investigation. If necessary, the strength or weakness of a witness's vision can be demonstrated through medical records. An in-court demonstration may also be considered.

The following excerpt from the cross-examination of a complainant establishes not only that the witness had been drinking but that, as a result, the witness was confused about certain events. Such confusion can be crucial in establishing reasonable doubt over aspects of a witness's testimony, particularly identification of the assailant.

Q. Were you, in your opinion, intoxicated when you left the Black Hole Bar?

A. Well, how do you define intoxication?

Q. I'm asking you.

A. Well, I don't know what you consider to be intoxicated.

Q. Would you consider yourself to be intoxicated?

A. Yes.

Q. Real intoxicated, real drunk?

---

[32] People v. Benson, 206 A.D.2d 674, 675, 614 N.Y.S.2d 808, 809 (1994), *appeal denied*, 84 N.Y.2d 1029, 647 N.E.2d 457, 623 N.Y.S.2d 185 (1995).

A. Well, what do you mean by real intoxicated?

Q. I'm just asking if you considered yourself intoxicated?

A. Yes.

Q. And while you were walking on the street and before you were assaulted, you were intoxicated also, correct?

A. Yes.

Q. And while you were walking, and just before you felt someone approach you from behind, you were lost, correct?

A. Yes.

Q. And, as a result of your intoxication, you were in a state of confusion, correct?

A. I was in a state of confusion when I was walking around outside and I couldn't find my way.

Q. Were you still in a state of confusion when you went into that apartment?

A. I was just scared, crying because I couldn't find my way and I wasn't sure what was going on.

Q. Were you hysterical?

A. I was crying.

Q. You were intoxicated, is that true?

A. Yes.

Q. So at the time of this incident you were crying, intoxicated, and confused, correct?

A. Yes.

§ 8.9 Lighting conditions.

An important piece of evidence often overlooked is the *actual* lighting condition at the time of the sexual assault (and not at the time of a subsequent visit to the scene). It should be remembered that lighting in a room may come not only from a table lamp or night light, but also from a clock radio or through a window from a parking lot or street light, the moon, or other external source. The investigation should determine the presence or absence of such possible lighting sources.

Another important factor to consider on the lighting issue is the ability of the human eye to function with little light. In certain situations, expert testimony may be helpful here, but an effective appeal to common sense also may develop this area.

Lighting is discussed in further detail in Chapter 13 at §§ 13.37–13-38, which deal with, among other things, the use of a representative of a utility company to explain lighting conditions at a particular location. Also, an expert with the proper qualifications might explain how much light the moon provided on a particular night.[33]

It may be important to determine just what the witness was doing prior to the time the observation was made. If the witness was sleeping, her eyes might not have adjusted to the lighting condition.

§ 8.10   The witness's perspective.

During the course of a sexual assault, the relative positions of the victim and assailant probably will not have remained constant. Much will depend upon the extent of the struggle and the nature of the sex acts. Also, in many sexual assaults, the assailant will attempt to avoid face-to-face contact, or his face will be covered. Thus, one cannot assume that, during a sexual encounter that lasted 20 minutes, the complainant had 20 minutes to observe the assailant.

§ 8.11   Opportunity to commit the crime.

If the defendant asserts an alibi as a defense, how close was the defendant's alibi location to the scene of the crime? Determine the different routes between the two locations that might have been available to a defendant on the night in question; the time it would have taken the defendant to travel those routes; the defendant's familiarity with the area in which the crime occurred; the means of transportation available to the defendant at the time, or were others able to assist the defendant in his movements.

§ 8.12   Description of assailant in general.

Attorneys and investigators often fail to understand the many components of a description. There are many areas in which complainants and witnesses may be able to provide descriptive information *if they are only asked.* Following are some of the points to consider in recalling the physical characteristics of an assailant:

(1)   Height — Should not be estimated; best to compare with a known individual.

(2)   Weight — Like height, should not be guessed at; there should be a reference for any estimate.

(3)   Build — Slender, fat, muscular, muscle tone.

(4)   Hair Color.

(5)   Hair Style.

(6)   Hair Density — Receding, thick, thin.

---

[33] *See* §   13.38.

(7)   Eyes — Color or other distinguishing aspects.

(8)   Glasses.

(9)   Eyebrows.

(10) Nose.

(11) Facial hair — Type of beard or mustache; does it fit a particular style?

(12) Mouth — Including description of lips, teeth, dental work.

(13) Scars — Including estimated size and shape.

(14) Moles or birthmarks — Including size and shape.

(15) Tattoos.

(16) Genitals — Circumcised? Any marks or disfigurements?

In addition to purely physical characteristics, there are other nontangible characteristics of an individual that can be explored:

(1)   Odors — Was there a smell that would indicate gasoline or some other type of work exposure? Was there a distinctive cologne? Was there some other unique smell exhibited by the individual?

(2)   Breath — Was there an odor of alcoholic beverages, or some particular food smell?

Another nontangible characteristic of an individual is his or her voice.

(1)   Was there any speech impediment or defect?

(2)   Was there a particular tone or accent, or particular words used?

(3)   Did the individual use good grammar? Was there difficulty articulating?

A final area to explore is the clothing and attire of the perpetrator:

(1)   Clothes — Can the witness remember colors, brand names, insignia, or any other identifying feature of the articles of clothing?

(2)   Jewelry — What kind of jewelry? Rings, earrings, watch (brand or type), necklace?

(3)   Belt — Was there a particular style of belt? At what hole was the belt creased?

(4)   Shoes — Style and condition of shoes. Casual, dress, or work shoes? Were they worn or fairly new? Were the laces in good condition?

A witness who is simply asked to describe an individual will likely provide information in only a few of the above areas. Most individuals, however, if adequately interviewed and directed to these particular areas, will be able to provide much more information concerning the identity of an assailant.

§ 8.13   Obtaining all descriptions provided by complainant.

One should obtain and review *all* descriptions of an assailant made by a witness. (*See* § 8.3.) This information should be sought in crime reports, investigation reports, teletypes, witness's or complainant's statements, tapes of police telecommunications, paramedic reports, hospital records, rape crisis or counseling records, and grand jury testimony. Each description should be compared with others for consistency.

All evidence of the *defendant's* actual description on the date in question should be obtained. This should be obtained through booking photos, arrest records, driver's license records and photos, employment records, family photos, and verbal descriptions from coworkers, friends, and family members. Police booking records (as opposed to photos) should also contain information on the defendant's description. This search should be done by both the prosecution and defense.

The prosecution should seek to establish that the description provided by the complainant matches in several ways that of the defendant as he appeared on the date in question. Defendants may change appearance — get hair cuts, trim facial hair, and change clothing styles prior to the time of the trial. In this regard, demonstrative evidence can be used by both the prosecution and the defense to establish their case. This is discussed more fully in the chapter on demonstrative evidence.[34]

§ 8.14   Utilizing inconsistencies in prior descriptions.

Before utilizing an inconsistency in a prior description by a witness, it is important to establish the circumstances under which the description was given. In the case of the complainant, the information may have been provided under less than ideal circumstances — the complainant will have undergone the trauma of the assault and also may have been without sleep for a long period of time. On the other hand, if the complainant had the opportunity to provide descriptive information and was desirous of doing so, but failed to do so, the foundation for this should be laid. This may be done as follows:

Q. And were you asked by the police investigator handling your case to furnish him with a description?

A. Yes, sir.

Q. And that was roughly how long after this incident occurred?

A. The evening of the rape.

Q. And he asked you questions about what had happened?

A. Yes, sir.

Q. And he was there for the purpose of investigating your complaint?

A. Yes, sir.

Q. And attempting to determine who had done what had occurred?

---

[34] *See* §§ 14.15, 14.34–14-35.

A. Yes, sir.

Q. And you related to him, did you not, as best you could, a description of the assailant?

A. Yes, sir.

Q. You were cooperating with him?

A. Yes, sir.

Q. You were giving him as much descriptive information as you could?

A. Yes, sir.

Q. And at no point were you attempting to hold anything back from him, were you?

A. No, sir.

Q. You weren't trying to mislead him?

A. No, sir.

Q. Or conceal anything from him?

A. No, sir.

Q. You were giving him as much descriptive information as you could?

A. Yes, sir.

Q. And giving it to him as accurately as you possibly could?

A. Yes, sir.

Q. And this descriptive information was the very evening that this took place?

A. Yes, sir.

Q. So, it would be fair to say that it was within hours of the event itself?

A. Yes, sir.

Q. Was your recollection at that time fresh?

A. Yes, sir.

Q. And was it vivid?

A. Yes, sir.

At this point, the foundation has been laid to confront the witness with any inconsistency. Cross-examining about the inconsistency without laying the foundation will minimize the effectiveness of the testimony.

The witness's opportunity to review his or her prior written statement should also be established before raising the inconsistency, as in the following:

Q. And on the occasion of your interview with the investigating officer, after you had spoken to him, he typed up a statement, is that correct?

A. Yes, sir.

Q. And at the conclusion of your interview with him, did he present you with a typewritten statement to review?

A. Yes, sir.

Q. Showing you Exhibit A for identification, do you recognize that?

A. Yes, sir.

Q. What is it?

A. This is the statement that I gave the police.

Q. And is that your signature on the bottom of each page?

A. Yes, sir.

Q. And it was witnessed by the investigator?

A. Yes, sir.

Q. And you had a chance to review it before you signed it, correct?

A. Yes.

Q. And did you read it before you signed it?

A. Yes.

Q. And did you make any corrections in the statement before you signed it?

A. No, sir.

Q. And does it in fact fairly reflect what you told the investigator concerning the description of the person you were involved with?

A. Yes, sir.

Q. Now, with respect to the description of that individual, did you tell the detective that . . .?

§ 8.15 Cross-examination of complainant based on differences between earlier description and defendant at time of trial.

After having the complainant testify on cross-examination that she was never in a better position to remember the traits of the assailant as she was immediately after the assault, the defense attorney should review any inconsistencies in the complainant's earlier description of the assailant as compared to the defendant as he sits in the courtroom. For example, if there is a discrepancy in height or hair color, have the defendant stand and ask the witness to admit that the defendant's height or hair color is not what she earlier described the assailant as possessing. If the defendant has a scar, and the complainant did not mention a scar in describing the assailant, have the witness describe the scar on the defendant. This use of an in-court display of the defendant for purposes of showing mistaken identification is discussed in greater detail in the chapter on demonstrative evidence. [35]

§ 8.16 Cross-examination by use of prior testimony of assailant concerning description.

Most complainants in sexual assault cases will have testified under oath at a preliminary hearing or a grand jury proceeding. That testimony should be compared with other descriptions of the assailant for inconsistencies and brought out on cross-examination of the complainant. In the following example, the witness is cross-examined concerning grand jury testimony. In the grand jury proceeding, the complainant testified that she was unable to provide any further description of the assailant. Such a response is very crucial should the complainant offer additional details at trial.

Q. Miss Dillon, now, do you recall testifying before a grand jury in connection with this case?

A. Yes, sir.

Q. Are you the same Mary Dillon who testified on October 3, 1992?

A. Yes, sir.

Q. On that occasion you testified right here in this courthouse, correct?

A. Yes, sir.

Q. And your testimony was under oath?

A. Yes, sir.

Q. And you took the same oath which you took today, correct?

A. Yes, sir.

Q. And there was a reporter taking down your testimony just as there is one now?

A. Yes.

Q. And you met with the prosecutor or members of his staff before you testified, correct?

A. Yes, sir. Of course.

Q. And you reviewed with him the testimony you were going to be expected to give before the grand jury?

A. Yes, sir.

Q. And you appreciated the importance of your appearance before that grand jury at that time, correct?

---

[35] *See* § 14.35.

A. Yes.

Q. And when you testified before that grand jury you were asked by the prosecutor, were you not, to give a full description of your assailant?

A. Yes, sir.

At this point, defense counsel had the witness relate the description of the assailant she provided in the grand jury proceeding.

Q. Were you asked after relaying those characteristics whether or not you could give any further characteristics?

A. Not that I recall.

Q. You don't recall being asked that question?

A. No, sir.

Q. Do you recall testifying before the grand jury and being asked the following question and making the following answer?

A. Yes.

Q. In addition to those characteristics, can you provide any further description of your assailant?

A. No. That's it.

§ 8.17 Prior identifications and investigative efforts to link the defendant to the complainant.

Many techniques are available to investigators to identify the perpetrator of a crime. These include the use of composites, drawings, photo spreads, showups, lineups, canine detection, voice identification, and hypnosis. The use of criminal profiling to identify a suspect, which is discussed in the chapter on expert testimony,[36] is sometimes used as an investigative lead, although this is unlikely to be admissible at trial. All of these efforts at obtaining an identification must be reviewed for suggestiveness. (Also, the *number* of the techniques used must be evaluated to determine whether their combined use becomes suggestive, where only one technique may not have been suggestive.)

There are many ways that investigative efforts at obtaining an identification may be unduly suggestive. Areas of inquiry can be ascertained by carefully reviewing the discovery materials suggested in § 8.3, as well as questioning of witnesses at a pretrial identification hearing. The precise wording of questions or statements of investigators to potential witnesses may not be set forth in reports. The suggested areas of discovery in § 8.3 also represent areas of inquiry at a pretrial identification hearing. An example of an unduly suggestive pretrial identification procedure that might lead to a reversal of a defendant's conviction is displaying four wanted posters to a rape victim, one of which she had earlier

---

[36] *See* §§ 11.29–11.33.

eliminated, another of which is the same poster as the eliminated one with only a slight modification, one poster that did not contain the heading "Wanted for Rape" that the other three posters did, and a poster of the defendant with the words "Wanted for Rape" printed in bold letters at the top and with details of the victim's rape below his picture.[37] The showing of only four posters in the context of this case is unduly suggestive to the defendant and highly prejudicial when the defendant is linked to the crime solely by the complainant's testimony.[38]

The use of particular wording in questioning a witness about identification also plays a role. In referring to eyewitness testimony, a different impression can be created by referring to a complainant's "choice" of the defendant in a photospread rather than the "identification" of the defendant.

§ 8.18   Stolen property and other circumstantial evidence relating to identification.

There are ways of linking a defendant to a sexual assault without a witness identifying a defendant. An effective way is to locate objects on, or associated with, the defendant that can be positively identified by the complainant. On the other hand, if property was taken from the victim, and it is not found in the possession of, or connected to, the defendant, especially if the defendant was taken into custody soon after an assault, this may create reasonable doubt as to the defendant's guilt.

Other circumstantial evidence may or may not link the defendant. Consider testimony from individuals that a defendant was seen dressed in a business suit at the time of a rape, whereas the assailant was described as wearing overalls. Circumstantially, this supports defendant's position that he is not the attacker. This is often done with sexual markings or characteristics of the defendant.[39]

In the following excerpt from a direct examination of a complainant, she identifies the apartment where the rape took place through a photograph. This apartment was connected to the defendant by other witnesses. Previously, when driven to the area of the rape by police, the complainant was unable to identify the building. At the time of the rape, the complainant was intoxicated and lost in an unfamiliar area of the city. However, just prior to trial, she walked the area and was able to identify the apartment.

Q. Did you have occasion two weeks ago to walk in the area of Devon Avenue?

A. Yes, I did.

---

[37] People v. Colas, 206 A.D.2d 183, 619 N.Y.S.2d 702 (1994), *appeal denied*, 85 N.Y.2d 907, 650 N.E.2d 1332, 627 N.Y.S.2d 330 (1995).

[38] *Id.*

[39] *See* § 14.35.

Q. Did you go to an area of Devon Avenue?

A. Yes, I did.

Q. Did you recognize anything there?

A. The apartment I was raped at.

Q. What did you recognize about it?

A. I recognized the stairway and the entranceway; how it went down.

Q. And do you recognize this photo (exhibit of the apartment connected to the defendant)?

A. Yes.

Q. What is it?

A. The apartment I was taken to and raped.

In the following direct testimony, the complainant identifies jewelry taken from her during the rape, which was recovered by the police and traced to the defendants.

Q. I would like to show you People's 33 for identification. Do you recognize that? What is that?

A. That's the necklace I was wearing.

Q. The necklace that you had on when you were in that apartment?

A. Yes.

Q. Is that the necklace that you gave to that tall strong woman?

A. Yes, it is.

Q. And the female defendant took it from you?

A. She took it from me.

Q. Is it in the same condition today as when it was taken from you?

A. Yes, it is.

Such testimony establishes powerful identification evidence, perhaps more persuasive than eyewitness identification.

§ 8.19   Use of hypnosis in developing details or suggesting information to a witness.

Hypnosis is sometimes used to elicit further information from a witness, particularly with respect to elements of a description of an assailant or other identification information concerning a crime, such as a license plate number. Through hypnosis, an attempt is made to have a witness concentrate on an event and retrieve information that he or she may have suppressed for a variety of reasons. The science of hypnosis has developed specific information and has assisted in the apprehension of criminals in many situations. In a way, it is merely another form of refreshing the memory of a witness; however, a great danger with hypnosis is that suggestion can play an important role in the recollection. Florida's Supreme Court has observed that "the great weight of scientific opinion appears to be that such a belief — that a subject can be made to re-experience a visual perception under hypnosis — is to be considered highly suspect if not clearly erroneous."[40]

It is important that the use of hypnosis in a case be disclosed. All information provided by a witness prior to hypnosis should be well-documented and compared with the additional information developed through hypnosis. Hypnosis of a witness should be recorded so that any element of suggestiveness can be evaluated.

Many appellate decisions on hypnosis-enhanced testimony have involved rape cases. The general rule emerging from these cases is that information developed through hypnosis is inadmissible. The Supreme Court of California has ruled that "the testimony of a witness who has undergone hypnosis for the purpose of restoring his memory of the events and issues is inadmissible as to all matters relating to those events, from the time of the hypnotic session forward."[41] This decision highlights many of the dangers relating to the suggestiveness of the procedure. The court noted that the hypnotized person "becomes extremely receptive to suggestions that he perceives as emanating from the hypnotist"[42] and that there is a strong desire on the part of the witness to please the hypnotist.[43]

New York has followed California in rejecting the admissibility of information developed through hypnosis.[44] Citing research in the field of hypnosis, the New York Court of Appeals noted that a person who recalls an incident under hypnosis will become more confident in subsequent recollections of that incident.[45]

The conclusion of most appellate decisions in this area is that hypnotically-induced statements are not admissible;[46] there is no *per se* rule of inadmissibility of hypnotically-refreshed testimony, and there are situations in which such testimony will be admitted.[47]

---

[40] Bundy v. State, 455 So. 2d 330, 342 (Fla. 1984), *cert. denied*, 479 U.S. 894 (1986).

[41] People v. Shirley, 31 Cal. 3d 18, 66–67, 181 Cal. Rptr. 243, 723 P.2d 1354, *cert. denied*, 459 U.S. 859 (1982).

[42] *Id.* at 63, 641 P.2d at 802, 181 Cal. Rptr. at 271.

[43] *Id.*

[44] People v. Hughes, 59 N.Y.2d 523, 453 N.E.2d 484, 466 N.Y.S.2d 255 (1983).

[45] *Id.* at 535, 453 N.E.2d at 489, 466 N.Y.S.2d at 260.

[46] *See* Thomas M. Fleming, Annotation, *Admissibility of Hypnotically Refreshed or Enhanced Testimony*, 77 A.L.R.4th 927 (1990).

[47] Biskup v. McCaughtry, 20 F.3d 245 (7th Cir. 1994) (upholding Wisconsin court's decision permitting hypnotically refreshed testimony in a case in which it was the victim's own decision to undergo the hypnosis, a decision that was not influenced by the prosecution).

There is emerging authority that "a witness who has undergone hypnosis is not barred from testifying to events which the court finds were recalled and related prior to the hypnotic session."[48] The effect of these rulings is that the prosecution must establish the information provided by a complainant before hypnosis. If this cannot be established, the testimony will be precluded, since the hypnosis session cannot be ruled out as the source of the information. Florida has suggested that the defendant has the burden of demonstrating that the hypnosis has rendered testimony so untrustworthy as to be inadmissible.[49] In Texas, the proponent must establish by clear and convincing evidence that hypnosis did not render the witness's post-hypnotic memory untrustworthy nor did it substantially impair the ability of the opponent to test the witness's recall by cross-examination.[50]

Many states that permit the use of pre-hypnosis testimony require that the prosecution give notice to the defense that the witness has been subjected to hypnosis. Then a pretrial hearing is held to determine the extent of the pre-hypnosis testimony and whether the hypnosis session was so suggestive as to taint the witness's pre-hypnosis recollections.[51] If the defense fails to request a pretrial hearing concerning the use of hypnosis after notice has been given, the defendant may be deemed to waive his right to a hearing on the issue and will be precluded from a hearing at the time of trial.[52] This, in effect, adopts procedures similar to the pretrial *Wade* hearing for pretrial photographic or lineup identification.

In a civil suit, a federal appeals court rejected hypnotically-induced testimony of an alleged victim of sexual abuse since such memories appeared to be the result of therapeutic hypnosis by an individual without adequate professional qualifications.[53] The court also noted that the therapist did not keep any record of the procedures utilized[54] and that *Daubert* was not directly applicable since the issue was whether the plaintiff was a competent witness by virtue of the hypnotically-refreshed recollection.[55]

---

[48] People v. Hayes, 49 Cal. 3d 1260, 1270, 265 Cal. Rptr. 132, 138, 783 P.2d 719, 725 (1989). *See also* State *ex rel.* Collins v. Superior Court, 132 Ariz. 180, 209, 644 P.2d 1266, 1295 (1982) (permitting several rape victims to testify as to information described and recalled prior to hypnosis); Drake v. State, 467 N.E.2d 686 (Ind. 1984); People v. Hughes, 59 N.Y.2d 523, 545, 453 N.E.2d 484, 495, 466 N.Y.S.2d 255, 266 (1983); State v. Beard, 194 W. Va. 740, 461 S.E.2d 486, 503 (1995).

[49] Bundy v. State, 455 So. 2d 330, 342 (Fla. 1984), *cert. denied*, 479 U.S. 894 (1986).

[50] State v. Merando, 127 S.W.3d 781 (Tex. Crim. App. 2004), *citing* Zani v. State, 758 S.W.2d 233 (Tex. Crim. App. 1988) (noting "hypersuggestibility, loss of critical judgment, confabulation, and memory cementing, are dangers that directly undercut the reliability of a witness's hypnotically enhanced testimony." *Id.* at 787.)

[51] *Hughes*, 59 N.Y.2d at 546, 453 N.E.2d at 495–96, 466 N.Y.S.2d at 260.

[52] People v. Hults, 76 N.Y.2d 190, 556 N.E.2d 1077, 557 N.Y.S.2d 270 (1990).

[53] Borawick v. Shay, 68 F.3d 597 (2d Cir. 1995), *cert. denied*, 517 U.S. 1229 (1996).

[54] *Id.* at 609.

[55] *Id.* at 610.

At the pretrial hearing, the trial court should take into consideration the witness's confidence in her recollections prior to hypnosis, the extent of the witness's belief in hypnosis to yield the truth, the extent of the hypnosis, the length of the hypnosis session, the nature and type of questioning utilized during hypnosis, the extent to which the hypnosis produced additional information, and "any other factors which [the] court may deem important based upon circumstances of a case which may artificially enhance the victim's confidence in her pre-hypnotic recollections, thereby impairing a defendant's ability to conduct a meaningful cross-examination." [56] The people's burden at such a hearing is to establish by clear and convincing evidence the reliability of the complainant's testimony and that the hypnosis does not substantially impair the defendant's ability to meaningfully cross-examine the witness. [57]

A third issue concerning hypnosis-enhanced testimony is the admissibility of such testimony on cross-examination of a complainant. Some courts find insufficient trustworthiness of evidence developed from hypnosis to permit its use for any truth-testing function, including that of cross-examination. [58] Even if the statement produced during hypnosis is inconsistent with the trial testimony of a witness, "because of the statement's unreliability, the inconsistency simply is not probative of the truth or falsity of the witness's subsequent trial testimony." [59] Other courts have also precluded use of hypnotically-induced statements on cross-examination. [60]

Any authority permitting the use of hypnosis-enhanced testimony should be carefully questioned, since most appellate decisions question the reliability of information developed through hypnosis. Given the current weight of opinion that such information is inadmissible, but that any information that can be documented as having been recollected by the witness prior to hypnosis is admissible, to the extent that court decisions may permit a greater use of hypnosis, those decisions should be challenged and a predicate laid for appellate review.

---

[56] *People v. Tunstall*, 63 N.Y.2d 1, 9, 468 N.E.2d 30, 34, *appeal denied* 73 N.Y.S.2d 791, 533 N.E.2d 681, 536 N.Y.S.2d 751 (1988).

[57] People v. Schwing, 9 A.D.3d 685, 779 N.Y.S.2d 816, *appeal denied*, 3 N.Y.3d 742, 820 N.E.2d 300, 786 N.Y.S.2d 821 (2004) ("Here, the hypnosis session lasted only 45 minutes, the questioning was not suggestive and very few additional details were revealed. Although the witness did not initially remember every detail of the shooting, her pre-hypnotic statements to the police were clear and confident and her trial testimony mirrored her pre-hypnotic recollection. As 'the extent of the witness's pre-hypnotic recollections establishes the boundaries of admissible testimony,' [citation omitted] the court properly balanced the applicable factors, and determined that the victim's wife could testify, but only about her pre-hypnotic recollections." [citations omitted.]).

[58] People v. Hults, 76 N.Y.2d 190, 556 N.E.2d 1077, 557 N.Y.S.2d 270 (1990).

[59] *Id.* at 198, 556 N.E.2d at 1082, 557 N.Y.S.2d at 275.

[60] Mills v. State, 322 Ark. 647, 910 S.W.2d 682 (1995) (upholding the preclusion of defense counsel's attempt on cross-examination to elicit statements made by the witness while under hypnosis).

§ 8.20   Composite and artist illustrations.

Identification techniques used by law enforcement agencies include a "composite" made from a witness's description of a perpetrator. A composite is a technique in which the witness is given various options that illustrate certain facial features in an attempt to develop an accurate picture of a suspect. The person preparing the composite may at the end of the selection process make other changes to the composite to better reflect the individual. Sometimes, a law enforcement agency will use an artist-illustrator to prepare an original drawing of the suspect. This requires greater skill and technique in preparing, but it also provides for a drawing that is not limited by the available facial features in a composite kit.

The composite or illustration is not likely to be a suggestive device unless the authorities have already identified a suspect and seek to match the composite or illustration to that individual. Usually, composites and illustrations are created in advance of the identification of a particular suspect. Experience indicates that for a composite or illustration to be as accurate as possible, it should be created immediately after the crime, when the witness's memory is still fresh.

On direct examination, a composite or illustration may be challenged by the defense as hearsay.[61] However, it may fall within an exception to the hearsay rule as assessing the accuracy of the witness's identification or as a prior consistent statement.[62] If a composite or drawing does not reflect the defendant's physical appearance, the defense may use it on cross-examination to impeach the witness who provided the information from which it was created, as one would use a prior inconsistent written or oral statement.

In the following excerpt, counsel offers a composite as an exhibit, laying a foundation to show that the witness participated in the composite's preparation, that it was not hurriedly created, and that the witness was satisfied with the finished product.

Q.   Showing you an exhibit which has been marked F for identification. That is the composite that was prepared in connection with the investigation into this case; is it not?

A.   Yes, it is.

Q.   This is a composite prepared based upon descriptive information furnished by you to the investigator handling your case?

A.   Yes, it is.

Q.   When was it prepared?

A.   A few hours after I was attacked.

---

[61] *See* § 8.30.

[62] *See* § 10.48, and *see generally* Thomas J. Goger, Annotation, *Admissibility in Evidence of Composite Picture or Sketch Produced by Police to Identify Offender,* 42 A.L.R.3d 1217 (1972).

Q. Now, in putting that composite together with the police artist, roughly how much time did the two of you spend together?

A. You mean how much time before it was completely finished?

Q. Yes.

A. Maybe an hour or so, hour and a half maybe.

Q. An hour and a half approximately?

A. Approximately, yes.

Q. All right. And does that photocopy fairly and accurately represent the composite as it was prepared by the investigator at that time based on the information and description you provided?

A. Yes, it does.

Q. And you looked at the composite when it was done?

A. Yes.

Q. And you were satisfied with it at that time?

A. Yes.

§ 8.21 Photographic arrays and lineups.

The pretrial suppression hearing is crucial to explore the facts that should be developed at trial concerning the photo array or lineup identification procedure. It is important to remember that this procedure may take place a substantial period of time after the assault.

Suggestiveness in the identification process can exist in many forms. The individuals used in a lineup or photo array may not be sufficiently representative and may not contain sufficient common characteristics. It is important to review not only the height and weight similarities of these individuals, but also areas of physical description such as clothing, glasses, and facial hair.

Also important, but not as easy to ascertain, are statements or comments by law enforcement personnel to a witness prior to identification of the defendant. Was the witness told that there had been a break in the case? Was the witness told that the person who attacked her might be in a group of photos that was about to be shown to her? Was the witness told that someone was in custody who was in the photos that she was about to be shown? Any suggestion that the assailant was among the group of individuals being presented to the complainant can render the lineup or photo identification less reliable. The number of photographs used in a photographic array is not crucial so long as the photographs or other procedures surrounding the identification process are not unduly suggestive.[63]

---

[63] United States v. Sanchez, 24 F.3d 1259 (10th Cir. 1994), *cert. denied*, 513 U.S. 1007 (1994).

Was there any pressure on the victim to help close the case? Why was the complainant told the purpose of the meeting with investigators? What was the complainant asked to do? Were there any nonverbal indicators in the course of the identification process? Did anyone point to, or nod in the direction of, a photo or an individual in the lineup? If individual photos of suspects were used, how were they presented? Was the defendant's photo on top? Was the process videotaped? If not, why not?

It should also be documented whether the complainant at any time previously had reviewed the array of photos and whether the defendant's photo was among them at that time. A complainant's repeated exposure to a defendant's photograph is not *per se* suggestive.[64] Such a practice, however, invites careful scrutiny and will be evaluated by a "totality of circumstances" standard in determining whether the identification should be suppressed.[65]

§ 8.22   Has the witness viewed the defendant between the time of the crime and the photo array or lineup?

Another avenue of suggestiveness in the identification process is to allow the complainant to see the defendant at some point in time between the occurrence of the crime and the identification procedure. Of course, the witness could have seen the defendant in the course of daily affairs or at a public event. It is also possible the complainant may have seen the defendant just prior to the lineup, perhaps in a waiting area of the police station. If the complainant has had the opportunity to see the defendant prior to the lineup, it can compromise the identification procedure.

The defendant's picture might have been displayed in the media. This can be a particular problem when law enforcement authorities arrest a suspect and supply his photograph to, or a photo or videotape of the defendant is taken by the news media and printed or broadcast. This may be a reason to close certain pretrial procedures to the public.[66] An example of this problem can be found in the Arizona Supreme Court's decision in *State v. Atwood*,[67] in which many eyewitnesses had one or more opportunities to view the defendant in the media prior to trial.[68] These included photographs of the defendant being arrested and transported in handcuffs, close-up photographs of his face, videotapes of him being arrested and escorted from a police vehicle by law enforcement officials, and videotape coverage of hearings. The identification testimony of two out of fourteen eyewitnesses was suppressed, with the appellate court upholding the trial court's decision that: "Whatever the witness's opportunity and ability to

---

[64] State v. Figueroa, 235 Conn. 145, 156–57, 665 A.2d 63, 72 (1995).

[65] *Id.*

[66] See discussion in Ch. 2.

[67] 171 Ariz. 576, 832 P.2d 593 (1992).

[68] *Id.* at 602, 832 P.2d at 619.

make their original observations and then to recall and testify about them, those observations cannot be free of influence from the subsequent viewings of the defendant and the various suggestive circumstances."[69]

The Arizona court's decision to suppress the testimony of some eyewitnesses but not others was based on the totality of circumstances approach. However, Arizona's Supreme Court has subsequently ruled that private suggestive identification procedures do not trigger the same reliability standards as when the state engages in suggestive procedures.[70] Other courts, too, have refused to suppress identification testimony of witnesses who have seen a defendant's picture in the media primarily on the theory that the procedure was not initiated by law enforcement officials or the witness was not influenced by the exposure.[71] Even though most courts will not suppress an identification as the Arizona court did, the issue still should be explored. While the defendant's exposure in the media may not create the *per se* exclusion of witness identification, it is nonetheless an important fact to consider at a pretrial *Wade* hearing as well as on cross-examination of the witness.

§ 8.23 Admissibility of negative identification testimony.

When identification of a defendant is at issue, it may be relevant that a witness or complainant did not identify other individuals who may have shared common distinguishing characteristics such as clothing, physical, racial, or gender characteristics. The theory is that just as in a lineup, the jury should be allowed to consider the witness's ability to identify the defendant or recognize the defendant while eliminating other similar suspects. When relevant, negative identification evidence may be admissible.[72]

---

[69] *Id.*

[70] State v. Nordstrom, 200 Ariz. 229, 240–42, 25 P.3d 717, 728–30 (2001), *cert. denied*, 534 U.S. 1046 (2001) (The Court noted that due process concerns could be implicated in the absence of state action, such as a situation where the defendant is somehow precluded from pointing out the weakness of the identification testimony.).

[71] United States v. Peele, 574 F.2d 489 (9th Cir. 1978); United States v. Zeiler, 470 F.2d 717 (3d Cir. 1972); United States v. Milano, 443 F.2d 1022 (10th Cir.), *cert. denied*, 404 U.S. 943 (1971); Bundy v. State, 455 So. 2d 330 (Fla. 1984), *cert. denied*, 479 U.S. 894 (1986); O'Connell v. State, 742 N.E.2d 943 (Ind. 2001) (holding victims' in-court identification were not based on an impermissibly suggestive procedure when they identified defendant in a television broadcast not arranged by police or prosecutors); Norris v. State, 265 Ind. 508, 356 N.E.2d 204 (1976); People v. Knight, 280 A.D.2d 937, 721 N.Y.S.2d 166, *appeal denied*, 96 N.Y.2d 864, 754 N.E.2d 1121, 730 N.Y.S.2d 38 (2001); People v. Hart, 208 A.D.2d 861, 618 N.Y.S.2d 381, *appeal denied*, 84 N.Y.2d 936, 645 N.E.2d 1233, 621 N.Y.S.2d 533 (1994) (viewing of defendant's photograph on a television program did not taint victim's lineup identification since photograph was identical to the photograph selected by complainant from hundreds the day after the crime).

[72] People v. Wilder, 93 N.Y.2d 352, 712 N.E.2d 652, 690 N.Y.S.2d 483 (1999); People v. Maldonado, 11 A.D.3d 294, 782 N.Y.S.2d 455, *appeal denied*, 4 N.Y.3d 746, 824 N.E.2d 59, 790 N.Y.S.2d 658 (2004) (ruling the probative value of receiving evidence of negative identification did not outweigh potential for prejudice because it was relevant to the issue of the identifying witness's reliability).

§ 8.24 Prior identification by means of group or mass lineup.

In-person identification of a suspect need not be by the traditional police precinct lineup. A suspect may be identified in a group of persons at a location other than a police station. In fact, a group procedure presents less of an issue in terms of suggestiveness and also allows the witness to view a greater number of individuals. In the following example, the complainant was called by a friend, a bartender, who told her that he thought that the man who attacked her might be in the bar at that moment. The complainant called the police and two officers took her to the bar. The court permitted this testimony on direct examination.

Q. Can you tell us what happened when you arrived at the Eight Ball Lounge?

A. I was asked to go inside to see if I could find the attacker.

Q. Will you tell us about how many people were inside at that time?

A. 75, a hundred people.

Q. Can you tell us, as you walked in, what you did?

A. I looked around and I spotted him.

Q. What did you do at that time?

A. I immediately told the officers and I ran out, out of the bar.

Q. And what happened then?

A. He was brought outside to see if I could identify him again and I did and I started to go after him.

Q. What did they do?

A. They restrained me.

Q. And that person that you identified in the Eight Ball Lounge on the evening of April 3, 1992, do you see him here today?

A. Yes, I do.

Q. Could you please point him out?

A. The man with the maroon shirt.

Q. The Defendant, James Jones?

A. Correct, yes.

During cross-examination, in the above case, the defense attorney attempted to point out the potential suggestiveness in the identification procedure.

Q. Do you recall being before the Grand Jury and being asked these questions and giving these answers: "Q" Do you recall several days later being accompanied by two representatives of the Police Department to the Eight Ball Lounge? "A" Yes, I do. "Q" And do you recall what it was that happened when you went inside the Eight Ball Lounge, when you were accompanied by those two officers? "A" Yes. "Q" Tell us what it was all about? "A" We walked into the bar and the bartender pointed out somebody and immediately I knew who it was. I just freaked out.'

A. Yes, I do.

Q. Well, you said, before the Grand Jury, that the bartender pointed out the Defendant to you. Was that Mark, the fellow that called you?

A. Yes, it was.

Q. And he told you, "I think the guy that did it is here"?

A. Yes, it was.

Q. So you relied on Mark's information that the person was there and he pointed him out to you, didn't he?

A. Well, not really.

Q. Didn't you say that Mark — Well, didn't you actually say that the bartender pointed someone out to you?

A. I looked around and I looked at Mark and I looked at him.

Q. But Mark pointed to him, didn't he?

A. Yes, he did.

Q. And that was before you made any identification on April 3rd at the Eight Ball Lounge, isn't it?

A. Mark did point to him, but that didn't mean anything to me.

Q. But Mark is the man who called you up and said to you, "I'm at Amelia's. Why don't you come up? The guy's here"?

A. Yes, he did. He didn't say he was there, he said he thought he would be there.

§ 8.25 Voice identification testimony.

Many courts permit voice identification testimony, and a witness need not be an expert in voice identification to offer a comparison of voices as long as there is a basis for the comparison. Federal Rules of Evidence 901 expressly permits use of lay opinion testimony to form a foundation for voice identification of a defendant.[73]

---

[73] Fed. R. Evid. 901:

(a)The requirement of authentication or identification as a condition precedent to admissibility is satisfied by evidence sufficient to support a finding that the matter in question is what its proponent claims. (b) Illustrations. By way of illustration only, and not by way of limitation, the following are examples of authentication or identification conforming with the requirements of this rule . . . . (5) Voice Identification. Identification of a voice, whether heard firsthand or through mechanical or electronic transmission or recording, by opinion based upon hearing the voice at any time under circumstances connecting it with the alleged speaker.

Voice identifications are subject to the same scrutiny and safeguards as eyewitness identification.[74] For example, playing only the suspect's voice is suggestive.[75] If both voice identification and visual identification procedures are utilized, it is better practice that the suspect not be in the same position in both the visual and audio identification procedure.[76] Suggestiveness is less of an issue when the parties know each other.[77] Even if the voice identification procedure is suggestive, it may be reliable if the complainant had adequate opportunity to hear her attacker.[78] Such factors include the fact that the assailant spoke several times during an assault lasting several minutes; the witness's degree of attention and ability to describe details of the assailant's voice; and the accuracy of the

---

[74] Government of the V.I. v. Sanes, 57 F.3d 338 (3d Cir. 1995) (differences in the voice array were not sufficiently significant to cause misidentification by sexual assault complainant); State v. Burnison, 247 Kan. 19, 795 P.2d 32 (1990); Commonwealth v. Miles, 420 Mass. 67, 648 N.E.2d 719 (1995) (upholding voice identification of defendant by rape complainant where all participants read the same passage and no suggestiveness was utilized in the identification procedure); State v. Gallagher, 286 N.J. Super. 1, 15, 668 A.2d 55, 62 (1995), cert. denied, 146 N.J. 569, 683 A.2d 1164 (1996); People v. Greco, 230 A.D.2d 23, 654 N.Y.S.2d 890, appeal denied, 90 N.Y.2d 858, 683 N.E.2d 1059, 661 N.Y.S.2d 185 (1997); People v. Carroll, 182 A.D.2d 693, 582 N.Y.S.2d 281, appeal denied, 80 N.Y.2d 902, 602 N.E.2d 235, 588 N.Y.S.2d 827 (1992). See generally Suzanne V. Estrella, Annotation, Admissibility of Evidence of Voice Identification of Defendant as Affected by Allegedly Suggestive Voice Lineup Procedures, 55 A.L.R.5th 423 (1998).

[75] United States v. Pheaster, 544 F.2d 353, 369–71 (9th Cir. 1976), cert. denied sub nom. Inciso v. United States, 429 U.S. 1099 (1977) (holding nonetheless that the witness's voice identification was reliable in this case); Macias v. State, 673 So. 2d 176 (Fla. Dist. Ct. App. 1996), review denied, 680 So. 2d 423 (Fla. 1996)

> Where the witness bases the identification on only part of the suspect's total personality, such as height alone, or eyes alone, or voice alone, prior suggestions will have most fertile soil in which to grow to conviction. This is especially so when the identifier is presented with no alternative choices; there is then a strong predisposition to overcome doubts and to fasten guilt upon the lone suspect . . . . The procedures used here for both pretrial voice identifications were impermissibly suggestive because in each instance defendant's voice was the only voice heard by the victim.

[76] Commonwealth v. DeMaria, 46 Mass. App. Ct. 114, 118, 703 N.E.2d 1203, 1206, review denied, 429 Mass. 1101, 709 N.E.2d 1119 (1999) ("Obviously, it would have been better had the authorities not called the defendant by the same number in both the visual and the voice lineups. The question, however, is not whether that was suggestive—we may assume it was—but whether it was so suggestive as to have deprived the defendant of due process of law.") Id. at 118, 703 N.E.2d at 1206.

[77] People v. Collins, 60 N.Y.2d 214, 456 N.E.2d 1188, 469 N.Y.S.2d 65 (1983).

[78] Gallagher, 286 N.J. Super. at 18–19, 668 A.2d at 64

> M.M. had ample opportunity to listen to her attacker's voice because she engaged him in conversation by asking him questions. She said she intently listened to his voice hoping that she could later identify him. Further, she described her attacker's voice to the police and the pretrial voice identification occurred only a few days after the incident. Moreover, M.M. never equivocated in her identification of defendant's voice as the voice of the assailant. Under the totality of circumstances, we are satisfied that there was no substantial likelihood of misidentification in M.M.'s identification of defendant's voice, both out-of-court and in-court.

victim's physical description of the assailant.[79] Massachusetts looks at five factors in determining whether a one-on-one out-of-court voice identification has been made under unnecessarily suggestive conditions.[80] These *Marini* factors are:

> (1) the witness who has a basis for making an identification by sight should not be asked to make a voice identification unless he requests to hear the voice; (2) one-on-one auditions should be avoided — the best approach is a lineup; (3) the witness should not view the suspect as he listens to the suspect's voice; (4) the words spoken by the suspect should not be the same as those heard by the witness at the scene of the crime; and (5) the voice identification should occur close to the time of the crime, the earlier the better.[81]

When a witness is asked to identify a suspect by his voice, a tape should be made of his statements which should then be repeated verbatim by other individuals. All of the voices should be repeated over again for the witness as many times as necessary. It may not be absolutely essential that all the individuals repeat the same words; however, doing so minimizes suggestiveness in the procedure, particularly if key words were articulated by the suspect.

A tape is better than a live vocal lineup since the tape can be preserved for review. While not always possible, the likelihood of suggestiveness is lessened when the person conducting the voice lineup does not know which voice is that of the suspect. Also, it is best if the witness not see the individuals speaking to ensure the voice identification is not tainted by a prior identification or visual cues.

When voice identification is the primary means of identification, or where there are questions concerning the reliability of the identification, cautionary instructions may be in order to guide the jury.[82] Conceivably, an expert may provide evidence of the memory and perception, factors that may affect a voice identification. A trial court may also preclude expert testimony comparing eyewitness and voice identification testimony on the ground that such expert testimony is of limited probative value and that the value of such testimony is outweighed by its waste of time and confusion.[83] A single extrajudicial voice identification may be insufficient to establish the element of identification, particularly if the jury

---

[79] *Macias*, 673 So. 2d at 181.

[80] Commonwealth v. Saunders, 50 Mass. App. Ct. 865, 744 N.E.2d 74 (2001).

[81] Commonwealth v. Marini, 375 Mass. 510, 378 N.E.2d 51 (1978).

[82] Jeffrey T. Walter, Annotation, *Cautionary Instructions to Jury as to Reliability of, or Factors to be Considered in Evaluating, Voice Identification Testimony,* 17 A.L.R.5TH 851 (1994).

[83] Government of the V.I. v. Sanes, 57 F.3d 338, 341 (3d Cir. 1995).

has no opportunity to hear the defendant's voice or other voices of the lineup from which the defendant was selected.[84]

§ 8.26 Shaping of testimony by law enforcement or prosecution contacts.

A witness's identification can be influenced through meetings with law enforcement or prosecutorial personnel. This is sometimes referred to as "shaping" of testimony. The nature of the meetings may need to be examined. A typical cross-examination in this area by defense counsel might be as follows:

Q. Miss Dillon, prior to testifying here today, did you meet with members of the investigation team or the prosecutor's office concerning your testimony?

A. Yes, sir.

Q. On how many occasions prior to trial would you say that you have met to discuss your testimony with the prosecutor?

A. Oh, approximately three times.

Q. During the lunch and recess you have been in the prosecutor's office, correct?

A. Yes, sir.

Q. And you were there all day yesterday?

A. Yes, sir.

Q. What about last week?

A. Once that I can recall, sir.

Q. When would that have been?

---

[84] People v. Scott, 283 A.D.2d 98, 728 N.Y.S.2d 474 (2001):

> Had such an exemplar been admitted into evidence, the jury would at least have had both the opportunity to hear for itself the supposedly distinctive character of the defendant's voice and, consequently, the opportunity to assess the reliability of the claim that the complaining witness was able to distinguish that voice from all others . . . . Had the People proved that their principal witness selected the defendant from a lineup consisting of other deep-voiced men, then the weight to be afforded to any evidence relating to such identification would certainly be stronger than if it were to appear that the defendant was instead chosen from a lineup in which every other participant had a voice noticeably higher than his own. As it stands, the record is silent as to the reliability of the voice-identification, and, aside from whether the silence of the record in this respect would warrant suppression of any evidence relating to the lineup identification as a matter of due process, [citation omitted] we find that, in the circumstances of this case, the People's failure, at the *Wade* hearing, to demonstrate more clearly the reliability of the identification procedure employed by the police resulted in a distinct failure of proof at the time of the later trial. *Id.* at 102-105; 728 N.Y.S.2d at 477-78.

A. Last Thursday.

Q. Roughly for how long?

A. Maybe an hour, hour and a half.

Q. And you have had occasion to discuss with members of the prosecutor's staff your testimony in this case, correct?

A. Yes, sir.

Q. And you have had a chance to discuss with the prosecutor's staff Mr. White's physical appearance, haven't you?

A. Yes, sir.

Q. You knew when you came into this court this morning, did you not, that Mr. White would be seated right here at counsel table, correct?

A. Uh, I wasn't sure.

Q. You didn't know that?

A. I don't know.

Q. You knew he was on trial?

A. Yes, sir.

Q. Did you know he would be in the courtroom?

A. Yes, sir.

Q. Had you discussed that fact with the District Attorney's Office or any of its members?

A. Not that I can recall.

Q. Did you review with any member of the prosecutor's staff how you would select or identify Mr. White at all in the course of your testimony in this case?

A. Uh, I don't believe so.

Q. Not at all?

A. Well, to an extent.

§ 8.27 Cross-examining the complainant with one too many questions.

There is the old adage that a trial attorney should never ask a witness a question to which he or she (the attorney) does not already know the answer. This rule, of course, is violated by both experienced and inexperienced lawyers, sometimes for good reason. Because of the numerous components of identification testimony, it is possible on cross-examination of a witness to flush out details that were omitted by the prosecution — for example, testimony that the complainant saw a scar on the assailant's face (which the defendant does not have) and about which the complainant was not asked on direct examination. (Remember, in cross-examining any witness about omissions in prior statements, the rule is that the matter should have been brought to the witness's attention in the course of the interview to be used as an inconsistency.)[85] In deciding how far to delve into unknown areas, consider the nature and extent of pretrial information, the nature and extent of the witness's sworn testimony at a preliminary hearing or grand jury proceeding, information supplied through investigation reports and, perhaps most important, the assessment of the witness as the trial testimony develops. This decision calls for an on-the-spot evaluation.

In the following excerpt from a defense attorney's cross-examination of a complainant, the ultimate in reversal of fortune occurs when this rape victim, who was unable to identify the defendant during pretrial procedures and who was not asked to identify the defendant during direct examination, was asked on cross-examination if she could identify anyone in the courtroom. She could indentify, and did — the two defendants. When defense counsel regained his composure, he attempted to lay a safety net by questioning the complainant as to whether the investigators had shown her several photos, one of which was of one of the defendants and whether she was unable to identify the defendant at that time. (This will be explored on cross-examination of this defendant's alibi witness, which is set forth in a subsequent section.)

Q. When you talked to the investigators, they had occasion to show you photographs of several individuals?

A. Correct.

Q. And you were asked if you could identify anyone as being your assailant, correct?

A. Yes.

Q. You didn't pick anyone out as being the assailants?

A. No.

Q. As you sit here today, you can't pick anyone out as being your assailants?

A. They're right there, (indicating).

At this point, counsel as well as most people in the courtroom were undoubtedly shocked. Further cross-examination on this point only emphasized the identification.

---

[85] People v. Bornholdt, 33 N.Y.2d 75, 88, 305 N.E.2d 461, 468, 350 N.Y.S.2d 369, 379–80 (1973), *cert. denied sub nom.* Victory v. New York, 416 U.S. 905 (1974) ("The weight of authority holds, however, that a witness may not be impeached simply by showing that he omitted to state a fact, or to state it more fully at a prior time. It need also be shown that at the prior time the witness' attention was called to the matter and that he was specifically asked about the facts embraced in the question propounded at trial." *Id.* at 88, 305 N.E.2d at 468). *See also* People v. Vega, 169 A.D.2d 586, 564 N.Y.S.2d 438 (1991) (a police officer's grand jury testimony failing to state that a vehicle was unoccupied did not constitute a prior inconsistent statement when he had not been specifically questioned about it).

Q. Now you can pick them out?

A. I never saw them before in person except for that night.

Q. You were never shown any pictures of Sammy White?

A. I don't know.

Q. Well, you were.

A. I never saw them in person until now.

Q. Do you see anyone in the courtroom that you say was your assailant?

A. Yes. Both of those two people right there (indicating).

Defense counsel then introduced the photographs that were shown to the complainant that included the photograph of defendant Sammy White. But this boomerangs as will be seen in the cross-examination of the defendant's alibi witness in § 8.41.

§ 8.28   Cross-examination of police investigators concerning identification.

In cross-examining police investigators regarding identification of the assailant, defense counsel usually attempts to develop avenues of investigation that could have been pursued but were not. Were all leads pursued by investigators? For example, did the investigators question neighbors or other individuals who may have seen the assailant? Did further investigation stop once a suspect was developed? Were all appropriate scientific and forensic avenues of investigation pursued? Defense counsel typically questions investigators about the failure to process properly the scene for fingerprints. There well may be good reasons why a scene or object was not dusted for fingerprints, but this explanation, if any, must be provided by the investigator.

Another issue to develop on cross-examination of a police investigator is the description of the assailant taken by the investigator from the complainant or other key identification witnesses. Establish the limited or incorrect nature of the description given to the investigator by the complainant. Perhaps the witness has supplemented her initial description with additional information. Note that the police investigator is trained to be careful and thorough. It should be developed that the investigator will record all the information provided concerning the assailant's description to assist in the investigation as well as to refresh his recollection or that of others should it be necessary. Establish that the police officer has training with respect to report taking and writing. Establish the importance of compiling all information concerning a description provided by a witness. It also should be developed that the police officer is trained to elicit as much information as possible from a complainant.

§ 8.29 In-court identification.

In most cases, the prosecution will have an identification witness identify the defendant in court. While usually this is no problem, in the trial involving the bombing of the World Trade Center, a witness identified a juror instead of the defendant. In-court identification can be enhanced by having the witness stand up and point to the defendant, or better still, leave the stand and touch him on the shoulder.

In-court identifications have been criticized as unduly suggestive, and there is authority that since a defendant is isolated at counsel's table, the in-court identification is inherently unfair, especially if the witness has not identified the defendant previously.[86] Most courts reject the argument that in-court identifications are unduly suggestive,[87] and a defendant may request that the defendant not sit next to the defense attorney at the counsel table or have others who fit the defendant's description also sit at the counsel table.[88] These special procedures are necessary, according to one court, where: "(1) identification is a contested issue; (2) the defendant has moved in a timely manner prior to trial for a lineup; and (3) despite that defense request, the witness has not had an opportunity to view a fair out-of-court lineup prior to his trial testimony or ruling on the fairness of the out-of-court lineup has been reserved."[89] In this decision, the court commented that the request should be made in advance of trial.

It should be noted that a "defendant does not have a constitutional right to participate in a lineup whenever he requests one," and thus it is at the discretion of the trial judge to grant one during trial.[90] Furthermore, when a defendant's appearance has changed or been altered, the in-court lineup may actually be an unfair procedure.[91]

Sometimes a witness will be asked to stand to identify an assailant. This may be considered an unduly suggestive identification procedure. However, some

---

[86] United States v. Hill, 967 F.2d 226, 232 (6th Cir. 1992).

[87] Satcher v. Pruett, 126 F.3d 561 (4th Cir. 1997), *cert. denied*, 522 U.S. 1010 (1997); Green v. State, 35 Md. App. 510, 520–21, 371 A.2d 1112, 1118 (1977).

[88] United States v. Archibald, 734 F.2d 938 (2d Cir. 1984), *modified, reh'g denied*, 756 F.2d 223 (2d Cir. 1984) (discussing in detail the problem of in-court identification and the various court decisions recommending in-court "line-ups" and stating that steps should be taken to insure fairness of in-court identification).

[89] United States v. Archibald, 756 F.2d 223, 224 (2d Cir. 1984).

[90] People v. Bradley, 154 A.D.2d 609, 609–10, 546 N.Y.S.2d 437 (1989), *appeal denied*, 75 N.Y.2d 810, 551 N.E.2d 1238, 552 N.Y.S.2d 560 (1990) (*citing* United States v. Williams, 436 F.2d 1166, 1168–69 (9th Cir. 1970), 402 U.S. 912 (1971)).

[91] People v. Powell, 105 A.D.2d 712, 714–16, 481 N.Y.S.2d 157, 160–61 (1984) (Titone dissenting), *aff'd*, 67 N.Y.2d 661, 490 N.E.2d 536, 499 N.Y.S.2d 669 (1986) (lengthy discussion of a defendant changing appearances for trial, possible approaches to in-court identification techniques, and case of a single photo shown to a ten-year-old witness at trial to identify a defendant).

courts find such a procedure justified for a witness under an infirmity, such as a child[92] or elderly sight-impaired witness.[93]

§ 8.30 Admission of a witness's prior identification and admissibility of prior identification when the witness forgets.

Under the Federal Rules of Evidence, a statement is not hearsay if the declarant testifies and is subject to cross-examination, and the statement is "one of identification of a person made after perceiving the person."[94] Various state and federal statutes permit the admission of a prior identification by a witness. In some states, however, such as New York, the use of prior identification testimony is severely restricted.[95] Under this view, admitting into evidence a police sketch of the suspect, based on a description by the complainant, is hearsay or double hearsay and not admissible unless under cross-examination a witness's account is attacked as a recent fabrication.[96] If the witness suffers from memory loss and is unable to remember the pretrial identification, the Supreme Court of the United States has held that the witness's pretrial identification is still admissible. The Court stated that the confrontation clause was not violated, since the witness appeared and was cross-examined. The confrontation clause does not insure the right of an effective or successful cross-examination. The Court felt that cross-examination demonstrating the witness's inability to remember the attack provided an adequate safeguard for the defendant.[97]

---

[92] Croy v. State, 247 Ga. App. 654, 545 S.E.2d 80 (2001).

[93] Hayslip v. State, 154 Ga. App. 835, 270 S.E.2d 61 (1980).

[94] FED. R. EVID. 801(d)(1)(C).

[95] N.Y. CRIM. PROC. LAW §§ 60.25 and 60.30. *See, e.g.*, People v. Quevas, 81 N.Y.2d 41, 611 N.E.2d 760, 595 N.Y.S.2d 721 (1993) (prosecution must establish why sexual assault complainant cannot make in-court identification as foundation for prior out-of-court identification; foundation must establish witness's lack of present recollection of defendant as the perpetrator). New York also does not permit testimony on the prosecution's direct case that a witness identified the defendant from a photographic array.

[96] People v. Maldonado, 97 N.Y.2d 522, 769 N.E.2d 1281, 743 N.Y.S.2d 389 (2002) (Court noted Hawaii and Massachusetts follow this view). Court also noted:

> When a jury examines a composite sketch, the temptation to inculpate or exonerate the defendant on the basis of the sketch is all but irresistible. A great many other people may also resemble the sketch, but only the defendant on trial sits before the jury. Despite any influence of the artist's interpretations or possibility that the sketch may be inaccurate, many jurors will be prone to conclude — if not exhorted to conclude — that because the defendant sitting before them matches the sketch, the defendant must be guilty. The prejudice of that circular logic is manifest and inescapable.

[97] United States v. Owens, 484 U.S. 554 (1988).

§ 8.31   Expert testimony on eyewitness identification background and opposing research.

The work of Loftus and Doyle (discussed in § 8.1) and the studies they cite is the underpinning of much of the psychological basis for expert testimony on eyewitness identification. Experts in the field of eyewitness identification can explain some of the variables in identifying individuals, such as the tendency to overestimate the length of time of events, the detrimental effect of high stress on the ability to remember, the tendency to focus attention on a weapon, the difficulty of identifying individuals of a different race, the tendency of individuals to unconsciously transfer identification from one setting to another, and that there is no necessary correlation between accuracy and a witness's confidence in an identification. Psychologists also can explain that the human mind does not record and reproduce events like a video recorder. Rather, the mind will collect all information it is able to record, but in recalling such information, it may be affected by information gathered after the event. Thus, viewing a composite drawing, artist's sketch, or photograph of a suspect after an event, as well as being exposed to other means of suggestiveness described in the preceding sections of this chapter, may influence the memory of an identification witness.

Belief in the helpfulness of expert testimony concerning eyewitness identification or the unreliability of eyewitness testimony is not necessarily universally embraced by psychologists. The two rationales for the use of expert psychological testimony, i.e., that jurors cannot discriminate adequately between accurate and inaccurate eyewitnesses and that jurors readily embrace eyewitness testimony, have been challenged as without basis in an article by Michael McCloskey and Howard E. Egeth. As to the helpfulness of expert eyewitness testimony, they conclude:

> As mentioned above, the expert psychological testimony reduced the jurors' overall willingness to believe eyewitnesses. However, the expert testimony had absolutely no effect on jurors' ability to discriminate accurate from inaccurate witnesses . . . . Expert testimony, on the other hand, may serve to increase juror skepticism but not to improve juror discrimination . . . we must conclude that at present there is no evidence that expert psychological advice improves juror evaluation of eyewitness testimony.[98]

---

[98] Michael McCloskey & Howard E. Egeth, *Eyewitness Identification: What Can a Psychologist Tell a Jury?*, AM. PSYCHOLOGIST, May 1983, at 550, 556. The article states that mistaken eyewitness identification is not a significant problem. It also notes that there is little data on the weight given to eyewitness testimony relative to other evidence and that it is difficult to determine what weight should be given different types of evidence. It also questions whether psychological studies in a laboratory can be extrapolated to real juries.

The problem of laboratory studies of eyewitness testimony and whether those results are transferable to the real world is emphasized in another article by John C. Yuille and Judith L. Cutshall, *A Case Study of Eyewitness Memory of a Crime*, 71 J. APPLIED PSYCHOL., 291–301 (1986). This analysis of the accuracy of eyewitnesses in a real-life crime made several conclusions that appear to contradict many laboratory studies. Among the conclusions of the study:

§ 8.32 Expert testimony on identification — Legal approaches to scientific reliability under *Daubert* and *Frye*.

Not all courts automatically accept the scientific reliability of expert testimony on eyewitness identification. One court rejected expert testimony on eyewitness identification testimony because the defendant did not offer evidence to establish the scientific reliability and acceptance of the expert's opinion.[99] Another court found such testimony did not meet the standard of "generally acceptable as reliable" after reviewing evidence presented by the defendant.[100] Unlike other areas of expert testimony, there is no difficulty establishing the general acceptance and reliability of the psychological theories forming the basis of expert testimony concerning eyewitness identification. Most courts that exclude expert testimony do so on the theory of Federal Rule of Evidence 403.

The legal parameters for the use and admissibility of expert testimony are set forth in detail in Chapter 11 in the discussion of the Supreme Court's decision in *Daubert v. Merrell Dow Pharmaceuticals, Inc.*[101] Interestingly, in that case the Court cited several times a Circuit Court of Appeals decision looking favorably upon the use of expert testimony concerning eyewitness identification.[102]

While courts may be directed to review prior holdings on the admissibility of expert testimony under the *Daubert* standard,[103] the result may remain the same. For example, one federal appeals court re-examined its view of expert testimony under *Daubert* and found that while the area of testimony involves

---

Most of the witnesses in this case were highly accurate in their accounts, and this continued to be true 5 months after the event . . . . Our finding of significantly higher accuracy rates among the five witnesses directly involved in the event suggests that details may be retained more vividly by those who participate in an event . . . . The passivity demanded of witnesses in laboratory research has precluded examining the effect of active involvement on subsequent recall; however, the possibility of such an effect in real-life witnessing situations should not be ignored. We suggest that the relatively high accuracy rates found in this study may have been due, in part, to factors usually absent in experimental research: a particularly salient event with obvious life and death consequences, and the opportunity for active involvement by some witnesses . . . . One of the more striking results was the lack of memory loss over time . . . . It does appear, however, that in this case stress had no negative effect on memory.

Id. at 299–300.

[99] Weatherred v. State, 15 S.W.3d 540 (Tex. Crim. App. 2000).

[100] People v. LeGrand, 196 Misc. 2d 179, 747 N.Y.S.2d 733 (Sup. Ct. 2002).

[101] 509 U.S. 579 (1993). *See* discussion in §§ 11.2–11.10.

[102] United States v. Downing, 753 F.2d 1224 (3d Cir. 1985).

[103] United States v. Smithers, 212 F.3d 306 (6th Cir. 2000) (finding trial court abused its discretion in rejecting expert testimony on eyewitness identification without a hearing); United States v. Amador-Galvan, 9 F.3d 1414 (9th Cir. 1993) (appellate court remanded for a *Daubert* hearing on whether expert testimony on reliability of eyewitness identification testimony should have been admitted).

scientific knowledge, the expert testimony fails under the second prong, namely that it does not assist the trier of fact.[104]

§ 8.33   Expert testimony on identification — Legal approaches to admissibility.

Traditionally, courts have been leery of expert testimony on eyewitness identification finding it is a subject within the knowledge of the jury, confusions, or an area which can be addressed by cross-examination.[105]

A few courts have a blanket prohibition against expert testimony on eyewitness identification. Tennessee's Supreme Court finds expert eyewitness identification testimony *per se* inadmissible because it is misleading, confusing, and within the common understanding of reasonable persons, and would not assist the trier of fact.[106] Few courts adhere to this exclusion of expert testimony as a matter of law.[107]

---

[104] United States v. Smith, 122 F.3d 1355, 1357–59 (11th Cir. 1997).

[105] McClendon v. Commissioner of Corr., 58 Conn. App. 436, 755 A.2d 238 (2000) (upholding exclusion of expert testimony in eyewitness identification since expert's conclusions were "nothing outside the common experience of mankind"); Commonwealth v. Simmons, 541 Pa. 211, 662 A.2d 621 (1995), *cert. denied*, 516 U.S. 1128 (1996) ("Here, appellant's expert would have testified generally about the reliability of eyewitness identification. Such testimony would have given an unwarranted appearance of authority as to the subject of credibility, a subject which an ordinary juror can assess. Moreover, appellant was free to and did attack the witness's credibility and point out inconsistencies of all the eyewitnesses at trial through cross-examination and in his closing argument. Thus, the trial court properly excluded appellant's proposed expert testimony." *Id.* at 231, 662 A.2d at 631.).

See generally Gregory S. Sarno, Annotation, *Admissibility, at Criminal Prosecution, of Expert Testimony on Reliability of Eyewitness Testimony*, 46 A.L.R.4th 1041 (1986).

[106] State v. Coley, 32 S.W.3d 831 (Tenn. 2000):

> [W]e are of the opinion that the subject of the reliability of eyewitness identification is within the common understanding of reasonable persons. Therefore, such expert testimony is unnecessary. It may mislead and confuse, and it could encourage the jury to abandon its responsibility as fact-finder. Such responsibility is a task reserved for and ably performed by the jury, aided by skillful cross-examination and the jury instruction promulgated in *Dyle* when appropriate. For these reasons, we find that general and unparticularized expert testimony concerning the reliability of eyewitness testimony, which is not specific to the witness whose testimony is in question, does not substantially assist the trier of fact.

Id. at 837–38.

[107] *See, e.g.*, United States v. Smith, 122 F.3d 1355 (11th Cir. 1997); State v. Gaines, 260 Kan. 752, 754-62, 926 P.2d 641, 645–49 (1996). *See also* Lenoir v. State, 77 Ark. App. 250, 72 S.W.3d 899 (2002) (holding that expert testimony concerning the reliability of eyewitness identification "is within the common knowledge and not beyond the ken of lay jurors and would tend to obfuscate rather than elucidate the issues and, therefore, is not a proper subject for expert testimony").

Most courts now hold that admission of expert testimony on the accuracy of eyewitness identification should not be summarily precluded but rather is a matter of the trial court's discretion and is not *per se* inadmissible.[108]

Most federal courts also take the position that the admissibility of expert testimony on eyewitness identification is a matter of discretion, since the factors surrounding eyewitness identification are within the knowledge of the jury and that such testimony can only further confuse the jury and would be helpful to the jury.[109]

Courts will look at the proof and issues of the case. Among the factors to consider is the court's discretion in admitting expert testimony on eyewitness identification is the strength of the identification testimony, including such factors as the opportunity and time to observe the assailant, whether the identification was based on the testimony of one or more witnesses, and the overall proof connecting the defendant to the crime.[110] When identification is weak or

---

[108] McMullen v. State, 714 So. 2d 368, 371 (Fla. 1998) (holding that "expert testimony should be excluded when the facts testified to are of such nature as not to require any special knowledge or experience in order for the jury to form its conclusions" but not summarily precluded); Johnson v. State, 272 Ga. 254, 526 S.E.2d 549 (2000); State v. Gaines, 260 Kan. 752, 926 P.2d 641 (1996); State v. Chapman, 410 So. 2d 689, 702 (La. 1981); State v. Kelly, 752 A.2d 188, 191 (Me. 2000) (in upholding denial of funds for defendant to obtain expert on eyewitness identification, Maine's Supreme Court noted that it has "repeatedly upheld the exclusion of expert testimony regarding eyewitness reliability as within the court's discretion"); Commonwealth v. Santoli, 424 Mass. 837, 680 A.2d 1116 (1997); State v. Miles, 585 N.W.2d 368, 371–72 (Minn. 1998) (upholding exclusion of expert testimony concerning reliability of eyewitness identification testimony, including problems associated with cross-racial identifications, since jury was given adequate instructions concerning eyewitness testimony); White v. State, 112 Nev. 1261, 926 P.2d 291 (1996); People v. Lee, 96 N.Y.2d 157, 750 N.E.2d 63, 726 N.Y.S.2d 361 (2001) (noting psychological studies regarding accuracy of eyewitness identification are not within the ken of the typical juror); People v. Mooney, 76 N.Y.2d 827, 559 N.E.2d 1274, 560 N.Y.S.2d 115 (1990); State v. Gardiner, 636 A.2d 710 (R.I. 1994); State v. Cheatam, 150 Wash. 2d 626, 81 P.3d 830 (2003) ("We conclude . . . instead, that where eyewitness identification of the defendant is a key element of the State's case, the trial court must carefully consider whether expert testimony on the reliability of eyewitness identification would assist the jury in asserting the reliability of eyewitness testimony. In making this determination, the court should consider the proposed testimony and the specific subjects involved in the identification to which the testimony relates, such as whether the victim and the defendant are of the same race, whether the defendant displayed a weapon, the effect of stress, etc." *Id.* at 649, 81 P.3d at 842.).

[109] United States v. Kime, 99 F.3d 870 (8th Cir. 1996), *cert. denied*, 519 U.S. 1141 (1997); United States v. Daniels, 64 F.3d 311, 315 (7th Cir. 1995), *cert. denied*, 516 U.S. 1063 (1996); United States v. Brien, 59 F.3d 274, 277 (1st Cir. 1995), *cert. denied*, 516 U.S. 953 (1995); United States v. Stevens, 935 F.2d 1380, 1397–1401 (3d Cir. 1991); United States v. Ruggiero, 928 F.2d 1289, 1304 (2d Cir. 1991), *cert. denied sub. nom.*, Gotti v. United States, 502 U.S. 938 (1991); United States v. Affleck, 776 F.2d 1451, 1458 (10th Cir. 1985) (court declined to receive testimony of memory expert relative to how well or how poorly people remember events over the course of time and the process of remembering); United States v. Fosher, 590 F.2d 381 (1st Cir. 1979); United States v. Amaral, 488 F.2d 1148, 1153 (9th Cir. 1973); United States v. Burrous, 934 F. Supp. 525, 527 (E.D.N.Y. 1996).

[110] Farrell v. State, 612 N.E.2d 124 (Ind. Ct. App.), *rev'd on other grounds*, 622 N.E.2d 488

problematic, it may be an abuse of discretion to preclude expert testimony on eyewitness identification.[111]

Arizona's Supreme Court has held that while typical jurors may be aware of many of the dangers of eyewitness identification, there were "many specific variables which affect the accuracy of identification" that are important and helpful to the jury.[112]

A third approach to admissibility (the first being *per se* inadmissible and the second being discretionary) is California's Supreme Court's decision in *People v. McDonald*,[113] a general case in the use of expert eyewitness identification testimony, which suggests such testimony should be admitted when proof of identification is weak. In a case without substantial corroboration of the identification testimony, the court held expert testimony from a psychologist should be admitted concerning the ability of an eyewitness to perceive, recall, and relate accurately events and factors that can affect the ability to perceive, such as fear, anxiety, and excitement. Neither of these decisions mandate the use of expert testimony concerning eyewitness identification, but they reflect greater willingness to find it necessary in particular situations than other state courts. Even under the liberal view of *McDonald*, California courts have found it within a trial court's discretion and functionally the equivalent of the discretionary view to preclude expert testimony on eyewitness identification, usually on the grounds that there was sufficient reliability in the eyewitness's identification or other evidence connecting the defendant with the crime or that the expert testimony would not be helpful given other physical evidence.[114] Some other courts follow *McDonald's* principles and hold that "[i]t shall be an abuse of discretion for a district court to disallow expert testimony on eyewitness testimony when no substantial corroborating evidence exists."[115]

(Ind. 1993) (noting that the exclusion of expert eyewitness testimony in this case was harmless error due to the strength of the identification testimony, but that courts should consider its introduction in cases involving eyewitnesses, the identification of a defendant by one or two eyewitnesses); Commonwealth v. Santoli, 424 Mass. 837, 680 A.2d 1116 (1997) ("It is significant, in deciding the principal issue on appeal, that the Commonwealth's case was not built solely on the eyewitness testimony of the victim." *Id.* at 839, 680 N.E.2d at 1117); State v. Percy, 156 Vt. 468, 595 A.2d 248 (1990), *cert. denied*, 502 U.S. 927 (1991) (court's preclusion of expert testimony by defendant on the effect of stress on the victim's perception acceptable when there is sufficient corroboration of identification of defendant; the court noted there may be cases where expert testimony on psychological aspects of eyewitness identification should be admitted).

[111] People v. Campbell, 847 P.2d 228 (Colo. Ct. App. 1992) (ruling that the expert testimony should have been admitted because of its reliability, because it was not misleading considering the facts of the case, and because it was more probative than prejudicial); Nations v. State, 944 S.W.2d 795 (Tex. Ct. App. 1997) (holding it was an abuse of discretion to preclude expert witness from identification testimony in rape case which involved reliability of eyewitness identification).

[112] State v. Chapple, 135 Ariz. 281, 293, 660 P.2d 1208, 1220 (1983).

[113] 37 Cal. 3d 351, 208 Cal. Rptr. 236, 690 P.2d 709 (1984).

[114] People v. Sanders, 51 Cal. 3d 471, 503–06, 273 Cal. Rptr. 537, 554–56, 797 P.2d 561, 578–80 (1990), *cert. denied*, 500 U.S. 948 (1991).

[115] State v. DuBray, 317 Mont. 377, 387, 77 P.3d 247, 255 (2003).

§ 8.34 Expert testimony on identification and court appointed experts on that topic.

A defendant, under the doctrine of *Ake v. Oklahoma*,[116] may have a qualified right to seek the appointment by the court of an expert on eyewitness identification. Many of the same principles discussed in that section apply to court appointed experts in the field of identification testimony on behalf of a defendant. In a sexual assault case, this is likely to depend on how important the identification issue is to the case, whether the prosecution will use an expert in hypnosis to support the complainant's testimony, and the specificity of the need established by the defendant in requesting an expert.[117]

§ 8.35 Special or cautionary instructions concerning eyewitness identification testimony.

Sometimes it is appropriate to request special or cautionary jury instructions concerning the reliability of eyewitness identification testimony. New York and Massachusetts have adopted such a rule in cases when identification of the defendant is a close issue.[118] The leading federal case advocating specific or expanded instructions on the factors influencing eyewitness identification is *United States v. Telfaire*.[119] The failure to provide an expanded charge on identification will not necessarily be error when in the context of all the evidence there is little chance that the failure to provide the expanded instruction is of significance.[120]

---

[116] 470 U.S. 68 (1985). *See also* discussion at § 11.52.

[117] Little v. Armontrout, 835 F.2d 1240, 1243 (8th Cir. 1987), *cert. denied*, 487 U.S. 1210 (1988) (In a sexual assault trial involving identification issues, the court held that "the denial of a state-provided expert on hypnosis to assist this indigent defendant rendered the trial fundamentally unfair and requires that the conviction be set aside."); People v. Fennell, 237 A.D.2d 459, 655 N.Y.S.2d 972, *appeal denied*, 89 N.Y.2d 1092, 682 N.E.2d 987, 660 N.Y.S.2d 386 (1997) (holding trial court acted within its discretion in denying defendant funds for an expert on eyewitness identification); People v. Anderson, 218 A.D.2d 533, 630 N.Y.S.2d 77, *appeal denied*, 87 N.Y.2d 844, 661 N.E.2d 1383, 638 N.Y.S.2d 602 (1995) (in denying defendant funds for an expert on eyewitness identification, court noted that such evidence is not beyond the ken of the average juror).

[118] State v. Warner, 230 Kan. 385, 635 P.2d 1236 (1981); Commonwealth v. Rodriguez, 378 Mass. 296, 301–02, 391 N.E.2d 889, 892–93 (1979) (suggesting the charge from United States v. Telfaire, 469 F.2d 552 (D.C. Cir. 1972)); People v. Whalen, 59 N.Y.2d 273, 279, 451 N.E.2d 212, 214–15, 464 N.Y.S.2d 454, 456–57 (1983).

[119] 469 F.2d 552 (D.C. Cir. 1972).

[120] People v. Knight, 87 N.Y.2d 873, 662 N.E.2d 256, 638 N.Y.S.2d 938 (1995) (holding that an expanded charge specifically instructing the jury that identification of the defendant had to be proven beyond a reasonable doubt is the "better practice" when identification is at issue; whether such a charge is required in a particular case is a m atter within the trial court's discretion); People v. Torres, 8 A.D.3d 123, 779 N.Y.S.2d 34, *appeal denied*, 3 N.Y.3d 712, 818 N.E.2d 682, 785 N.Y.S.2d 40 (2004) (noting the court's instruction to the jury requiring them to prove identity beyond a reasonable doubt included much of the same information that would be contained in a typical expanded identification charge). *See also* State v. Vinge, 81 Haw. 309, 916 P.2d 1210

Examples of such an expanded charge, which outlines the potential unreliability of identification testimony, is set forth in Appendix M of this book, including the charge suggested in *Telfaire*. There is some research that suggests the charge from *Telfaire* may be confusing for a jury and that the instruction on identification should be clearer and more understandable. The second charge in Appendix M is a modified version of the *Telfaire* charge.[121] In lieu of expert testimony, which it finds *per se* inadmissible, Tennessee holds that special instructions on eyewitness identification, focusing on the role of the jury in evaluating relevant factors, should be given to the jury. Such a jury charge is also included in Appendix M.[122]

Loftus and Doyle also suggest instructions on time estimates, eyewitness confidence, and good faith mistake.[123] Special instructions have been cited as one alternative to expert testimony on the subject.[124] Most courts, however, do not find it necessary for a court to provide a detailed charge or cautionary instructions on eyewitness identification, but that a jury should scrutinize eyewitness identification testimony with extreme care.[125]

A jury instruction that states "You may take into account . . . the strength of the identification" is likely to be improper since it suggests that the confidence

---

(1996); People v. Page, 6 A.D.3d 553, 774 N.Y.S.2d 403, *appeal denied*, 3 N.Y.3d 645, 816 N.E.2d 206, 782 N.Y.S.2d 416 (2004); People v. Daniels, 225 A.D.2d 632, 639 N.Y.S.2d 96, *appeal denied*, 670 N.E.2d 1351, 647 N.Y.S.2d 719 (1996); People v. Davis, 208 A.D.2d 989, 617 N.Y.S.2d 220 (1994), *appeal denied*, 84 N.Y.2d 1030, 647 N.E.2d 458, 623 N.Y.S.2d 186 (1995).

[121] ELIZABETH F. LOFTUS & JAMES M. DOYLE, EYEWITNESS TESTIMONY: CIVIL AND CRIMINAL 333–37 (3d ed. 1997).

[122] State v. Coley, 32 S.W.2d 831 (Tenn. 2000):

> [W]e have concluded that requiring trial courts to admit this type of expert evidence [on eyewitness identification] is not the answer to the [eyewitness identification] problem. We believe that the problem can be alleviated by a proper cautionary instruction to the jury which sets forth the factors to be considered in evaluating eyewitness testimony. Such instruction, coupled with vigorous cross-examination and persuasive argument by defense counsel dealing realistically with the shortcomings and trouble spots of the identification process, should protect the rights of the defendant and at the same time enable the courts to avoid problems involved in the admission of expert testimony on this subject.

Id. at 837.

[123] *Id.* at 343.

[124] United States v. Smith, 122 F.3d 1355 (11th Cir. 1997), *cert. denied*, 522 U.S. 1021 (1997) ("Of course, defendants who want to attack the reliability of eyewitness recollection are free to use the powerful tool of cross-examination to do so. They may also request jury instructions that highlight particular problems in eyewitness recollection. Smith did in the present case and was successful in getting the district court to instruct the jury about cross-racial identification, potential bias in earlier identifications, delay between the event and the time of identification and stress." *Id.* at 1359.).

[125] *See, e.g.*, United States v. Tipton, 11 F.3d 602 (6th Cir. 1993), *cert. denied*, 512 U.S. 1212 (1994); People v. Fuller, 791 P.2d 702, 707 (Colo. 1990).

of a person's identification "is a valid indicator of the accuracy of the recollection."[126]

§ 8.36   Expert testimony and jury instruction on cross-racial identification.

There is some research which suggests a witness may have increased difficulty making accurate identification of individuals of another race.

Cross-racial identification may also be subject to a cautionary instruction. New Jersey's Supreme Court, in a robbery and sexual assault case, held that a jury should be instructed on the problem of cross-racial identification when the identification of the defendant is based largely or solely on one witness and there is little corroborating evidence of the eyewitness identification.[127]

Some courts permit expert testimony on eyewitness identification including the issue of cross-racial identification.[128]

On the theory that there is not general agreement in the scientific community about the extent of "own-race" bias, a court may preclude expert testimony on cross-racial identification.[129] A court may also find the issue within jurors'

---

[126] Commonwealth v. Santoli, 424 Mass. 837, 845, 680 N.E.2d 116, 1121 (1997); People v. Jouvert, 289 A.D.2d 40, 733 N.Y.S.2d 608 (2001), *appeal denied*, 97 N.Y.2d 756, 769 N.E.2d 362, 742 N.Y.S.2d 616 (2002); People v. Torres, 282 A.D.2d 481, 722 N.Y.S.2d 414, *appeal denied*, 96 N.Y.2d 908, 756 N.E.2d 94, 730 N.Y.S.2d 806 (2001); People v. Ramos, 282 A.D.2d 278, 723 N.Y.S.2d 352, *appeal denied*, 96 N.Y.2d 906, 756 N.E.2d 92, 730 N.Y.S.2d 804 (2001) (holding trial court's instruction on factors to consider in eyewitness identification adequately covered issue).

[127] State v. Cromedy, 158 N.J. 112, 727 A.2d 457 (1999) (The decision also cites some other authority for such an instruction when there is no corroborating evidence and there is a question of the reliability of the eyewitness identification.).

[128] People v. Drake, 188 Misc. 2d 210, 728 N.Y.S.2d 636 (Sup. Ct. 2001) (court upheld expert testimony on eyewitness identification to inform jury of role of violence and stress, weapon focus, media attention, assimilation of post event information, filling in phenomenon, motivation, delay in identification, lack of correlation between witness confidence and reliability, and cross-racial identification); State v. Echols, 128 Ohio App. 3d 677, 716 N.E.2d 728 (1998) (defendant's conviction was reversed because trial court abused its discretion in refusing to sever counts of indictment involving multiple incidents, as well as trial court's ruling precluding testimony by an eyewitness identification expert. The court concluded:

> Further, Dr. Fulero's testimony would have been very helpful to the jury because his knowledge, as demonstrated by his deposition, was outside the scope of a layperson's knowledge and could dispel misconceptions about eyewitness identification. Dr. Fulero's testimony included information regarding the confidence of an eyewitness in his identification being unrelated to the accuracy of the identification; the manner in which memory functions; the inverse relationship of stress and accuracy of identification; the effect of familiarity of an individual in a different context on identification, and the inaccuracy of cross-racial identification, to name a few examples.

Id. at 697, 716 N.E.2d at 742).

[129] People v. Carrieri, 4 Misc. 3d 307, 777 N.Y.S.2d 627 (Sup. Ct. 2004) ("Thus, the court concludes that the procedural safeguards, to wit, cross-examination, summation, and a *Daniels* charge, combined with the life experience of jurors, are sufficient tools for a jury to rationally decide if the accused has been accurately identified.") *Id.* at 309, 777 N.Y.S.2d at 629.

general knowledge and life experience,[130] or adequately dealt with by questioning of the witness,[131] or general instructions on identification.[132]

As an acceptable alternative to a jury instruction on cross-racial identification, many courts permit counsel to comment on the topic in closing argument, and it may be reversible error to preclude a defendant from commenting on cross-racial identification in closing.[133]

§ 8.37   The notice of alibi, disclosure of alibi evidence, people's reciprocal discovery obligations, burden of proof, and jury instructions on alibi.

An important component to an identification defense may be the alibi. Strictly speaking, an alibi is a "defense based on the physical impossibility of a defendant's guilt by placing a defendant in a location other than the scene of the crime at the relevant time."[134] An alibi need not cover the whole period

---

[130] Commonwealth v. Walker, 421 Mass. 90, 96, 653 N.E.2d 1080 (1995) (upholding trial court's refusal to allow a defendant to present expert testimony concerning the unreliability of cross-racial identifications, since trial judge "could reasonably have concluded in his discretion that the subject of cross-racial identifications was not 'one on which the opinion of an expert would have been of assistance to the jury.' " *quoting* Commonwealth v. Francis, 390 Mass. 89, 98, 453 N.E.2d 1204 (1983); People v. Carrieri, 4 Misc. 3d 307, 777 N.Y.S.2d 627 (Sup. Ct. 2004).

[131] People v. Mathien, 276 A.D.2d 302, 714 N.Y.S.2d 28 (2000), *appeal denied*, 96 N.Y.2d 736, 745 N.E.2d 1026, 722 N.Y.S.2d 803 (2001) (holding trial court properly precluded defendant's expert testimony on cross-racial identification).

[132] Lenoir v. State, 77 Ark. App. 250, 72 S.W.3d 899 (2002) (finding no violation of due process in trial court's failure to give instruction on cross-racial identification); State v. Miles, 585 N.W.2d 368, 371–72 (Minn. 1998).

[133] People v. Sanders, 11 Cal. 4th 475, 46 Cal. Rptr. 2d 751, 905 P.2d 420, 435 (1995) (holding that defendant had not been prejudiced by trial court's refusal of expert testimony on eyewitness identification because defense counsel had been allowed to argue the problems of cross-racial identification in closing argument); State v. Wiggins, 74 Conn. App. 703, 813 A.2d 1056, 1059 (2003) ("closing argument may be employed to demonstrate the problems that might arise as a result of cross-racial identification"); Smith v. State, 388 Md. 468, 880 A.2d 288 (2005) (In citing defendant's Sixth Amendment Right to Counsel, court held defendant was improperly restricted in arguing the problems of cross-racial identification. Defense counsel clearly was entitled to challenge Ms. Crandall's "educated" identification of the defendants by arguing to the jury that her identification should not be accorded the weight that she credited to her own ability to identify them. At this juncture, the extent to which own-race bias affects eyewitness identification is unclear based on the available studies addressing this issue, so that we cannot state with certainty that difficulty in cross-racial identification is an established matter of common knowledge. Here, however, the victim's identification of the defendants was anchored in her enhanced ability to identify faces. Under these circumstances, defense counsel should have been allowed to argue the difficulties of cross-racial identification in closing argument.

Therefore, we conclude that the trial court erred in refusing to allow defense counsel to comment on cross-racial identification in closing argument.).

[134] Noble v. Kelly, 246 F.3d 93, 98 n.2 (2d Cir. 2001), cert. denied, 534 U.S. 886 (2001), *citing* Black's Law Dictionary (7th ed. 1999).

of time during which the crime may have occurred, but issues may arise when the "alibi" evidence covers some time period near the time the crime was committed. To the extent the proposed "alibi" evidence is not tied to the alleged time of the offense, it may be subject to preclusion because it is of minimal probative value.[135] Defining whether the defendant's evidence is "alibi evidence" may also determine whether it must be disclosed in a "notice of alibi."

As discussed more fully in Chapter 1 concerning pretrial discovery, there are situations where the prosecution is entitled to discovery from a defendant. One of these is the notice of alibi. Most states require that, if the prosecution makes a demand, the defense is required to submit a notice of alibi within a particular time period. Such statutes have withstood constitutional scrutiny and have been repeatedly upheld by many courts.[136] A court may also order a defendant to disclose to the prosecution records or documents that the defendant intends to offer in support of the defendant's alibi.[137] Many statutory notice of alibi provisions also include a duty on the part of the prosecution to provide the names and addresses of rebuttal witnesses to the defendant's alibi.

While a jury may expect to hear an alibi on the part of a defendant when the defense of mistaken identification is asserted, there is no duty to provide an alibi. Merely challenging the complainant's testimony as to the time of a sexual assault does not necessarily require the filing of a notice of alibi.[138] The failure to give an alibi instruction when the proof reasonably supports such a defense may be reversible error.[139] If an alibi is offered, generally the prosecution has the burden of disproving it beyond a reasonable doubt, and a judge must unequivocally state during the jury charge that this burden is on the prosecution.[140] A jury charge can shift this burden of proof if the charge is framed in terms of "if the alibi evidence is true," or "if there is evidence tending to prove an alibi," or some similar language that implies that the burden of proof has somehow shifted to the defense.[141] However, alibi evidence, like any other evidence, need not be believed by the trier of fact. Thus, even if the prosecution offers no rebuttal to a defendant's alibi, a jury is free to disbelieve the alibi.[142]

---

[135] *See,* e.g., People v. Harrison, 23 A.D.3d 689, 803 N.Y.S.2d 291 (2005).

[136] Ferdinand S. Tinio, Annotation, Validity and Construction of Statute Requiring Defendant in Criminal Case to Disclose Matter as to Alibi Defense, 45 A.L.R.3D 958 (1986).

[137] People v. Sirmons, 242 A.D.2d 883, 662 N.Y.S.2d 645 (1997) ("The discovery order in this case prevented the surprise at trial that would have resulted from undisclosed evidence belatedly offered to support defendant's alibi defense. Such discovery furthers the legislative policy of enabling the People to prepare to meet that defense." Id. at 884, 662 N.Y.S.2d at 646).

[138] State v. Baron, 80 Haw. 107, 118, 905 P.2d 613, 624 (1995).

[139] State v. Rodriguez, 192 Ariz. 58, 961 P.2d 1006 (1998).

[140] People v. Victor, 62 N.Y.2d 374, 465 N.E.2d 817, 477 N.Y.S.2d 97 (1984).

[141] People v. Victor, 62 N.Y.2d 374, 465 N.E.2d 817, 477 N.Y.S.2d 97 (1984).

[142] People v. Bigelow, 106 A.D.2d 448, 442 N.Y.S.2d 541 (1984).

§ 8.38 Prosecution's use of notice of alibi to impeach and commenting on defendant's failure to call an alibi witness.

The notice of alibi document is an important document. Because it is prepared with the defendant's participation and is a declaration by the defendant in the course of a legal proceeding, the prosecution may use the notice of alibi to impeach the defendant either on the basis of an informal judicial admission or a prior inconsistent statement.[143]

If the defendant withdraws his notice before trial, the prosecution may not cross-examine the defendant about the notice of alibi.[144] The Federal Rules of Criminal Procedure, as well as many states' rules, allow a defendant to withdraw an alibi notice without being cross-examined on the notice.[145]

When there is no claim of bad faith or prejudice to the prosecution, the prosecution can not introduce a defendant's notice of alibi, which was "disavowed" but not "withdrawn," and which conflicts with the defendant's alibi witnesses who give a new alibi relating to a different time frame.[146] Of course, the prosecution can still request preclusion or an adjournment to investigate. Nonetheless, the defendant's notice of alibi may permit the prosecution to comment concerning a defendant's failure to produce an available alibi witness. A defendant's "failure to call an alibi witness who was available, who, it may be inferred, had material information favorable to the defendant, and whose testimony would not be trivial or cumulative," can be properly brought to the jury's attention.[147] While a defendant has no burden to produce an alibi, the

---

[143] State v. Irving, 114 N.J. 427, 436-38, 555 A.2d 575, 580-81 (1989) (noting that notice of alibi can be used to cross-examine or rehabilitate defendant's credibility); People v. Rodriguez, 2 A.D.3d 296, 770 N.Y.S.2d 38 (2003), *appeal granted*, 2 N.Y.3d 745, 810 N.E.2d 924, 778 N.Y.S.2d 471 (2004) (allowing prosecution to introduce redacted copy of alibi notice into evidence solely for purpose of impeaching two alibi witnesses); People v. Shuff, 168 A.D.2d 348, 564 N.Y.S.2d 132 (1990), *appeal denied*, 77 N.Y.2d 967, 573 N.E.2d 589, 570 N.Y.S.2d 501 (1991) ("defendant's cross-examination on the notice [of alibi] appropriately served to test the defendant's faithfulness to his obligation to testify truthfully").

[144] People v. Brown, 98 N.Y.2d 226, 235, 774 N.E.2d 186, 746 N.Y.S.2d 422 (2002).

[145] FED. R. CRIM. P. 12.1[f]; CONN. SUPER. CT. RULES § 40-25; MASS. RULES CRIM. PROC. RULE 14[b][1]; D.C. SUPER. COURT RULE 12.1[f]; S.D. CODIFIED LAWS § 6.23A-9-6.

[146] People v. Rodriguez, 3 N.Y.3d 462, 821 N.E.2d 122, 787 N.Y.S.2d 697 (2004).

[147] State v. Irving, 114 N.J. 427, 436-38, 555 A.2d 575, 580-81 (1989) (noting that notice of alibi can be used to cross-examine or rehabilitate defendant's credibility); People v. Ramirez, 208 A.D.2d 384, 617 N.Y.S.2d 17 (1994) (missing witness instruction proper with respect to defendant's wife, who was included in defendant's notice of alibi); People v. Shuff, 168 A.D.2d 348, 564 N.Y.S.2d 132 (1990), *appeal denied*, 77 N.Y.2d 967, 573 N.E.2d 589, 570 N.Y.S.2d 501 (1991) ("defendant's cross-examination on the notice [of alibi] appropriately served to test the defendant's faithfulness to his obligation to testify truthfully."); People v. Whitmore, 123 A.D.2d 336, 506 N.Y.S.2d 231, *appeal denied*, 68 N.Y.2d 919, 501 N.E.2d 613, 508 N.Y.S.2d 1040 (1986).

prosecution may comment and refer to a defendant's statements concerning his whereabouts at or about the time of the crime without necessarily improperly commenting upon the defendant's failure to produce proof. The law concerning such an argument is discussed in § 15.4.

§ 8.39 Preclusion of alibi due to defendant's failure to provide notice.

Courts generally have the power to preclude a defendant from presenting an alibi when the statutory notice has not been provided to the prosecution. Absent extenuating circumstances, it is difficult to find a reasonable excuse in the middle of trial for having failed to give a notice of alibi. In oft-quoted language of the Supreme Court of the United States in *Williams v. Florida*,[148] "given the ease with which an alibi can be fabricated, the State's interest in protecting itself against an eleventh hour defense is both obvious and legitimate" Later, the Supreme Court upheld the right of a trial court to preclude the testimony of defense witnesses when a defendant does not comply with statutory discovery requirements.

> A trial judge may certainly insist on an explanation for a party's failure to comply with a request to identify his or her witnesses in advance of trial. If that explanation reveals that the omission was willful and motivated by desire to obtain a tactical advantage that would minimize the effectiveness of cross-examination and the ability to include rebuttal evidence, it would be entirely consistent with the purposes of the Compulsory Process Clause simply to exclude the witness' testimony.[149]

When there is no reasonable excuse for the delay or failure to file a notice for alibi, the result will be preclusion of the defendant's alibi witnesses. Preclusion is deemed an appropriate remedy, since the prosecution will be forced to disprove the alibi without an adequate opportunity to investigate it.[150] The

---

[148] 399 U.S. 78, 81-82 (1970).

[149] Taylor v. Illinois, 484 U.S. 400, 415 (1988).

[150] Watley v. Williams, 218 F.3d 1156 (10th Cir. 2000), *cert. denied,* 531 U.S. 1089 (2001); Geske v. State, 770 So.2d 252 (Fla. Dist. Ct. App. 2000) (holding trial court properly struck defendant's late notice of alibi); Harrison v. State, 644 N.E.2d 1243, 1254 (Ind. 1995), *cert. denied,* 519 U.S. 933 (1996); People v. Travis, 443 Mich. 668, 677-80, 505 N.W.2d 563 (1993); People v. Watson, 269 A.D.2d 755, 704 N.Y.S.2d 396, *appeal denied,* 95 N.Y.2d 806, 733 N.E.2d 246, 711 N.Y.S.2d 174 (2000) (defendant precluded from introducing alibi defense due to late notice and failure to provide reason for late notice); People v. Parson, 268 A.D.2d 208, 704 N.Y.S.2d 8 (2000), *on recons., appeal denied,* 95 N.Y.2d 837, 735 N.E.2d 424, 713 N.Y.S.2d 144 (2000) ("The court properly exercised its discretion in precluding defendant from eliciting alibi testimony from a witness as to whom a notice of alibi was not served until approximately nine months after service of the People's demand for a notice of alibi, given that defendant would have had sufficient information about the witness, who allegedly was his personal friend and co-worker for years prior to his arrest, at the conception of the case."); People v. Biavaschi, 265 A.D.2d 268, 697 N.Y.S.2d 53 (1999), *appeal denied,* 94 N.Y.2d 916, 729 N.E.2d 1155, 708 N.Y.S.2d 356 (2000); People

late entry of counsel may be insufficient to avoid preclusion, especially if the prosecution is not in a position to adequately investigate the alibi.[151]

There are limits to preclusion, however. If the notice of alibi is given before trial, but the defense has difficulty in locating a witness at time of trial, a reasonable continuance may be afforded.[152] One of the most important limitations upon preclusion is that the defendant himself cannot be precluded from testifying concerning his alibi even if there has not been compliance with the notice of alibi provisions, nor can a defendant's testimony be stricken or a jury charge be given to disregard the defendant's own alibi testimony as a sanction for failing to comply with the notice requirement.[153]

§ 8.40 Cross-examination of the alibi witness.

A good alibi defense is difficult to overcome. However, a poor alibi defense or an effective cross-examination of an alibi witness can provide support to the prosecution's case.

The first point to consider in cross-examining an alibi witness is bias on the part of the witness. This involves an examination of the relationship of the witness

---

v. Himmel, 252 A.D.2d 273, 686 N.Y.S.2d 504, *appeal denied,* 93 N.Y.2d 899, 711 N.E.2d 987, 689 N.Y.S.2d 711 (1999) (upholding trial court's preclusion of defendant's attempt at trial to use his employment records during time period in which one of the incidents is alleged to have occurred since defendant did not file a notice of alibi and was seeking to use such evidence to establish an alibi); People v. Aviles, 234 A.D.2d 466, 652 N.Y.S.2d 48 (1996), *appeal denied,* 89 N.Y.2d 983, 678 N.E.2d 1358, 656 N.Y.S.2d 742 (1997); People v. Rene, 223 A.D.2d 733, 637 N.Y.S.2d 453, *appeal denied,* 87 N.Y.2d 1024, 666 N.E.2d 1071, 644 N.Y.S.2d 157 (1996); People v. Alvarez, 223 A.D.2d 401, 636 N.Y.S.2d 331, *appeal denied,* 88 N.Y.2d 980, 672 N.E.2d 612, 649 N.Y.S.2d 386 (1996); People v. Smith, 208 A.D.2d 965, 618 N.Y.S.2d 577 (1994) (defendant accused of rape and sodomy properly precluded from presenting alibi witnesses on the ground that the defendant did not provide adequate notice nor sufficient reason for failure to comply with notice requirement); People v. Brown, 167 A.D.2d 847, 562 N.Y.S.2d 254 (1990).

[151] People v. Mensche, 276 A.D.2d 834, 714 N.Y.S.2d 377, *appeal denied,* 95 N.Y.2d 966, 745 N.E.2d 404, 722 N.Y.S.2d 484 (2000):

> Although the late entry of defense counsel into the case may provide the required reasonable excuse for delay in service of the notice of alibi here, the tardiness of the notice of alibi prejudiced the People's ability to adequately investigate defendant's claims prior to trial. Further, the tardiness of the service of the notice of alibi was not cured when defendant renewed his application to present the alibi witness based upon his contention that the People had, in fact, interviewed those witnesses, since County Court properly found the notice facially inadequate because it failed to advise the People of the places at which defendant claimed to be at the time of the commission of the crimes, hampering the People's opportunity to thoroughly investigate defendant's claim. Accordingly, County Court's denial of defendant's application to present alibi witnesses was not an abuse of discretion.

[152] People v. Foy, 32 N.Y.2d 473, 299 N.E.2d 664, 346 N.Y.S.2d 245 (1973).

[153] Alicea v. Gagnon, 675 F.2d 913 (7th Cir. 1982); Walker v. Hood, 679 F. Supp. 372, 381 (S.D.N.Y.), *aff'd,* 854 F.2d 1315 (2d Cir. 1988); People v. Hampton, 696 P.2d 765 (Colo. 1985); *Contra* State v. Burroughs, 117 Wis. 2d 293, 344 N.W.2d 149 (1984).

to the defendant. A classic example would be parent or spouse. If the witness is a friend, the nature and extent of that friendship should be explored, including the types of activities the defendant and the friend engage in on a regular basis. Friendship or love can produce a strong desire to assist someone in trouble.

A primary area of inquiry is the point at which the alibi witness first became aware of (1) the charges against the defendant, and (2) the date and time of the crime. Another basic issue to pursue is the *reason* the witness remembers the day and time in question. Was there an unusual event related to the date and time in question? How much time elapsed between the day of the event and date on which the witness was first asked to recall the day of the event? Was the day of the event just a routine day for the witness? For example, if the alibi witness is a fellow employee with whom the defendant works five days a week, and the event occurred on one of those days, why is the witness able to distinguish that day from any other day? If it was an evening and defendant and the witness went out for coffee, how many times a week do the two of them go out for coffee? How many weeks had they been going out for coffee prior to the date in question, and how many weeks after the date in question have they been going out for coffee? To test the witness's memory, inquiry can then be made about details of other dates and times when the witness and defendant went to get coffee.

Also to be explored is when the alibi witness first came forward with the alibi. Did the witness make any effort to inform the police, the grand jury, or the prosecutor's office of the alibi? When did the witness first tell *anyone* about the alibi. When did the witness first realize that he or she was going to be an alibi witness? Some jurisdictions require that a foundation be laid through a hearing outside the presence of the jury before a witness can be cross-examined concerning his or her failure to timely inform law enforcement authorities of exculpatory information such as an alibi.[154] Under this rule, the prosecution should establish the following foundation:

1. That the alibi witness was aware of the charges against the defendant for a sufficient period of time before trial to communicate with investigators or other law enforcement officials;

2. That the alibi witness knew he possessed exculpatory information or helpful information to the defendant;

---

[154] State v. Bryant, 202 Conn. 676, 705–06, 523 A.2d 451–52 (1987); Davis v. State, 344 Md. 331, 686 A.2d 1083 (1996)

We hold that, before the prosecution may cross-examine an alibi witness regarding his or her pretrial silence, it must lay a foundation. The foundation consists of establishing the existence of a relationship between the witness and the defendant, or circumstances, such that it would be the natural response of the witness to act to exonerate the defendant, a relationship and/or circumstances of such a nature that, if the witness possessed evidence exculpating the defendant, he or she would disclose it immediately to law enforcement authorities. This is sufficient to give rise to an apparent inconsistency between the witness's pretrial silence and his or her testimony at trial.

3. That the alibi witness had such a relationship with the defendant that he or she would be reasonably expected to have a motive to help exonerate the defendant;

4. That the alibi witness was capable of or knew how to communicate the alibi information to investigators or law enforcement officials.

After the foundation has been laid, the defense may explain why an alibi witness failed to come forward. Only then "the jury could infer that the witness's pretrial silence is inconsistent with his or her trial testimony."[155]

Some courts do not require the prosecutor to lay any particular foundation before questioning an alibi witness's failure to come forward before trial.[156] This may be true even though the silence was on the advice of counsel.[157] Under this view, unlike those requiring a foundation:

> A witness (unlike a defendant) has no right to refuse to give information to official investigators. Such advice of counsel may help to explain the conduct but does not necessarily remove the inconsistency when it would otherwise be natural for the alibi witness to inform the State's investigators. Thus, the advice of counsel may be a circumstance that would lead the court to limit, rather than discontinue, cross-examination.[158]

An alibi witness should also be asked with whom he discussed the alibi information between the day of the event and the time he first came forward. Contacts between the alibi witness, the defendant, defense investigators, attorneys, and family members should also be explored to develop what has been discussed with respect to the alibi. It should be determined if any efforts were expended to develop or elaborate on an alibi by the defendant or any of his representatives.

Another area of cross-examination of an alibi witness pertains to collateral details concerning the time the witness was with the defendant. This is particularly important if there are multiple alibi witnesses, since this may develop inconsistencies in their stories. Such collateral details would include what was discussed, what people were wearing, the weather, how the event began and ended, etc. Additional collateral details to bring up on cross-examination may be suggested by the alibi witness's testimony on direct examination; however, alibi witnesses tend to provide little detail on direct examination concerning the time spent with the defendant. On the other hand, if there are several alibi witnesses, as each witness testifies, he or she may suggest areas of inquiry for subsequent alibi witnesses.

---

[155] Davis v. State, 344 Md. 331, 346, 686 A.2d 1083, 1090 (1996).

[156] People v. Phillips, 217 Mich. App. 489, 494, 552 N.W.2d 487, 490 (1996), *appeal denied*, 456 Mich. 865, 568 N.W.2d 683 (1997); Hines v. State, 38 S.W.3d 805 (Tex. Ct. App. 2001).

[157] State v. Silva, 131 N.J. 438, 621 A.2d 17 (1993).

[158] *Id.* at 448, 621 A.2d at 22.

§ 8.41 Example of cross-examination of alibi witness.

The following cross-examination of an alibi witness demonstrates several techniques to bring out information described in the preceding section. The alibi witness is the girlfriend of a defendant on trial for rape. Charged also is a female co-defendant. Defendant's girlfriend claims to have been working with the defendant between 5:00 p.m. and 9:00 p.m. on the evening of the rape. Afterward, she claims they went to a supermarket to cash her check and then to a lounge for an hour or so, and then returned to their apartment at about 11:00 p.m. They went to bed at about 2:00 a.m. or 3:00 a.m. The cross-examination begins by having the witness establish that the defendant was associated with the female co-defendant, thus adding to the plausibility that the two defendants would be together at the time of the crime.

Q. How often would you see Jane McBride, the co-defendant?

A. Not very often.

Q. Where would you see her?

A. At my house, or once we went to her house. Sammy and I went to her house.

Q. When you say her house, was that Kathy Davis'?

A. No.

Q. Where was her house?

A. 146 Devon Avenue.

Q. Do you know when it was that you first met Jane McBride?

A. It was after Thanksgiving and I knew that she hadn't been here that long.

Q. And the first time you met her, was she with Sammy White?

A. Sammy White and Diane.

Q. And how many times in the next two to three months would you see her?

A. Not often.

Q. When you say not often, once a month? Once a week?

A. I can just say not often.

In the next area of inquiry, the prosecutor obtains testimony from the witness, who was not married to the defendant when the rape occurred, that during the weeks before the night of the crime, the defendant was not at home with the witness every night.

Q. And you knew Kathy Davis, correct?

A. Yes.

Q. And you knew that Sammy would stay there?

643

A. Yes.

Q. Sammy started staying with you overnight beginning in October, right?

A. And November.

Q. Was it just weekends or were there other nights also?

A. Sometimes he would stay during the week.

In the following, the prosecutor probes the basis for the witness's ability to remember the date in question. The day of the alibi was a Friday, which was the day the witness claims was her payday.

Q. Now, you would work at Acme with Sammy White, correct?

A. Yes.

Q. Was that every day of the week?

A. Every day during the weekday.

Q. So Monday through Friday?

A. Monday through Friday.

Q. And was Sammy White also working Monday through Friday with you?

A. Yes.

Q. And would you have been working Monday through Friday prior to December 14, 1990?

A. Yes.

Q. And when you would go to work, was that at the hospital?

A. Yes.

Q. Was that every day you were doing that week?

A. Yes.

Q. That week?

A. Yes.

Q. And when would you get paid?

A. We got paid on the Friday but some weeks we could get our checks earlier. It depends. But Friday was the payday.

Q. And was the payday different from the date you got your check?

A. I don't understand.

Q. O.K. You would get paid, and there's a date on the check, right?

A. Yes.

Q. Is that the date that you would pick up your check?

A. Yes.

Q. The date on the check?

A. Sometimes.

Q. Do you know if this Friday was the date that you were paid?

A. Right.

Q. Is that correct?

A. Yes.

The following deals with the bias of the alibi witness and her relationship with the defendant. This is a basic area of cross-examination.

Q. Now, you are the girlfriend of the defendant, Sammy White, correct?

A. Yes.

Q. And you love him, correct?

A. Yes.

Q. As his girlfriend, you would help him if he had a problem?

A. Yes.

Another basic area of cross-examination is to establish when the witness was first aware of the charges against the defendant.

Q. You were aware of the charges against Sammy when he was arrested in April, 2001, correct?

A. Yes.

Q. And he told you what those charges were?

A. Yes.

Q. And that was the first time you were aware of the charges against your boyfriend, Sammy?

A. Yes.

The alibi witness is then questioned about the contacts she had with the defendant between the day of the rape and the date of the trial. Discussions between the witness and the defendant concerning the alibi testimony are also established.

Q. Now, you, of course, have seen Sammy at the jail, correct?

A. Yes.

Q. You go up and visit him?

A. Yes.

Q. How many times would you say you have discussed the events of December 14 and 15 with Sammy White?

A. I can't really say how many times.

Q. More than a dozen?

A. Several, I don't know how many.

Q. And you have had a chance to talk to him about the charges, correct?

A. Yes.

Q. Your visits have included discussions about the things you have testified to, correct?

A. Yes.

Q. More than once or twice?

A. Yes.

The prosecutor begins to use the alibi witness's testimony to deal with issues concerning the complainant's description of the defendant. One of the issues in dispute is the defendant's height and weight. In the following, the witness identifies the handwriting of the defendant on an employment application form that lists his height and weight, information that is closer to the description provided by the complainant.

Q. Now, has he written you since then?

A. Yes.

Q. You would recognize his writing if you saw it?

A. Yes.

Q. And it would be fair to say you have seen his writing on more than one or two occasions?

A. Yes.

Q. Showing you People's 35 for identification. Do you recognize the writing on that document?

A. Yes.

Q. Whose writing is it?

A. Sammy's.

Q. And have you filled out a form like that also?

A. Yes. This is an employment application.

Q. And an employment application for Acme, correct?

A. Right.

Q. And you recognize the information under the box that says employment application, under applicant Sammy White — do you see that line that says Sammy White?

A. Yes.

Q. And that appears to you, from your experience, to be the handwriting of Sammy White, correct?

A. Yes.

A. PROSECUTOR: Your Honor, at this time I'm going to offer the information concerning the height and weight of Sammy White.

A. DEFENDANT'S ATTORNEY: I object to that, your Honor. No foundation if it's coming in as a business record.

A. THE COURT: It is coming in as an admission of the defendant.

A. DEFENDANT'S ATTORNEY: He's not testifying and I object to that.

A. THE COURT: It's his handwriting.

A. DEFENDANT'S ATTORNEY: Can I be heard out of the presence of the jury?

A. THE COURT: Come up here.

The following proceedings transpired at the bench out of the hearing of the jury.

Q. THE COURT: Mr. Donald, your objection is based on the fact there is no foundation?

A. DEFENDANT'S ATTORNEY: Yes.

Q. THE COURT: Overruled. Received. When it goes to the jury, it shall be redacted. (People's Exhibit 35 for identification was received and marked in evidence.)

A. PROSECUTOR: Your Honor, can I read the portion of People's 35 that has been admitted?

Q. THE COURT: You may.

A. PROSECUTOR: "Applicant. Sammy White. Height: 5 feet, 9 inches. Weight: 142 pounds."

Q. DEFENDANT'S ATTORNEY: Judge, I object. It's immaterial. We have his height on that photo.

A. THE COURT: Overruled.

The witness is then questioned about details surrounding the alibi, including her claim that the defendant slept for 11 hours after a normal workday.

Q. Now, Mrs. White, can you tell us what time it was that you went to bed on the morning of December 15, 1990?

A. 3 a.m.

Q. And what time do you say that Sammy went to bed on the morning of December 15, 1990?

A. Around 1 a.m.

Q. And what time did you get up on on December 15, 1990?

A. After noon.

Q. Do you know what time in the afternoon?

A. No.

Q. Sometime after 12:00, though, is when you got up?

A. Yes.

Q. And when you got up sometime after noon, was your boyfriend still sleeping in your bed?

A. He was in the bed.

Q. Was he awake?

A. I'm not sure.

Q. But he was in your bed sometime after 12:00, correct?

A. Right.

Q. You, yourself, did not wake up from the time you went to bed, sometime between 1 and 3 and the time you got up after noon, is that correct?

A. Maybe.

Q. Do you have any recollection of having wakened anytime from the moment you went to bed until you got up sometime in the afternoon?

A. No.

Q. Do you have any recollection of Sammy White waking you up at any time from the moment you first went to bed until you got up sometime in the afternoon?

A. No.

Q. So it would be at least 11 hours from the time you say Mr. White went to bed until you saw him get up, is that correct?

A. Correct.

Q. Eleven hours?

A. Yes.

Documentary evidence that contradicts a witness's testimony is an effective technique. Here it is used when the prosecutor returns to cross-examine the witness concerning the reason she is sure of the date in question. This relates to her testimony that the day of the rape was a payday for her. The prosecutor confronts her with her paycheck for that week, which is not dated the day of the crime.

Q. Now, your payday was not December 14, was it?

A. Yes. We got paid on Fridays.

Q. But that's not the day that you are officially paid, is it?

A. Yes.

Q. Is that the date of your check?

A. Yes.

Q. Showing you People's Exhibit 37 for identification. Do you recognize that?

A. Yes; it's a check from Acme.

Q. Is that a paycheck of yours?

A. Yes.

Q. Does that refresh your recollection as to the payday that you had on or, about, or near December 14?

A. I guess it could be. I guess it is.

Q. Well, what was the date of the check you got paid that week?

A. It's dated the 12th.

Q. December 12?

A. December 12; yeah.

Q. Not the 14th?

A. The 14th is not on here.

Q. Is that your endorsement on the back?

A. Yes.

Q. And you went to Safeway to cash it?

A. Yes. Just because the check was dated the 12th — does it say that I cashed it on the 14th?

Q. Does it refresh your recollection looking at the exhibit? If it does —

A. This says that it was processed on the 18th. So I could have — the check could be dated the 12th and I could have cashed it anytime between the 12th and the 18th.

Q. There's no question now as you sit here that the payday that you were given your check was December 14th?

A. You asked me what our payday was and I told you we got paid on Friday. The checks can come in between Tuesday and Friday. We got paid on Friday. If your check is there on Tuesday, you can get it. If your check is there on Wednesday, you can get it. If it's there on Thursday, if you ask for it. Other than that, you get paid on Friday.

In the following, the witness is again questioned about the description of the defendant, the goal being to confirm aspects of the complainant's description.

Q. During the period that you knew Sammy White did you ever see him have different style mustaches?

A. No.

Q. Did you ever see him have a smaller mustache than other times?

649

A. He might trim it around his lip.

Q. Did he have a goatee at one time?

A. Yes.

Q. And there were times he didn't have a goatee, correct?

A. He always had hair on his face.

Q. How about his chin?

A. Not always on his chin but he always had this, (indicating).

Q. Sometimes did he have hair on his chin?

A. When he needed to shave.

Q. Did you ever see him sport a goatee?

A. I told you he always had hair here, (indicating).

Q. You're indicating like where —

A. Here. (Indicating). Sometimes he would let it go here, (indicating).

Q. That's my question. Sometimes he would let it go on the chin, is that correct?

A. Yes.

Q. And then sometimes he would shave it?

A. Well, he would let it go on the chin but that's it. Then he would shave it sometimes. Sometimes he would shave it.

The complainant in this case had been unable to identify the defendant's photograph when it was shown to her with others by investigators. The complainant, however, when asked on cross-examination by the defendant's attorney whether she was able to identify anyone in the courtroom as her assailant, pointed to the defendant and his female co-defendant. (This testimony is set forth in § 8.27 above.) To challenge the in-court identification on cross-examination, the defendant's attorney introduced into evidence the photo array that was shown to the complainant to establish that she had been given the opportunity by the police to identify the defendants, but was unable to do so. The complainant responded on cross-examination that the first time she saw the individuals who assaulted her was that day in the courtroom, and that the defendants in the courtroom were her assailants.

In the following excerpt, the alibi witness is shown the same photograph of the defendant that was displayed to the complainant by the police (and which the complainant was unable to identify). The prosecutor then has the alibi witness establish that she has never seen the defendant look as he does in the photograph and that that is not the way he looked during the month in question. (The photo used by the police in the photo array was taken much earlier than the date of the crime.) Thus the alibi witness bolsters the credibility of the complainant significantly.

650

Q. Looking at Defendant's Exhibit C-6. Do you recognize that person?

A. I've never seen him like that.

Q. You've never seen him like that?

A. No.

Q. So would you agree that the photo — do you recognize that as being Sammy White?

A. Yes. May I see it?

Q. Is that Sammy White?

A. Yes.

Q. Is that the way he looked in December 2000?

A. No.

Q. Is the way he looks today similar to how he looked in December, 2000?

A. Yes.

In the following, the alibi witness is cross-examined on a prior statement to investigators that the defendant had told her that he was with the co-defendant on the night in question and that the defendant had told her that the co-defendant had assaulted and robbed the complainant. In impeaching the witness with this statement, the prosecutor takes time to develop an adequate foundation, establishing that the witness had given the statement freely and voluntarily, and had read and signed it, and that the witness was aware of the crime for which the defendant was charged and the date upon which it was committed.

Q. Now, I think you said you spoke to someone by the name of Peter Carmichael, correct?

A. Right.

Q. And you know what his job is, correct?

A. Right.

Q. His job is as a detective with the Albany Police Department, correct?

A. Yes.

Q. He contacted you in May of 1991, correct?

A. Yes.

Q. And at the time that he contacted you, you knew that he was investigating rape charges against Sammy White, correct?

A. Well, he told me that once. Yes.

Q. You knew that because Detective Carmichael told you that, correct?

A. Yes.

Q. Now, before Detective Carmichael ever contacted you, you were aware that in April 1991 Sammy White had been charged with rape, correct?

A. That's when I first found out.

Q. That's the first time you found out, correct? In April of 2001, correct?

A. Yes.

Q. It was after that Detective Carmichael contacted you, correct?

A. Yes.

Q. It was several weeks after that, correct?

A. Yes.

Q. When you went to see Detective Carmichael you went voluntarily, correct?

A. Yes.

Q. You met him, correct?

A. Yes.

Q. There had been phone calls before you went to the Albany Police Department to give a statement, correct?

A. Yes.

Q. And the questions that Detective Carmichael was asking you had to do with what happened on December 14 and 15, 2000, correct?

A. Yes.

Q. And you knew when Detective Carmichael was questioning you this is what he wanted to know, correct?

A. Yes.

Q. And you told him that the week before December 14 you had a party, correct?

A. A bowling party with my job.

Q. And you told him that, correct?

A. Yes.

Q. And you told him that you would give a statement, correct?

A. Yes.

Q. And you gave Detective Carmichael a sworn statement, correct?

A. Yes.

Q. A statement under oath, correct?

A. Yes. (Document was duly marked People's Exhibit 38 for identification.)

Q. Looking at People's 38 for identification, do you recognize that document?

A. Yes.

Q. Would you review it for a moment, please?

A. Yes.

Q. Have you had a chance to review it?

A. Yes.

Q. Does it have your signature on it?

A. Yes.

Q. Is that the original statement?

A. It looks like it.

Q. Does that have your initials on it at the end of the last typed sentence?

A. Yes.

Q. Those are your initials?

A. Yes.

Q. And do you see Detective Carmichael's name on it?

A. Yes.

Q. You gave him this sworn statement on May 12, 2001, correct?

A. Yes.

Q. At 8:25 a.m., correct?

A. Yes.

Q. And you read it before you signed it, right?

A. Yes.

Q. And do you recall telling Detective Carmichael on May 12, 2001, in a sworn statement, that Sammy told you that Jane McBride and him had been together one night or morning and that they saw this white girl on or around Devon Avenue, and that Jane wanted to get her? Did you say that to Detective Carmichael?

A. It's written down. I don't remember telling him that.

Q. Did you tell Detective Carmichael that Sammy White told you they ended up in a place "unknown to me because Sammy didn't really tell me the details?" Did you say that to Detective Carmichael?

A. If it's here. I don't remember telling him that.

Q. Did you tell Detective Carmichael that Sammy told you this white girl was said to be quite drunk? Did you say that to Detective Carmichael?

A. I guess so.

Q. Did you tell Detective Carmichael that Sammy told you when they got to wherever they took her, Jane began to slap her around and also took some jewelry from her? Did you say that to Detective Carmichael on May 12, 2001?

A. I guess I did.

Q. Did you tell Detective Carmichael a few weeks back after Sammy had initially been arrested, about the rape, sodomy, and unlawful imprisonment, "Sammy came to see me" and you talked about the date these things were supposed to have taken place? Did you say that to Detective Carmichael?

A. I guess I did. It's written here.

Q. Did you tell Detective Carmichael that Sammy White was with you and Bobby Jones, and Cindy Gibson.

A. Yes.

Q. Did you give those names to the defendant's attorney?

A. Yes.

Q. You never gave the name of your daughter as being with you that night, did you?

A. I never gave the name of Cary either when I told the detective that I could remember what we did on Saturday night. I couldn't remember what we did on that Friday night. He told me to call him back when I remembered, and I called him back and I told him.

Q. Did you ever mention the name of your daughter to Detective Carmichael in that statement?

A. No.

Q. Did you ever mention the name of Cary?

A. No. Because I told him about the Saturday night. Not Friday night.

Q. And then it was the weekend of December 8, correct, that you were speaking about?

A. Yes.

Q. And not only had the police given you the date involved but Sammy White had spoken to you about the date, correct?

A. Yes.

Q. You had spoken to Sammy White about what you were doing on the night in question before you even spoke to Detective Carmichael, correct?

A. No.

Q. Didn't you tell Detective Carmichael, in your statement a few weeks back after he had initially been arrested for the rape, robbery, and sodomy, and unlawful imprisonment, Sammy came to see me and we talked about

the date that these things were supposed to have taken place on? Isn't that what you told Detective Carmichael?

A. I might have.

Q. And then you told Detective Carmichael, in your sworn statement, "I really don't remember what happened to Sammy White later that night. I can't honestly say if he stayed over with me or not?" Isn't that what you told Detective Carmichael in May of 2001?

A. Maybe.

Q. Is that what is in your sworn statement?

A. That's what it says.

A. PROSECUTOR: No further questions.

A. REDIRECT EXAMINATION BY DEFENDANT'S ATTORNEY:

Q. When you allegedly gave the statement to Detective Carmichael, this was May 12?

A. That's what it says on the statement.

Q. Did they give you a copy of that statement?

A. No.

Q. What, if anything, did Carmichael tell you where he got that information from?

A. He told me that he knows that Sammy was there and I told him he wasn't. He said yes, he was, and he went on like that a couple of times and then he told me I'm going to get him off the streets because he has too many women.

CHAPTER 9

AIDS AND SEXUAL ASSAULT

§ 9.1 Overview of AIDS and sexual assault.

Increasingly, courts are addressing issues related to the Human Immunodeficiency Virus (HIV), the causative agent of Acquired Immune Deficiency Syndrome (AIDS). Recent legislation has sought to deal with mandated testing of sexual offenders for AIDS, disclosure of results of AIDS testing to victims, and the role of AIDS as a factor in sentencing or dismissal of an indictment.

HIV is generally accepted as being spread in three ways: (1) through sexual contact, (2) through blood or blood products, or (3) from a mother to child during pregnancy or birth. Casual contact has not been shown to transmit HIV, and some courts have acknowledged that HIV cannot be transmitted through saliva.[1] The

---

[1] Thomas v. Atascadero, Unified Sch. Dist., 662 F. Supp. 376, 380 (C.D. Cal. 1986); Glover v. E. Neb. Cmty. Office of Retardation, 686 F. Supp. 243, 249, 251 (D. Neb. 1988), *aff'd*, 867 F.2d 461 (8th Cir.), *cert. denied*, 493 U.S. 932 (1989).

Centers for Disease Control and Prevention (CDC) have concluded that "the potential for salivary transmission of HIV is remote."[2] In one of the first studies of its kind, researchers at the CDC have reported that sexual transmission of the HIV infection among children is not only under-reported and perhaps under-recognized, but also that a link exists between child sexual abuse and HIV.[3] The researchers recommend that health care professionals consider sexual abuse as a possible means of transmission of the virus when a child is diagnosed with the HIV virus.[4]

Controversy over how HIV can be transmitted can be found in appellate review of prosecutions for assault or similar crimes involving biting of the victim by an HIV-infected defendant. While courts have found insufficient evidence in the records before them that HIV is *probably* transmitted by a human bite,[5] and that such transmission has not been established as a "scientific fact,"[6] they have found other reasons, including the theoretical possibility of transmission, to sustain a conviction.[7]

The risk of HIV transmission in sexual assault cases involving a transfer of bodily fluids has been conservatively estimated at two per 1,000 contacts, and

---

[2] U.S. Dept. Of Health AND Human Services, Public Health Service, Centers for Disease Control, Guidelines for; Prevention of Transmission of Human Immunodeficiency Virus and Hepatitis-B Virus to Health-Care and Public-Safety Workers 10 (February 1989).

[3] Mary Lou Lindegren et al., *Sexual Abuse of Children: Intersection with the HIV Epidemic*, 102 Pediatrics E46 (1998).

[4] Mary Lou Lindegren et al., *Sexual Abuse of Children: Intersection with the HIV Epidemic*, 102 Pediatrics E46 (1998).

[5] United States v. Sturgis, 48 F.3d 784 (4th Cir.), *cert. denied*, 516 U.S. 833 (1995) (HIV-infected defendant's teeth qualify as a dangerous weapon); United States v. Moore, 846 F.2d 1163, 1167–68 (8th Cir. 1988) (on a case of biting a corrections officer, the court held that the defendant's mouth and teeth were used as a deadly and dangerous weapon, even though the evidence did not support a finding that defendant's bite could have transmitted AIDS).

[6] Brock v. State, 555 So. 2d 285, 288 (Ala. Crim. App. 1989) (holding there was insufficient evidence of a human bite to cause serious physical injury as defined by law).

[7] Scroggins v. State, 198 Ga. App. 29, 34, 401 S.E.2d 13, 18 (1990)

> [P]eculiar circumstances of this case, including the dearth of scientific knowledge as to the precise ways and means of transmitting this disease, support a finding that, by his deliberately biting another and injecting saliva into the blood stream while knowing he was infected with the AIDS virus, appellant's assault amounted to such wanton and reckless disregard as to whether he might transmit the disease, that the jury could infer a malicious intent, i.e., to murder[.]

State v. Haines, 545 N.E.2d 834, 841 (Ind. Ct. App. 1989) (defendant's belief that he could kill victim was sufficient to support attempted murder charge; "the medical evidence showed that transmission by bites or contact with blood was at least possible, and to a degree that exceeded a merely theoretical or speculative chance"); State v. Smith, 262 N.J. Super. 487, 621 A.2d 493 (1993) (holding that even if a bite cannot transmit AIDS, defendant's belief was sufficient to support attempted murder charge; possibly of transmission sufficient for jury's findings); Weeks v. State, 834 S.W.2d 559 (Tex. Ct. App. 1992) (noting that inconclusiveness of evidence on impossibility of transmitting HIV through saliva was sufficient to support attempted murder charge).

two per 100 or greater risk "if other factors were present, such as violence producing trauma and blood exposure or the presence of inflammatory or ulcerative [sexually transmitted diseases]."[8]

Testimony that the risk of transmission is greatly increased if the HIV-infected person has an open wound lesion, sore, or gum disease in the mouth through which blood can be transferred into the bloodstream of another person adds weight to the argument that a person's bite or spittle is a deadly weapon.[9]

Current testing for HIV detects antibodies created by the immune system in response to HIV; however, while these tests are considered as generally reliable, there is a period of time during which an individual may be infected with, and capable of transmitting the virus yet will produce negative test results. Generally, it is suggested that individuals who are concerned about their HIV status be tested three months and six months after a possible transmission event to determine whether they are positive or negative for the virus. The three-month test would give some indication of whether the virus was contracted prior to the transmission event, and it is generally accepted that the transmission of the virus will be detected within six months. A positive HIV individual will not necessarily transmit the virus in all situations of sexual contact. Vaginal intercourse is less likely to result in the transmission of the virus than anal intercourse, but the possibility still exists.

Individuals may carry HIV without any symptoms. Thus, they may be unaware they have the virus, a fact that may be crucial under certain statutes criminalizing the exposure of another individual to the virus.

Some states have sought to enhance the penalties for individuals who engage in sexual crimes when positive with HIV, while other states have sought to develop new crimes to deal with individuals who commit sexual assault or engage in acts of prostitution when HIV-positive knowledge is an element.

It is still unclear whether post-exposure treatment helps. If treatment is performed, it should be done within one or two hours of exposure. The approximate 30-day treatment of anti-retroviral drugs also produces severe side effects.

§ 9.2 Potentially prejudicial references to AIDS or defendant's HIV status.

One issue is whether a defendant is prejudiced by the jury learning of a defendant's HIV status through newspaper reports, or through the improper introduction of testimony concerning the defendant's HIV status during trial. For example, a complainant's testimony that "I still worry about if I got AIDS from

---

[8] Lawrence O. Gostin et al., *HIV Testing, Counseling, and Prophylaxis After Sexual Assaults,* 271 JAMA 1436, 1437 (1994).

[9] *Scroggins,* 198 Ga. App. at 37, 401 S.E.2d at 20 (1990).

him" may be unduly prejudicial to a defendant.[10] A newspaper story on defendant's infliction of AIDS may be prejudicial depending on jurors' exposure to the article.[11] References by a defendant to a victim about whether or not he has AIDS is not necessarily prejudicial.[12]

Gratuitously suggesting a defendant's HIV status may be prejudicial and reversible.[13] Sometimes the subject of AIDS weaves itself indirectly into a trial, as when a prosecutor makes an unnecessary connection between the AIDS epidemic and the defendant in summation.[14] One court has permitted withholding the identities of victims in an HIV assault case from the jury, although the defendant was given their names.[15]

Another court has permitted a prosecutor to argue the anxiety of a sexual assault victim's awaiting the results of AIDS testing even when there was no proof of AIDS, on the theory that the jury could infer that the complainant would undergo health screens, "particularly in light of the defendant's admission of his attempted sexual liaison with a prostitute."[16] Then, too, referencing a defendant's HIV status may be necessary to support charges of attempted murder or assault with a deadly weapon.[17] In one case, the court upheld the admission of testimony concerning the complainant's post-rape medical efforts to prevent transmission of the AIDS virus, which included the negative side effects and unproven effectiveness of AZT treatment, since this evidence could be relevant to whether the complainant would have consented to unprotected sex with the defendant.[18]

---

[10] State v. Corella, 79 Haw. 255, 900 P.2d 1322 (1995) (noting that on remand trial court should carefully scrutinize relevance of complainant's statement, "I still worry about if I got AIDS from him.").

[11] State v. Degree, 114 N.C. App. 385, 391, 442 S.E.2d 323, 326–27 (1994) (holding that trial juror's exposure to a newspaper story that the defendant had AIDS did not require mistrial where only one juror had seen the article and formed no opinion jeopardizing the defendant's right to a fair trial).

[12] State v. Powers, 163 Vt. 98, 655 A.2d 712 (1994) (admitting into evidence a letter defendant wrote in which he lied about having AIDS was not unfairly prejudicial to defendant on the ground that it was likely to incite irrational fears among the jurors).

[13] *But see* State v. Gray, 958 P.2d 37 (Kan. 1998) (reversing defendant's conviction because of several improper comments of prosecutor, including the suggestion that defendant was infected with HIV); Commonwealth v. Martin, 424 Mass. 301, 676 N.E.2d 451 (1997); State v. Mastracchio, 612 A.2d 698, 702–04 (R.I. 1992) (cross-examining defendant's witness about his positive HIV status not proper, but not reversible in this case). Franklin v. State, 986 S.W.2d 349, 356–57 (Tex. Ct. App. 1999) (upholding prosecution's proof through child protective worker that defendant, his wife, and victim were all HIV-positive on the theory it was circumstantial proof of defendant's guilt), *rev'd on other grounds*, 12 S.W.3d 473 (Tex. Crim. App. 2000).

[14] People v. Fearnot, 200 A.D.2d 583, 606 N.Y.S.2d 288 (1994), *rev'd. on other grounds*.

[15] State v. Ferguson, No. 21329-0-II, 1999 Wash. App. LEXIS 1905 (Nov. 5, 1999), *remanded*, 15 P.3d 1271 (2001).

[16] Harris v. State, 996 S.W.2d 232 (Tex. Ct. App. 1999).

[17] State v. Monk, 132 N.C. App. 248, 511 S.E.2d 332, 338, *review denied*, 350 N.C. 845 (1999).

[18] Parks v. State, 241 Ga. App. 381, 526 S.E.2d 893 (1999).

The sexual assault charge may also be joined with HIV specific charges. One appellate court has also held that an HIV charge need not be severed from other charges because of undue prejudice particularly where a complainant's knowledge of a defendant's HIV status is relevant to the issue of consent. [19]

How AIDS defendants are treated in the courtroom raises issues of prejudice also. [20] Separating an HIV-infected defendant from his attorney and placing him in leg irons and telling jurors they may not examine articles of clothing without gloves because they may not be safe is not necessarily prejudicial in the eyes of the Supreme Judicial Court of Massachusetts. [21] The court noted defense counsel's lack of objection to some of the judge's conduct, and that a cautionary instruction could have brought further attention to the AIDS issue. [22] The court suggested that if it appears AIDS will be an issue in the trial, the court should allow full voir dire on the issue. [23] In that case, the court also held that the complainant's testimony that the defendant told her he had tested HIV positive and had AIDS may be admissible and relevant to the complainant's fear and consent.

The prejudicial nature of any testimony referencing AIDS may require a limiting instruction. A defendant's conviction was reversed when the prosecution introduced evidence that the defendant stated he was HIV-positive but did not allow the defendant to rebut that statement with test results showing him to be HIV-negative. [24] The evidence of defendant's statement that he was HIV-positive was offered ostensibly to show defendant's motive for the rape. However, the court noted that the prejudicial effect of a statement that the defendant was HIV-positive outweighed its probative value. [25]

---

[19] People v. Dembry, 91 P.3d 431 (Colo. Ct. App. 2003) (ruling trial court did not abuse its discretion when it denied defendant's motion for severance of attempted manslaughter and sexual assault charges on the basis that the jury heard highly prejudicial evidence of his HIV status); State v. Deal, 319 S.C. 49, 459 S.E.2d 93 (1995).

[20] Johnson v. State, 699 N.E.2d 746, 750 (Ind. Ct. App. 1998) (providing jury with rubber gloves not necessarily prejudicial to defendant since "jurors might well be uncomfortable or unwilling to examine, without protection, items which allegedly contain his bodily fluids," and rubber gloves "may have been offered to protect the evidence itself"). *But see* Wiggins v. State, 315 Md. 232, 554 A.2d 356, 359–62 (1989) (improper for judge to provide jurors with rubber gloves during trial since it suggested defendant had AIDS).

[21] Johnson v. State, 699 N.E.2d 746 (Ind. Ct. App. 1998) (it was reasonable to provide jury with rubber gloves to handle sexual assault evidence); Commonwealth v. Martin, 424 Mass. 301, 676 N.E.2d 451 (1997); State v. Monk, 132 N.C. App. 248, 511 S.E.2d 332, 338, *review denied*, 350 N.C. 845, 539 S.E.2d 1 (1999) (trial court's decision to permit jurors to wear rubber gloves while handling evidence in trial where proof of defendant's HIV status was presented was found to be "proper exercise of 'reasonable control' over the presentation of evidence").

[22] Commonwealth v. Martin, 424 Mass. 301, 676 N.E.2d 451 (1997).

[23] Commonwealth v. Martin, 424 Mass. 301, 306, 676 N.E.2d 451, 455 (1997).

[24] Yazid Abunaaj v. Commonwealth, 28 Va. App. 47, 502 S.E.2d 135 (1998).

[25] *Id.* at 57, 502 S.E.2d at 140.

The fact that a defendant is suffering from a life-threatening disease, i.e., he is HIV positive, does not open the door to questioning on that fact on the theory that this is evidence that the defendant intended to commit the crime for which he was charged because he had nothing to lose by committing them in the absence of any evidence to support that theory.[26]

Even a victim's HIV-positive condition has been withheld from the jury on the grounds that its highly prejudicial effect outweighs any probative value. A rape victim's HIV status is protected under Arkansas' rape-shield statute because: "[w]hile it is possible to contract HIV through blood transfusions or other means, the public generally views it as a sexually-transmitted disease. In the minds of the jurors, evidence that [the victim] was HIV-positive would be tantamount to evidence of her prior sexual behavior."[27]

§ 9.3   AIDS as a factor in bail.

A defendant's HIV status can be a factor in arguing for reduced bail or release on recognizance, since AIDS is generally considered fatal, and depending on the stage of the illness, the defendant may be greatly restricted in physical movement. Many jurisdictions that must sustain the financial burden of treating inmates prefer that inmates with serious diseases such as AIDS be released to avoid the financial pressure on the correctional institution. A defendant with AIDS also may argue that his health status provides additional incentive to remain in contact with friends and family.

A defendant who wishes to raise the AIDS issue as a bail consideration must deal with the reality that doing so publicizes his disease. Bail proceedings are generally a matter of public record and are held in open court. It is possible that an argument may be made for the limited closure of a bail proceeding prior to raising this issue.[28]

Under its statute requiring HIV testing of sexual-offenders, Missouri orders a court to include as part of a defendant's pretrial release a bond amount that "shall be sufficient to cover the cost of any post-trial HIV testing ordered by the court."[29] Missouri requires that a sexual offender pay for the cost of HIV testing, which is taxed to the defendant as costs in the criminal proceeding.[30]

The prosecution, however, may wish to use the AIDS argument in denying a defendant's right to bail. Here the prosecutor may argue that an HIV-positive

---

[26] People v. Felix-Torres, 281 A.D.2d 649, 721 N.Y.S.2d 415 (2001), *remanded on other grounds* (Trial court allowed prosecution to question defendant whether he had a life-threatening disease. If defendant replied, "No," prosecution was to be allowed to ask the defendant if he is HIV positive. While error, it was harmless in this case, but remand was necessary to resolve an issue relating to the failure to disclose certain reports).

[27] Fells v. State, 2005 Ark. LEXIS 246 at *7 (Apr. 21, 2005).

[28] *See* § 2.2.

[29] Mo. Rev. Stat. § 191.663.

[30] *Id.*

person has a greater incentive to flee or that the possibility of HIV transmission increases the seriousness of the offense. A prosecutor also may claim that an AIDS test be conducted as a prerequisite for release on bail, although at least one court has rejected this as a prerequisite,[31] and it would appear difficult to sustain this as a justifiable bail criterion.

§ 9.4 Issues in the application of traditional assault statutes to criminalize sexual conduct by HIV-positive individuals.

Apart from specific statutes dealing with HIV-infected persons engaging in sexual relations, some prosecutions based on an individual's HIV status utilize traditional assault crimes and theories. Some of the issues on use of traditional assault statutes involve intent, causation, the likelihood of serious physical injury or death from the behavior, and the definition of dangerous instrument or deadly weapon.

Some assault prosecutions have an element of a deadly weapon. The teeth or mouth have been held to be a dangerous instrument or deadly weapon.[32] However, some jurisdictions hold that teeth are not a dangerous instrument, even when the defendant is HIV-positive.[33] A hypodermic needle may be a dangerous instrument when a defendant threatens his victim with the needle and states that it contains the deadly HIV virus, regardless of whether the prosecution can prove the existence of the HIV virus in the needle.[34] A penis and bodily fluids in a sexual assault prosecution involving an HIV-infected person can be deadly weapons.[35]

Some sexual assault prosecutions have included some form of reckless endangerment charge that alleges that a defendant engaged in reckless conduct

---

[31] People ex rel. Glass v. McGreevy, 134 Misc. 2d 1085, 1086, 514 N.Y.S.2d 622, 623 (1987). ("The County Court here has effectively denied bail to the petitioner by requiring a negative 'AIDS' test as a condition to release on bail. . . . The court finds it was improper and an abuse of discretion . . . to impose a condition of a negative AIDS test prior to release on bail.").

[32] United States v. Sturgis, 48 F.3d 784 (4th Cir.), cert. denied, 516 U.S. 833 (1995) (HIV-infected defendant's teeth qualify as a dangerous weapon); United States v. Moore, 846 F.2d 1163, 1167–68 (8th Cir. 1988) (in a case of biting a corrections officer, the court held that the defendant's mouth and teeth were used as a deadly and dangerous weapon, even though the evidence did not support a finding that defendant's bite could have transmitted AIDS).

[33] Brock v. State, 555 So. 2d 285 (Ala. Crim. App. 1989) (reversing conviction of first-degree assault when an HIV-positive defendant bit a prison official because there was no evidence presented at trial that HIV can be transmitted through a human bite); State v. Bachelor, 6 Neb. Ct. App. 426, 575 N.W.2d 625 (1998); People v. Owusu, 93 N.Y.2d 398, 712 N.E.2d 1228, 690 N.Y.S.2d 863 (1999). See also Carlton D. Stansbury, Deadly and Dangerous Weapons and AIDS: The Moore Analysis is Likely to be Dangerous, 74 Iowa L. Rev. 951 (1989).

[34] State v. Ainis, 317 N.J. Super. 127, 721 A.2d 329 (1998); People v. Nelson, 215 A.D.2d 782, 627 N.Y.S.2d 412 (1995).

[35] State v. Monk, 132 N.C. App. 248, 511 S.E.2d 332, 335–36, review denied, 350 N.C. 845 (1999); Najera v. State, 955 S.W.2d 698 (Tex. Ct. App. 1997).

that placed a victim at risk of physical injury by knowingly engaging in relations when the defendant was aware of his HIV status.[36] A defendant stating to someone he has AIDS and then biting that person supports an inference the defendant intended to infect his victim with a deadly disease.[37] The defendant's knowledge of his HIV status can also be shown through his statements to third parties, and such disclosures to third persons can be a waiver of the defendant's medical condition, authorizing the prosecution to gain access to the defendant's confidential medical records.[38]

A defendant may be convicted of assault in the first degree for attempting to kill his child or cause physical injury by infecting him with the HIV virus.[39] The defendant's threats are relevant to establishing the intent to injure the potential victim.[40]

---

[36] Hancock v. Commonwealth, 998 S.W.2d 496 (Ky. Ct. App. 1998) (defendant convicted of wanton endangerment for exposing victim to HIV or AIDS). People v. Hawkrigg, 138 Misc. 2d 764, 525 N.Y.S.2d 752 (1988).

[37] Hall v. Commonwealth, 1997 Va. App. LEXIS 782 at *6 (Va. Ct. App. Dec. 30, 1997).

[38] *Hawkrigg, above* note 36. *See also* People v. Dempsey, 242 Ill. App. 3d 568, 610 N.E.2d 208 (1993) (defendant's conviction for knowing the transmission of HIV virus raised issues of privilege, but any error was harmless since defendant's knowledge was established through other witnesses). The court noted:

> Dr. Hyde's testimony regarding defendant's medical condition and treatment was essentially cumulative to that given by defendant's mother and sister and by the defendant himself. Defendant's mother testified for the State that upon returning to Marion, defendant's blood was tested for HIV. The mother was present in Dr. Hyde's office when Dr. Hyde informed defendant that he was infected with HIV and prescribed medication for the condition. Defendant cross-examined the mother at length about defendant's treatment with Dr. Hyde. One of defendant's sisters testified in the defendant's case that defendant was treated by Dr. Hyde and that defendant had frequent blood tests performed. The sister was present on two separate occasions when Dr. Hyde explained to defendant that his blood tests indicated he was positive for HIV. She testified that defendant had been prescribed AZT, a drug commonly prescribed for HIV. Finally, defendant himself testified to his medical condition and his treatment by Dr. Hyde. Defendant gave blood samples to be tested for HIV. Defendant was advised that the first blood test had been positive for HIV. Defendant was advised that he was infected with HIV. Defendant was prescribed AZT to fight the infection. Defendant knew that AZT was prescribed to people infected with HIV. Dr. Hyde never told defendant that he was cured.

Id. at 593–94, 610 N.E.2d at 224.

[39] State v. Stewart, 18 S.W.3d 75 (Mo. Ct. App. 2000) (upholding conviction of phlebotomist with access to HIV virus who injected son with HIV virus to avoid child support).

[40] *Id.* The *Stewart* court noted:

> Defendant said [to the child's mother], 'I told you that when I leave, I'm going to leave for good and I'm not going to leave any loose ends or ties behind.' Defendant said, 'you won't need to look me up for child support anyway because your child is not going to live that long.' Mother asked what Defendant meant by that and he replied, 'don't worry about it. I just know that he is not going to live to see the age

A major issue in many assault statutes is the element that the act would be likely to produce "great bodily injury," "serious physical injury," or similar level of injury. One California appellate court found no likelihood of infection when there is evidence in the trial record to support an inference that "one or two individual incidents of unprotected sex between an HIV-positive male and an uninfected female would result in transmission of HIV to the female."[41] Other courts have noted the importance of addressing the probability of injury in evaluating risk of serious physical injury.[42]

Usually, but not always, successful assault based convictions require showing that the defendant was a known carrier of the HIV virus.[43]

Spitting has been held to possibly transmit HIV and thus support an attempted murder charge when there is testimony in the records to support this theory.[44] Biting, as well as spitting, has also been held to pose a sufficient risk of injury to uphold either a reckless endangerment or assault-based conviction.[45] A defendant's statement to a victim during an encounter that "I'm HIV positive, let go of me, let go of me" supports a felony menacing charge even if the victim is not sure if the statement is a threat, warning, or ruse, since the focus of the

---

of five.' Defendant said that if Mother tried to find him, he could have her taken care of and that nobody would be able to trace it back to him.

18 S.W.3d at 83.

[41] Brock v. State, 555 So. 2d 285, 287–88 (Ala. Crim. App. 1989) (reversing defendant's conviction for assault when there was no proof about likelihood of HIV transmission); Guevara v. Superior Court, 62 Cal. App. 4th 864, 869, 73 Cal. Rptr. 2d 421 (1998) (court cited medical journal articles that stated that risk of HIV transmission through unprotected vaginal intercourse is fairly low).

[42] State v. Smith, 902 S.W.2d 313 (Mo. Ct. App. 1995) (defendant was charged with felonious restraint which included the element of exposing a person to a substantial risk of serious physical injury. However, the prosecution offered no evidence that the defendant had the AIDS virus and there was no proof that the defendant could have passed a virus on to the victim; court noted that it was important in a felonious restraint prosecution to emphasize the ability of the defendant to inflict a particular injury).

[43] Commonwealth v. Brown, 413 Pa. Super. 421, 605 A.2d 429 (1992) (upholding aggravated assault conviction of HIV-infected inmate who flung fecal material at guard); Weeks v. State, 834 S.W.2d 559, 562–65 (Tex. Ct. App. 1992), subsequent appeal sub nom., Weeks v. Scott, 55 F.3d 1059 (5th Cir. Tex. 1995) (upholding attempted murder conviction of HIV-infected inmate who spat in face of guard).

[44] Weeks v. Scott, 55 F.3d 1059 (5th Cir. Tex. 1995). See also State v. Haines, 545 N.E.2d 834, 839–41 (Ind. Ct. App. 1989) (holding attempted murder charge improperly dismissed since there was more than speculative chance that HIV could be transmitted through biting, or contact with blood; all that state had to prove was that defendant did all that he believed necessary to brag about intended result).

[45] Burk v. State, 223 Ga. App. 530, 478 S.E.2d 416 (1996) (upholding conviction of defendant who bit police officer knowing he was HIV-positive and had AIDS); Scroggins v. State, 198 Ga. App. 29, 401 S.E.2d 13 (1990) (upholding defendant's conviction for assault and assault with intent to murder for biting a police officer); State v. Haines, 545 N.E.2d 834 (Ind. Ct. App. 1989) (upholding attempted murder conviction of defendant who spit, bit, scratched, and threw blood at a police officer while knowing he was HIV-positive).

crime is the defendant's intent, not the victim's actual reaction.[46] The likelihood of serious injury or harm in an HIV-infected person engaging in sexual contact need only be more than speculative or a remote possibility to support an assault-based charge.[47]

The United States Court of Appeals for the Armed Forces takes the position that an HIV-infected servicemember engaging in unprotected sex is likely to produce "death or grievous bodily harm" and be guilty of an aggravated assault.[48] In such a prosecution for engaging in unprotected sexual intercourse while infected with the HIV virus, the prosecution need not prove that the complainant was aware of the defendant's infection, and the complainant's consent to sexual relations is not a defense since the consent is not to the risk of infection.[49]

The issue of causation is tied to the element of intent in a prosecution such as attempted murder. Maryland's highest court in *Smallwood v. State* holds that a defendant's HIV-positive status alone is insufficient evidence to convict a defendant of attempted murder in connection with a rape case — there must be a specific intent to kill.[50] Before an intent to kill may be inferred based solely upon the defendant's exposure of a victim to a risk of death, it must be shown that the victim's death would have been a natural and probable result of the defendant's conduct. It is for this reason that a trier of fact may infer that a defendant possessed an intent to kill when firing a deadly weapon at a vital part of the human body.

The Maryland court noted death by AIDS is clearly one natural possible consequence of exposing someone to a risk of HIV infection, even on a single occasion. It is less clear that death by AIDS from that single exposure is a sufficiently probable result to provide the sole support for an inference that the person causing the exposure intended to kill the person who was exposed. The Maryland court in *Smallwood* noted that while the risk to which Smallwood his victims when he forced them to engage in unprotected sexual activity must not be minimized, the State presented no evidence from which it can reasonably be concluded that death by AIDS is a probable result of Smallwood's actions to the same extent that death is the probable result of firing a deadly

---

[46] People v. Shawn, 107 P.3d 1033, 1035 (Colo. Ct. App. 2004), *cert. denied*, 2005 Colo. LEXIS 55 (Jan. 31, 2005).

[47] United States v. Weatherspoon, 49 M.J. 209 (C.A.A.F. 1998).

[48] United States v. Bygrave, 46 M.J. 491 (C.A.A.F. 1997).

[49] *Id. See also* United States v. Schoolfield, 40 M.J. 132 (C.M.A. 1994), *cert. denied*, 513 U.S. 1178 (1995) (In *Schoolfield,* the United States Court of Military Appeals upheld defendant's conviction for assault based on a theory of criminal liability that the defendant (HIV positive) assaulted his victims by intentionally having unprotected sex with them. The court also held that a specific intent to infect the victim with the HIV virus or expose her to it was not required, only "a general intent to have unprotected sexual intercourse." *Id.* at 136); State v. Hinkhouse, 139 Or. App. 446, 912 P.2d 921 (1996) (upholding defendant's conviction for attempted murder for engaging in unprotected intercourse with several individuals).

[50] Smallwood v. State, 343 Md. 97, 680 A.2d 512 (1996).

weapon at a vital part of someone's body. Without such evidence, it concluded that death by AIDS was not sufficiently probable to support an inference that Smallwood intended to kill his victims in the absence of other evidence indicative of an intent to kill.[51]

It noted that other jurisdictions' decisions supporting such a prosecution had such additional evidence, such as statements of the defendant relevant to intent. Thus, a defendant's statement of intent to kill and stabbing the victim with a needle, coupled with expert testimony on the likelihood of HIV transmission, may support an attempted murder charge.[52]

When the victim is infected with the HIV virus from the defendant, then a prosecution based on the element of causing serious bodily injury is sustainable.[53] Such prosecutions can raise the issue of causation, that is, whether the victim may have had sexual relations with another person infected with HIV.[54] Prosecutions based on actually producing an HIV infection will open the door to an exploration of the complainant's sexual history to possibly explain the positive medical findings. (*See* §§ 5.34–35.) Convicting an HIV-negative person of assaultive behavior for telling his biting victim that he has AIDS is not possible where a statute requires acting knowingly since there would be insufficient evidence to establish that the defendant intentionally attempted to cause physical injury with an intent to pass the HIV infection when the defendant never had the infection and the victim never contracted the disease.[55] "Absent the disease being demonstrated, the knowledge element of the offense is lacking," held the appellate court.[56] Another issue in the prosecution of individuals for "attempted extreme indifference murder" is the defendant's mental state. For example, an HIV-positive sex offender's conviction for attempted "extreme indifference murder" for engaging in unprotected sex with his step-daughter, even though he knew he was HIV-positive, was reversed because in the view of one court the crime of extreme indifference murder applies only to indiscriminate killings and not a crime which is directed against a specific person.[57]

---

51 *Id.* at 105–107, 680 A.2d at 516.

52 *See also* State v. Schmidt, 771 So. 2d 131 (La. Ct. App. 2000), *cert. denied*, 535 U.S. 905 (2002) (upholding defendant physician's attempted murder conviction based on evidence he injected his girlfriend with HIV virus); State v. Caine, 652 So. 2d 611 (La. Ct. App.), *cert. denied*, 661 So. 2d 1358 (1995) (defendant's attempted murder conviction upheld when proof established that defendant stabbed victim with a needle attached to syringe with a clear liquid and stated to her that he would "give" her AIDS. Although the syringe was not found, "there was a stray possibility that the needle was infected with the virus since the defendant is infected with the HIV virus," and the defendant's body indicated repeated needle usage. Expert testimony established that contact between needle and victim was sufficient to infect her with the HIV virus).

53 Zule v. State, 802 S.W.2d 28 (Tex. Ct. App. 1990).

54 *Id.* at 33.

55 State v. Reif-Hill, No. 72864, 1998 Ohio App. LEXIS 5404 (Nov. 12, 1998), *appeal denied*, 85 Ohio St. 3d 1440, 708 N.E.2d 208 (1999).

56 *Id.* at *10.

57 People v. Perez, 972 P.2d 1072 (Colo. Ct. App. 1998), *cert. denied*, No. 98SC752, 1999 Colo. LEXIS 200 (Mar. 1, 1999).

§ 9.5 Special statutes targeting sexual relations by persons infected with HIV.

Some states have sought to develop specific crimes for persons who engage in sexual acts when infected with HIV. One issue in many of these statutes is establishing that the defendant is aware of his or her HIV status. Most of the statutes set forth a requirement that the defendant know of his HIV status. Another issue is whether such statutes criminalize protected behavior such as consensual relations between adults who have full knowledge of the risks and consequences of their actions. Some statutes have been amended to permit relations between individuals with knowledge and consent of a person's HIV status. [58]

Under a representative statute, it has been held that a "grave and unjustifiable risk" of transmitting the disease exists even if the victim remains uninfected. [59] The statistical risk of infection is not pivotal; it is the seriousness of the consequences. [60] The courts in Tennessee, Washington, and Louisiana have also followed this line of reasoning when rejecting an HIV-positive defendant's claim that the statute requires the actual transfer of or contact with bodily fluids. The word "exposure" has been interpreted broadly to require only that the victim was subjected to a risk of contact. [61] The constitutionality of such a statute has been upheld. [62] Among the special state statutes for criminal sexual activity by individuals afflicted with the HIV virus:

Ark. Code Ann. § 5-14-123:

(b) A person commits the offense of exposing another to human immunodeficiency virus if the person knows he or she has tested positive for human immunodeficiency virus and exposes another person to human immunodeficiency virus infection through the parenteral transfer of blood or blood products or engages in sexual penetration with another person without first having informed the other person of the presence of human immunodeficiency virus.

Cal. Health & Safety Code § 120291:

(a) Any person who exposes another to the human immunodeficiency virus (HIV) by engaging in unprotected sexual activity when the infected person

---

[58] Mo. Rev. Stat. § 191.677.1(2).

[59] State v. Bowens, 964 S.W.2d 232 (Mo. Ct. App. 1998).

[60] *Id.* at 237.

[61] State v. Roberts, 844 So. 2d 263 (La. 2003) (upholding defendant's conviction of intentional exposure to AIDS virus when the prosecution proved a rape occurred even though no seminal fluid was found during the rape kit examination); State v. Bonds, 2005 Tenn. Crim. App. LEXIS 1043 at *22 (Sept. 22, 2005) (concluding "the word 'exposure' requires something less than actual contact with bodily fluids"); State v. Stark, 66 Wash. App. 423, 435, 832 P.2d 109 (1992) (finding "expose" to mean "engaging in conduct that can cause another person to become infected with the virus").

[62] State v. Mahan, 971 S.W.2d 307 (Mo. 1998) (holding such language to not be unconstitutionally broad).

knows at the time of the unprotected sex that he or she is infected with HIV, has not disclosed his or her HIV-positive status, and acts with the specific intent to infect the other with HIV, is guilty of a felony punishable by imprisonment in the state prison for three, five, or eight years. Evidence that the person had knowledge of his or her HIV-positive status, without additional evidence, shall not be sufficient to prove specific intent.

(b) As used in this section, the following definitions shall apply:

(1) "Sexual activity" means insertive vaginal or anal intercourse on the part of an infected male, receptive consensual vaginal intercourse on the part of an infected woman with a male partner, or receptive consensual anal intercourse on the part of an infected man or woman with a male partner.

(2) "Unprotected sexual activity" means sexual activity without the use of a condom.

(c) (1) When alleging a violation of subdivision (a), the prosecuting attorney or grand jury shall substitute a pseudonym for the true name of the victim involved. The actual name and other identifying characteristics of the victim shall be revealed to the court only in camera, and the court shall seal that information from further revelation, except to defense counsel as part of discovery.

(2) All court decisions, orders, petitions, and other documents, including motions and papers filed by the parties, shall be worded so as to protect the name or other identifying characteristics of the victim from public revelation.

(3) Unless the victim requests otherwise, a court in which a violation of this section is filed shall, at the first opportunity, issue an order that the parties, their counsel and other agents, court staff, and all other persons subject to the jurisdiction of the court shall make no public revelation of the name or any other identifying characteristics of the victim.

(4) As used in this subdivision, "identifying characteristics" includes, but is not limited to, name or any part thereof, address or any part thereof, city or unincorporated area of residence, age, marital status, relationship to defendant, and race or ethnic background.

Fla. Stat. § 384.24:

(2) It is unlawful for any person who has human immunodeficiency virus infection, when such person knows he or she is infected with this disease and when such person has been informed that he or she may communicate this disease to another person through sexual intercourse, to have sexual intercourse with any other person, unless such other person has been informed of the presence of the sexually transmissible disease and has consented to the sexual intercourse.

Ga. Code Ann. § 16-5-60:

Reckless conduct causing harm to or endangering the bodily safety of another; conduct by HIV infected persons.

669

. . .

(c) A person who is an HIV infected person who, after obtaining knowledge of being infected with HIV:

(1) knowingly engages in sexual intercourse or performs or submits to any sexual act involving the sex organs of one person and the mouth or anus of another person and the HIV infected person does not disclose to the other person the fact of that infected person's being an HIV infected person prior to that intercourse or sexual act;

. . .

(3) offers or consents to perform with another person an act of sexual intercourse for money without disclosing to that other person the fact of that infected person's being an HIV infected person prior to offering or consenting to perform that act of sexual intercourse;

(4) solicits another person to perform or submit to an act of sodomy for money without disclosing to that other person the fact of that infected person's being an HIV infected person prior to soliciting that act of sodomy is guilty of a felony and, upon conviction thereof, shall be punished by imprisonment for not more than ten years.

Idaho Code § 39-601:

It shall be unlawful for anyone infected with [venereal diseases that include HIV and AIDS] to knowingly expose another person to the infection of such diseases.

Idaho Code § 39-608:

Transfer of body fluid which may contain the HIV virus — Punishment — Definitions — Defenses

(1) Any person who exposes another in any manner with the intent to infect or, knowing that he or she is or has been afflicted with acquired immunodeficiency syndrome (AIDS), AIDS related complexes (ARC), or other manifestations of human immunodeficiency virus (HIV) infection, transfers, or attempts to transfer any of his or her body fluid, body tissue, or organs to another person is guilty of a felony and shall be punished by imprisonment in the state prison for a period not to exceed fifteen (15) years, by fine not in excess of five thousand dollars ($5,000), or by both such imprisonment and fine.

(2) Definitions. As used in this section:

(a) "Body fluid" means semen (irrespective of the presence of spermatozoa), blood, saliva, vaginal secretion, breast milk, and urine.

(b) "Transfer" means engaging in sexual activity by genital-genital contact, oral-genital contact, anal-genital contact; or permitting the use of a hypodermic syringe, needle, or similar device without sterilization; or giving, whether or not for value, blood, semen, body tissue, or organs to a person, blood bank, hospital, or other medical care facility for purposes of transfer to another person.

(3) Defenses:

(a) Consent. It is an affirmative defense that the sexual activity took place between consenting adults after full disclosure by the accused of the risk of such activity.

(b) Medical advice. It is an affirmative defense that the transfer of body fluid, body tissue, or organs occurred after advice from a licensed physician that the accused was noninfectious.

Ill. Comp. Stat. ch. 720, 5/12-16.2:

Criminal Transmission of HIV.

(a) A person commits criminal transmission of HIV when he or she, knowing that he or she is infected with HIV:

(1) engages in intimate contact with another;

. . .

(c) Nothing in this Section shall be construed to require that an infection with HIV has occurred in order for a person to have committed criminal transmission of HIV.

Ind. Code § 35-42-2-6:

Battery by body waste.

(a) As used in this section, "corrections officer" includes a person employed by:

(1) the department of correction;

(2) a law enforcement agency; or

(3) a county jail; or

(4) a circuit, superior, county, probate, city or town court.

(b) As used in this section, "human immunodeficiency virus (HIV)" includes acquired immune deficiency syndrome (AIDS) and AIDS related complex.

(c) A person who knowingly or intentionally in a rude, insolent, or angry manner places blood or another body fluid or waste on a law enforcement officer or a corrections officer identified as such and while engaged in the performance of official duties or coerces another person to place blood or another body fluid or waste on the law enforcement officer or corrections officer commits battery by body waste, a Class D felony. However, the offense is:

(1) a Class C felony if the person knew or recklessly failed to know that the blood, bodily fluid, or waste was infected with:

(A) hepatitis B;

(B) HIV; or

(C) Tuberculosis.

(3) a Class A felony if:

(A) the person knew or recklessly failed to know that the blood, bodily fluid, or waste was infected with HIV; and

(B) the offense results in the transmission of HIV to the other person.

Iowa Code § 709C.1:

Provides for the criminal transmission of HIV virus if a person, knowing that the person's HIV status is positive, engages in intimate contact with another, transfers, donates, or provides blood or bodily fluids. Also, the statute criminalizes dispensing, delivering, exchanging, or selling non-sterile intravenous or intramuscular drug paraphernalia previously used by the HIV-infected person. It is an affirmative defense that the person exposed consented to the exposure.

Ky. Rev. Stat. Ann. § 510.320:

(2) A defendant charged with an offense pursuant to this chapter, which has sexual intercourse or deviate sexual intercourse as an element, or has sexual contact as an element when the circumstances of the case demonstrate a possibility of transmission of human immunodeficiency virus, shall upon initial court appearance on the charge, be informed by the judge of the availability of human immunodeficiency virus testing. The judge shall also notify the victim of the offense, or parent or guardian of the victim, that the defendant has been so notified.

(3) When a defendant has been convicted of any offense in subsection (2) of this section, other provisions of law to the contrary notwithstanding, the sentencing court, regardless of any prior human immunodeficiency virus test, shall order the defendant to undergo a human immunodeficiency virus test, under the direction of the Cabinet for Health and Family Services.

La. Rev. Stat. § 14:43.5:

Intentional Exposure to AIDS Virus.

A. No person shall intentionally expose another to any acquired immunodeficiency syndrome (AIDS) virus through sexual contact without the knowing and lawful consent of the victim.

B. No person shall intentionally expose another to any acquired immunodeficiency syndrome (AIDS) virus through any means or contact without the knowing and lawful consent of the victim.

C. No person shall intentionally expose a police officer to any AIDS virus through any means or contact without the knowing and lawful consent of the police officer when the offender has reasonable grounds to believe the victim is a police officer acting in the performance of his duty.

D. For purposes of this Section, the following words have the following meanings:

(1) "Means or contact" is defined as spitting, biting, stabbing with an AIDS contaminated object, or throwing of blood or other bodily substances.

Md. Code Ann. § 18-601.1:

Exposure of other individuals — By individual with human immunodeficiency virus.

(a) Prohibited act. — An individual who has the human immunodeficiency virus may not knowingly transfer or attempt to transfer the human immunodeficiency virus to another individual.

(b) Penalty. — A person who violates the provisions of this section is guilty of a misdemeanor and on conviction is subject to a fine not exceeding $2,500 or imprisonment not exceeding three years or both.

Mich. Comp. Laws § 333.5210:

Sexual penetration as felony; definition.

Sec. 5210. (1) A person who knows that he or she has or has been diagnosed as having acquired immunodeficiency syndrome or acquired immunodeficiency syndrome related complex, or who knows that he or she is HIV infected, and who engages in sexual penetration with another person without having first informed the other person that he or she has acquired immunodeficiency syndrome or acquired immunodeficiency syndrome related complex, or is HIV infected, is guilty of a felony.

(2) As used in this section, "sexual penetration" means sexual intercourse, cunnilingus, fellatio, anal intercourse, or any other intrusion, however slight, of any part of a person's body or of any object into the genital or anal openings of another person's body, but emission of semen is not required.

Mo. Rev. Stat. § 191.677:

It shall be unlawful for any individual knowingly infected with HIV to:

(1) Be or attempt to be a blood, blood products, organ, sperm, or tissue donor, except as deemed necessary for medical research; or

(2) Act in a reckless manner by exposing another person to HIV without the knowledge and consent of that person to be exposed to HIV, in one of the following manners:

(a) Through contact with blood, semen, or vaginal secretions in the course of oral, anal, or vaginal sexual intercourse; or

(b) By the sharing of needles; or

(c) By biting another person or purposely acting in any other manner which causes the HIV-infected person's semen, vaginal secretions, or blood to come into contact with the mucous membranes or nonintact skin of another person.

Mont. Code Ann. § 50-18-112:

Infected person not to expose another to sexually transmitted disease.

A person infected with a sexually transmitted disease may not knowingly expose another person to infection.

N. Rev. Stat. Ann. 441A.300 (2004):

§ 441A.300. Confinement of person whose conduct may spread acquired immunodeficiency syndrome.

A person who is diagnosed as having acquired immunodeficiency syndrome who fails to comply with a written order of a health authority, or who engages in behavior through which the disease may be spread to others, is, in addition to any other penalty imposed pursuant to this chapter, subject to confinement by order of a court of competent jurisdiction.

N.J. Stat. Ann. § 2C:34-5:

Diseased person committing an act of sexual penetration.

a. A person is guilty of a crime of the fourth degree who, knowing that he or she is infected with a venereal disease such as chancroid, gonorrhea, syphilis, herpes virus, or any of the varieties or stages of such diseases, commits an act of sexual penetration without the informed consent of the other person.

b. A person is guilty of a crime of the third degree who, knowing that he or she is infected with human immune deficiency virus (HIV) or any other related virus identified as a probable causative agent of acquired immune deficiency syndrome (AIDS), commits an act of sexual penetration without the informed consent of the other person.

N.D. Cent. Code § 12.1-20-17:

Transfer of body fluid that may contain the human immunodeficiency virus — Definitions — Defenses — Penalty

1. As used in this section, unless the context otherwise requires:

(a) "Body fluid" means semen, irrespective of the presence of spermatozoa; blood; or vaginal secretion.

(b) "Transfer" means to engage in sexual activity by genital-genital contact, oral-genital contact, or anal-genital contact, or to permit the reuse of a hypodermic syringe, needle, or similar device without sterilization.

2. A person who, knowing that that person is or has been afflicted with acquired immune deficiency syndrome, afflicted with acquired immune deficiency syndrome related complexes, or infected with the human immunodeficiency virus, willfully transfers any of that person's body fluid to another person is guilty of a class A felony.

3. It is an affirmative defense to a prosecution under this section that if the transfer was by sexual activity, the sexual activity took place between consenting adults after full disclosure of the risk of such activity and with the use of an appropriate prophylactic device.

674

Ohio Rev. Code Ann. § 3701.81:

Spreading contagion

(A) No person, knowing or having reasonable cause to believe that he is suffering from a dangerous, contagious disease, shall knowingly fail to take reasonable measures to prevent exposing himself to other persons, except when seeking medical aid.

(B) No person, having charge or care of a person whom he knows or has reasonable cause to believe is suffering from a dangerous, contagious disease, shall recklessly fail to take reasonable measures to protect others from exposure to the contagion, and to inform health authorities of the existence of the contagion.

(C) No person, having charge of a public conveyance or place of public accommodation, amusement, resort or trade, and knowing or having reasonable cause to believe that persons using such conveyance or place have been or are being exposed to a dangerous, contagious disease, shall negligently fail to take reasonable measures to protect the public from exposure to the contagion, and to inform health authorities of the existence of the contagion.

Okla. Stat. Tit. 21, § 1192.1:

Knowingly engaging in conduct reasonably likely to transfer HIV virus

A. It shall be unlawful for any person knowing that he or she has Acquired Immune Deficiency Syndrome (AIDS) or is a carrier of the human immunodeficiency virus (HIV) and with intent to infect another, to engage in conduct reasonably likely to result in the transfer of the person's own blood, bodily fluids containing visible blood, semen, or vaginal secretions into the bloodstream of another, or through the skin or other membranes of another person, except during in utero transmission of blood or bodily fluids, and:

(1) the other person did not consent to the transfer of blood, bodily fluids containing blood, semen, or vaginal secretions; or

(2) the other person consented to the transfer but at the time of giving consent had not been informed by the person that the person transferring such blood or fluids had AIDS or was a carrier of HIV.

B. Any person convicted of violating the provisions of this section shall be guilty of a felony, punishable by imprisonment in the custody of the Department of Corrections for not more than five (5) years.

S.C. Code Ann. § 44-29-145:

Penalty for exposing others to Human Immunodeficiency Virus.

It is unlawful for a person who knows that he is infected with Human Immunodeficiency Virus (HIV) to:

(1) knowingly engage in sexual intercourse, vaginal, anal, or oral, with another person without first informing that person of his HIV infection;

675

(2) knowingly commit an act of prostitution with another person;

(3) knowingly sell or donate blood, blood products, semen, tissue, organs, or other body fluids;

(4) forcibly engage in sexual intercourse, vaginal, anal, or oral, without the consent of the other person, including one's legal spouse; or

(5) knowingly share with another person a hypodermic needle, syringe, or both, for the introduction of drugs or any other substance into, or for the withdrawal of blood or body fluids from the other person's body without first informing that person that the needle, syringe, or both, has been used by someone infected with HIV.

A person who violates this section is guilty of a felony and, upon conviction, must be fined not more than five thousand dollars or imprisoned for not more than ten years.

Tenn. Code Ann. § 39-13-109:

Criminal exposure to HIV — Defenses — Penalty:

(a) A person commits the offense of criminal exposure of another to HIV when, knowing that such person is infected with HIV, such person knowingly:

(1) Engages in intimate contact with another;

(2) Transfers, donates, or provides blood, tissue, semen, organs, or other potentially infectious body fluids or parts for transfusion, transplantation, insemination, or other administration to another in any manner that presents a significant risk of HIV transmission; or

(3) Dispenses, delivers, exchanges, sells, or in any other way transfers to another any nonsterile intravenous or intramuscular drug paraphernalia.

(b) As used in this section:

(1) "HIV" means the human immunodeficiency virus or any other identified causative agent of acquired immunodeficiency syndrome;

(2) "Intimate contact with another" means the exposure of the body of one person to a bodily fluid of another person in any manner that presents a significant risk of HIV transmission; and

(3) "Intravenous or intramuscular drug paraphernalia" means any equipment, product, or material of any kind which is peculiar to and marketed for use in injecting a substance into the human body.

(c) It is an affirmative defense to prosecution under this section, which must be proven by a preponderance of the evidence, that the person exposed to HIV knew that the infected person was infected with HIV, knew that the action could result in infection with HIV, and gave advance consent to the action with that knowledge.

(d) Nothing in this section shall be construed to require the actual transmission of HIV in order for a person to have committed the offense of criminal exposure of another to HIV.

(e) Criminal exposure of another to HIV is a Class C felony.

Tenn. Code Ann. § 39-13-516:

Aggravated Prostitution.

(a) A person commits aggravated prostitution when, knowing that such person is infected with HIV, the person engages in sexual activity as a business or is an inmate in a house of prostitution or loiters in a public place for the purpose of being hired to engage in sexual activity;

(b) For the purposes of this section, "HIV" means the Human Immunodeficiency Virus or any other identified causative agent of Human Immunodeficiency Virus;

(c) Nothing in this section shall be construed to require that an infection with HIV has occurred in order for a person to have committed aggravated prostitution; (d) Aggravated prostitution is a Class C felony.

Utah Code Ann. § 26-6-5.

Willful introduction of communicable disease a misdemeanor.

Any person who willfully or knowingly introduces any communicable or infectious disease into any county, municipality, or community is guilty of a Class A misdemeanor, except as provided in Section 76-10-1309.

Wash. Rev. Code § 9A.36.011

Assault in the first degree.

(1) A person is guilty of assault in the first degree if he or she, with intent to inflict great bodily harm:

(b) Administers, exposes, or transmits to or causes to be taken by another, poison, the human immunodeficiency virus as defined in chapter 70.24 RCW, or any other destructive or noxious substance; or

(2) Assault in the first degree is a Class A felony.

§ 9.6 Constitutionality of HIV in statutes criminalizing sexual activity by HIV-infected person.

Statutes making AIDS a factor in criminal charges against a defendant, as set forth in § 9.5, raise numerous constitutional issues.

Louisiana's Court of Appeals has rejected the constitutionality challenge to its intentional exposure to the AIDS virus statute due to vagueness of the statute on the grounds that an innocent person could violate the statute without being aware of his HIV status.[63] The court held that criminalizing the exposure of

---

[63] State v. Gamberella, 633 So. 2d 595, 602 (La. App. 1 Cir.), *appeal denied*, 640 So. 2d 1341 (La. 1994); State v. Serrano, 715 So. 2d 602 (La. Ct. App. 1998) (holding Louisiana statute criminalizing intentional exposure to AIDS virus was not unconstitutionally vague because there is no such thing as "AIDS virus"); State v. Ferguson, No. 21329-0-II, 1999 Wash. App. LEXIS 1905 (Nov. 5, 1999), *rev'd on other grounds*, 142 Wash.2d 631 (2001) (court found that statute

someone with HIV "through sexual contact" was not vague and that "sexual contact," while including sexual acts such as kissing that are incapable of transmitting the virus, "unambiguously describes the unlawful conduct with sufficient particularity and clarity."[64] The court added that while the statute may cover conduct that cannot transmit the virus, "considering the uncertainty of the medical community concerning all aspects of this disease, the statute is narrowly drawn to further the state's compelling interest."[65] Nonetheless, the Louisiana legislature amended the statute to cover intentional exposure through "any means or contact," including "spitting, biting, stabbing with an AIDS-contaminated object, or throwing blood or other bodily substances."[66]

In the Louisiana case, the defendant also raised the argument that the statute breached the right to privacy as well as the right of an HIV-infected person to engage in sexual activities. But the court held that the right of privacy, which is a limited right, does not shield all private sexual acts:

> No one can seriously doubt that the state has a compelling interest in discouraging the spread of the HIV virus. Forcing an infected person to inform all of his sexual partners so the partner can make an informed decision prior to engaging in sexual activity furthers the state's interest in preventing the spread of the virus. Defendant argues the statute is not the least restrictive means which could have been chosen to accomplish the state's purpose. According to defendant, some absolutely safe forms of sexual contact are illegal under the statute. Defendant also appears to complain that the statute does not go far enough. The statute does not prohibit unprotected sexual intercourse with an infected person nor does it criminalize other methods of transmission (perinatal transmissions and blood-to-blood transmissions). However, merely because the statute does not go as far as it could to discourage the spread of the virus does not result in the current version's being viewed as an invasion of privacy.[67]

---

criminalizing as an assault exposing another person to HIV did not violate equal protection clause of United States or Washington State Constitutions, holding:

> [The statute] did not single out for unequal treatment a class of persons infected with HIV, or a class of persons infected with contagious and deadly diseases. It criminalized, for example, the conduct of a healthy, non-infected medical worker who, with the required intent, injects a patient with someone else's HIV-contaminated bodily fluids. It criminalized, for another example, the conduct of a healthy, non-infected drug user who, with the required intent, injects another with an HIV-contaminated needle. It criminalized, for a third example, the conduct of a healthy, non-infected prisoner who, with the required intent, throws at a prison guard the HIV-contaminated bodily fluids of a cellmate. We conclude that the statute applied equally to infected and non-infected defendants, and that it did not create a suspect or semi-suspect class.

Id. at *13–14).

[64] *Id.* at 603.

[65] *Id.* at 604.

[66] La. Rev. Stat. § 14:43.5. *See* § 9.5.

[67] *Gamberella,* 633 So. 2d at 604.

The Illinois Supreme Court has rejected a constitutional challenge to the crime of knowingly transmitting HIV on the basis of vagueness, free speech, and infringement on the right of intimate association.[68] As to the latter, the court held:

> Additionally, the defendants' cases do not infringe on any supposed right of intimate association as claimed. In fact, we know of no such right. The facts are that in the first of the two cases, the victim did not know that his sexual partner had HIV. In the second of the two cases, the HIV transmission charge is appendant to a charge of forcible rape. It is preposterous to argue that the statute constitutes a violation of either of the defendants' supposed right to intimate association in these situations.[69]

The court left open the possibility that there may be a situation where "the statute might open the innocent conduct of others to possible prosecution," but held that that would have to be reviewed on another set of facts.

An intermediate Michigan appeals court has upheld the constitutionality of two Michigan statutes which make it a crime to fail to inform a sexual partner that one has AIDS or is HIV-positive, analogizing that drunken drivers who do not intend to kill may be criminally responsible when causing death while driving intoxicated.[70] The court noted the parallel causal relationship between a defendant who drives while intoxicated resulting in a person's death and a person with AIDS or HIV engaging in sexual activity which may end another person's life.[71] The court observed that a "defendant's ostensible right to withhold her HIV status from her sexual partners is not an absolute right when balanced against the state's 'unqualified interest' in preserving human life."[72]

§ 9.7 HIV or AIDS as factors in plea bargaining or dismissal of charges.

The fact that most individuals who test positive for HIV will contract AIDS would seem to provide a defendant with a significant basis to argue that he should receive a reduced sentence or a favorable plea bargain. Among the factors to weigh in this consideration is the cost of AIDS treatment and whether the state wishes to sustain this burden. The physical limitations placed upon the defendant by the disease may be another factor. On the other hand, prosecutors may argue that a defendant who is HIV-positive represents a greater threat to the community should he or she commit further offenses.

---

[68] People v. Russell, 158 Ill. 2d 23, 630 N.E.2d 794 (1994), *cert. denied sub nom.*, Lunsford v. Illinois, 513 U.S. 828 (1994).

[69] *Id.* at 26, 630 N.E.2d at 796.

[70] People v. Jensen, 231 Mich. App. 439, 586 N.W.2d 748 (1998).

[71] 231 Mich. App. at 454, 586 N.W.2d at 755.

[72] 231 Mich. App. 456–57, 586 N.W.2d at 756.

An affidavit setting forth the medical facts concerning the prognosis for an HIV-positive accused also has been used as a basis to argue for dismissal of charges. At least one trial court has dismissed an indictment in the interest of justice based on AIDS-inflicted defendant's frailty where he had no significant criminal record; however, the appellate court suggested that this action be used sparingly and that a "complete showing" of the gravity of the defendant's condition should be established before such a dismissal.[73]

§ 9.8 HIV or AIDS as a factor in sentencing.

HIV status can be considered as a factor in sentencing.[74] HIV status may also be a factor in the conditions that a court sets for a defendant's probation. These conditions may include mandatory counseling or education dealing with AIDS.[75] Testing of a defendant may be included by statute as a part of a defendant's sentence.[76] A defendant may also be ordered to pay the costs of his HIV testing.[77]

It is not unusual for a defendant's deteriorated physical condition to be considered by a court in determining a sentence, but courts also have disregarded or minimized physical condition as a factor in sentencing. Courts have so far been reluctant to use a defendant's AIDS status by itself to reduce an otherwise appropriate sentence, including the provisions of the federal sentencing guidelines.[78] One federal judge has decided that a defendant's HIV status may be

---

[73] People v. Moye, 302 A.D.2d 610, 755 N.Y.S.2d 307 (2003) (holding defendant's serious physical ailments, mainly related to AIDS, did not warrant "the extraordinary remedy of dismissal of the indictment in the furtherance of justice"); People v. McAlister, 280 A.D.2d 556, 720 N.Y.S.2d 391, *appeal denied*, 96 N.Y.2d 803, 750 N.E.2d 83, 726 N.Y.S.2d 381 (2001); Santamaria v. Kelly, 280 A.D.2d 536, 720 N.Y.S.2d 182 (2001); People v. Lawson, 198 A.D.2d 71, 603 N.Y.S.2d 311 (1993), *aff'd sub nom.* People v. Herman L., 83 N.Y.2d 958, 639 N.E.2d 404, 615 N.Y.S.2d 865 (1994).

[74] Alan Stephen, *Transmission or Risk of Transmission of Human Immunodeficiency Virus (HIV) or Acquired Immunodeficiency Syndrome (AIDS) as Basis for Prosecution or Sentencing in Criminal or Military Discipline Case,* 13 A.L.R.5TH 628 (1993).

[75] *See, e.g.,* People v. Henson, 231 Cal. App. 3d 172, 282 Cal. Rptr. 222 (1991).

[76] *See, e.g.,* Neb. Rev. Stat. § 29-2290.

[77] *See* S.C. Code §§ 16-3-740, 16-15-255.

[78] United States v. Mayes, No. 97-6504, 1999 U.S. App. LEXIS 11105 (6th Cir. May 26, 1999); Negron v. United States, 2002 U.S. Dist. LEXIS 6921 (Apr. 17, 2002) (upholding court's refusal to depart downward in defendant's sentence since such refusal is a justifiable exercise of discretion); United States v. Streat, 22 F.3d 109, 112 (6th Cir. 1994) (noting that § 5H1.4 of the federal sentencing guidelines justifies downward departure for "extraordinary physical impairment," but declining to decide whether AIDS alone or in conjunction with other physical disabilities will permit a downward departure under the guidelines); United States v. DePew, 751 F. Supp. 1195, 1199 (E.D. Va. 1990), *aff'd,* 932 F.2d 324 (4th Cir.), *cert. denied,* 502 U.S. 873 (1991) (in a case involving a defendant convicted of conspiracy to hidings and conspiracy to exploit a 12-year-old in a sexually explicit "sex-snuff" film, the trial court held that "defendant's AIDS affliction warrants sympathy, but not a departure" from sentencing guidelines).

the basis for leniency under the federal sentencing guidelines, but has also noted the wide disparity in federal courts' treatment of a defendant's HIV status as a factor in sentencing.[79] The decision provides a good review of federal court decisions' treatment of HIV or AIDS as a factor in a defendant's sentence.[80] One federal court noted the defendant's HIV status, as well as his vulnerability as a sex offender in prison, in support of a downward departure from federal sentencing guidelines.[81] Some federal courts take the position that a defendant is entitled to a downward departure in sentencing guidelines only when the AIDS disease has progressed to such an advanced stage as to constitute an extraordinary physical impairment.[82] Several New York courts have taken the position that affliction with the HIV virus "standing alone" does not warrant a reduction in an otherwise appropriate sentence.[83] Other state courts have also declined to reduce a defendant's sentence because of a defendant's HIV status.[84]

---

[79] United States v. Hammond, 37 F. Supp. 2d 204 (E.D.N.Y. 1999).

[80] 37 F. Supp. 2d at 209.

[81] United States v. Ruff, 998 F. Supp. 1351 (M.D. Ala. 1998).

[82] United States v. Woody, 55 F.3d 1257, 1275 (7th Cir.), *cert. denied*, 516 U.S. 889 (1995); United States v. Thomas, 49 F.3d 253, 261 (6th Cir. 1995).

[83] People v. Roy, 248 A.D.2d 566, 669 N.Y.S.2d 907 (1998); People v. Salmons, 210 A.D.2d 512, 620 N.Y.S.2d 1008 (1994), *appeal denied*, 85 N.Y.2d 866, 648 N.E.2d 805, 624 N.Y.S.2d 385 (1995); People v. Alvira, 209 A.D.2d 628, 619 N.Y.S.2d 126 (1994); People v. Kellar, 199 A.D.2d 703, 605 N.Y.S.2d 486 (1993), *appeal denied*, 83 N.Y.2d 854, 634 N.E.2d 987, 612 N.Y.S.2d 386 (1994); People v. Reyes, 198 A.D.2d 449, 605 N.Y.S.2d 907 (1993), *appeal denied*, 83 N.Y.2d 809, 633 N.E.2d 500, 611 N.Y.S.2d 145 (1994); People v. Perez, 181 A.D.2d 922, 581 N.Y.S.2d 846, *appeal denied*, 80 N.Y.2d 836, 600 N.E.2d 648, 587 N.Y.S.2d 921 (1992).

[84] State v. Abrams, 706 So. 2d 903 (Fla. Dist. Ct. App. 1998)

> With regard to the other reason, we have found no authority to indicate that a defendant's HIV-positive status alone constitutes a valid reason for departure from the guidelines. A defendant's need for specialized treatment for physical disability and amenability to treatment is a valid reason for departure. *See* Fla. R. Crim. P. 3.990. There is no evidence in the record, however, that Mr. Abrams requires specialized treatment for HIV that cannot be provided through the Department of Corrections. We, therefore, reverse Mr. Abrams' sentence and remand for resentencing within the guidelines.

Id. at 904; People v. Williams, 301 Ill. App. 3d 210, 703 N.E.2d 133 (1998) (upholding trial court's sentence in rejecting defendant's claim that trial judge failed to consider defendant's HIV status); State v. Lee, 735 So. 2d 715 (La. Ct. App. 1999) (holding that defendant's HIV status was "purely subjective" to justify deviation from a statutorily mandated sentence); State v. Lee, 699 So. 2d 461 (La. Ct. App. 1997) ("we decline to consider in this case, his HIV positive medical condition as a mitigating factor for sentencing purposes because of the defendant's long and serious criminal and anti-social history. Status as HIV positive is not a legislatively recognized mitigating factor for sentencing or for deviation from the mandatory minimum sentence prescribed under the Habitual Offender Law."); Lindsay v. State, 720 So. 2d 182 (Miss. 1998) (declining to alter defendant's sentence on ground that trial judge was not aware of defendant's HIV status and therefore was unaware of defendant's life expectancy); State v. Woller, 189 Wis. 2d 490, 527 N.W.2d 398, *reported in full*, 1994 Wisc. App. LEXIS 1417 (Wis. Ct. App. 1994) (rejecting defendant's claim that his sentence should be modified due to the potential impact of his HIV status upon his health

Some statutes specifically permit a court to consider a defendant's HIV status. California's penal code allows enhancement of a sentence when a defendant commits certain sexual assaults with knowledge of having AIDS or the human immunodeficiency virus.[85] The statute has been held to not violate either the equal protection or Eighth Amendment prohibition against cruel and criminal punishment.[86]

The fact that a defendant was aware of his infection at the time he engaged in sexual activity can be the type of "deliberate cruelty to a victim during the commission of a crime" to constitute an aggravating circumstance justifying an enhanced sentence.[87] Other courts, too, have held that a defendant's infliction with HIV at the time of a sexual assault is a type of circumstance surrounding a crime that a court can consider in sentencing, since the defendant's conduct placed the sexual assault victim at risk of contracting AIDS and can be cited as a reason for going outside sentencing guidelines.[88] While it can be argued

---

and questions as to whether the correctional system was equipped to handle his health needs); State v. Iglesias, 185 Wis. 2d 117, 517 N.W.2d 175, 177 (1994) (in sentencing defendant convicted for her role in engaging two 14-year-old girls to work as prostitutes, court was sensitive to the defendant's diagnosis as HIV positive but felt that the medical condition was counterbalanced by the seriousness of her crimes and the goal of deterrence).

[85] Charges may also be elevated to a felony when a defendant has tested positive for HIV on a previous conviction and was informed of such positive results. See Cal. Penal Code § 12022.85 (rape and other sexual offenses); Cal. Penal Code § 647f (2004); Ind. Code § 35-38-1-7.1 (permitting defendant's HIV-positive status to be an aggravating factor in imposing consecutive terms if an epidemiologically risk of transmission is established).

[86] Guevara v. Superior Court, 62 Cal. App. 4th 864, 73 Cal. Rptr. 2d 421 (1998).

[87] State v. Farmer, 116 Wash. 2d 414, 805 P.2d 200 (1991) (basing the enhancement of sentence on the guidelines for sentencing that state among the aggravating circumstances "the defendant's conduct during the commission of the current offense manifested deliberate cruelty to the victim," (citing Wash. Rev. Code § 9.94A.390(2)(a))).

[88] United States v. Blas, 360 F.3d 1268 (11th Cir. 2004) (upholding upward departure because defendant's conduct — "exposure of a young victim to a potentially fatal disease through sexual relations — took the conviction out of the heartland of cases."); United States v. Jones, 44 M.J. 103, 104 (1996) (finding defendant's medical condition subjected victim to a fatal disease and thus was relevant as an aggravating circumstance in defendant's sentencing); State v. Lewis, 123 Idaho 336, 848 P.2d 394 (1993) (court considered defendant's HIV status at two of sexual assault cases a factor in defendant's sentence); State v. Richmond, 708 So. 2d 1272 (La. 1998) (noting the judge considered that defendant committed the crime after knowing she was HIV positive); State v. Richmond, 734 So. 2d 33, 38–39 (La. Ct. App. 1999) (upholding enhancement of defendant's sentence based in part on the fact that "the defendant committed the offense after she knew that she was HIV-positive"). Perkins v. State, 559 N.W.2d 678 (Minn. 1997) (upholding trial court's greater-than-triple durational departure from sentencing guidelines where the defendant knew he was infected with the AIDS virus, threatened the victim, and inflicted gratuitous injuries as part of the sexual assaults; record demonstrated that defendant knew he had AIDS when he committed the offense. Court noted that passing HIV to a defenseless victim equaled giving the victim a "death sentence."); State v. Guayante, 99 Or. App. 649, 783 P.2d 1030 (1989), appeal denied, 309 Or. 522, 789 P.2d 1386 (1990); Sellers v. State, 1996 Tex. App. LEXIS 1736 (April 29, 1996) (rejecting defendant's argument that defendant's HIV status should not be considered

that for a court to enhance a defendant's sentence under this theory, it must be shown that the defendant was aware of his HIV status at the time of the sexual assault. At least one court has upheld additional sentencing in a sexual assault conviction even though there was no proof that the defendant knew at the time of the crime that he was infected with HIV.[89]

Tennessee's statutes permit sentence enhancement if the defendant was HIV-positive at the time of a certain offense.[90] This has been interpreted to permit enhancement even without the defendant's knowledge of his HIV status. However, the mere possibility that HIV may have been transmitted to a victim during a crime should not be considered in the defendant's sentence in the view of one Tennessee appellate court.[91]

Another argument for enhanced sentencing of an HIV-positive sexual offender is future dangerousness. The basis of this argument is that the defendant is a threat to others because of his ability to transmit a deadly disease to others. However, the potential dangerousness of a defendant is more likely to be determined by the person's criminal history rather than the person's HIV status. An HIV-infected person is no more or less likely to hurt others than a convicted robber is to rob again. On the other hand, an HIV-infected offender may continue to commit crimes because he or she has "nothing to lose." An offender may also continue to engage in criminal or "high-risk" behavior out of revenge because that is how the offender contracted AIDS, or some other animus. Sentencing should be based on individual characteristics rather than group characteristics or traits such as race, ethnicity, socioeconomic status, or medical condition.

---

in sentencing because it is an unadjudicated extraneous offense, i.e., exposing intentionally another to AIDS or HIV and holding that a defendant's AIDS "status at the time of the offense is especially relevant in circumstances like those here where there is evidence that appellant's bodily fluids entered the victim's mouth"); Hunter v. State, 799 S.W.2d 356 (Tex. Ct. App. 1990) (noting that the defendant's conduct was criminalized under Texas law, and that the intentional and nonconsensual transfer of bodily fluids by an HIV-positive individual was a crime under Texas law).

[89] Cooper v. State, 539 So. 2d 508 (Fla. Crim. App.), *review denied*, 548 So. 2d 662 (Fla. 1989); State v. Woller, 189 Wis. 2d 490, 527 N.W.2d 398, *reported in full*, 1994 Wis. App. LEXIS 1417 (1994) (there was no showing that defendant was HIV positive at the time of the offense, but trial court did not use defendant's HIV status as a basis for its sentence).

[90] Tenn. Code § 39-13-521; State v. Pipkin, 1997 Tenn. Crim. App. LEXIS 1216 (Dec. 4, 1997) ("In addition to the fact that defendant was not tested for HIV until the day prior to the sentencing hearing, there is no proof in the record that the defendant knew he was infected with the HIV virus at the time of the offense. However, this does not prevent application of the fact of a positive test for HIV in consideration of consecutive sentencing under Tennessee Code Annotated § 40-35-115(b)(5)." *Id.* at* 19–20).

[91] State v. Cage, C.C.A. No. 01C01-9605-CC-00179, 1999 Tenn. Crim. App. LEXIS 62, at *39 (Jan. 26, 1999) ("[W]e do not agree with the trial court that the possible transmission of the HIV virus during the rape established that appellant was a dangerous offender whose behavior indicates little or no regard for human life and who has no hesitation committing a crime in which the risk to human life is high. While this may have been true if appellant actually had the HIV virus and knew that he had the virus, there is no evidence in the record that appellant had any sexually transmitted disease.").

A number of reasons have been cited by defendants for not increasing their sentences because of their HIV status. A defendant may not have known he was HIV-positive at the time of an offense. It may be argued that the victim did not contract the virus, that the defendant did not understand how the virus was transmitted, or that he did not engage in any activity with intent to cause harm.[92] These are all factors to consider in keeping a defendant's sentence within guidelines.[93]

There are situations where a defendant may argue that HIV status should mitigate punishment. In Colorado, a defendant's voluntary submission to HIV testing can be used to mitigate his sentence.[94] A defendant may also argue that since AIDS is virtually a death sentence itself, there is little additional punishment that can be meted out to a defendant. An individual with advanced AIDS is also less likely to be physically able to assault another individual. Since a correctional system must provide medical care and treatment to ill inmates, including those with AIDS, there may be financial incentives for the state to treat AIDS patients in a less costly outpatient setting. Furthermore, detention centers housing HIV-positive inmates may have difficulty providing medical assistance to these inmates while maintaining security and safety. A defendant's AIDS status has been successfully used to argue for dismissal of charges.[95] In any event, if a case for special consideration is argued, a proper record should be made that sets forth any special facts that would make the defendant's case unique. Prosecutors should recognize the possible sensitive nature of a defendant's HIV status in order to avoid a possible downward departure on sentencing. The 5th Circuit Court of Appeals reversed a district court's decision to depart downward-ing from the sentencing range when the prosecutor disclosed in open-court that the defendant was HIV-positive.[96]

§ 9.9 Reasons and grounds for compelling a defendant or suspect to undergo a test for HIV.

The compelled testing of a suspect or defendant for HIV in sexual assault charges is a developing area of law. It is also an emotional issue for many sexual assault victims. While such testing is not invasive and only involves the withdrawal of a small amount of blood, there is a concern as to whether such testing can be done before conviction and the fact that it would lead to the disclosure of an individual's private medical facts.

---

[92] State v. Stark, 66 Wash. App. 423, 832 P.2d 109 (1992).

[93] Id.

[94] Colo. Rev. Stat. § 18-3-415.

[95] People v. Wong, 227 A.D.2d 852, 642 N.Y.S.2d 396 (1996) (defendant's AIDS status, to-gether with other factors, warranted dismissal of indictment against defendant); People v. Lawson, 198 A.D.2d 71, 603 N.Y.S.2d 311 (1993), aff'd sub nom. People v. Herman L., 83 N.Y.2d 958, 639 N.E.2d 404, 615 N.Y.S.2d 865 (1994).

[96] United States v. Castillo, 430 F.3d 230 (5th Cir. 2005).

Testing an accused for HIV is not going to establish the crime, since the fact that an accused is infected will not prove the infection was transmitted to the victim.[97] Also, such testing does not necessarily provide a victim with truly reassuring information. There can be a significant period of time before an HIV person will test positive. During this period, a person who is indeed infected will, nonetheless, test negative. A victim cannot conclude from a negative test that she or he has not been exposed to the virus and may be capable of transmitting HIV to others. While public health organizations have advocated voluntary HIV testing to facilitate education, counseling, and behavior modification, exposure to HIV through sexual assault distinguishes it from activities such as intravenous drug use or consensual sexual relations.[98] The difference is summarized as follows:

> Because the survivor's exposure starts with a wrong, the accused owes the survivor a duty to limit the harm caused by the assault. Sexual assault causes ongoing harm, including the continuing fear of HIV infection, which can postpone or limit recovery. It is this dynamic and ongoing nature of the harm that suggests that public policy should do everything possible to limit future harm and to preserve the health of the survivor and his or her partners and children. It is fundamentally unfair to place all the burden of limiting future harm on the survivor. In the case of sexual assault, survivors usually bear the whole burden of continuing anxiety and protecting themselves, partners, and families. If testing the accused could limit future harm to the survivor and ease the burden of unfairness, it would provide a persuasive argument for involuntary testing of the accused.[99]

The arguments advanced for compulsory testing of a defendant accused of sexual assault, even though the results will not provide definitive answers to a victim, are: (1) the potential clinical benefit to a survivor of prompt prophylaxis therapies, should progress be made in HIV prophylaxis and presymptomatic clinical treatment of HIV; (2) the public health benefit to survivors and their partners, including aiding in decisions on starting a family by providing some

---

[97] *In re* Michael WW., 203 A.D.2d 763, 611 N.Y.S.2d 47 (1994). In a family court proceeding where a law guardian sought to have the accused submit to a blood test, the court held:

> It is not insignificant in this regard that even Michael stated that his abuser wore a condom during the alleged penetration. . . . In short, the only way to determine whether Michael has been infected, and to allay his fears if he has not, is to test Michael himself, and there is no reason why that course should not be pursued at this time. If Michael does test positively, that unfortunate result may provide some evidence that he was abused, thus tending to establish the allegations of the petition to a much greater degree than would a test of Roy; it may also provide probable cause, coupled with the remainder of the allegations of the petition, for testing Roy to determine whether he was possibly the source of Michael's infection.

[98] Lawrence O. Gostin et al., *HIV Testing, Counseling, and Prophylaxis after Sexual Assault,* 271 Jama. 1436, 1439 (1994).

[99] *Id.*

guidance as to the extent to which precautions should be taken; and (3) the psychological benefit to the survivor.[100]

Courts have accepted the argument that a negative result from an HIV test of a defendant can help decrease the anxiety of a complainant, even if it is not a guarantee that there has been no exposure, and a positive result can assist a victim in making certain treatment decisions, such as undertaking possible prophylactic courses of treatment or undergoing experimental drug therapy.[101]

> There are compelling reasons to order testing of a defendant accused of rape for the HIV virus, namely to help the victim 'to reduce anxiety and to receive proper psychological and medical treatment' even though the 'rape victim cannot conclude from her own negative HIV results that her assailant did not expose her to the virus since seroconversion, the process by which the immune system generates antibodies and the time at which HIV infection may be identified, which typically occurs three to six months after exposure and up to fourteen months in some persons.'[102]

Another court has noted that there is "considerable medical utility" in HIV testing of a defendant "even if the test does not test positive" and that a positive test of a person who may have infected a victim could dictate additional or more extensive monitoring of the victim than if there were negative results.[103] It has also been noted that the substantial interest of the government in stopping the transmission of HIV can be a basis for the compelled testing of a defendant.[104]

§ 9.10 HIV testing of defendant under Violence Against Women Act.

Under the 1994 Violence Against Women Act, sexual assault victims have the right to obtain, at federal government expense, testing for sexually-transmitted diseases, as well as court-ordered testing of defendants for HIV. The complainant

---

[100] *Id.* at 1441–42.

[101] Virgin Islands v. Roberts, 756 F. Supp. 898, 903 (D.V.I. 1991), *aff'd without op.*, 961 F.2d 1567 (3d Cir. 1992); State *ex rel.* J.G., 151 N.J. 565, 701 A.2d 1260 (1997).

[102] United States v. Ramirez-Burgos, 1994 U.S. Dist. LEXIS 4564 at 3–4 (D.P.R. Mar. 9, 1994).

[103] Johnetta J. v. Municipal Court, 218 Cal. App. 3d 1255, 1266, 267 Cal. Rptr. 666, 671–72 (1990) (quoting from testimony before the trial court):

> Allaying the fears of a patient can be a significant factor in treating that patient. Anxiety itself can cause or complicate medical problems and it can impede recovery. Where a fatal disease is involved, having access to all information bearing on the question of possible exposure can be of great assistance in relieving a patient's anxiety. Having all relevant information about potential exposure to HIV also assists a patient in determining the extent to which that patient wishes to make changes in his or her lifestyle taking into account the potential exposure, such as changes in diet and exercise, as well as whether it is necessary to take precautions in intimate relationships.

[104] *Roberts,* 756 F. Supp. at 904.

may petition the federal court for testing of the defendant when the defendant has been charged in Federal or state courts. Under the law:

> The Attorney General or the head of another department or agency that conducts an investigation of a sexual assault shall pay, either directly or by reimbursement of payment by the victim, the cost of a physical examination of the victim which an investigating officer determines was necessary or useful for evidentiary purposes. The Attorney General shall provide for the payment of the cost of up to two anonymous and confidential tests of the victim for sexually-transmitted diseases, including HIV, gonorrhea, herpes, chlamydia, and syphilis, during the 12 months following sexual assaults that pose a risk of transmission, and the cost of a counseling session by a medically trained professional on the accuracy of such tests and the risk of transmission of sexually-transmitted diseases to the victim as the result of the assault. A victim may waive anonymity and confidentiality of any tests paid for under this section.[105]

The basis for a court order is set forth as follows:

> Court order. The victim of an offense of the type referred to in subsection (a) may obtain an order in the district court of the United States for the district in which charges are brought against the defendant charged with the offense, after notice to the defendant and an opportunity to be heard, requiring that the defendant be tested for the presence of the etiologic agent for acquired immune deficiency syndrome, and that the results of the test be communicated to the victim and the defendant. Any test result of the defendant given to the victim or the defendant must be accompanied by appropriate counseling.[106]

The Federal law does not violate the Fourth Amendment's prohibition against unreasonable searches according to one appeals court.[107] However, the same court ruled that the law requires a court to make certain findings.[108] The law "requires that there be probable cause to believe that the subject of the search has sexually assaulted the victim in a manner which creates a risk of transmission of HIV."[109]

The showing required is as follows:

Showing required. To obtain an order under paragraph (1), the victim must demonstrate that:

(A) the defendant has been charged with the offense in a State or Federal court, and if the defendant has been arrested without a warrant, a probable cause determination has been made;

---

[105] 42 U.S.C. § 10607(c)(7).

[106] 42 U.S.C. § 14011(b)(1).

[107] United States v. Ward, 131 F.3d 335 (3d Cir. 1997).

[108] *Id.*

[109] *Id.* at 341.

(B) the test for the etiologic agent for acquired immune deficiency syndrome is requested by the victim after appropriate counseling; and

(C) the test would provide information necessary for the health of the victim of the alleged offense and the court determines that the alleged conduct of the defendant created a risk of transmission, as determined by the Centers for Disease Control and Prevention, of the etiologic agent for acquired immune deficiency syndrome to the victim.[110]

§ 9.11 Statutes providing for the testing of accused or convicted sex offenders.

In addition to Federal law (§ 9.10), several states have enacted legislation compelling defendants to undergo testing for HIV. A sample of a motion and order to compel a defendant to undergo an HIV test is set forth in Appendix E. The following is an outline of state statutes dealing with HIV testing of accused or convicted offenders.

ARIZONA

Permits a victim or the parent or guardian of a minor victim of a sexual offense or "significant exposure" to petition prosecutor to request that defendant be tested. If defendant is convicted, the parent or guardian of the minor "shall" petition court for an order requiring the defendant to be tested. (Ariz. Rev. Stat. § 13-1415)

ARKANSAS

Victim may request testing of arrested defendant. Court shall order testing of a convicted defendant upon request of the victim. (Ark. Code Ann. § 16-82-101)

CALIFORNIA

Provides that "the court shall order every person convicted" of designated sexual offenses to submit to a blood test for evidence of AIDS. (Cal. Penal Code § 1202.1)

Provides for AIDS testing and education for a person convicted of soliciting or engaging in prostitution. (Cal. Penal Code § 1202.6)

Provides for search warrant application to test for HIV for those charged with a crime where bodily fluids may have been transferred. (Cal. Penal Code § 1524.1)

Provides for testing of individuals charged with certain designated sex crimes if requested by a victim and court finds probative cause of transfer of bodily fluids. (Cal. Health & Safety Code § 121055)

---

[110] 42 U.S.C. § 14011(b)(2).

COLORADO

Permits AIDS testing of any defendant bound over for trial on sexual offense or convicted of sexual offense. (Colo. Rev. Stat. § 18-3-415)

CONNECTICUT

Provides for HIV testing of defendant convicted of enumerated sexual assault crimes at the request of the crime victim (Conn. Gen. Stat. § 54-102(h))

FLORIDA

Court shall order HIV testing of person charged with sexual offense. These HIV test results are not admissible in any criminal or juvenile proceeding. (Fla. Stat. Ann. § 960.003)

GEORGIA

Permits the victim of an "AIDS transmitting crime" to request that prosecuting agency test an individual charged with such a crime. If the accused declines to submit to the test, the court, "upon a showing of probable cause that the person arrested for the offense committed the alleged crime and significant exposure occurred, may order the test." Results are sealed and may not be used by state "in any criminal proceeding arising out of the alleged offense." AIDS testing is mandatory upon a verdict or plea of guilty to these crimes and for all individuals committed to a correctional institution. (Ga. Code § 17-10-15; Ga. Code § 42-5-52.1; Ga. Code § 15-11-66.1 (relating to children involved with committing delinquent acts constituting AIDS transmitting crimes); (Ga. Code § 31-22-9.1) (defining terms involved in AIDS testing statutes).

HAWAII

Provides for victim's right to request that a defendant convicted of sexual assault offenses be tested for HIV and for counseling of both victim and defendant before and after testing and if convicted person does not voluntarily consent to the HIV test or fails to take HIV test, court may order defendant to submit to the test. (Haw. Rev. Stat. § 325-16.5)

IDAHO

Defines AIDS and ARC (AIDS Related Complex) and manifestation of HIV as a venereal disease. Testing required of confined or imprisoned sex offenders whether convicted or not and release of results to victim if requested by the victim. (Idaho Code §§ 39-601, 39-604)

ILLINOIS

Permits the prosecution, at the request of the victim in certain designated sexual assault crimes, after a finding at a preliminary hearing that the defendant has committed the crime, to seek an order compelling the accused to be tested for HIV. Results of test to be kept strictly confidential by the medical personnel

689

involved and personally delivered in a sealed envelope to the victim and to the judge. It is in the judge's discretion to determine to whom, if anyone, the results should be revealed; however, the identity of the victim shall not be disclosed. (Ill. Comp. Stat. Ch. 720, § 5/12-18).

INDIANA

Court shall order testing of a convicted offender. Positive test results shall be reported to the victim. (Ind. Code §§ 35-38-1-10.5, 35-38-1-10.6)

IOWA

Provides that the county attorney may request an order requiring a defendant to submit to an HIV test, provided the defendant has been convicted in the sexual assault that involved a significant exposure defined in § 915.40 as "contact of the victim's ruptured or broken skin or mucous membranes with the blood or bodily fluids, other than tears, saliva, or perspiration of the convicted offender . . . or penetration of the convicted or alleged offender's penis into the victim's vagina or anus, contact between the mouth and genitalia, or contact between the genitalia of the offender or alleged offender and the genitalia or anus of the victim," and the defendant has been requested to provide consent for the testing and has refused to provide such consent. The court shall then conduct a hearing "in an informal manner," which shall be *in camera* and not released to the public. (Iowa Code § 915.42(5)(a))

Authorizes a court order to test defendant only if the petitioner or victim proves by a preponderance of the evidence that the sexual assault constituted a significant exposure. (Iowa Code §§ 915.40, 915.42(6)(a)).)

KENTUCKY

Provides for testing of defendants convicted of prostitution offenses. (Ky. Rev. Stat. § 529.090)

LOUISIANA

Requires a person indicted by a grand jury for a sexual offense to undergo testing for AIDS and HIV. (La. Code Crim. Proc. Ann. art. 499)

MAINE

Provides that a victim may request testing of a convicted offender and the convicted offender be informed of the test results. (Me. Rev. Stat. Ann § 19203-F)

MICHIGAN

Provides for testing of convicted sex offenders and results given to the victim if she has requested them. (Mich. Comp. Laws § 333.5129)

MISSISSIPPI

Provides for testing of convicted sex offenders who are imprisoned in a state correctional facility. Victims or their spouses shall be notified of results. (Miss. Code §§ 99-19-201, 99-19-203)

MISSOURI

Convicted sex offenders shall be tested and must pay for the testing. (Mo. Rev. Stat. § 191.663)

MONTANA

Convicted sex offenders may be tested at the request of a victim. (Mont. Code § 46-18-256)

NEBRASKA

Convicted sex offenders may be tested at the request of a victim as part of the defendant's sentence. (Neb. Rev. Stat. § 29-2290)

NEVADA

Requires testing for sexually-transmitted disease, including HIV, "as soon as practicable" after arrest for crime involving "sexual penetration of the victim's body." Results shall be disclosed to the victim. (Nev. Rev. Stat. § 441A.320)

NEW JERSEY

Provides for HIV testing of adult or juvenile offender, if (1) in the course of the commission of the offense, including the immediate flight thereafter or during any investigation or arrest related to that offense, a law enforcement officer, the victim, or other person suffered a prick from a hypodermic needle, provided there is probable cause to believe that the defendant is an intravenous user of controlled dangerous substances; or (2) in the course of the commission of the offense, including the immediate flight thereafter or during any investigation or arrest related to that offense, a law enforcement officer, the victim, or other person had contact with the defendant which involved or was likely to involve the transmission of bodily fluids. (N.J. Stat. §§ 2A:4A-43.4, 2C:43-2.3a)

NEW YORK

Permits a victim, or if victim is an infant or incompetent, that person's representative, to request HIV testing when a defendant is convicted of certain enumerated felony sexual assault crimes where an act of "sexual intercourse" or "deviate sexual intercourse" occurred. (N.Y. Crim. Proc. Law § 390.15)

NORTH CAROLINA

"If a judicial official conducting an initial appearance or first appearance hearing finds probable cause that an individual was exposed to the defendant in a manner that poses a significant risk of transmission of the AIDS virus or Hepatitis B by such defendant, the judicial official shall order the defendant to be detained for a reasonable period of time, not to exceed 24 hours, for investigation by public health officials and for testing for AIDS virus infection and Hepatitis B infection if required by public health officials. . . ." (N.C. Gen. Stat. § 15A-534.3)

NORTH DAKOTA

Mandates testing for convicted offenders. (N.D. Cent. Code § 23-07-07.5)

OHIO

Testing for HIV shall be performed upon individuals accused of certain sexual assaults with results provided to the victim upon request. The results are not admissible in a prosecution arising out of the transaction leading to the charge. "If the test result is negative, and the charge has not been dismissed or if the accused has been convicted of the charge or a different offense arising out of the same circumstances as the offense charged, the court shall order that the test be repeated not earlier than three months nor later than six months after the original test." Detailed provisions pertaining to the confidentiality and disclosure of HIV information are set forth in Section 3701.243. (Ohio Rev. Code §§ 2907.27, 3701.243)

OKLAHOMA

Provides for court order of individuals arrested for sex offenses and results provided to the victim. (Okla. Stat. tit. 63 § 1-524)

OREGON

Court shall seek consent of convicted defendant to submit to HIV testing. If defendant fails to consent and victim requests testing, court may order the testing. Section 137.076 provides for testing of convicted offenders including sexual abuse. Costs of testing to be paid for by defendant. (Or. Rev. Stat. §§ 135.139, 137.076)

RHODE ISLAND

Mandates testing for convicted sex offenders. (R.I. Gen. Laws § 11-34-10)

SOUTH CAROLINA

Mandates testing for convicted sex offenders. (S.C. Code Ann. § 16-3-740)

SOUTH DAKOTA

Provides for a victim or law enforcement official to request to the state's attorney that a defendant be tested for HIV, that a search warrant be obtained for the purpose of taking a blood sample, and that the court may issue such an order "if the court finds probable cause to believe that the defendant or the juvenile committed the offense and that there was an exchange of blood, semen, or other bodily fluids" between the defendant and victim. The victim or law enforcement official will be provided with the results of the test. The victim may also request the testing for himself or herself. The results of the test may not be used to establish a defendant's guilt or innocence of a charge and may not be used to determine a juvenile status as a delinquent. (S.D. Codified Laws §§ 23A-35B-2 to 23A-35B-5)

TENNESSEE

Provides for testing of certain convicted sex offenders upon request of the victim. (Tenn. Code § 39-13-521)

TEXAS

Individuals indicted for certain sex offenses may be compelled to undergo testing "to show or help show whether the person has a sexually-transmitted disease or . . . AIDS or . . . HIV. . . ." The court may direct the person to undergo the procedure or test on its own motion or on the request of the victim of the alleged offense. (Tex. Crim. Proc. Code § 21.31)

VIRGINIA

"As soon as practicable following arrest" of certain sex offenses, the prosecutor, after consulting with the victim, may request testing of the defendant. If the defendant refuses, the court may order the testing after a finding of probable cause that the defendant has committed the crime. Upon conviction, the court may order the defendant to undergo testing, even if testing had been previously ordered. Test results are not admissible as evidence in any criminal proceeding. (Va. Code § 18.2-62)

WASHINGTON

Provides for mandatory HIV testing and post-test counseling of all individuals convicted of designated sexual offenses. (Wash. Rev. Code § 70.24.340)

WEST VIRGINIA

Provides for the compelled testing of individuals convicted of designated sexual assaults and prostitution and that the court shall not release such a convicted offender from custody and revoke any order admitting the defendant to bail until the HIV testing and counseling has been completed. If the test results are negative, the court has authority to order further HIV testing of the convicted offender. The prosecuting attorney must inform the victim, or parent or guardian of the victim, at the earliest stage of the proceedings, of the availability of HIV-related testing. (W. Va. Code § 16-3C-2)

WISCONSIN

Permits a district attorney (in specifically enumerated criminal actions) to apply for a court-ordered HIV test of the defendant when there is probable cause to believe that the defendant "has significantly exposed" a victim to the HIV virus. (Wis. Stat. § 968.38)

§ 9.12   Constitutionality of statutes pertaining to HIV or AIDS testing of accused or convicted defendants.

Statutes that mandate the testing of individuals charged with or convicted of certain sexual offenses raise constitutional issues, particularly under the Fourth Amendment or Due Process Clause. Most courts have held that HIV testing is reasonable. As Georgia Supreme Court holds, "the Government's interest outweighs the interest of the individual" and that controlling AIDS is a valid purpose of testing statutes. [111] Part of the state's compelling interest is "making information available when it directly affects the physical and mental well-being of survivors of sexual assault." [112] The Massachusetts Supreme Court has also found that the involuntary taking of blood samples from defendants does not violate the Fourth Amendment. [113] It noted that the limited distribution of the data collected reasonably eliminates concerns about improper or wrongful disclosure of the information. [114] Federal courts have also found the collection of DNA information or DNA databases does not violate the Fourth Amendment. [115]

It is important that a court have probable cause to believe the accused or convicted sex offender has exposed the victim to a risk of possible HIV transmission without any showing that the defendant may be infected. When such a showing is made, the constitutionality of HIV testing statutes has been upheld as not violating due process, equal protection, or *ex post facto* clauses of the Constitution. [116] Testing statutes have also been upheld on the grounds that the results are not used for prosecution of the defendant. [117] The Missouri Supreme

---

[111] Adams v. State, 269 Ga. 405, 498 S.E.2d 268 (1998) (noting that Government has been particularly concerned with the needs and rights of crime victims). *See also* Johnetta J. v. Municipal Court, 218 Cal. App. 3d 1255, 1267, 267 Cal. Rptr. 666, 672–73 (1990).

[112] State *ex rel.* J.G., 151 N.J. 565, 581, 701 A.2d 1260, 1267 (1997).

[113] Landry v. Attorney General, 429 Mass. 336, 709 N.E.2d 1085 (1999), *cert. denied*, 528 U.S. 1073 (2000).

[114] Landry, 429 Mass. at 352–53, 709 N.E.2d at 95.

[115] Kruger v. Erickson, 875 F. Supp. 583, 588–589 (D. Minn. 1995), *aff'd*, 77 F.3d 1071 (8th Cir. 1996); Ryncarz v. Eikenberry, 824 F. Supp. 1493, 1498–99 (E.D. Wash. 1993).

[116] State v. Superior Court, 187 Ariz. 411, 930 P.2d 488 (1996) (Arizona statute which requires juvenile sex offender to be tested upon request of victim does not violate constitutional search and seizure protections); Fosman v. State, 664 So. 2d 1163 (Fla. Ct. App. 1995) ("We conclude that where there is probable cause to believe that a person has committed sexual battery and transmitted bodily fluids to the victim, there is no reasonable expectation of privacy in regard to having a blood test for HIV, the results of which are disclosed only to the victim and to public health authorities."); Adams v. State, 269 Ga. 405, 498 S.E.2d 268 (1998); People v. Adams, 149 Ill. 2d 331, 597 N.E.2d 574 (1992); State *ex rel.* J.G., 151 N.J. 565, 701 A.2d 1260 (1997); People v. J.G., 171 Misc. 2d 440, 655 N.Y.S.2d 783 (1996) (holding mandatory HIV testing of a convicted sex offender is neither an unreasonable search and seizure nor an *ex post facto* violation); State v. Parr, 182 Wis. 2d 349, 365, 513 N.W.2d 647, 652 (1994).

[117] Fosman v. State, 664 So. 2d 1163, 1166–67 (Fla. Ct. App. 1995); Adams v. State, 269 Ga. 405, 408, 498 S.E.2d 268 (1998); State *ex rel.* J.G., 151 N.J. 565, 587, 701 A.2d 1260, 1271 (1997).

Court has upheld the constitutionality of its statute making it a felony to knowingly expose others to HIV through sexual contact as being neither over-broad nor vague.[118] However, the court noted that defendant's argument that the statute criminalizes certain conduct which may be constitutionally protected (e.g., a pregnant woman knowing she is infected could be subject to prosecution if she gave birth, or heterosexual contact between an HIV-positive person and "a willing and informed partner") could be raised by someone in that category should they be prosecuted, but that the defendant in the instant appeal did not have standing to raise such a challenge.[119] With respect to the ambiguity of the statute, the court noted that this constitutional analysis should be made on the facts of the case, and that in the case on appeal the defendant had engaged in unprotected sex despite verbal warnings from the public health counselor and had signed a statement that he was aware of the law.[120] Subsequent to the crime charged in this case, Missouri revised its law to require that a defendant acted in a "reckless manner" by exposing others to HIV through contact with blood, semen, or vaginal fluid, or by sharing drug needles as opposed to knowingly exposing others to HIV through sexual contact.[121]

Washington's Supreme Court has upheld the constitutionality of that state's mandated testing of convicted sexual offenders as not violative of defendant's privacy rights and within the "special needs" requirement for such testing.[122] It noted that such testing can benefit offenders by making them aware of their HIV status and provides offenders with the opportunity to obtain treatment.[123] The court also noted the compelling interest of the state in such testing in that the tests assisted in prison and probation management of offenders as well as dealt with the mental anguish and anxiety of a sexual assault victim.[124]

An intermediate California appellate court upheld the constitutionality of California's Proposition 96, which called for statutory provisions for mandatory AIDS blood testing by applying the "special need" analysis upholding searches in "context involving special circumstances making no warrant or probable cause requirements impractical."[125] However, there may well be limits to the

---

[118] State v. Mahan, 971 S.W.2d 307 (Mo. 1998).

[119] 971 S.W.2d at 311.

[120] 971 S.W.2d at 311–12.

[121] See § 9.5; Mo. Rev. Stat. § 191.677.

[122] In re Juveniles A, B, C, D, E, 121 Wash. 2d 80, 847 P.2d 455 (1993).

[123] Id. at 88, 847 P.2d at 458.

[124] Id. at 94, 847 P.2d at 461.

[125] Johnetta J. v. Municipal Court, 218 Cal. App. 3d 1255, 1272–73, 267 Cal. Rptr. 666, 676 (1990) (noting that its decision was based on an analysis of (1) "whether the blood testing scheme arises from a 'special need' beyond the needs of ordinary law enforcement, and (2) if so, whether the intrusion of compulsory blood testing for AIDS, without probable cause or individualized suspicion that the AIDS virus will be found in the tested person's blood, is justified by that need." Id. at 1273, 267 Cal. Rptr. at 677.). See also People v. C.S., 222 Ill. App. 3d 348, 583 N.E.2d

applicability of some of the testing provisions. For example, California's mandatory testing requirement cannot be applied to attempted sexual activities, such as attempted forcible sodomy or attempted forcible oral copulation, since they are not offenses specifically designated in the statute as among those subject to mandatory testing.[126]

In general, testing of convicted criminals presents fewer issues of intrusion upon individual rights since there is an implicit finding that the defendant has engaged in sexual contact with a victim.[127] Washington's Supreme Court notes that there are fewer restrictions in testing a convicted criminal and that "for sexual offenders in particular, their expectation of privacy in bodily fluids is greatly diminished because they have engaged in a class of criminal behavior which presents the potential of exposing others to the AIDS virus."[128]

§ 9.13   Non-statutory basis to compel testing of defendant for HIV.

Attempts to obtain a defendant's blood can be made even when there is no statutory provision for such blood testing. AIDS testing may be part of a plea agreement. However, it may be a breach of a plea agreement for the prosecution to seek HIV testing at the time of sentence when it was not part of the plea bargain.[129]

Courts have differed in their determination as to whether traditional discovery procedures are available to mandate the testing of a defendant for HIV. The United States district court in the Virgin Islands has permitted the testing of an unconvicted defendant for HIV for the benefit of a rape victim.[130] An intermediate New York appellate court, despite the absence of statutory authority, found no violation of a defendant's constitutional rights when he was directed to undergo an AIDS test upon the request of the victim.[131] And a New York trial

---

726 (1991), *appeal denied*, 146 Ill. 2d 636, 602 N.E.2d 461 (1992) (upholding the constitutionality of the Illinois statute requiring mandatory HIV testing of individuals convicted of certain drug offenses since "the testing requirement of § 5-5-3(H) directly addresses the public health concerns surrounding the spread of HIV among intravenous drug users. It does not compel an oppressive treatment but rather requires mere submission to a minimally intrusive medical technique involving virtually no risk, trauma, or pain." *Id.* at 354, 583 N.E.2d at 730.).

[126] People v. Jillie, 8 Cal. App. 4th 960, 11 Cal. Rptr. 2d 107 (1992).

[127] Jones v. Murray, 962 F.2d 302, 307 (4th Cir. 1992), *cert. denied*, 506 U.S. 977 (1992).

[128] *See, e.g.*, People v. Griffin, 233 A.D.2d 616, 650 N.Y.S.2d 42 (1996), *appeal denied*, 89 N.Y.2d 1012, 680 N.E.2d 624, 658 N.Y.S.2d 250 (1997); *In re* Juveniles A, B, C, D, E, 121 Wash.2d 80, 92, 847 P.2d 455, 460 (1993).

[129] State v. Abbott, 79 Haw. 317, 901 P.2d 1296 (1995).

[130] United States v. Ramirez-Burgos, 1994 U.S. Dist. LEXIS 4564 at 3–4 (D.P.R. Mar. 9, 1994); Virgin Islands v. Roberts, 756 F. Supp. 898 (D.V.I. 1991), *aff'd without op.*, 961 F.2d 1567 (3d Cir. 1992).

[131] People v. Cook, 143 A.D.2d 486, 532 N.Y.S.2d 940, *appeal denied*, 73 N.Y.2d 786, 533 N.E.2d 676, 536 N.Y.S.2d 746 (1988).

court has held that a defendant can be forced to undergo an AIDS test when a crime lab refused to examine a rape kit because the defendant had declared that he had AIDS.[132] However, a New York intermediate appellate court has held that a prosecutor's motion under a discovery statute to obtain blood for an HIV test from a defendant charged with rape and sodomy was not for the purpose of developing evidence, and an order mandating the test was outside the authorized powers of a trial court.[133]

If the prosecution seeks to develop evidence of the defendant's HIV infection to establish an element of a crime, such as attempted murder due to the defendant's HIV infection, a court may then have a basis to order testing under the prosecution's right to non-testimonial evidence.[134]

§ 9.14 Legal issues in compelling a defendant or suspect to undergo a test for HIV.

Statutes providing for the testing of defendants vary as to whether the testing may be performed before or after conviction, as well as to the scope of the sex offenses to which the statutes apply. Some states mandate testing only at the request of a victim. Some apply only to acts of intercourse or sodomy, whereas others apply to crimes such as sexual abuse where only touching between the victim and defendant may have been involved.

The prerequisite of a testing statute must be satisfied. If the request for testing does not establish the transmission of bodily fluids from one person to another, it is improper to order testing of the defendant.[135]

If a statute provides that there is probable cause to believe there was a transfer of bodily fluids, one court has found that standards were met if a defendant tries to penetrate a victim, regardless of whether the record establishes that the defendant was erect.[136] The practical advice from these cases is that prosecutors should make sure the plea allocation or trial testimony is developed to support an application for HIV testing.

---

[132] People v. Durham, 146 Misc. 2d 913, 553 N.Y.S.2d 944 (1990).

[133] John Doe v. Connell, 179 A.D.2d 196, 583 N.Y.S.2d 707 (1992) (noting that the prosecution had cited "no statutory authority that grants jurisdiction to county court either to compel a defendant in a criminal action to submit to a blood test for the purpose of determining his HIV status or to direct disclosure of the results of that test where, as here, the test results were not for use in any aspect of the criminal action." *Id.* at 199, 583 N.Y.S.2d at 709–10).

[134] People v. Rodriguez, 214 A.D.2d 347, 625 N.Y.S.2d 20, *appeal denied*, 86 N.Y.2d 740, 655 N.E.2d 718, 631 N.Y.S.2d 621 (1995) (defendant was properly compelled to undergo an AIDS blood test as this evidence was material to a charge of attempted murder).

[135] James v. State, 695 So. 2d 863 (Fla. Ct. App. 1997); State v. Johnson, 131 Idaho 808, 964 P.2d 675 (1998) (reversing trial court's order compelling defendant to undergo HIV testing since prosecution's expert did not establish the likelihood that defendant's saliva had transmitted to the police officer who was bitten by defendant; rejected argument that "common sense" was that saliva would be transmitted by a bite, particularly where defendant's bite was over clothing).

[136] People v. Caird, 63 Cal. App. 4th 578, 73 Cal. Rptr. 2d 799 (1998).

An intermediate California appellate court has held that the involuntary AIDS or HIV testing statute is strictly limited by statute and that a failure to comply with a requirement of the statute that the victim file a written request will nullify an AIDS testing order.[137] Similarly, if the statute requires a hearing, the failure to hold a hearing and make a finding of probable cause required by statute will invalidate an AIDS testing order.[138] It is also true that since the HIV testing requirement is not penal in nature, it may apply to pleas after the effective date of the statute.[139]

The California Supreme Court has also distinguished the right of a defendant in objecting on appeal to an involuntary HIV testing for insufficiency of the evidence and lack of probable cause. Upholding the general rule, a defendant must timely object to the absence of an express finding of probable cause or docket notation when challenging an HIV testing order.[140] A defendant, however, may challenge an order directing submission to a blood test for insufficiency of the evidence even when he has failed to make an appropriate objection in the trial court because involuntary HIV testing is conditional upon sufficient evidence to support the implied finding of probable cause.[141]

Not all defects in procedure are fatal. A court's failure to include a mandated HIV test in its sentencing order does not preclude the court from subsequently ordering the HIV test after the defendant commences his sentence.[142]

Many statutes require only that there be probable cause that a defendant committed an enumerated offense to trigger the right to HIV testing. The fact that a defendant is acquitted of the enumerated offense does not necessarily preclude a mandated HIV test.[143] Sometimes courts must look to the circumstances of the plea or crime to determine whether or not the defendant is subject to mandatory testing. For example, a defendant who pleads guilty to rape while acting in concert may be compelled to undergo testing even though acting in

---

[137] People v. Guardado, 40 Cal. App. 4th 757, 47 Cal. Rptr. 781 (1995).

[138] Id.

[139] People v. Doe, 169 Misc. 2d 29, 642 N.Y.S.2d 996 (1996).

[140] People v. Stowell, 31 Cal. 4th 1107, 79 P.3d 1030, 6 Cal. Rptr. 3d 723 (2003) (holding that appeal of an HIV testing order requires a timely objection to the absence of an express finding of probable cause).

[141] People v. Butler, 31 Cal. 4th 1119, 79 P.3d 1036, 6 Cal. Rptr. 3d 730 (2003) (holding a defendant may challenge an order directing submission to a blood test for insufficiency of the evidence even when he has failed to make an appropriate objection in the trial court). *See also*, People v. Harward, 2004 Cal. App. Unpub. LEXIS 5582; People v. Newton, 2004 Cal. App. Unpub. LEXIS 17.

[142] People v. Barriga, 54 Cal. App. 4th 67, 62 Cal. Rptr. 2d 502 (1997) (trial court could order statutorily requested blood test for convicted defendant after defendant commenced his sentence since trial court had the inherent power to correct its unauthorized sentence that omitted order for HIV test).

[143] State v. Parr, 182 Wis. 2d 349, 364, 513 N.W.2d 647, 652, *review denied*, 520 N.W.2d 90 (1994).

concert is not an enumerated offense subjecting a defendant to testing since the defendant has thereby admitted to "raping" the victim.[144] Similarly, a defendant's conviction for the continuous sexual abuse of a child may not be an enumerated offense but encompasses sexual acts which are the subject of mandatory testing.[145] However, other courts may strictly construe a statute to apply only to specified offenses or only offenses committed after the statute became effective.[146] For example, if a defendant is indicted on a rape charge, but pleads guilty to attempted sexual abuse, which is not a designated offense in the statute for the mandated testing of convicted offenders, a court lacks authority to order an HIV test.[147] Thus, the prosecution's plea reduction may affect the ability to order HIV testing of a defendant.

Sometimes it is necessary to look beyond the named conviction to see if the facts underlying the plea or conviction support the conduct triggering HIV testing.[148] While a court may be able to look behind a defendant's convictions to determine if a jury necessarily found a defendant to have committed an offense justifying HIV testing, if it is unclear what acts the jury relied upon to reach its verdict, an AIDS testing order may be stricken.[149] The fact that an HIV test may provide little valuable information to the victim, because the test was 18 months after the crime, does not necessarily defeat a victim's right to have a defendant tested.[150]

§ 9.15 Disclosure of test results.

Once a defendant is tested for AIDS, the next question is to what extent this information can be disclosed or made available to others. Where a defendant is compelled to undergo HIV testing, some of the state statutes provide for limited access to the test results. (*See* § 9.11.)

Under the federal HIV testing statute, (§ 9.10), test results are to be disclosed only to the victim, or victim's parents or guardian, or the person tested.[151] The

---

[144] People v. Frausto, 36 Cal. App. 4th 712, 42 Cal. Rptr. 2d 540 (1995).

[145] People v. Adames, 54 Cal. App. 4th 198, 62 Cal. Rptr. 2d 631, *review denied*, No. S061382, 1997 Cal. LEXIS 3866 (June 25, 1997).

[146] *In re* Khonsavanh S., 67 Cal. App. 4th 532, 79 Cal. Rptr. 2d 80 (1998) (holding defendant's conviction for gang-style killings did not fall within specified circumstances for compelled HIV testing of criminal suspects); People v. Jillie, 8 Cal. App. 4th 960, 11 Cal. Rptr. 2d 107 (1992); People v. Doe, 169 Misc. 2d 29, 642 N.Y.S.2d 996 (1996); State v. Foster, 81 Wash. App. 508, 915 P.2d 567 (1996).

[147] Donald P. v. Palmieri, 668 N.Y.S.2d 218 (1998).

[148] People v. Doe, 169 Misc.2d 29, 642 N.Y.S.2d 996 (1996).

[149] People v. Barron, 34 Cal. App. 4th 1003, 40 Cal. Rptr. 660 (1995) (decision subsequently withdrawn from publication. *See* 1995 Cal. App. LEXIS 415 and 1995 Cal. LEXIS 4955).

[150] Isom v. State, 722 So. 2d 237 (Fla. Dist. Ct. App. 1998).

[151] 42 U.S.C. § 14011(b)(5).

victim may disclose the results to a "medical professional, counselor, family member, or sexual partner(s) the victim may have had since the attack."[152] The results may not be used as evidence in any criminal trial.[153] This is true with most states' statutes providing for the testing of defendants.

New York has a statute that broadly applies to disclosure of all confidential HIV-related information.[154]

(1) Notwithstanding any other provision of law, no court shall issue an order for the disclosure of confidential HIV-related information, except a court of record of competent jurisdiction in accordance with the provisions of this section.

(2) A court may grant an order for disclosure of confidential HIV-related information upon an application showing: (a) a compelling need for disclosure of the information for the adjudication of a criminal or civil proceeding; (b) a clear and imminent danger to an individual whose life or health may unknowingly be at significant risk as a result of contact with the individual to whom the information pertains; (c) upon application of a state, county, or local health officer, a clear and imminent danger to the public health; or (d) that the applicant is lawfully entitled to the disclosure and the disclosure is consistent with the provisions of this article.

The above statute also provides for sealing of records pertaining to the proceeding and notice of proceedings to individuals affected by application. The court may also, under Section 2785 (6)(d) of the statute, include such other measures as it deems necessary to limit any disclosures not authorized by its order.

The propriety of statutory disclosure provisions has been successfully challenged. An Illinois statute providing for the disclosure of HIV test results to the state's attorney was deemed without justification and against the public interest when testing was mandated for a defendant convicted for drug-related charges.[155] The state should demonstrate a reason for needing the results, such as where the information is necessary for a specific prosecution.[156]

As part of a criminal prosecution, a prosecutor may be able to subpoena existing HIV information of a defendant under a statute providing for release of such information when a compelling need is established.[157]

---

[152] *Id.*

[153] 42 U.S.C. § 14011(b)(6).

[154] N.Y. Pub. Health Law § 2785.

[155] People v. C.S., 222 Ill. App. 3d 348, 583 N.E.2d 726 (1991), *appeal denied*, 146 Ill. 2d 636, 602 N.E.2d 461 (1992).

[156] *Id.* at 355–56, 583 N.E.2d at 731.

[157] Weaver v. State, 66 Ark. App. 249, 990 S.W.2d 572, *cert. denied* 528 U.S. 913 (1999) (upholding prosecutor's use of aubpoena to obtain records pertaining to defendant's HIV status in a prosecution for exposing another person to HIV; John B. v. Superior Court, 121 Cal. App. 4th 1000, 18 Cal. Rptr. 3d 48 (2004) (finding the trial court did not abuse its discretion in compelling

It is important to insure that appropriate safeguards are in place for the confidentiality of test results. These provisions can be included in the order directing testing if they are not covered by a statute. Prison inmates and convicted offenders have a constitutional right of privacy that protects them from unwarranted disclosure of their HIV status, even if the HIV testing can be mandated.[158] This right of privacy can be violated when a state prison system transfers HIV-positive inmates to a particular facility.[159] When there has been an unlawful disclosure of an individual's HIV test results by a public official, there may be a violation of individual's constitutional right to privacy under 42 U.S.C. § 1983.[160]

It is possible that a complainant's HIV status may be inadvertently disclosed to the defense. This may happen when such HIV status set forth in medical records is disclosed by the prosecution. One court dealing with this scenario granted the people a protective order redacting information pertaining to the HIV status of the complainant from all discovery material.[161] The same court ordered the prosecution to arrange for a physician or health officer to inform the defendant that he may have come into contact with a person who was infected with HIV without naming the individual.[162] The court noted that generally the victim's HIV status will generally not be relevant or discoverable.[163] However, the court would not prohibit a defense attorney who learned of the complainant's HIV status, such as through information inadvertently disclosed, from truthfully answering a client's question about whether or not the complainant is HIV positive.[164]

---

disclosure of the defendant's medical records that may contain information about his HIV status); *In re* Gribetz, 159 Misc. 2d 550, 605 N.Y.S.2d 834 (1994) (limiting disclosure of test results in this prosecution for reckless endangerment and assault only to the prosecutor directly involved in the case).

[158] Nolley v. County of Erie, 776 F. Supp. 715, 731 (W.D.N.Y. 1991).

[159] Doe v. Coughlin, 697 F. Supp. 1234, 1236–37 (N.D.N.Y. 1988).

[160] Hillman v. Columbia County, 164 Wis. 2d 376, 474 N.W.2d 913 (1991) (holding that oral communication among jail employees and inmates concerning an inmate's HIV status violated confidentiality provisions of a Wisconsin statute limiting dissemination of test results for the presence of HIV and that summary judgment was improperly granted as to individual defendants based on qualified immunity doctrine, but that the county government was not shown to have demonstrated a deliberate indifference to the inmate's rights). *See generally* Annotation, *State Statutes or Regulations Expressly Governing Disclosure of Fact That Person Has Tested Positive for Human Immunodeficiency Virus (HIV) or Acquired Immunodeficiency Syndrome (AIDS)*, 12 A.L.R.5TH 149 (1993).

[161] People v. Pedro M., 165 Misc. 2d 710, 630 N.Y.S.2d 208 (N.Y. Crim. Ct. 1995).

[162] *Id.*

[163] *Id.*

[164] *Id.* at 719, 630 N.Y.S.2d at 215.

CHAPTER 10

HEARSAY

§ 10.1   Introduction.

Hearsay is one of the most frequently encountered evidentiary issues in sexual assault trials, particularly in trials involving children. Children often are unavailable to testify at trial, and the prosecution frequently seeks to use a child's prior statements. The United States Supreme Court's decision in *Crawford v. Washington*,[1] discussed in § 10.45, alters the legal landscape of sexual assault cases, particularly since it precludes use of statements previously permitted under special statutes pertaining to introduction of child hearsay.

When hearsay issues are anticipated in a trial, it is important to determine what, if any, pretrial motions are necessary to protect against inadmissible evidence. While many hearsay exceptions are well known, they often have been applied differently in sexual assault cases because of the nature of the crime and the fact that children are frequently involved. The Supreme Court of the United States

---

[1] 541 U.S. 36 (2004).

has recognized that the right to confront witnesses is not absolute and must be balanced against other legal and societal values. The Court has noted: "We have attempted to harmonize the goal of the [Confrontation] Clause — placing a limit on the kind of evidence that may be received against a defendant — with a societal interest in accurate fact finding, which may require consideration of out-of-court statements."[2] Hearsay admitted under firmly rooted exceptions (such as the excited utterance and medical treatment exceptions) to the hearsay rule do not constitute a violation of a defendant's right of confrontation.[3] *Crawford* represents a return to a more traditional application of the hearsay rule.

In sexual assault trials, the hearsay exceptions can be particularly important when the victim does not testify. Furthermore, the admission of hearsay will be particularly important if the proof is not overwhelming. Thus, the application of the hearsay rule in sexual assault trials has resulted in a significant body of law.

Unfortunately, the interpretation of the various hearsay exceptions has not been uniform. There have been wide variations among the jurisdictions as courts have struggled to apply long-standing rules to relatively new legal applications, such as out-of-court statements of children who may not be competent to testify.

It is also important to remember that whether a statement qualifies for admission as an exception under the hearsay rule is only the initial issue. Other issues may affect admissibility. In many trials, there are multiple admissions of hearsay that must be evaluated to see if they are unnecessarily cumulative.[4] This has become a particular issue in child sexual assault trials where there is little or no court testimony from the child complainant. It is discussed further in § 10.52.

Statements must also be reviewed to see if their probative value is outweighed by their prejudicial effect. Even when all criteria for the admissibility of evidence are met, limiting instructions should be provided when the hearsay is offered for a limited purpose. (*See* § 10.14).

While hearsay may be objectionable, there could be tactical reasons not to object to its introduction. It may open the door to other hearsay statements that are favorable to a party, such as other statements a child made regarding her medical history that negate allegations of abuse. Finally, practitioners should note that unobjected hearsay can support a conviction and have the same effect as legally admissible evidence. Hearsay also may not be objectionable when a party

---

[2] Bourjaily v. United States, 483 U.S. 171, 182 (1987).

[3] Bourjaily v. United States, 483 U.S. 171, 182 (1987).

[4] *See, e.g.*, State v. Tizard, 897 S.W.2d 732 (Tenn. Crim. App. 1994) (In reviewing the use of prior consistent hearsay statements of a sexual assault complainant, court noted that there was concern with "unnecessarily cumulative" evidence. "Thus, trial courts should be mindful of the need to limit credibility bolstering evidence to that which they in their discretion, determine will not be unduly prejudicial to the opponent of such evidence." *Id.*).

opens the door to hearsay testimony. For example, a defense attorney who inquires of a complainant's mother about what caused the child to inform her of the rape opens the door on redirect examination to hearsay statements of the complainant.[5]

§ 10.2　Hearsay defined — what is an assertion and statements made as operative legal facts.

Federal Rule of Evidence 801 represents a generally accepted definition of hearsay.[6] Hearsay is a statement, other than one made by the declarant while testifying at the trial or hearing, offered in evidence to prove the truth of the matter asserted. A statement is (1) an oral or written assertion or (2) nonverbal conduct of a person if it is intended by the person as an assertion. A declarant is a person who makes a statement. Hearsay within hearsay is not excluded under the hearsay rule "if each part of the combined statement conforms with an exception to the hearsay rule."[7] This principle is often applied to statements and information contained in business or medical records.

A major problem in the definition of hearsay, often encountered in sexual assault situations, is the word "assert." While "assert" plays a significant role in the definition of hearsay, the word itself is not defined. Another problematic area frequently encountered is whether the statement is actually offered to prove the truth of a matter or for some other purpose. In reality, the effect on the trier of the fact may be the same, but courts go to great lengths in making such a distinction.

Statements made as part of the operative legal facts — or issue — forming the basis of a claim, charge, or defense, are considered verbal acts and not hearsay. Thus, in a witness tampering prosecution arising out of a sexual abuse trial, a witness' repetition of statements made to her by another on behalf of the defendant were admissible as verbal acts establishing that the defendant was attempting to discourage a witness from testifying.[8]

§ 10.3　Reasons for the hearsay rule.

While it is not unusual for courts to lament the unreliability of hearsay statements, hearsay is often admitted. Traditionally, several objections have been raised to the use of hearsay.[9] The hearsay rule excludes out-of-court statements offered for the truth of the matter asserted because of four general areas of risk in the out-of-court declaration: those are (1) insincerity, (2) faulty perception,

---

[5] Levy v. State, 724 So. 2d 405 (Miss. 1998).

[6] FED. R. EVID. 801.

[7] FED. R. EVID. 805.

[8] State v. Charger, 2000 SD 70, 611 N.W.2d 221 (2000).

[9] 2 MCCORMICK ON EVIDENCE § 245, at 93 (4th ed. 1992).

(3) faulty memory and (4) faulty narration, each of which decreases the reliability of the inference from the statement made to the conclusion for which it is offered.[10] The history and reasons for the hearsay rule are discussed at length in Justice Scalia's opinion in *Crawford v. Washington*.[11] Under the Anglo-American system of trial, the hearsay statement is made without the benefit of any oath. This is particularly true of child hearsay, which may be from a declarant who is incapable of providing an oath. Also, the fact that the statement is made out-of-court deprives the court and jury the opportunity to observe the declarant and, lastly, out-of-court statements are not subject to cross-examination at trial. Despite these objections, many factors have led to the admission of hearsay.

In sexual assault trials, certain out-of-court statements may, in fact, be more reliable than those made in court due to the nature of the crime and the circumstances under which the statements were made. Some of these factors are ultimately involved in the examination of the admissibility of statements under the residual exception of the hearsay rule, as set forth in Federal Rule of Evidence 803(24), which must now be viewed in the context of *Crawford*. The practical problem with hearsay is the lack of opportunity to cross-examine the declarant.

While cross-examination might not be an ultimate test of reliability, it certainly plays a crucial role. As one court has noted in declining to accept hearsay statements of a child, hearsay is not acceptable since it cannot be cross-examined, but also, in many situations, it provides details that a witness cannot.[12] At trial, the litigator must argue to the court the legal grounds that hearsay should not be accepted. However, if the objected evidence to hearsay is also admitted, the attorney should also point out to the jury why the statement, while admitted into evidence, should not be viewed by the jury with the same force and effect as other testimony. The jury should be made to understand why the admitted hearsay should be believed and whether the lack of cross-examination undermines its reliability. Too often attorneys fail to agressively attack before the jury as they do before the court the inherent problems in accepting hearsay.

§ 10.4 Non-assertive conduct, such as child's crying or other behaviors.

An initial question is whether the out-of-court statement or conduct is hearsay. The usual issue is whether the statement or conduct is an assertion. An utterance, writing, or nonverbal conduct that is not assertive is not hearsay. Many utterances are not intentional expressions of fact or opinion, such as greetings, pleasantries, expressions of joy, sadness, or such other emotions. Thus a child's shaking, trembling, or crying is admissible since it is non-assertive conduct. Non-assertive

---

[10] *See, e.g.,* Headley v. Tilghman, 53 F.3d 472,477 (2d Cir. 1995).

[11] 541 U.S. 36 (2004).

[12] Commonwealth v. Haber, 351 Pa. Super. 79, 505 A.2d 273 (1986).

conduct is usually "an uncontrollable action or reaction."[13] Testimony that a child appeared to be happy that her mother was in the hospital, wondered where her younger sister was, and was upset that the defendant might be at the hospital was not hearsay because these acts were not assertions.[14] Non-assertive conduct may be circumstantial evidence of a fact; a typical reason for offering it.

A common area of hearsay issue in sexual assault cases concerns victim behavior or conduct at a particular point in time as testified to by a third party, such as the victim's reactions while being questioned by a police officer.[15] For example, testimony of a child's crying when questioned by her mother about a defendant's conduct does not constitute assertive conduct.[16] Similarly, a mother's testimony that her child became frightened of the house in which the child was sexually assaulted is not an assertion.[17] Non-assertive conduct may be testimony by complainant's mother as to her mental health and demeanor, such as she was "frightened, sad, unhappy, and confused" and that "she had trouble sleeping at night and rarely left the house."[18] The key to the admission of such testimony is that while it was offered for the truth of the conduct, it was not assertive in nature by the declarant, thus falling outside the scope of the hearsay rule. This should be compared with the examples set forth in § 10.6 regarding assertive nonverbal conduct.

Another fundamental question is whether the declarant intended the utterance to be assertive. There are other issues after that determination is made. The non-assertive utterance is still subject to the rule of relevance. An example of apparent hearsay that is not hearsay would be an abuse victim's stepmother's testimony that the victim's "actual story never varied." Non-assertive conduct may include a witness who heard a little girl's voice say, "Daddy, don't!" because no "matter" is asserted in the statement.[19] It would seem such testimony may not be hearsay, but may be bolstering the victim's testimony.[20] The testimony may also be objectionable as unduly prejudicial and cumulative.

[13] 2 MCCORMICK ON EVIDENCE § 250, at 107 (4th ed. 1992).

[14] State v. Weaver, 608 N.W.2d 797, 804–05 (Iowa 2000).

[15] People v. Chitwood, 148 Ill. App. 3d 730, 499 N.E.2d 992 (1986), *appeal denied*, 505 N.E.2d 356 (1987).

[16] People v. Davis, 139 Mich. App. 811, 363 N.W.2d 35 (1984). *See also* Cole v. United States, 327 F.2d 360 (9th Cir. 1964).

[17] People v. Jackson, 203 Ill. App. 3d 1, 560 N.E.2d 1019, *appeal denied*, 135 Ill. 2d 562, 564 N.E.2d 843 (1990). *See also In re* Dependency of Penelope B., 104 Wash. 2d 643, 709 P.2d 1185 (1985).

[18] State v. Martin, 38 Conn. App. 731, 741, 663 A.2d 1078, 1084 (1995), *appeal denied*, 237 Conn. 921, 676 A.2d 1376, *cert. denied*, 519 U.S. 1044 (1996) (noting that non-assertive conduct such as running to hide or shaking and trembling is not hearsay and that an out-of-court statement is not hearsay when offered to illustrate circumstantially the declarant's then present state of mind).

[19] State v. Gifford, 595 A.2d 1049, 1052 (Me. 1991), *cert. denied*, 502 U.S. 1040 (1992).

[20] United States v. Provost, 875 F.2d 172, 176 (8th Cir. 1989).

Determining whether a statement is assertive is often necessary in sexual assault cases. The victim's behavior, especially soon after an assault, may or may not be assertive. (*See* § 10.10.) Children's statements and behavior must also be evaluated for their assertive nature, especially when playing with dolls.

§ 10.5   Non-assertive conduct while sleeping or unconscious.

An area of testimony often encountered in sexual assault cases involves statements or conduct, particularly by child victims, while sleeping or unconscious. [21] Court rulings in these areas revolve heavily around a finding of whether or not the conduct by the declarant was intentional or assertive. Thus, utterances by a child when asleep consisting of "Arne, stop!" and "Arne, don't!" were held to be involuntary verbal reactions of a child rather than conscious, intentional assertions and, therefore, admissible. [22] The argument often made in support of the admissibility of such hearsay is that nightmares are a common symptom of sexual abuse. [23] For example, a child's therapist may utilize a nightmare as a basis of expert opinion that the victim's behavior is consistent with sexual abuse. [24] Previous decisions that upheld statements made by a child during nightmares under a special child hearsay statute can now be challenged under *Crawford.* [25]

Other courts have adopted a more cautious view of statements made by child sexual abuse victims during their sleep. For example, a New York intermediate appellate court held that statements made by a child sex abuse victim during sleep were admissible as hearsay. However, on appeal, the state's highest court

---

[21] *See* Jay M. Zitter, Annotation, *Admissibility of Evidence Concerning Words Spoken While Declarant was Asleep or Unconscious,* 14 A.L.R.4TH 802 (1982).

[22] State v. Stevens, 58 Wash. App. 478, 794 P.2d 38, *review denied,* 115 Wash. 2d 1025, 802 P.2d 128 (1990); State v. Dunlap, 239 Wis. 2d 423, 620 N.W.2d 398 (2000), *aff'd,* 250 Wis. 2d 466, 640 N.W.2d 112 (2002) (child's father testified about child's nightmares about defendant returning home and telling her parents. Court held this evidence was not improperly received into evidence. "Although we do agree that the nightmare evidence was in fact hearsay, it falls into the category of mental and emotional condition evidence, admissible as an exception to the hearsay rule pursuant to Wis. Stat. § 908.03(3)." *Id.* at 408, 620 N.W.2d at 411.).

[23] State v. Stevens, 58 Wash. App. 478, 794 P.2d 38, 45, *review denied,* 115 Wash.2d 1025, 802 P.2d 128 (1990). *See also* State v. Burress, 1995 Neb. App. LEXIS 141 (Apr. 18, 1995) (mother's testimony of child's nightmares and other behaviors admissible as to her state of mind, emotion, sensation, or physical condition, and such evidence can be interpreted by jury "to mean the child was under stress" without expert testimony interpreting the behavior).

[24] United States v. Calogero, 44 M.J. 697 (C.G.C.C.A. 1996), *aff'd,* 46 M.J. 423 (C.A.A.F. 1997). The propriety of such an expert opinion is discussed in Chapter 11. *See also* People v. Leske, 937 P.2d 821 (Colo. Ct. App. 1996) (holding that to the extent admission's hearsay testimony concerning child's nightmare was improper, the error was harmless).

[25] *See, e.g.,* State v. Brown, 953 S.W.2d 133 (Mo. Ct. App. 1997) (involving nightmares of six-year-old child huddled in the corner of her bed, distraught and panicked, at the time of statements).

ruled that any errors in the admission of such statements were harmless without further addressing the legal issues involved in such statements. [26]

An example of non-assertive conduct appears in the following direct examination of the mother in a case involving alleged child sexual abuse.

Q. Prosecutor: After Mr. Van Meter left your home, has the child had any emotional problems?

A. Mother: Yes.

Q. Prosecutor: Could you just describe that briefly for the Court please?

A. Mother: Terrible temper tantrums and nightmares screaming at night. She said that Earl was under her bed and he was going to get her. Sucking her thumb, wetting her pants, and what we call be-bopping . . . where she sits like — she sits on the couch and she bangs her head on the wall.

Q. Prosecutor: Has the child been in therapy for those things?

A. Mother: Yes ma'am. [27]

The appellate court permitted this testimony as relevant evidence without discussing the hearsay issues involved. This testimony is an example of the type of non-assertive conduct often seen in sexual assault cases, especially by children. A court may permit the testimony not as proof of a rape, but simply to show the child was mumbling in her sleep and having nightmares. [28]

A key question in analyzing the admissibility of such declarations is to determine their meaning, significance, and relevance. If the statements do not relate to the defendant, they have no relevance. If the statements are unclear as

---

[26] People v. DiFabio, 170 A.D.2d 1028, 566 N.Y.S.2d 172 (1991), *aff'd*, 79 N.Y.2d 836, 588 N.E.2d 80, 580 N.Y.S.2d 182 (1992). *See also* State v. Posten, 302 N.W.2d 638, 641–42 (Minn. 1981):

> The real issue is whether this evidence was sufficiently trustworthy. We believe that each case has to be considered on its own. It may be that generally evidence of this sort would be untrustworthy. Here, however, we are not dealing with a conniving person who was out to get someone by faking a bad dream, but with a child who obviously had suffered. The length of time between the last of the defendant's acts and the first of the sleep statements was only a few days. Finally, and we think importantly, the trial court knew that this was not the only evidence against defendant and that the evidence likely was going to be used primarily for corroborative purposes. If this were the only evidence connecting defendant to the crime, we would say that it was insufficient to support a conviction. But it was just one of a number of items of evidence offered in support of complainant's testimony. Under all these circumstances, the error, if any, was harmless.

[27] Van Meter v. State, 743 P.2d 385, 392 (Alaska App. 1987).

[28] State v. Cramer, 57 Conn. App. 452, 457, 749 A.2d 60, 64–65, *appeal denied*, 253 Conn. 924, 754 A.2d 797 (2000) (where child's mother testified to changes in her daughter's personality in month following alleged assault, when daughter would say in middle of night, "No, stop it," court held this was not offered for its truth or to prove defendant raped child, but rather to show child was mumbling in sleep and having nightmares).

to their meaning and reflect only a general anxiety or distress, they would lack significance and relevance.

A child may be cross-examined about her dreaming, but this does not justify introducing into evidence a note with hearsay references about a dream.[29]

§ 10.6 Hearsay, assertive conduct, and the use of dolls or drawings.

Witnesses often refer to gestures or actions of a person, such as when a police officer testifies that a victim "pointed" to the defendant as the person who attacked her when shown suspects shortly after the commission of the crime. Such testimony is obviously hearsay since it is assertive (pointing to someone) and is offered for its truth (that the defendant is the attacker). However, hearsay is also encountered in other situations and must be carefully evaluated for its propriety and prejudice. Thus, when a police officer testifies about a child victim's physical gestures during an interview and provides details of the child's sexual abuse, he is offering hearsay testimony.[30] So strong is the potential for prejudice from this type of hearsay that its admission can lead to reversible error.[31]

It is not unusual to have a child use dolls as a means of communicating acts of sexual abuse. However, once a witness begins to describe what a child has done with the dolls, such testimony becomes hearsay. It seems clear that any testimony concerning what a sexual assault victim has explained through use of dolls represents assertive conduct and should be considered inadmissible hearsay.[32] Similarly, testimony about a child's out-of-court anatomical drawings is hearsay.[33]

Yet, there is a school of thought that views the use of dolls, as well as a child's behavior and anxiety in certain situations, as non-assertive conduct and is therefore admissible. This view is best represented by the Supreme Court of Washington in *In re Dependency of Penelope B.*[34] In holding such conduct to be non-assertive and admissible, the court wrote:

> [T]he child's utterances showing precocious knowledge of explicit sexual matters and certain private names for male and female genitalia, as testified

---

[29] State v. Miller, 2001 ND 132, 631 N.W.2d 587 (2001).

[30] People v. Fowler, 240 Ill. App. 3d 442, 608 N.E.2d 390 (1992).

[31] People v. Fowler, 240 Ill. App. 3d 442, 608 N.E. 2d 390 (1992).

[32] People v. Bowers, 801 P.2d 511 (Colo. 1990); Souder v. Commonwealth, 719 S.W.2d 730, 734 (Ky. 1986); State v. D.R., 109 N.J. 348, 356–57, 537 A.2d 667, 671 (1988); State v. Mayfield, 302 Or. 631, 733 P.2d 438 (1987).

[33] United States v. Knox, 46 M.J. 688 (N.M.C.C.A. 1997) (finding child's drawings — given to expert witnesses for interpretation — were not admissible under any traditional hearsay exception); Hellstrom v. Commonwealth, 825 S.W.2d 612, 615 (Ky. 1992).

[34] 104 Wash. 2d 643, 709 P.2d 1185 (1985). *See also* United States v. Short, 790 F.2d 464, 467 (6th Cir. 1986).

to by witnesses, are examples of non-assertive utterances which are not hearsay and are admissible.

Another example is the testimony of a therapist. The therapist testified that Penelope was playing with an anatomically correct male doll and on her own, as she was playing, "pushed the doll toward [the other therapist], within maybe one or two feet [of the therapist's] face and said something like either 'put this in your mouth' or 'suck me'. And at that point she was holding the penis of the doll in her hand." This was a combination of non-assertive verbal and non-verbal conduct; it was not hearsay and was admissible.

Other examples of non-assertive conduct by the child, as testified to by others, included the following: Penelope's moods fluctuating between openness and evasiveness; her uncomfortableness in handling the anatomically correct dolls and not wanting to undress the male doll; her fearfulness and anxiety in different contexts; her defensiveness when asked about "her secret"; her barricading herself behind furniture or stuffed toys when talked to; and when, at not seeing her father someplace where she had expected to see him, her fear that he was in jail. None of this was hearsay testimony and it was admissible.[35]

In *Penelope B.*, the inadmissible hearsay occurred when the therapist asked questions of the child about her play with the dolls, such as who had done that to her, and testified to the child's answers or conduct in response to these questions.[36]

Such testimony has previously been admissible under the residual exception to the hearsay rule.[37] Since testimony of a child's use of dolls to describe sexual acts is hearsay, it is incumbent on the trial court to make particularized findings of reliability and trustworthiness under the residual hearsay exception.[38] Introducing a child's drawings to an interviewer, which describes sexual abuse, is improper hearsay and reversible error when proof of guilt rests heavily on the child's testimony.[39] However, *Crawford* has limited this theory of admissibility.

---

[35] *In re* Dependency of Penelope B., 104 Wash. 2d 643, 654–55, 709 P.2d 1185, 1192 (1985).

[36] *In re* Dependency of Penelope B., 104 Wash. 2d 643, 657, 709 P.2d 1185, 1194 (1985).

[37] United States v. Ellis, 935 F.2d 385 (1st Cir. 1991), *cert. denied*, 540 U.S. 839 (1991); People v. Barger, 251 Ill. App. 3d 448 (1993). *See also* discussion under § 10.42. *But see* People v. Mitchell, 215 Ill. App. 3d 849, 855, 576 N.E.2d 78, 82–83 (Ill. App. Ct. 1991) (admitting the testimony of a complainant's mother concerning her daughter; illustrating to a prosecutor, with anatomically correct dolls, acts of sexual abuse).

[38] Kansas v. Bratt, 250 Kan. 264, 273, 824 P.2d 983, 990 (1992).

[39] State v. Presley, 2003 Ohio App. LEXIS 5401 (Nov. 13, 2003):

We agree with defendant's contention that the diagram created by Josie and her corresponding statements to [the Detective] qualified as hearsay and were improperly admitted at trial. Josie created the diagram during the course of her interview with [the detective] in an effort to explain her allegations. Josie then made statements describing the diagram and what it represented. Both the diagram and the statements were out-of-court assertions by Josie to [the detective].

Id. at 16–17.

§ 10.7 State of mind of victim.

Classic hearsay exceptions can find their way into many sexual assault trials. One involves hearsay testimony on the state of mind of a complaining witness. Testimony concerning what the victim said at such a time might be offered by either side to show the victim's state of mind was such that they would or would not be inclined to report the crime. Statements made by a victim in the period of time between the alleged crime and the report thereof might be helpful in establishing a particular state of mind that a party feels establishes the reason why the victim would or would not have reported the event, or would or would not have behaved in a particular way in the company of the defendant or others. Such testimony generally will not present significant hearsay issues.

To explain a victim's denial of molestation, it is permissible for the victim to testify as to what the defendant's attorney said to her, since this would relate to her state of mind at the time of the denial, rather than the truth of any of the attorney's assertions.[40] An example of the state-of-mind exception to the hearsay rule in a rape case was testimony that the victim stated that "she was not feeling very well, she had a terrible headache," and that "she had to go to work early the next morning and she needed to go home because she had a terrible headache and she needed to get some sleep."[41] Such a statement was admissible to show the victim's lack of consent to sexual intercourse, since it showed that her plans were not to go with the defendant.[42] While the declarant may have falsely spoken, this possibility is not enough to defeat admission under a hearsay exception.[43]

Another example is testimony by a mother about her child's nightmares, in addition to bed wetting, complaint of pain on her bottom, requesting frequent baths, and fear of remaining in the family home which is admissible as to the complainant's state of mind, emotion, sensation, or physical condition.[44]

Testimony by a person whom a victim called during a crime concerning that person's experience at a rape crisis center where the two had met, is relevant as to why that person called the police after speaking with the victim and as to the victim's state of mind at the time of the crime.[45]

---

[40] United States v. Payne, 944 F.2d 1458, 1472 (9th Cir. 1991) (permitting questions of victim about whether anyone had questioned her about being abused and her response that the defendant's attorney had questioned her about the abuse but that she denied the abuse because she couldn't admit it in front of the defendant and his wife).

[41] People v. Rowland, 4 Cal. 4th 238, 841 P.2d 897, 14 Cal. Rptr. 2d 377 (1992).

[42] People v. Rowland, 4 Cal. 4th 238, 841 P.2d 897, 14 Cal. Rptr. 2d 377 (1992).

[43] People v. Rowland, 4 Cal. 4th 238, 841 P.2d 897, 14 Cal. Rptr. 2d 377 (1992).

[44] State v. Burress, 1995 Neb. App. LEXIS 141 (Apr. 18, 1995).

[45] People v. Fields, 87 N.Y.2d 821, 660 N.E.2d 1134, 637 N.Y.S.2d 355 (1995).

The hearsay statement of the witness may help explain the delay in reporting the crime.[46]

It is important to carefully analyze a statement to determine if portions may be admissible and portions inadmissible under the state-of-mind theory. For example, while being treated for a rape eight days before she was allegedly murdered by the defendant, the victim told her doctor that she was "afraid sometimes" because her husband had threatened to kill her.[47] The portion of the statement that she was "afraid sometimes" was admissible as reflecting the victim's then-existing state of mind; the remainder of the statement was rather "an assertion of *why* she was afraid" and thus not a statement of memory and belief and therefore inadmissible.[48] A statement by a child that she did not want to return to her father because "he gets drunk and thinks I'm his wife" does not reveal or express the complainant's fear or state of mind and is also a product of a question, and thus would not fall within the state of mind exception.[49]

Statements by a developmentally disabled victim three days after a sexual assault to her swimming instructor asking how she can say "no" if the incidents with the defendant happen again is relevant to her state of mind, since this "reflected her then-existing concern about refusing unwanted sexual encounters."[50]

Statements of a victim to bystanders that she had been raped may be admissible to explain the complainant's emotional condition or to explain why the witnesses stopped the complainant on the highway late at night and took her to the police.[51] These types of statements may be outside the prompt outcry or excited utterance exception,[52] but they may be admissible under the state-of-mind exception. Such an approach can emasculate the hearsay restrictions on a victim's report of a crime under the prompt outcry and excited utterance exceptions. Admission of such testimony should be balanced by its potential prejudicial effect. Material may be offered in the name of the state of mind of the victim, but in reality, it is an attempt to establish the facts. For example, it would be inadmissible hearsay to admit a diary entry of an alleged sexual assault victim that was written some time after the event, since such statements would not be made under the

[46] People v. Mayo, 284 A.D.2d 111, 726 N.Y.S.2d 32, *appeal denied*, 97 N.Y.2d 639, 761 N.E.2d 4, 674 N.Y.S.2d 499 (2001) (upholding admission of witness, nine years old at time of shooting and 18 when she came forward to authorities, of statements made to her by her mother and grandmother as relevant to her state of mind and why she did not come forward earlier).

[47] United States v. Joe, 8 F.3d 1488 (10th Cir. 1993), *cert. denied*, 510 U.S. 1184 (1994).

[48] United States v. Joe, 8 F.3d 1488, 1492-93 (10th Cir. 1993), *cert denied*, 510 U.S. 1184 (1994).

[49] United States v. Tome, 61 F.3d 1446, 1453–54 (10th Cir. 1995).

[50] State v. Scherzer, 301 N.J. Super. 363, 423, 694 A.2d 196, 225, *appeal denied*, 151 N.J. 466, 700 A.2d 878 (1997).

[51] United States v. Norquay, 987 F.2d 475, 479 (8th Cir. 1993).

[52] *See* §§ 10.13–10.19 and 10.20–10.26.

stress of the event, and the victim's state of mind at the time the diary entries were made would not be relevant.[53]

The state-of-mind exception cannot be used to automatically permit testimony of the victim's response to questions of why she is upset, which triggers testimony of the complainant's report of rape,[54] and the complainant's report of sexual abuse is irrelevant to a third party's state of mind, such as a child's mother.[55] The exception is not designed to prove a past fact. Any state-of-mind testimony must be relevant. A victim's state of mind hours after an assault would not ordinarily be relevant; however, if the victim made statements at that time inconsistent with her trial testimony, her state of mind may then be relevant to explain her inability to articulate fully or accurately, and any state-of-mind testimony, even if properly an exception, should be evaluated for its unnecessarily prejudicial effect.[56] It is important to remember that the state-of-mind exception justifies hearsay declarations to explain the declarant's state of mind and not to prove the conduct of another. Thus, a complainant's statements about what she feared defendant would do to her are inadmissible to establish what the defendant did.[57] Likewise, the state-of-mind exception cannot be used to prove the identity of the assailant.[58] The statements may be admissible under another hearsay exception.[59]

---

[53] State v. Smith, 241 Neb. 311, 488 N.W.2d 33 (1992). *See also* People v. Seiver, 187 A.D.2d 683, 590 N.Y.S.2d 248 (1992), *appeal denied*, 81 N.Y.2d 976, 615 N.E.2d 235, 598 N.Y.S.2d 778 (1993) (noting a victim's diary reporting sexual abuse was not relevant to victim's state of mind or state of mind of teacher to whom she gave diary).

[54] McGrew v. State, 673 N.E.2d 787 (Ind. Ct. App. 1996) (Complainant's response to questions of why she was upset, which indicated that defendant raped her, were not admissible under the state-of-mind exception since victim's state of mind was not relevant to any material issue. "The state-of-mind exception does not include statements of memory or belief to prove the fact remembered."); State v. Bubeck, 1997 Wash. App. LEXIS 367, *review denied*, 133 Wash. 2d 1011, 946 P.2d 401 (1997) (noting that exception for a declarant's then-existing state of mind or emotional state "does not allow statements concerning the declarant's past mental or emotional states, and is not intended to allow the admission of a statement as circumstantial evidence of the occurrence of an event or the doing of an act before the declarant's statement. In addition, the declarant's mental or emotional state must be at issue.").

[55] People v. Barrieau, 229 A.D.2d 664, 645 N.Y.S.2d 350 (1996).

[56] Shepard v. United States, 290 U.S. 96, 102–04 (1933) (The prosecution offered murder victim's hearsay statement that "Dr. Shepard has poisoned me." This may have been an appropriate exception to the hearsay rule to refute the victim's suicidal state of mind, but was too prejudicial to the defendant (her husband, Dr. Shepard)).

[57] State v. Fulminante, 193 Ariz. 485, 975 P.2d 75 (1999) (finding hearsay statements of victim such as "he's going to kill me," "I'm afraid he's going to kill me," or statements of belief about defendant's future conduct are not within state-of-mind exception).

[58] State v. Fulminante, 193 Ariz. 485, 975 P.2d 75 (1999).

[59] State v. Aesoph, 2002 SD 71, 647 N.W.2d 743 (2002) (Court upheld admission of prior statements of victim expressing her fear of defendant, since they were excited utterances and to rebut defendant's claim of accidental death. Furthermore, "[t]he court appropriately instructed the jury to consider the statements only for the purpose of ascertaining 'whether [the victim's] death was an accident' and not 'in determining whether . . . Aesoph is guilty.' ").

§ 10.8 State of mind of police officers or hearsay to show effect of statements on investigation.

Other evidence often included in the state-of-mind exception to hearsay testimony is testimony by police officers describing why they responded to a location. This is sometimes called the "mental input" theory, that is, the out-of-court statement offered for the purpose of showing the effect of the declaration on the individual who hears it.[60] Thus, a police officer may testify to what they were told by a dispatcher, bystander, witness, or complainant to explain why the police officer responded or behaved as they did.[61] Such testimony is offered

---

[60] EDWARD J. IMWINKELRIED, COURTROOM CRIMINAL EVIDENCE § 1004, at 337–40 (3d ed. 1998). *See also* 2 MCCORMICK ON EVIDENCE § 249, at 104 (4th ed. 1992)

> In criminal cases, an arresting or investigating officer should not be put in the false position of seeming just to have happened upon the scene; he should be allowed some explanation of his presence and conduct. His testimony that he acted 'upon information received,' or words to that effect, should be sufficient. Nevertheless, cases abound in which the officer is allowed to relate historical aspects of the case, replete with hearsay statements in the form of complaints and reports, on the ground that he was entitled to give the information upon which he acted. The need for the evidence is slight, the likelihood of misuse great.

[61] Nash v. United States, 405 F.2d 1047, 1053 (8th Cir. 1969); Brandon v. State, 839 P.2d 400, 408 (Alas. Ct. App. 1992) (Defendant cross-examined police officer as to why he had not dusted certain items for fingerprints. On redirect examination, prosecutor could elicit a heavy response that victim had already identified her attacker since the victim's out-of-court statement was offered to explain the officer's investigative actions); People v. O'Garra, 16 A.D.3d 251, 791 N.Y.S.2d 538, *appeal denied*, 5 N.Y.3d 766, 834 N.E.2d 1271, 801 N.Y.S.2d 261, *cert. denied*, 126 S. Ct. 627 (2005) (The court properly exercised its discretion in admitting a tape of a 911 call made by a nontestifying declarant who had placed the call for the victim, who had been too nervous to place the call herself. The call contained descriptions of the robbers and of the getaway car. It was clear to the jury that the caller was not an identifying witness, and the court gave careful limiting instructions advising the jury that the tape was not admitted for its truth, but as background information explaining police actions); People v. Baez, 7 A.D.3d 633, 777 N.Y.S.2d 162 (2004) (upholding testimony of description of the perpetrator contained in a radio report overheard by the arresting officer and his partner and was properly admitted to explain the officers' presence at the scene); People v. Smith, 248 A.D.2d 148, 670 N.Y.S.2d 762 (1998) ("The complainant's statement to the arresting officer was properly admitted as background evidence, to complete the narrative of events and explain why the officer took the actions that he did."); People v. Gonzalez, 223 A.D.2d 653, 636 N.Y.S.2d 846, *appeal denied*, 88 N.Y.2d 848, 667 N.E.2d 344, 644 N.Y.S.2d 694 (1996)

> There is no merit to the defendant's contention that Detective Robert Cortes' testimony, which referred to a complaint report, was inadmissible hearsay. Upon arriving at the scene of the crime, in addition to speaking with the complainant, Officer Noel Ortiz spoke with an unidentified Hispanic male. The conversations were incorporated into the complaint report. The detective's testimony that he referred to the complaint report before picking up the defendant was not offered for its truth, but to demonstrate how the defendant was apprehended 1 ½ months after the incident. Therefore, the testimony was not inadmissible hearsay [citation omitted].

State v. Thomas, 61 Ohio St. 2d 223, 232, 400 N.E.2d 401, 407–408 (1980); State v. Williams, 115 Ohio App. 3d 24, 44, 684 N.E.2d 358, 371(1996).

for the limited purpose of explaining the officer's actions and is subject to a limiting instruction. In this situation, the dispatched information was not offered for the truth of such information. Similarly, a statement that provides the impetus for an investigation or investigative action is not offered for the truth of the matter asserted.[62] Unnecessary, excessive, or prejudicial[63] use of the hearsay, such as

---

[62] United States v. Freeman, 816 F.2d 558, 563 (10th Cir. 1987); United States v. Love, 767 F.2d 1052, 1063 (4th Cir. 1985), *cert. denied*, 474 U.S. 1081 (1986); People v. Gayfield, 261 Ill. App. 3d 379, 633 N.E.2d 919, *appeal denied*, 157 Ill. 2d 511, 642 N.E.2d 1291 (1994)

> When a police officer testifies to the fact that he had a conversation with an individual and that he subsequently acted thereon without revealing the substance of the conversation, that testimony does not amount to hearsay. [citation omitted] Testimony recounting the steps taken in a police investigation is admissible and does not violate the Sixth Amendment, even if a jury would conclude that the police began looking for a defendant as a result of what a non-testifying witness told them, as long as the testimony does not gratuitously reveal the substance of their statements and so inform the jury that they told the police that the defendant was responsible for the crime.

Id. at 389–90, 633 N.E.2d at 927; People v. Tosca, 98 N.Y.2d 660 (2002) (holding police officer's testimony concerning unidentified cab driver's report of recent encounter with armed defendant properly admitted not for truth but background for officer's confronting defendant); People v. Newland, 6 A.D.3d 330, 775 N.Y.S.2d 308, *appeal denied*, 3 N.Y.3d 679, 817 N.E.2d 835, 784 N.Y.S.2d 17 (2004):

> The court properly admitted a police officer's brief testimony that, while canvassing for possible witnesses to a burglary, he spoke to a person across the street from the site of the burglary, who was not a witness to the crime, and that, as a result of an unspecified conversation with this person, he searched a shopping cart left directly outside the burglarized premises and found papers bearing defendant's name. Even assuming that this testimony conveyed an implicit assertion by a non-testifying declarant, it was not received for its truth, but as background evidence to complete the narrative of events and explain why the officer looked in the cart.

People v. Jackson, 298 A.D.2d 144, 747 N.Y.S.2d 768 (2002), *appeal denied*, 99 N.Y.2d 583, 785 N.E.2d 740, 755 N.Y.S.2d 718 (2003) (Evidence concerning an uncalled eyewitness's description of defendant was properly admitted, not for its truth, but as background information to explain the police actions leading to defendant's arrest and to prevent speculation by the jury [citations omitted]. Moreover, any possible prejudice arising from the testimony was averted by the court's extensive limiting instructions.); State v. Loose, 994 P.2d 1237 (Utah 2000) (holding victim's hearsay essential for jury to understand how allegations against the defendant arose); State v. Bryant, 965 P.2d 539 (Utah 1998) (holding that victim's statements as testified to by police officer were admissible to explain officer's investigative actions, such as not taking the complainant to the hospital and why the detectives asked that a certain item be fingerprinted and why the complainant's clothes were in their current condition).

[63] United States v. Williams, 358 F.3d 956, 963–64 (D.C. Cir. 2004) ("To the extent that the testimony was offered as 'background' information, the testimony is inadmissible because its considerable prejudicial effect substantially outweighed its minimal probative value . . ." since context could be provided without prejudicial reference to suspects as armed); United States v. Malik, 345 F.3d 999, 1001 (8th Cir. 2003) ("evidence may not be admitted for the non-hearsay purpose of explaining an investigation where the propriety of the investigation is not a relevant issue at trial"); United States v. Becker, 230 F.3d 1224, 1229 (10th Cir. 2000) ("The government's identification of a relevant non-hearsay use for such evidence, however, is insufficient to justify its admission if the jury is likely to consider the statement for the truth of what was stated with

hearsay on a "controversial" issue of the case, is not necessarily cured by a limiting instruction.[64]

While hearsay testimony of individuals who are not available to testify may be admissible to explain why a police officer handcuffed it is essential that such hearsay testimony be accompanied by a limiting instruction that the hearsay is offered only to explain the officer's actions and is not to be considered on the issue of defendant's guilt or innocence.[65] Furthermore, a defendant can invite the hearsay testimony by questioning, which creates a "material gap" in a police officer's testimony or a "selective portrayal" of events.[66] However, testimony by officers establishing background for their actions, such as police dispatch information, is easily subject to misuse. If the testimony does not have a valid non-hearsay purpose, it can easily lead to reversible error.

Offering into evidence a statement for the truth of the matter under the guise of the declarant's state of mind violates the hearsay rule. Testimony by a police officer that a complainant did not want to speak with him because the defendant, her boyfriend, was outside and that she feared that the boyfriend would beat her up if she were seen speaking with the police officer may not be used to "prove the underlying facts upon which the fear is based," since those facts should be established by other non-hearsay evidence.[67] Thus, the hearsay is not justified to explain the officer's conduct.

---

significant resultant prejudice"), *cert. denied*, 532 U.S. 1000 (2001); United States v. Cass, 127 F.3d 1218 (10th Cir. 1997), *cert. denied*, 522 U.S. 1138 (1998) (noting that extensive use of the exception was prejudicial, but harmless); United States v. Forrester, 60 F.3d 52, 59 (2d Cir. 1995) ("The government's identification of a relevant non-hearsay use for such evidence, however, is insufficient to justify its admission if the jury is likely to consider the statement for the truth of what was stated with significant resultant prejudice."); United States v. Sallins, 993 F.2d 344 (3d Cir. 1993) (discussing authorities permitting hearsay background information, but holding that such use of hearsay must be strictly scrutinized):

> Whether a disputed statement is hearsay frequently turns on the purpose for which it is offered. If the hearsay rule is to have any force, courts cannot accept without scrutiny an offering party's representation that an out-of-court statement is being introduced for a material non-hearsay purpose. Rather, courts have a responsibility to assess independently whether the ostensible non-hearsay purpose is valid. The facts of the present case undermine the government's position that testimony regarding the police radio call was admissible as background. . . . Not only was the testimony regarding the radio call inadmissible to show background, it clearly was not offered for that purpose. The absence of a tenable nonhearsay purpose for offering the contents of the police radio call establishes that the evidence could have been offered only for its truth value. [citation omitted].

[64] United States v. Martin, 897 F.2d 1368, 1372 (6th Cir. 1990) (finding "limiting instructions can be an inadequate safeguard" where background testimony was highly prejudicial); United States v. Tussa, 816 F.2d 58 (2d Cir. 1987) (holding limiting instruction did not prevent error from hearsay, which addressed a highly material issue).

[65] People v. Rivera, 96 N.Y.2d 749, 748 N.E.2d 1060, 725 N.Y.S.2d 264 (2001).

[66] People v. Rivera, 96 N.Y.2d 749, 748 N.E.2d 1060, 725 N.Y.S.2d 264 (2001).

[67] State v. Canady, 80 Haw. 469, 476, 911 P.2d 104, 111 (1996).

§ 10.9   Testimony including hearsay to explain subsequent conduct of one who heard the statement.

May a witness testify to what the witness told someone to suggest the reason for that person's actions? For example, a child's hearsay statements may explain why the child's mother began an investigation.[68] Consider a defendant's attorney cross-examining a complainant about the circumstances under which she made her complaint of sexual abuse:[69]

Q.   Did she [stepmother] ask you about it first or did you just go tell her first?

A.   She asked me.

Q.   And what did she ask you?
PROSECUTION. Objection, calls for hearsay.
THE COURT. It's overruled.

A.   Should I answer?
THE COURT. Yes.

A.   What was the question?

Q.   What did [stepmother] ask you?

A.   She asked me if anything had happened 'cause she heard on the phone that someone had told her about —
PROSECUTION. Objection, hearsay.
THE COURT. Sustained as to what someone else heard on the phone. That's secondary hearsay. As to what she asked is another matter, and I allow that in. That objection is sustained. Ask your next question, Counselor.

The defendant's attorney is seeking testimony that the complainant's mother initiated an inquiry about abuse because the mother heard that "other kids" had been abused, thereby suggesting abuse to the complainant and explaining the reason for the report of abuse against the defendant.

The court reversed the defendant's conviction in this case, since the trial court improperly precluded this testimony as hearsay. The appellate court noted:

> A statement offered to explain the subsequent conduct of one who heard the statement is not inadmissible hearsay. . . . This questioning was proper and not within the hearsay rule if it sought to explain why [the complainant] might have fabricated her story of sexual abuse on the bus. Since the allegation of abuse came as a response to [the complainant's] mother's questioning of [the complainant] as to where she got money, the circumstances surrounding that questioning are relevant.[70]

---

[68] United States v. Farley, 992 F.2d 1122 (10th Cir. 1993).

[69] State v. Foust, 920 S.W.2d 949 (Mo. Ct. App. 1996).

[70] State v. Foust, 920 S.W.2d 949, 954 (Mo. Ct. App. 1996).

Testimony that repeats hearsay statements is often encountered. An example can be seen in the discussion of the "mental input theory" in the preceding section. Another example is testimony offered by the prosecution by a mother testifying that she reported to the police that her child told her of abuse, or a doctor testifying that he reported to a child abuse hotline that a child had been abused by a particular person. The theory underlying the admission of such testimony is to explain the conduct of the person hearing the statement. However, the admissibility of such statements still requires that the statement be relevant, material, and that its probative value not be outweighed by its prejudice.

§ 10.10   Complainant's demeanor or behavior after alleged sexual assault.

Separate and apart from a complainant's statements is the complainant's demeanor soon after the sexual assault. As a general rule, a complainant's behavior, personality, emotional, and mental and physical condition after a sexual assault is admissible and outside the hearsay rule.[71] Whether offered by the prosecution or defendant, it is usually offered to establish whether a sexual assault did or did not take place. The theory supporting the admission of such evidence is that it is circumstantial evidence to support a lack of consent or to bolster the credibility of the complainant.[72]

---

[71] Markgraf v. State, 12 P.3d 197 (Alas. Ct. App. 2000) (holding police officer permitted to testify that complainant appeared to be fearful when he interviewed her since this testimony went to her state of mind); State v. Cummings, 148 Ariz. 588, 716 P.2d 45 (1985); State v. Brown, 59 Conn. App. 243, 247–48, 756 A.2d 860, 863–84, *appeal dismissed*, 256 Conn. 740, 775 A.2d 980 (2001) (holding testimony of victim's aunt that victim was crying and feared being alone following assault were non-hearsay observations); Street v. United States, 602 A.2d 141 (D.C. 1992); Hennings v. State, 532 N.E.2d 614 (Ind. 1989); Simmons v. State, 504 N.E.2d 575 (Ind. 1987) (admitting evidence of rape complainant's increasing fear of going out after the assault); Commonwealth v. Scanlon, 412 Mass. 664, 671, 592 N.E.2d 1279, 1284 (1992) (Testimony that victim was "hysterical" and "punching the wall and the kitchen table" were admissible observations of complainant's demeanor at time she reported incident); Commonwealth v. Thatch, 39 Mass. App. Ct. 904, 653 N.E.2d 1121, *review denied*, 421 Mass. 1105, 656 N.E.2d 1258 (1995); State v. Burke, 719 S.W.2d 887 (Mo. Ct. App. 1986); People v. Biavaschi, 265 A.D.2d 268, 269, 697 N.Y.S.2d 53, 55 (1999), *appeal denied*, 94 N.Y.2d 916, 729 N.E.2d 1155, 708 N.Y.S.2d 356 (2000) (holding that child's behavioral changes after alleged sexual assault, including attempt to hurt herself, was relevant testimony); People v. Mejia, 221 A.D.2d 182, 633 N.Y.S.2d 157 (1995), *appeal denied*, 87 N.Y.2d 975, 664 N.E.2d 1268, 642 N.Y.S.2d 205 (1996) (given the defendant's questioning of whether or not a sexual assault took place, complainant's emotional condition, crying, and sobbing, were relevant to material issues of case); People v. Jettoo, 205 A.D.2d 555, 614 N.Y.S.2d 265, *appeal denied*, 83 N.Y.2d 1004, 640 N.E.2d 153, 616 N.Y.S.2d 485 (1994); State v. Schmidt, 288 S.C. 301, 342 S.E.2d 401 (1986); State v. Shaw, 149 Vt. 275, 542 A.2d 1106 (1987) (admitting testimony that before sexual assault complainant was outgoing and she became withdrawn and oppressed afterwards).

[72] State v. Thomas, 130 Ariz. 432, 636 P.2d 1214 (1981); State v. Baron, 80 Haw. 107, 117, 905 P.2d 613, 623 (1995), *rev'd on other grounds* (permitting testimony that complainant "looked real sad and [she was] crying and [she] had a hard time talking"; defendant contended this testimony

There is less agreement on how long after an event a complainant's behavior and demeanor are relevant. There is authority admitting such testimony many months after an alleged assault.[73] If the changes in behavior "commenced immediately or shortly after the rape and continued to the time described, it is more likely to be relevant and material."[74]

While such testimony may be relevant, it still may be reversible error to admit such testimony when its prejudicial effect outweighs its probative value.[75] The testimony may be precluded, unless the victim's consent to the sexual assault is disputed.[76] If the testimony is objected to and is not precluded, one approach on cross-examination of such testimony is to suggest other possible causes of the behavior.

Furthermore, post-incident behavior may be offered by a defendant to show that it was inconsistent with a sexual assault.[77] It is precisely the interpretation of post-incident behavior that leads to expert testimony in the area of Rape Trauma Syndrome or Child Sexual Abuse Accommodation Syndrome, as discussed in Chapter 11.

---

was irrelevant to whether she was sexually assaulted); State v. Apilando, 79 Haw. 128, 900 P.2d 135 (1995), *rev'd on other grounds* ("First, although we recognize that there was no objection to officer Kimura's testimony regarding the complainant and her teddy bear, we believe that the officer's observations of the complainant's appearance and demeanor at the hospital were relevant and served as circumstantial evidence regarding whether her behavior was consistent with a child of her age who had experienced a recent upsetting event." *Id.* at 141, 900 P.2d at 148); People v. Williams, 223 Ill. App. 3d 692, 585 N.E.2d 1188, 1193 (1992) (permitting victim's past assault, physical, and psychological charges to help establish offense occurred); Simmons v. State, 504 N.E.2d 575, 581 (Ind. 1987) (holding victim's post-rape behavior probative of fact of rape); Dickerson v. Commonwealth, 174 S.W.3d 451 (Ky. 2005) (noting that evidence of victim's emotional injuries were more relevant given defendant's position that no sexual assault occurred); Parker v. State, 156 Md. App. 252, 268–74, 846 A.2d 485, 494–98, *cert. denied*, 382 Md. 347, 855 A.2d 350 (2004) (holding evidence of complainant's behavior in weeks following sexual assault was not too ambiguous and equivocal to be relevant and was relevant to show the attack did occur and there was a lack of consent); State v. Seiter, 949 S.W.2d 218, 223 (Mo. Ct. App. 1997).

[73] State v. Phillips, 670 S.W.2d 28 (Mo. Ct. App. 1984) (rape victim's behavior eight months after assault relevant).

[74] Street v. United States, 602 A.2d 141, 144 (D.C. Ct. App. 1992).

[75] State v. Alexander, 303 S.C. 377, 401 S.E.2d 146 (1991) (complainant's testimony was that since rape she lost a lot of sleep, lost her appetite, got emotionally upset easily, could not concentrate, and had to purchase a gun to protect herself).

[76] Yatalese v. State, 991 S.W.2d 509, 554 (Tex. Ct. App. 1999).

[77] *See, e.g.*, Kitchens v. State, 898 P.2d 443, 448 (Alaska Ct. App. 1995); Larson v. State, 102 Nev. 448, 725 P.2d 1214 (1986) (complainant's smiling after alleged assault relevant to consent); People v. Zazversky, 193 Misc. 2d 347, 750 N.Y.S.2d 493 (2002) (permitting defendant to introduce testimony from child complainant's teacher, principal, and school nurse that there were no changes in child's demeanor or behavior, nor any complaints of abuse during the time period of the alleged abuse).

§ 10.11   Testimony concerning victim's prior description or composite of defendant.

Ordinarily, a witness may not testify concerning his or her own prior out-of-court statements.[78] In such a situation, the witness and declarant are the same. Such testimony may also be objectionable as bolstering and subject to the rules of prior consistent statements.[79]

During the prosecution's case-in-chief, a complaining witness may be asked to testify regarding the description of the assailant that she originally provided to the law enforcement authorities. Such testimony can appear to be hearsay as well as bolstering. However, in *People v. Huertas*,[80] the New York Court of Appeals held that a victim who made an in-court identification of the defendant could, on direct examination, testify as to the description of the assailant she gave police. The court held that such testimony bears on the accuracy and reliability of her ability to observe and recall her assailant and that such testimony relates to the jury charge criteria for evaluating a victim's description. As such, the testimony is admissible for a nonhearsay purpose and falls outside the hearsay rule. Certainly, the theory underlying the decision, namely that a witness' prior description of an event is relevant in determining her credibility, would permit a whole area of testimony traditionally inadmissible. However, courts seem to place particular weight on the fact that proper jury instructions direct the jury to evaluate the witness' in-court identification in relation to their initial description of the assailant. It also may be proper for a police officer to testify to a victim's statement that the defendant was the one who raped her if the victim is present in court and subject to cross-examination so that the jury can assess her credibility.[81]

Many courts hold that a composite sketch provided by a complainant is hearsay[82] or double hearsay.[83] When offered to counteract a defendant's attack on the witness' identification, it is considered "bolstering" and therefore inadmissible.[84] It may be admissible, however, as a prior consistent statement.

---

[78] State v. Webb, 1997 Tenn. Crim. App. LEXIS 188 at *26 (Feb. 27, 1997).

[79] *See* § 10.48.

[80] 75 N.Y.2d 487, 553 N.E.2d 992, 554 N.Y.S.2d 444 (1990).

[81] Commonwealth v. Sanders, 260 Pa. Super. 358, 394 A.2d 591 (1978). *See also* FED. R. EVID. 801(d)(1)(c), which defines as nonhearsay a prior statement of identification if the declarant testifies at trial and is subject to cross-examination. *See also* Chapter 8.

[82] State v. Motta, 66 Haw. 254, 260–61, 659 P.2d 745, 749–50 (1983); Commonwealth v. McKenna, 355 Mass. 313, 244 N.E.2d 560 (1969); People v. Coffey, 11 N.Y.2d 142, 145 (1962); Commonwealth v. Morris, 522 Pa. 533, 541, 564 A.2d 1226, 1230 (1989). *See generally, Admissibility of Evidence of Composite Picture or Sketch Produced by Police to Identify Offender*, 25 A.L.R.5TH 672 (2002).

[83] People v. Turner, 91 Ill. App. 2d 436, 444, 235 N.E.2d 317, 320 (1968).

[84] People v. Maldonado, 97 N.Y.2d 522, 769 N.E.2d 1281, 743 N.Y.S.2d 389 (2002).

§ 10.12 Defendant's state of mind.

The parties may wish to offer hearsay testimony concerning a defendant's state of mind. The Federal Rules of Evidence provide the following exception to the hearsay rule:

> A statement of the declarant's then existing state of mind, emotion, sensation, or physical condition (such as intent, plan, motive, design, mental feeling, pain, and bodily health), but not including a statement of memory or belief to prove the fact remembered or believed. . . .[85]

Witnesses may testify to a defendant's statements when the defendant's state of mind or frame of mind is relevant. For example, a child or other witnesses may testify to the defendant's past statements concerning the nutritional value of oral sex.[86] However, in one case, a rape conviction was overturned because of the prosecution's introduction of a letter written by the defendant to the victim after the crime, since there were no admissions made by the defendant, nor was the letter relevant to defendant's state of mind.[87]

One court has even permitted a victim's hearsay statements as to the defendant's motive and intent,[88] or to establish the defendant's state of mind at the time of the offense.[89]

A defendant may wish to present hearsay testimony on his state of mind at the time he made admissions to the police.[90] This testimony may be excluded if it is unreliable or self-serving, or if a defendant has "had time to manufacture the contents of the conversation."[91]

---

[85] FED. R. EVID. 803(3).

[86] People v. Edkin, 210 A.D.2d 808, 621 N.Y.S.2d 395 (1994), *appeal denied*, 85 N.Y.2d 937, 651 N.E.2d 924, 627 N.Y.S.2d 999 (1995).

[87] People v. Singh, 186 A.D.2d 285, 288, 588 N.Y.S.2d 573, 576 (1992). *See also* People v. Robles, 201 A.D.2d 591, 609 N.Y.S.2d 803, *appeal denied*, 83 N.Y.2d 876, 635 N.E.2d 305, 613 N.Y.S.2d 136 (1994) (holding that defendant should have been allowed to introduce hearsay testimony to show defendant's state of mind, but that error was harmless).

[88] Abraha v. State, 271 Ga. 309, 518 S.E.2d 894 (1999) (murder victim's statements to her close friends regarding reluctance about a marriage the defendant was arranging for her was an apparent motive for killing her; court noted the hearsay statements were necessary since declarant was deceased, and declarant lacked any motive to fabricate statements); People v. Cody, 260 A.D.2d 718, 689 N.Y.S.2d 245, *appeal denied*, 93 N.Y.2d 1002, 717 N.E.2d 1084, 695 N.Y.S.2d 747 (1999) (holding victim's hearsay statements as to why she intended to leave defendant as relevant to defendant's motive and intent).

[89] City of Willard v. Semer, 2000 Ohio App. LEXIS 5314 (Nov. 17, 2000) (reversing defendant's conviction due to trial court's failure to permit defendant and his girlfriend to testify to alleged victim's acts or threats of violence, which were relevant to defendant's state of mind at the time of the offense).

[90] United States v. Miller, 874 F.2d 1255, 1264–65 (9th Cir. 1989), *cert. denied*, 510 U.S. 894 (1993).

[91] United States v. Miller, 874 F.2d 1255, 1265 (9th Cir. 1989), *cert denied*, 510 U.S. 894 (1993).

There may be times when the defendant wishes to demonstrate his state of mind and invoke this exception, especially in sexual assault crimes dealing with intent.[92] For example, refusing a grant of immunity may be admissible as consciousness of innocence.[93] In sexual abuse statutes requiring intent of sexual gratification, and attempted crimes requiring that the defendant intended to commit the particular crime, a defendant's state of mind may be relevant. It would also be relevant in cases of a psychiatric defense or possibly the defendant's state of mind during police questioning. A defendant's cooperation with the police, such as in agreeing to undergo tests or procedures, must be analyzed for the purpose for which it is offered. For example, in a rape prosecution, testimony of a defendant's acquiescence to undergo DNA testing was clearly assertive conduct offered to prove his innocence and not properly admitted as "consciousness of innocence."[94] It was also unreliable, nonverbal conduct since it was self-serving in nature.[95] Such cooperation by a defendant has been viewed as not making any fact or consequence more probable than not,[96] and simply self-serving.[97] Yet, some courts hold that a defendant's offer to take "a polygraph and DNA tests" is relevant to a defendant's state of mind if the defendant believes the test or analysis is "possible, accurate, and admissible."[98]

§ 10.13   Prompt outcry or fresh complaint delay or lack of complaint.

A traditional hearsay exception in sexual assault cases involves the "prompt outcry" or "fresh complaint" (sometime also called "first complaint") of a victim

---

[92] For an excellent discussion on the use of hearsay on behalf of a defendant, *see* Edward J. Imwinkelried, Exculpatory Evidence §§ 14-1 to 14-8 (1990).

[93] United States v. Biaggi, 909 F.2d 662, 689–91 (2d Cir. 1990), *cert. denied*, 499 U.S. 904 (1991).

[94] People v. Jardin, 154 Misc. 2d 172, 584 N.Y.S.2d 732 (Sup. Ct. 1992).

[95] People v. Jardin, 154 Misc. 2d 172, 584 N.Y.S.2d 732 (Sup. Ct. 1992).

[96] People v. Torres, 289 A.D.2d 136, 734 N.Y.S.2d 174 (2001), *appeal denied*, 97 N.Y.2d 762, 769 N.E.2d 369, 742 N.Y.S.2d 623 (2002) (The court properly exercised its discretion in precluding defendant from eliciting various instances of his cooperation with the police, offered as "consciousness of innocence" evidence. A person involved in criminal activity has a strong incentive to feign nonchalance upon contact with the authorities, and such conduct would constitute a self-serving assertion of innocence that would constitute inadmissible hearsay); State v. Drinkard, 909 S.W.2d 13 (Tenn. Crim. App. 1995) (holding that trial court properly excluded evidence that defendant had consented to the taking of blood or hair samples on theory that such evidence did not make the existence of any fact or consequence more probable or less probable than it would have been without such evidence).

[97] United States v. Cianci, 378 F.3d 71, 106–07 (1st Cir. 2004), *cert. denied*, 126 S. Ct. 421 (2005). *See also* Rollins v. State, 2005 Ark. LEXIS 293.

[98] State v. Santana-Lopez, 2000 WI App 122, 613 N.W.2d 918 (2000) (remanding case for determination whether defendant believed DNA could detect sexual assaults of which he was charged and, if so, whether error was harmless). *See also* United States v. Moolick, 53 M.J. 174 (C.A.A.F. 2000) (upholding defendant's denial of rape soon after he was accused and in a state of excitement should have been admitted as an excited utterance).

of the assault. Generally, this involves the testimony of the first person to whom the outcry or complaint was made. It may be in writing, such as the complainant's statement given to the police shortly after the assault.[99]

The prompt outcry witness need not be the intended recipient of the victim's report of sexual assault.[100] There is no requirement that any certain level of detail be provided by the complainant to trigger the prompt complaint exception.[101]

The witness can testify to the victim's demeanor and physical condition as discussed in the preceding section, as well as to the contents of the prompt complaint. The theory underlying the admission of such testimony is that individuals are more likely to be credible in a report of sexual assault if they promptly make such complaint. However, studies have suggested that many sexual assault victims do not come forward promptly because of the traumatic consequences of a sexual assault.[102] There can be confusion, disbelief, emotional trauma, and physical discomfort that interferes with a victim's reporting of an assault. There also may be a fear of the reporting process itself or the legal system.

While complaints of sexual assault have increased, these crimes are still underreported. Nevertheless, courts believe that admission of prompt outcry testimony remains of value because "our judicial process cannot remove from every juror all subtle biases or illogical views of the world. The fresh-complaint rule responds to those jurors on their own terms."[103] As can be seen in many cases, the courts have broadened the time frame and applicability of the prompt complaint doctrine when applying it to children.

The prosecution cannot introduce under the constancy of accusation doctrine evidence created by the state in preparation for trial, such as videotape interviews of the complainant, and the introduction of such clearly improper hearsay can be reversible error.[104]

The amount of detail permitted, as well as the effect of admission of the outcry statement, varies greatly between jurisdictions. The exception has withstood

---

[99] State v. Bispham, 48 Conn. App. 135, 708 A.2d 604 (1998); Commonwealth v. Graves, 35 Mass. App. Ct. 76, 616 N.E.2d 817 (1993); People v. Newsome, 222 A.D.2d 530, 635 N.Y.S.2d 247 (1995), *appeal denied*, 87 N.Y.2d 1022, 666 N.E.2d 1070, 644 N.Y.S.2d 156 (1996) ("Under the circumstances of this case, a note written by the complainant to her mother was sufficiently prompt to be admitted into evidence pursuant to the prompt outcry exception to the hearsay rule [citation omitted].").

[100] Commonwealth v. Allen, 40 Mass. App. Ct. 458, 469, 665 N.E.2d 105, 113 (1996).

[101] State v. Beliveau, 237 Conn. 576, 678 A.2d 924, 932–33 (1996).

[102] *See, e.g.*, Ann W. Burgess and Linda L. Holmstrom, *Rape Trauma Syndrome*, 131 AMER. J. OF PSYCHIATRY 981 (1974); Roland Summit, M.D., *The Child's Sexual Abuse Accommodations Syndrome*, 7 CHILD ABUSE & NEGLECT 177–192 (1983).

[103] State v. Hill, 121 N.J. 150, 164, 578 A.2d 370, 377 (1990) (containing an excellent review of the origins and legal history of the prompt outcry doctrine). *See also* State v. Battle, 39 Conn. App. 742, 667 A.2d 1288 (1995), *appeal denied*, 237 Conn. 922, 676 A.2d 1357, *cert. denied*, 519 U.S. 955 (1996).

[104] State v. Marshall, 246 Conn. 799, 717 A.2d 1224 (1998).

constitutional scrutiny and been found to not violate the right to confrontation. [105] Some jurisdictions have restricted the exception. For example, Tennessee has eliminated the fresh complaint doctrine in cases involving child victims. [106]

Just as the complainant's demeanor, behavior, and prompt outcry may help corroborate a sexual assault, the lack of a complaint or changes in behavior or demeanor of a complainant may be relevant and probative as to whether a sexual assault occurred, particularly in the absence of physical evidence or admission. [107] A jury may consider a victim's delay in reporting a sexual assault in assessing the witness's credibility. [108] Also, the failure to make a prompt complaint is a principle on which a defendant may not only comment, but also request a jury instruction to that effect. [109] Instructing a jury that it may not consider delay in determining credibility may be reversible error. [110]

§ 10.14   Effect of admission and need for limiting instruction.

The effect of admission of prompt outcry testimony varies widely. On rare occasions the initial complaint is viewed as substantive evidence. [111] Because

---

[105] State v. Troupe, 237 Conn. 284, 677 A.2d 917 (1996) (holding that prompt outcry evidence does not violate the right to confrontation).

[106] State v. Livingston, 907 S.W.2d 392 (Tenn. 1995).

[107] People v. Zazversky, 193 Misc. 2d 347, 750 N.Y.S.2d 493 (2002) (permitting defendant to call child complainant's teacher, principal, and nurse to show no complaint of abuse made during time period of the alleged abuse).

[108] People v. Brown, 8 Cal. 4th 746, 762, 883 P.2d 949, 958, 35 Cal. Rptr. 2d 407 (1994); State v. Owen, 40 Conn. App. 132, 135, 669 A.2d 606, 609, appeal denied, 673 A.2d 114, 676 A.2d 1376 (1996); Roberts v. State, 242 Ga. App. 621, 624, 530 S.E.2d 535, 539 (2000); Love v. Commonwealth, 18 Va. App. 84, 89, 441 S.E.2d 709, 713 (1994).

[109] State v. Troupe, 237 Conn. 284, 677 A.2d 917 (1996); Commonwealth v. Jones, 449 Pa. Super. 58, 672 A.2d 1353 (1996):

> Although we acknowledge the lower court was not required to instruct the jury on the issue of the lack of a prompt complaint *verbatim* from the standard jury instruction, we find that the instruction given by the court did not adequately and clearly present the issue to the jury. Nowhere in its instruction did the lower court inform the jury that S.B.'s delay in making a complaint should be considered in deciding *whether the act occurred with or without her consent.* In fact, the instruction could have been reasonably interpreted by the jury as bolstering the victim's credibility since it provided: Lack of prompt complaint is something that you can consider but by itself *it doesn't mean that the event didn't occur.* To the contrary, the law is that lack of a prompt complaint should cause the jury to look more critically upon the credibility of the victim. [citation omitted]

Id. at 68, 672 A.2d at 1357–58.

[110] State v. P.H., 178 N.J. 378, 840 A.2d 808 (2004) (reversing defendant's conviction for trial court's refusal to instruct jury on victim's delay in assessing her credibility and noting "the fact that many child sexual abuse victims delay in reporting such offenses does not mean that such delay is irrelevant to an evaluation of an alleged victim's credibility."); People v. Derrick, 96 A.D.2d 600, 465 N.Y.S.2d 292, 293 (1983). *See* Chapter 16.

[111] State v. Valentine, 668 So. 2d 383, 387 (La. Ct. App. 1996); Nelson v. State, 137 Md. App.

a fresh complaint is generally admitted only for corroborative purposes and is not evidence-in-chief, it is not a true hearsay exception. In many states, the prompt outcry testimony does not constitute evidence-in-chief of the defendant's guilt, but is admissible for the limited purpose of rebutting the adverse inference that the jury may draw from the failure to make a timely complaint.[112] It is admissible in this view to establish not the truth of the complaint but only to show that a complaint was made.[113]

California's Supreme Court revisited the issue of the fresh-complaint doctrine and determined that the admission of evidence of a victim's complaint should be admissible for a limited, non-hearsay purpose:

> [namely], to establish the fact of, and the circumstances surrounding, the victim's disclosure of the assault to others — whenever the fact that the disclosure was made and the circumstances under which it was made are relevant to the trier of fact's determination as to whether the offense occurred.[114]

In making this determination, the timing of the complaint, the circumstances under which it was made and whether it was spontaneous or in response to questions are not necessarily determinative of the admissibility of the evidence, and the "freshness" and the "volunteered" natures of the complaint are not essential prerequisites to the admissibility of such evidence.[115]

Tennessee has held that in cases involving child victims, neither the fact of the complaint nor details of the complaint are admissible under the prompt outcry exception.[116]

It is imperative that the jury be instructed as to the limited purpose for which the testimony is being admitted.[117] Failing to provide a contemporaneous

---

402, 422, 768 A.2d 738, 749 (2001); Gallegos v. State, 918 S.W.2d 50, 53–54 (Tex. Ct. App. 1996) (under Texas prompt outcry rule, TEX. CODE CRIM. PROC. ANN. art. 38.072, complaint is substantive evidence admissible for truth of the matter asserted).

[112] State v. Beliveau, 237 Conn. 576, 678 A.2d 924, 933 (1996) ("This testimony is admissible for the limited purpose of ascertaining the credibility of the victim's own testimony."); State v. Woodard, 146 N.H. 221, 769 A.2d 379 (2001); People v. Zurak, 168 A.D.2d 196, 571 N.Y.S.2d 577, *appeal denied*, 79 N.Y.2d 834, 588 N.E.2d 112, 580 N.Y.S.2d 214 (1991), *cert. denied*, 504 U.S. 941 (1992).

[113] People v. Grady, 229 A.D.2d 503, 646 N.Y.S.2d 275, *appeal denied*, 89 N.Y.2d 864, 675 N.E.2d 1240, 653 N.Y.S.2d 287 (1996).

[114] People v. Brown, 8 Cal. 4th 746, 35 Cal. Rptr. 2d 407, 883 P.2d 949 (1994).

[115] People v. Brown, 8 Cal. 4th 746, 35 Cal. Rptr. 2d 407, 883 P.2d 949 (1994).

[116] State v. Livingston, 907 S.W.2d 392 (Tenn. 1995).

[117] State v. Eged, 48 Conn. App. 283, 289, 709 A.2d 39, 43 (1998) (holding defendant entitled to a limiting instruction with respect to limited purpose of fresh complaint testimony); Commonwealth v. Trowbridge, 419 Mass. 750, 760, 647 N.E.2d 413, 421 (1995) (holding it is insufficient to instruct jury that prompt complaint can be used only to corroborate without further definition and clarification that such testimony is not substantive evidence); Commonwealth v. Licata, 412 Mass. 654, 591 N.E.2d 672 (1992).

limiting instruction may be reversible error.[118] If the defendant introduces or elicits evidence of a victim's silence to prove a rape did not occur, the prosecutor may request a charge to the jury that a woman may respond to rape in a variety of ways.[119]

§ 10.15   Testimony generally limited to fact of complaint.

The majority of courts limit prompt outcry testimony to the fact and time of a complaint sufficient to connect the occurrence complained of with the crime charged, including time and place, but usually not details such as the name or description of the attacker or location of the attack.[120] Some courts restrict the testimony to the fact of the complaint and require the victim to testify first to the facts of the sexual assault.[121]

---

[118] Commonwealth v. Brouillard, 40 Mass. App. Ct. 448, 665 N.E.2d 113 (1996)

> The defendants complain that they suffered a substantial risk of a miscarriage of justice because there were no contemporaneous fresh complaint instructions during any of the four fresh complaint witness['s] direct testimony. The only contemporaneous instruction came during the cross-examination of the third fresh complaint witness, Miles Tarter. In addition, the defendants complain that the word 'corroborate' was not defined for the jury, thus rendering the fresh complaint instruction ineffective. We do not agree that the judge failed to make clear the meaning of 'corroborate.' However, we do find that the lack of contemporaneous fresh complaint instructions also independently created a substantial risk of a miscarriage of justice.

Id. at 455, 665 N.E.2d at 118.

[119] State v. Hill, 121 N.J. 150, 166, 578 A.2d 370, 378 (1990).

[120] Williams v. United States, 756 A.2d 380 (D.C. 2000) ("report of rape rule" permits testimony by witness that complainant stated a sexual crime occurred and detail necessary to identify crime); State v. Woodard, 146 N.H. 221, 226, 769 A.2d 379, 384 (2001) ("We caution that on direct examination of the victims, such evidence should be limited to the fact of the complaint and circumstances giving rise to it."); People v. McDaniel, 81 N.Y.2d 10, 611 N.E.2d 265, 595 N.Y.S.2d 364 (1993); People v. Rice, 75 N.Y.2d 929, 554 N.E.2d 1265, 555 N.Y.S.2d 677 (1990); People v. Terrence, 205 A.D.2d 301, 612 N.Y.S.2d 571, *appeal denied*, 84 N.Y.2d 873, 642 N.E.2d 337, 618 N.Y.S.2d 18 (1994) (even though prompt outcry testimony included some details such as the fact that victim was beaten and verbally abused, such limited detail did not unduly prejudice defendant); People v. Harris, 132 A.D.2d 940, 518 N.Y.S.2d 269 (1987); Dawkins v. State, 346 S.C. 151, 551 S.E.2d 260 (2001); Jolly v. State, 314 S.C. 17, 20, 443 S.E.2d 566, 568 (1994); State v. Kendricks, 891 S.W.2d 597 (Tenn. 1994) (holding that prompt complaint testimony is limited to fact of the complainant and details are admissible only once complainant's credibility is attacked); State v. Alexander, 64 Wash. App. 147, 151, 822 P.2d 1250 (1992). *See also* OR. REV. STAT. § 40.460 (18a)(a).

[121] State v. William C., 267 Conn. 686, 841 A.2d 1144 (2004) (limiting prompt outcry evidence to fact and timing of complaint and stating that victim must have first testified concerning the facts of the sexual assault and the identity of the person to whom the incident was reported); State v. Troupe, 237 Conn. 284, 677 A.2d 917 (1996) (only fact and timing of victim's complaint admissible; before such evidence is received the victim must have first testified concerning facts of sexual assault and the identity of the person to whom the assault was reported); State v. Orhan, 52 Conn. App. 231, 726 A.2d 629 (1999) (finding that prosecution had established through circumstantial evidence that mother was the person to whom child had complained, even though

Only a few courts permit details of the assault. Massachusetts, in modifying its fresh complaint doctrine to a "first complaint" doctrine, still permits testimony of details of the complaint to provide maximum information to the jury and to avoid speculation as to what was said.[122] The complainant may also testify to the details of the first complaint and why the complaint was made at that particular time.[123]

Minnesota also permits details of the sexual assault.[124] A court may permit the identification of the defendant as the perpetrator to connect the occurrence complained of with the offense charged.[125] These details are to include those that are necessary to identify the crime; however, this has been interpreted to permit significant details, such as a mother's testimony that her child pointed to her genitals and said, "He put a thing there."[126]

A five-year-old's statement identifying the perpetrator made eight to ten hours after the assault was found to be a fresh complaint, even though made in response to questioning, when the report of the rape was made at the first reasonable opportunity.[127] However, this approach does not reflect most interpretations of the fresh-complaint doctrine. Even when a statute permits details of the crime and acts as a prompt outcry, it may be improper to include as part of those details

---

victim had not identified her as the person to whom she had told details since explicit identification of the person to whom prompt report made is not a necessary prerequisite to prompt outcry testimony); State v. Eged, 48 Conn. App. 283, 289, 709 A.2d 39, 42–43 (1998).

[122] Commonwealth v. King, 445 Mass. 217, 244, 834 N.E.2d 1175, 1198 (2005). *See also* Commonwealth v. Quincy Q., 434 Mass. 859, 874, 753 N.E.2d 781, 795 (2001); Commonwealth v. Licata, 412 Mass. 654, 591 N.E.2d 672 (1992); Commonwealth v. Moreschi, 38 Mass. App. Ct. 562, 649 N.E.2d 1132 (1995).

[123] Commonwealth v. King, 445 Mass. 217, 244, 834 N.E.2d 1175, 1198 (2005).

[124] State v. Blohm, 281 N.W.2d 651 (Minn. 1979).

[125] Nelson v. State, 137 Md. App. 402, 768 A.2d 738 (2001), (*citing* Cole v. State, 83 Md. App. 279, 293–94, 574 A.2d 326, 333 (1990)); Commonwealth v. Stohr, 361 Pa. Super. 293, 522 A.2d 589 (1987).

[126] Galindo v. United States, 630 A.2d 202, 209 (D.C. Cir. 1993):

> The mother's testimony that the child pointed to her genitals and said 'he put a thing there' was admissible to show that the child reported a sexual offense. In the absence of actual impeachment of the complainant, limited details regarding the complainant's report to her mother are admissible to show that a complainant was describing a sexual assault. The complainant in this case was a three-year-old and, understandably, had a limited sexual vocabulary. The mother's testimony that the complainant first said that 'he has put a thing there' did not clearly indicate that the complainant was describing a sexual assault. The limited additional details regarding the complainant's statements — that the complainant said 'here, mommy' while 'pointing to her private parts' to indicate the 'thing' with which appellant touched her, and where he touched her — simply indicated that the act complained of was a sexual assault.

Id. at 209.

[127] State v. Adams, 394 So. 2d 1204, 1212 (La. 1981).

other information, such as why the victim delayed reporting, the fears of the victim, or the behavior of victims in general.[128]

Tennessee's Supreme Court overruled its prior holding concerning the admissibility of the "fresh complaint" and now permits details of the incident to be presented only when the victim's credibility has been attacked, analogizing its admissibility to the use of prior consistent statements. The fact of the complaint is still admissible as part of the prosecution's case-in-chief.[129] This same Court has also held "that in cases where the victim is a child, neither the fact of the complaint nor the details of the complaint to a third party is admissible under the fresh complaint doctrine."[130] Connecticut's Supreme Court now restricts prompt complaint testimony to the fact and timing of the victim's complaint and permits details of the sexual assault only to the extent "necessary to associate the victim's complaint with the pending charge, including, for example, the time and place of the attack or the identity of the alleged perpetrator."[131]

However, there may be reversible error when the fresh complaint testimony exceeds the scope of the complainant's testimony. Adding "substantively" to the complainant's testimony by a description of acts and abuse not testified to by the complainant may be prejudicial error.[132] The outcry details should not include hearsay concerning uncharged conduct.[133] Illinois has codified the hearsay exception pertaining to the complaint of a child victim of sexual assault, including

---

[128] People v. Fowler, 240 Ill. App. 3d 442, 450–51, 608 N.E.2d 390, 395–96 (1992).

[129] State v. Kendricks, 891 S.W.2d 597 (Tenn. 1994).

[130] State v. Livingston, 907 S.W.2d 392 (Tenn. 1995). *See also* State v. Speck, 944 S.W.2d 598 (Tenn. 1997) (holding that while prompt outcry testimony was improperly received, it did not improperly or unduly affect the verdict).

[131] State v. Troupe, 237 Conn. 284, 677 A.2d 917 (1996).

[132] Commonwealth v. Flebotte, 417 Mass. 348, 630 N.E.2d 265 (1994). *Compare* Corbett v. State, 130 Md. App. 408, 746 A.2d 954, *cert. denied*, 359 Md. 31, 753 A.2d 3 (2000) (child victim's prior statement was not admissible as a "prompt complaint" and admission of details of statement was reversible error since this exceeded scope of prompt complaint and was only direct evidence of elements of crime, and prompt complaint was also inconsistent with the victim's trial testimony that she did not remember events); Commonwealth v. Kirkpatrick, 423 Mass. 436, 668 N.E.2d 790 (1996) (prompt outcry witness's testimony went beyond scope of outcry rule, but did not "inject into the case a form of abuse that had not already been brought to the jury's attention" and was a relatively insignificant piece of testimony and thus not reversible error); Commonwealth v. Gichel, 48 Mass. App. Ct. 206, 209, 718 N.E.2d 1262, 1265 (1999), *review denied*, 430 Mass. 1113, 723 N.E.2d 33 (2000) (while fresh complaint testimony need not match victim's testimony exactly, it is permissible for fresh complaint witness to testify about details of event that victim had not testified to more generally; court held error in this case of additional detail in prompt complaint testimony was not significant in context of case); State v. Buscham, 360 N.J. Super. 346, 823 A.2d 71 (App. Div. 2003) (The prejudicial error in the prompt outcry witness' going beyond the fact of the complaint was compounded by the prosecutor's reference to the details in summation and seeking to use the testimony to bolster the victim's credibility — precisely how prompt outcry testimony should not be used).

[133] People v. Johnson, 296 Ill. App. 3d 53, 693 N.E.2d 1224 (1998).

details of the complaint when reliability is demonstrated.[134] Illinois' Supreme Court has interpreted this statute as requiring that the age requirement applies to the age of the child at the time of the outcry, not the age of the victim when the assault occurs.[135] Texas' prompt outcry statute requires "more than a general allusion that sexual abuse is going on" and should "describe the offense in some discernible manner."[136] The proper outcry witness is the first person other than the defendant to whom the child made a statement describing the sexual assault "in some discernible manner."[137] The outcry witness need not provide a date of the disclosure. Because of *Crawford*, a victim's outcry statement may be inadmissible, unless the child testifies.[138]

§ 10.16 Application to various types of sexual assault.

Most states will permit the prompt outcry or fresh complaint doctrine not only as to rape but also as to other forms of sexual assault, such as sodomy and sexual abuse.[139] Some jurisdictions do not apply the exception to all charges of sexual assault. Virginia had limited the fresh complaint doctrine to rape and attempted

---

[134] ILL. ANN. STAT. ch. 725, 5/115-10:

> (a) In a prosecution for a physical or sexual act perpetrated upon or against a child under the age of 13, including but not limited to prosecutions for violations of §§ 12-13 through 12-16 of the Criminal Code of 1961, the following evidence shall be admitted as an exception to the hearsay rule: (1) testimony by such child of an out of court statement made by such child that he or she complained of such act to another; and (2) testimony of an out of court statement made by such child describing any complaint of such act, or matter, or detail pertaining to any act which is an element of an offense which is the subject of a prosecution for a sexual act perpetrated upon a child. (b) Such testimony shall only be admitted if: (1) The court finds in a hearing conducted outside the presence of the jury that the time, content, and circumstances of the statement provide sufficient safeguards of reliability; and (2) The child either: (A) Testifies at the proceeding; or (B) Is unavailable as a witness and there is corroborative evidence of the act which is the subject of the statement. (C) If a statement is admitted pursuant to this section, the court shall instruct the jury that it is for the jury to determine the weight and credibility to be given the statement and that, in making the determination, it shall consider the age and maturity of the child, the nature of the statement, the circumstances under which the statement was made, and any other relevant factors. (D) The proponent of the statement shall give the adverse party reasonable notice of his intention to offer the statement and the particulars of the statement.

[135] People v. Holloway, 177 Ill. 2d 1, 682 N.E.2d 59 (1997).

[136] Smith v. State, 131 S.W.3d 928, 930–31 (Tex. Ct. App. 2004) (interpreting TEX. CODE CRIM. PROC. art. 38.072).

[137] Smith v. State, 131 S.W.3d 928, 931 (Tex. Ct. App. 2004).

[138] Martinez v. State, 178 S.W.3d 806, 810 n.14 (Tex. Crim. App. 2005); Chapman v. State, 150 S.W.3d 809 (Tex. Ct. App. 2004), *review denied*, 2005 Tex. Crim. App. LEXIS 527 (Apr. 6, 2005).

[139] Commonwealth v. Brenner, 18 Mass. App. Ct. 930, 465 N.E.2d 1229 (1984); State v. Balles, 47 N.J. 331, 221 A.2d 1 (1966), *cert. denied*, 388 U.S. 461 (1967).

rape cases and precluded it in other sexual assault crimes, but has amended its statute pertaining to prompt outcry to include other sexual assault charges.[140]

The principles of fresh complaint may, under some circumstances, be applied when there are references to nonsexual offenses charged along with sexual assault. However, the use of the fresh complaint evidence may be limited to the sexual assault charge and the defendant entitled to a jury instruction as to the prompt outcry's limited purpose[141] or entitled to an instruction that the prompt outcry testimony may be used to impeach as well as corroborate the complainant's testimony.[142]

§ 10.17 Timeliness of complaint.

Over time, the fresh-complaint doctrine has evolved into a *reasonably* fresh complaint doctrine. More and more, the promptness of a complaint is measured not only in terms of time, but also by the reasons for the delay.[143] Whether a complaint was made "at the first suitable opportunity" will be judged on whether the victim was limited because of threats, fear, or other circumstances.[144] Massachusetts has modified its prompt complaint doctrine into a "first complaint," which renders delay in disclosing a complaint, not a reason to exclude the complaint but simply one factor for the jury to consider in weighing the complaint's testimony.[145] "Freshness has no bearing on its admission."[146] The

---

[140] Kauffmann v. Commonwealth, 8 Va. App. 400, 382 S.E.2d 279 (1989). *See* VA. CODE ANN. § 19.2-268.2.

[141] Commonwealth v. Moreschi, 38 Mass. App. Ct. 562, 566–69, 649 N.E.2d 1132, 1135–37, *review denied*, 420 Mass. 1106, 652 N.E.2d 145 (1995) (Prompt complaint witnesses permitted to testify about complainant's statements of defendant's assaults upon her prior to rape which were tied together by "unity of time, place and circumstance."); State v. Jones, 1995 Tenn. Crim. App. LEXIS 827 at *14 (Oct. 4, 1995) (conviction reversed for trial judge's failure to give limiting instruction).

[142] State v. Ali, 233 Conn. 403, 660 A.2d 337 (1995) (upholding defendant's argument that "because the trial court did not caution the jury that constancy of accusation testimony can be used to impeach as well as to corroborate the victim's testimony, and because the trial court failed in its other instructions to charge the jury that in assessing her credibility it could consider any contradictions, inconsistencies, or falsities in the victim's out-of-court statements, the court failed to provide a proper balance to the instructions." *Id.* at 421, 660 A.2d at 346).

[143] Gaerin v. State, 159 Md. App. 527, 860 A.2d 396 (2004) (holding "that promptness is a flexible concept, tied to the circumstances of the particular case. . . . Promptness is not defeated by some delay in the reporting, so long as the delay is adequately explained.").

[144] People v. Shelton, 1 N.Y.3d 614, 808 N.E.2d 1268, 777 N.Y.S.2d 9 (2004) (using this standard, court upheld an 81-year-old victim's complaint of rape less than 24 hours after it had taken place was prompt. The court determined it was proper to consider that the rape occurred late at night, that defendant warned victim not to tell anyone, and that defendant lived in the same building as the victim).

[145] Commonwealth v. King, 445 Mass. 217, 242, 834 N.E.2d 1175, 1197 (2005).

[146] Commonwealth v. King, 445 Mass. 217, 242, 834 N.E.2d 1175, 1197 (2005).

Massachusetts holding reflects the evolution of the standard for admissibility of the first complaint into an evaluation of the circumstances for the delay and taking the evaluation from the court and placing it in the hands of the jury. Such circumstances may include the age of the victim and whether they were in a hospitable environment. Did the defendant continue to have the victim under their control? Was the victim among strangers and there was no one in whom the victim could confide? If the defendant threatened the victim, was the victim within the defendant's reach?[147] While timeliness is a component of the fresh complaint principle, it "depends upon an assessment of all the facts and circumstances."[148] The majority of cases that have expanded the time period encompassing the prompt outcry or fresh complaint exceptions involve children. A five-year-old girl's report to her mother, father, and aunt of a rape several days after the event was timely where the evidence showed that the child was reluctant to tell her family what happened to her because she thought she had done something wrong and feared she would be punished.[149] And a four-year-old's statements identifying the defendant two days after she was assaulted qualified under the fresh complaint doctrine where the circumstances indicated that the report was made at the first opportunity the child had to speak to a close family member.[150] A victim's developmental disability is also a factor to consider in the timeliness of the complaint.[151] Some examples showing the range of acceptable time in making a fresh complaint include one day after a sexual assault of a seven-year-old,[152] one week,[153] one month,[154] several months,[155]

---

[147] *See, e.g.*, People v. O'Sullivan, 104 N.Y. 481, 10 N.E. 880 (1887); Commonwealth v. Rodriguez, 343 Pa. Super. 486, 495 A.2d 569 (1985) (holding that a 14-year-old child's complaint six days after the event was timely where the victim told his mother when he was in a hospital and feared telling her because he would be sent to a boy's home).

[148] State v. Kendricks, 891 S.W.2d 597, 605 (Tenn. 1994).

[149] State v. Sanders, 691 S.W.2d 566 (Tenn. Crim. App. 1984).

[150] State v. Noble, 342 So. 2d 170 (La. 1977).

[151] Commonwealth v. Bryson, 2004 Pa. Super. 405, 860 A.2d 1101 (2004), *appeal denied* 583 Pa. 658, 875 A.2d 1072 (2005) (holding mentally disabled victim, with IQ of 59, did not report the sexual assault to defendant's sister or anyone in household, did not tell her family, but reported it when she went to school the following day).

[152] Nelson v. State, 137 Md. App. 402, 768 A.2d 738 (2001) (upholding as a prompt report 13-year-old complainant's complaint to school counselor day after alleged sexual assault); People v. Aguirre, 262 A.D.2d 175, 692 N.Y.S.2d 325, 326, *appeal denied*, 94 N.Y.2d 819, 724 N.E.2d 381, 702 N.Y.S.2d 589 (1999)

> The court properly admitted outcry testimony from various individuals. Regarding the first incident in question, in light of the victim's young age and expressed fear of retribution if she disclosed the sexual attack, the complainant's report to her best friend, made the day following this incident, constituted prompt outcry that was properly admitted as an exception to the hearsay rule. The same principles apply to the complainant's report to a trusted adult, made during the week following the second and third attacks. [citations omitted]

People v. Lussier, 205 A.D.2d 910, 613 N.Y.S.2d 466, *appeal denied*, 83 N.Y.2d 1005, 640

one year,[156] or even two years or more.[157] Usually prompt complaints admitted after a period of time involved an element of fear or intimidation.

N.E.2d 154, 616 N.Y.S.2d 486 (1994), *cert. denied,* 513 U.S. 1078 (1995) (Court properly permitted as prompt outcry or delayed outcry child's statement, made to his sister the day after the assault, that he did not want to go back to work because defendant had tried to penetrate him); People v. Bonilla, 200 A.D.2d 369, 606 N.Y.S.2d 201, *appeal denied,* 83 N.Y.2d 849, 634 N.E.2d 982, 612 N.Y.S.2d 381 (1994) (child's statement to her sister one day after incident properly admitted as a prompt outcry due to child's age and fear of defendant); People v. Thomas, 176 A.D.2d 470, 574 N.Y.S.2d 551 (1991). *But compare* Turtle v. State, 600 So. 2d 1214 (Fla. Dist. Ct. App. 1992) (court found a 12-year-old's complaint one day after the event too tardy to qualify as a prompt complaint).

[153] People v. Rodriguez, 284 A.D.2d 952, 728 N.Y.S.2d 597, *appeal denied,* 96 N.Y.2d 924, 758 N.E.2d 667, 732 N.Y.S.2d 641 (2001) (upholding statement to school social worker nine days after assault given proof that her fear of defendant prevented her from coming forward earlier).

[154] People v. Meacham, 152 Cal. App. 3d 142, 158, 199 Cal. Rptr. 586 (1984).

[155] Commonwealth v. Allen, 40 Mass. App. Ct. 458, 665 N.E.2d 105 (1996) (Complaint three to four months after alleged abuse was reasonably prompt "[g]iven the children's fear of reprisals from the defendant, and the reasonableness of their belief that their own father could gain access to them, the victims' complaints were reasonably made." *Id.* at 469, 655 N.E.2d at 112); Terry v. Commonwealth, 24 Va. App. 627, 484 S.E.2d 614, 615–18 (1997) (upholding 12-year-old victim's complaint ten months after sexual assault).

[156] State v. Romero, 59 Conn. App. 469, 757 A.2d 643, *appeal denied,* 255 Conn. 919, 763 A.2d 1043 (2000) (noting that delay is only one factor to be considered by the trier of fact); Commonwealth v. Amirault, 404 Mass. 221, 535 N.E.2d 193 (1989); Commonwealth v. Kruah, 47 Mass. App. Ct. 341, 346, 712 N.E.2d 1182, 1187 (1999) (in case involving prompt complaint testimony, where defendant who held position of leadership in community was charged with threatening victim's life 15 months earlier, court found that 15-month delay was reasonable, noting: "Circumstances that have traditionally justified delayed reporting include the victim's age and relationship to the defendant; the defendant's knowledge of the location of the victim's residence; and the victim's feelings of shame, fear, intimidation, guilt, and belief that the complaint will not be believed or treated seriously."); State v. L.P., 352 N.J. Super. 369, 800 A.2d 207, *cert. denied,* 174 N.J. 546, 810 A.2d 65 (2002):

> Statements made nearly a year after the last of several alleged assaults were made within a reasonable time required for admission under the fresh complaint rule and admissible 'in view of the continuing aura of intimidation under which the child lived until four months before she told her foster mother and another girl.'
>
> Moreover, the introduction of evidence of an alleged child sexual abuse victim's initial complaints, even if made a significant time after the abuse, is especially appropriate in a case where the State relies upon CSAAS evidence to explain why the victim did not complain about the alleged abuse shortly after it occurred.

352 N.J. Super. at 383, 800 A.2d at 215; Villalon v. State, 805 S.W.2d 588 (Tex. Ct. App. 1991).

[157] Commonwealth v. Lavoie, 47 Mass. App. Ct. 1, 710 N.E.2d 1011, *review denied,* 430 Mass. 1106, 717 N.E.2d 1015 (1999) (upholding admission of prompt outcry made 26 months after sexual assault given defendant's coercive relationship with his daughter and that child was out of defendant's control for only two weeks before the complaint was made); Commonwealth v. Hyatt, 31 Mass. App. Ct. 488, 579 N.E.2d 1365 (1991) (holding a report two years after the event acceptable since the 13-year-old victim was concerned about disturbing her sister's relationship with the defendant, whom her sister married one month after the incident, and the victim was fearful she would not be believed. She finally disclosed the assault to a male who had been making sexual advances toward her).

The prompt outcry may cover details provided over several days on the theory that it may take a child a period of time to complete the outcry.[158] Where a complaint may not be particularly timely, yet admitted as a prompt complaint, it is best to argue to the jury the weight to be given to the disclosure and the effect of the delay. Courts are often inclined to look at the lengthy period of time as a factor that affects credibility rather than admissibility.[159] California's Supreme Court has held that under this exception, the freshness of the complaint is not an essential prerequisite to the admissibility.

Nonetheless, there are limits as to how long after an event a complaint of sexual abuse may be made and still fall within the prompt outcry exception. Ten hours may be too long a delay, especially when the complainant had the opportunity to report the event to others.[160] Even without objection, admission of testimony under the fresh complaint doctrine seven years after the event, created a substantial miscarriage of justice requiring a reversal of conviction.[161] Written evidence, such as in a victim's diary, may cause difficulty in qualifying as a prompt outcry since the written nature of the statement would usually reflect the untimeliness of the complaint.[162]

§ 10.18 Multiple witnesses to prompt outcry or first complaint.

Arguments against admitting multiple witness' testimony of a prompt outcry or fresh complaint include the fact that it generally is not logical to have more than one fresh complaint, that it permits bolstering of the witness's testimony, and that it is cumulative. As with other hearsay exceptions, there is the issue of whether the prompt complaint in addition to other hearsay of the complainant is prejudicial. (*See* § 10.52.) Such repeated hearsay testimony has been held improper.[163] Nonetheless, prompt complaint testimony does not usually provide

---

[158] Zinger v. State, 899 S.W.2d 423 (Tex. Ct. App. 1995), *rev'd on other grounds*, 932 S.W.2d 511 (Tex. Crim. App. 1996).

[159] *See, e.g.*, People v. Brown, 8 Cal. 4th 746, 883 P.2d 949, 35 Cal. Rptr. 2d 407 (1994); State v. Valentine, 668 So. 2d 383, 387 (La. Ct. App. 1996); Commonwealth v. King, 445 Mass. 217, 834 N.E.2d 1175 (2005); Herron v. Commonwealth, 208 Va. 326, 330, 157 S.E.2d 195, 198 (1967).

[160] Seagrave v. State, 768 So. 2d 1121 (Fla. Dist. Ct. App. 2000) (finding admission of 12-year-old's outcry ten hours after event was harmless error).

[161] Commonwealth v. Perreira, 38 Mass. App. Ct. 901, 644 N.E.2d 253 (1995). *See also* Commonwealth v. Shiek, 42 Mass. App. Ct. 209, 675 N.E.2d 805, *review denied*, 424 Mass. 1107, 678 N.E.2d 1334 (1997) (reversing defendant's conviction for improper admission of prompt complaint testimony of a 13-year-old, 32 months after sexual assault, since there was no compelling reason for the delay and defendant did not reside with declarant, nor did she testify that she was threatened by him).

[162] People v. Seiver, 187 A.D.2d 683, 590 N.Y.S.2d 248 (1992), *appeal denied*, 81 N.Y.2d 976, 615 N.E.2d 235, 598 N.Y.S.2d 778 (1993); People v. Singh, 186 A.D.2d 285, 288, 588 N.Y.S.2d 573, 576 (1992).

[163] Perry v. State, 593 So. 2d 620 (Fla. Dist. Ct. App. 1992). *See also* the discussion on the prejudicial effect of multiple hearsay statements in § 10.52.

details of the assault, unlike other hearsay exceptions, and therefore is less prejudicial.

The trial court may determine whether multiple prompt outcries are irrelevant or unfairly prejudicial.[164] The greater the number of fresh complaint witnesses, the more likely such testimony will be viewed by a jury as substantive evidence.[165] For example, admitting testimony of a report of a rape by the complainant to a detective three and one-half hours after the crime and after the victim's complaint to her mother and another police officer, was considered reversible error because it was too all-encompassing to be a prompt complaint in light of the earlier complaints.[166]

Other courts see no reason to limit the number of prompt complaint witnesses or limit the witnesses to the first one.[167] For example, recent outcry testimony of a victim's mother, which duplicated a police officer's testimony to the same effect, was deemed not improper.[168] Even the testimony of seven prompt outcry witnesses has been held not prejudicially cumulative.[169]

§ 10.19   Effect of questioning victim.

A fact that can affect the admissibility of a fresh complaint is whether the complaint is in response to questioning. Generally, the fact that the victim was questioned must be viewed in the context of the report and will not alone defeat the complaint's admissibility.[170] However, "pointed, inquisitive, and coercive

---

[164] State v. Hill, 121 N.J. 150, 168, 578 A.2d 370, 380 (1990).

[165] Commonwealth v. Brouillard, 40 Mass. App. Ct. 448, 456–57, 665 N.E.2d 113, 119 (1996) (reversing defendant's conviction, for among other reasons, admission of multiple fresh complaint witnesses).

[166] Commonwealth v. King, 445 Mass. 217, 245, 834 N.E.2d 1175, 1199 (2005); Commonwealth v. Green, 487 Pa. 322, 409 A.2d 371 (1979).

[167] Gaerian v. State, 159 Md. App. 527, 860 A.2d 396 (2004); Parker v. State, 156 Md. App. 252, 846 A.2d 485 (2004) (permitting prompt outcry testimony, even though police officer testified to a similar and earlier complaint); Nelson v. State, 137 Md. App. 402, 768 A.2d 738 (2001) (upholding admission of multiple prompt reports by complainant); State v. Wiest, 2001 ND 150, 632 N.W.2d 812 (2001) (finding that "mere repetition" of child's hearsay statement does not make them unduly prejudicial).

[168] People v. Ravenell, 133 A.D.2d 354, 519 N.Y.S.2d 255 (1987).

[169] State v. Zoravali, 34 Conn. App. 428, 439–41, 641 A.2d 796, 802–03, *appeal denied*, 230 Conn. 906, 644 A.2d 921 (1994).

[170] People v. Brown, 8 Cal. 4th 746, 35 Cal. Rptr. 2d 407, 883 P.2d 949 (1994) (holding that whether or not the complaint was volunteered spontaneously or made in response to questions is not a prerequisite to admissibility of such evidence); People v. Harris, 134 Ill. App. 3d 705, 480 N.E.2d 1189 (1985); State v. Hill, 121 N.J. 150, 167, 578 A.2d 370, 379 (1990); State v. Kendricks, 891 S.W.2d 597, 605 (Tenn. 1994) (Tennessee's Supreme Court takes the position that questioning does not automatically disqualify a statement for admission under the prompt outcry rule but that "the nature, type, and purpose of the questioning should be considered by the trial court to determine if the statements actually constituted a legitimate 'complaint'. [citations omitted] If the questioning is neither coercive nor suggestive, the statements may be safely admitted. If

interrogation" will decrease the reliability of the fresh complaint, and the trial court should examine the nature of the questioning, the victim's age, the setting of the disclosure, and the victim's relationship to the questioner (*e.g.*, a police officer, a friend, or a counselor) in determining whether to admit a complaint that is the product of questioning.[171]

§ 10.20 Excited utterance.

A well-founded hearsay exception is the "excited utterance," which is often encountered in sexual assault trials. The Federal Rules of Evidence has codified the generally accepted definition of an excited utterance, which is a "statement relating to a startling event or condition made while the declarant was under the stress of excitement caused by the event or condition."[172] The excited utterance is part of the *res gestae*, a generic term that encompasses four distinct exceptions to the hearsay rule: (1) declarations as to present bodily condition; (2) declarations of present mental status and emotions; (3) excited utterances; and (4) declarations of present sense impressions.[173] The *res gestae* terminology is not heuristic; as one court has noted, "*res gestae* has gone the way of the great auk, the passenger pigeon, and high-button shoes."[174]

The trial court must initially determine the admissibility of an excited utterance. The burden is on the party offering the hearsay declaration to establish that the statement was made under the stress and excitement of the shocking event without lapses. A three-year-old's identification of his attacker, 20 minutes after the attack, is admissible as an excited utterance when the child has been continuously crying before making the identification.[175] The classic examples of an excited utterance in a sexual assault case are those statements made by a victim shortly after an assault while they are emotional and upset.[176] A complainant's statement

---

the questioning is clearly leading or overly suggestive, however, the resulting statement would not, in all likelihood, be the victim's product"); Herron v. Commonwealth, 208 Va. 326, 330, 157 S.E.2d 195, 198 (1967).

[171] State v. Hill, 121 N.J. 150, 167, 578 A.2d 370, 379 (1990).

[172] FED. R. EVID. 803(2).

[173] Commonwealth v. Blackwell, 343 Pa. Super. 201, 494 A.2d 426 (1985).

[174] People v. Orduno, 80 Cal. App. 3d 738, 744, 145 Cal. Rptr. 806, 809 (1978), *cert. denied*, 439 U.S. 1074 (1979).

[175] United States v. Sowa, 34 F.3d 447, 452–53 (7th Cir. 1994), *cert. denied*, 513 U.S. 1117 (1995).

[176] State v. Parkinson, 128 Idaho 29, 909 P.2d 647 (1996); Dearing v. State, 100 Nev. 590, 592, 691 P.2d 419, 420–21 (1984); People v. Torres, 175 A.D.2d 635, 572 N.Y.S.2d 269, *appeal denied*, 78 N.Y.2d 1082, 583 N.E.2d 958, 577 N.Y.S.2d 246 (1991)

> Here, the Sheriff's deputies were patrolling the park when they observed defendant and the complainant on the ground near a parked car. They then heard the complainant screaming that she was being raped. Defendant ran away, and the complainant ran to one of the deputies and told him what had happened. Under those circumstances, the statements complainant made to the deputy that defendant raped her, had been

made in a hospital emergency room shortly after a sexual assault may also qualify as an excited utterance.[177]

An assault victim's statements to an emergency room physician, not in response to a question, identifying her attacker, may qualify as an excited utterance.[178]

A rape victim's statements shortly before dying from the assault may be admissible as an excited utterance.[179] The excited utterance exception derives its trustworthiness from the emotional shock of an event that limits the reflective process and lessens the likelihood of fabrication.[180] The main criteria by which to determine whether a statement falls within the excited utterance exception is whether, at the time the utterance was made, the declarant was under the stress and influence of an external event sufficient to still his or her reflective faculties and prevent the opportunity for deliberation; the nature of the startling event; the amount of time that elapsed between the occurrence and the statement; and the activities of the declarant between the event and statement (to ascertain whether there was significant opportunity to be untruthful).[181] Theoretically, these criteria would preclude the admission of statements that were the product of deliberation or reflection; however, in sexual assault cases, many of these criteria are substantially relaxed.

A knife-point rape is clearly a startling event likely to deprive the declarant of reflective thought,[182] as is an attempted rape during a burglary.[183] Other situations may not be as clear, as discussed in sections to follow.

The startling event may be subsequent to the event about which the excited utterance relates. Thus, a child's statements naming the defendant as the one who hurt her, made while experiencing pain upon urination, qualifies as an excited utterance since "the victim's painful urination was a sufficiently serious and startling event under the rule."[184] When there is no evidence of the witness'

---

hitting her, and did not ejaculate, were properly received by the trial court. In our view, complainant's statements, beyond the mere complaint of rape, were precipitated by a startling event and were made with the requisite spontaneity so as to justify their admission into evidence [as an excited utterance].

177 Johnson v. State, 699 N.E.2d 746, 748–49 (Ind. Ct. App. 1998).

178 Oldman v. State, 998 P.2d 957 (Wyo. 2000).

179 People v. Vega, 225 A.D.2d 890, 639 N.Y.S.2d 511, *appeal denied*, 88 N.Y.2d 943, 670 N.E.2d 461, 647 N.Y.S.2d 177 (1996) (adult rape victim's statement, prior to her death, made immediately after she was found below overpass but hours after sexual assault qualified as excited utterance); Jolly v. State, 314 S.C. 17, 443 S.E.2d 566 (1994).

180 State v. Taylor, 66 Ohio St. 3d 295, 300, 612 N.E.2d 316, 320 (1993).

181 State v. Stover, 126 Idaho 258, 263, 881 P.2d 553, 558 (1994); People v. Edwards, 47 N.Y.2d 493, 392 N.E.2d 1229, 419 N.Y.S.2d 45 (1979).

182 State v. Crawford, 672 So. 2d 197, 202–03 (La. Ct. App.), *review denied*, 679 So. 2d 1379 (1996).

183 State v. Moore, 1998 Tenn. Crim. App. LEXIS 443 (Apr. 9, 1998).

184 State v. Gordon, 952 S.W.2d 817, 821 (Tenn. 1997) (holding startling event was not rape,

state of mind at the time of the statements, and the startling event is remote from the actual abuse, the statements may not be admissible as excited utterances.[185]

There is a "clear judicial trend to liberalize the requirements for an excited utterance when applied to young children victimized by sexual assaults."[186] Thus, a child's statement one hour after an assault can still qualify as an excited utterance.[187]

A reflection of the expanding definition of the excited utterance exception in child sexual assault cases is seen in the custody case of *Morgan v. Foretich*,[188] in which excited-utterance statements were made hours after the abuse. The Fourth Circuit Court of Appeals held:

> One attempt to deal with this problem has been a recognition that the time lapse to be considered in these cases is not simply the time between the abuse and the declaration. Rather, courts must also be cognizant of the child's first real opportunity to report the incident. Plaintiff's declaration of July 20, 1986 has been proffered with absolutely no reference to the time of abuse or the child's first opportunity to speak of the abuse and therefore cannot qualify as an excited utterance. However, the first four statements proffered by the plaintiffs were made within three hours of the child's first opportunity to speak with her mother . . . . All of the statements offered by plaintiffs were made before Hillary was four years old, and it is virtually inconceivable that a child of this age would have either the extensive knowledge of sexual activities or the desire to lie about sexual abuse that would be required to fabricate a story such as the one told by Hillary. Hillary's tender years greatly reduce the likelihood that reflection and fabrication were involved. An examination of Hillary's physical and mental state shows that she was nearly hysterical in the moments immediately preceding most of these statements. There can be little doubt but that she was acting under the stress of the situation. Hillary's method of giving these statements consisted of touching herself sexually and speaking in a vocabulary that definitely belonged to a child which adds a 'ring of verity to her declarations.'[189]

---

but pain suffered while urinating following the rape); Esser v. Commonwealth, 38 Va. App. 520, 566 S.E.2d 876 (2002) (holding startling event for child need not be sexual assault, and in this case startling event was child being told by mother that she was required to return to work and child was to be returned to the place of her assault and her attacker).

[185] R.C. v. Commonwealth, 101 S.W.3d 897 (Ky. 2002).

[186] State v. Wagner, 30 Ohio App. 3d 261, 263, 508 N.E.2d 164, 166 (1986); State v. Huntington, 216 Wis. 2d 671, 682, 575 N.W.2d 268, 273 (1998) (noting the need for hearsay of child sexual assault victims who may refuse or be unable to testify).

[187] Territory of Guam v. Ignacio, 10 F.3d 608, 614 (9th Cir. 1993) (holding that child's statement made to defendant's wife, one hour after she had left the child with the defendant, "Auntie Lin, Uncle Ton touched my pee-pee" held to be an excited utterance since the child was still under the stress of the startling event).

[188] 846 F.2d 941 (4th Cir. 1988).

[189] Morgan v. Foretich, 846 F.2d 941, 947–48 (4th Cir. 1988). *See also* United States v. Nick, 604 F.2d 1199, 1204 (9th Cir. 1979).

Another factor to evaluate in determining whether or not a statement qualifies as an excited utterance and whether the declarant had the opportunity for "studied reflection" is whether or not declarant has given different accounts of the incident.[190] Statements by an alleged crime victim identifying the defendant as an attacker, made while crying hysterically and repeatedly asking whether he was going to die, are admissible as an excited utterance even if the declarant later denies being attacked by the defendant and swears that he never made any statements identifying the defendant.[191] Such excited utterances may be more reliable than later versions of the event after the declarant has had time to contrive or misrepresent events.[192]

§ 10.21 Victim's behavior.

One of the circumstances to look at in evaluating a statement offered as an excited utterance is the declarant's behavior. A critical factor in determining the spontaneity requirement is the emotional response of the declarant. This involves evaluating the nature of the startling event and the intensity of the declarant's response.[193] Justification for the exception disappears as the emotional excitement of the declarant subsides.[194] The failure of a victim to appear upset, speak nervously "or otherwise [behave] in a manner showing that she was under the stress of an exciting event" can demonstrate a lack of reliability to justify receiving the statement as a spontaneous utterance.[195] If the victim is in an emotional state, such as crying or agitated, this fact helps support the claim that the declarant's statement was influenced by the startling event.[196]

---

[190] People v. Pette, 251 A.D.2d 600, 674 N.Y.S.2d 768 (1998) (reversing defendant's conviction due to improper admission into evidence of statements in medical records which were neither admissible under medical records exception nor excited utterance exception and which inculpated the defendant).

[191] People v. Fratello, 92 N.Y.2d 565, 706 N.E.2d 1173, 684 N.Y.S.2d 149 (1998), *cert. denied*, 526 U.S. 1068 (1999); State v. Williamson, 100 Wash. App. 248, 996 P.2d 1097 (2000).

[192] People v. Fratello, 92 N.Y.2d 565, 706 N.E.2d 1173, 684 N.Y.S.2d 149 (1998), *cert. denied*, 526 U.S. 1068 (1999).

[193] State v. Smith, 909 P.2d 236 (Utah 1995)

> Usually the most difficult issue in determining the admissibility of an excited utterance is whether the statement was uttered with a spontaneity produced by emotional excitement to a degree that provides a warrant of trustworthiness. The determination requires an evaluation of a variety of factors, including the nature of the startling event and the intensity of the excitement or other emotional effect on the declarant. The statement need not be strictly contemporaneous with the startling event to be spontaneous, as is the case with the 'present sense impression' exception. . . .

Id. at 240.

[194] State v. Smith, 909 P.2d 236 (Utah 1995).

[195] Commonwealth v. Whelton, 428 Mass. 24, 696 N.E.2d 540 (1998) (but holding that error was harmless in this case).

[196] Johnson v. State, 326 Ark. 430, 934 S.W.2d 179 (1996), *rev'd on other grounds* (murder

Merely being upset may not be enough to meet the requirements for admissibility. Not every statement by an excited person is an excited utterance, since the declarant's "excited" reactions may be due to a variety of reasons, such as retelling the incident rather than the stress of the event.[197] If the statements were made by an upset person after deliberation and reflection, for example, the statement is not an excited utterance.[198]

Generally, while a victim's excited appearance helps to establish that the statement was made under the influence of a startling event, the absence of an excited appearance does not, in and of itself, preclude the admission of excited utterance testimony. The fact that a declarant's demeanor was unremarkable is not dispositive of the inquiry as to whether he or she was under the stress of excitement, and there is no requirement that the declarant must have been emotionally overpowered by the event.[199] Nervous excitement is not necessarily manifested by hysteria, crying, or other obvious ways in which it is usually demonstrated, but it may be shown in many ways that reflect a person's age, experience, and psychological make-up.[200] A seven-year-old's statements three or four hours after being sexually abused would qualify as an excited utterance, even though the child is engaged in normal childhood play.[201]

---

victim's six-year-old daughter's scared and hyperactive behavior provided foundation for admission of her statement as excited utterance); Weaver v. State, 271 Ark. 853, 612 S.W.2d 324, *cert. denied*, 452 U.S. 963 (1981); State v. Parkinson, 909 P.2d 647, 654 (Idaho Ct. App. 1996) (complainant was in tears and appeared to be distraught when she had described sexual abuse to her brother a few minutes after the incident had occurred); Commonwealth v. Alvarado, 36 Mass. App. Ct. 604, 634 N.E.2d 132, *review denied*, 418 Mass. 1106, 639 N.E.2d 1081 (1994) (victim's statement to responding police officers that defendant hit and bit her admissible as an excited utterance based upon the observations of disarray in the apartment, the declarant's emotional state, the bite marks on her body, her statement that the assault had just occurred, and the short time period between the call for police and the officers' response); People v. Luke, 8 A.D.3d 203, 779 N.Y.S.2d 194, *appeal denied* 3 N.Y.3d 740, 820 N.E.2d 290, 786 N.Y.S.2d 820 (2004) (finding it proper to admit a testifying victim's statement to a social worker as an excited utterance when victim acted hysterical and distraught after being brutally beaten); State v. Binion, 947 S.W.2d 867, 873 (Tenn. Crim. App. 1996) (holding 15-year-old's shaking and crying when she told her cousin and mother about sexual assault constituted evidence of strain and excitement from event); State v. Sims, 77 Wash. App. 236, 890 P.2d 521 (1995) (police officer properly allowed to repeat domestic violence complainant's statement given the foundation that she was crying, upset and made statement right after the incident; her hesitancy did not negate the spontaneity).

[197] West Valley City v. Hutto, 5 P.3d 1, n.8 (Utah Ct. App. 2000) (reversing defendant's conviction due to erroneous admission of domestic violence and complainant's statements to a police officer, after traveling six blocks to her mother's house and six hours before speaking to officer and responding to questions in the familiar environment of her mother's house).

[198] State v. Bowles, 1998 Ohio App. LEXIS 1889 *13–15 (Apr. 28, 1998).

[199] State v. Hobby, 9 Neb. App. 89, 95–96, 607 N.W.2d 869, 876 (2000) (holding demeanor of victim who was upset, nervous, withdrawn, and uncomfortable reflected nervous excitement and shock of assault); Commonwealth v. Sanford, 397 Pa. Super. 581, 589, 580 A.2d 784, 788 (1990).

[200] State v. Ramos, 203 N.J. Super. 197, 496 A.2d 386 (1985).

[201] People v. Hackney, 183 Mich. App. 516, 455 N.W.2d 358 (1990).

Because of the U.S. Supreme Court's decision in *Crawford v. Washington*,[202] discussed in § 10.45, hearsay statements, which are testimonial and include a statement "in response to structured police questioning" are inadmissible because of the lack of opportunity to cross-examine the declarant.[203] However, some courts have held that comments and statements made during on-scene interviewing, usually brief and used in assessing a situation, or made under stress and excitement, do not violate *Crawford*.[204] For a further discussion of the factors involved in this assessment, see § 10.45.

§ 10.22 Effect of questioning declarant.

Another consideration in assessing the admissibility of an excited utterance is whether the statement was the product of questioning.[205] That the declaration is in response to inquiries does not preclude a statement from being an excited utterance, but most courts will look at many factors in the context of the questioning in determining the admissibility of such statements. Questions by a witness or police officer do not automatically defeat statements as an excited utterance.[206] The circumstances of the questioning must be evaluated. A

---

[202] 541 U.S. 36 (2004).

[203] Crawford v. Washington, 541 U.S. 36, 53, n.4 (2004).

[204] In People v. Bradley, 22 A.D.3d 33, 799 N.Y.S.2d 472 (2005):

> Where the purpose of the inquiry is to gain familiarity with the situation confronting a police officer to determine what happened, the officer is making only a preliminary investigatory inquiry. Thus, the response is not the product of a structured police interrogation and should not be regarded as testimonial. However, where the purpose of the inquiry is to gather incriminating evidence against a particular individual, the officer is advancing a potential prosecution, and the response takes on a testimonial character. . . . Applying this test to the facts at bar, it is clear that the responding police officer merely posed a general question to elicit information needed to evaluate the circumstances and take appropriate action. The officer testified that he was responding to a 'call for help' and apparently did not know whether the cause of the victim's injury was accidental or criminal. He asked a preliminary and nonspecific question, not calculated to elicit incriminating evidence. Until he heard the victim's response, he was not even aware that defendant was the particular person to be targeted for investigation. Because the officer was merely making a preliminary inquiry, not performing a quasi-prosecutory function at the time he posed the question, the answer he received cannot be characterized as testimonial.

Id. at 42–43, 799 N.Y.S.2d at 480; State v. Forrest, 164 N.C. App. 272, 596 S.E.2d 22 (2004).

[205] Zitter, Jay M., *When is Hearsay Statement "Excited Utterance" Admissible Under Rule 803(2) of Federal Rules of Evidence,* 155 A.L.R. FED. 583 (1999). Annotation, Wade R. Habeeb, *Fact That Rape Victim's Complaint or Statement was Made in Response to Questions as Affecting Res Gestae Character,* 80 A.L.R.3D 369 (1977).

[206] State v. Peite, 122 Idaho 809, 839 P.2d 1223 (1992); People v. Fratello, 92 N.Y.2d 565, 706 N.E.2d 1173, 684 N.Y.S.2d 149 (1998), *cert. denied,* 526 U.S. 1068 (1999) (holding that the fact that statements were made in response to questioning and that there was an approximately ten-minute interval from the event until the declaration to a police officer does not impair a statement's admissibility since neither of the factors detracted from the statement's spontaneity under the

statement can be an excited utterance where a police officer asks a ten-year-old victim: "What happened?"[207] Questions that did not call for reflection by a child-declarant, even though the child did not tell her sitter (the defendant's wife), her sister, or her mother immediately after the event, did not defeat the spontaneous nature of her statement.[208] The types of questions that may be considered not to call for reflection include an occasional "what?", "where?", "kissed you where?", "what else happened?", and "he did what?"[209] A victim's 911 call to the police following her abduction qualified as an excited utterance, even though some statements were in response to questions.[210] However, statements by a victim in response to "suggestive comments and questioning" by an eyewitness will lack the inherent reliability to qualify as an excited utterance.[211]

The age of the declarant may affect the willingness of a court to accept an utterance in response to questioning. The statements of a child in response to persistent questioning can be admissible on the theory of his or her limited reflective power and inability to understand the implications of the attack. This theory was articulated by an Ohio court in upholding as excited responses displays of sexual acts through anatomical dolls by a three-year-old in response to repeated questioning by his mother and a police detective hours and days after the event:

> The limited reflective powers of a three-year-old, coupled with his inability to understand the enormity or ramifications of the attack upon him, sustain the trustworthiness of his communications. As a three-year-old, truly in the age of innocence, he lacked the motive or reflective capacities to prevaricate the circumstances of the attack. Furthermore, the immediacy of each communication, considered in light of the available opportunities to express himself, satisfies the requirement of spontaneity.[212]

---

circumstances); State v. Scott, No. 01C01-9708-CR-00331, 1999 Tenn. Crim. App. LEXIS 758, at *36–39 (July 28, 1999) (holding that rape victim's statements to police officer, while still under stress of the incident, made in response to police officer's questions still qualify as excited utterance).

[207] People v. Jackson, 203 Ill. App. 3d 1, 560 N.E.2d 1019 (1990). *See also* State v. Bowler, 892 S.W.2d 717 (Mo. Ct. App. 1994) (fact that 12-year-old was questioned prior to making statement did not detract from the excited nature of her statement since the circumstances surrounding the victim's utterance demonstrated she was "still under the influence of the unusual event and was in an agitated state of mind").

[208] Commonwealth v. Sanford, 397 Pa. Super 581, 592, 580 A.2d 784, 789-90 (1990).

[209] Commonwealth v. Sanford, 397 Pa. Super 581, 592, 580 A.2d 784, 789-90 (1990).

[210] Commonwealth v. Blackwell, 343 Pa. Super. 201, 494 A.2d 426 (1985).

[211] People v. Fenner, 283 A.D.2d 516, 727 N.Y.S.2d 117 (2001) (reversing defendant's conviction due to erroneous admission of hearsay statements).

[212] State v. Wagner, 30 Ohio App. 3d 261, 263, 508 N.E.2d 164, 167 (1986). *See also* State v. Smith, 909 P.2d 236 (Utah 1995) (child's statement a day and a half later in response to "somewhat leading" questions qualified as excited utterance).

The lack of suggestive or persistent questioning may be a factor in evaluating admissibility.[213] However, at a certain point, repetitive or suggestive questioning will deprive a statement of its spontaneity. A grandmother's repeated questioning of a child regarding what happened[214] and similar aggressive interrogation can defeat the excited utterance exception.[215]

§ 10.23   Time lapse between startling event and utterance.

There is no fixed time period as to when a statement loses its excited nature. Courts tend to look at many factors and emphasize that time is but one.[216] In many sexual assault cases, it appears that courts focus on the nature of the sexual assault and the age of the declarant as a reason to expand the traditional view that an excited utterance must be made immediately after the event. For example, one hour does not remove the excited utterance exception under the Federal Rules of Evidence, especially when a child is involved.[217] A 15-year-old's statements one-half hour after a sexual assault are sufficiently prompt in the context of a sexual assault.[218] Courts are willing to acknowledge that it is reasonable to expect that a child will be "confused and uncertain" after a sexual assault, that a child will not tell certain individuals, and that a child's inconsistent demeanor, conduct, and facial expressions can reflect the stress of the event as well as the confusion

---

[213] People v. Smith, 456 Mich. 543, 553, 581 N.W.2d 654, 658 (1998) (upholding admission of 16-year-old's statements ten hours after assault and questioning of complainant).

[214] Souder v. Commonwealth, 719 S.W.2d 730, 734 (Ky. 1986).

[215] Felix v. State, 109 Nev. 151, 849 P.2d 220, 239–240 (1993). *See also* People v. Farmer, 47 Cal. 3d 888, 765 P.2d 940, 254 Cal. Rptr. 508, *cert. denied*, 490 U.S. 1107 (1989); People v. Edwards, 47 N.Y.2d 493, 498–99, 392 N.E.2d 1229, 1232, 419 N.Y.S.2d 45 (1979).

[216] State v. Sanchez-Lahora, 9 Neb. Ct. App. 621, 639–41, 616 N.W.2d 810, 824–25 (2000), *rev'd on other grounds, aff'd*, 261 Neb. 192, 622 N.W.2d 612 (2001) (holding that under all the circumstances, i.e., a complainant crying and to the point that she could not speak at times, neighbor's testimony of complainant's statements after she walked four to five blocks qualified as an excited utterance); People v. Fratello, 92 N.Y.2d 565, 706 N.E.2d 1173, 684 N.Y.S.2d 149 (1998), *cert. denied*, 526 U.S. 1068 (1999) (holding that the fact that statements were made in response to questioning and that there was an approximate ten-minute interval from the event until the declaration to a police officer does not impair a statement's admissibility since neither of the factors detracted from the statement's spontaneity under the circumstances); People v. Nelson, 266 A.D.2d 725, 698 N.Y.S.2d 755 (1999), *appeal denied*, 95 N.Y.2d 801, 733 N.E.2d 241, 711 N.Y.S.2d 169 (2000) (holding 911 call made ten to 15 minutes after crime admissible since victim "still under the excitement precipitated by event"); State v. Tribble, 2000 Ohio App. LEXIS 5665 (Dec. 1, 2000) (holding trial court could best assess that complainant's statements to responding officer were excited utterances made in response to stress of event and time was but one factor for court to consider). *See generally* W. A. Harrington, Annotation, *Time Element as Affecting Admissibility of Statement or Complaint Made by Victim of Sex Crime as Res Gestae, Spontaneous Exclamation, or Excited Utterance*, 89 A.L.R.3D 102 (1979).

[217] Wheeler v. United States, 211 F.2d 19, 24 (D.C. Cir. 1953), *cert. denied*, 347 U.S. 1019 (1954).

[218] United States v. Rivera, 43 F.3d 1291 (9th Cir. 1995) (15-year-old's statement concerning abuse made to her mother at least one-half hour after intercourse occurred fell within excited utterance exception).

and uncertainty surrounding the event.[219] A seven-year-old's statement telling a neighbor about a sexual assault three or four hours earlier, even though the victim had engaged in normal childhood play in the interim may qualify as an excited utterance.[220] A ten-year-old rape victim's statement two hours after the assault can also be considered an excited utterance.[221] Similarly, a four-year-old's statement to his mother concerning an act of sodomy when the mother returned home from shopping was deemed an excited utterance based on an evaluation of the victim's reluctance to describe the incident and the circumstances surrounding the assault.[222] Also, in a case involving a three-year-old who did not report being sexually assaulted by his teacher until five hours after the incident, the child's statement was held admissible as an excited utterance on the theory that the fact that the child was quiet and withdrawn up until the time he made the statement demonstrated that his delay in reporting was the product of the event rather than deliberation.[223]

In *People v. Smith*,[224] the Michigan Supreme Court found a 16-year-old's statements ten hours after the sexual abuse to be excited utterances. The court noted the complainant's actions during the time period included taking an hour-long bath with the water running, pacing, and pounding his fist in his hand, uncharacteristically sleepy on the couch, and crying.[225] These actions "describe a continuing level of stress arising from the assault that precluded any possibility of fabrication," despite the ten-hour delay.[226]

A child's emotional reaction to recounting details of an event can trump the passage of time.[227]

---

[219] United States v. Donaldson, 58 M.J. 477 (C.A.A.F. 2003) (statement of three-year-old sexual assault victim held admissible despite 11–12 hour lapse between assault and the statement, because the statement was made during the child's first opportunity alone with a trusted adult); Commonwealth v. Sanford, 397 Pa. Super. 581, 593, 580 A.2d 784, 790 (1990), *appeal denied*, 527 Pa. 586, 588 A.2d 508 (1991); State v. Boruff, No. E1999-00274-CCA-R3-CD, 2000 Tenn. Crim. App. LEXIS 244 (Mar. 17, 2000), *appeal denied*, 2002 Tenn. LEXIS 133 (Mar. 11, 2002) (holding three-year-old sexual assault victim's statements made approximately 40 minutes after event qualified as excited utterance).

[220] People v. Hackney, 183 Mich. App. 516, 455 N.W.2d 358 (1990).

[221] State v. Kaytso, 684 P.2d 63, 64 (Utah 1984) (*per curiam*).

[222] People v. Van Patten, 125 A.D.2d 827, 509 N.Y.S.2d 926 (1986).

[223] People v. Nevitt, 135 Ill. 2d 423, 553 N.E.2d 368 (1990), *on remand*, 228 Ill. App. 3d 888, 593 N.E.2d 797 (1992).

[224] 456 Mich. 543, 581 N.W.2d 654 (1998).

[225] People v. Smith, 456 Mich. 543, 552-53, 581 N.W.2d 654, 658 (1998).

[226] People v. Smith, 456 Mich. 543, 553, 581 N.W.2d 654, 658 (1998).

[227] State v. Siler, 101 Ohio St. 3d 1489, 805 N.E.2d 539, *appeal denied*, 2004 Ohio 2569, 809 N.E.2d 34 (2004) (allowing as admissible hearsay child's statement to police describing defendant's use of rope in killing, because such recollection caused the child to cry and shift his attention back to the house where he felt his mother should be, even though it was made eight hours after her murder).

The combination of a child's youth, limited terminology, and the distress of the assault can greatly reduce the likelihood of reflection and fabrication.[228] A telephone call to the police seven and one-half hours after a rape was admissible as an excited utterance where, during the interim, the victim had been hiding in a boatyard under a tarp, thinking that her attacker was looking for her.[229] A 16-year-old's statements to her sister that she was raped by her father made the day after an assault and after she had contact with several other people, including coworkers and other family members, was deemed an excited utterance because of the "shame, embarrassment, and stress associated with rape, particularly of a child by a father."[230] This expands the excited utterance exception to the level of the prompt reasoning outcry exception, *i.e.*, the first reasonably available opportunity to report the rape. In a nonsexual assault prosecution, a four-year-old child's excited utterance implicating a defendant in a murder was admissible even though made 12 hours after the crime where there was no reason to believe that premeditation, design, or reflection produced the statement.[231] Many courts have upheld the admission of a child's excited utterances many hours after a murder.[232]

---

[228] United States v. Farley, 992 F.2d 1122, 1126 (10th Cir. 1993). *See also* United States v. Iron Shell, 633 F.2d 77, 83 (8th Cir. 1980), *cert. denied*, 450 U.S. 1001 (1981); United States v. Nick, 604 F.2d 1199, 1204 (9th Cir. 1979); People v. Cobb, 108 Mich. App. 573, 310 N.W.2d 798 (1981) (child's statement one day after witnessing the death of his sister was admissible as an excited utterance where the child was still under the excitement of the tragic event).

[229] State v. Guizzotti, 60 Wash. App. 289, 803 P.2d 808 (1991).

[230] Heflin v. State, 643 So. 2d 512 (Miss. 1994) (proof demonstrated this was the first reasonable opportunity for the complainant to tell someone she trusted. As [the victim] put it, "anything short of this would have been dangerous"). *See also* United States v. Rivera, 43 F.3d 1291 (9th Cir. 1995) (admitting as excited utterance statements made one-half hour after the assault by a 15-year-old complainant when viewed in the context of her semi-hysterical state and the physical abuse and death threats she and her family had received).

[231] Gross v. Greer, 773 F.2d 116 (7th Cir. 1985).

[232] Johnson v. State, 326 Ark. 430, 934 S.W.2d 179 (1996), *rev'd. on other grounds* (murder victim's six-year-old daughter's statements about murder nine hours after murder admissible as excited utterance); People v. Trimble, 5 Cal. App. 4th 1225, 7 Cal. Rptr. 2d 450 (1992) (upholding an excited utterance when a two and one-half-year-old child's statement that her father murdered her mother, made two days after the event, was admissible where she had been in the house with the defendant for the two days); Corn v. State, 796 So. 2d 641 (Fla. Dist. Ct. App. 2001) (finding murder witness' statement two to 20 hours after murder qualified as excited utterance); Barnett v. State, 757 So. 2d 323 (Miss. Ct. App. 2000) (four-year-old child's statements approximately six hours after he awoke and discovered mother had been stabbed and dragged into car trunk were made while still under excitement of event); State v. Siler, 2003 Ohio App. LEXIS 5091 (Oct. 24, 2003), *appeal denied*, 101 Ohio St. 3d 1489, 805 N.E.2d 539 (2004) (holding three-year-old's statements about a murder eight hours after witnessing mother's death is still a time period during which child would be under shock of startling event); State v. Sims, 348 S.C. 16, 558 S.E.2d 518 (2000) (Police officer was permitted to testify that child told him defendant was in home at time his mother was murdered:

> In this case, a five-year-old child possibly saw his mother being attacked and, at the very least, was left alone with his severely injured mother whom he could not wake,

Some cases have gone so far as to suggest that days may elapse between the event and the declaration.[233] The violence of the attack and its psychological effects may be factors to weigh in the time lapse.[234]

For example, an adult woman's statements made to a police officer 30 minutes after an assault qualifies as an excited utterance. She had been looking for police officers during the period and was in an excited state when she encountered one.[235]

An assault victim sleeping for 20 minutes does not necessarily defeat the timeliness requirement of the exception.[236]

Courts sometimes grant more leeway in admitting excited utterances days after an event if the declarant suffers from a developmental disability.[237]

Furthermore, Virginia has ruled the "startling event" requirement under the excited utterance exception does not have to be the actual crime, but rather can be a related occurrence causing such a reaction even days afterwards.[238] A related occurrence giving rise to an excited utterance is found when the victim's mother told her two days after the assaults that she would be returned to the place where the assaults occurred and supervised by her attacker.[239] The statements made by the victim to her mother were construed as excited utterances and thus negated the existence of spontaneity required for application of the exception.[240] Even after the witness complains of the sexual assault to one person, a statement to a second person may qualify as an excited utterance when the declarant is still under the stress of the event.[241] Statements of defendant's domestic violence

---

    until he made his way outside to be found by a neighbor. Under these circumstances, we find the stress of excitement from those events lasts a longer period of time than would be likely to occur if the son had been an adult.
State v. Sims, 348 S.C. 16, 22, 558 S.E.2d 518, 521 (2000)).

[233] State v. Rogers, 109 N.C. App. 491, 501, 428 S.E.2d 220, 226, *cert. denied*, 334 N.C. 625, 435 S.E.2d 348 (1993), *cert. denied*, 511 U.S. 1008 (1994), *citing* State v. Smith, 315 N.C. 76, 86, 337 S.E.2d 833, 841 (1985) (finding excited utterance by five-year-old child, three days after sexual assault); *In re* Michael, 119 Ohio App. 3d 112, 694 N.E.2d 538 (1997) (holding two-week delay between alleged sexual abuse and child's statements a permissible delay).

[234] State v. Smith, 909 P.2d 236 (Utah 1995) (Six-year-old child's statements a day and a half after assault were an excited utterance "owing to the violence of the attack and the specific psychological response of the six-year-old victim . . . ." *Id.* at 242 (child was not communicating with others during this period except to ask for pain pills)).

[235] Reyes-Contreras v. United States, 719 A.2d 503 (D.C. 1998).

[236] State v. Kinross, 906 P.2d 320, 323 (Utah 1995) (citing cases).

[237] State v. Taplette, 519 So. 2d 854 (La. 1988) (admitting statements made seven days after the assault, where the court found developmentally disabled victim made disclosure at what *she perceived* was her first reasonable opportunity).

[238] Esser v. Commonwealth, 38 Va. App. 520, 566 S.E.2d 876 (2002).

[239] Esser v. Commonwealth, 38 Va. App. 520, 525, 566 S.E.2d 876, 879 (2002).

[240] Esser v. Commonwealth, 38 Va. App. 520, 525, 566 S.E.2d 876, 879 (2002).

[241] State v. Leonard, 2000 Tenn. Crim. App. LEXIS 924 (Dec. 1, 2000) (holding child's report

by a deceased victim seeking refuge from defendant's assaultive behavior are excited utterances given evidence of stress precipitated by trauma of being beaten. The startling event in this case is not the crime charged.[242]

§ 10.24   Limits on the time period between startling event and declaration.

The cases cited in the last section demonstrate the necessity of establishing the foundation for the admissibility of excited utterances made well after an event occurs. Many court decisions conclude that there is no excited utterance under comparable time intervals between the event and declaration cited in the preceding section. For example, cases in the previous section suggest that 20 minutes is a short enough time period for a victim to still be under the influence of the "startling event." On the other hand, 20 minutes between the startling event and the declaration is held to be sufficient time for an alleged victim of domestic violence to contemplate, reflect, and deliberate about the incident and is not reasonably contemporaneous with the event, thus defeating the foundational requirement for an excited utterance in one case.[243] A general argument that a victim is distraught is insufficient to justify a lengthy interval between the sexual assault and declaration.[244] It is the offering party's burden to establish the statement's spontaneous nature and that it was made under the stress of the event.[245] A child's statements before scheduled visits to her father that she did not want to visit him and did not like him do not qualify as an excited utterance.[246] A victim's statement to a police officer one day after the attack

of sexual assault to mother, made after child had told someone else, qualified as an excited utterance, despite the passage of some period of time since child was still under the stress of the sexual assault).

[242] People v. Vega, 3 A.D.3d 239, 771 N.Y.S.2d 30 *appeal denied* 2 N.Y.3d 766, 811 N.E. 2d 46, 778 N.Y.S.2d 784 (2004).

[243] State v. Ortiz, 74 Haw. 343, 359, 845 P.2d 547, 549, *review denied*, 74 Haw. 650, 849 P.2d 81 (1993) (However, another statement in the same case was admitted as an excited utterance when the complainant's physical condition of crying and holding her face indicated that the alleged offense occurred immediately prior to the declaration, her physical condition supported a conclusion that the statement was the result of the defendant's actions, and third, there was a very short time span between the event and the statement which did not give the declarant time to reflect on her statement).

[244] *See, e.g.*, State v. Burroughs, 328 S.C. 489, 500–01, 492 S.E.2d 408, 412–13 (1997) (finding error in admission of victim's statements hours after she returned home when witness testified she composed herself after attack and decided how to tell her husband about assault).

[245] State v. Taylor, 103 N.M. 189, 704 P.2d 443 (1985); State v. Paster, 524 A.2d 587 (R.I. 1987); State v. Bubeck, 1997 Wash. App. LEXIS 367, *review denied*, 133 Wash. 2d 1011, 946 P.2d 401 (1997) (rape complainant's statement not an excited utterance when removed in time and complainant had talked to enough people to indicate the time and opportunity for reflection and fabrication).

[246] Commonwealth v. Trowbridge, 419 Mass. 750, 758, 647 N.E.2d 413, 420 (1995) (child's tearful statements to her first grade teacher on Friday afternoon prior to scheduled visits with her father that she did not want to visit her daddy and she didn't like her daddy did not qualify as a spontaneous utterance).

and after she had been "calmed down" by the officer is not an excited utterance.[247] A statement to a police officer one to one and one-half hours after an assault, after the declarant spoke to her parents and another officer, is too long after the startling event and affords the declarant an opportunity to reflect.[248] If the declarant is no longer under the influence of the startling event and can urge a family member to calm down, this too disqualifies the statement as an excited utterance.[249] One hour after a rape is too long for a statement to be an excited utterance when two victims "had time to think about their actions and to invent an excuse about their late arrival at the dorm with alcohol on their breath."[250] Courts will focus on the ability to deliberate prior to the declaration.[251] Statements made by a victim while seeking an order of protection ordinarily evidences an opportunity to reflect or fabricate.[252]

Similarly, a complainant's statements to her friends after traveling some distance, ordering a drink,[253] or "sobering up" after a crime and then reporting a sexual assault[254] do not qualify as an excited utterance. When the prosecution fails to establish sufficiently specific reasons or grounds justifying the delayed utterance, the statement should be inadmissible. Furthermore, the prosecution must establish when the event took place and the time period between the event and declaration to show that the statements were made under the stress of an event, even when the age of the declarant would justify a statement made hours

---

[247] State v. Bargas, 52 Wash. App. 700, 763 P.2d 470 (1988) *review denied*, 112 Wash. 2d 1005 (1989).

[248] Cartwright v. State, 242 Ga. App. 825, 531 S.E.2d 399 (2000).

[249] People v. Fenner, 283 A.D.2d 516, 727 N.Y.S.2d 117 (2001)

> The victim's subsequent statements to his brother and girlfriend were made after the victim was no longer under the influence of excitement, and was capable of urging his brother to remain calm. The fact that he whispered the allegation that the defendant was the shooter in his brother's ear, and told his girlfriend he would tell her who did it 'later' indicates he was capable of concealment from personnel in the ambulance. This constituted further evidence that he was capable of studied reflection.

[250] United States v. Sherlock, 962 F.2d 1349, 1365 (9th Cir. 1992), *cert. denied sub nom.*, Charley v. United States, 506 U.S. 958 (1992).

[251] United States v. Marrowbone, 211 F.3d 452 (8th Cir. 2000) (holding a teenage sexual assault victim's statements made about three hours after event not an exited utterance, since teenager had ability to deliberate and fabricate and "[t]his particular teenager also had reason to fabricate because making a charge of molestation might enable him to avoid a night in jail for being intoxicated" and declarant's actions did not show continuous excitement or stress); People v. Johnson, 1 N.Y.3d 302, 804 N.E.2d 402, 772 N.Y.S.2d 238 (2003) (holding victim's statement to police, "He stabbed me, he stabbed me," made a full hour after the startling event, was made after declarant had ability to engage in reasoned reflection and deliberation. Declarant was alert and oriented and should not have been admitted as an excited utterance, but error was harmless).

[252] State v. Bauer, 598 N.W.2d 352, 366–67 (Minn. 1999) (finding error was harmless in context of all the evidence).

[253] McGrew v. State, 673 N.E.2d 787 (Ind. Ct. App. 1996), *aff'd*, 682 N.E.2d 1289 (Ind. 1997).

[254] State v. Carter, 1998 Minn. App. LEXIS 87 at *13–14 (Jan. 27, 1998).

after a sexual assault.[255] Of course, if the prosecution has not identified the time at which the assault took place, it may be difficult to establish an excited utterance. Courts have clearly placed limits on statements made several days after an assault. For example, while statements of a mentally retarded victim with a mental capacity of a six-to seven-year-old, made the morning after an alleged rape, qualify as excited utterances, her statements made four days later are not admissible as excited utterances.[256] Hearsay declarations of sexual abuse by a child more than one year after the abuse and only after substantial prodding and suggestive questioning will not be admitted as excited utterances.[257]

A sexual assault victim's diary entry made several days after the assault is not an excited utterance, since it is not made under the stress of an event.[258] Ordinarily, writing down a statement will deprive it of its spontaneous character; however, it is possible, such as in the case of a suicide note, that a written statement will qualify as an excited utterance.[259]

§ 10.25   Subject of the declaration.

An excited utterance should be evaluated to ensure that its content relates to the event that triggered the startling reaction. The Federal Rules of Evidence require that the statement be one "relating to a startling event or condition."[260] Any extraneous information or comments would make the statement not truly an excited utterance. This can form the basis for an objection to a statement's admissibility. However, there may be gray areas, such as the statement by a victim, "You guys better find the guy before I kill him."[261]

Admissibility of the utterance can be affected by a declaration that is not clearly related to the crime charged. For example, a nontestifying child's statement: "Yes, right after Foster put his tinkler in my mouth, I did," required testimony by the child's mother as to her opinion as to what the child meant by "tinkler." Such opinion testimony interpreting the excited utterance is improper and reversible error.[262]

While the excited utterance should ordinarily be about or relate to a startling event, the event need not be the crime charged. It may be any relevant event,

---

[255] State v. Jano, 524 So. 2d 660 (Fla. 1988).

[256] Cole v. State, 307 Ark. 41, 818 S.W.2d 573 (1991).

[257] Felix v. State, 109 Nev. 151, 179, 849 P.2d 220, 239–40 (1993).

[258] State v. Smith, 241 Neb. 311, 488 N.W.2d 33 (1992); People v. Singh, 186 A.D.2d 285, 288, 588 N.Y.S.2d 573, 576 (1992).

[259] United States v. O'Brien, 51 F.2d 37 (4th Cir. 1931).

[260] FED. R. EVID. 803(2).

[261] United States v. Barrett, 937 F.2d 1346 (8th Cir. 1991).

[262] Oldham v. State, 167 Tex. Crim. 644, 322 S.W.2d 616 (1959).

although courts are divided on whether there must be independent evidence of the event. [263]

For example, the startling event may be an occurrence or consequence related to the sexual assault. [264]

Sometimes a complainant's expression of feeling may qualify as an excited utterance. Thus, a 14-year-old complainant's statement to a friend that he did not want the defendant near him because he was feeling sick was admissible as an excited utterance when made contemporaneously with the assault. [265]

§ 10.26 Multiple statements of excited utterance.

As with the prompt outcry, there can be multiple excited utterances, and such declarations can be properly admitted. [266] Nevertheless, multiple spontaneous declarations should be evaluated to determine whether such testimony is necessary, cumulative, or unduly prejudicial. While a statement may qualify for admission into evidence as an excited utterance, there may be other grounds for its preclusion from evidence.

The admission of multiple hearsay statements under different hearsay exceptions is particularly an issue with non-testifying or non-responsive child witnesses. The potential prejudice in the admission of multiple hearsay statements is discussed in § 10.52.

---

[263] Janet Boeth Jones, Annotation, *Necessity, in Criminal Prosecution, of Independent Evidence of Principal Act to Allow Admission, Under Res Gestae or Excited Utterance Exception to Hearsay Rule, of Statement Made at Time of, or Subsequent to, Principal Act,* 38 A.L.R.4th 1237 (1985).

[264] United States v. Napier, 518 F.2d 316, 318 (9th Cir. 1975) (holding that complainant seeing defendant's picture seven weeks after assault was a startling event); State v. Johnson, 2003 Tenn. Crim. App. LEXIS 1074 (Dec. 23, 2003) (concluding the statement of a father made shortly after learning of his son's sexual abuse qualified as an excited utterance as such discovery "undoubtedly qualified as a startling event"); State v. Snider, 2000 Tenn. Crim. App. LEXIS 642 (Aug. 18, 2000) (allowing victim's mother to testify about statements the victim made to her was not an error and qualified as excited utterances as the victim was still under the stress of having bled on the toilet seat after the defendant molested her); State v. Gordon, 952 S.W.2d 817, 821 (Tenn. 1997) (holding that pain suffered while urinating after rape was a startling event, justifying complainant's statement identifying defendant); Esser v. Commonwealth, 38 Va. App. 520, 525–27, 566 S.E.2d 876, 878–80 (2002) (complainant's statement made when she believed she was to be returned to the place where she was assaulted and to control of person who had assaulted her was sufficiently trustworthy to be admitted as an excited utterance).

[265] Commonwealth v. Capone, 39 Mass. App. Ct. 606, 659 N.E.2d 1196, *review denied*, 422 Mass. 1106, 663 N.E.2d 576 (1996).

[266] People v. Kulakowski, 135 A.D.2d 1119, 523 N.Y.S.2d 288 (1987), *appeal denied*, 70 N.Y.2d 1007, 521 N.E.2d 1085, 526 N.Y.S.2d 942, *appeal denied*, 72 N.Y.2d 912, 528 N.E.2d 1234, 532 N.Y.S.2d 761 (1988).

§ 10.27   Availability and competency of declarant.

The Supreme Court of the United States has ruled that the prosecution does not have to produce or demonstrate the unavailability of the declarant to justify evidence received under a well-rooted hearsay exception, such as the excited utterance,[267] and other courts follow this rule.[268] However, a state court may not follow the United States Supreme Court holding of *White v. Illinois* and require a showing of the declarant's unavailability pursuant to its own state constitution.[269] Some courts have required the prosecution to produce the declarant at trial to demonstrate his or her competency on the theory that a hearsay declaration by an incompetent person is inadmissible.[270] Ohio's Supreme Court has held that hearsay statements "must meet the same basic requirements as live witness testimony" and that competency of the declarant must be established as

---

[267] White v. Illinois, 502 U.S. 346 (1992).

[268] Morgan v. Foretich, 846 F.2d 941, 946 (4th Cir. 1988) (admitting excited utterances of child, even though child was incompetent to testify); Gross v. Greer, 773 F.2d 116 (7th Cir. 1985); United States v. Nick, 604 F.2d 1199, 1202 (9th Cir. 1979); People v. Daily, 49 Cal. App. 4th 543, 552, 56 Cal. Rptr. 2d 787, 792, *review denied*, No. S056947, 1996 Cal. LEXIS 7288 (Dec. 23, 1996) ("It is well established that the spontaneous hearsay declarations of minors who were not competent to testify in court concerning sexual molestation are admissible pursuant to Evidence Code § 1240."); People v. Orduno, 80 Cal. App. 3d 738, 145 Cal. Rptr. 806, 808 (1978), *cert. denied*, 439 U.S. 1074 (1979); Reyes-Contreras v. United States, 719 A.2d 503, 507 (D.C. 1998) ("We now make explicit . . . that no showing of a declarant's unavailability for trial is required under the Confrontation Clause of the Sixth Amendment to the Constitution of the United States before a spontaneous utterance may be admitted into evidence as an exception to the hearsay rule."); Commonwealth v. Whelton, 428 Mass. 24, 696 N.E.2d 540 (1998); Commonwealth v. Napolitano, 42 Mass. App. Ct. 549, 558, 678 N.E.2d 447, 453, *review denied*, 425 Mass. 1104, 682 N.E.2d 1361 (1997) (noting that even if the excited utterance exception were subject to the unavailability requirement it would have been fulfilled in this case because of declarant's recantation of prior accusations: "Exculpatory testimony for the defendant made her practically unavailable as a witness for the prosecution. She was effectively unavailable in the same sense that a declarant who refuses to testify based upon the assertion of her Constitutional privilege against self-incrimination is considered unavailable, so that the declarant's reliable hearsay statements may then be admitted as evidence."); State v. Bellotti, 383 N.W.2d 308 (Minn. Ct. App. 1986); State v. Rogers, 109 N.C. App. 491, 498, 428 S.E.2d 220, 224, *cert. denied*, 334 N.C. 625, 435 S.E.2d 348 (1993), *cert. denied*, 511 U.S. 1008 (1994); State v. Campbell, 299 Or. 633, 705 P.2d 694 (1985) (unnecessary for child witness to testify as precondition to admission of prompt complaint testimony).

[269] State v. Ortiz, 74 Haw. 343, 845 P.2d 547, *recons. denied*, 74 Haw. 650, 849 P.2d 81 (1993) ("A showing of the declarant's unavailability is necessary to promote the integrity of the fact-finding process and to insure fairness to defendants. Although excited utterances have certain guarantees of reliability, we also recognize that the right to confront an accuser should not be abandoned simply because the alleged incriminating statement was made spontaneously. Thus, we choose to follow the Supreme Court test set forth in *Roberts*." *Id.* at 362, 845 P.2d at 549); State v. Moore, 334 Or. 328, 49 P.3d 785 (2002) (Oregon's Supreme Court, citing its constitution and past decisions, holds: "Before the state may introduce into evidence a witness's out-of-court declarations against a criminal defendant, the state must produce the witness at trial or demonstrate that the witness is unavailable to testify." *Id.* at 341, 49 P.3d at 792).

[270] People v. Sullivan, 117 A.D.2d 476, 504 N.Y.S.2d 788 (1986).

a prerequisite to admissibility.[271] However, the Ohio court specifically excepted excited utterances from this rule.[272] The competency must be at the time of the statement.[273]

If a court requires competency at the time of the event, it may be critical to establish when the event occurred, which may be difficult for some child witnesses.[274] It may also be essential for the proponent of a hearsay statement to establish that a declarant had personal knowledge of the information contained in the statement as well as the declarant's competency.[275] It would appear, however, that most jurisdictions do not require a showing of competency prior to the admission of the excited utterance.[276] Nonetheless, in those states that do permit the admission of testimony by individuals who have not been produced or who are incompetent to testify at trial, this could be an argument against the admission of the proffered excited utterance.

A child's statement admitted under a special hearsay exception may[277] or may

---

[271] State v. Said, 71 Ohio St. 3d 473, 475, 477, 644 N.E.2d 337, 339–41 (1994).

[272] State v. Said, 71 Ohio St. 3d 473, 477 n.1, 644 N.E.2d 337, 340 n.1 (1994). *See* State v. Burnette, 125 Ohio App. 3d 278, 708 N.E.2d 276 (1998).

[273] State v. Said, 71 Ohio St. 3d 473, 477, 644 N.E.2d 337, 341 (1994); State v. Street, 122 Ohio App. 3d 79 (1997) (upholding preclusion of child's testimony and hearsay statements due to child's incompetence); State v. Ungerer, 1996 Ohio App. LEXIS 2947 (June 5, 1996) (reversing defendant's conviction, in part, because trial court admitted child's hearsay statements under medical treatment and excited utterance exception even though trial court found she was not competent at time she made them); State v. Vaughn, 106 Ohio App. 3d 775 (1995) (finding that child was competent at the time hearsay statements were made and implying such competency was a prerequisite for admission of hearsay statements made under medical treatment exception of hearsay rule).

[274] *In re* Dependency of A.E.P., 135 Wash. 2d 208, 956 P.2d. 297 (1998)

> If the trial court has no idea when the alleged event occurred, the trial court cannot begin to determine whether the child had the mental ability at the time of the alleged event to receive an accurate impression of it. . . . [T]he court should have determined whether the child has the capacity at the time of the event to receive an accurate impression of the event. This would have required the trial court to fix a time period of the alleged abuse. Absent this critical information, and despite the high level of deference accorded to the trial court's competency findings, we are compelled to hold the trial court abused its discretion in finding A.E.P. competent to testify.

Id. at 225, 956 P.2d at 225–26.

[275] Commonwealth v. Crawford, 417 Mass. 358, 363–64, 629 N.E.2d 1332, 1335 (1994).

[276] State v. Waddell, 351 N.C. 413, 421–22, 527 S.E.2d 644, 650 (2000) (child's incompetence as witness did not render child's out-of-court statements unreliable); Simmers v. State, 943 P.2d 1189 (Wyo. 1997) (upholding admission of child's hearsay statements to social worker even though child was not competent to testify). *See generally,* Jay M. Zitter, Annotation, *Admissibility of Testimony Concerning Spontaneous Declarations Made by One Incompetent to Testify at Trial,* 15 A.L.R.4TH 1043 (1982).

[277] Carpenter v. State, 786 N.E.2d 696 (Ind. 2003):

> Added to these difficulties, we note that during the competency determination at the

not[278] require as part of a finding of reliability that the child is competent to testify. However, statements under these exceptions may be inadmissible as a result of the Supreme Court decision in *Crawford v. Washington*.[279]

§ 10.28   Present-sense impression.

The present-sense impression permits introduction of a "statement describing or explaining an event or condition made while the declarant was perceiving the event or condition, or immediately thereafter."[280] This exception does not necessarily require a startling event, and the declarant need not be involved in the event. This exception is seen in sexual assault litigation, often in the context of 911 calls for assistance. The present-sense impression requires that a declarant see an event and make an observation about it to another person present at the time of the event or so shortly thereafter that the declarant is unlikely to misstate the observation. For example, a child's statement during a bath that her "pee-pee hurt," made while the child experiences the pain, comes within the present-sense impression exception.[281] Theoretically, reliability of the statement is assumed

---

> hearing, A.C. was asked three times in different ways whether she understood the difference between the truth and a lie. A.C. responded that she did not. It was on this basis that the trial court found that she was incompetent to be a witness in the case and unavailable to testify at trial. While it is certainly true that the protected person statute provides that a statement or videotape made by a child incapable of understanding the nature and obligation of an oath is nevertheless admissible if the statute's requirements are met, there is a degree of logical inconsistency in deeming reliable the statements of a person who cannot distinguish truth from falsehood.

786 N.E.2d at 704.

[278] State v. C.J., 148 Wash. 2d 672, 63 P.3d 765 (2003):

> [T]he legislature did not intend to exclude the hearsay statements of a child who is incompetent to testify, so long as the statute's requirements of reliability and corroboration are satisfied. It is equally clear that the legislature did not intend . . . an additional finding that a child declarant understood the difference between a truthful statement and a false statement at the time the statement was made, or that he understood his obligation to speak truthfully about the incident . . .
>
> We also note that a finding that the child victim is incompetent to testify at trial does not make the hearsay statements unreliable [citations omitted] . . . Admissibility under the statute does not depend on whether the child is competent to take the witness stand, but on whether the comments and circumstances surrounding the statement indicate it is reliable.

Id. at 679, 63 P.3d at 771.

[279] 541 U.S. 36 (2004). *See* § 10.45.

[280] FED. R. EVID. 803(1).

[281] Territory of Guam v. Ignacio, 10 F.3d 608, 614 (9th Cir. 1993) (While the child victim's older sister was giving her a regularly scheduled bath on the evening of the alleged sexual abuse, complainant would not allow her sister to wash her vaginal area, complaining that "her pee-pee hurt." Since the victim made the statements while she was experiencing the pain, they come within the present-sense exception).

by the closeness of the statement to the event and the fact that the observation is made to another person. In the following example from a rape case, the hearsay testimony of the defendant's girlfriend that, while looking into the window of the crime scene, she saw a sock and stated that it was the defendant's sock, was offered by a police officer:[282]

Q. Officer, did you have occasion to go to 5739 Knox Street on the morning of September 26th, 1986?

A. Yes, I did.

Q. What time did you arrive there?

A. About eight o'clock, eight something, like that, in the morning.

Q. While you were there, did you have occasion to see somebody named Ruth Holley?

A. Yes, I did.

Q. How do you know her?

A. I know Ruth. I be knowing her for a long time because I work that district.

Q. Now, is this the mother, Ruth Holley, or the daughter?

A. The daughter.

Q. Now, where was it that you saw the daughter, Ruth Holley?

A. I was going to the crime scene at that address when Ruth came up to the crime scene where I was.

Q. What happened when she came up there?

A. She came up to the crime scene and she was talking to me and she asked me what were we doing, and I was telling her we were guarding the scene on account of a rape. She was peeping through the window, trying to look through the door.

Q. What window was it that she was trying to peep into?

A. I believe it was the front window.

Q. What door was she looking into?

A. It was like a hallway with a vestibule, and this was to the right as you enter the apartment.

Q. So, was she looking into the room where the crime allegedly occurred?

A. Yes.

Q. What happened as she was looking into the window or the door?

A. She told me that they are her boyfriend's socks, that it was her boyfriend's socks that was on the bed in the room of the window she was looking into.

---

[282] Commonwealth v. Harper, 419 Pa. Super. 1, 6–7, 614 A.2d 1180, 1182–83 (1992), *appeal denied*, 533 Pa. 649, 624 A.2d 109 (1993).

Q. How did she say that?

A. She said, "I think these are Irving's. Those are my boyfriend's socks laying on that bed."

Q. I am going to show you what was marked Commonwealth Exhibit Six. Is this one of the socks laying on the bed?

A. That seems to be the sock.

Q. Now, do you know who her boyfriend is?

A. No, I don't recall him.

Q. You don't know?

A. No.

Q. But, she said, she did say, "my boyfriend, Irving"?

A. Yes.

Q. Did she use any other word?

A. Not that I can recall.

In finding this hearsay to be within the present-sense impression exception of the hearsay rule, the court held that a startling occurrence is not required, but the utterance must be "instinctive rather than deliberate," and Holley's statement was a contemporaneous verbalization of her having observed the sock on the bed when she looked into the room, with no opportunity for retrospective thought.[283] The majority of jurisdictions follow Federal Rule of Evidence 803(1), which does not require the declarant's unavailability as a prerequisite to the use of present-sense impression evidence.

§ 10.29   911 transmissions by victims, and identified and unidentified callers.

The present-sense impression exception permits the introduction into evidence of 911 calls of a rape victim made contemporaneously with or immediately after the event.[284] The statement during the call must describe or explain the event

---

[283] Commonwealth v. Harper, 419 Pa. Super. 1, 8, 614 A.2d 1180, 1183 (1992), *appeal denied*, 533 Pa. 649, 624 A.2d 109 (1993) (*citing* Commonwealth v. Coleman, 458 Pa. 112, 117, 326 A.2d 387, 389 (1974)).

[284] State v. Crawford, 672 So. 2d 197 (La. Ct. App.), *cert. denied*, 679 So. 2d 1379 (La. 1996); People v. Buie, 86 N.Y.2d 501, 658 N.E.2d 192, 634 N.Y.S.2d 415 (1995) (admitting 911 tape of victim describing unfolding events); People v. Williams, 244 A.D.2d 587, 665 N.Y.S.2d 87 (1997), *appeal denied*, 91 N.Y.2d 899, 691 N.E.2d 1039, 669 N.Y.S.2d 13 (1998) (sexual assault complainant's 911 call admissible as an excited utterance); People v. Palmer, 237 A.D.2d 311, 655 N.Y.S.2d 380, *appeal denied*, 90 N.Y.2d 862, 683 N.E.2d 1063, 661 N.Y.S.2d 189 (1997); People v. Holton, 225 A.D.2d 1020, 640 N.Y.S.2d 707, *appeal denied*, 88 N.Y.2d 986, 672 N.E.2d 619, 649 N.Y.S.2d 393 (1996) (attempted robbery victim's 911 call immediately after incident admissible as present-sense impression) (*citing* United States v. Medico, 557 F.2d 309, 313, 315

prompting it, and the declarant must have perceived the event being described as well as being substantially contemporaneous with the event.[285] The greater the delay between the event and the statement, the less likely the statement will qualify as a present-sense impression.[286]

Statements of unidentified callers and bystanders who provide information concerning a crime are admissible as present-sense impressions if their descriptions are sufficiently corroborated by other evidence.[287]

Of course, an event must be established by other proof, since Federal Rule of Evidence 803(1) requires that the statement describe an event or condition, which is usually not an issue in a sexual assault trial where the complainant testifies. This corroboration depends on the circumstances of each case. It is in the discretion of the trial court as to whether the declarant has sufficient personal knowledge or whether sufficient corroboration exists. This requirement of some other evidence is followed by most courts.[288]

If the content of a 911 call is not sufficiently corroborated by a witness' testimony or other evidence, it may be inadmissible. For example, a defendant may be precluded from offering into evidence a 911 tape, offering a description of the perpetrator, when there has been no testimony presented to support the substance and content of the information in the call; it is insufficient that the

---

(2d Cir.), *cert. denied*, 434 U.S. 986 (1977)); People v. Lewis, 222 A.D.2d 1058, 635 N.Y.S.2d 872 (1995), *appeal denied*, 87 N.Y.2d 1021, 666 N.E.2d 1069, 644 N.Y.S.2d 154 (1996) (upholding admission into evidence of sexual assault complainant's 911 call placed shortly after the attack as an excited utterance); State v. Guizzotti, 60 Wash. App. 289, 803 P.2d 808 (1991). *See generally*, Stuart D. Murray, Annotation, *Admissibility of Tape Recording or Transcript of "911" Emergency Telephone Call*, 3 A.L.R.5TH (1992).

[285] United States v. Campbell, 782 F. Supp. 1258 (N.D. Ill. 1991).

[286] People v. Kello, 96 N.Y.2d 740, 746 N.E.2d 166, 723 N.Y.S.2d 111 (2001) (finding two and one-half hour time period was too long for reflection to justify admission of 911 caller's statements that she had in view "the guy that did it," but error was harmless since defendant raised only a common law hearsay objection and not an objection based on his right of confrontation under the Sixth Amendment); People v. Breland, 292 A.D.2d 460, 740 N.Y.S.2d 345, *appeal denied*, 98 N.Y.2d 649, 772 N.E.2d 610, 745 N.Y.S.2d 507 (2002) (holding the trial court improperly classified tape recording of complainant's police telephone call as an excited utterance "based on the surrounding circumstances, including the amount of time that elapsed before the telephone call, the complainant's actions in the interim, and the lack of serious physical injury to the complainant . . . ." Error was not harmless in light of weight of evidence).

[287] People v. Brown, 80 N.Y.2d 729, 734–35, 610 N.E.2d 369, 594 N.Y.S.2d 696 (1993) (also noting that some states do not require any corroboration at all) (*citing* State v. Flesher, 286 N.W.2d 215, 218 (Iowa 1979); People v. Cobenais, 301 A.D.2d 958, 755 N.Y.S.2d 736, *appeal denied*, 99 N.Y.2d 653, 790 N.E.2d 291, 760 N.Y.S.2d 117 (2003) (holding complainant husband's 911 call, which included her cries and agitated comments in the background, relevant to her state of mind and element of forcible compulsion); People v. Richardson, 300 A.D.2d 13, 751 N.Y.S.2d 14 (2002), *appeal denied*, 99 N.Y.2d 584, 785 N.E.2d 742, 755 N.Y.S.2d 720 (2003).

[288] *See also* United States v. Blakey, 607 F.2d 779, 785 (7th Cir. 1979).

hearsay statements were unprompted and made at or about the time of the reported event.[289]

A call by a victim made ten minutes after an event may not be sufficiently contemporaneous,[290] although courts do not adopt an arbitrary time period, but rather focus on the circumstances of the statements, such as the opportunity for reflection or to falsify. A phone call made five minutes after the assailant fled and after the victim spoke to her friends may still be made under the influence of the event.[291] Since the present-sense impression does not require unavailability of the declarant for its admission, a victim can testify in person in addition to presenting the taped call.[292]

Some courts go beyond this and require corroboration by an "equally percipient witness" at the scene who had an opportunity to view the events in question.[293]

The fact that the 911 dispatcher questions the victim does not defeat the "excited utterance" nature of a victim's call when the proof establishes that the declarant's statements were not the product of reflection and deliberation.[294] A 911 call may also be admissible as an excited utterance.[295]

Crawford raised the issue whether 911 calls would still be admissible when the declarant was not available for cross-examination. In *Davis v. Washington* the Supreme Court further defined "testimonial statement" and held that a statement made by a victim to a 911 operator was part of an "ongoing emergency" and not for evidence-gathering purposes and therefore admissible in trial.[296] In distinguishing testimonial and non-testimonial statements generated by questioning, the Court noted:

> Statements are non-testimonial when made in the course of police interrogation under circumstances objectively indicate that there is no such ongoing

---

[289] People v. Vasquez, 88 N.Y.2d 561, 670 N.E.2d 1328, 647 N.Y.S.2d 697 (1996).

[290] United States v. Cain, 587 F.2d 678 (5th Cir. 1979).

[291] People v. Simpson, 238 A.D.2d 611, 656 N.Y.S.2d 765, *appeal denied*, 90 N.Y.2d 910, 686 N.E.2d 234, 663 N.Y.S.2d 522 (1997).

[292] People v. Hughes, 228 A.D.2d 618, 645 N.Y.S.2d 493, *appeal denied*, 88 N.Y.2d 987, 672 N.E.2d 619, 649 N.Y.S.2d 393 (1996).

[293] State v. Case, 100 N.M. 714, 676 P.2d 241 (1984).

[294] United States v. Joy, 192 F.3d 761 (7th Cir. 1999), *cert. denied*, 530 U.S. 1250 (2000).

[295] People v. Wine, 279 A.D.2d 424, 719 N.Y.S.2d 847, *appeal denied*, 96 N.Y.2d 805, 750 N.E.2d 85, 726 N.Y.S.2d 383 (2001) (The tape recordings of the complainant's 911 calls were properly introduced into evidence as excited utterances [citation omitted]. Clearly, the first call, made immediately after the robbery, was made under the excitement and shock of the gunpoint robbery. The record also supports the court's finding that the second call, 15 minutes later, was still made under the influence of the startling event, and that the complainant did not have a significant opportunity to deviate from the truth while he waited for the police to arrive [citation omitted]). *See also* People v. Mendez, 279 A.D.2d 434, 720 N.Y.S.2d 65, *appeal denied*, 96 N.Y.2d 832, 754 N.E.2d 212, 729 N.Y.S.2d 452 (2001).

[296] Davis v. Washington, 124 S. Ct. 2266 (2006).

emergency, and that the primary purpose of the interrogation is to establish or prove past events potentially relevant to later prosecution.[297]

Because the operator in *Davis* elicited answers that were necessary to resolve an ongoing emergency, the 911 call was properly admitted as non-testimonial hearsay despite the witness not attending trial and the defendant not having an opportunity for cross-examination.[298] The Court noted the 911 call may include the identity of the assailant when such information is the product of a limited inquiry to identify the assailant to determine if the perpetrator was a violent felon.

Apparently concerned that a police officer might take advantage of the rulings and use 911 calls or crime scene emergencies to "generate testimonial statements," the court added that the entirety of a 911 call or a crime scene statement might not be admissible if a police interrogation is initiated after the emergency subsides.[299]

Admission of 911 calls can raise hearsay within hearsay issues if the present-sense impression or some other hearsay exception does not apply to the call placed.[300]

§ 10.30   Hearsay, unavailability rule, and use of prior testimony.

The Federal Rules of Evidence permit the use of former testimony of an available witness if given "at another hearing of the same or different proceeding, or in a deposition taken . . . in the course of the same or another proceeding," and the party against whom the testimony is offered had the opportunity to develop the testimony by direct, cross, or redirect examination.[301]

The use of testimony from a prior legal proceeding is hearsay and invokes the requirement that the declarant be unavailable at the trial at which the testimony is sought to be introduced.[302] Not only must the witness be unavailable, there must also be facts from which a trial court may determine that a good-faith effort has been made to secure the witness's presence at trial. Thus, a prosecutor who asserts without any documentary support that a victim was subpoenaed and provided with a plane ticket and witness fee, and then did not

---

[297] Davis v. Washington, 124 S. Ct. 2266, 2273–2274 (2006).

[298] Davis v. Washington, 124 S. Ct. 2266, 2276 (2006).

[299] Trial courts "should redact or exclude the portions of any statements that have become testimonial, as they do, for example, with unduly prejudicial portions of otherwise admissible evidence."126 S. Ct. 2266, 2277.

[300] *See, e.g.,* United States v. Sallins, 993 F.2d 344, 347–48 (3d Cir. 1993).

[301] FED. R. EVID. 804(b)(1). Subsections (2), (3), (4), and (5) state that statements under belief of impending death, a statement against interest, and a statement of personal or family history are not excluded by the hearsay rule if the declarant is unavailable as a witness. Subsection (5) is a "catchall" exception applicable to statements that have "guarantees of trustworthiness" comparable to the provisions of Rule 803(24).

[302] Ohio v. Roberts, 448 U.S. 56 (1980).

contact the state with any excuse for her absence, does not sufficiently demonstrate a good-faith effort to justify use of the prior testimony in a sexual assault
trial.[303] Cases which held that if a sufficient showing is made that a child will
be traumatized by testifying at a further proceeding, or that a complainant's prior
testimony may be admissible at a later trial[304] are now subject to challenge under
the Supreme Court's holding in *Crawford v. Washington*.[305]

§ 10.31 Medical treatment exception and applicability to sexual assault trials.

Statements made to a physician for care and treatment are generally recognized
as an exception to the hearsay rule. This is so, regardless of whether the
information is in response to questions and regardless of the spontaneity of the
medical history provided. This exception has particular application in sexual
assault trials, since it often provides inculpatory evidence from a victim who may
be too young to testify or provide additional testimony concerning the identification of the perpetrator or other details of a sexual assault that bolster the
prosecution's case. As set forth in the Federal Rules of Evidence, the medical
examination exception permits:

> Statements made for purposes of medical diagnosis or treatment and describ-
> ing medical history, or past or present symptoms, pain or sensations, or the
> inception or general character of the cause or external source thereof insofar
> as reasonably pertinent to diagnosis or treatment.[306]

Some states, such as California, have a special hearsay statute that applies to
children's statements made for medical diagnosis and treatment.[307]

The medical treatment exception to the hearsay rule is a firmly-rooted
exception and, according to the Supreme Court of the United States in *White
v. Illinois*,[308] when testimony is properly admitted under this exception, no
further guarantees of trustworthiness are required. In *White*, the Court approved
the trial court's admission into evidence of five witnesses who relayed statements
made by a nontestifying child as spontaneous declarations and within the medical

---

[303] State v. Archie, 171 Ariz. 415, 831 P.2d 414 (1992).

[304] Commonwealth v. Bourgeon, 439 Pa. Super. 355, 654 A.2d 555 (1994), *appeal denied*, 542
Pa. 657, 668 A.2d 1121 (1995).

[305] 541 U.S. 36 (2004).

[306] FED. R. EVID. 803(4).

[307] CAL. EVID. CODE § 1253 (provides, in substance, that hearsay statements of a child victim
describing any act, or attempted act, of child abuse or neglect are admissible if the statement was
made for purposes of medical diagnosis or treatment and describes medical history as reasonably
pertinent to diagnosis or treatment. These statements must be trustworthy under California Evidence
Code § 1252).

[308] 502 U.S. 346 (1992). *See also* Tracy A. Buteman, Annotation, *Admissibility of Statements
Made for Purposes of Medical Diagnosis or Treatment as Hearsay Exception Under Rule § 803(4)
of the Uniform Rules of Evidence*, 38 A.L.R.5TH 433 (1996).

diagnosis exception. Nonetheless, a state court may still require a finding of trustworthiness or reliability, unlike the holding in *White*. One Michigan court[309] has reviewed ten factors in establishing the trustworthiness of a child's hearsay statement that it applies to statements offered under the medical treatment exception:

(1)   the age and maturity of the declarant;

(2)   the manner in which the statements are elicited;

(3)   the manner in which the statements are phrased;

(4)   the terminology of the child compared with children of a similar age;

(5)   the reason for the examination;

(6)   the timing of the examination in relation to the abuse;

(7)   the timing of the examination in relation to the trial;

(8)   the type of examination;

(9)   the relation of the declarant; and

(10) the evidence of any motive to fabricate.[310]

In addition, reliability in this situation can be established by other evidence, including results of the medical examination.[311]

Other hearsay exceptions may apply to statements made to medical personnel. For example, statements made by a rape complainant arriving in an emergency room by ambulance and still in a state of excitement and shock, may make her statements fall within the excited utterance as well as the medical treatment exceptions.[312]

The following testimony and examination by the court shows the type of questions that need to be addressed in establishing that a medical history is necessary for medical care and treatment and thus admissible under the medical treatment exception. The medical examination involved a child who was four years of age at the time of trial, competent to testify, but unable to answer questions effectively. The questioning also points out issues pertaining to the use of dolls by the child and medical history provided by the child's father.

PROSECUTOR:

Q.   As part of your examination, did you have the opportunity to obtain any history from the child?

---

[309] People v. McElhaney, 215 Mich. App. 269, 545 N.W.2d 18 (1996), *appeal denied*, 454 Mich. 853, 558 N.W.2d 726 (1997).

[310] People v. McElhaney, 215 Mich. App. 269, 280-82, 545 N.W.2d 18, 25-26 (1996), *appeal denied*, 454 Mich. 853, 558 N.W.2d 726 (1997).

[311] People v. McElhaney, 215 Mich. App. 269, 282, 545 N.W.2d 18, 26 (1996), *appeal denied*, 454 Mich. 853, 558 N.W.2d 726 (1997).

[312] Johnson v. State, 699 N.E.2d 746, 748–49 (Ind. Ct. App. 1998).

A. Yes, I did, from the child and her father.

Q. Can you tell us what you got as medical history from the child?

THE COURT: All right, gentlemen. Please approach the bench. (Bench conference.)

THE COURT: Let the record reflect we are out of the hearing of the jury.

EXAMINATION BY THE COURT:

Q. Doctor, with respect to the history that you took from the child and from the father, was that history necessary for your diagnosis or your care and treatment of the child?

A. I am not sure how to answer that.

Q. Well, would you have been able to diagnose and treat the child without knowing what this matter was about?

A. Yes.

Q. You would have. All right. What is meant by that is, if nobody told you what this matter was about, you could not go ahead and diagnose — you could not treat the child?

A. Without the history I would not have done the — not have tested as I did. I used a special rape kit that I would not have used without the history.

Q. So that the history was necessary, then, for diagnosis?

A. Yes, I presume the history was necessary.

Q. Doctor, if you had been told that the child was sexually abused, that would have been a sufficient history for you to do an examination, wouldn't it?

A. Yes.

(Author's Note: This would depend upon the definition of sexual abuse, such as touching of vaginal, oral, or anal intercourse.)

Q. You would not have needed to talk to the child if you had been told that the child had been sexually abused?

A. Somebody would have been — would speak to the child, but I would have done the same tests.

Q. Somebody had to tell you something?

A. Yes.

Q. Otherwise you could have treated the child for a cold; is that correct?

A. Right.

Q. If you hadn't known that she was sexually abused, you wouldn't —

A. I would not have done the tests.

Q. You would not have given her whatever tests you gave her; is that correct?

A. That's correct.

Q. It so happens you spoke to the child, and you spoke to the child's father; is that correct?

A. Yes.

Q. And they were the ones that told you what the history was?

A. That's correct.

Q. All right.

(Author's Note: It would be important to separate, if possible, what was provided by the child and father and then determine to what extent, if necessary, the history by the father is admissible.)

Q. Some dolls were shown that day; correct?

A. Yes.

Q. Doctor, you didn't need the dolls to get a history, did you? In other words, if you were told that the child was sexually abused, that's all you needed of a history to make the examination; isn't that right?

A. I am not sure I understand.

Q. What I am getting at is this: You didn't need the dolls to conduct the examination. You needed the knowledge that this child had been sexually abused, and on that basis you conducted an investigation; is that correct?

A. Yes.

Q. All right.

A. I didn't use the dolls. The social worker did.

Q. But they were used in your presence, but it didn't make any difference as far as your examination?

A. I still would have done the same.

BY THE COURT:

Q. That was the way the child spoke; isn't that correct?

A. Yes.

Q. I mean, she shows you — whoever was there — what happened?

A. She showed mostly to the social worker. My history was obtained chiefly from the child's father.

Q. But you saw what the child did with respect to the dolls?

A. I didn't see the whole doll-showing.

Q. You saw some of it. And were there certain words spoken by the child that you put into your history?

A. What I recorded is my history from the father because the social worker did most of the child interview.

Q. The father told you that the child told him that she had been touched?

A. That's correct.

(Author's Note: Does the medical treatment exception encompass double hearsay? Can a parent provide medical history or is it limited to a patient?[313] Is it the type of information reasonably relied upon by experts in the field to form opinions?[314] Does the fact that the child's father provided the history demonstrate the child did not understand the need for treatment, thus negating the basis for treatment exception?)[315]

THE COURT: Whatever he saw is admissible.

DEFENDANT'S ATTORNEY: I object. I will submit that I don't have any problem with the doctor testifying that he had an allegation of sexual abuse and therefore he tested the child. Anything else was not necessary. All he needed was to hear that the child was sexually abused, and on that basis he conducted a test, which is entirely proper. And we are now going to hear conversations that this child gave to the social worker. I don't think that information is necessary to medical care and treatment. I can't cross-examine this child. And the social worker's interview is extremely prejudicial and has absolutely no probative value because it does not pertain directly to the history.

THE COURT: The history wasn't given to you by the social worker, was it?

THE WITNESS: No, this is direct from the child's father.

DEFENDANT'S ATTORNEY: But on the dolls, I believe that was done by the social worker.

THE COURT: But he was present at the time.

DEFENDANT'S ATTORNEY: I understand, but it's not part of the history. I don't think it has anything to do with the history.

THE COURT: It certainly seems to me that if that's the way the child talks, by demonstrating with dolls as to what happened, that it's certainly necessary for a doctor to know what happened before he can start his examination.

---

[313] *See* § 10.33.

[314] *See* §§ 10.37–10.38, discussing the concept of information necessary for care and treatment in the context of the perpetrator's identity. *See also* United States v. Farley, 992 F.2d 1122, 1125 (10th Cir. 1993) (permitting a psychologist to testify to a child's hearsay statements under Federal Rules of Evidence 703, discussed in Chapter 11. The psychologist "testified that she had relied upon [the victim's] comments during their interview as well as the drawings made by D.C. to arrive at her opinion. . . . Therefore, Rule 703 would allow the expert to testify regarding the information, even if the evidence would not otherwise be admissible. [citation omitted] The judge issued a proper warning to the jury explaining that the testimony was being received for the limited purpose of laying a foundation for the doctor's opinion.").

[315] *See* § 10.32.

§ 10.32 Need for children to understand purpose of medical treatment.

One of the theoretical underpinnings of the medical treatment exception to the hearsay rule is that the reliability is assured by the likelihood that a patient believes that appropriate treatment will flow from an honest rendition of his or her medical history,[316] or as stated by another authority, "A fact reliable enough to serve as a basis for a diagnosis is also reliable to escape hearsay prescription."[317]

Some courts have challenged the application of the patient-motivation component of the hearsay exception in children.[318] "Because of their young age, sexually abused children may not always grasp the relation between their statements and receiving effective medical treatment."[319] Many of these courts suggest that there should be a showing that the child understood the need to tell the truth to the doctor.[320] If the record does not demonstrate that the child understood the need to tell the truth and the purpose of the examination, a conviction may be jeopardized if the medical history hearsay played a significant role in the trial or proof was less than overwhelming. In one case, a conviction was reversed when there was no showing the child knew the person examining her was a doctor.[321]

Some courts have challenged a child patient's understanding of the need for medical treatment when the examination is part of the investigatory process. If the child believes that the examination is for investigatory rather than medical

---

[316] 2 MCCORMICK ON EVIDENCE § 277, at 246–47 (4th ed. 1992).

[317] 4 WEINSTEIN'S EVIDENCE § 803(4)[01] (1994).

[318] State v. Storch, 66 Ohio St. 3d 280, 612 N.E.2d 305 (1993).

[319] State v. Robinson, 153 Ariz. 191, 199, 735 P.2d 801, 809 (1987) (upholding the admission of the child's medical history because the record clearly showed the victim's motive in making the statements).

[320] United States v. Sumner, 204 F.3d 1182 (8th Cir. 2000) (reversing defendant's conviction because child's statements to doctor gave few indications of trustworthiness and understanding of purpose of doctor's examination; child mostly nodded in response to doctor's questions during examination); Olesen v. Class, 164 F.3d 1096, 1098 (8th Cir. 1999) (*citing* United States v. White, 11 F.3d 1446, 1449 (8th Cir. 1993); United States v. Barrett, 8 F.3d 1296, 1300 (8th Cir. 1993); United States v. Avila, 27 M.J. 62, 66 (C.M.A. 1988); Oldsen v. People, 732 P.2d 1132 (Colo. 1986); Begley v. State, 483 So. 2d 70, 73–74 (Fla. Dist. Ct. App. 1986);Cassidy v. State, 74 Md. App. 1, 536 A.2d 666, *cert. denied,* 312 Md. 602, 541 A.2d 965 (1988); People v. Meeboer, 439 Mich. 310, 484 N.W.2d 621 (1992); State v. Waddell, 351 N.C. 413, 527 S.E.2d 644 (2000); State v. Hinnant, 351 N.C. 277, 287, 523 S.E.2d 663, 669 (2000), *cert. denied,* 125 S. Ct. 1846 (2005); State v. Watts, 141 N.C. App. 104, 539 S.E.2d 37 (2000) (reversing defendant's conviction because record lacked evidence that child understood her statements to medical personnel were medically motivated and that she appreciated importance of truthful statements); Jenkins v. Commonwealth, 254 Va. 333, 492 S.E.2d 131 (1997) ("Because the patient in this case was a two-year old child who could not appreciate the need for furnishing reliable information, we decline to apply the exception here." *Id.* at 339, 492 S.E.2d at 11.).

[321] Ring v. Erickson, 983 F.2d 818 (8th Cir. 1993).

purposes, the child's statements may lack the necessary foundation for admission.[322] One court has noted that when a child makes statements to a person procured by a governmental agency, the prosecution has a heavier burden in establishing that the child's statements were made for purposes of medical treatment, and that the prosecution must "affirmatively demonstrate the child made the statements understanding that they would further the diagnosis and possible treatment of the child's condition."[323]

Many courts apply a less rigorous requirement for a child's understanding of the need for medical treatment. These courts look at circumstances to infer a child's understanding of the need for medical treatment. For example, proof that the child experienced a traumatic event, was taken to a hospital or clinic for a medical examination, possibly in discomfort, and the child then makes statements to emergency room personnel, is sufficient evidence to support a finding that the child understood the need to be truthful.[324]

---

[322] United States v. Henry, 42 M.J. 593 (A.C.C.A. 1995) (presence of investigators during a medical examination may have suggested to child that examination "was part of the investigatory process rather than for the purpose of receiving medical treatment" and therefore statements made during such examination were not properly received under the medical treatment exception of the hearsay rule).

[323] State v. Carol, 89 Wash. App. 77, 86, 948 P.2d 837, 842 (1997). *See also* State v. Wade, 136 N.H. 750, 622 A.2d 832 (1993); R.S. v. Knighton, 125 N.J. 79, 96, 592 A.2d 1157, 1166 (1991); State v. Waddell, 351 N.C. 413, 527 S.E.2d 644 (2000); State v. Hinnant, 351 N.C. 277, 523 S.E.2d 663 (2000).

[324] United States v. Norman T., 129 F.3d 1099 (10th Cir. 1997), *cert. denied*, 523 U.S. 1031 (1998):

> Although the victim was young, there is evidence to support the district court's determination the statements were reasonably pertinent to diagnosis or treatment. The victim was complaining of pain. She had been to the hospital many times before because her brother needed asthma treatments. She knew the nurse and had talked with her before. When he first met with the victim, the doctor discussed with her the difference between telling the truth and telling a lie. And, the doctor described patient history as the 'predominant part of reaching [a] diagnosis,' and confirmed for the trial court the type of information he obtained from a patient. Furthermore, the victim testified and was subject to cross-examination by Norman T.'s attorney. The opportunity to cross-examine the out-of-court declarant helps ensure the fairness and integrity of the proceedings where hearsay testimony has been admitted.

Id. at 1105–06.; Virgin Islands v. Morris, 42 V.I. 135, 191 F.R.D. 82 (1999) (finding minor's age, six years old, did not negate reliability of medical treatment exception, and circumstances of case established an awareness that child understood she went to hospital for medical treatment related to sexual assault); Commonwealth v. Sanford, 397 Pa. Super. 581, 595, 580 A.2d 784, 794 (1990), *appeal denied*, 527 Pa. 586, 588 A.2d 508 (1991); State v. Gordon, 952 S.W.2d 817 (Tenn. 1997):

> We conclude that the evidence was sufficient to warrant an inference that the conditions of Tenn. R. Evid. 803(4) were met. First, the victim cried out at her grandparents' home with pain on urination shortly after being alone with the defendant. The victim's mother was called; the victim was taken home and bathed and again cried out from pain while trying to urinate. Her mother examined her and observed evidence of injury inside the vagina. The victim identified the defendant as the cause

The Tenth Circuit Court of Appeals has specifically rejected the Eighth Circuit's requirement that the proponent of the hearsay statement demonstrate that the child understood the medical importance of being truthful.[325] The child's age, personal characteristics, and other circumstances of the making of the medical history statement can go to the weight of the hearsay testimony rather than its admissibility.[326] In addition to these circumstances, another element of

> of the injury. The child was then immediately taken about 9:00 p.m. to a hospital for treatment, then referred to another hospital where she stayed until 3:00 a.m. She refused to be treated because of the pain. She was referred for treatment to Our Kids Clinic, where she went the next morning at 8:00 a.m. for examination. The victim gave a history and was examined within 12 hours of the initial incident. The nurse practitioner testified the purpose of the history was for proper diagnosis and treatment, and that she relied on the history for that purpose. The questioning by the psychologist was not suggestive or leading. The content of the victim's statement suggests no motive by the victim other than that of seeking medical treatment. The physical examination revealed injury to the vagina within the previous 24 hours. There was no evidence of improper influence on the child, nor evidence of any other factor affecting the victim's trustworthiness. No investigative agency had been involved to that point, and no investigative referral had been made. The motive was to seek medical treatment. Half the night was consumed in this continuing quest, which was resumed early the following day.

Id. at 823; State v. Writer, 2003 Tenn. Crim. App. LEXIS 519, *appeal denied*, 2003 Tenn. LEXIS 1044 (Oct. 27, 2003):

> We also find that the victim made statements to Dr. Heise for the purpose of medical diagnosis and treatment. Although Dr. Heise received the defendant's case pursuant to a referral from Children Services, he indicated that his purpose in examining the victim was to ensure the victim's well-being and that he was not obligated to any purpose other than the welfare of the victim. Furthermore, after examining the victim, Dr. Heise had the victim tested for several sexually transmitted diseases and referred him to a local counseling service, thereby treating aspects of the victim's physical and mental health. Thus, we find that Dr. Heise's purpose was more than to merely evaluate the victim's condition, but to treat him as well.

Id. at *20; State v. Pearson, 238 Wis. 2d 95, 617 N.W.2d 677, *review denied*, 239 Wis. 2d 773, 621 N.W.2d 629 (2000).

[325] United States v. Edward J., 224 F.3d 1216 (10th Cir. 2000).

[326] United States v. George, 960 F.2d 97 (9th Cir. 1992); Doe v. Doe, 644 So. 2d 1199, 1206 (Miss. 1994) (recognizing that a pre-school child may make statements to a physician that are consistent with the purpose of promoting treatment); State v. Stinnett, 958 S.W.2d 329 (Tenn. 1997) (Court found circumstances that six-year-old child understood her statements were for purposes of diagnosis and treatment.

> At the time the statements were made, RM was six years old and old enough to understand that the physician was examining her to determine whether there was injury or trauma and to treat her for such, if necessary. She used childlike terms in describing body parts and the sexual abuse to each physician. In addition, her statements to both physicians and her testimony at trial were internally and comparatively consistent in all pertinent respects. Further, she was examined immediately after the allegations were made and nearly four years prior to trial. Moreover, there is no indication that RM was motivated to be untruthful to the doctors.

the foundation may be whether the physician informed the child of the purpose of the examination or the role of the medical history in treatment. [327] A factor may also be whether the child verbalized an understanding of the purpose and importance of providing an accurate history to the doctor. [328]

One court has proposed a preliminary inquiry to evaluate the medical history testimony in light of several factors to determine if the child's medical history should be received. If the trial court finds that the child's statements were improperly influenced by another, the product of suggestive or leading questioning, or any other factor that adversely affects the history's reliability, the statements should be precluded. [329] The same court recognizes that most young children probably cannot seek treatment on their own, and that the motivational requirement of the medical history must be viewed in context, i.e., "the initial desire to seek treatment may be absent, but the motivation certainly can arise once the child has been taken to the doctor," and that an overly strict motivational requirement would preclude the application of the medical examination exception to child witnesses. [330] A further factor for the court to consider is the physician's professional reliance on the history for diagnosis and treatment, a factor that alone may not indicate reliability, but that may be afforded some weight. [331] If the record demonstrates no other motivation than medical diagnosis and treatment, and the physician and declarant are available for cross-examination, there may be no error on admitting the child's hearsay statements to the doctor without a hearing or voir dire to determine whether the child was seeking medical care

Id. at 332; Owen v. State, 902 P.2d 190 (Wyo. 1995) (citing Betzle v. State, 847 P.2d 1010 (Wyo. 1993)) (holding that while a child may be too young to know what is relevant to medical treatment, the child's statements are still reliable in the context of seeking medical treatment).

[327] United States v. Cox, 45 M.J. 153 (C.A.A.F. 1996), cert. denied, 117 S. Ct. 961 (1997) (The requirement that the child understand the purpose of the treatment and examination need not be based on testimony of the child, but can be provided by a counselor who explained to the children why they were being examined, which provides a basis for showing that the children expected to receive a medical benefit by providing the history); United States v. Ureta, 44 M.J. 290 (C.A.A.F. 1996), cert. denied, 117 S. Ct. 692 (1997) (holding that trial judge's finding that declarant had "an actual expectation of receiving medical treatment" was supported by declarant's age and intelligence, physician's identifying himself as a physician, hospital setting of the examination, the examination conducted and physician explaining why information needed); United States v. Dean, 31 M.J. 196 (C.M.A. 1990), cert. denied, 499 U.S. 906 (1991); State v. Ochoa, 576 So. 2d 854, 856 (Fla. Dist. Ct. App. 1991).

[328] State v. Ulis, 1994 Ohio App. LEXIS 3217 (July 22, 1994) (child complainant understood significance of visit to medical facility when, in response to nurse's question as to why she was there, she responded that her private parts hurt); State v. Logan, 105 Or. App. 556, 806 P.2d 137 (1991).

[329] State v. Dever, 64 Ohio St. 3d 401, 410, 596 N.E.2d 436, 444 (1992), cert. denied, 507 U.S. 919 (1993). See also State v. Burnette, 125 Ohio App. 3d 278, 708 N.E.2d 276 (1998).

[330] State v. Denver, 64 Ohio St.3d 401, 410, 596 N.E.2d. 436, 443-44 (1992), cert denied, 507 U.S. 919 (1993).

[331] State v. Denver, 64 Ohio St.3d 401, 411, 596 N.E.2d. 436, 444-45 (1992), cert denied, 507 U.S. 919 (1993). See also State v. Burgess, 1996 Ohio App. LEXIS 4887 (Nov. 8, 1996).

and treatment.[332] A victim's denial of sexual contact or physical injury may also demonstrate that the patient is not motivated to seek medical treatment.[333] While the common law criteria of treatment-seeking motive and physician reliance may be required for admission of the medical treatment exception, one appeals court finds that in the absence of the criteria, the statements may be admissible when possessing particularized guarantees of trustworthiness.[334]

§ 10.33   Medical history provided by a parent.

Sometimes physicians rely on the medical history provided by a child's parent or guardian in providing treatment, particularly with very young or nonverbal patients. Such a history may constitute double hearsay. Some courts have been willing to extend the medical treatment exception to statements of medical history provider by parents in the case of a very young or nonverbal patient.[335] Statements by a child victim made to a mother may be admissible on the theory that young children cannot directly seek medical treatment and must rely on a

---

[332] State v. Noble, 90 Ohio St. 3d 1403, 734 N.E.2d 834 (2000); State v. Kelly, 93 Ohio App. 3d 257, 264, 638 N.E.2d 153, 157 (1994).

[333] State v. Schauer, 90 Ohio St. 3d 1414, 735 N.E.2d 454 (2000):

> Based upon the testimony of Dr. Cotton and the victim, we are unable to conclude that her motives in speaking to Dr. Cotton were akin to those of a patient seeking treatment. First, the fact that the victim initially denied any sexual contact indicates that the victim was not motivated to speak with Dr. Cotton by a desire for proper diagnosis and treatment. Additionally, the fact that the victim denied any injury and stated that she did not wish to have a pelvic exam reflects that her state of mind was not that of a patient seeking diagnosis or treatment. Rather, the victim had already diagnosed herself and determined that she did not need treatment.

Id. at *9–10.

[334] State v. Massengill, 62 P.3d 354, 133 N.M. 263 (2002), *cert. denied*, 133 N.M. 126, 61 P.3d 835 (2003).

[335] Lovejoy v. United States, 92 F.3d 628 (8th Cir. 1996) (admitting hearsay statements of mother providing medical history for her 13-year-old blind and verbally impaired child); Galindo v. United States, 630 A.2d 202, 210 (D.C. 1993)

> Under the medical diagnosis exception to the hearsay rule, statements made by a patient for purposes of obtaining medical treatment are admissible for their truth because the law is willing to assume that a declarant seeking medical help will speak truthfully to medical personnel. *See* Sullivan v. United States, 404 A.2d 153, 158 (D.C. 1979). We find no principled basis in the instant case not to apply the same rationale to a parent who brings a very young child to a doctor for medical attention; the parent has the same incentive to be truthful, in order to obtain appropriate medical care for the child . . . . The mother's statements to the doctor did not suggest a deliberate attempt to lay a foundation for expert testimony at a trial, *see Sullivan, supra*, 404 A.2d at 158–59, but rather suggested a mother's natural concern about her child's condition and health.

In re Lucas, 94 N.C. App. 442, 446–47, 380 S.E.2d 563, 566 (1989); State v. Bauman, 98 Or. App. 316, 779 P.2d 185 (1989).

caretaker for treatment.[336] Under this view, the main rationale for admitting such statements is whether the statements resulted in the child receiving a diagnosis and treatment.

One federal appeals court has noted that while most statements to a doctor by a parent of an injured child might "easily qualify" under the medical treatment exception, "a parent's statement to a doctor identifying the assailant in a child molestation case must be treated as suspect."[337] If it can be shown from "the context and content of the statements that they were made for the purpose of medical diagnosis or treatment," the parent's statements identifying the offender may be admissible.[338] The same court noted that not "all statements made by a parent or a guardian to a doctor are made for medical purposes, even if they are made in a clinical setting" and noted that several statements of a parent made to a physician concerning a child's sexual abuse on a second visit did not qualify for the medical treatment exception.[339] Statements to a parent, with no showing that the child believed they would lead to medical treatment, do not qualify as an exception under the medical history exception.[340]

§ 10.34 Statements to consulting physicians.

The medical history exception to hearsay statements may not apply when the examination was conducted as a social services or law-enforcement investigative consultation rather than for treatment or diagnosis.[341] The issue can arise when

---

[336] Matthews v. State, 106 Md. App. 725, 741, 666 A.2d 912, 920 (1995); State v. Rogers, 109 N.C. App. 491, 503, 428 S.E.2d 220, 227, *cert. denied*, 334 N.C. 625, 435 S.E.2d 348 (1993), *cert. denied*, 511 U.S. 1008 (1994); State v. Brisco, 2000 Ohio App. LEXIS 3835 (Aug. 24, 2000) (holding seven-year-old child's sexual assault trial involving that parent's statements to physician contained in medical records were admissible since "a child's parent can give a medical professional information for medical diagnosis and treatment of the child." *Id.* at *10); State v. Huntington, 216 Wis. 2d 671, 575 N.W.2d 268 (1998) ("Young children cannot independently seek out medical attention, but must rely on their caretakers to do so. A parent's interest in obtaining necessary medical care for a child demonstrates fundamental indicia of reliability." Court noted such statements must still be accompanied by guarantees of trustworthiness. *Id.* at 693–94, 575 N.W.2d at 277.); Hayes v. State, 935 P.2d 700 (Wyo. 1997) (holding that physician properly relied on statements made by child to other individuals rather than direct interview of child).

[337] United States v. Yazzie, 59 F.3d 807, 813 (9th Cir. 1995).

[338] United States v. Yazzie, 59 F.3d 807, 813 (9th Cir. 1995).

[339] United States v. Yazzie, 59 F.3d 807, 813 (9th Cir. 1995). *See also* discussion of Tennessee Supreme Court's requirement of an evidentiary hearing prior to admitting statements under the medical treatment exception in § 10.40.

[340] State v. McGraw, 137 N.C. App. 726, 529 S.E.2d 493, *review denied*, 352 N.C. 360, 544 S.E.2d 554 (2000).

[341] Felix v. State, 109 Nev. 151, 195–96, 849 P.2d 220, 250 (1993); Commonwealth v. Fink, 2002 Pa. Super. 32, 791 A.2d 1235 (2002) (remanding to trial court for hearing to determine if statements to physician, examining child at request of child welfare agency, were for purposes of diagnosis and treatment). *See also* cases cited in the notes 317 and 318.

a child is taken to a physician who is part of a sexual abuse investigation team. This may limit the admissibility of statements, because the purpose of the examination is to determine if abuse occurred and, if so, to identify the perpetrator.[342] Other courts give heightened scrutiny to statements made to medical providers who are provided as part of a governmental investigative program. Part of the skepticism is based on the child's possible lack of understanding the medical benefit of the examination,[343] an issue discussed in the previous section.

Likewise, statements by a nine-year-old child to her physician do not qualify as a medical history exception when they were made three days before trial and for the purpose of preparing and presenting the prosecution's rape trauma syndrome at trial and no diagnosis is made by the doctor.[344] On the other hand, some courts have applied the hearsay exception to statements made to a doctor who was consulted only for the purpose of providing expert testimony in a criminal prosecution,[345] and to statements made to a social worker who was

---

[342] Jones v. State, 600 So. 2d 1138, 1138–39 (Fla. Dist. Ct. App. 1992).

[343] United States v. Henry, 42 M.J. 593 (A.C.C.A. 1995) (upholding trial court's decision to preclude admission of statements made during a medical examination, at which investigators were present, which appeared to be "inextricably intertwined with a criminal investigation" and there was no showing that the child understood she was undergoing an examination to receive a medical benefit instead of an examination as part of the criminal investigation); State v. Brauner, 782 So. 2d 52 (La. Ct. App. 2001), *writ denied*, 811 So. 2d 920 (2002) (victim's statements to doctor were inadmissible hearsay because purpose of exam was to find evidence of sexual assault, but defendant's counsel failed to object); State v. Lawrence, 752 So. 2d 934 (La. Ct. App. 1999), *writ denied*, 764 So. 2d 962 (La. 2000) (statements made by victim to a consulting doctor exceeded scope of medical treatment exception since principal reason for examination was forensic and conducted 18 months after sexual assault, but error was harmless); Gohring v. State, 967 S.W.2d 459 (Tex. Ct. App. 1998)

> While this assumption [of truthfulness to receive effective medical treatment] might be valid where the person to whom the statement is made is a recognized medical professional, there is no basis for such an assumption where, as here, the individual to whom the statement is made is an investigator for CPS, not a recognized medical professional. Even if a part of the witness's duties for the State included the possibility of referral for medical treatment or possible counseling with the child, as suggested by the State, there is no showing the child would have had any appreciation of that fact. Without the child appreciating that any statement made to the witness was for the purpose of medical treatment, there is no basis for the statement having the trustworthiness upon which this exception is based.

Id. at *7–8; State v. Carol, 89 Wash. App. 77, 948 P.2d 837 (1997) (reversing defendant's conviction because there was no showing that child understood the need for accurate and truthful information to counselor provided as part of investigative process).

[344] State v. Stafford, 317 N.C. 568, 574, 346 S.E.2d 463, 467 (1986).

[345] United States v. Whitted, 994 F.2d 444, 448 (8th Cir. 1993), *adhered to, on reh'g, remanded*, 11 F.3d 782, 787 (8th Cir. 1993) (*citing* United States v. Iron Thunder, 714 F.2d 765, 772–73 (8th Cir. 1983)); State v. Isenberg, 148 N.C. App. 29, 36–39, 557 S.E.2d 568, 573–75 (2001), *review denied, appeal dismissed*, 355 N.C. 288, 561 S.E.2d 268 (2002) (fact that child was examined by physician at request of detective did not disqualify child's statements under medical treatment

part of an investigative child protection team.[346]

Most courts do not distinguish between statements made to a treating physician as opposed to a consulting physician,[347] and some states that once maintained the distinction have eliminated it by statute. The Kentucky Rules of Evidence, for example, eliminated the distinction between an "examining" and "treating" physician.[348]

However, former Supreme Court Justice Powell, sitting as a Court of Appeals judge in the case of *Morgan v. Foretich*,[349] noted his concern about applying the exception to statements made to a consulting physician:

> The professional objectivity of a physician for treatment may well be greater than that of a witness employed and paid to testify as an expert. More importantly, the veracity of the declarant's statements to the physician is less certain where the statements need not have been made for purposes of promoting treatment or facilitating diagnosis in preparation for treatment.[350]

A North Carolina court suggested the following factors be used to determine if a medical examination was for medical diagnosis or treatment:

1. whether the examination was requested by persons involved in the prosecution of the case;

---

exception given context and conduct of examination); State v. Writer, 2003 Tenn. Crim. App. LEXIS 519, *appeal denied*, 2003 Tenn. LEXIS 1044 (Oct. 27, 2003):

> We also find that the victim made statements to Dr. Heise for the purpose of medical diagnosis and treatment. Although Dr. Heise received the defendant's case pursuant to a referral from Children Services, he indicated that his purpose in examining the victim was to ensure the victim's well-being and that he was not obligated to any purpose other than the welfare of the victim. Furthermore, after examining the victim, Dr. Heise had the victim tested for several sexually transmitted diseases and referred him to a local counseling service, thereby treating aspects of the victim's physical and mental health. Thus, we find that Dr. Heise's purpose was more than to merely evaluate the victim's condition, but to treat him as well.

Id. at *20.

[346] *In re* Lucas, 94 N.C. App. 442, 380 S.E.2d 563 (1989); State v. Jones, 89 N.C. App. 584, 367 S.E.2d 139 (1988).

[347] United States v. Farley, 992 F.2d 1122, 1125 (10th Cir. 1993); Morgan v. Foretich, 846 F.2d 941, 950 (4th Cir. 1988); United States v. Iron Thunder, 714 F.2d 765, 773 (8th Cir. 1983) (holding "that no treatment was contemplated or given does not prevent application of the Rule 803(4) exception"); United States v. Iron Shell, 633 F.2d 77, 83 (8th Cir. 1980), *cert. denied*, 450 U.S. 1001 (1981); State v. Fitzgerald, 39 Wash. App. 652, 658, 694 P.2d 1117, 1121–22 (1985) ("A qualified physician, whether treating the patient or examining a person solely to enable the doctor to testify at trial, may relate what the patient told her regarding the nature or cause of the injury insofar as it pertains to treatment or diagnosis and not fault.").

[348] *See, e.g.*, Garrett v. Commonwealth, 48 S.W.3d 6 (Ky. 2001).

[349] 846 F.2d 941, 952 (4th Cir. 1988) (Powell, J., concurring in part and dissenting in part).

[350] 846 F.2d 941, 952 (4th Cir. 1998).

2. the proximity of the examination to the victim's initial diagnosis;

3. whether the victim received a diagnosis or treatment as a result of the examination; and

4. the proximity of the examination to the trial date.[351]

Another court in the same state held that a physician consulted solely for trial cannot utilize the medical treatment exception.[352]

An appeals court decision, *United States v. Renville*,[353] outlined a two-part criteria for admission of the medical hearsay exception: "First, the declarant's motive in making the statement must be consistent with the purposes of promoting treatment; and second, the content of the statement must be such as is reasonably relied on by a physician in treatment or diagnosis."[354]

Federal Rule of Evidence 803(4) and its state variations generally blur the distinction between treating and nontreating physicians in most situations, including nonsexual assault cases.

§ 10.35 Unavailability of declarant.

White v. Illinois[355] clearly states that the declarant need not be produced at trial nor must the declarant be found to be unavailable in order to permit the introduction of hearsay testimony under the medical treatment exception. Some states permit hearsay testimony, even though the declarant is available as a witness.[356] Most states follow the *White* rule of not requiring a showing of unavailability. That fact, together with the fact that there need be no particular showing of trustworthiness and that such evidence is evidence-in-chief, make the medical treatment exception one of the most potent pieces of hearsay testimony in child sexual assault trials.

Even when a child can not remember what the defendant has done to her, and thus may be unavailable as a witness, statements under the medical treatment exception may be admissible.[357]

---

[351] State v. Jones, 89 N.C. App. 584, 591, 367 S.E.2d 139, 144 (1988).

[352] State v. Rogers, 109 N.C. App. 491, 502, 428 S.E.2d 220, 226, *cert. denied*, 334 N.C. 625, 435 S.E.2d 348 (1993), *cert. denied*, 511 U.S. 1008 (1994) (noting that "[s]tatements made to a physician for the sole purpose of preparing and presenting the state's case at trial are not admissible under the medical treatment exception").

[353] 779 F.2d 430 (8th Cir. 1985).

[354] 779 F.2d 430, 436 (8th Cir. 1985).

[355] 502 U.S. 346 (1992). *See also* § 10.27.

[356] WYO. RULE EVID. 803(4).

[357] United States v. McHorse, 179 F.3d 889, 900 (10th Cir. 1999), *cert. denied*, 528 U.S. 944 (1999) (holding that child's out-of-court statements falling within the medical treatment exception were admissible, even though child was seven years old at time of trial and testified she could not remember what defendant had done to her since these hearsay statements were admissible under a "firmly rooted" exception to the hearsay rule).

However, individual states may impose greater requirements on the use of hearsay exceptions. For example, some states request a hearing on availability of the declarant or a showing of necessity and reliability before admitting an out-of-court declaration against a defendant.[358] There may also be limitations on the use of multiple hearsay statements. (*See* § 10.51.). The availability of the complainant for cross-examination may support admissibility of the medical treatment hearsay.[359]

§ 10.36   Scope of medical history.

A significant issue in applying the medical treatment exception to the hearsay rule is the scope of information in the victim's medical history under the exception. It is important that the trial attorney examine the history carefully to make sure which portions are properly part of the exception.[360] Many courts have taken the position that, for proper treatment, the medical history in sexual assault cases requires details of the assault, including the type, nature, and extent of sexual intercourse.[361] Furthermore, statements by the offender, such as "don't tell anyone," are important to the medical history in treating the psychological manifestations of the assault.[362] Details such as the perpetrator's threat to kill the victim's family have been deemed an admissible part of medical history and relevant to the victim's state of mind and emotional condition.[363] Details such as how, when, and where the act occurred will generally be relevant absent a

---

[358] *See, e.g.*, State v. Ortiz, 74 Haw. 343, 845 P.2d 547 (1993) (requiring a showing of declarant's unavailability before admitting hearsay statement); State v. Lopez, 122 N.M. 459, 926 P.2d 784 (1996) (holding that New Mexico does not follow *White*, "Thus, when a hearsay declarant is not present for cross-examination at trial, the confrontation clause of the New Mexico constitution requires a showing that he or she is unavailable." *Id.* at 464, 926 P.2d at 789.); State v. Storch, 66 Ohio St. 3d 280, 612 N.E.2d 305 (1993) (questioning the analysis of *White v. Illinois* and calling for a pretrial ruling on the availability of the child, and questioning a child's ability to understand the necessity of telling the truth).

[359] United States v. Norman T., 129 F.3d 1099, 1106 (10th Cir. 1997), *cert. denied*, 118 S. Ct. 1322 (1998).

[360] State v. Ochoa, 576 So. 2d 854 (Fla. Dist. Ct. App. 1991).

[361] Clausen v. State, 50 Ark. App. 149, 901 S.W.2d 35 (1995); State v. McFadden, 318 S.C. 404, 458 S.E.2d 61 (1995) (complainant's history that she had been raped falls within medical history exception).

[362] United States v. Cherry, 938 F.2d 748 (7th Cir. 1991).

[363] People v. Rushing, 192 Ill. App. 3d 444, 548 N.E.2d 788 (1989), *appeal denied*, 131 Ill. 2d 565, 553 N.E.2d 400 (1990) (interpreting ILL. COMP. STAT. ch. 725, § 5/115-13: "In a prosecution for violation of §§ 12-13, 12-14, 12-15, or 12-16 of the Criminal Code of 1961, statements made by the victim to medical personnel for purposes of medical diagnosis or treatment including descriptions of the cause of symptoms, pain or sensations, or the inception or general character of the cause or external source thereof insofar as reasonably pertinent to diagnosis or treatment shall be admitted as an exception to the hearsay rule").

reason for their exclusion.[364] However, some courts have limited the descriptions of the acts and other details of the medical history.[365]

It must also be determined to what extent details about the complainant or her medical history are relevant. For example, a statement that the complainant never had a menstrual cycle may be relevant to the physician's determination of the reason for finding blood.[366] Tennessee's Supreme Court holds that a trial court should conduct an evidentiary hearing and make an affirmative finding outside the presence of the jury to determine if a proper foundation exists for admission of a statement under the medical treatment exception.[367] This inquiry, according to the Tennessee Court, should include all circumstances of the statements, including whether they were in response to leading and suggestive questions, factors affecting trustworthiness such as the context of a custody battle or family feud, or the child's motive for treatment and the content of the statements and whether they are reasonably pertinent to diagnosis or treatment.[368]

This scope of medical history is also addressed in the chapter on medical testimony.[369]

§ 10.37 Statements identifying perpetrator held admissible.

An often-cited case that sets forth the arguments for admitting the identity of the abuser in a victim's medical history is *United States v. Renville*,[370] which holds that a proper diagnosis of a child's psychological problems requires identifying the perpetrator. If the perpetrator is not a member of the immediate household, but will still have access to the child in the future, thereby allowing the sexual abuse to continue, the hearsay testimony identifying the perpetrator may be admissible.[371] If the abuser is part of the child's household, part of the treatment will involve removing the perpetrator from the household. Knowing that the child's abuser is a household member is important in the emotional and psychological treatment to be provided to the child. Such knowledge may also

---

[364] People v. Roy, 201 Ill. App. 3d 166, 558 N.E.2d 1208 (1990); People v. Edwards, 261 A.D.2d 899, 690 N.Y.S.2d 807, *appeal denied*, 93 N.Y.2d 1017, 719 N.E.2d 937, 697 N.Y.S.2d 576 (1999) (upholding admission of statement by victim in medical records that victim assaulted by a gun as relevant to diagnosis and treatment).

[365] People v. Smith, 129 A.D.2d 1005, 514 N.Y.S.2d 304 (1987); State v. Burroughs, 328 S.C. 489, 501, 492 S.E.2d 408, 413 (1997) (holding defendant's statement to complainant that he wanted a hug before he assaulted her not "reasonably pertinent" to diagnosis and treatment).

[366] State v. Rossier, 672 A.2d 455, 457 (R.I. 1996).

[367] State v. McLeod, 937 S.W.2d 867 (Tenn. 1996).

[368] State v. McLeod, 937 S.W.2d 867 (Tenn. 1996).

[369] *See* Chapter 12.

[370] 779 F.2d 430, 435–39 (8th Cir. 1985).

[371] Hennington v. State, 702 So. 2d 403 (Miss. 1997); Doe v. Doe, 644 So. 2d 1199, 1206 (Miss. 1994) (upholding admission of medical history testimony identifying perpetrator who is not a member of child's household, where visitation was at issue).

be relevant in a case involving a sexually-transmitted disease. Where the defendant is not a member of the child's household, it may be impermissible to introduce hearsay testimony identifying the perpetrator. Michigan takes the position that statements of identification are admissible when a foundation is laid that such statements are needed by the physician, are reliable, and the patient understood the necessity and importance of telling the truth.[372] Some jurisdictions require an on-the-record finding that these foundational requirements have been met.[373] Without such a showing, the statements of identification should be precluded from evidence.[374]

On the theory that the name of the perpetrator is relevant to treatment of the mental and emotional aspect of sexual abuse, most federal courts permit medical history testimony identifying the defendant,[375] as have many state courts.[376]

---

[372] People v. Meeboer, 439 Mich. 310, 484 N.W.2d 621 (1992):

> A physician should also be aware of whether a child will be returning to an abusive home. This information is not needed merely for "social disposition" of the child, but rather to indicate whether the child will have the opportunity to heal once released from the hospital. Statements by sexual assault victims to medical health care providers identifying their assailants can, therefore, be admissible under the medical treatment exception to the hearsay rule if the court finds the statement sufficiently reliable to support that exception's rationale.

Id. at 329–30, 484 N.W.2d at 629. *See also* § 10.32.

[373] Eakes v. State, 665 So. 2d 852, 866–67 (Miss. 1995) (instructing trial courts to make on-the-record findings of satisfaction of the two-part test as set forth in main text).

[374] People v. Meeboer, 439 Mich. 310, 484 N.W.2d 621 (1992), *above* note 367.

[375] United States v. Pacheco, 154 F.3d 1236 (10th Cir. 1998), *cert. denied*, 525 U.S. 1112 (1999) (holding identity of defendant, victim's mother's boyfriend, pertinent to care and treatment, since he had an "intermittent relationship" with child's mother); United States v. Tome, 61 F.3d 1446, 1450 (10th Cir. 1995), *rev'd on other grounds*; Territory of Guam v. Ignacio, 10 F.3d 608, 613 (9th Cir. 1993) (noting that while the complainant's statement to the doctor as to who caused her injuries was properly admissible, the child's statement to the social worker was not admissible under this theory, though statements were not made in the course of medical treatment); United States v. Longie, 984 F.2d 955, 959 (8th Cir. 1993); United States v. George, 960 F.2d 97, 99 (9th Cir. 1992); United States v. Provost, 875 F.2d 172 (8th Cir. 1989), *cert. denied*, 493 U.S. 859 (1989); Morgan v. Foretich, 846 F.2d 941, 948–50 (4th Cir. 1988); United States v. Shaw, 824 F.2d 601, 608 (8th Cir. 1987), *cert. denied*, 484 U.S. 1068 (1988); United States v. Iron Shell, 633 F.2d 77, 82–85 (8th Cir. 1980), *cert. denied*, 450 U.S. 1001 (1981).

[376] Kuhn v. State, 1993 Ark. App. LEXIS 107 (Feb. 17, 1993); Stallnacker v. State, 19 Ark. App. 9, 715 S.W.2d 883 (1986) (psychological impact particularly important because source of child's abdominal pains was nerves. "Prevention of recurrence of the injury is a paramount consideration in the treatment of children who have been sexually abused in the home. This is not, however, merely an aspect of medical or psychological treatment. [Physicians must] prevent an abused child from being returned to an environment in which he or she cannot be adequately protected from recurrent abuse." *Id.* at 12, 715 S.W.2d at 885.); State v. Robinson, 153 Ariz. 191, 735 P.2d 801 (1987); People v. Brodit, 61 Cal. App. 4th 1312, 1331, 72 Cal. Rptr. 2d 154, 164–65 (1998); People v. Galloway, 726 P.2d 249 (Colo. App. 1986); State v. Cruz, 56 Conn. App. 763, 746 A.2d 196, *appeal granted*, 253 Conn. 901, 753 A.2d 938 (2000); People v. Falaster, 273 Ill. App. 3d 694, 702, 653 N.E.2d 467, 473, *appeal granted*, 163 Ill. 2d 570, 657 N.E.2d 629 (1995);

An additional argument in favor of admitting such testimony is that physicians in most states have a duty to report suspected cases of child abuse and that without information as to the suspect's identity, a physician cannot perform this duty.[377]

Failure to articulate the basis for admission can result in reversible error, since an appellate court may not speculate as to the identity of the perpetrator for the admission of testimony.[378]

§ 10.38 Statements identifying perpetrator held not admissible.

Courts have refused to admit the portion of a victim's medical history that identifies the perpetrator for reasons relating to the specific fact pattern of a case, as well as because of a general objection that such testimony is not appropriate under the medical treatment exception. Some courts challenge the principle that statements identifying the perpetrator are relevant to the child's psychological and thus overall medical condition. One Maryland court attacks the premise that the declarant in a child sexual assault examination has only a motive to tell the truth when there is as much a social disposition as medical result at issue and holds:

> In stretching outward their list of a physician's responsibilities and in pushing forward with their definition of 'medical treatment and diagnosis,' the expansionists have left behind, abandoned and forgotten, the state of mind of the declarant. . . . Physical self-survival dictates revealing even embarrass-ing truth to avoid the risk of the wrong medicine or the needless operation.

Barnett v. State, 757 So. 2d 323 (Miss. Ct. App. 2000) (four-year-old victim's statement identifying mother's boyfriend as attacker admissible as utterance relevant to diagnosis and treatment even though not a sexual assault); State v. Youngs, 141 N.C. App. 220, 540 S.E.2d 794 (2000), *review denied*, 353 N.C. 397, 547 S.E.2d 430 (2001); State v. Woody, 124 N.C. App. 296, 477 S.E.2d 462 (1996) (holding that child's identification of the perpetrator was pertinent to the psychological and emotional problems resulting from the sexual assault); State v. Dever, 64 Ohio St. 3d 401, 413–14, 596 N.E.2d 436, 446 (1992), *cert. denied*, 507 U.S. 919 (1993); State v. Elkins, 2000 Ohio. App. LEXIS 4670 (Sept. 27, 2000), *dismissed, discretionary appeal not allowed*, 91 Ohio St. 3d 1429, 741 N.E.2d 893 (2001) (holding child's statements identifying perpetrator admissible since there was no indication her statements were the product of "external, suggestive influences"); State v. Burgess, 1996 Ohio App. LEXIS 4887 (Nov. 8, 1996); State v. Vosika, 83 Or. App. 298, 731 P.2d 449 (1987); State v. Stinnett, 958 S.W.2d 329 (Tenn. 1997) ("In the instant case, each physician testified that the examination was for the purpose of diagnosis and treatment. The fact that the perpetrator was RM's stepfather, who resided in the same household, was pertinent to the diagnosis and treatment of an emotional or psychological injury suffered as a result of the abuse." *Id.* at 333.); State v. Livingston, 907 S.W.2d 392, 397 (Tenn. 1995); State v. Ackerman, 90 Wash. App. 477, 953 P.2d 816 (1998); State v. Ashcraft, 71 Wash. App. 444, 456–57, 859 P.2d 60, 67 (1993); Oldman v. State, 998 P.2d 957, 961–62 (Wyo. 2000) (holding statement of victim of domestic assault identifying perpetrator relevant to diagnosis and treatment); Blake v. State, 933 P.2d 474, 477 (Wyo. 1997); Stephens v. State, 774 P.2d 60, 72 (Wyo. 1989); Goldade v. State, 674 P.2d 721, 725 (Wyo. 1983), *cert. denied*, 467 U.S. 1253 (1984).

[377] State v. Vosika, 83 Or. App. 298, 731 P.2d 449, 453 (1987).

[378] *See, e.g.*, Commonwealth v. Sanford, 397 Pa. Super. 581, 597, 580 A.2d 784, 792 (1990), *appeal denied*, 527 Pa. 586, 588 A.2d 508 (1991).

Presupposing a declarant conscious of the probable consequences of his assertions, the imperative to speak truthfully is not nearly so strong when the anticipated result is a social disposition. The temptation to influence the result may, indeed, run in quite the opposite direction. Truthful answers as to the identity of its abuser may well wrench a child from the reassuring presence of its mother or father or both. It is highly unlikely that there operates in an infant declarant a compelling desire to bring about such a result.[379]

Florida takes the view that a child's statements identifying the perpetrator are not admissible under the medical treatment exception and are more properly covered by the state's special child hearsay statute.[380] Pennsylvania's Supreme Court holds that "statements regarding the identity of an assailant or abuser are of legal and not of medical significance."[381] It concluded that if statements identifying a perpetrator were admissible for the psychological and emotional treatment of a child,

> . . . everything said by the patient in the context of being questioned for the purposes of psychological treatment and diagnosis would be admissible under the medical treatment exception. This would destroy the "pertinent to medical treatment" requirement. The Commonwealth's position renders the "pertinent to medical treatment" requirement meaningless as a standard for judicial analysis.[382]

Another argument is that the identity of the perpetrator in a child sexual abuse case is not relevant when the perpetrator is not a member of the immediate household and exercises only infrequent visitation, even though the perpetrator is the victim's natural father.[383] Even if a court admits testimony concerning the identity of a perpetrator who is a member of the child's household on the

---

[379] Cassidy v. State, 74 Md. App. 1, 38, 536 A.2d 666, 684, *cert. denied*, 312 Md. 602, 541 A.2d 965 (1988).

[380] State v. Jones, 625 So. 2d 821, 825–26 (Fla. 1993).

[381] Commonwealth v. Smith, 545 Pa. 487, 494, 681 A.2d 1288, 1292 (1996).

[382] Commonwealth v. Smith, 545 Pa. 487, 496, 681 A.2d 1288, 1292-93 (1996).

[383] Johnson v. State, 666 So. 2d 784, 795 (Miss. 1995); Jones v. State, 606 So. 2d 1051, 1056–57 (Miss. 1992) (acknowledging the theory of *Renville*, but strictly construing requirement that the statements of a child abuse victim under the medical history statement pertaining to identity of a perpetrator require that the abuser be a member of the victim's immediate household); Commonwealth v. D.J.A., 2002 Pa. Super. 176, 800 A.2d 965 (2002):

> While sexual abuse carries with it the danger of contracting a sexually transmitted disease, a child's statement identifying the perpetrator cannot obviate that danger, nor can such a statement, standing alone, determine whether the child should be tested and/or treated for a sexually transmitted disease. Thus, we find no error in the trial court's finding the child's statement in this case inadmissible.

Id. at 35, 800 A.2d at 977. State v. Writer, 2003 Tenn. Crim. App. LEXIS 519, *appeal denied*, 2003 Tenn. LEXIS 1044 (Oct. 27, 2003) (finding that testimony identifying defendant, with whom child did not live but routinely visited, in physician's testimony about child's medical history was volunteered by child and not "imperative" to child's well being, but error was harmless).

theory that such information is relevant to diagnosis and treatment of the emotional and psychological injury of the child, admission of other hearsay statements to the physician, such as feelings about the abuse, not properly encompassed within this or another hearsay exception, can lead to reversal of a defendant's conviction.[384]

Some courts hold that the admission of testimony concerning the identity of the perpetrator as part of medical history is reversible error simply because statements regarding who caused injuries are irrelevant to medical diagnosis and treatment.[385] A statement by a child that "daddy twisted my arm" was deemed inadmissible by an Arizona court under the medical treatment exception, since it was not reasonably pertinent to diagnosis or treatment.[386]

Courts offer a variety of other reasons for finding identity of the assailant not properly part of medical history. Some courts hold that to permit the examining physician to testify with respect to a victim's statements regarding the location of an alleged attack or identity of the perpetrator constitutes impermissible bolstering of evidence.[387] If the record reveals that the examination was more for the purpose of substantiating an allegation, such as "investigative consultation," it is less likely to be an examination for diagnosis and treatment and may fail to meet the criteria of the medical treatment exception justifying admission of the identity of the perpetrator.[388] A court has also reversed a conviction for

[384] State v. Livingston, 907 S.W.2d 392 (Tenn. 1995).

[385] People v. Sexton, 162 Ill. App. 3d 607, 617, 515 N.E.2d 1359, 1366 (1987); People v. Taylor, 153 Ill. App. 3d 710, 721, 506 N.E.2d 321, 329 (1987); People v. Hackney, 183 Mich. App. 516, 455 N.W.2d 358 (1990); State v. Bellotti, 383 N.W.2d 308, 312 (Minn. App. 1986); State v. Massengill, 62 P.3d 354, 361 (N.M. Ct. App. 2002), *cert. denied*, 133 N.M. 126, 61 P.3d 835 (2003); People v. Brown, 262 A.D.2d 328, 689 N.Y.S.2d 652, *appeal denied*, 94 N.Y.2d 820, 724 N.E.2d 382, 702 N.Y.S.2d 590 (1999); Commonwealth v. D.J.A., 2002 Pa. Super. 176, 800 A.2d 965, 975–77 (2002), *appeal denied*, 579 Pa. 700, 857 A.2d 677 (2004) (rejecting argument that danger of child contracting venereal disease justified permitting statement identifying perpetrator under medical treatment exception); State v. Veluzat, 578 A.2d 93 (R.I. 1990); State v. Brown, 286 S.C. 445, 447, 334 S.E.2d 816, 817 (1985); State v. Wetherbee, 156 Vt. 425, 435, 594 A.2d 390, 395 (1991); State v. Fitzgerald, 39 Wash. App. 652, 694 P.2d 1117, 1122 (1985) (holding error harmless).

[386] State v. Reidhead, 146 Ariz. 314, 705 P.2d 1365 (1985).

[387] People v. Harris, 132 A.D.2d 940, 941, 518 N.Y.S.2d 269 (1987), *appeal after remand*, 151 A.D.2d 981, 542 N.Y.S.2d 71, *appeal denied*, 74 N.Y.2d 810, 545 N.E.2d 882, 546 N.Y.S.2d 568 (1989).

[388] Jones v. State, 600 So. 2d 1138, 1138–39 (Fla. Dist. Ct. App. 1992)

The state's argument [that the identity of the perpetrator is admissible under the medical treatment exception] is flawed, however, since the examining physicians were providing services for the child protection team, one of the physicians being the director of the team at the time of the examination. While treatment for the disease should result naturally from the examination, the true and only initial purpose of the examination was to determine whether sexual abuse had occurred and, if so, the identity of the individual responsible for it.

Id. at 1139; Felix v. State, 109 Nev. 151, 196, 849 P.2d 220, 250 (1993).

sexual abuse because the record failed to demonstrate that the identity of the assailant was a relevant inquiry of the doctor for the psychological well-being and safety of the child, thus emphasizing the importance of a factual predicate for the admission of such testimony. [389] Other courts stress the reliability of the statement identifying the perpetrator. If the patient does not understand the need to be truthful, the statement identifying an assailant may not be admissible. [390]

Even if a jurisdiction accepts the concept that identity of a perpetrator is relevant to the child's overall well-being, and to prevent future abuse, it may disallow such testimony when the identification was not "made with an understanding that it was imperative to the child's well-being." [391]

Similarly, if the physician does not explain that identifying the abuser is pertinent to diagnosis and treatment, there may be an inadequate foundation for the hearsay statements identifying the defendant. [392] The importance of establishing the circumstances and context of the examination in evaluating admissibility can be seen where a child approaches a physician months after the alleged abuse, and it is unclear whether the medical examination is performed to substantiate

---

[389] Commonwealth v. Sanford, 397 Pa. Super. 581, 580 A.2d 784 (1990).

[390] See § 10.32; People v. Meeboer, 439 Mich. 310, 484 N.W.2d 621 (1992):

> While the inquiry into the trustworthiness of the declarant's statement is just one prong of the analysis under MRE 803(4), it is very important that the understanding to tell the truth to the physician be established. Factors related to trustworthiness guarantees surrounding the actual making of the statement include: (1) the age and maturity of the declarant, (2) the manner in which the statements are elicited (leading questions may undermine the trustworthiness of a statement), (3) the manner in which the statements are phrased (childlike terminology may be evidence of genuineness), (4) use of terminology unexpected of a child of similar age, (5) who initiated the examination (prosecutorial initiation may indicate that the examination was not intended for purposes of medical diagnosis and treatment), (6) the timing of the examination in relation to the assailant (the child is still suffering pain and distress), (7) the timing of the examination in relation to the trial (involving the purpose of the examination), (8) the type of examination (statements made in the course of treatment for psychological disorders may not be as reliable), (9) the relation of the declarant to the person identified (evidence that the child did not mistake the identity), and (10) the existence of or lack of motive to fabricate. [footnotes omitted]

Id. at 324–25, 484 N.W.2d at 627.

[391] State v. Writer, 2003 Tenn. Crim. App. LEXIS 519 at *26 (June 10, 2003).

[392] United States v. Gabe, 237 F.3d 954 (8th Cir. 2001)

> Here, the government presented no evidence that V.G. repeated her accusation to Dr. Jones for purposes of medical diagnosis or treatment. Given the context, V.G.'s statement identifying Gabe as her abuser to Dr. Jones is no more reliable than her initial accusation to agent Weir, which the district court properly excluded because V.G. was available to testify at trial. In these circumstances, V.G.'s hearsay declaration identifying Gabe as the abuser to Dr. Jones is, like most such identity statements, inadmissible under Rule 803(4).

Id. at 958.

an allegation of abuse or because the child is in need of treatment or protection.[393] In some cases, it may be impermissible to elicit information as to the details of how a defendant molested a victim.[394]

§ 10.39 Statements to nonphysicians.

As a general rule, to qualify as a statement under the medical treatment exception, the statement does not have to be provided to a medical doctor; it can be provided to nurses,[395] ambulance drivers, and even members of the family.[396] Statements made to an interviewer of a hospital child abuse intervention team may also qualify under the exception.[397] Generally, federal[398] and state[399] courts have permitted the medical treatment exception to be applied to

[393] People v. DePlanche, 183 Mich. App. 685, 455 N.W.2d 395 (1990).

[394] People v. Knapp, 139 A.D.2d 931, 527 N.Y.S.2d 914, 915 (1988); State v. Gallagher, 150 Vt. 341, 554 A.2d 221, *cert. denied*, 488 U.S. 995 (1988).

[395] Lovejoy v. United States, 92 F.3d 628 (8th Cir. 1996); People v. Falaster, 273 Ill. App. 3d 694, 700, 653 N.E.2d 467, 472, *appeal granted*, 163 Ill. 2d 570, 657 N.E.2d 629 (1995); People v. Hackney, 183 Mich. App. 516, 455 N.W.2d 358 (1990); State v. Alcalan-Paria, 1995 Minn. App. LEXIS 1468 (Nov. 28, 1995); State v. Crozier, 2001 Ohio App. LEXIS 693 (Feb. 21, 2001) (holding statements to nurse were admissible as statements made for purpose of medical diagnosis or treatment; court also noted child was examined and cross-examined under oath); State v. Hunter, 926 S.W.2d 744 (Tenn. Crim. App. 1995) (holding that statements to nurse practitioners fall within medical treatment exception when they were the basis of the medical history relied on for treatment); Gregory v. State, 56 S.W.3d 164 (Tex. Ct. App. 2001), *cert. denied*, 538 U.S. 978 (2003) (holding statements may be made to a nurse and fall within hearsay exception for purpose of medical diagnosis and treatment; court noted Texas has allowed other non-physicians to testify under this exception); State v. Huntington, 216 Wis. 2d 671, 694, 575 N.W.2d 268, 278 (1998) (holding exception applies to nurses "on staff" with a physician).

[396] 2 MCCORMICK ON EVIDENCE § 277, at 248 (4th ed. 1992).

[397] State v. Mayer, 146 Or. App. 86, 932 P.2d 570 (1997), *rev'd on other grounds*.

[398] United States v. Tome, 61 F.3d 1446, 1451 (10th Cir. 1995) (noting that for a hearsay statement to be admissible under Rule 803(4), the statement need not necessarily have been made to a physician; however, statements to caseworker must be made for purposes of diagnosis and treatment, which was not demonstrated in this case); United States v. Balfany, 965 F.2d 575 (8th Cir. 1992); Morgan v. Foretich, 846 F.2d 941 (4th Cir. 1988); United States v. Cox, 42 M.J. 647 (A.F.C.C.A. 1995) (statements given to a social worker or other non-physician health professional for such a purpose are admissible under Military Rule of Evidence 803(4)).

[399] State v. Robinson, 153 Ariz. 191, 735 P.2d 801 (1987); People v. Oldsen, 697 P.2d 787 (Colo. App. 1984); State v. Martin, 38 Conn. App. 731, 663 A.2d 1078 (1995) (statements made by a victim to a mental health professional at a hospital were properly admitted under the medical treatment exception); Drumm v. Commonwealth, 783 S.W.2d 380 (Ky. 1990); People v. Hackney, 183 Mich. App. 516, 455 N.W.2d 358 (1990); State v. Altgilbers, 109 N.M. 453, 786 P.2d 680 (1989); State v. Bullock, 320 N.C. 780, 360 S.E.2d 689 (1987); State v. Moore, 2001 Ohio App. LEXIS 653 (Feb. 7, 2001) (holding it is not necessary for person diagnosing or treating declarant to be a physician); State v. Vaughn, 106 Ohio App. 3d 775 (1995) (Statements made during a psychological examination of a sexual assault victim are admissible to the same extent as those to a treating physician, "provided that the purpose of the psychological examination is the diagnosis and treatment of the victim's psychological condition, rather than the gathering of evidence against

statements to therapists, psychologists, and social workers, finding that Federal Rule of Evidence 803(4) applies to treatment sought for emotional and psychological injuries. [400]

Some states have amended their medical record exception to include statements made for purposes of emotional and mental treatment, thus including statements made to psychologists and counselors. [401] Some state statutes refer to statements made to "medical personnel," [402] with a warning that this exception should not be an open invitation to admit all evidence of any statements made to health care providers. The Nevada Supreme Court has limited such testimony to licensed psychologists or psychiatrists and a showing that the patient understood the need to speak truthfully and the statements were reasonably necessary for treatment or diagnosis of the patient. [403] Other courts, too, have found error when a child's

---

the accused." *Id.* at *6.); State v. Hunter, 926 S.W.2d 744 (1995) (noting that the exception will apply to non-physicians when the purpose of the interview is to take the medical history from the victim for purposes of treatment); Macias v. State, 776 S.W.2d 255, 258–59 (Tex. Ct. App. 1989); *In re* Dependency of Penelope B., 104 Wash. 2d 643, 655–56, 709 P.2d 1185 (1985) (holding child's statements to child psychiatrist admissible under medical history exception); State v. Nelson, 138 Wis. 2d 418, 406 N.W.2d 385 (1987); Simmers v. State, 943 P.2d 1189 (Wyo. 1997):

> The State properly laid its foundation prior to the hearsay testimony in question. The social worker was SS's counselor, and she testified that the statements were made for the purpose of diagnosis and treatment. The statements described the inception and general character of the external source of SS's symptoms, were reasonably pertinent to her diagnosis and treatment, and were consistent with the purpose for which the witness became involved with the victim. Further, the social worker relied upon the statements for diagnosis and treatment. Therefore, in accordance with our previous cases, the trial court properly admitted the social worker's testimony concerning statements SS made to her during treatment.

Id. at 1197.

[400] United States v. Balfany, 965 F.2d 575 (8th Cir. 1992); United States v. Cox, 42 M.J. 647 (A.F.C.C.A. 1995) (statements given to a social worker or other non-physician health professional for such a purpose are admissible under Military Rule of Evidence 803(4)); State v. Cruz, 56 Conn. App. 763, 746 A.2d 196, *appeal granted*, 253 Conn. 901, 753 A.2d 938 (2000) (holding that statements to social worker were admissible since social worker "was in the chain of medical diagnosis and treatment, and not solely [made to her] because she was a social worker"); Horner v. State, 129 S.W.3d 210, 216–20 (Tex. Ct. App. 2004) (hospital social worker's qualifications and work established her connection to medical treatment of child and thus child's statement about sexual abuse qualified under medical treatment exception and child could have "appreciated that the effectiveness of treatment depended on the accuracy of the information she provided.").

[401] MISS. R. EVID. 803(4) ("For purposes of this rule, the term 'medical' refers to emotional and mental health as well as physical health." According to the comment to Rule 803(4), "the amendment . . . . is a recognition that medical diagnosis and treatment may encompass mental and emotional conditions as well as physical conditions.").

[402] ILL. COMP. STAT. ch. 725, § 5/115-13.

[403] Felix v. State, 109 Nev. 151, 194–96, 849 P.2d 220, 249–50 (1993) (rejecting the admission of the proposed testimony in this case because examination was an investigative consultation rather than for treatment or diagnosis).

statement is admissible without the foundation of a treatment motive.[404]

Some jurisdictions have viewed the medical treatment exception as not applicable to statements made to a non-physician or counselor of a sexual abuse victim.[405] While statements to a non-physician may arguably fall within the medical treatment exception, if the statements to a caseworker or other person are part of the medical diagnosis or treatment of the child or go beyond a recitation of prior symptoms, the medical treatment exception is inapplicable and the statements are simply hearsay.[406] Statements made to non-physicians as part of a child abuse investigative protocol may also not qualify.[407] For example, an intake social worker for a governmental social services agency who conducts an interview in the presence of a police officer, gathering information for the investigation, is not collecting statements that qualify under the medical treatment exception.[408] Courts denying application to non-physicians usually find that the exception is based on the need to tell the truth to a doctor, but not a counselor.

Finding that not only is there a question as to whether children understand the need to tell the truth but also that psychological problems are less subject to verification than physical ones, courts have refused to extend the medical history exception to psychologists[409] and social workers.[410] These decisions reject extending the exception to mental health workers when medical treatment is not the goal of the interview and the history is provided for mental health rather than medical purposes. However, statements made to non-physicians have been held to fall within the medical treatment exception when the non-physician obtains the history as part of medical treatment.[411] The focus is why the victim's

---

[404] *See also* State v. Bates, 140 N.C. App. 743, 538 S.E.2d 597 (2000) (finding error in trial court's admission of child's hearsay statements to psychologist when interview did not possess a treatment motive, child did not know why she was at interview, and psychologist did not make clear that child needed treatment, and did not emphasize need to be truthful).

[405] State v. Zimmerman, 121 Idaho 971, 829 P.2d 861 (1992); State v. Harris, 247 Mont. 405, 808 P.2d 453 (1991).

[406] United States v. Tome, 61 F.3d 1446, 1451 (10th Cir. 1995); Jenkins v. Commonwealth, 254 Va. 333, 339, 492 S.E.2d 131, 134 (1997).

[407] Gohring v. State, 967 S.W.2d 459 (Tex. Ct. App. 1998) (holding statements "not admissible in the case of a social worker employed as a child abuse investigator unless there is a showing both that there is a medical care component to the worker's employment and that the declarant is aware of that medical care component." *Id.* at 463.).

[408] State v. Woods, 2004 Ohio 2700 (2004) (finding error harmless).

[409] State v. Barone, 852 S.W.2d 216 (Tenn. 1993).

[410] Territory of Guam v. Ignacio, 10 F.3d 608, 613 (9th Cir. 1993) (noting that child's statements to the social worker were not admissible where the record did not support that the child's statements were made to the social worker in the course of medical treatment — complainant was referred to social worker by the physician after the physician's examination); Sharp v. Commonwealth, 849 S.W.2d 542, 545 (Ky. 1993) (*citing* Souder v. Commonwealth, 719 S.W.2d 730, 734 (Ky. 1986)) ("There is no recognized exception to the hearsay rule for social workers or the results of their investigation.").

[411] Commonwealth v. Smith, 545 Pa. 487, 494, 681 A.2d 1288, 1292 (1996) (admitting state-

statements were given;[412] the fact that this information may be used later for mental health purposes does not preclude their introduction under the medical treatment exception.[413]

Sometimes the medical history is taken by a non-physician and then repeated by the testifying physician. This may be objectionable as double hearsay.[414] However, statements made to a non-physician after a medical exam cannot be admitted under the medical treatment exception, since there is no motivation of medical treatment.[415]

§ 10.40   Need for hearing to determine admissibility of hearsay statements.

Many jurisdictions are requiring or suggesting a pre-trial hearing to determine admissibility of hearsay statements. In some jurisdictions, the issue may involve availability of the declarant. (*See* §§ 10.27 and 10.35.).

Tennessee's Supreme Court has held that a trial court should conduct an evidentiary hearing and affirmative finding outside the presence of the jury to determine if a proper foundation exists for admission of a statement under the medical treatment exception.[416] This inquiry, according to the Tennessee Court, should include all circumstances of the statements including whether they were a response to leading and suggestive questions, factors affecting trustworthiness, such as the context of a custody battle or family feud, or the child's motive for treatment and the content of the statements and whether they are reasonably pertinent to diagnosis or treatment.[417]

In some jurisdictions a preliminary hearing on the admissibility of the medical history must be requested, and failure to do so may be considered a waiver of the issues surrounding the medical treatment exception.[418] In any event, the foundational requirements for the medical treatment exception as outlined in this chapter should be established by the trial testimony.

---

ments made to social worker under medical treatment exception only when social worker was providing information to physician for child's medical care and treatment); State v. Hunter, 926 S.W.2d 744 (Tenn. Crim. App. 1995).

[412] Commonwealth v. Smith, 545 Pa. 487, 494, 681 A.2d 1288, 1292 (1996) (statements made to social worker were admissible since they were provided as part of the medical professional's policy of having the clinic social worker obtain medical history from the victim prior to diagnosis and treatment; focus is not so much upon who received "[t]he statements as to why they were given." *Id.* at 747).

[413] State v. Hyde, 1996 Tenn. Crim. App. LEXIS 494 at *42 (July 31, 1996).

[414] State v. Naucke, 829 S.W.2d 445, 457–58 (Mo. 1992).

[415] State v. Waddell, 351 N.C. 413, 527 S.E.2d 644 (2000).

[416] State v. McLeod, 937 S.W.2d 867 (Tenn. 1996).

[417] State v. McLeod, 937 S.W.2d 867 (Tenn. 1996).

[418] State v. Childers, 1996 Ohio App. LEXIS 5761 at *21 (Dec. 19, 1996).

§ 10.41   Residual hearsay exception.

Unlike the aforementioned exceptions to the hearsay rule, which are known as "firmly-rooted" exceptions, the residual exception does not have a history of reliability nor of traditional acceptance.[419] The Federal Rules of Evidence permit the admission of a hearsay statement, even though it does not qualify under one of the other exceptions, under the following conditions:

> A statement not specifically covered by Rule 803 or 804 but having equivalent circumstantial guarantees of trustworthiness, is not excluded by the hearsay rule, if the court determines that

(A) the statement is offered as evidence of a material fact;

(B) the statement is more probative on the point for which it is offered than any other evidence which the proponent can procure through reasonable efforts; and

(C) the general purposes of these rules and the interests of justice will best be served by the admission of the statement into evidence. However, a statement may not be admitted under this exception unless the proponent of it makes known to the adverse party sufficiently in advance of the trial or hearing to provide the adverse party with a fair opportunity to prepare to meet it, the proponent's intention to offer the statement and the particulars of it, including the name and address of the declarant.[420]

The Federal Rules of Evidence also apply to military proceedings.[421]

To be admissible under the residual exception, the proffered statement must thus meet five requirements: trustworthiness, materiality, probative importance, the interests of justice, and notice. Congress intended that the residual hearsay exception would be used very rarely, and only in exceptional circumstances.[422]

The residual hearsay exception also has reasonable necessity requirements. The possibility that a witness may lie or change their story does not justify the necessity requirement.[423]

The statutes may impose a duty to provide notice before the statements can be used. Failure to comply with the notice requirement may be reversible error.[424] The residual exception, or a modification, is set forth in many states'

---

[419] Daniel P. Jones, Annotation, *Uniform Rule 803(24): The Residual Hearsay Exception,* 51 A.L.R.4TH 999 (1987).

[420] Federal Rule of Evidence 807.

[421] Effective June 1, 1999, Federal Rule of Evidence 807 became applicable to military proceedings in place of Military Rule of Evidence 803(24) by virtue of Military Rule of Evidence 1102. *See also* Matter of Cornfield, 365 F.Supp.2d 271 (E.D.N.Y. 2004), *aff'd* 156 Fed. Appx. 343 (2d Cir. 2005) ("The test for admissibility under Rule 807 is onerous and the exception should only be invoked in exceptional circumstances." *Id.* at 278.).

[422] United States v. Tome, 61 F.3d 1446 (10th Cir. 1995) ("Courts must use caution when admitting evidence under Rule 803(24), for an expansive interpretation of the residual exception would threaten to swallow the entirety of the hearsay rule"); Huff v. White Motor Corp., 609 F.2d 286, 291 (7th Cir. 1979) [citations omitted].

[423] State v. Marshall, 45 Conn. App. 66, 694 A.2d 816, 822 (1997).

[424] Commonwealth v. Crossley, 711 A.2d 1025 (Pa. Super. Ct. 1998).

evidence codes. It has been used extensively in the child sexual abuse area as a means of introducing hearsay statements that would otherwise be precluded. Some states have added special statutory hearsay provisions for child sexual assault trials, some of which include the residual exception.

One California court has suggested that a court can create child hearsay exception without statutory authority, although that case involved a child dependency proceeding.[425]

§ 10.42   Residual hearsay exception and sexual assault cases.

In sexual assault cases, the trustworthiness requirement generates the greatest inquiry. In *Idaho v. Wright*,[426] the Supreme Court of the United States provided a detailed evaluation of the criteria for the admissibility of hearsay statements under the residual exception in child abuse cases. The Idaho appellate court had ruled that a child's statements to a pediatrician during an interview were not trustworthy because: the interview was not videotaped, the doctor used leading questions, and the doctor was aware beforehand that the child may have been sexually abused. The Supreme Court noted that the reliability requirement for the admission of hearsay statements requires either that the statement fall within a firmly-rooted exception or is supported by "a showing of particularized guarantees of trustworthiness."[427] Some of the factors the Court suggested be considered in determining the admissibility of hearsay statements by a child complainant are: (1) spontaneity and consistent repetition, (2) the mental state of the declarant, (3) the use of terminology unexpected of a child of similar age, and (4) the absence or presence of a motive to fabricate.[428] It held that the guarantee of trustworthiness could not be established by evidence that corroborates the truth of the statement, such as medical evidence.[429] Even after

---

[425] *In re* Carmen O., 28 Cal. App. 4th 908, 33 Cal. Rptr. 2d 848, *modified, reh'g denied*, 29 Cal. App. 4th 981A (1994), *review denied*, 1995 Cal. LEXIS 146 (Jan. 5, 1995). (The court felt that a child hearsay exception had been impliedly recognized and that it was time to give it the name of "child dependency exception" to the hearsay rule. The court utilized the traditional areas for examining the reliability of a hearsay statement under the residual hearsay exception. The court also noted: "While expansion of a child hearsay exception may well also be appropriate for criminal child abuse cases, we obviously do not reach that subject." *Id.* at 922, 33 Cal. Rptr. 2d at 856. The court noted the difference between criminal and dependency cases by noting that in a criminal case, the issue is the guilt of the defendant, whereas in a dependency case the subject is the well-being of the victim. It cited comments from *In re* Kailee B., 18 Cal. App. 4th 719, 22 Cal. Rptr. 2d 485 (1993). In that case, the court noted that while it may be true in criminal cases, it is better that ten guilty people escape rather than one innocent suffer, "few, if any, would agree it is better that 10 pedophiles be permitted to continue molesting children than that 1 innocent parent be required to attend therapy sessions in order to discover why his infant daughter was falsely making such appalling accusations against him." *Id.* at 727, 22 Cal. Rptr. 2d at 490).

[426] 497 U.S. 805 (1990).

[427] Idaho v. Wright, 497 U.S. 805, 816 (1990) (*citing* Ohio v. Roberts, 448 U.S. 56, 66 (1980)).

[428] Idaho v. Wright, 497 U.S. 805, 816 (1990).

[429] Idaho v. Wright, 497 U.S. 805, 816 (1990).

Crawford, in considering the admissibility of nontestimonial hearsay, courts may continue to take into account the circumstances indicating the reliability of a hearsay statement, in accordance with *Wright* and *Roberts.*

A crucial requirement is that the reliability of the hearsay statement must be established by the circumstances surrounding the making of the statement and not by other evidence at trial.[430] For example, the trial court in *Wright*, in admitting the hearsay testimony, relied on factors such as the physical evidence of abuse, the opportunity of the defendant to commit the offense, and an older daughter's corroborating identification, all of which related to other evidence corroborating the act and not to the circumstances under which the statement was made.[431] Even a defendant's confession could not be used to establish trustworthiness under this analysis.[432] However, eyewitness testimony may help provide corroboration of the declarant's statements,[433] and some courts will permit a defendant's confession or admission[434] or medical evidence[435] to be corroborating evidence under a child's hearsay statements.

The Supreme Court also noted that the failure to videotape the interview was not a litmus test for determining the reliability and trustworthiness of the statement nor were the statements presumptively unreliable on the ground that the child was found incompetent to testify at trial.[436] Rather, in examining the circumstances of the making of the statement, the Court found them to be unreliable due to the manner in which the physician conducted the interview, which the Court felt involved sufficient prompting to defeat the trustworthiness of the statement.

Noting that leading questions do not necessarily render responses untrustworthy, a federal appeals court subsequent to *Wright* admitted hearsay testimony

---

[430] State v. D.G., 157 N.J. 112, 723 A.2d 588 (1999) (noting that corroborating evidence may not be used to support a finding of trustworthiness).

[431] Idaho v. Wright, 497 U.S. 805, 826 (1990). *See also* United States v. Tome, 61 F.3d 1446, 1452 (10th Cir. 1995) ("Moreover, other evidence that corroborates truth of a hearsay statement is not a circumstantial guarantee of a declarant's trustworthiness.").

[432] The Supreme Court of Nevada has refused to follow this approach and holds that corroborating evidence should not be excluded in making a reliability determination that does not involve federal confrontation clause considerations. *See* Felix v. State, 109 Nev. 151, 199–200, 849 P.2d 220, 252 (1993) (noting that there was no corroboration of a child's fantastic allegations of killing of animals and humans at a day care center).

[433] State v. Reed, 173 Or. App. 185, 193–97, 21 P.3d 137, 142–44 (2001) (hearsay statements of unavailable child sufficiently corroborated and reliable given the testimony of declarant's brother that he saw defendant naked with a blanket over the unavailable child, even though the child's corroborating testimony did not correspond to any of the charged incidents).

[434] Seagrave v. State, 768 So. 2d 1121 (Fla. Ct. App. 2000).

[435] State v. C.J., 148 Wash. 2d 672, 63 P.3d 765 (2003) (holding that corroboration of hearsay statements under child hearsay statute may be provided by both direct and circumstantial evidence, including medical evidence and "precocious sexual knowledge").

[436] Idaho v. Wright, 497 U.S. 805, 818–819, 824 (1990).

under the residual exception when it found no leading questions and no motive to fabricate on the part of the declarant.[437]

The Court's ruling in *Wright* would question earlier decisions that found trustworthiness based on findings pertaining to physical or medical evidence,[438] and some courts have indicated a willingness to reexamine holdings in cases involving the residual exception.[439] The statements of an adult victim of domestic violence identifying the perpetrator may also be admissible for the same reasons as with child sexual assault victims, *i.e.*, to prevent the recurrence of injury.[440]

§ 10.43 Factors to consider in evaluating reliability and admissibility.

Among "contamination errors" that can occur in child interviews and diminish the reliability of children's statements are:

> Systems contamination (outside information gained from police or other sources); cross-contamination (using information gained from other children during therapy with another child); concertizing (repetitive, leading discussions creating false memories in the child); assuming incidents occurred and following a preconceived agenda; coercive questioning; and ignoring or discounting a child's denials.[441]

South Dakota's Supreme Court lists the following factors to consider when assessing the reliability of a child's hearsay statements:

> (1) the child's age and maturity; (2) the nature and duration of the abuse; (3) the relationship of the child to the offender; (4) the coherence of the statement, bearing in mind that young children may sometimes describe incidents in age-appropriate language and in a disorganized manner; (5) the child's capacity to observe, retain, and communicate information; (6) the nature and character of the statement itself, considering the child's developmental limitations in understanding and describing sexual behavior; (7) any motivation of the child to make a false allegation or a false denial; (8) the child's susceptibility to suggestion and the integrity of the situation under which the statement was obtained; and (9) all the circumstances under which the statement was made.[442]

---

[437] United States v. George, 960 F.2d 97 (9th Cir. 1992).

[438] *See, e.g.*, United States v. Cree, 778 F.2d 474 (8th Cir. 1985).

[439] United States v. Gomez-Lemos, 939 F.2d 326 (6th Cir. 1991).

[440] State v. Sims, 77 Wash. App. 236, 890 P.2d 521 (1995).

[441] State v. Babayan, 106 Nev. 155, 787 P.2d 805 (1990).

[442] State v. Cates, 2001 SD 99, 632 N.W.2d 28, 34 (2001).

The use of nonleading and open-ended questions is a common factor used in evaluating trustworthiness.[443] A suggestive interview may imperil the reliability of a child hearsay statement. Expert testimony and evidence of leading and suggestive questioning can establish unreliability.[444] Suggestiveness may also affect the competency requirement of some statutes of a memory sufficient to retain an independent recollection of the event.[445] Some use of leading questions may be permissible.[446] For example, the fact that a four-year-old child's out-of-court statements were made in response to questions does not necessarily render the child's hearsay statements unreliable when there is no indication that the child was coached or prodded into making the statements.[447] This is discussed further at the end of this section and in Chapter 11.

Bootstrapping of statements is not permitted. For example, the fact that two children make the same statements in two days does not establish reliability and trustworthiness of the statement at the time it is made.[448] This runs afoul of the *Wright* proscription against using corroborating evidence to establish trustworthiness and reliability. Theoretically, using another child's statements that have not been established as reliable and trustworthy begs the question of reliability and trustworthiness of the statement at the time it was made.

Not only should the offered statement be reviewed, but also earlier statements should be examined for "continuity in subsequent statements" because of research that shows that children's memories are better in the first interview than later interviews.[449]

---

[443] United States v. Grooms, 978 F.2d 425, 427 (8th Cir. 1992); State v. Brown, 953 S.W.2d 133 (Mo. Ct. App. 1997) (holding questioning child in a non-coercive environment a factor in hearsay statement's reliability:

> With regard to the witnesses who testified as to L.M.'s out-of-court statements, they appear to be elicited with non-suggestive techniques. Dr. Howenstine asked open-ended questions, and did not force L.M. to talk about a subject with which she was uncomfortable. Officer Wooderson-Stanley may have made some interviewing errors, but L.M. was not questioned in a coercive environment, nor was she pushed to respond in any specific way. . . . Neither child was questioned in a coercive environment, and it appears that at least most of the witness'[s] questioning was either only in response to a spontaneous remark or was left open so as to not lead the child.

Id. at 140.); State v. Clark, 91 Wash. App. 69, 954 P.2d 956 (1998) (questioning was neither leading or suggestive, suggesting reliability of the statement).

[444] Felix v. State, 109 Nev. 151, 164–65, 849 P.2d 220, 230 (1993).

[445] Petcu v. Dept. of Social and Health Servs. (*In re* Dep. of A.E.P.), 135 Wash. 2d 208 (1998).

[446] State v. Smith, 158 N.J. 376, 730 A.2d 311, 319 (1999) (New Jersey Supreme Court found that while some of the questions were slightly leading in nature, they were not unduly suggestive and "the use of leading questions to facilitate an examination of child witnesses who are hesitant, evasive, or reluctant is not improper").

[447] State v. Cardosi, 122 Ohio App. 3d 70, 701 N.E.2d 44 (1997).

[448] Swan v. Peterson, 6 F.3d 1373, 1380 (9th Cir. 1993).

[449] Felix v. State, 109 Nev. 151, 183, 849 P.2d 220, 241 (1993).

The consistency of a child's statements is often cited as evidence of reliability.[450] The fact that the child's out-of-court statements are inconsistent with the victim's trial testimony does not establish unreliability.[451] Another factor is the explicit and detailed nature of the statement compared with the developmental level of the child and the victim's emotional condition at the time of the statements. The child's explicit language and terminology is a factor that can be used to assess trustworthiness and reliability, since it may reflect knowledge of sexual acts beyond the usual experience of a child in that age category, and may be reflective of candor rather than coaching.[452]

The fact that the statements were made spontaneously is a factor indicating reliability of a statement.[453] Reliability is present when a child's statements were "basically unrehearsed . . . in the language of childhood about events of which she could have known only through direct experience," and the child's demeanor was "at least consistent with the thesis of believability."[454]

---

[450] United States v. Grooms, 978 F.2d 425–27 (8th Cir. 1992); United States v. Ureta, 44 M.J. 290 (C.A.A.F. 1996), *cert. denied*, 519 U.S. 1059 (1997); Mikler v. State, 829 So. 2d 932, 2002 Fla. App. LEXIS 14591, *reh'g denied*, 2002 Fla. App. LEXIS 17528 (Nov. 12, 2002) (determining it unnecessary to require corroboration of an 11-year-old victim's taped out-of-court statement, since its reliability was clearly established by the victim's responsive and expansive articulation of the incident and because the statement was made on the same day as the incident); Hennington v. State, 702 So. 2d 403, 418 (Miss. 1997); Eakes v. State, 665 So. 2d 852, 866 (Miss. 1995) (noting consistency of allegations against defendant by children); State v. Costa, 11 S.W.3d 670 (Mo. 1999), *transfer denied, cert. denied*, 530 U.S. 1282 (2000) (holding that child's consistent repetition of statements was evidence of reliability).

[451] State v. Werneke, 958 S.W.2d 314 (Mo. Ct. App. 1997) (holding it is not uncommon for child sex abuse victim's testimony to contain some variations, contradictions, and lapses in memory).

[452] United States v. Dorian, 803 F.2d 1439, 1445 (8th Cir. 1986); State v. Larson, 472 N.W.2d 120, 125–27 (Minn. 1991); State v. Redman, 916 S.W.2d 787 (Mo. Ct. App. 1996) (analyzing the use of terminology criteria, court noted "that when assessing content-reliability, courts must examine whether the child's knowledge of the subject matter, rather than the child's particular vocabulary or words, is unexpected in a child of similar age." *Id.* at 792.); State v. Stuart, 2001 Ohio App. LEXIS 1566 at *10, *dismissed, discretionary appeal not allowed*, 92 Ohio St. 3d 1445, 751 N.E.2d 483 (2001), *cert. denied*, 535 U.S. 929 (2002) (holding among one of the factors in establishing reliability of child's hearsay statements was the sexually explicit nature of five-year-old's statements).

[453] United States v. Tome, 61 F.3d 1446, 1453 (10th Cir. 1995) (hearsay statements should not have been admitted under residual exception because, among other reasons, they were not spontaneously made). *See also* Swan v. Peterson, 6 F.3d 1373, 1381 (9th Cir. 1993); Morgan v. Foretich, 846 F.2d 941, 948 (4th Cir. 1988); People v. Barger, 251 Ill. App. 3d 448, 624 N.E.2d 405 (1993); State v. Brown, 953 S.W.2d 133 (Mo. Ct. App. 1997) (noting that spontaneity of child's statements were a factor in the reliability of the out-of-court statements); State v. J.C.E., 235 Mont. 264, 274, 767 P.2d 309, 315 (1988) (noting that statements to a therapist were not spontaneously made); Bockting v. State, 109 Nev. 103, 109, 847 P.2d 1364, 1368 (1993); State v. Stuart, 2001 Ohio App. LEXIS 1566 at *10, *dismissed, discretionary appeal not allowed*, 92 Ohio St. 3d 1445, 751 N.E.2d 483 (2001), *cert. denied*, 535 U.S. 929 (2002).

[454] State v. Donegan, 265 N.J. Super. 180, 187, 625 A.2d 1147, 1150 (1993).

Some courts note the limited reflective process of a young child as a factor in determining trustworthiness of declaration. [455]

A lack of spontaneity or emotional display may reflect unreliability of the statement. [456] A factor to consider is the time period between the statements made and the alleged abuse. [457] Statements made one year after the alleged sexual assault may not possess the guarantee of trustworthiness required by the exception. [458]

While recording a statement may be insufficient to establish its reliability, [459] some courts view the recording of a statement as evidence of trustworthiness and reliability. The recording allows expert opinion on the suggestiveness of the interview. There is also authority that failing to record the statement or portion of the interview may be a factor in precluding admission of the statement. [460] Statements made after a gap in a videotape may lack reliability even if the statements are recorded. [461] A court may find "an additional safeguard" in evaluating reliability of a child's hearsay statement if the declarant testifies. [462]

---

[455] State v. Ashford, 2001 Ohio App. LEXIS 583 (Feb. 16, 2001) (four-year-old's statement, while crying and visibly upset, with no evidence that child was coached or subject to influence, qualified as an excited utterance).

[456] United States v. Turning Bear, 357 F.3d 730 (8th Cir. 2004) (videotaped interview of child's alleged sexual abuse not found trustworthy to satisfy a hearsay exception where over two months had lapsed from the alleged abuse and the child was not found to have a strong motivation to tell the truth); Territory of Guam v. Ignacio, 10 F.3d 608, 613–14 (9th Cir. 1993) (concluding that the child's out-of-court statement was not reliable because it "was not spontaneous, . . . [and was not] accompanied by an emotional display that would indicate that she was telling the truth and the record does not support a finding that the child used terminology unexpected of a child of similar age or that the child lacked motive to fabricate evidence).

[457] Carpenter v. State, 786 N.E.2d 696 (Ind. 2003):

> We find that the testimony recounting A.C.'s statements to her mother and grandfather and her videotape interview failed to exhibit sufficient indications of reliability as the protected person statute requires because of the combination of the following circumstances: there was no indication that A.C.'s statements were made close in time to the alleged molestations, the statements themselves were not sufficiently close in time to each other to prevent implantation or cleansing, and A.C. was unable to distinguish between truth and falsehood.

Id. at 704.

[458] United States v. Tome, 61 F.3d 1446, 1453 (10th Cir. 1995).

[459] State v. Frazier, 2001 SD 19, 622 N.W.2d 246 (2001) (reversing defendant's conviction due to failure to establish inherent reliability of out-of-court statements and why cross-examination of declarant would be unnecessary or superfluous; fact that statement was recorded is insufficient indicator of reliability).

[460] United States v. Cabral, 43 M.J. 808 (A.F.C.C.A. 1996), *aff'd*, 47 M.J. 268 (C.A.A.F. 1997), *cert. denied*, 522 U.S. 1114 (1998) (the failure to record all of the interview, including "rapport" building sessions, may tip the scales against admitting hearsay under the residual exception).

[461] State v. D.G., 157 N.J. 112, 723 A.2d 588 (1999) (finding unreliable those portions of child's videotape statements made after a seven-minute gap in the interview of child by investigators).

[462] Baker v. State, 228 Ga. App. 32, 33, 491 S.E.2d 78, 80 (1997); State v. Brown, 953 S.W.2d 133 (Mo. Ct. App. 1997).

A child's play with anatomical dolls is hearsay, but usually within the scope of the residual and special child hearsay exceptions.[463] Moreover, courts also have relied on testimony, sometimes by experts, concerning a child's interactions and play with anatomically correct dolls and drawings to corroborate trustworthiness.[464] One court noted that a child's spontaneous demonstration with the dolls "inspired confidence" in the reliability of the child's statements,[465] However, some courts have also noted that the child's handling of the dolls must be established as trustworthy.[466] However, this may also be evidence of a pressure tactic.[467]

Courts have also examined the motive of the declarant to falsify or distort the testimony and the stress of excitement from the incident in evaluating trustworthiness.[468] This is similar to the analysis used in evaluating excited utterance declarations. For example, a child who continued insisting that the events occurred even though the declarant's mother did not want the defendant prosecuted, and the victim bore no animus toward the defendant and did not accuse the defendant of other types of sexual conduct when questioned about them, reflects a lack of motive.[469] Similarly, a victim's statement made in a confidential conversation will be evidence that the declarant had no motive to lie about her feelings.[470]

While the relationship between the declarant and witness is a fact to consider, a witness associated with the police, prosecutor or social services does not automatically make the hearsay statements unreliable.[471] As to the circumstances surrounding the testimony of a witness to a child's statement regarding a sexual assault, the Montana Supreme Court suggests the following should be considered:

---

[463] People v. Fowler, 240 Ill. App. 3d 442, 451, 608 N.E.2d 390, 396 (1992); Bockting v. State, 109 Nev. 103, 109–10, 847 P.2d 1364, 1368 (1993).

[464] United States v. Grooms, 978 F.2d 425, 427 (8th Cir. 1992); United States v. Ellis, 935 F.2d 385, 393–94 (1st Cir.), cert, denied, 502 U.S. 869 (1991) (admissible even though play with dolls not recorded); Souder v. Commonwealth, 719 S.W.2d 730 (Ky. 1986); State v. Mayes, 251 Mont. 358, 825 P.2d 1196 (1992); State v. Deanes, 323 N.C. 508, 374 S.E.2d 249, 256 (1988), cert, denied, 490 U.S. 1101 (1989); State v. Wagner, 30 Ohio App. 3d 261, 508 N.E.2d 164 (1986).

[465] Bockting v. State, 109 Nev. 103, 847 P.2d 1364, 1368 (1993).

[466] State v. Bratt, 250 Kan. 264, 273, 824 P.2d 983, 990 (1992). See also §§ 10.6 and Chapter 11 and discussion of anatomical dolls in Chapter 14 and Appendix G.

[467] State v. Costa, 11 S.W.3d 670 (Mo. Ct. App. 1999), cert. denied, 530 U.S. 1282 (2000) (finding use of anatomical dolls in interviewing child was evidence of a "pressure tactic," but that consistency of statements helped statements meet test of trustworthiness).

[468] State v. Larson, 472 N.W.2d 120, 125–27 (Minn. 1991); Hennington v. State, 702 So. 2d 403, 418 (Miss. 1997); State v. Clark, 91 Wash. App. 69, 954 P.2d 956 (1998) ("In short, the evidence supports no motive to lie in making the hearsay statements, but instead suggests a motive for E to lie when she testified at trial." Id. at 78.); State v. Huntington, 216 Wis. 2d 671, 687–88, 575 N.W.2d 268, 275 (1998). See also Swan v. Peterson, 6 F.3d 1373, 1381 (9th Cir. 1993).

[469] Bockting v. State, 109 Nev. 103, 111, 847 P.2d 1364, 1369 (1993).

[470] State v. Williams, 117 N.M. 551, 561, 874 P.2d 12, 22 (1994).

[471] State v. Clark, 91 Wash. App. 69, 954 P.2d 956 (1998).

(a) The witness's relationship to the child.

(b) Whether the relationship between the witness and the child might have an impact on the trustworthiness of the hearsay statement.

(c) Whether the witness might have a motive to fabricate or distort the child's statement.

(d) The circumstances under which the witness heard the child's statement, including the timing of the statement in relation to the incident at issue and the availability of another person in whom the child could confide.[472]

Using the above criteria, the Montana Court found that a therapist is predisposed to confirm what the patient reports, that the trustworthiness of the statement is adversely affected by the fact that a patient is a child, and that "in general, the circumstances in which a therapist hears a child's statement about sexual abuse are not such that a hearsay statement by the therapist will possess circumstantial guarantees of trustworthiness."[473]

If an expert is going to offer an opinion that a child's statement is trustworthy, a foundation should be laid to establish the reliability of the expert's methodology.[474] Courts have allowed expert testimony on trustworthiness evaluations of residual hearsay testimony such as:

> It would be almost impossible for [Mechelle] to fabricate an entire incident of such complexity as the one which [Mechelle] describes . . . and which is the subject of the charges against the accused. . . . [The victim] is "very honest," if for no other reasons than because she does not have the inhibitions that would cause others to hold back information and because she lacks the degree of creativity required to be deceitful.[475]

However, a defendant may not rely on expert testimony involving his polygraph results to evaluate the reliability of the hearsay statement.[476] Another court utilizing expert testimony as one basis for reliability and trustworthiness, after summarizing many of the factors discussed in this section as yardsticks to use in evaluating statements offered under the residual hearsay exception, concluded:

> Finally, we find the following equivalent circumstantial guarantees of trustworthiness: (1) the child's statement was taken by two persons, both of whom were called to explain the circumstances surrounding its recordation;

---

[472] State v. Harris, 247 Mont. 405, 415, 808 P.2d 453, 458–59 (1991) (*citing* State v. J.C.E., 235 Mont. 264, 274, 767 P.2d 309, 315 (1988)).

[473] State v. Harris, 247 Mont. 405, 415, 808 P.2d 453, 458-59 (1991).

[474] State v. Nelson, 777 P.2d 479 (Utah 1989).

[475] United States v. Lyons, 36 M.J. 183, 187 (C.M.A. 1992).

[476] State v. Gregory, 80 Wash. App. 516, 520–21, 910 P.2d 505, 507–08, *review denied*, 129 Wash. 2d 1009, 917 P.2d 129 (1996) (appellate court refused to consider defendant's polygraph results in assessing reliability of child's hearsay statements). *See* Chapter 11 on use and reliability of polygraph examinations.

(2) prior to taking the statement, an agent impressed upon the child the importance of telling the truth and the child swore to tell the truth; (3) the child was speaking from first hand knowledge; (4) no cogent motivation for the child to lie was suggested; (5) about two weeks after making the statement to NIS, the child was examined by a clinical psychologist who testified that child's symptoms were consistent with a sexually-abused child, that the child confirmed the acts of sodomy by his father, that the child expressed no ill will to his father, and that he was in fact concerned his father would be punished; (6) the same psychologist also testified that he had listened to the audiotapes of the NIS interview, that at the time the child was a very pressured little boy, but from a clinical and structural point, his basic personality and integrity were quite intact, and that from his evaluations the child would not create anything out of his own fantasy or make statements that did not have some objective validity; (7) the child was available to testify; and (8) the child's statement and the appellant's own confession which preceded it were mutually corroborating.[477]

While not every statement will possess all these factors, it is important that as many areas as possible be assessed in offering or objecting to statements offered under the residual hearsay exception.

Even when there are circumstantial guarantees of trustworthiness, the other criteria of the residual exception must be satisfied, such as the necessity for the statement. When a child is available to testify to material elements of the offense, the residual hearsay statements are not the most probative proof and become cumulative testimony.[478] Where a victim's 15-year-old brother was present at the time of the event and could testify as to what occurred, hearsay statements of the victim to a therapist were no more reliable or probative than the testimony of the brother.[479]

The following summarizes most of the criteria courts have considered in assessing reliability and trustworthiness of statements under the residual hearsay exception.

1. The questioning process, whether leading and suggestive questions were used, and the extent to which the complainant agreed with the questioner.

2. Whether the statements were recorded.

3. When the statements were made in relation to the assailant.

4. The spontaneity of the statements and lack of coaching of the child.

5. The consistency of the statements.

6. Explicit and detailed nature of the statements compared with the developmental level of the child.

---

[477] United States v. Martindale, 36 M.J. 870, 881 (N-M.C.M.R. 1993).
[478] State v. Harris, 247 Mont. 405, 413–14, 808 P.2d 453, 458 (1991).
[479] State v. Nelson, 777 P.2d 479 (Utah 1989).

7. The bias or motive of the declarant.

8. The cognitive and mental capacities of the declarant, including the child's competency.

9. The use of age-appropriate language.

10. The age of the child.

11. The relationship of the witness to the child and whether that relationship affects the reliability of the reported statement.

12. Expert testimony on reliability and testimony of the statements.

13. Availability of other more probative proof of facts contained in hearsay statement.

14. The child's general character.

15. Whether more than one person heard the statements.

16. Whether the statement contains express assertions about past fact.

17. Whether cross-examination could show the child's lack of knowledge.

18. Whether there is only a remote possibility the child's recollection was faulty.

19. Whether the circumstances surrounding the statement are such that there is no reason to suppose the child misrepresented the defendant's involvement. [480]

Only the circumstances surrounding the making of the statement are to be considered. As noted earlier, pursuant to *Idaho v. Wright*, [481] evidence corroborating the statement, such as medical evidence of a sexual contact, may not be considered in determining reliability and trustworthiness.

§ 10.44 Availability of declarant.

While the Court in *Wright* did not require the declarant to testify as a predicate for the admission of the hearsay statements made pursuant to traditional exceptions to the hearsay rule, the Supreme Court's decision in *Crawford* (§ 10.3) does not permit "testimonial" hearsay statements, unless the declarant testifies. Before *Crawford*, the fact that the declarant testified and was available for cross-examination weighed in favor of admissibility, [482] even if the victim recanted the accusation at trial [483] or the victim testified but was not able to remember details or was not totally responsive to the questioning. [484] Unavailability was

---

[480] *See, e.g.*, State v. Anthony, 1996 Wash. App. LEXIS 747 (Dec. 16, 1996).

[481] 497 U.S. 805 (1990).

[482] United States v. Dunn, 851 F.2d 1099 (8th Cir. 1988).

[483] United States v. Renville, 779 F.2d 430, 438 (8th Cir. 1985).

[484] United States v. Spotted War Bonnet, 933 F.2d 1471 (8th Cir. 1991) (holding that a defen-

not an indispensable prerequisite to admission under the residual exception, but an important factor to evaluate. The trend in both state and federal courts had been not to make admissibility dependent on unavailability.[485]

As noted in § 10.35, some states require a finding of unavailability under their own constitution. However, analysis of hearsay statements under the residual hearsay exception must be viewed in light of *Crawford*.

§ 10.45   *Crawford v. Washington, Davis v. Washington* and the right of confrontation and sexual assault trials and forfeiture of right of confrontation.

The United States Supreme Court in *Crawford v. Washington*[486] in a far reaching decision affecting many of the hearsay exceptions utilized in sexual assault trials, established a new standard for evaluating hearsay evidence and redefining the Confrontation Clause. The court's decision overruled its previous holding in *Ohio v. Roberts,*[487] which has often been used in support of many child hearsay exceptions. The Court replaced *Roberts'* "reliability" standard with a bright line rule based on the Confrontation Clause. This test led to a long line of cases and varying concepts of what constitutes a reliable and trustworthy statement. "Where testimonial statements are involved," Justice Scalia wrote, "we do not think the Framers meant to leave the Sixth Amendment's protection to the vagaries of the rules of evidence, much less to amorphous notions of 'reliability.' "[488] "Admitting statements deemed reliable by a judge is fundamentally at odds with the right of confrontation."[489] After *Crawford*, "testimonial statements of a witness who [does] not appear at trial" may not be admitted or used against a criminal defendant unless the declarant is "unavailable to testify, and the defendant ha[s] had a prior opportunity for cross examination."[490] The Court's decision does not bar the use of testimonial statements offered for purposes other than establishing the truth of the matter asserted.[491] The decision

---

dant's right of confrontation had not been abridged when a child witness could not remember the underlying events upon which the pretrial statement was based and, hence, could not be cross-examined on them); United States v. St. John, 851 F.2d 1096 (8th Cir. 1988); United States v. Shaw, 824 F.2d 601 (8th Cir. 1987), *cert. denied*, 484 U.S. 1068 (1988); United States v. Lyons, 36 M.J. 183 (C.M.A. 1992) (17-year-old retarded and hearing-impaired victim testified, but had severe difficulty responding to questions).

[485] *See, e.g.*, Bockting v. State, 109 Nev. 103, 107, 847 P.2d 1364, 1366 (1993).

[486] 541 U.S. 36 (2004).

[487] 448 U.S. 56 (1980).

[488] *Crawford,* 541 U.S. at 61

[489] *Crawford,* 541 U.S. at 61

[490] *Crawford*, 541 U.S. at 54.

[491] *Crawford* at 59. *See also* People v. Reynoso, 2 N.Y.2d 820, 814 N.E.2d 456, 781 N.Y.S.2d 289 (2004) (finding testimony of co defendant's statements to detective were admissible to establish the detective's state of mind rather than for their truth and thus the hearsay did not fall within

also does not bar the use of testimonial statements when the declarant appears for cross examination at trial.[492] (However, in considering the admissibility of nontestimonial hearsay, courts may continue to take into account the circumstances indicating the reliability of a hearsay statement, in accordance with *Roberts.*)

The Court's Confrontation Clause requirement for hearsay applies only to testimonial statements. It left for "another day" a comprehensive definition of "testimonial statement," but noted "at a minimum [it includes] prior testimony at a preliminary hearing, before a grand jury, or at a former trial; and . . . police interrogations. These are the modern practices with closest kinship to the abuses at which the Confrontation Clause was directed."[493] Under the Confrontation Clause, the foundation to use such testimonial evidence requires that the accused had a prior opportunity to question the declarant and that the declarant is unavailable at trial. The circumstances surrounding the making of the statement assist in the evaluation of the hearsay statement more than how the statement is categorized. For example, a spontaneous declaration or excited utterance may or may not fall within *Crawford.* Justice Scalia specifically cited the example of "statements of a child victim to an investigating police officer," which he describes as testimonial.[494] This analysis implies that when law enforcement officials play a role in the production of the statement, this is a factor that suggests a testimonial statement.

The statements in *Crawford* involved a wife's tape recorded statements to the police implicating her husband in an assault and attempted murder case involving a man the defendant believed had tried to murder his wife. At trial, the wife was unavailable to testify because of the marital privilege. The prosecution utilized a special hearsay provision, and the trial court admitted the statement because it was "reliable" and "trustworthy." Because many sexual assault and domestic violence cases involve witnesses unavailable for a variety of reasons (e.g. incompetency, unwillingness, or "emotionally unavailable") and their hearsay statements are substituted for their testimony, *Crawford* plays an important role. It clearly overrules and questions the validity of many previous holdings, particularly in the child hearsay area. Many of the state statutes permitting the use of child hearsay statements by non-testifying declarants were upheld on the basis of the Court's decision in *Roberts* and are likely overruled

---

reach of *Crawford* holding); People v. Ruis, 11 A.D.3d 714, 784 N.Y.S.2d 558, *appeal denied,* 4 N.Y.3d 747, 824 N.E.2d 61, 790 N.Y.S.2d 660 (2004) ("Here, the investigating officer was permitted to testify that after speaking with an eyewitness who did not testify at trial and obtaining from the eyewitness a photograph of the defendant, the officer investigated further and the defendant subsequently was apprehended in Costa Rica. This testimony was properly admitted for the purpose of explaining the sequence of events leading to the defendant's apprehension.").

[492] *Crawford,* 541 U.S. at 59.

[493] *Id.* at 68.

[494] *Id.* at 58.

by *Crawford.* Hearsay admitted under the theory that the statement is reliable and trustworthy now does not fit within the Confrontation Clause standard of *Crawford.* Statements made to a multidisciplinary child abuse team and introduced into evidence under a child hearsay exception may violate the Confrontation Clause, since they are structured statements given under circumstances that they would be used at trial.[495] This approach has support from the court's reasoning in *Crawford* that "[a]n accuser who makes a formal statement to government officers bears testimony in a sense that a person who makes a casual remark to an acquaintance does not."[496] It is not the government's intent in arranging the interview or where the interview took place or who employed the interview that is determinative, but rather the reasonable belief that the statement would be available for use at trial or testimonial in nature.[497] A key question is, "Did the declarant have a reason to expect that his statements would be used in a future judicial proceeding?"[498] Some courts, contrary to others, find that

---

[495] People v. Sisavath, 118 Cal. App. 4th 1396, 13 Cal. Rptr. 3d 753 (2004). *See also* People v. T.T. (*In re* T.T.), 351 Ill. App. 3d 976, 815 N.E.2d 789 (2004) (holding that "where [a social worker] works at the behest of and in tandem with the State's Attorney with the intent and purpose of assisting in the prosecutorial effort, [the social worker] functions as an agent of the prosecution." *Id.* at 990, 815 N.E.2d at 801); Snowden v. State, 156 Md. 64, 867 A.2d 314 (2005) ("Moreover, we find that the structure, location, and style of the interviews actually support the notion that the children's interviews were a formal and structured interrogation where the responses reasonably would be expected to be used at a later trial. The fact that the interviews were conducted by a licensed sexual abuse investigator, rather than a police officer, is of little persuasive weight in our analysis." *Id.* at 85, 867 A.2d at 326); Flores v. State, 120 P.3d 1170, 1178-79 (Nev. 2005).

[496] *Crawford,* 541 U.S. at 51.

[497] *Sisavath,* 118 Cal. App. 4th at 1402-03, 13 Cal. Rptr. 3d at 758; Snowden v. State, 385 Md. 64 at 87, 867 A.2d at 327 ("[W]here an objective person in the position of the declarant would be aware that the statement-taker is an agent of the government, governmental involvement is a relevant, and indeed weighty, factor in determining whether any statements made would be deemed testimonial in nature.")

[498] United States v. Saget, 377 F.3d 223, 229 (2d Cir. 2004), *cert. denied,* 543 U.S. 1079 (2005); Commonwealth v. Gonsalves, 445 Mass. 1, 833 N.E.2d 549 (2005):

> In light of our definition of 'testimonial statements,' the judges of the Commonwealth must remain engaged gatekeepers, evaluating any out-of-court statements offered without benefit of confrontation. First, the judge must determine whether the statement is part of an affidavit, deposition, confession, or prior testimony at a preliminary hearing, before a grand jury, or at a former trial, or if it was procured through law enforcement interrogation (which does not include emergency questioning by law enforcement to secure a volatile scene or determine the need for or provide medical care). If so, it is per se testimonial and the confrontation clause applies. The statement is inadmissible unless the declarant testifies at trial or formally is unavailable and previously was subject to cross-examination. If the statement is not per se testimonial, the judge still must conduct a further fact-specific inquiry regarding whether a reasonable person in the declarant's position would anticipate the statement's being used against the accused in investigating and prosecuting the crime. As we have indicated above, judges are well suited to conduct this inquiry with respect to statements made to a police officer engaged in the community caretaking function

the health care provider's relationship with law enforcement or a multidisciplinary team in gathering evidence for possible prosecution may render the statements to the health care provider testimonial.[499]

Another view is that child abuse investigative interviews are not for the purpose of preserving testimony for trial but primarily for the health and welfare of the child or that the child may be too young to understand the legal system or that they may be giving statements for a legal proceeding.[500] Some courts hold that statements made to a physician for medical diagnosis or treatments are presumptively nontestimonial.[501]

---

or while securing a volatile scene. If the judge concludes the statement is testimonial, the confrontation clause governs its admissibility. The statement is inadmissible unless the declarant testifies at trial or formally is unavailable and previously was subject to cross-examination. If judge finds that an out-of-court statement is not testimonial, then the Commonwealth's rules of evidence alone govern admissibility, usually in relation to hearsay.

[499] Medena v. State, ___ Nev. ___, 131 P.3d 15 (2006) (finding error in the admission of such testimony harmless).

[500] State v. Bobadilla, 709 N.W. 2d 243 (Minn. 2006) (holding statements made by a three-year-old child sexual abuse victim in an interview with a county child protection worker with a law enforcement officer present were not testimonial); Flores v. State, ___ Nev. ___, 120 P.3d 1170, 1178–79 (2005) (finding statements to child protective worker and police investigator to be testimonial); State v. Brigham, ___ NC App. ___, 632 S.E.2d 498, 506 (2006) (holding child less than three years of age would not understand statements to doctor would be used at trial); State v. Edinger, 2006 Ohio 1527:

Although each factual situation must be judged on its own merits, the facts of this case lead this court to conclude that the statements P.S. made to the social worker are non-testimonial. (1) The social worker was not a governmental officer or employee. She was an employee of the Child Advocacy Center, which is part of Children's Hospital. The fact that the social worker was, in essence, a member of a team does not, in and of itself, make the social worker a government official absent a more direct and controlling police presence. (2) The social worker testified that her function in interviewing P.S. was solely for medical treatment and diagnosis and not to develop testimony for trial. (3) The forms used were prepared by the hospital and the social worker did not act at the direction of the police. (4) Although the police were permitted to watch the interview, they did not control the process. (5) The police were not overtly present and the child was not made aware of their presence. These procedures do not constitute the functional equivalent of a police interrogation.

[501] United States v. Peneaux, 432 F.3d 882, 896 (8th Cir. 2005), *cert. denied,* 2006 U.S. LEXIS 5930 (U.S. Oct. 2, 2006); People v. Vigil, 127 P.3d 916 (Colo. 2006):

The doctor was not a government official who produced the child's statements with a purpose of developing testimony for trial, nor was the police officer involved in producing the statements with a purpose of developing testimony for trial. . . . Turning now to the application of the objective witness test to the statements the child made to the doctor, we analyze the circumstances surrounding the statements to determine whether an objective witness in the position of the child would believe that his statements would be used at trial. We hold that no objective witness in the position of the child would believe that his statements to the doctor would be used at trial. Rather, an objective seven-year-old child would reasonably be interested in feeling

It may make a difference if a government person "initiated, participated, or was involved in" the statements at issue.[502]

One court specifically held that a domestic violence victim's statements to the police, ten minutes after arriving at the scene, while bleeding, moaning and crying, were admissible at trial after she took the stand and stated, "I don't want to testify no more!"[503] The statements to the police were deemed nontestimonial under the excited utterance exception.

Even traditional hearsay exceptions, sometimes called "firmly rooted" exceptions, must be reviewed to determine if the statements they encompass are testimonial in nature. There is a reference in Crawford that the holding in *White v. Illinois,* dealing with the spontaneous declaration and medical treatment exceptions to the hearsay rule, may be at tension with the Confrontation Clause requirement.[504] Federal[505] and state[506] courts, since *Crawford* have admitted statements under the excited utterance exception, finding they were non testimonial in nature.

The Supreme Court has clarified some of the ambiguity surrounding the admissibility of 911 calls under *Crawford* and whether 911 calls would still be admissible when the declarant is not available for cross-examination. In *Davis v. Washington,* the Supreme Court further defined "testimonial statement" and held that a statement made by a victim to a 911 operator was part of an "ongoing emergency" and not for evidence-gathering purposes and therefore admissible in trial.[507] In distinguishing testimonial and nontestimonial statements generated by questioning, the Court noted:

> better and would intend his statements to describe the source of his pain and his symptoms. In addition, an objectively reasonable seven-year-old child would expect that a doctor would use his statements to make him feel better and to formulate a medical diagnosis. He would not foresee the statements being used in a later trial.

Id. at 924, 926); State v. Scacchetti, 711 N.W.2d 508 (Minn. 2006) (court noted that given child's age it was not clear child understood purpose of questions); Foley v. State, 914 So.2d 677 (Miss. 2005); State v. Vaught, 268 Neb. 316, 318-19, 682 N.W.2d 284, 286-87 (2004).

[502] Scacchetti, 711 N.W.2d at 518. *See also* People v. Geno, 261 Mich. App. 624, 683 N.W.2d 687, *appeal denied,* 471 Mich. 921, 688 N.W.2d 829 (2004).

[503] Fowler v. State, 809 N.E.2d 960 (Ind. Ct. App. 2004).

[504] *Crawford,* 541 U.S. at 1368 n.8. *See* §10.31 for a discussion of the *White* holding.

[505] Leavitt v. Arave, 371 F.3d 663, 683–84 n.22 (9th Cir. 2004), *cert. denied,* 125 S. Ct. 2540 (2005) (reasoning that victim's excited utterance in emergency call to police was not "testimonial" because the victim, not the police, initiated their interaction and she was "in no way being interrogate" but instead "sought their help in ending a frightening intrusion into her home").

[506] State v. Forrest, 164 N.C. App. 272, 596 S.E.2d 22 (2004), *aff'd.,* 359 N.C. 424, 611 S.E.2d 883 (2005) (holding victim's statements to police after assault were nontestimonial in nature since they were made immediately after her rescue by police with no time for reflection or thought, were initiated by the victim, and she "immediately abruptly started talking", was nervous, shaking, and crying and her demeanor never changed during the conversation with the police officer).

[507] Davis v. Washington, 126 S. Ct. 2266 (2006).

Statements are non-testimonial when made in the course of police interrogation under circumstances objectively indicating that the primary purpose of the interrogation is to enable police assistance to meet an ongoing emergency. They are testimonial when the circumstances objectively indicate that there is no such ongoing emergency, and that the primary purpose of the interrogation is to establish or prove past events potentially relevant to later prosecution.[508]

Because the operator in *Davis* elicited answers that were necessary to resolve an ongoing emergency, the 911 call was properly admitted as non-testimonial hearsay despite the witness not attending trial and the defendant not having an opportunity for cross-examination.[509] The Court noted the 911 call may include the identity of the assailant when such information is the product of a limited inquiry to identify the assailant to determine if the perpetrator was a violent felon.

Apparently concerned that a police officer might take advantage of the rulings and use 911 calls or crime scene emergencies to "generate testimonial statements," the court added that the entirety of a 911 call or a crime scene statement might not be admissible if a police interrogation is initiated after the emergency subsides.[510]

Under the *Davis* definition of testimonial statements, the Court contrasted the facts of the 911 call with a police interview of the victim conducted at her home when police responded to a report of a domestic disturbance. After initially denying any assault by her husband, the complainant signed an affidavit accusing him of assault. She wrote:

> Broke our Furnace & shoved me down on the floor into the broken glass.
> Hit me in the chest and threw me down. Broke our lamps & phone. Tore
> up my van where I couldn't leave the house. Attacked my daughter.

The police testified to her statements and affidavit when she refused to testify. The Court found that the statements taken by the police officer took place some time after the events described were over, and the statements were "neither a cry for help nor the provision of information enabling officers immediately to end a threatening situation."[511] It analyzed:

> It is entirely clear from the circumstances that the interrogation was part of an investigation into possibly criminal past conduct . . . There was no emergency in progress; the interrogating officer testified that he had heard no arguments or crashing and saw no one throw or break anything. When the officers first arrived, [the victim] Amy told them that things were fine,

---

[508] Davis v. Washington, 126 S. Ct. 2266, 2273–2274 (2006).

[509] Davis v. Washington, 126 S. Ct. 2266, 2276 (2006).

[510] Trial courts "should redact or exclude the portions of any statement that have become testimonial, as they do, for example, with unduly prejudicial portions of otherwise admissible evidence." *Id.* at 2277.

[511] *Id.* at 2279.

and there was no immediate threat to her person. When the officer questioned Amy for the second time, and elicited the challenged statements, he was not seeking to determine (as in Davis) "what is happening," but rather "what happened." Objectively viewed, the primary, if not indeed the sole, purpose of the investigation was to investigate a possible crime – which is, of course, precisely what the officer *should* have done. [512]

At a crime scene, there may be nontestimonial statements from a victim or witness given to the police in response to inquiries necessary to defuse the danger to themselves and the potential victim.

The Court noted that if it can be demonstrated the defendant was involved in procuring or coercing the declarant's silence, the defendant "forfeits the constitutional right to confrontatio" and the otherwise inadmissible hearsay may be admissible. [513] The court suggested that the proponent should establish the forfeiture by a preponderance-of-evidence standard. [514] Other courts have recognized that a defendant forfeits his right of confrontation when his actions render the witness unavailable. [515]

Trial practitioners must beware of the pitfalls to objecting to hearsay statements. As noted in §10.54, a general hearsay objection, an evidentiary objection, does not preserve an objection based on the Constitutional Confrontation Clause. The objection that the hearsay statement violates the Confrontation Clause must be specifically stated on the record to preserve the objection. However, one court found that a *Crawford* violation affected the "fairness, integrity or public reputation of judicial proceedings." A court may nonetheless acknowledge that unconstitutionally inadmissible hearsay testimony, providing the heart of the prosecution's case is plain error requiring vacating a conviction even in the absence of an objection based on the right of confrontation. [516] Yet the improper admission of hearsay under a special child hearsay statute may be harmless when

---

[512] *Id.* at 2278.

[513] *Id.* at 2280. ("But when defendants seek to undermine the judicial process by procuring or coercing silence from witnesses and victims, the *Sixth Amendment* does not require courts to acquiesce. While defendants have no duty to assist the State in proving their guilt, they *do* have the duty to refrain from acting in ways that destroy the integrity of the criminal-trial system.")

[514] *Id.*

[515] People v. Moore, 117 P.3d 1 (Colo. Ct. App. 2004), *cert. denied,* 2004 Colo. LEXIS 772 (concluding that the defendant forfeited his right to claim a confrontation violation in connection with the admission of the victim's statements into evidence since he was responsible for her death); State v. Meeks, 277 Kan. 609, 88 P.3d 789 (2004); Gonzalez v. State, 153 S.W.3d 603 (Tex. Ct. App. 2004).

[516] United States v. Bruno, 383 F.3d 65 (2d Cir. 2004) (finding plain error in admission of co conspirator's plea, which was inadmissible based on *Crawford* and had not been decided at time of trial).

the hearsay does not relate to a major issue or element of the case[517] is cumulative[518] or there is overwhelming evidence of guilt.[519]

Also, it should be noted that the Confrontation Clause protection benefits a criminal defendant and not the prosecution. Thus, "unconstitutional" hearsay provisions may be available for a defendant to utilize.

§ 10.46 Necessity of findings.

In general, the trustworthiness of a child's out-of-court statement should be specifically determined by the trial judge.[520] It is imperative that affirmative findings of reliability are made justifying the admission of hearsay testimony under the residual or catchall exception to the hearsay rule. The requirement is set forth in many states' residual hearsay statutes. Even if a defendant does not request a hearing or object to the hearsay evidence, the failure of the trial court to make findings of reliability may require reversal of a defendant's conviction.[521] Appellate courts may require an adequate factual predicate to uphold the admission of such testimony.[522] It is improper to place the burden on the defendant to show unreliability.[523] In one case, a police detective was permitted

---

[517] State v. Herrmann, 2004 S.D. 53, 679 N.W.2d 503 (2004) (holding child's statements, even if impermissible under *Crawford,* did not identify the defendant and overwhelming DNA evidence rendered it harmless error).

[518] Purvis v. State, 829 N.E.2d 572 (Ind. Ct. App. 2005), *appeal denied,* 841 N.E.2d 180 (Ind. 2005), *cert. denied,* 2006 LEXIS 2345 (Mar. 20, 2006).

[519] T.P. v. State, 911 So.2d 1117 (Ala. Crim. App. 2004) (holding trial court erred in admitting the statements of the victim to the social worker because they were "testimonial hearsay" that violated defendant's Confrontation Clause rights since defendant did not have a chance to cross-examine the victim regarding them, but also found the error in admitting them was harmless given the other evidence in the case); People v. Vigil, 127 P.3d 916 (Colo. 2006); Medina v. State, ___ Nev. ___, 131 P.3d 15 (2006).

[520] Quevedo v. State, 113 Nev. 35, 930 P.2d 750 (1997); State v. Smith, 315 N.C. 76, 94, 337 S.E.2d 833, 845 (1985).

[521] Quevedo v. State, 113 Nev. 35, 930 P.2d 750 (1997); State v. D.G., 157 N.J. 112, 723 A.2d 588 (1999) (remanding to trial court for hearing on whether there was adequate basis for judge's admission of hearsay statements because trial court failed to conduct hearing and make findings); State v. Hirschkorn, 2002 ND 36, 640 N.W.2d 439 (2002) (The Supreme Court of North Dakota granted defendant a new trial, even in the absence of a hearsay objection by defendant as to the testimony of a mother and forensic interviewer about what the child told them. In applying the abuse of discretion standard of review to the trial court's evidentiary rulings under N.D.R. Ev. 803(24), the court found a lack of factual support, including credibility, to allow admission of the child's hearsay statements. This court set out a three-prong test for determining whether its admission into evidence constitutes "obvious error." Here, the defendant has the burden of showing: (1) error, (2) that is plain, and (3) that affects substantial rights); State v. Miller, 2001 N.D. 132, 631 N.W.2d 587 (2001); English v. State, 982 P.2d 139 (Wyo. 1999) (holding that trial court failed to make appropriate record to support its decision admitting child's hearsay statements).

[522] State v. Bratt, 250 Kan. 264, 273, 824 P.2d 983, 990 (1992); Felix v. State, 109 Nev. 151, 849 P.2d at 240 (hearing required to establish reliability).

[523] Felix v. State, 109 Nev. 151, 849 P.2d at 244.

to testify as to statements made by a child victim describing various ways her father had abused her. The child could not remember the abuse but could remember telling the police. While the victim may have been an unavailable witness because of her inability to remember details, the trial court made no such finding, nor did it make any specific findings on the record of trustworthiness, materiality, probative value, the interest of justice, or notice with respect to the hearsay testimony, and the appellate court thus reversed the defendant's conviction.[524]

In some situations, a court may apply a harmless error analysis to the failure of the trial court to make findings of reliability.[525]

§ 10.47   Is hearsay problem obviated when declarant testifies?

An issue dividing courts is whether hearsay issues are eliminated when the declarant testifies at trial. Sometimes a court will require that a party seeking to use an out-of-court statement as substantive evidence from a testifying declarant establishes a foundation from the declarant that the statements were made, even if the declarant cannot recall all the details of the out-of-court statement.[526] However, it may be insufficient to just call the witness to the stand to claim that the out-of-court statements are no longer hearsay since the declarant is testifying.[527] Some courts take the position that the opportunity to question the declarant eliminates the prejudice sought to be avoided by the hearsay rule.[528]

---

[524] Quimby v. State, 604 So. 2d 741 (Miss. 1992).

[525] Braunstein v. State, 118 Nev. 68, 40 P.3d 413 (2002) (finding that the failure to conduct a trustworthiness hearing does not warrant automatic reversal and that courts should apply a harmless error analysis to hearsay statements admitted without a hearing. "When applying a harmless error analysis to hearsay statements admitted without a hearing . . . the question of prime importance is whether or not the child to whom the hearsay statements are attributed testified at trial. If the child did testify and was subject to cross-examination, then no useful purpose is served by requiring . . . automatic reversal. An inquiry into the harm caused by the error is more appropriate." *Id.* at 420).

[526] Timmons v. State, 584 N.E.2d 1108, 1111 (Ind. 1992).

[527] Timmons v. State, 584 N.E.2d 1108, 1111 (Ind. 1992).

[528] Galindo v. United States, 630 A.2d 202, 209 (D.C. Cir. 1993) (referring to the fact that the victim testified in upholding trial court's admission of details of crime admitted under prompt-outcry exception); Griffin v. State, 243 Ga. App. 282, 531 S.E.2d 175, *cert. denied*, 2000 Ga. LEXIS 660 (Sept. 8, 2000) (any error in admission of child's hearsay statement was mitigated by child testifying under oath and being subject to cross-examination); People v. Hyland, 212 Mich. App. 701, 538 N.W.2d 465 (1995) ("Because the nine-year-old was the declarant testifying at the trial or hearing, her statement was not hearsay." *Id.* at 708, 538 N.W.2d at 468.); State v. Chappell, 97 Ohio App. 3d 515, 535, 646 N.E.2d 1191, 1203 (1994) (holding that when the defense has a chance to fully cross-examine a victim, hearing is no more prejudicial than the victim's testimony); Commonwealth v. Rakes, 398 Pa. Super. 440, 446–47, 581 A.2d 212, 216 (1990), *appeal denied*, 589 A.2d 690 (1991); Commonwealth v. Fanelli, 377 Pa. Super. 555, 572, 547 A.2d 1201, 1210 (1988), *appeal denied*, 523 Pa. 641, 565 A.2d 1165 (1989); State v. Bubeck, 1997 Wash. App. LEXIS 367, *review denied*, 133 Wash. 2d 1011, 946 P.2d 401 (1997) (holding that because child

Similarly, if the hearsay declaration falls within a firmly rooted exception, it may not be necessary to produce the declarant,[529] and the Confrontation Clause is not violated if the declarant is produced and unable to recall the event in question.[530]

Another view is that a testifying declarant provides "an additional safeguard" in a hearsay statement, a factor to consider in determining the propriety or prejudice of the hearsay testimony.[531]

The exact parameters of the approach that hearsay is obviated when the declarant testifies are yet to be determined. If the declarant is available and testifies, to what extent must he or she be able to answer questions on cross-examination? Suppose a child is available but refuses to answer questions or "freezes" while being questioned? How effective a cross-examination must be provided by the testifying declarant? At least in the case of prior statements of identification under Federal Rule of Evidence 801(d)(1)(c), the Supreme Court of the United States has ruled that the witness need not recall the incident or facts surrounding the identification.[532]

Other courts have held that a child witness need not be able to recall details of events or respond to all questions to satisfy the confrontation clause.[533] A

---

complainant testified about rape at trial erroneous admission of her hearsay statements would not violate confrontation clause). *See also* KAN. STAT. ANN. § 60-460, which states:

> Evidence of a statement which is made other than by a witness while testifying at the hearing, offered to prove the truth of the matter stated, is hearsay evidence and inadmissible except: (a) *Previous statements of persons present.* A statement previously made by a person who is present at the hearing and available for cross-examination with respect to the statement and its subject matter, provided the statement would be admissible if made by declarant while testifying as a witness. (emphasis added).

[529] *See* §§ 10.27 and 10.35.

[530] United States v. McHorse, 179 F.3d 889, 899–901 (10th Cir.), *cert. denied*, 528 U.S. 944 (1999) (upholding admission into evidence of hearsay statements made pursuant to medical treatment exception, even though seven-year-old child could not remember events surrounding incident).

[531] Baker v. State, 228 Ga. App. 32, 33, 491 S.E.2d 78, 80 (1997). *See also* Commonwealth v. Whelton, 428 Mass. 24, 696 N.E.2d 540 (1998) (holding the error in recalling a statement as an excited utterance minimized by the opportunity to cross-examine declarant); State v. Brown, 953 S.W.2d 133 (Mo. Ct. App. 1997) (child declarant's availability for cross-examination a factor to consider in the reliability of the hearsay testimony).

[532] United States v. Owens, 484 U.S. 554 (1988). *See also* Delaware v. Fensterer, 474 U.S. 15, 20 (1985) ("Generally speaking, the Confrontation Clause guarantees an opportunity for effective cross-examination, not cross-examination that is effective in whatever way, and to whatever extent, the defense might wish."). *See also* discussion of *Owens*, on identification, in § 8.30.

[533] Bear Stops v. United States, 339 F.3d 777 (8th Cir. 2003), *cert. denied*, 540 U.S. 1094 (2003):

> 'Because Bear Stops had the opportunity to cross-examine the child witnesses, there is no Confrontation Clause violation from the admission of the alleged hearsay

child's recantation of prior allegations does not defeat the admissibility of a hearsay statement when the child takes the stand and can be cross-examined about the alleged acts — and out-of-court statements. [534] The theory behind the Federal Rules of Evidence placing prior consistent statements outside the scope of the hearsay rules is that the declarant is testifying.

More courts follow the traditional view that the hearsay character of a proffered out-of-court assertion is not changed by the declarant testifying at trial. The issue can arise not only with a child's statements, but also with a child's play with dolls or drawings. In rejecting the theory that a child's out-of-court drawings were admissible because the victim testified, the Kentucky Supreme Court stated:

> The error in admitting this hearsay was not cured when [the victim] identified and explained the statements in court subject to cross-examination. The evidence remains objectionable because the declarant was not subject to cross-examination at the time the statements were made, nor was the declarant a witness before the jury when they were made. These conditions are necessary to insure the statements were originally made without improper influence or suggestion and to give the jury the opportunity to observe the demeanor of the declarant while making the statement. These are the dangers of hearsay, which are not eliminated by providing the declarant at trial. They can only be eliminated by not introducing the out-of-court statement (the drawing) into evidence. [535]

---

evidence, and we find it unnecessary to consider whether the statements fell within any recognized hearsay exception.'

Bugh v. Mitchell, 329 F.3d 496 (6th Cir. 2003) (Four-year-old child's hearsay statements were admitted at trial and child testified. She answered non-verbally through much of her questioning and did not remember in response to many questions. Despite her memory failure, court found defendant had an adequate confrontation of the child witness and inquiry into reliability of hearsay statements was not required).

While the mere physical presence of a child victim on the witness stand does not necessarily eliminate *Confrontation Clause* concerns, we will not second-guess the state court trial judge's determination that Robin was mature enough to testify and to be cross-examined. Counsel had the opportunity to cross-examine Robin, and this opportunity served to satisfy Bugh's confrontation rights. Robin's inability to recall many of the details surrounding her statements does not lead us to conclude otherwise.

Id. at 509; United States v. Spotted War Bonnet, 933 F.2d 1471 (8th Cir.), *cert. denied*, 502 U.S. 1101 (1991) (finding no denial of right of confrontation where child testified, but could not recall events set forth in a pretrial statement); State v. Guerra, 834 So. 2d 1206, 1216–17 (La. Ct. App. 2002), *writ denied*, 842 So. 2d 398 (La. 2003) (holding in a case interpreting use of a child's videotaped statement that statutory requirement that child be available was met by child taking stand even though answers were not responsive; significantly, this was not a case where child refused to testify).

[534] State v. Clark, 139 Wash. 2d 152, 985 P.2d 377 (1999).

[535] Hellstrom v. Commonwealth, 825 S.W.2d 612, 615 (Ky. 1992). *See also* State v. Martin, 356 So. 2d 1370, 1374 (La. 1978).

One court holds that mere availability of a witness for questioning does not make a hearsay statement admissible, particularly where the hearsay consists of unsworn oral statements.[536]

§ 10.48 Prior consistent statements as exception to hearsay rule.

A prior consistent statement is generally inadmissible as self-serving hearsay. However, the following exception to the rule, which is followed in many states and is often encountered in sexual assault trials, is set out in Federal Rule of Evidence Rule 801:

> (d) Statements which are not hearsay. A statement is not hearsay if — (1) Prior statement by witness. The declarant testifies at the trial or hearing and is subject to cross-examination concerning the statement, and the statement is . . . (B) consistent with the declarant's testimony and is offered to rebut an express or implied charge against the declarant of recent fabrication or improper influence or motive.[537]

Thus, under this exception, the declarant must testify and be subject to cross-examination, and the prior statement must be consistent with the declarant's trial testimony and rebut an express or implied charge of fabrication, improper influence, or motive. If the declarant does not testify, a predicate for the admission of the prior consistent statement has not been met.[538]

The fact that a child testifies, but is unresponsive to certain questions, does not defeat the requirement that they must be subject to examination, as long as the witness is able to answer some questions about the prior statement.[539] The nature of the cross-examination should be considered; the questions may be too complicated for a child to answer. For example, a child may refuse to answer several questions because she did not know a word used in the questions.[540] The requirement of availability for cross-examination would require more than the mere presence of the witness, but the context of the cross-examination and the nature and extent of the nonresponsiveness should be evaluated.

Some jurisdictions will require more than merely placing a witness on the stand who is under oath and responding to questions. One court has held that utilization of a prior statement under its state law, unlike federal law,

---

[536] Nucci v. Proper, 95 N.Y.2d 597, 744 N.E.2d 128, 721 N.Y.S.2d 593 (2001).

[537] FED. R. EVID. 801(d)(1)(B).

[538] United States v. Bordeaux, 400 F.3d 548 (8th Cir. 2005) (reversing defendant's conviction in part because prior consistent statements were admitted into evidence, even though child did not testify at trial).

[539] United States v. Tome, 3 F.3d 342, 347–49 (10th Cir. 1993), *rev'd on other grounds*, 513 U.S. 150 (1995). This issue is also discussed in the following section, § 10.47, notes 532-533.

[540] United States v. Tome F.3d 342, 348 (10th Cir. 1993), *rev'd on other grounds*, 513, U.S. 150 (1995).

. . . requires, as a guarantee of the trustworthiness of a prior inconsistent statement, that the witness be subject to cross-examination about the subject matter of the prior statement, that is, that the witness be capable of testifying substantively about the event, allowing the trier of fact to meaningfully compare the prior version of the event with the version recounted at trial before the statement would be admissible as substantive evidence of the matter stated therein.[541]

The prior statement offered must be consistent with the witness's trial testimony. When the statement supplies significant additional information such as the time, place, and frequency of sexual acts that are not part of a victim's testimony, the admission of the prior statement is reversible error.[542] On the other hand, perfect consistency is not necessarily required.[543] The statement may contain some new or additional information, but should be substantially similar.[544]

Improper influence can be suggested by cross-examination about the number of contacts or discussions a complainant has had with the prosecutor, law enforcement officials, case workers, or family members.[545] A classic example

---

[541] State v. Canady, 80 Haw. 469, 480–81, 911 P.2d 104, 115–16 (1996).

[542] Commonwealth v. Smith, 402 Pa. Super. 257, 586 A.2d 957 (1991).

[543] Van Meter v. State, 743 P.2d 385 (Alaska Ct. App. 1987); Sorensen v. State, 895 P.2d 454 (Wyo. 1995) (Complainant's testimony of "having sex," which defendant equated with intercourse, is consistent with prior statement by her that defendant had touched her private parts. "The fact that the testimony is susceptible to different interpretations is not relevant so long as one interpretation is consistent. If there is a question as to the consistency of the statements, the proper place to divine the witness'[s] meaning is during cross-examination, not on appeal.").

[544] State v. Goforth, 170 N.C. App. 584, 614 S.E.2d 313 (2005), cert. denied 359 N.C. 859, 619 S.E.2d 854 (2005).

[545] United States v. Cherry, 938 F.2d 748 (7th Cir. 1991); Bing v. State, 23 Ark. App. 19, 740 S.W.2d 156 (1987) (prior statement permitted to rebut inference that sexual abuse allegation was the result of contact between victim, her parents, and prosecutor); State v. Hydock, 51 Conn. App. 753, 770–71, 725 A.2d 379, 389, appeal denied, 248 Conn. 921, 733 A.2d 846 (1999) (holding that cross-examination suggesting that child was testifying not from memory but from a suggestion of other members of family opened the door to prior consistent statement); Begley v. State, 483 So. 2d 70, 73 (Fla. Dist. Ct. App. 1986) (child's prior consistent statement admissible because "an effort was made to impeach the child's credibility by charging that her testimony had been improperly influenced by both her mother and the state. The admission of her statement to her mother lessened the force of the impeaching evidence by showing the victim had made a consistent statement before she allegedly had been improperly influenced by the state. Therefore, her prior consistent statement was admissible to rebut this implied charge."); State v. Capper, 539 N.W.2d 361, 366 (Iowa 1995) (defense counsel's suggestions on cross-examination of children, that they changed their story after pre-trial depositions, opened the door to their prior consistent statements); People v. Wilens, 198 A.D.2d 463, 603 N.Y.S.2d 585 (1993), appeal denied, 83 N.Y.2d 812, 633 N.E.2d 503, 611 N.Y.S.2d 148 (1994) (social worker's testimony of child rape victim's prior consistent statement given prior to her grand jury testimony admissible to rehabilitate child after defendant's attorney suggested the child had been influenced by prosecutor in her testimony); State v. Brisco, 2000 Ohio App. LEXIS 3835 (Aug. 24, 2000) (holding defense attorney's questioning

would be cross-examination suggesting that a victim had been coached by social service caseworkers or counselors,[546] or their mother.[547]

Cross-examination that a victim was influenced by her contacts with the police, investigators, or the prosecutor opens the door to the admission of a prior consistent statement.[548] Similarly, suggesting that a victim changed her testimony concerning penetration to conform to the prosecution's superseding indictment opens the door to the victim's prior statements.[549] Suggesting that a victim had told her aunt or mother something different from what she testified opens the door to a prior consistent statement for corroborative purposes.[550] Some courts relax the traditional requirements for introduction of a prior consistent statement in sexual assault cases.[551]

---

child about the number of people who questioned her, and that interviews helped child "remember stuff" "amounted to an implied charge of recent fabrication" justifying introduction of prior consistent statement); Commonwealth v. McEachin, 371 Pa. Super. 188, 537 A.2d 883, *appeal denied*, 520 Pa. 603, 553 A.2d 965 (1988); State v. Thaxton, 2000 Tenn. Crim. App. LEXIS 770 (Oct. 10, 2000) (child's statement to protective services worker admissible as a prior consistent statement to rebut child's statement to a neighbor that defendant had never touched the victim); Lacey v. State, 803 P.2d 1364 (Wyo. 1990).

[546] United States v. Red Feather, 865 F.2d 169, 171 (8th Cir. 1989); United States v. Robles, 53 M.J. 783, 793–94 (A.F.C.C.A. 2000) (allegation of improper influence and fabrication of testimony are raised when counsel emphasizes a child told her story "over and over" and that investigators and therapists suggested answers and facts to child justified admitting child's prior consistent statements to rebut what was in effect a change of recent fabrication and improper influence); People v. Litzenberger, 234 A.D.2d 947, 652 N.Y.S.2d 912 (1996) (admitting victim's prior consistent statement because of defense suggestion she had been influenced by a caseworker).

[547] State v. Jeffcoat, 350 S.C. 392, 565 S.E.2d 321 (2002):

> We agree with the State that defense counsel raised the issue of improper influence or 'coaching' by asking Victim whether she 'practiced' before testifying and whether anyone had told her what to say. Counsel specifically inquired whether Victim had talked to Mother about what she was going to say in court and whether the solicitor told Victim 'what things to say in the courtroom.' These questions impliedly charged improper influences by Mother and the prosecution.

Id. at 397, 565 S.E.2d at 324.

[548] Van Meter v. State, 743 P.2d 385, 389 (Alaska App. 1987); Joines v. State, 264 Ga. App. 558, 591 S.E.2d 454, 1508 (2003), *cert. denied*, 2004 Ga. LEXIS 299 (Mar. 29, 2004) (holding cross-examination of victim suggesting victim had fabricated dates and that she was coached by prosecutor about dates permitted introduction of victim's prior consistent statement).

[549] United States v. Barrett, 937 F.2d 1346 (8th Cir.), *cert. denied*, 502 U.S. 916 (1991).

[550] State v. Livingston, 907 S.W.2d 392, 398 (Tenn. 1995).

[551] Parker v. State, 581 So. 2d 1211 (Ala. Crim. App. 1990); People v. Eppens, 979 P.2d 14 (Colo. 1999); State v. Pollitt, 205 Conn. 61, 530 A.2d 155 (1987) (holding no requirement of recent fabrication to rehabilitate a sexual assault witness without prior consistent statement); Commonwealth v. Hunzer, 2005 PA Super. 13, 868 A.2d 498, *appeal denied*, 2005 Pa. LEXIS 1756, 880 A.2d 1237 (2005) (finding cross-examination of child about her inconsistent statements and defendant's denial that he placed his finger and tongue in child's vagina created an inference of recent fabrication justifying admission of child's prior consistent statements).

Tennessee has taken a more liberal approach to the prior consistent statement rule, allowing the prior consistent statement when the honesty or accuracy of the complainant's account is challenged.[552] Some courts will allow the prior consistent statement, even if the complainant is cross-examined about a delay in reporting.[553]

Use of a prior consistent statement to rehabilitate a witness who has been impeached with a prior inconsistent statement may be permissible, particularly if the witness is a child.[554]

Cross-examining a victim about her intention to bring a civil suit against the defendant to receive crime victim compensation money invokes a motive post-dating the sexual assault allegation in the view of one court.[555]

There should be a sufficient foundation to admit the statements. Introducing a victim's handwritten notes and describing the defendant's abuse of her is reversible error when they are introduced before cross-examination, and the defense did not suggest the complainant's testimony was recently fabricated, improperly influenced, or motivated.[556]

Only statements antedating the alleged influencing of a sexual assault victim are admissible as a prior consistent statement.[557] If the prior consistent statement is improperly used on direct examination of the victim, a curative instruction should be given by the court.[558]

Some courts take a more restricted view of when a prior consistent statement can be admitted as a recent fabrication and limit the admission to the charge of recent fabrication by the witness, which means the witness made up a false story well after the event.[559] This limits significantly the areas of cross-examination that will trigger the right to introduce prior consistent statements.

Many courts take the view that asserting that a victim was lying or fabricating all along does not avoid application of the prior consistent statement exception.

---

[552] State v. Livingston, 907 S.W.2d 392, 398 (Tenn. 1995), *above* note 550. *See also* State v. Jones, 2001 Tenn. Crim. App. LEXIS 356 at *6–15 (May 7, 2001) (holding child's prior consistent statement admissible in evaluating victim's credibility, but not as evidence of matters asserted in it, given the defense counsel's attempt to impeach her).

[553] Shamsuddeen v. State, 255 Ga. App. 326, 565 S.E.2d 544 (2002) (finding trial court did not err in admitting the victim's prior consistent statement when defendant placed in issue the victim's veracity by cross-examining her about the delay in reporting the incident, as well as her drug and alcohol use the weekend the crime took place).

[554] Monday v. State, 792 So. 2d 1278 (Fla. Ct. App. 2001) (noting the propriety of court's decision to allow use of prior consistent statement on the issue of the date of the offense, an issue for which the witness was impeached, particularly in light of the age of the impeached witness).

[555] State v. Kholi, 672 A.2d 429, 438 (R.I. 1996).

[556] Miller v. Commonwealth, 77 S.W.3d 566 (Ky. 2002).

[557] People v. McDaniel, 81 N.Y.2d 10, 611 N.E.2d 265, 595 N.Y.S.2d 364 (1993).

[558] People v. McDaniel, 81 N.Y.2d 10, 611 N.E.2d 265, 595 N.Y.S.2d 364 (1993).

[559] *See, e.g.*, People v. Davis, 44 N.Y.2d 269, 376 N.E.2d 901, 405 N.Y.S.2d 428 (1978).

Once the implication of improper influence on the part of a prosecuting attorney is made, the door is opened to the prior consistent statement.[560] On the other hand, the door is not opened to a prior consistent statement merely because the witness made a prior inconsistent statement. A prior inconsistent statement that is an attack on credibility and that does not suggest recent fabrication or improper influences does not allow the introduction of prior consistent statements.[561] For example, suggesting that a victim wants to "get even" does not necessarily allow introduction of a prior consistent statement.[562]

Under the majority view, to be admissible, the prior consistent statement must have been made prior to the time of the alleged motive to fabricate or the alleged improper influence.[563] The United States Supreme Court in *Tome v. United*

[560] State v. Scheffelman, 250 Mont. 334, 820 P.2d 1293, 1296 (1991).

[561] Woodard v. State, 269 Ga. 317, 320, 496 S.E.2d 896, 899 (1998) (holding that for prior consistent statement to be admitted, affirmative charges of recent fabrication, improper influence or improper motive must be raised during cross-examination; otherwise, admission of prior consistent statement constitutes bolstering); State v. Palabay, 9 Haw. App. 414, 428, 844 P.2d 1, 8–9 (1992), *cert. denied*, 74 Haw. 652, 849 P.2d 81 (1993) ("[T]he fact that complainant was impeached when defendant testified to facts that contradicted her version of the facts . . . does not amount to a 'prior consistent statement' of complainant so as to constitute an attack on her credibility."); Commonwealth v. Zukoski, 370 Mass. 23, 27, 345 N.E.2d 690, 693 (1976); State v. Mensing, 297 Mont. 172, 991 P.2d 950 (1999) (questioning victim about inconsistencies in her testimony and implying that memory was faulty as a result of drinking alcohol and smoking marijuana on night in question did not open door to prior consistent statement although error was harmless); Commonwealth v. Jubilee, 403 Pa. Super. 589, 597–98, 589 A.2d 1112, 1116, *appeal denied*, 529 Pa. 617, 600 A.2d 534 (1991) (reversing defendant's conviction because of the prejudicial effect of bolstering the victim's testimony through prior consistent statements); State v. Livingston, 907 S.W.2d 392, 398 (Tenn. 1995) (mildly questioning on cross-examination child's disagreements with the defendant did not open the door to admission of prior consistent statement); State v. Mainiero, 189 Wis. 2d 80, 102, 525 N.W.2d 304, 313 (1994) (Court improperly admitted complainant's prior consistent statement since cross-examination of complainant probed whether complainant had ever complained of sexual intercourse with the defendant, which was not an express or implied charge of recent fabrication or improper influence or motive. However, such improper admission of prior consistent statement evidence was harmless error).

[562] Fields v. Commonwealth, 905 S.W.2d 510 (Ky. Ct. App. 1995) (holding defense witness's testimony that victim vowed to "get even" did not allow introduction of prior consistent statement).

[563] United States v. Miller, 874 F.2d 1255, 1271–74 (9th Cir. 1989); State v. Martin, 135 Ariz. 552, 663 P.2d 236 (1983) (holding that court erred in admitting prior consistent statements of child without determining when alleged motive to fabricate began); Phillips v. State, 241 Ga. App. 764, 527 S.E.2d 604 (2000) (reversing defendant's conviction due to admission of child's prior consistent statement which was not made before time of alleged improper motive of child's antagonism toward grandmother after grandmother was appointed guardian); People v. Buckley, 43 Ill. App. 3d 53, 356 N.E.2d 1113 (1976); Caley v. State, 650 N.E.2d 54 (Ind. Ct. App. 1995) (holding that prior consistent statement must have been made prior to the alleged motive to fabricate; however, in this case the error did not substantially prejudice defendant's rights); Fields v. Commonwealth, 905 S.W.2d 510 (Ky. Ct. App. 1995); Owens v. State, 666 So. 2d 814, 816 (Miss. 1995); State v. Scheffelman, 250 Mont. 334, 820 P.2d 1293, 1297 (1991); People v. Davis, 44 N.Y.2d 269, 277, 376 N.E.2d 901, 405 N.Y.S.2d 428 (1978); State v. Jeffcoat, 350 S.C. 392, 565 S.E.2d 321 (2002).

States[564] followed the common law principle that to be admissible, a prior consistent statement should be made prior to any improper influence or motive to lie. It notes that because prior consistent statements can be used as substantive evidence, it is all the more important that evidentiary preconditions be met before admitting statements under the prior consistent statement rule. This decision brings all federal courts in line with the common law requirement that prior consistent statements be made prior to the time of the alleged motive to fabricate or the alleged improper influence. It forces a review of those courts that had permitted prior consistent statements of sexual assault complainants under a "rule of completeness theory."[565] The *Tome* decision, however, did not address whether the hearsay statements would have been admissible under the residual hearsay exception or some other exception.

A general attack on witness credibility does not open the door to a prior consistent statement under *Tome*.[566] If motive to fabricate exists at the time of the prior consistent statement, it may be reversible error to admit the statement.[567]

Wyoming does not follow the Supreme Court ruling in *Tome*, and permits a prior consistent statement without showing the statement was made prior to the motive to fabricate.[568]

Prior consistent statements can be used for other purposes, such as explaining the context of an inconsistent statement offered by an adversary. In this situation, the prior consistent statement is being used to respond to an attack on the witness's credibility and will not be substantive evidence.[569] For example, FBI reports of a 12-year-old rape victim's interview were admissible to demonstrate consistencies when the same reports were used to attack the victim on cross-examination for inconsistencies in her testimony.[570] The theory supporting admissibility is that the entire police reports explain the significance of the inconsistencies and provide the broader context of the alleged inconsistent statements.[571] If the suggestion is that a child's protective worker influenced

---

[564] 513 U.S. 150 (1995).

[565] *See, e.g.*, State v. Sharp, 180 Wis. 2d 640, 511 N.W.2d 316 (1993).

[566] Thomas v. United States, 41 F.3d 1109, 1119 (7th Cir. 1994) (noting that a party may "impeach for lack of credibility without going so far as to charge recent fabrication"); Lancaster v. State, 43 P.3d 80, 90–92 (Wyo. 2002).

[567] United States v. Collicott, 92 F.3d 973 (9th Cir. 1996) (reversing defendant's conviction because of prosecution's "windfall of inadmissible evidence" through hearsay offered as prior consistent statement).

[568] Lancaster v. State, 2002 WYO 45, 43 P.3d 80 (2002); Beartusk v. State, 6 P.3d 138 (Wyo. 2000).

[569] *See* note 561.

[570] United States v. Payne, 944 F.2d 1458 (9th Cir. 1991), *cert. denied*, 503 U.S. 975 (1992).

[571] Monday v. State, 792 So. 2d 1278 (Fla. Ct. App. 2001) (noting prior consistent statements had greater value because witness was a child and helped explain contradictions in her testimony

the victim to make the complaint, the prior statement offered to rebut that allegation must have been made prior to the victim's contact with the protective worker. A police officer who is cross-examined about facts that he omitted in his grand jury testimony but testified to at trial can be rehabilitated by the prior consistent statements in his reports, *i.e.*, the facts omitted in grand jury testimony were included in his reports.[572] Some courts have held that the prior consistent statements must be made even before the witness could have anticipated their use at trial.[573]

However, admitting a prior consistent statement to explain the context of the statement does not necessarily open the door to the entire statement of the complainant. It is improper to admit into evidence the complainant's entire statement when it contains a prejudicial or detailed statement about the defendant's conduct which does not bear on the issues raised on cross-examination.[574] Most courts hold that, under Rule 801, prior statements are admitted as substantive evidence.[575] Other courts admit a prior consistent statement for the jury to consider on the issue of credibility and not for its truth.[576] When a court admits a prior consistent statement to rehabilitate a witness or only on the issue of credibility, a limiting jury instruction may be required.[577] Another factor in admissibility of a prior consistent statement may be whether the prior consistent statement is more probative than prejudicial.[578]

---

concerning the date of the offense. *Id.* at 1471); State v. Hennessey, 142 N.H. 149, 697 A.2d 930 (1997) (admitting complainant's prior consistent statements in police reports as a result of defense counsel's attacks on inconsistencies in victim's testimonies and police reports); State v. Martin, 138 N.H. 508, 643 A.2d 946 (1994) (holding that sexual assault victim's prior consistent statement was properly admitted to provide jury with a "broader context from which to evaluate the victim's credibility after the defendant had used inconsistent portions of her prior statements to impeach her. That the defense also intended for the inconsistent portions of the statements to contribute to its theory of recent fabrication or motive does not preclude the state from introducing a more complete version of those very statements for purely rehabilitative purposes, even if the statements do not predate the motive to fabricate." *Id.* at 514, 643 A.2d at 950.).

[572] People v. Stanley, 135 A.D.2d 910, 522 N.Y.S.2d 309 (1987).

[573] Commonwealth v. Hutchinson, 521 Pa. 482, 487, 556 A.2d 370, 372 (1989).

[574] State v. Bingham, 124 Idaho 698, 864 P.2d 144 (1993).

[575] United States v. Miller, 874 F.2d 1255, 1271–74 (9th Cir. 1989). *But see Payne*, 944 F.2d at 1458 (9th Cir. 1991) *cert. denied*, 503 U.S. 975 (1992); United States v. Brennan, 798 F.2d 581, 587–88 (2d Cir. 1986); United States v. Harris, 761 F.2d 394, 398–400 (7th Cir. 1985) (both holding that Rule 801 statements may be admitted for substantive evidence or credibility depending on circumstances); Donaldson v. State, 244 Ga. App. 89, 534 S.E.2d 839 (2000).

[576] State v. Valentine, 240 Conn. 395, 412–13, 692 A.2d 727, 737 (1997); State v. Woody, 124 N.C. App. 296, 303, 477 S.E.2d 462, 465 (1996) (holding that prior consistent statement in North Carolina "is admissible to strengthen his/her credibility"); Moore v. Commonwealth, 222 Va. 72, 79, 278 S.E.2d 822, 826 (1981).

[577] United States v. White, 11 F.3d 1446, 1449 (8th Cir. 1993) (limiting instruction required when prior consistent statement admitted to rehabilitate witness and not as substantive evidence); State v. Jones, 2001 Tenn. Crim. App. LEXIS 356 at *15 (May 7, 2001).

[578] Smith v. State, 255 Ga. 685, 341 S.E.2d 451 (1986); Lancaster v. State, 43 P.3d 80, 92–93 (Wyo. 2002).

§ 10.49   Prior inconsistent statements as exception to hearsay rule.

Many child sexual assault victims recant their allegations or deny any abuse at all. Rule 801 permits prior inconsistent statements as follows:

> (d) Statements which are not hearsay: A statement is not hearsay if (1) Prior statement by witness. The declarant testifies at the trial or hearing and is subject to cross-examination concerning the statement, and the statement is (A) inconsistent with the declarant's testimony, and was given under oath subject to the penalty of perjury at a trial, hearing, or other proceeding, or in a deposition.[579]

If a victim denies the sexual assault, generally the victim can be impeached of the prior inconsistent statement.[580] However, some courts hold that when a witness cannot remember an event, that testimony is not "inconsistent" with a prior written statement unless the trial court makes a preliminary finding that the witness's lack of memory is feigned or actual.[581] Because of the frequency of recantation in child sexual abuse cases, this is a significant exception.

Most courts will allow the prior inconsistent statement, if admissible, to be substantive evidence of the facts in the statement, if the declarant testifies and is subject to cross-examination. It is insufficient to make the declarant available for cross-examination without actually calling the declarant.[582] Excessive use of this hearsay exception prior to the witness being called may be improper.[583]

The United States Supreme Court has held that admission of a prior inconsistent statement for substantive purposes does not violate the confrontation

---

[579] FED. R. EVID. 801(d)(1)(A). *See also* CAL. EVID. CODE § 1235; ILL. ANN. STAT. ch. 725, para. 5/115-10.

[580] State v. Thomason, C.C.A. No. 02C01-9903-CC-00086, 2000 Tenn. Crim. App. LEXIS 229 (Mar. 7, 2000).

[581] Corbett v. State, 130 Md. App. 408, 746 A.2d 954, *cert. denied*, 359 Md. 31, 753 A.2d 3 (2000).

[582] State v. Moran, 151 Ariz. 378, 728 P.2d 248 (1986); People v. Jones, 105 Cal. App. 3d 572, 164 Cal. Rptr. 605 (1980) (holding in a rape prosecution that use of prior inconsistent statements as substantive evidence is proper under California constitution; prior statement involved extrajudicial confession of defendant's brother who testified as defense witness); People v. Manson, 71 Cal. App. 3d 1, 139 Cal. Rptr. 275 (1977), *cert. denied*, 435 U.S. 953 (1978); Montoya v. People, 740 P.2d 992 (Colo. 1987); Carswell v. State, 179 Ga. App. 56, 345 S.E.2d 66 (1986) (admitting as substantive evidence videotaped statement describing instances of sexual molestation which were recanted at trial); State v. Clark, 83 Haw. 289, 926 P.2d 194 (1996) (holding defendant's wife's prior inconsistent statement to detective that he stabbed her admissible as substantive evidence of guilt where wife testified that she made the prior statement, that it was a lie and statement was tape recorded); State v. Ganotisi, 79 Haw. 342, 902 P.2d 977 (1995) (holding step-daughter's prior inconsistent statement admissible at trial when defendant had adequate opportunity to cross-examine her); People v. Sambo, 197 Ill. App. 3d 574, 554 N.E.2d 1080 (1990); Dausch v. State, 616 N.E.2d 13 (Ind. 1993); Patterson v. State, 324 N.E.2d 482 (Ind. 1975); LaPierre v. State, 108 Nev. 528, 836 P.2d 56 (1992) (holding child's prior inconsistent statement admissible for impeachment and as substantive evidence).

[583] Modesitt v. State, 578 N.E.2d 649 (Ind. 1991).

clause.[584] The same decision noted the importance of the declarant testifying in court and being available for cross-examination on the out-of-court and in-court statements in which case "the usual dangers of hearsay are largely non-existent where the witness testifies at trial."[585] Generally, before impeaching a witness with a prior inconsistent statement, the party offering the prior statement must establish the prior statement was made by the witness.[586] If the witness admits the prior inconsistent statement, usually the prior statement is not admissible.[587] Many of these decisions are based on prior statements, which are in writing, recorded, or otherwise reliable.[588] Prior oral statements are likely to lack the reliability for admission as evidence. Admitting a prior inconsistent statement that is not in writing or recorded may be reversible error.[589] A parent's signature

---

[584] California v. Green, 399 U.S. 149, 165 (1970).

[585] California v. Green, 399 U.S. 149, 155 (1970).

[586] People v. Robinson, 267 A.D.2d 1031, 700 N.Y.S.2d 892 (1999) (holding that before sexual assault victim's prior inconsistent statement, defendant was requested to inform witness of circumstances of making statement and inquire whether she in fact made it); Garza v. State, 18 S.W.3d 813, 821 (Tex. Ct. App. 2000).

[587] See, e.g., State v. Noble, 90 Ohio St. 3d 1403, 734 N.E.2d 834 (2000).

[588] State v. Whelan, 200 Conn. 743, 513 A.2d 86, cert. denied, 479 U.S. 994 (1986)

> We, therefore, adopt today a rule allowing the substantive use of prior written inconsistent statements, signed by the declarant, who has personal knowledge of the facts stated, when the declarant testifies at trial and is subject to cross-examination. The hazard of error is greatly lessened with respect to prior inconsistent written statements signed by the declarant. Errors in transcription are rare and methods of detecting and establishing forgery or alterations are widely available. [citation omitted]. Prior oral statements of a witness, easily manufactured and often difficult to rebut, should not be used to prove an element of a crime essential to guilt. Although the requirement that prior statements be written and signed by the declarant is not an absolute guaranty of reliability, it does provide significant assurance of an accurate rendition of the statement and that the declarant realized it would be relied upon.

Id. at 753–54, 513 A.2d at 92; Mickel v. Pennsylvania Bd. of Prob. & Parole, 810 A.2d 728 (Pa. Commw. Ct. 2002).

[589] Commonwealth v. Wilson, 550 Pa. 518, 707 A.2d 1114 (1998)

> We hold, . . . when the prior inconsistent statement is a contemporaneous verbatim recording of a witness' statement, the recording of the statement must be an electronic, audiotaped, or videotaped recording in order to be considered as substantive evidence. This will ensure that the requisite degree of reliability demonstrated will be similar to instances in which the statement was given under oath at a formal legal proceeding or the statement is reduced to a writing signed and adopted by the declarant. Since the questions and answers contained in the police report introduced into evidence in this case were not recorded on audiotape or videotape, the evidence was improperly admitted.

Id. at 527, 707 A.2d at 1118; Commonwealth v. Brady, 510 Pa. 123, 507 A.2d 66 (1986); Commonwealth v. Sopota, 403 Pa. Super. 1, 587 A.2d 805, appeal denied, 528 Pa. 629, 598 A.2d 283 (1991); Gelhaar v. State, 41 Wis. 2d 230, 163 N.W.2d 609 (1968), cert. denied, 399 U.S. 929 (1970).

in a statement in place of a child declarant's, who can not read or write, may not satisfy the foundational requirement for use of a prior inconsistent statement.[590] For instance, introducing a summary of a police officer's interview notes is admissible. Other courts permit the use of prior inconsistent statements only for impeachment purposes.[591]

New York restricts the use of prior inconsistent statements of a witness on direct examination only when the "witness in a criminal proceeding gives testimony upon a material issue of the case which tends to disprove the position of such party, and then only on the issue of credibility."[592] Furthermore, if the witness's testimony does not tend to disprove the position of the party who called the witness, the prior statement may not be used to refresh the recollection of the witness in any way that discloses the statement's contents to the jury.[593] When a prior inconsistent statement is admitted for impeachment or a limited purpose, it is not substantive evidence and cannot support a conviction for sexual assault if the victim recants the allegation and there is no other evidence of the offense.[594] When, under the rules of the jurisdiction, a party uses a prior inconsistent statement for impeachment purposes only, a cautionary instruction should be given the jury so that it is clear that the prior extrajudicial statement is not to be considered for its truth.[595] Limiting instructions are more effective

---

[590] State v. Corbin, 61 Conn. App. 496, 765 A.2d 14 (2001). *See also* Noel v. Commonwealth, 76 S.W.3d 923 (Ky. 2002) (impeaching by prior inconsistent statement requires witness to be asked if he made statement and time and place person to whom the declaration was made).

[591] State v. Williams, 204 Conn. 523, 529 A.2d 653 (1987); State v. Corbin, 61 Conn. App. 496, 511–15, 765 A.2d 14, 24–26 (2001), *aff'd in part and rev'd in part*, 260 Conn. 730, 799 A.2d 1056 (2002) (reversing one count of defendant's convictions for sexual assault because trial court improperly permitted use of child's prior inconsistent statement as substantive evidence); State v. Hach, 2001 Ohio App. LEXIS 10 (Jan. 3, 2001) (holding trial court properly excluded defendant from offering complainant's prior inconsistent statement about rape to her mother since defendant was seeking to offer it for the truth of the matter asserted and not just her credibility); State v. Hancock, 109 Wash. 2d 760, 748 P.2d 611 (1988); State v. Reece, 637 S.W.2d 858 (Tenn. 1982); State v. Blake, 197 W. Va. 700, 706, 478 S.E.2d 550, 556 (1996).

[592] N.Y. Crim. Proc. Law § 60.35(1)(2).

[593] N.Y. Crim Proc. Law § 60.35(3).

[594] People v. Zurak, 168 A.D.2d 196, 571 N.Y.S.2d 577, *appeal denied*, 79 N.Y.2d 834, 588 N.E.2d 112, 580 N.Y.S.2d 214 (1991), *cert. denied*, 504 U.S. 941 (1992).

[595] United States v. Garcia, 530 F.2d 650 (5th Cir. 1976); People v. Montgomery, 22 A.D.3d 960, 803 N.Y.S.2d 228 (2005) (holding that sexual abuse victim's prior inconsistent statement was admissible only for impeachment, not affirmative evidence of guilt and counsel's failure to object rendered his representation deficient); People v. Mills, 302 A.D.2d 141, 145, 750 N.Y.S.2d 230, 233 (2002), *appeal granted*, 99 N.Y.2d 587, 785 N.E.2d 745, 755 N.Y.S.2d 723 (2003) (In a domestic violence homicide prosecution of defendant wife, trial court properly permitted use of wife's prior grand jury testimony as a prior inconsistent statement when she "could not recall" details of her prior testimony, and jury was properly instructed that such questioning was for the "sole purpose of evaluating credibility" and that wife's prior testimony was not to be considered "legal evidence" in the case); People v. Patterson, 203 A.D.2d 597, 611 N.Y.S.2d 217 (1994); State v. Arnold, 133 Or. App. 647, 893 P.2d 1050 (1995) (reversing defendant's conviction due to failure to provide limiting instruction with use of prior inconsistent statement); State v. Reece, 637 S.W.2d 858 (Tenn. 1982); Royal v. Commonwealth, 234 Va. 403, 362 S.E.2d 323 (1987).

if given at the time evidence is presented rather than in the court's final charge. Depending on the nature of the prior inconsistent statement, it may be plain error not to give an immediate limiting instruction. [596]

If the prior statement contains both consistent and inconsistent statements, the offering party must edit the statement, whether in writing or on a videotape, to locate the inconsistent portions rather than offer the entire statement. [597]

§ 10.50 Conviction based solely on complainant's prior inconsistent statement.

Most jurisdictions will uphold a conviction based on the testimony of a single witness, *i.e.*, the complainant. However, several jurisdictions that permit a prior inconsistent statement as substantive evidence will not sustain a conviction supported only by a prior inconsistent statement. [598] In reversing a particular defendant's convictions, one court explained why a sexual abuse defendant's conviction could not be supported solely by a prior inconsistent statement:

> It is clear to this court today, that because there is an absence of adequate safeguards to assure reliability, a conviction based solely on a prior statement, though admissible via statute, falls short of due process protection.
>
> One reason for this is the lack of trustworthiness in the atmosphere where the prior out-of-court statement was procured. A less than impartial questioner could, hypothetically, maneuver the witness into giving an inaccurate statement. [citation omitted.]
>
> Additionally, the jury may draw unreliable inferences from its mistrust of the declarant's present demeanor. The demeanor may have been equally poor at the time she made the prior statement, but that demeanor is hidden from the critical eyes of the present trier of facts. A witness'[s] unsatisfactory trial demeanor should not provide a sufficient basis to permit conviction solely on that witness'[s] prior unobserved statement. Another danger is that people tend to believe the prior statements rather than the in-court repudiation. [citation omitted.] However, the danger of unreliability is inherent in the substantive evidentiary use of any out-of-court assertion and never more so than with the use of a prior inconsistent statement, the truth of which the

---

[596] Jones v. United States, 385 F.2d 296 (D.C. Cir. 1967).

[597] Willover v. State, 70 S.W.3d 841 (Tex. Crim. App. 2002) ("When a trial judge is presented with a proffer of evidence containing both admissible and inadmissible statements and the proponent of the evidence fails to segregate and specifically offer the admissible statements, the trial court may properly exclude all of the statements." *Id.* at 847.).

[598] Thompson v. State, 769 P.2d 997 (Alaska Ct. App. 1989); Acosta v. State, 417 A.2d 373 (Del. 1980); State v. Green, 667 So. 2d 756 (Fla. 1995) (child's statement under Florida's residual hearsay exception insufficient standing alone to sustain a criminal conviction); State v. Moore, 485 So. 2d 1279, 1281 (Fla. 1986); State v. Allien, 366 So. 2d 1308, 1311 (La. 1978); Commonwealth v. Costello, 411 Mass. 371, 582 N.E.2d 938 (1991); State v. White Water, 194 Mont. 85, 634 P.2d 636 (1981).

declarant denies at trial. When the trier of fact decides to believe a witness'[s] prior statement rather than the in-court contradiction, that decision often is based solely on guess or intuition, not credible facts. This inherent danger is compounded when that prior inconsistent statement is the only prosecution evidence against the accused, and becomes the sole basis for conviction. [599]

This rule will not necessarily prohibit a conviction based solely on hearsay. If the hearsay has a sufficient showing of reliability, such as with an excited utterance, the hearsay declaration may support a conviction, even if the hearsay is contradicted by the declarant's trial testimony. [600]

§ 10.51   Hearsay admitted without objection.

It is important that any objection to hearsay testimony be stated on the record, since the failure to object will usually be considered a waiver. [601] In some situations, an appellate court may determine whether the improperly admitted hearsay was error harmless beyond a reasonable doubt. [602] Generally, hearsay admitted without objection is not plain error. [603] However, the general rule is that hearsay admitted without objection may be properly considered in determining and establishing facts of the case and used to support a conviction or a finding

---

[599] State v. Pierce, 906 S.W.2d 729, 735–36 (Mo. Ct. App. 1995).

[600] Williams v. State, 714 So. 2d 462 (Fla. Ct. App. 1997)

> In this case, the trial judge conducted a hearing outside the presence of the jury during which she heard the testimony of the victim and her son. She also listened to the trial testimony of Officer Hunter and to the tape-recorded 911 calls made by the victim and her son. She evaluated the testimony and concluded that the state had established the predicate necessary to admit the statements in question as excited utterances. We can find no error in her analysis. These excited utterances were, on their own, sufficient to deny the defendant's motions for judgment of acquittal and to send the case to the jury. The victim's conflicting statements, like those of her son, presented the jury with a choice of which statements to believe. Their guilty verdict clearly illustrates their determination that Ms. Davis' statements to Officer Hunter, immediately after the violent altercation with the defendant, and her son's hysterical telephone call to the 911 operator, were more credible than their trial testimony.

Id. at 466. *See also*, Anderson v. State, 655 So. 2d 1118 (Fla. 1995), *cited* by the court in *Williams*.

[601] United States v. Wake, 948 F.2d 1422, 1434 (5th Cir. 1991), *cert. denied*, 504 U.S. 975 (1992); United States v. Fernandez, 772 F.2d 495, 499 (9th Cir. 1985); Anderson v. State, 718 N.E.2d 1101, 1102 (Ind. 1999); People v. Shook, 294 A.D.2d 710, 743 N.Y.S.2d 573, *appeal denied*, 98 N.Y.2d 702, 776 N.E.2d 10, 747 N.Y.S.2d 421 (2002) (affirming admission of victim's complaint of sexual abuse through the testimony of another child witness with whom victim confided where defendant failed to object at trial to the admissibility of this testimony, never moved to strike it, nor sought an appropriate limiting instruction); State v. Cly, 1998 Wash. App. LEXIS 148 at *4 (Feb. 2, 1998) (holding failing to object to nurse practitioner's testimony of child's statements waived review of issue).

[602] United States v. Payne, 944 F.2d 1458 (9th Cir. 1991), *cert. denied*, 503 U.S. 975 (1992).

[603] State v. Brown, 912 S.W.2d 643 (Mo. Ct. App. 1995) ("Hearsay evidence offered without objection is not plain error. . . .").

of the fact proved by the hearsay statement.[604] The majority of courts will treat hearsay admitted without objection as probative as other competent evidence.[605] For example, testimony to support the element of force could be provided by the unobjected to hearsay testimony of a child's mother who testified that the child complainant told her that the defendant held her down, even if the child's testimony did not establish force, since "the hearsay testimony was admissible as substantive evidence of the crime where there was no objection raised."[606] However, the same court noted that unobjected to hearsay is not admissible when it is the only evidence of the offense or an essential element of the offense or it is contradicted by the declarant at trial.[607] Texas' rules of evidence provide that hearsay admitted without objection shall not be denied probative value because it is hearsay.[608] A minority view is that hearsay admitted without objection lacks probative value to establish any fact. Permitting unobjected hearsay to support a fact proven by the hearsay statement in child sexual assault cases is particularly significant, since there may be little or no other direct proof of a defendant's guilt when a child does not testify or testifies as an unsworn witness.[609]

Furthermore, an error in admitting hearsay testimony in a sexual abuse trial may be harmless if the hearsay is cumulative to other testimony to which the defendant did not object.[610]

When the hearsay admitted without objection falls within a residual hearsay requiring a hearing and findings before admitting the hearsay, the failure to conduct a hearing, even if the hearsay is admitted without objection of the defendant, may result in reversal of a defendant's conviction.[611]

---

[604] EDWARD J. IMWINKELRIED, COURTROOM CRIMINAL EVIDENCE § 1006 at 273; WHARTON'S CRIMINAL EVIDENCE § 265 (C. Torcia, ed. 1986); 2 MCCORMICK ON EVIDENCE § 245 at 96 (4th ed. 1992); 30 AM. JUR. 2d *Evidence* § 1103 (1967). *See, e.g.*, People v. Parker, 46 A.D.2d 699, 360 N.Y.S.2d 99 (1974).

[605] Nelson v. State, 1999 Alas. App. LEXIS 130 (Nov. 10, 1999) ("Hearsay that is received without objection is competent evidence."); Jones v. State, 332 Ark. 617, 621, 967 S.W.2d 559 (1998); Sears v. Curtis, 147 Conn. 311, 317, 160 A.2d 742, 745 (1960); People v. Parker, 46 A.D.2d 699, 360 N.Y.S.2d 99 (1974); Baughan v. Commonwealth, 206 Va. 28, 31, 141 S.E.2d 750, 753 (1965) (holding that hearsay testimony that is admitted without objection may "properly be considered by the trial court and given its natural probative effect"); State v. Whisler, 61 Wash. App. 126, 139, 810 P.2d 540 (1991) ("Hearsay evidence admitted without objection may be considered by the trier of fact or the appellate court for its probative value.").

[606] State v. Straughter, 727 So. 2d 1283, 1287 (La. Ct. App. 1999), *writ denied*, 747 So. 2d 14 (1999).

[607] State v. Straughter, 727 So.2d 1283, 1286–87 (La. Ct. App. 1999), *writ denied*, 747 So.2d 14 (1999) (*citing* State v. Allien, 366 So. 2d 1308, 1312 (La. 1978)).

[608] TEX. R. CRIM. EVID. 802.

[609] Howell Mill/Collier Assoc. v. Pennypacker's, Inc., 194 Ga. App. 169, 171, 390 S.E.2d 257, 260 (1990).

[610] United States v. Peneaux, 432 F.3d 882, (8th Cir. 2005); United States v. Gabe, 237 F.3d 954, 958–59 (8th Cir. 2001).

[611] Quevedo v. State, 113 Nev. 35, 930 P.2d 750 (1997).

§ 10.52   Admission of multiple hearsay statements.

When hearsay testimony is improperly admitted at trial, an appellate court will review the issue in the context of whether its admission was harmless beyond a reasonable doubt.[612] This is especially true when there is proof in addition to the complainant's testimony or the complainant was available for effective cross-examination.[613] However, in child sexual abuse cases where a victim may not testify, may not be sworn, or may be unable to be effectively cross-examined, there is a greater danger that the fairness of the trial will be impaired by the admission of improper hearsay, especially if there are multiple admissions of hearsay statements or proof of guilt is not overwhelming. There are also issues of sufficiency of evidence when a preliminary hearing[614] or grand jury[615] determination is based on hearsay. Hawaii permits hearsay in a grand jury proceeding when direct testimony is unavailable, but requires that the hearsay not be deliberately used in place of better evidence to improve the case for indictment.[616] However, the Federal Rules permit the use of hearsay in the grand jury and an indictment may be based solely on hearsay testimony.[617]

Appellate courts reverse convictions for child sexual abuse because of the cumulative prejudicial effect of multiple hearsay. In *Felix v. State*,[618] in a lengthy discussion of the application of hearsay rule to child sexual abuse cases, the Nevada Supreme Court overturned the defendant's conviction where the victim's allegations were repeated six times by different witnesses and on a videotape of her preliminary hearing testimony.[619] Other courts, too, have noted the prejudicial impact of improperly admitted hearsay in child sexual abuse cases, usually in the context of the residual exception of the hearsay rule or cumulative and repetitive hearsay.[620] The likelihood of reversal is also greater when proof

---

[612] United States v. Echeverry, 759 F.2d 1451, 1457 (9th Cir. 1985).

[613] United States v. Ellis, 935 F.2d 385, 393 (1st Cir. 1991).

[614] Commonwealth *ex rel.* Buchanan v. Verbonitz, 525 Pa. 413, 581 A.2d 172 (1990), *cert. denied*, 499 U.S. 907 (1991) (where seven-year-old victim did not testify, hearsay admitted at preliminary hearing not under a hearsay exception was insufficient to establish prima facie case).

[615] Many states prohibit the use of hearsay in grand jury proceedings except in limited situations. *See, e.g.*, N.Y. CRIM. PROC. LAW § 190.30(1) (rules of evidence for grand jury are the same as "criminal proceedings in general").

[616] *See* State v. Murphy, 59 Haw. 1, 575 P.2d 448 (1978).

[617] United States v. Taylor, 154 F.3d 675, 681 (7th Cir.), *cert. denied*, 525 U.S. 1060 (1998) (noting that under federal rules, an indictment may be based solely on hearsay testimony and that "an otherwise valid indictment cannot be challenged on the ground that the grand jury based it on inadequate or incompetent evidence").

[618] 109 Nev. 151, 849 P.2d 220 (1993).

[619] Felix v. State, 109 Nev. 151, 849 P.2d 220, 254 (1993).

[620] United States v. Tome, 61 F.3d 1446 (10th Cir. 1995)

In this case, the erroneously admitted hearsay evidence was extremely compelling. A.T.'s statements to Rocha and Ecklebarger were the most detailed accounts of the abuse presented at trial. As discussed earlier, these statements vividly described a

of defendant's guilt is not overwhelming,[621] or the hearsay statement is the foundation of the prosecution's case.[622]

The admission of multiple hearsay statements may also make reversal of a defendant's conviction more likely when there is another error in the proceedings. For example, if the defendant is precluded from presenting proof of a child's prior allegations, which resulted in no findings of abuse, then the effect of multiple hearsay will be more carefully scrutinized.[623]

Any hearsay statement, even if admissible, will be subject to the rule that its probative value must be balanced against its prejudicial effect.[624] One area of prejudicial effect is multiple hearsay statements of a complainant. There is also authority that, even when hearsay is admissible, it is improper to admit multiple hearsay statements because of the danger of unfair prejudice from the presentation of multiple hearsay statements or the bolstering of the victim's in-court testimony.[625]

---

particular instance of abuse with great specificity and in graphic terms. They painted a rather brutal picture of defendant. By comparison, the victim's own testimony at trial was not nearly as articulate or comprehensive in its description of the abuse. Moreover, most of the prosecution's remaining evidence concerned not the abuse itself — nor the abuser's identity — but medical evidence that A.T. had suffered penetration.

Id. at 1455. *See, e.g.*, State v. Thompson, 167 Ariz. 230, 235, 805 P.2d 1051, 1056 (1990), *on reh'g*, 169 Ariz. 471, 820 P.2d 335 (1991); Turtle v. State, 600 So. 2d 1214 (Fla. Dist. Ct. App. 1992) (reversing defendant's conviction in part on improperly admitted prompt-outcry hearsay testimony); People v. Fowler, 240 Ill. App. 3d 442, 608 N.E.2d 390 (1992); Traver v. State, 568 N.E.2d 1009, 1013–14 (Ind. 1991); Souder v. Commonwealth, 719 S.W.2d 730 (Ky. 1986); State v. Seever, 733 S.W.2d 438, 441 (Mo. 1987) (*en banc*); People v. Shay, 210 A.D.2d 735, 620 N.Y.S.2d 189 (1994), *appeal denied*, 85 N.Y.2d 980, 653 N.E.2d 636, 629 N.Y.S.2d 740 (1995); State v. Arnold, 133 Or. App. 647, 893 P.2d 1050 (1995) (reversing defendant's conviction because improper hearsay provided a "full story" not available through any other witness); State v. Livingston, 907 S.W.2d 392, 397 (Tenn. 1995).

[621] People v. Fowler, 240 Ill. App. 3d 442, 608 N.E.2d 390 (1992); Commonwealth v. Brouillard, 40 Mass. App. Ct. 448, 457, 665 N.E.2d 113, 119 (1996) (noting the case depended entirely on the credibility of the complainant, the emotional nature of the fresh complaint testimony that the court failed to provide a limiting instruction); People v. Phillips, 190 A.D.2d 1065, 594 N.Y.S.2d 1014 (1993); People v. Seiver, 187 A.D.2d 683, 590 N.Y.S.2d 248 (1992), *appeal denied*, 81 N.Y.2d 976, 615 N.E.2d 235, 598 N.Y.S.2d 778 (1993) (reversing defendant's conviction because of improperly admitted hearsay in the nature of a prompt outcry and victim's diary).

[622] State v. Wetherbee, 156 Vt. 425, 594 A.2d 390 (1991).

[623] State v. E.B., 348 N.J. Super. 336, 791 A.2d 1124, *cert. denied*, 174 N.J. 192, 803 A.2d 1163 (2002) ("Nevertheless we cannot ignore the extra weight which a jury might well be inclined to give a story heard five times in different forms, by different witnesses, and in different modes as opposed to a denial heard only once from a single witness." Court went on to reverse defendant's conviction in light of the multiple hearsay and trial court's preclusion of testimony concerning child's prior unsubstantiated complaints of sexual abuse).

[624] *See, e.g.*, State v. Mayfield, 302 Or. 631, 641–42, 733 P.2d 438, 445 (1987).

[625] State v. Ali, 233 Conn. 403, 660 A.2d 337 (1995) ("[B]ecause the trial court did not caution the jury that constancy of accusation testimony can be used to impeach as well as to corroborate the victim's testimony, and because the trial court failed in its other instructions to charge the

The admission of multiple hearsay statements is also discussed in the context of fresh complaint testimony (*See* §§ 10.18 and 10.26).

The admission of multiple hearsay testimony of a victim may be permissible when "the hearsay testimony is not completely duplicative of and had probative value beyond the victim's own testimony."[626] Such prejudice may be alleviated with multiple hearsay statements when the trial court repeatedly provides instructions limiting the use of hearsay,[627] or when there may be additional reasons for the different pieces of hearsay testimony.[628]

There is some authority that multiple hearsay statements are admissible in response to a defendant's attack on the inconsistencies of the complainant's statements.[629] This premise contradicts the approach of those courts that find weaknesses in the state's proof as increasing the prejudice of multiple hearsay statements.

§ 10.53   Need for and effect of limiting instruction.

As noted many times in this chapter, admissible hearsay may be admissible for a limited purpose. When evidence is admissible for one purpose but not admissible for another purpose, "the court, upon request, shall restrict the evidence to its proper scope and instruct the jury accordingly."[630] Admitting scores of out-of-court statements without limiting instructions is error.[631] Prompt

jury that in assessing her credibility it could consider any contradictions, inconsistencies or falsities in the victim's out-of-court statements, the court failed to provide a proper balance to the instructions." *Id.* at 422, 660 A.2d at 346.); Perry v. State, 593 So. 2d 620 (Fla. Dist. Ct.), *appeal denied*, 602 So. 2d 942 (1992) (*citing* Kopko v. State, 577 So. 2d 956 (1991)). *Contra* State v. Pardo, 582 So. 2d 1225 (Fla. Dist. Ct. 1991); People v. Peck, 285 Ill. App. 3d 14, 674 N.E.2d 440 (1996) (reversing defendant's conviction due to improper admission of ten hearsay statements of two child witnesses); Commonwealth v. Trowbridge, 419 Mass. 750, 761, 647 N.E.2d 413, 421 (1995); Commonwealth v. Almeida, 42 Mass. App. Ct. 607, 679 N.E.2d 561, *review denied*, 425 Mass. 1105, 682 N.E.2d 1362 (1997) (reversing defendant's conviction because of multiple improperly admitted hearsay statements of the complainant in a case where victim's credibility at issue); ("Although there is no *per se* rule of how many fresh complaint witnesses may testify, the repetition of fresh complaint testimony creates a risk that the jury will use the details of the fresh complaints as substantive evidence that the crime actually occurred."); State v. Tizard, 897 S.W.2d 732 (Tenn. Crim. App. 1994); *In re* Dependency of Penelope B., 104 Wash. 2d 643, 656, 709 P.2d 1185, 1193 (1985) (noting that testimony under the medical history exception is subject to objection as unnecessarily cumulative and prejudicial).

[626] State v. Gollaher, 905 S.W.2d 542, 546 (Mo. Ct. App. 1995).

[627] Commonwealth v. Lamontagne, 42 Mass. App. Ct. 213, 675 N.E.2d 1169, *review denied*, 424 Mass. 1106, 678 N.E.2d 1333 (1997).

[628] State v. Pardo, 582 So. 2d 1225 (Fla. Dist. Ct. 1991); State v. Garrett, 76 Wash. App. 719, 726, 887 P.2d 488, 492 (1995) (noting that some of the hearsay established that complainant made complaint not just to family members, but third parties also).

[629] State v. Huntington, 216 Wis. 2d 671, 695–96, 575 N.W.2d 268, 278–79 (1998).

[630] FED. R. EVID. 105.

[631] United States v. Cass, 127 F.3d 1218, 1222–23 (10th Cir. 1997), *cert. denied*, 522 U.S. 1138 (1998).

complaint testimony without an appropriate limiting instruction can in itself lead to a reversal of conviction.[632] Reference is also made to the need for a limiting instruction to accompany the admission of hearsay under the prompt complaint (*See* § 10.14) or prior consistent or inconsistent statements (*See* §§ 10.47–10.49).

Even if the hearsay is admissible, its admission may require a limiting instruction. The Supreme Court of the United States has recognized that a properly admissible hearsay statement may be so prejudicial that a limiting instruction would be ineffective, and that "when the risk of confusion is so great as to upset the balance of advantage, the evidence goes out."[633] Thus, in some situations, improperly admitted hearsay may be so prejudicial that the error cannot be cured by a cautionary instruction.[634]

§ 10.54 Objecting to hearsay and the failure to provide limiting instruction.

The importance of making a record of a party's objection to out-of-court statements or to a request for a limiting instruction cannot be over-emphasized. A general objection may not preserve various challenges to scope and admissibility of hearsay,[635] and also may not preserve the issue of a failure to provide a limiting instruction unless there is a specific request for one.[636] Failing to object

---

[632] State v. Buscham, 360 N.J. Super. 346, 823 A.2d 71 (2003). Court reversed defendant's conviction because prompt complaint testimony went beyond fact of complaint and court provided no limiting instruction on how the jury should consider such testimony:

> An additional protection afforded to a defendant under the fresh complaint doctrine, beyond the limited scope of permissible testimony, is the necessity of a trial court instructing the jury how to utilize fresh complaint evidence.

> Trial courts should instruct the jury of the limited role that fresh-complaint evidence should play in its consideration of the case. The trial court should make clear that a fresh complaint does not bolster the victim's credibility or prove the underlying truth of the sexual assault charges but merely dispels the inference that the victim was silent. (*citing* State v. Bethune, 121 N.J. 137, 146, 148, 578 A.2d 364, 369 (1990)).

Id. at 359, 578 A.2d at 79.

[633] Shepard v. United States, 290 U.S. 96, 104 (1933). *See above* note 55.

[634] People v. Stanaway, 446 Mich. 643, 521 N.W.2d 557 (1994), *cert. denied*, 513 U.S. 1121 (1995) (Defendant's conviction for sexually assaulting a 14-year-old girl reversed because of improper impeachment of a prosecution witness with highly prejudicial hearsay testimony).

[635] People v. Sanders, 238 A.D.2d 215, 656 N.Y.S.2d 255 (1997); State v. Marr, 731 A.2d 690 (R.I. 1999).

[636] Gray v. Busch Entm't Corp., 886 F.2d 14, 16 (2d Cir. 1989) (concerning a business record that was admissible only with a limiting instruction and was not admitted for the truth of the matter asserted. "No such instruction was given. We believe that the wholesale objection made at trial did not preserve this point, however."); United States v. Garcia, 530 F.2d 650, 656 (5th Cir. 1976) (holding that failure to give a limiting instruction is reversible only if there is plain error); United States v. Bamberger, 456 F.2d 1119, 1131–32 (3d Cir. 1972) ("We hold that under the instant circumstances, where no instruction was requested or given as to the relevancy of the seized goods, it was not clear error under Fed. R. Crim. P. 52(b) to receive this evidence.").

to the hearsay statement can result not only in a waiver of appellate review, it may also allow the statement to be admitted as substantive evidence. The basis of any objection must be accurate, *clearly* articulated, and brought to the court's attention. An ill-founded hearsay objection can also fail to preserve for review the improper admission of hearsay.[637]

Once a hearsay objection is lodged and overruled, it is essential to note the additional objection that although the statement may fall within a hearsay exception, the statement should be precluded because its probative value is outweighed by its prejudicial effects, if such an effect can be demonstrated. This is a separate basis for objection.

Objecting on the grounds of hearsay will not necessarily preserve an objection based on the constitutional right to confrontation, and a confrontation objection should therefore be clearly articulated when it is a basis for objecting to the out-of-court statement.[638] The filing of a motion *in limine* seeking to preclude hearsay testimony may also be insufficient to preserve the issue for appeal.[639] When a hearsay error affects the "fairness, integrity or public reputation of judicial proceedings," a court may nonetheless acknowledge that unconstitutionally inadmissible hearsay testimony, providing the heart of the prosecution's case,

---

[637] Lewis v. Kendrick, 944 F.2d 949 (1st Cir. 1991); Vasquez v. State, 287 Ark. 468, 702 S.W.2d 411 (1986) ("We have long held that a party cannot change the grounds for an objection on appeal."); People v. Qualls, 55 N.Y.2d 733, 734, 431 N.E.2d 634, 635, 447 N.Y.S.2d 149, 150 (1981) ("The defendant's objection at trial was solely on the ground that the evidence constituted improper bolstering. That was insufficient to preserve for our review the contentions now advanced that the evidence constituted inadmissible hearsay and that its introduction violated the defendant's constitutional right of confrontation. . . .").

[638] United States v. Dukagjini, 326 F.3d 45, 60 (2d Cir. 2002) ("We adhere to the principle that, as a general matter, a hearsay objection by itself does not automatically preserve a Confrontation Clause claim."); People v. Kello, 96 N.Y.2d 740, 746 N.E.2d 166, 723 N.Y.S.2d 111 (2001) (holding hearsay objection did not preserve an objection based on Sixth Amendment's right of confrontation and noting that statutory or common law hearsay exceptions may not satisfy mandate of confrontation clause); People v. Perez, 9 A.D.3d 376, 779 N.Y.S.2d 584 (2004) ("The defendant contends that the trial court improperly admitted hearsay testimony, which implied that a nontestifying witness implicated him in a murder, depriving him of his constitutional right to confront the witnesses against him. Although the defendant objected to the testimony at issue, he did not specify the ground now raised on appeal. Therefore, the issue of whether he was deprived of his right of confrontation is unpreserved for appellate review."); State v. Gove, 148 Wis. 2d 936, 940–41, 437 N.W.2d 218, 220 (1989); State v. Nelson, 138 Wis. 2d 418, 439, 406 N.W.2d 385, 393–94 (1987).

[639] United States v. Archdale, 229 F.3d 861 (9th Cir. 2000):

Appellant's contention that the mere filing of a *motion in limine* preserves for appeal the issue of the admissibility of the evidence to which the motion is directed without merit. Absent a thorough examination of the objection raised in the *motion in limine* and an explicit and definitive ruling by the district court that the evidence is admissible, a party does not preserve the issue of admissibility for appeal absent a contemporaneous objection. *Id.* at 864.

is plain error requiring vacating a conviction, even in the absence of an objection based on the right of confrontation.[640]

---

[640] United States v. Bruno, 383 F.3d 65 (2d Cir. 2004) (finding plain error in admission of co-conspirator's plea, which was inadmissible based on *Crawford*, discussed in § 10.45, which had not been decided at time of trial).

§ 11.1 Introduction.

One of the most important areas in sexual assault cases involves the use of expert testimony, especially behavioral psychological testimony. Quite often issues arising out of the use of expert mental health testimony relate to profile testimony offered by both the prosecution and the defense. Expert mental health testimony is often subjected to the scientific standard of admissibility; when "personal experience is used as a basis for generalized statements regarding the behavior of sexually-abused children as a class, the testimony crosses over to scientific testimony regarding a profile or syndrome, whether or not the term is used."[1] Such profile testimony is generally offered to show that a victim or a defendant has certain characteristics that would qualify them to be a victim of sexual assault or an abuser or nonabuser.

Other areas commonly encountered in sexual assault trials are the "rape trauma syndrome" and the "child sexual abuse accommodation syndrome" to explain the behaviors of victims. The extensive use of expert testimony in these areas has resulted in substantial appellate law. Many of these principles apply to other areas of expert testimony. For example, in a case involving sexual abuse by a physician during a medical examination, expert testimony concerning proper medical procedures can be relevant to show that the sexual contact was not accomplished for medical purposes.[2] The parameters of expert medical testimony are also discussed in Chapter 12.

§ 11.2   The *Daubert* standard.

For generations, the admission of scientific testimony was governed in large part by the so-called *Frye* standard,[3] which required as a foundation for the admission of expert scientific testimony that the theory be generally accepted as reliable in the relevant scientific community. The following often-quoted excerpt sets forth the essence of this standard:

> Just when a scientific principle or discovery crosses the line between experimental and demonstrable stages is difficult to define. Somewhere in this twilight zone the evidential force of the principle must be recognized, and while courts will go a long way in admitting expert testimony deduced from a well-recognized scientific principle or discovery, the thing from which the deduction is made must be sufficiently established to have gained general acceptance in the particular field in which it belongs.[4]

General acceptance under *Frye* focuses on the underlying methodology used to generate the expert's opinion — not the ultimate conclusion.[5] General acceptance does not require universal acceptance, consensus, or a majority.[6] If the underlying methodology is generally relied on by experts in the field, the jury may consider an opinion even if the conclusion is novel. Only "novelty" of a scientific principle, test or technique requires a *Frye* evidentiary hearing.[7]

---

[1] State v. Jones, 71 Wash. App. 798, 818, 863 P.2d 85, 97 (1993), *review denied*, 124 Wn. 2d 1018, 881 P.2d 254 (1994).

[2] State v. Tizard, 897 S.W.2d 732 (Tenn. Crim. App. 1994).

[3] Frye v. United States, 293 F. 1013 (D.C. Cir. 1923).

[4] Frye v. United States, 293 F. 1013, 1014 (D.C. Cir. 1923)

[5] Donaldson v. Central Ill. Pub. Serv. Co., 199 Ill. 2d 63, 78, 767 N.E.2d 314, 324 (2002).

[6] Donaldson v. Central Ill. Pub. Serv. Co., 199 Ill. 2d 63, 77–78, 767 N.E.2d 314, 324 (2002).

[7] Donaldson v. Central Ill. Pub. Serv. Co., 199 Ill. 2d 63, 77–78, 767 N.E.2d 314, 324 (2002).

For years, many state courts and a few federal courts used the *Frye* standard for the admissibility of scientific testimony; however, in 1993, the Supreme Court of the United States, in *Daubert v. Merrell Dow Pharms., Inc.*,[8] held that the Federal Rules of Evidence supersedes *Frye*, which significantly broadened the criteria for the admission for expert testimony. The Court noted that the Federal Rules take a "general approach of relaxing . . . traditional barriers to opinion testimony,"[9] but that Rule 702 anticipated "some degree of regulation of the subjects and theories about which an expert may testify."[10]

In *Daubert*, the plaintiffs in a civil suit against a pharmaceutical company sought to offer expert testimony relating to opinions that could not be shown to be generally accepted as reliable, in particular because the experts' findings had not been published or subjected to peer review. In overturning the *Frye* standard, the Supreme Court started with Federal Rule of Evidence 402, which states that "all relevant evidence is admissible,"[11] and particularly noted that Rule 702 specifically deals with testimony by experts: "If scientific, technical, or other specialized knowledge will assist the trier of fact to understand the evidence or to determine a fact in issue, a witness qualified as an expert by knowledge, skill, experience, training, or education, may testify thereto in the form of an opinion or otherwise."[12]

Rule 702, according to the Supreme Court, eliminates the requirement of general acceptance in the scientific community. However, Rule 702 also sets forth some of the standards that must be applied to the admission of expert testimony. For example, the subject of an expert's testimony must be "scientific, technical, or other specialized knowledge." The Court noted that the word "scientific" implies a grounding in the methods and procedures of science. This can be a particularly important requirement when examining the admissibility of expert testimony in sexual assault trials where expert testimony may not have scientific grounding. On the other hand, "specialized knowledge" implies a broader net for admissible expert testimony. The word "knowledge" connotes more than subjective belief or unsupported speculation.[13] The term applies to any body of known facts or to any body of ideas from such facts or accepted as truths on good grounds.[14] The scientific knowledge requirement provides a standard of evidentiary reliability.[15] However, "it would be unreasonable to conclude that

---

[8] Daubert v. Merrell Dow Pharmaceuticals, Inc., 509 U.S. 579 (1993).

[9] Daubert v. Merrell Dow Pharmaceuticals, Inc., 509 U.S. 579, 588 (1993) (*citing* Beech Aircraft Corp. v. Rainey, 488 U.S. 153, 169 (1988)).

[10] Daubert v. Merrell Dow Pharmaceuticals, Inc., 509 U.S. 579, 589 (1993).

[11] Fed. R. Evid. 402.

[12] Fed. R. Evid. 702.

[13] Daubert v. Merrell Dow Pharmaceuticals, Inc., 509 U.S. 579, 590 (1993).

[14] Daubert v. Merrell Dow Pharmaceuticals, Inc., 509 U.S. 579, 590 (1993).

[15] Daubert v. Merrell Dow Pharmaceuticals, Inc., 509 U.S. 579, 590 (1993).

the subject of scientific testimony must be 'known' to a certainty; arguably there are no certainties in science."[16]

Rule 702 also requires that the proposed expert testimony "assist the trier of fact to understand the evidence or to determine a fact in issue," that is, will it be helpful to the trier in fact?[17] The interplay of these two requirements is provided by the example of the phases of the moon. While there is perhaps sufficient scientific knowledge about whether a moon was full on a particular night, testimony that the moon was full on a particular night and that this fact is related to a person behaving irrationally on that night would not satisfy the helpfulness standard of Rule 702.[18]

To summarize *Daubert*, it requires four areas of evidentiary analysis and reliability for the admissibility of an expert opinion: (1) testing, (2) peer review, (3) rate of error, and (4) general acceptance. Then, the expert testimony must pass the relevancy test (Rule 702); its probativeness must outweigh any prejudice, confusion, or be misleading to the jury (Rule 403), and it must not rely on inadmissible hearsay unless of a type reasonably relied upon by experts in the field (Rule 703).

§ 11.3 Factors to consider in assessing scientific knowledge.

The Supreme Court set forth a list of factors that the trial courts should consider in assessing the reliability of proposed expert testimony. One is whether the theory or technique has been tested. A second is whether the theory or technique has been subjected to peer review and publication — although this will not necessarily be dispositive of reliability. Well-grounded, innovative theories may be too new or of too limited interest to be published, the Court observed, but submission for the scientific community's scrutiny increases reliability by increasing the likelihood that errors or flaws in the theory or methodology will be detected.[19] Third, in the case of scientific technique, the "potential rate of error" and the existence and maintenance of standards are factors to consider.[20] The *Frye* standard of general acceptance is still a factor to consider, although not the exclusive standard, to assess reliability. Even under the *Frye* standard, general acceptance does not require universal acceptance. The principle of general acceptance still has bearing on whether the knowledge is scientific, and widespread acceptance by the scientific community is relevant in considering reliability.[21] "Broad statements of general scientific acceptance, without accompanying support, are insufficient to meet the burden of establishing such acceptance."[22]

---

[16] Daubert v. Merrell Dow Pharmaceuticals, Inc., 509 U.S. 579, 590–91.

[17] Daubert v. Merrell Dow Pharmaceuticals, Inc., 509 U.S. 579, 591 (1993).

[18] Daubert v. Merrell Dow Pharmaceuticals, Inc., 509 U.S. 579, 591 (1993).

[19] Daubert v. Merrell Dow Pharmaceuticals, Inc., 509 U.S. 579, 592.

[20] Daubert v. Merrell Dow Pharmaceuticals, Inc., 509 U.S. 579, 594.

[21] Daubert v. Merrell Dow Pharmaceuticals, Inc., 509 U.S. 579, 595.

[22] Saulpaugh v. Krafte, 5 A.D.3d 934, 774 N.Y.S.2d 194, *appeal denied*, 3 N.Y.3d 610, 820 N.E.2d

The Supreme Court noted that the "focus, of course, must be solely on principles and methodology, not on the conclusions that they generate."[23] The Court also noted that scientific testimony must also be tested by the principles of Rule 703, which provides that expert opinions based on otherwise inadmissible hearsay should be admitted only if the basis for the opinions are "of the type reasonably relied upon by experts in the particular field forming opinions or inferences upon the subject."[24]

Perhaps the strongest limitation in the use of expert testimony, and one that is often cited directly or indirectly in the use of expert testimony in sexual assault trials, is the principle of Rule 403, which permits the exclusion of relevant evidence "if its probative value is substantially outweighed by the danger of unfair prejudice, confusion of the issues, or misleading the jury."[25] This limitation has particular significance in many areas of expert opinion offered in sexual assault trials.

On remand from the United States Supreme Court, the Circuit Court of Appeals in *Daubert* amplified the criteria that courts will use to analyze whether experts' testimony is based on scientifically valid principles.[26] On remand, the Court of Appeals rejected the opinions of plaintiff's experts. The court considered whether their opinions grew "naturally and directly out of research they have conducted independent of the litigation, or whether they have developed their opinions expressly for purposes of testifying."[27] While noting there may be situations where an expert may have performed more work in the courtroom than in the lab, it noted that "testimony proffered by an expert . . . based directly on legitimate, pre-existing research unrelated to the litigation provides the most persuasive basis for concluding that the opinions he expresses [are] 'derived by the scientific method.' "[28] It noted that an expert testimony can be buttressed by showing that the opinions grew out of prelitigation research or that the research has been subjected to peer review.[29] The United States Supreme Court in *Kumho Tire Co. v. Carmichael*[30] held that not all, or even one, of the four *Daubert* standards (testing, peer review, error rates, and scientific susceptibility) must be satisfied for expert testimony to be admissible, whether in cases of expert

---

292, 786 N.Y.S.2d 813 (2004) (rejecting an expert medical opinion, which was not supported by "controlled studies, clinical data, medical literature, peer review, or supportive proof" establishing general acceptance).

[23] Daubert v. Merrell Dow Pharmaceuticals, Inc., 509 U.S. 579, 595.

[24] Fed. R. Evid. 703.

[25] Fed. R. Evid. 403.

[26] Daubert v. Merrell Dow Pharms., Inc., 43 F.3d 1311 (9th Cir.), *cert. denied*, 516 U.S. 869 (1995).

[27] Daubert v. Merrell Dow Pharmaceuticals, Inc., 43 F.3d 1311, 1317.

[28] Daubert v. Merrell Dow Pharmaceuticals, Inc., 43 F.3d 1311.

[29] Daubert v. Merrell Dow Pharmaceuticals, Inc., 43 F.3d 1311, 1317–18.

[30] Kumho Tire Co. v. Carmichael, 526 U.S. 137, 150–51 (1999).

testimony based on scientific or non-scientific evidence. Under *Kumho*, the trial judge has considerable latitude in determining admissibility of expert testimony and noted that appellate courts should give trial judges "considerable leeway" in determining the admissibility of expert testimony.[31] In *Kumho*, while the Supreme Court rejected the expert testimony of a tire failure expert as not meeting the threshold standards for the admissibility of expert testimony, the Court noted that expert conclusions may be based on methodologies consistent with the prevailing norms of a field of study as long as the opinions are "from a set of observations based on extensive and specialized experience."[32]

§ 11.4   Determination of admissibility and need for preliminary determining or hearing.

The trial judge must determine the admissibility of expert testimony. In *Daubert*, the Court noted that this would be at the outset.[33] This somewhat ambiguous guidance means, primarily, that the trial judge must rule on the testimony before it is admitted. The federal rules note that preliminary questions concerning the qualifications of a witness, the existence of privilege, or the admissible evidence are determined by the court.[34] Also, Rule 403 states that the trial court is not bound by the rules of evidence in dealing with the admissibility of evidence unless privileges are at issue. The burden of proof for the admissibility of expert testimony is a preponderance of evidence.[35] It is important given the significant legal issues raised by the introduction of expert testimony in sexual assault trials that counsel aggressively present admissibility issues to the trial court and make a clear record of any objections to the admission of the expert testimony to avoid waiving appellate review of the propriety of the expert testimony. By virtue of the United States Supreme Court's decision in *Kumho Tire Co. v. Carmichael*,[36] trial judges are given considerable leeway in determining the admissibility of all forms of expert testimony, both scientific and non-scientific, and permitted to "avoid unnecessary 'reliability' proceedings in ordinary cases where the reliability of an expert's methods is properly taken for granted."[37] The Court specifically noted that experts who have traditionally testified in areas of expert testimony should not be subject to protracted objections or *Daubert* hearings.[38]

---

[31] Kumho Tire Co. v. Carmichael, 526 U.S. 137, 152 (1999).

[32] Kumho Tire Co. v. Carmichael, 526 U.S. 137, 156.

[33] Daubert v. Merrell Dow Pharmaceuticals, Inc., 509 U.S. 579, 592.

[34] Fed. R. Evid. 104(a).

[35] Daubert v. Merrell Dow Pharmaceuticals, Inc., 509 U.S. 579, 592 n.10 (*citing* Bourjaily v. United States, 483 U.S. 171, 175–76 (1987)).

[36] Kumho Tire Co. v. Carmichael, 526 U.S. 137.

[37] Kumho Tire Co. v. Carmichael, 526 U.S. 137, 152.

[38] Kumho Tire Co. v. Carmichael, 526 U.S. 137, 152.

§ 11.5 Practical considerations in the *Daubert* decision — Focusing on principles, methodology, and reasoning.

By increasing the considerations for the admission of expert testimony, *Daubert* also increases the opportunities of the trial lawyer to argue admission or preclusion of expert testimony. In addition to making sure that the trial court decides the issue of admissibility and makes adequate findings for appellate review, other issues stem from the *Daubert* decision. First of all, the *Daubert* decision applies only to federal courts and those states that have adopted the Federal Rules of Evidence. It is up to individual state courts to decide whether to follow *Daubert*. While most states do follow the *Frye* standard, counsel can also argue that the *Frye* standard should be abandoned in those states and argue that general acceptance in the scientific community is not an appropriate standard for the admission of expert testimony. A party wishing to propose expert testimony should make sure that its experts are familiar with the criteria set forth in *Daubert* and can present testimony showing how those criteria are met by the proposed testimony. Finally, and perhaps significantly, whereas in the past the *Frye* standard addressed only one area of inquiry, namely general acceptance within the scientific community, *Daubert* opens the door to several other areas to be considered in determining whether to admit expert testimony, such as whether the testimony is based upon scientific, technical, or other specialized knowledge. The Court took pains to note that the word "knowledge" connotes more than subjective belief or unsupported speculation.[39]

In a post-*Daubert* decision, the Seventh Circuit Court of Appeals noted in rejecting proffered expert testimony that "if experts cannot tie their assessment of data to known scientific conclusions, based on research or studies, then there is no comparison for the jury to evaluate, and the experts' testimony is not helpful to the jury."[40] The court further noted that personal experiments or observations of the expert who testified were insufficient to establish scientific knowledge.[41]

Another post-*Daubert* decision emphasized that even under the *Daubert* standard, an expert's methodology must have a scientific basis or be rejected, and the party offering the expert's opinion must establish that basis.[42]

Daubert also highlights the significance of evaluating expert testimony in light of Rule 403 concerning the disqualification of relevant testimony due to potential prejudice, and Rule 703 requiring that expert testimony using hearsay data be of "a type reasonably relied upon by experts in the particular field."

---

[39] Daubert v. Merrell Dow Pharmaceuticals, Inc., 509 U.S. 579, 590.

[40] Porter v. Whitehall Lab., 9 F.3d 607, 614 (7th Cir. 1993).

[41] Porter v. Whitehall Lab., 9 F.3d 607, 614 (7th Cir. 1993).

[42] O'Conner v. Commonwealth Edison Co., 13 F.3d 1090 (7th Cir.), *cert. denied*, 512 U.S. 1222 (1994) (rejecting expert's opinion as lacking scientific basis in a civil case involving expert testimony by plaintiff concerning cataracts caused by unsafe levels of radiation).

§ 11.6 *Daubert*, *Frye*, and applicability to psychological and mental health testimony.

The United States Supreme Court in *Kumho Tire Company v. Carmichael*[43] held that all types of expert testimony are subject to the *Daubert* principles of relevance and reliability gatekeeping. The Court concluded that a trial judge's "gatekeeping" responsibility "applies not only to testimony based on 'scientific' knowledge, but also to testimony based on 'technical' and 'other specialized' knowledge."[44] The Supreme Court specifically rejected the holdings of some courts that *Daubert* applied only in cases where an expert "relies on the application of scientific principles."[45] Courts have cited *Kumho Tire* for the proposition that a mental health expert should not comment on the credibility of a sexual assault victim when there is no showing of reliability for this type of expert analysis.[46] While *Kumho* appears to supersede decisions which hold that expert testimony often seen in sexual assault cases is not subject to the *Daubert* reliability standards, not all courts have applied it to mental health or behavioral testimony.[47]

Even in a civil lawsuit, expert testimony on psychological evaluations in a child abuse case must conform to *Daubert* standards. In analyzing the admissibility of psychological testimony in a child abuse case, the 8th Circuit Court of Appeals has held that expert psychological testimony in child abuse cases should be both scientifically valid and properly applied to the facts and issue.[48] Among

---

[43] Kumho Tire Co. v. Carmichael, 526 U.S. 137 (1999).

[44] Kumho Tire Co. v. Carmichael, 526 U.S. 137, 147.

[45] Kumho Tire Co. v. Carmichael, 526 U.S. 137, 146.

[46] United States v. Velarde, 214 F.3d 1204 (10th Cir. 2000), *cert. denied*, 541 U.S. 1069 (2004) (reversing defendant's conviction due to trial court's failure to conduct reliability hearing with respect to expert's testimony on whether complainant's statements and behaviors are consistent with her having been sexually abused; reversal was required because "little other evidence suggested sexual abuse had occurred"); United States v. Charley, 189 F.3d 1251 (10th Cir. 1999), *cert. denied*, 528 U.S. 1098 (2000). *See also* Roise v. State, 7 S.W.3d 225 (Tex. Ct. App. 1999) (holding trial court improperly admitted expert testimony without findings of reliability, interpreting photos of children, "arousal analysis" and harm to children portrayed, but error was harmless given proof of guilt).

[47] *See, e.g.*, United States v. Bighead, 128 F.3d 1329 (9th Cir. 1997) (holding expert testimony on characteristics of sexual abuse victims, such as delayed disclosure, does not fall within *Daubert* standards for admissibility of expert testimony); State v. Lente, 119 P.3d 737 (N.M. Ct. App.), *cert. denied*, 119 P.3d 1265 (2005) (noting that New Mexico courts have not applied *Daubert* to all expert testimony); Nenno v. State, 970 S.W.2d 549 (Tex. Crim. App. 1998) (finding that, "When addressing fields or study aside from the hard sciences, such as the social sciences or fields that are based primarily upon experience and training as opposed to the scientific method, *Kelly's* requirement of reliability applies but with less rigor than to the hard sciences." When soft sciences are at issue, the trial court should inquire: "(1) whether the field of expertise is a legitimate one, (2) whether the subject matter of the expert's testimony is within the scope of that field, and (3) whether the expert's testimony properly relies upon and/or utilizes the principles involved in the field." Nenno v. State, 970 S.W.2d 549, 561 (Tex. Crim. App. 1998)).

[48] Gier by & Through Gier v. Educational Serv. Unit No. 16, 66 F.3d 940 (8th Cir. 1995).

the reasons that the appellate court offered for rejecting the expert testimony in a civil suit by a child who was allegedly abused in a school, the court noted the following weaknesses in the expert's testimony: (1) there was no validation of the experts' methodology with respect to mentally-disabled children; (2) the experts' checklist was insufficient on its own to make a determination of abuse; (3) there were no guidelines for the interviewing of the child; and (4) the experts did not follow their own protocol which they had submitted to the court. [49] The court found that this was "precisely the type of analysis the decision in *Daubert* would appear to contemplate." [50]

Some courts even before *Daubert* had difficulty applying the *Frye* standard to mental health testimony, preferring to focus on reliability rather than general acceptance, noting that medical opinions on injury causation or diagnoses are not based on absolute certainty. [51] The fact that a theory is new, emerging, or relatively untested is not enough to deny admission of psychological testimony if reliability is shown. [52]

Some courts apply a scientific reliability standard to psychological testimony or the "soft sciences." Yet, there are conflicting court decisions in applying scientific reliable standards.

Also, while an expert may rely on material not in evidence, the material must be a kind ordinarily accepted by experts in the field. An expert's opinion lacks legal foundation when based upon unreliable studies, theories, premises, or tests. [53] The application of this principle can be seen with the polygraph; generally an expert may not base an opinion on a polygraph test. [54] The issue arises particularly with new or novel evidence.

§ 11.7 *Frye* and *Daubert* applicability to psychological and mental health testimony — Expert testimony on complainant, victim, or defendant behaviors: pattern or profile evidence.

General acceptance and reliability of psychological testimony may be required by some courts when expert testimony is offered to show that a complainant's behavior is consistent with that of a sexual assault victim, [55] and it may be

---

[49] Grier by & Through Gier v. Educational Serv. Unit No. 16, 66 F.3d 940 (8th Cir. 1995).

[50] Grier by & Through Gier v. Educational Serv. Unit No. 16, 66 F.3d 940, 943 (8th Cir. 1995).

[51] People v. Cegers, 7 Cal. App. 4th 988, 998, 9 Cal. Rptr. 2d 297, 303 (1992) (reversing a defendant's conviction where the trial court precluded testimony on defendant's suffering from "confusional arousal syndrome" at time of crime).

[52] People v. Cegers, 7 Cal. app. 4th 988, 998, 9 Cal. Rptr. 2d 297, 303 (1992).

[53] *See* §§ 11.57 and 11.66.

[54] People v. Angelo, 88 N.Y.2d 217, 666 N.E.2d 1333, 644 N.Y.S.2d 460 (1996).

[55] Hadden v. State, 690 So. 2d 573 (Fla. 1997) ("We hold that upon proper objection prior to the

reversible error to fail to conduct a *Daubert* hearing on expert testimony that a complainant's statements and behaviors are consistent with having been sexually abused.[56] This objection should be registered separate and apart from other objections to such testimony, such as prejudice or improper reference upon the credibility of a witness.[57]

One court distinguishes between an expert testifying that a victim's symptoms were more consistent with the symptoms of children who have been sexually abused than with children who witness physical abuse of their mother, since such an opinion is a more positive statement that abuse occurred.[58] The court noted that such testimony lacked foundation, and no *Daubert* finding of reliability was undertaken by the trial court.

Some courts will not permit without establishing scientific reliability, a defense expert to testify that a victim's post-incident demeanor was inconsistent with the "usual" emotional reactions exhibited by trauma victims, particularly given the variability in victims' reactions.[59]

Some courts have found expert testimony on a victim's behavior to meet the standards of scientific reliability.[60]

This is also discussed in other sections in this chapter on expert testimony.

Two courts have suggested the following 12 criteria as a framework of questions to ask regarding the validity of profile evidence under the standard for the admissibility of scientific testimony:

1. If there is a control group, what criteria are used to determine whether a child in that group has been, in fact, sexually abused?

2. Do children react in similar ways to sexual abuse?

3. Do older children react differently to sexual abuse than do younger children?

---

introduction of a psychologist's expert testimony offered to prove the alleged victim of sexual abuse exhibits symptoms consistent with one who has been sexually abused, the trial court must find that the psychologist's testimony is admissible under the standard for admissibility of novel scientific evidence announced in *Frye*. . . ."); Irving v. State, 705 So. 2d 1021 (Fla. Ct. App. 1998) (reversing defendant's conviction due to expert's testimony that victim's behavior demonstrated sexual abuse based on "projective tests", a diagnostic criteria that must pass *Frye* test); State v. Foret, 628 So. 2d 1116, 1127 (La. 1993) (holding that psychological syndrome theories are practically untestable and fail *Daubert's* threshold test of reliability).

[56] United States v. Velarde, 214 F.3d 1204 (10th Cir. 2000); Roise v. State, 7 S.W.3d 225 (Tex. Ct. App. 1999).

[57] Hadden v. State, 690 So. 2d 573 (Fla. 1997).

[58] United States v. Charley, 189 F.3d 1251 (10th Cir. 1999), *cert. denied*, 528 U.S. 1098 (2000) (holding such testimony erroneously admitted but harmless error).

[59] People v. Wells, 118 Cal. App. 4th 179, 12 Cal. Rptr. 3d 762 (2004).

[60] *See, e.g.*, Crawford v. State, 754 So. 2d 1211 (Miss. 2000) (holding expert's description of victim's behavior as common with that of sexually-abused child, met *Frye* standard and was properly admitted by trial court).

4.   Is there a typical reaction, or a typical set of reactions manifested by child victims of sexual abuse?

5.   Must a child react typically to be believed?

6.   Was the syndrome developed on the assumption that the children studied were in fact molested?

7.   Can the syndrome, developed as a therapeutic aid, be used as a truth-seeking device?

8.   Is the syndrome described in DMS III?

9.   Is the symptomology, when described by different experts and manifested by different victims, precise?

10. Have the symptoms of those children known to be sexually abused been compared to those of children known not to have been sexually abused?

11. Do reactions of children to sexual abuse vary according to the child's relationship to the perpetrator?

12. Is there agreement in the community as to which combinations of symptoms comprise the syndrome? How many? Which ones?[61]

The principle also applies to a defendant's expert. The expert opinion may not be based on "unreliable" data. A defendant who seeks to offer a "pattern, profile, theory, or syndrome" to portray a pattern of behavior must establish its general acceptance or reliability.[62] Experts should not be permitted "to parade before the jury non-testifying experts' publications about a theoretical profile, without a reliability foundation."[63]

Some courts do not believe that it is appropriate to conduct a hearing on the reliability of evidence in the field of psychology and that *Daubert* does not apply to the "soft" sciences.[64]

§ 11.8   Reliability based on personal experience of witness and medical opinions on diagnoses subject to *Frye* or *Daubert* analysis.

However, in some situations involving expert medical testimony, the personal experience of the expert may form a valid basis for the expert opinion.[65] For

---

[61] Beaulieu v. State, 671 So. 2d 807 (Fla. Ct. App. 1996).

[62] People v. Wernick, 89 N.Y.2d 111, 674 N.E.2d 322, 651 N.Y.S.2d 392 (1996) (rejecting defendant's effort to offer expert testimony of neonaticide, a term used to describe a mother killing her newborn within 24 hours of birth).

[63] People v. Wernick, 89 N.Y.2d 111, 117–18, 674 N.E.2d 322, 325, 651 N.Y.S.2d 392, 395 (1996).

[64] Moore v. Ashland Chem. Inc., 126 F.3d 679 (1997) (holding *Daubert* criteria applicable only to "hard" sciences); State v. Whaley, 305 S.C. 138, 406 S.E.2d 369 (1991).

[65] Gregory v. State, 56 S.W.3d 164, 180 (Tex. Ct. App. 2001), *cert. denied*, 538 U.S. 978 (2003) (upholding nurse's ability to give opinions concerning genital injuries, court noted experience alone can provide a sufficient basis for expert testimony).

example, a physician may testify that ordinarily there are no physical findings in child sexual abuse cases based on his personal experience, and that in greater than 50 percent of sexual abuse cases there is an absence of findings.[66] Quite often, medical diagnoses are not held to a *Frye* or *Daubert* standard. For example, the battered child syndrome (§ 11.37) and shaken baby syndrome are not usually governed by *Frye* or *Daubert* analysis.[67] Expert testimony by a physician concerning the amount of time between the alleged shaking of the deceased child and the onset of symptoms is supported by medical literature and does not require a *Frye* hearing.[68] Also, a pathologist's 75 autopsies constitutes sufficiently reliable experience under *Daubert* to render an opinion that a bullet wound was consistent with a certain body position.[69] The Kansas Supreme Court holds that *Frye* does not apply to "pure opinion" testimony, which it defines as expert opinions developed based on the expert's own experience and observation.[70] It holds that *Frye* does apply to expert opinion based on a new or novel scientific principle, formula, or procedure developed by others.[71] Yet another court finds a pathologist may testify that a victim was alive when police officers arrived at a scene, but not that a gag in her mouth stopped her from crying out, since the latter opinion was "not based on scientific method or study and is outside his area of expertise."[72]

A counselor's personal experience may be insufficient to meet the standard of scientific reliability to testify about victim behaviors.[73] This is designed to

---

[66] State v. Malroit, 2000 Ohio App. LEXIS 5169 at *17–19 (Nov. 8, 2000), *dismissed, discretionary appeal not allowed*, 91 Ohio St. 3d 1460, 743 N.E.2d 400, 2001 Ohio LEXIS 660 (2001).

[67] Commonwealth v. Passarelli, 2001 Pa. Super. 377, P25–26, 789 A.2d 708, 714–16 (2001), *affirmed*, 573 Pa. 372, 825 A.2d 628 (2003).

[68] People v. Scoon, 303 A.D.2d 525, 756 N.Y.S.2d 100, *appeal denied*, 100 N.Y.2d 624, 799 N.E.2d 631, 767 N.Y.S.2d 408 (2003).

[69] Deering v. Reich, 183 F.3d 645, 654, *cert. denied*, 528 U.S. 1021 (1999).

[70] Kuhn v. Sandoz Pharms. Corp., 270 Kan. 443, 14 P.3d 1170 (2000).

[71] Kuhn v. Sandoz Pharms. Corp., 270 Kan. 443, 14 P.3d 1170 (2000).

[72] Schieber v. City of Philadelphia, 2000 U.S. Dist. LEXIS 16084, *summary judg. granted in part, summary judg. denied in part*, 2001 U.S. Dist. LEXIS 5887 (May 9, 2001).

[73] *See, e.g.*, Fowler v. State, 958 S.W.2d 853 (Tex. Ct. App. 1997) (A domestic violence counselor's opinions, based solely on personal experience, are subject to a scientific reliability standard. The court held:

> Our review of the record reveals that the State failed to present sufficient evidence of the validity of the scientific theories underlying Gregory's testimony and the validity of the techniques used to apply the theories. Apart from establishing her qualifications and experience, not a single *Kelly* factor was met. The evidence does not show whether Gregory's theories are accepted as valid, nor whether a single piece of literature has been written to support her testimony. Likewise, whether Gregory has ever conducted research to test the validity of her theories or been subjected to peer review does not appear in the record. Whether or not the underlying theory and technique could be clearly explained is also unknown, considering that no attempt was made. In short, we find that the State, as the proponent of this evidence, failed to make an adequate

eliminate "unsubstantiated, unsupported opinion."[74]

§ 11.9   *Frye, Daubert* and applicability to psychological and mental health testimony — Actuarial assessments and expert opinion on prediction of future dangerousness.

Some courts still do not apply the *Frye* test to various actuarial assessments in the sexual abuse field, which seek to predict dangerousness of an offender,[75] while other courts require that general acceptance of the actuarial instruments in the psychological and psychiatric communities be established.[76]

§ 11.10   Applicability to psychological testing on *Miranda* rights, interviewing techniques.

When a defense expert offers psychological testimony that a defendant lacks the comprehension to understand *Miranda* warnings based on psychological tests administered by the expert, the court must determine the reliability and acceptance of the tests.[77]

---

showing of a valid underlying scientific theory, a valid technique applying the theory, or that any technique at all was applied in the present case. As a result, we find that the expert testimony fails to meet the *Kelly* test for admissibility and thus was improperly admitted.

Fowler v. State, 958 S.W.2d 853, 864 (Tex. Ct. App. 1997)).

[74] Fowler v. State, 958 S.W.2d 853, 862 (Tex. Ct. App. 1997).

[75] State *ex rel.* Romley v. Fields, 201 Ariz. 321, 35 P.3d 82 (2001) (holding in a Sexually Violent Person's Act hearing "that the use of actuarial models by mental health experts to help predict a person's likelihood of recidivism is not the kind of novel scientific evidence or process to which *Frye* applies." Decision cites with approval, State v. Varela, 178 Ariz. 319, 325–26, 873 P.2d 657, 663–64 (1993), which held *Frye* inapplicable to the general characteristics of child sexual abuse victims); People v. Erbe (*In re* Erbe), 344 Ill. App. 3d 350, 800 N.E.2d 137 (2003); State v. Holz (*In re* Holz), 653 N.W.2d 613 (Iowa Ct. App. 2002).

[76] People v. Bolton (*In re* Bolton), 343 Ill. App. 3d 1223, 800 N.E.2d 128 (2003); People v. Hargett (*In re* Hargett), 786 N.E.2d 557, 272 Ill. Dec. 18 (Ill. App. Ct. 2003); People v. Taylor, 335 Ill. App. 3d 965, 782 N.E.2d 920 (2002) (holding use of MNSOST, RRASOR (Minnesota Sex Offender Screening Tool, Raped Risk Assessment of Sexual Offense) and STATIC-99 methods to assess defendant's risk of re-offending required a *Frye* hearing.).

[77] People v. Rogers, 247 A.D.2d 765, 669 N.Y.S.2d 678, *appeal denied,* 91 N.Y.2d 976, 695 N.E.2d 725, 672 N.Y.S.2d 856 (1998); Salazar v. State, 127 S.W.3d 355 (Tex. Ct. App. 2004) (finding defendant's expert's testimony on evaluating interviewing techniques of children, using "content-based interview analysis" to address suggestiveness of interviews was not admissible and subject to *Daubert* analysis, because defendant did not establish its general acceptance and expert's opinions were also not sufficiently tied to case, and potential rate of error was great).

§ 11.11　Rape trauma syndrome and post-traumatic stress disorder.

One of the most frequently encountered areas of expert testimony in sexual assault trials is that of the "rape trauma syndrome." The theory was first set forth in 1974 in a report by Burgess and Holmstrom,[78] which was based on a year-long study conducted at an emergency room at a Boston hospital of all women who reported being raped. The syndrome tends to identify both acute and long-term reactions of victims of forcible rape. According to the authors, the syndrome consists of a two-phase reaction. The initial reaction is acute and causes tremendous disorganization in the victim's lifestyle, many physical symptoms, and fear. Immediately after an attack there are two main emotional responses seen in victims. One is a feeling of fear, anger, and anxiety expressed in behavior such as crying, sobbing, smiling, restlessness, and tenseness. Other individuals may present a more controlled style in which feelings are masked or hidden. There are also somatic reactions during the first several weeks, which can include physical trauma from the assault itself, skeletal muscle tension (which can include headaches, fatigue, and sleep pattern disturbances), gastrointestinal irritability, and genital or urinary disturbance. Burgess and Holmstrom also identify emotional reactions in the acute phase such as humiliation, embarrassment, anger, desire for revenge, and self-blame. There is also a fear of physical violence or death.

As time passes, certain other changes take place in victims. Many will take other steps to ensure their safety, such as changing their residence or phone number. Victims also may experience nightmares and a fear of indoors, of outdoors, of being alone, of crowds, and of having people behind them. Also, during the attempt to reorganize their lives, many women will experience problems relating to their sexuality and have difficulty resuming normal sexual relations.

In identifying the syndrome, clinicians hope to help victims who may not have reported their sexual assault and yet carry with them significant medical and physical problems related to the assault.

The mental health community has generally accepted the rape trauma syndrome as a valid diagnosis. Evidence of this can be seen in the American Psychiatric Association's inclusion of rape as one of the stressors that can lead to the "post-traumatic stress disorder" (PTSD) in *The Diagnostic and Statistical Manual of Mental Disorders,*[79] the basic classification and definition handbook of psychiatric and psychological disorders. This book contains the generally accepted

---

[78] Ann W. Burgess & Linda L. Holmstrom, *Rape Trauma Syndrome*, 131 Am. J. Psychiatry 981 (1974).

[79] American Psychiatric Association, Diagnostic and Statistical Manual of Mental Disorders (4th ed., 2000) (hereinafter DSM IV). This is a basic book and should be consulted during the attorney's preparation for the direct or cross-examination of mental health experts.

definitions and the criteria for diagnosing psychiatric and psychological conditions. It is used by psychiatrists, psychologists, and social workers in their daily practices. The cautionary statement at the beginning of the manual warns that it is designed primarily as a treatment tool and that it does not "encompass all the conditions that may be legitimate objects of treatment or research efforts."[80]

A previous edition of the Manual (DSM III-R) had described the "distressing event" in PTSD as "outside the range of usual human experience." This has been changed. DSM IV begins its definition of PTSD as follows:

> The essential feature of Post-traumatic Stress Disorder is the development of characteristic symptoms following exposure to an extreme traumatic stressor involving direct personal experience of an event that involves actual or threatened death or serious injury, or other threat to one's physical integrity; or witnessing an event that involves death, injury, or a threat to the physical integrity of another person; or learning about unexpected or violent death, serious harm, or threat of death or injury experienced by a family member or other close associate (Criterion A1). The person's response to the event must involve intense fear, helplessness, or horror (or in children, the response must involve disorganized or agitated behavior) (Criterion A2). The characteristic symptoms resulting from the exposure to the extreme trauma include persistent re-experiencing of the traumatic event (Criterion B), persistent avoidance of stimuli associated with the trauma and numbing of general responsiveness (Criterion C), and persistent symptoms of increased arousal (Criterion D). The full symptom picture must be present for more than 1 month (Criterion E), and the disturbance must cause clinically significant distress or impairment in social, occupational, or other important areas of functioning (Criterion F).

> Traumatic events that are experienced directly include, but are not limited to, military combat, violent personal assault (sexual assault, physical attack, robbery, mugging), being kidnapped, being taken hostage, terrorist attack, torture, incarceration as a prisoner of war or in a concentration camp, natural or manmade disasters, severe automobile accidents, or being diagnosed with a life-threatening illness. For children, sexually-traumatic events may include

---

[80] American Psychiatric Association, Diagnostic and Statistical Manual of Mental Disorders (4th ed., 2000) at xxxii-xxxiii:

> Cautionary Statement: The specified diagnostic criteria for each mental disorder are offered as guidelines for making diagnoses, since it has been demonstrated that the use of such criteria enhances agreement among clinicians and investigators. The proper use of these criteria requires specialized clinical training that provides both a body of knowledge and clinical skills.

> These diagnostic criteria and the DSM-III-R classification of mental disorders reflect a consensus of current formulations of evolving knowledge in our field but do not encompass all the conditions that may be legitimate objects of treatment or research efforts.

developmentally inappropriate sexual experiences without threatened or actual violence or injury.[81]

The manual outlines very specific criteria for the diagnosis of this disorder, including how the trauma is re-experienced, how stimuli associated with the event are avoided, the persistent symptoms that will be exhibited by the victim, and the duration of these symptoms.[82]

PTSD is the psychological umbrella for rape trauma syndrome and "battered-woman syndrome," which also is frequently encountered in sexual assault trials. The main problem from a scientific reliability perspective is that the signs and symptoms of PTSD have many potential causes other than abuse or assault. This is a primary and fertile area for the cross-examination of expert testimony in these cases.

Some courts permit testimony of rape trauma syndrome and post-traumatic stress disorder, but only by a physician and not other mental health professionals, such as a social worker.[83] Other courts may permit a social worker to testify to the diagnosis of post-traumatic stress disorder or symptoms of rape accommodation syndrome.[84] The fact that a social worker is "non-certified" does not necessarily preclude the social worker from testifying as an expert.[85]

§ 11.12 When admissible.

Courts have recognized rape trauma syndrome as one of the possible stressors in PTSD, and the syndrome is generally accepted in the scientific community.[86]

---

[81] American Psychiatric Association, Diagnostic and Statistical Manual of Mental Disorders (4th ed., 2000) at 424.

[82] American Psychiatric Association, Diagnostic and Statistical Manual of Mental Disorders (4th ed., 2000) at 427–29.

[83] Perez v. State, 25 S.W.3d 830 (Tex. Ct. App. 2000).

[84] United States v. Raya, 45 M.J. 251 (C.A.A.F. 1996); Kansas Stat. § 65-6319 was amended to permit certain licensed clinical social workers to diagnose and treat mental disorders specified in diagnostic and statistical manual of mental disorder. *See* Welch v. State, 270 Kan. 229, 13 P.3d 882 (2000).

[85] Harnett v. State, 38 S.W.3d 650 (Tex. Ct. App. 2000).

[86] Discepolo v. Gorgone, 399 F. Supp. 2d 123 (D. Conn. 2005); People v. Taylor, 75 N.Y.2d 277, 552 N.E.2d 131, 552 N.Y.S.2d 883 (1990); State v. Hall, 330 N.C. 808, 819, 412 S.E.2d 883, 889 (1992); State v. Bidinost, 71 Ohio St. 3d 449, 644 N.E.2d 318 (Ohio 1994) ("Accordingly, we are convinced that post-traumatic stress disorder in children has gained sufficient recognition in the psychiatric profession to be considered a proper subject for expert testimony."); State v. Bidinost, 71 Ohio St. 3d 449, 644 N.E.2d 318, 323 (Ohio 1994)); State v. Kinney, 171 Vt. 239, 762 A.2d 833 (2000) (finding rape trauma syndrome sufficiently reliable since methodologies admissible under previous evidentiary standards are admissible under *Daubert* absent affirmative evidence of unreliability); Chapman v. State, 2001 Wyo. 25, P16–19, 18 P.3d 1164, 1171–72 (2001) (Court found that PTSD has achieved general acceptance in fields of psychiatry and psychology, but there are limitations on how it may be used. It may be used to explain a victim's behavior, but not to establish that abuse occurred.). *Contra* Prickett v. State, 220 Ga. App. 244, 469 S.E.2d

Most jurisdictions will allow testimony on rape trauma syndrome and PTSD when they involve specific behaviors or issues raised at trial. For example, evidence of rape trauma syndrome is commonly admitted to explain a victim's delay in reporting a sexual assault when delay is an issue.[87] The syndrome is also proper to show why a victim could not identify her assailant immediately after her assault[88] and to rebut a defendant's contention that the rape victim's memory loss was due to intoxication rather than the trauma of rape.[89] Testimony of post-traumatic stress disorder may be admissible to rebut the defense's suggestions made during cross-examination that the complainant "was a troubled teenager, whose medical problems were related to menstruation, and whose unhappy homelife could lead to false claims of rape."[90] The diagnosis of post-traumatic stress disorder in a child may also help to explain an abused child's behavior.[91]

Expert testimony can explain why a rape victim who knows her assailant may be fearful of identifying him and less likely to report the rape. This behavior

---

371 (1996) (noting that Georgia courts have not necessarily accepted the scientific basis of rape trauma syndrome and PTSD and that a trial court should conduct a hearing to determine acceptance in the particular field in which it belongs). *See generally* Gregory G. Sarno, Annotation, *Admissibility, and Criminal Prosecution of Expert Testimony on Rape Trauma Syndrome*, 42 A.L.R. 4TH 879 (1985).

[87] United States v. Peel, 29 M.J. 235, 241 (C.M.A. 1989), *cert. denied*, 493 U.S. 1025 (1990); People v. Fasy, 829 P.2d 1314 (Colo. 1992) (expert permitted to testify that victim's delay in reporting assault was consistent with PTSD); People v. Hampton, 746 P.2d 947 (Colo. 1987) (permitting expert testimony to explain why victims are reluctant to report sexual assault by someone known to them; in this case the victim waited 89 days to report the rape); Hutton v. State, 339 Md. 480, 663 A.2d 1289 (1995); Commonwealth v. Mamay, 407 Mass. 412, 421, 553 N.E.2d 945, 951 (1990) (expert permitted to testify that victims in a trusted relationship may return to the perpetrator); State v. Doan, 498 N.W.2d 804 (Neb. 1993); People v. Taylor, 75 N.Y.2d 277, 552 N.E.2d 131, 552 N.Y.S.2d 883 (1990); State v. Kinney, 171 Vt. 239, 762 A.2d 833 (2000) (upholding expert testimony that rape trauma syndrome accounts for a victim's delay in reporting assault and what victims "may experience such as difficulty in interpersonal relationships, guilt, shame, and sexual dysfunction" and that victims do not usually resist by force but rather through verbal protests); State v. Noyes, 157 Vt. 114, 596 A.2d 340 (1991).

[88] People v. Taylor, 75 N.Y.2d 277, 552 N.E.2d 131, 552 N.Y.S.2d 883 (1990). *See also* People v. Maymi, 198 A.D.2d 153, 603 N.Y.S.2d 862 (1993), *appeal denied*, 82 N.Y.2d 927, 632 N.E.2d 489, 610 N.Y.S.2d 179 (1994) (Expert testimony regarding rape trauma syndrome was admissible to assist the jury in understanding that the fact that the victim told her boyfriend about the rape the day after it occurred, but refrained from telling her mother and the police until two weeks later was consistent with "patterns of response exhibited by rape victims" (*citing* People v. Taylor) and was not admitted for purposes of bolstering the victim's testimony. The testimony also assisted the jury by explaining that the victim experienced psychological stress that was not apparent from her testimony. Thus, it supplied the jury with an explanation as to why someone who had been raped appeared to act in a manner inconsistent with such an incident. Any prejudice was dissipated when the court instructed the jury, both after the expert finished testifying and in its main charge, that the testimony was not offered for the truth of the allegations).

[89] State v. Staples, 120 N.H. 278, 282, 415 A.2d 320, 322 (1980).

[90] Commonwealth v. Hudson, 417 Mass. 536, 541, 631 N.E.2d 50, 53 (1994).

[91] State v. Bidinost, 71 Ohio St. 3d 449, 644 N.E.2d 318, 323 (1994).

is not within the ordinary understanding of the jury, and the rape trauma syndrome can provide a scientifically-accepted theory to explain such conduct.

The following is an example of expert testimony used to explain that a sexual assault victim may provide a disoriented "sparse version of the events" and be unable to recount the details of the trauma immediately after an assault.[92]

> **Q.** Is it common to have someone in the early stages of their admission to your hospital — as was this victim — is it common for that person not to be able to tell you all the details of the event that brought them there?
>
> **A.** Yes.
>
> **Q.** Okay. Is it common for them to tell you, what it is that they tell you, out of chronological sequence?
>
> **A.** Yes.
>
> **Q.** And is it common for portions of the events to come to them at a later time as they proceed through the trauma and the recovery from the trauma?
>
> **A.** Very common.

Illinois, by statute, permits testimony by a qualified expert relating to any recognized and accepted form of post-traumatic stress syndrome.[93] However, this statute has been limited by the Supreme Court of Illinois, which has held that the prosecution cannot use the statute unless either the victim consents to an examination by an expert chosen by the defendant or the prosecution offers the expert testimony without having the victim examined by an expert.[94]

Other uses of PTSD or the rape trauma syndrome include establishing the lack of consent and that such behavior is "consistent with" these conditions,[95]

---

[92] State v. Freeney, 228 Conn. 582, 590, 637 A.2d 1088, 1092 (1994).

[93] ILL. COMP. STAT. ch. 725, § 5/115-7.2. *See* People v. Nelson, 203 Ill. App. 3d 1038, 561 N.E.2d 439 (1990), *appeal denied*, 136 Ill. 2d 551, 567 N.E.2d 339 (1991); People v. Roy, 201 Ill. App. 3d 166, 558 N.E.2d 1208 (1990), *appeal denied*, 136 Ill. 2d 552, 567 N.E.2d 340 (1991), *cert. denied*, 502 U.S. 1071 (1992). *See* §§ 1.17 to 1.19 for a discussion on a defendant's right to a psychological examination of a complainant.

[94] People v. Wheeler, 151 Ill. 2d 298, 311, 602 N.E.2d 826, 832 (1992).

[95] United States v. Carter, 26 M.J. 428 (C.M.A. 1988) (admitting testimony of Rape Trauma Syndrome to show "improbability" of consent); State v. Huey, 145 Ariz. 59, 699 P.2d 1290, 1294 (1985); Toro v. State, 642 So. 2d 78 (Fla. Ct. App. 1994) (admitting expert's testimony that child's behaviors of a "sense of danger," sleep disturbance, decrease in occupational function (i.e., going to school), making poor choices about her friends, decreased interest in events or activities in general, irritability, anger, poor concentration, hyper vigilance, and exaggerated startled response (i.e., jumping when someone walked up behind her and touched her) was evidence that child suffered from "Post-Traumatic Stress Disorder" and that expert believed source of the trauma was sexual abuse; however, court questioned whether it may be time to re-examine the use of such evidence in Florida courts); State v. Marks, 231 Kan. 645, 647 P.2d 1292 (1982) ("[i]f the presence of Rape Trauma Syndrome is detectable and reliable as evidence that a forcible assault did take place, it is relevant when a defendant argues the victim consented to sexual intercourse. As such

although this would not be in line with the weight of authority or the intended scope of the rape trauma syndrome, as noted in the following section.

The Supreme Court of New Mexico reviewed the admissibility of expert testimony in light of the Supreme Court's decision in *Daubert*. It held that PTSD testimony is valid, probative, and not unduly prejudicial, and it is admissible to show that a complainant's symptoms are "consistent with" (but not "caused by") a sexual assault.[96] Citing *Daubert*, the Court said, "there is no requirement that a scientific technique or method prove conclusively what it purports to prove."[97]

The New Mexico Court, in commenting on other courts' distinction in admitting PTSD testimony to explain a victim's reaction but not to establish the abuse, observed:

> Allowing an expert to testify that PTSD symptoms are a common reaction to sexual assault for the purpose of rebutting the defense that the victim's reactions to the alleged incident are inconsistent with sexual assault is no different from allowing the expert to testify that the alleged victim's symptoms are consistent with sexual abuse. Although the Court of Appeals and some other courts maintain a bright-line distinction between these two purposes for the admissibility of PTSD testimony, we see no logical difference. Both of these purposes for which PTSD evidence is offered rest on the valid scientific premise that victims of sexual abuse exhibit identifiable symptoms. Either the PTSD diagnosis is a valid scientific technique for identifying certain symptoms of sexual abuse or it is not. Expert testimony in these two cases show that it is valid.[98]

However, the Court did make a distinction between PTSD and rape trauma syndrome (RTS), which many courts do not. It held that RTS expert testimony

---

an expert's opinion does not invade the province of the jury. It is merely offered as any other evidence, with the expert subject to cross-examination and the jury left to determine its weight." State v. Marks, 231 Kan. 645, 654, 647 P.2d 1292, 1299 (1982)); Hutton v. State, 339 Md. 480, 663 A.2d 1289 (1995) (noting that while PTSD testimony is admissible where the defense is that the victim consented to sexual intercourse, it is improper to admit such testimony to prove that sexual abuse occurred); Acuna v. State, 332 Md. 65, 629 A.2d 1233 (1993) (PTSD admissible where expert connects it to crime charged); State v. Allewalt, 308 Md. 89, 517 A.2d 741 (1986) (permitting testimony about PTSD to establish consent); State v. Liddell, 211 Mont. 180, 685 P.2d 918 (1984); State v. Schumpert, 312 S.C. 502, 435 S.E.2d 859 (1993) (holding that expert testimony and behavioral evidence are admissible as rape trauma evidence to prove a sexual offense occurred where the probative value of such evidence outweighs its prejudicial effect); State v. McCoy, 179 W. Va. 223, 366 S.E.2d 731 (1988) ("qualified expert testimony regarding rape trauma syndrome is relevant and admissible in a prosecution for rape where the defense is consent. The expert may testify that the alleged victim exhibits behavior consistent with Rape Trauma Syndrome, but the expert may not give an opinion, expressly or implicitly, as to whether or not the alleged victim was raped." State v. McCoy, 179 W. Va. 223, 229, 366 S.E.2d 731, 737 (1988)).

[96] State v. Alberico, 116 N.M. 156, 861 P.2d 192 (1993).

[97] State v. Alberico, 116 N.M. 156, 172, 861 P.2d 192, 208.

[98] State v. Alberico, 116 N.M. 156, 174, 861 P.2d 192, 210.

is inadmissible because "it is not part of the specialized manual DSM III-R like PTSD is, even though there is evidence in the record that RTS is generally accepted by psychologists just like PTSD is."[99] This is a distinction without much difference and is more of a semantic exercise. The New Mexico Court also precluded a PTSD expert from identifying the alleged perpetrator, commenting that the victim is telling the truth, and identifying the cause of the complainant's PTSD symptoms.[100]

Expert testimony on post-traumatic stress disorder and comments upon the credibility of the complainant may be permissible when elicited on cross-examination by defense counsel.[101]

When the defense suggests another source as the "triggering event" for the complainant's symptoms, this may open the door to the expert's eliminating other causes.[102]

§ 11.13   Limitations on admissibility.

It should be remembered that rape trauma syndrome was developed as a therapeutic tool and not as a test to determine the existence of a rape. Therefore, any attempt to establish that a rape took place by offering RTS testimony is impermissible, since there is no scientific basis for such a conclusion. While an expert can testify on RTS to rebut misconceptions about presumed behavior of a rape victim, an expert cannot testify that the symptoms exhibited by a rape victim prove that a rape in fact occurred.[103] Sometimes the same effect can be

---

[99] State v. Alberico, 116 N.M. 156, 176, 861 P.2d 192, 212.

[100] State v. Alberico, 116 N.M. 156, 176, 861 P.2d 192, 212.

[101] Taylor v. Commonwealth, 21 Va. App. 557, 562–63, 466 S.E.2d 118, 120–21 (1996).

[102] Ward v. Commonwealth, 264 Va. 648, 653, 570 S.E.2d 827, 830 (2002).

[103] People v. Bledsoe, 36 Cal. 3d 236, 203 Cal. Rptr. 450, 681 P.2d 291 (1984); Hutton v. State, 339 Md. 480, 663 A.2d 1289 (1995); People v. Beckley, 434 Mich. 691, 456 N.W.2d 391, 409–10 (1990); State v. Saldana, 324 N.W.2d 227, 229–30, 232 (Minn. 1982) (Expert's opinion that an alleged rape victim suffered from RTS was inadmissible on the issue of consent. The counselor for sexual assault victims testified that she had met the alleged victim 10 days after the alleged rape and had counseled her for a 10-week period. The counselor stated her opinion that the victim suffered from RTS and that the victim had been sexually assaulted and raped. Further, she related that the victim could not have fantasized the rape. This testimony was unduly prejudicial to the defendant.); State v. Scherzer, 301 N.J. Super. 363, 694 A.2d 196, *appeal denied*, 151 N.J. 466, 700 A.2d 878 (1997) (holding that prosecution's expert improperly expressed opinion that complainant suffers from rape trauma syndrome but that error was harmless in this case); State v. W.L., 292 N.J. Super. 100, 678 A.2d 312 (1996) (reversing defendant's conviction in part because of prosecution's expert testimony that the complainant's post-traumatic stress disorder was "not inconsistent" with a victim of sexual abuse); People v. Taylor, 75 N.Y.2d 277, 552 N.E.2d 131, 552 N.Y.S.2d 883 (1990); People v. Graham, 251 A.D.2d 426, 674 N.Y.S.2d 120 (1998); State v. Chavis, 141 N.C. App. 553, 540 S.E.2d 404 (2000) (holding psychologist in testifying about victim's PTSD should not have stated that the assault by defendant on date in question was the "triggering event" of her PTSD, but error was not prejudicial); State v. Hensley, 120 N.C. App. 313, 462 S.E.2d 550 (1995) (defendant granted a new trial because of expert testimony that the

produced by stating that the existence of the syndrome established the act of sexual penetration. This, in effect, also states that a particular event took place and is impermissible.[104]

Reversible error was found where RTS was used to help explain why a victim could not identify her attacker two weeks after the attack, but could identify him four years later, since this would improperly enhance the victim's credibility.[105] This, however, is an area in which state courts have expressed different views; some courts will permit such testimony when a delay in identification has been raised as an issue, and there is a showing that RTS helps explain this delay.[106] When an expert witness comments directly on the credibility of a witness by stating in effect that the victim suffered RTS as a consequence of the incident with a defendant, or that the victim did not fantasize about the rape, testimony that a victim suffers from RTS carries with it the implication that the complainant has been raped and is being truthful, and this is improper expert opinion testimony.[107]

Similarly, testimony concerning PTSD can be admissible in the same case for one purpose but not another. For example, testimony about PTSD may be proper to explain why a complainant delayed in reporting the sexual abuse, but not to state that the victim's nightmares, flashbacks, and intrusive memories were the results of sexual abuse and that it is common for these symptoms to appear after a victim has left the abuser, since the effect of such testimony is to prove that the alleged acts of abuse took place.[108]

Another argument sometimes made against admitting expert testimony concerning sexual assault is that the average layman is familiar with the crime of rape and its emotional and behavioral effects. This argument has been accepted by one court, which reversed the defendant's rape conviction because it found that the jury was well-qualified to form its own conclusions concerning behavioral issues surrounding the rape.[109]

Some courts object to testimony on the rape trauma syndrome because it suggests that the only cause of the victim's symptoms is rape.[110] Certainly, the

victim's post-traumatic stress disorder was caused by "sexual abuse that he received, was the victim of, specifically anal penetration"); State v. Black, 109 Wash. 2d 336, 745 P.2d 12 (1987).

[104] Hutton v. State, 339 Md. 480, 663 A.2d 1289 (1995) ("Testimony by an expert that the alleged victim suffered from PTSD as a result of sexual abuse goes beyond the limits of proper expert expression." Hutton v. State, 339 Md. 480, 504, 663 A.2d 1289, 1301 (1995)); State v. Bowman, 104 N.M. 19, 715 P.2d 467 (1986).

[105] Commonwealth v. Gallagher, 519 Pa. 291, 547 A.2d 355 (1988).

[106] See, e.g., People v. Taylor, 75 N.Y.2d 277, 552 N.E.2d 131, 552 N.Y.S.2d 883 (1990).

[107] State v. Taylor, 663 S.W.2d 235 (Mo. 1984).

[108] People v. Singh, 186 A.D.2d 285, 588 N.Y.S.2d 573 (1992).

[109] Reichard v. State, 510 N.E.2d 163 (Ind. 1987).

[110] State v. Roles, 122 Idaho 138, 832 P.2d 311, 318 (Idaho Ct. App. 1992); State v. Gettier, 438 N.W.2d 1, 6 (Iowa 1989); State v. Allewalt, 308 Md. 89, 517 A.2d 741, 751 (1986).

term "rape trauma" has more potential prejudice and impact than the term "post-traumatic stress," the latter not implying any particular cause.

The rape trauma syndrome may or may not be used to explain why a victim behaved in a particular way during the course of a sexual assault. In *People v. Bennett*,[111] the complainant alleged that she was sexually assaulted by a state trooper after being stopped for a traffic violation. She testified that she followed the trooper to his station, waited while he entered the station and returned, whereupon he assaulted her. At trial, the prosecutor elicited from his expert, Dr. Ann Burgess, who first described the rape trauma syndrome, that, assuming the fact pattern testified to by the complainant, such a woman "would comply" and would not try to get away in her own car because of fear and stress concerning what else her attacker might do. The New York Court of Appeals noted that since this testimony about a hypothetical woman, and women generally, who would submit without resistance to a sexual assault as a means of self-preservation, concerns the victim's behavior during the sexual assault rather than after it, it is not part of the rape trauma syndrome and should not be admitted unless two requirements are met: "the evidence has the requisite scientific basis," and "its potential value outweighs the possibility of undue prejudice to defendant or interference with the jury's province to determine credibility."[112]

On the other hand, Connecticut's highest court has permitted expert testimony to explain a complainant's conduct during a sexual assault — why she failed to call for help and why she did not attempt to escape.[113]

In *Bennett*, it is interesting to note that the New York Court of Appeals articulates a *Daubert* framework in examining the use of expert testimony. While it does not preclude the use of expert testimony to describe a victim's behavior during a sexual assault, the court notes that the use of rape trauma syndrome for this purpose has not previously been approved by the courts. However, the court is willing to consider such testimony, if there is a "scientific basis" for it, which must be established before the testimony is admitted. A court may require a hearing to establish the scientific basis for an expert opinion based on rape trauma syndrome.[114]

Testimony that children exhibit the post-traumatic stress symptoms of victims of abuse is generally improper, since there is no one characteristic or group of

---

[111] People v. Bennett, 79 N.Y.2d 464, 593 N.E.2d 279, 583 N.Y.S.2d 825 (1992). The trial testimony of the expert, Dr. Burgess, is set forth in Appendix N.

[112] People v. Bennett, 79 N.Y. 2d 464, 473, 593 N.E.2d 279, 285, 583 N.Y.S.2d 825, 831.

[113] State v. Freeney, 228 Conn. 582, 637 A.2d 1088 (1994). *See also* People v. Iniguez, 7 Cal. 4th 847, 872 P.2d 1183, 30 Cal. Rptr. 2d 258 (1994) (California Supreme Court, in defining fear necessary to constitute force, relied on expert testimony on rape trauma syndrome that described the "variety of ways" victims respond *during* a rape).

[114] Prickett v. State, 220 Ga. App. 244, 469 S.E.2d 371 (1996) (noting that Georgia courts have not necessarily accepted the scientific basis of rape trauma syndrome and PTSD and that a trial court should conduct a hearing to determine acceptance in the particular field in which it is being offered).

characteristics that can be relied on for such a conclusion.[115] The symptoms of the disorder are "not like a fingerprint in that it can clearly identify the perpetrator of the crime."[116] There are similar problems with the use of the "child sexual abuse accommodation syndrome."

§ 11.14 Child sexual abuse accommodation syndrome (CSAAS).

One of the most often used, misused, and cited syndromes in sexual assault trials is the child sexual abuse accommodation syndrome developed by Roland Summit, M.D.[117] According to Dr. Summit, there are five phases that a victim of child sexual abuse will encounter: (1) secrecy; (2) helplessness; (3) entrapment and accommodation; (4) delayed, conflicted, or unconvincing disclosure; and (5) retraction. The first two phases exist before or during the abuse, while the last three are stages that the victim can be expected to experience and represent behavior not within the normal experience of most adults.

In the secrecy phase, the child develops a secret with the offender, and the secrecy is the source of fear in the promise of safety. The child may be told not to tell anyone for fear of the consequences of telling a parent or other adult. The consequences may be those to be suffered by the victim, such as being spanked or sent to an orphanage, or fear of the consequences to the offender, who may be a loved one. As part of the secrecy phase, victims will feel that they will be blamed for what happened or that there may be retaliation on the part of the offender. There is also the fear of the loss of love or attention or the benefits bestowed by the offender.

In the next stage of helplessness, the adult uses his authoritarian relationship with the child to overcome the child's instinct of self-protection and disclosure, since children are required to be obedient to those adults who care for them and whom they trust. It is the betrayal of trust by the adult that leads a child to feel helpless when confronted by sexual abuse.

In the third phase of entrapment and accommodation, the child learns to accept the abuse and tries to survive, since there is no way out and no perceived solution. When a parent or other trusted figure is involved in the abuse, the child will feel that they have few options and must do whatever is necessary to maintain love and acceptance by the trusted offender. There is a feeling of no place to turn and that the best must be made of the relationship, which includes protecting

---

[115] State v. Ballard, 855 S.W.2d 557 (Tenn. 1993).

[116] Mitchell v. Commonwealth, 777 S.W.2d 930, 932 (Ky. 1989); State v. Hensley, 120 N.C. App. 313, 462 S.E.2d 550 (1995) (admission of post-traumatic stress syndrome testimony improperly suggested that the victim suffered a sexual assault by anal penetration and that the defendant committed the offense).

[117] Roland Summit, *The Child's Sexual Abuse Accommodations Syndrome*, 7 Child Abuse & Neglect 177–192 (1983); Roland J. Summit, *Abuse of the Child Sexual Abuse Accommodation Syndrome*, J. Child Sexual Abuse 153–63 (1992).

a parent or guardian and engaging in other behaviors for psychological survival. Male victims of child sexual abuse may engage in aggressive or antisocial behavior or may even rationalize that they are exploiting the relationship for their own benefit. The use of drugs is a common form of accommodating the sexual abuse.

In the fourth stage of the syndrome, disclosure occurs. It may be delayed, or persuasive, or conflicting. This is because the child fears that they will not be believed and will sense the disbelief in the adult who hears the report of abuse. Disclosure is also affected by the fact that many of the victims have also engaged in delinquency or other antisocial behavior, which can cloud the message of the reported abuse. The disclosure may be incomplete because the child or adolescent fears humiliation or punishment for reporting the abuse. The difficulties and complexities of the disclosure are also increased if the disclosure is accidental or made by a third party. When disclosure is accidental, the child is even less ready to deal with the consequences, and the results are greater inconsistencies and complications in the child's admissions.

Lastly, the child is likely to retract the report of abuse. It is this phase that is often the subject of expert testimony in child sexual abuse trials. Frequently, many of the initial fears in reporting the abuse are realized, such as loss of the loved one through removal of the victim or the offender, loss of family relationships, abandonment by friends and loved ones, and other conflicts. Often the retraction is the result of the fear of breaking up the family or destroying a reputation or relationship. Thus, the child who comes forward may find it easier to retract the allegation than continue with the disclosure.

It is important to note that it was not the purpose of the original study on CSAAS to establish signs or symptoms that were diagnostic of child sexual abuse. "Thus, any attempt to show that a child had been abused because he exhibits some signals of CSAAS is an improper usage of Dr. Summit's theory."[118]

§ 11.15 Acceptance as scientific tool.

Any form of syndrome testimony must be evaluated for its reliability and the field in which it is reliable. Since CSAAS was never designed to be diagnostic of child sexual abuse, its use for that purpose can be challenged.[119] Courts have recognized that CSAAS is not generally accepted as a scientific tool or as an accurate means of determining whether someone has been sexually abused.[120] The Supreme Court of Utah has summarized the view of many courts:

---

[118] Hall v. State, 611 So. 2d 915, 919 (Miss. 1992) (however, the court permitted testimony on the common behavior of sexually-abused children); Roland J. Summit, *Abuse of the Child Sexual Abuse Accommodation Syndrome*, J. Child Sexual Abuse 153–63 (1992).

[119] *See generally*, Elizabeth Trainor, Annotation, *Admissibility of Expert Testimony on Child Sexual Abuse Accommodation Syndrome (CSAAS) in Criminal Case*, 85 A.L.R.5th 585 (2001).

[120] Lantrip v. Commonwealth, 713 S.W.2d 816 (Ky. 1986); State v. Foret, 628 So. 2d 1116 (La. 1993); State v. Black, 537 A.2d 1154 (Me. 1988); Commonwealth v. Dunkle, 529 Pa. 168, 602 A.2d 830 (1992). *See also* §§ 11.16–18.

[T]he child abuse profile consists of a long list of vague and sometimes conflicting psychological characteristics that are relied upon to establish the fact of injury in a specific case as well as the cause. And neither the record nor our independent research demonstrates that there is general acceptance of child abuse profile evidence as a determinant of abuse either by the legal community, as noted above, or by the scientific community, as discussed below.

Not only is there a lack of any consensus about the ability of the profile to determine abuse, but the scientific literature raises serious doubts as to the reliability of profile testimony when used for forensic purposes to demonstrate that abuse actually occurred. Scholars acknowledge that no uniformly identifiable psychological profile applies to sexually-abused children as a class. They make two related points. First, children may have widely varying reactions to abuse, so that "typicality" is hard to determine. The truth of this proposition is attested to by the fact that existing profiles use very general descriptive terms, such as "guilt" or "anxiety" or "nightmares" to describe the characteristics of abused children. For similar reasons, some lists of characteristics of abused children include contrasting traits, such as "regressive behavior" and "pseudo-mature behavior", "acting out". . . . The second criticism directed at profiles is that psychological characteristics often said to be indicative of abuse may also describe persons suffering from a wide range of emotional problems unrelated to sexual abuse.[121]

Arguing in summation that CSAAS establishes abuse may be reversible error.[122]

Because CSAAS is not like medical opinion testimony, which is based on generally recognized and accepted interpretation of medical findings (*e.g.,* the "battered-child syndrome") most courts have been unwilling to accept CSAAS as a diagnostic tool.[123] Because CSAAS has a limited therapeutic purpose and

---

[121] State v. Rimmasch, 775 P.2d 388, 401 (Utah 1989) [footnote and citations omitted].

[122] *See* § 15.17.

[123] State v. Rimmasch, 775 P.2d 388, 395 (Utah 1989) (trial court erroneously relied on court acceptance of battered-child syndrome in admitting profile evidence concerning victims). *Contra* State v. Edward Charles L., 183 W. Va. 641, 398 S.E.2d 123 (1990):

> There is no valid reason that a physician cannot give an opinion based on physical findings that a person has been sexually assaulted. Similarly, there is no valid reason a psychologist or psychiatrist should not be allowed to give an opinion based on objective findings as to whether an individual, most particularly a child, has been sexually assaulted. It is true that such an expert opinion aids the victim's verisimilitude, but it is a fair and proper basis for doing so and the probative value of such testimony far outweighs any potential for unfair prejudice. Furthermore, whether a person has been sexually assaulted is not the ultimate issue for a jury. The ultimate issue is whether the defendant committed the assault.

State v. Edward Charles L., 183 W. Va. 641, 659, 398 S.E.2d 123, 141 (1990) (The battered-child syndrome is discussed in § 11.37).

not a predictive one, "the evidence must be tailored to the purpose for which it is being received."[124] However, the fact that a syndrome has a therapeutic origin does not necessarily render it unreliable for trial purposes.[125] As will be seen in subsequent sections, the CSAAS does have a role in explaining certain behaviors that a jury may not understand, such as a victim's delay in reporting or recantation. Thus, it is important to distinguish the purpose for which the testimony is offered and clearly establish its parameters. It is also important to remember that if the testimony of an expert that certain traits do identify sexually-abused children is not objected to, there may be no right to appeal the propriety of such testimony.[126]

The Texas Court of Appeals reversed a conviction where a social worker testified in rebuttal concerning the child sexual abuse accommodation syndrome.[127] In particular, the court was critical of a non-medical witness testifying about findings made by a pediatric psychiatrist.[128] Utilizing *Daubert* factors, the court also noted that Dr. Summit's findings had never been subjected to "scientific examination" and the record was silent as to a "rate of error" or existence of literature supporting the underlying theory.[129]

§ 11.16 Testimony offered to establish that a particular child was or was not sexually abused.

Generally, expert testimony in a criminal trial that a person has "indicators," "syndromes," "patterns," or "clinical features" is indicative of sexual abuse and is improper opinion testimony when it leads to the conclusion that a particular child was sexually abused.[130] This includes testimony by a child protective

---

[124] People v. Bowker, 203 Cal. App. 3d 385, 249 Cal. Rptr. 886, 891 (1988). *See also* State v. Ballard, 855 S.W.2d 557 (Tenn. 1993).

[125] People v. Taylor, 75 N.Y.2d 277, 552 N.E.2d 131, 552 N.Y.S.2d 883 (1990) (referring to the rape trauma syndrome).

[126] United States v. St. Pierre, 812 F.2d 417 (8th Cir. 1987).

[127] Perez v. State, 25 S.W.3d 830 (Tex. Ct. App. 2000).

[128] Perez v. State, 25 S.W.3d 830 (Tex. Ct. App. 2000).

[129] Perez v. State, 25 S.W.3d 830, 836–38 (Tex Ct. App. 2000).

[130] People v. Bowker, 203 Cal. App. 3d 385, 249 Cal. Rptr. 886 (1988); Steward v. State, 652 N.E.2d 490, 499 (Ind. 1995); State v. Foret, 628 So. 2d 1116 (La. 1993) (It is improper to use child sexual abuse accommodation syndrome to establish that the child, in expert's opinion, was telling the truth about being the victim of sexual abuse. This opinion was based on the detailed accounts of the abuse provided by the child, the child's feelings of disgust and sadness, the victim's claim that the defendant was possessive of her and did not want her to be with other boys, the victim's feelings that she had done something wrong, and the fact that the defendant had told her to keep the molestations a secret); State v. Black, 537 A.2d 1154 (Me. 1988); Commonwealth v. LaCaprucia, 41 Mass. App. Ct. 496, 671 N.E.2d 984, *review denied*, 424 Mass. 1102, 674 N.E.2d 674 (1996) (defendant's convictions were reversed because trial judge improperly admitted expert testimony on characteristics of an incestuous family as well as other testimony directly linking characterization of sexually-abused children to the complainants. The court noted that the

worker that the child's sexual abuse was confirmed.[131] The error is not avoided if the expert does not use the term "syndrome" during testimony. The problem can develop when the expert examines a child, and questions about the patterns of abuse juxtaposed with questions about the complainant have the effect of vouching for the complainant's credibility.[132] A defendant, too, cannot apply general aspects of sexual abuse to a specific case since this, too, would comment on the witness's credibility,[133] nor offer expert testimony that an allegation is false as a result of "transferred abuse."[134] An expert may not testify to the propensity of children who are the subject of parental custody and visitation conflicts to falsify allegations of abuse.[135] If there is any attempt to transform inadmissible hearsay into reliable scientific evidence or relate symptoms establishing that a victim was abused, it is still reversible error.[136]

Problems also develop where the expert testimony is properly admitted to explain a delay in reporting the abuse, but the expert continues to testify that the victim's nightmares, flashbacks, and intrusive memories of abuse by the defendant are symptoms of post-traumatic stress disorder of a child sexual abuse victim.[137] Such testimony is prejudicial in that it tends to establish that the alleged acts took place.[138] Similarly, expert testimony that a child victim's asking about AIDS and "hitting himself against a wall," and the child's behavior with anatomically correct dolls, which consisted of replacing their clothing and hitting them in the head, is how victims comport themselves, is inadmissible because it "constitutes an impermissible comparison of the complainant's behavior with

---

"inadmissible profile evidence had the effect of identifying the defendant as a person likely to commit incestuous sexual abuse, and the complainants as children who testified truthfully to the occurrence of sexual abuse." Commonwealth v. LaCaprucia, 41 Mass. App. Ct. 496, 499, 671 N.E.2d 984, 987, *review denied*, 424 Mass. 1102, 674 N.E.2d 674 (1996)); People v. Pullins, 145 Mich. App. 414, 378 N.W.2d 502 (1985); State v. Cressey, 628 A.2d 696 (N.H. 1993); State v. W.L., 278 N.J. Super. 295, 650 A.2d 1035 (1995); State v. J.Q., 252 N.J. Super. 11, 33–35, 599 A.2d 172, 184–85 (1991), (citing articles), *aff'd*, 130 N.J. 554, 617 A.2d 1196 (1993); State v. Milbradt, 305 Or. 621, 756 P.2d 620 (1988); Commonwealth v. Dunkle, 529 Pa. 168, 602 A.2d 830, 832–36 (1992) (holding that expert testimony on CSAAS is not permissible for any purpose, including delay and recantation); State v. Hudnall, 293 S.C. 97, 359 S.E.2d 59 (1987); State v. Ballard, 855 S.W.2d 557 (Tenn. 1993); State v. Rimmasch, 775 P.2d 388, 401–02 (Utah 1989).

[131] Putnam v. State, 231 Ga. App. 190, 498 S.E.2d 340 (1998).

[132] Commonwealth v. Brouillard, 40 Mass. App. Ct. 448, 665 N.E.2d 113 (1996); Commonwealth v. Rather, 37 Mass. App. Ct. 140, 148–149 n.4, 638 N.E.2d 915, 920 (1994).

[133] Lunberry v. State, 231 Ga. App. 706, 500 S.E.2d 625 (1998).

[134] United States v. Weisbeck, 48 M.J. 570, 575 (A.C.C.A. 1998).

[135] Floray v. State, 720 A.2d 1132 (Del. 1998).

[136] Hellstrom v. Commonwealth, 825 S.W.2d 612, 614 (Ky. 1992) (as to CSAAS, "neither the syndrome nor the symptoms that comprise the syndrome have recognized reliability in diagnosing child sexual abuse as a scientific entity").

[137] People v. Singh, 186 A.D.2d 285, 588 N.Y.S.2d 573 (1992) (defendant's conviction was reversed even though testimony was not objected to).

[138] People v. Singh, 186 A.D. 2d 285, 588 N.Y.S. 2d 573 (1992).

that commonly associated with victims of these crimes."[139] This leads to the issue of admissibility of expert opinions that a victim's behavior is "consistent with" sexual abuse. In some situations, a curative instruction will prevent reversible error resulting from an expert's impermissible opinion testimony that a child was sexually abused.[140]

§ 11.17   Expert and lay testimony relating to credibility of victim.

The Federal Rules of Evidence do not prohibit an expert opinion just because it "embraces an ultimate issue to be decided by the trier of fact."[141] Nevertheless, opinion evidence is still subject to other rules of admissibility, such as prejudice, reliability, and relevance. Opinion testimony on credibility is usually permitted. (As a general rule, a witness — lay or expert — cannot state that a person "was sexually assaulted," although an exception to this rule permits the statement when physical findings are involved.)[142] Opinions about sexual abuse victims' denials and recantations ordinarily require training, observations, and experience not within the common knowledge of the general public and are not admissible as lay witness testimony.[143] Clearly, testimony from an expert, whether a physician or a psychologist, that a particular victim has been sexually abused,[144] is believable or credible,[145] as well as testimony to the effect that the expert could

---

[139] People v. Mercado, 188 A.D.2d 941, 592 N.Y.S.2d 75 (1992).

[140] Sewell v. State, 244 Ga. App. 449, 452, 536 S.E.2d 173, 177 (2000).

[141] Fed. R. Evid. 704(a): Except as provided in subdivision (b), testimony in the form of an opinion or inference otherwise is not objectionable because it embraces an ultimate issue to be decided by the trier of fact. Subdivision (b) relates to expert opinion on the mental state or condition of a defendant.

[142] See Chapter 12.

[143] State v. Gonzalez, 150 N.H. 74, 834 A.2d 354 (2003) (holding such testimony erroneously admitted as lay witness testimony, but that error was harmless). See also State v. Tierney, 150 N.H. 339, 347–48, 839 A.2d 38, 45–46 (2003) (reversing defendant's conviction in part due to prosecution presenting expert testimony on dynamics of intra-familial abuse).

[144] Odom v. State, 243 Ga. App. 227, 531 S.E.2d 207 (2000) (holding psychiatric testimony that child was sexually abused improper, but not reversible due to overwhelming evidence of guilt); Commonwealth v. Colin C., 419 Mass. 54, 643 N.E.2d 19 (1994) (testimony by child psychiatrist and expert in child abuse who had conducted physical examinations and clinical interviews of complainants who testified about the effect of sexual abuse on children, and the psychological dimensions of disclosure, and that in her opinion the complainants had been sexually abused was tantamount to an expert opinion that the children's claims of sexual abuse were likely true and reversed defendant's conviction); State v. Jones, 1994 Tenn. Crim. App. LEXIS 587 (Sept. 15, 1994) (reversing defendant's conviction where physician testified that while unable to find any physical evidence, of abuse, based on the child's statements to her mother, he found that the child's story was believable and that the abuse had occurred and he recommended immediate counseling); State v. Van Matre, 777 P.2d 459 (Utah 1989).

[145] United States v. Knox, 46 M.J. 688 (N.M.C.C.A. 1997) (holding improper social worker's testimony that child's drawings led her to believe the child); People v. Roscoe, 168 Cal. App. 3d 1093, 1098–99, 215 Cal. Rptr. 45, 48–49 (1985); Barlow v. State, 270 Ga. 54, 507 S.E.2d 416 (1998); State v. Batangan, 71 Haw. 552, 799 P.2d 48 (1990) (holding improper testimony

"see no reason why [the victim] would not be telling the truth in this matter"[146] or that a child is "a forthright-type person"[147] are clearly improper and reversible when there are strong issues of credibility (which is particularly true in child sexual abuse cases where the testimony consists solely, or is based in large part, on the child's testimony). The same rules apply to expert testimony offered by a defendant.[148]

Furthermore, testimony that the expert can evaluate whether a child is telling the truth about being sexually abused when he interviews a child — even if he does not explicitly testify that the plaintiff was "truthful" or "believable"[149] — as well as any aspect of a psychologist's testimony that may give the impression that he believes the victim, can be viewed as a comment on the credibility of the child and is reversible error.[150]

Testifying that a child is unavailable to testify about traumatic events in front of a person of whom she is extremely fearful and who was responsible for the trauma is in effect an expert vouching for a child's credibility.[151]

The Idaho Court of Appeals noted that while neither an expert nor lay witness should comment on the credibility of a witness, an expert's opinion concerning a witness's credibility will be afforded greater weight and be more prejudicial than such testimony by a lay witness. It noted:

by a psychologist that the victim was telling the truth about being abused, implying she was believable, and that she had been abused by the defendant); State v. Plaskett, 271 Kan. 995, 1031, 27 P.3d 890, 913–14 (2001) (finding detective's comment on child's credibility together with other errors required reversal in a case where two girls' credibility was pivotal to prosecution's case); Bohnert v. State, 312 Md. 266, 278–79, 539 A.2d 657, 663 (1988) (finding reversible error in social worker's testimony that child sex abuse victim was telling the truth); State v. Bellotti, 383 N.W.2d 308 (Minn. Ct. App. 1986); Townsend v. State, 103 Nev. 113, 734 P.2d 705 (1987); State v. Aguallo, 318 N.C. 590, 350 S.E.2d 76 (1986); State v. Dempsey, 340 S.C. 565, 532 S.E.2d 306 (2000) (expert improperly commented that he believed complainant, but error was not reversible in this case).

[146] United States v. Azure, 801 F.2d 336, 339–341 (8th Cir. 1986). *See generally* Annotation, *Necessity and Admissibility of Expert Testimony as to Credibility of Witness*, 20 A.L.R.3d 684 (1968); State v. Milbradt, 305 Or. 621, 756 P.2d 620 (1988) (testimony by expert that there was no evidence of deception by victim and victim could not lie without being tripped up).

[147] Felix v. State, 109 Nev. 151, 203, 849 P.2d 220, 255 (1993).

[148] Heidelberg v. State, 36 S.W.3d 668, 675–76 (Tex. Ct. App. 2001) (holding trial court properly precluded defendant's psychologist from testifying that complainant's allegations were "false and lacking in veracity" since this was an opinion on the truthfulness of the witness).

[149] State v. Batangan, 71 Haw. 552, 799 P.2d 48 (1990).

[150] *But see,*Pena v. State, 247 Ga. App. 211, 542 S.E.2d 630 (2000) (finding no error in expert's testimony of how she determines whether a child is truthful during an interview); Davison v. Commonwealth, 18 Va. App. 496, 445 S.E.2d 683 (1994) (defendant's conviction reversed when prosecution's expert, a "therapist," testified that the child's recantation should be disbelieved and offered an opinion as to why the child's testimony should be believed and not a prior inconsistent statement); State v. Wetherbee, 156 Vt. 425, 594 A.2d 390 (1991).

[151] Cunningham v. State, 801 So. 2d 244, 247–48 (Fla. Ct. App. 2001).

We do not believe that in this case a mother's testimony that she believes her child, or an adult friend's testimony that she believes the victim, would have any more than a marginal effect on the jury's determination of the credibility of the victim. The danger of experts testifying regarding credibility lies in the perception by the jury that the expert is a detached, neutral party who has no stake or interest in the litigation. Experts often possess special knowledge or training, giving their opinions of credibility great weight in the minds of jurors. Such weight is not afforded the lay witness who obviously sides with one party.[152]

An expert's opinion that a child did not exhibit "behaviors that point to having been manipulated" expresses an opinion on truthfulness of a child witness.[153] Testimony that three victims in a case were able to distinguish reality from fantasy and truth from falsity improperly bolstered a victim's testimony and was improper.[154] However, some courts permit testimony to the effect that a child is not "suggestible" or "coached," finding that such testimony is not a comment on the child's truthfulness.[155] Testimony or comments about a victim's demeanor when being interviewed may[156] or may not[157] be an improper comment on

[152] Reynolds v. State, 126 Idaho 24, 30, 878 P.2d 198, 204 (1994).

[153] Schutz v. State, 957 S.W.2d 52 (Tex. Crim. App. 1997) (reversing defendant's conviction due to erroneous admission of expert testimony on child's credibility).

[154] United States v. Binder, 769 F.2d 595, 601–02 (9th Cir. 1985).

[155] United States v. Cacy, 43 M.J. 214, 217 (C.A.A.F. 1995); People v. Jones, 851 P.2d 247 (Colo. Ct. App. 1993); Morris v. State, 268 Ga. App. 325, 601 S.E.2d 804, cert. denied, 2004 Ga. LEXIS 989 (Oct. 25, 2004) (permitting psychologist to testify that there was nothing in demeanor of victim to rule out abuse); State v. Wilson, 247 Kan. 87, 98–99, 795 P.2d 336, 343–44 (1990) (permitting social worker's testimony that child was "coached" given the child's level of detail, vocabulary, sentence construction and consistency over time); Burns v. State, 122 S.W.3d 434 (Tex. Ct. App. 2003) (finding psychologist's testimony that child's answering questions on tests in an open, non-defensive and truthful manner was not a comment on the child's truthfulness; comments on child's ability to be manipulative is appropriate and "jury was instructed that her testimony only went to what the test showed and did not extend to any other character trait or truthfulness of anything except for the particular test"); State v. Adams, 5 P.3d 642 (Utah 2000) (affirmed the opinion of the intermediate appeals court decision cited in main text). State v. Adams, 955 P.2d 781 (Utah Ct. App. 1998) (The trial court permitted testimony that victim was not capable of being coached. This opinion was based on the expert's background, training and psychological tests administered to the complainant, as well as a review of educational records. The appellate court held this opinion was based on objective information and was not a subjective credibility determination).

[156] State v. Lawrence, 752 So. 2d 934 (La. Ct. App. 1999) (holding police officer's testimony that victim's statements were "consistent and detailed" and her descriptions of victim's "demeanor" improperly commented on credibility, but error was harmless).

[157] State Supreme Court v. Oscarson, 176 Vt. 176, 2004 Vt. 4, 845 A.2d 337 (2004) (holding physician's testimony that five-year-old child knew the difference between truth and falsehood, and child's demeanor when questioned and the protocols he followed in interviewing child, was not vouching for child's credibility); Cook v. State, 7 P.3d 53 (Wyo. 2000) (holding deputy's testimony of his evaluation of individuals' demeanor during investigation to evaluate their credibility was not an opinion on victim's credibility). See also Robinson v. State, 151 Md. App. 384,

credibility. Nonetheless, most courts are chary of such testimony, and it may be difficult to avoid an inference that the expert is stating that the child is truthful.

Comments on the credibility of sexually-abused children as a class are also clearly improper and form the basis of many reversed convictions. Examples of the type of statements by experts in the course of their testimony that can lead to reversible error include: 90 percent of children receiving treatment in the expert's sex abuse program had told the truth,[158] a young child could not fantasize about a sexual act,[159] "very rarely do [sexually-abused children] lie," the "incidence of lying among children is very low, less than three percent," and if the child was not asked any questions, then the child's spontaneous response "declaring 'who it was [who sexually abused her]' " and the "physical findings and the behavioral indicators can only support what the child says."[160] A police officer's testimony that "in 90% of the cases I investigate, there is a delay in reporting" is improper testimony of the habit of other abused children as a class in the guise of empirical evidence and improperly supports inference that child

---

394–95, 827 A.2d 167, 173–74, *cert. denied*, 377 Md. 276, 833 A.2d 32 (2003) (finding reversible error in the admission of police officer's statement that the victim did not report anything "inconsistent" since this testimony invaded the province of the jury, but error was harmless).

[158] Powell v. State, 527 A.2d 276, 279–280 (Del. 1987). *See also* State v. Lindsey, 149 Ariz. 472, 720 P.2d 73, 75 (1986) (expert may not provide opinion testimony as to percentage of victims who are truthful in their initial reports of abuse despite subsequent recantation).

[159] State v. Brotherton, 384 N.W.2d 375, 378 (Iowa 1986).

[160] State v. Williams, 858 S.W.2d 796 (Mo. Ct. App. 1993). *See also* Commonwealth v. Trowbridge, 419 Mass. 750, 759, 647 N.E.2d 413, 420 (1995) (finding harmless error expert's testimony that child's inconsistencies not unusual among child victims); People v. Peterson, 450 Mich. 349, 537 N.W.2d 857 (1995) (expert testimony about percentage of children who lie about sexual abuse was improper but harmless in this case); State v. Bush, 164 N.C. App. 254, 595 S.E.2d 715 (2004) (reversing defendant's conviction due to physician's testimony that child was sexually abused, based only on child's history without physical findings:

The practical effect of Dr. Russo's testimony was to give [the child's] story a stamp of credibility by an expert in pediatric gynecology . . . [the physician's] diagnosis did not only go to the credibility of [the child's] allegation of sexual abuse, but conclusively stated that defendant had sexually abused [the child].

Commonwealth v. Cepull, 390 Pa. Super. 167, 568 A.2d 247, *appeal denied*, 525 Pa. 624, 578 A.2d 411 (1990) (holding prejudicial testimony that result of research studies showed that only three percent of all women who reported being sexually abused had lied)); State v. Jones, 1994 Tenn. Crim. App. LEXIS 587 (Sept. 15, 1994) (Pediatrician's testimony that although there was no physical evidence supporting the charge, his opinion was based on the age of the child and the nature of the complaints, the incidents had to be believed, and that a child of age four would not "make up stories and tell fibs and things like that" were improper comments on the credibility of the victim and invaded the province of the jury. The court noted "a pediatrician's ability to ascertain the truthfulness of an alleged child sexual abuse victim is not certain or reliable enough to substantially assist the jury in determining the issue of credibility." State v. Jones, 1994 Tenn. Crim. App. LEXIS 587, *21 (Sept. 15, 1994)); State v. Rammel, 721 P.2d 498, 501 (Utah 1986).

was sexually abused.[161] Other qualifications of the percentage of truthful sexual assaults are also improper.[162]

Also, expert testimony that sufferers of post-traumatic stress syndrome disorder generally do not fabricate claims of sexual abuse,[163] testimony by an expert that in her 16 years she only had one child lie to her about sexual abuse,[164] expert testimony concerning the general credibility of children based on references to studies on the percentage of sexual abuse victims who tell the truth,[165] and expert testimony and the general credibility of eight-year-old children who claim to have been sexually abused are all improper.[166] Also, an example of a form of impermissible indirect comment on credibility is a physician's statement that in taking a child's history, "there was no evidence of leading or coaching or fantasizing" about the sexual abuse, and the child was "obviously telling you about what happened to her body."[167] Some courts permit the prosecution to present testimony on interviewing techniques. *See* §§ 11.40–41 for the defense use of such testimony.[168]

Courts have also occasionally permitted testimony commenting on the credibility of the victim directly or on the class of child sexual abuse victims generally. One court permitted a pediatrician to testify on the credibility of children in general because the expert was in "a better position than the trier of fact to have an opinion on the credibility of children who report sexual abuse," since the comment on credibility was a general one and not a specific comment on the credibility of the testifying victim.[169] This testimony may be helpful to the jury

---

[161] Miller v. Commonwealth, 77 S.W.3d 566, 571–72 (Ky. 2002).

[162] Snowden v. Singletary, 135 F.3d 732, 737–39 (11th Cir. 1998), *cert. denied*, 525 U.S. 963 (1998) (granting a habeas petition in part because expert testified that 99.5% of children tell the truth regarding sexual abuse allegations); State v. Kinney, 171 Vt. 239, 762 A.2d 833, 843–45 (2000) (holding testimony by expert that at least 98% of rapes reported actually occurred was improper but harmless).

[163] State v. Catsam, 148 Vt. 366, 534 A.2d 184 (1987).

[164] State v. Myers, 382 N.W.2d 91 (Iowa 1986).

[165] Commonwealth v. Cepull, 390 Pa. Super. 167, 568 A.2d 247 (1990). *See also* Commonwealth v. McNeely, 368 Pa. Super. 517, 534 A.2d 778, 779 (1987).

[166] Commonwealth v. Seese, 512 Pa. 439, 517 A.2d 920 (1986).

[167] State v. Keller, 315 Or. 273, 844 P.2d 195 (1993). *See also* State v. Brotherton, 384 N.W.2d 375, 378–79 (Iowa 1986) (holding improper expert's opinion that three-to four-year-old children do not have the ability to fantasize a sexual experience); Commonwealth v. Carter, 9 Mass. App. Ct. 680, 403 N.E.2d 1191 (1980) (holding trial court erred in failing to strike doctor's testimony that child was telling the truth), *aff'd*, 383 Mass. 873, 417 N.E.2d 438 (1981).

[168] Roebuck v. State, 261 Ga. App. 679, 583 S.E.2d 523 (2003) (holding that expert could comment on interview techniques designed to avoid coaching or interference).

[169] State v. Oliver, 85 N.C. App. 1, 12, 354 S.E.2d 527, 534, *appeal denied*, 320 N.C. 174, 358 S.E.2d 64 (1987). *See also In re* Lucas, 94 N.C. App. 442, 380 S.E.2d 563 (1989) (permitting the following testimony by the examining pediatrician of a three-year-old complainant: Q. "Have you made any studies with references to the truthfulness of young children, specifically under the age of five years or so?" A. "That the younger children certainly can be altered, but basically

and proper as long as not commenting on the complainant's credibility.[170]

Some courts also permit an expert to comment on credibility in a child sexual abuse case when the child victim testifies and the victim's credibility is attacked.[171] For example, the Montana Supreme Court permitted testimony that children make up stories of sexual abuse less than 5 percent of the time, that the victim was sexually assaulted, that the victim was telling the truth, and that the victim had been "traumatized and physically abused by someone,"[172] but only when the victim testifies at trial,[173] and credibility is brought into question.[174]

---

the ability to tell, to create testimony, artificially, especially in the area as sensitive as this, is for the most part, ought to be pretty foreign to the child of preschool [age] as a rule." *In re* Lucas, 94 N.C. App. 442, 450, 380 S.E.2d 563, 568 (1989)).

[170] Commonwealth v. Mamay, 407 Mass. 412, 421, 553 N.E.2d 945 (1990) (expert testimony to explain the behavior of sexual assault victims permissible when phrased in terms of victims generally, and does not relate to the credibility of the testifying victims); People v. Brown, 7 A.D.3d 726, 777 N.Y.S.2d 508, *appeal denied*, 3 N.Y.3d 671, 817 N.E.2d 827, 784 N.Y.S.2d 9 (2004) (upholding expert testimony to explain complainant's intellectual limitations in aftermath of the crime; when the expert was challenged as to complainant's truthfulness on cross-examination, this opened the door to prosecutor's redirect examination and the question of whether the complainant was capable of fabricating such an elaborate lie and maintaining it over a period of time and his opinion that the victim was intellectually incapable of doing so); State v. Bright, 131 N.C. App. 57, 505 S.E.2d 317, *appeal denied*, 349 N.C. 366, 525 S.E.2d 180 (1999) (permitting prosecution's physician to testify that when he interviewed the complainant she "was very able to describe what happened to her with careful detail and without making any inconsistencies, whatsoever. I believe that she was a reliable informant." The theory supporting admission of such testimony was that the doctor was not saying the child was truthful, but rather that she was able to provide reliable answers to questions about the source of her injuries).

[171] State v. Steffes, 269 Mont. 214, 228, 887 P.2d 1196, 1204 (1994); State v. Geyman, 224 Mont. 194, 729 P.2d 475 (1986). *See also* State v. Timperio, 38 Ohio App. 3d 156, 528 N.E.2d 594 (1987) (The court permitted testimony by psychologist that she had been treating the victim for two years, that the victim exhibited symptoms symptomatic of a child who has been sexually abused, and that the history related by the child was significant because a child of her years did not have the capacity to make up such a story. The psychologist qualified as an expert witness and was allowed to give her opinion that the child was sexually abused and to give her basis for arriving at that opinion).

[172] State v. Geyman, 224 Mont. 194, 729 P.2d 475 (1986). *Compare* State v. Brodniak, 221 Mont. 212, 718 P.2d 322 (1986) (not permitting testimony concerning the percentage of false accusations). *See also* State v. Bachman, 446 N.W.2d 271, 276 (S.D. 1989) (allowing testimony that child's allegations were truthful). *But see* McCafferty v. Solem, 449 N.W.2d 590 (S.D. 1989), *habeas corpus* proceeding; McCafferty v. Leapley, 944 F.2d 445 (8th Cir. 1991), *cert. denied*, 503 U.S. 911 (1992).

[173] State v. J.C.E., 235 Mont. 264, 269, 767 P.2d 309, 312–13 (1988).

[174] State v. Hall, 244 Mont. 161, 797 P.2d 183 (1990). This requirement was strictly construed in State v. Harris, 247 Mont. 405, 410, 808 P.2d 453, 455–56 (1991):

In the present case, although Robby testified at trial, his credibility was not attacked by defendant. Defendant did not denigrate Robby's credibility in an opening statement or cross-examine him when he took the stand. The only time she touched on the issue of credibility was during the cross-examination of Robby's mother when she asked

The door to credibility opinion can be opened by a defendant's strategy and questioning. If the defense questions a police officer about whether there was sufficient basis for the charges based just on a nine-year-old's allegations, it opens the door to comments by the police officer pertaining to the reliability or credibility of the child.[175] In a Minnesota case, cross-examining a complainant's mother in an attempt to establish that the victim was not truthful, and that the mother did not believe her daughter, opened the door to the prosecution to question its expert as to whether he believed the child's allegations of abuse were truthful.[176] Inartful cross-examination can also elicit otherwise improper expert opinion on a child's credibility.[177] For example, challenging a physician on whether he was "fooled" by the history given by the child can open the door to the expert's opinion on credibility.[178]

A defendant who questions a doctor about victim credibility in an attempt to explore another issue, such as the victim's mental state, risks a damaging answer and the inability to pursue the questioning. In *State v. Chapman*,[179] the defense, on cross-examination, asked the examining physician if the victim had been too distraught to make an accurate identification. When the doctor replied in the

---

if Robby had at first denied the abuse. The State, however, had opened the door to this line of questioning by bringing the matter up on direct. Because Robby's credibility was not called into question by defendant, the District Court committed reversible error by allowing the psychotherapist to comment directly on his trustworthiness.

[175] Condon v. State, 597 A.2d 7 (Del. 1991). *See also* United States v. Plenty Arrows, 946 F.2d 62 (8th Cir. 1991).

[176] State v. Myers, 359 N.W.2d 604, 611 (Minn. 1984); State v. Collins, 163 S.W.3d 614 (Mo. Ct. App. 2005) (finding defendant's strategy opened the door to expert's comments about child's "hallmark of credibility").

[177] United States v. Rivera, 43 F.3d 1291, 1295 (9th Cir. 1995); Commonwealth v. O'Brien, 35 Mass. App. Ct. 827, 626 N.E.2d 892, 896, *review denied*, 417 Mass. 1102, 631, N.E.2d 58 (1994); State v. Baymon, 108 N.C. App. 476, 483–84, 424 S.E.2d 141, 145 (1993), *aff'd*, 336 N.C. 748, 446 S.E.2d 1 (1994); Taylor v. Commonwealth, 21 Va. App. 557, 466 S.E.2d 118 (1996) (clinical social worker's testimony that she believed the victim was telling the truth and had been sexually assaulted was permissible when elicited upon cross-examination by defense counsel).

[178] United States v. Rivera, 43 F.3d 1291 (9th Cir. 1995) (defendant opened the door to the prosecution's questioning of a physician concerning the child's credibility when the defendant tried to demonstrate through cross-examination of the physician that the complainant provided a false history of the incident and thereby "fooled" her into making an incorrect diagnosis of nonconsensual intercourse); People v. Brown, 7 A.D.3d 726, 777 N.Y.S.2d 508, *appeal denied*, 3 N.Y.3d 671, 817 N.E.2d 827, 784 N.Y.S.2d 9 (2004) (upholding expert testimony to explain complainant's intellectual limitations in aftermath of the crime; when the expert was challenged as to complainant's truthfulness on cross-examination, this opened the door to prosecutor's redirect examination and the question of whether the complainant was capable of fabricating such an elaborate lie and maintaining it over a period of time and his opinion that the victim was intellectually incapable of doing so); State v. Lyons, 725 A.2d 271, 275 (R.I. 1999) (defense attorney's questioning of physician about taking what patient says at "face value" opened the door to comment by physician that "very rarely are children making up these stories").

[179] State v. Chapman, 410 So. 2d 689 (La. 1981).

negative, the defense asked: "Do you feel that the identification may have been somewhat prejudicial to Mr. Chapman?" and "Doctor, do you remember telling me when I interviewed you last week that you would have hated like hell to have been brought in like [the defendant] was for identification?"[180] However, the court sustained the prosecution's objections to the defendant's questions, since they sought "to elicit [the] gynecologist's opinion concerning the mental state of the victim," which was an area outside the doctor's field of expertise.[181] This decision points out the importance of reviewing expert testimony on both direct and cross-examination to insure that the witness has been properly qualified in the field or area to which an opinion question is addressed.[182] A defendant's expert, too, can be held to the same proscriptions in commenting on a victim's credibility. An opinion on the percentage of false sexual assault complaints must have an adequate and reliable foundation and not be based on anecdotal information.[183]

Sometimes courts will permit testimony that children in general do not lie, on the theory that there was a failure to object to such testimony or that such testimony did not relate to the particular victim's testimony at trial.[184] While a court may permit testimony on the credibility of child sexual abuse victims in general, it will generally find impermissible direct comments on the testifying child's credibility. Such an indirect comment can be made when an expert witness testifies he had not picked up anything to suggest the child had been told what to say or been coached.[185] At times, the reference to credibility of the child may be so obscure and isolated in the context of the trial to be improper but not reversible.[186] Failing to object can result in a failure to preserve the issue of

---

[180] State v. Chapman, 410 So. 2d 689, 701–02(La. 1981).

[181] State v. Chapman, 410 So. 2d 689, 702(La. 1981).

[182] Bussey v. Commonwealth, 697 S.W.2d 139 (Ky. 1985); People v. Beckley, 434 Mich. 691, 456 N.W.2d 391 (1990).

[183] State v. Parkinson, 128 Idaho 29, 909 P.2d 647 (1996).

[184] United States v. Rivera, 43 F.3d 1291 (9th Cir. 1995) (defendant's failure to object to doctor's testimony that complainant did not falsify the rape waived any objection to such testimony on appeal. Defendant's objection was to foundation, and that the testimony was "totally subjective." There was no objection on other grounds such as improper bolstering. Thus, on appeal the court would only review such testimony under a "plain error" standard.); State v. Guidry, 647 So. 2d 502, 508 (La. Ct. App. 1994); State v. Price, 165 S.W.3d 568 (Mo. Ct. App. 2005); State v. Stevens, 58 Wash. App. 478, 794 P.2d 38 (1990).

[185] State v. Baymon, 108 N.C. 476, 424 S.E.2d 141 (1993).

[186] United States v. Provost, 875 F.2d 172, 176 (8th Cir.), cert. denied, 493 U.S. 859 (1989) (In this case, a physician, referring to the child's history of sexual abuse and a "triggering mechanism" stated, "I think what is an elementary basic thing is that whether or not they were contingent in time they both occurred and the memory of taking the shower and washing the semen off her body triggered the memory of the other intrusion into her private space and that she then was responding to the shower and the fact that something else happened in the shower." While not sanctioning the testimony that both events "occurred," the appellate court found that the reference was isolated and not so prejudicial in the context of the trial.); Engram v. State, 341

improper comment on credibility or the ultimate issue of whether a complainant was raped.[187] Not only is it important to object if any reference is made to the credibility of the victim in general, but it is also important not to open the door to such testimony on cross-examination of an expert.

When proof is not overwhelming or the only direct evidence of guilt is supplied by the child victim, a court is even more likely to reverse a conviction where there has been an improper expert opinion on the child's credibility.[188]

§ 11.18 Testimony that a particular child's or victim's behavior, signs, symptoms, or characteristics are consistent with sexual abuse.

Courts vary widely in how they view expert testimony that a victim displays signs, symptoms, behavior, or characteristics consistent with sexual abuse. When the opinion is based on physical or medical evidence, the opinion is usually admissible. This can be seen in expert testimony on the battered-child syndrome (§ 11.37) and medical evidence related to sexual assault (Chapter 12). There may

---

Ark. 196, 15 S.W.3d 678 (2000); People v. Cox, 197 Ill. App. 3d 1028, 557 N.E.2d 288 (1990) (physician commented on rape victim's credibility but the error was harmless in light of a confession from defendant); State v. Braun, 787 P.2d 1336 (Utah 1990) (reference to credibility of complainant did not mandate reversal where there was other physical evidence of guilt).

[187] United States v. Rivera, 43 F.3d 1291 (9th Cir. 1995); Schaefer v. State, 695 So. 2d 656 (Ala. Crim. App. 1996); Allgire v. State, 575 N.E.2d 600 (Ind. 1991); State v. Stribley, 532 N.W.2d 170 (Iowa Ct. App. 1995); Baine v. State, 604 So. 2d 249, 255 (Miss. 1992); State v. Butler, 24 S.W.3d 21 (Mo. Ct. App. 2000) (holding that admissibility of an expert's opinion only an issue when timely and specific objection has been made); State v. Malroit, 2000 Ohio App. LEXIS 5169 (Nov. 8, 2000), *appeal denied*, 91 Ohio St. 3d 1460, 743 N.E.2d 400 (2001) (holding that since there was no objection by defendant, there was no plain error in psychologist's testimony that child presented in a credible way since the testimony "was not based on his belief in Bryan's statements but rather conclusions drawn from his observations of Bryan's behavior." State v. Malroit, 2000 Ohio App. LEXIS 5169, *16–17 (Nov. 8, 2000), *appeal denied*, 91 Ohio St. 3d 1460, 743 N.E.2d 400 (2001)); State v. Ross, 152 Vt. 462, 568 A.2d 335 (1989) (improper expert opinion on victim's credibility will not result in reversal unless the court's failure to exclude the testimony *sua sponte* constituted plain error).

[188] United States v. Knox, 46 M.J. 688 (N.M.C.C.A. 1997); State v. Butler, 36 Conn. App. 525, 651 N.E.2d 1306 (1995) (defendant's conviction reversed when social worker testified that complainant was not "fabricating or making up the story." Court held this opinion required reversal of defendant's conviction "since the entire case turned on the issue of the credibility of the victim . . . [and the expert's] testimony vouching for the truthfulness of the victim affected the outcome of the trial and denied the defendant his right to a fair trial." State v. Butler, 36 Conn. App. 525, 532, 651 N.E.2d 1306, 1310 (1995)); Smith v. State, 674 So. 2d 791 (Fla. Ct. App. 1996), *review denied*, 684 So. 2d 1352 (Fla. 1996) (holding that court erred in allowing prosecution's expert to testify that she believed that child had been sexually abused and that defendant was perpetrator); State v. Plaskett, 271 Kan. 995, 1031, 27 P.3d 890, 913–14 (2001) (finding detective's comment on child's credibility, together with other errors, required reversal since case involved "words of the two girls against the defendant's"); State v. Catsam, 148 Vt. 366, 372, 534 A.2d 184, 188 (1987).

be situations where a court will permit an expert, such as a police officer, to testify that certain physical evidence is consistent with a victim's story.[189] Many courts permit an expert to testify that a victim's behavioral characteristics are "consistent with" sexual abuse or behavior observed in sexually-abused children,[190] and that such testimony is not an opinion on the credibility of the witness and does not answer the ultimate issue before the jury.

---

[189] Satterwhite v. State, 212 Ga. App. 543, 442 S.E.2d 5 (1994) (upholding police investigator's testimony that physical evidence found at the scene "conformed to the victim's story. Although an expert witness may not testify as to his opinion of the victim's truthfulness, 'the witness may . . . express an opinion as to whether medical or other objective evidence in the case is consistent with the victim's story.' " Satterwhite v. State, 212 Ga. App. 543, 544, 442 S.E.2d 5, 6 (1994), *citing* State v. Oliver, 188 Ga. App. 47, 50–51, 372 S.E.2d 256 (1988)).

[190] United States v. Antone, 981 F.2d 1059, 1062 (9th Cir. 1992); United States v. Hadley, 918 F.2d 848 (9th Cir. 1990); United States v. Wright, 53 M.J. 476 (C.A.A.F. 2000) (upholding trial judge's allowing expert to testify whether or not complainant's traits consistent with sexual abuse and that her decision not to report and her reactions, though inconsistent, were not unusual for a sexual assault victim); United States v. Stroh, 46 M.J. 643 (A.F.C.C.A. 1997); United States v. Raya, 45 M.J. 251 (C.A.A.F. 1996); United States v. Calogero, 44 M.J. 697 (C.G.C.C.A. 1996) (expert testified that victim's symptoms and "her clinical presentation in the hospital and subsequent to the hospital was consistent with a person who had been a victim of sexual abuse"); United States v. Cacy, 43 M.J. 214 (C.A.A.F. 1995); State v. Butler, 36 Conn. App. 525, 651 A.2d 1306 (1995) (While the court reversed defendant's conviction because of social worker's improper comment that child did not fabricate or make up the story, expert testimony concerning behavioral characteristics exhibited by victims of sexual abuse may be relevant, particularly where expert testifies that the behavioral symptoms exhibited by children who have been abused are also exhibited by children who may not have been sexually abused); Roebuck v. State, 261 Ga. App. 679, 583 S.E.2d 523 (2003); Brownlow v. State, 248 Ga. App. 366, 544 S.E.2d 472, *cert. denied*, 2001 Ga. LEXIS 539 (June 25, 2001) (upholding expert testimony that child's behaviors were consistent with abuse since this does not provide the jury a direct answer to the ultimate issue, but leaves the ultimate issue or conclusion for the jury); Odom v. State, 243 Ga. App. 227, 531 S.E.2d 207 (2000) (permitting witness to testify about behavior consistent with allegations of sexual abuse); Fleener v. State, 648 N.E.2d 652 (Ind. Ct. App. 1995), *aff'd*, 656 N.E.2d 1140 (Ind. 1995); Brady v. State, 540 N.E.2d 59 (Ind. Ct. App. 1989) (upholding expert testimony that victim's behavior was "consistent with" those commonly observed in sexually-abused children); People v. Beckley, 434 Mich. 691, 456 N.W.2d 391 (1990); Crawford v. State, 754 So. 2d 1211 (Miss. 2000) (holding expert's description of victim's behavior as common with that of sexually-abused child, met *Frye* standard and was properly admitted by trial judge); State v. Matthews, 37 S.W.3d 847 (Mo. Ct. App. 2001) (upholding expert testimony that child exhibited behaviors consistent with that of a sexually-abused child); State v. Gollaher, 905 S.W.2d 542 (Mo. Ct. App. 1995); State v. Rogers, 992 P.2d 229 (Mont. 1999) (medical expert's "comparisons of objectively obsessive behavior" not with those of other women who have been raped and his opinion that complainant's behavior was "very consistent" with women who have reported to be raped does not constitute an opinion on credibility); People v. Lemanski, 217 A.D.2d 962, 630 N.Y.S.2d 174 (1995) (CSAAS testimony admissible to show that victim's conduct consistent with syndrome); State v. Kennedy, 320 N.C. 20, 32, 357 S.E.2d 359, 366 (1987) (holding such testimony would be helpful to the jury in understanding the behavior patterns of sexually-abused children and in assessing the credibility of the victim); State v. Isenberg, 148 N.C. App. 29, 34, 557 S.E.2d 568, 572 (2001) (finding testimony that child's behavior consistent with that of sexually-abused child was not an opinion that child was sexually abused); State v. Fitch, 2003 Ohio App. LEXIS 230 (Jan. 17, 2003); State v. Stowers, 81 Ohio St. 3d 260, 690 N.E.2d 881 (1998); State v. Morgan, 326 S.C. 503,

There may also be a statute permitting testimony that a victim's behavior is consistent with a sexual assault victim. [191] In upholding a social worker's opinion that a child's behavioral changes of bedwetting, loss of appetite, hyperactivity, nightmares, wetting and soiling her pants, and chewing her fingers until they were raw were behavioral indicators consistent with abuse and did not improperly bolster child's testimony, one court explained:

> Common experience teaches us that a sexual offense can cause behavioral and personality changes in the complainant. Evidence of such changes renders the occurrence of the offense more probable than it would be without such evidence. This evidence is, therefore, relevant. [citations omitted] The probative value of this evidence has been weighed against its potentially prejudicial effect to determine whether to exclude the evidence. The relative trustworthiness of observations of change by disinterested experts and those by interested kin is included in this determination. The determination has been and is to permit kin as well as experts to testify about their observations. [192]

The main objections to expert testimony that a complainant's characteristics or behaviors are "consistent with" sexual abuse is that it is too close to an opinion that the abuse occurred or the complainant is a victim and that it bolsters the complainant's testimony. Thus, many courts reject the "consistent with" opinion

---

485 S.E.2d 112 (1997); State v. Trotter, 322 S.C. 537, 473 S.E.2d 452 (1996); Zinger v. State, 899 S.W.2d 423 (Tex. Ct. App. 1995) (psychologist's testimony that complainant's behavior was consistent with post-traumatic stress disorder admissible to help jury understand the evidence); State v. Loose, 994 P.2d 1237 (Utah 2000) (upholding prosecution expert's testimony that child's behaviors were "consistent with children who may have been sexually abused"); State v. Kallin, 877 P.2d 138 (Utah 1994) (holding that the manifestation of certain behavioral symptoms may have some probative value as circumstantial evidence and that a victim's behavior of sleeplessness, poor appetite, fear of the victim's grandfather, clinging to her mother, and a urination accident were symptoms consistent with sexual abuse; on cross-examination, expert noted that there were causes other than sexual abuse, such as other psychological trauma or the complainant's recent withdrawal from the prescription of Ritalin); State v. Edward Charles L., 183 W. Va. 641, 398 S.E.2d 123 (1990) (holding expert may offer opinion based on objective findings that child was sexually abused, but not whether expert believes child or that sexual abuse was committed by the defendant); State v. Dunlap, 250 Wis. 2d 466, 640 N.W.2d 112 (2002); State v. Huntington, 216 Wis. 2d 671, 575 N.W.2d 268 (1998) (physicians permitted to testify that child's difficulty at school, failure to report abuse, and inability to recant exact dates were all properly consistent with sexual abuse); State v. Jensen, 147 Wis. 2d 240, 432 N.W.2d 913 (1988) (upholding expert opinion that the child complainant's behavior was "consistent with" the behavior of children who are sexual abuse victims); Frenzel v. State, 849 P.2d 741 (Wyo. 1993), cert. denied, 522 U.S. 959 (1997) (expert testimony on CSAAS is admissible to explain why a victim's specific behavior might be incorrectly construed as inconsistent with an abuse victim's rebuttal attack on the victim's credibility; here expert was permitted to testify that complainant's recantation was "consistent with a pattern of sexual abuse").

191 Nev. Rev. Stat. 50.345 ("In any prosecution for sexual assault, expert testimony is not inadmissible to show that the victim's behavior or mental or physical condition is consistent with the behavior or condition of a victim of sexual assault.").

192 State v. Silvey, 1994 Mo. App. LEXIS 862 at *18–19 (May 31, 1994), aff'd, 894 S.W.2d 662, 670–71 (Mo. 1995).

as an attempt to use vague symptomatology or general behavioral characteristics to establish victimization.[193] One court distinguishes between an expert testifying

[193] United States v. Armstrong, 53 M.J. 76, 81 (C.A.A.F. 2000) (where prosecution asked expert if victim's characteristics and symptoms were consistent with those of victim of sexual abuse and expert responded they were "highly indicative" of being sexually abused by her father, this was deemed reversible error in light of lack of other evidence to support testimony of complainant who "appear[s] to live in a fantasy world and 'may be prone to perceptual inaccuracies' "); State v. Moran, 151 Ariz. 378, 728 P.2d 248, 255 (1986); Hadden v. State, 690 So. 2d 573 (Fla. 1997) ("[W]e hold that at the present time, a psychologist's opinion that a child exhibits symptoms consistent with what has come to be known as 'child sexual abuse accommodation syndrome' (CSAAS) has not been proven by a preponderance of scientific evidence to be generally accepted by a majority of experts in psychology. Therefore, such opinions (which we will refer to as 'syndrome testimony') may not be used in a criminal prosecution for child abuse."); Irving v. State, 705 So. 2d 1021 (Fla. Dist. Ct. App. 1998) (holding it reversible error to permit expert to testify that child exhibited behavior "consistent with" sexual abuse); Dennis v. State, 698 So. 2d 1356 (Fla. Dist. Ct. App. 1997); Ball v. State, 651 So. 2d 1224 (Fla. Dist. Ct. App. 1995) (reversing defendant's conviction due to expert's testimony that child's behaviors were consistent with those of sexually-abused children constituted a "seal of approval" for complainant and "a highly prejudicial stamp of condemnation for the alleged perpetrator"); Audano v. State, 641 So. 2d 1356 (Fla. Dist. Ct. App. 1994) (reversing defendant's conviction in part because of expert testimony that the alleged victim's disclosure is "more consistent with a true allegation of sexual abuse"); Steward v. State, 652 N.E.2d 490 (Ind. 1995); State v. Foret, 628 So. 2d 1116 (La. 1993); Commonwealth v. Federico, 425 Mass. 844, 683 N.E.2d 1035 (1997); Commonwealth v. Brouillard, 40 Mass. App. Ct. 448, 665 N.E.2d 113 (1996); Commonwealth v. Perkins, 39 Mass. App. Ct. 577, 658 N.E.2d 975 (1995) (defendant's conviction reversed because of prosecution's expert testimony that child's behavior was not inconsistent with sexual abuse; court held that such testimony "would inescapably have the same impact on the jury as a direct reference to and comparison with the child witnesses in the case." Commonwealth v. Perkins, 39 Mass. App. Ct. 577, 583, 658 N.E.2d 975, 979 (1995)); Commonwealth v. Richardson, 38 Mass. App. Ct. 384, 648 N.E.2d 445 (1995) (police officer's testimony improperly suggested that complainant's behavior conformed to or was consistent with the general characteristics of a sexually-abused child); Commonwealth v. Rather, 37 Mass. App. Ct. 140, 148–49 n.4, 638 N.E.2d 915, 920 (1994) (juxtaposing questions about the patterns of abuse with questions about complainant can have the effect of vouching for complainant's credibility); State v. Doan, 498 N.W.2d 804 (Neb. 1993) (Expert testimony on post-traumatic stress disorder is admissible to explain that an alleged victim's behavior or symptoms are consistent with rape or sexual abuse and to rebut the implied or expressed defense assertion that an alleged victim is lying); State v. Cressey, 137 N.H. 402, 628 A.2d 696 (1993) (noting there is little difference between expert testimony that a child's symptoms are "consistent with" sexual abuse and testimony that the child was sexually abused); State v. W.L., 292 N.J. Super. 100, 678 A.2d 312 (1996) (reversing defendant's conviction in part because of prosecution's expert testimony that the complainant's post-traumatic stress disorder was "not inconsistent" with a victim of sexual abuse); People v. Graham, 251 A.D.2d 426, 674 N.Y.S.2d 120 (1998) (reversing defendant's conviction due to expert's testimony that complainant's symptoms were consistent with patterns of response exhibited by proven rape victims); People v. Seaman, 239 A.D.2d 681, 657 N.Y.S.2d 242 (1997), appeal dismissed, 91 N.Y.2d 954, 694 N.E.2d 881, 671 N.Y.S.2d 712 (1998) (reversing defendant's conviction in part because of expert's testimony that any one of victim's behavioral changes may not be indicativeof sexual abuse but the pattern of changes "fit somebody that has been sexually traumatized"); People v. Shay, 210 A.D.2d 735, 620 N.Y.S.2d 189 (1994), appeal denied, 85 N.Y.2d 980, 653 N.E.2d 636, 629 N.Y.S.2d 740 (1995) (defendant's conviction reversed where trial court admitted expert testimony regarding child sexual abuse syndrome, which showed that "the victim's behavior was consistent with patterns of response exhibited by victims

that a victim's symptoms were more consistent with the symptoms of children who have been sexually abused than with children who witness physical abuse of their mother, since such an opinion is a more positive statement that abuse occurred.[194] The court noted that such testimony lacked foundation, and no *Daubert* finding of reliability was made by the trial court. In some situations, it may be reversible error to fail to conduct a *Daubert* hearing on expert testimony that a complainant's statements and behaviors are consistent with having been sexually abused.[195]

Some courts will not permit without establishing scientific reliability, a defense expert to testify that a victim's post incident demeanor was inconsistent with the "usual" emotional reactions exhibited by trauma victims, particularly given the variability in victims' reactions.[196] Such testimony is not relevant to correct any myth or misconception about children who have been molested.[197]

For example, an expert who testified that eating disorders, problems in sleeping, regression, sexual symptomatology, and the development of fears in several children in a day-care center were "consistent with" a child being sexually abused improperly provided testimony that a particular event took place.[198] The phrase "consistent with" in an expert's testimony is a red flag that the expert is attempting to establish that an event took place, rather than explain behavior.

Michigan's Supreme Court in a lengthy discussion of the admission of expert testimony in child sexual abuse cases has concluded that "consistent with" testimony is admissible only on rebuttal after a defendant opens the door to such testimony by attacking a sexual victim's behavior or reactions. It holds:

> Unless a defendant raises the issue of the particular child victim's post-incident behavior or attacks the child's credibility, an expert may not testify that the particular child victim's behavior is consistent with that of a sexually abused behavior. Such testimony would be improper because it comes too

---

of proven sexual abuse . . . in our view, county court erred in permitting this testimony because it went beyond explaining specific behavior that might be unusual or beyond the ken of a jury but rather had the effect of tending to prove that the crimes took place."); Commonwealth v. Emge, 381 Pa. Super. 139, 553 A.2d 74 (1988); State v. Roderigues, 656 A.2d 192 (R.I. 1995) (developing on cross-examination of social worker called by defendant that complainant's behaviors were "entirely consistent" with that of a sexually-abused child bolstered complainant's testimony and required reversal of defendant's conviction).

[194] United States v. Charley, 189 F.3d 1251 (10th Cir. 1999), *cert. denied*, 528 U.S. 1098 (2000) (holding such testimony erroneously admitted but harmless error).

[195] United States v. Velarde, 214 F.3d 1204 (10th Cir. 2000). *See also* Roise v. State, 7 S.W.3d 225 (Tex. Ct. App. 1999).

[196] People v. Wells, 118 Cal. App. 4th 179, 12 Cal. Rptr. 3d 762 (2004), *review denied*, 2004 Cal. LEXIS 7513 (Aug. 11, 2004).

[197] People v. Wells, 118 Cal. App. 4th 179, 189, 12 Cal. Rptr. 3d 762, 770 (2004), *review denied*, 2004 Cal. LEXIS 7513 (Aug. 11, 2004).

[198] State v. Michaels, 264 N.J. Super. 579, 625 A.2d 489 (1993), *aff'd*, 136 N.J. 299, 642 A.2d 1372 (1994).

close to testifying that the particular child is a victim of sexual abuse. . . .
When the credibility of the particular victim is attacked by a defendant, we
think it is proper to allow an explanation by a qualified expert regarding the
consistencies between the behavior of that victim and other victims of child
sexual abuse.[199]

For example, the Michigan Supreme Court upheld prosecution testimony that
a complainant's behaviors were consistent with sexual abuse when the defense
did not accuse the complainant of intentionally lying, but raised the issue in the
defendant's opening by arguing that complainant's post-incident behavior and
emotional problems affected her ability to recount and describe the sexual
abuse.[200]

§ 11.19 Expert testimony on CSAAS to explain victim's behavior such as delay in reporting, recantation, incomplete disclosure, courtroom or emotional reactions, difficulty providing details, inconsistencies in complainant's statements.

While expert testimony cannot be used to establish that an event occurred or
that certain behaviors are consistent with the abuse taking place, it is generally
acceptable to use expert testimony for rehabilitative purposes when issues
concerning the victim's behavior or reactions such as delaying the disclosure or
recanting the accusation are raised at trial. When the defense seeks to establish
that the complainant's conduct is inconsistent with abuse and, therefore, the claim
of abuse is false, expert testimony may be admitted to explain such conduct.
Since these areas of behaviors may not be understood by the average juror, expert
testimony can assist a jury in evaluating credibility. This is, in fact, a major
exception to the general rule precluding expert testimony on CSAAS, since the
issue of delay in reporting and recantation is often raised by the defense at trials.
Such testimony will be acceptable even when there are specific references to
CSAAS. The key point is that such testimony is offered merely for rehabilitative
purposes and not direct evidence of abuse.[201]

One of the most common and significant areas in which expert testimony has
been permitted is as a rehabilitative tool to explain why many sexual abuse
victims, particularly children, delay their disclosure by weeks, months, and

---

[199] People v. Peterson, 450 Mich. 349, 373–75, 537 N.W.2d 857, 868–69 (1995) (noting that
if the defense does not argue that the victim's behavior is not consistent with that of a typical
child sexual abuse victim, admission of such testimony is error. People v. Peterson, 450 Mich.
349, 376–377, 537 N.W.2d 857, 869 (1995)). *See also* Frenzel v. State, 849 P.2d 741 (Wyo. 1993),
cert. denied, 522 U.S. 959 (1997).

[200] People v. Lukity, 460 Mich. 484, 596 N.W.2d 607 (1999).

[201] People v. Bowker, 203 Cal. App. 3d 385, 249 Cal. Rptr. 886 (1988).

sometimes years,[202] and why they have difficulty reporting sexual abuse and

[202] United States v. Bighead, 128 F.3d 1329 (9th Cir. 1997); United States v. Tsinnijinnie, 91 F.3d 1285, 1289 (9th Cir. 1996) (expert testimony admissible "to explain why children may be intimidated by physical abuse and deterred from complaining against the abuser, sometimes for long periods of time"); People v. Salas, 30 Cal. App. 4th 417, 36 Cal. Rptr. 2d 374 (1994) (expert testimony properly admitted to contradict defense theory that complainant's long delayed report of molestation was a fabrication designed to get rid of a stepfather she disliked); People v. Patino, 26 Cal. App. 4th 1737, 32 Cal. Rptr. 2d 345, *appeal denied*, 1994 Cal. LEXIS 6132 (Nov. 16, 1994); People v. Baenziger, 97 P.3d 271 (Co. 2004) (upholding expert testimony on rape trauma syndrome to explain why victim initially failed to call for help during the assault, disclose the assault to the defendant's mother, her family or the police); State v. Christiano, 228 Conn. 456, 637 A.2d 382 (1994) (noting that when such testimony is offered, a cautionary instruction should be provided that the expert testimony is not offered to prove the abuse, but only as an aid to the jury in understanding the victim's behavior). *See also* Wheat v. State, 527 A.2d 269, 274 (Del. 1987) (limiting such testimony to victims of *intra-familial* abuse and permitting with respect to adult rape victims); Siharath v. State, 246 Ga. App. 736, 541 S.E.2d 71 (2000) (upholding social worker's expert testimony that it was not unusual for a child to endure sexual abuse and keep the fact a secret, even when there is a safe outlet to report the abuse); State v. Torregano, 875 So. 2d 842 (La. Ct. App. 2004) (permitting physician to testify as an expert qualified to address delayed disclosure of sexual abuse); People v. Peterson, 450 Mich. 349, 537 N.W.2d 857 (1995) (upholding admission of expert testimony on victim's delayed reporting abuse as part of prosecution's case-in-chief); State v. Bowler, 892 S.W.2d 717 (Mo. Ct. App. 1994) (physician permitted to testify on redirect examination about whether the victim's delay in reporting the incidents was typical of the behavior of victims of sexual abuse); People v. DeCosta, 146 N.H. 405, 772 A.2d 340 (N.H. 2001) (while holding expert may testify regarding tendency of victims to delay disclosure of abuse, court cautioned "trial courts to be vigilant in ensuring that an expert's testimony does not cross the line into the impermissible realm of vouching for the victim's credibility"); People v. Carroll, 95 N.Y.2d 375, 740 N.E.2d 1084, 718 N.Y.S.2d 10 (2000), *rev'd on other grounds* (upholding expert testimony which explained why a victim of sexual abuse would delay in reporting a sexual assault); People v. Higgins, 12 A.D.3d 775, 784 N.Y.S.2d 232 (2004), *appeal denied*, 4 N.Y.3d 764, 825 N.E.2d 139, 792 N.Y.S.2d 7 (2005) (permitting expert to explain victim behaviors, which may be unusual or hard to understand, such as delay, even though expert never met or treated victim); People v. Herington, 11 A.D.3d 931, 782 N.Y.S.2d 214 (2004), *appeal denied*, 4 N.Y.3d 799, 828 N.E.2d 90, 795 N.Y.S.2d 174 (2005); People v. Doherty, 305 A.D.2d 867, 762 N.Y.S.2d 432, *appeal denied*, 100 N.Y.2d 580, 796 N.E.2d 482, 764 N.Y.S.2d 390 (2003) (upholding testimony of expert in child abuse accommodation syndrome to explain delay in reporting); People v. Kukon, 275 A.D.2d 478, 711 N.Y.S.2d 870, *appeal denied*, 95 N.Y.2d 936, 744 N.E.2d 148, 721 N.Y.S.2d 612 (2000) (holding prosecution's psychiatric expert properly permitted to explain why a victim would delay in reporting a crime as long as it is accompanied by limiting instructions); People v. Brown, 270 A.D.2d 496, 705 N.Y.S.2d 300, *appeal denied*, 95 N.Y.2d 832, 735 N.E.2d 419, 713 N.Y.S.2d 139 (2000) (holding prosecution properly presented expert testimony on rape trauma syndrome to explain complainant's three-week delay in reporting crime); People v. Thompson, 267 A.D.2d 602, 699 N.Y.S.2d 770 (1999), *appeal denied*, 94 N.Y.2d 953, 731 N.E.2d 627, 710 N.Y.S.2d 10, 95 N.Y.2d 805, 733 N.E.2d 246, 711 N.Y.S.2d 174 (2000) (upholding expert testimony on rape trauma syndrome to explain why a victim may be reluctant to identify a sexual attacker); People v. McGuinness, 245 A.D.2d 701, 665 N.Y.S.2d 752 (1997) (holding child sexual abuse syndrome testimony admissible to show why victim may not immediately report the abuse); People v. DeLong, 206 A.D.2d 914, 615 N.Y.S.2d 168 (1994); People v. Daniels, 185 A.D.2d 894, 586 N.Y.S.2d 1017, *appeal denied*, 80 N.Y.2d 974, 605 N.E.2d 879, 591 N.Y.S.2d 143 (1992); State v. Carpenter, 147 N.C. App. 386, 556 S.E.2d 316 (2001) (finding masters level social worker, with experience interviewing sexually-abused children,

870

their feelings of guilt.[203] However, testimony by a police officer that "in 90% of the cases I investigate, there is a delay in reporting" is improper expert testimony, because it offers empirical evidence of the habit of the class of sexual abuse victims with the inference that "one fabrication should not arise from the fact that the [complainant] delayed reporting the sexual abuse."[204] Explaining a child's delay in reporting may require expert testimony.[205] Another acceptable area of expert testimony is to explain, in response to the defendant's effort to

qualified to give expert testimony why delayed and incomplete disclosures are not uncommon in child abuse cases); State v. Moore, 2001 Ohio App. LEXIS 653 (Feb. 7, 2001); State v. Trotter, 317 S.C. 411, 453 S.E.2d 905 (1995), *modified, aff'd*, 322 S.C. 537, 473 S.E.2d 452 (1996) (court upheld the admission of expert testimony as to why it was not unusual or unimaginable for a victim of incest to delay reporting for 22 years and also maintain a relationship with an offender); State v. Cates, 2001 SD 99, 5, 632 N.W.2d 28, 32 (2001); State v. Edelman, 1999 SD 52, 593 N.W.2d 419, 422–24 (1999) (upholding prosecution expert's testimony that sexually-abused children typically delay disclosure of abuse and may at first only disclose a small part of what occurred); State v. Leggett, 164 Vt. 599, 664 A.2d 271 (1995) ("The expert testified that children who are sexually abused by a family member are more likely to delay reporting the incident than are children who are abused by strangers. The expert noted that children fear the disruption to family relationships created by their revelation, and that many experience feelings of shame and guilt. The expert did not state that the victim in this case was truthful, nor did he comment on her veracity in any way." *Id.* at 600, 664 A.2d at 272); State v. Hicks, 148 Vt. 459, 535 A.2d 776 (1987); State v. Petrich, 101 Wash. 2d 566, 575, 683 P.2d 173, 180 (1984); State v. Claflin, 38 Wash. App. 847, 852, 690 P.2d 1186, 1190 (1984), *appeal denied*, 183 Wash. 2d 1014 (1985) (noting that expert may explain delay and use statistical probability in support of that opinion when there is an inadequate foundation for such statistics); Frenzel v. State, 849 P.2d 741 (Wyo. 1993), *cert. denied*, 118 S. Ct. 388 (1997).

[203] Martin v. State, 205 Ga. App. 591, 422 S.E.2d 876 (1992); State v. Myers, 359 N.W.2d 604 (Minn. 1984), court noted:

A young child subjected to sexual abuse, however, may for some time be either unaware or uncertain of the criminality of the abuser's conduct. As Dr. Bell testified, uncertainty becomes confusion when an abuser who fulfills a caring-parenting role in the child's life tells the child that what seems wrong to the child is, in fact, all right. Because of the child's confusion, shame, guilt, and fear, disclosure of the abuse is often long delayed. When the child does complain of sexual abuse, the mother's reaction frequently is disbelief, and she fails to report the allegations to the authorities. By explaining the emotional antecedents of the victim's conduct and the peculiar impact of the crime on other members of the family, an expert can assist the jury in evaluating the credibility of the complaint.

Martin v. State, 205 Ga. App. 591, 610, 422 S.E.2d 876 (1992); State v. Myers, 359 N.W.2d 604 (Minn. 1984).

[204] Miller v. Commonwealth, 77 S.W.3d 566, 571–72 (Ky. 2000):

Thus, a party cannot introduce evidence of the habit of a class of individuals either to prove that another member of the class acted the same way under similar circumstances or to prove that the person was a member of that class because he/she acted the same way under similar circumstances. Rudzinski's testimony as to her observation of the habits of sexually-abused children, as a class, should have been excluded as irrelevant.

[205] Commonwealth v. Fredette, 56 Mass. App. Ct. 253, 263–64, 776 N.E.2d 464 (2002).

discredit a complainant, the complainant's remaining with, or expressing love or affection for an alleged abuser.[206] The expert testimony can rebut the inference raised by the defense that because a victim appeared to be happy when he or she was with the defendant, he or she must have fabricated the story of abuse.[207] The expert also can help explain the reason for timing and sequencing inconsistencies in a victim's testimony,[208] or the difficulty remembering details, dates, time, the number of incidents,[209] the child's courtroom reactions,[210] the victim's lack of emotion while testifying,[211] inconsistencies or lies in the victim's statements after the assault,[212] and sexual "acting out" by the complainant.[213]

---

[206] United States v. Johns, 15 F.3d 740, 743 (8th Cir. 1994); Rodriquez v. State, 741 P.2d 1200 (Alaska Ct. App. 1987); *In re* K.A.S., 585 N.W.2d 71, 76–77 (Minn. Ct. App. 1998) (upholding social worker's testimony concerning how abused children usually behave including the failure to report and inconsistent versions of the abuse); People v. White, 229 A.D.2d 610, 645 N.Y.S.2d 562 (1996) (upholding admission of expert testimony of social worker to explain why the behavior of a child victim of sexual abuse may appear unusual to the average juror); People v. Page, 166 A.D.2d 886, 560 N.Y.S.2d 546 (1990), *appeal denied*, 77 N.Y.2d 842, 568 N.E.2d 659, 567 N.Y.S.2d 210 (1991).

[207] State v. McMillan, 69 Ohio App. 3d 36, 590 N.E.2d 23 (1990). *See also* People v. Krause, 187 A.D.2d 1019, 591 N.Y.S.2d 650 (1992), *appeal denied*, 81 N.Y.2d 842, 611 N.E.2d 780, 595 N.Y.S.2d 741 (1993) (admitting CSAAS testimony where limited to psychological and emotional reactions of victims).

[208] State v. Black, 537 A.2d 1154 (Me. 1988).

[209] People v. Grant, 241 A.D.2d 340, 659 N.Y.S.2d 474, *appeal denied*, 90 N.Y.2d 1011, 688 N.E.2d 1390, 666 N.Y.S.2d 106 (1997) (permitting expert testimony on the child's "reluctance to testify and inability to remember minor details of the incident"); People v. Sanchez, 200 A.D.2d 363, 606 N.Y.S.2d 185, *appeal denied*, 83 N.Y.2d 1007, 640 N.E.2d 156, 616 N.Y.S.2d 488 (1994) (expert testimony concerning child sexual abuse accommodation syndrome "relevant to explain why the victim had difficulty pinpointing dates, failed to initially disclose the abuse, and her reaction to courtroom procedure"); State v. Ryan, 2005 SD 5073, 699 N.W.2d 471 (2005) (holding proper expert's testimony "that trauma, as well as age, can affect a child's ability to remember and testify" and that how adult phrases affects a child's ability to understand questions); State v. Huntington, 216 Wis. 2d 671, 575 N.W.2d 268 (1998) (physician permitted to explain child's inability to remember number of times sexually abused).

[210] People v. Sanchez, 200 A.D. 2d 363, 606 N.Y.S. 2d 185, *appeal denied*, 640 N.E. 2d 156, 616 N.Y.S. 2d 488 (1994).

[211] Sexton v. State, 529 So. 2d 1041, 1048 (Ala. Crim. App. 1988); People v. Lopez, 187 A.D.2d 533, 589 N.Y.S.2d 920, *appeal denied*, 81 N.Y.2d 843, 611 N.E.2d 781, 595 N.Y.S.2d 742 (1993); State v. Middleton, 294 Or. 427, 657 P.2d 1215 (1983).

[212] United States v. Bighead, 128 F.3d 1329 (9th Cir. 1997) (permitting expert testimony on inconsistencies in child victim's testimony); United States v. Halford, 50 M.J. 402 (C.A.A.F. 1999); Simmons v. State, 504 N.E.2d 575 (Ind. 1987); State v. McLain, 249 Mont. 242, 815 P.2d 147 (1991).

[213] State v. Jones, 71 Wash. App. 798, 863 P.2d 85 (1993) ("[T]he use of generalized profile testimony, whether from clinical experience or reliance on studies in the field, to prove the existence of abuse is insufficient under *Frye*. However, such testimony may be used to rebut an inference that certain behaviors of the victim, such as sexual acting out, are inconsistent with abuse." State v. Jones, 71 Wash. App. 798, 820, 863 P.2d 85, 98–99 (1993)).

The expert may explain the progressive nature of disclosure of the abuse, the confusion a child has about details of the abuse, including the time frame and who was present, the reporting of the assault to a trusted person not connected with the scene, and the role of fear, embarrassment, or guilt in reporting the abuse.[214] Child sexual abuse syndrome testimony can also explain why a victim initially claimed she was raped by a stranger instead of the defendant, her stepfather.[215] Attacking a victim's credibility also can open the door to testimony by expert witnesses that the victim's behavior was "typical" of that normally found in sexually-abused children.[216] On the other hand, Pennsylvania restricts the use of expert testimony in sexual assault trials and does not permit testimony even on the issue of the reasons for a victim's delay in reporting,[217] while South Dakota permits expert testimony explaining the general characteristics of sexually-abused children.[218]

Another use of rehabilitative expert testimony is to explain why it is not unusual for a child to recant allegations that they were abused by someone, particularly a family member.[219]

---

[214] State v. McKinney, 2005 SD 73, 699 N.W.2d 471 (2005) (permitting forensic viewer to explain how age, trauma, and developmental level of child affects child's ability to recount stories, understand questions and time that may lead to "inconsistencies" in child's testimony); State v. Dunlap, 250 Wis. 2d 466, 489–90, 640 N.W.2d 112, 123 (2002) (holding expert testimony was proper, since it was not offered as substantial evidence of guilt, but in response to defendant's cross-examination, inconsistencies in complainant's testimony, and her reporting behavior).

[215] People v. Houston, 250 A.D.2d 535, 673 N.Y.S.2d 425, appeal denied, 92 N.Y.2d 983, 706 N.E.2d 752, 683 N.Y.S.2d 764 (1998).

[216] United States v. Rivera, 43 F.3d 1291 (9th Cir. 1995) (defendant's cross-examination of prosecution's physician, suggesting that she had been "fooled" by the complainant into making an incorrect diagnosis of nonconsensual intercourse opened the door to prosecution's physician stating that, in her opinion, the complainant did not fake the rape); People v. Reinhardt, 188 Mich. App. 80, 469 N.W.2d (1991), appeal denied, 439 Mich. 999, 484 N.W.2d 657 (1992).

[217] Commonwealth v. Balodis, 560 Pa. 567, 747 A.2d 341, cert. denied, 531 U.S. 817 (2000) (also noting that improper nature of this type of opinion testimony not cured by cautionary instructions). See, e.g., Commonwealth v. McCleery, 439 Pa. Super. 378, 654 A.2d 566 (1995) (reversing defendant's conviction, following the Pennsylvania line of authority that expert testimony is not admissible to explain the delay in reporting by child sexual abuse victims); Commonwealth v. Garcia, 403 Pa. Super. 280, 588 A.2d 951 (1991), appeal denied, 524 Pa. 656, 604 A.2d 248 (1992) (rejecting as improper bolstering pediatrician's testimony concerning general reasons for children's delay in reporting sexual abuse and, specifically, that one child delayed reporting due to fear and a previous sexual assault and that second child was threatened with death, if he reported abuse).

[218] State v. Cates, 2001 S.D. 99, 632 N.W.2d 28, 36 (2001).

[219] United States v. Halford, 50 M.J. 402 (C.A.A.F. 1999); Oliver v. United States, 711 A.2d 70 (D.C. 1998) (expert explained that children recant because of status of abuser as trusted individual or questioning by a significant adult who disbelieves the child); Sexton v. State, 529 So. 2d 1041, 1048 (Ala. Crim. App. 1988); State v. Moran, 151 Ariz. 378, 728 P.2d 248 (1986); People v. Dunnahoo, 152 Cal. App. 3d 561, 577, 199 Cal. Rptr. 796, 804 (1984); State v. Spigarolo, 210 Conn. 359, 556 A.2d 112, cert. denied, 493 U.S. 933 (1989); People v. Gallow, 171 A.D.2d 1061, 569 N.Y.S.2d 530, appeal denied, 77 N.Y.2d 995, 575 N.E.2d 406, 571 N.Y.S.2d 920 (1991);

The testimony explaining victim behaviors need not always be by a mental health expert.[220] A police officer, based on his experience with child victims and training, can testify that it is "normal" for children who have been abused to initially deny the abuse when confronted.[221]

A lay witness, such as a child's parents, may be able to testify how the defendant's abuse affected their children's lives.[222]

When expert testimony on CSAAS is properly admitted for one purpose, such as explaining the victim's inconsistent statements or threats to retract the allegations, or on the inference that the victim fabricated the complaint in some jurisdiction, it may be reversible if the expert testimony goes beyond an explanation and states that the child's behaviors are consistent with those of a child who has been sexually abused.[223] While this distinction may seem fine, it is increasingly being made by appellate courts.

§ 11.20   Expert testimony on CSAAS as part of case-in-chief.

Once a challenge has been raised to the victim's credibility, which triggers the use of CSAAS for rehabilitative purposes, the prosecution need not wait until rebuttal to offer such evidence, but rather may present CSAAS as part of its case-in-chief.[224] Connecticut permits the state to "introduce expert testimony that

State v. Moore, 2001 Ohio App. LEXIS 653 (Feb. 7, 2001); Davenport v. State, 806 P.2d 655 (Okla. Crim. App. 1991) (admitting CSAAS testimony as a form of rebuttal to explain recantation and retraction, but not as direct evidence, and not as evidence that a particular child was abused); State v. Middleton, 294 Or. 427, 657 P.2d 1215 (1983); State v. Petrich, 101 Wash. 2d 566, 575–76, 683 P.2d 173, 179–80 (1984). *But see* Davison v. Commonwealth, 18 Va. App. 496, 445 S.E.2d 683 (1994) (expert's explanation of complainant's recantation was improper because it included the opinion that victim's trial testimony should be believed and victim's prior inconsistent statement disbelieved).

[220] *See* § 11.44.

[221] People v. Turner, 241 Ill. App. 3d 236, 608 N.E.2d 906 (1993) (*citing* Illinois statute on admissibility of rape trauma syndrome referred to in § 11.12).

[222] State v. Wagner, 2004 Ohio 3941, 2004 Ohio App. LEXIS 3583 at *49–55 (July 26, 2004).

[223] State v. Chamberlain, 137 N.H. 414, 628 A.2d 704 (1993); State v. R.B., 183 N.J. 308, 873 A.2d 511 (2005) (emphasizing that expert testimony on CSAAS should be "carefully circumscribed" solely to explain to the jury why it is not uncommon for sexually-abused children, without reference to the child victim in that case, to delay reporting their abuse and why many children, again without reference to the child victim in that case, recant allegations of abuse and deny the events at issue. State v. R.B., 183 N.J. 308, 329, 873 A.2d 511, 524–525 (2005)); *See also* People v. Singh, 186 A.D.2d 285, 588 N.Y.S.2d 573 (1992). This is discussed in § 11.18.

[224] People v. Patino, 26 Cal. App. 4th 1737, 1745, 32 Cal. Rptr. 2d 345, 349 (1994), *appeal denied*, 1994 Cal. LEXIS 6132 (Nov. 16, 1994); People v. Sanchez, 208 Cal. App. 3d 721, 735–36, 256 Cal. Rptr. 446, 454, *cert. denied*, 493 U.S. 921 (1989); People v. Peterson, 450 Mich. 349, 375, 537 N.W.2d 857, 868–69 (1995); State v. Grecinger, 569 N.W.2d 189, 193 (Minn. 1997) (state may use battered-woman syndrome once victim's credibility is attacked in opening or cross-examination and need not wait for rebuttal); State v. McWilliams, 1995 Neb. App. LEXIS 334 (Oct. 24, 1995) ("Even though the rationale behind PTSD evidence is to rehabilitate abused chil-

explains in general terms the tendencies of minors to delay in reporting incidents of abuse once the victim has testified and there has been testimony introducing the alleged dates of abuse and reporting" as part of the state's case-in-chief.[225]

Expert rehabilitative testimony can be offered during the prosecution's case-in-chief when the victim recants at trial or where the issue has been raised by the defense.[226] The following is an example of such testimony:

Q. You mentioned that she [victim] appeared angry to you.

A. Yes.

Q. Is anger a typical response in adolescence for someone who has been subjected to sexual molestation?

A. Yes it is, they carry it on their shoulder like a flag.

Q. In your experience as a psychologist and particularly working with adolescents, are people very reluctant to report this sort of incident?

A. Very reluctant.

Q. Doctor, in your experience, what would trigger reporting of an incident?

A. Of those that have been reported to me, it has been either anger, or something has occurred and the child is upset or angry with their parents and they come in . . . .

Q. In your experience, is it common for victims to recant their story at some point down the line?

A. Yes.

Q. What exactly are the dynamics, the things that come into play when you have someone who has reported that molestation has occurred and then recants on that same report?

A. The biggest problem seems to be that the youngster seems to feel that they are responsible for holding their family together, and if the family falls apart it's their responsibility, and they are the guilty party. They are between a rock and hard place. Anything they seem to do seems to be wrong and most look for the easiest way out; the easiest way out is to

---

dren's testimony, it is not necessary for defense counsel to attack the child's veracity before such evidence can be introduced." State v. McWilliams, 1995 Neb. App. LEXIS 334, *16 (Oct. 24, 1995)); People v. Herington, 11 A.D.3d 931, 782 N.Y.S.2d 214 (2004), *appeal denied*, 4 N.Y.3d 799, 828 N.E.2d 90, 795 N.Y.S.2d 174 (2005) (permitting prosecution to introduce expert testimony on why a child might not immediately report sexual abuse as part of People's case-in-chief).

225 State v. Cardany, 35 Conn. App. 728, 730–32, 646 A.2d 291, 294, *appeal denied*, 231 Conn. 942, 653 A.2d 823 (1994).

226 People v. Bowker, 203 Cal. App. 3d 385, 393–94, 249 Cal. Rptr. 886, 891–92 (1988); People v. Dempsey, 242 Ill. App. 3d 568, 610 N.E.2d 208 (1993) (evidence of CSAAS admissible when defense questions the credibility of a victim due to recantation, delayed reporting, and inconsistency, which could be explained by the expert testimony; here cross-examination of the complainant raised the issue of recantation).

go back to the way things were, seeing it all the way through is for them a very frightening experience, and so they try to back out.[227]

Some courts do not allow rehabilitative testimony on direct or rebuttal.[228] Some courts do not permit expert testimony on recantation and other behaviors of sexual abuse victims,[229] unless the victim's credibility has been attacked.[230]

§ 11.21   Expert testimony on victim behaviors by defendant.

A defendant, too, may present expert testimony on recantation. In *State v. St. George*, the Wisconsin Supreme Court overturned a defendant's conviction due to the trial court's preclusion of defendant's expert testimony, rebutting prosecution's expert testimony that no scientific basis exists to conclude whether a recanted accusation is truthful in a particular situation.[231]

§ 11.22   Expert testimony on CSAAS or explaining victim behaviors and need for limiting instruction.

When expert testimony is presented to explain a delay in reporting, recantation, or some other aspect of a complainant's actions or behavior, the trial court should ensure the testimony is not viewed by the jury as substantive evidence of guilt or some other improper purpose. Many courts have held that such expert testimony must be accompanied by a limiting instruction.[232]

---

[227] State v. Moran, 151 Ariz. 378, 383, 728 P.2d 248, 253 (1986).

[228] Newkirk v. Commonwealth, 937 S.W.2d 690 (Ky. 1996).

[229] People v. Simpkins, 297 Ill. App. 3d 668, 697 N.E.2d 302, *appeal denied*, 181 Ill. 2d 586, 706 N.E.2d 502 (1998) (holding such expert testimony is a direct comment on a child's believability).

[230] People v. Nelson, 203 Ill. App. 3d 1038, 561 N.E.2d 439 (1990), *appeal denied*, 136 Ill. 2d 551, 567 N.E.2d 339 (1991); Hosford v. State, 560 So. 2d 163 (Miss. 1990).

[231] State v. St. George, 252 Wis. 2d 499, 643 N.W.2d 777 (2002).

[232] Commonwealth v. Dockham, 405 Mass. 618, 542 N.E.2d 591 (1989) (noting it is good practice to use limiting instruction with expert testimony to explain victim behaviors); Commonwealth v. Richardson, 38 Mass. App. Ct. 384, 648 N.E.2d 445 (1995) (noting that if testimony is offered by an expert, it should be accompanied by appropriate limiting instructions); State v. W.L., 278 N.J. Super. 295, 650 A.2d 1035 (1995) (noting that the misuse of CSAAS testimony in this case was heightened by the failure of the trial court to provide a limiting instruction concerning the proper use of such expert testimony); People v. Archer, 232 A.D.2d 820, 649 N.Y.S.2d 204 (1996), *appeal denied*, 90 N.Y.2d 938, 687 N.E.2d 653, 664 N.Y.S.2d 756 (1997) (noting that while expert testimony improperly correlated the alleged victim's behavior with that of known victims of sexual abuse, the testimony was harmless error in part because trial court gave limiting instruction that the expert could not render an opinion on the issue of whether the victim was sexually abused); State v. Hensley, 120 N.C. App. 313, 317, 462 S.E.2d 550, 552 (1995); State v. Trotter, 317 S.C. 411, 453 S.E.2d 905, *modified, aff'd by*, 322 S.C. 537, 473 S.E.2d 452 (1996) (appellate court noted with approval trial court's limiting instruction concerning the expert testimony about the behavior of the complainant); State v. Dunlap, 239 Wis. 2d 423, 434–40, 620 N.W.2d 398, 407–08 (2000) (noting that a limiting instruction would have gone "a long way" to prevent the jury from

California has held that due to the potential prejudice to the defendant from expert testimony on CSAAS, the court must, on the admission of such testimony, *sua sponte* render a limiting jury instruction that: "(1) such evidence is admissible solely for the purpose of showing the victim's reactions as demonstrated by the evidence are not inconsistent with having been molested, and (2) the expert's testimony is not intended and should not be used to determine whether the victim's molestation claim is true."[233] While a limiting instruction is helpful and appropriate when expert testimony is offered to explain a victim's behaviors, the defendant's failure to request one may negate any reversible error.[234] An appropriate limiting instruction by a trial court can render harmless improper expert testimony concerning the child sexual abuse accomodation syndrome.[235] While it may be helpful to provide the limiting instruction at the time the expert testimony is presented, it is not necessarily reversible error for the court to provide the instruction only in its final charge[236] or only at the time the testimony is admitted.[237] Some courts that do not favor expert testimony to explain victim's behavior or reactions also hold that the problematic nature of such testimony is not cured by cautionary instructions.[238]

The CSAAS charge should not "place a child sexual assault victim's silence or delayed disclosure beyond the jury's consideration" when determining witness credibility.[239] The following instruction is recommended by the New Jersey Supreme Court to balance the role of a delayed reporting, explained by a prompt outcry instruction, with expert testimony on CSAAS so as to take away from the jury's consideration its evaluation of the delay as a factor in assessing credibility:

> The law recognizes that stereotypes about sexual assault complainants may lead some of you to question [complaining witness's] credibility based solely on the fact that [he or she] did not complain of the alleged abuse sooner. You may not

---

"going astray" in preventing prejudice from prosecution's expert testimony); Frenzel v. State, 849 P.2d 741, 749 (Wyo. 1993), *cert. denied*, (1997) (when requested, a limiting instruction concerning the limited purpose of CSAAS testimony should be provided).

[233] People v. Housley, 6 Cal. App. 4th 947, 959, 8 Cal. Rptr. 2d 431, 438–39 (1992); People v. McGuinness, 245 A.D.2d 701, 665 N.Y.S.2d 752 (1997); People v. Abrams, 232 A.D.2d 240, 649 N.Y.S.2d 5, *appeal denied*, 88 N.Y.2d 1066, 674 N.E.2d 340, 651 N.Y.S.2d 410 (1996).

[234] State v. Goforth, 170 N.C. App. 584, 614 S.E.2d 313, 316, *cert. denied*, 619 S.E.2d 854 (2005); Alicea v. State, 13 P.3d 693, 699 (Wyo. 2000).

[235] People v. Archer, 232 A.D.2d 820, 649 N.Y.S.2d 204 (1996), *appeal denied*, 89 N.Y.2d 1087, 682 N.E.2d 982, 660 N.Y.S.2d 381 (1997).

[236] People v. Yovanov, 69 Cal. App. 4th 392, 81 Cal. Rptr. 2d 586 (1999), *review denied*, No. S076812, 1999 Cal. LEXIS 2358 (Apr. 14, 1999).

[237] State v. J.A., 337 N.J. Super. 114, 121, 766 A.2d 782, 78, *cert. denied*, 169 N.J. 606, 782 A.2d 424 (2001) (holding no requirement that the limiting instruction be repeated by the court in its final charge).

[238] Commonwealth v. Balodis, 560 Pa. 567, 747 A.2d 341, *cert. denied*, 531 U.S. 817 (2000).

[239] State v. P.H., 178 N.J. 378, 396, 840 A.2d 808, 819 (2004).

automatically conclude that [complaining witness's] testimony is untruthful based only on [his or her] silence/delayed disclosure. Rather, you may consider the silence/delayed disclosure along with all of the other evidence including [complaining witness's] explanation for [his or her] silence/delayed disclosure when you decide how much weight to afford to [complaining witness's] testimony. You also may consider the expert testimony that explained that silence is, in fact, one of the many ways in which a child may respond to sexual abuse.

Accordingly, your deliberations in this regard should be informed by the testimony you heard concerning child abuse accommodation syndrome. [240]

In the absence of expert testimony by the prosecution, the court suggests this instruction absent the last two sentences.

§ 11.23   Polygraph, *Frye*, *Daubert*, and scientific reliability and admissibility of polygraph results.

Many courts still do not permit the results of a polygraph test to be admitted for any purpose whatsoever, whether as substantive evidence or on the issue of witness credibility,[241] and it is not error to refuse to admit a defendant's polygraph expert's testimony in a child sexual abuse prosecution.[242] The main reason for excluding the results of polygraph examination is the unreliability of the test. A crude precursor of the polygraph test was the basis for the *Frye* test for the admissibility of expert testimony.[243]

In 2003, the National Academy of Sciences, a private group of scientists and engineers who advise the federal government on scientific and technical matters, issued its report on the polygraph, including a review of the different techniques, the science underlying the technique, and the literature on its reliability.[244] It is an excellent resource for attorneys who are facing forensic issues relating to the polygraph. The report concluded that "basic scientific knowledge on psychophysiology offers support for expecting polygraph testing to have some diagnostic

---

[240] State v. P.H., 178 N.J. 378, 400, 840 A.2d 808, 821 (2004) (The court reversed the defendant's conviction because "[h]ere, the instructions given at trial were contradictory and confusing. Worse, they improperly suggested that, when undertaking to evaluate the credibility of an alleged child victim of sexual assault, jurors could not consider for any purpose the child's delay in reporting the alleged abuse." State v. P.H., 178 N.J. 378, 400, 840 A.2d 808, 822 (2004)).

[241] People v. Anderson, 637 P.2d 354, 358 (Colo. 1981); People v. Leone, 25 N.Y.2d 511, 255 N.E.2d 696, 307 N.Y.S.2d 430 (1969); Crawford v. State, 617 S.W.2d 925 (Tex. Crim. App. 1980), *cert. denied*, 452 U.S. 931 (1981).

[242] Haakanson v. State, 760 P.2d 1030 (Alaska Ct. App. 1988).

[243] Frye v. United States, 293 F. 1013 (D.C. Cir. 1923). *See* § 11.2.

[244] *See National Research Council of the National Academies, The Polygraph and Lie Detection* (2003), available at http://www.nap.edu/openbook/0309084369/html.

value, at least among naïve examinees."[245] Another excellent resource for attorneys are two books by Richard Matte.[246]

Despite advances in the use of the polygraph, the United States Supreme Court in *United States v. Scheffer* held that the Military Rules of Evidence *per se* exclusion of polygraph evidence does not abridge the defendant's Sixth Amendment right to present a defense.[247] The Court reasoned that there was no consensus on the reliability of polygraph evidence and that it would distract the jury in its guilt or innocence determination.[248] Some federal courts have adopted a *per se* rule excluding polygraph evidence,[249] questioning the polygraph's reliability,[250] or leaving it to the discretion of a district court under *Daubert*.[251]

Some federal courts find polygraph evidence still not admissible, even under *Daubert*. After a *Daubert* hearing, one circuit court of appeals, which previously reversed a defendant's conviction because of a *per se* exclusion of polygraph evidence, upheld the trial court's determination on remand that polygraph evidence did not meet the reliability standard of *Daubert*, that defects in the test given the defendant undermined the test's relevance, and that the test's prejudice outweighs its probative value.[252] While finding that there was peer review of the polygraph and studies of its accuracy, the studies did not establish an error rate transferable to real life situations, given variables in the polygraph examiner, a subject's ability to employ countermeasures and the setting of the exam.[253] It noted the trial court's findings "that there is no known error rate for real-life polygraph exams,"[254] that polygraph testimony did not meet the general acceptance[255] test, and that no standards control the administration of polygraph

---

[245] *See National Research Council of the National Academies, The Polygraph and Lie Detection* 101, (2003), available at http://www.nap.edu/openbook/0309084369/html.

[246] James Allan Matte, Ph.D., *Examination and Cross-Examination of Experts in Forensic Psychophysiology Using the Polygraph* (2000); James Allan Matte, Ph.D., *Forensic Psychophysiology Using the Polygraph* (1996).

[247] United States v. Scheffer, 523 U.S. 303 (1998).

[248] United States v. Scheffer, 523 U.S. 303 (1998).

[249] United States v. Ruhe, 191 F.3d 376 (4th Cir. 1999); United States v. Sanchez, 118 F.3d 192, 197 (4th Cir. 1997); Rowland v. United States, 840 A.2d 664, 673 (D.C. Cir. 2004), *citing* Procter v. United States, 728 A.2d 1246, 1249, *amended on reh'g in immaterial part*, 747 A.2d 134 (D.C. 1999) (calling polygraph results "untrustworthy").

[250] United States v. Reed, 147 F.3d 1178, 1183 (9th Cir. 1998); United States v. Messina, 131 F.3d 36, 42 (2d Cir. 1997), *cert. denied*, 523 U.S. 1088 (1998); United States v. Kwong, 69 F.3d 663, 668 (2d Cir. 1995), *cert. denied*, 517 U.S. 1115 (1996); United States v. Robbins, 197 F.3d 829 (7th Cir. 1999); United States v. Orians, 9 F. Supp. 2d 1168 (D. Ariz. 1998).

[251] United States v. Posado, 57 F.3d 428, 434 (5th Cir. 1995).

[252] United States v. Cordoba, 194 F.3d 1053 (9th Cir. 1999), *cert. denied*, 529 U.S. 1081 (2000).

[253] United States v. Cordoba, 194 F.3d 1053, 1059 (9th Cir. 1999), *cert. denied*, 529 U.S. 1081 (2000).

[254] United States v. Cordoba, 194 F.3d 1053, 1060 (9th Cir. 1999), *cert. denied*, 529 U.S. 1081 (2000).

[255] United States v. Cordoba, 194 F.3d 1053, 1060–1061 (9th Cir. 1999), *cert. denied*, 529 U.S. 1081 (2000).

exams.[256] In the instant case, the court noted no tape or video was made of the pre-test interview, the machine was not calibrated and among the "relevant" questions only one was truly relevant; the report was drafted before the test and included numerous errors.[257]

A thorough discussion of the history of the polygraph's test and its admissibility is set forth in *United States v. Piccinonna*.[258] *Piccinonna* affirmed a defendant's conviction when the prosecution did not stipulate to the techniques for using a polygraph.[259] However, the court noted that polygraph technology and techniques have improved and are not *per se* inadmissible.[260] It stated also that, at least in the Eleventh Circuit, polygraph testimony will be admissible:

> [w]hen both parties stipulate in advance as to the circumstances of the test and as to the scope of its admissibility. The stipulation as to circumstances must indicate that the parties agree on material matters such as the manner in which the test is conducted, the nature of the questions asked, and the identity of the examiner administering the test. The stipulation as to scope of admissibility must indicate the purpose or purposes for which the evidence will be introduced.[261]

Piccinonna also went on to permit polygraph evidence to impeach or corroborate the testimony of a witness at trial where adequate notice to the opposing party has been provided, where the opposing party has had a reasonable opportunity to have its polygraph expert administer a comparable test, and where the expert testimony will be limited by the Federal Rules of Evidence for the admissibility of corroboration or impeachment testimony, namely Rule 608, which permits evidence of truthful character only after the witness's character has been attacked.[262]

There are state statutes that preclude polygraph evidence unless stipulated.[263]

---

[256] United States v. Cordoba, 194 F.3d 1053, 1061–1062 (9th Cir. 1999), *cert. denied*, 529 U.S. 1081 (2000).

[257] United States v. Cordoba, 194 F.3d 1053, 1062 (9th Cir. 1999), *cert. denied*, 529 U.S. 1081 (2000).

[258] United States v. Piccinonna, 885 F.2d 1529 (11th Cir. 1989).

[259] United States v. Piccinonna, 885 F.2d 1529 (11th Cir. 1989).

[260] United States v. Piccinonna, 885 F.2d 1529 (11th Cir. 1989).

[261] United States v. Piccinonna, 885 F.2d 1529, 1536 (11th Cir. 1989).

[262] Fed. R. Evid. 608(a) provides:

> Opinion and reputation evidence of character. The credibility of a witness may be attacked or supported by evidence in the form of opinion or reputation, but subject to these limitations: (1) the evidence may refer only to character for truthfulness or untruthfulness, and (2) evidence of truthful character is admissible only after the character of the witness for truthfulness has been attacked by opinion or reputation evidence or otherwise.

[263] Cal. Evid. Code § 351.1: "(a) Notwithstanding any other provision of law, the results of a polygraph examination, the opinion of polygraph examiner, or any reference to an offer to take, failure to take, or taking of a polygraph examination, shall not be admitted into evidence in any criminal proceeding . . .unless all parties stipulate to the admission of such results."

Some state courts continue to reject polygraph evidence under both *Daubert* and *Frye*.[264]

Some state courts require a hearing on the reliability of polygraph evidence rather than relying on a *per se* exclusion.[265]

---

[264] People v. Wilkinson, 33 Cal. 4th 821, 94 P.3d 551 (2004) (reversing intermediate appeals court decision remanding case for *Kelly/Frye* hearing, since legislatively enacted *per se* rule excluding polygraph evidence is not arbitrary or disproportionate); State v. Porter, 241 Conn. 57, 92–95, 698 A.2d 739, 758–59 (1997); State v. Perry, 139 Idaho 520, 81 P.3d 1230 (2003) (The Supreme Court of Idaho reversed a trial court decision to permit the defendant to introduce results of his polygraph examination. Court concluded that polygraph lacked sufficient reliability under *Daubert* and:

> In this case, the results of the polygraph are useful to bolster Perry's credibility but do not provide the trier of fact with any additional information that pertains to Perry's case. The fact of whether the alleged act occurred is for the jury to decide. [citation omitted] Additionally, credibility questions are left to the trier of fact, in this case a jury. [citation omitted] The polygraph results in this case do not help the trier of fact to find facts or to understand the evidence. . . . To admit these results is an attempt to substitute the credibility determination appropriate for the jury, with Dr. Honts' interpretation of the alleged involuntary physiological results from the polygraph examination. Dr. Honts usurps the role of the jury as the ultimate finder of credibility.
>
> Therefore, this Court holds Dr. Honts' testimony as well as the polygraph results, inadmissible and reverses the decision of the district court. Perry's constitutional right to present a defense will not be infringed upon by this Court's holding. Perry will be able to present all of the relevant details of the charge from his perspective and will not be precluded from introducing factual evidence; the exclusion merely bars the introduction of expert opinion testimony that would bolster Perry's credibility. [citations omitted]

State v. Perry, 139 Idaho 520, 525, 81 P.3d 1230, 1235 (2003). *See also* People v. Wallace, 97 P.3d 262 (Colo. Ct. App. 2004), *cert. denied*, 2004 Colo. LEXIS 605 (Aug. 16, 2004):

> Even assuming that the polygraph evidence met the requirements of CRE 702, we agree with the trial court that introduction of the evidence would invade the province of the jury and influence its decision regarding witness credibility . . . even though the *Frye* standard has been modified . . . [we] conclude that the trial court was correct in refusing to admit the polygraph evidence under CRE 403, without deciding whether the polygraph evidence otherwise may have satisfied CRE 702.

State v. Shively, 268 Kan. 573, 999 P.2d 952 (2000) (holding polygraph results too unreliable despite advances in computerization of polygraph scoring); People v. Gormely, 222 A.D.2d 521, 635 N.Y.S.2d 256 (1995), *appeal denied*, 87 N.Y.2d 973, 664 N.E.2d 1265, 642 N.Y.S.2d 202 (1996) (finding that the defendant did not offer proper foundation of scientific reliability for introduction of defense expert's testimony which was based on the result of a polygraph examination taken at the time of the defendant's interrogation); State v. Weatherspoon, 1998 N.D. 148, 583 N.W.2d 391 (1998); Marcum v. State, 983 S.W.2d 762, 765 (Tex. Ct. App. 1998). *See also* State v. Schatz-Sousa, 1998 Wash. App. LEXIS 425 (Mar. 23, 1998); State v. Beard, 194 W. Va. 740, 461 S.E.2d 486 (1995).

[265] In the Interest of Robert R., 340 S.C. 242, 531 S.E.2d 301 (2000).

The Supreme Court did not discuss whether stipulated polygraph results are admissible, particularly in a non-jury proceeding, such as a pretrial hearing.[266] States will admit polygraph evidence if the parties stipulate to its admission or if other conditions are met, such as a showing of the qualifications of the expert administering the test and reliability of the test.[267] Even when there is a stipulation to admit polygraph results as evidence, there may be disputes as to interpretation of the stipulation. For example, if a defendant and prosecutor agree to polygraph testing and inconclusive results void the stipulation, do "inconclusive" results on the victim's polygraph results permit a second testing of the victim? One appellate court ruled that a trial court committed reversible error in permitting polygraph results that a victim was telling the truth after the inconclusive results were admitted over the defendant's objections.[268]

The Supreme Court has not ruled whether stipulated polygraph results are admissible, particularly in a non-jury proceeding, such as a pretrial hearing.[269] States will admit polygraph evidence if the parties stipulate to its admission or if other conditions are met, such as a showing of the qualifications of the expert administering the test and reliability of the test.[270]

---

[266] *See, e.g.,* United States v. Posado, 57 F.3d 428 (5th Cir. 1995) (holding that polygraph evidence is not *per se* inadmissible in light of the admissibility standards of *Daubert;* trial judge should determine reliability and whether the polygraph evidence will be helpful or relevant for purposes of suppression hearing).

[267] State v. Valdez, 91 Ariz. 274, 283–84, 371 P.2d 894, 900 (1962); People v. Trujillo, 67 Cal. App. 3d 547, 136 Cal. Rptr. 672, 676 (1977); Williams v. State, 378 A.2d 117, 120 (Del. 1977); State v. Fain, 116 Idaho 82, 774 P.2d 252 (1989); State v. Lucero, 86 N.M. 686, 526 P.2d 1091 (1974) (requiring not only stipulation but also proof of polygraph operator's qualifications, validity of tests on subject, and reliability of test procedures used; *Lucero's* stipulation requirement was released in State v. Dorsey, 88 N.M. 184, 539 P.2d 204 (1975)); State v. Jackson, 57 Ohio St. 3d 29, 37, 565 N.E.2d 549, 558 (1991); State v. Woo, 84 Wash. 2d 472, 527 P.2d 271 (1974); Cullin v. State, 565 P.2d 445, 453–59 (Wyo. 1977) (setting forth the stipulation agreement used in the case); *In re* Dependency of K.R., 128 Wash. 2d 129, 147, 904 P.2d 1132, 1141 (1995).

[268] State v. Rucker, 2000 Ohio App. LEXIS 3819 (Aug. 25, 2000).

[269] *See, e.g.,* United States v. Posado, 57 F.3d 428 (5th Cir. 1995) (holding that polygraph evidence is not *per se* inadmissible in light of the admissibility standards of *Daubert;* trial judge should determine reliability and whether the polygraph evidence will be helpful or relevant for purposes of suppression hearing).

[270] Foster v. State, 285 Ark. 363, 687 S.W.2d 829 (1985); State v. Valdez, 91 Ariz. 274, 283–84, 371 P.2d 894, 900 (1962); People v. Trujillo, 67 Cal. App. 3d 547, 136 Cal. Rptr. 672, 676 (1977); Williams v. State, 378 A.2d 117, 120 (Del. 1977); Lockett v. State, 258 Ga. App. 178, 180–81, 573 S.E.2d 437 (2002); State v. Fain, 116 Idaho 82, 774 P.2d 252 (1989); State v. Dorsey, 88 N.M. 184, 539 P.2d 204 (1975)); State v. Lucero, 86 N.M. 686, 526 P.2d 1091 (1974) (requiring not only stipulation but also proof of polygraph operator's qualifications, validity of tests on subject, and reliability of test procedures used; *Lucero's* stipulation requirement was released in State v. Jackson, 57 Ohio St. 3d 29, 37, 565 N.E.2d 549, 558 (1991); *In re* Dependency of K.R., 128 Wash. 2d 129, 147, 904 P.2d 1132, 1141 (1995); State v. Woo, 84 Wash. 2d 472, 527 P.2d 271 (1974); Cullin v. State, 565 P.2d 445, 453–59 (Wyo. 1977) (setting forth the stipulation agreement used in the case).

A risk for a defendant in agreeing to allow a polygraph result to be used is that an unfavorable result can be admitted.[271] This may include unfavorable testimony as to how the defendant may have tried to distort the results of the exam.[272] Even if there is a stipulation to admit polygraph results, it is error to preclude defendant's expert's testimony as to his disagreement with the state's expert's interpretation.[273] Any ambiguity in the stipulation is likely to be resolved against the state.[274]

Even when there is a stipulation to admit polygraph results as evidence, there may be disputes as to interpretation of the stipulation. For example, if a defendant and prosecutor agree to polygraph testing and inconclusive results void the stipulation, do "inconclusive" results on the victim's polygraph results permit a second testing of the victim? One appellate court ruled that a trial court committed reversible error in permitting polygraph results that a victim was telling the truth after the inconclusive results were admitted over the defendant's objections.[275]

New Mexico is unique in making polygraph evidence generally admissible without stipulation or major restriction, although the examination must be recorded.[276] Even though New Mexico's Supreme Court did not find general acceptance of the polygraph, it found sufficient reliability under *Daubert* factors of testability, peer review and publication, rate of error and maintenance of standards controlling the technique.[277] It relied in large part on the report of the National Academy of Sciences on the polygraph report,[278] which found the polygraph to have diagnostic reliability among "naïve examiners," supported by peer-review studies, a rate of error, although there were ways in which the accuracy of the polygraph could be affected and there was a lack of its general acceptance in the scientific community. The New Mexico court noted that "[o]ften the same government officials who vigorously oppose the admission of exculpatory polygraphs of the accused find polygraph testing to be reliable enough to use in their own decision-making."[279]

---

[271] United States v. Oliver, 525 F.2d 731 (8th Cir. 1975), *cert. denied*, 424 U.S. 973 (1976); Lockett v. State, 258 Ga. App. 178, 573 S.E.2d 437 (2002) (holding no error in child molestation trial in admission into evidence of defendant's polygraph results, since defendant was bound by his stipulation to allow polygraph results into evidence even though court found polygraph tests unreliable).

[272] Horne v. State, 273 Ga. App. 132, 134, 614 S.E.2d 243, 245 (2005).

[273] State v. Elliott, 121 Wash. App. 404, 88 P.3d 435 (2004).

[274] State v. Elliott, 121 Wash. App. 404, 88 P.3d 435 (2004).

[275] State v. Rucker, 2000 Ohio App. LEXIS 3819 (Aug. 25, 2000).

[276] N.M. RULE EVID. § 11-707.

[277] Lee v. Martinez, 136 N.M. 166, 96 P.3d 291 (2004).

[278] *See* http://www.nap.edu/openbook/0309084369/html.

[279] Lee v. Martinez, 136 N.M. 166, 181, 96 P.3d at 291, 306 (2004).

There are standards for evidentiary polygraph examinations established by the American Polygraph Association,[280] which are similar to those in the New Mexico statutes.[281] These include calibration of the machine, standards with respect to pre-test interview and questions asked, recording of the examination as well as a "quantitative" or numerical evaluation of the results as opposed to subjective factors (sometimes called global assessment), which utilizes factors such as body languages and gestures.[282]

There are a variety of extrinsic factors that affect polygraph accuracy. Sometimes, the examiner's results are checked by quality control officers (as are most federally-administered polygraph exams) who will request a re-examination if there is a doubt about the examiner's conclusions. At times, courts are leery of privately commissioned polygraph exams.[283]

As with other areas of expert testimony, the expert must have the appropriate credentials to render an opinion on a polygraph test. If the expert has experience with polygraph testing but has not remained current on developments in the field, he will be precluded from testifying on the grounds of his lack of qualifications.[284] It may be reversible error to preclude the defendant from presenting testimony concerning the interpretation of the prosecution's polygraph results.[285]

Modifications of the *per se* exclusionary rule for polygraph evidence do not limit the trial court's ability to exclude polygraph testimony on other grounds, such as Federal Rule of Evidence 702 as to whether the testimony will assist the trier of fact, Rule 401 concerning relevancy of testimony, and, probably the most important limitation, Rule 403 pertaining to whether the testimony's probative value is outweighed by the danger of unfair prejudice or confusion.[286] Even under this view, which permits expert testimony of the polygraph for

---

[280] *See American Polygraph Association, Division III: APA Standards of Practice* (Jan. 10, 1999), available at <http://www.polygraph.org/standards.htm>.

[281] New Mexico Rule Evid. § 11-707.

[282] *See* NAS Report, *supra* note 278.

[283] United States v. Ross, 412 F.3d 771 (7th Cir. 2005) ("Indeed, courts have routinely rejected unilateral and clandestine polygraph examinations like the one taken here, citing concern that a test taken without the government's knowledge is unreliable because it carries no negative consequences, and probably won't see the light of day if a defendant flunks." [citations omitted] *Id.* at 773.

[284] United States v. Taylor, 154 F.3d 675 (7th Cir.), *cert. denied*, 525 U.S. 1060 (1998) (noting that expert used "stock" questions rather than questions tailored to circumstances of case and used a subjective visual scoring technique rather than an objective numerical scoring system which therefore affected the reliability of the test as well as the probative value of the expert's opinion).

[285] State v. Elliott, 121 Wash. App. 404, 88 P.3d 435 (2004) (reversing defendant's rape conviction because defendant did not voluntarily and knowingly waive his constitutional right to call a witness to testify about the meaning of the polygraph test results, and trial court erred in refusing to allow defendant's expert to testify about this interpretation of the testing, which was constitutional error).

[286] United States v. Piccinonna, 885 F.2d 1529, 1536 (11th Cir. 1989).

impeachment or corroboration, the expert testimony can be precluded if the expert's qualifications are unacceptable, the test procedure was unfairly prejudicial, or the questions were irrelevant or improper,[287] or will not assist the trier of fact.[288]

§ 11.24   Credibility and uses of the polygraph — Bail, plea bargaining and of complainant in sexual assault case and admissibility of defendant's offer to undergo polygraph.

The polygraph can play several different roles in a sexual assault case. Apart from its admissibility at trial, it can be used as an investigative tool by law enforcement, as a negotiating tool between prosecutor and defense attorney to determine whether to bring charges, and in other pretrial matters. For example, a polygraph examination may be utilized by a defendant to support a bail application or to determine the weakness of the prosecution's proof[289] or a motion dismissing charges. Even when a polygraph report is used to support such a motion, it may be rejected as unreliable because the questions placed to the suspect are not dispositive of guilt or innocence.[290] A court is not required to consider the polygraph at a pre-trial or post-trial proceeding and may reject the polygraph report as unworthy of credit.[291] Sometimes, the polygraph is used by prosecutors as well as defense attorneys to assess the case and as a tool in plea bargaining. When the polygraph is used by a defendant for pretrial purposes, it does not open the door for the prosecution to test the defendant — the prosecutor has no right to test a defendant by means of a polygraph. However, it may open the door to the prosecution's use of statements made by defendant to the polygrapher.[292]

The polygraph also can be used with complaining witnesses and victims; however, most children are too young to test by polygraph. Some states statutorily prohibit the use of a polygraph as a law enforcement investigative tool in

---

[287] United States v. Piccinonna, 885 F.2d 1529, 1537.

[288] United States v. Canter, 338 F. Supp. 2d 460 (S.D.N.Y. 2004) (holding polygraph questions offered by defendant as part of his case were not probative of defendant's guilt or innocence and would not assist the trier of fact).

[289] United States v. Bellomo, 944 F. Supp. 1160 (S.D.N.Y. 1996) (noting that "[t]he polygraph evidence is properly considered on this application despite its long established inadmissibility in criminal trials, because the rules of evidence do not apply in detention hearings under the Bail Reform Act, 18 U.S.C. § 3142(f)").

[290] United States v. Bellomo, 944 F.Supp 1160, 1164–1166.

[291] United States v. Messina, 131 F.3d 36, 41–42 (2d Cir. 1997), *cert. denied*, 523 U.S. 1088 (1998).

[292] People v. Welch, 51 Cal. App. 4th 1128, 60 Cal. Rptr. 2d 116 (1996) (permitting prosecution to use admission made by rape defendant during his polygraph examination and contained in a report turned over to the prosecution).

questioning a sexual assault victim as a prerequisite to the filing of criminal charges.[293] The practice of polygraphing victims by police is not as prevalent as it once was. Today, it is more likely that a law enforcement agency will test a victim only with the complainant's consent and when a polygraph is also administered to the suspect.

Law enforcement agencies do routinely use the polygraph as an interview tool, however, and statements made during a polygraph examination, particularly during the pretest interview, are admissible. Before performing the actual polygraph test, an extensive interview is conducted with the subject; this is known as the pretest interview, which is considered an essential part of the polygraph examination.

Occasionally, a court will permit a defendant's offer to take a polygraph test on a "conscience of innocence" theory. However, most courts[294] follow the rule that polygraph examinations are inadmissible unless their use is stipulated to by the parties, so that a defendant's offer to submit to a polygraph test has no probative value, and there is no error in refusing to admit a defendant's offer to take the test.[295] Other courts also find it proper to delete or preclude references to a defendant's offer to take a polygraph.[296] Yet, evidence from the prosecution that a defense witness refused a police-administered polygraph examination, while improper, may be a harmless error.[297]

§ 11.25   Use of polygraph as part of probation or supervised release and sentencing and motion for new trial.

The level of reliability required for a polygraph (or penile plethysmograph) is not as high when used for probation, supervised release or treatment or making

---

[293] *See, e.g.*, Conn. Gen. Stat. § 54-86; N.Y. Crim. Proc. Law § 160.45:

> (1) No district attorney, police officer or employee of any law enforcement agency shall request or require any victim of a sexual assault crime to submit to any polygraph test or psychological stress evaluator examination. (2) As used in this section, "victim of a sexual assault crime" means any person alleged to have sustained an offense under article one hundred thirty or § 255.25 of the penal law.

[294] State v. Santana-Lopez, 237 Wis. 2d 332, 613 N.W.2d 918 (2000), *citing* State v. Hoffman, 64 Wis. 2d 62, 74–76, 218 N.W.2d 342, 348 (1974).

[295] State v. Campbell, 904 S.W.2d 608 (Tenn. Crim. App. 1995) (fact that accused "offered to take, took, or refused to take a polygraph examination cannot be admitted as evidence." State v. Campbell, 904 S.W.2d 608, 615 (Tenn. Crim. App. 1995)).

[296] Rollins v. State, 2005 Ark. LEXIS 293 (2005) (upholding trial court's redaction in accused rapist's videotaped statement of his offer to take polygraph); Kremer v. State, 514 N.E.2d 1068 (Ind. 1987); Kosmas v. State, 316 Md. 587, 592, 560 A.2d 1137, 1140 (1989); State v. Weatherspoon, 1998 ND 148, 583 N.W.2d 391 (1998) (holding trial court properly deleted references to defendant's willingness to take a polygraph examination which were contained in defendant's statement to investigators).

[297] Rowland v. United States, 840 A.2d 664 (D.C. Cir. 2004).

an arrest[298] as it is when used as trial evidence.

Several courts permit probation to use a polygraph as a tool to monitor a sex offender's compliance with conditions of probation.[299]

While the requirement to pass a polygraph as a tool of supervised release does raise Fifth Amendment issues, most of these same courts find that a defendant can still invoke the Fifth Amendment in response to polygraph questions.[300] As long as there are no consequences to the invocation of the Fifth Amendment, the probationer may be compelled to lie under polygraph testing.[301] Nonetheless, some courts maintain their prohibition against the use of polygraph examination results in revocation proceedings.[302]

Some courts hold that a polygraph examination should not be utilized in enhancing a defendant's sentence.[303] A sentencing court may also reject the

---

[298] Gomez v. Atkins, 296 F.3d 253, 264 n.8 (4th Cir. 2002), *cert. denied*, 537 U.S. 1159 (2003) (holding polygraph results may be relied on in evaluating probable cause); Johnson v. Schneiderheinz, 102 F.3d 340, 342 (8th Cir. 1996) (permitting polygraph results to be part of officer's probable cause for arrest).

[299] United States v. York, 357 F.3d 14 (1st Cir. 2004) (noting that court would not issue "a blanket decision on propriety of polygraph testing as a tool of supervised release" given paucity of record on issue of polygraph's reliability); United States v. Taylor, 338 F.3d 1280, 1284 (11th Cir.), *cert. denied*, 540 U.S. 1066 (2003); United States v. Zinn 321 F.3d 1084, 1092 (11th Cir.), *cert. denied*, 540 U.S. 839 (2003) (finding no error in trial court's delegation of authority to a probation officer for overseeing defendant's mental health treatment, including administering polygraph tests administered as part of treatment); United States v. Lee, 315 F.3d 206, 217 (3d Cir.), *cert. denied*, 540 U.S. 858 (2003); United States v. Powers, 59 F.3d 1460, 1471 n.13 (4th Cir. 1995), *cert. denied*, 516 U.S. 1077 (1996); *In the Matter of D.S.*, 160 Ohio App. 3d 552, 828 N.E.2d 143 (2005):

> Because it is reasonably related to rehabilitating the offender, has a relationship to the crime committed and serves the statutory ends of probation, we continue to find that submission to a polygraph examination is a reasonable requirement of probation.

In the Matter of D.S., 160 Ohio App. 3d 552, 562, 828 N.E.2d 143, 151 (2005). *Ex parte* Renfro, 999 S.W.2d 557 (Tex. Ct. App. 1990); State v. Riles, 135 Wash. 2d 326, 957 P.2d 655 (1998). *See generally*, Anne M. Payne, Annotation, *Propriety of Conditioning Probation on Defendant's Submission to Polygraph or Other Lie Detector Testing*, 86 A.L.R.4th 709 (1991).

[300] United States v. York, 357 F.3d 14, 27 (court noted defendant would be entitled to a hearing before any penalty can be imposed for defendant's invocation of Fifth Amendment in response to polygraph questions).

[301] State v. Gaither, 196 Or. App. 131, 100 P.3d 768 (2004) (holding statements to probation officer should have been suppressed if it was clear that defendant's probation would be revoked for failure to answer a question).

[302] White v. Commonwealth, 41 Va. App. 191, 583 S.E.2d 771 (2003) (finding polygraph "wholly unreliable").

[303] State v. Shaneyfelt, 2005 Iowa App. LEXIS 138 (Feb. 24, 2005) (remanding accused child molester's sentence due to judge's reliance on defendant's failed polygraph report). Court held:

> We find it particularly problematic that the district court relied on a failed polygraph examination as a factor to assess Shaneyfelt's credibility and justify the sentence. The record contains scant information about the polygraph administered in this case.

polygraph results as "flat out wrong."[304]

A more relaxed standard permits use of "favorable polygraphs" on behalf of capital defendants at sentencing.[305] Attempts have been made to use the results of a polygraph to support a motion for a new trial based on a child's recantation.[306]

§ 11.26   Reference to polygraph examination during trial or police testimony concerning interview of defendant.

Statements made by a defendant during a polygraph examination are admissible pursuant to the same rules as other statements of a defendant.[307] This includes statements made by him to his own polygrapher contained in a report turned over to the prosecution.[308]

What reference, if any, may be made to a polygraph test or its results during a trial? Courts have varied widely on this. One court has permitted the introduction of the fact that the defendant failed a polygraph test to explain why the law enforcement authorities did not conduct a more thorough examination.[309] Some courts will permit the prosecution to introduce polygraph results to rebut a claim by a defendant that his confession was the result of coercion;[310] however, when testimony has been admitted under these circumstances, it is for a very limited purpose. For example, in *Tyler v. United States*,[311] the defendant confessed to

---

The only record reference to the examination appears in the PSI report which does not indicate (1) the qualifications of the examiner, (2) the technique employed by the examiner, or (3) evidence tending to establish the reliability of the technique employed by the examiner. The PSI report merely asserts that Shaneyfelt voluntarily took and failed a polygraph examination.

State v. Shaneyfelt, 2005 Iowa App. LEXIS 138 (Feb. 24, 2005).

[304] United States v. Messina, 131 F.3d 36 (2d Cir. 1997), *cert. denied*, 523 U.S. 1088 (1998).

[305] State v. Porter, 241 Conn. 57, 137, 698 A.2d 739, 779 (1997); Height v. State, 278 Ga. 592, 604 S.E.2d 796 (2004) ("Therefore, we conclude that Georgia's general ban on the admission of polygraph test results absent the parties' stipulation should not be applied automatically in the sentencing phase of a capital case so as to prevent the defendant from presenting a favorable polygraph test result." Height v. State, 278 Ga. 592, 595, 604 S.E.2d 796, 798 (2004)); State v. Pierce, 138 S.W.3d 820, 826 (Tenn. 2004).

[306] *See, e.g.*, United States v. Rouse, 410 F.3d 1005, 1011 (8th Cir. 2005) (finding trial court did not abuse its discretion in finding polygraph did not meet "accepted polygraph testing procedure" and therefore results were not reliable).

[307] Cal. Evid. Code 351.1(b): "Nothing in this section is intended to exclude from evidence statements made during a polygraph examination which are otherwise admissible."

[308] People v. Welch, 51 Cal. App. 4th 1128, 60 Cal. Rptr. 2d 116 (1996).

[309] United States v. Hall, 805 F.2d 1410 (10th Cir. 1986).

[310] United States v. Johnson, 816 F.2d 918, 923 (3d Cir. 1987); United States v. Kampiles, 609 F.2d 1233, 1245 (7th Cir. 1979), *cert. denied*, 446 U.S. 954 (1980).

[311] Tyler v. United States, 193 F.2d 24 (D.C. Cir. 1951), *cert. denied*, 343 U.S. 908 (1952). *See also* United States v. Willis, 41 M.J. 435 (C.A.A.F. 1995) (statements made during polygraph

the crime after being told that his reactions during the polygraph indicated to the examiner that he was not telling the truth. This fact was held admissible "as revealing circumstances leading to the confession,"[312] with the court giving a limiting instruction admonishing the jury that the testimony was admitted only on the issue of whether the confession was voluntary.[313] However, when all the questions and answers of the polygraph examination are brought into evidence, and there is no limitation on the testimony concerning the polygraph examination, and the expert testimony is not "narrowly tailored to limit the prejudicial effect of such evidence," a defendant's conviction may be reversed because of the prejudicial impact.[314] There is no probative value in admitting such testimony to set the scene for the defendant's statements, particularly where the voluntary nature of the statements is not challenged by the defendant, but only the statements' reliability.[315] When a defendant's statements are at the heart of the prosecution's case, the error in permitting extensive testimony concerning the polygraph examination is not cured by a limiting instruction, and the defendant's conviction must be reversed.[316]

Not all courts will permit reference to the fact that a defendant was told he failed a polygraph test and then confessed. Montana condemned the use of a polygraph to obtain a defendant's confession in a case involving a defendant accused of sexually molesting his 11-year-old daughter. The defendant confessed to the crime when he was told by police at the conclusion of a polygraph examination that he had lied.[317] The Montana Supreme Court said:

> [W]e strongly condemn the tactics used by the officers in this case to coerce defendant's confession. Prior to this charge, defendant had no criminal record and did not have experience with police interrogation. The officers misled defendant into believing that the results of the test were legitimate and admissible in order to induce a confession. The State maintains that the officers' conduct in this case is an acceptable tactic, and that the use of a polygraph test is an effective tool for investigative purposes.

examination did not create an impermissible inference that defendant took and failed polygraph, even in light of Military Rule of Evidence 707, which precludes any reference to the results of a polygraph examination).

[312] Tyler v. United States, 193 F.2d 24, 31 (D.C. Cir. 1951), *cert. denied*, 343 U.S. 908 (1952).

[313] Tyler v. United States, 193 F.2d 24, 31 (D.C. Cir. 1951), *cert. denied*, 343 U.S. 908 (1952).

[314] United States v. Miller, 874 F.2d 1255, 1260–62 (9th Cir. 1989), *cert. denied*, 510 U.S. 894 (1993) (holding also that the defendant was properly precluded from calling a psychologist as an expert on the issue of the impact of being told that one has failed a polygraph examination).

[315] United States v. Miller, 874 F.2d 1255, 1260-1262 (9th Cir. 1989), *cert denied*, 510 U.S. 894 (1993).

[316] United States v. Miller, 874 F.2d 1255, 1260-1262 (9th Cir. 1989), *cert. denied*, 510 U.S. 894 (1993); United States v. Murray, 784 F.2d 188, 189 (6th Cir. 1986) (holding that a curative instruction did not "unring the bell" of inadmissible polygraph evidence).

[317] State v. Craig, 262 Mont. 240, 864 P.2d 1240 (1993).

Regardless of its acceptability among the police, it is not acceptable to this Court for the police to use the results of a polygraph examination to tell a defendant that he lied in order to extract a confession. Nor can we say that the polygraph was used for investigative purposes in this case. [The officer] testified that the purpose of telling defendant that he lied was to elicit a statement. . . . In light of the lack of trustworthiness of the results of polygraph tests . . . polygraph evidence shall not be allowed in any proceeding in a court of law in Montana. The only acceptable lie detection methods in Montana court proceedings reside with the court in bench trials, the jury in jury trials, and the skill of counsel in cross-examination in all trials. . . . We also condemn the use of the results of polygraph examinations to elicit or coerce a confession from defendants. [318]

Sometimes a passing reference to a polygraph test is not so prejudicial to require a new trial if the jury can not infer that the witnesses passed or failed the test. [319] Sometimes, it is reversible error to do so. [320] A defendant may, however, refer to an investigator's asking him to take a polygraph in support of his defense that his statements were involuntary, on the theory his will was overborne by aggressive interrogation tactics, without opening the door to a prosecutor's cross-examination of the defendant of the reasons for refusing to take the polygraph. [321]

§ 11.27 Polygraph and special jury instructions with respect to polygraph testimony.

When admitted into evidence, some courts have suggested that a special jury instruction should be required when polygraph results are admitted. [322] To what extent such an instruction should go beyond the general instruction on expert testimony [323] is debatable and some courts find no authority for such an instruction. [324]

---

[318] State v. Craig, 262 Mont. 242-243, 864 P.2d 1240, 1242 (1993).

[319] Peters v. State, 357 Ark. 297, 166 S.W.3d 34 (2004) (finding no reversible error in rape case in witness's reference to defendant missing a polygraph test); Albury v. State, 835 So. 2d 1208, 1209 (Fla. Ct. App. 2003); Jasso v. State, 112 S.W.3d 805, 813–14 (Tex. Ct. App. 2003) (finding improper reference to polygraph test harmless and that defendant did not timely object).

[320] State v. Smith, 2004 Ohio App. LEXIS 646 (Feb. 13, 2004) (reversing defendant's rape conviction in part due to prejudicial reference to incomplete polygraph examination by police officer and in defendant's written statement, since this was plain error).

[321] People v. Uriah, 261 A.D.2d 848, 691 N.Y.S.2d 216 (1999) (reversing defendant's conviction as a result of prosecutor's questioning defendant that he refused polygraph because "you knew that you had done it, and they could tell you were lying on a polygraph").

[322] See, e.g., State v. Trotter, 110 Ariz. 61, 514 P.2d 1249 (1973).

[323] See § 16.5.

[324] Lockett v. State, 258 Ga. App. 178, 573 S.E.2d 437 (2002):

Lockett provides no authority — and we are aware of none — that would require the trial court to provide limiting instructions at the time the polygraph evidence was

However, if an improper reference is made to a polygraph exam, the jury should be instructed to disregard the reference. For example, if the prosecution elicits testimony that a defense witness refused a polygraph, the court might instruct the jury as to why other witnesses were not asked to take a polygraph and that polygraph evidence is inadmissible. [325]

§ 11.28 Expert testimony on CSAAS and RTS as substantive evidence of guilt.

As noted in previous sections, CSAAS and RTS testimony is used for rehabilitative and not substantive purposes. New Jersey's court emphasizes "the overarching principle that CSAAS expert testimony cannot be allowed as substantive proof to establish guilt or innocence." [326]

Profiles, such as drug courier profiles, cannot be used as substantive evidence of guilt. [327] In criminal sexual assault trials, expert mental health testimony may have limited value as the sole evidence of a material element of a crime. In *People v. Zurak,* [328] the prosecutor attempted to use expert testimony to establish the element of sexual contact when the victim refused to testify to the abuse at trial. The jury convicted the defendant, but the expert testimony was the only proof that established sexual contact. (Because New York law does not permit the use of prior statements or direct evidence except in narrowly defined situations, [329] the prosecution could not use the victim's original statement alleging abuse.) The appellate court reversed defendant's conviction on this count, disapproving the use of psychological opinion evidence to supply proof of a specific element of a sex crime charged. [330]

§ 11.29 Testimony by prosecution that defendant fits profile of an abuser.

The prosecution may offer testimony through its expert that persons who abuse children or commit other sexual crimes have certain characteristics or that there

admitted absent a request from the defendant. In any event, the trial court properly instructed the jury with respect to the polygraph results during its general charge, which eviscerates Lockett's claim of error.

Lockett v. State, 258 Ga. App. 178, 181, 573 S.E.2d 437, 441 (2002).

[325] Rowland v. United States, 840 A.2d 664, 673 (D.C. 2004).

[326] State v. R.B., 183 N.J. 308, 328-29, 873 A.2d 511, 524 (2005).

[327] United States v. McDonald, 933 F.2d 1519, 1521 (10th Cir. 1991), *cert. denied,* 502 U.S. 897 (1991).

[328] People v. Zurak, 168 A.D.2d 196, 571 N.Y.S.2d 577 (1991), *appeal denied,* 79 N.Y.2d 834, 588 N.E.2d 112, 80 N.Y.S.2d 214, *cert. denied,* 504 U.S. 941 (1992).

[329] N.Y. Crim. Proc. Law § 60.35.

[330] People v. Zurak, 168 A.D.2d 196, 199, 571 N.Y.S.2d 577, 579–80, *appeal denied,* 79 N.Y.2d 834, 588 N.E.2d 112 (1991).

are typical circumstances under which child sexual abuse or sexual assaults take place. Most courts have followed the rule that evidence that only describes the characteristics of the typical offender has no relevance as to whether an accused committed the crime in question.[331] This includes testimony based on psychological tests that a defendant is likely to engage in deviant conduct.[332] Testimony of an expert that classifies a defendant as a "power rapist" was prejudicial, since the issue for the jury is whether there was a rape, not characteristics of the rapist.[333] According to an Oregon court, a statement that a nonviolent child abuser is usually a male and unrelated to the child is a very vague and general grouping and highly prejudicial.[334] Another reference that can result in reversible error is testimony that, in "85–90 percent of sexual abuse cases, the child is molested by someone they already know."[335]

A complaint against the use of profile evidence or group characteristic evidence is that it places before the jury the forbidden inference that the defendant has a propensity to commit the crime for which he is charged, and that it has a tendency to introduce percentages or characteristics pertaining to sexual abuse or assaults that have not been accepted in the scientific community or shown to be scientifically reliable.[336] In fact, so unreliable and prejudicial is profile testimony of abusers or group characteristics that it may be forbidden even when the defendant places his character in issue.[337] The same problem is presented by prosecution testimony that the defendant fits the profile of a pedophile — someone who has a sexual preference for children.[338] Particularly prejudicial is testimony as to the large number of children typically victimized by a pedophile.[339] Thus, courts have clearly come down on the side of not allowing

---

[331] State v. Clements, 770 P.2d 447, 454 (Kan. 1989).

[332] State v. W.L., 278 N.J. Super. 295, 304, 650 A.2d 1035, 1040 (1995) (prosecutor improperly presented psychological testimony concerning a psychologist's administration of the Child Abuse Potential Inventory, which included the psychologist's opinion that the defendant's responses on this test indicated to him that the defendant's "faking good index" was "highly elevated" indicating that "he wasn't giving us honest answers with regard to that test" and led to the prosecutor's conclusion and summation that the defendant was the "type of individual" who was likely to engage in "deviant conduct").

[333] Reichard v. State, 510 N.E.2d 163, 166 (Ind. 1987).

[334] State v. Hansen, 304 Or. 169, 743 P.2d 157 (1987).

[335] State v. Petrich, 101 Wash. 2d 566, 683 P.2d 173 (1984).

[336] State v. McMillan, 69 Ohio App. 3d 36, 590 N.E.2d 23 (1990).

[337] State v. McMillan, 69 Ohio App. 3d 36, 590 N.E.2d 23 (1990).

[338] Turtle v. State, 600 So. 2d 1214, 1221 (Fla. Dist. Ct. App. 1992); State v. Hester, 114 Idaho 688, 760 P.2d 27 (1988); Dyer v. Commonwealth, 816 S.W.2d 647 (Ky. 1991); Brewington v. State, 802 S.W.2d 691, 692 (Tex. Crim. App. 1991) (en banc).

[339] Buzzard v. State, 669 N.E.2d 996 (Ind. Ct. App. 1996) (holding that testimony concerning characterization of pedophiles, including that the "average pedophile will molest 247 children in their lifetime," coupled with prosecutor's argument that defendant met definition of pedophile warranted reversal of defendant's conviction).

the prosecution to offer profile testimony that the defendant meets certain characteristics of molesters or testimony concerning some of the common characteristics of those who molest children.[340] This is also discussed in § 6.48.

Profile testimony may be quite subtle, as in the following social worker's testimony concerning the "grooming process" of child molesters, which led to reversal of a defendant's conviction:

> [The term "grooming process"] has been applied to what we would call a process of victimization. . . . [W]hat is basically meant by that is that in most cases where sexual abuse happens, it isn't something that just happens out of the blue. Generally there is a period of time where the person who intends to abuse the child gradually gets the child to feel more comfortable and may gradually sexualize the relationship or form a bond with the child so that the child will either not understand that what's happening to them is wrong or the child will not tell anyone about it after it happens.[341]

This testimony in effect identified the defendant, who met some of these characteristics, with a group more likely to commit the charged crime. The testimony suffers from the same objections as other profile testimony offered by the prosecution concerning defendants.

When the behavior of those who abuse children is couched in terms of an explanation of physical findings — such as why only a small tear in the hymen was found in one of the victims — the court may allow the testimony.[342] The following is such a response, not objected to at trial, and is an example of testimony that must be carefully scrutinized for its impermissible references to profile testimony:

> A person who wants to have sex with or to accomplish penile-vagina penetration with a child may be one of two kinds of people. He may be a person who is too wound up in his own needs or so angry that he doesn't care how much it hurts the child at all. In that case, you can have a very

---

[340] Haakanson v. State, 760 P.2d 1030 (Alaska Ct. App. 1988); Hall v. State, 15 Ark. App. 309, 692 S.W.2d 769 (1985); Flanagan v. State, 625 So. 2d 827 (Fla. 1993) (holding that while admission of such testimony was harmless, it was irrelevant as background information, inadmissible for failing to meet the *Frye* test to the extent it was offered as substantive evidence of guilt and constituted an impermissible attack on the defendant's character); Phillips v. State, 589 So. 2d 1360 (Fla. Dist. Ct. App. 1991) (holding that such testimony was reversible error); People v. Bradley, 172 Ill. App. 3d 545, 526 N.E.2d 916, *appeal denied*, 123 Ill. 2d 560, 535 N.E.2d 404 (1988); State v. Clements, 244 Kan. 411, 770 P.2d 447 (1989); State v. Hansen, 304 Or. 169, 743 P.2d 157 (1987); State v. Rimmasch, 775 P.2d 388 (Utah 1989); State v. Percy, 146 Vt. 475, 507 A.2d 955 (1986), *appeal after remand*, 156 Vt. 468, 595 A.2d 248, *cert. denied*, 502 U.S. 927 (1991); State v. Maule, 35 Wash. App. 287, 667 P.2d 96 (1983) (reversing conviction where expert testified "that the majority of sexual abuse cases involved 'a male parent figure, in those cases that would involve a father figure, biological parents are in the majority'").

[341] State v. Braham, 67 Wash. App. 930, 933, 841 P.2d 785, 787 (1992).

[342] Underwood v. State, 309 S.C. 560, 425 S.E.2d 20 (1992).

violent rape. You can have significant damage to the child which requires a surgical repair.

That is not — that is — a lot of people feel that that's the common kind of sexual abuse of children. That's not true.

Very prominently, people who want to become sexually involved with children are people who want and need the children to like them, to trust them, and to come back for more.

If you hurt a child very badly, that child is going — another adult is going to find out more likely. The child isn't going to come back, and you will be discovered. Therefore, many people who want to be sexually involved with children are careful of the children with whom they become sexually involved. [343]

Even though the argument can be made that the above testimony is to explain physical findings, it is not like the "battered-child syndrome," which is a syndrome accepted and based on physical findings. [344] Such testimony is more logically viewed as profile testimony, and failing to object to it may render a trial court less likely to strike it or issue appropriate limiting instructions, and render an appellate court less likely to reverse. However, testimony offered in the name of *modus operandi* (§ 11.33) or other theories (§§ 11.30, and 11.32) come very close to providing profile evidence, which is one objection that may be lodged to expert testimony offered under these theories.

§ 11.30   Testimony by defense concerning general characteristics or profile of offender and use of penile plethysmograph.

The defense may seek to offer testimony concerning the characteristics or profile of those who molest or abuse children or commit other sexual crimes to establish that the defendant could not be the guilty party. Typically, the defense wishes to offer expert testimony that the defendant does not exhibit those psychological or personality characteristics normally associated with offenders. While such testimony goes to the ultimate issue of the defendant's guilt, it usually is rejected because it has not been shown to be reliable or have a scientific basis or because it can have a highly prejudicial effect. One federal court of appeals has noted that there is no scientific treatise that recognizes the acceptability of such testimony. [345] Most courts follow the same line of thinking concerning reliability and have rejected profile testimony concerning traits of molesters or rapists offered by the defense. [346] This is true whether the opinion is based on

---

[343] Underwood v. State, 309 S.C. 560, 425 S.E.2d 20, 22.

[344] *See* § 11.37.

[345] United States v. St. Pierre, 812 F.2d 417, 420 (8th Cir. 1987).

[346] Hawkins v. State, 549 So. 2d 552 (Ala. 1989) (upholding trial court's rejection of expert

a psychological evaluation alone or in conjunction with a penile plethysmograph test, a device that measures an individual's sexual arousal in response to sexually explicit photographs of varying age groups.[347] The use of profile testimony has been offered in other situations by the defense and usually rejected. In the well-known case of Army Green Beret Jeffrey McDonald, the defense sought to offer testimony from a psychiatrist that the defendant was possessed of "a personality configuration inconsistent with the outrageous and senseless murders of [his]

---

testimony that defendant did not exhibit pedophile tendencies); State v. Tucker, 165 Ariz. 340, 798 P.2d 1349 (Ariz. App. 1990); State v. Person, 20 Conn. App. 115, 564 A.2d 626 (1989), *appeal granted in part*, 213 Conn. 811, 568 A.2d 796, *aff'd*, 215 Conn. 653, 577 A.2d 1036 (1990), *cert. denied*, 498 U.S. 1048 (1991); Turtle v. State, 600 So. 2d 1214 (Fla. Dist. Ct. App. 1992); Wyatt v. State, 578 So. 2d 811 (Fla. Dist. Ct. App.), *review denied*, 587 So. 2d 1331 (1991); Gilstrad v. State, 215 Ga. App. 180, 450 S.E.2d 436 (1994); State v. Parkinson, 128 Idaho 29, 909 P.2d 647 (1996); People v. Wheeler, 216 Ill. App. 3d 609, 159 Ill. Dec. 266, 575 N.E.2d 1326 (1991), *appeal granted*, 142 Ill. 2d 664, 164 Ill. Dec. 926, 584 N.E.2d 138, *and rev'd on other grounds*, 151 Ill. 2d 298, 602 N.E.2d 826 (1992); State v. Hulbert, 481 N.W.2d 329 (Iowa 1992); Tungate v. Commonwealth, 901 S.W.2d 41 (Ky. 1995); Pendleton v. Commonwealth, 685 S.W.2d 549 (Ky. 1985); Kanaras v. State, 54 Md. App. 568, 460 A.2d 61 (1983); People v. Watkins, 176 Mich. App. 428, 440 N.W.2d 36 (1989); State v. Fitzgerald, 382 N.W.2d 892 (Minn. Ct. App. 1986); State v. Cavaliere, 140 N.H. 108, 663 A.2d 96 (1995); State v. Cavallo, 88 N.J. 508, 443 A.2d 1020 (1982); State v. Michaels, 264 N.J. Super. 579, 625 A.2d 489 (1993), *aff'd*, 136 N.J. 299, 642 A.2d 1372 (1994); People v. Berrios, 150 Misc. 2d 229, 568 N.Y.S.2d 512 (Sup. Ct. 1991); State v. Gallup, 98 Or. App. 211, 779 P.2d 169 (1989); State v. Campbell, 904 S.W.2d 608 (Tenn. Crim. App. 1995); Williams v. State, 649 S.W.2d 693 (Tex. Ct. App. 1983); State v. Miller, 709 P.2d 350, 352 (Utah 1985) (observing that jury would shift its attention from whether defendant had committed crime to whether prosecution had proven that he fit the psychological profile of child abuser); State v. Friedrich, 135 Wis. 2d 1, 398 N.W.2d 763 (1987). *See generally* Gregory G. Sarno, Annotation, *Admissibility of Expert Testimony as to Criminal Defendant's Propensity Towards Sexual Deviation*, 42 A.L.R.4TH 937 (1985).

347 United States v. Powers, 59 F.3d 1460, 1471–73 (4th Cir. 1995), *cert. denied*, 516 U.S. 1077 (1996) (Court properly precluded defense expert's testimony that he did not demonstrate the psychological profile of a fixated pedophile since the defendant did not offer evidence to link the non-proclivity for pedophilia with the non-proclivity for incest abuse, the crime for which he was on trial; court also noted that the results of a "penile plethysmograph test" were inadmissible since they failed to meet the scientific validity prong for test of admission of expert evidence); R.D. v. State, 706 So. 2d 770 (Ala. 1997), *cert. denied*, 525 U.S. 829 (1998) (holding that trial court properly excluded results of the Derogatis Sexual Functioning Inventory, the penile plethysmograph and Minnesota Multiphasic Personality Inventory to demonstrate that defendant did not meet characteristics of a child sex abuser); State v. Kallin, 877 P.2d 138, 141–42 (Utah 1994) (upholding trial court's refusal to permit defense expert to testify that the defendant did not exhibit the symptoms of a pedophile. Trial court had also ruled that the defense expert's reliance on a "penile plethysmograph *[sic]* was not supported by evidence of reliability sufficient to warrant admission." State v. Kallin, 877 P.2d 138, 142 (Utah 1994)); *In re* Marriage of Parker, 91 Wash. App. 219, 957 P.2d 256 (1998) (holding a father cannot be required to undergo a plethysmograph test as part of a parenting evaluation since the device is not generally accepted as a reliable measure of sexual deviancy).

family."[348] The testimony was rejected for want of a basis and because it would be prejudicial and misleading to the jury.[349]

Similarly, attempts to use the Minnesota Multiphasic Inventory (MMPI) as an assessment device to determine whether a defendant committed the crime charged is not permitted. While the MMPI is a generally accepted psychological test for evaluating individuals' personalities and establishing their emotional state at the time of testing, it has not been shown to be scientifically reliable or useful to determine whether a person committed a particular act.[350] Thus, the MMPI-2 can not be used by a psychologist as the basis for an opinion that the defendant is not an exhibitionist.[351]

A major exception to the rule precluding expert testimony as to whether a defendant matches the particular traits or profile of those who molest children occurred in a 1989 California case. In *People v. Stoll*,[352] the Supreme Court of California reversed a conviction in which the trial court rejected testimony offered by the defense that the defendant showed no signs of deviance or abnormality based upon interviews and interpretation of standardized personality tests by defense psychologists because such evidence bore on the defense claim that the acts did not occur. The defense psychologist offered testimony that his interpretation of interviews of the defendant as well as his interpretation of psychological test results of tests administered to the defendant led him to the "professional opinion" that the defendant "has a *normal personality function*, likely has [had] throughout her lifetime, and . . . is falsely charged in this matter." The expert also noted that, since the defendant has "[not] engaged in the past in sexual deviancy of any kind . . . [and] shows no indications of deviancy in any other personality function . . . especially [in light of] a low indication for anti-social or aggressive behavior, I must conclude that it is unlikely . . . she would be involved in the events she's been charged with."[353] This opinion was based in large part on psychological tests designed to measure personality function — the Minnesota Multiphasic Personality Inventory and the Millon Clinical Multiaxial Inventory (MCMI) — which have been in existence

---

[348] United States v. MacDonald, 688 F.2d 224, 227 (4th Cir. 1982), *cert. denied*, 459 U.S. 1103 (1983).

[349] United States v. MacDonald, 688 F.2d 224, 227 (4th Cir. 4982), *cert. denied* 459 U.S. 1103 (1983).

[350] Byrd v. State, 593 N.E.2d 1183 (Ind. 1992). The MMPI has been admitted on other issues in criminal trials, such as the defendant's ability to assist in his own defense; People v. Bowman, 141 Mich. App. 390, 367 N.W.2d 867 (1985), and on the issue of competency, State v. Skjonsby, 417 N.W.2d 818 (N.D. 1987).

[351] United States v. Huberty, 53 M.J. 369 (C.A.A.F. 2000), *cert. denied*, 531 U.S. 1100 (2001) (noting defendant was unable to establish the scientific community's general acceptance of the expert's opinion).

[352] People v. Stoll, 49 Cal. 3d 1136, 783 P.2d 698, 265 Cal. Rptr. 111 (1989).

[353] People v. Stoll, 49 Cal. 3d 1136, 1149, 783 P.2d 698, 705, 265 Cal. Rptr. 111, 118 (1989) (alteration in original).

for a long period of time and are relied on regularly in the field of psychology. The court felt no need to apply the *Frye* standard for purposes of evaluating their reliability.[354] (It should be noted that similar uses of psychological tests such as the MMPI, the Thematic Apperception Test and the Rohrschach Inkblot Test have been challenged and criticized.)[355] The Court also relied heavily in its decision upon California Evidence Code § 1102, finding that it permits the introduction of expert opinion of the defendant's good character to demonstrate the defendant's noncommission of the offense.[356]

A subsequent decision has somewhat tempered *Stoll* by noting that the defense must show the *reliability* of testimony of an opinion that a defendant was not a sexual deviant or did not match the profile of a pedophile.[357]

A Tennessee appellate court has also permitted the use of psychological testimony to demonstrate that a defendant does not exhibit "characteristics attributable to child sexual abusers when administered well-accepted, standardized tests designed to measure psychological profiles."[358] The court permitted such profile testimony on the grounds that it was admissible as evidence of the character trait of sexual proclivity.[359] In Wisconsin, it may be reversible error to preclude a defendant from presenting expert testimony that the defendant does not meet the profile of a person with a sexual disorder and is unlikely to molest a child.[360] The theory underlying such expert testimony is that it assists the jury in determining whether the defendant committed the offense and is admissible as part of the defendant's right to present character evidence.[361] Wisconsin's

---

[354] People v. Stoll, 49 Cal. 3d 1136, 1157, 783 P.2d 698, 711, 265 Cal. Rptr. 111, 124 (1989)

[355] Jay Ziskin and David Faust, *Coping with Psychiatric and Psychological Testimony* (4th ed. 1988); Lee Coleman, *The Reign of Error* (1994).

[356] Cal. Evid. Code § 1102. This section provides "In a criminal action, evidence of the defendant's character or a trait of his character in the form of an opinion or evidence of his reputation is not made inadmissible by section 1101 if such evidence is: (a) Offered by the defendant to prove his conduct in conformity with such character or trait of character." This language, however, does not appear to differ significantly from Federal Rules of Evidence 405: "Methods of Proving Character (a) Reputation or opinion. In all cases in which evidence of character or a trait of character of a person is admissible, proof may be made by testimony as to reputation or by testimony in the form of an opinion. On cross-examination, inquiry is allowable into relevant specific instances of conduct."

[357] People v. Ruiz, 222 Cal. App. 3d 1241, 272 Cal. Rptr. 368 (1990) (remanding to the trial court to permit the defendant to establish that testimony that a defendant did not meet the profile of a pedophile was reliable).

[358] State v. Jones, 1994 Tenn. Crim. App. LEXIS 587 at *48 (Sept. 15, 1994) (The defendant's expert relied on the MMPI; the Wexler Adult Intelligence Scale, a widely-used IQ test; the California Psychological Inventory; the Emotions Profile Index; and the Psychological Screening Inventory.).

[359] State v. Jones, 1994 Tenn. Crim. App. LEXIS 587 at *51. *See also* Nolte v. State, 854 S.W.2d 304 (Tex. Ct. App. 1993).

[360] *See also* State v. Kaminski, 228 Wis. 2d 509, 597 N.W.2d 773 (1999); State v. Richard A.P., 223 Wis. 2d 777, 589 N.W.2d 674 (1998), *review denied*, 225 Wis. 2d 489, 554 N.W.2d 383 (1999).

[361] State v. Kaminski, 228 Wis. 2d 509, 597 N.W.2d 773 (1999); State v. Richard A.P., 223 Wis. 2d 777, 589 N.W.2d 674 (1998), *review denied*, 225 Wis. 2d 489, 554 N.W.2d 383 (1999).

Supreme Court holds such evidence admissible pursuant to both principles of character evidence and expert testimony.[362] However, it holds that such evidence must be carefully evaluated for its relevance, probative value, and potential for unfair prejudice or confusion, and the trial court should make a determination on the admissibility of such evidence.[363] If the defendant's expert testifies implicitly or explicitly to facts of the crime, the court may compel the defendant to undergo a psychological examination by the prosecution.[364] This requires the defense to disclose its expert's opinions and the basis of those opinions, such as the results of standardized tests.

If an expert is used to testify to defendant's character, such testimony may open the door to testimony otherwise precluded. For example, a defense psychologist who testifies on direct examination that the defendant had been non-violent "throughout his life" opens the door to the defendant's prior bad acts that the trial court had previously ruled inadmissible.[365]

§ 11.31   Expert testimony concerning defendant's mental state.

While under the Federal Rules of Evidence, an expert may not opine whether the defendant "did or did not have the mental state or condition constituting an element of the crime," it may explain that the defendant has a "typical belief system" on delusion, which prevented defendant from forming the requisite intent.[366]

Psychological tests may be used in conjunction with clinical interviews to provide information and opinions that may be relevant to a defendant's mental state or level of functioning. A psychological evaluation, as opposed to a profile,

---

[362] State v. Davis, 254 Wis. 2d 1, 645 N.W.2d 913 (2002).

[363] State v. Davis, 254 Wis. 2d 1, 645 N.W. 2d 913 (2002). *See also* State v. Walters, 269 Wis. 2d 142, 675 N.W.2d 778 (2004) (emphasizing that admission of such testimony is purely discretionary, must be on pertinent character traits and must be weighed against its potential prejudice, confusion, and potential for delay: "the record supports the circuit court's conclusion that the minimal probative value of Walters's proffered expert testimony was substantially outweighed by the danger that the issues would be confused and the jury would be misled. The circuit court determined first that although relevant, the evidence was minimally probative." Court also noted that defendant's expert testified that tests assess personality, which can be altered by alcohol. This minimized the probative value of the testimony given the defendant's long history of alcohol use).

[364] State v. Davis, 254 Wis. 2d 1, 645 N.W. 2d 913 (2002). (However, if the expert testifies using only standardized tests to form an opinion, then the state may not be able to examine the defendant).

[365] People v. Fardan, 82 N.Y.2d 638, 628 N.E.2d 41, 607 N.Y.S.2d 220 (1993).

[366] Fed. R. Evid. 704(b):

No expert witness testifying with respect to the mental state or condition of a defendant in a criminal case may state an opinion or inference as to whether the defendant did or did not have the mental state or condition constituting an element of the crime charged or of a defense thereto. Such ultimate issues are matters for the trier of fact alone.

is more likely to be admissible, since it relies on well established and accepted psychological testing. Psychological evaluations and opinions often rely upon the diagnoses, definitions, and criteria of DSM IV *(Diagnostic and Statistical Manual of Mental Disorders)*, published by the American Psychiatric Association. However, use of DSM IV diagnosis and criteria "may not be wholly relevant to legal judgments," warns a cautionary statement at the beginning of the manual.[367]

The Minnesota Multiphasic Personality Inventory (MMPI) is a recognized psychological test dealing with scales that may reflect the pathology of an abuser, such as antisocial behavior, poor judgment, and poor impulse control. The MMPI and related tests are often used as a basis for forensic psychological opinions.

Psychological testimony may be relevant and admissible when a defendant's intent is at issue. It is important to remember that expert testimony "does not depend on whether the witness has personal knowledge of a defendant or a defendant's particular characteristics."[368] A thorough background in the MMPI and psychological testimony is a predicate to effective direct and cross-examination of such expert testimony.[369]

Many sexual assault crimes have intent as an element, such as attempted rape or sexual abuse. Sexual abuse may require an intent of sexual gratification to

---

[367] United States v. Finley, 301 F.3d 1000 (9th Cir. 2002) (reversing defendant's conviction for failure to admit such testimony, which court found met *Daubert* standard even though expert assumed defendant's truthfulness in his interviews, and such opinion did not "necessarily compel" a conclusion about defendant's *mens rea*; court noted expert did not rely "solely" on defendant's statements, but also utilized psychological tests). *See also* United States v. Shay, 57 F.3d 126, 133 (1st Cir. 1995) (holding defendant should have been permitted to present expert testimony that he suffered a mental disorder leading him to grandiose, self-incriminating lies). American Psychiatric Association, Diagnostic and Statistical Manual of Mental Disorders (4th ed., 2000) at xxvii:

> The purpose of DSM IV is to provide clear descriptions of diagnostic categories in order to enable clinicians and investigators to diagnose, communicate about, study, and treat the various mental disorders. It is to be understood that inclusion here, for clinical and research purposes, of a diagnostic category such as Pathological Gambling or Pedophilia does not imply that the condition meets legal or other nonmedical criteria for what constitutes mental disease, mental disorder, or mental disability. The clinical and scientific considerations involved in categorization of these conditions as mental disorders may not be wholly relevant to legal judgments, for example, that take into account such issues as individual responsibility, disability determination, and competency.

[368] People v. Aphaylath, 68 N.Y.2d 945, 502 N.E.2d 998, 510 N.Y.S.2d 83 (1986) (reversing defendant's conviction for murder because of trial court's preclusion of expert testimony concerning stress and disorientation encountered by Laotian refugees in attempting to assimilate into the American culture, where the sole basis for the court's ruling was that expert was not going to be able to testify to anything specifically relating to the defendant).

[369] *See* Kenneth S. Pope, James N. Butcher & Joyce Seelen, *The MMPI, MMPI-2, and MMPI-A in Court: Assessment, Testimony, and Cross-Examination for Expert Witnesses and Attorneys* (1993).

satisfy the element of sexual gratification. In other areas of the law, a psychologist's opinion that a defendant suffered from an "objectively ascertainable organic brain injury" has been deemed relevant on the issue of the defendant's state of mind and, therefore, admissible.[370] However, one must be careful not to run afoul of the proscriptions of Rule 704(b),[371] which prohibits an expert from giving "an opinion or inference as to whether the defendant did or did not have the mental state or condition constituting an element of the crime charged or of a defense thereto." The actual conclusion must be left to the jury. However, the expert can provide information concerning the defendant's condition or diagnosis to assist it in that conclusion. The expert testimony can also help the jury understand lay witness testimony concerning the defendant's emotional state of mind or behavior;[372] but counsel must be particularly careful to document the reliability of the findings, opinions, or conclusions of the expert or of the particular diagnosis. If an attorney is not prepared to set forth the scientific and psychological basis for the testimony, it will easily be disallowed. Furthermore, scientific knowledge in the area of psychology is changing, and court opinions on psychological tests from ten years ago may well be outdated for evaluating the admissibility of new theories. However, they may still be required to pass a reliability test. (*See* § 11.10.)

§ 11.32　Admissibility of other forms of profile testimony: criminal profiling, sexual homicide, psychological autopsies, the effects of abuse.

There are other situations where courts have, on occasion, admitted evidence of profiling or some form of profiling. In a murder prosecution in which the defense was that the defendant did not intend to kill anyone, testimony was admissible by a psychologist, who concluded that the circumstances of the crime, which involved the killing of two teenagers, indicated a rare pathological condition known as *piquerism*, which is the realization of sexual satisfaction from penetrating a victim by "sniper activity" or by stab or bite wounds.[373] Such profiling of the defendant was not improper because it was relevant to the defense he raised, and the subject of the expert's testimony "concerned a behavioral phenomenon not within the common knowledge of the average juror and requiring professional knowledge."[374]

---

[370] United States v. McBride, 786 F.2d 45 (2d Cir. 1986) (holding that testimony as to defendant's brain injury should have been admissible on the question of her intent and whether she was able to understand that she was part of a bank fraud scheme).

[371] Fed. R. Evid. 704(b).

[372] United States v. McBride, 786 F.2d 45, 50 (2d Cir. 1986).

[373] People v. Drake, 129 A.D.2d 963, 514 N.Y.S.2d 280, *appeal denied*, 70 N.Y.2d 799, 516 N.E.2d 1229, 522 N.Y.S.2d 116 (1987), *appeal denied*, 71 N.Y.2d 895, 523 N.E.2d 311, 527 N.Y.S.2d 1004 (1988).

[374] People v. Drake, 129 A.D.2d 963, 965, 514 N.Y.S.2d 280, 281.

One of the more popular forms of profile testimony is that performed by the FBI's Behavioral Sciences Unit, which was popularized in the motion picture *Silence of the Lambs*. Other law enforcement agencies also utilize behavioral profiling, which is an assessment of the crime through reviews of police reports, pathological findings, medical reports, and any other relevant information that would produce a profile of the offender. It is often used by law enforcement authorities in focusing on suspects or narrowing a list of potential suspects. An attempt is made to determine whether there is an order to the events of the crime that is consistent with recognized patterns of criminal behavior and the individuals who would engage in such particular behavior. When such testimony is limited to "signature aspects" of a crime that links it to similar crimes, such testimony may be permissible.[375] It may also provide testimony about the crime scene without identifying the person or characteristics of the person committing the crime.[376] It may also provide the basis for testimony that a murder was a sexually motivated homicide.[377]

A police officer may in some situations be qualified to give an opinion "as to what happened" based on a review of the crime scene, physical evidence, and experience in crime scene reconstruction.[378] Any attempt to use profile evidence in a criminal trial that attempts to link the general characteristics of serial murders or rapists to a particular defendant is of little probative value and extremely prejudicial, since it provides evidence of guilt not by someone with direct knowledge of a crime but by a behavioral analysis of the defendant's

---

[375] United States v. Rogers, 769 F.2d 1418 (9th Cir. 1985) (allowing an FBI expert to testify to signature aspect of bank robberies); Pennell v. State, 602 A.2d 48 (Del. 1991); State v. Russell, 125 Wash. 2d 24, 69–72, 882 P.2d 747, 777–778 (1994), *cert. denied*, 514 U.S. 1129 (1995) (upholding the admission of testimony by FBI experts in "crime scene analysis" regarding the rarity of posing of bodies after death; once the defense had raised the issue as to whether multiple crimes were related to each other, the prosecution was permitted to ask the experts in "crime scene analysis" whether the crimes were related to another and had been committed by one person).

[376] United States v. Meeks, 35 M.J. 64 (C.M.A. 1992) (permitting FBI investigator to analyze physical aspects of a crime scene, but not give opinion that any particular individual committed crime nor the physical characteristics of the person who committed crime); Simmons v. State, No. CR-97-0768, 2000 Ala. Crim. App. LEXIS 98, at *28–29 (Apr. 28, 2000), *cert. denied, Ex parte Simmons*, 797 So. 2d 1186, *cert. denied*, 534 U.S. 932 (2001) (where FBI agent testified that homicide was sexually motivated, court upheld this testimony and stated it was not profile evidence and that "crime-scene analysis and victimology are reliable fields of specialized knowledge"; noting that such testimony was relevant to establish killer's intent to derive sexual gratification from sexual abuse, which is element of predicate felony sexual abuse, court drew distinction between profile testimony that identifies person with certain characteristics as more likely to have committed crime and testimony about physical evidence of a crime that reveals certain characteristics about the offense).

[377] State v. Stevens, 78 S.W.3d 817, 835 (Tenn. 2002), *cert. denied*, 537 U.S. 1115 (2003) (upholding trial court's decision to permit expert testimony that murder was a sexual homicide).

[378] Almond v. State, 274 Ga. 348, 553 S.E.2d 803 (2001) (permitting police officer to express opinion whether scene and evidence was "consistent with a hypothetical sequence of events surrounding the shooting").

characteristics.[379] Crime scene analysis testimony is a form of profile testimony offered under the name of "linkage-analysis" testimony. Such testimony lacks sufficient reliability and is therefore inadmissible.[380] One problem with "linkage-analysis" is that the field involves only a small group of people and lacks peers to review or duplicate their work.[381] Several courts have rejected, or questioned, "profiler" testimony because of the lack of databases, statistics, and methodology to support the technique.[382] If there are sufficient unique, distinct, or unusual aspects to a crime, other acts may be admissible as signature crime evidence.

One court has permitted expert testimony as to the traits and characteristics of perpetrators of sexual homicides and to further testify that the defendant's writings and drawings were consistent with a typical perpetrator.[383] The court held that the sexual homicide evidence elicited from the expert is generally accepted within the forensic community.[384] Such testimony explains "the seemingly inexplicable" behavior to the jury.[385] The expert was able to interpret the defendant's writings and drawings, and was able to explain to presumably law-abiding jurors the role of rehearsal fantasy and trigger mechanisms, which are relatively unique to perpetrators of sexual homicide.[386]

Courts are likely to reject the attempts to offer through expert testimony multiple criminal acts, which have as many differences as similarities. While "crime scene analysis" and "linkage-analysis" may assist in the investigation of

---

[379] Pennell v. State, 602 A.2d 48, 55 (Del. 1991).

[380] State v. Fortin, 178 N.J. 540, 586–590, 843 A.2d 974, 1000–02 (2004); cf. Simmons v. State, No. CR-97-0768, 2000 Ala. Crim. App. LEXIS 98 (Apr. 28, 2000), cert. denied, Ex parte Simmons, 797 So. 2d 1186 (2001).

[381] State v. Fortin, 178 N.J. 540, 543, 843 A.2d 974, 1000–02 (2004).

[382] People v. Mertz, 218 Ill. 2d 1, 842 N.E.2d 618, 299 Ill. Dec. 581 (2005) (declining to determine if profiler's testimony was properly presented before jury since any error in its admission was harmless); State v. Fortin, 178 N.J. 540, 587–90, 843 A.2d 974, 1000–02 (2004) (reversing defendant's conviction because profiler's opinion was not supported by methodology and databases); State v. Stevens, 78 S.W.3d 817, 836 (Tenn. 2002), cert. denied, 537 U.S. 1115 (2003) (rejecting FBI profiler testimony because of lack of showing of reliability and methodology).

[383] Masters v. People, 58 P.3d 979 (Colo. 2002):

> Dr. Meloy opined that sexual homicides are often preceded by a "triggering mechanism" or "precipitating event" that causes the perpetrator to transform his fantasies into action. Although the trial court prohibited Dr. Meloy from testifying that any particular event in Defendant's life was a triggering mechanism, he was allowed to testify hypothetically as to the types of occurrences that could serve as a trigger mechanism. One such hypothetical example was a conflict or confrontation with adult women in positions of authority in an employment or educational environment. The jury was left to draw the inference that Defendant's confrontation with his teacher was the precipitating event for Ms. Hettrick's murder itself.

Masters v. People, 58 P.3d 979, 1004 (Colo. 2002).

[384] Masters v. People, 58 P.3d 979, 989 (Colo. 2002).

[385] Masters v. People, 58 P.3d 979, 1002 (Colo. 2002).

[386] Masters v. People, 58 P.3d 979, 996-97 (Colo. 2002).

cases, these techniques do not yet have sufficient reliability to permit expert testimony that an individual who committed one crime committed another, without establishing that the other crimes meet the traditional yardstick for signature evidence.[387]

In an Ohio prosecution for rape and involuntary manslaughter, the court reversed a conviction based on the admission of a criminal profile, because it was not shown that such evidence was reliable or would be helpful to the jury, and that the testimony established, in effect, a prejudicial stereotype.[388] Such profile testimony is particularly prejudicial if it presents testimony concerning the character traits of the accused, such as anger, revenge, hostility, and difficulty in relationships with women in relation to the individual who actually committed the crime.[389]

On the other hand, there may be some unique circumstances in which offshoots of psychological profiles may be relevant and admissible. For example, in a Florida case where a mother was charged with child abuse in causing her 17-year-old daughter to earn money as a strip dancer, which led to such stress that the daughter committed suicide, the court found relevant testimony in the form of a 'psychological autopsy', which helped prove that the defendant was guilty of such abuse.[390] Here, the focus of the expert testimony was the effect of the abuse upon the victim. Such testimony may not necessarily be relevant, however, even if accepted or reliable.[391] Some courts may find a "suicide profile" reliable enough to use as a basis for declaring a person committed suicide.[392]

There are other situations where expert testimony of the crime's affect on a victim is admissible.

For example, if there are charges pertaining to the endangerment of the child's welfare, expert psychological testimony may be presented to explain how children who have been repeatedly sexually abused are likely to suffer psychologically, which is an element of the crime charged.[393]

---

[387] Masters v. People, 58 P.3d 979, 989 (Colo. 2002).

[388] State v. Roquemore, 85 Ohio App. 3d 448, 620 N.E.2d 110 (1993).

[389] State v. Roquemore, 85 Ohio App. 3d 448, 620 N.E.2d 110 (1993).

[390] Jackson v. State, 553 So. 2d 719 (Fla. Dist. Ct. App. 1989).

[391] *Compare* Sysyn v. State, 756 So. 2d 1058 (Fla. Dist. Ct. App. 2000), *review denied*, 773 So. 2d 57 (Fla. 2000) (noting "psychological autopsy" testimony is accepted in the field of psychiatry to evaluate a suicide; it is not necessarily relevant when a defendant raises self-defense in a homicide trial).

[392] State v. Guthrie, 2001 SD 61, 627 N.W.2d 401 (2001) (holding in a murder trial that under *Daubert* standard, given the state of psychological knowledge, a suicide profile alone could not be used by an expert to declare with scientific certainty that a person did or did not commit suicide, but error was harmless in this case).

[393] People v. Keindl, 68 N.Y.2d 410, 502 N.E.2d 577, 509 N.Y.S.2d 790 (1986).

§ 11.33 Profiling compared to *modus operandi* and expert testimony explaining the behavior of child molesters and pedophiles.

There are situations in which courts will permit testimony concerning *modus operandi* testimony to explain actions of defendants, particularly when unique characteristics, conduct, or language require an expert's explanation.[394] A somewhat analogous situation is a lay witness giving an opinion under Federal Rule of Evidence 701 as to his understanding of abbreviated and ambiguous references on a tape recorded conversation between himself and another person.[395]

A similar case in permitting testimony of child molesters and pedophiles is in *United States v. Cross*,[396] in which the Eleventh Circuit Court of Appeals permitted testimony from an FBI agent, who was an expert in the area of child sexual exploitation. In *Cross*, a child pornography prosecution, the FBI agent testified that certain photos would be of interest to pedophiles — persons with a sexual preference for children. The defense contended that the photos were "nude studies" rather than child pornography, and the defendant had a legitimate purpose in having them in that they were related to the casting of a legitimate film in which he was involved. The FBI agent was permitted to testify that pedophiles "derive sexual satisfaction from and collect even such ostensibly non-sexual nude photographs of children. . . . [T]hese kinds of pictures, rather than more graphic ones, are frequently published in magazines distributed to pedophiles in an attempt to circumvent laws against obscenity and child pornography."[397] The court held that such testimony was relevant to a critical issue in the case, that is, whether the defendant obtained the photos with the intention of using them to produce and distribute child pornography. Another part of the *modus operandi* testimony was that pedophiles often employed the term "nude studies" as a code word to refer to non-obscene photos of children.[398] The court noted that use of such expert testimony is akin to allowing an expert to testify on the meaning of "gambling jargon" in recorded telephone conversations.[399]

---

[394] United States v. Anderson, 851 F.2d 384, 392–93 (D.C. 1988) (relating to expert testimony on the behaviors or *modus operandi* of pimps), *cert. denied*, 488 U.S. 1012 (1989); United States v. Burchfield, 719 F.2d 356–358, (11th Cir. 1983) (*per curiam*) (relating to counterfeiting activities).

[395] United States v. De Peri, 778 F.2d 963, 977 (3d Cir. 1985), *cert. denied sub. nom.*, Pecic v. United States, 475 U.S. 1110 (1986) and *cert. denied sub. nom.*, Katz v. United States, 476 U.S. 1159 (1986). Rule 701 permits opinion testimony by lay witnesses as follows: "If the witness is not testifying as an expert, the witness'[s] testimony in the form of opinions or inferences is limited to those opinions or inferences which are (a) rationally based on the perception of the witness and (b) helpful to a clear understanding of the witness'[s] testimony or the determination of a fact in issue."

[396] United States v. Cross, 928 F.2d 1030 (11th Cir. 1991), *cert. denied*, 502 U.S. 985 (1991).

[397] United States v. Cross, 928 F.2d 1030, 1050 (11th Cir. 1991), *cert denied*, 502 U.S. 985 (1991).

[398] United States v. Cross, 928 F.2d 1030, 1050 (11th Cir. 1991), *cert denied*, 502 U.S. 985 (1991).

[399] United States v. Cross, 928 F.2d 1030, 1050 (11th Cir. 1991), *cert denied*, 502 U.S. 985 (1991) (*citing* United States v. Alfonso, 552 F.2d 605 (5th Cir.), *cert. denied*, 434 U.S. 857 (1977)

Similarly, a federal postal inspector familiar with child pornography and its subculture can testify that the terms "miniature erotica," "Lolita," and "Wonderboy" are terms used by the child pornography subculture.[400]

Under this theory, the expert may explain the significance and meaning of the defendant's screen name, "Chicken Hawk," as follows:

Q. What sort of a name is "Chicken Hawk?"

A. It's actually a combination of two words or two slang phrases. In the parlance of those people who are involved in the sexual exploitation of children, chicken generally refers to a young boy typically probably under the age of 12. A hawk would be someone who goes after a chicken, so a chicken hawk would be someone who is interested in young boys)[401]

It should be noted that the testimony implies the defendant is a person who had sexual relations with children and even though there were no such charges, the court noted the potential prejudice in such testimony and such testimony must be carefully weighed against its potential prejudice.[402]

One court permitted an expert to explain that the following e-mail was an attempt to "entice" or "encourage" a child to engage in sex:

I was hoping that you would send me some more good pix before I left . . . . I hope that everything is working out with your 9 yo. Have you f?#%&? her yet? If so, do you have pix? . . . . Man you are not going to believe it when I adopt that little girl and send you pix of her and me as I promised. I am going to do everything to her that you can imagine. And you will be the first to see, I promise you that much. I hope that you can find it in your heart to send me more pix as you have in the past week or so. If you send me more pix, I will be eternally grateful, and reward you greatly. Please send me more!![403]

The expert may certify that newsgroup file names "Preteen" and "Lolita" reflect child pornography themes and were found on files associated with defendant's newsgroup browser programs.[404]

The court in *Cross* also permitted testimony on the nature of the defendant's relationship with an undercover agent and the reasons why and how they would cooperate in a "complex, risky, criminal conspiracy although they had never met

---

[400] United States v. Byrd, 31 F.3d 1329 (5th Cir. 1994), *cert. denied*, 514 U.S. 1052 (1995).

[401] United States v. Campos, 221 F.3d 1143 (10th Cir. 2000).

[402] United States v. Campos, 221 F.3d 1143 (10th Cir. 2000) (The court noted that sexual exploitations did not necessarily encompass sexual relations and that the defendant did not challenge this testimony as improper character evidence under Rule 404. United States v. Campos, 221 F.3d 1143 (10th Cir. 2000)).

[403] United States v. Hays, 62 M.J. 158, 165–66 (C.A.A.F. 2005).

[404] United States v. Murray, 52 M.J. 423 (C.A.A.F. 2000).

and knew little about one another."[405] It should be noted that this testimony, while called *modus operandi* testimony, does bear similarities to criminal profile testimony; however, it is much more limited in nature than profile testimony offered to identify someone as a victim of child sexual abuse. This testimony — which relates to an area of expertise that has been found reliable — rather than stating the conclusion that the defendant was guilty of a crime, explains conduct that a lay jury might not otherwise understand.

Following the reasoning of *Cross*, other courts have permitted expert testimony concerning the general characteristics and techniques of child molesters to explain otherwise "innocent" or ambiguous behavior.[406] This is admissible as the "*modus operandi*" of child molesters, such as spending large amounts of time in relationships with children, probing a child's needs and interests and satisfying them, engaging in certain compulsive behaviors and how molesters find and seduce their victims.[407] The qualified expert may testify as to the typology, identification, characteristics, and strategies of sexual offenders, in particular "preferential sexual offenders", as well as the characteristics and behavior of child victims of sexual abuse.[408] Such testimony is not considered profile testimony or improper character testimony, especially when it rebuts the defense of "innocent intent and fabrication."[409] However, expert testimony in a child pornography case that certain photographs "promote sexual impulses and sexual fantasies" and that the "particular" children in the photographs would be affected later in life in their sexual identity and relationships has been deemed unreliable and unsupported speculation.[410]

---

[405] United States v. Cross, 928 F.2d 1030, 1050 n. 65 (11th Cir. 1991), *cert. denied*, 502 U.S. 985 (1991).

[406] United States v. Romero, 189 F.3d 576 (7th Cir. 1999), *cert. denied*, 529 U.S. 1011 (2000) (noting the expert's opinion "was critical in dispelling from the jurors' minds the widely held stereotype of a child molester as 'a dirty old man in a wrinkled raincoat' who snatches children off the street as they wait for the school bus." United States v. Romero, 189 F.3d 576, 584 (7th Cir. 1999), *cert. denied*, 529 U.S. 1011 (2000)). *See also* United States v. Hayward, 359 F.3d 631, 636–37 (3d Cir. 2004) (holding expert's testimony did not remove determination of element of defendant's intent on charge of transporting minor with intent to engage in criminal sexual activity; testimony explained "motives and practices of an acquaintance molester" and *modus operandi* of child molesters to find and seduce their victims).

[407] United States v. Romero, 189 F.3d 576, 585 (7th Cir. 1999), *cert denied*, 529 U.S. 1011 (2000). *See also* United States v. Huberty, 53 M.J. 369, 373 (C.A.A.F. 2000), *cert. denied*, 531 U.S. 1100 (2001) (upholding government expert's testimony as to defendant's manipulative behavior consistent with defendant having groomed victim to have sex with him); People v. Ackerman, 257 Mich. App. 434, 669 N.W.2d 818 (2003).

[408] United States v. Long, 328 F.3d 655 (D.C. Cir. 2003), *cert. denied*, 540 U.S. 1075 (2003) (holding expert's testimony was "for a permissible purpose, namely to identify the behavior and actions of child molesters and explain their *modus operandi*, the prosecution adduced considerable other evidence of Long's pedophilia, and the jury was instructed that the weight to be given to [expert's] testimony was for the jurors to determine"; United States v. Long, 328 F.3d 655, 668 (D.C. Cir. 2003), *cert. denied*, 540 U.S. 1075 (2003)).

[409] United States v. Long, 328 F.3d 655, 667 (D.C. Cir. 2003), *cert denied*, 540 U.S. 1075 (2003).

[410] Roise v. State, 7 S.W.3d 225 (Tex. Ct. App. 1999), *cert. denied*, 531 U.S. 895 (2000).

There is concern that the type of testimony as outlined in this section provides a profile of an offender that suggests the defendant is a molester. The difference between testimony that explains the motives and behaviors of an offender and victim and profile testimony can be subtle.[411]

§ 11.34 Child-battering profiles or batterer's profile.

A syndrome that must be distinguished from others in the areas of child abuse is the "child maltreatment syndrome" or "battering-parent syndrome." These syndromes tend to focus on the conduct and behaviors of those who abuse children. The child maltreatment syndrome has not been properly recognized and accepted, and it is not admissible.[412] This profile tends to focus on the family characteristics, patterns, and risk profile of those who are likely to abuse their children. If the testimony does not implicate the defendant, it may be acceptable. For example, if the expert describes a "dysfunctional family" and that the victim is abused by someone, not necessarily the defendant, this may be permissible.[413] On the other hand, when the testimony targets the defendant, courts have ruled that expert testimony on child-battering profiles are prejudicial and do not meet the relevancy test because the fact that a defendant fits a profile does not prove that he committed the crime.[414]

Testimony by a physician that "overwhelmingly, the most likely person to kill a child is going to be his or her own biological parent" places a "statistical probability that [the defendant] committed the offense" and thus is impermissible profile evidence.[415] On the other hand, the physician may rely on subjective factors, such as the "behavior of parents" and "inconsistent history" in conjunction with the physical examination in giving an opinion that the cause of death is "homicide or inflicted child abuse," given the expert's testimony that the methodology is relied on by experts in the field of forensic pediatrics.[416]

Sometimes the battering-parent profile, which sounds like it might be related to the battered-child syndrome, is offered by a party to introduce otherwise

---

[411] United States v. Forrest, 429 F.3d 73 (4th Cir. 2005) (finding such testimony "troubling" but holding any error was harmless and not resolving whether such testimony was unduly prejudicial or met standard of scientific reliability).

[412] McCartney v. State, 262 Ga. 156, 414 S.E.2d 227 (1992). *See also* State v. Steward, 34 Wash. App. 221, 660 P.2d 278 (1983) (rejecting expert testimony about the alleged propensity of babysitting boyfriends to abuse their girlfriends' children).

[413] United States v. Pagel, 45 M.J. 64 (C.A.A.F. 1996) (expert's description of a "dysfunctional family" explained victim's counter-intuitive behaviors and that she was abused by someone, not necessarily the defendant).

[414] United States v. Diaz, 59 M.J. 79 (C.A.A.F. 2003) (reversing defendant's conviction due to physician's testimony that child was a victim of homicide perpetrated by the defendant); Commonwealth v. Day, 409 Mass. 719, 569 N.E.2d 397 (1991); State v. Conlogue, 474 A.2d 167 (Me. 1984).

[415] United States v. Traum, 60 M.J. 226 (C.A.A.F. 2004) (finding error was harmless).

[416] United States v. Traum, 60 M.J. 226 (C.A.A.F. 2004).

inadmissible profile testimony. This profile, unlike the battered-child syndrome, is not a recognized medical diagnosis, being based on neither physical findings nor any generally and accepted medical or scientific principle. A conviction has been reversed because of highly prejudicial testimony that child abuse injuries are often inflicted by either live-in or babysitting boyfriends, because such testimony has no scientific basis.[417] Prosecution attempts to introduce testimony of a battering-parent profile have been rejected by appellate courts.[418] An attempt by a defendant to offer a battering-parent profile to show the defendant does not meet the profile and therefore is not guilty of the abuse charge is likely to be similarly treated.[419] Also impermissible is an expert's description of a defendant as meeting a "batterer's profile" of an abusive male.[420] Testimony concerning "separation violence" and that batterers have a propensity to kill those whom they have abused is also inadmissible profile testimony.[421]

§ 11.35 Battered-woman syndrome.

The "battered-woman syndrome," which is a subgroup of the broader "post-traumatic stress disorder," is an attempt to explain the dynamics of women who are physically abused by the men they live with and why they engage in certain behaviors, such as never leaving or taking steps to stop the abuse. The continuation of abuse is explained in part by the theory of "learned helplessness" — the inability to control the violence and a resulting dependence upon the abuser — and a false hope that someday the situation will improve. According to Dr. Lenore Walker, a leading proponent of the battered-woman syndrome theory, the woman must go through the battering cycle twice with a man to be labeled a battered woman.[422] The victim will accept her beatings because she believes that she is responsible for them and feels that her best chance for survival is to maintain the relationship. Since this is behavior that many jurors would not understand, most courts have permitted expert testimony on the syndrome, particularly when the woman is a defendant and claims self-defense or duress.[423]

---

[417] State v. Steward, 34 Wash. App. 221, 660 P.2d 278 (1983).

[418] Sanders v. State, 251 Ga. 70, 303 S.E.2d 13 (1983) (admission deemed harmless error); Sloan v. State, 70 Md. App. 630, 522 A.2d 1364, *appeal denied,* 310 Md. 276, 528 A.2d 1287 (1987). *See generally* Gregory E. Sarno, Annotation, *Admissibility at Criminal Prosecution of Expert Testimony on Battering Parent Syndrome,* 43 A.L.R.4th 1203 (1986).

[419] Hoosier v. State, 612 So. 2d 1352 (Ala. Crim. App. 1992); People v. Neer, 129 A.D.2d 829, 513 N.Y.S.2d 566, *appeal denied,* 70 N.Y.2d 652, 516 N.E.2d 1233, 522 N.Y.S.2d 120 (1987).

[420] Commonwealth v. Roche, 44 Mass. App. Ct. 372, 380, 691 N.E.2d 946, 952 (1998).

[421] Ryan v. State, 988 P.2d 46 (Wyo. 1999) (noting lack of scientific evidence basis for such testimony).

[422] Lenore Walker, *The Battered Woman Syndrome* (1984).

[423] *Ex parte Hill,* 507 So. 2d 554, 555 (Ala. Crim. App. 1986), *cert. denied,* 507 So. 2d 558 (Ala. 1987); Ibn-Tamas v. United States, 407 A.2d 626 (D.C. 1979), *aff'd,* 455 A.2d 893 (D.C. 1983); People v. Humphrey, 13 Cal. 4th 1073, 921 P.2d 1, 56 Cal. Rptr. 2d 142 (1996) (holding battered-woman syndrome admissible in deciding the reasonableness as well as the existence of

Battered person syndrome evidence may also be admissible to justify the actions of a male charged with hitting a family member. The defense may not be available when the defendant is charged with a reckless, as opposed to an intentional, crime.[424]

The expert may be precluded, however, from testifying on the accused's state of mind at the time of the crime's commission.[425] A Massachusetts court has held that the syndrome can be considered by a jury on the issue of whether a defendant shared her husband's intent to jointly abuse a child, but not on the issue of whether the defendant had the specific intent to commit the abuse herself, without the assistance of her husband.[426]

Federal appeals courts have also addressed whether or not evidence of battered-woman's syndrome is admissible in a case where duress is raised as a defense. The 5th Circuit has developed a *per se* rule excluding expert testimony that may be characterized as addressing the battered-woman's syndrome.[427] Another federal court has held that the syndrome may be admitted to support a defense of duress in much the same way that it is admissible in a self-defense claim,

---

defendant's belief that killing was necessary); People v. Romero, 8 Cal. 4th 728, 883 P.2d 388, 35 Cal. Rptr. 2d 270 (1994); Smith v. State, 247 Ga. 612, 277 S.E.2d 678 (1981); People v. Minnis, 118 Ill. App. 3d 345, 356–57, 455 N.E.2d 209, 217–218 (1983); State v. Anaya, 438 A.2d 892 (Me. 1981); State v. Kelly, 97 N.J. 178, 196, 478 A.2d 364, 372 (1984); People v. Torres, 128 Misc. 2d 129, 488 N.Y.S.2d 358 (Sup. Ct. 1985); State v. Koss, 49 Ohio St. 3d 213, 551 N.E.2d 970 (1990) (requiring defendant to establish that she is a battered wife); Bechtel v. State, 840 P.2d 1 (Okla. Crim. App. 1992); State v. Dillon, 528 Pa. 417, 598 A.2d 963 (1991); State v. Allery, 101 Wash. 2d 591, 682 P.2d 312 (1984). *See generally* Cynthia Lynn Barnes. Annotation, *Admissibility of Expert Testimony Concerning Domestic Violence Syndromes to Assist Jury in Evaluating Victim's Testimony or Behavior*, 57 A.L.R.5TH 315 (1998) and James O. Pearson, Jr., Annotation, *Admissibility of Expert or Opinion Testimony on Battered Wife or Battered Women Syndrome*, 18 A.L.R.4th 1153 (1992).

[424] People v. Colberg, 182 Misc. 2d 798, 701 N.Y.S.2d 608 (Co. Ct. 1999) (holding battered person syndrome evidence available to father charged with hitting his adult son since such testimony relevant to defense of justification); Duran v. State, 990 P.2d 1005 (Wyo. 1999) (battered-woman syndrome is used to explain elements of self-defense and is not relevant to charge of reckless homicide).

[425] People v. Erickson, 57 Cal. App. 4th 1391, 67 Cal. Rptr. 2d 740 (1997), *review denied*, 1998 Cal. LEXIS 234 (Jan. 14, 1998) ("[I]t would be a dramatic departure for the Legislature to permit use of battered-women's syndrome to predict the actual state of mind of a particular individual at a given moment." People v. Erickson, 57 Cal. App. 4th 1391, 1400, 67 Cal. Rptr. 2d 740, 746 (1997), *review denied*, 1998 Cal. LEXIS 234 (Jan. 14, 1998)); State v. Richardson, 525 N.W.2d 378 (Wis. Ct. App. 1994) (the court found out that testimony concerning battered-woman syndrome should have been admitted "so long as it does not include the expert's *conclusions* about the battered person's actual beliefs at the time of the offense, about the reasonableness of those beliefs or about the person's state of mind before, during or after the criminal act" and does not comment on the defendant's state of mind at the time of the crime. State v. Richardson, 525 N.W.2d 378, 382 (Wis. Ct. App. 1994)); Witt v. State, 892 P.2d 132, 138 (Wyo. 1995).

[426] Commonwealth v. Lazarovick, 410 Mass. 466, 574 N.E.2d 340 (1991).

[427] United States v. Willis, 38 F.3d 170 (5th Cir. 1994), *cert. denied*, 515 U.S. 1145 (1995).

since both defenses seek to demonstrate that the defendant acted reasonably in response to a fear of death or bodily injury. Some state courts have held that evidence of battered-woman's syndrome is relevant to a defendant's intent to commit a crime insofar as it relates to the defendant's ability to make decisions and to protect her children.[428]

Many states address the admissibility of the battered-women's syndrome by statute. Many of these statutes allow expert testimony on the syndrome, but only when offered by a defendant, usually in support of a self-defense claim.[429] Oklahoma has statutory authority for receiving such expert testimony by either the prosecution or defense.[430] California specifically precludes use of the syndrome, referred to as "intimate partner battering", when offered against a defendant to prove the act of abuse that forms the basis of the criminal charge.[431]

On behalf of the prosecution, the battered-woman syndrome may also be relevant in a sexual assault prosecution. Walker's study of over 400 battered women revealed that 59 percent reported being forced to engage in sexual acts

---

[428] State v. Mott, 183 Ariz. 191, 901 P.2d 1221 (1995); Barrett v. State, 675 N.E.2d 1112, 1116 (Ind. Ct. App. 1996).

[429] Georgia Code § 16-3-21(d)(2) (permits expert testimony in a prosecution for murder or manslaughter, when defendant raises a defense of justification, of "relevant facts and circumstances relating to the family violence or child abuse that are the bases of the expert's opinion"); La. Code Evid. Ann. art § 404a(2); Md. Code Ann. Cts. & Jud. Proc. § 10-916; Mo. Ann. Stat. § 563.033; Nev. Rev. Stat. § 48.061; Ohio Rev. Code Ann. § 19.06; Tex. Code Crim. Proc. Ann. art. § 38.36(b)(2) (permits testimony in prosecution for murders when jurisdiction raised as a defense of "relevant expert testimony regarding the condition of the mind of the defendant at the time of the offense, including those relevant facts and circumstances relating to family violence that are the basis of the expert's opinion"); Utah Crim. Code § 76-2-402(5)(e) (permits defendant in murder prosecution to present evidence of "any patterns of abuse or violence in the parties' relationship" when self-defense at issue); Wyo. Stat. § 6-1-203.

[430] Okla. Stat. Ann. tit. 22, § 40.7: "In an action in a court of this state, if a party offers evidence of domestic abuse, testimony of an expert witness concerning the effects of such domestic abuse on the beliefs, behavior and perception of the person being abused shall be admissible as evidence."

[431] Cal. Evid. Code § 1107:

> Admissibility of expert evidence regarding intimate partner battering, (a) In a criminal action, expert testimony is admissible by either the prosecution or the defense regarding intimate partner battering, including the physical, emotional, or mental effects upon the beliefs, perceptions, or behavior of victims of domestic violence, except when offered against a criminal defendant to prove the occurrence of the act or acts of abuse which form the basis of the criminal charge. (b) The foundation shall be sufficient for admission of this expert testimony if the proponent of the evidence establishes its relevancy and the proper qualifications of the expert witness. Expert opinion testimony on intimate partner battering and its effects shall not be considered a new scientific technique whose reliability is unproven. (c) For purposes of the section, "abuse" is defined as provided in Section 6203 of the Family Code, and "domestic violence" is defined in Section 6211 of the Family Code and may include acts defined in Section 242, subdivision (e) of Section 243, Section 262, 273.5, 273.6, 422, or 653m of the Penal Code. (d) This section is intended as a rule of evidence only and no substantive change affecting the Penal Code is intended.

by the men they lived with, even though at other times, the men could also engage in loving and caring relations.[432] A woman raped by her husband or boyfriend can offer testimony of the syndrome to explain her behaviors. In *State v. Ciskie*,[433] the victim testified that she had been raped at least four times over a period of 23 months. The prosecution was permitted to present testimony of the battered-woman syndrome to explain why she remained in the relationship and failed to report the rapes. Courts will routinely permit an expert to use the syndrome to explain the dynamics of a sexual assault victim's relationship.[434] This includes testimony to explain the rape victim's behavior before, during, and after the rape and how such conduct is not inconsistent with a sexual assault.[435] However, the expert was precluded from testifying that she believed the rapes to be the stressors that initiated the process in post-traumatic stress disorder, since this would constitute testimony that a rape had in fact occurred.[436]

A very typical application of the battered-woman syndrome is to explain the recantation of an allegation of abuse.[437] If a victim recants her grand jury

---

[432] Lenore Walker, *The Battered Woman Syndrome* 47–48, (1984). *See also* Diane Russell, *Rape in Marriage* 87-101 (1982).

[433] 110 Wash. 2d 263, 751 P.2d 1165 (1988).

[434] Commonwealth v. Goetzendanner, 42 Mass. App. Ct. 637, 679 N.E.2d 240, *review denied*, 425 Mass. 1105, 682 N.E.2d 1362 (1997) (battered-woman syndrome admissible in rape case to explain behavioral characteristics of typical victims of battering); People v. Christel, 449 Mich. 578, 537 N.W.2d 194 (1995) (expert testimony concerning battered-woman's syndrome may be admissible in a sexual assault prosecution when it is directly related to factual premises of the case and to explain a complainant's actions such as repeated physical abuse, accompanied by minimization of the abuse, delays in reporting abuse or recantation of allegations of abuse, although in this case the court noted that the factual predicate for the admission of the expert testimony did not exist).

[435] Russell v. State, 934 P.2d 1335 (Alaska Ct. App. 1997) (expert testimony on battered-woman testimony relevant to explain rape victim's behavior before, during and after sexual assault and how such conduct was not inconsistent with allegation of rape).

[436] State v. Ciskie, 110 Wash.2d 263, 279, 751 P.2d 1165, 1173 (1988).

[437] People v. Gadlin, 78 Cal. App. 4th 587, 92 Cal. Rptr. 2d 890, *review denied*, No. S087205, 2000 Cal. LEXIS 4716 (June 2, 2000) (holding expert testimony on effects of domestic battery on a victim was properly admitted, even though victim did not recant at trial, to explain victim's recantation of a prior incident and her decision to resume the relationship with the defendant before the charged incident); People v. Dillard, 45 Cal. App. 4th 1417, 53 Cal. Rptr. 2d 456 (1996); People v. Lafferty, 9 P.3d 1132 (Colo. 1999), *cert. denied*, 2000 Colo. LEXIS 1164 (Oct. 10, 2000) (holding battered-woman syndrome expert testimony proper to explain victim's recantation); State v. Borrelli, 227 Conn. 153, 629 A.2d 1105 (1993); Nixon v. United States, 728 A.2d 582 (D.C. 1999), *cert. denied*, 528 U.S. 1098 (2000) (holding battered-woman syndrome to be generally accepted and relevant to explain complainant's recantation); State v. Clark, 83 Haw. 289, 926 P.2d 194, 203–04 (testimony on battered-woman syndrome was properly admitted to explain victim's disavowal of her earlier allegation that her husband had stabbed her), *cert. denied*, 83 Haw. 545, 928 P.2d 39 (1996); Dausch v. State, 616 N.E.2d 13 (Ind. 1993); State v. Grecinger, 569 N.W.2d 189, 195 (Minn. 1997); People v. Ellis, 170 Misc. 2d 945, 650 N.Y.S.2d 503 (Sup. Ct. 1996) (holding evidence of battered-woman syndrome admissible to explain complainant's "recantation or minimization" of earlier allegations); State v. Bahn, 218 Wis. 2d 164, 578 N.W.2d 208 (1998)

testimony concerning a sexual assault and the manner in which injuries were inflicted on her, a jury would be permitted to hear that the victim's behavior is part of the syndrome.[438]

The expert can explain why a victim would report abuse, recant the allegation, and then testify in accordance with her initial report.[439] Following is testimony from such a case.

Q. Do you ever run into victims who refuse to testify against their batterers?

A. Well, based on the battered-women's syndrome, it is the battered-woman's perception, reasonable perception, that another beating is inevitable. And that all of our assistance, meaning the criminal justice system, counselors, our assistance will not be effective in stopping the violence. It hasn't been in the past for her, and so it is her reasonable belief that to testify against the batterer and not — versus showing him loyalty, being a wonderful actress in making sure that he believes she won't testify, that she will lie for him, she will do whatever it takes, is a life-saving coping skill for her. I hear law enforcement officers tell me all the time, battered women, they lie and they're great actresses. And my response is always, "they better be great actresses. Their life may depend on it."

Q. Why, in your experience, might a woman who's a victim of domestic violence protect the batterer, based on your knowledge of the models and your research and your experience in this area?

A. Well, the same reason. It's very important for her to prove loyalty, to focus on his needs and to make sure that he understands that she is in his camp at all times. Also because of the psychological terrorism that I referred to earlier. At some point she may have literally bonded with

---

("The State presented expert testimony that this case involved 'battered-woman's' syndrome. Evidence of the parties' relationship was relevant to this theory and helped to place the victim's recantation of some of her accusations against Bahn into context. A psychotherapist testified regarding the features of this syndrome and the 'cycle of violence' which can include the victim's recantation of her accusations and delays in reporting episodes of abuse. The evidence of previous sexual assaults was also relevant to Bahn's knowledge of the victim's lack of consent on the occasions charged in the information. We conclude that there was a logical or rational connection between the other acts evidence and facts of consequences to the determination of the action being tried." *Id.* at *9–10); State v. Schaller, 199 Wis. 2d 23, 544 N.W.2d 247 (1995) (prosecution experts in domestic violence testified in sexual assault trial that women in abusive domestic relationships commonly recant; this did not entitle defendant to examine complainant since the prosecution experts did not examine her as basis of their opinion); State v. Bednarz, 179 Wis. 2d 460, 507 N.W.2d 168 (1993). *But see* State v. Stringer, 271 Mont. 367, 897 P.2d 1063 (1995) (battered-woman syndrome rejected to explain recantation because of inadequate foundation demonstrating that witness was a battered spouse).

[438] Arcoren v. United States, 929 F.2d 1235 (8th Cir. 1991), *cert. denied*, 502 U.S. 913 (1991).

[439] State v. Griffin, 564 N.W.2d 370 (Iowa 1997).

the batterer and believes his perceptions that it is all her fault. That he is omnipotent in her life and that it's her job to protect him.[440]

As with other areas of expert testimony in sexual assault cases, battered-woman syndrome can explain why a battered woman would not report an assault,[441] why the victim would return to her batterer,[442] why a victim would minimize her abuse or injuries,[443] or inconsistencies in the victim's testimony and previous statements to the police.[444] Thus, the syndrome is not limited to cases in which it is offered to bolster a claim of self-defense.[445] Even prior to the coining of the phrase "battered-woman syndrome," expert testimony concerning prostitutes, physical beatings, rapes, psychological stress, and post-traumatic stress disorder was admissible to explain why women would voluntarily submit to an abuser's requests and fail to escape, cry out for help, or report the abuse.[446]

---

[440] State v. Griffin, 564 S.W.2d 370, 374–75 (Iowa 1997) ("The witness did not offer an opinion on Dee Dee's credibility, but instead testified concerning the medical and psychological syndrome present in battered women generally. We think this expert testimony was appropriate and conclude the district court did not abuse its discretion by admitting it. Griffin's contention to the contrary is without merit.").

[441] Alvarado v. State, 257 Ga. App. 746, 572 S.E.2d 18 (2002) (holding that "expert testimony regarding battered person's syndrome was admissible because the reasons why a battered woman would not leave the abuser or report his abuse are beyond the ken of the average layman" and was admissible even if the testimony may have placed his character in issue); State v. Grecinger, 569 N.W.2d 189 (Minn. 1997) (holding battered-woman testimony necessary to explain the "complexity" of and "reasons" for victim's behavior); State v. Allevy, 101 Wn. 2d 591, 682 P.2d 312 (1984) ("We find that expert testimony explaining why a person suffering from the battered woman syndrome would not leave her mate, would not inform police or friends, and would fear increased aggression against herself would be helpful to a jury in understanding a phenomenon not within the competence of an ordinary lay person." State v. Allevy, 101 Wn. 2d 591, 597, 682 P.2d 312, 316 (1984)).

[442] Trujillo v. State, 953 P.2d 1182 (Wyo. 1998) (expert's testimony relevant to explain for the jury victim's "continuing return to the abusive environment").

[443] State v. Searles, 141 N.H. 224, 680 A.2d 612 (1996) ("Given this testimony, we cannot say the trial court abused its discretion in concluding that evidence had been presented from which a jury could reasonably find that the victims had minimized their injuries and the defendant's actions, and that this minimization would likely be puzzling to the lay observer. In these circumstances, expert testimony about domestic violence syndrome could provide a reasonable explanation for the victims' changed accounts of their injuries and the events in question." State v. Searles, 141 N.H. 224, 228–229, 680 A.2d 612, 616 (1996)).

[444] Scugoza v. State, 949 S.W.2d 360 (Tex. Ct. App. 1997).

[445] Arcoren v. United States, 929 F.2d 1235 (8th Cir. 1991), cert. denied, 502 U.S. 913 (1991) ("It would seem anomalous to allow a battered woman, where she is a criminal defendant, to offer this type of expert testimony in order to help the jury understand the action she took, yet deny her that same opportunity when she is the complaining witness and/or victim and her abuser is the criminal defendant." (citing State v. Frost, 242 N.J. Super. 601, 612, 577 A.2d 1282, 1287 (1990). Arcoren v. United States, 929 F.2d 1235, 1241 (8th Cir. 1991), cert. denied, 502 U.S. 913 (1991)).

[446] United States v. Winters, 729 F.2d 602 (9th Cir. 1984).

Preparation for dealing with the battered-woman syndrome requires uncovering all documented, reported, and alleged acts of violence between the parties. Investigation should not be limited to formal discovery. Interviews with friends, relatives, and coworkers can often shed light on the relationship, as can a police department's call history to a particular address, employment, and medical records. Preparation also includes questioning, during jury selection, prospective jurors who may have experience with, or feelings about, battered women.

§ 11.36   Objections to battered-woman syndrome.

A fundamental issue in presenting battered-woman syndrome is establishing that the person about which the expert testimony is offered is in fact a battered person. The foundation can be laid by testimony of the battered woman. Unless there is an adequate foundation to demonstrate the complainant is a battered spouse, the expert testimony is objectionable.[447] This usually requires proof that the victim experienced two cycles of abuse.[448] This includes proof establishing the abusive behavior, and linking the abuser's actions with the defendant's behavior.[449]

---

[447] State v. Stringer, 271 Mont. 367, 897 P.2d 1063 (1995) (defendant's conviction reversed because there was inadequate foundation to show that complainant was a battered spouse; thus testimony as to why she recanted was irrelevant).

[448] State v. Stringer, 271 Mont. 367, 897 P2d 1063 (1995).

[449] People v. Gomez, 72 Cal. App. 4th 405, 415–16, 85 Cal. Rptr. 2d 101 (1999), *review denied*, No. S079856, 1999 Cal. LEXIS 6135 (Sept. 1, 1999) (holding evidence of battered woman syndrome irrelevant since there was no evidence of prior abuse); People v. Bryant, 278 A.D.2d 7, 717 N.Y.S.2d 136 (2000), *appeal denied* 96 N.Y.2d 757, 748 N.E.2d 1079, 725 N.Y.S.2d 283 (2001):

> The court did not improvidently exercise its discretion in denying the defense application to call an expert witness on battered women's syndrome on the ground that, under all the circumstances, defendant did not lay a sufficient foundation [citations omitted] or make an adequate offer of proof. We note that there was overwhelming evidence that defendant personally inflicted vicious abuse and severe injuries upon the deceased, her four-year-old child, entirely of her own volition and ill-will toward the child, and that the purported abuser, defendant's husband, was not even present during some of this abuse. The People's theory that defendant failed to protect the child from abuse by defendant's husband was only a minor component of the case.

People v. Bryant, 278 A.D.2d 7, 717 N.Y.S.2d 136, 137 (2000), *appeal denied* 96 N.Y.2d 757, 748 N.E.2d 1079, 725 N.Y.S.2d 283 (2001); People v. Herrera, 219 A.D.2d 511, 631 N.Y.S.2d 660, *appeal denied*, 87 N.Y.2d 847, 661 N.E.2d 1387, 638 N.Y.S.2d 605 (1995) (upholding trial court's rejection of defendant's offer of testimony of psychologist with respect to the battered-woman syndrome since defendant did not lay a foundation regarding the co-defendant's alleged abusive behavior toward her and therefore "the psychologist's diagnosis would not have been based on admissible evidence"); State v. Ogden, 168 Or. App. 249, 6 P.3d 1110, *on recons.* 169 Or. App. 469, 6 P.3d 1109 (2000), *rev. denied*, 331 Or. 692, 26 P.3d 149 (2001) ("[A]t trial, the state failed to establish a critical link between the expert's testimony about why a battered woman might choose to remain in an abusive relationship and why this complainant did so. Specifically, the

However, another view is that a prior episode of domestic violence is not a prerequisite to expert testimony, which is limited to why a victim of domestic violence may make inconsistent statements about the abuse and return to the perpetrator.[450] While testimony concerning battered-woman's syndrome may be helpful in explaining a woman's behavior during a sexual assault or post-incident behavior, there must be sufficient similarities between the victim's characteristics and those of the syndrome. For example, expert testimony concerning the syndrome should not be admitted when the complainant testifies that the relationship ended one month before the sexual assaults and did not attempt to hide, deny, or delay reporting the instant sexual assault, but rather sought immediate medical attention.[451]

When testimony of the battered-woman's syndrome is offered to explain why the victim failed to attempt an escape from the defendant, delayed reporting, or a victim's reactions, it is not substantive evidence that the crime occurred, similar to expert testimony that offers the same type of explanation under the umbrella of rape trauma syndrome or CSAAS testimony.[452] It is logical, as one court held, that it is error to fail "to give the jury limiting instructions on the difference between substantive use and limited use" of battered-woman syndrome testimony.[453] Limiting instructions are favored by many courts.[454] This, too, is consistent with the holding of many courts when CSAAS is used for rehabilitative purposes.[455]

---

state did not establish that complainant suffers from BWS. If complainant does not suffer from BWS, then testimony about that subject seemingly has no bearing on complainant's behavior." State v. Ogden, 168 Or. App. 249, 256, 6 P.3d 1110, 1114, *on recons.* 169 Or. App. 469, 6 P.3d 1109 (2000), *rev. denied*, 331 Or. 692, 26 P.3d 149 (2001)).

[450] People v. Brown, 33 Cal. 4th 892, 94 P.3d 574 (2004) (permitting expert testimony on reactions and behaviors of domestic violence victims when only one incident of abuse has occurred, particularly where as in this case there was evidence that parties were in a "cycle of violence;" "[t]here is no rule requiring a preliminary finding that the charged act of abuse occurred before the jury can consider" the expert's testimony); State v. Niemeyer, 55 Conn. App. 447, 452–453, 740 A.2d 416, 420 (1999), *aff'd in part, rev'd in part*, 258 Conn. 510, 782 A.2d 658 (2001).

[451] People v. Christel, 449 Mich. 578, 537 N.W.2d 194 (1995) (Michigan's Supreme Court noted that "[t]he prosecution's contention that she remained in the relationship despite the abuse does not by itself make it relevant and helpful to a material issue." People v. Christel, 449 Mich. 578, 597, 537 N.W.2d 194, 204 (1995)).

[452] *See* §§ 11.11–11.20.

[453] State v. Ellis, 280 N.J. Super. 533, 544–45, 656 A.2d 25, 30–31 (1995).

[454] People v. Lafferty, 9 P.3d 1132 (1999), *appeal denied*, 2000 Colo. LEXIS 1164 (Oct. 10, 2000) (noting that trial court properly gave trial jury a limiting instruction that battered-woman syndrome expert testimony was not to establish victim credibility, but rather why victim's version of the event had changed over time); Nixon v. United States, 728 A.2d 582 (D.C. 1999), *cert. denied*, 528 U.S. 1098 (2000) (noting that it would have been better practice for trial court to have given limiting instruction as to purpose for introduction of battered-woman syndrome testimony). *See also* People v. Christel, 449 Mich. 578, 199, 537 N.W.2d 194, 199 (1995) ("On request, the trial judge may deem a limiting instruction appropriate" when evidence of battered-woman's syndrome is offered).

[455] *See* § 11.22.

Objections to the use of the battered-woman syndrome include that it is not "scientific" and not reliable enough to permit expert testimony. There is little in the way of scientific data on battered women and the correlation between battering and rape or homicide. Some courts have cited this criticism in rejecting the syndrome.[456] Another objection to the battered-woman syndrome is that it is irrelevant to a defendant's duress defense where the battered-woman syndrome testimony deals with the defendant's subjective perceptions.[457] A pretrial motion may address objections to this testimony. Still another objection that can be raised is that the subject matter of the testimony is within the knowledge and understanding of a jury. It can also be argued in a rape case that it is not relevant to the material issue of rape and is prejudicial, in that it brings out prior uncharged behavior on the part of the defendant and that the prejudicial effect of such testimony outweighs its probative effect. While battered-woman syndrome testimony may explain the victim's behavior, it should not present characteristics of the abuser, which place the defendant's character in issue. For example, it is improper for the expert to state that "these men frequently have been in trouble with the police on past occasions," and "frequently, there is a history of alcohol or drug abuse" with batterers.[458] Another objection may relate to the qualifications of the witness providing the opening, such as a police officer.[459] Care must be taken to avoid misusing the battered woman syndrome as a purpose for which it was designed. For example, it is improper to use the syndrome to bolster the credibility of an eyewitness to a crime[460] who did not report a victim's death for years.[461]

---

[456] Hawthorne v. State, 470 So. 2d 770, 773 (Fla. Dist. Ct. 1985) (upholding trial court's determination that Dr. Walker's theories are not sufficiently developed and that the "depth of study in their field has not yet reached the point where an expert witness can give testimony with any degree of assurance that the state of the art will support an expert opinion"); Buhrle v. State, 627 P.2d 1374 (Wyo. 1981).

[457] United States v. Willis, 38 F.3d 170, 174–77 (5th Cir. 1994), *cert. denied*, 515 U.S. 1145 (1995) (However, court did allow into evidence all objective evidence of the batterer's violent nature). *But see* United States v. Marenghi, 893 F. Supp. 85 (D. Me. 1995), *aff'd*, 109 F.3d 28 (1st Cir. 1997) ("Providing the jury with information of specific incidents of abuse while providing no information about how such treatment can, over time, establish a dynamic where the threat of abuse hovers over every interaction between the individuals, even if such threat is not always articulated, would give the jury only half of the story." United States v. Marenghi, 893 F. Supp. 85, 95 (D. Me. 1995), *aff'd*, 109 F.3d 28 (1st Cir. 1997)).

[458] Parrish v. State, 237 Ga. App. 274, 514 S.E.2d 458, *cert. denied*, No. S99C1069, 1999 Ga. LEXIS 523 (June 4, 1999) (holding that expert's testimony, while improper, was harmless).

[459] State v. Stillday, 646 N.W.2d 557, 562–63 (Minn. Ct. App. 2002) (upholding lay witness opinion testimony of police officer on battered women, but noting defendant's lack of objection).

[460] 745 A.2d at 528 (noting specifically that in other cases, such as *Pennell*, cited in note 378 in main volume, the other acts had sufficient unique characteristics to qualify admission of the expert's testimony as signature evidence).

[461] People v. Howard, 305 Ill. App. 3d 300, 712 N.E.2d 380, *appeal denied*, 185 Ill. 2d 646, 720 N.E.2d 1099 (1999).

§ 11.37 Battered-child syndrome, profiling, and CSAAS.

The "battered-child syndrome" has neither a legal nor a scientific connection to the "child sexual abuse accommodation syndrome" (CSAAS) and other syndromes commonly seen in sexual assault trials. The battered-child syndrome has been accepted by the medical profession as a diagnostic tool to determine if a child is the subject of abuse rather than accidental injury.[462] The syndrome is used in connection with young children, usually less than three years of age, and is generally based on a finding of multiple injuries in various stages of healing that are inconsistent with the explanation for the injuries offered by the parent or caretaker of the child. The Supreme Court of the United States has reviewed expert testimony based on on the battered-child syndrome, noting its scientific basis and reliability.[463] The syndrome also has been accepted and approved overwhelmingly by both state and federal courts.[464]

The syndrome may involve a simple episode of abuse, but more often reflects abuse and neglect over a period of time. The type and distribution of injuries

---

[462] C. Henry Kempe, Frederic N. Silverman, Brandt F. Steele, William Droegemueller & Henry K. Silver, *The Battered Child Syndrome*, 181 J.A.M.A 17 (1962).

[463] Estelle v. McGuire, 502 U.S. 62 (1991).

[464] United States v. Boise, 916 F.2d 497, 503–04 (9th Cir. 1990), *cert. denied*, 500 U.S. 934 (1991); United States v. Bowers, 660 F.2d 527 (5th Cir. 1981); Eslava v. State, 473 So. 2d 1143 (Ala. Crim. App. 1985); State v. Hernandez, 167 Ariz. 236, 805 P.2d 1057 (1990); People v. Jackson, 18 Cal. App. 3d 504, 95 Cal. Rptr. 919 (1971); State v. Dumlao, 3 Conn. App. 607, 491 A.2d 404 (1985); Smith v. State, 247 Ga. 612, 277 S.E.2d 678 (1981); People v. Peters, 224 Ill. App. 3d 180, 586 N.E.2d 469, 166 Ill. Dec. 511 (1991), *appeal allowed*, 144 Ill. 2d 640, 591 N.E.2d 28, 169 Ill. Dec. 148 (1992), *aff'd*, 153 Ill. 2d 218, 180 Ill. Dec. 124, 606 N.E.2d 1201 (1992); State v. Heath, 264 Kan. 557, 957 P.2d 449 (1998); State v. Conlogue, 474 A.2d 167, 172 (Me. 1984); Commonwealth v. Day, 409 Mass. 719, 724, 569 N.E.2d 397 (1991); State v. Durfee, 322 N.W.2d 778 (Minn. 1982); Schleret v. State, 311 N.W.2d 843 (Minn. 1981); Bludsworth v. State, 98 Nev. 289, 646 P.2d 558 (1982); State v. Moorman, 286 N.J. Super. 648, 670 A.2d 81 (1996); State v. Aguayo, 114 N.M. 124, 129, 835 P.2d 840, 845 (1992); People v. Henson, 33 N.Y.2d 63, 304 N.E.2d 358, 349 N.Y.S.2d 657 (1973); State v. Phillips, 328 N.C. 1, 399 S.E.2d 293 (1991), *cert. denied*, 501 U.S. 1208 (1991); Commonwealth v. Rodgers, 364 Pa. Super. 477, 528 A.2d 610, *appeal denied*, 518 Pa. 638, 542 A.2d 1368 (1988); State v. Durand, 465 A.2d 762, 768–69 (R.I. 1983); State v. Lopez, 306 S.C. 362, 412 S.E.2d 390 (1991) (noting that the battered-child syndrome has been developed as a result of extensive research and is an accepted medical diagnosis); State v. Holland, 346 N.W.2d 302 (S.D. 1984) (noting that all elements of the syndrome need not be presented before admitting such testimony); State v. Tanner, 675 P.2d 539 (Utah 1983) (noting the syndrome consists of "a brief set of narrow, specific, and predominantly physical symptoms" that constitute an accepted medical diagnosis suggesting that the cause of the injuries in question was not accidental. "The concept of the Battered-Child Syndrome is grounded in scientific research and is widely accepted in the medical community" and "all courts which have addressed the question have affirmed the admission of expert medical testimony regarding the presence of the Battered-Child Syndrome." State v. Tanner, 675 P.2d 539, 542–544 (Utah 1983)); Price v. Commonwealth, 18 Va. App. 760, 766, 446 S.E.2d 642, 1640 (1994); State v. Janes, 121 Wash. 2d 220, 850 P.2d 495 (1993) (syndrome admissible to aid defendant's claim of self-defense); State v. Toennis, 52 Wash. App. 176, 758 P.2d 539, *review denied*, 111 Wash. 2d 1026 (1988); State v. Mulder, 29 Wash. App. 513, 629 P.2d 462 (1981).

are factors used in making the diagnosis.[465] Since the syndrome is a generally recognized medical diagnosis, it had not been qualified under the test for the admissibility of expert testimony.[466] The syndrome helps explain that a child did not die by accidental means. The expert may explain that changing histories is part of the syndrome and that the physical findings are not consistent with the history or explanation offered by the defendant.[467] The syndrome does not permit the expert to testify that the injuries were caused by any particular person or class of persons as a general rule.[468] Even though it does not identify the person who inflicted those injuries, it is admissible "on the question of the intent with which the person who caused the injuries acted."[469] This includes establishing the element of depravity of the defendant's conduct.

One issue with the battered-child syndrome is the admission of old or prior injuries that are usually part of the syndrome, and whether a court will require evidence connecting those injuries to the defendant. The general rule requiring prior acts of the defendant to be established by a particular level of proof is discussed in Chapter 6. Despite some language in *Estelle v. McGuire* implying that the defendant need not be connected to the prior injuries,[470] some courts require sufficient proof connecting the prior injuries to the defendant.[471] This

---

[465] C. Henry Kempe, Frederic N. Silverman, Brandt F. Steele, William Droegemueller & Henry K. Silver, *The Battered Child Syndrome*, 181 J.A.M.A 17, 18 (1962).

[466] United States v. Boise, 916 F.2d 497, 503 (9th Cir. 1990), *cert denied*, 500 U.S. 934 (1991).

[467] State v. Heath, 264 Kan. 557, 957 P.2d 449 (1998) (holding doctor's testimony that defendant's statement to police is not consistent with deceased child's injuries is not improper comment on defendant's credibility); State v. Butterfield, 128 Or. App. 1, 874 P.2d 1339 (1994) (noting that a caretaker's changing explanations of the cause of the child's injuries is part of the battered-child syndrome, and that such testimony is not inadmissible because it may imply that the defendant was not telling the truth, since such expert testimony was not a direct comment on the credibility of the defendant).

[468] State v. Wilkerson, 295 N.C. 559, 570, 247 S.E.2d 905, 911 (1978).

[469] Estelle v. McGuire, 502 U.S. 62, 69 (1991).

[470] Estelle v. McGuire, 502 U.S. 62 (1991) ("When offered to show that certain injuries are a product of child abuse, rather than accident, evidence of prior injuries is relevant even though it does not purport to prove the identity of the person who might have inflicted those injuries." Estelle v. McGuire, 502 U.S. 62, 68 (1991)).

[471] United States v. Boise, 916 F.2d 497, 502 (9th Cir. 1990), *cert. denied*, 500 U.S. 934 (1991) (holding that deceased child's prior injuries are admissible only if "jury could reasonably conclude that the injuries occurred and that Boise inflicted them"); People v. Oaks, 169 Ill. 2d 409, 455–56, 662 N.E.2d 1328, 1348–49, *cert. denied*, 519 U.S. 873 (1996) (connecting deceased child's prior injuries to defendant should be established by more than "mere suspicion" but not beyond a reasonable doubt); Clemens v. State, 610 N.E.2d 236, 242 (Ind. 1993) (holding there must be "sufficient evidence" to support a finding that defendant inflicted prior injuries upon child but proof may be circumstantial and not direct); State v. Guyette, 139 N.H. 526, 658 A.2d 1204 (1995) (trial court erred in admitting evidence of child's prior injuries which could not be connected to the defendant and testimony concerning battered-child syndrome. The court noted:

Nor in a criminal context can we accept the State's premise that the more intentional

standard of proof varies from jurisdiction to jurisdiction, much as it does for prior acts' evidence. Some of these decisions permit circumstantial evidence connecting the prior injuries to the defendant.[472] Admission of the battered-child syndrome should be accompanied by appropriate limiting instructions so the jury is instructed as to the specific purpose of the testimony and so that the jury does not view evidence of prior injuries as propensity evidence or evidence of defendant's bad character.[473]

Some courts have permitted battered-child syndrome as a defense in a parricide case or killing of another family member.[474] The evidence may also be

> prior injuries a child has sustained, the more probable that the current injury is intentional or non-accidental. . . . By contrast, if the State could prove that there was a nexus between the defendant and the prior intentional injuries, such evidence might be relevant and highly probative of whether the defendant purposely scalded her son.

State v. Guyette, 139 N.H. 526, 529, 658 A.2d 1204, 1207 (1995)); State v. Moorman, 286 N.J. 648, 670 A.2d 81 (1996) ("clear and convincing" evidence established that defendant committed prior acts of physical abuse upon child); State v. Pierce, 326 S.C. 176, 485 S.E.2d 913 (1997) (reversing defendant's child homicide conviction due to prosecution's failure to establish by clear and convincing evidence that deceased child's previous injuries were inflicted by the defendant); Pavlick v. Commonwealth, 27 Va. App. 219, 497 S.E.2d 920 (1998) (following *Huddleston* standard that jury find by a preponderance of the evidence that defendant inflicted prior injuries to deceased child, but that this credibility determination is to be made by jury and not trial court); State v. Norlin, 134 Wash. 2d 570, 951 P.2d 1131 (1998) (holding that in child abuse prosecutions evidence of prior injuries are admissible only if they are connected to the defendant by a preponderance of the evidence).

[472] Clemens v. State, 610 N.E.2d 236, 242 (Ind. 1993); Pavlick v. Commonwealth, 27 Va. App. 219, 497 S.E.2d 920 (1998)

> "We find that the evidence that appellant was the cause of the child's prior injuries was not inherently incredible. The record established that the child had received rib injuries prior to the fatal shaking. While the child's mother and the child's paternal grandmother were the only individuals, other than appellant, who had been alone with the child during the time frame in which the rib fractures were inflicted, both testified that they had never shaken the child. Appellant maintained that he had not caused the prior injuries. The jury was entitled to consider and resolve this conflict in the evidence against appellant." Pavlick v. Commonwealth, 27 Va. App. 219, 230, 497 S.E.2d 920, 925 (1998);

> "In short, a number of incidents that may well have resulted in the prior injuries that the doctors found Nicholas had sustained prior to the June 1 incident occurred during times when Norlin was alone with the child. Furthermore, there was no evidence at trial that any other person had been alone with Nicholas when these incidents occurred. Neither was there evidence of any other incidents that could have caused the arm, ankle, and rib injuries testified to by the physicians. Although this evidence can only be described as circumstantial, it was sufficient to connect Norlin to Nicholas' injuries by a preponderance of the evidence." State v. Norlin, 134 Wash. 2d 570, 583, 951 P.2d 1131, 1137 (1998).

[473] *See e.g.*, State v. Moorman, 286 N.J. Super. 648, 670 A.2d 81 (1996).

[474] State v. Hines, 303 N.J. Super. 311, 324, 696 A.2d 780, 787 (1997); State v. Nemeth, 82 Ohio St. 3d 202, 694 N.E.2d 1332 (1998); Commonwealth v. Kacsmar, 421 Pa. Super. 64, 617 A.2d 725 (1992), *appeal denied*, 536 Pa. 640, 639 A.2d 25 (1994); State v. Janes, 121 Wash. 2d 220, 850 P.2d 495 (1993) (*en banc*).

admissible under statutes which permit a defendant to present evidence of familial violence or other abuse, such as battered-woman syndrome, in defense or mitigation of a charge.[475] However, a battered-child syndrome case is defined differently than in a case in which injuries inflicted on a child is at issue. (It may also be referred to as "child abuse syndrome" or a form of post-traumatic stress disorder.)[476]

§ 11.38 Parental-alienation syndrome and sex-abuse legitimacy scale.

The "parental-alienation syndrome" was developed by the psychiatrist Richard A. Gardner.[477] Gardner uses the term to describe a disturbance in which a child is obsessed with the deprecation and criticism of a parent to an unjustified or exaggerated extent. In the view of the child suffering from the syndrome, one parent may engage in negative behavior, while the other parent can do no wrong. There is both a conscious brainwashing of the child and also an array of subconscious and unconscious factors on the part of the preferred parent that influences the child's alienation. According to the syndrome, the child will be strongly influenced by the loved parent and may even engage in behavior similar to the loved parent, using phrases and expressions learned from the loved parent.

Gardner divides the syndrome into three categories: severe, moderate, and mild. A child suffering from the syndrome will speak with hatred about a parent and may justify the alienation with memories of minor altercations with that parent. The hatred may also extend to relatives and loved ones of the hated parent. The syndrome also suggests that there is a lack of ambivalence on the part of the child about the relationship; that is, the hated parent is all bad and the loved parent is all good, when in reality, as in all relationships there are the good moments and bad moments.

Gardner believes that it is within the context of this parental-alienation syndrome that many allegations of child sexual abuse occur, particularly in custody disputes. Gardner believes that the syndrome, together with the desire of women to seek an additional weapon in custody disputes and the zealousness of sex abuse investigators, have led to the increased incidents of allegations of sexual abuse in intra-familial situations. Gardner contends that many normal behaviors that are often taken as evidence of child abuse — nightmares, tantrums, masturbation, depression, obsessive-compulsive rituals, conduct disorders, antisocial behavior, hyperactivity, attention deficit disorder, and gastrointestinal complaints — have a variety of causes and have nothing to do with sexual

---

[475] See § 11.35.

[476] See § 11.14.

[477] Richard A. Gardner, *True and False Accusations of Sexual Abuse* (1992); Richard A. Gardner, *The Sex Abuse Legitimacy Scale* (1987); Richard A. Gardner, *The Parental Alienation Syndrome and the Differentiation Between Fabricated and Genuine Child Sex Abuse* (1987).

abuse.[478] As a means of assessing legitimate and fabricated allegations of child sexual abuse, Gardner has developed the "sex abuse legitimacy scale",[479] which attempts to provide objective criteria for determining true versus fabricated cases of abuse. To date, Gardner's syndrome and scale have not been accepted as expert testimony in any criminal trial in the United States, although his theories and opinions have been permitted in family court and custody proceedings.[480] Also, many of the bases of the syndrome have been used in trials as a basis for other expert's opinions or for argument by counsel. Similar expert testimony or opinion on the propensity of children who are the subject of parental custody or visitation conflicts to falsify allegations of abuse is likewise inadmissible.[481]

§ 11.39 Expert psychological testimony on child development.

An area where expert psychological testimony may be admissible and helpful is the field of child development. A psychologist may be able to testify as to the language skills and developmental differences between children and their emotional, cognitive, social, and behavioral stages of growth. Children do not communicate in sentence structure and vocabulary in the same manner as adults. In this sense, their testimony must sometimes be interpreted, just as the testimony of a witness speaking a foreign language or using sign language. This is particularly true where children, particularly preschoolers, do not have the concept of time and cannot answer questions about when an event took place or when an event took place in relation to another event.[482] Thus, asking a young child how many times something took place or when in relation to a particular event something took place will not likely result in an accurate answer; they simply cannot think in those terms. Similarly, a psychologist can explain that some children cannot understand the concept of causation, and, therefore, they

---

[478] Richard A. Gardner, *Sex Abuse Hysteria: Salem Witch Trials Revisited* (1991).

[479] Richard A. Gardner, *The Sex Abuse Legitimacy Scale* (1987).

[480] Page v. Zordan, 564 So. 2d 500 (Fla. Dist. Ct. App. 1990) (refusing to admit "sex abuse legitimacy scale" since it was not shown to be generally accepted); Tungate v. Commonwealth, 901 S.W.2d 41 (Ky. 1995) (Gardner's proposed testimony concerning his 24 "indicators for pedophilia" upon which he would opine that the defendant was unlikely to be engaged in pedophilic acts did not satisfy the standard of relevance and scientific reliability); People v. Fortin, 289 A.D.2d 590, 735 N.Y.S.2d 819 (2001), *appeal denied*, 97 N.Y.2d 754, 769 N.E.2d 360, 742 N.Y.S.2d 614 (2002) (holding that parental-alienation syndrome does not have general acceptance in the professional community to justify its admission as evidence); Krebsbach v. Gallagher, 181 A.D.2d 363, 587 N.Y.S.2d 346, *appeal denied*, 81 N.Y.2d 701, 610 N.E.2d 388, 594 N.Y.S.2d 715 (1992); People v. Loomis, 172 Misc. 2d 265, 658 N.Y.S.2d 787 (County Ct. 1997) (defendant not entitled to examine complainants to see if their allegations motivated by "parent alienation syndrome").

[481] Floray v. State, 720 A.2d 1132 (Del. 1998).

[482] State v. Weaver, 117 N.C. App. 434, 451 S.E.2d 15 (1994) (upholding trial court's admission into evidence of expert testimony as to the age at which children begin to understand dates. Expert testified, "we certainly don't expect children . . . to be able to name dates, or to give more than a general approximation of how many times something happened, you know, if it is more than, say, one time." State v. Weaver, 117 N.C. App. 434, 439, 451 S.E.2d 15, 18 (1994)).

may not be able to deal with the questions of why and how. The expert may be able to explain memory problems connected with a sexual assault to explain inconsistent statements.[483] Expert testimony may also explain to the jury the victim's perception of reality.[484] Expert testimony may also be offered concerning a developmentally-disabled person's ability to remember. Testimony that a developmentally-disabled person has "an incredible memory and that her ability to recall is almost picture-perfect" is not necessarily an opinion or a comment regarding the truth of the allegations, but helps to explain background of the complainant, which may be helpful to the jury concerning developmental disabilities of the witness.[485]

An expert may help explain a child's reaction to the courtroom setting and explain the anxiety a courtroom can create and how it can affect the child's ability to answer questions. New York's highest court holds admissible expert testimony on child development and the victim's reactions to courtroom procedures.[486]

§ 11.40   Expert testimony concerning interviewing techniques, interviews, or cognitive abilities of child complainants.

Increasingly, testimony has been offered on behalf of defendants in child sexual abuse litigation concerning the suggestiveness of pretrial interviews and questioning of child victims. Such testimony can establish that the investigatory or interview techniques utilized with child witnesses "were so suggestive that they give rise to a substantial likelihood of irreparably false recollection of material facts bearing on defendant's guilt."[487] Some courts have not found such expert

---

[483] State v. Barber, 120 N.C. App. 505, 512–13, 463 S.E.2d 405, 410 (1995), *review denied*, 342 N.C. 896, 467 S.E.2d 906 (1996) (prosecution expert, a police investigator, permitted to testify that victim's inconsistent statements were memory problems associated with sexual assault victimization because the defendant opened the door by questioning investigator's techniques).

[484] Fleener v. State, 648 N.E.2d 652 (Ind. Ct. App. 1995), *aff'd*, 656 N.E.2d 1140 (Ind. 1995).

[485] *See, e.g.*, United States v. Reynolds, 77 F.3d 253 (8th Cir. 1996).

[486] People v. Cintron, 75 N.Y.2d 249, 267, 551 N.E.2d 561, 552 N.Y.S.2d 68 (1990). *See also* § 11.19.

[487] State v. Michaels, 136 N.J. 299, 320–21, 642 A.2d 1372, 1383 (1994). *See also* Sheldon v. State, 796 P.2d 831 (Alaska Ct. 1990); People v. Diefenderfer, 784 P.2d 741, 753 (Colo. 1989); Timmons v. State, 584 N.E.2d 1108 (Ind. 1992) (holding that trial court properly allowed defendant's expert to discuss interview bias, and properly limited such testimony to the extent it was cumulative); State v. Erickson, 454 N.W.2d 624 (Minn. Ct. App. 1990); State v. Foust, 920 S.W.2d 949 (Mo. Ct. App. 1996) ("As this court and others have recognized, children are susceptible to suggestive interview techniques and the circumstances surrounding the questioning of the child is a proper subject of inquiry." State v. Foust, 920 S.W.2d 949, 955 (Mo. Ct. App. 1996)); State v. Sargent, 738 A.2d 351, 144 N.H. 103 (1999) (holding defendant should have been permitted to present expert testimony on the possibility of false memory implantation with child witnesses through improper and suggestive interviewing techniques); Felix v. State, 109 Nev. 151, 849 P.2d 220 (1993); People v. Michael M., 162 Misc. 2d 803, 618 N.Y.S.2d 171 (Sup. Ct. 1994); State v. Hadfield, 788 P.2d 506 (Utah 1990). *See generally*, Brent G. Filbert, Annotation, *Admissibility of Expert Testimony as to Proper Techniques for Interviewing Children or Evaluating Techniques Employed in Particular Case*, 87 A.L.R.5th 693 (2001).

testimony helpful or appropriate, since it provides information that can be developed on cross-examination or is within the common knowledge of jurors for which an expert is not required. **488** The Eighth Circuit Court of Appeals has

---

488 Washington v. Schriver, 255 F.3d 45, 59–60 (2d Cir. 2001) (upholding on habeas review state court exclusion of expert on suggestibility of children in forensic sexual abuse interviews, for among other reasons, "We essentially agree with both the trial court and the Appellate Division that the basic idea that young children can be suggestible is 'not beyond the knowledge of the jurors,' " and because defense counsel on cross-examination explored the potential suggestibility of the children); Ahmed v. United States, 856 A.2d 560 (D.C. 2004), *cert. denied*, 544 U.S. 955 (2005) (defendant sought to offer testimony by child psychologist on whether child's account was consistent with the way children remember events. Court upheld preclusion of such testimony, since it was not beyond ken of the average layman and because defendant's attorney sufficiently highlighted child's inconsistencies); Shumate v. Newland, 75 F. Supp. 2d 1076, 1087–88 (N.D. Cal. 1999) (holding in federal *habeas corpus* proceeding trial judge did not violate due process or right to present a defense by excluding defendant's expert testimony concerning effect of interview techniques on child witnesses); People v. Wilson, 246 Ill. App. 3d 311, 320–322, 615 N.E.2d 1283, 1288–89, *appeal denied*, 152 Ill. 2d 578, 622 N.E.2d 1225 (1993) (Defendant offered expert testimony concerning children's cognitive abilities and "proclivities to invent accusations to please their elders." "In refusing to allow defendant's expert to testify, the trial court noted that the expert testimony would unduly emphasize the children's testimony at trial, would reveal only general information about children as opposed to knowledge that defendant could argue to the jury without the aid of an expert. We agree. The limited cognitive abilities of children are well known, and any jury can be expected to take that factor into account when determining a child's credibility. The proffered expert testimony on this point would have provided no useful information to the jury.") *See also* State v. James, 211 Conn. 555, 560 A.2d 426 (1989) (holding trial court properly exercised discretion in excluding defendant's expert psychological testimony on credibility of child witnesses since jurors were equally capable of assessing this issue without expert testimony, analogizing this area to expert testimony on eyewitness identification); State v. Ellis, 669 A.2d 752 (Me. 1996) ("Defendant was entitled to explore the interviewing techniques that were used and to argue to the jury that they may have influenced the children's testimony. Defendant was not entitled to have his argument buttressed by the presentation of common knowledge in the form of an expert scientific opinion." State v. Ellis, 669 A.2d 752, 753 (Me. 1996)); People v. Johnston, 273 A.D.2d 514, 709 N.Y.S.2d 230, *appeal denied*, 95 N.Y.2d 935, 744 N.E.2d 148, 721 N.Y.S.2d 612 (2000) (The *Johnston* court upheld the trial court's preclusion of a defense expert on children's susceptibility to suggestive interrogation:

> Moreover, there is support in this record for County Court's additional basis for precluding defendant's expert on the ground that such opinions had not received general acceptance in the field of psychology . . . . Finally, although the expert did not testify, defendant had an opportunity to challenge the interview techniques used with the victims on cross-examination and he was not unduly prevented from presenting this defense.

People v. Johnston, 273 A.D.2d 514, 518, 709 N.Y.S.2d 230, 236, *appeal denied*, 95 N.Y.2d 935, 744 N.E.2d 148, 721 N.Y.S.2d 612 (2000); *See* People v. Kanani, 272 A.D.2d 186, 709 N.Y.S.2d 505, *appeal denied*, 95 N.Y.2d 935, 744 N.E.2d 148, 721 N.Y.S.2d 612 (2000); People v. Wilson, 255 A.D.2d 612, 679 N.Y.S.2d 732 (1998), *appeal denied*, 93 N.Y.2d 981, 716 N.E.2d 1113, 695 N.Y.S.2d 68 (1999) (issue whether child victims' testimony was tainted went to children's credibility and reliability, which were issues reserved for trier of fact and did not necessitate pretrial hearing to determine whether testimony was tainted by suggestive questioning); People v. Washington, 238 A.D.2d 263, 657 N.Y.S.2d 24 (1997) ("The court properly denied defendant's request to present the testimony of an expert on the susceptibility of young children to suggestion.

held that a trial court can limit the expert's testimony to the general ways "in which adults influence children's memories and the possible impact on their credibility" without the expert offering an opinion on a particular child's credibility.[489] When the jury has the opportunity to review the interviewing techniques in the case, such as the social influences on a child at the time of the accusations, and the jury observes the child testifying, it is not necessarily prejudicial to preclude expert testimony on whether interviewers employed a "practice of suggestibility" in interviewing the complainant.[490] As with expert testimony on eyewitness identification, a court may take the position that such testimony is more helpful and appropriate when proof of guilt is marginal and the defendant comes forward with evidence of suggestiveness in the interview process.[491] A court may review the adequacy of corroborating evidence and the significance of the child's testimony in determining whether or not expert testimony on suggestive interview techniques should be admitted.[492] These positions adopt many of the arguments utilized for and against the admission of expert testimony on eyewitness identification.

Courts have recognized the following areas as possible evidence of improper or suggestive interview techniques that may be addressed by expert testimony.[493]

This subject was not beyond the knowledge of the jurors, and, in any event, the child revealed the incident prior to any prodding or questioning by anyone and any deficiencies in her memory, and the effects of any suggestibility were presented to the jury through cross-examination and summations and were the subject of proper jury instructions" People v. Washington, 238 A.D.2d 263, 264, 657 N.Y.S.2d 24, 25 (1997)); People v. Jones, 185 Misc. 2d 899, 714 N.Y.S.2d 876 (Sup. Ct. 2000) (holding that issues surrounding law enforcement interviewing of child victim could be adequately explored at a pretrial competency hearing or during cross-examination of child or investigators).

[489] United States v. Rouse, 111 F.3d 561, 572 (8th Cir. 1997) (*en banc*).

[490] United States v. Rouse, 111 F.3d 561, 572 (8th Cir. 1997) (*en banc*).

[491] State v. Biezer, 947 S.W.2d 540 (Mo. Ct. App. 1997); People v. Michael M., 162 Misc. 2d 803, 618 N.Y.S.2d 171 (Sup. Ct. 1994).

[492] United States v. Reynolds, 77 F.3d 253 (8th Cir. 1996)

"We need not reach the issue of whether the evidence was reliable, as the trial court held a Daubert hearing and properly determined that, although testimony-concerning memory and suggestibility was admissible, testimony concerning interviewing techniques was not relevant to Reynolds' case. The trial court so determined because of the absence of evidence suggesting the victim had been interviewed, and because the victim's mother observed the sexual abuse and immediately confirmed her observation with the victim. Thus, under Daubert's requirements that expert testimony be reliable and relevant, [citation omitted], the testimony concerning interviewing techniques was properly excluded." United States v. Reynolds, 77 F.3d 253, 255 (8th Cir. 1996)); United States v. Kibler, 43 M.J. 725 (A.C.C.A. 1995), *cert. denied*, 523 U.S. 1011 (1998).

[493] Felix v. State, 109 Nev. 151, 849 P.2d 220, 230 (1993); State v. Babayan, 106 Nev. 155, 162, 787 P.2d 805, 811 (1990); State v. Michaels, 136 N.J. 299, 309–10, 642 A.2d 1372, 1377 (1994).

- the use of leading questions;

- incessant questioning;

- praise, rewards, tone of voice, bribes, or threats;

- preconceived notions of what happened by the interviewer;

- vilification of the defendant;

- systems contamination (outside information gained from police or other sources);

- cross-contamination (using information gained from other children during interviews or therapy);

- lack of control over outside influences upon children, such as parents, peers, or other interviewers; and

- the lack of spontaneous or voluntary recall of facts by the child.

However, some courts hold that leading questions are not necessarily improper, nor does the use of leading questions establish unduly suggestive interviewing.[494]

Increasingly, courts are suggesting that it may be reversible error to preclude testimony concerning the proper methods for interviewing young children in sexual abuse investigations. The failure to admit such testimony may be error.[495] One Wisconsin court noted:

---

[494] State v. Smith, 158 N.J. 376, 390, 730 A.2d 311, 319 (1999); Alicea v. State, 13 P.3d 693 (Wyo. 2000), *reh'g denied*, 2000 Wyo. LEXIS 235 (Dec. 19, 2000)

> Although leading questions were asked by all interviewers, there was no evidence that those interviewers assumed the existence of the criminal conduct, and, as we set out above, the use of leading questions is not improper in this context. While all interviewers were authority figures of various sorts, the record does not suggest that their status as such was used to coerce information from the children.

Alicea v. State, 13 P.3d 693, 697–698 (Wyo. 2000), *reh'g denied*, 2000 Wyo. LEXIS 235 (Dec. 19, 2000).

[495] State v. Speers, 209 Ariz. 125, 130–131, 98 P.3d 560, 565–67 (2004), *review denied*, 2005 Ariz. LEXIS 60 (May 24, 2005) (holding trial court erred, as a matter of due process, in excluding expert testimony as to improper investigatory child interviews, including suggestiveness of interview techniques, finding that it was accepted by the scientific community and subject matter was not necessarily familiar to jurors); State v. Malarney, 617 So. 2d 739, 740 (Fla. Dist. Ct. App. 1993) (defendant's conviction reversed due to failure of trial court to permit expert testimony concerning unreasonably suggestive interview techniques); Barlow v. State, 270 Ga. 54, 507 S.E.2d 416 (1998) (holding "that the defendant in a child molestation case is entitled to introduce expert testimony for the limited purpose of providing the jury with information about proper techniques for interviewing children and whether the interviewing techniques actually utilized were proper" and the failure to do so in this case was reversible error); Pyron v. State, 237 Ga. App. 198, 514 S.E.2d 51 (1999) (reversing defendant's conviction due to trial court's failure to permit expert testimony on child interviewing techniques in a case alleging physical abuse of a child); State v. Sloan, 912 S.W.2d 592 (Mo. Ct. App. 1995) (Trial court improperly precluded defense expert testimony on faulty techniques or methods in interviewing and dealing with child witness, particularly when the prosecution elicited testimony about the experience of its witnesses in dealing

Expert testimony as to the principles behind suggestive questioning and how interviewers are able to create false reports by questioning children in a manner that is directed to obtain answers that interviewers desire is knowledge that is not within the ordinary experience of a lay juror. [The defendant] proposes that the child had been exposed to leading questioning and may have changed her account of the incident accordingly. Whether this happened is a question for the jury to decide, but how this may have happened should be addressed by a witness who is qualified to explain the process.[496]

Another Wisconsin court has suggested that "it may be an erroneous exercise of discretion to deny an indigent defendant's request for permission to hire an expert for testimony on the issue of suggestive interview techniques used with a young child witness" when the defendant demonstrated a particularized need for such expert testimony.[497]

with children); State v. Sargent, 144 N.H. 103, 738 A.2d 351 (1999) (reversing defendant's conviction and finding defendant presented sufficient evidence of improper interview techniques to warrant defendant's proposed testimony on suggestiveness of interviews); State v. Gersin, 76 Ohio St. 3d 491, 668 N.E.2d 486 (1996) (Ohio Supreme Court holds that "a defendant in a child sexual abuse case may present testimony as to the proper protocol for interviewing child victims regarding their abuse. . . . Special interviewing processes are necessary to get information from child victims, who are often immature, inarticulate, frightened, and confused about the abuse they have received. Most jurors lack the knowledge of accepted practices in interviewing child victims, and expert testimony on the issue is therefore admissible."); State v. Ungerer, 1996 Ohio App. LEXIS 2947 (June 5, 1996) (reversing defendant's conviction, in part, for court's failure to allow defendant to present expert testimony on interview techniques used in case); State v. Wigg, 2005 VT 91, 889 A.2d 233, 2005 Vt. LEXIS 170 (2005) (concluding "categorical exclusion" of defendant's expert testimony on how interviews of complainant failed to satisfy the scientifically-suggested protocol for accurate interviewing of children was error but harmless); State v. St. George, 252 Wis. 2d 499, 643 N.W.2d 777 (2002) (reversing defendant's conviction because of trial court's exclusion of the testimony of defendant's expert witness about recantation, and interview techniques denied the defendant his constitutional right to present evidence central to his defense. The court noted:

Second, Dr. Stonefeld's testimony was relevant to a material issue in this case: the credibility of Kayla and the defendant. Indeed credibility was central to both the State's prosecution and the defendant's claim of innocence. Both the defendant and Kayla took the stand and denied the alleged sexual contact. In order to succeed in the prosecution, the State had to introduce Kayla's contradictory out-of-court statements and attempt to show why her statements accusing the defendant were more reliable than those denying he assaulted her. The State had to explain why her answers would change depending on the circumstances under which the statements were made.

State v. St. George, 252 Wis. 2d 499, 531, 643 N.W.2d 777, 790 (2002); State v. Wortman, 191 Wis. 2d 362, 530 N.W.2d 70 (1995) (error was harmless due to weight of evidence against the defendant). *See also* State v. Willis, 151 Wash. 2d 255, 264, 87 P.3d 1164, 1168 (2004) (finding that generally expert testimony on interviewing techniques of children is admissible but that the facts of this case did not support the expert testimony since child's statements were made before the possible tainted interviewing techniques).

[496] State v. Wortman, 191 Wis. 2d 362, 530 N.W.2d 70 (1995).

[497] State v. Kirschbaum, 195 Wis. 2d 11, 25–26, 535 N.W.2d 462, 467, *review denied*, 537 N.W.2d 591 (1995).

Another court has suggested, after reversing defendant's convictions on other grounds, that the trial court utilize traditional yardsticks for the admissibility of expert testimony in deciding whether expert testimony on interviewing techniques should be admissible, such as: 1) whether the testimony will assist the trier of fact to understand the evidence or determine a fact in issue, 2) whether the issue requires scientific, technical, or specialized knowledge not generally within the knowledge of the average juror, 3) whether the testimony is based on data or facts of a type reasonably relied upon by experts in the field, 4) the probative value of the testimony weighed against the possible prejudice or confusion by admitting the testimony, and 5) whether the testimony invades the province of the jury.[498] The age of the complainant and the quantity of proof may be other factors to consider in admitting expert testimony on suggestive questioning. One court that reversed a defendant's sexual assault conviction because of the trial court's preclusion of expert testimony on interviewing techniques of the child complainants[499] upheld the preclusion of such testimony in another case when the victims were older, lessening their susceptibility to suggestion and were not "double-learned" during interviews.[500] Expert testimony on interviewing techniques employed with a child witness may be particularly relevant when the prosecution has "clothed" its experts with expertise in dealing with children.[501]

Once a court accepts that expert testimony is appropriate as to interview procedures, the scope of that testimony must be defined. One court allowed an expert to testify to general procedures in interviewing sexual abuse complainants, but precluded her opinions with respect to the validity and reliability of the interviews conducted in the case because she had "very little first-hand experience working with sexually-abused children."[502] This seems to be consistent with decisions following the *Daubert* and post-*Daubert* decisions concerning the admissibility and reliability of expert testimony. Another court permitted general testimony on the proper interview techniques with child sexual assault complainants but precluded the expert's comments on the specific questions used during the interview, since it would appear an inappropriate comment on the credibility of the child as a result of the interview procedures.[503] A court may reject expert testimony on the susceptibility of children to suggestion if there is no foundation of general reliability or acceptance of the expert's theories.[504] One federal circuit

---

[498] State v. Jones, 1994 Tenn. Crim. App. LEXIS 587 (Sept. 15, 1994).

[499] State v. Sloan, 912 S.W.2d 592 (Mo. Ct. App. 1995).

[500] State v. Biezer, 947 S.W.2d 540 (Mo. Ct. App. 1997).

[501] State v. Sloan, 912 S.W.2d 592, 596–97 (Mo. Ct. App. 1995).

[502] State v. Steffes, 887 P.2d 1196, 1205 (Mont. 1994).

[503] Commonwealth v. Allen, 40 Mass. App. Ct. 458, 463, 665 N.E.2d 105, 109, *review denied*, 423 Mass. 1104, 667 N.E.2d 1159 (1996).

[504] Nelson v. State, No. A-6358, No. 4147, 1999 Alas. App. LEXIS 130 (Nov. 10, 1999) (upholding trial court's denial of a taint hearing since defendant did not establish consensus or acceptance in scientific community of defense experts' opinions); People v. Johnston, 273 A.D.2d 514,

court of appeals notes that the expert "may explain to the jury the dangers of implanted memory and suggestive practices when interviewing or questioning child witnesses, but may not opine as to a child witness's credibility."[505]

It should also be remembered that the issue of the interviewing techniques utilized with children can also be developed through cross-examination of investigators or interviewers involved in the investigation and interview of the child complainants.[506]

§ 11.41　Suggestiveness in interviewing and right to pre-trial taint hearing or competency hearing.

Some courts hold that the issue of suggestiveness in the investigatory interviews of children requires a pretrial suggestibility "taint" hearing.[507] When the

---

709 N.Y.S.2d 230, *appeal denied*, 95 N.Y.2d 935, 744 N.E.2d 148, 721 N.Y.S.2d 612 (2000) (upholding trial court's rejection of defendant's expert testimony on children's susceptibility to suggestive interrogation on grounds that subject matter was within jurors' common knowledge and experience and "on the ground that such opinions had not received general acceptance in field of psychology"); People v. Kanani, 272 A.D.2d 186, 709 N.Y.S.2d 505, *appeal denied*, 95 N.Y.2d 935, 744 N.E.2d 148, 721 N.Y.S.2d 612 (2000); Salazar v. State, 127 S.W.3d 355 (Tex. Ct. App. 2004) (finding defendant's expert's testimony on evaluating interviewing techniques of children, using "content-based interview analysis" to address suggestiveness of interviews was not admissible and subject to *Daubert* analysis, because defendant did not establish its general acceptance and expert's opinions were also not sufficiently tied to case, and potential rate of error was great).

[505] United States v. Rouse, 111 F.3d 561, 571 (8th Cir. 1997) (*en banc*). *See also* Morris v. Burnett, 319 F.3d 1254, 1269 (10th Cir. 2003) (noting that appeals court may have permitted cross-examination of investigator concerning investigative and interview techniques, but error was not reversible since questions were of marginal relevance).

[506] Timmons v. State, 584 N.E.2d 1108, 1113 (Ind. 1992); Pendleton v. Commonwealth, 83 S.W.3d 522, 525–26 (Ky. 2002); People v. Hudy, 73 N.Y.2d 40, 535 N.E.2d 250, 538 N.Y.S.2d 197 (1988) (reversing defendant's conviction due to trial court's failure to permit cross-examination of investigating officers concerning the manner in which complainants were first questioned); State v. Leak, 1998 Ohio App. LEXIS 1654 (Mar. 27, 1998) (The court held that Ohio does not provide for a pretrial hearing as in New Jersey, but that the issue of suggestive or coercive interviews can be approached through testimony on proper interview techniques or cross-examination. But, the court noted:

> "The practical difficulty in following this approach lies in the fact that the rules of discovery ordinarily do not extend to interview technique information. Absent voluntary disclosure by the prosecutor, a defendant's only alternative is to proceed by subpoena, witness by witness, to learn what happened. The court may cut this effort off as a mere fishing expedition, absent some evidence that the statements that the witness related were the product of coercive or suggestive interview techniques. That is the same threshold showing required in *Michaels*. The only real difference is that it is conducted during the trial, before the jury, rather than pretrial before the court. However, that creates a risk of prejudice that some defendants may not wish to endure."

State v. Leak, 1998 Ohio App. LEXIS 1654, at *7–8 (Mar. 27, 1998)).

[507] *See, e.g.*, United States v. Cabral, 43 M.J. 808 (A.F.C.C.A. 1996), *aff'd*, 47 M.J. 268 (C.A.A.F.

proof is that a child did not know what a "secret touch" was until the interviewer told her, that the interviewer helped the child to remember "things" and otherwise planted sexual information in a child's mind, a defendant may be entitled to a hearing on whether the child's testimony has been improperly influenced.[508] Without making a "non-speculative" threshold showing of suggestiveness, a defendant may not be entitled to a pretrial hearing on interview techniques of a child.[509]

Some courts hold that when sufficient evidence of suggestiveness or tainting of a child's testimony is presented, a competency hearing should be held rather than a pretrial taint hearing.[510] The defendant, under this approach, is not entitled

1997); United States v. Geiss, 30 M.J. 678 (A.F.C.M.R. 1990), *review denied*, 32 M.J. 45 (C.M.A. 1990) (both courts holding that evidence of suggestive or coercive interviewing went to the credibility of the child's testimony and not admissibility); State v. Michaels, 136 N.J. 299, 320–21, 642 A.2d 1372, 1383 (1994); People v. Michael M., 162 Misc. 2d 803, 618 N.Y.S.2d 171 (Sup. Ct. 1994).

[508] State v. Carol, 89 Wash. App. 77, 91–92, 948 P.2d 837, 845 (1997).

[509] Commonwealth v. Allen, 40 Mass. App. Ct. 458, 462, 665 N.E.2d 105, 108, *review denied*, 423 Mass. 1104, 667 N.E.2d 1159 (1996); People v. Wolff, 2002 Mich. App. LEXIS 2307 (Dec. 27, 2002) (holding defendant did not offer sufficient proof to trigger a pretrial inquiry into suggestive interviewing); State v. Michaels, 136 N.J. 299, 320, 642 A.2d 1372, 1383 (1994) (holding that defendant is required to offer "some evidence" that the complainant's statements were the product of suggestive or coercive questioning; then the prosecution must show by clear and convincing evidence the reliability of the child's statements); People v. Nickel, 14 A.D.3d 869, 788 N.Y.S.2d 274, *appeal denied*, 4 N.Y.3d 834, 829 N.E.2d, 682, 796 N.Y.S.2d 89 (2005) (noting that even though there is no specific authority for a pretrial taint hearing, court may order one if "non-speculative showing of any undue suggestion" is made); People v. Kemp, 251 A.D.2d 1072, 674 N.Y.S.2d 525, *appeal denied*, 92 N.Y.2d 900, 702 N.E.2d 849, 680 N.Y.S.2d 64 (1998); People v. Bimonte, 185 Misc. 2d 390, 712 N.Y.S.2d 829 (Crim. Ct. 2000); People v. Michael M., 162 Misc. 2d 803, 618 N.Y.S.2d 171 (Sup. Ct. 1994); State v. Willis, 113 Wash. App. 389, 395–96, 54 P.3d 184, 186–87 (2002) (while holding "that the propriety and effect of specific interview techniques on children in sex abuse cases may be a proper subject for expert testimony so long as the witness has proper qualifications, relies on generally accepted theories and the proffered testimony is helpful to the trier of fact," in this case the trial court properly precluded the defendant's expert as not "helpful" to the jury, since he was unable to give an opinion, because there was "no verbatim record" of the questioning process, acknowledged that different experts use different definitions of leading questions, that leading questions are sometimes unavoidable, that preschoolers are difficult to interview, and that there are no generally agreed techniques appropriate for all children); State v. Kirschbaum, 195 Wis. 2d 11, 535 N.W.2d 462 (1995), *review denied*, 537 N.W.2d 591 (1995).

[510] Commonwealth v. Delbridge, 578 Pa. 641, 855 A.2d 27 (2003) (Despite Pennsylvania's long standing opposition to expert's testimony in child abuse case, it may be relevant in determining competency of a child witness and "whether the child's memory has been so infected by the implantation of distorted memories so as to make it difficult for the child to distinguish fact from fantasy." Commonwealth v. Delbridge, 578 Pa. 641, 647, 855 A.2d 27, 30 (2003)); State v. Carol M.D., 97 Wash. App. 355, 983 P.2d 1165, 1166 (1999), *review pending sub nom*, State v. Doggett, 2000 Wash. LEXIS 270 (Mar. 24, 2000) ("We therefore withdraw the portion of our earlier opinion that directed the superior court to conduct a 'taint' hearing. Instead, on retrial, the court shall conduct a competency hearing to determine whether the State subjected M.D. to coercive and improper

to such a hearing when no evidence is presented of undue suggestiveness or coercion in the interview process,[511] and the court has a sufficient basis to determine competency. A defendant must justify a need for a competency hearing to address suggestiveness by clear and convincing evidence.[512] When a defendant establishes at a pretrial taint hearing that unduly suggestive interview techniques were utilized, the prosecution may be precluded from utilizing any testimony derived from the suggestive interview.

The circumstances of a crime, including the age of the victim, competence of the witness, and whether or not sexual contact is conceded, is a factor to consider in granting a taint hearing.[513] Other avenues of addressing the issue of suggestiveness may negate the necessity of a pretrial hearing. For example, reliability must be shown for statements under a residual or special child-hearsay

tactics that rendered her incapable of testifying accurately at trial about what happened to her."); English v. State, 982 P.2d 139, 146–47 (Wyo. 1999) (among reasons why court reversed defendant's conviction was failure to conduct competency hearing when there was sufficient evidence to trigger competency hearing; among factors court noted was young age of five-year-old child, circumstances in questioning of child, including fact that child's mother was acting under assumption that defendant had touched child, and use of leading questions, as well as rewards used to pressure child and fact that child's initial statements were not spontaneous).

[511] Pendleton v. Commonwealth, 83 S.W.3d 522, 525–26 (Ky. 2002) (upholding trial court's finding of child's competency without conducting a pretrial taint hearing); Commonwealth v. Adkinson, 442 Mass. 410, 420–21, 813 N.E.2d 506, 515 (2004) (finding defendant's request for hearing on suggestiveness of interviews on theory that children were not competent to testify properly denied, since judge was in position to determine competency and there was no reason to upset judge's decision); People v. Jones, 185 Misc. 2d 899, 714 N.Y.S.2d 876 (Sup. Ct. 2000); State v. Olah, 146 Ohio App. 3d 586, 2001 Ohio 1641, 767 N.E.2d 755 (2001), appeal denied, 94 Ohio St. 3d 1485, 763 N.E.2d 1184 (2002) (holding court did not abuse discretion in finding child competent and not holding a pretrial taint hearing); Alicea v. State, 13 P.3d 693, 696–98 (Wyo. 2001) (defendant failed to establish "some evidence" to warrant a competency hearing. Some evidence means a quantity more than one or a scintilla that would lead to a conclusion of incompetency. Leading questions are not necessarily improper); Ryan v. State, 988 P.2d 46, 58 (Wyo. 1999).

[512] Commonwealth v. Delbridge, 578 Pa. 641, 664, 855 A.2d 27, 40 (2003).

[513] State v. Scherzer, 301 N.J. Super. 363, 694 A.2d 196, appeal denied, 151 N.J. 466, 700 A.2d 878 (1997) (In a sexual assault prosecution based on the complainant's inability to consent, appeals court upheld denial of a suggestibility hearing.

"This is not a case, such as Michaels, where young children have given statements about extraordinary sexual acts that the defendants say never occurred. Nor, where one child's statement was used to pressure other children into molding their statements to conform to those of their peers. Here, M.G. described the same events in the Scherzer basement that Paul, a defense witness, described, with the main difference being in those aspects reflecting on the participants' state of mind. Although M.G.'s trial testimony shows that she was susceptible to leading questions, mere susceptibility is not enough to make a threshold showing that M.G.'s statements were the result of suggestive interview techniques."

State v. Scherzer, 301 N.J. Super. 363, 466, 694 A.2d 196, 246–247, appeal denied, 151 N.J. 466, 700 A.2d 878 (1997)).

exception. At a hearing to establish reliability of the hearsay statement, the court may consider the issue of suggestiveness as part of the reliability determination.[514]

§ 11.42 Expert testimony about a child's use of anatomically correct dolls and art therapy.

Some experts claim to be able to interpret a child's drawings in the same fashion that some experts claim to interpret a child's play with dolls. The theory holds that certain graphical traits involving the use of line, form, color, and content will vary from the norm in children who have been abused. In a Kentucky case, an expert testified that the child's drawings led him to believe that the child was sexually abused because of the child's depiction of the father (the defendant) as having special importance (due to his greater size and fuller form); the child's heavy shading of the father's genital area; the caption "Dad" written in the area of the father's penis; and the positioning of family members and an odd line across the father's torso.[515] On appeal, the court found the admission of this expert testimony reversible error because "art therapy has not achieved status as a recognized science for diagnostic purposes in child sexual abuse cases."[516] The court added:

> We do not hold, however, that testimony respecting art therapy is inadmissible as a matter of law — nor that it will fail to achieve general acceptance in the future in such cases. We simply hold that in this case, the Commonwealth failed to establish the necessary predicate of foundation, reliability, and relevance.[517]

If expert testimony is expected on a child's use of anatomically correct dolls, the defense may want to obtain its own expert to review the proposed evidence to support a motion to restrict its use.

Anatomically correct dolls are used both before and during trial to assist a child in communicating about sexual acts or sexual abuse.[518] Some experts have observed a child playing with anatomical dolls and have rendered an opinion, based on the child's interactions with the dolls, as to whether the child has been sexually abused. This approach is especially used with children who may be too young or too traumatized to describe what happened. It should be noted that testimony concerning such events may be challenged as hearsay[519] as well as an attempt to obtain statements from an incompetent child witness. A problem

---

[514] *In re* Dependency of A.E.P., 135 Wash. 2d 208, 230, 956 P.2d 297, 307 (1998).

[515] Staggs v. Commonwealth, 877 S.W.2d 604 (1994).

[516] Staggs v. Commonwealth, 877 S.W.2d 604, 606 (1994).

[517] Staggs v. Commonwealth, 877 S.W.2d 604, 606 (1994).

[518] *See* Chapter 14.

[519] *See* Chapter 10.

with the use of dolls, which is also discussed elsewhere in this book,[520] is that the dolls themselves may be suggestive of sexual issues, since they contain sexual organs that are not usually found on ordinary dolls, and because these sexual organs may be disproportionate in size to the rest of the doll's body. The dolls thereby may "load the dice" and increase the likelihood that sexual activities will be discussed.

Most courts will not permit expert testimony that a child has been sexually abused based on an expert's observations of that child playing with anatomically correct dolls because it has not been established that the technique is scientifically reliable or generally accepted within the psychological community.[521] Testimony that a child's handling of the dolls demonstrating what occurred or corroborates sexual abuse is improper because it is testimony that the abuse or fact occurred.[522]

Expert testimony that a child sex abuse victim's behavior with dolls — such as the way a child removed a doll's clothes or the way she hit the adult doll in the head as she was leaving the evaluation room — is consistent with that of a child sexual abuse victim and is inadmissible on the question as to whether the child was actually abused.[523]

An affidavit by psychologists in support of such a motion is set forth in Appendix G.

§ 11.43 Expert testimony on recovered or repressed memories.

The trauma of sexual abuse or assault can cause individuals to repress memory of the event until brought out through some form of psychotherapy. Memories are recovered through a variety of techniques, including hypnosis, guided imagery, and discussion of family memorabilia such as toys, report cards, or photographs. Some therapists will pose questions or interpret dreams for possible signs of abuse.

The key source of information for mental health experts dealing with repressed memory is a book entitled *The Courage to Heal*.[524] This book has been called the Bible by those working in the field of repressed memories, however, attorneys should be aware of certain questionable comments in the book such as: "If you

---

[520] *See* Chapter 14 and Appendix G for a more detailed discussion of some of the concerns involving the use of anatomical dolls.

[521] United States v. Gillespie, 852 F.2d 475 (9th Cir. 1988); *In re* Amber B. 191 Cal. App. 3d 682, 236 Cal. Rptr. 623 (1987).

[522] People v. Garrision, 187 Mich. App. 657, 468 N.W.2d 321 (1991); State v. Scherzer, 301 N.J. Super. 363, 411, 694 A.2d 196, 219, *appeal denied*, 151 N.J. 466, 700 A.2d 878 (1997) (holding that prosecution's expert should not have testified based on victim's drawings, but that error was harmless in this case).

[523] People v. Mercado, 188 A.D.2d 941, 942, 592 N.Y.S.2d 75 (1992).

[524] Ellen Bass & Laura Davis, *The Courage to Heal* (1988).

are unable to remember any specific instances like the ones mentioned above but still have a feeling that something abusive happened to you, it probably did."[525] Another statement is:

> You may think you don't have memories, but often as you begin to talk about what you do remember there emerges a constellation of feelings, reactions and recollections that add up to substantial information. To say "I was abused" you don't need the kind of recall that would stand up in a court of law. Often the knowledge that you were abused starts with a tiny feeling, and intuition . . . soon your feelings are valid. So far no one we've talked to thought she might have been abused, and then later discovered that she hadn't been. The progression always goes the other way, from suspicion to confirmation. If you think you were abused and your life shows the symptoms, then you were.[526]

As repressed memory advocates increased in number, efforts began to extend the statutes of limitations for the filing of civil cases, and some efforts are under way to alter the criminal statutes to allow prosecution for the late discovery of sexual abuse. Most states, but not all, now limit prosecution to a fixed number of years, such as five.

Wyoming has no statute of limitations for felonies. Some states have extended their sexual assault statute of limitations which facilitates prosecution based on recovered memories.[527]

Repressed memory also tends to find its way into allegations of ritualistic abuse, that is, allegations of bizarre rituals usually involving acts of sexual molestation that take place in the context of satanic cultism.

Civil lawsuits involving claims of repressed memories of sexual abuse have been brought 10, 20, and even 30 years after the fact. There are civil law decisions upholding the use of expert testimony based on repressed memories.[528] However, a witness, even in a civil lawsuit, cannot refer to his or her own repressed memories without accompanying expert testimony.[529] Repressed memories were

---

[525] Ellen Bass & Laura Davis, *The Courage to Heal*, 21 (1988).

[526] Ellen Bass & Laura Davis, *The Courage to Heal*, 22 (1988).

[527] *See, e.g.*, Colo. Rev. Stat. § 16-5-401 (6)(7) (period of time for which a person may be prosecuted for certain sexual assaults when victim is under 15 years of age extended by seven years); Ind. Code § 35-41-4-2(c) (period to prosecute certain sexual assaults extends until victim reaches 31 years of age).

[528] Hoult v. Hoult, 57 F.3d 1 (1st Cir. 1995) (expert permitted to explain plaintiff's recovered memories of sexual abuse); Isely v. Capuchin Province, 877 F. Supp. 1055 (E.D. Mich. 1995), *motion granted, claim dismissed, motion denied*, 880 F. Supp. 1138 (E.D. Mich. 1995) (expert permitted to testify about her theories of repressed memory and of plaintiff's behavior as consistent with someone suffering from repressed memory, but not whether she believes plaintiff).

[529] Shahzade v. Gregory, 923 F. Supp. 286, 287 (D. Mass. 1996); Barrett v. Hyldburg, 127 N.C. App. 95, 487 S.E.2d 803 (1997) ("Moreover, even assuming plaintiff were not to use the term 'repressed memory' and simply testified she suddenly in 1993 remembered traumatic incidents

the heart of the successful criminal prosecution in 1989 for a murder that occurred 20 years earlier. The key witness against the defendant was his daughter, who was eight years old at the time of the murder of her childhood friend, whom the daughter claimed had been sexually assaulted by the defendant. The daughter testified that she witnessed the murder, but that her memory of it had been repressed for over 20 years. However, the conviction was reversed based on the unreliability of repressed memories.[530]

Another criminal case that was heavily based upon recovered memory involved the claim of Paul Ingram of Olympia, Washington.[531] This case contains a fascinating history of allegedly repressed ritualistic abuse and should be reviewed by anyone handling a criminal charge of sexual assault based on recovered memory.

At this time there is no significant legal authority in this country permitting the use of repressed memory testimony or expert testimony concerning repressed memories. There is little, if any, data to support the theory of a traumatized person recovering his or her memory of an event well in the past. Not only must expert testimony in this area be carefully scrutinized, so should any witness whose testimony is based on recovered memories. There has been substantial literature critically reviewing the repressed memory theory.[532]

Courts have held that if a witness is to testify to a revived recovery memory, the trial judge should hold a preliminary evidentiary hearing outside the presence of the jury to determine the reliability of such testimony.[533] A witness cannot testify to his or her own memories without expert testimony to establish the reliability of such testimony. For example, a mother of a sexual abuse complainant cannot testify that her child had repressed memories of sexual abuse by the

---

from her childhood, such testimony must be accompanied by expert testimony on the subject of memory repression so as to afford the jury a basis upon which to understand the phenomenon and evaluate the reliability of testimony derived from such memories." Barrett v. Hyldburg, 127 N.C. App. 95, 101, 487 S.E.2d 803, 806 (1997)).

[530] Franklin v. Duncan, 884 F. Supp. 1435 (N.D. Cal. 1995), aff'd, 70 F.3d 75 (9th Cir. 1995). For a full discussion of the use of repressed memory in this case, see Harry N. MacLean, Once Upon a Time: A True Story of Memory, Murder and the Law (1993).

[531] The Ingram case is thoroughly chronicled in Lawrence Wright, Remembering Satan-Part I, The New Yorker, May 17, 1993, at 60 and Remembering Satan-Part II, The New Yorker, May 24, 1993, at 54. See also Lawrence Wright, Remembering Satan (1994).

[532] Elizabeth F. Loftus & Katherine Ketcham, The Myth of Repressed Memory (1994); Richard Ofshe & Ethan Watters, False Memories, Psychotherapy and Sexual Hysteria (1994); Elizabeth F. Loftus & Katherine Ketcham, Witness for the Defense (1991); Hollida Wakefield & Ralph Underwager, Uncovering Memories of Alleged Sexual Abuse: The Therapists Who Do It, in 4 Issues in Child Abuse Accusations 197-213 (1992) (surveying psychological studies in the area of recovered memory that may assist those involved in the forensic use of recovered memory).

[533] State v. Walters, 142 N.H. 239, 698 A.2d 1244 (1997); State v. Hungerford, 142 N.H. 110, 697 A.2d 916 (1997); Commonwealth v. Crawford, 452 Pa. Super. 354, 682 A.2d 323, appeal granted, 548 Pa. 625, 693 A.2d 965 (1997); State v. Quattrocchi, 681 A.2d 879 (R.I. 1996).

defendant.[534] New Hampshire's Supreme Court, in a criminal sexual assault prosecution, expresses the view that a trial court should determine the competency of a witness testifying based on a recovered repressed memory as well as the scientific reliability of the process by which the memory is recovered.[535] It noted that the testimony of a witness testifying with a recovered memory cannot be understood without the assistance of expert testimony.[536] Such a witness's memory has undergone a physiological process unlike ordinary memory with which an average juror would be familiar.[537] Such testimony must rise to the threshold level of reliability to be admissible.[538] This reliability must be as to both the witness's memory and the expert explaining the phenomenon.[539] The New Hampshire court concluded:

> Furthermore, the Court finds that the techniques used in the course of psychotherapy in both cases were highly suggestive. Because the memories in the instant cases were recovered during therapy or while the witness was engaged in therapy, we ordinarily would proceed to examine more closely the circumstances of the therapeutic environment, as discussed earlier. Our review of the memories without regard to the suggestiveness of the therapeutic process, however, convinces us that they do not pass our test of reliability. The phenomenon of recovery of repressed memories has not yet reached the point where we may perceive these particular recovered memories as reliable.[540]

If such testimony based on a revived memory is received, one might think the defense should be permitted to present expert testimony on the reliability of recovered repressed memories.

However, the Pennsylvania Supreme Court reversed the intermediate appellate court which so held and ruled that the trial court properly precluded the defendant from presenting expert testimony on repressed memory when the prosecution did not introduce expert testimony on repressed memory or argue that the witness's memory had been revived.

The American Psychological Association's Working Group on Investigation of Memories of Childhood Abuse issued an interim report summarizing its view

---

[534] *In re* State v. Kelly, 118 N.C. App. 589, 596, 456 S.E.2d 861, 868, *review denied*, 341 N.C. 422, 461 S.E.2d 764 (1995).

[535] State v. Hungerford, 142 N.H. 110, 697 A.2d 916 (1997).

[536] State v. Hungerford, 142 N.H. 110, 120, 697 A.2d 916, 921 (1997).

[537] State v. Hungerford, 142 N.H. 110, 120, 697 A.2d 916, 922 (1997).

[538] State v. Hungerford, 142 N.H. 110, 121, 697 A.2d 916, 922 (1997).

[539] State v. Hungerford, 142 N.H. 110, 121, 697 A.2d 916, 922 (1997).

[540] State v. Hungerford, 142 N.H. 110, 133, 697 A.2d 916, 929–930 (1997); Commonwealth v. Crawford, 553 Pa. 195, 718 A.2d 768 (1998) (Because the issue of revived repressed memory was never an issue that needed to be resolved, the determination of the witness's credibility was properly left to the jury. However, the decision in effect permitted a witness's testimony based upon his repressed memory of a murder.).

of the current research literature on both trauma and memory and reached four conclusions:[541]

- Most people who were sexually abused as children remember all or part of what happened to them.

- However, it is possible for memories of abuse that have been forgotten for a long time to be remembered. The mechanism(s) by which such delayed recall occur(s) is/are not currently well understood.

- It is also possible to construct convincing pseudo memories for events that never occurred. The mechanism(s) by which these pseudo memories occur(s) is/are not currently well understood.

- There are gaps in our knowledge about the processes that lead to accurate and inaccurate recollections of childhood abuse.

The APA's Board of Directors also noted that therapists "must approach questions of childhood abuse from a neutral position."[542]

A social worker may be qualified to testify to the dissociative memory loss experienced by trauma victims, which may lend to the delayed recovery and disclosure of a traumatic memory.[543] However, the same expert may not be qualified to testify how a trauma victim stores and retrieves, or disassociates a traumatic memory, because such testimony involves the physical functioning of the brain, requiring scientific and medical expertise.[544]

§ 11.44 Qualification of experts — social workers, care workers, counselors, and victim advocates.

The threshold issue in any expert testimony is whether the expert is properly qualified. The Federal Rules of Evidence state that a witness is qualified as an expert by "knowledge, skill, experience, training or education."[545] Whether a witness is qualified as an expert is a preliminary question for the court to decide.[546] There is no formal requirement that a court certify a witness as an expert.[547] Sometimes, experience alone may be sufficient to qualify a witness in the area of sexual abuse,[548] even if the expert has never testified in the subject

[541] *Working Group on Investigation of Memories of Childhood Abuse*, American Psychological Association, November 11, 1994.

[542] *Working Group on Investigation of Memories of Childhood Abuse*, American Psychological Association, November 11, 1994.

[543] Commonwealth v. Frangipane, 433 Mass. 527, 533–34, 744 N.E.2d 25, 31 (2001).

[544] Commonwealth v. Frangipane, 433 Mass. 527, 535-36, 744 N.E.2d 25, 31-32 (2001).

[545] Fed. R. Evid. 702.

[546] United States v. Stifel, 433 F.2d 431, 438 (6th Cir. 1970), *cert. denied*, 401 U.S. 994 (1971).

[547] People v. Gordon, 202 A.D.2d 166, 608 N.Y.S.2d 192, *appeal denied*, 83 N.Y.2d 911, 637 N.E.2d 284, 614 N.Y.S.2d 393 (1994) (*citing* United States v. Bartley, 855 F.2d 547, 552 (8th Cir. 1988)).

[548] People v. Turner, 241 Ill. App. 3d 236, 608 N.E.2d 906 (1993).

area, but has experience.[549] While not often seen, it is possible that an expert may derive knowledge solely from reading, without any experience at all.[550] Furthermore, some individuals who might not qualify as experts may be qualified to give an opinion on patterns of behavior in abuse as a lay witness under Federal Rule of Evidence 701, such as a caseworker with extensive experience.

An expert may be precluded from testifying, although experienced in the subject matter of the expert opinion, if he has not remained current on developments in the field.[551]

The expert need not necessarily be licensed in the state in which they are testifying to qualify as an expert witness.[552]

Furthermore, some individuals who might not qualify as experts may be qualified to give an opinion on patterns of behavior in abuse as a lay witness under Federal Rule of Evidence 701, such as a caseworker with extensive experience.[553]

While opposing counsel may want to stipulate to an expert's qualifications, particularly experts who are well qualified, it is best to let the jury hear the expert's qualifications. Areas to consider in qualifying the expert in a sexual assault case are:

(1) Education, including training or field placement dealing with children or sexual assault;

(2) Thesis work/licensing/publications/employment history;

(3) Specialty and areas of expertise;

(4) Course of employment;

(5) Professional organizations;

(6) Professional conduct with offenders or victims, including number seen or treated;

---

[549] State v. Wommack, 770 So. 2d 365 (La. Ct. App. 2000) (permitting oral surgeon to testify to bite-mark evidence based on his experience and training even though he had never testified as expert in the field).

[550] I McCormick on Evidence, § 13, at 54–5 (4th ed. 1992).

[551] United States v. Taylor, 154 F.3d 675, 683 (7th Cir.), *cert. denied*, 525 U.S. 1060 (1998) (precluding defense expert from testifying regarding polygraph test because he had not remained current on developments in polygraph testing nor made any effort to update or refine where he found his technique).

[552] Mitchell v. Mitchell, 830 So. 2d 755, 757–59 (Ala. Civ. App. 2002) (holding psychologist need not be licensed in state to testify as an expert witness).

[553] Hall v. State, 611 So. 2d 915, 919 (Miss. 1992). *See also* Farley v. People, 746 P.2d 956 (Colo. 1987) (permitting opinion as a lay witness from rape counselor that victim's reactions were consistent with having been raped since the opinion was based upon the witness's observations and experience, and not just information provided by the victim). *Contra* State v. Bowman, 84 N.C. App. 238, 352 S.E.2d 437 (1987) (police officer not qualified as lay witness to give opinion that child could not fantasize about sex).

(7) Familiarity with research and developments, including conferences or training sessions attended; and

(8) Prior experience in offering testimony in court, listing those courts in which the expert has been accepted as a witness.

However, the fact that an expert has qualified as a witness on a previous occasion does not automatically qualify that expert as a witness in subsequent cases.[554]

It has been suggested that an expert testifying in the field of child sexual abuse should possess the following qualifications: (1) extensive first-hand experience with sexually abused and nonsexually-abused children; (2) thorough and up-to-date knowledge of the professional literature on child sexual abuse; and (3) objectivity and neutrality about individual cases as required of other experts.[555] Under these criteria, an expert who has not worked with nonsexually-abused children would be disqualified as an expert on the theory that without such experience the expert's opinions on symptoms or behavior of abused individuals would not have context or be based upon a standard.[556]

An expert should be tendered as an expert and qualified in the specific field.[557] Where the prosecution offered expert testimony from a forensic psychiatrist that a defendant's behavior was inconsistent with that of someone suffering from the "battered-woman syndrome," it was error to receive such testimony when the psychiatrist admitted that he was not an expert on the subject of battered women.[558] Lack of experience with sexual assault victims may disqualify a witness as expert.[559] Social workers with master's degrees,[560] child abuse

---

[554] Englehart v. Jeep Corp., 122 Ariz. 256, 594 P.2d 510 (1979).

[555] State v. Scheffelman, 250 Mont. 334, 342, 820 P.2d 1293, 1298 (1991) (*citing* John Meyers, *Expert Testimony in Child Sexual Abuse Litigation*, 68 Neb. L. Rev. 1, 12 (1989)).

[556] State v. Scheffelman, 250 Mont. 334, 342, 820 P.2d 1293, 1298 (1991).

[557] State v. Hall, 330 N.C. 808, 412 S.E.2d 883 (1992).

[558] People v. Barrett, 189 A.D.2d 879, 592 N.Y.S.2d 766 (1993).

[559] Prickett v. State, 220 Ga. App. 244, 246, 469 S.E.2d 371, 374 (1996) (counselor not qualified to testify in area of rape trauma syndrome or post-traumatic stress disorder since there was no showing witness had "special knowledge" or expertise in these areas).

[560] United States v. Raya, 45 M.J. 251 (C.A.A.F. 1996) (social worker qualified to be expert in the field of rape trauma); United States v. Peel, 29 M.J. 235 (C.M.A. 1989). *But see* State v. Willis, 256 Kan. 837, 888 P.2d 839 (1995) (master's level social worker not qualified to give expert testimony concerning Rape Trauma Syndrome or Post-Traumatic Stress Disorder; such testimony must be provided by a witness specially trained in the field of psychiatry; State v. Willis, 256 Kan. 837, 846–847, 888 P.2d 839, 845 (1995)); *Ex parte Hill*, 553 So. 2d 1138 (Ala. 1989); State v. Spigarolo, 210 Conn. 359, 556 A.2d 112, *cert. denied*, 493 U.S. 933 (1989); Siharath v. State, 246 Ga. App. 736, 541 S.E.2d 71 (2000) (holding witness with masters degree in child and family studies and social work, and with experience in field of child sexual abuse qualified in area of forensic evaluation); Commonwealth v. Frangipane, 433 Mass. 527, 744 N.E.2d 25 (2001) (holding masters level social worker qualified to testify to dissociative memory loss experienced by trauma victims, which may lead to the delayed recovery and disclosure of a traumatic memory, but *not* qualified to testify to how a trauma victim stores and retrieves, or dissociates a traumatic memory,

caseworkers,[561] individuals with a master's degree in counseling,[562] master's degree in behavioral sciences or human services,[563] rape crisis counselors,[564] outreach advocates who work with victims of domestic violence,[565] and victim services counselors[566] have all been accepted as expert witnesses. A "non-certified" social worker is not necessarily precluded from testifying as an expert.[567] However, some courts do not permit social workers to testify to medical diagnosis or theories such as the rape trauma syndrome[568] or child sexual abuse accommodation syndrome.[569] A teacher of human sexuality who provides

because such testimony involves the physical functioning of the brain, requiring scientific and medical expertise); Hall v. State, 611 So. 2d 915, 920 (Miss. 1992); State v. Carpenter, 147 N.C. App. 386, 393–94, 556 S.E.2d 316, 321–22 (2001), *cert. denied*, 536 U.S. 983 (2002) (holding masters level social worker with experience training in field of child sexual abuse, qualified to render expert testimony explaining that delayed and incomplete disclosures are not unusual in child abuse cases and complainants may continue to associate with an alleged abuser); Dennis v. State, 178 S.W.3d 172 (Tex. Ct. App. 2005) (master's level social worker, with 35 years of practice, working primarily with abused children, qualified to render expert testimony); State v. Hicks, 148 Vt. 459, 461–62, 535 A.2d 776 (1987); Taylor v. Commonwealth, 21 Va. App. 557, 466 S.E.2d 118 (1996).

[561] State v. Guidry, 647 So. 2d 502, 508 (La. Ct. App. 1994) (mental health counselor with Master's degree in psychology and experience counseling sexually-abused children qualified as an expert in the field of counseling abused children); People v. Foreman, 161 Mich. App. 14, 23–24, 410 N.W.2d 289 (1987).

[562] State v. French, 233 Mont. 364, 760 P.2d 86 (1988).

[563] Mulvihill v. State, 177 S.W.3d 409 (Tex. Ct. App. 2005) (noting expert's experience and training with sexual abuse victims).

[564] People v. Page, 166 A.D.2d 886, 560 N.Y.S.2d 546 (1990), *appeal denied*, 77 N.Y.2d 842, 659, 567 N.Y.S.2d 210 (1991); People v. Whitehead, 142 A.D.2d 745, 531 N.Y.S.2d 48 (1988); Butler v. State, 892 S.W.2d 138 (Tex. Crim. App. 1994).

[565] State v. Cardany, 35 Conn. App. 728, 646 A.2d 291, *appeal denied*, 231 Conn. 942, 653 A.2d 823 (1994).

[566] R.D. v. State, 706 So. 2d 770 (Ala. Crim. App. 1997); State v. Isenberg, 148 N.C. App. 29, 557 S.E.2d 568 (2001) (licensed professional counselor, with masters in education and experience with children with behavioral problems related to sexual abuse, qualified to give expert testimony on behaviors of sexually-abused children).

[567] Harnett v. State, 38 S.W.3d 650 (Tex. Ct. App. 2000) (Licensing in and of itself does not determine whether a witness may render an expert opinion. Thus, a teacher with a degree in special education, who works with other professionals such as psychologists, psychiatrists, and medical doctors to assess intellectual and physical abilities can testify to a complainant's cognitive and mental capacity to connect to or understand the consequences of a sexual act and utilize psychological testing as part of that assessment); State v. Kelley, 1 P.3d 546, 549–51 (Utah 2000).

[568] Kan. Stat. § 65-6319 was amended to permit certain licensed clinical social workers to diagnose and treat mental disorders specified in diagnostic and statistical manual of mental disorder). *See* also Welch v. State, 270 Kan. 229, 13 P.3d 882 (2000); State v. Willis, 256 Kan. 837, 888 P.2d 839 (1995) (reversing defendant's conviction due to social worker testifying about post-traumatic stress disorder).

[569] Perez v. State, 25 S.W.3d 830 (Tex. Ct. App. 2000) (reversing defendant's conviction due to social worker testifying about pediatric and psychiatric theories of child sex abuse accommodation syndrome).

mental health counseling to victims and offenders may be qualified to provide expert testimony on the reactions of sex abuse victims, such as their tendency to delay disclosure.[570]

§ 11.45 Qualifications of physicians.

A physician with a background in sexual abuse may also be qualified to provide opinions on the behaviors or traits of sexual abuse of victims.[571]

This may allow the attorney to call one fewer expert and avoid possible contradiction of opinions, as well as the additional expense of a second expert. The qualifications of physicians and nurses, as well as limits in testimony, is discussed in Chapter 12.[572]

§ 11.46 Qualifications of police officers as experts.

Many jurisdictions have also recognized that police officers may be qualified by virtue of their training and experience to provide expert testimony concerning the reactions of sexual abuse victims.[573]

---

[570] State v. DeCosta, 146 N.H. 405, 772 A.2d 340 (2001).

[571] United States v. Stroh, 46 M.J. 643 (A.F.C.C.A. 1997) (pediatrician permitted to testify not only about child hymenal injuries but also that child exhibited common behavior of sexually-abused children in the six-to 11-year-old group such as delayed reporting, recurrent nightmares, bed-wetting, low self-esteem, poor school performance, antisocial behavior, and excessive masturbation); People v. Carney, 222 A.D.2d 1006, 636 N.Y.S.2d 524 (1995), *appeal denied*, 88 N.Y.2d 877, 668 N.E.2d 422, 645 N.Y.S.2d 451 (1996) (permitting a pediatrician whose training and experience were in evaluating and treating patients for physical and sexual abuse to testify as an expert); State v. Bowman, 84 N.C. App. 238, 352 S.E.2d 437 (1987) (physician permitted to testify as to child's delayed reporting of abuse); State v. Huntington, 216 Wis. 2d 671, 575 N.W.2d 268 (1998) (physician permitted to explain complainant's difficulties in school, delay in reporting and difficulty providing specific dates).

[572] *See* Chapter 12.

[573] People v. Dunnahoo, 152 Cal. App. 3d 561, 577, 199 Cal. Rptr. 796, 804 (1984); Condon v. State, 597 A.2d 7, 11 (Del. 1991) (permitting police officer to testify about victims' gradual disclosure of sexual abuse); People v. Turner, 241 Ill. App. 3d 236, 608 N.E.2d 906 (1993) (citing the Illinois statute on admissibility of the rape trauma syndrome, referred to in §§ 11.11–11.13); Commonwealth v. Richardson, 423 Mass. 180, 667 N.E.2d 257 (1996) (police officer's extensive training, education and experience in investigating allegations of sexual assault and interviewing children qualified him as an expert); State v. Sandberg, 406 N.W.2d 506, 511 (Minn. 1987); State v. Logan, 1996 Ohio App. LEXIS 4394 (Oct. 3, 1996), *appeal dismissed*, 77 Ohio St. 3d 1544, 674 N.E.2d 1184 (1997) (police detective qualified to testify to general characteristics of approximately two hundred rape victims to be interviewed); State v. Auxter, 1994 Ohio App. LEXIS 5622 (Dec. 16, 1994) (court properly admitted the testimony of a former police officer with experience in sexual abuse investigations and currently employed as a director of a juvenile detention center to testify on why it was normal for juvenile victims to initially deny acts of molestation); State v. McMillan, 69 Ohio App. 3d 36, 47, 590 N.E.2d 23, 30 (1990); Scadden v. State, 732 P.2d 1036, 1046–47 (Wyo. 1987). *Contra* State v. Bowman, 84 N.C. App. 238, 352 S.E.2d 437 (1987) (police officer not qualified as lay witness to give opinion that child could not fantasize about sex).

Police officers are often permitted to interpret facts and situations which are not within the knowledge or experience of the average juror.[574] Thus, law enforcement witnesses are permitted to interpret behaviors, such as the "innocent" or legal collection of photographs of children or the words and expressions used in those accused of exploiting children.[575] Sometimes, the police officer will give an "opinion" without being considered an expert by the court. For example, a police officer is permitted to give an opinion as to what is contained on a defendant's hard drive; his use of the word "examined" does not necessarily convert the witness to an expert.[576] A police officer may also provide lay witness testimony about the characteristics of battered women.[577] A police officer may also be qualified to give a lay witness or expert opinion on the age of a child in a photograph or image.[578]

§ 11.47 Sample qualification of police officer as expert.

As noted in the previous section, police officers may qualify as expert witnesses. The following is an excerpt from one case where a police officer was qualified as an expert and demonstrates how easily an expert can be qualified.[579] The witness's training and experience can be developed further if necessary and to show the jury the witness's background, even if not required to be legally qualified as an expert.

Q. The prosecutor: Also, with respect to your training, can you tell us something about your training as a sexual assault officer?

A. The witness: Yes, sir. In 1994, I began investigating sexual assaults until 1998, at which time I was promoted. Then I resumed sexual assault investigations in 2001.

Q. The prosecutor: Do you have any specialized training, or is it all on-the-job training?

A. The witness: I've taken numerous seminars and courses on sexual assault, child sexual assault, and my own experience.

Q. The prosecutor: As I understand it, you've taken courses specifically on child sexual assault?

---

[574] United States v. Harris, 192 F.3d 580 (6th Cir. 1999) ("Courts have overwhelmingly found police officers' expert testimony admissible where it will aid the jury's understanding of an area, such as drug dealing, not within the experience of the average juror." United States v. Harris, 192 F.3d 580, 598 (6th Cir. 1999), *citing* United States v. Thomas, 74 F.3d 676, 682 (6th Cir. 1996)).

[575] *See* § 11.33.

[576] Boone v. State, 811 So. 2d 402 (Miss. Ct. App. 2001). *See also*, McDonald v. State, 249 Ga. App. 1, 548 S.E.2d 361 (2001).

[577] State v. Stillday, 646 N.W.2d 557, 562–63 (Minn. Ct. App. 2002).

[578] *See* Chapter 12.

[579] Commonwealth v. Richardson, 423 Mass. 180, 183, 667 N.E.2d 257, 261 (1996).

A. The witness: Yes, sir.

Q. The prosecutor: Have you had an opportunity to investigate other allegations of child sexual assault?

A. The witness: Many.

A. [Sidebar conference.]

Q. The prosecutor: Sergeant, how many years have you been with the Sexual Assault Unit?

A. The witness: Again, from 1994 to 1998 and then from '01 until the present.

Q. The prosecutor: When did you become a sergeant detective?

A. The witness: In '01.

Q. The prosecutor: Can you tell us, what are the functions and responsibilities of a sergeant detective?

A. The witness: My responsibilities are I am the night commander. I supervise the detectives who investigate sexual assaults.

Q. The prosecutor: And how many detectives do you supervise?

A. The witness: Six.

Q. The prosecutor: Do you also still conduct investigations, yourself?

A. The witness: Yes, I do.

Q. The prosecutor: How many investigations have you conducted of alleged sexual assaults on children?

A. The witness: Hundreds.

Q. The prosecutor: During conducting those investigations, have you had an opportunity to speak with the complainants, themselves?

A. The witness: Always.

§ 11.48   Hearing to determine qualifications or propriety of expert testimony.

Counsel can request a hearing to determine the qualifications of the expert or whether the expert's opinion is proper. Sometimes a hearing may be requested under *Daubert* or *Frye*. While such a hearing may not be required, it may offer certain tactical advantages beyond possibly precluding the expert's testimony. The court may limit the extent of the expert's opinion, minimizing the potential damage of the testimony. It also allows an attorney to be better prepared to cross-examine the expert since the attorney knows exactly some, if not all, of the expert's testimony. It also allows counsel to assess the expert's demeanor in deciding the most effective cross-examination approach.

§ 11.49   Required level of certainty in expert opinion.

Traditionally, it was felt that expert opinion had to be rendered with reasonable certainty and that the failure to do so rendered such testimony inadmissible. Reasonable degree of certainty is usually defined as more probably than not and more than mere speculation, possibility, or surmise. However, the more contemporary trend is that the verbal straightjacket of reasonable degree of certainty is no longer required for the admission of expert testimony. The Federal Rules of Evidence do not require that expert opinions be made with any particular degree of certainty or probability. Thus, the opinion that hairs found on an article connected with a crime "could have come" from the defendant is admissible, with the lack of certainty going to the weight of the testimony.[580] All that is required to satisfy the accepted standard of reliability is a reasonable degree of confidence in the expert's conclusion.[581] The failure of an expert to phrase an opinion in terms of reasonable scientific certainty does not deprive that opinion of evidentiary value, even if phrased in terms of "possible," "could," or "strong suspicion."[582] However, when an expert expresses opinion testimony in terms of "possibility," "could be," "likely," "I think," or "suggests," it is a lightning rod for cross-examination on the witness' uncertainty and the opinion's lack of reliability.

---

[580] United States v. Cyphers, 553 F.2d 1064, 1072 (7th Cir. 1977), *cert. denied*, 434 U.S. 843 (1977); State v. Riley, 568 N.W.2d 518 (Minn. 1997) (upholding ballistic expert's testimony that to a reasonable degree of scientific certainty a particular handgun was the source of shell casings, even though expert could not conclusively state that shells could not have come from any other gun).

[581] Matott v. Ward, 48 N.Y.2d 455, 399 N.E.2d 532, 423 N.Y.S.2d 645 (1979).

[582] United States v. Cyphers, 553 F.2d 1064 (7th Cir. 1977), *cert. denied*, 434 U.S. 843 (1977) ("Alternatively, defendants argue that the testimony was inadmissible because it was not 'to' a reasonable scientific certainty. As we understand their rather opaque argument, defendants appear to be saying that an expert's opinion testimony must be expressed in terms of a reasonable scientific certainty in order to be admissible. There is no such requirement." *Id.* at 1072.); People v. Jackson, 18 Cal. App. 3d 504, 95 Cal. Rptr. 919 (1971); Floray v. State, 720 A.2d 1132 (Del. 1998); State v. Stribley, 532 N.W.2d 170 (Iowa Ct. App. 1995) (Doctor's testimony that a "notch" he observed in the posterior of child's hymen indicated "strong suspicion" of trauma to hymen was admissible opinion even though doctor could not state opinion with reasonable degree of medical certainty since Iowa law permits expert opinions as to probable or merely possible causation); People v. Forsha, 151 A.D.2d 875, 542 N.Y.S.2d 847 (1989) (pathologist's testimony on child's cause of death was admissible even though opinion was not stated "with expression of words with reasonable medical certainty"); State v. Sibert, 98 Ohio App. 3d 412, 648 N.E.2d 861 (1994) (expert's testimony phrased in terms of his "professional opinion" can demonstrate sufficient certainty of his conclusions); State v. Warness, 77 Wash. App. 636, 893 P.2d 665 (1995) (Odontologist's testimony in rape case was that bite mark was "consistent with" complainant's assertion that she bit defendant. "Expert testimony couched in terms of 'could have,' 'possible,' or 'similar' is uniformly admitted at trial. The lack of certainty goes to the weight to be given the testimony, not to its admissibility. This is so, in part, because the scientific process involved often allows no more certain testimony." State v. Warness, 77 Wash. App. 636, 643, 893 P.2d 665, 669 (1995), *quoting* State v. Lord, 117 Wn. 2d 829, 822 P.2d 177 (1991), *cert. denied*, 506 U.S. 856, 113 S.Ct. 164 (1992)).

§ 11.50   Source of experts.

Traditional sources of experts in the field of sexual abuse and sexual assault include legal publications, especially jury verdict reporters such as the Jury Verdict Research Reporter (which reports on civil cases and includes the experts used by the parties); individuals who have testified as experts in cases in which similar issues have been raised; authors of publications in the field; and referrals from fellow attorneys. With the advent of computerized legal research libraries such as WESTLAW and LEXIS, it is also possible to search for similar cases in other states and jurisdictions in which experts have testified. LEXIS also contains specific libraries relating to experts and medical issues. The Association of Trial Lawyers of America (ATLA) also provides a list of experts in particular areas.[583] Another source of experts is brochures for continuing legal education programs and seminars in the field of sexual assault. If an expert is located but is not available, he or she may be able to refer the attorney to other expert witnesses in the field.

There are also nontraditional sources of experts, such as local counseling agencies that deal with victims and offenders. Also, there are therapists and counselors who do not deal exclusively with sex crimes victims and offenders but who have gained experience in treating these patients or clients. These include alcohol and substance abuse counselors, social service counselors, counselors for the homeless, counselors for runaways, and jail counselors. Another possible nontraditional source of experts on mental health issues related to sexual assault litigation are churches and houses of worship. A parish priest may be able to testify from his experience in dealing with victims or offenders on highly relevant issues. Just like an automobile mechanic who may be more qualified than an automotive engineer to provide testimony about a particular vehicle, priest and counselors who deal first-hand with victims and offenders may offer more impressive testimony on relevant mental health issues than an expert from academia.

If an expert is called who is actually treating a victim or defendant or who has been consulted by the party, it opens the door to the release of all treatment records of the expert, as well as to cross-examination concerning communications by the victim or defendant.[584] The potential consequences of waiving the privilege in this situation should be carefully evaluated. It may also affect the therapist-patient relationship to have the therapist testify fully in open court. Submitting records to another expert for review is an option.

---

[583] Association of Trial Lawyers of America, 1050 31st St., N.W., Washington, D.C. 20007-4499; telephone (800) 424–2725.

[584] *See, e.g.*, United States v. Alvarez, 519 F.2d 1036, 1045–46 (3d Cir. 1975) (holding government can not obtain defendant's pretrial communications to psychiatrist consulted by defendant unless defendant calls psychiatrist as witness). *See, e.g.*, State v. Scheffelman, 250 Mont. 334, 820 P.2d 1293 (1991) (holding rape victim's records should be reviewed by court if expert testifies that victim shared characteristics consistent with sexual abuse victims).

§ 11.51   Qualifications of prosecutors as experts.

One court has allowed an assistant district attorney who handles rape cases to explain the lack of physical injury to a rape victim to rebut defense expert testimony of a physician that usually there is some physical evidence or physical injury as a result of a rape.[585] A prosecutor may be able to testify to the reactions and demeanor of a witness, but not whether the witness is credible and accurate when he testifies at a preliminary hearing, and when the defendant places the witness' veracity in question and the witness testifies that the reason he gave "semi-true" testimony at the preliminary hearing was the result of fear.[586] But a prosecutor testifying in a sexual assault case on any issue relating to credibility of a witness is likely to raise the issue of a member of the prosecution team or office unfairly bolstering the credibility of a witness.[587]

§ 11.52   Court-appointed experts to assist defendant.

The Supreme Court of the United States has held that an indigent defendant whose sanity at the time of an offense is "seriously in question" must be provided

---

[585] State v. Washington, 229 Kan. 47, 622 P.2d 986 (1981) (noting also potential prejudice in allowing a prosecuting attorney to testify in a criminal proceeding).

[586] Commonwealth v. Randall, 2000 Pa. Super. 212, 758 A.2d 669, *appeal denied*, 2000 Pa. LEXIS 2707, 764 A.2d 1067 (2000).

[587] State v. Baron, 80 Haw. 107, 905 P.2d 613 (1995). The court noted:

> In this case, the gist of Prosecutor's testimony focused on her professional experience with sexual assault victims. She testified about the interview process with alleged sexual assault victims, and specifically, that it is common for the alleged victims to disclose additional facts during the interview process. Further, she testified that she made the decision as to whether charges should be filed and that she decided to present the case to the grand jury. It is clear that Prosecutor's testimony was rendered in her professional capacity as a deputy prosecuting attorney and that her testimony no doubt supported the complainant's testimony.
>
> The presentation of Prosecutor's testimony exceeded the bounds of responsible prosecutorial conduct. As the initial prosecutor who reviewed the case, she testified that she made the determination to charge Appellant. Therefore, by bringing charges, she impliedly found the complainant's allegations to be truthful. As this case was a case that concerned the credibility of the complainant, the testimony of Prosecutor unfairly influenced the jury.
>
> Prosecutors are subject to certain prohibitions as officers of the court. It is patently unfair for the prosecution to call as a witness another member of the prosecuting team, albeit not the trial attorney, in effect to bolster the credibility of a witness. To allow the testimony would create a combustible conflict of interest in the criminal justice system, which would be impossible to contain. Consequently, we hold that the trial court abused its discretion by not precluding the testimony of Prosecutor. The prejudice to Appellant is patently clear and warrants a reversal in this case. We therefore vacate the guilty verdicts and remand the case to the circuit court for a new trial.

State v. Baron, 80 Haw. 107, 116, 905 P.2d 613, 622 (1995).

the assistance of a psychiatrist to prepare an effective defense.[588] Holding that the state must "assure that the defendant has a fair opportunity to present his defense,"[589] the Court noted that a psychiatrist, among other things, could help interpret psychological information and data for a defendant,[590] something fundamental in many sexual assault trials. The Court limited its holding to those criminal proceedings in which a defendant's mental condition is "at issue."[591] Nevertheless, expertise in psychology and mental health is at the core of many issues in sexual assault litigation, particularly in cases involving children.

Most states have a statutory provision similar to 18 U.S.C. § 3006A(e), which provides that indigent defendants shall receive the assistance of all experts "necessary for adequate representation."[592] Some provisions allow the defendant to select the expert. Nevertheless, the general rule would be that a defendant

---

[588] Ake v. Oklahoma, 470 U.S. 68, 70 (1985). *See also* People v. Lawson, 163 Ill. 2d 187, 644 N.E.2d 1172 (1994) (holding that trial court should have provided defendant with an expert in fingerprint and shoeprint analysis in light of the importance of such evidence in this capital murder prosecution).

[589] Ake v. Oklahoma, 470 U.S. 68, 76 (1985).

[590] Ake v. Oklahoma, 470 U.S. 68, 81 (1985).

[591] Ake v. Oklahoma, 470 U.S. 68, 82 (1985).

[592] 18 U.S.C. § 3006A(e):

> Services Other Than Counsel: (1) Upon request. Counsel for a person who is financially unable to obtain investigative, expert, or other services necessary for adequate representation may request them in an *ex parte* proceeding, that the services are necessary and that the person is financially unable to obtain them, the court, or the United States magistrate [United States magistrate judge] if the services are required in connection with a matter over which he has jurisdiction, shall authorize counsel to obtain the services. (2) Without prior request. (A) Counsel appointed under this section may obtain, subject to later review, investigative, expert, and other services without prior authorization if necessary for adequate representation. Except as provided in subparagraph (B) of this paragraph, the total cost of services obtained without prior authorization may not exceed $300 and expenses reasonably incurred. (B) The court, or the United States magistrate [United States magistrate judge] (if the services were rendered in a case disposed of entirely before the United States magistrate [United States magistrate judge]), may, in the interest of justice, and upon the finding that timely procurement of necessary services could not await prior authorization, approve payment for such services after they have been obtained, even if the cost of such services exceeds $300. (3) Maximum amounts. Compensation to be paid to a person for services rendered by him to a person under this subsection, or to be paid to an organization for services rendered by an employee thereof, shall not exceed $1,000, exclusive of reimbursement for expenses reasonably incurred, unless payment in excess of that limit is certified by the court, or by the United States magistrate [United States magistrate judge] if the services were rendered in connection with a case disposed of entirely before him, as necessary to provide fair compensation for services of an unusual character or duration, and the amount of the excess payment is approved by the chief judge of the circuit. The chief judge of the circuit may delegate such approval authority to an active circuit judge.

does not have the right to any expert of his or her choice and denial of expert assistance is a matter of the court's discretion.[593]

The Federal Rules permit the court on its own motion or on the motion of any party to appoint experts.[594] Under the Federal Rules, courts have broad discretion in granting applications for the appointment of expert witnesses.[595] Although a party may suggest the name of an expert, a party will have little control over whom the court will appoint, and this should be considered in making a request, the outcome of which cannot be known. Counsel wishing to obtain a court-appointed expert must show a reasonable probability that the expert will aid the defendant or "establish necessity."[596]

A bald assertion that a defendant needs an expert is insufficient to trigger the right to the appointment of one.[597] The defendant should show that there is "a reasonable probability that an expert would aid in his defense and that denial would result in an unfair trial."[598] For example, a request for a private investigator must establish how the investigator can specifically assist the defendant.[599] However, at least one court has noted the importance of requiring

---

[593] People v. Lane, 195 A.D.2d 876, 600 N.Y.S.2d 848, *appeal denied*, 82 N.Y.2d 850, 627 N.E.2d 524, 606 N.Y.S.2d 602 (1993).

[594] Fed. R. Evid. 706 provides:

> (a) Appointment. The court may on its own motion or on the motion of any party enter an order to show cause why expert witnesses should not be appointed, and may request the parties to submit nominations. The court may appoint any expert witnesses agreed upon by the parties, and may appoint expert witnesses of its own selection. An expert witness shall not be appointed by the court unless he consents to act. A witness so appointed shall be informed of his duties by the court in writing, a copy of which shall be filed with the clerk, or at a conference in which the parties shall have opportunity to participate. A witness so appointed shall advise the parties of his findings, if any; his deposition may be taken by any party; and he may be called to testify by the court or any party. He shall be subject to cross-examination by each party, including a party calling him as a witness. (b) Compensation. Expert witnesses so appointed are entitled to reasonable compensation in whatever sum the court may allow. . . . (c) Disclosure of appointment. In the exercise of its discretion, the court may authorize disclosure to the jury of the fact that the court appointed the expert witness.

[595] United States v. Schultz, 431 F.2d 907, 910 (8th Cir. 1970).

[596] United States v. Gunkle, 55 M.J. 26, 31 (C.A.A.F. 2001).

[597] Caldwell v. Mississippi, 472 U.S. 320 (1985); State v. Mason, 82 Ohio St. 3d 144, 1998 Ohio 370, 694 N.E.2d 932 (1998); State v. Ulis, 1994 Ohio App. LEXIS 3217 (July 22, 1994) (upholding trial court's decision declining to provide defendant funds for a medical expert in a child sexual assault case).

[598] McCafferty v. Solem, 449 N.W.2d 590 (S.D. 1989), *habeas corpus proceeding*; McCafferty v. Leapley, 944 F.2d 445 (8th Cir. 1991), *cert. denied*, 503 U.S. 911 (1992).

[599] Lewis v. Government of Virgin Islands, 77 F. Supp. 2d 681 (D.V.I. 1999), *aff'd*, 215 F.3d 1314 (3d Cir. 2000) (refusing to appoint a private investigator for defendant in rape case because defendant "did not explain what factual issues the investigator would explore, how those issues pertained to his defense, or why counsel could not perform the desired investigation"); State v.

how an expert may be helpful to a defendant without the opportunity to have an expert "articulate and explain the need for an expert."[600] Some courts have also required that a defendant establish not only the relevance of the expert's testimony, but also the proposed expert's identity, his or her proposed fee, and show that the defendant is unable to afford the services of an expert. Courts may even require a defendant to consider less expensive alternatives, such as subpoenaing experts, despite authority to the effect that experts cannot be forced to render opinions.[601] (Some experts will refuse to testify in sexual assault cases under any circumstances; others may decline to testify for a party, but will become involved if appointed by the court.)

Defendants generally do not prevail in obtaining court-appointed experts if the expert is requested to provide an opinion in an inadmissible area, such as whether the defendant fits the profile of a sexual abuser.[602] However, one court has ruled that a defendant should not automatically be denied expert psychological witnesses to rebut the inference he is a pedophile simply because it may be an expert opinion on character.[603] If the expert sought is in an area which the court deems within the ken of the average juror, funds for an expert may be denied.[604] Also, a defendant may not be able to request the court to provide an expert to determine a child's competence to testify.[605] Where a court appointed one expert upon the motion of both parties, the defense could not request that a second expert be appointed to examine the victim on the grounds that the first expert had been called by the prosecution on a number of occasions, in the absence of proof that this fact compromised the first expert's opinion.[606]

Fletcher, 125 N.C. App. 505, 481 S.E.2d 418, *review denied*, 346 N.C. 285, 487 S.E.2d 560, *cert. denied*, 522 U.S. 957 (1997) (upholding trial court's denial of a private investigator to conduct surveillance of sexual assault claimant due to behavior related to defendant's evidence since defendant made no showing that there was a reasonable likelihood that it would materially assist the defendant in the preparation of his defense or that without such assistance the defendant would more likely than not receive an unfair trial).

[600] United States v. Kreutzer, 59 M.J. 773, 777 n.4 (A.C.C.A. 2004), *aff'd*, 61 M.J. 293 (C.A.A.F. 2005).

[601] State v. Hebel, 174 Ill.App.3d 1, 34, 527 N.E.2d 1367, 1389 (1988).

[602] United States v. St. Pierre, 812 F.2d 417 (8th Cir. 1987).

[603] United States v. Parker, 2005 CCA LEXIS 340 (Oct. 18, 2005) (noting in this case there were other grounds for trial judge to have denied request, such as timelines, sufficiency of basis of request, and failure to demonstrate need or admissibility under *Daubert*).

[604] State v. Kelly, 752 A.2d 188, 191–92 (Me. 2000) (finding defendant's request for expert on issue of cross-racial identification would not be a subject matter helpful to jury); People v. Anderson, 218 A.D.2d 533, 630 N.Y.S.2d 77, *appeal denied*, 87 N.Y.2d 844, 661 N.E.2d 1383, 638 N.Y.S.2d 602 (1995) (denying defendant funds for expert in eyewitness identification on grounds this is a topic within knowledge of the ordinary juror).

[605] People v. Gallow, 171 A.D.2d 1061, 569 N.Y.S.2d 530, *appeal denied*, 77 N.Y.2d 995, 575 N.E.2d 406, 571 N.Y.S.2d 920 (1991).

[606] United States v. Provost, 875 F.2d 172, 175 (8th Cir.), *cert. denied*, 493 U.S. 859 (1989).

One military court holds that a court should not permit the prosecution to have an expert qualified in the medical specialty at issue while providing the defendant with a generalist.[607] Thus, the court followed a principle that the defense be provided an expert comparably qualified to the prosecution's experts, particularly where the prosecution challenges the qualifications of the expert appointed the defendant.[608] However, in a sexual assault case, a defendant is not necessarily prejudiced or denied due process by the appointment of two nurses, one with a background in obstetrics and gynecology and one with a background in sexual assault, instead of a medical doctor.[609]

The fact that the State uses a psychologist or psychiatrist in its case does not necessarily trigger a defendant's right to such an expert.[610]

A general request for an expert to assist on interviewing techniques of children or the behavior of sexual assault victims are often denied on the basis of insufficient bases for the request.[611]

However, a defendant may raise an issue in the interviewing techniques utilized in an investigation and it may be reversible error to deny the defendant funds for an expert to explore the reliability of a child's statements.[612] In this situation, a court held that the defendant need not identify the expert he wants.[613] A

---

[607] United States v. Warner, 62 M.J. 114 (C.A.A.F. 2005) (The court interpreted Article 46 of the Uniform Code of Military Justice, which states that "the trial counsel, the defense counsel, and the court-martial shall have equal opportunity to obtain witnesses and other evidence. . . ."; *See* 10 U.S.C. § 846.

[608] United States v. Warner, 62 M.J. 114 (C.A.A.F. 2005).

[609] United States v. Rogers, 2005 CCA LEXIS 143 (Apr. 19, 2005).

[610] Koerschner v. State, 116 Nev. 1111, 13 P.3d 451 (2000).

[611] Coalson v. State, 251 Ga. App. 761, 555 S.E.2d 128 (2001) (holding defendant made insufficient showing how defendant's trial would be rendered fundamentally unfair if he were not provided with court funds for an expert on interviewing techniques of children and whether child's behavior is consistent with that of an abused child; court also noted the state did not utilize an expert); Smith v. State, 131 S.W.3d 928 (Tex. Ct. App. 2004) (holding trial court did not abuse its discretion in denying defendant's motion for funds to obtain an expert witness to determine whether the child was fantasizing, being misinterpreted, or coached, since there was no evidence to support the necessity of the request).

[612] State v. Carol, 89 Wash. App. 77, 948 P.2d 837 (1997) (holding trial court erred in denying defendant's funds for an expert on "false memory syndrome" given questions about the reliability of child's memory and accusations).

[613] People v. Lawson, 163 Ill. 2d 187, 644 N.E.2d 1172 (1994). In *Lawson*, the Illinois Supreme Court held:

> While we reject the notion that an accused is not entitled to funds for expert assistance unless he identifies the specific expert and provides an estimate of the costs involved, we believe that defendant identified a specific expert by stating unequivocally and repeatedly that he needed a shoeprint and fingerprint expert to examine and compare fingerprints and shoeprints found at the crime scene and to assist in the preparation of a defense, as well as in the cross-examination of the State's similar expert. The trial court would not have been more assisted in deciding defendant's request for reasonable funds by the provision of a particular expert's name or his price.

People v. Lawson, 163 Ill. 2d 187, 230, 644 N.E.2d 1172, 1192 (1994).

defendant is usually not entitled to a court-appointed expert for issues relating to sentencing.[614] A defendant's right to a DNA expert is discussed in the chapter on DNA and scientific evidence.[615]

§ 11.53 Prosecution's access to defense experts and information given to defense experts by defendant.

A basic rule is that a party may examine the information or documents reviewed by the opposing party's experts. When a defendant's expert interviews a defendant as part of the expert's review, statements made to the defendant's expert may be used on cross-examination of the defendant, even if the expert is not called by the defendant.[616]

Defense counsel must be aware that in some situations experts whom they retain also may be available to the prosecution as prosecution witnesses. This can be seen in Federal Rules of Criminal Procedure that addresses the reciprocal discovery of expert witness evidence. This is particularly true when mental health or psychiatric testimony is an issue. While the government may be entitled to medical reports that a defendant intends to use at trial, *communications* by defendant to a psychiatrist retained by defense counsel to aid in the preparation for a defense would generally be considered privileged as long as the psychiatrist is not called as a witness.[617] Furthermore, if the defendant's statements to a mental health expert were relied upon by the expert in forming opinions to which the expert testified, these statements are not protected and are a proper subject of cross-examination of the expert.[618]

A witness is not the property of a party to a suit, and the fact that one party has conferred with a witness or paid for his or her expert advice does not render that witness incompetent to testify for the other party. Courts have permitted the prosecution to call defense-retained experts when the expert's opinion refers to nontestimonial evidence. When courts permit the prosecution to use defense experts, it is usually where the opinion is not "inextricably intertwined with communications which passed between" the defendant and his or her attorney.[619]

---

[614] State v. Goodall, 2000 Ohio App. LEXIS 3017 (July 6, 2000) (denying defendant's request for a psychological expert in connection with a sexual predator hearing).

[615] *See* Chapter 13.

[616] People v. Crow, 28 Cal. App. 4th 440, 448–53, 33 Cal. Rptr. 2d 624, 628–31 (1994) (defendant provided prosecutor a report of his expert, who determined defendant did not match profile of a child molester; defendant could be impeached with inconsistencies between his trial testimony and statements to the expert even though expert did not testify at trial).

[617] United States v. Alvarez, 519 F.2d 1036, 1045–46 (3d Cir. 1975). *See also* Miller v. District Court of Denver, 737 P.2d 834 (Colo. 1987).

[618] People v. Coleman, 48 Cal. 3d 112, 151–52, 255 Cal. Rptr. 813, 835, 768 P.2d 32, 54 (1989), *cert. denied*, 494 U.S. 1038 (1990).

[619] United States v. Pipkins, 528 F.2d 559, 564 (5th Cir. 1976), *cert. denied*, 426 U.S. 952 (1976); United States v. Kendrick, 331 F.2d 110, 115 (4th Cir. 1964); People v. Speck, 41 Ill. 2d 177,

§ 11.54 Direct examination of expert.

Many experts have limited courtroom experience and many experts are not communicators. One noted communications expert makes the following observations about expert witnesses:

> They have no knowledge of the jury's needs or mind set. They do not understand, as you do what sways a jury in one direction or another, or keeps the jury's attention. Their main goal is to explain in great detail, in their own occult language, what they know and care about greatly. They've devoted their lives to their field. They love it and understand it. It doesn't occur to them that other people not only do not understand, but really don't care, or could even be bored by it. So, they can go on at great length in this loving monologue about drafts and graphs and numbers and cells, never even looking up to see that the jury has long since fallen asleep.[620]

Remember this in preparing and presenting expert testimony. It is the attorney's responsibility to make sure the expert's testimony is presented as clearly as possible.

The following is a basic approach to the direct examination of an expert.

1. *Present persuasive credentials, not lengthy credentials.*

Credentials need not always be lengthy, but they should be persuasive. When an expert's credentials contain something that will be particularly significant in the mind of the jury, it is sometimes helpful to begin the credentialing process in the opening statement. Also, lengthy credentials at the beginning of the direct examination of the expert can be boring or distracting. After some initial background information, it is sometimes helpful to work in additional information concerning the expert's background in support of an opinion question. For example:

Q. And Doctor Caldwell, how significant is it when a child reports sexual abuse by a parent or guardian and then recants that allegation several months later?

A. It is part of the dynamics of being a sexually-abused child that there will be pressures and contradictory emotional feelings leading a child to recant his allegations; it is not at all unusual for victims who report sexual abuse to recant the allegations.

Q. And doctor, in how many cases of sexual abuse have you worked with victims who have reported sexual abuse?

200, 242 N.E.2d 208, 221 (1968), *rev'd on other grounds,* 403 U.S. 946 (1971) (permitting the prosecution to use defendant's fingerprint expert); People v. Greene, 153 A.D.2d 439, 552 N.Y.S.2d 640 (1990), *appeal denied,* 76 N.Y.2d 735, 557 N.E.2d 1193, 558 N.Y.S.2d 897 (1990), *cert. denied,* 498 U.S. 947 (1990) (permitting the prosecution to use defendant's expert opinion concerning nontestimonial evidence of a palm print).

[620] Sonya Hamlin, *What Makes Juries Listen* 272 (1985).

A. Over 500.

Q. And is recantation of abuse something you have seen in your experience in the reporting of sexual abuse?

A. Most definitely.

Here, the expert's experience is highlighted in responding to an important opinion question. While the expert could have been asked about the number of cases he has seen or worked with, it has more weight and value in the context of explaining a particular finding or opinion.

While it is important to present persuasive credentials, the credentials should not be exaggerated or presented in a pretentious fashion. Inflation of credentials on direct examination opens the door to an effective cross-examination that can nullify the value of the expert's opinion.

2. Explain materials reviewed.

It is important to show the nature and extent of the expert's experience or familiarity with the facts of the case. This can be through the review of important documents or records or through contact with individuals who are important to the case. This also gives counsel the opportunity to highlight information or evidence that may be significant. For example, if the expert indicates that he or she has reviewed a child victim's school records, it would be helpful to follow up and ask the expert the significance of the records or what one would expect to find or not find in school records.

3. Get to the expert's opinion early and be short, direct, and to the point.

While the expert has the jury's attention, and after minimal credentialing, the expert can be asked his or her opinion concerning the major issue in dispute. This also helps the jury understand why the witness has been called. This approach follows the principles of primary and recency. Generally, few witnesses can command the jury's attention for long periods of time. Jurors will lose interest in the absence of the most compelling of testimony. Experts cannot afford to lose valuable time while they have the jury's attention; therefore, it is important that the key points be brought out early.

Eliminate from direct examination nonessential information and leave certain explanations for cross-examination. Good photographs, medical illustrations, and other demonstrative evidence can assist in this goal.[621] If necessary, use redirect examination to allow further explanation. Use short and leading questions on direct examination to get to the point. Long narrative questions and answers should be avoided; they are difficult to follow, and they dilute the impact of the expert's testimony. If necessary, interrupt the witness and ask him or her to repeat or explain answers. Feel free to ask: "What do you mean by that?"

---

[621] The basis for using such demonstrative evidence is discussed in Chapter 14.

or "I didn't understand that, would you repeat that?" Not only does this clarify the opinion, it allows the message to be repeated for greater impact on the jurors, and, in addition, some jurors find it reassuring to know that the attorney also had difficulty following the expert.

4. Have findings and opinions expressed in understandable and memorable terms.

This is crucial; if the opinion is not understood and remembered, it is of no value. Psychological and medical terms should be explained, preferably with lay terms. The meaning of legal terms such as "reasonable medical certainty" and "reasonable psychological certainty" should be clear to both the expert and the jurors. Analogies and examples to which a jury can relate are helpful. This should be discussed in advance with the expert. When possible, the expert should "show and tell" with a piece of visual or demonstrative evidence. Demonstrative evidence can be as simple as a blow up of a statement or a chart, but something that the jury can take with them to identify and remember the witness. The use of demonstrative evidence by experts is discussed more fully in Chapter 14, particularly the use of illustrations, drawings, and models.

5. Key opinions should be presented with persuasive and compelling language.

The expert should avoid words that suggest uncertainty, such as "I think this could be corrected by" or "I believe," or "despite contrary opinion in the field." These phrases at best dilute the opinion in the eyes of the jury and at worst open the expert to cross-examination. Know in advance how the expert will present his or her opinions.

6. Use hypothetical questions cautiously.

Hypothetical questions can be effective, but often they are unwieldy and difficult to follow. They frequently are objected to for assuming facts not in evidence. A hypothetical question is easier to follow if the expert, instead of assuming facts, is asked to assume an exhibit, such as a statement, medical record, tape recording, or photograph, which the jury can see or hear. However, the hypothetical question can sometimes be used effectively to summarize important facts in the case that you want the jury to remember. If a hypothetical question is going to be used, the expert should be briefed on the law governing its use and informed of the objections that can be raised on direct examination and the ways it can be challenged on cross-examination.

7. Consider having expert comment on the opinions of the opponent's expert.

Comments by your expert on the opinions of your opponent's expert can help develop points to raise on your cross-examination of that expert. The comments may relate to the opponent's expertise. For example, a child psychologist testifying on direct may comment that his or her opinions on child development and behavior are particularly within the expertise of child psychology, as opposed to the field of the opposing party's expert (e.g., social work or counseling, or general psychology). The expert need not even directly refer to the opposing expert, just make an observation. However, this should not be done at the expense of weakening or complicating your expert's direct testimony. One expert may also attack another's methodology and techniques.[622]

If the court permits, you may want your expert to be in court while the opposing expert testifies so that he or she can comment directly on the testimony without resorting to hypothetical questions.

§ 11.55   Practical and tactical considerations in the use of experts.

The area of evidence must be carefully evaluated to ensure that your expert witness will be able to give an opinion on the desired subject. There are many rules and exceptions to rules concerning the use of expert testimony in sexual assault trials. Fine distinctions are often made in determining the propriety of testimony by mental health and psychological experts.

The use of experts can open unwanted doors. When a party presents an expert in one area, it may open the door for the opposition's expert in another area. The opposition may be able to present expert testimony that was previously precluded. Inexperienced experts are particularly prone to open doors (or be a source of surprising testimony).

The use of experts can also close doors. By calling on an expert in a particular field or subspecialty that is subject to challenge, a party may close the door to an effective cross-examination of an opposing expert in that field.

Another consideration is whether your expert will hurt rather than help your position. This can occur if the expert has difficulty communicating clearly and effectively. While experts may be academically qualified in their field, they may not be forensically experienced to communicate and convince. The expert's opinion must make sense to the jury. Expert opinions, even those that may pass the *Daubert* standard of admissibility, can create doubts in the minds of the jurors as to their validity, particularly under the scrutiny of a talented cross-examiner. Theories and opinions also may appear stronger in a report or a medical journal than under the pressure of a courtroom cross-examination.

As a tactical consideration, it is sometimes more effective to present information gained from experts, particularly information concerning victim behavior and the dynamics of a sex crime through direct and cross-examination of lay witnesses together with argument to the jury. Sometimes, issues involving a victim's delay in reporting a sexual assault, or the recantation of allegations of sexual abuse, can be better presented by the attorney trying the case. Armed with

---

[622] Alberts v. Wickes Lumber Co., 1995 U.S. Dist. LEXIS 13657 (Sept. 15, 1995).

an understanding of the dynamics of such victim behavior, counsel, through careful questioning, can bring out testimony in such a way that the victim or another witness becomes the expert. This also may be true in the case of a defendant who is able to take the stand and through careful direct examination explain some of the dynamics of his situation.

An expert also can be retained merely to observe and advise — to see how the case develops during trial and advise as to whether necessary issues are being raised and how they should be handled.

§ 11.56 Preparation of expert for cross-examination.

If not an experienced witness, the expert should always be briefed as to how the legal system operates in the courtroom. This should include a general discussion of the rules of procedure, the format for questioning, the role of expert testimony, and the legal standards for expert testimony.

Even experienced expert witnesses need to be aware that there are many variables in trials. Procedures may vary from courtroom to courtroom and from judge to judge, particularly the parameters of expert testimony and direct examination and cross-examination. The peculiarities of the trial judge concerning an expert's freedom to explain answers or concerning limitations on repetitive questions should be made known to the expert. Even the nuances of the layout of the particular courtroom should be explained to an expert. Is it a courtroom where the expert must keep his voice raised for the jury to hear, or is there a speaker system for the expert's testimony? Will the judge end testimony promptly at a particular time regardless of whether the expert has finished testifying? Will the expert be expected to have made arrangements to stay over?

An expert should be thoroughly briefed on any prior testimony in the proceeding on which he or she might be questioned. Ignorance of case facts is one of the most significant vulnerabilities of an expert witness. It is especially important that the expert be familiar with all records and documents in evidence and not appear surprised. Similarly, the expert should be thoroughly familiar with all materials he or she has reviewed and any materials in the possession of opposing counsel upon which he or she may be cross-examined. The expert must be prepared to disclose facts, notes, and records contained in his or her file. This is supported by most state disclosure rules and the Federal Rules.[623] This includes especially any notes and reports provided by or made by the expert. Many inexperienced experts are not aware that notes and records they have generated must be produced and provided to the opposing counsel for purposes

---

[623] Fed. R. Evid. 705:

Disclosure of Facts or Data Underlying Expert Opinion. The expert may testify in terms of opinion or inference and give reasons therefor without prior disclosure of the underlying facts or data, unless the court requires otherwise. The expert may in any event be required to disclose the underlying facts or data on cross-examination.

of cross-examination. Comments made in those notes or letters from the attorney can be the subject of fertile cross-examination, especially when the expert is not prepared.

An expert should also be prepared to answer questions concerning his or her work history and expertise. Is there something in the expert's background that can be used to discredit him or her? Has the expert frequently appeared only for one side or the other in sexual assault cases? Has the expert ever been involved in controversial matters? Has the expert been involved in litigation? Has the expert ever lost a job or been forced to terminate employment? And, of course, the expert must also be prepared to answer questions concerning compensation or payment — in a forthright and direct manner and not be evasive.

The expert should be warned about compound and "suggestive" questions on cross-examination. He or she also should be prepared for hypothetical questions on cross-examination and understand the legal theory underpinning hypothetical questions. It is common on cross-examination of an expert to be asked about other causes of events or possibilities, and the expert should be prepared to answer these questions.

The expert should be counseled to not venture into areas outside his or her expertise. Venturing beyond one's expertise under cross-examination can destroy the validity of one's entire testimony on direct. An experienced attorney will inform the expert of the main goals of his or her testimony and where the limits are.

Experts should also be prepared to deal with the "learned treatise exception" to the hearsay rule and how learned treatises are used by opposing counsel on cross-examination. The learned treatise exception is a potent weapon in the hands of an experienced cross-examiner. (*See* § 11.76–11.77.) If unprepared for the foundational requirements for this exception to the hearsay rule, the expert may be discredited without the opposition ever calling an expert to the stand.

Finally, counsel should determine where the expert might be cross-examined successfully — the possible areas of weakness in the testimony. The expert should then be candidly confronted with these and prepared as much as possible.

It is in the course of preparing an expert for cross-examination that counsel is most likely to ascertain the serious pitfalls in calling a particular expert as a witness. These pitfalls seldom appear in discussions over the telephone or in reviewing the expert's report. Often it is only after careful preparation of an expert for cross-examination that counsel can make a truly informed decision as to whether that expert should be called as a witness at the trial.

§ 11.57   Basis of expert testimony and expert opinion based upon hearsay information, studies, and non-record facts.

An expert can testify to matters that are within the expert's personal knowledge. That is to say, the expert can testify to findings made in the process of a physical examination or to statements made directly to the expert. An expei can also base his or her opinion on facts assumed to be true as set forth by the trial testimony, which is usually accomplished in the form of a hypothetical question. There is no requirement that the expert have personal knowledge of the facts underlying the expert's opinion, but may instead rely on the facts in evidence. [624]

Opinions based on personal knowledge, facts, or exhibits in evidence do not generally present significant issues at trial — at least with regard to the basis for those opinions — other than whether the expert did in fact personally observe the facts upon which the opinion is based, or whether the facts in evidence are as the hypothetical question states them to be.

Many issues are raised by an expert opinion that is based upon hearsay information or non-record facts. The Federal Rules of Evidence permit an expert to provide an opinion on the facts and data not admissible in evidence "if of a type reasonably relied upon by experts in the particular field."[625] Many states follow the same rule.[626] "Facts or data that are otherwise inadmissible shall not be disclosed to the jury by the proponent of the opinion or inference unless the court determines that their probative value in assisting the jury to evaluate the expert's opinion substantially outweighs their prejudicial effect."[627] While a psychiatrist may rely on statements from interviewers as material accepted in the profession as reliable, use of such out-of-court statements before the jury may violate the defendant's right to confrontation under *Crawford*.[628] For example, an expert may rely on a well-established psychological test when rendering an opinion.[629] A typical problem occurs when an expert witness

---

[624] People v. Miller, 91 N.Y.2d 372, 694 N.E.2d 61, 670 N.Y.S.2d 978 (1998).

[625] Fed. R. Evid. 703:

> The facts or data in the particular case upon which an expert bases an opinion or inference may be those perceived by or made known to the expert at or before the hearing. If of a type reasonably relied upon by experts in the particular field in forming opinions or inferences upon the subject, the facts or data need not be admissible in evidence in order for the opinion or inference to be admitted.

[626] *See, e.g.*, Tex. R. Evid. 703; Dennis v. State, 178 S.W.3d 172 (Tex. Ct. App. 2005) (upholding social worker's testimony, whose opinion on sexually-abused child was based on information given her).

[627] Fed. R. Evid. 703.

[628] People v. Goldstein, 6 N.Y.3d 119, 843 N.E.2d 727, 810 N.Y.S.2d 100 (2005) (reversing defendant's conviction and holding prosecution psychiatrist's use of statements obtained from witnesses were testimonial statements used in violation of *Crawford*);

> The facts or data in the particular case upon which an expert bases an opinion or inference may be those perceived by or made known to the expert at or before the hearing. If of a type reasonably relied upon by experts in the particular field in forming opinions or inferences upon the subject, the facts or data need not be admissible in evidence in order for the opinion or inference to be admitted.

[629] State v. Kelley, 2000 Ut. 41, 1 P.3d 546 (2000) (complainant's incapacity to and consent

justifies a statement by testifying that other experts have come to the same conclusion as the witness with respect to a particular issue. The Federal Rules of Evidence do not permit an expert witness to circumvent the rules of hearsay by testifying that other experts, not present in the courtroom, corroborate the expert's views[630] on cross-examination. The court may limit questioning concerning information on a report not received in evidence.[631]

The expert may rely on police reports.[632] A psychiatrist may testify to a defendant's statements contained in a police report to inform the jury of the basis of his opinion. Such hearsay testimony of the expert is not presented for the truth of the statement.[633] A physician in a sexual assault case may rely on the medical reports of others, even though the doctor did not examine the victim in forming an opinion.[634] Relying on another's "facts" as opposed to opinions is not always simple. However, a medical report prepared as part of litigation may not be the type of report reasonably relied upon by an expert.[635] An expert cannot base

---

to or understand consequences of a sexual act established by special education teacher who worked with professionals such as psychologists, psychiatrists, and doctors to determine individuals' intellectual and physical abilities, and he could also utilize psychological testing, such as IQ tests, as part of that assessment since such testing is "reasonably relied on by experts in that particular field." State v. Kelley, 2000 Ut. 41, 1 P.3d 546, 551 (2000)).

[630] United States v. Grey Bear, 883 F.2d 1382, 1392–93 (8th Cir. 1989), *cert. denied*, 493 U.S. 1047 (1990) (holding that defendant was not improperly restricted by the court's ruling that expert witness could not state that the opinions of two other pathologists agreed with his own); State v. Jones, 325 S.C. 310, 479 S.E.2d 517 (1996) (noting that while not reversible error in this case, prosecution's expert should not have referred to a non-testifying physician's opinion which confirmed the testifying expert's opinion).

[631] People v. Laracuente, 21 A.D.3d 1389, 801 N.Y.S.2d 676 (2005).

[632] State v. Russell, 125 Wash. 2d 24, 73–74, 882 P.2d 747, 778–79 (1994), *cert. denied*, 514 U.S. 1129 (1995) (permitting expert to testify based on hearsay police reports; disclosure of this information is in the discretion of the trial court under Federal Rule 705).

[633] People v. Wright, 266 A.D.2d 246, 697 N.Y.S.2d 667, *appeal denied*, 94 N.Y.2d 831, 724 N.E.2d 394, 702 N.Y.S.2d 602 (1999).

[634] State v. Kelley, 945 S.W.2d 611 (Mo. Ct. App. 1997) ("Dr. Beal testified that he reviewed medical records from Dr. Cook and Dr. Russell and investigative reports provided by DFS. Dr. Beal agreed that these were the type of documents upon which he and other experts normally rely in making medical determinations and arriving at their medical conclusions. Dr. Beal's opinion was that C.K. suffered multiple episodes of sexual assault. . . ." *Id.* at 615).

[635] United States v. Tran Trong Cuong, 18 F.3d 1132 (4th Cir. 1994)

> The government argues that an expert witness may consult other experts, books and treatises on the subject and may consider hearsay in reaching his opinion. However, this misses the point. Essentially, the defendant is subjected to the testimony of a witness whom he may not cross-examine, and Dr. MacIntosh bolstered his testimony by claiming that an outstanding doctor, who is also a lawyer and president of the Medical Society, agrees with him. In the present record, there is no indication that the medical report of Dr. Stevenson was 'of a type reasonably relied upon by experts in a particular field in forming opinions or inferences upon the subject.' Even if this foundation had been properly laid, which it was not, it would still have been improper for Dr. MacIntosh to state that the two medical opinions were essentially the same.

an opinion on a medical report contained in a police investigation report when the physician was under no duty to review the criminal file and render an opinion concerning medical questions.[636] The outside sources of information must be "reasonably relied upon by experts in the particular field," and while the expert is usually permitted to make this decision in providing his testimony, the lack of reasonableness can be developed upon cross-examination to set the basis for appellate review. Essentially, "an expert witness may not testify as to the opinions of another expert in the same field."[637] For example, testimony by an expert that he consulted with the author of a book who agreed with his opinion does not fall within the rule permitting an expert to rely upon nonadmissible evidence, since the expert testifying is "acting as a conduit for the other doctor's opinion."[638] Nor should the medical expert testify to a study not introduced into evidence when offered as proof of the facts on the study.[639] An expert may be precluded from providing an expert opinion on DNA evidence when that opinion is based on DNA test results which have not been introduced into evidence.[640] This is particularly so if the expert does not have any personal knowledge of the DNA test or the test results.[641] An expert should not give an opinion based substantially on the reports of others which are not in evidence.[642] However, a DNA expert may rely on a DNA database containing data on DNA profiles, since such studies are of a type automatically relied upon in the DNA expert's field.[643] What non-record evidence is automatically relied on by experts in a field is in some situations a matter of judicial discretion.

Mental health experts, as well as other experts, often rely on tests or reports that may not be generally accepted within their professional community. For

---

> In addition to the problems of hearsay and Stevenson's report being used to vouch for the opinion of MacIntosh, it is doubtful if Dr. Stevenson's report would qualify as data 'of a type reasonably relied upon by experts in the particular field.' The Stevenson report was prepared at the request of the prosecution and thereby is a forensic opinion or report in a criminal case. We question whether Dr. MacIntosh usually relies upon forensic medical opinions or reports in forming his opinions in his field of expertise — family medicine.

United States v. Tran Trong Cuong, 18 F.3d 1132, 1143 (4th Cir. 1994)).

[636] People v. Ruff, 185 A.D.2d 454, 457, 586 N.Y.S.2d 327, 330 (1992), aff'd, 81 N.Y.2d 330, 615 N.E.2d 611, 599 N.Y.S.2d 221 (1993).

[637] State v. Chapman, 410 So. 2d 689, 704 (La. 1981); People v. Jones, 73 N.Y.2d 427, 539 N.E.2d 96, 541 N.Y.S.2d 340 (1989).

[638] State v. Towne, 142 Vt. 241, 246–47, 453 A.2d 1133, 1135 (1982).

[639] People v. Beckwith, 289 A.D.2d 956, 734 N.Y.S.2d 770 (2001) (holding medical expert improperly testified to a study not introduced into evidence since it was hearsay and offered as proof of facts contained in the study but error was harmless).

[640] Leonard v. State, 269 Ga. 867, 506 S.E.2d 853 (1998).

[641] Leonard v. State, 269 Ga. 867, 506 S.E.2d 853 (1998).

[642] Leonard v. State, 269 Ga. 867, 506 S.E.2d 853 (1998).

[643] Hills v. Commonwealth, 32 Va. App. 479, 528 S.E.2d 730, reh'g remanded, 33 Va. App. 442, 534 S.E.2d 337 (2000).

example, in sexual assault cases, some experts will base an opinion on a child's use of anatomically correct dolls, which may not always be acceptable evidence.[644] The expert may be relying on recovered memories.[645] In fact, a myriad of psychological tests is available but not widely used or recognized. These may be subject to a *Frye* or *Daubert* hearing.[646] An expert should be challenged if he or she attempts to use such tests as a basis for an opinion. This is where a thorough discovery process is helpful as is requesting a voir dire of the expert before he or she gives opinion testimony.

Experts rely on "studies" to support their opinion, some of which are unpublished. These should be checked out and, if necessary, brought to trial, especially studies that the expert himself has performed. Unless an expert produces nonpublished studies in the courtroom, they should not be permitted as a basis for the expert's opinion. An expert cannot simply refer to "studies" and "the literature" as to whether a child is capable of fabricating an allegation.[647]

An expert may be precluded from relying on his own out-of-court test which the court finds unreliable.[648] For example, one area of expert testimony much less common than rape trauma and Child Sexual Abuse Accommodation Syndrome, but with similarities to them, is traumagenic dynamics. Traumagenic dynamics analyzes sexual abuse in terms of four trauma-causing factors: traumatic sexualization, which refers to a child's sexuality being affected in developmentally inappropriate ways resulting from sexual abuse; betrayal, which refers to a child's discovery that someone upon whom they are dependent has caused harm; and powerlessness and stigmatization, when badness, shame, and guilt become part of the child's self-image. Traumagenic dynamics has been held by one court not to have reached such a state of development so as to permit an expert to form an opinion based on the theory.[649]

---

[644] *See* § 11.42.

[645] *See* § 11.43.

[646] People v. Rogers, 247 A.D.2d 765, 669 N.Y.S.2d 678, *appeal denied*, 91 N.Y.2d 976, 695 N.E.2d 725, 672 N.Y.S.2d 856 (1998) (holding that defendant's psychologist in sexual assault case could not rely on psychological tests which did not pass the *Frye* test to establish defendant's "lack of comprehension, vocabulary, and suggestibility," and defendant's lack of understanding *of Miranda* warnings).

[647] United States v. King, 35 M.J. 337 (C.M.A. 1992) (noting that in certain situations an expert may refer to the studies, findings, and conclusions of others but should not ascend the witness stand and commence spouting hearsay generally. *Id.* at 341).

[648] State v. Zerla, 1994 Ohio App. LEXIS 5864 (Dec. 22, 1994), *appeal denied*, 72 Ohio Ct. 3d 1407, 647 N.E.2d 495 (1995) (court properly precluded a microbiologist from testifying concerning his own tests involving four couples to determine how long sperm could be recovered from the oral cavity since the tests were found by the trial court to be "casual, unscientific and somewhat bizarre").

[649] Sorensen v. State, 895 P.2d 454 (Wyo. 1995).

One issue under *Crawford* is whether an expert can rely on hearsay information, such as a child's statements made to the experts, when that evidence would be otherwise inadmissible and the child does not testify.[650]

§ 11.58   Expert testimony based on learned treatise.

An important tool in both direct and cross-examination of experts is the "learned treatise" exception to the hearsay rule. The Federal Rules of Evidence[651] and some states permit experts to refer to learned treatises as part of their direct testimony. Not all states follow this rule. One problem is that it automatically opens the door to cross-examination on that treatise, since the expert has explicitly recognized the work as authoritative, which is one of the prerequisites to allowing the use of a learned treatise. (*See* §§ 11.76 and 11.77.)

§ 11.59   Checklist for challenging the legal basis of the expert's opinion.

As discussed extensively in this chapter, there are many areas of an expert opinion that can be improper. Sometimes the expert's testimony appears proper when first offered, but diverges into objectionable areas as the witness continues to testify. Also, an answer on direct examination may contain both admissible and inadmissible testimony. These situations require prompt objections. If improper areas can be anticipated in advance, a motion *in limine* might be appropriate.

A summary of some of the legal objections to expert testimony in sexual assault cases is that the expert's opinion:

(1)   Fails to meet the *Daubert* or *Frye* standard of reliability and acceptability;

(2)   The expert is not qualified in the area in which he or she is offering an opinion;

(3)   Is in an area on which an expert may not comment, such as credibility;

(4)   Is based on inadmissible or improper evidence, or insufficient foundation, such as a child's use of dolls, a nontestifying expert's opinion, hearsay, or inadmissible statement of a defendant or other witness, or is based on a test which does not meet the standard of reliability and acceptability;

(5)   Has no legal basis, such as a physician who testifies that a child has been sexually assaulted based solely on history without corroborative physical findings;

---

[650] United States v. Farley, 992 F.2d 1122, 1125 (10th Cir. 1993) (holding that an expert who testified that she relied upon the child's statements during their interview, as well as drawings made by the child, to arrive at her opinion is permissible under Federal Rule 703, as long as the judge instructs the jury that the testimony was received for a limited purpose of laying a foundation for the expert's opinion).

[651] Fed. R. Evid. 803(18).

(6)　May mislead or confuse the jury;

(7)　Is cumulative;

(8)　Is an issue on which the average juror does not need expert testimony;

(9)　Creates a substantial danger of undue prejudice; and

(10)　May be admissible, but a cautionary or limiting instruction should be provided.

§ 11.60　Cross-examination of expert witnesses.

The cross-examination of an expert witness should begin with a thorough research of the expert's background, credentials, experience level, and prior testimony, and all notes and reports prepared by the expert in connection with the case. In particular, the expert's experience is important. Has the expert had experience with the particular issues and problems addressed in this case? Has the expert's experience been limited to a small area? Has the expert dealt primarily (or exclusively) with just victims or defendants? Has the expert had experience primarily on a theoretical or research basis rather than a first-hand clinical basis? Has the expert's experience with the subject of the testimony primarily been as an expert witness? Is the expert's experience outdated given the substantial advances in the field of sexual assault?

The background of experts can be checked out, particularly through the use of computerized data banks. Computer databases such as **LEXIS**, **WESTLAW**, and **MEDLINE** provide quick access to background credentials and experiences of expert witnesses. They also can be used to find cases in which the expert has previously testified and, perhaps, has been cited as authority in appellate decisions. Particular decisions can be reviewed for relevant insights as to the expert, including whether his or her qualifications or testimony has been challenged, and also permits counsel to get in touch with attorneys who have had courtroom experience with the expert and request transcripts of relevant testimony. As previously noted, the Association of Trial Lawyers of America (ATLA) also possesses a data bank on experts.[652]

The expert should be evaluated before trial (if possible) or during direct examination for potential weaknesses. What is the extent of the knowledge of the expert on the issues about which he or she is testifying? Is the expert of sharp intelligence? What is the expert's personality — timid, overbearing, pompous, hostile, quick to anger? Uncovering potential areas of weakness in the expert may change the focus of the cross-examination.

Cross-examination of an expert should be dictated to a certain extent on whether the cross-examiner is also calling an expert. An attack on the theories or field upon which the expert bases his or her opinion will be counterproductive

---

[652] *See* § 11.50.

if the cross-examiner is planning to call an expert in the same field who will rely on the same methodology. Similarly, attacking an expert as being a paid professional witness is counterproductive if the cross-examiner will be calling an expert witness with a similar background.

§ 11.61   Challenging the expert's credentials.

The credentials of an expert should only be challenged when there is a substantial reason to do so. If there is, counsel may wish to request a voir dire of the expert outside the presence of the jury. The voir dire permits counsel and the court to focus on the expert's credentials, which a court is less likely to do after the expert has already been placed on the witness stand. A challenge to the expert's credentials can be woven into the cross-examination, although by then the court usually has already ruled on the expert's qualifications.

Many experts are qualified to testify as an expert in one area, but not in other areas, a challenge often overlooked even by experienced attorneys.

Questioning credentials should be carefully weighed. One approach is to note that the expert may be qualified in the area, but lacks background on the issues for which the expert is providing an opinion. For example:

Q. Doctor, you have spent your 20 years as a psychologist specializing in alcohol rehabilitation, correct?

A. Yes.

Q. And what percentage of your patients are children?

A. Perhaps one percent.

Q. What percent were less than 14?

A. Less than one percent.

Q. And how many children have you treated in the past 20 years for sexual abuse?

A. Well, I don't treat sexual abuse, but I've seen these children.

Q. And has any physician or doctor ever referred a child to you for treatment of sexual abuse?

A. No, they wouldn't.

Q. Would you?

A. No, but. . . .

§ 11.62   Challenging the certainty of the expert's opinion.

Listen carefully to the expert's testimony to see if the expert's answers suggest uncertainty — for example, by hesitating or by the use of certain equivocal words, such as "could" or "might" — so you can create doubt in the jury's minds: "So your testimony is that this event *could* be caused by . . .”; *“Might be* means maybe not, correct?”; “You hesitated in answering, you must be uncertain.” Repeat the equivocal words in subsequent questions and in your closing argument.

In the following example, the cross-examiner attacks the expert’s conclusion by questioning the basis of the opinion, that it is not supported by the records, and then highlights the uncertainty of the expert’s answers.

Q. Is there anything in the proof or records that you have reviewed that indicates that anybody grabbed the child by the thigh?

A. I am making this as a reasonable supposition.

Q. You are speculating, correct?

A. Yes, indeed.

Q. You have no proof to support that?

A. Except that I have seen it elsewhere.

Q. In other cases?

A. Yes, sir.

Q. But not this case, correct?

A. Correct.

This cross-examination also makes the expert and jury focus on the facts of the case at hand and not other cases, as an expert may be prone to do.

Many expert opinions are phrased in terms of findings or behavior being “consistent with” an incident of sexual abuse or assault.[653] This calls for cross-examination questions that point out that the opinion may mean just the opposite of what the expert is suggesting, or something else entirely.

Q. Let me ask you this, Doctor: You say that based on the history you received that your findings are consistent with the possibility of intercourse, correct?

A. Based on the history, my findings, right, yes.

Q. Now, isn’t it a fair statement that your findings, or absence of findings, are equally consistent with the absence of sexual intercourse?

A. Yes.

Q. No question about that?

A. Right, yes, true.

Q. So, bedwetting is consistent with not being an abused child also, correct?

---

[653] *See* § 11.18 and Chapter 12 for discussion of the admissibility of this area of expert testimony.

A. Yes.

Q. And bedwetting would also be consistent with a child who is undergoing stress at school?

A. Yes.

Q. And won't this child's school records reflect that Todd was having serious problems with fellow students and teachers during this period?

This is also discussed in Chapter 12.

§ 11.63   Challenging the expert's bias and fees.

The bias of a witness testifying as an expert can be explored through the expert's prior work experience or through the expert having consulted or testified on behalf of a particular party in similar proceedings.[654] The interest of a witness in a case has a bearing upon that witness's credibility, expert or lay. Thus, it is proper to question an expert on cross-examination as to the compensation he or she has received for litigation work.[655] While questioning the expert about fees may be proper, an argument that the expert is relying on defense counsel for employment or that the prosecutions' experts are more reliable because they are not paid may be improper when there is no evidence that the expert was motivated to lie or to draw a favorable conclusion based on the relationship with defense counsel or future employment.[656] The expert witness also can be questioned concerning unprofessional conduct or professional negligence.[657] Allegations of misconduct by an expert may be discovered through searches of computer databases as well as through licensing authorities in the states in which the expert is licensed.

---

[654] Russell G. Donaldson, Annotation, *Propriety of Cross-Examining Witness Regarding His Status as Professional Witness*, 39 A.L.R.4th 742 (1985).

[655] Russell G. Donaldson, Annotation, *Propriety of Cross-Examining Witness Regarding His Status as Professional Witness*, 39 A.L.R.4th 742 (1985). Collins v. Wayne Corp., 621 F.2d 777 (5th Cir. 1980); Keating v. Dominick's Finer Foods, 224 Ill. App. 3d 981, 985, 587 N.E.2d 57, 60 (1992); Wrobleski v. de Lara, 353 Md. 509, 526, 727 A.2d 930, 938 (1999) (holding that expert may be cross-examined as to whether expert earns "a significant portion or amount of income from applying that expertise in a forensic setting and is thus in the nature of a 'professional witness.' If there is a reasonable basis for a conclusion that the witness may be a 'professional witness,' the party may inquire both into the amount of income earned in the recent past from services as an expert witness and into the approximate portion of the witness's total income derived from such services."). *See also* Spino v. John S. Tilley Ladder Co., 448 Pa. Super. 327, 671 A.2d 726 (1996), *aff'd on other grounds*, 548 Pa. 286, 696 A.2d 1169 (1997). 1 McCormick on Evidence § 13, at 57 (4th ed. 1992).

[656] State v. Smith, 167 N.J. 158, 770 A.2d 255 (2001) (reversing defendant's conviction because of prosecutor's attack on defendant's experts and in particular, comment that the experts may have "shaded their testimony" in the hopes of future employment).

[657] George L. Blum, Annotation, *Propriety of Questioning Expert Witness Regarding Specific Incidents or Allegations of Expert's Unprofessional Conduct or Professional Negligence*, 11 A.L.R.5th 1 (1993).

There are also situations where it is proper to cross-examine an expert concerning opinions expressed in the expert's writings which relate to the charges. For example in a sexual assault trial, it has been held proper for a prosecutor to cross-examine a defense expert in a child sexual abuse trial about the expert's statements made in a magazine entitled *Padika,* "an Amsterdam pedophilia journal, in which he appeared to endorse pedophilia as an acceptable and reasonable lifestyle."[658] The court held that such views are relevant to the expert's credentials and "his objectivity in cases involving the sexual abuse of children."[659]

In all areas of attack that are outside the scope of the expert's opinion in the case, it is important that the cross-examination be directed to a *significant* credibility problem. Cross-examination concerning fees earned for testifying or the expert's misconduct have impact only if they reflect a substantial amount of money or a substantial misdeed. Otherwise, the cross-examiner runs the risk of being viewed in the eyes of the jury as a pettifogger.

The following cross-examination delves into bias suggested by an expert's history of consulting and testifying on behalf of the prosecution in sexual assault cases.

Q. Now, Doctor, this is not the first time you have testified in a courtroom, is it?

A. No, it's not.

Q. It is not the first time you have testified on behalf of this prosecutor in a sexual assault trial, is it?

A. No, it's not.

Q. It's not the first time you have testified on behalf of the prosecution in a sexual assault case, is it?

A. No, it's not.

Q. In addition to testifying, you also consult and review, do you not?

A. Yes, I do.

Q. Can you tell us, in 2003 how many times did you consult a prosecutor's office asserting your opinion on the behaviors of a person alleging sexual abuse?

A. I'm not sure, perhaps a couple of dozen times.

In the following, the financial component of the expert's relationship to the prosecution is explored.

---

[658] Commonwealth v. Perkins, 39 Mass. App. Ct. 577, 581, 658 N.E.2d 975, 978 (1995), *rev'd on other grounds, review denied,* 422 Mass. 1104, 601 N.E.2d 935 (1996).

[659] Commonwealth v. Perkins, 39 Mass. App. Ct. 577, 581, 658 N.E.2d 975, 978 (1995), *rev'd on other grounds, review denied,* 422 Mass. 1104, 601 N.E.2d 935 (1996).

Q. Over the past five years, on approximately how many cases have you been consulted by either the prosecution or social services agency seeking to establish an act of sexual abuse?

A. Several hundred.

Q. And on how many occasions have you testified in criminal or family court?

A. It's hard to remember, a fair number of times.

Q. More than several times?

A. Yes.

Q. Every time you consult, you are paid for your time, are you not?

A. Yes.

Q. Every time you review, you are paid for your time, are you not?

A. The majority, yes, yes.

Q. You were not subpoenaed here to testify, were you?

A. No, I was not.

Q. You are being paid to come here and testify; is that correct?

A. That is a correct statement that you make.

Q. Now, you were retained by the prosecution in this case; correct?

A. Yes, that's correct.

Q. Now, in connection with your assistance to the prosecution of this case, you are being paid, is that correct?

A. Yes, I'm being paid for my time.

Q. And your time to this point in time is being reimbursed at what rate?

A. At 125 dollars an hour.

Q. How many hours have you involved yourself in the defense of this case?

A. Since the inception?

Q. Yes.

A. About 10 hours.

Q. Could you check your records?

A. Well, there's been a few more hours since I computed the time.

Q. So it's closer to 20 hours?

A. Yes.

Q. In addition to being paid for those 20 hours, you are also being paid for testifying here today, are you not?

A. Yes.

Q. Can you tell us what you are being paid for testifying here today?

A. Well, they give me the same rate to a maximum of three thousand dollars if I stay all day.

Q. Now, what percentage of your income would come from consulting, reviewing or testifying?

A. Approximately 20 percent.

This approach will not be effective if the expert has not been *significantly* involved as a paid consulting expert. If you believe that the opponent's expert derives a substantial amount of income from testifying or consulting, you may wish to subpoena the expert's income or business records.

§ 11.64　Questioning the evasive expert on issues of financial remuneration.

Some experts are evasive when questioned about financial remuneration for their consulting or testifying. In that situation counsel may want to notify the expert before he testifies that he will be asking questions about his financial compensation and wants to provide the expert time to review his records. The attorney will then be prepared to effectively continue the line of questioning as in the following example:

Q. Can you tell us how much you have received as compensation for services in this case?

A. I don't know.

Q. Can you tell the jury how much you have received in the last two years for reviewing, consulting and testifying in court?

A. I have no idea.

Q. During the lunch break did I tell you that one of the questions I would ask you this afternoon would be how much money you have received in this case?

A. I couldn't tell you.

Q. My question is did I come up to you during lunch?

A. Yes.

Q. Did I say I would like you to check, to check with your office and the defense so you would be able to answer that question?

A. I asked. I have no record, myself.

Q. Doctor, you have been asked that question in other criminal trials, haven't you?

A. Yes.

Q. And every time you are asked that question you tell the jury you don't know how much you have been paid in a case, right?

A. Yes.

Q. Do you have records or not?

A. I have no records.

Q. No records.

A. No. That's the truth. Come and see my office.

Q. Do you file tax returns?

A. Yes.

Q. You don't have to keep records of how much you get paid?

A. Yes. I should. I think that — well, sorry.

Apart from the issue of financial interest, this line of cross-examination establishes evasiveness on the part of the witness. The fairness of the inquiry is highlighted by having warned the expert of the inquiry prior to testifying.

§ 11.65   Cross-examination concerning mistakes, errors or lies by expert.

When an expert testifies falsely, it may lead to reversal of a defendant's conviction when it involves a significant issue in the trial and there is a reasonable likelihood the false testimony affected the judgment of the jury. For example, in the trial of Andrea Yates, who asserted an insanity defense in connection with charges of murdering her five children, the prosecution's psychiatrist testified that he was a consultant to the television program *Law and Order*, a program watched regularly by the defendant. The psychiatrist testified regarding a *Law and Order* episode with a similar fact pattern, in which the defendant mother asserted an insanity defense. However, no such episode ever aired. The expert's false statement became material when the prosecutor emphasized, as suggested by their expert, that the defendant viewed the episode and argued both in cross-examination of the defendant's psychiatric expert and in summation that the defendant learned from it that she could kill her children and "get away with it."[660] While several experts testified that Ms. Yates was not responsible for the killings, the court noted that "had the jury known prior to their deliberations in the guilt-innocence phase of the trial, that Dr. Dietz's testimony regarding the 'Law and Order' episode was false, the jury would likely have considered him, the State's only mental health expert, to be less credible." As a result, a retrial was ordered.[661] The expert's error can be used in subsequent trials in which the expert testifies, since it may be probative of the expert's "fallibility."[662]

---

[660] Yates v. State, 171 S.W.3d 215, 218–19 (Tex. Ct. App. 2005), *review denied, In re* Yates, 2005 Tex. Crim. App. LEXIS 1926 (Nov. 9, 2005).

[661] Yates v. State, 171 S.W.3d 215, 218–19 (Tex. Ct. App. 2005), *review denied, In re* Yates, 2005 Tex. Crim. App. LEXIS 1926 (Nov. 9, 2005) at 222, n.6.

[662] United States v. Purkey, 428 F.3d 738, 758 (8th Cir. 2005) (but holding error in failing to permit the cross-examination was harmless).

§ 11.66 Challenging basis of opinions and pointing out additional information.

Much mental health testimony is based upon psychological tests or theories that have not been thoroughly established and fully accepted by the profession. An example is the use of anatomically correct dolls by children to describe possible sexual abuse or assault.[663] The expert may concede such; if not, he or she may be confronted by learned treatises and articles on the subject. This is discussed further in the following section.

An expert opinion may not, in whole or in part, be based on an unreliable test such as a polygraph test.[664] It is also fundamental that an expert opinion that is not supported by facts and is based upon speculation has an inadequate basis for admission. For example, testimony concerning the effects of cocaine use and alcohol upon a complainant when it is not sufficiently established whether the complainant ingested cocaine or alcohol lacks a sufficient basis or foundation to be admissible.[665] If the cross-examiner wishes to cross-examine the expert concerning hearsay records or reports of another expert, the cross-examiner should first lay a foundation as to whether or not the expert relied on those diagnoses or records or reviewed them.[666] In the absence of a proper foundation, a court may preclude cross-examination about the hearsay reports.[667]

In sexual assault cases, an expert's inadequate knowledge of the field in general or the issues of the particular case can sometimes be done by confronting the expert with earlier testimony of the complainant or defendant or with medical records and other documents that are already before the jury. This can be particularly effective since the jury is well aware of these facts and often will be surprised to learn that the expert is not.

The accuracy of the information forming the basis of the expert's opinion can also be challenged. In the following example, a medical expert is testifying from a review of a rape victim's medical records. The cross-examiner is seeking to show that when a nontreating expert bases his or her opinions solely on medical or psychological records without examining the patient or discussing her case with other medical personnel involved, the expert's testimony may be flawed.

Q. Your opinions today are based upon the victim's medical records you have reviewed, correct?

---

[663] See § 11.42.

[664] People v. Angelo, 208 A.D.2d 939, 618 N.Y.S.2d 77 (1994), aff'd, 88 N.Y.2d 217, 666 N.E.2d 1333, 644 N.Y.S.2d 460 (1996). See discussion of the varying views concerning the admissibility of polygraph results in § 11.23.

[665] People v. Benson, 206 A.D.2d 674, 614 N.Y.S.2d 808 (1994), appeal denied, 84 N.Y.2d 1029, 647 N.E.2d 457, 623 N.Y.S.2d 185 (1995).

[666] United States v. Halford, 50 M.J. 402 (C.A.A.F. 1999) (upholding trial court's refusal to permit defense counsel to cross-examine prosecution's expert concerning opinions of other experts who had different diagnoses of sexual assault victim).

[667] United States v. Halford, 50 M.J. 402 (C.A.A.F. 1999).

A. Yes.

Q. Prior to testifying today, you have made no effort to contact the physicians, nurse or whoever made the entries in the chart to discuss with them the accuracies or inaccuracies in the record, correct?

A. Correct.

Q. And in addition to the medical record, have you based your opinion on any additional information?

A. No, sir.

Q. When was the first time that you reviewed the medical record of the complainant?

A. On morning last.

Q. And is it not a fact that the medical records sometimes contain inadequate information?

A. Very frequently, sir.

Q. You have made that observation; correct?

A. I have.

Q. Based on your years of experience?

A. I have, indeed.

Q. And that can be information which is omitted?

A. Correct.

Q. And it could be information which is not correctly recorded in the record; is that correct?

A. Yes, sir.

Q. And can we agree that can be done either intentionally or unintentionally, those inaccuracies?

A. Yes, most certainly.

The cross-examiner should again ask the expert exactly to whom he spoke (apparently no one) and to whom he did not speak in forming the opinion.

Many experts in sexual assault trials testify without having any contact with the victim, basing their opinions simply on records, a practice that has been compared to "seeing but several frames of a motion picture."

Q. You've never talked to any of the children in this case, any of the children who were at the defendant's home; is that correct?

A. That's correct.

Q. You've never personally spoken to any of the parents?

A. No.

Q. And the only information you have as to what the children may have said outside of the social services interviews was a police report that you read that was written a year ago; is that correct?

A. Correct.

Q. But you have no idea what each child would have said outside the interviews since last year other than those police reports and the interviews?

A. That's correct.

A similar approach may be taken with any piece of evidence that the expert is unaware of or has not reviewed, especially psychological tests, the accuracy of which can be challenged on a general level.

Q. Let me ask you this. Do psychological tests always apply to how someone performs in the real world?

A. It's not a one-to-one correlation, no.

Q. People can take a test like an aptitude test for college and not do well in college, right?

A. Correct.

Q. And that's true with a lot of psychological testing, correct?

A. Yes.

Q. And the WAIS IQ test doesn't tell someone how someone performs in the real world, correct?

A. That's correct. This is the best estimate we have.

Q. It's an estimate, is that what you said?

A. Yes.

Q. And a psychological test is subject to interpretation, correct?

A. Yes.

§ 11.67　Challenging the basis of the expert's opinion — The subjective report of a complainant or defendant.

Quite often, a mental health expert relies on the information provided by a complainant or defendant. The expert will usually rely on the accuracy and truthfulness of their statements. This assumption is usually not acknowledged on direct examination.

In the following example, the expert's reliance on the interview, or history, provided by the subject is highlighted by the expert's reliance on past psychological history — a history of deception and manipulation.

The expert also failed to record the interview, or otherwise fully and accurately note the patient's statements, also suggesting another reason to question the reliability of the history.

The cross-examination is also effective because at the same time it shows the expert to either be not fully aware of his subject's history or that he has not fully disclosed important parts of the history on direct examination.

Q. Doctor, I think you said that you relied on past psychological records in making your diagnosis, correct?

A. In part.

Q. And relying on those records is a basis of your opinion, correct?

A. Yes.

Q. And you testified to those opinions on direct examination, correct?

A. Yes, I did.

Q. And you testified as to your recollections as to what those past records stated, correct?

A. Correct.

Q. You also testified that a basis of your opinion was the interview you conducted with Sammy, who you were asked to evaluate?

A. Yes.

Q. There were three interviews, correct?

A. Correct.

Q. At the time those interviews were conducted, who was present?

A. It was just myself and Sammy.

Q. Did you make any audio or videotape recording of that interview?

A. No, I did not.

Q. Were you aware that you were being consulted for the purposes of possibly testifying in a criminal trial?

A. Yes.

Q. You knew the importance of documenting what Sammy said to you?

A. Yes.

Q. You knew it would be an important part of your opinion?

A. Yes.

Q. Were you aware that it was important to document thoroughly and accurately the information given to you by Sammy at that time?

A. I was aware that I needed to make notes to formulate a report on.

Q. In your opinion was it important to know whether or not the person you were interviewing had been truthful in the past?

A. Yes.

Q. Was it important to know whether or not that person had lied in sworn statements in the past?

A. It would be a piece of information, certainly, that I would consider.

Q. Were you given any information by the defense that Sammy had lied in school and on employment applications?

A. I was unaware of any specific lies that he made about employment.

Q. Did you review any employment applications or records which were sworn to by him?

A. Yes.

Q. And on the employment application, did you observe any lies on the part of Sammy?

A. There were some inconsistencies that I noted between what he told me and specific dates, specific —

Q. Were there lies?

A. I don't know if they were lies.

Q. Are you aware of any lies as you sit here on that stand?

A. No.

Q. Are you aware of any indications in any of the medical records that you reviewed that Sammy had lied to medical professionals in the past?

A. I know that he has minimized on various occasions reports that he has had these altered states of consciousness and also that he has minimized his use of drugs.

Q. He's minimized. Is that your testimony?

A. Yes.

Q. And minimize means not providing all the information, correct?

A. That's correct.

Q. Are you aware of specific entries in the medical records that you reviewed that indicated Sammy had feigned illness?

A. Not volitionally feigned, no, I'm not aware of a specific entry about that.

Q. Are you aware of entries in the medical records that you reviewed that showed that this defendant had been labeled manipulative or deceptive?

A. Oh, certainly.

Q. And how many doctors have labeled him manipulative or deceptive in the records?

A. At least three.

Q. Did you make any notation in any of your notes about the references in the medical records that he had of this person you were interviewing to be manipulative or deceptive?

A. No.

Q. And does your report refer to Sammy's history of deception and manipulation?

A. No.

§ 11.68 Questioning the expert concerning the expert's notes, reports or actions.

It is essential to obtain, preferably before trial, copies of all of the opposing expert witness' notes and reports. These may contain information that contradicts the expert's opinion. In the following example, a psychiatrist testifying for the defense claims that the defendant is incapable of understanding and waiving his *Miranda* rights due to his lack of intelligence. However, the expert's notes of the defendant's comments to a psychologist are used to discredit that opinion:

Q. Now, Mr. Wayne indicated to your unit at the jail that he could read and write to a certain extent.

A. I believe so, yes.

Q. He had also indicated to you that he can play cards, correct?

A. As I reviewed the notes, I believe I read them to be that he watched people playing cards and chess. I'm not sure if he was engaged in card-playing.

Q. Doesn't one of your notes from November 15th, 2003, say that the defendant kept busy on the tier by watching TV, praying, and playing cards?

A. If that's what the note says.

Q. And he's also made references and used the word "purgatory," correct?

A. Yes, he has.

Q. In proper context, correct?

A. As a form of punishment I believe he talks about it, yes.

Q. And that's certainly something that he has indicated in discussions according to your notes, correct?

A. Yes. He has quite an interest in religious topics.

Q. And your notes indicated he could recount biblical events in chronological sequence, correct?

A. Yes.

The psychologist is then cross-examined. He also contends that the defendant was not competent to give up *Miranda* rights. The prosecutor confronts the expert with his own conduct, in having the defendant sign a waiver of medical confidentiality forms.

Q. In the course of your work did you have occasion to ask Mr. Wayne to sign authorization forms?

A. Authorization for release of information from previous providers, yes.

Q. Correct?

A. Yes.

Q. And that was an authorization requesting him to give up certain legal privileges he had, correct?

A. The right to confidentiality of his records.

Q. And that is a legal right he has, correct?

A. I believe, yes.

Q. And in doing your job it was important that you ask him to give up that right, correct?

A. We asked him if we could collect additional information.

Q. To collect that information he had to give up his right to medical confidentiality, correct?

A. Yes.

Q. And it was your decision to present and accept his consent to do so, correct?

A. Yes.

Q. And in your opinion it was proper for Mr. Wayne to give up his right to medical confidentiality and have him sign forms to that effect, correct?

A. At that time I felt so, yes.

This cross-examination was very effective because the expert is, in effect, impeaching himself. It shows the importance of obtaining and carefully reviewing the notes, records, and reports involved in an expert's work. If any notes and records were not kept, this should be pursued.

Q. Did you keep all of your rough notes from your interviews?

A. No.

Q. Did you destroy any notes from your interviews?

A. Only the rough notes that went into forming the typewritten report.

Q. And those are notes which formed the bases of your opinions, correct?

A. That was the information I collected in longhand, which was then transcribed into a typed report.

Q. And who destroyed those notes?

A. I threw them away.

Q. And when was it you threw away those notes?

A. After I dictated the report.

Q. And they don't exist anymore, any place, do they?

A. Hopefully not.

Q. Did you tape-record that interview at which you made notes which you threw out?

A. No, I did not.

Q. So, there is no way of knowing exactly what David said to you, correct?

A. No.

§ 11.69 Challenging the expert's opinion with raw data of the expert's psychological tests (IQ test).

A psychological expert's own test data can be explored for information that may contradict the expert's opinion. To do this, all raw data and psychological testing material must be obtained through discovery or subpoena. In the following example, the expert's opinion that the defendant is incapable of comprehending *Miranda* rights is challenged with information from the standard intelligence test the expert used as a basis of his opinion.

Q. As part of the intelligence test, did you ask Mr. Wayne who Martin Luther King was?

A. Yes.

Q. What was his answer?

A. His answer was, "Politician for equal rights."

Q. And those were his words, weren't they?

A. That is correct.

Q. And that was used in response to a question, correct?

A. Yes.

Q. He had no difficulty understanding your question?

A. Of who was Martin Luther King, no.

Q. He had no difficulty formulating a response, correct?

A. Correct.

Q. And he associated the name of the individual with equal rights, correct?

A. Correct.

Q. And he's the one who used the words "equal rights," correct?

A. Yes. Those are his words.

Q. Now, you also asked him, "How many miles was Paris from New York," is that correct?

A. Yes.

Q. Is that the correct question on the IQ test?

A. Yes.

Q. And what was his answer?

A. "3,500."

Q. Is that the correct answer?

A. That's an acceptable answer, yes.

Q. He understood your question, correct?

A. Yes.

Q. He didn't say, "I don't understand what you're asking me?"

A. That's correct.

Q. The answer means he has some sense of geography, correct?

A. That's correct.

Q. He has some sense of numbers, correct?

A. Correct.

Q. And is that one of the more advanced questions on that examination?

A. It's item number 23 out of 29.

Q. And he answered the question as to how many senators there are in the U.S. Senate?

A. Yes.

Q. No problem understanding your question?

A. Evidently not.

Q. That requires an understanding of the concept of government, doesn't it?

A. I would say not.

Q. It requires an understanding of elected officials?

A. Somewhat.

Q. But in many situations he had no difficulty understanding your question and providing appropriate responses, correct?

A. Yes. He can recall information on the subtest.

Q. Is there a question, "With whose name is the theory of relativity most often associated?"

A. Yes, there is.

Q. Did Mr. Wayne answer that question?

A. Yes, he did.

Q. What was his answer?

A. "Einstein."

Q. Is that the correct answer?

A. Yes, it is.

Q. And these answers were provided by a man you contend suffers from moderate verbal retardation and cannot understand *Miranda* rights?

A. Yes.

§ 11.70 Challenging the expert's opinion with raw data of expert's psychological tests (MMPI test).

In the following example, the expert psychologist is questioned about results in the commonly used Minnesota Multiphasic Personality Inventory test that he administered to his patient. It is one of the few psychological tests that has a built-in scale to determine what psychologists call malingering and others call lying.

The expert fails to note in his report or direct examination that his patient scored far above the cutoff for malingering. By omitting this finding, the expert's bias is also implicitly raised as an issue. It is significant to note that this cross-examination would not have been possible unless the cross-examiner had forced disclosure of the psychologist's raw data of the tests he administered.

Q. The MMPI test assesses different areas, correct?

A. Yes.

Q. These areas are measured by scales, correct?

A. Yes.

Q. There are objective measures of these areas of assessment, or scales, correct?

A. Yes.

Q. And the F scale is one scale that is used to determine malingering in patients, correct?

A. Yes.

Q. And the other scale is called the Goff dissimulation index, correct?

A. Yes.

Q. Which is the F minus K scale, correct?

A. Correct.

Q. And in this case you did give him a raw score on the F scale of what?

A. I would have to look at the profile. It was at the 99th percentile.

Q. People's 38.

THE COURT: Let the record reflect that the witness is reviewing People's 38 for identification.

A. There is a raw score of 26.

Q. And what does that translate into?

A. It's a T score of over 120. It's many standard deviations above the norm.

Q. You're familiar with the phrase faking bad, correct?

A. Correct.

Q. And if one fakes bad, they try to appear more impaired or worse than they are, correct?

A. That's true.

Q. Now, one scale that you look at is the F scale for that, correct?

A. It's one thing that you would consider, yes.

Q. And what score level would one have to have to be considered faking bad?

A. Well, independent of the K, any F scale above a — over, say, three standard deviations above the norm would imply that the person might be dissimulating.

Q. Dissimulating means failing, right?

A. Yes.

Q. What T score?

A. Well, there's different cut-offs. There's not one. Different people would suggest different levels.

Q. What level are you saying, Doctor?

A. Anything over a T score of 80.

Q. Anything?

A. I would begin to become suspect.

Q. Anything over a T score of 80 suggests malingering, correct?

A. The possibility of malingering.

Q. It suggests faking bad, correct?

A. The possibility of faking bad.

Q. And the F scale score of T equals 120 is consistent with faking bad, isn't it?

A. It implies that, yes.

Q. In fact, you can't get much higher than 120 in terms of a T score for that faking bad scale, can you?

A. No, you can't get much higher than that.

Q. It's off the chart, isn't it?

A. It's not exactly off the chart, but it's right at the very top of it.

Q. In addition, you can look at the F minus K scale, correct?

A. Yes.

Q. And that's the second way on the MMPI of looking for fakers and malingerers, right?

A. Yes.

Q. And did you compute or can you compute?

A. You would subtract 14 from 26 and get a positive 12.

Q. And above what number?

A. A lot of people consider above positive seven or positive nine would be a significant discrepancy between the two.

Q. And that score in this case for this patient on the F minus K scale is consistent with someone faking bad, correct?

A. It could be.

Q. The F minus K scale score with Sammy is consistent with faking bad, isn't it?

A. Yes.

Q. Because of the score in the test you administered, correct?

A. Correct.

Q. And those are the two main scales on that MMPI test that seek to determine whether someone is presenting honestly, correct?

A. Yes, those are the two main indicators that one uses.

Q. And both those scores are evidence that Sammy was not being truthful, correct?

A. Yes.

Q. You never indicated those conclusions of your administration of the MMPI in your report, did you?

A. No.

§ 11.71 Challenging the expert's procedures or theories.

Experts can be questioned on the reliability of their procedures or theories, a particularly important area of cross-examination in new and developing areas of expertise and mental health testimony. Cross-examination can develop the failure of the prosecution's experts to use more reliable testing techniques.[668] Failure to permit such cross-examination can be reversible error.[669]

The Supreme Court of the United States has held that a defendant's constitutional rights were not violated where, on cross-examination, an expert witness could not remember which procedure of three he had used to reach his opinion regarding evidence that linked the defendant to the scene of the crime.[670] While leaving open the possibility that there could be a fact pattern where a witness's memory lapse violates the Confrontation Clause of the Constitution, the Court held that "Generally speaking, the Confrontation Clause guarantees an *opportunity* for effective cross-examination, not cross-examination that is effective in whatever way, and to whatever extent the defense might wish."[671] But the court remanded the case to the state court to determine if the opinion was properly received on state evidentiary grounds. The state court reversed the defendant's conviction because of the expert's "inability to establish a sufficient basis for his opinion."[672] As discussed in § 11.57, an expert's opinion may not be based on non-reliable tests. Even if accepted by the trial court, the cross-examiner may still challenge the tests or data. This decision, based on evidentiary rather than constitutional grounds, highlights the importance of scrutinizing the basis of expert opinions in general and the procedures used by the expert in particular.

§ 11.72   Use of leading questions to develop an area of cross-examination.

One approach to the cross-examination of the expert witnesses is to ask leading questions. This is especially true of a "runaway" expert witness who tries to control the flow of information. In these cases, try to limit the witness to "yes" or "no" answers and proceed slowly.

To the extent possible, favorable responses from the expert witness should be secured early. The questions should also be easily understood by the jury, with technical language kept at a minimum.

The following excerpt is a good example of leading questions used by the defense in a rape case where a physician testified that the only medical findings on examining the vagina of the ten-year-old victim was a slight "redness." The questions used allow the cross-examiner to limit the expert's answers and emphasize the defense's position.

---

[668] Commonwealth v. Rodriguez, 378 Mass. 296, 308, 391 N.E.2d 889, 896 (1979).

[669] People v. Watkins, 157 A.D.2d 301, 310–12, 556 N.Y.S.2d 541, 547 (1990) (reversing defendant's conviction where trial court limited cross-examination of the procedures used by a police chemist).

[670] Delaware v. Fensterer, 474 U.S. 15 (1985) (involving testimony by expert microscopist concerning his opinion that hairs found at a murder scene were forcibly removed).

[671] Delaware v. Fensterer, 474 U.S. 15, 20 (1985).

[672] Fensterer v. State, 509 A.2d 1106, 1109–10 (Del. 1986).

Q. Now, you have indicated that you found some evidence of skin redness; is that correct?

A. Erythema.

Q. That was external to the vagina?

A. That's right.

Q. And erythema is simply redness?

A. Right.

Q. As I understand it, it was only slight?

A. Right.

Q. And as I understand your testimony, that redness could be caused by a number of different factors?

A. Yes, it could.

Q. It can be caused by itching or scratching or rubbing of yourself?

A. Yes,

Q. It can be caused by a disease or sickness?

A. Yes, it could.

Q. It can be caused by a child's uncleanliness in the genital area?

A. Yes, it could.

Q. So any number of factors could be involved in this process; is that correct?

A. Yes.

Q. And, in any event, it was only slight?

A. Right.

Q. All right. And you can't say as you sit there now what the cause of it was?

A. No, you can't.

Q. All you can say is that it was slight and it was there?

A. Right.

Q. But what it was, we have no idea?

A. Right.

When using leading questions, it is important to avoid appearing too imperious or petulant in demanding "yes or no" answers from the expert. Rather than get in a fight over how the question should be answered, try rephrasing the question. Break the question down and try to reach an agreement on the wording. Fighting with an expert can make the cross-examiner appear out of control and defensive. But stay on track until you get to your destination.

§ 11.73   Establishing areas of agreement on cross-examination.

Sometimes it is helpful to begin the cross-examination of an expert by developing areas of agreement. This can be done by questions such as, "Can we agree that. . .?" or "You admit that. . .?" It is helpful in establishing testimony, and it also suggests to the jurors that the cross-examiner does not wish to totally discredit the witness. Sometimes areas of agreement also can be reached for the closing argument.

Areas of agreement which usually are obtained with leading questions can encompass facts of the case, definitions of terms, or principles of medicine or psychology.

In the following example taken from a child abuse case, an agreement is established on the many possible explanations of certain child behaviors:

Q. Can we agree, doctor, that the Child Sexual Abuse Accommodation Syndrome was never meant to determine if a child was sexually abused?

A. Yes.

Q. Can we agree that many children who are not sexually abused exhibit the behaviors you have described?

A. Yes.

Q. Can we agree that many children who have not been sexually abused have nightmares?

A. Yes.

Q. Can we agree that many events may cause a nightmare?

A. Yes.

Q. Can we agree that a nightmare can be a normal event for a child?

A. Yes.

Q. Can we agree that a lack of appetite can have many causes?

A. Yes.

Q. Can we agree that a lack of appetite can be a physical problem?

A. Yes.

Q. Can we agree that many children who have not been sexually abused have nightmares and loss of appetite?

A. Yes.

§ 11.74   Challenging the nonresponsive expert.

A common problem on cross-examination of expert witnesses, particularly with experts who specialize in court testimony, is their desire to provide long, nonresponsive answers. These experts prefer to discuss their theories and opinions rather than answer the cross-examiner's question. They tend not to answer questions with "yes or no" and show a dislike for leading questions.

There are several techniques that can be used to deal with a nonresponsive expert witness. One is to state early on that you will be asking questions that can be answered with either a "yes" or "no," but if the witness feels that a question cannot be so answered, the expert should say so, and you will rephrase the question.

Q. Doctor, you have been in court before, haven't you?

A. Yes, indeed.

Q. And do you understand that I will ask you questions?

A. Yes.

Q. My questions will be designed to elicit a "yes or no" answer and if you can't answer "yes or no," please say so and I will rephrase my question.

Another technique is to restate the question with words to the effect: "Excuse me, but perhaps you did not hear my question." Or "Excuse me, but perhaps you did not understand my question." If the expert persists, the simple device of repeating the question will highlight the expert's obstinacy. Another way of highlighting that the expert's answer is unresponsive is to ask the court reporter to read the question back.

In the following example, the cross-examiner repeats the question when it is not answered responsively and emphasizes this unresponsiveness by statements that alert the jury.

Q. What professional journal or professional book supports your view that the MMPI can be used to determine if someone has sexually molested a child?

A. Well, that's a technique that would be explained in any introduction to psychological testing. You can use it with many tests. It's not limited to the MMPI. It's done routinely.

Q. Maybe my question wasn't clear. Not the technique, but what professional journal or book supports the use of the MMPI to determine if someone has sexually molested a child?

A. Well, there are a variety of sources that talk about looking at the profiles of groups of individuals to assess the likelihood of certain behaviors.

Q. Let me ask the question once again. Can you tell us what book in the field of psychology states that it is accepted practice to use any form of psychological testing to determine whether or not someone has sexually molested a child?

A. There is no way that a psychological test can do that. You will not find a book that will say you can use MMPI or any other psychological test to determine if a person is a molester or not.

Q. Let me try that question a fourth time. Is there any book that says you can use any combination of tests or interpretation of their results to determine if someone has sexually molested a child?

A. Not to determine it, no.

The above technique emphasizes the cross-examiner's point that there is no authority to support the use of psychological tests to determine if someone is or is not a child molester. At the same time, the expert's credibility is challenged, not only because there is no support for the use of the psychological tests in this manner, but also because of the expert's evasiveness in answering the questions.

Generally, appealing to the court to ask that the expert respond to the cross-examiner's question is not effective. Many judges will refuse to order an expert witness to respond to leading questions without permitting the expert to expand or explain the answers. Opposing attorneys can also object to such a request on the grounds that the cross-examiner is refusing to allow the expert to provide a full answer. A judge's refusal to respond affirmatively to a request to direct the expert to answer a question will only compound the problem. Appealing to the court for an intervention may emphasize the attorney's inability to control the expert and his or her ineffectiveness in cross-examination.[673]

§ 11.75   Challenging an expert with prior testimony.

An expert can be cross-examined with the expert's prior sworn testimony from other cases. This is effective when on a major issue, and the contradiction between the instant and prior testimony is clear or dramatic. When using this technique, it is important to first commit the expert to an answer. It is also helpful to use the expert's own words from the prior testimony in the foundation question to magnify the inconsistency, as demonstrated in the following example.

Q. And in giving an opinion as to the cause and manner of death wouldn't you agree that the pathologist who conducts the autopsy is in the best position to render an opinion?

A. Not always.

Q. Have you ever given a different answer under oath to that question, Doctor?

A. Probably not.

Q. I would like to ask you if you were asked the following question and made the following answer, under oath, in the case of People v. Doe, in Berkshire in June 2004. "Question: Would it be fair to say, Doctor,

---

[673] For an excellent discussion on controlling the runaway witness and cross-examination in general, *See* Larry S. Pozner & Rogers J. Dodd, Cross Examination: Science and Techniques, 2nd Ed. 19.01–48 (2004).

that you have made determinations of a cause of death of an individual without actually being present at the autopsy?" "Answer: I have, but I think it is far better to be at the autopsy. There is absolutely nothing like being present. Nothing." Did you give that answer to that question under oath?

A. Yes.

§ 11.76   Learned treatise exception on direct and cross-examination.

Many jurisdictions do not permit the cross-examination of an expert witness by means of a textbook, treatise or professional article unless the expert either relied on it during direct examination or recognizes it as an authority. Federal Rule of Evidence 803(18) also reflects the rule of the majority of states in defining the use of learned treatises or articles on direct or cross-examination:

> Learned treatises. To the extent called to the attention of an expert witness upon cross-examination or relied upon by the expert witness in direct examination, statements contained in published treatises, periodicals, or pamphlets on a subject of history, medicine, or other science or art, established as a reliable authority by the testimony or admission of the witness or by other expert testimony or by judicial notice. If admitted, the statements may be read into evidence but may not be received as exhibits.

The Federal Rule differs from the minority view in the following ways: (1) reliability of the treatise may be established by an expert other than the cross-examined expert; (2) the treatise may be used on direct examination as well as cross; and (3) its use is not limited to credibility, but may be used as substantive evidence. Many states follow the Federal Rule, allowing a learned treatise to be used regardless of whether a cross-examined expert recognizes it as authoritative as long as it is established as authoritative by some other means. When a learned treatise or article is used, the entire article or treatise is not admitted into evidence — only the relevant part. When a sufficient foundation is laid by the expert on direct examination, the expert may cite and read from the authority or treatise as a basis of the opinion.[674] An example of the learned treatise exception in a sexual assault trial is a physician referring to illustrations from a medical publication to explain medical findings.[675] Likewise, illustrations from a medical treatise may be used on cross-examination of the expert or on direct of the opposing party's expert who challenges the first physician's opinions.[676] The learned treatise may also be in the form of a video tape. For example, a training video produced by the American College of Obstetrics and Gynecologists

---

[674] Harman v. Commonwealth, 898 S.W.2d 486, 490–91 (Ky. 1995).

[675] State v. Henry, 1996 S.D. 108, 554 N.W.2d 472 (1996).

[676] State v. Henry, 1996 S.D. 108, 554 N.W.2d 472 (1996).

may qualify as a learned treatise.[677] This is so, even though the treatise or videotape contains language, it is not a "standard of care" or not for use in litigation.[678] Nonetheless, such a videotape or treatise is not necessarily admissible "wholesale." Any unduly prejudicial or irrelevant references should be redacted from the learned treatise.[679]

The minority view finds statements from a learned treatise on direct examination to be hearsay and permits the use of the learned treatise only on the issue of credibility of the expert and not as substantive proof. Under this view, an expert may not refer to authorities and treatises in direct examination except for a limited purpose of explaining the basis of an opinion of the expert.[680]

This requires the expert to acknowledge the treatise as authoritative. If the expert does not acknowledge the book as authoritative, it may not be used as authority.[681] The expert may not be willing to do this, particularly if the expert is aware that such an acknowledgment would open the door to cross-examination.

Some courts limit the use of the learned treatise to cross-examination of an expert, but allow authoritativeness to be established not only by the witness being cross-examined, but also by judicial notice or other experts in the field.[682] However, even though an expert does not explicitly concede an author on treatise as authoritative, the witness may implicitly do so and open the door to use of the treatise on cross-examination.[683] If after acknowledging the authoritativeness of a book edited by a physician and that the witness consulted the chapter written by that physician in formulating his opinion, it is "unduly prejudicial" if the cross-examiner confronts the expert with passages not from the same book and chapter

---

[677] Constantino v. Herzog, 203 F.3d 164, 171 (2d Cir. 2000) ("We see no reason to deprive a jury of authoritative learning simply because it is presented in a visual, rather than printed, format.").

[678] Constantino v. Herzog, 203 F.3d 164, 175 (2d Cir. 2000).

[679] Constantino v. Herzog, 203 F.3d 164, 175 (2d Cir. 2000).

[680] Aldridge v. Edmunds, 561 Pa. 323, 334, 750 A.2d 292, 298 (2000).

[681] People v. Laracuente, 21 A.D.3d 1389, 1391, 801 N.Y.S.2d 676, 678 (2005) (holding trial court properly limited cross-examination of medical examiner with respect to a text not established as authoritative); Labate v. Plotkin, 195 A.D.2d 444, 600 N.Y.S.2d 144 (1993); State v. Malroit, 2000 Ohio App. LEXIS 5169 (Nov. 8, 2000), appeal denied, 91 Ohio St. 3d 1460, 743 N.E.2d 400 (2001) (In a child sexual abuse case, the defendant's physician was properly precluded from referring to specific medical treatises or articles. The court noted:

> Beyond the hearsay problem, learned treatises are inadmissible because the opinions or conclusions contained therein are unverifiable, the technical language may not be understood by most jurors, the opinions or conclusions would be admitted into evidence without an oath of truthfulness, and the opposing party would be unable to cross-examine the person who gave the opinion or conclusion.

Id. at 110–11. Robinson v. Warner-Lambert, 998 S.W.2d 407 (Tex. Ct. App. 1999).

[682] Coats v. Hickman, 11 S.W.3d 798, 303 (Mo. Ct. App. 1999); Freshwater v. Scheidt, 86 Ohio St. 3d 260, 714 N.E.2d 891 (1999) (noting a court may take judicial notice of Gray's Anatomy); Ohio R. Evid. 706.

[683] See § 11.77.

written by that physician.[684] If a treatise is used on cross-examination, the same learned treatise can be displayed and read on redirect examination to rehabilitate the expert.[685]

When an expert does not readily accept a book, treatise, or individual as authoritative, the following section presents some approaches to deal with this situation.

When the use of learned treatise is limited to credibility, a party is entitled to a limiting instruction.[686]

Great care must be taken to insure that statements used from a learned treatise are not out of context and that there is not another statement more damaging to the cross-examiner's position in the same treatise.

Just because a medical article has been published does not establish it as a reliable authority.[687] Not all books in a field are necessarily recognized as authoritative. For example, there was no error in refusing to allow a defendant's attorney to cross-examine a prosecution expert on the "false accusation syndrome" as set forth in a book when the book was not shown to be a standard treatise in the expert's area of expertise.[688] Assuming that a publication qualifies under the learned treatise exception, its use and content can be limited by the trial court on the grounds of relevancy.[689]

Another point that may be developed through the use of the learned treatise exception is that the expert has conveniently overlooked opposing data or research that was not helpful to the expert's opinion. While the expert may not agree with the opinion in the text or treatise being used on cross-examination, the expert may agree that there is at least a difference of opinion by recognized experts in the field.

§ 11.77   Cross-examination of an expert who refuses to recognize any text as authoritative.

The following excerpt is from a cross-examination of an expert who refuses to accept any text as authoritative.[690] The fact that the expert must acknowledge

---

[684] Watkins v. Labiak, 6 A.D.3d 426, 774 N.Y.S.2d 340 (2004).

[685] Hinkle v. Cleveland Clinic Found., 159 Ohio App. 3d 351, 823 N.E.2d 945 (2004).

[686] The authority for such an instruction under the Federal Rules of Evidence is Rule 105:

Limited Admissibility. When evidence which is admissible as to one party or for one purpose but not admissible as to another party or for another purpose is admitted, the court, upon request, shall restrict the evidence to its proper scope and instruct the jury accordingly.

See also Aldridge v. Edmunds, 561 Pa. 323, 333, 750 A.2d 292, 297 (2000).

[687] Meschino v. North American Drager, Inc., 841 F.2d 429, 434 (1st Cir. 1988).

[688] Fitzgerald v. State, 193 Ga. App. 76, 78, 386 S.E.2d 914 (1989).

[689] State v. Chapman, 410 So. 2d 689, 703 (La. 1981).

[690] This testimony taken from Jacober v. St. Peter's Med. Ctr., 128 N.J. 475, 481–83, 608 A.2d

a learned treatise as authoritative before he or she can be cross-examined on its contents is essential in those states that do not follow the Federal Rules of Evidence.

Q. Am I right, Doctor, that what you are telling us is that you do not accept this textbook as one of the standard texts in the field of neonatology?

A. It's a standard text, but I don't think it's authoritative, if that's what you're getting at.

Q. Do you accept your own writing as authoritative?

A. Only for me.

Q. So that, essentially, I gather what you're saying is that if I were to ask you if anything that was written in medical literature is authoritative on the subject in which it addresses, you would have to say no?

A. It depends what you mean by authoritative. If you mean this is the way it's supposed to be done. . . .

Q. Generally accepted in the profession.

A. I don't believe that. I think those textbooks are one man's opinion. They're constantly revised, they're never up to date, and I don't believe that they're that type of authority. Medicine doesn't recognize authorities this way.

Q. And am I right that in forming your opinion and testifying here today, you are making no reference whatsoever to any medical literature?

A. That's correct.

Q. Did you, yourself, write a chapter in this book entitled; [sic] Neonatal/ Perinatal Medicine, Diseases of the Fetus and Infant, edited by Richard E. Behrman?

A. Yes.

Q. Do you accept this book as one of the standard and authoritative textbooks in the field?

A. No.

Q. Even though you, yourself, are an author in the first edition of this book?

A. That's correct.

The following is from the cross-examination of another expert in the same trial who refused to acknowledge a standard textbook as authoritative:

Q. Do you recognize this as one of the standard treatises in the field?

304, 308–309 (1992). This testimony, and the problem of expert witnesses refusing to recognize any source as authoritative, was a basis for the New Jersey Supreme Court adopting Federal Rule of Evidence 803(18), which does not require the witness being cross-examined to acknowledge the treatise as authoritative.

A. It's a standard textbook, yeah.

Q. By standard, Doctor, do you mean standard in that it is recognized in the field by other practitioners as an authoritative source for reference?

A. Well, I don't think any textbook is really authoritative, it has a set of opinions that some clinicians would agree with and others would be very controversial. Authoritative sort of sounds to me as though it implies that one opinion is the correct opinion that's expressed in a particular book, and that's simply not the way that any textbook is written.

In these situations, counsel can try the following questions to gain acknowledgment of the treatise as authority or emphasize to the jury the obstinacy of the witness.

Q. Now, Doctor, you have testified in court before today?

Q. And therefore you are familiar with the fact that unless you recognize as authoritative for a standard in the field a book or article that I ask you about I cannot use it in my cross-examination of you. Correct?

Q. Do you know or have you ever heard of the author or book?

Q. Do other professionals in the field consider [name of publication] a reliable authority on the subject?

Q. Is there any author or book on the subject of your expert testimony that you recognize as authoritative?

Q. When you studied for your professional licensing exams, did you study from a textbook?

Q. Which one?

If the witness has not published anything himself in the field, the following questions might be helpful:

Q. You do not recognize as authoritative any of the authors or books I have cited, is that correct?

Q. Are you an authority?

Q. Have you written any textbooks or articles in the field?

An issue to be aware of in using learned treatises on cross-examination is that authoritative texts usually have several editions. Some experts will point out that the cross-examiner's text is not the latest edition or that the edition being used was not in effect at the time of the events upon which the expert is providing an opinion.

An expert may implicitly accept a treatise as authoritative while explicitly stating it is not an authority. For example, by stating that the author is a "respected colleague" "with very good experience" whose "opinion and his experience" he valued and had "invited him to write a chapter in a textbook" in the field and had relied on the author's opinion in his daily practice as well as his court testimony, a witness implicitly makes the author an expert even if the witness refuses to accept the author's work as authoritative.[691]

§ 11.78   Conclusion.

The cross-examination of the expert witness should be outlined in advance after determining the most effective approaches. The outline should include cross-references to important documents, reports, and prior testimony.

Cross-examination of experts is particularly vulnerable to the "one-too-many questions" mistake. When a favorable response is secured, it is important that the expert not be permitted to recuperate by further questioning along the same lines. Thus, the adage of "do not gild the lily" should be kept in mind, especially with an expert who is no stranger to the witness stand.

---

[691] Freshwater v. Scheidt, 86 Ohio St. 3d 260, 268–69, 714 N.E.2d 891, 897 (1999) (noting that experts should not be able "to adroitly evade cross-examination simply by avoiding such words as 'rely' or 'authority' or any forms of these words." Freshwater v. Scheidt, 86 Ohio St. 3d 260, 269, 714 N.E.2d 891, 897 (1999)).